Weiss Ratings'
Guide to Banks

Weiss Ratings'
Guide to Banks

A Quarterly Compilation of Health
Insurance Company Ratings and Analyses

Spring 2021

GREY HOUSE PUBLISHING

Weiss Ratings
4400 Northcorp Parkway
Palm Beach Gardens, FL 33410
561-627-3300

Published by Grey House Publishing, Inc., located at 4919 Route 22, Amenia, NY 12501; telephone 518-789-8700. Grey House Publishing neither guarantees the accuracy of the data contained herein nor assumes any responsibility for errors, omissions or discrepancies. Grey House Publishing accepts no payment for listing; inclusion in the publication of any organization, agency, institution, publication, service or individual does not imply endorsement of the publisher.

4919 Route 22
PO Box 56
Amenia, NY 12501-0056

Edition No. 121, Spring 2021

ISBN: 978-1-64265-871-2
ISSN: 2158-5962

Contents

Terms and Conditions

Date of Data Analyzed: September 30, 2020
Data Source: Call Report data provided by SNL Financial.

Welcome to Weiss Ratings'
Guide to Banks

Most people automatically assume their bank will survive, year after year. However, prudent consumers and professionals realize that in this world of shifting risks, the solvency of financial institutions can't be taken for granted. After all, your bank's failure could have a heavy impact on you in terms of lost time, lost money (in cases of deposits exceeding the federal insurance limit), tied-up deposits, lost credit lines, and the possibility of being shifted to another institution under not-so-friendly terms.

If you are looking for accurate, unbiased ratings and data to help you choose a commercial bank, savings bank, or savings and loan for yourself, your family, your company or your clients, Weiss Ratings' Guide to Banks gives you precisely what you need.

Weiss Ratings' Mission Statement

Weiss Ratings' mission is to empower consumers, professionals, and institutions with high quality advisory information for selecting or monitoring a financial services company or financial investment.

In doing so, Weiss Ratings will adhere to the highest ethical standards by maintaining our independent, unbiased outlook and approach to advising our customers.

Why rely on Weiss Ratings?

Weiss Ratings provides fair, objective ratings to help professionals and consumers alike make educated financial decisions.

At Weiss Ratings, integrity is number one. Weiss Ratings never takes a penny from rated companies for issuing its ratings. And, we publish Weiss Safety Ratings without regard for institutions' preferences. Our analysts review and update Weiss ratings each and every quarter, so you can be sure that the information you receive is accurate and current – providing you with advance warning of financial vulnerability early enough to do something about it.

Other rating agencies focus primarily on a company's current financial solvency and consider only mild economic adversity. Weiss Ratings also considers these issues, but in addition, our analysis covers a company's ability to deal with severe economic adversity in terms of a sharp decline in the value of its investments and a drop in the collectability of its loans.

Our use of more rigorous standards stems from the viewpoint that a financial institution's obligations to its customers should not depend on favorable business conditions. A bank must be able to honor its loan and deposit commitments in bad times as well as good.

Weiss's rating scale, from A to F, is easy to understand. Only a few outstanding companies receive an A (Excellent) rating, although there are many to choose from within the B (Good) category. A large group falls into the broad average range which receives C (Fair) ratings. Companies that demonstrate marked vulnerabilities receive either D (Weak) or E (Very Weak) ratings. So, there's no numbering system, star counting, or color-coding to keep track of.

How to Use This Guide

The purpose of the *Guide to Banks* is to provide consumers, businesses, financial institutions, and municipalities with a reliable source of banking industry ratings and analysis on a timely basis. We realize that the financial safety of a bank is an important factor to consider when establishing a relationship. The ratings and analysis in this Guide can make that evaluation easier when you are considering:

- A checking, merchant banking, or other transaction account
- An investment in a certificate of deposit or savings account
- A line of credit or commercial loan
- Counterparty risk

The rating for a particular company indicates our opinion regarding that company's ability to meet its obligations – not only under current economic conditions, but also during a declining economy or in an environment of increased liquidity demands.

To use this Guide most effectively, we recommend you follow the steps outlined below:

Step 1   To ensure you evaluate the correct company, verify the company's exact name as it was given to you. It is also helpful to ascertain the city and state of the company's main office or headquarters since no two banks with the same name can be headquartered in the same city. Many companies have similar names but are not related to one another, so you will want to make sure the company you look up is really the one you are interested in evaluating.

Step 2   Turn to Section I, the Index of Banks, and locate the company you are evaluating. This section contains all federally-insured commercial banks and savings banks. It is sorted alphabetically by the name of the company and shows the main office city and state following the name for additional verification.
If you have trouble finding a particular institution or determining which is the right one, consider these possible reasons:

- You may have an incorrect or incomplete institution name. There are often several institutions with the same or very similar names. So, make sure you have the exact name and proper spelling, as well as the city in which it is headquartered.
- You may be looking for a *bank holding company*. If so, try to find the exact name of the main bank in the group and look it up under that name.

Step 3   Once you have located your specific company, the first column after the state shows its current Weiss Safety Rating. Turn to *About Weiss Safety Ratings* for information about what this rating means. If the rating has changed since the last edition of this Guide, a downgrade will be indicated with a down triangle ▼ to the left of the company name; an upgrade will be indicated with an up triangle ▲.

Step 4   Following the current Weiss Safety Rating are two prior ratings for the company based on year-end data from the two previous years. Use this to discern the longer-term direction of the company's overall financial condition.

Step 5   The remainder of Section I; provides insight into the areas our analysts reviewed as the basis for assigning the company's rating. These areas include size, capital adequacy, asset quality, profitability, liquidity, and stability. An index within each of these categories represents a composite evaluation of that particular facet of the company's financial condition. Refer to the Critical Ranges In Our Indexes table for an interpretation of which index values are considered strong, good, fair, or weak. In most cases, lower-rated companies will have a low index value in one or more of the indexes shown. Bear in mind, however, that Weiss Safety Rating is the result of a complex qualitative and quantitative analysis which cannot be reproduced using only the data provided here.

Step 6   If the company you are evaluating is not highly rated and you want to find a bank with a higher rating, turn to the page in Section II that has your state's name at the top. This section contains Weiss Recommended Banks by State (rating of A+, A, A- or B+) that have a branch office in your state. If the main office telephone number provided is not a local telephone call or to determine if a branch of the bank is near you, consult your local telephone Yellow Pages Directory under "Banks," "Savings Banks," or "Savings and Loan Associations." Here you will find a complete list of the institution's branch locations along with their telephone numbers.

Step 7   Once you've identified a Weiss Recommended Company in your local area, you can then refer back to Section I to analyze it.

Step 8   In order to use Weiss Safety Ratings most effectively, we strongly recommend you consult the *Important Warnings and Cautions* listed. These are more than just "standard disclaimers." They are very important factors you should be aware of before using this Guide. If you have any questions regarding the precise meaning of specific terms used in the Guide, refer to the Glossary.

Step 9   Make sure you stay up to date with the latest information available since the publication of this Guide. For information on how to set up a rating change notification service, acquire follow-up reports, check ratings online or receive a more in-depth analysis of an individual company, call 1-877-934-7778 or visit www.weissratings.com.

About Weiss Safety Ratings

The Weiss Ratings are calculated based on a complex analysis of hundreds of factors that are synthesized into five indexes: capitalization, asset quality, profitability, liquidity and stability. Each index is then used to arrive at a letter grade rating. A weak score on any one index can result in a low rating, as financial problems can be caused by any one of a number of factors, such as inadequate capital, non-performing loans and poor asset quality, operating losses, poor liquidity, or the failure of an affiliated company.

Our **Capitalization Index** gauges the institution's capital adequacy in terms of its cushion to absorb future operating losses under adverse business and economic scenarios that may impact the company's net interest margin, securities' values, and the collectability of its loans.

Our **Asset Quality Index** measures the quality of the company's past underwriting and investment practices based on the estimated liquidation value of the company's loan and securities portfolios.

Our **Profitability Index** measures the soundness of the company's operations and the contribution of profits to the company's financial strength. The index is a composite of five sub-factors: 1) gain or loss on operations; 2) rates of return on assets and equity; 3) management of net interest margin; 4) generation of noninterest-based revenues; and 5) overhead expense management.

Our **Liquidity Index** evaluates a company's ability to raise the necessary cash to satisfy creditors and honor depositor withdrawals.

Finally, our **Stability Index** integrates a number of sub-factors that affect consistency (or lack thereof) in maintaining financial strength over time. These include 1) risk diversification in terms of company size and loan diversification; 2) deterioration of operations as reported in critical asset, liability, income and expense items, such as an increase in loan delinquency rates or a sharp increase in loan originations; 3) years in operation; 4) former problem areas where, despite recent improvement, the company has yet to establish a record of stable performance over a suitable period of time; and 5) relationships with holding companies and affiliates.

In order to help guarantee our objectivity, we reserve the right to publish ratings expressing our opinion of a company's financial stability based exclusively on publicly available data and our own proprietary standards for safety.

Each of these indexes is measured according to the following range of values.

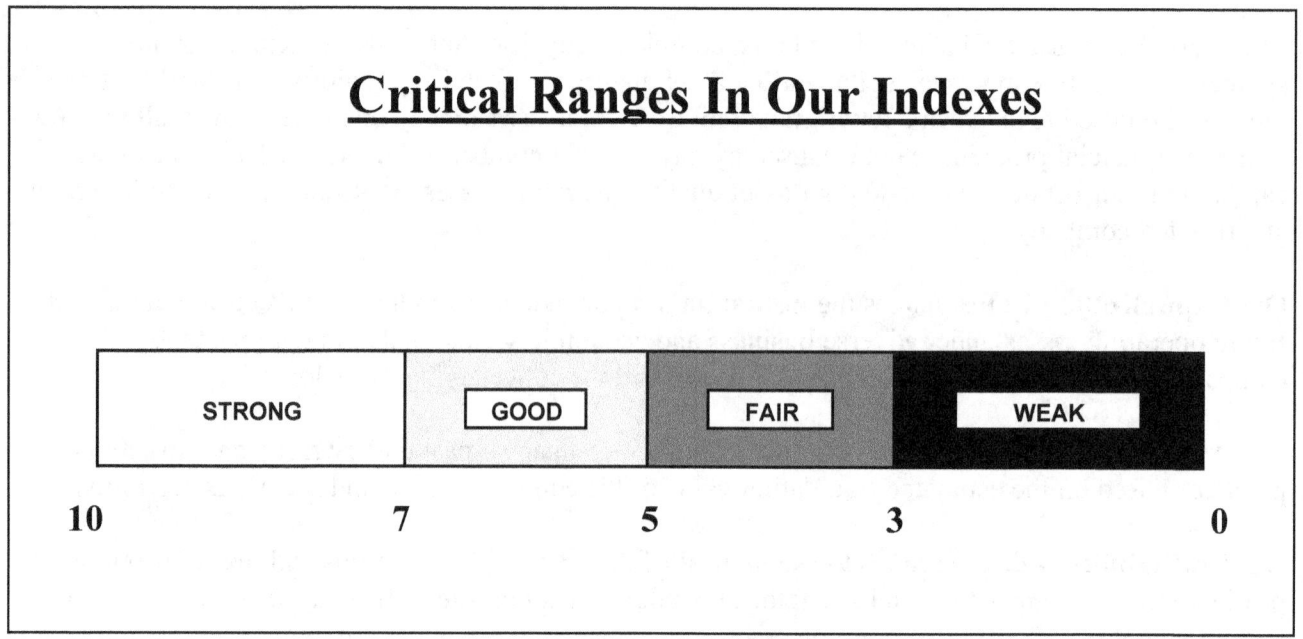

Finally, the indexes are combined to form a composite company rating which is then verified by one of our analysts. The resulting distribution of ratings assigned to all banks looks like this:

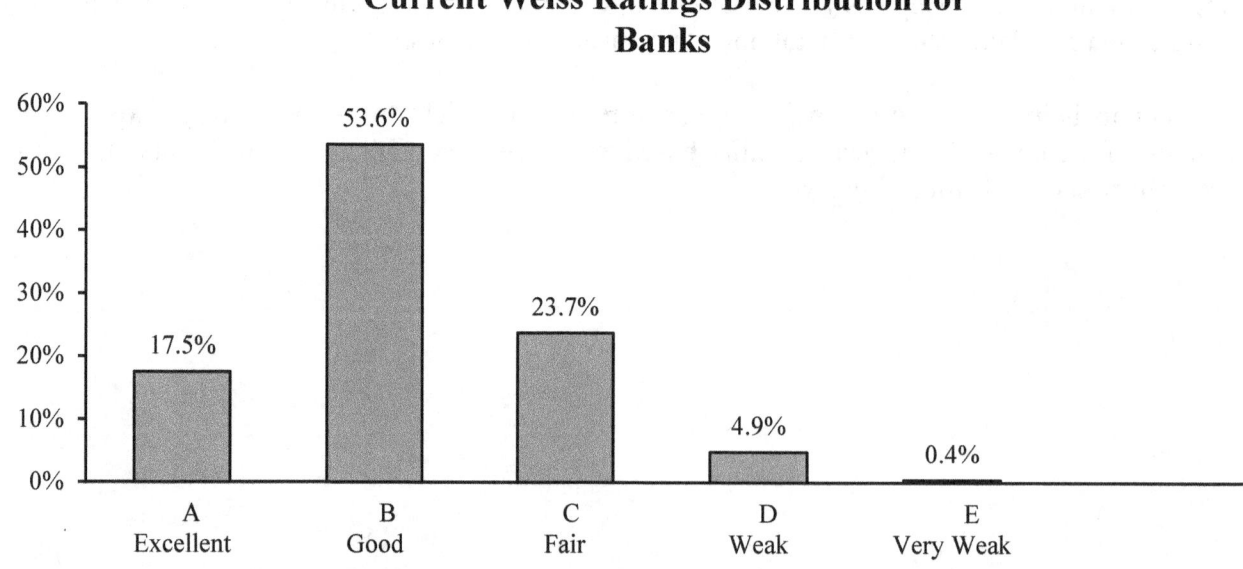

What Our Ratings Mean

A **Excellent.** The institution offers excellent financial security. It has maintained a conservative stance in its business operations and underwriting practices as evidenced by its strong equity base, high asset quality, steady earnings, and high liquidity. While the financial position of any company is subject to change, we believe that this institution has the resources necessary to deal with severe economic conditions.

B **Good.** The institution offers good financial security and has the resources to deal with a variety of adverse economic conditions. It comfortably exceeds the minimum levels for all of our rating criteria, and is likely to remain healthy for the near future. Nevertheless, in the event of a severe recession or major financial crisis, we feel that this assessment should be reviewed to make sure that the company is still maintaining adequate financial strength.

C **Fair.** The institution offers fair financial security, is currently stable, and will likely remain relatively healthy as long as the economic environment remains relatively stable. In the event of a severe recession or major financial crisis, however, we feel this company may encounter difficulties in maintaining its financial stability.

D **Weak.** The institution currently demonstrates what, in our opinion, we consider to be significant weaknesses which could negatively impact depositors or creditors. In the event of a severe recession or major financial crisis, these weaknesses could be magnified.

E **Very Weak.** The institution currently demonstrates what we consider to be significant weaknesses and has also failed some of the basic tests that we use to identify fiscal stability. Therefore, even in a favorable economic environment, it is our opinion that depositors or creditors could incur significant risks.

F **Failed.** The institution has been placed under the custodianship of regulatory authorities. This implies that it will be either liquidated or taken over by another financial institution.

+ The **plus sign** is an indication that the institution is in the upper third of the letter grade.

- The **minus sign** is an indication that the institution is in the lower third of the letter grade.

U **Unrated.** The institution is unrated due to the absence of sufficient data for our ratings.

Peer Comparison of Bank Safety Ratings

Weiss Ratings	Veribanc	Bauer Financial	IDC Financial	Bankrate.com	Lace Financial
A+, A, A-	Green, Three Stars w/ Blue Ribbon recognition	5 stars, 4 stars	201-300	1, Five stars	A+, A
B+, B, B-	Green, Three Stars w/out Blue Ribbon recognition	3 ½ stars	166-200	2, Four stars	B+
C+, C, C-	Green Two Stars, Yellow Two Stars	3 stars	126-165	3, Three stars	B, C+
D+, D, D-	Green one star, Yellow one star, Green no stars	2 stars	76-125	4, Two stars	C, D
E+, E, E-	Yellow no stars, Red no stars	1 star	1-75	5, One star	E

Important Warnings and Cautions

1. **A rating alone cannot tell the whole story.** Please read the explanatory information contained here, in the section introductions and in the appendix. It is provided in order to give you an understanding of our rating philosophy as well as to paint a more complete picture of how we arrive at our opinion of a company's strengths and weaknesses. In addition, please remember that our safety rating is not an end-all measure of an institution's safety. Rather, it should be used as a "flag" of possible troubles, suggesting a need for further research.

2. **Safety ratings shown in this directory were current as of the publication date.** In the meantime, the rating may have been updated based on more recent data. Weiss Ratings offers a notification service for ratings changes on companies that you specifiy. For more information call 1-877-934-7778 or visit www.weissratings.com.

3. **When deciding to do business with a financial institution, your decision should be based on a wide variety of factors in addition to Weiss Safety Rating.** These include the institution's pricing of its deposit instruments and loans, the fees you will be charged, the degree to which it can help you meet your long-term planning needs, how these costs/benefits may change over the years, and what other choices are available to you given your current location and financial circumstances.

4. **Weiss Safety Ratings represent our opinion of a company's insolvency risk.** As such, a high rating means we feel that the company has less chance of running into financial difficulties. A high rating is not a guarantee of solvency nor is a low rating a prediction of insolvency. Weiss Safety Ratings are not deemed to be a recommendation concerning the purchase or sale of the securities of any bank that is publicly owned.

5. **All firms that have the same Weiss Safety Rating should be considered to be essentially equal in safety.** This is true regardless of any differences in the underlying numbers which might appear to indicate greater strengths. Weiss Safety Rating already takes into account a number of lesser factors which, due to space limitations, cannot be included in this publication.

6. **A good rating requires consistency.** If a company is excellent on four indicators and fair on one, the company may receive a fair rating. This requirement is necessary due to the fact that fiscal problems can arise from any *one* of several causes including poor underwriting, inadequate capital resources, or operating losses.

7. **Our rating standards are more conservative than those used by other agencies.** We believe that no one can predict with certainty the economic environment of the near or long-term future. Rather, we assume that various scenarios – from the extremes of double-digit inflation to a severe recession – are within the range of reasonable possibilities over the next one or two decades. To achieve a top rating according to our standards, a company must be adequately prepared for the worst-case reasonable scenario, without impairing its current operations.

8. **We are an independent rating agency and do not depend on the cooperation of the companies we rate.** Our data are derived, from quarterly financial statements filed with federal regulators. Although we seek to maintain an open line of communication with the companies being rated, we do not grant them the right to influence the ratings or stop their publication. This policy stems from the fact that this Guide is designed for the protection of our customers.

9. **Inaccuracies in the data issued by the federal regulators could negatively impact the quality of a company's Safety Rating.** While we attempt to find and correct as many data errors as possible, some data errors inevitably slip through. We have no method of intercepting fraudulent or falsified data and must take for granted that all information is reported honestly to the federal regulatory agencies.

10. **Institutions that operate exclusively or primarily as a trust company may have skewed financial information.** Due to the nature of their business, these companies often record high profit levels compared to other more "traditional" banks. Trust companies can usually be recognized by the initials "TC" or "& TC" in their names.

11. **This Guide does not cover nonbank affiliates of banking companies.** Although some nonbank companies may be affiliated with the banks cited in this Guide, the firms are separate corporations whose financial strength is only partially dependent on the strength of their affiliates.

12. **There are many companies with the same or similar sounding names, despite no affiliation whatsoever.** Therefore, it is important that you have the exact name, city, and state of the institution's headquarters before you begin to research the company in this Guide.

13. **Affiliated companies do not automatically receive the same rating.** We recognize that a troubled institution may expect financial support from its parent or affiliates. Weiss Safety Ratings reflect our opinion of the measure of support that may become available to a subsidiary bank, if the subsidiary were to experience serious financial difficulties. In the case of a strong parent and a weaker subsidiary, the affiliate relationship will generally result in a higher rating for the subsidiary than it would have on a stand-alone basis. Seldom, however, would the rating be brought up to the level of the parent.

    This treatment is appropriate because we do not assume the parent would have either the resources or the will to "bail out" a troubled subsidiary during a severe economic crisis. Even when there is a binding legal obligation for a parent corporation to honor the obligations of its subsidiary banks, the possibility exists that the subsidiary could be sold and lose its parental support. Therefore, it is quite common for one affiliate to have a higher rating than another. This is another reason why it is especially important that you have the precise name of the company you are evaluating.

14. **This publication does not include foreign banking companies, or their U.S. branches.** Therefore, our evaluation of foreign banking companies is limited to those U.S. chartered domestic banks owned by foreign banking companies. In most cases, the U.S. operations of a foreign banking company are relatively small in relation to the overall size of the company, so you may want to consult other sources as well. In any case, do not be confused by a domestic bank with a name which is the same as – or similar to – that of a foreign banking company. Even if there is an affiliation between the two, we have evaluated the U.S. institution based on its own merits.

Section I

Index of Banks

An analysis of all rated

U.S. Commercial Banks and Savings Banks

Institutions are listed in alphabetical order.

Section I Contents

This section contains Weiss Safety Ratings, key rating factors, and summary financial data for all U.S. federally-insured commercial banks and savings banks. Companies are sorted in alphabetical order, first by company name, then by city and state.

Left Pages

1. **Institution Name**

   The name under which the institution was chartered. If you cannot find the institution you are interested in, or if you have any doubts regarding the precise name, verify the information with the bank itself before proceeding. Also, determine the city and state in which the institution is headquartered for confirmation. (See columns 2 and 3.)

2. **City**

   The city in which the institution's headquarters or main office is located. With the adoption of intrastate and interstate branching laws, many institutions operating in your area may actually be headquartered elsewhere. So, don't be surprised if the location cited is not in your particular city.

   Also use this column to confirm that you have located the correct institution. It is possible for two unrelated companies to have the same name if they are headquartered in different cities.

3. **State**

   The state in which the institution's headquarters or main office is located. With the adoption of interstate branching laws, some institutions operating in your area may actually be headquartered in another state.

4. **Safety Rating**

   Weiss rating assigned to the institution at the time of publication. Our ratings are designed to distinguish levels of insolvency risk and are measured on a scale from A to F based upon a wide range of factors. See *About Weiss Safety Ratings* for specific descriptions of each letter grade.

   Highly rated companies are, in our opinion, less likely to experience financial difficulties than lower rated firms. See *About Weiss Safety Ratings* for more information. Also, please be sure to consider the warnings regarding the ratings' limitations and the underlying assumptions.

5. **Prior Year Safety Rating**

   Weiss rating assigned to the institution based on data from December 31 of the previous year. Compare this rating to the company's current rating to identify any recent changes.

6. **Safety Rating Two Years Prior**

   Weiss rating assigned to the institution based on data from December 31 two years ago. Compare this rating to the ratings in the prior columns to identify longer term trends in the company's financial condition.

| 7. | **Total Assets** | The total of all assets listed on the institution's balance sheet, in millions of dollars. This figure primarily consists of loans, investments (such as municipal and treasury bonds), and fixed assets (such as buildings and other real estate). |

Overall size is an important factor which affects the company's ability to diversify risk and avoid vulnerability to a single borrower, industry, or geographic area. Larger institutions are usually, although not always, more diversified and thus less susceptible to a downturn in a particular area. Nevertheless, do not be misled by the general public perception that "bigger is better." Larger institutions are known for their inability to quickly adapt to changes in the marketplace and typically underperform their smaller brethren.

8. One Year Asset Growth

The percentage change in total assets over the previous 12 months. Moderate growth is generally a positive since it can reflect the maintenance or expansion of the company's market share, leading to the generation of additional revenues. Excessive growth, however, is generally a sign of trouble as it can indicate a loosening of underwriting practices in order to attract new business.

9. Commercial Loans/ Total Assets

The percentage of the institution's asset base invested in loans to businesses. Commercial loans are the traditional bread and butter of commercial banks, although many have increased their business lending in recent years.

10. Consumer Loans/ Total Assets

The percentage of the institution's asset base invested in loans to consumers, primarily credit cards. Consumer lending has grown rapidly in recent years due to the high interest rates and fees institutions are able to charge. On the down side, consumer loans usually experience higher delinquency and default rates than other loans, negatively impacting earnings down the road.

11. Home Mortgage Loans/ Total Assets

The percentage of the institution's asset base invested in residential mortgage loans to consumers, excluding home equity loans. Savings banks have traditionally dominated mortgage lending.

This type of loan typically experiences lower default rates. However, the length of the loan's term can be a subject for concern during periods of rising interest rates.

12. Securities/ Total Assets

The percentage of the institution's asset base invested in securities, including U.S. Treasury securities, mortgage-backed securities, and municipal bonds. This does not include securities the institution may be holding on behalf of individual customers.

Although securities are similar to loans in that they represent obligations to pay a debt at some point in the future, they are a more liquid investment than loans and usually present less risk of default. In addition, mortgage-backed securities can present less credit risk than holding mortgage loans themselves due to the diversification of the underlying mortgages.

13. Capitalization Index

An index that measures the adequacy of the institution's capital resources to deal with potentially adverse business and economic situations that could arise. It is based on an evaluation of the company's degree of leverage compared to total assets as well as risk-adjusted assets. See the Critical Ranges In Our Indexes for a description of the different critical levels presented in this index.

14. Leverage Ratio

A regulatory ratio defined by the federal banking regulators as core (tier 1) capital divided by tangible assets. This ratio answers the question: How much does the institution have in stockholders' equity for every dollar of assets? Thus, the Leverage Ratio represents the amount of actual "capital cushion" the institution has to fall back on in times of trouble. We feel that this is the single most important ratio in determining financial strength because it provides the best measure of an institution's ability to withstand losses.

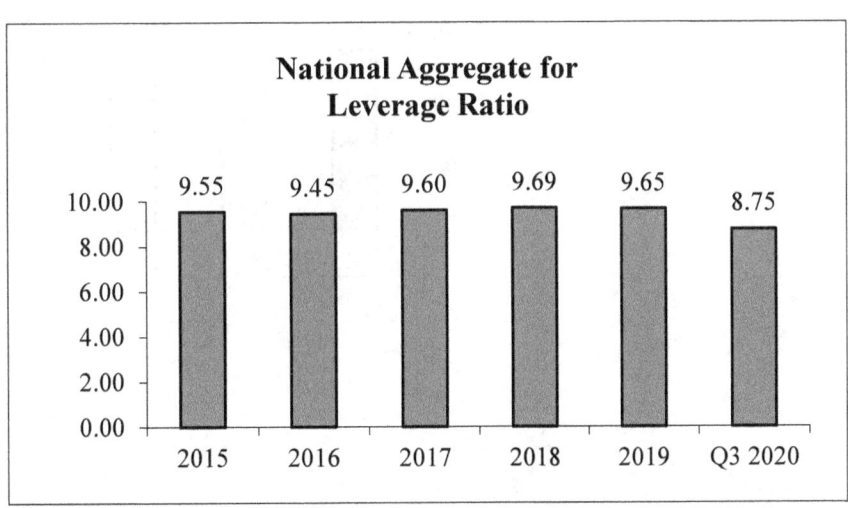

15. Risk-Based Capital Ratio

A regulatory ratio defined by the federal banking regulators as total (tier 1 + tier 2) capital divided by risk-weighted assets. This ratio addresses the issue that not all assets present the same level of credit risk to an institution. As such, all assets and certain off-balance sheet commitments are assigned to risk categories based on the level of credit risk they pose and then weighted accordingly to arrive at risk-weighted assets.

For instance, assets with virtually no risk, such as cash and U.S. Treasury securities, are risk-weighted at 0% and therefore, not included in the calculation. Assets with low risk, for example, high quality mortgage-backed securities and state and municipal bonds, are partially weighted at 20%.

Those assets possessing moderate risk, such as residential mortgages and state and local revenue bonds are partially weighted at 50%. And finally, assets considered to possess "normal" or "high" risk, including certain off-balance sheet commitments such as unfunded loans, are risk-weighted at 100%. The summation of these categories of risk-weighted assets results in the figure used in the denominator of this ratio.

Please be aware that not all banks and savings banks are required to report risk-weighted assets as defined by the federal regulators. Consequently, we have estimated this figure when necessary based on estimates used by the regulators themselves.

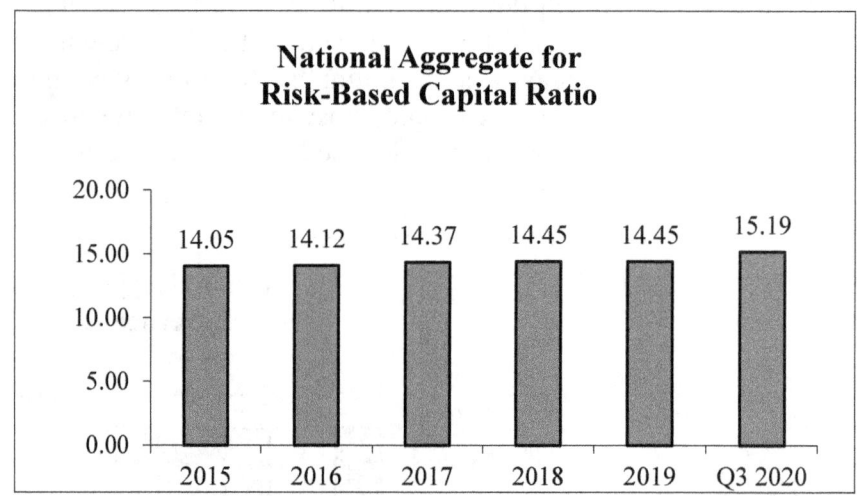

National Aggregate for Risk-Based Capital Ratio

1. **Asset Quality Index**

An index that measures the quality of the institution's past underwriting and investment practices, as well as its loss reserve coverage. See the Critical Ranges In Our Indexes for a description of the different critical levels presented in this index.

2. **Adjusted Nonperforming Loans/ Total Loans**

The percentage of the institution's loan portfolio which is either past due on its payments by 90 days or more, or no longer accruing interest due to doubtful collectability plus a portion of all restructured loans, less government guaranteed GNMA loans and those loans protected by the FDIC. This ratio is affected primarily by the quality of the institution's underwriting practices and the prosperity of the local economies where it is doing business. While only a portion of these loans will actually end up in default, a high ratio here will have several negative consequences including increased loan loss provisions, increased loan collection expenses, and decreased interest revenues.

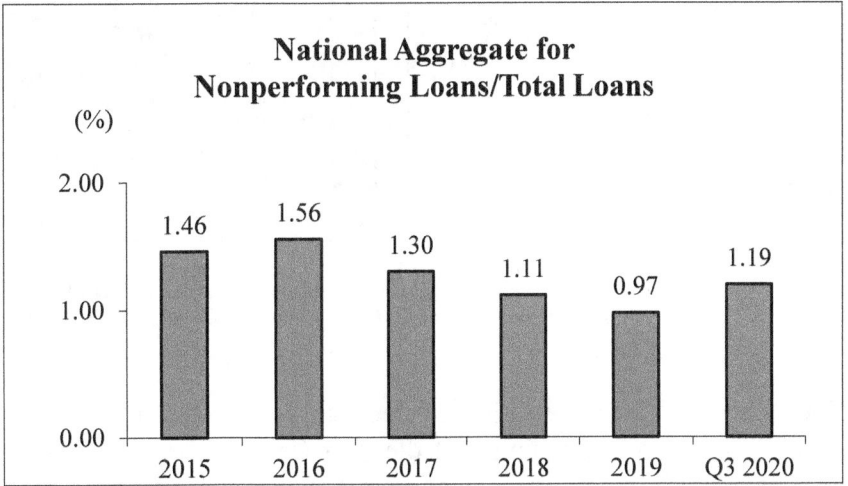

National Aggregate for Nonperforming Loans/Total Loans

(%)

1.46	1.56	1.30	1.11	0.97	1.19
2015	2016	2017	2018	2019	Q3 2020

[1]Nonperforming loans were adjusted in 2011 to include a portion of all restructured loans, less government guaranteed GNMA loans and those loans protected by the FDIC.

3. Adjusted Nonperforming Loans/ Capital

The percentage of past due 90 days and nonaccruing loans plus a portion of all restructured loans, less government guaranteed GNMA loans and those loans protected by the FDIC to the company's core (tier 1) capital plus reserve for loan losses. This ratio answers the question: If all of the bank's significantly past due and nonaccruing loans were to go into default, how much would that eat into capital? A large percentage of nonperforming loans signal imprudent lending practices which are a direct threat to the equity of the institution.

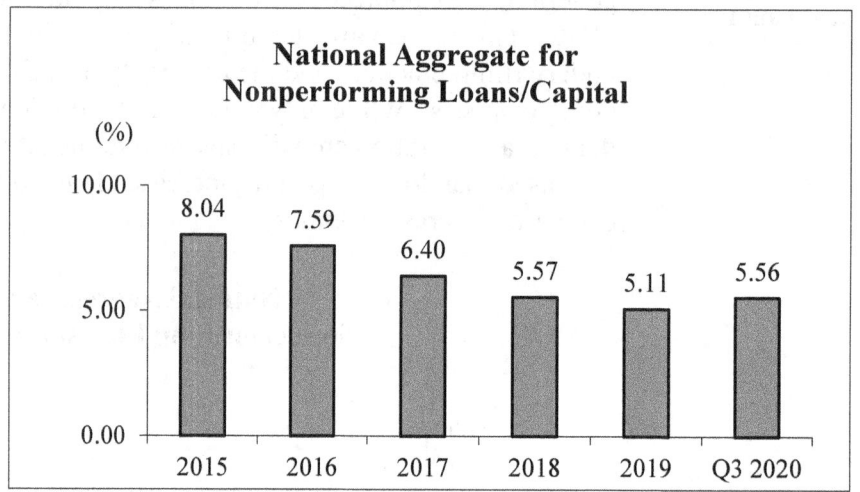

[1] Nonperforming loans were adjusted in 2011 to include a portion of all restructured loans, less government guaranteed GNMA loans and those loans protected by the FDIC.

4. Net Charge-offs/ Average Loans

The ratio of foreclosed loans written off the institution's books since the beginning of the year (less previous write-offs that were recovered) as a percentage of average loans for the year. This ratio answers the question: What percentage of the bank's past loans have actually become uncollectible? Past loan charge-off experience is often a very good indication of what can be expected in the future, and high loan charge-off levels are usually an indication of poor underwriting practices.

5. Profitability Index

An index that measures the soundness of the institution's operations and the contribution of profits to the company's financial strength. It is based on five sub-factors: 1) gain or loss on operations; 2) rates of return on assets and equity; 3) management of net interest margin; 4) generation of noninterest-based revenues; and 5) overhead expense management. See the Critical Ranges In Our Indexes for a description of the different critical levels presented in this index.

6. Net Income

The year-to-date net profit or loss recorded by the institution, in millions of dollars. This figure includes the company's operating profit (income from lending, investing, and fees less interest and overhead expenses) as well as nonoperating items such as capital gains on the sale of securities, income taxes, and extraordinary items.

7. Return on Assets   The ratio of net income for the year (year-to-date quarterly figures are converted to a 12-month equivalent) as a percentage of average assets for the year. This ratio, known as ROA, is the most commonly used benchmark for bank profitability since it measures the company's return on investment in a format that is easily comparable with other companies.

Historically speaking, a ratio of 1.0% or greater has been considered good performance. However, this ratio will fluctuate with the prevailing economic times. Also, larger banks tend to have a lower ratio.

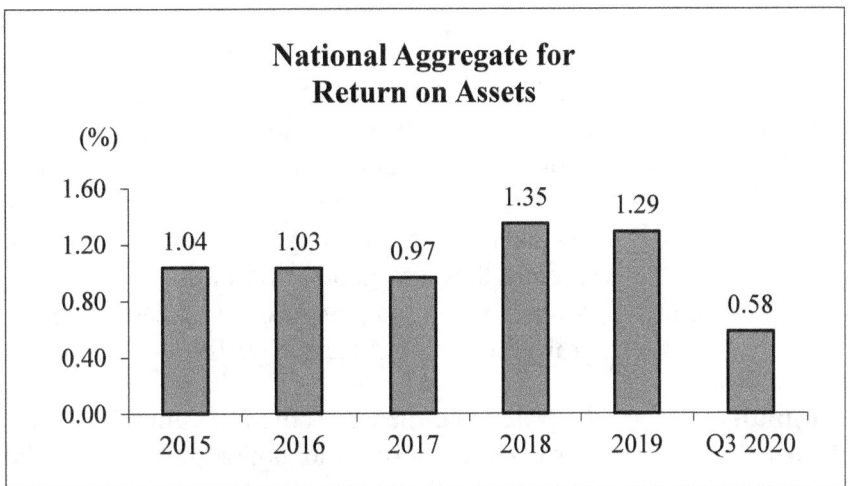

8. Return on Equity   The ratio of net income for the year (year-to-date quarterly figures are converted to a 12-month equivalent) as a percentage of average equity for the year. This ratio, known as ROE, is commonly used by a company's shareholders as a measure of their return on investment. It is not always a good measure of profitability, however, because inadequate equity levels at some institutions can result in unjustly high ROE's.

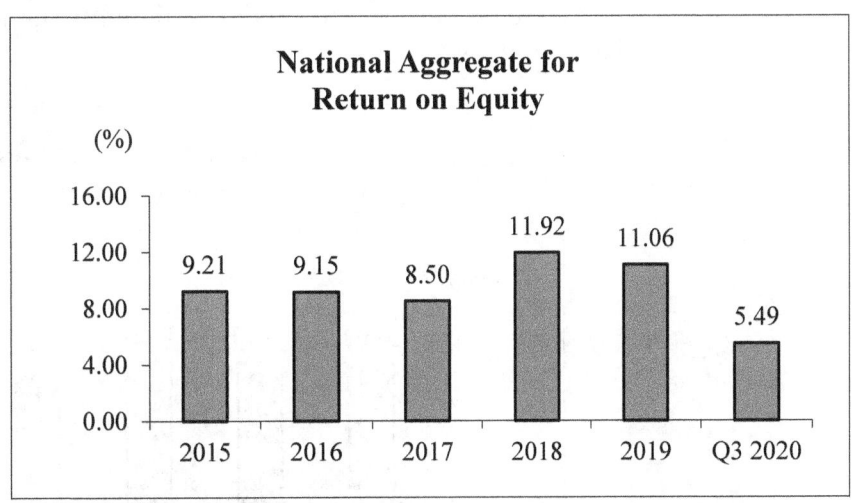

9. **Net Interest Spread**

The difference between the institution's interest income and interest expense for the year (year-to-date quarterly figures are converted to a 12-month equivalent) as a percentage of its average revenue-generating assets. Since the margin between interest earned and interest paid is generally where the company generates the majority of its income, this figure provides insight into the company's ability to effectively manage interest spreads.

A low Net Interest Spread can be the result of poor loan and deposit pricing, high levels of non-accruing loans, or poor asset/liability management.

10. **Overhead Efficiency Ratio**

Total overhead expenses as a percentage of total revenues net of interest expense. This is a common measure for evaluating an institution's ability to operate efficiently while keeping a handle on overhead expenses like salaries, rent, and other office expenses. A high ratio suggests that the company's overhead expenses are too high in relation to the amount of revenue they are generating and/or supporting. Conversely, a low ratio means good management of overhead expenses which usually results in a strong Return on Assets as well.

11. **Liquidity Index**

An index that measures the institution's ability to raise the necessary cash to satisfy creditors and honor depositor withdrawals. It is based on an evaluation of the company's short-term liquidity position, including its existing reliance on less stable deposit sources. See the Critical Ranges In Our Indexes for a description of the different critical levels presented in this index.

12. **Liquidity Ratio**

The ratio of short-term liquid assets to deposits and short-term borrowings. This ratio answers the question: How many cents can the institution easily raise in cash to cover each dollar on deposit plus pay off its short-term debts? Due to the nature of the business, it is rare (and not expected) for an established bank to achieve 100% on this ratio. Nevertheless, it serves as a good measure of an institution's liquidity in relation to the rest of the banking industry.

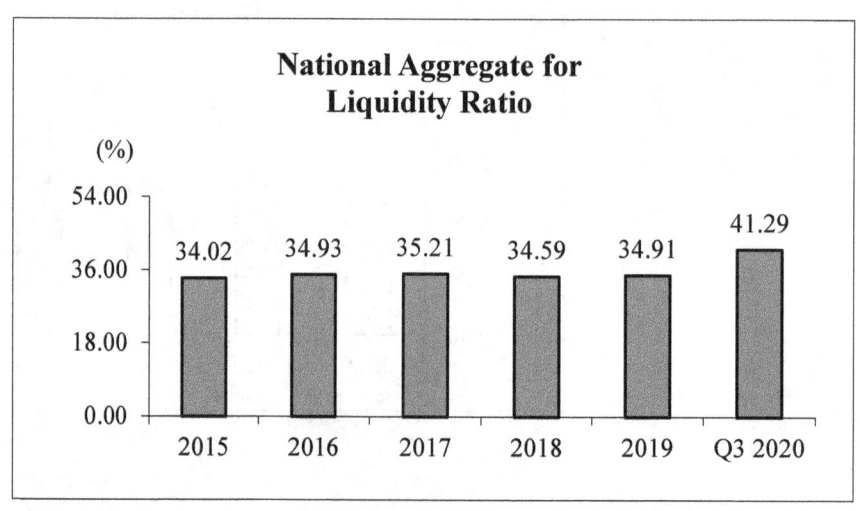

13. Hot Money Ratio

The percentage of the institution's deposit base that is being funded by jumbo CDs and brokered deposits. Jumbo CDs (high-yield certificates of deposit with principal amounts of at least $100,000) and brokered deposits (pooled funds sold by brokers seeking the highest interest rate available) are generally considered less stable (and more costly) and thus less desirable as a source of funds.

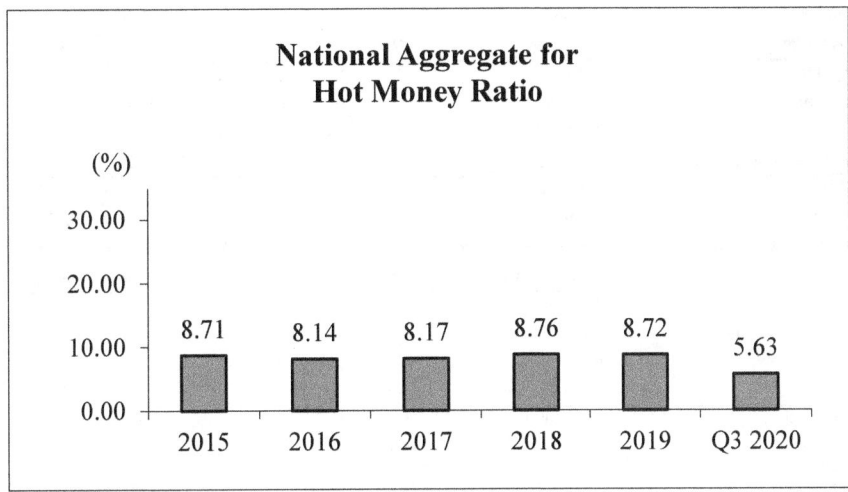

14. Stability Index

An index that integrates a number of factors such as 1) risk diversification in terms of company size and loan diversification; 2) deterioration of operations as reported in critical asset, liability, income and expense items, such as an increase in loan delinquency rates or a sharp increase in loan originations; 3) years in operation; 4) former problem areas where, despite recent improvement, the company has yet to establish a record of stable performance over a suitable period of time; and 5) relationships with holding companies and affiliates. See the Critical Ranges In Our Indexes for a description of the different critical levels presented in this index.

Name	City	State	Rating	2019 Rating	2018 Rating	Total Assets ($Mil)	One Year Asset Growth	Asset Mix (As a % of Total Assets) Commercial Loans	Consumer Loans	Mortgage Loans	Securities	Capitalization Index	Leverage Ratio	Risk-Based Capital Ratio
1st Advantage Bank	Saint Peters	MO	C	C	C	135.7	23.97	24.7	0.0	7.3	1.7	7.7	9.7	13.1
1st Bank	Broadus	MT	A-	A-	A-	52.4	10.57	5.2	1.5	0.5	0.0	7.1	9.1	24.6
▼ 1st Bank in Hominy	Hominy	OK	D+	C-	D+	42.8	6.05	12.3	10.0	9.5	28.1	6.7	8.7	0.0
▼ 1st Bank of Sea Isle City	Sea Isle City	NJ	C	C+	C	271.1	10.51	1.1	0.1	45.0	5.0	9.1	10.4	20.9
1st Bank Yuma	Yuma	AZ	B+	B+	B	473.9	33.48	13.7	0.2	2.1	8.2	6.1	8.1	14.7
1st Cameron State Bank	Cameron	MO	C	C	C-	64.0	11.56	0.6	1.6	21.8	31.1	6.5	8.5	26.5
1st Capital Bank	Salinas	CA	B+	B+	B-	749.0	17.50	20.8	0.0	15.5	8.0	7.9	9.6	15.4
▲ 1st Colonial Community Bank	Cherry Hill	NJ	C+	C+	C+	596.3	9.40	11.2	0.4	34.9	16.5	8.0	9.7	17.7
1st Community Bank	Sherrard	IL	C	C	C	68.3	6.00	6.0	2.0	10.7	7.6	8.0	9.7	0.0
1st Constitution Bank	Cranbury	NJ	B	B	B	1843.5	37.37	28.9	0.1	9.1	12.3	5.8	9.3	11.6
▲ 1st Equity Bank	Skokie	IL	C-	C-	D	141.6	48.66	15.5	0.1	17.0	0.1	10.0	15.2	23.0
1st Federal Savings Bank of SC, Inc.	Walterboro	SC	B-	B-	C+	116.3	19.09	0.1	1.2	53.1	6.4	6.6	8.6	18.7
1st Financial Bank USA	Dakota Dunes	SD	C	C	C	633.1	-3.77	0.8	60.4	1.6	11.9	10.0	28.3	35.0
1st National Bank	Lebanon	OH	C+	C	C	258.4	32.09	5.2	0.7	25.8	11.4	5.9	7.9	14.0
1st Security Bank of Washington	Mountlake Terrace	WA	A-	A	A	2053.8	21.25	9.6	17.8	25.8	8.7	7.2	10.7	0.0
1st Source Bank	South Bend	IN	A-	A-	A-	7294.0	9.31	50.1	1.9	5.4	14.9	9.1	10.9	14.2
1st State Bank	Saginaw	MI	B-	B-	C+	408.5	40.09	42.8	0.2	4.5	3.9	5.6	7.6	13.3
▲ 1st State Bank of Mason City	Mason City	IL	C+	C+	B-	30.8	21.61	0.7	4.8	10.5	44.0	10.0	11.2	0.0
1st Summit Bank	Johnstown	PA	B-	B	B	1224.8	11.52	11.6	2.5	23.1	44.3	7.6	9.4	18.6
▲ 1st Trust Bank, Inc.	Hazard	KY	C	C-	C	249.3	-8.09	17.8	2.2	19.4	3.2	6.9	9.1	0.0
1st United Bank	Faribault	MN	A-	A-	B	172.6	20.57	12.3	1.5	5.6	40.7	8.5	10.0	0.0
▲ 21st Century Bank	Loretto	MN	A-	B+	B+	617.9	21.37	30.1	0.1	8.3	9.3	10.0	11.2	18.4
22nd State Bank	Louisville	AL	D	D-	C-	168.0	24.43	13.2	1.6	22.0	6.3	7.0	9.0	13.0
5Star Bank	Colorado Springs	CO	B+	A-	A-	380.9	51.94	13.2	0.1	7.8	0.3	10.0	12.1	0.0
AB&T	Albany	GA	B	B	B-	235.8	23.11	24.5	1.5	16.2	0.7	6.2	8.3	12.9
▲ Abacus Federal Savings Bank	New York	NY	B-	B-	B-	359.8	7.31	1.0	0.0	59.4	1.4	10.0	11.8	23.3
Abbeville Building & Loan	Abbeville	LA	C+	B-	B-	58.7	9.62	0.0	0.0	47.2	2.1	10.0	27.7	17.0
Abbeville First Bank, SSB	Abbeville	SC	D+	C	C	96.7	22.93	9.3	1.0	37.6	28.8	6.4	8.4	0.0
AbbyBank	Abbotsford	WI	C+	B-	B-	614.9	16.67	7.3	0.4	12.4	17.5	5.2	7.8	11.2
Abington Bank	Abington	MA	B-	B-	C+	592.8	2.66	3.1	0.1	38.0	8.6	10.0	11.7	18.0
Academy Bank, N.A.	Kansas City	MO	A-	A-	A-	2341.1	44.59	22.6	0.7	9.9	10.3	10.0	12.0	18.1
ACB Bank	Cherokee	OK	D+	D+	C	125.8	-3.21	9.4	1.8	10.2	17.5	6.9	10.9	0.0
Access Bank	Omaha	NE	B	B	B	766.0	20.07	22.7	0.3	9.3	5.9	7.2	10.3	12.7
AccessBank Texas	Denton	TX	C	B-	B-	504.5	18.92	19.5	1.6	11.5	7.7	8.2	9.8	14.0
ACNB Bank	Gettysburg	PA	B+	A-	B+	2489.2	44.56	11.2	0.6	17.3	13.2	7.3	9.2	14.2
Adams Bank & Trust	Ogallala	NE	B+	B+	B	975.3	18.19	12.2	1.5	12.1	2.3	6.2	10.0	0.0
Adams Community Bank	Adams	MA	C	C	C	706.9	14.35	4.0	1.2	67.1	6.6	6.0	8.1	14.8
Adams County Bank	Kenesaw	NE	B	B	C+	202.3	12.52	5.1	0.8	3.1	33.4	7.3	9.4	0.0
Adams State Bank	Adams	NE	B+	B+	B+	56.3	10.00	5.5	3.9	13.4	6.7	10.0	17.7	0.0
Adirondack Bank	Utica	NY	C-	C	C	1012.4	12.27	16.0	0.9	21.1	28.1	5.2	7.2	17.5
Adirondack Trust Co.	Saratoga Springs	NY	B	B	B	1460.0	21.23	13.8	1.5	12.1	14.1	6.8	8.8	16.8
ADP Trust Co., N.A.	Wilmington	DE	U			35.2	116.25	0.0	0.0	0.0	42.6	10.0	95.4	555.6
Adrian Bank	Adrian	MO	A	A-	B-	153.5	7.69	6.0	4.9	8.9	29.7	10.0	11.5	21.1
▼ Adrian State Bank	Adrian	MN	C	C+	C	58.6	13.25	4.2	0.9	2.5	4.5	6.0	9.3	0.0
Affiliated Bank, N.A.	Bedford	TX	B-	B	B	1238.2	30.26	24.5	0.4	17.2	0.0	9.1	10.4	16.7
AIG Federal Savings Bank	Wilmington	DE	U	U	U	38.3	1.84	0.0	0.0	0.0	85.4	10.0	97.9	0.0
AimBank	Littlefield	TX	A-	A-	B	1851.8	19.78	12.4	0.9	11.0	26.0	8.1	9.7	0.0
Alamerica Bank	Birmingham	AL	D	D	D+	15.4	-25.91	13.5	1.6	6.2	3.7	10.0	12.9	19.5
Alamosa State Bank	Alamosa	CO	A-	A-	A-	317.8	19.79	6.5	2.9	5.6	25.8	7.2	9.1	0.0
Albany Bank and Trust Co., N.A.	Chicago	IL	B+	A-	B+	686.2	12.42	8.2	0.1	3.4	6.6	10.0	15.1	0.0
Alden State Bank	Sterling	KS	C-	C	C-	21.3	6.74	8.6	6.0	15.2	19.4	10.0	11.2	24.1
Alden State Bank	Alden	MI	A-	A-	B+	249.7	14.59	9.7	2.5	15.4	4.5	10.0	11.5	0.0
Alden State Bank	Alden	NY	B-	B-	B-	402.8	16.27	7.5	0.7	44.4	13.5	10.0	12.0	19.6
Alerus Financial, N.A.	Grand Forks	ND	A-	A-	A-	2897.2	30.17	25.8	2.7	21.0	17.1	7.1	9.0	13.7
Algonquin State Bank	Algonquin	IL	C-	C	D+	150.6	12.54	6.1	16.2	11.3	24.0	8.6	10.6	0.0
All America Bank	Oklahoma City	OK	B-	B-	C+	458.9	1.29	5.9	2.4	16.6	11.8	7.4	9.3	13.2
Allegiance Bank	Houston	TX	B-	C+	B-	5964.7	21.67	22.2	0.7	10.9	11.1	8.0	9.6	15.4
Alliance Bank	Francesville	IN	A	A-	B+	343.4	10.77	11.1	0.3	4.1	30.6	10.0	12.2	19.6
Alliance Bank	Topeka	KS	B+	B+	B	129.4	16.90	22.8	2.2	17.2	3.4	8.3	10.1	0.0
Alliance Bank	Saint Paul	MN	B	B	B	734.6	15.24	24.0	0.8	3.6	10.0	8.1	9.8	13.6

Asset Quality Index	Adjusted Non-Performing Loans as a % of Total Loans	as a % of Capital	Net Charge-Offs / Avg Loans	Profitability Index	Net Income ($Mil)	Return on Assets (R.O.A.)	Return on Equity (R.O.E.)	Net Interest Spread	Overhead Efficiency Ratio	Liquidity Index	Liquidity Ratio	Hot Money Ratio	Stability Index
7.3	0.02	na	0.00	3.3	0.7	0.72	7.42	3.47	75.0	1.8	11.5	19.8	4.7
8.9	0.00	na	0.00	9.8	1.3	3.26	32.58	3.50	60.9	5.7	60.2	10.0	7.0
2.3	4.20	na	-0.07	3.4	0.2	0.63	7.05	3.62	80.4	3.3	46.2	19.6	3.7
7.3	0.63	na	-0.03	2.4	0.5	0.27	2.43	3.39	92.9	5.1	34.2	6.9	5.1
7.9	0.32	na	0.03	6.2	3.9	1.18	13.12	3.97	65.6	5.4	35.4	5.5	5.8
7.7	0.91	na	0.00	2.2	0.1	0.23	2.50	2.58	89.0	5.9	52.3	7.1	4.0
8.1	0.29	na	-0.02	4.2	2.9	0.56	5.54	3.65	67.8	4.9	11.8	2.2	6.7
4.9	1.46	na	0.77	3.6	2.7	0.60	7.13	3.11	69.8	2.6	10.1	14.6	5.5
6.6	0.19	na	0.00	2.7	0.2	0.39	3.81	3.36	87.6	2.0	26.6	21.5	5.3
4.3	1.57	na	0.02	5.6	12.3	0.98	8.48	3.68	57.9	2.2	9.3	17.9	9.1
3.0	3.67	na	0.00	4.5	1.0	0.98	6.72	3.12	66.4	0.9	24.7	44.7	8.3
7.6	0.59	na	0.05	4.6	0.8	0.95	10.58	3.44	73.6	4.5	34.3	10.6	4.3
2.4	4.17	8.7	3.65	9.4	8.1	1.69	6.31	15.94	80.7	0.6	23.6	37.5	8.3
4.3	1.63	11.9	0.02	7.1	4.3	2.47	30.97	2.47	63.8	1.6	23.7	25.3	4.3
6.6	0.44	na	-0.01	9.4	28.4	2.00	18.07	4.10	48.9	1.5	11.5	13.4	10.0
5.5	1.26	7.1	0.13	5.8	58.2	1.11	9.37	3.36	56.6	3.1	14.5	9.4	10.0
3.7	1.83	na	-0.04	4.6	2.6	0.92	11.41	3.40	62.3	5.1	23.8	2.5	4.5
6.5	3.34	na	0.08	2.7	0.1	0.48	3.77	2.15	79.0	5.7	84.3	13.3	4.8
8.6	0.46	2.7	0.12	3.7	6.2	0.72	7.29	2.71	67.5	3.3	25.8	16.5	7.8
3.4	1.30	na	0.82	2.8	0.8	0.41	4.56	3.10	68.6	0.7	14.4	40.6	4.4
8.0	0.19	na	0.00	5.8	1.4	1.15	8.64	3.28	59.8	6.8	54.0	2.5	7.5
7.2	0.29	na	0.00	6.4	5.3	1.20	10.59	4.11	51.1	2.1	10.0	3.0	7.5
1.5	6.27	na	0.03	0.5	-0.6	-0.53	-5.63	3.66	101.5	0.9	19.2	36.8	3.2
7.4	0.11	0.6	0.02	4.2	1.7	0.68	5.49	3.36	60.9	2.7	31.2	18.4	7.9
7.1	0.08	na	-0.03	4.9	1.6	0.97	10.50	3.71	63.0	4.8	21.9	4.2	5.4
9.2	0.33	na	0.00	3.4	1.6	0.58	4.38	3.09	77.2	0.7	17.6	31.9	7.9
4.3	1.00	na	0.18	2.8	0.1	0.30	1.08	4.24	83.7	1.6	10.7	22.1	7.2
7.2	2.17	na	0.01	2.1	0.4	0.61	5.87	2.88	79.0	3.3	35.2	16.9	3.7
4.0	6.12	na	0.91	4.3	3.6	0.83	9.86	3.12	64.8	1.8	24.7	18.9	5.2
6.4	0.51	na	0.03	3.7	2.5	0.57	3.62	3.58	68.4	1.9	25.0	20.4	6.8
6.3	1.77	na	0.23	3.5	6.1	0.36	2.96	2.88	74.4	1.1	20.8	33.6	8.0
1.5	2.60	na	1.85	3.2	0.4	0.44	4.03	4.14	51.0	0.7	16.1	43.1	5.8
5.6	0.66	4.2	0.01	5.8	6.0	1.21	10.15	4.10	63.7	4.0	20.8	6.1	7.7
3.6	1.38	na	0.67	3.1	1.4	0.38	3.75	3.88	71.9	1.8	18.1	20.7	6.3
7.2	0.62	na	0.22	4.5	12.0	0.70	6.80	3.49	64.5	3.7	15.4	11.1	8.5
7.3	0.40	na	0.05	6.4	8.6	1.27	12.16	4.22	65.3	2.8	20.2	15.6	8.2
5.4	0.94	na	0.01	3.1	2.6	0.52	5.75	2.99	75.8	3.6	12.6	8.5	5.6
5.3	0.00	na	0.00	5.7	2.0	1.37	14.61	2.72	45.2	0.8	13.0	26.9	6.2
8.4	0.00	na	-0.03	5.2	0.5	1.16	6.17	3.62	62.6	3.8	44.1	15.5	8.4
4.9	1.95	13.7	0.00	2.6	2.1	0.30	3.92	3.16	78.2	3.3	17.1	10.2	4.9
8.2	0.20	1.0	0.00	4.0	7.3	0.72	6.97	2.97	66.8	5.3	29.6	7.8	8.5
10.0	na	na	na	6.3	12.4	56.71	64.05	0.31	20.5	4.0	na	0.0	6.4
6.7	0.70	na	-0.08	8.9	2.6	2.28	18.79	3.98	47.1	4.4	30.4	9.9	8.5
2.7	0.89	na	-0.03	7.3	0.7	1.72	18.10	4.03	52.1	2.1	25.5	19.5	6.4
7.4	0.32	0.8	0.00	4.2	6.6	0.80	6.22	3.88	68.7	1.6	21.5	26.8	9.2
10.0	na	na	na	9.5	2.0	7.08	7.32	0.99	36.4	4.0	na	100.0	6.7
7.6	0.77	na	0.02	6.8	23.4	1.68	14.97	4.22	55.1	2.6	23.6	18.8	9.2
1.7	2.00	34.8	-0.14	0.0	-1.3	-9.40	-60.76	2.93	1362.4	0.8	29.1	56.3	3.4
8.7	0.05	na	0.03	7.1	3.4	1.60	15.74	3.31	50.0	4.5	36.6	11.6	7.7
7.5	0.40	na	0.00	4.3	3.1	0.64	4.12	2.66	65.2	2.6	39.0	24.8	8.5
8.7	0.00	na	0.04	1.2	0.0	0.06	0.53	2.86	104.8	3.3	43.6	16.9	5.4
7.7	3.76	na	-0.13	6.2	2.1	1.26	10.27	4.19	56.6	4.9	36.8	9.2	7.6
3.4	3.38	na	0.04	6.6	3.5	1.24	10.19	3.86	52.9	3.8	23.5	10.9	7.4
7.5	0.26	1.5	0.15	9.2	38.0	1.89	17.51	3.58	66.9	4.7	18.4	4.9	9.3
7.5	0.34	na	0.00	2.6	0.8	0.71	6.16	3.00	89.3	5.0	21.7	3.1	5.5
4.3	0.81	na	0.05	6.8	5.6	1.61	16.44	4.43	56.9	3.2	12.8	12.7	6.8
4.8	1.09	na	0.12	4.4	32.6	0.79	5.55	4.15	59.9	1.6	19.2	20.1	9.5
7.5	1.32	na	0.00	7.1	4.1	1.67	12.46	3.61	57.7	5.7	45.3	7.4	8.9
7.4	0.84	na	0.00	5.0	0.8	0.87	8.28	3.84	62.3	1.9	24.7	20.6	6.6
4.4	1.00	6.4	0.00	6.3	5.5	1.09	10.35	3.53	60.9	3.1	15.5	13.4	9.0

Name	City	State	Rating	2019 Rating	2018 Rating	Total Assets ($Mil)	One Year Asset Growth	Commercial Loans	Consumer Loans	Mortgage Loans	Securities	Capitalization Index	Leverage Ratio	Risk-Based Capital Ratio
Alliance Bank	Cape Girardeau	MO	B+	B+	B+	300.0	9.89	13.4	1.8	17.2	1.6	7.1	12.1	0.0
Alliance Bank	Sulphur Springs	TX	B-	B-	B-	1082.2	11.33	8.2	1.0	12.0	38.8	7.7	9.5	16.0
Alliance Bank	Mondovi	WI	B	B	B-	196.5	4.54	3.5	3.1	16.5	19.6	8.0	9.7	0.0
Alliance Bank & Trust Co.	Gastonia	NC	C+	C+	D+	180.3	19.79	20.7	0.6	5.7	9.1	5.7	8.0	11.5
Alliance Bank Central Texas	Woodway	TX	C+	C+	C+	350.9	10.20	9.9	2.0	27.4	12.5	6.7	8.7	13.0
Alliance Community Bank	Petersburg	IL	C+	C+	B-	299.3	9.85	5.5	4.7	14.9	30.9	8.1	9.7	18.2
Alliant Bank	Madison	MO	B+	B+	B+	173.5	7.21	10.6	0.9	24.2	5.1	9.9	10.9	17.4
▲ Allied First Bank,sb	Oswego	IL	B-	C	C-	142.0	37.09	12.2	1.8	52.3	5.8	10.0	13.1	0.0
AllNations Bank	Calumet	OK	D-	D	D	43.5	-3.33	7.0	1.5	2.4	24.6	9.7	10.8	0.0
Ally Bank	Sandy	UT	B	B+	A-	174591.0	4.50	16.9	36.5	9.1	15.8	8.6	10.1	14.9
▲ Alma Bank	Astoria	NY	D+	D	D-	1228.0	3.16	14.7	0.1	3.0	3.7	8.3	9.9	13.9
Alpine Bank	Glenwood Springs	CO	A-	A-	A-	5131.0	33.58	8.5	0.7	17.5	13.8	6.4	8.4	13.6
▼ Alpine Capital Bank	New York	NY	A-	A	A-	249.5	-3.31	8.4	1.7	1.2	30.4	10.0	21.4	32.1
Altabank	American Fork	UT	A	A	A	3175.2	29.93	8.3	0.3	3.4	35.4	9.5	10.7	18.8
Altamaha Bank and Trust Co.	Vidalia	GA	B	B	B-	212.4	24.68	18.0	3.2	13.2	21.8	8.7	10.1	15.0
Alton Bank	Alton	MO	B+	B+	B+	81.1	25.07	5.6	7.0	15.4	20.4	9.4	13.7	14.5
Altoona First Savings Bank	Altoona	PA	B-	B	B	267.3	15.18	8.1	3.8	25.4	13.5	10.0	12.8	0.0
▲ Alva State Bank & Trust Co.	Alva	OK	C+	C	C+	416.0	2.55	9.1	1.7	2.5	16.9	10.0	13.8	17.4
Amalgamated Bank	New York	NY	B	B	B-	6626.2	31.71	9.6	2.7	20.3	29.6	5.4	7.4	14.0
Amalgamated Bank of Chicago	Chicago	IL	B	B	C+	915.8	2.77	1.8	3.7	3.8	16.5	10.0	11.1	17.7
Amarillo National Bank	Amarillo	TX	B+	B+	A-	6354.2	17.90	30.9	13.7	4.6	3.9	6.5	9.3	12.1
Ambler Savings Bank	Ambler	PA	B	B	B	441.3	6.43	5.8	0.0	43.7	19.9	10.0	12.5	27.5
Amboy Bank	Old Bridge	NJ	B	B-	B-	2546.3	9.17	5.0	0.0	11.9	14.3	10.0	14.3	19.2
▼ Amerant Bank, N.A.	Coral Gables	FL	D+	C+	C+	7969.3	1.46	15.0	2.4	4.4	17.3	8.2	9.8	13.6
Amerant Trust, N.A.	Coral Gables	FL	U	U	U	9.3	2.38	0.0	0.0	0.0	51.0	10.0	96.7	177.0
Amerasia Bank	Flushing	NY	A	A-	A	719.1	5.62	5.0	0.1	18.6	0.3	10.0	12.9	17.4
America's Community Bank	Blue Springs	MO	B-	C+	C+	33.2	6.39	5.9	1.6	32.6	0.8	10.0	11.2	15.5
American B&T of the Cumberlands	Livingston	TN	B+	B	B-	286.2	12.45	8.6	4.3	30.2	1.2	7.4	9.3	15.6
▼ American Bank	Bozeman	MT	B+	A-	A-	524.1	15.33	16.4	0.2	9.9	7.3	6.0	8.9	0.0
American Bank	Wagoner	OK	C	C+	C	35.7	23.17	0.8	4.0	2.0	41.5	10.0	19.8	0.0
American Bank	Allentown	PA	B+	B+	B	720.4	10.86	17.5	0.1	10.6	7.5	8.2	10.2	13.5
▲ American Bank & Trust	Huron	SD	A-	B	B	1057.8	13.95	17.1	1.3	2.9	16.0	7.5	9.4	12.9
American Bank & Trust Co.	Opelousas	LA	A-	A-	A-	207.9	10.75	12.6	3.0	26.6	10.1	10.0	11.6	0.0
American Bank & Trust Co., Inc.	Bowling Green	KY	B	B	B	510.7	19.85	13.0	0.9	18.5	6.9	5.1	8.0	11.0
▲ American Bank & Trust Co., Inc.	Covington	LA	C	C	C	203.7	13.44	10.7	1.4	25.3	0.1	5.1	8.6	0.0
American Bank and Trust Co.	Tulsa	OK	B+	A-	B+	299.4	31.26	17.1	0.1	2.8	23.6	8.8	10.2	0.0
American Bank and Trust Co., N.A.	Davenport	IA	C+	C+	C+	429.7	16.62	9.5	0.7	16.1	14.7	7.4	9.3	15.3
American Bank Center	Dickinson	ND	B-	B-	B-	1820.3	20.17	10.1	14.9	4.1	26.6	6.5	8.6	12.8
▼ American Bank of Baxter Springs	Baxter Springs	KS	C+	B-	B	122.2	19.78	6.9	0.8	8.9	41.5	9.0	10.3	0.0
American Bank of Beaver Dam	Beaver Dam	WI	B	B-	C+	180.9	20.66	5.4	1.1	14.8	16.6	8.3	9.9	0.0
American Bank of Commerce	Wolfforth	TX	B	B	B	1185.1	22.04	18.1	0.4	9.7	28.2	6.6	8.6	15.0
American Bank of Missouri	Wellsville	MO	B-	B	B	477.3	20.88	18.5	0.1	23.5	4.5	6.4	9.5	12.1
▲ American Bank of Oklahoma	Collinsville	OK	C	C	C+	348.4	11.12	20.9	7.3	14.6	1.3	4.8	7.8	10.9
American Bank of the Carolinas	Monroe	NC	D-			65.8	64.92	24.9	1.2	7.0	11.2	9.8	30.8	0.0
American Bank of the North	Nashwauk	MN	B	B-	C-	630.8	19.81	17.7	1.3	11.4	13.6	5.3	7.3	12.4
American Bank, N.A.	Le Mars	IA	C+	C+	C+	379.7	15.96	12.9	1.2	3.8	1.9	8.4	9.9	13.7
American Bank, N.A.	Corpus Christi	TX	C	B-	B	1936.7	27.75	23.4	0.8	6.3	20.4	6.3	8.3	12.8
American Bank, N.A.	Dallas	TX	B	B	C+	127.3	52.71	19.3	29.7	1.2	16.8	7.4	10.3	0.0
American Bank, N.A.	Waco	TX	B-	B	B	525.8	17.65	17.8	1.1	22.5	8.2	8.0	9.7	15.1
American Business Bank	Los Angeles	CA	B	B	B-	3321.4	42.45	30.8	0.3	0.6	28.8	5.0	7.0	14.5
American Commerce Bank, N.A.	Bremen	GA	B-	B-	C+	394.1	16.13	5.2	0.9	19.5	0.0	10.0	12.0	16.0
American Community Bank	Glen Cove	NY	B-	B	B	238.6	5.99	12.1	0.6	15.1	9.7	9.8	12.2	0.0
American Community Bank & Trust	Woodstock	IL	B+	B+	B+	786.0	35.32	37.3	0.1	6.4	13.1	5.7	10.1	0.0
American Community Bank of Indiana	Saint John	IN	B-	B-	B-	256.7	13.25	13.6	0.4	24.8	2.5	6.7	8.7	13.6
▼ American Continental Bank	City of Industry	CA	B+	A-	B+	299.2	11.52	6.4	0.0	27.9	1.4	10.0	12.1	17.3
▲ American Eagle Bank	South Elgin	IL	C+	C-	C-	256.8	-6.36	5.1	51.4	8.0	5.1	5.7	9.0	11.5
American Equity Bank	Minnetonka	MN	D	D+	D	63.8	23.63	40.3	0.5	31.0	0.0	9.6	10.8	0.0
American Exchange Bank	Elmwood	NE	B+	B	B-	55.4	19.83	23.7	1.6	8.4	22.6	9.7	10.8	0.0
▲ American Exchange Bank	Henryetta	OK	B-	B-	B-	75.4	11.39	5.0	8.1	38.0	5.9	10.0	11.0	0.0
▲ American Exchange Bank	Lindsay	OK	A-	B+	B+	73.6	-1.33	8.6	4.2	4.9	61.8	10.0	11.5	0.0

Asset Quality Index	Adjusted Non-Performing Loans as a % of Total Loans	as a % of Capital	Net Charge-Offs Avg Loans	Profitability Index	Net Income ($Mil)	Return on Assets (R.O.A.)	Return on Equity (R.O.E.)	Net Interest Spread	Overhead Efficiency Ratio	Liquidity Index	Liquidity Ratio	Hot Money Ratio	Stability Index
6.9	0.27	na	0.11	5.0	2.2	1.02	8.28	3.97	66.4	2.5	8.6	15.7	8.1
8.3	0.66	na	0.14	4.4	8.8	1.14	9.93	3.23	70.1	5.4	31.7	8.2	8.8
4.6	1.16	6.0	-0.01	6.4	2.1	1.47	14.45	3.61	58.9	3.8	28.7	12.0	7.1
3.7	0.99	na	-0.14	3.9	0.9	0.72	8.65	4.14	74.8	4.8	23.4	4.3	4.5
8.4	0.08	na	0.01	3.4	1.6	0.63	7.06	3.43	76.8	2.0	22.3	20.0	5.1
3.6	1.98	na	0.02	4.5	2.5	1.14	8.75	3.37	64.9	5.2	42.4	9.3	7.0
7.1	0.27	1.8	0.16	5.5	1.6	1.34	12.48	4.03	70.3	2.5	19.8	16.3	7.3
7.3	2.86	na	0.09	8.6	3.5	3.75	31.23	2.96	92.6	1.6	14.6	16.2	7.0
0.3	13.64	na	1.84	0.3	-0.1	-0.30	-2.71	3.68	116.5	5.1	24.7	2.8	3.5
4.3	1.78	8.1	0.66	4.9	1142.0	0.90	9.14	3.13	46.7	2.4	29.9	18.9	9.9
1.5	5.43	23.5	0.22	2.1	2.2	0.23	2.33	2.89	82.8	0.6	9.4	36.5	8.1
8.2	0.66	3.3	0.04	6.4	39.3	1.20	12.88	4.12	63.5	6.2	30.1	1.8	8.1
6.5	3.18	na	0.00	5.3	1.7	0.89	4.33	2.64	74.1	4.7	72.6	13.9	9.4
7.3	0.52	na	0.16	9.2	33.5	1.64	13.12	3.97	51.8	4.8	14.3	3.8	10.0
5.3	1.73	na	0.17	5.1	1.6	1.13	10.28	4.71	69.8	2.5	21.4	17.0	6.5
4.8	0.82	na	0.22	5.2	0.6	1.03	7.47	3.88	66.9	1.8	21.7	21.2	7.1
5.8	1.72	na	0.11	2.7	0.5	0.24	1.78	3.28	75.1	2.1	30.3	23.1	7.4
2.7	5.14	na	1.44	5.3	3.7	1.20	8.84	3.84	44.1	1.9	28.0	24.2	7.6
5.2	1.91	12.2	0.22	4.0	32.4	0.72	8.74	3.13	62.0	6.0	29.8	3.1	6.5
8.6	0.21	na	0.23	3.5	2.6	0.40	3.81	3.53	84.7	4.6	28.4	6.1	6.2
4.7	0.62	4.3	0.82	6.1	62.6	1.38	13.04	3.47	52.1	2.7	14.9	14.5	10.0
8.6	0.81	na	0.07	3.8	2.2	0.70	5.34	2.84	68.2	2.7	13.0	15.4	7.4
4.1	5.59	13.2	-0.02	7.4	31.3	1.70	11.49	3.04	48.6	3.8	25.3	13.7	10.0
4.3	1.46	9.0	0.56	1.5	-5.6	-0.09	-0.90	2.52	68.7	1.2	20.4	24.0	8.2
10.0	na	na	na	9.5	0.1	1.82	1.90	2.22	91.5	4.0	na	0.0	3.0
7.4	0.29	na	0.00	9.8	9.7	1.83	14.63	4.12	38.7	0.6	9.8	44.6	9.5
8.5	0.47	na	0.00	3.9	0.2	0.91	8.02	4.08	73.2	1.0	12.1	31.3	6.6
8.3	0.07	na	0.11	7.8	4.3	2.10	23.37	3.36	56.6	1.3	29.0	34.9	6.4
8.5	0.35	na	0.17	4.8	3.2	0.91	9.34	4.06	67.8	5.7	32.0	1.9	6.9
10.0	0.00	na	0.00	1.5	0.0	0.07	0.36	2.74	97.3	7.2	100.3	7.1	6.4
6.1	0.86	3.6	-0.07	6.1	6.6	1.27	12.39	2.92	46.0	2.5	3.2	15.4	7.7
7.9	0.08	na	0.00	7.5	13.8	1.78	17.30	3.91	51.1	3.3	15.3	12.6	9.9
8.7	0.07	na	0.01	6.5	2.4	1.63	13.28	3.93	59.7	4.3	23.2	8.1	7.5
6.3	0.79	5.1	0.06	5.4	3.9	1.10	13.27	3.36	59.7	1.9	24.3	21.3	6.1
5.0	0.72	na	0.17	3.7	1.0	0.65	8.27	4.80	79.2	1.3	12.0	21.1	4.3
9.0	0.00	na	0.21	4.7	1.8	0.87	7.98	3.09	61.4	2.7	37.9	22.5	5.5
5.4	1.26	na	-0.03	3.2	2.1	0.72	7.06	3.13	78.9	3.8	25.7	10.3	4.3
4.0	2.23	11.1	0.45	7.0	18.0	1.37	14.37	3.66	60.1	3.3	9.9	11.2	7.7
7.3	2.09	na	0.00	3.2	0.6	0.63	5.53	2.47	84.1	2.8	38.0	20.4	6.9
5.7	1.30	na	-0.05	6.2	1.7	1.39	13.23	3.64	64.4	5.4	36.7	5.7	5.3
7.1	1.34	4.8	-0.02	4.6	8.5	1.01	10.67	3.11	67.7	4.5	28.6	12.0	7.4
8.1	0.21	1.2	0.06	4.5	2.8	0.86	8.29	3.52	61.8	0.9	7.8	29.2	5.9
4.1	0.84	6.8	0.03	4.9	3.2	1.22	16.33	4.45	76.0	1.0	16.2	32.7	3.5
8.6	0.00	na	0.00	0.0	-1.7	-4.19	-11.19	2.70	230.3	4.8	50.3	12.9	0.3
4.1	1.04	na	na	3.6	0.6	0.00	0.00	na	59.1	5.0	21.7	2.7	6.5
3.8	0.67	5.2	0.00	7.8	5.0	1.82	17.37	3.10	46.1	2.0	16.1	15.9	7.7
7.4	0.05	na	1.34	2.5	4.5	0.34	3.82	3.11	78.4	6.1	36.2	4.7	7.4
6.7	0.02	na	0.59	4.4	0.8	0.98	7.08	5.46	61.9	1.4	31.3	30.5	5.5
8.0	0.01	na	0.17	4.2	3.1	0.86	8.65	3.70	73.1	3.2	20.8	13.5	6.9
8.5	0.13	1.0	0.03	4.6	19.5	0.87	11.72	3.08	57.5	6.1	27.7	1.2	6.4
3.6	2.86	na	0.00	5.6	2.9	1.03	8.95	3.36	54.0	0.8	16.5	32.0	7.4
7.5	0.00	na	0.00	3.6	1.1	0.63	5.07	3.64	74.9	3.4	13.3	11.9	7.9
8.4	0.09	na	-0.01	4.8	5.1	0.97	8.80	3.02	54.9	3.4	22.6	12.8	6.7
5.4	0.70	na	0.15	4.1	1.5	0.82	9.25	3.33	67.2	2.7	14.9	15.6	5.3
8.8	0.03	na	0.02	4.8	1.5	0.69	5.40	2.76	64.5	1.0	27.5	53.0	8.2
5.5	0.19	na	0.28	5.0	2.1	1.02	11.92	3.26	55.1	0.6	12.8	41.5	4.4
5.5	0.50	na	0.34	2.8	0.3	0.75	6.34	4.52	87.4	0.9	8.1	27.3	4.2
8.4	0.00	na	-0.21	7.0	0.7	1.81	16.95	3.73	57.5	3.6	28.5	13.1	7.1
4.1	1.80	na	0.07	4.3	0.5	0.91	8.11	5.17	73.4	3.9	20.6	10.2	6.1
9.2	0.00	na	0.17	6.3	0.9	1.57	13.49	3.69	55.3	6.5	70.9	7.2	7.2

Name	City	State	Rating	2019 Rating	2018 Rating	Total Assets ($Mil)	One Year Asset Growth	Comm- ercial Loans	Cons- umer Loans	Mort- gage Loans	Secur- ities	Capital- ization Index	Lever- age Ratio	Risk- Based Capital Ratio
▼ American Express National Bank	Sandy	UT	C+	B-	B+	134472.9	11.90	18.5	45.6	0.0	14.2	8.6	10.1	18.3
American Federal Bank	Fargo	ND	B	B	B+	678.0	6.93	9.0	0.8	15.1	7.6	6.9	8.9	14.2
American First National Bank	Houston	TX	A-	A-	B+	2047.0	9.43	6.6	0.3	3.3	3.3	7.6	11.2	13.0
American Heritage Bank	Clovis	NM	B+	B+	B	105.9	11.28	10.6	0.3	8.2	32.8	9.4	10.6	15.8
▲ American Heritage Bank	Sapulpa	OK	B	B-	B-	1424.2	26.71	7.4	2.2	12.3	53.0	6.7	8.7	22.3
American Heritage National Bank	Long Prairie	MN	A-	A-	A-	448.9	24.33	15.0	0.3	7.7	10.0	8.5	10.0	17.2
American Interstate Bank	Elkhorn	NE	A	A	A	108.8	-1.07	9.7	0.6	21.3	0.0	10.0	18.7	0.0
American Investors Bank and Mortgage	Eden Prairie	MN	B-	B-	B-	93.4	28.56	0.3	0.2	16.8	14.7	7.9	10.0	13.2
American Metro Bank	Chicago	IL	C+	C+	C	85.9	5.53	3.5	0.0	20.3	0.0	9.7	10.8	19.4
American Momentum Bank	College Station	TX	B+	B+	A-	2657.3	60.18	22.0	0.3	9.0	6.3	8.3	9.8	14.0
American Nation Bank	Ardmore	OK	B	B	B	505.6	14.58	3.0	3.7	17.0	30.7	7.8	9.6	0.0
American National Bank	Oakland Park	FL	A-	A-	A-	393.0	30.67	23.5	0.0	1.5	7.1	10.0	12.3	20.4
American National Bank	Omaha	NE	B+	B	B	4636.5	17.04	20.1	16.9	5.3	19.2	6.8	8.8	12.5
▲ American National Bank & Trust	Wichita Falls	TX	B+	B	B+	1063.5	29.78	7.2	2.2	7.9	7.9	8.4	10.1	13.7
American National Bank and Trust Co.	Danville	VA	B+	B+	A-	2886.8	18.24	16.8	0.3	9.9	12.1	7.4	9.2	13.9
▲ American National Bank of Minnesota	Brainerd	MN	B+	B-	B	333.7	10.96	11.3	2.6	32.9	1.3	9.3	10.5	15.8
American National Bank of Mount Pleasant	Mount Pleasant	TX	A-	A-	B+	122.1	17.70	9.9	7.8	13.4	41.1	9.9	10.9	0.0
American National Bank of Texas	Terrell	TX	B+	B+	B	4100.2	26.10	12.8	0.6	10.2	26.1	6.9	8.9	15.3
▲ American National Bank-Fox Cities	Appleton	WI	A	A-	B+	343.4	14.23	26.7	0.3	4.8	18.1	10.0	12.9	0.0
American Plus Bank, N.A.	Arcadia	CA	A-	A-	B+	576.3	1.83	12.3	1.6	13.4	3.4	10.0	15.1	0.0
American Pride Bank	Macon	GA	B+	A-	B+	209.4	7.30	4.0	0.1	4.3	4.7	10.0	13.9	17.0
American River Bank	Rancho Cordova	CA	B	B	B	858.5	18.94	11.8	3.2	3.3	31.1	6.3	8.3	0.0
American Riviera Bank	Santa Barbara	CA	B	B	B	930.2	33.39	20.9	0.0	11.2	7.9	6.5	8.5	13.1
American Savings Bank	Tripoli	IA	B+	B+	B+	54.6	8.43	5.0	1.6	11.1	34.0	10.0	19.5	0.0
American Savings Bank, F.S.B.	Honolulu	HI	B+	B+	B+	8075.8	13.18	12.4	2.3	30.1	23.4	6.3	8.4	0.0
American State Bank	Osceola	IA	B+	B+	B+	248.9	13.03	16.9	3.7	10.4	21.3	6.9	8.9	0.0
American State Bank	Sioux Center	IA	C+	C	C	1078.7	13.71	19.4	1.6	3.2	1.0	8.9	10.5	14.1
American State Bank	Arp	TX	C	C+	C+	503.3	14.33	21.3	2.8	19.9	3.7	4.9	8.3	10.9
American State Bank & Trust Co	Williston	ND	B+	B+	B+	620.9	-0.43	10.7	3.5	5.1	48.1	10.0	12.1	23.3
American State Bank & Trust Co.	Wichita	KS	B	B	B	770.8	18.94	12.3	2.2	4.8	21.5	6.9	10.1	0.0
American State Bank of Grygla	Grygla	MN	B-	B-	C+	61.4	4.10	8.9	5.4	10.5	13.4	8.7	10.1	19.2
American Trust and Savings Bank	Lowden	IA	C+	B-	B-	34.6	6.27	3.0	1.6	0.3	27.6	10.0	18.8	54.3
Americana Community Bank	Sleepy Eye	MN	C+	C+	C	138.8	8.72	19.6	0.4	6.9	14.9	5.8	7.8	12.6
AmeriFirst Bank	Montgomery	AL	B-	C+	C	207.3	11.86	19.0	1.7	14.9	7.3	8.0	10.1	13.3
Ameriprise Bank, FSB	Minneapolis	MN	U	U	U	7291.5	159.60	0.0	1.2	0.3	86.8	5.8	8.5	11.6
Ameris Bank	Atlanta	GA	B+	B+	B+	19786.0	11.94	12.5	6.0	19.6	5.6	8.7	10.3	13.9
AmeriServ Financial Bank	Johnstown	PA	C+	C+	C+	1246.0	7.63	17.0	1.4	12.8	15.8	6.1	9.1	11.8
▲ AmeriState Bank	Atoka	OK	C+	C+	C+	313.3	12.85	10.8	5.7	15.6	2.8	9.0	10.3	0.0
AMG National Trust Bank	Greenwood Village	CO	A-	A-	A-	556.5	18.07	3.2	3.7	2.9	32.1	7.8	9.5	13.9
Amistad Bank	Del Rio	TX	A-	A-	B+	39.6	37.29	7.3	0.5	4.8	9.7	10.0	11.1	0.0
Amory Federal S&L Assn.	Amory	MS	D+	D+	C-	79.6	-2.07	0.0	0.9	61.1	4.5	10.0	13.0	31.1
Anahuac National Bank	Anahuac	TX	B+	B+	B+	219.0	22.23	7.2	3.7	8.3	48.2	8.1	9.7	21.7
ANB Bank	Denver	CO	B+	B+	B+	3194.4	22.50	13.4	0.3	13.0	32.9	5.8	7.8	15.7
Anchor Bank	Juno Beach	FL	C	C	C	162.8	13.63	16.4	1.5	11.9	6.4	4.2	9.3	0.0
Anchor D Bank	Texhoma	OK	B+	B+	B+	227.6	-1.09	8.4	4.6	5.2	30.7	10.0	11.5	15.5
Anchor State Bank	Anchor	IL	C+	C+	C+	25.7	58.00	45.1	1.0	0.5	5.6	10.0	24.1	39.8
Anderson Brothers Bank	Mullins	SC	B-	C+	C+	1158.0	36.74	12.5	25.8	12.9	4.8	5.9	7.9	12.6
Anderson State Bank	Oneida	IL	B	B	B-	97.4	8.67	3.0	1.9	4.1	33.7	10.0	15.0	40.9
▲ Andes State Bank	Lake Andes	SD	C-	D+	D+	24.0	7.46	4.6	5.2	5.1	8.2	10.0	11.7	0.0
Andover Bank	Andover	OH	B-	B-	B	508.7	18.87	3.6	0.7	28.2	41.9	5.9	7.9	17.1
Andover State Bank	Andover	KS	C+	C+	C+	132.0	17.81	28.3	1.0	13.7	2.3	5.3	7.3	11.6
Andrew Johnson Bank	Greeneville	TN	A-	A-	B+	428.8	12.00	10.1	0.9	26.0	10.1	8.9	10.2	15.9
Androscoggin Savings Bank	Lewiston	ME	C+	C+	C+	1275.4	16.07	14.5	0.1	23.9	8.0	8.2	9.8	13.9
Angelina Savings Bank, SSB	Lufkin	TX	C+	C+	C+	74.9	13.00	10.3	17.6	19.1	0.0	6.0	8.1	17.4
Anna State Bank	Anna	IL	B+	B+	B+	95.6	14.21	2.2	1.8	19.4	49.5	10.0	14.3	0.0
Anna-Jonesboro National Bank	Anna	IL	B+	B+	B	239.6	9.07	5.2	3.5	24.3	40.7	10.0	13.3	30.7
Anstaff Bank	Green Forest	AR	B-	B	B	824.7	18.04	10.1	3.2	16.3	14.8	6.3	8.6	12.0
Anthem Bank & Trust	Plaquemine	LA	C	C	C-	164.8	4.84	18.2	1.4	18.9	16.6	8.3	9.8	16.8
Antwerp Exchange Bank Co.	Antwerp	OH	B-	B-	B	132.7	13.70	7.3	4.8	21.9	20.5	7.6	9.4	13.8
▼ ANZ Guam, Inc.	Hagatna	GU	C	B-	C+	380.9	18.03	8.8	0.2	4.7	0.0	10.0	12.8	0.0

Asset Quality Index	Adjusted Non-Performing Loans as a % of Total Loans	as a % of Capital	Net Charge-Offs Avg Loans	Profitability Index	Net Income ($Mil)	Return on Assets (R.O.A.)	Return on Equity (R.O.E.)	Net Interest Spread	Overhead Efficiency Ratio	Liquidity Index	Liquidity Ratio	Hot Money Ratio	Stability Index
2.6	3.96	11.6	2.84	10.0	3066.3	3.07	30.11	6.07	55.6	3.1	40.8	2.2	10.0
7.2	0.18	na	0.18	6.6	7.8	1.59	18.31	4.41	61.0	2.8	3.6	9.3	7.1
6.8	0.15	na	0.06	7.0	20.3	1.37	12.48	3.59	46.5	0.7	12.9	52.0	9.7
5.6	1.63	na	-0.02	6.2	0.9	1.24	10.40	3.88	62.0	3.4	44.5	19.2	7.7
8.8	0.62	na	0.08	4.8	11.5	1.20	12.54	3.51	65.5	3.2	18.5	13.6	7.9
8.2	0.22	0.7	0.00	6.4	3.8	1.21	10.70	3.46	54.2	5.1	29.6	4.7	7.3
8.6	0.00	0.0	-0.18	10.0	2.4	2.97	15.53	4.54	36.8	4.3	25.1	8.4	10.0
9.8	0.00	na	-0.16	3.7	0.4	0.56	5.08	3.87	76.3	1.4	15.9	25.9	5.8
4.3	3.96	13.2	-0.02	3.2	0.3	0.56	5.06	3.86	83.0	1.3	30.6	48.3	6.1
4.9	1.15	na	0.02	5.5	14.2	0.75	5.49	3.76	65.4	4.2	19.1	8.5	10.0
7.1	0.13	na	0.23	4.7	4.0	1.11	11.04	3.24	62.0	1.7	36.1	40.0	6.3
7.4	0.00	na	0.00	6.4	3.1	1.14	8.71	3.63	56.1	4.6	25.5	6.2	8.0
6.0	0.64	na	0.12	7.0	54.2	1.70	17.35	3.94	48.9	2.1	19.9	7.2	9.2
5.4	0.48	6.3	0.00	5.8	8.7	1.18	10.86	3.70	59.7	2.5	16.2	8.7	9.5
7.6	0.19	1.0	0.03	5.3	23.0	1.14	8.84	3.41	52.1	3.7	18.9	11.5	9.9
5.6	0.93	5.6	0.00	5.8	3.4	1.41	13.42	4.56	68.4	1.0	9.4	17.7	6.9
8.4	0.00	na	0.11	6.0	1.3	1.44	12.03	3.85	65.4	2.2	36.1	28.7	7.9
8.2	0.55	2.5	0.03	4.7	26.3	0.94	9.90	3.31	68.0	4.5	14.4	5.6	8.1
7.6	0.34	na	0.02	9.2	5.3	2.15	15.60	3.73	46.1	0.9	22.2	19.4	9.5
7.2	0.00	na	0.18	7.8	5.2	1.23	8.28	3.47	34.9	0.6	13.3	50.3	9.8
4.4	1.23	na	0.00	4.5	1.3	0.85	5.97	4.18	70.1	0.8	16.7	32.7	9.1
6.8	1.23	na	0.00	4.7	5.4	0.90	8.11	3.57	57.2	4.4	26.4	7.7	7.7
8.2	0.05	na	0.01	4.9	5.0	0.81	8.47	4.07	66.2	4.9	20.9	3.7	6.1
8.2	0.00	na	0.02	5.9	0.5	1.33	6.54	3.30	52.2	4.6	60.8	15.2	9.1
6.1	1.17	6.6	0.41	4.1	41.9	0.73	7.95	3.33	65.5	4.9	19.8	3.7	7.8
5.0	1.16	na	0.10	7.1	2.8	1.55	16.30	3.95	59.4	2.1	20.5	18.8	7.3
3.9	1.75	na	0.24	6.8	12.3	1.58	13.98	3.22	48.3	1.5	13.2	20.2	8.6
4.5	0.71	na	0.13	3.6	3.5	0.96	10.23	4.00	78.9	1.7	13.8	21.5	5.6
5.2	2.94	na	0.14	9.7	10.7	2.28	18.20	3.55	44.0	6.0	42.1	4.3	9.8
4.6	0.95	na	-0.01	3.9	3.8	0.72	5.40	3.36	70.2	3.9	23.2	10.4	8.0
6.5	0.00	na	0.32	5.1	0.6	1.28	11.89	3.84	67.6	5.8	38.0	4.1	6.2
9.4	1.26	na	-0.85	2.4	0.1	0.30	1.58	2.93	89.6	6.8	88.6	7.9	6.7
3.9	1.52	na	-0.03	3.9	0.6	0.64	7.74	3.57	74.5	3.6	20.1	7.9	4.5
5.5	1.27	5.3	-0.01	4.3	1.3	0.84	8.17	4.26	71.0	2.8	16.0	15.2	5.7
10.0	0.22	na	2.81	5.1	38.9	0.88	12.55	1.71	39.6	8.6	95.7	0.0	8.5
4.6	1.37	5.7	0.15	6.7	183.1	1.29	9.23	3.83	55.2	3.7	7.5	8.3	9.8
8.2	0.27	na	0.04	3.3	4.6	0.51	5.72	3.35	78.5	2.7	8.8	15.0	7.1
3.8	2.31	na	0.25	5.7	3.2	1.40	15.40	4.13	68.3	1.8	29.5	25.7	6.3
8.5	0.19	na	0.00	9.2	7.0	1.67	16.09	2.21	67.8	7.6	63.4	0.2	8.2
7.6	0.02	na	-0.02	7.8	0.4	1.49	12.04	4.72	66.6	4.0	34.9	13.2	7.0
8.1	0.56	na	0.10	0.5	-0.2	-0.26	-1.96	1.80	111.7	1.9	42.0	51.5	5.5
8.8	0.12	na	-0.09	5.0	2.8	1.61	16.82	3.41	71.0	3.2	42.6	19.9	7.2
8.0	0.52	3.3	0.18	5.1	26.4	1.21	14.56	3.52	64.8	6.2	31.1	2.5	7.6
6.8	0.30	na	-0.01	2.9	0.3	0.29	3.16	3.61	91.9	1.4	17.8	26.7	4.7
7.2	0.00	na	0.30	5.5	3.1	1.84	15.86	3.47	66.9	0.9	23.1	33.3	7.8
8.3	0.00	na	0.00	2.9	0.1	0.35	1.73	3.36	78.5	2.7	22.1	16.0	6.9
4.3	0.79	6.5	0.82	7.8	10.7	1.39	16.21	6.60	62.9	1.7	21.6	22.0	6.8
9.3	0.13	na	0.00	4.5	0.8	1.11	7.10	2.65	57.9	6.1	72.6	10.0	8.0
4.5	7.42	na	-0.17	3.7	0.1	0.71	6.16	3.07	78.4	2.5	51.8	28.2	3.7
8.0	0.49	na	-0.01	3.9	3.0	0.88	8.91	2.90	73.2	4.9	36.0	8.6	5.3
5.1	0.44	na	0.00	4.1	0.7	0.71	9.48	3.78	68.3	3.5	3.3	10.5	4.4
6.4	0.72	3.5	0.10	5.6	3.2	1.03	9.75	4.20	65.9	4.1	20.5	9.0	6.7
7.0	0.70	na	0.00	3.7	6.5	0.76	7.27	3.34	69.6	1.7	17.2	8.2	7.7
4.8	2.06	na	0.10	3.9	0.4	0.68	7.66	4.08	78.3	5.6	45.7	7.0	4.0
8.4	1.54	na	0.05	4.4	0.6	0.91	6.25	3.00	62.1	3.3	49.4	20.0	7.7
6.8	1.95	na	0.07	4.7	1.6	0.90	6.28	3.72	63.3	3.8	37.4	15.0	6.7
5.4	0.72	na	0.01	5.6	7.8	1.33	14.27	3.64	61.4	1.7	16.2	21.7	7.2
5.0	1.89	na	0.00	3.2	0.7	0.60	5.81	3.62	85.8	1.6	23.1	25.1	6.3
4.5	1.08	na	0.10	3.6	0.5	0.51	5.24	3.57	83.2	3.9	23.6	10.1	5.9
7.0	2.83	na	2.51	0.8	-2.4	-0.92	-6.60	1.84	132.3	7.3	88.4	5.9	7.3

Name	City	State	2019 Rating	2018 Rating	2018 Rating	Total Assets ($Mil)	One Year Asset Growth	Asset Mix (As a % of Total Assets)				Capital-ization Index	Lever-age Ratio	Risk-Based Capital Ratio
								Comm-ercial Loans	Cons-umer Loans	Mort-gage Loans	Secur-ities			
▲ Apex Bank	Camden	TN	B-	B-	C-	872.8	47.55	3.7	1.1	58.8	0.2	10.0	11.1	0.0
Apollo Bank	Miami	FL	B-	B-	C	838.4	12.27	9.1	2.0	12.3	20.1	7.5	9.4	14.0
Apollo Trust Co.	Apollo	PA	B+	B+	B	167.7	5.59	4.1	1.8	46.6	17.8	9.9	11.0	19.1
▼ Apple Bank for Savings	New York	NY	C	B-	C+	16332.1	8.10	31.1	0.1	0.6	22.0	5.1	7.1	13.7
Apple Creek Banking Co.	Apple Creek	OH	B-	B-	C+	168.5	17.49	14.6	0.3	21.9	8.2	5.7	7.7	12.0
Apple River State Bank	Apple River	IL	A-	A-	B	448.2	24.32	10.8	2.5	10.9	30.0	7.8	9.5	16.2
Applied Bank	Wilmington	DE	A	A	A	185.1	-5.07	10.8	0.0	2.7	0.0	10.0	23.5	61.0
Aquesta Bank	Cornelius	NC	B-	B	B-	687.4	36.16	31.2	0.0	4.3	4.5	7.2	9.1	14.6
▲ Arbor Bank	Nebraska City	NE	C+	C	C-	465.4	32.16	27.0	1.2	9.7	6.7	5.2	7.2	11.9
Arcola First Bank	Arcola	IL	C+	B-	B-	119.4	7.53	2.4	0.4	2.6	80.3	10.0	11.0	24.0
Argentine Federal Savings	Kansas City	KS	C	C	C	56.2	1.11	0.0	0.4	48.8	30.1	10.0	13.6	0.0
Arizona Bank & Trust	Phoenix	AZ	B+	B+	B+	1039.3	49.48	28.2	0.8	5.6	27.3	6.3	8.3	12.3
▲ Arkansas County Bank	De Witt	AR	A-	B	B-	179.2	-0.99	5.4	2.1	18.5	21.3	10.0	11.7	0.0
Arlington State Bank	Arlington	MN	B+	B+	C+	59.7	18.01	4.7	1.4	2.3	30.8	8.0	9.7	24.7
Armed Forces Bank, N.A.	Fort Leavenworth	KS	A-	A-	B+	1167.8	4.00	9.9	0.4	8.8	17.9	10.0	15.0	23.5
Armor Bank	Forrest City	AR	C-	C	C	187.4	97.40	17.2	0.9	10.2	15.9	10.0	12.0	16.4
Armstrong Bank	Muskogee	OK	B-	B-	B-	2103.6	105.14	8.8	3.1	15.4	20.9	7.2	9.2	14.7
Armstrong County Building and Loan Assn.	Ford City	PA	C	C	C	90.1	3.74	0.0	0.8	51.4	35.0	10.0	14.5	35.3
Aroostook County Federal S&L Assn.	Caribou	ME	B-	C+	B-	149.1	10.99	15.0	11.1	46.8	14.7	9.2	10.5	16.3
Arrowhead Bank	Llano	TX	A-	A-	B	213.5	10.64	4.4	3.6	22.0	15.1	8.8	10.2	18.0
Arthur State Bank	Union	SC	B+	B+	B	601.8	17.67	10.5	1.2	28.6	10.9	6.5	8.5	13.2
Artisans' Bank	Wilmington	DE	C	C	C	605.7	11.67	5.8	0.1	16.6	25.0	6.5	8.5	12.1
Arundel Federal Savings Bank	Glen Burnie	MD	C-	C	C+	443.9	2.92	0.4	0.1	60.4	13.6	10.0	15.1	0.0
▼ Arvest Bank	Fayetteville	AR	C+	B-	B-	24028.6	24.30	13.5	7.1	16.0	22.6	5.8	7.8	12.7
Ascent Bank	Helena	MT	B	B	C+	86.2	49.14	31.3	0.8	13.9	2.0	9.7	10.8	19.3
Ashton State Bank	Ashton	IA	B	B	B+	50.1	0.93	7.9	2.4	9.7	25.6	10.0	12.8	0.0
Ashton State Bank	Ashton	NE	D-	D-	D-	19.7	-3.44	2.4	1.4	0.2	0.5	7.6	10.5	13.0
Asian Bank	Philadelphia	PA	B-	B-	C+	271.2	18.47	4.7	0.0	13.8	2.4	6.4	8.4	13.6
▲ Asian Pacific National Bank	San Gabriel	CA	C	C	C+	58.6	4.80	0.4	0.0	6.3	3.4	10.0	17.5	0.0
▲ Aspire Bank	Fargo	ND	C	D+	C	54.2	33.22	34.6	0.7	9.6	0.2	5.4	9.1	11.3
Associated Bank, N.A.	Green Bay	WI	B-	B	B-	34651.8	6.45	17.9	0.9	23.2	15.5	7.1	9.0	12.9
Associated Trust Co., N.A.	Milwaukee	WI	U	U	U	68.6	7.37	0.0	0.0	0.0	1.5	10.0	87.8	157.7
Astra Bank	Scandia	KS	B-	B-	C+	349.6	21.92	11.2	0.9	8.9	36.8	6.5	8.5	13.8
▼ Atascosa Bank	Pleasanton	TX	B-	B	B-	93.8	5.32	3.0	2.2	2.8	57.0	8.8	10.2	0.0
Athol Savings Bank	Athol	MA	C+	B-	C+	506.8	13.00	4.3	1.7	36.8	22.2	10.0	12.5	22.0
Atkins Savings Bank & Trust	Atkins	IA	B+	B+	B+	111.5	15.11	9.6	3.4	11.6	29.2	10.0	12.5	0.0
Atlanta National Bank	Atlanta	IL	B-	B-	C+	70.9	19.49	2.5	3.2	9.8	58.5	10.0	12.2	30.4
Atlantic Capital Bank, N.A.	Atlanta	GA	B+	B+	B	2923.5	21.25	32.3	5.1	1.0	15.7	10.0	11.5	15.6
Atlantic Community Bankers Bank	Camp Hill	PA	C+	B-	B	775.1	-5.57	2.1	0.1	2.4	16.8	10.0	12.8	25.1
▼ Atlantic Union Bank	Richmond	VA	B	B+	B+	19882.8	14.30	17.8	3.3	8.0	15.4	7.4	9.5	12.8
▼ Auburn Banking Co.	Auburn	KY	B-	B	C+	91.5	12.94	9.5	3.4	21.8	19.2	6.1	8.6	11.8
Auburn Savings Bank, FSB	Auburn	ME	C	C	C	89.1	10.43	10.2	0.8	53.4	5.9	7.6	9.4	14.6
▲ Auburn State Bank	Auburn	NE	A-	A-	A-	201.5	14.36	3.8	1.0	9.2	37.1	10.0	16.7	0.0
AuburnBank	Auburn	AL	B+	A-	B+	938.0	13.59	7.5	0.8	9.2	34.2	9.1	10.4	18.8
Audubon State Bank	Audubon	IA	A-	B+	B	126.6	6.43	8.6	2.6	11.8	6.0	7.7	9.5	14.7
Austin Bank, Texas N.A.	Jacksonville	TX	A	A	A-	2179.0	18.24	12.6	5.1	20.9	9.3	10.0	13.1	0.0
Austin Capital Bank SSB	Austin	TX	B+	B+	B+	226.5	77.43	1.5	57.6	18.4	0.8	6.0	8.0	37.5
Austin County State Bank	Bellville	TX	B+	B+	B+	256.2	38.67	30.7	1.3	21.5	9.0	7.4	9.3	14.7
Auto Club Trust, FSB	Dearborn	MI	D-	D-	D	585.4	4.57	0.0	21.9	21.6	44.1	7.4	9.3	14.8
Availa Bank	Carroll	IA	B+	B+	B+	1266.5	18.58	12.0	0.5	8.4	20.1	5.1	8.4	0.0
AVB Bank	Broken Arrow	OK	B-	B	B	443.2	15.21	17.5	0.3	19.9	8.2	7.6	9.4	14.1
Avidbank	San Jose	CA	B+	B+	B	1441.0	29.54	29.2	0.1	0.6	2.8	6.4	9.3	12.0
Avidia Bank	Hudson	MA	C+	B	B	2005.2	20.80	32.1	0.5	18.0	11.5	6.5	8.5	13.3
Axiom Bank, N.A.	Maitland	FL	C	C+	B-	674.5	-1.52	16.7	14.8	17.8	0.0	10.0	12.5	16.9
▼ Axos Bank	San Diego	CA	B+	A-	A-	12426.1	14.23	7.2	2.8	36.8	1.9	6.8	8.8	12.7
▼ b1Bank	Baton Rouge	LA	C+	B	B-	3956.6	78.00	23.9	1.2	10.5	13.8	2.7	9.1	0.0
BAC Community Bank	Stockton	CA	B	B	B	755.9	17.20	13.3	1.1	4.8	22.5	6.8	9.4	0.0
BAC Florida Bank	Coral Gables	FL	B+	B+	B	2266.8	-0.18	1.3	0.3	51.6	9.1	9.4	10.6	19.7
▲ Badger Bank	Fort Atkinson	WI	A	A-	B+	159.2	16.48	7.8	1.0	28.1	15.7	10.0	12.7	0.0
Baker-Boyer National Bank	Walla Walla	WA	B+	B+	B	680.3	12.22	12.5	0.6	12.3	22.1	6.6	8.7	18.4

| Asset Quality Index | Adjusted Non-Performing Loans | | Net Charge-Offs | Profitability Index | Net Income ($Mil) | Return on Assets (R.O.A.) | Return on Equity (R.O.E.) | Net Interest Spread | Overhead Efficiency Ratio | Liquidity Index | Liquidity Ratio | Hot Money Ratio | Stability Index |
	as a % of Total Loans	as a % of Capital	Avg Loans										
4.3	1.27	15.3	0.06	10.0	16.5	2.94	23.17	6.12	37.9	0.7	17.4	27.4	9.6
4.1	1.89	na	0.01	4.1	4.4	0.76	7.75	2.96	67.9	4.3	35.1	12.0	6.7
8.4	0.13	na	0.03	5.5	1.4	1.13	10.44	4.30	69.1	4.6	13.9	3.5	6.8
7.5	0.23	2.7	0.00	2.5	31.9	0.27	3.13	1.87	74.5	1.4	18.4	23.7	6.6
7.5	0.02	0.1	0.21	5.5	1.3	1.09	13.93	4.53	66.9	4.9	19.6	3.3	4.2
8.3	0.21	na	0.00	6.1	4.5	1.51	14.72	3.04	58.2	3.7	30.8	13.4	6.5
9.3	0.00	na	0.00	5.6	1.2	0.94	3.97	2.78	80.2	7.8	70.9	0.2	9.4
4.7	1.37	12.7	0.06	4.0	3.5	0.76	8.39	3.19	62.4	3.4	9.3	11.2	5.3
4.9	0.45	na	0.01	5.6	4.2	1.34	17.97	3.80	72.1	4.1	10.7	7.0	4.1
10.0	0.00	na	0.00	3.4	0.6	0.71	5.65	2.35	72.6	5.9	57.3	9.8	7.2
10.0	0.25	na	0.00	2.2	0.1	0.25	1.82	2.93	88.0	2.0	40.2	38.4	7.0
7.1	0.10	0.7	0.11	7.8	9.8	1.45	15.68	4.04	53.4	5.2	20.5	2.1	7.5
5.5	1.67	na	0.13	6.4	2.0	1.56	13.19	4.32	63.8	3.5	24.0	12.6	7.7
3.7	0.56	na	0.16	3.9	0.4	0.84	7.75	3.31	72.6	6.2	64.4	7.1	6.1
7.3	0.66	na	0.08	9.5	15.6	1.89	11.05	3.09	77.4	6.1	37.9	5.6	8.7
7.2	0.09	na	0.40	1.4	-0.1	-0.04	-0.39	3.29	83.3	2.5	15.5	16.7	5.6
4.3	2.42	12.2	0.11	6.1	16.5	1.20	11.91	3.69	62.7	3.3	34.1	19.3	10.0
8.7	0.36	na	-0.01	2.1	0.1	0.21	1.46	1.40	79.9	2.2	47.2	38.5	6.8
5.4	0.56	na	0.02	3.8	0.9	0.80	7.47	3.17	70.5	2.2	27.0	19.5	5.8
8.7	0.00	0.0	0.00	6.1	2.2	1.44	13.76	3.88	60.7	5.7	37.9	4.3	6.0
5.5	1.29	6.2	0.00	6.0	5.2	1.23	13.46	4.44	65.2	5.0	22.0	3.0	6.0
5.4	0.95	na	0.00	2.5	1.2	0.27	2.89	2.98	83.3	3.6	31.1	13.9	6.0
5.9	2.46	na	-0.11	1.8	0.3	0.08	0.55	2.03	97.1	1.9	27.6	24.8	7.4
4.3	1.46	6.9	0.30	2.7	37.4	0.23	2.19	3.22	82.1	6.1	30.4	3.0	8.3
5.8	0.93	na	0.00	4.2	0.4	0.73	6.34	4.04	69.6	4.2	32.1	11.5	6.0
6.0	0.00	4.3	1.01	4.1	0.3	0.78	5.84	3.06	61.0	2.7	36.0	19.9	8.0
0.0	7.32	na	0.00	0.5	0.0	-0.28	-2.64	4.06	98.5	1.7	20.8	21.9	3.1
4.8	0.78	na	0.00	4.5	1.7	0.88	10.60	3.15	60.5	1.1	27.4	39.3	5.5
9.4	0.00	na	0.00	2.0	0.1	0.24	1.39	2.79	91.1	2.5	58.6	52.5	7.3
7.9	0.00	na	-0.02	5.5	0.5	1.57	18.36	4.03	55.8	3.2	12.5	12.6	4.5
5.4	1.03	5.6	0.40	4.3	248.8	0.97	8.41	2.55	61.3	4.1	14.0	3.2	9.8
7.3	na	0.0	na	10.0	12.2	24.87	29.00	1.08	74.3	4.0	319.9	0.0	5.7
6.1	0.33	na	0.21	5.1	3.1	1.24	12.39	4.04	68.1	4.7	25.2	5.2	5.8
9.9	0.00	na	0.00	3.8	0.5	0.71	6.62	2.22	64.3	6.8	96.4	9.0	5.4
8.7	0.69	3.1	0.02	1.6	0.1	0.02	0.16	2.67	85.3	3.6	41.7	14.9	7.0
5.1	0.40	na	0.67	6.6	1.3	1.66	12.76	3.20	45.3	3.0	42.8	22.8	7.9
9.3	0.81	na	0.03	3.4	0.3	0.65	4.95	2.84	74.3	5.8	61.2	9.2	6.2
7.2	0.83	2.1	0.13	4.1	15.8	0.74	5.65	3.41	52.3	5.0	21.0	0.3	9.4
9.0	0.32	0.9	0.00	2.5	1.1	0.16	1.24	1.96	84.6	2.9	42.6	23.7	7.5
6.1	0.36	1.9	0.09	4.2	110.4	0.79	5.40	3.38	58.0	3.9	14.8	9.4	9.6
5.9	1.03	na	-0.01	6.3	0.9	1.40	15.70	3.76	64.9	1.8	19.3	20.6	5.7
4.0	2.33	na	0.08	3.1	0.3	0.44	5.03	3.50	85.0	1.0	9.6	30.3	4.4
9.0	0.41	na	0.07	5.6	2.0	1.42	8.33	3.20	51.5	2.3	20.3	18.3	8.4
8.9	0.12	na	-0.03	4.0	5.0	0.76	6.66	3.00	67.8	3.8	31.3	12.9	7.4
7.2	0.53	na	0.01	7.8	1.6	1.76	14.66	3.88	48.8	2.9	19.7	12.8	8.6
6.6	0.89	4.0	0.15	7.7	20.8	1.35	9.73	4.34	59.1	4.0	17.5	9.4	10.0
6.3	0.00	na	0.00	8.0	2.9	2.21	25.63	4.64	84.3	3.8	15.4	10.0	5.6
6.1	0.10	na	-0.01	5.8	2.2	1.37	15.52	4.43	63.2	0.8	14.6	35.1	6.2
5.5	0.85	3.5	0.05	0.0	-6.6	-1.53	-14.33	1.27	161.1	0.8	26.0	41.4	6.0
7.3	0.26	1.5	0.00	4.5	7.8	0.89	8.32	3.19	68.4	3.6	22.9	12.7	9.1
7.2	0.15	na	0.43	3.8	1.9	0.58	5.98	4.24	67.4	2.6	14.9	16.0	5.6
8.0	0.03	0.2	0.06	5.3	7.4	0.77	7.71	3.94	68.5	4.0	29.7	14.7	8.2
6.0	1.04	na	0.15	3.3	7.7	0.54	5.64	3.50	77.7	1.4	21.1	7.0	7.6
4.6	1.57	na	0.08	0.3	-3.4	-0.66	-4.62	2.95	121.5	0.8	17.4	44.5	7.7
4.5	1.53	14.2	0.26	9.8	167.4	1.84	19.98	4.37	37.8	1.7	10.0	11.6	8.9
6.7	0.31	3.2	0.06	4.6	21.2	0.87	7.90	4.08	65.2	1.7	11.6	20.7	8.9
5.5	0.85	na	-0.03	5.5	6.8	1.27	12.16	3.71	63.1	5.2	26.8	3.1	7.3
6.3	2.25	10.2	0.20	5.3	17.0	1.00	9.72	2.86	56.2	1.9	30.2	42.1	8.9
7.4	1.08	na	-0.01	9.1	2.0	1.82	13.92	3.71	53.9	4.8	31.9	7.5	7.7
7.1	0.85	na	0.00	4.3	4.2	0.86	9.42	3.46	79.9	6.4	43.2	1.8	6.6

Name	City	State	2019 Rating	2018 Rating	Total Assets ($Mil)	One Year Asset Growth	Asset Mix (As a % of Total Assets) Commercial Loans	Consumer Loans	Mortgage Loans	Securities	Capitalization Index	Leverage Ratio	Risk-Based Capital Ratio
▲ Balboa Thrift and Loan Assn.	Chula Vista	CA	B	B-	B-	331.7	2.05	0.0	73.8	0.9	0.0	8.7	13.1	0.0
Baldwin State Bank	Baldwin City	KS	B-	C+	B-	88.1	12.84	7.3	2.9	29.1	24.6	8.6	10.1	0.0
Ballston Spa National Bank	Ballston Spa	NY	B-	B-	C+	667.3	15.62	9.7	4.4	30.2	9.8	7.0	9.0	13.5
Baltic State Bank	Baltic	OH	C	C+	B+	87.0	21.42	4.7	2.6	33.6	7.6	5.2	7.2	11.5
Banc of California, N.A.	Santa Ana	CA	C-	C	B-	7725.3	-10.16	8.4	0.1	15.8	16.1	10.0	12.2	18.1
BancCentral, N.A.	Alva	OK	C	C	C	507.8	-3.24	15.6	1.3	3.1	25.9	5.7	8.4	11.5
BancFirst	Oklahoma City	OK	A-	A-	A-	8760.6	15.98	23.0	4.1	11.1	6.2	7.4	9.3	15.1
Banco Do Brasil Americas	Miami	FL	C+	C+	C+	710.6	8.67	2.1	0.6	45.8	1.4	7.9	9.6	0.0
Banco Popular de Puerto Rico	San Juan	PR	C-	C-	D+	55262.0	31.79	6.0	9.6	12.6	36.1	5.2	7.2	18.0
Bancorp Bank	Wilmington	DE	B	B	B-	6180.4	24.93	8.8	21.6	0.8	20.5	6.5	8.5	14.5
BancorpSouth Bank	Tupelo	MS	B+	B+	B+	23557.3	18.60	11.9	0.9	17.1	24.0	6.6	8.6	14.2
Bandera Bank	Bandera	TX	B+	B+	B	75.5	7.25	5.1	3.5	30.0	14.3	8.8	10.2	0.0
▼ Banesco USA	Coral Gables	FL	C	B-	B-	1989.1	8.36	12.5	0.0	16.2	23.5	5.9	7.9	13.3
Bangor Savings Bank	Bangor	ME	B-	B-	B-	5571.7	21.20	11.1	0.5	26.4	20.5	6.3	8.4	14.1
▲ BANK	Wapello	IA	B+	C+	C+	100.4	8.24	15.8	5.2	17.4	0.0	10.0	12.8	0.0
▼ Bank & Trust Co.	Litchfield	IL	B-	B	B-	397.1	16.36	10.6	5.8	12.4	22.7	7.8	9.5	14.8
Bank 1st	West Union	IA	A	A	A-	149.4	23.53	3.7	2.0	13.6	30.3	10.0	13.7	0.0
Bank 21	Carrollton	MO	B-	C+	B-	148.3	0.32	13.0	1.1	35.6	3.1	6.3	8.3	13.5
BANK 34	Alamogordo	NM	C+	C+	C+	464.8	20.81	14.7	0.0	8.2	11.6	7.1	9.0	12.7
Bank and Trust, SSB	Del Rio	TX	B+	B+	B+	482.8	13.12	7.9	2.4	34.2	15.0	6.4	8.5	19.2
▲ Bank First, N.A.	Manitowoc	WI	B+	B	B	2639.3	22.33	19.5	1.1	16.7	6.7	6.0	9.3	11.7
Bank Five Nine	Oconomowoc	WI	C+	C+	B-	1373.6	10.00	11.8	0.1	12.6	9.5	8.0	9.6	16.2
Bank Forward	Hannaford	ND	B+	B	B	817.1	24.78	11.9	2.6	8.7	3.2	5.5	8.8	0.0
Bank Independent	Sheffield	AL	B	B	B	1917.5	12.36	21.2	1.1	12.0	3.3	6.7	8.7	14.0
Bank Iowa	West Des Moines	IA	B-	B	B	1606.1	18.57	10.9	0.7	7.5	21.8	6.7	9.0	12.3
▼ Bank Leumi USA	New York	NY	B-	B	B	7351.9	7.98	26.6	0.0	0.4	18.5	9.7	11.1	14.8
Bank Michigan	Brooklyn	MI	D+	C-	D	126.1	21.87	22.8	0.1	12.0	8.2	6.1	8.2	12.5
Bank Midwest	Spirit Lake	IA	B	B-	B-	1084.2	15.44	26.9	0.5	5.9	7.7	6.7	8.7	12.6
Bank Northwest	Hamilton	MO	A-	A-	A-	182.3	13.96	18.0	1.9	11.1	10.1	6.5	8.7	0.0
▲ Bank of Abbeville & Trust Co.	Abbeville	LA	B	B-	B-	190.9	10.03	13.8	1.8	14.7	25.4	10.0	15.8	0.0
Bank of Advance	Advance	MO	A	A-	B+	356.2	8.32	8.8	6.1	29.4	13.1	10.0	13.4	0.0
▼ Bank of Alapaha	Alapaha	GA	B-	B+	B+	205.7	16.29	18.7	6.5	16.4	17.9	8.0	9.7	17.8
Bank of Alma	Alma	WI	A+	A	A-	276.3	13.28	4.5	0.7	6.0	26.6	10.0	42.8	69.1
Bank of America California, N.A.	San Francisco	CA	A-	A-	A-	22254.0	66.53	0.0	0.0	35.6	0.0	8.0	9.7	45.7
Bank of America, N.A.	Charlotte	NC	B+	B+	B	2157008.0	18.98	13.7	7.0	10.5	26.4	5.7	7.7	14.6
▲ Bank of Anguilla	Anguilla	MS	C	C-	C-	157.0	4.22	6.1	4.3	7.2	20.1	8.6	10.1	13.8
Bank of Ann Arbor	Ann Arbor	MI	A-	A-	A-	2219.8	29.52	24.3	0.5	4.8	3.4	8.8	10.4	14.0
Bank of Baker	Baker	MT	C	B-	C	169.1	19.88	14.3	0.9	1.8	11.8	9.0	10.3	0.0
▲ Bank of Bartlett	Bartlett	TN	C+	C+	C	427.6	21.54	19.0	2.3	24.9	17.3	5.6	7.6	15.6
Bank of Bearden	Bearden	AR	B+	B+	B	67.3	23.75	7.4	2.6	6.5	11.9	8.9	10.3	0.0
Bank of Beaver City	Beaver	OK	B-	B	B	134.5	4.69	15.5	2.8	12.9	33.9	10.0	11.2	0.0
Bank of Belle Glade	Belle Glade	FL	C+	B-	C+	126.4	27.27	9.6	0.3	9.9	34.1	5.8	7.8	23.0
Bank of Belleville	Belleville	IL	C+	C+	C+	299.3	32.44	25.6	0.9	11.5	14.7	5.8	7.8	12.0
Bank of Bennington	Bennington	NE	B-	B-	C	169.5	16.23	24.9	1.3	10.2	8.5	9.7	10.8	14.8
Bank of Bennington	Bennington	VT	C+	B	B	496.5	17.18	7.3	0.1	51.2	13.8	8.8	10.2	0.0
Bank of Benoit	Benoit	MS	C-	C-	C-	21.1	20.98	2.0	14.1	0.1	21.9	10.0	18.3	50.0
Bank of Billings	Billings	MO	B-	B-	C+	65.2	11.40	22.2	3.7	25.8	0.0	7.1	9.6	0.0
Bank of Bird-in-Hand	Bird in Hand	PA	B	B	B	532.4	17.65	7.0	0.1	23.5	0.0	10.0	13.2	15.7
Bank of Blue Valley	Overland Park	KS	B+	B+	B	1424.3	5.79	19.7	1.1	2.0	33.2	9.7	10.8	16.3
Bank of Bluffs	Bluffs	IL	C+	B-	B-	59.5	9.47	3.1	4.6	15.2	24.7	10.0	13.2	0.0
Bank of Botetourt	Buchanan	VA	B-	B	C+	586.7	21.08	9.6	3.5	26.0	2.7	6.5	9.3	0.0
▼ Bank of Bourbonnais	Bourbonnais	IL	B+	A-	B+	80.3	17.98	3.0	0.3	9.5	0.8	9.1	10.4	19.9
Bank of Bozeman	Bozeman	MT	C+	C+	C+	99.9	28.98	18.2	0.8	12.1	10.1	6.3	8.4	12.2
Bank of Brenham, N.A.	Brenham	TX	B	B	B+	551.1	21.06	3.9	0.8	6.5	76.5	9.4	10.6	0.0
Bank of Brewton	Brewton	AL	B-	C+	B	55.2	16.77	18.0	4.1	4.1	43.9	10.0	22.0	0.0
Bank of Bridger, N.A.	Bridger	MT	B	B	B	678.7	27.94	9.4	2.1	6.9	43.1	6.9	8.9	18.4
▲ Bank of Brodhead	Brodhead	WI	A-	B+	B+	233.9	48.58	8.9	2.0	12.6	22.1	10.0	12.6	0.0
Bank of Brookfield-Purdin, N.A.	Brookfield	MO	B-	B-	B-	91.4	3.41	5.2	1.5	4.9	52.4	10.0	12.3	37.1
▼ Bank of Brookhaven	Brookhaven	MS	B	B+	B+	188.6	13.62	8.2	2.4	13.6	38.9	9.2	10.5	17.9
Bank of Buffalo	Buffalo	KY	B	B	B	74.2	0.96	1.0	6.0	24.6	39.5	10.0	11.5	19.5

Asset Quality Index	Adjusted Non-Performing Loans as a % of Total Loans	as a % of Capital	Net Charge-Offs Avg Loans	Profitability Index	Net Income ($Mil)	Return on Assets (R.O.A.)	Return on Equity (R.O.E.)	Net Interest Spread	Overhead Efficiency Ratio	Liquidity Index	Liquidity Ratio	Hot Money Ratio	Stability Index
4.7	0.40	na	1.23	5.5	2.4	0.97	7.65	6.36	51.0	0.4	10.1	71.6	6.5
6.4	0.63	na	0.02	4.5	0.7	1.10	10.44	2.93	64.1	5.0	37.3	9.0	5.3
6.3	0.39	na	0.01	3.9	3.7	0.78	9.10	3.38	70.9	4.2	12.8	6.8	5.6
8.9	0.02	na	0.00	3.1	0.3	0.47	6.16	3.99	85.7	1.8	23.3	15.6	4.1
6.2	1.27	6.5	0.06	1.5	2.4	0.04	0.34	3.18	84.7	3.4	22.2	12.5	7.6
1.7	3.13	38.2	0.20	2.0	4.0	1.04	10.29	3.47	91.0	0.8	17.9	34.9	6.4
5.8	1.38	7.9	0.06	6.2	60.1	0.96	9.04	3.65	56.7	5.1	22.5	4.3	8.9
8.1	0.32	na	0.01	3.6	3.0	0.60	5.36	3.23	74.9	2.1	30.5	23.5	7.1
1.9	8.98	30.8	0.89	5.4	338.0	0.96	11.10	3.54	60.1	5.4	30.7	7.5	7.0
5.6	0.85	4.9	0.10	7.4	62.9	1.43	16.65	3.47	58.0	1.6	27.8	0.0	5.6
5.5	0.85	4.2	0.14	5.0	159.3	0.95	7.82	3.40	63.0	4.0	14.6	8.7	10.0
8.2	0.04	na	0.03	4.7	0.5	0.95	8.87	3.44	74.4	5.5	48.8	8.9	7.3
6.8	1.35	7.5	0.03	2.6	6.7	0.47	5.51	3.35	73.3	2.1	27.8	23.3	7.4
7.6	0.60	3.6	0.01	4.0	32.1	0.83	8.39	3.20	70.3	4.1	9.7	4.4	7.4
6.0	1.04	na	0.00	6.2	1.2	1.62	13.29	3.86	66.6	2.3	17.5	16.4	7.1
4.5	1.66	8.7	0.05	3.8	1.8	0.65	6.35	3.24	61.6	1.8	22.0	22.7	6.2
8.5	0.01	na	0.01	6.4	1.4	1.38	9.61	3.65	60.2	5.6	48.6	8.6	8.7
5.0	0.14	na	0.30	6.5	1.9	1.68	20.29	3.31	60.7	2.9	11.3	14.3	6.2
6.5	0.90	na	0.02	2.8	1.1	0.35	3.59	3.81	75.4	2.4	14.0	13.0	5.0
8.6	0.08	na	0.01	5.9	5.0	1.47	15.26	3.90	67.2	3.9	22.9	10.5	6.3
6.1	0.87	5.8	0.04	7.7	28.9	1.58	13.85	3.81	48.1	3.9	6.7	7.7	9.0
5.3	1.18	na	0.04	7.8	17.5	1.84	18.40	3.97	63.3	1.8	15.9	17.8	8.0
5.7	0.37	3.6	-0.02	6.2	8.0	1.36	14.12	3.67	71.6	1.9	22.7	12.7	7.7
4.7	0.89	11.2	0.25	5.0	12.7	0.92	10.04	4.46	72.3	2.9	22.8	14.6	7.9
5.5	1.26	9.6	0.04	4.1	11.1	0.98	10.29	3.35	66.8	2.7	14.3	15.8	8.4
4.5	2.27	13.4	0.35	3.4	33.3	0.61	5.23	3.38	63.3	2.8	24.3	12.6	9.1
3.5	1.32	na	0.13	0.0	-0.6	-0.73	-8.63	3.41	110.0	0.8	16.0	26.6	2.6
7.7	0.15	na	0.02	5.8	8.1	1.08	11.31	4.11	64.0	2.8	17.5	11.4	8.7
8.1	0.17	1.3	0.01	10.0	3.4	2.59	29.20	4.73	43.1	3.7	13.3	10.5	7.1
7.6	2.98	na	-0.03	3.9	1.0	0.75	4.60	3.03	71.2	3.9	38.1	14.8	7.3
7.2	0.72	na	0.12	9.7	5.8	2.20	17.07	4.53	53.2	1.8	10.8	19.5	9.3
5.9	0.40	na	1.04	3.1	0.5	0.35	3.34	3.10	74.6	1.4	26.1	29.5	5.7
8.9	2.46	na	0.00	9.8	5.4	2.49	6.15	3.83	13.3	7.0	71.8	5.2	9.7
6.6	4.13	11.4	-0.03	6.8	151.0	1.08	9.95	1.93	22.3	7.7	70.8	0.0	8.5
6.2	0.96	3.3	0.43	4.9	9411.0	0.62	5.97	2.39	57.4	7.1	51.3	1.6	9.0
2.8	2.47	na	0.33	4.3	1.2	1.03	11.03	4.14	69.1	1.0	15.1	29.7	3.8
7.1	0.73	4.8	0.09	7.6	20.5	1.34	13.03	3.98	46.1	5.2	24.1	5.0	9.8
1.4	6.28	na	0.65	7.4	1.9	1.60	15.51	3.78	45.9	5.6	35.6	3.8	7.0
3.3	2.71	na	0.36	4.2	2.4	0.81	9.57	4.44	75.3	4.8	14.9	3.7	4.0
8.6	0.07	na	-0.02	4.5	0.4	1.03	9.25	3.11	63.4	4.7	52.5	13.4	6.2
8.3	0.08	na	1.06	2.9	0.8	0.75	6.42	3.77	87.0	2.2	28.5	20.1	6.5
8.4	1.90	na	0.00	3.1	0.5	0.54	6.28	2.24	73.0	6.4	61.3	7.8	4.3
8.4	0.00	na	0.03	4.5	2.2	1.09	14.53	2.52	59.6	1.6	11.6	21.4	3.8
8.1	0.00	na	-0.06	4.6	1.2	1.02	8.51	4.04	72.4	4.8	17.1	3.7	6.2
7.5	0.64	2.8	0.29	3.3	1.8	0.53	5.00	2.87	68.3	3.3	21.9	13.2	6.1
7.3	0.03	na	0.20	1.4	0.0	0.03	0.23	3.35	89.5	3.5	83.1	29.0	4.5
3.1	1.08	6.0	-0.05	4.4	0.3	0.64	4.67	4.86	80.3	3.6	15.2	11.2	6.4
8.7	0.03	na	0.00	4.3	2.9	0.78	6.55	2.76	58.9	3.7	14.5	10.3	7.5
7.5	0.30	1.2	-0.03	6.0	13.1	1.32	8.97	4.06	57.6	5.7	28.5	4.5	8.5
7.0	0.75	na	0.09	2.3	0.1	0.25	1.76	3.54	85.3	4.3	35.5	11.7	6.7
5.9	0.56	na	0.17	4.2	3.3	0.80	8.53	3.38	63.9	1.4	18.0	26.8	6.0
7.6	0.00	na	-0.01	2.0	0.1	0.12	1.11	2.34	93.5	2.4	39.8	28.1	6.3
4.3	1.31	9.1	-0.14	3.6	0.2	0.35	3.50	4.29	79.5	1.9	24.7	20.6	5.9
9.0	0.78	0.8	0.06	5.0	7.2	1.93	13.35	2.62	46.8	2.8	56.7	40.2	7.9
8.3	1.28	2.2	0.01	4.0	0.3	0.88	3.76	4.43	80.0	6.5	65.2	5.5	6.6
7.6	0.77	na	0.12	5.2	5.1	1.05	10.18	3.69	57.2	4.8	32.8	8.0	6.6
8.3	1.04	na	-0.06	5.4	1.8	1.14	8.00	3.36	58.6	3.2	43.3	20.0	7.8
9.5	0.00	na	0.00	3.7	0.5	0.75	5.77	2.64	70.8	6.0	63.0	8.3	7.2
8.6	0.00	na	0.02	4.2	1.2	0.89	8.09	3.21	69.5	3.4	36.5	16.9	6.6
6.6	0.93	na	-0.16	5.9	0.7	1.32	11.11	3.16	52.7	2.2	41.8	25.6	7.8

Name	City	State	2019 Rating	2018 Rating	Rating	Total Assets ($Mil)	One Year Asset Growth	Asset Mix (As a % of Total Assets)				Capital- ization Index	Lever- age Ratio	Risk- Based Capital Ratio
								Comm- ercial Loans	Cons- umer Loans	Mort- gage Loans	Secur- ities			
Bank of Burlington	Burlington	CO	B+	B+	B	73.8	13.41	22.3	0.8	0.0	14.9	10.0	12.2	0.0
Bank of Cadiz and Trust Co.	Cadiz	KY	B-	B-	B-	134.6	14.41	2.7	2.4	19.9	28.7	6.2	8.3	16.5
Bank of Calhoun County	Hardin	IL	C+	C+	C	72.4	8.42	1.4	2.4	31.0	8.9	7.2	9.1	0.0
Bank of Camilla	Camilla	GA	B+	B+	B+	116.6	11.57	7.3	1.2	15.1	24.0	10.0	14.8	0.0
Bank of Canton	Canton	MA	B	B	B	721.8	12.08	6.9	0.2	25.6	8.1	10.0	11.4	16.7
Bank of Carbondale	Carbondale	IL	B	B+	B+	261.6	6.26	12.5	1.6	15.2	29.7	10.0	12.8	0.0
Bank of Cashton	Cashton	WI	B+	A-	A-	118.6	23.04	20.8	1.9	10.1	12.0	7.8	9.5	15.0
Bank of Castile	Castile	NY	B	B	B	1782.7	20.20	15.8	0.5	14.0	17.4	6.2	8.2	12.6
Bank of Cattaraugus	Cattaraugus	NY	C-	D+	D+	25.3	5.55	6.8	8.0	15.5	36.1	7.1	9.1	19.9
Bank of Cave City	Cave City	AR	B-	B-	C+	144.7	18.64	7.2	3.7	16.2	20.1	6.6	8.7	16.9
Bank of Central Florida	Lakeland	FL	B+	B+	B	790.6	54.45	21.8	1.4	9.4	8.0	5.3	7.3	15.3
Bank of Charles Town	Charles Town	WV	B-	B-	B-	630.8	24.92	11.1	1.2	29.5	8.4	7.1	9.1	15.4
Bank of Charlotte County	Phenix	VA	A-	A-	A-	154.7	10.72	5.1	2.8	32.5	14.1	10.0	13.5	20.4
Bank of Cherokee County	Hulbert	OK	C+	C+	C+	134.9	15.71	7.7	7.9	23.0	1.3	6.1	8.1	14.0
Bank of Chestnut	Chestnut	IL	D	D	D	18.5	2.11	4.1	9.2	33.3	17.8	8.2	9.8	0.0
Bank of Clarendon	Manning	SC	A	A	A-	311.9	12.40	8.5	2.5	10.7	25.1	10.0	12.9	0.0
Bank of Clarke County	Berryville	VA	B+	B+	B	1065.3	26.14	12.6	1.7	20.5	14.3	7.5	9.3	13.6
Bank of Clarks	Clarks	NE	C+	C+	C+	39.1	-0.08	5.8	12.4	4.8	3.3	8.6	10.6	13.8
Bank of Clarkson	Clarkson	KY	B+	B+	B+	131.3	8.82	1.5	5.3	25.3	18.8	10.0	13.3	21.7
Bank of Cleveland	Cleveland	TN	A	A-	C+	330.3	18.52	8.5	0.5	17.5	1.0	10.0	14.2	20.0
Bank of Clovis	Clovis	NM	A-	A-	B+	248.7	19.75	13.1	2.7	12.9	33.7	10.0	11.6	25.2
Bank of Colorado	Fort Collins	CO	A-	A-	A-	5327.0	20.31	11.0	0.7	10.6	28.2	6.7	8.7	14.8
Bank of Columbia	Columbia	KY	B-	B	C+	172.2	19.82	11.9	4.5	16.1	16.0	5.8	9.3	0.0
Bank of Commerce	Ammon	ID	A	A	A	1514.1	20.66	16.6	0.7	2.1	6.7	10.0	14.6	18.7
Bank of Commerce	Chanute	KS	B	B-	B-	362.8	100.41	9.1	3.4	16.1	29.0	7.0	9.0	16.5
Bank of Commerce	White Castle	LA	B-	B-	B-	59.6	0.11	11.0	2.5	9.1	23.3	10.0	12.2	0.0
Bank of Commerce	Greenwood	MS	A-	A-	B	654.9	20.04	10.5	2.1	16.1	36.2	8.1	9.8	0.0
Bank of Commerce	Chelsea	OK	A-	B+	B	183.0	23.42	13.8	7.3	14.3	8.5	9.9	10.9	18.3
Bank of Commerce	Chouteau	OK	C+	C+	C	40.9	7.11	6.6	3.1	14.3	28.7	6.4	8.4	20.9
Bank of Commerce	Duncan	OK	D+	C-	D+	354.9	14.65	18.6	1.1	4.0	8.0	5.9	10.3	0.0
Bank of Commerce	Rawlins	WY	A-	A-	A-	151.6	8.25	11.5	1.5	15.2	35.9	10.0	11.9	22.0
Bank of Commerce & Trust Co.	Crowley	LA	C+	B-	B-	357.5	17.92	5.5	1.6	5.0	71.4	10.0	11.6	0.0
Bank of Commerce and Trust Co.	Wellington	KS	B-	B-	B-	88.0	10.48	7.1	5.4	16.2	32.7	6.6	8.6	16.3
Bank of Cordell	Cordell	OK	B+	B+	B-	39.1	4.41	12.2	1.0	41.5	0.0	10.0	11.6	0.0
Bank of Coushatta	Coushatta	LA	B	B	B	246.3	9.97	4.7	1.2	14.5	50.7	7.7	9.8	0.0
Bank of Crocker	Waynesville	MO	C+	C+	B-	134.3	7.50	5.7	1.7	12.2	28.2	10.0	11.2	25.4
Bank of Crockett	Bells	TN	B+	B+	B+	200.9	13.17	8.7	2.7	6.2	51.9	7.5	9.4	16.3
Bank of Dade	Trenton	GA	A-	A-	B+	124.5	14.98	1.4	4.3	24.5	48.7	9.1	10.4	23.6
Bank of Dawson	Dawson	GA	B+	A-	B+	127.5	3.00	6.1	3.0	16.0	18.6	10.0	18.8	0.0
Bank of Deerfield	Deerfield	WI	A	A-	B+	172.8	11.50	10.4	1.3	29.4	5.5	10.0	12.4	16.4
Bank of Delight	Delight	AR	A-	A-	B+	156.5	17.40	9.9	1.8	14.9	8.3	10.0	12.6	0.0
Bank of Delmarva	Salisbury	MD	C+	C	C-	948.9	19.76	7.1	0.2	12.4	6.5	6.0	8.0	12.8
Bank of Denton	Denton	KS	C	C	C	19.0	3.61	3.6	7.6	31.7	15.4	10.0	18.3	0.0
Bank of Denver	Denver	CO	B-	C+	B-	252.0	8.64	0.4	4.1	9.9	22.3	6.6	8.7	14.7
Bank of DeSoto, N.A.	Desoto	TX	A-	A-	B	230.3	27.34	12.1	11.1	17.6	1.0	7.0	9.0	0.0
Bank of Dickson	Dickson	TN	B-	B	B	258.6	8.53	5.5	1.7	35.3	40.2	10.0	11.5	0.0
▲ Bank of Dixon County	Ponca	NE	A-	B+	B-	103.8	14.55	10.8	5.6	14.8	11.5	10.0	12.0	19.3
Bank of Doniphan	Doniphan	NE	B	B	B-	125.3	9.62	13.4	2.4	7.2	24.4	7.7	9.5	13.3
▼ Bank of Dudley	Dublin	GA	B+	A-	B	253.0	16.27	12.8	3.8	13.0	10.1	10.0	11.9	0.0
Bank of Eastern Oregon	Heppner	OR	D	D+	C	692.8	43.51	19.9	0.5	3.3	2.1	1.4	9.1	0.0
Bank of Easton	North Easton	MA	B-	B-	B-	175.6	13.88	0.0	0.4	40.4	22.4	9.5	10.7	0.0
Bank of Edison	Edison	GA	C-	C	C	56.7	13.18	7.9	5.2	11.6	29.8	6.7	8.7	14.2
Bank of Edmonson County	Brownsville	KY	B+	B	B-	232.9	6.89	2.0	2.6	25.3	24.6	10.0	11.4	19.5
Bank of Elgin	Elgin	NE	A-	B+	B+	63.2	11.66	7.0	1.1	0.5	4.1	10.0	14.2	0.0
Bank of Elk River	Elk River	MN	B+	B+	B	565.3	26.00	25.4	1.8	7.5	26.0	5.9	7.9	15.5
▲ Bank of England	England	AR	A	B+	B	586.0	24.39	5.1	0.6	51.1	7.4	10.0	17.2	20.0
Bank of Erath	Erath	LA	B-	B	B	105.1	5.67	10.7	2.2	18.6	10.9	10.0	13.0	0.0
Bank of Estes Park	Estes Park	CO	A-	A-	B+	155.6	11.50	0.9	0.0	12.6	20.4	8.1	9.7	0.0
Bank of Eufaula	Eufaula	OK	C+	C+	B-	99.6	5.28	2.5	5.9	13.7	47.6	10.0	13.3	0.0
Bank of Evergreen	Evergreen	AL	B-	B-	C+	63.4	4.97	15.2	3.0	19.0	30.1	10.0	13.3	0.0

Asset Quality Index	Adjusted Non-Performing Loans as a % of Total Loans	as a % of Capital	Net Charge-Offs Avg Loans	Profitability Index	Net Income ($Mil)	Return on Assets (R.O.A.)	Return on Equity (R.O.E.)	Net Interest Spread	Overhead Efficiency Ratio	Liquidity Index	Liquidity Ratio	Hot Money Ratio	Stability Index
8.6	0.00	na	0.00	5.4	0.6	1.28	9.63	3.52	60.7	2.3	33.5	23.4	7.7
6.7	0.58	3.1	0.16	3.1	0.5	0.58	6.51	2.94	81.3	4.2	49.2	16.5	4.3
7.9	0.82	na	0.00	3.3	0.3	0.54	5.43	3.05	75.8	4.9	39.6	10.3	4.9
7.1	2.28	na	-0.08	4.2	0.7	0.89	5.58	3.88	75.2	1.6	23.1	24.8	8.2
5.7	1.02	na	0.00	4.0	3.9	0.74	6.89	3.42	75.2	4.2	11.4	4.3	6.7
3.4	5.66	na	0.05	5.5	2.1	1.14	8.76	3.04	56.3	5.0	25.6	3.5	7.1
8.5	0.15	na	0.05	6.7	1.3	1.55	14.91	3.68	54.4	3.7	36.8	15.0	7.1
7.9	0.43	3.7	0.00	5.6	13.5	1.09	13.08	3.49	52.2	3.4	11.1	6.8	6.8
6.4	1.13	na	0.06	3.5	0.1	0.58	6.94	4.51	86.2	5.3	23.3	1.0	4.1
5.2	0.89	na	0.14	4.1	0.9	0.88	9.71	3.85	71.4	1.7	19.2	19.1	5.6
8.6	0.03	na	-0.01	4.8	4.4	0.89	11.57	3.60	49.7	4.8	35.1	3.9	5.4
7.7	0.31	na	-0.06	3.7	2.8	0.65	7.04	3.19	72.1	3.2	22.4	13.9	5.6
7.6	1.31	4.1	0.00	5.2	1.1	0.97	6.57	4.09	72.3	3.6	21.5	11.7	8.3
4.6	0.99	na	0.03	3.2	0.5	0.54	6.49	4.10	87.0	2.4	25.6	18.4	4.6
3.0	3.07	14.3	0.08	2.1	0.0	0.10	1.02	3.72	92.4	2.2	20.3	18.3	3.6
8.8	0.44	na	0.02	5.6	2.6	1.14	8.40	3.39	63.5	5.0	35.7	7.8	7.8
7.3	0.87	na	-0.17	5.7	8.8	1.20	12.14	3.80	66.6	4.2	22.1	9.9	8.0
3.9	0.26	5.2	0.18	4.5	0.2	0.77	7.39	4.43	73.2	3.8	16.1	9.9	6.5
6.3	2.58	6.1	0.00	7.9	1.4	1.51	11.04	4.09	58.7	3.4	32.5	15.3	8.5
7.6	0.60	na	0.22	8.6	3.6	1.52	10.76	4.00	56.2	4.5	21.2	6.3	9.0
8.6	0.78	na	-0.44	7.0	2.6	1.45	12.03	4.10	58.1	3.7	35.0	14.7	7.0
7.6	0.62	3.7	0.00	6.3	44.8	1.22	12.39	3.32	56.2	4.8	25.1	7.8	8.6
3.4	2.04	na	0.02	7.6	2.1	1.73	17.54	4.13	58.3	1.8	24.4	22.7	7.5
8.4	0.26	1.0	0.06	9.8	19.6	1.85	12.60	4.05	39.1	5.2	38.9	11.1	10.0
8.8	0.00	na	0.00	5.6	3.5	1.34	15.74	3.60	58.7	3.1	16.9	13.8	5.2
5.5	1.39	7.8	0.03	3.2	0.2	0.48	3.91	3.57	86.6	2.2	21.3	18.6	6.2
7.4	0.18	na	0.05	6.8	6.6	1.48	13.26	3.30	46.5	2.8	27.7	16.7	7.0
7.1	0.22	na	0.06	5.2	1.3	1.00	8.62	4.98	71.5	3.0	25.1	14.9	6.5
9.3	0.03	na	0.04	3.0	0.1	0.45	5.28	3.70	87.6	5.3	37.4	7.1	4.5
1.7	3.11	na	0.18	4.9	3.0	1.19	10.51	3.80	62.5	1.6	21.2	25.1	7.5
8.9	0.03	na	-0.01	6.2	1.5	1.38	11.34	4.03	57.6	1.7	19.7	23.2	7.9
6.2	4.01	na	0.02	2.5	0.7	0.28	2.47	1.99	81.8	5.2	44.7	10.0	5.5
4.9	0.65	na	0.01	4.1	0.7	1.11	11.85	3.90	83.5	3.4	31.5	15.0	5.7
8.6	0.00	na	-1.27	9.8	0.8	2.73	24.23	5.51	62.2	0.6	7.5	35.5	7.0
4.8	3.60	na	0.38	4.7	2.1	1.16	11.59	3.03	65.1	1.9	17.2	19.8	6.8
5.5	3.44	10.9	-0.07	2.9	0.6	0.59	4.93	2.74	84.3	3.7	45.6	18.0	6.3
9.0	0.01	na	0.01	7.0	2.2	1.55	13.75	3.61	47.5	1.9	29.8	26.1	7.0
5.5	1.71	na	-0.27	7.4	1.6	1.77	15.81	3.91	59.1	5.2	41.2	9.1	8.0
5.1	4.15	na	0.45	7.3	1.6	1.66	8.87	4.19	57.1	1.8	27.9	26.2	8.8
8.5	0.64	na	0.00	10.0	3.5	2.84	23.47	3.65	47.9	0.4	9.6	44.1	9.1
7.5	0.47	na	0.47	5.1	1.3	1.09	8.65	2.98	53.4	1.3	21.6	29.6	9.3
4.7	1.55	7.8	0.21	3.7	3.1	0.48	5.12	3.60	66.4	2.6	32.2	17.2	6.0
6.7	1.40	na	-0.09	3.6	0.1	0.77	4.12	3.29	72.8	4.9	30.6	4.4	6.6
7.3	0.08	na	0.18	3.9	1.3	0.70	7.42	3.64	75.7	4.0	14.6	8.4	6.1
6.9	0.47	na	0.26	7.7	2.5	1.60	16.18	6.15	60.5	2.9	44.1	25.2	6.4
5.3	3.42	na	0.01	3.7	1.3	0.72	5.82	3.05	73.5	4.2	39.8	14.1	7.4
7.0	0.42	na	0.26	6.0	0.9	1.17	9.66	3.95	56.6	2.2	20.3	18.3	7.3
8.0	0.00	na	0.00	4.7	1.0	1.05	9.89	3.96	69.7	3.7	16.1	10.6	6.8
6.7	0.97	na	0.09	4.9	1.6	0.90	7.21	4.29	67.4	4.1	22.4	9.1	7.1
2.4	2.02	na	0.00	5.5	4.3	1.02	11.39	4.96	71.2	4.9	22.6	3.6	5.5
9.0	0.43	na	0.00	3.6	0.8	0.62	5.51	2.14	64.0	3.2	50.5	25.2	6.3
4.2	2.56	15.7	0.37	3.3	0.4	0.88	9.96	3.60	81.1	2.1	21.2	19.1	4.2
5.8	2.93	na	0.11	5.0	2.0	1.17	9.98	3.38	66.5	1.6	28.8	29.6	8.3
6.9	0.00	na	-0.01	9.6	1.1	2.34	15.81	3.85	48.0	4.6	24.1	6.0	9.2
7.3	0.00	na	-0.01	5.6	4.9	1.27	13.82	3.95	62.7	4.9	33.7	7.7	6.6
7.0	1.19	3.7	-0.01	9.7	36.7	9.51	69.70	2.54	78.2	1.0	16.3	30.8	9.8
5.1	1.37	11.6	0.51	3.2	0.3	0.43	3.24	4.31	81.4	2.4	26.2	18.6	7.0
9.4	0.00	0.0	0.00	5.3	1.2	1.18	10.89	3.65	67.9	6.8	53.4	2.5	6.9
7.7	1.52	na	0.15	3.2	0.5	0.68	4.76	3.39	72.0	3.6	46.7	18.0	5.9
5.4	2.70	na	2.02	3.1	0.2	0.39	2.82	3.81	74.3	2.5	36.7	24.6	6.1

Name	City	State	2019 Rating	2018 Rating	Rating	Total Assets ($Mil)	One Year Asset Growth	Asset Mix (As a % of Total Assets)				Capital-ization Index	Lever-age Ratio	Risk-Based Capital Ratio
								Comm-ercial Loans	Cons-umer Loans	Mort-gage Loans	Secur-ities			
Bank of Farmington	Farmington	IL	B-	B-	B-	198.2	9.86	15.4	2.6	12.1	24.1	9.6	10.7	17.4
Bank of Fayette County	Piperton	TN	B-	B-	B-	748.0	13.41	6.6	6.6	29.0	6.6	6.4	9.2	0.0
Bank of Feather River	Yuba City	CA	B+	A-	B+	184.4	35.93	21.5	0.1	2.3	0.0	3.0	9.6	0.0
Bank of Fincastle	Fincastle	VA	C	D+	D-	267.0	20.14	23.1	0.4	17.1	5.7	9.8	10.8	16.2
Bank of Forest	Forest	MS	B+	B+	B+	224.0	10.17	6.4	3.8	8.8	33.9	10.0	12.6	0.0
Bank of Frankewing	Frankewing	TN	B+	B+	B+	344.1	13.56	10.3	3.9	16.7	6.6	8.8	10.7	0.0
Bank of Franklin	Meadville	MS	B+	A-	B+	168.6	15.40	10.4	3.9	18.5	27.6	8.8	10.2	0.0
Bank of Franklin County	Washington	MO	C+	C+	C	296.9	8.71	17.9	2.1	15.2	13.6	3.8	8.6	0.0
Bank of George	Las Vegas	NV	A	A	B+	430.3	37.53	16.2	0.0	1.2	0.7	10.0	12.4	0.0
▲ Bank of Gibson City	Gibson City	IL	B-	C+	C	105.4	22.13	6.4	3.8	10.1	17.3	6.0	8.0	12.8
Bank of Gleason	Gleason	TN	B+	B+	B+	119.1	5.79	8.3	7.3	12.2	42.8	10.0	22.7	39.3
Bank of Glen Burnie	Glen Burnie	MD	C-	C	C	430.9	12.38	8.1	19.3	18.0	26.6	7.2	9.2	12.7
▲ Bank of Grain Valley	Kansas City	MO	A	A-	A-	103.4	10.24	13.6	0.8	16.7	12.0	10.0	20.4	0.0
Bank of Grand Lake	Grove	OK	B-	B-	B-	210.2	14.79	7.4	2.5	21.9	19.2	4.7	6.7	12.3
Bank of Grandin	Grandin	MO	C+	B-	B-	182.6	8.12	12.6	7.2	11.3	28.8	10.0	14.8	18.5
Bank of Gravette	Gravette	AR	C	C+	C+	133.9	-1.47	5.5	2.2	20.7	8.1	5.9	9.2	0.0
Bank of Greeley	Greeley	KS	B	B	B	38.9	1.57	6.5	3.5	15.9	7.4	10.0	13.3	0.0
Bank of Greeleyville	Greeleyville	SC	B+	B+	C+	103.6	17.25	18.4	7.0	12.0	17.9	10.0	11.6	0.0
Bank of Greene County	Catskill	NY	B+	B+	B+	1796.1	27.67	9.9	0.3	19.8	38.0	6.2	8.3	16.2
Bank of Guam	Hagatna	GU	C+	C+	C+	2366.7	21.73	13.2	8.8	6.3	25.1	5.4	7.4	13.8
Bank of Gueydan	Gueydan	LA	B-	B	B-	79.2	5.96	4.2	6.2	0.8	61.9	10.0	20.5	0.0
Bank of Halls	Halls	TN	B	B	B	102.2	19.19	10.1	2.0	5.8	39.0	7.0	9.0	15.3
▲ Bank of Hamilton	Hamilton	ND	B-	C+	C-	22.0	16.54	2.1	2.9	0.0	3.3	8.0	9.7	0.0
Bank of Hancock County	Sparta	GA	B	B+	B+	81.4	11.20	4.5	4.7	13.1	58.8	10.0	19.8	0.0
Bank of Hartington	Hartington	NE	B	B-	C+	108.5	15.02	12.4	1.7	4.8	23.1	6.9	8.9	13.9
Bank of Hawaii	Honolulu	HI	B	B	B	20081.1	13.82	6.7	5.2	23.4	32.3	4.5	6.5	12.8
Bank of Hays	Hays	KS	B	B	B-	312.6	23.03	20.5	1.8	7.8	30.5	7.6	9.4	0.0
Bank of Hazelton	Hazelton	ND	B	B	B-	53.7	-2.04	4.1	0.8	0.7	22.5	9.0	10.3	0.0
▲ Bank of Hazlehurst	Hazlehurst	GA	C-	D+	D	112.6	-5.18	12.1	2.5	8.4	27.5	10.0	13.1	24.6
Bank of Hemet	Riverside	CA	A	A-	B+	854.6	18.32	1.9	0.0	0.2	8.0	8.4	9.9	14.7
▼ Bank of Herrin	Herrin	IL	C+	B-	B-	277.4	10.79	13.6	1.3	11.1	23.7	7.2	9.1	14.1
Bank of Hillsboro, N.A.	Hillsboro	IL	B+	B	B-	442.4	22.66	10.5	0.8	7.7	21.2	7.2	10.1	0.0
Bank of Hindman	Hindman	KY	C+	C+	C	267.8	26.69	6.9	1.1	10.9	50.1	6.1	8.1	0.0
Bank of Holland	Holland	NY	B-	B-	B-	166.0	15.27	4.0	1.7	42.8	24.0	5.7	7.7	13.3
▲ Bank of Holly Springs	Holly Springs	MS	B	B	B-	266.2	8.99	13.0	6.5	22.1	13.4	10.0	13.1	0.0
Bank of Holyrood	Holyrood	KS	B	B	B+	66.4	4.81	21.4	5.1	21.1	9.4	10.0	14.6	23.0
Bank of Hope	Los Angeles	CA	B	B	B	16731.7	8.79	17.0	0.2	4.4	12.3	9.4	11.1	14.5
Bank of Houston	Houston	MO	D	D-	D-	45.0	43.25	38.4	0.4	6.0	3.4	8.5	10.0	15.4
Bank of Houston, N.A.	Houston	TX	D+	D+	C	264.4	120.33	31.1	0.5	10.3	1.5	10.0	15.0	0.0
Bank of Hydro	Hydro	OK	A-	A	B+	131.4	8.60	9.5	1.8	32.6	0.6	8.6	11.5	0.0
Bank of Iberia	Iberia	MO	C	C	D+	60.2	8.21	2.0	4.7	24.0	13.6	6.8	8.8	17.9
Bank of Idaho	Idaho Falls	ID	B-	B-	B-	578.8	24.08	23.0	1.5	7.2	18.7	7.7	9.4	14.5
Bank of Jackson	Jackson	TN	B	B-	B-	221.8	15.87	10.4	1.2	6.8	59.6	7.2	9.2	19.4
Bank of Jackson Hole	Jackson	WY	B+	B	C+	1178.0	29.08	10.9	0.3	15.6	9.3	6.7	8.7	13.8
Bank of Jamestown	Jamestown	KY	B-	B-	B-	217.4	5.75	5.2	0.9	10.4	25.0	8.9	11.4	14.0
Bank of Kampsville	Kampsville	IL	B	B	B	117.3	7.68	2.5	7.1	17.3	33.3	10.0	17.1	0.0
▲ Bank of Kaukauna	Kaukauna	WI	B-	C	D+	116.5	19.36	30.8	1.5	9.6	3.5	7.4	9.3	15.0
Bank of Kilmichael	Kilmichael	MS	B+	B+	B+	208.7	18.92	12.2	4.7	12.2	31.8	6.9	8.9	0.0
▼ Bank of Kirksville	Kirksville	MO	B	B+	B	436.4	1.32	3.8	0.5	13.7	38.4	10.0	12.1	39.3
Bank of Kremlin	Kremlin	OK	B-	B-	C+	325.9	9.27	15.3	1.7	6.3	8.0	9.3	10.5	0.0
▼ Bank of Labor	Kansas City	KS	C-	C	C	781.2	25.50	18.8	0.1	2.4	43.7	5.2	7.2	13.6
Bank of LaFayette, Georgia	Lafayette	GA	B	B	B	290.1	12.35	2.6	6.0	19.0	55.9	10.0	12.3	30.7
Bank of Lake Mills	Lake Mills	WI	A-	A-	B+	245.3	7.55	4.0	16.6	28.9	8.7	10.0	12.3	17.7
Bank of Lake Village	Lake Village	AR	A-	A-	B+	72.5	9.35	8.5	1.6	4.2	20.7	10.0	12.0	21.9
Bank of Landisburg	Landisburg	PA	B+	B+	B+	333.8	11.18	2.3	1.7	40.9	18.3	10.0	17.4	0.0
Bank of Lewellen	Lewellen	NE	C+	C+	B-	25.0	10.79	3.1	1.0	0.0	22.1	10.0	25.3	0.0
Bank of Lexington, Inc.	Lexington	KY	B	B	B	314.3	26.14	1.0	0.1	31.2	4.0	9.1	10.4	19.5
Bank of Lincoln County	Fayetteville	TN	A-	A-	B	177.4	21.47	9.6	1.2	9.7	7.7	10.0	11.7	0.0
Bank of Lindsay	Lindsay	NE	C+	C+	C+	72.5	-0.17	6.9	1.7	0.4	2.5	9.1	12.1	14.2
Bank of Little Rock	Little Rock	AR	B-	B-	C-	236.6	20.00	12.9	1.8	33.6	26.6	8.3	9.9	0.0

Asset Quality Index	Adjusted Non-Performing Loans		Net Charge-Offs Avg Loans	Profitability Index	Net Income ($Mil)	Return on Assets (R.O.A.)	Return on Equity (R.O.E.)	Net Interest Spread	Overhead Efficiency Ratio	Liquidity Index	Liquidity Ratio	Hot Money Ratio	Stability Index
	as a % of Total Loans	as a % of Capital											
6.3	2.17	na	0.01	3.8	0.9	0.65	5.83	3.64	73.7	2.3	22.1	18.1	6.6
5.1	0.52	na	0.06	6.3	6.8	1.30	14.19	4.04	57.0	0.7	14.6	35.0	6.2
8.3	0.00	na	-0.01	6.8	1.5	1.16	12.10	4.23	56.6	1.7	12.7	20.1	6.1
5.4	1.37	na	-0.22	3.0	0.8	0.45	3.77	3.68	82.9	3.4	12.5	11.9	4.0
7.2	0.48	1.8	0.10	5.3	2.0	1.23	9.11	3.88	68.4	2.8	37.4	21.1	8.0
5.7	0.97	na	-0.06	5.0	1.9	0.77	7.01	3.74	70.3	1.0	25.4	34.3	7.6
7.2	0.29	na	0.07	4.7	1.0	0.84	7.74	3.96	73.6	2.8	24.1	16.1	6.6
4.6	1.91	8.5	0.42	4.1	1.6	0.76	8.51	3.85	64.6	3.4	19.5	12.5	5.1
6.9	0.00	na	0.00	7.5	3.6	1.27	10.65	3.96	63.4	3.2	17.0	13.1	9.3
6.5	0.92	na	0.06	5.6	0.8	1.10	9.90	3.55	51.4	3.6	19.8	11.3	6.3
8.7	0.47	na	0.27	4.8	1.0	1.16	4.94	3.52	64.7	4.8	71.4	17.2	8.1
3.0	1.81	13.1	0.07	2.9	1.3	0.43	4.74	3.18	85.9	4.9	35.6	8.4	3.5
9.0	0.00	na	0.00	7.1	1.2	1.62	7.57	3.79	57.2	5.9	48.6	7.1	9.4
5.0	0.91	na	0.01	4.5	1.7	1.11	15.47	3.27	67.9	2.6	29.3	14.9	4.5
4.1	11.68	na	0.20	5.2	1.6	1.18	7.88	3.76	60.7	1.9	28.4	25.2	8.3
3.7	0.83	na	-0.05	2.4	0.3	0.26	1.86	3.60	88.7	1.5	11.5	23.7	6.6
8.7	0.00	na	-0.16	5.2	0.4	1.21	9.18	3.23	63.1	4.7	42.6	12.1	7.4
6.8	1.66	na	0.13	4.9	0.8	1.04	8.05	4.34	74.1	3.5	31.8	14.6	7.0
9.1	0.47	2.9	0.04	5.2	12.8	1.05	13.44	3.11	55.3	5.0	5.2	0.8	7.1
4.3	1.48	9.9	0.25	3.3	8.5	0.52	6.44	3.98	79.0	2.9	21.8	16.5	6.1
6.7	5.20	5.4	-0.74	3.7	0.4	0.70	3.46	2.73	69.1	4.2	86.8	23.6	6.7
4.6	3.71	na	-0.01	4.5	0.7	0.91	9.01	3.04	64.2	2.6	33.7	20.0	6.9
9.1	0.00	na	-0.16	0.4	0.0	-0.91	-8.70	1.58	101.4	7.5	88.9	1.2	5.8
9.1	0.42	na	0.06	3.3	0.4	0.62	2.85	3.78	87.0	6.1	70.5	9.8	7.7
8.2	0.00	na	0.00	5.5	1.1	1.34	14.95	4.23	67.1	3.7	14.6	10.3	6.1
7.8	0.63	3.7	0.09	4.4	102.4	0.72	10.73	2.83	54.3	4.2	19.6	8.4	5.9
7.2	0.21	1.1	-0.01	6.1	2.5	1.17	11.68	3.52	50.5	1.9	23.6	21.5	5.3
7.8	0.00	na	0.00	4.7	0.5	1.14	10.68	3.19	62.4	4.3	55.5	16.2	6.2
2.2	7.20	na	1.14	2.2	0.2	0.21	1.45	3.87	75.8	4.7	23.3	5.1	6.1
7.4	0.00	na	0.00	9.8	14.1	2.43	22.33	4.05	40.7	5.2	24.6	1.8	8.9
4.9	1.39	na	0.13	2.5	0.0	0.01	0.08	3.93	65.5	4.8	23.0	4.6	6.0
5.4	3.59	na	-0.03	6.0	3.6	1.19	10.94	3.43	55.8	2.4	15.6	17.0	6.3
4.1	2.75	na	-0.01	3.4	1.3	0.69	6.59	2.41	65.2	2.5	42.7	28.8	5.4
6.4	0.53	na	0.05	4.4	1.0	0.83	10.30	3.51	69.7	4.0	24.8	10.0	4.8
4.5	2.23	na	0.10	6.3	2.8	1.40	10.57	4.19	66.1	1.1	12.0	28.9	9.5
4.6	2.01	8.9	0.79	5.7	0.6	1.20	8.09	3.65	52.9	1.2	28.8	31.6	7.4
5.2	1.00	2.9	0.08	4.6	94.0	0.77	5.44	3.10	52.7	1.1	16.9	24.8	10.0
6.0	0.00	na	0.00	0.0	-0.5	-1.62	-14.33	5.21	121.1	3.5	10.5	10.9	3.0
8.1	0.00	na	0.01	2.4	0.7	0.45	2.46	4.13	76.3	1.5	15.1	24.0	6.5
7.1	0.01	na	0.02	9.4	2.0	2.08	18.24	4.40	53.7	1.2	9.1	27.8	8.8
5.5	1.43	na	0.53	3.0	0.3	0.58	6.26	4.03	89.2	4.3	46.8	14.6	4.0
4.4	1.84	na	0.02	4.2	2.7	0.73	6.79	4.39	75.9	5.0	10.4	1.4	6.1
8.6	0.67	na	0.06	4.6	1.8	1.12	10.17	3.01	62.1	3.5	53.1	22.7	6.0
8.1	0.90	na	0.00	5.8	8.0	1.04	11.07	3.53	60.1	5.3	29.4	7.7	8.2
8.1	0.61	na	0.00	4.5	1.6	0.99	8.58	3.34	62.3	1.7	14.4	21.3	6.6
7.4	0.88	na	0.01	4.2	0.7	0.86	4.89	2.89	64.3	4.8	52.1	13.8	8.1
5.7	2.79	na	-0.09	7.7	1.6	2.09	21.96	3.87	73.4	3.6	17.7	5.1	5.3
6.5	1.28	na	0.06	6.7	2.5	1.64	17.58	4.14	58.6	2.2	25.9	19.5	6.3
6.9	3.58	na	0.24	3.4	2.3	0.68	5.48	1.91	68.3	5.2	40.6	8.7	7.8
3.9	0.71	na	0.00	6.5	4.4	1.76	14.51	4.38	50.8	1.0	15.7	30.6	7.7
5.6	2.26	6.7	2.24	1.0	-0.5	-0.10	-1.30	3.23	87.7	5.9	48.6	6.8	3.8
6.8	2.56	na	-0.01	3.2	1.1	0.49	3.90	2.67	76.1	4.0	35.4	13.4	6.4
6.6	0.20	1.2	0.00	8.4	3.3	1.80	14.60	4.34	67.0	1.9	11.0	14.1	8.7
7.6	0.47	na	0.18	6.3	0.7	1.38	10.92	4.40	60.7	3.0	14.5	12.4	6.8
6.2	4.49	na	0.00	4.7	2.2	0.94	5.32	3.34	61.3	2.5	21.4	17.2	8.2
8.9	0.00	na	0.00	3.9	0.2	0.88	3.43	3.36	68.4	5.3	60.4	12.1	6.2
9.3	0.00	na	0.00	3.6	1.7	0.78	7.36	3.10	70.9	2.4	38.6	17.1	6.6
7.7	1.20	na	0.00	8.5	1.7	1.40	11.49	4.65	59.0	1.7	29.7	28.5	8.1
6.9	0.02	0.1	0.13	3.3	0.3	0.52	4.42	3.03	82.7	0.6	6.9	20.1	6.4
3.8	2.18	na	0.42	5.3	2.1	1.29	12.52	3.49	85.1	4.8	26.5	5.3	5.0

Name	City	State	2019 Rating	2018 Rating	Rating	Total Assets ($Mil)	One Year Asset Growth	Asset Mix (As a % of Total Assets)				Capital-ization Index	Lever-age Ratio	Risk-Based Capital Ratio
								Comm-ercial Loans	Cons-umer Loans	Mort-gage Loans	Secur-ities			
Bank of Locust Grove	Locust Grove	OK	B	B	B	45.8	14.21	29.5	36.8	3.5	9.5	8.0	11.5	0.0
Bank of Louisiana	New Orleans	LA	D+	C-	D-	84.3	8.95	0.4	3.8	31.5	1.8	3.5	7.8	10.3
Bank of Louisiana	Louisiana	MO	B-	B-	C+	56.0	4.04	14.0	1.7	14.3	22.6	8.5	10.0	16.9
Bank of Lumber City	Lumber City	GA	C	C	C	25.5	8.46	10.8	10.3	13.9	14.5	10.0	15.1	0.0
Bank of Luxemburg	Luxemburg	WI	C+	C+	B-	465.0	20.22	18.0	1.4	12.9	16.9	6.8	8.8	13.3
Bank of Madison	Madison	GA	A-	A-	B+	287.0	28.00	9.3	0.6	12.9	15.1	10.0	11.9	16.8
▲ Bank of Magnolia Co.	Magnolia	OH	A-	B	B-	91.9	12.63	9.4	4.2	24.3	18.7	10.0	11.6	26.5
Bank of Maple Plain	Maple Plain	MN	A-	A-	B+	95.8	10.18	11.1	1.2	14.7	35.1	10.0	12.6	25.8
Bank of Marin	Novato	CA	A-	A-	A-	2975.2	14.78	12.3	0.8	5.5	18.1	8.8	10.2	15.5
▼ Bank of Marion	Marion	VA	B+	A-	B	485.2	25.75	6.2	2.8	31.5	32.5	9.0	10.4	19.9
Bank of Mauston	Mauston	WI	A	A	A	342.3	13.99	5.8	1.7	7.9	37.8	10.0	12.5	20.6
Bank of Maysville	Maysville	KY	B+	B+	B+	142.1	11.88	1.0	1.0	26.5	37.1	10.0	16.1	28.6
Bank of Mead	Mead	NE	B	B	B-	28.8	5.70	10.4	5.1	18.4	31.0	10.0	11.8	0.0
Bank of Milan	Milan	TN	B-	B-	B-	83.7	5.76	12.2	1.2	19.0	26.8	6.4	8.4	0.0
Bank of Millbrook	Millbrook	NY	B-	B		273.4	19.17	5.0	1.1	19.5	33.9	8.8	10.2	25.5
Bank of Milton	Milton	WI	B+	B	B	156.4	25.10	8.1	1.6	18.6	20.7	6.5	8.7	12.1
Bank of Mingo	Williamson	WV	C-	C-	C-	109.7	30.01	12.6	6.8	29.5	8.3	7.7	9.7	13.1
▲ Bank of Missouri	Perryville	MO	A-	B+	B+	2411.9	33.95	13.4	2.4	18.4	18.6	8.7	10.2	14.1
Bank of Monroe	Union	WV	A-	A-	A-	170.7	17.77	7.4	2.8	24.3	23.2	10.0	13.2	23.6
Bank of Montana	Missoula	MT	A-	A-	B+	162.3	72.60	30.5	2.1	4.8	0.0	6.7	8.7	18.7
Bank of Montgomery	Montgomery	IL	C-	D	C-	43.0	5.16	9.2	1.6	11.1	37.8	7.2	9.1	26.6
Bank of Monticello	Monticello	GA	B+	B+	B	132.8	21.79	10.6	5.7	23.7	15.3	8.6	10.1	0.0
▲ Bank of Monticello	Monticello	MO	A-	A-	B+	120.3	7.48	8.1	3.8	9.8	21.5	10.0	11.7	0.0
▼ Bank of Morton	Morton	MS	B-	B+	B+	75.0	8.98	4.4	6.8	35.1	18.2	10.0	14.0	0.0
Bank of Moundville	Moundville	AL	C-	C-	C	100.9	7.91	10.4	2.2	14.0	52.1	7.8	9.5	22.4
Bank of New Cambria	New Cambria	MO	C+	B	B-	33.7	9.51	2.1	0.6	5.4	26.6	10.0	13.1	24.3
Bank of New England	Salem	NH	A-	B	C+	1058.6	2.87	7.6	0.0	0.2	1.1	10.0	15.4	0.0
Bank of New Glarus	New Glarus	WI	B-	B-	B-	360.6	16.44	20.5	1.6	10.5	15.7	8.7	10.7	14.0
Bank of New Hampshire	Laconia	NH	B-	B-	B-	1984.3	14.09	11.1	2.2	28.8	11.2	5.4	9.0	0.0
Bank of New Madrid	New Madrid	MO	A-	A-	A-	108.4	9.91	3.2	2.4	19.6	33.9	9.4	10.9	0.0
Bank of New York Mellon	New York	NY	B	B	B	349432.0	14.91	0.5	0.0	0.2	43.7	4.8	6.9	17.4
Bank of New York Mellon Trust Co., N.A.	Los Angeles	CA	U	U	U	1478.5	8.67	0.0	0.0	0.0	10.0	10.0	69.5	420.6
Bank of Newington	Newington	GA	B-	C+	C	159.6	9.70	9.9	2.0	21.7	0.7	6.7	8.7	13.8
Bank of Newman Grove	Newman Grove	NE	C+	C	C-	37.0	6.58	0.4	2.9	0.0	32.1	10.0	11.2	16.2
Bank of O'Fallon	O'Fallon	IL	A-	A-	A-	341.0	9.42	8.2	5.0	40.3	5.8	10.0	13.5	25.0
Bank of Oak Ridge	Oak Ridge	LA	C	B-	C+	62.8	19.08	19.1	0.5	11.4	5.5	8.7	10.1	14.0
Bank of Oak Ridge	Oak Ridge	NC	C+	B-	B-	545.7	16.90	21.3	0.9	15.1	8.5	5.1	9.2	0.0
Bank of Ocean City	Ocean City	MD	A-	A-	A-	501.1	30.87	8.9	0.3	13.3	10.7	6.7	8.7	15.1
Bank of Odessa	Odessa	MO	B+	B+	B+	307.6	14.65	9.9	3.4	39.5	15.0	10.0	16.7	27.9
Bank of Okolona	Okolona	MS	C	C-	C	222.2	10.60	20.9	4.5	13.3	23.8	8.0	9.7	0.0
Bank of Old Monroe	Old Monroe	MO	A	A	A	484.2	23.58	14.3	0.4	7.7	30.2	10.0	14.7	0.0
▼ Bank of Ontario	Ontario	WI	C+	B	C+	54.4	8.20	5.9	3.9	28.8	8.6	10.0	11.8	0.0
Bank of Orchard	Orchard	NE	B-	B-	B-	29.5	19.95	3.5	4.6	0.1	27.7	10.0	13.8	0.0
▼ Bank of Orrick	Orrick	MO	C-	C-	C-	38.7	14.25	0.9	2.0	16.5	49.2	7.2	9.2	21.7
Bank of Palmer	Palmer	KS	C+	C+	C+	48.3	6.73	1.9	3.9	7.7	46.6	9.0	10.4	0.0
▲ Bank of Pensacola	Pensacola	FL	C	C	C-	114.5	31.98	9.7	1.0	18.7	21.8	10.0	11.4	0.0
Bank of Perry County	Lobelville	TN	B	C+	C+	187.5	8.80	7.0	13.8	39.2	4.1	7.1	9.1	0.0
Bank of Pontiac	Pontiac	IL	A-	A-	B+	620.6	10.90	15.8	4.0	20.6	12.3	10.0	12.9	19.6
Bank of Prague	Prague	NE	A-	A-	B	32.5	10.42	15.2	10.1	1.0	17.4	10.0	13.9	0.0
Bank of Prairie Du Sac	Prairie Du Sac	WI	A+	A+	A+	531.2	19.99	14.4	0.4	6.4	29.9	10.0	14.1	21.0
Bank of Prairie Village	Prairie Village	KS	A-	A-	B+	124.1	20.65	13.5	0.8	21.1	19.0	9.2	10.4	0.0
Bank of Princeton	Princeton	NJ	B+	B+	A-	1549.8	12.33	13.4	0.0	8.0	5.2	10.0	12.3	16.4
Bank of Protection	Protection	KS	B+	B	B	73.2	10.88	6.4	2.8	6.1	16.5	10.0	14.9	20.7
Bank of Rantoul	Rantoul	IL	B	B-	B-	248.6	7.61	17.1	0.5	1.9	43.1	9.0	10.4	0.0
Bank of Richmondville	Cobleskill	NY	B-	B-	B-	164.4	7.52	2.8	5.4	31.0	27.0	10.0	11.1	23.7
Bank of Ripley	Ripley	TN	B	B	B	246.3	12.99	0.8	7.5	7.1	53.8	10.0	14.6	28.0
▲ Bank of Romney	Romney	WV	B+	B	B-	338.6	10.50	3.5	5.4	40.6	21.4	10.0	11.6	0.0
Bank of Salem	Salem	AR	B+	B+	B	160.5	11.82	11.1	5.1	21.5	4.1	9.4	10.6	0.0
Bank of Salem	Salem	MO	B-	B-	C+	116.6	13.43	2.8	3.8	28.9	25.0	7.3	9.2	0.0
Bank of San Francisco	San Francisco	CA	B+	A-	B+	662.4	83.46	37.3	0.0	21.4	0.0	6.2	8.2	16.4

Asset Quality Index	Adjusted Non-Performing Loans as a % of Total Loans	as a % of Capital	Net Charge-Offs Avg Loans	Profitability Index	Net Income ($Mil)	Return on Assets (R.O.A.)	Return on Equity (R.O.E.)	Net Interest Spread	Overhead Efficiency Ratio	Liquidity Index	Liquidity Ratio	Hot Money Ratio	Stability Index
3.6	1.35	na	0.22	9.2	0.5	1.64	13.33	5.58	54.9	1.6	13.4	22.8	6.8
1.6	3.35	na	0.10	2.5	-0.3	-0.53	-5.92	3.95	126.7	6.0	38.6	2.4	5.3
4.6	3.91	na	-0.09	1.8	0.1	0.15	1.40	3.47	92.1	2.4	23.7	17.8	5.6
7.0	2.17	na	0.00	2.6	0.1	0.30	1.92	5.08	92.9	4.0	44.6	15.7	6.2
3.8	1.82	7.7	0.01	7.0	4.7	1.48	16.15	3.90	56.7	3.9	27.0	11.3	4.9
7.0	0.64	na	0.01	6.9	2.9	1.53	12.35	4.51	61.2	3.6	12.6	10.5	7.4
9.0	0.38	1.5	-0.13	7.3	1.2	1.90	15.88	4.42	62.3	5.8	36.3	3.4	6.1
9.2	0.50	na	-0.05	5.5	0.9	1.30	9.51	3.57	60.8	5.4	45.1	8.3	7.8
8.1	0.65	2.1	0.00	5.9	22.9	1.07	9.10	3.65	55.5	5.5	24.4	2.7	9.8
6.3	0.41	4.4	0.10	5.0	3.4	1.06	8.81	4.15	68.4	4.8	28.3	6.3	6.1
8.1	0.73	na	0.07	9.8	7.1	2.94	22.21	3.85	38.5	3.1	31.9	16.9	8.7
8.6	0.20	na	0.01	4.1	0.9	0.86	4.62	3.49	71.1	4.3	33.5	11.5	7.9
8.6	0.00	na	0.00	4.8	0.2	0.95	7.73	3.63	62.6	5.4	32.9	4.4	6.7
7.9	0.00	na	-0.12	3.8	0.4	0.73	7.90	3.54	74.7	4.4	42.4	13.7	5.6
7.8	0.75	na	0.03	3.7	1.4	0.73	6.85	2.76	71.2	6.6	49.6	2.4	5.5
8.6	0.00	na	0.00	8.9	2.3	2.15	22.39	3.99	48.6	3.1	27.7	15.1	6.5
6.4	0.94	na	0.17	1.9	0.1	0.09	0.91	3.91	95.1	0.9	20.4	24.1	2.9
6.1	1.07	3.5	0.13	8.0	26.7	1.73	14.39	4.45	58.1	3.8	11.0	9.2	9.2
8.7	0.75	1.8	0.08	5.5	1.3	1.08	8.05	3.59	67.8	3.6	35.6	15.6	8.3
8.3	0.00	na	0.00	10.0	3.8	4.04	42.80	3.57	32.2	4.8	43.8	10.4	7.4
8.9	0.00	na	-0.55	3.1	0.3	0.79	8.13	2.67	81.4	5.3	68.8	13.2	2.7
5.1	0.96	5.7	0.17	6.8	1.5	1.62	15.25	4.33	58.3	4.3	24.6	8.2	6.5
6.1	0.58	na	0.14	7.5	1.6	1.78	15.51	4.15	53.1	2.8	19.9	15.4	7.8
1.7	2.57	na	0.17	9.1	1.1	2.01	13.65	4.90	60.3	2.0	30.6	25.9	9.3
9.3	0.04	na	0.01	2.1	0.3	0.40	3.81	2.32	89.6	1.8	26.4	24.5	5.2
7.3	0.00	na	0.01	2.3	0.1	0.23	1.69	3.13	91.2	6.7	62.6	3.9	6.8
6.7	0.96	na	0.00	9.1	11.5	1.52	9.91	3.86	39.0	0.7	12.2	14.1	10.0
4.3	2.04	na	0.06	8.6	4.1	1.63	14.29	3.74	50.9	4.0	26.7	10.3	6.9
7.3	0.44	na	0.01	4.5	13.2	0.94	9.21	3.81	58.7	3.6	9.6	4.8	8.5
9.0	0.01	na	0.03	5.2	0.9	1.17	10.15	3.75	66.3	2.0	18.5	19.6	8.2
9.3	0.37	0.3	-0.02	4.3	1960.0	0.81	9.44	0.96	68.5	6.5	55.4	1.5	7.2
6.5	na	0.0	na	10.0	152.1	14.12	17.18	1.07	44.3	9.9	192.3	0.0	6.3
5.6	1.05	na	0.28	6.0	1.3	1.13	13.00	4.79	63.6	1.3	20.4	29.7	5.1
3.5	0.13	na	0.00	2.0	0.0	0.09	0.78	2.74	95.1	4.8	42.6	11.6	5.6
8.7	0.12	0.7	0.02	6.0	3.7	1.52	10.77	2.80	48.2	1.5	25.7	27.9	8.6
8.4	0.02	na	0.01	2.5	0.1	0.27	2.66	3.72	86.4	1.0	18.7	32.6	5.2
4.7	1.32	8.1	0.01	4.2	2.8	0.73	7.20	3.75	64.3	1.0	13.6	23.5	6.8
8.9	0.40	na	0.02	6.3	4.0	1.27	12.85	3.26	49.9	5.2	39.7	8.6	5.8
6.4	0.59	6.4	0.18	7.7	3.3	1.47	8.57	3.57	37.5	2.1	10.6	17.8	7.5
3.4	1.23	na	0.02	4.5	1.4	0.83	8.09	3.88	77.5	1.6	34.0	34.3	7.3
8.7	0.39	na	0.00	9.9	12.3	3.70	24.90	4.34	42.5	4.5	29.7	6.6	9.5
2.2	8.34	na	0.64	4.4	0.1	0.13	1.06	4.54	77.1	1.4	11.1	24.1	8.5
9.1	0.00	na	0.48	3.7	0.2	0.88	6.31	2.94	69.3	5.3	85.8	15.6	6.5
5.5	1.90	na	0.00	2.1	0.1	0.47	4.53	3.44	96.8	5.8	54.5	4.9	4.8
5.9	0.00	na	-0.13	3.7	0.3	0.77	6.99	3.16	73.8	5.8	53.4	7.6	5.7
9.4	0.21	na	-0.01	3.0	0.4	0.50	4.04	2.47	74.0	4.5	56.7	16.6	5.1
5.2	0.72	na	0.02	7.6	2.3	1.66	18.24	4.33	57.5	1.4	14.6	20.4	7.2
6.2	1.50	na	0.18	7.1	6.2	1.41	11.01	3.62	49.7	3.5	17.8	10.9	7.7
7.6	0.00	na	0.00	9.4	0.5	2.09	14.92	4.27	59.7	4.6	32.8	9.4	8.6
8.7	0.38	1.1	-0.01	9.5	6.7	1.80	11.72	3.37	38.8	5.9	44.7	5.8	10.0
8.9	0.00	na	0.09	6.7	1.3	1.52	13.20	3.77	55.1	3.2	27.6	15.1	7.1
6.1	0.83	3.1	0.09	4.2	9.7	0.86	6.45	3.42	60.5	1.5	9.3	15.1	8.9
6.4	0.01	na	0.00	8.2	1.0	1.78	11.58	4.21	50.9	1.8	18.7	20.9	7.1
5.1	1.86	na	0.02	8.1	3.7	2.06	18.03	3.88	44.1	2.5	18.8	15.6	8.2
6.4	0.82	5.3	-0.02	3.5	0.6	0.57	4.90	3.65	78.2	4.5	28.3	8.0	6.3
4.9	4.46	10.0	0.87	4.1	1.7	0.94	5.77	3.61	79.3	4.0	49.9	17.7	6.9
5.3	2.44	na	0.07	5.5	2.7	1.15	10.48	3.78	61.4	1.6	21.8	13.7	6.1
5.0	0.91	5.1	0.07	9.1	2.5	2.19	20.29	4.50	53.9	1.5	25.5	25.7	7.3
5.9	0.87	na	-0.04	4.0	0.8	0.90	9.49	3.37	66.9	3.5	26.9	13.3	5.2
8.0	0.20	2.0	0.00	4.5	2.9	0.74	9.01	3.43	51.6	1.5	20.9	18.3	5.8

Name	City	State	Rating	2019 Rating	2018 Rating	Total Assets ($Mil)	One Year Asset Growth	Comm- ercial Loans	Cons- umer Loans	Mort- gage Loans	Secur- ities	Capital- ization Index	Lever- age Ratio	Risk- Based Capital Ratio
Bank of San Jacinto County	Coldspring	TX	B	B	B	46.8	15.30	4.1	2.5	21.3	13.5	10.0	13.8	0.0
Bank of Santa Clarita	Santa Clarita	CA	B+	B+	B	392.0	23.80	16.9	0.4	1.4	2.7	9.5	10.6	17.0
Bank of South Carolina	Charleston	SC	A-	A	A-	528.9	16.79	9.4	0.9	14.4	25.6	8.0	10.0	0.0
Bank of South Texas	Pharr	TX	B-	B-	C+	136.2	-1.36	5.1	1.2	19.6	4.7	9.2	10.5	0.0
Bank of Southern California, N.A.	San Diego	CA	B-	B	C+	1575.3	87.75	42.9	0.4	5.8	1.6	7.3	9.2	15.9
▼ Bank of Southside Virginia	Carson	VA	B+	A	B+	613.1	8.65	5.3	15.3	4.3	27.7	10.0	17.6	0.0
Bank of Springfield	Springfield	IL	C-	C-	C-	1246.5	18.15	26.4	0.5	8.7	4.3	6.2	8.5	11.9
Bank of St. Elizabeth	Saint Elizabeth	MO	A-	A-	B+	181.7	19.01	5.6	6.5	41.4	0.0	8.3	9.9	15.7
Bank of St. Francisville	Saint Francisville	LA	B	B	B-	174.6	21.13	13.8	2.1	16.5	8.4	6.2	9.7	0.0
Bank of Star Valley	Afton	WY	A-	B+	B	289.8	27.02	8.5	5.8	8.5	34.0	7.5	9.4	13.7
Bank of Steinauer	Steinauer	NE	C	C	D+	12.9	9.83	3.7	9.9	38.3	0.0	8.9	10.3	0.0
Bank of Stockton	Stockton	CA	B+	A	A-	3850.2	16.23	9.8	7.6	4.9	18.5	10.0	15.1	17.0
Bank of Stronghurst	Stronghurst	IL	C+	C+	C+	80.3	8.23	4.2	1.7	5.9	60.2	10.0	15.8	0.0
Bank of Sun Prairie	Sun Prairie	WI	B-	B	B+	492.7	13.36	11.9	0.9	8.3	8.7	8.8	11.4	14.0
Bank of Sunset and Trust Co.	Sunset	LA	B+	B+	B	170.2	14.66	19.1	0.5	22.8	8.0	7.1	9.1	0.0
Bank of Tampa	Tampa	FL	B+	B+	B+	2546.2	35.86	25.8	2.4	3.9	18.9	5.4	7.4	14.1
Bank of Tennessee	Kingsport	TN	B	B	B	1605.5	11.74	16.0	0.4	19.0	10.6	6.2	8.8	11.9
Bank of Tescott	Tescott	KS	B+	A-	B	420.4	8.56	4.2	1.8	20.6	24.8	10.0	14.1	20.1
Bank of Texas	Midland	TX	A-	A-	A-	420.0	10.53	26.1	0.1	2.2	1.2	9.4	13.2	14.5
Bank of the Bluegrass & Trust Co.	Lexington	KY	A-	A-	B+	296.5	11.61	6.9	0.5	19.9	18.4	10.0	11.1	0.0
Bank of the Federated States of Micronesi	Pohnpei	FM	A-	A-	B+	187.7	5.73	7.9	7.6	0.9	24.2	10.0	12.6	44.7
Bank of the Flint Hills	Wamego	KS	B-	B-	C+	343.6	13.29	22.6	1.7	14.3	9.6	4.1	9.3	0.0
Bank of the James	Lynchburg	VA	C+	B-	B-	849.5	19.90	17.2	1.7	14.0	9.4	6.1	8.1	12.3
Bank of the Lowcountry	Walterboro	SC	B	B	B-	252.6	8.34	7.0	1.1	11.9	34.1	9.0	10.3	0.0
Bank of the Mountains, Inc.	West Liberty	KY	C	C-	C-	76.3	5.50	8.6	18.4	26.2	8.5	9.3	10.5	16.5
Bank of the Orient	San Francisco	CA	B-	B-	B+	931.7	0.47	4.1	0.0	18.5	1.5	8.9	10.5	0.0
Bank of the Pacific	Aberdeen	WA	A-	A-	B+	1160.7	22.94	17.8	4.7	8.3	10.9	7.7	9.4	15.2
Bank of the Panhandle	Guymon	OK	A-	A-	A-	196.6	19.92	13.1	1.0	6.9	24.2	10.0	11.8	16.9
▲ Bank of the Rockies	White Sulphur Spring	MT	C-	C-	C	182.2	19.70	14.3	1.7	8.0	11.8	8.0	9.7	14.3
▼ Bank of the Sierra	Porterville	CA	B+	A-	A-	3199.6	21.39	6.7	0.2	5.1	18.0	5.8	10.3	0.0
▲ Bank of the South	Pensacola	FL	C	C	C-	83.2	4.28	4.5	0.1	4.1	47.0	10.0	17.4	0.0
Bank of the Southwest	Roswell	NM	B	B	B	190.3	21.81	28.5	4.4	12.3	0.0	5.5	7.5	14.1
Bank of the Valley	Bellwood	NE	C	C	C-	364.5	19.47	8.6	1.9	5.1	9.4	5.2	8.0	11.1
Bank of the West	San Francisco	CA	B-	B	B	96304.6	5.80	15.4	15.2	8.8	23.1	8.6	10.0	14.6
Bank of the West	Thomas	OK	A-	A	A-	151.8	4.79	10.8	0.4	6.8	0.0	9.0	13.1	0.0
Bank of the West	Grapevine	TX	B	B	B	630.1	27.71	19.7	0.4	7.3	5.0	6.2	8.2	13.8
Bank of Tioga	Tioga	ND	C+	C+	B-	356.2	6.76	4.1	0.9	3.1	73.4	7.9	9.6	19.4
Bank of Travelers Rest	Travelers Rest	SC	B+	B+	B	1005.7	26.38	10.1	3.3	11.7	23.2	6.8	8.8	16.0
▲ Bank of Turtle Lake	Turtle Lake	ND	B	B-	C-	58.0	6.45	10.8	1.2	0.3	8.6	7.6	11.3	0.0
Bank of Utah	Ogden	UT	A	A	B+	1780.5	23.64	13.8	0.3	2.2	7.2	10.0	11.7	16.4
Bank of Utica	Utica	NY	B-	A-	B+	1297.5	14.31	6.0	0.3	0.2	79.7	10.0	19.3	0.0
Bank of Vernon	Vernon	AL	A-	A-	B+	194.9	19.64	24.1	1.6	13.0	11.9	10.0	13.6	0.0
Bank of Versailles	Versailles	MO	B	B	B	290.9	10.67	0.9	0.6	59.2	0.0	10.0	12.8	0.0
▼ Bank of Vici	Vici	OK	C-	C+	C-	37.2	6.66	19.9	12.5	2.2	14.4	10.0	12.8	0.0
Bank of Walker County	Jasper	AL	C+	C	C+	79.0	9.88	14.1	2.9	22.8	10.8	8.1	10.3	0.0
▲ Bank of Washington	Washington	MO	C-	D	D	828.3	14.85	33.1	0.5	6.1	4.8	10.0	12.1	15.3
Bank of Western Oklahoma	Elk City	OK	B-	B-	B-	328.5	5.26	13.0	0.7	14.3	11.0	5.6	7.6	11.6
Bank of Weston	Weston	MO	B	B	B-	169.6	14.76	10.9	0.7	15.1	17.4	6.1	8.1	13.7
▲ Bank of Whittier, N.A.	Whittier	CA	B-	C+	B-	107.5	49.33	7.2	0.4	10.3	0.0	10.0	16.3	0.0
Bank of Wiggins	Wiggins	MS	B+	B+	B+	179.8	7.06	8.1	4.7	15.2	38.6	10.0	17.0	0.0
Bank of Winnfield & Trust Co.	Winnfield	LA	B-	B-	B	148.6	7.96	11.0	3.7	14.9	30.1	10.0	13.1	28.3
Bank of Winona	Winona	MS	B	B	B	134.0	9.03	5.0	2.8	18.4	46.2	9.1	10.4	14.6
Bank of Wisconsin Dells	Wisconsin Dells	WI	A-	A-	B	715.5	21.42	11.4	0.2	6.0	12.7	8.5	10.8	13.8
Bank of Wolcott	Wolcott	IN	B+	A-	B	192.9	13.36	5.6	0.9	10.3	31.3	10.0	11.0	0.0
Bank of Wrightsville	Wrightsville	GA	B-	B-	C	66.8	16.78	11.6	2.3	9.9	29.1	8.0	9.6	0.0
▼ Bank of Wyandotte	Wyandotte	OK	D+	C-	C-	13.2	3.45	20.0	12.6	11.6	28.6	7.7	9.4	15.4
Bank of Yates City	Yates City	IL	C-	C-	C-	71.1	0.57	9.5	6.8	22.5	25.6	6.6	8.6	0.0
Bank of Yazoo City	Yazoo City	MS	B	B	B	264.4	9.80	12.2	1.7	17.2	33.7	10.0	11.7	0.0
▼ Bank of York	York	SC	B	B+	B-	259.7	13.51	7.7	2.2	8.6	17.0	9.0	10.3	0.0
Bank of Zachary	Zachary	LA	C+	B-	B-	298.8	24.73	11.2	1.5	28.6	29.9	6.7	8.7	18.0

Asset Quality Index	Adjusted Non-Performing Loans		Net Charge-Offs	Profitability Index	Net Income ($Mil)	Return on Assets (R.O.A.)	Return on Equity (R.O.E.)	Net Interest Spread	Overhead Efficiency Ratio	Liquidity Index	Liquidity Ratio	Hot Money Ratio	Stability Index
	as a % of Total Loans	as a % of Capital	Avg Loans										
9.7	0.00	na	0.00	3.9	0.3	0.80	5.57	3.73	81.3	5.8	75.9	11.9	6.4
5.4	0.54	2.8	0.00	5.1	2.4	0.91	8.17	2.87	53.8	1.5	21.0	18.7	6.2
6.0	1.99	6.8	-0.05	7.9	4.9	1.37	12.64	3.95	59.7	5.3	28.9	2.9	8.3
4.0	1.88	na	0.39	4.6	0.6	0.56	4.40	5.50	82.7	1.8	34.3	30.7	7.9
7.6	0.08	na	-0.05	4.6	7.3	0.79	7.34	3.79	58.3	3.6	9.6	9.0	7.9
8.0	0.37	na	0.04	4.9	4.2	0.93	5.17	3.26	66.8	7.0	66.4	4.6	9.6
1.6	3.06	26.0	0.57	4.5	7.5	0.88	9.87	3.62	67.8	4.8	13.7	3.9	6.6
7.7	0.19	na	0.01	8.9	2.7	2.16	18.81	4.45	57.3	2.5	21.0	17.2	8.7
5.1	1.29	na	0.61	4.8	1.4	1.12	11.15	4.36	67.5	2.6	12.8	15.6	6.2
7.7	0.95	na	0.07	6.8	3.0	1.53	15.28	3.41	53.0	3.7	41.1	16.9	7.5
6.8	0.50	na	0.00	3.8	0.1	0.79	7.72	4.21	79.5	4.5	21.0	5.9	4.3
7.9	0.49	0.9	0.02	3.7	0.6	0.02	0.13	3.61	43.8	6.6	48.7	5.5	10.0
9.2	0.33	0.5	0.00	2.7	0.3	0.49	2.83	2.55	86.8	4.9	62.8	14.3	7.4
3.8	0.83	na	0.08	5.0	3.6	1.01	8.88	3.56	66.2	3.3	11.0	12.1	7.6
8.6	0.13	na	0.00	5.3	1.3	1.09	11.86	3.70	63.7	1.3	12.7	24.8	5.8
7.5	0.45	2.8	0.05	4.1	12.4	0.74	8.92	3.21	60.8	6.5	32.6	0.8	7.1
7.4	0.46	3.6	0.05	6.1	16.8	1.47	16.33	3.91	61.1	4.3	10.9	5.9	8.4
4.5	3.73	16.1	0.21	5.6	4.1	1.32	9.17	3.45	56.1	1.5	23.1	27.0	9.3
7.2	0.00	na	0.00	7.8	5.2	1.67	13.18	2.88	39.8	0.8	23.8	53.3	9.0
8.6	1.91	na	-0.02	5.7	2.6	1.24	10.35	3.59	64.9	3.7	29.3	12.1	8.1
8.0	2.87	na	0.25	5.6	1.7	1.22	8.21	3.68	63.9	7.1	83.6	6.4	8.4
7.9	0.19	na	0.05	4.9	2.8	1.14	11.77	3.84	64.3	2.4	15.0	16.4	5.9
6.8	0.46	3.5	0.05	3.4	3.6	0.60	6.95	3.36	76.2	3.3	18.7	11.4	5.4
6.6	2.22	na	-0.01	4.2	1.5	0.84	7.60	3.29	68.4	4.0	45.0	16.5	6.7
3.1	1.54	na	-0.11	4.1	0.3	0.61	5.74	5.23	84.5	1.7	15.4	21.4	5.8
3.6	1.63	10.3	-0.22	4.7	7.6	1.07	10.42	3.10	59.7	1.3	20.8	28.5	5.7
7.7	0.22	1.3	0.09	5.8	8.1	1.05	8.99	3.98	67.6	4.8	20.1	4.3	9.6
6.6	1.28	na	-0.07	6.8	2.2	1.59	12.67	3.82	58.4	2.4	33.5	21.3	8.5
3.0	2.08	na	-0.43	5.3	1.5	1.15	10.93	5.17	77.9	4.8	30.9	7.2	6.9
6.4	0.63	2.8	0.05	7.3	28.0	1.33	10.71	4.03	55.7	2.8	15.1	13.3	9.7
9.7	0.00	na	0.00	1.6	0.0	0.06	0.35	2.37	96.4	7.0	73.3	3.8	6.0
7.6	0.04	na	0.09	4.8	1.3	1.01	12.29	5.80	78.9	5.2	24.3	1.8	4.5
3.5	0.65	na	0.00	4.1	2.8	1.13	13.38	3.28	69.3	0.7	9.1	21.1	4.6
4.9	1.07	4.0	0.17	3.3	396.6	0.55	3.90	2.67	64.0	4.4	24.3	4.5	9.8
5.6	0.80	na	0.00	9.2	2.1	1.86	14.21	4.54	56.7	1.0	13.2	32.2	9.5
5.0	0.38	4.8	0.04	5.3	5.3	1.27	14.24	3.90	68.2	4.2	22.1	8.2	5.7
8.4	0.03	na	1.82	4.3	5.1	1.94	19.69	2.68	65.3	2.9	61.8	22.8	6.6
8.5	1.07	na	0.10	5.7	9.2	1.35	14.21	3.29	60.6	5.0	38.9	12.0	7.6
3.5	0.47	na	0.02	5.5	0.4	1.04	8.77	4.36	65.8	1.7	17.7	22.8	6.8
7.1	0.03	na	0.00	9.7	21.4	1.79	14.01	3.98	50.4	4.6	15.5	4.4	10.0
10.0	2.46	na	0.14	4.5	8.6	0.93	4.79	1.95	36.2	4.5	81.9	24.5	9.8
8.5	0.43	na	0.24	6.8	1.6	1.17	8.14	3.51	60.5	2.4	30.2	19.9	7.7
6.9	2.57	na	0.01	4.9	2.1	1.02	7.86	3.14	56.9	4.0	18.9	9.3	7.3
0.1	4.74	na	0.01	3.4	0.2	0.62	4.78	4.06	86.5	2.5	38.4	26.2	6.5
4.7	0.79	na	0.07	3.9	0.5	0.80	7.62	4.30	80.5	1.2	26.8	34.0	6.6
2.5	3.66	na	0.01	7.2	9.9	1.71	13.33	3.77	57.6	2.1	11.3	15.8	8.5
5.7	0.28	4.3	0.04	7.2	3.9	1.61	19.17	4.25	58.3	0.8	13.2	36.2	7.3
5.4	1.49	9.4	0.21	5.1	1.4	1.16	14.01	3.77	68.1	3.1	25.7	14.6	5.7
8.8	0.00	na	-0.14	7.1	1.0	1.64	10.20	1.12	52.0	3.1	68.9	56.2	7.4
8.4	0.44	na	0.12	4.2	1.1	0.83	4.77	3.68	75.1	3.5	52.8	21.6	7.8
7.1	1.31	na	-0.01	3.7	0.8	0.76	6.04	3.29	77.7	4.5	45.5	13.8	6.1
6.7	0.96	na	0.25	5.2	1.2	1.26	10.90	3.77	65.2	4.5	44.5	13.5	6.7
7.3	0.40	na	0.00	8.6	7.4	1.51	12.93	3.90	43.6	2.4	14.9	9.3	8.7
4.6	2.28	na	0.09	7.0	2.4	1.64	14.57	3.58	55.0	4.5	45.5	13.5	8.2
6.3	0.78	na	0.09	4.7	0.5	1.10	11.11	3.78	69.8	4.2	35.4	12.7	5.2
4.9	2.37	na	-0.02	3.7	0.1	0.65	6.82	5.42	87.6	3.6	29.2	9.8	3.0
2.4	2.61	na	1.60	0.7	-0.3	-0.54	-5.96	3.29	87.3	3.5	29.1	13.8	4.2
8.9	0.00	na	0.02	3.8	1.5	0.78	6.77	3.30	74.2	3.0	25.9	15.2	6.3
6.2	1.99	na	-0.01	3.1	0.9	0.46	4.06	2.61	79.9	6.3	58.3	7.7	6.6
5.9	0.86	na	0.02	3.6	1.4	0.67	7.24	3.98	78.9	3.5	23.1	12.2	4.9

Name	City	State	2019 Rating	2018 Rating	Rating	Total Assets ($Mil)	One Year Asset Growth	Commercial Loans	Consumer Loans	Mortgage Loans	Securities	Capitalization Index	Leverage Ratio	Risk-Based Capital Ratio
Bank of Zumbrota	Zumbrota	MN	B+	B+	B	181.4	9.73	15.8	3.4	10.8	12.1	8.6	12.1	13.8
Bank OZK	Little Rock	AR	A-	A-	B+	26888.3	14.89	3.5	9.6	3.0	12.9	10.0	13.4	15.3
Bank Plus	Estherville	IA	C+	B-	C	133.1	2.93	4.6	1.8	6.4	8.9	3.9	9.1	0.0
Bank Rhode Island	Providence	RI	B-	B	B	3191.7	28.97	24.1	0.0	8.6	11.2	5.6	7.6	11.9
Bank Star	Pacific	MO	B	B	B-	153.5	13.44	15.7	2.1	25.1	11.2	5.3	8.9	0.0
Bank, N.A.	McAlester	OK	A-	A-	B+	436.1	15.57	5.7	2.5	13.6	35.7	8.9	10.3	0.0
Bank3	Memphis	TN	C-	D+	D-	337.3	46.21	37.1	0.7	6.0	7.2	4.0	10.0	0.0
▼ Bank7	Oklahoma City	OK	B+	A	A	972.4	17.75	41.2	0.2	3.8	0.0	8.9	10.7	14.1
bankcda	Coeur d'Alene	ID	B+	A-	B-	179.9	30.72	23.1	0.6	3.8	29.6	7.9	10.5	0.0
BankChampaign, N.A.	Champaign	IL	B+	B+	B	260.2	15.80	17.7	0.1	16.1	9.4	7.0	9.0	15.6
BankCherokee	Saint Paul	MN	B	B-	B-	342.9	24.66	26.1	0.4	10.9	19.8	5.9	7.9	16.1
Bankers Trust Co.	Des Moines	IA	B	B	B-	5627.9	14.40	22.0	0.4	8.0	13.2	5.9	9.0	11.7
▲ Bankers' Bank	Madison	WI	B+	B	B	1033.0	38.14	1.0	0.5	6.8	7.4	8.1	9.7	15.5
Bankers' Bank of Kansas	Wichita	KS	B+	B+	B+	206.7	21.04	21.5	8.5	3.5	1.2	10.0	13.6	22.0
Bankers' Bank of Kentucky, Inc.	Frankfort	KY	C-	C+	C+	95.0	-29.37	2.0	0.0	2.1	1.1	9.0	10.3	36.8
Bankers' Bank of the West	Denver	CO	B+	A-	B+	454.5	18.69	8.7	0.0	0.2	3.8	10.0	11.0	17.7
BankFinancial, N.A.	Olympia Fields	IL	B+	B+	A-	1604.3	7.71	23.6	0.1	2.2	0.6	8.7	10.1	0.0
BankFirst	Norfolk	NE	B+	B+	B+	814.2	7.98	6.2	2.7	6.7	18.4	7.3	10.2	12.8
BankFirst Financial Services	Macon	MS	B	B	B	1682.2	32.11	13.5	1.5	16.6	17.6	6.7	8.7	14.0
BankFlorida	Jupiter	FL	D	D-	D	143.9	58.38	13.9	0.0	17.6	2.5	10.0	15.2	25.1
BankGloucester	Gloucester	MA	C+	C+	C	329.4	18.26	9.3	0.2	37.7	2.2	5.8	7.8	12.9
▼ BankIowa of Cedar Rapids	Cedar Rapids	IA	C+	B	B	770.9	12.94	14.0	1.5	14.7	14.8	7.3	10.2	0.0
▼ BankNewport	Middletown	RI	B	B+	B	2006.0	14.41	14.4	2.9	25.6	12.8	8.6	10.1	14.5
▲ BankNorth	Arthur	ND	C	C	C+	414.3	0.74	10.9	1.2	2.6	1.6	7.4	10.6	12.8
BankORION	Orion	IL	B	B	B-	572.6	19.87	10.2	2.2	15.2	31.4	9.0	10.3	0.0
▼ BankPacific, Ltd	Hagatna	GU	C-	C+	B-	179.2	23.44	5.4	24.6	31.1	0.6	8.7	10.1	17.4
BankPlus	Belzoni	MS	B+	B+	B+	4545.2	53.27	15.3	1.6	14.6	9.6	6.5	8.5	12.8
BankSouth	Dothan	AL	B+	A-	A-	195.9	7.51	8.1	1.3	32.6	25.4	10.0	19.6	0.0
BankSouth	Greensboro	GA	A-	A-	A-	971.8	35.81	8.9	0.5	38.2	2.4	8.4	9.9	14.0
BankStar Financial	Elkton	SD	B-	B-	B-	215.2	6.80	12.0	2.0	14.5	13.1	6.4	8.4	13.2
BankTennessee	Collierville	TN	B-	B	C+	355.5	14.16	16.5	2.2	26.2	5.7	6.4	8.9	12.1
BankUnited, N.A.	Miami Lakes	FL	B+	B+	B+	34895.9	6.15	14.2	0.0	17.1	26.4	7.8	9.5	14.4
BankVista	Sartell	MN	C+	C	C-	536.6	59.52	43.4	1.6	8.6	2.4	5.1	7.2	11.0
Bankwell Bank	New Canaan	CT	B-	B	B	2191.3	18.07	13.7	0.0	5.8	5.0	7.9	9.6	13.6
BANKWEST	Rockford	MN	B+	B+	B+	198.0	28.81	16.6	1.1	8.1	25.7	6.1	8.1	14.4
▼ Bankwest of Kansas	Goodland	KS	B+	B+	B	135.3	22.29	2.3	1.0	2.0	8.1	9.5	10.7	17.1
BankWest, Inc.	Pierre	SD	C-	C	C	1250.8	13.74	8.9	8.1	5.7	17.6	8.2	10.0	13.5
Banner Bank	Walla Walla	WA	B+	B+	B+	14347.0	21.64	15.9	0.8	6.4	15.0	7.5	9.3	13.3
Banner Banks	Birnamwood	WI	B-	B-	B-	110.9	11.91	2.4	0.4	7.0	27.6	10.0	11.3	0.0
Banner Capital Bank	Harrisburg	NE	C	C+	B-	211.0	11.56	13.7	3.1	4.3	5.4	5.2	9.4	11.1
Banterra Bank	Eldorado	IL	B-	B-	B-	2234.7	19.79	25.3	23.0	4.6	20.1	5.3	8.2	11.2
Bar Harbor Bank & Trust	Bar Harbor	ME	B	B	B	3857.1	6.84	9.0	0.3	28.1	15.7	7.1	9.1	13.0
Bar Harbor S&L Assn.	Bar Harbor	ME	B-	B-	B	101.9	-1.46	0.0	0.5	57.2	5.0	10.0	11.8	26.5
Baraboo State Bank	Baraboo	WI	B	B	B	491.5	27.20	11.9	0.9	6.8	7.9	8.7	10.2	15.1
Barclays Bank Delaware	Wilmington	DE	C+	C	C	31016.0	-9.96	0.5	67.0	0.0	0.4	10.0	15.1	23.8
Barrington Bank & Trust Co., N.A.	Barrington	IL	B	B	B	3506.0	34.63	24.1	15.2	37.4	3.3	7.1	12.4	12.5
Barwick Banking Co.	Barwick	GA	D+	D	D	20.7	71.52	9.4	1.9	0.1	43.5	10.0	36.2	104.1
Basile State Bank	Basile	LA	B-	B-	C+	65.9	16.29	2.6	8.1	35.7	1.3	9.0	10.4	0.0
Bath Savings Institution	Bath	ME	A	A	A-	1097.5	12.91	8.6	0.8	25.7	23.3	10.0	15.0	24.7
Bath State Bank	Bath	IN	B-	B-	B-	193.5	18.10	3.8	1.6	17.2	14.1	7.2	9.1	0.0
Battle Creek State Bank	Battle Creek	NE	B-	B-	B-	37.9	11.55	53.3	1.4	2.0	13.3	10.0	11.9	16.4
Baxter State Bank	Baxter Springs	KS	C	C+	C+	25.4	-0.07	2.2	8.3	33.2	10.7	10.0	20.7	0.0
Bay Bank	Green Bay	WI	B+	B+	B	123.3	19.08	21.0	3.8	12.0	16.5	10.0	12.7	23.4
Bay Port State Bank	Bay Port	MI	C+	C+	C-	119.3	8.96	11.0	2.1	18.5	1.3	5.4	7.4	12.2
Bay State Savings Bank	Worcester	MA	C	C	C	465.2	9.47	7.9	0.9	46.6	1.9	6.8	8.8	13.2
Baybank	Gladstone	MI	C+	C	C	117.2	9.97	22.9	10.8	18.0	17.3	6.1	8.9	0.0
▲ BayCoast Bank	Swansea	MA	C+	C+	C	2168.6	16.67	12.8	2.9	17.5	10.4	4.5	8.3	10.7
▲ BayVanguard Bank	Sparrows Point	MD	B+	B	C+	415.5	39.69	6.5	3.0	44.3	1.8	10.0	15.2	23.2
▼ BBVA USA	Birmingham	AL	C-	C+	C+	102042.3	10.95	18.5	6.9	13.7	15.3	6.1	8.1	14.0
BCB Community Bank	Bayonne	NJ	B-	B-	C+	2841.3	0.62	8.7	0.0	18.0	4.2	6.1	9.4	0.0

Asset Quality Index	Adjusted Non-Performing Loans as a % of Total Loans	as a % of Capital	Net Charge-Offs Avg Loans	Profitability Index	Net Income ($Mil)	Return on Assets (R.O.A.)	Return on Equity (R.O.E.)	Net Interest Spread	Overhead Efficiency Ratio	Liquidity Index	Liquidity Ratio	Hot Money Ratio	Stability Index
5.7	0.69	na	-0.40	8.2	2.8	2.09	16.74	3.65	55.0	2.7	16.2	14.0	8.0
6.0	0.30	1.2	0.16	6.4	171.4	0.90	5.54	3.79	42.9	1.0	20.2	29.6	10.0
5.3	0.03	na	0.00	5.0	1.2	1.22	11.09	3.85	61.8	2.1	6.9	12.0	6.9
5.3	0.72	na	0.01	2.9	3.7	0.17	1.46	2.89	63.1	2.8	11.5	11.5	7.7
7.9	0.00	na	0.06	4.8	1.1	0.95	9.10	4.45	64.6	3.4	7.2	11.5	6.4
5.7	1.02	na	0.12	7.8	6.1	1.95	17.78	3.77	53.0	5.2	50.7	11.7	7.8
8.2	0.02	na	0.00	2.4	1.7	0.83	7.51	3.32	76.2	1.0	22.0	16.7	4.4
3.9	2.33	16.7	0.00	9.9	14.5	2.07	19.45	5.18	36.5	1.4	9.7	18.4	8.7
7.6	0.85	na	-0.03	4.0	0.8	0.64	5.67	3.73	79.4	5.7	32.3	1.7	6.2
7.7	0.32	na	0.00	5.1	2.4	1.23	12.84	3.34	69.2	1.3	18.3	22.0	6.4
6.1	0.80	na	-0.01	5.1	2.5	1.08	12.86	3.50	63.4	5.8	34.0	2.0	4.6
6.6	1.01	4.4	0.11	4.9	37.3	0.94	9.88	2.97	58.9	3.3	13.5	12.4	8.6
6.8	0.93	na	0.01	6.9	10.1	1.48	14.92	1.94	57.1	3.6	48.3	15.4	7.0
7.3	0.84	na	0.27	5.1	1.4	0.94	6.56	3.51	77.6	1.1	26.7	11.8	7.1
9.4	0.00	na	0.00	2.6	0.7	0.32	6.36	0.60	67.0	7.4	65.9	0.0	7.1
8.7	0.13	na	-0.01	4.4	4.4	1.29	11.57	2.56	80.7	2.3	45.9	25.9	7.5
8.3	0.22	na	-0.01	4.1	7.6	0.66	6.18	3.13	72.1	5.0	32.7	10.6	8.2
3.7	1.79	na	-0.02	8.8	9.8	1.68	14.44	3.75	41.7	3.1	11.3	12.9	9.2
5.2	1.19	na	0.07	4.3	11.2	0.99	9.27	3.40	64.7	3.3	13.4	12.9	8.6
7.0	0.77	na	-0.04	0.0	-1.3	-1.46	-12.22	2.49	148.8	1.9	40.3	21.9	4.6
3.4	3.01	na	0.24	3.7	1.3	0.56	6.88	3.64	76.4	2.0	20.8	19.7	4.0
3.3	2.91	na	0.09	4.0	4.8	0.87	7.98	2.82	68.6	2.7	17.1	13.2	7.6
5.0	1.93	na	0.19	4.3	12.0	0.84	7.79	3.28	66.6	3.1	18.4	14.0	8.6
2.7	0.88	na	0.01	8.5	6.2	1.99	16.30	5.15	59.0	3.1	10.6	13.3	9.2
5.1	2.25	na	-0.01	4.0	3.3	0.86	7.17	3.01	64.8	4.1	31.6	11.7	7.4
0.0	5.39	32.2	0.20	3.0	0.4	0.33	3.06	4.86	87.4	5.4	28.0	1.9	4.8
6.6	0.54	4.4	0.11	5.4	32.7	1.09	12.72	4.04	69.1	3.7	11.8	10.5	7.3
9.1	0.09	na	0.03	5.0	1.6	1.13	5.51	3.35	62.4	3.0	36.0	18.7	8.9
6.5	0.45	na	0.05	9.2	18.1	2.96	29.60	3.93	69.7	3.7	9.5	10.0	8.3
4.2	1.15	na	0.01	5.6	2.1	1.33	13.77	3.86	58.6	1.2	8.9	22.5	6.9
3.9	1.92	na	0.17	3.8	1.3	0.51	5.09	3.90	72.6	1.9	8.5	18.9	6.6
5.7	1.03	8.3	0.25	3.4	129.5	0.51	5.80	2.42	49.3	1.5	16.6	10.7	8.5
5.1	0.27	na	0.08	5.4	3.4	1.05	14.65	3.55	60.5	1.5	6.1	20.3	4.1
4.8	1.10	6.6	0.00	3.7	8.6	0.56	6.00	2.89	59.8	1.3	22.4	33.9	7.9
6.4	1.09	3.8	0.10	5.4	1.6	1.26	13.78	3.71	68.0	6.5	47.3	2.7	6.0
4.9	0.00	na	0.00	4.7	0.9	0.88	7.61	4.65	58.4	2.1	38.6	8.4	7.3
1.8	2.59	23.9	0.88	3.9	5.0	0.55	5.39	3.65	72.2	3.4	17.0	6.0	9.4
7.2	0.32	1.7	0.07	4.7	79.8	0.80	6.39	3.94	62.4	5.2	23.1	4.2	9.9
7.2	2.17	na	0.28	3.7	0.7	0.80	6.69	2.58	74.9	6.4	66.2	8.6	6.9
2.8	1.41	9.0	0.01	4.1	1.4	0.91	9.15	3.70	68.8	0.7	5.5	31.2	5.8
5.2	0.55	na	0.09	6.1	22.4	1.45	15.33	3.51	57.1	3.1	17.1	11.5	8.8
6.0	0.67	3.8	0.09	4.7	27.9	0.99	8.39	3.04	62.9	1.8	16.3	10.7	8.1
6.5	2.04	na	0.00	3.3	0.4	0.50	4.27	2.08	74.5	1.4	31.6	40.7	6.6
5.2	1.36	na	-0.06	5.0	3.1	0.97	8.93	3.22	62.0	4.1	26.6	9.3	7.4
3.0	1.38	5.4	4.37	2.5	-198.0	-0.80	-4.90	7.74	52.6	3.3	40.1	9.8	9.1
5.0	0.61	5.4	0.25	9.9	84.2	3.99	29.51	2.79	61.7	2.6	5.6	7.3	8.3
9.7	0.06	0.0	0.07	0.0	-0.2	-1.45	-7.99	1.73	283.3	7.3	107.2	5.8	2.1
3.8	2.19	na	0.01	8.3	0.8	1.73	16.34	4.97	66.3	2.5	32.1	20.2	7.7
9.0	0.21	0.9	0.00	8.2	12.3	1.65	10.98	3.51	61.4	3.7	23.4	9.9	10.0
6.5	0.87	na	0.03	5.1	1.7	1.23	12.96	3.65	72.1	1.8	20.9	21.4	5.9
7.8	0.39	2.3	0.00	3.2	0.1	0.45	3.68	3.08	75.5	0.9	22.1	36.4	6.6
2.2	6.41	19.3	0.04	3.1	0.1	0.44	1.90	4.98	91.7	6.2	38.5	1.6	6.2
5.7	1.52	5.2	0.01	5.7	0.9	1.02	7.73	3.90	73.3	2.9	28.2	16.1	7.7
4.6	0.83	na	-0.01	4.1	0.7	0.76	10.34	4.11	71.5	2.0	15.6	18.9	4.8
3.6	1.97	na	0.00	3.1	1.6	0.48	5.40	3.06	78.3	2.2	6.6	14.7	5.6
3.9	2.60	na	0.09	5.5	1.0	1.14	12.27	4.47	62.7	2.3	23.0	18.2	5.9
7.3	0.54	na	0.01	4.1	12.2	0.84	9.82	3.26	77.3	1.9	14.2	16.2	7.0
6.5	1.96	5.4	0.00	5.2	3.0	1.05	6.16	3.90	60.6	1.9	8.9	18.7	6.7
3.2	2.02	11.2	0.66	0.4	-2265.7	-3.08	-28.26	2.74	156.3	5.0	27.7	4.4	8.2
5.2	0.98	5.8	-0.03	3.8	14.9	0.67	7.16	2.79	58.9	1.3	10.7	26.8	7.7

Name	City	State	Rating	2019 Rating	2018 Rating	Total Assets ($Mil)	One Year Asset Growth	Asset Mix (As a % of Total Assets)				Capital-ization Index	Lever-age Ratio	Risk-Based Capital Ratio
								Comm-ercial Loans	Cons-umer Loans	Mort-gage Loans	Secur-ities			
BCBank, Inc.	Philippi	WV	B-	C+	C+	151.2	6.35	8.8	2.9	16.7	14.8	7.1	9.3	0.0
Beach Bank	Fort Walton Beach	FL	D-	D-	E	568.8	15.77	16.8	0.3	14.4	3.4	8.7	10.2	14.3
▼ Beacon Business Bank, N.A.	San Francisco	CA	C+	B	C+	161.1	14.59	15.9	0.0	5.2	8.3	9.7	10.8	21.0
Beacon Community Bank	Charleston	SC	D	D	D	261.3	148.76	23.4	0.5	33.7	4.1	10.0	13.7	18.8
Beal Bank USA	Las Vegas	NV	C	C+	C-	8291.5	71.31	33.9	0.0	1.7	28.2	10.0	29.3	29.5
Beal Bank, SSB	Plano	TX	C	C+	C-	2040.3	28.03	12.4	0.4	24.6	27.3	10.0	24.1	34.7
Beardstown Savings s.b.	Beardstown	IL	C+	C+	C	60.4	15.77	5.0	10.2	40.1	19.5	9.6	10.7	18.9
Beauregard Federal Savings Bank	DeRidder	LA	B+	B+	B+	71.1	7.13	5.7	6.6	34.8	5.7	10.0	17.1	0.0
Bedford Federal Savings Bank	Bedford	IN	B	B	B	160.2	20.84	7.1	2.0	39.2	0.0	9.9	11.0	0.0
Bedford Loan & Deposit Bank	Bedford	KY	B	B	B-	100.2	6.67	0.5	5.5	33.5	31.8	10.0	13.5	24.8
Belgrade State Bank	Belgrade	MO	B	B	B-	318.3	15.70	7.6	4.5	26.8	14.1	6.9	8.9	16.1
▲ Bell Bank	Fargo	ND	A-	B+	B+	8224.8	31.26	21.6	1.9	17.4	0.6	8.5	10.1	13.8
▲ Bellevue State Bank	Bellevue	IA	A-	A-	B+	130.6	8.41	13.1	5.0	19.9	8.5	10.0	14.7	0.0
▲ Belmont Bank & Trust Co.	Chicago	IL	B+	C+	B-	732.2	37.23	20.2	0.6	6.0	17.6	9.1	10.4	18.0
Belmont Savings Bank	Bellaire	OH	B-	B	B	398.5	5.75	4.4	2.0	14.6	60.9	10.0	18.1	0.0
▲ Belmont Savings Bank, SSB	Belmont	NC	C+	C+	B-	95.5	3.54	0.0	0.0	67.7	1.1	10.0	20.2	0.0
▲ Belt Valley Bank	Belt	MT	B+	B	B	69.5	7.52	4.6	2.8	29.4	4.0	10.0	14.9	0.0
Benchmark Bank	Plano	TX	B+	B+	B+	820.3	15.02	10.6	2.3	18.7	0.1	5.7	8.7	11.5
Benchmark Community Bank	Kenbridge	VA	A-	A-	A-	807.0	15.22	11.1	1.8	34.1	4.9	8.0	9.7	15.7
Bendena State Bank	Bendena	KS	B-	B-	B-	74.2	10.44	6.6	2.2	11.6	15.3	7.8	9.5	14.4
▼ Beneficial State Bank	Oakland	CA	D	C-	C-	1201.1	13.72	24.4	11.9	3.2	10.3	5.5	9.3	0.0
Bennington State Bank	Salina	KS	B-	B-	C+	822.3	16.47	15.1	0.9	14.7	28.1	9.6	10.8	17.8
Benton County State Bank	Blairstown	IA	B	B	B	50.2	11.58	2.8	0.1	5.1	17.0	10.0	13.8	0.0
Benton State Bank	Benton	WI	C-	C-	D+	70.5	7.63	8.5	4.2	27.5	1.3	5.6	9.3	0.0
▼ Berkshire Bank	Boston	MA	C	B-	B-	12607.8	-6.64	16.5	2.4	18.6	15.3	7.0	9.0	14.3
Berkshire Bank	New York	NY	B-	B	B	686.4	6.78	1.1	0.1	6.1	13.5	10.0	17.5	37.1
Bessemer Trust Co.	New York	NY	A	A	B+	945.0	8.96	10.3	27.9	0.0	31.2	8.2	9.8	21.6
Bessemer Trust Co. of California, N.A.	San Francisco	CA	U	U	U	12.5	10.33	0.0	0.0	0.0	56.8	10.0	100.	0.0
Bessemer Trust Co. of Delaware, N.A.	Wilmington	DE	U	U	U	25.7	11.74	0.0	0.0	0.0	44.4	10.0	97.7	0.0
Bessemer Trust Co., N.A.	New York	NY	A	A	A-	2318.5	25.93	6.3	11.1	0.0	38.1	8.9	10.3	37.4
Better Banks	Peoria	IL	B-	B-	C+	331.1	14.05	6.9	27.4	17.9	20.1	6.4	8.4	13.7
Beverly Bank & Trust Co., N.A.	Chicago	IL	B	B	B	1761.9	11.13	34.7	13.0	2.4	6.3	6.4	9.8	12.0
Big Bend Banks, N.A.	Marfa	TX	B+	A-	A-	176.1	29.05	1.8	2.1	1.7	78.1	10.0	12.1	41.3
Big Horn Federal Savings Bank	Greybull	WY	C+	C+	C+	299.6	15.29	12.1	2.2	8.8	31.4	8.3	9.9	21.7
Bippus State Bank	Huntington	IN	B+	B	B-	215.0	17.23	18.3	2.4	13.0	11.2	9.8	11.1	14.8
▲ Bison State Bank	Bison	KS	C	D	D	16.3	14.58	17.3	5.5	32.6	3.1	9.1	10.4	0.0
Black Hills Community Bank, N.A.	Rapid City	SD	B-	B	B-	382.6	19.76	15.4	0.3	7.9	7.6	3.9	9.2	0.0
Black Mountain Savings Bank, SSB	Black Mountain	NC	C+	C+	C+	39.0	-5.19	0.0	0.5	68.1	0.0	10.0	13.4	0.0
Black River Country Bank	Black River Falls	WI	B+	B+	B+	89.9	13.87	7.1	3.6	31.6	9.6	8.9	10.3	17.0
▲ Blackhawk Bank	Beloit	WI	B	B	B-	1121.9	15.32	26.1	1.7	9.2	28.1	7.1	9.1	15.0
Blackhawk Bank & Trust	Milan	IL	B+	A-	B+	1554.2	12.54	10.1	0.7	6.6	50.4	9.8	10.9	0.0
BLC Community Bank	Little Chute	WI	A	A-	A-	315.0	4.94	20.1	0.3	10.4	16.2	9.7	10.8	16.4
▼ Blissfield State Bank	Blissfield	MI	C+	B-	C+	106.0	7.50	9.0	2.6	15.5	37.2	9.8	10.9	16.3
Bloomsdale Bank	Bloomsdale	MO	A-	B+	B+	302.6	32.72	15.7	1.5	13.7	24.3	6.2	8.2	14.9
▼ Blue Foundry Bank	Rutherford	NJ	C-	C+	C+	1924.1	8.36	2.9	0.0	34.7	12.2	9.6	10.7	20.8
Blue Grass Federal S&L Assn.	Paris	KY	B-	B-	C	35.3	-0.74	6.5	2.5	48.4	14.2	10.0	24.8	0.0
Blue Grass Savings Bank	Blue Grass	IA	B	B	B	209.5	5.31	10.9	0.7	17.4	39.0	10.0	15.0	27.3
Blue Grass Valley Bank	Blue Grass	VA	C+	C+	D+	48.7	12.30	5.7	5.2	28.3	6.2	9.9	11.0	0.0
Blue Ridge Bank	Walhalla	SC	C-	C+	C+	151.7	15.81	1.5	1.4	26.8	21.2	7.0	9.0	0.0
Blue Ridge Bank and Trust Co.	Independence	MO	C+	C	C	627.8	11.62	19.9	11.6	4.2	15.0	7.4	9.2	13.7
▲ Blue Ridge Bank, N.A.	Martinsville	VA	B-	C+	C+	1516.2	106.20	29.0	3.0	24.8	7.2	5.9	7.9	12.6
Blue Sky Bank	Pawhuska	OK	B	B	B+	420.8	79.22	26.4	1.2	4.2	16.9	6.1	11.0	0.0
BlueHarbor Bank	Mooresville	NC	A-	A-	B+	312.0	30.10	12.3	0.2	14.3	6.5	10.0	11.6	15.9
Bluestone Bank	Raynham	MA	C+	C+	C+	712.2	14.33	7.0	2.6	34.5	19.1	6.9	8.9	15.9
▲ Bluff View Bank	Galesville	WI	A	A-	A-	121.0	14.87	10.0	2.1	12.7	11.6	10.0	18.2	21.1
▼ BMO Harris Bank N.A.	Chicago	IL	C+	B	B-	151532.9	9.14	25.1	4.6	5.1	21.4	7.4	9.3	14.2
BMO Harris Central N.A.	Roselle	IL	U	U	U	8.0	0.77	0.0	0.0	0.0	0.0	10.0	87.0	444.9
BMW Bank of North America	Salt Lake City	UT	A-	A-	A-	11443.3	8.61	0.6	76.0	0.0	21.4	10.0	13.7	15.5
BNA Bank	New Albany	MS	A-	A-	A-	615.0	17.14	6.2	3.9	23.0	33.6	10.0	11.5	18.9
▼ BNB Bank	Bridgehampton	NY	B	B+	B+	6322.0	33.49	24.4	0.4	7.4	9.0	6.0	8.1	13.2

Asset Quality Index	Adjusted Non-Performing Loans as a % of Total Loans	as a % of Capital	Net Charge-Offs Avg Loans	Profitability Index	Net Income ($Mil)	Return on Assets (R.O.A.)	Return on Equity (R.O.E.)	Net Interest Spread	Overhead Efficiency Ratio	Liquidity Index	Liquidity Ratio	Hot Money Ratio	Stability Index
6.1	1.40	na	0.03	4.6	1.0	0.95	10.60	4.26	72.3	4.3	17.4	7.1	5.3
7.7	0.27	na	-0.04	0.0	-2.0	-0.48	-3.30	2.95	105.1	1.6	13.5	23.1	2.9
6.2	1.94	na	0.00	1.6	-0.2	-0.17	-1.48	3.41	104.3	4.5	36.3	11.0	7.8
8.6	0.00	na	0.00	0.0	-0.9	-0.63	-4.43	3.01	100.9	0.8	9.2	31.1	1.5
0.3	30.28	52.1	1.15	9.2	106.6	2.13	6.22	5.25	51.2	2.0	37.3	10.2	8.1
1.7	21.33	34.8	0.11	8.3	21.4	1.62	6.06	6.32	56.9	3.0	65.9	10.5	7.0
2.8	2.38	na	0.27	4.1	0.3	0.74	6.64	3.88	72.3	3.5	35.0	15.9	5.1
6.1	1.39	na	0.03	6.6	0.6	1.14	6.59	4.59	73.9	4.5	43.0	12.9	9.5
6.7	0.75	na	0.01	4.8	1.1	1.01	9.24	3.46	66.5	2.7	27.5	17.5	6.2
7.4	1.31	na	0.05	4.1	0.6	0.82	5.73	3.86	74.8	4.2	33.6	12.0	8.0
6.8	0.06	na	0.29	5.1	2.4	1.06	11.61	4.33	68.3	1.7	19.7	22.3	4.7
7.9	0.21	1.3	0.02	6.6	69.6	1.20	11.77	3.55	59.5	4.5	6.0	3.1	8.8
5.6	1.16	na	0.20	9.1	1.8	1.83	12.60	3.73	38.7	4.1	26.4	9.7	10.0
7.1	0.17	na	0.05	8.1	7.2	1.50	15.46	3.79	38.5	2.0	33.6	27.5	7.4
7.2	3.35	na	0.03	2.9	1.3	0.45	2.27	2.66	79.0	3.5	60.6	27.4	7.4
9.9	0.60	na	0.00	2.6	0.3	0.38	1.89	3.06	83.2	0.9	24.0	46.0	7.6
5.3	1.55	na	-0.03	9.6	0.9	1.72	11.47	4.75	52.1	2.5	18.2	16.9	8.4
6.0	0.40	na	-0.13	6.1	6.7	1.15	13.04	3.69	79.8	4.5	13.3	4.8	6.8
7.3	0.25	na	0.03	6.9	7.7	1.35	13.35	4.35	64.9	4.0	15.1	8.4	7.2
4.4	0.61	4.1	0.00	7.1	0.8	1.60	15.78	3.83	58.0	3.8	14.3	9.9	6.9
5.1	1.00	6.8	0.18	0.4	-7.6	-0.88	-8.32	3.97	118.8	3.3	18.9	13.2	7.4
5.0	3.37	na	0.77	7.8	10.3	1.74	15.10	3.09	43.5	2.8	15.2	14.8	8.8
5.1	0.00	na	0.00	5.5	0.4	1.10	7.69	3.60	60.9	2.8	38.4	21.5	7.5
4.0	1.53	9.7	0.00	4.9	0.6	1.21	13.09	4.47	73.8	1.5	17.0	23.4	3.7
5.8	0.74	5.1	0.46	1.1	-522.9	-5.21	-47.25	2.77	256.1	1.6	21.3	20.0	7.2
9.0	1.67	na	0.03	1.8	-0.4	-0.08	-0.45	2.68	83.0	5.2	64.2	14.6	8.4
7.3	0.00	na	0.00	9.5	20.8	2.93	31.58	1.40	70.9	5.9	31.0	0.0	8.5
10.0	na	na	na	9.5	0.8	9.10	9.21	1.13	66.2	4.0	na	0.0	7.0
10.0	na	na	na	9.5	8.2	47.18	53.36	1.39	66.0	4.0	na	0.0	7.0
7.5	0.00	na	0.00	9.5	58.1	3.75	27.56	1.07	86.0	7.1	41.3	0.0	8.8
4.6	0.62	na	0.08	4.2	2.1	0.91	9.08	3.50	70.4	2.7	23.7	16.2	5.9
6.0	0.69	4.3	0.04	4.2	8.4	0.66	6.35	3.08	64.9	2.0	9.2	9.9	7.8
9.8	0.00	na	1.27	5.0	1.5	1.23	9.16	3.18	63.5	6.3	57.2	7.4	8.0
5.3	2.38	na	0.17	3.1	1.0	0.47	4.54	3.39	80.6	5.3	47.0	10.5	5.7
5.0	0.78	na	0.58	9.3	3.7	2.44	21.99	4.09	52.1	4.1	11.7	7.3	8.3
8.0	0.31	na	-0.29	4.1	0.1	0.70	6.79	4.40	86.6	4.6	34.6	7.5	3.2
6.3	0.44	na	-0.01	5.9	3.9	1.47	15.36	3.68	58.0	1.2	14.7	29.0	6.3
10.0	0.00	na	0.00	2.3	0.1	0.32	2.44	2.88	85.4	1.4	31.8	41.8	5.8
8.2	0.03	na	0.02	6.4	1.0	1.54	14.50	3.94	58.8	2.0	21.6	19.8	7.5
4.7	1.56	7.7	0.77	5.1	7.7	0.98	8.96	3.94	63.1	5.0	21.2	4.1	8.4
7.9	0.89	na	-0.12	5.1	12.7	1.17	9.41	2.72	52.2	2.8	18.1	15.8	9.3
7.4	0.02	0.1	0.00	7.7	4.6	2.08	17.96	2.74	45.6	1.3	17.6	14.2	9.8
3.8	3.32	na	0.00	2.4	0.6	0.76	6.94	3.10	84.0	5.9	54.0	8.9	6.9
6.5	0.55	na	0.00	10.0	6.2	3.08	34.60	3.81	35.6	1.9	25.5	22.4	6.9
8.0	0.83	4.9	0.00	0.5	-16.6	-1.15	-10.52	2.21	166.9	2.1	27.2	29.3	8.8
8.1	0.42	na	0.10	2.0	-0.3	-1.13	-4.33	3.49	131.0	2.2	38.1	30.8	6.2
6.7	1.54	na	0.51	4.7	1.5	0.97	6.35	2.60	46.0	3.0	48.7	23.7	8.3
3.9	3.12	na	-0.07	3.8	0.2	0.64	5.77	3.52	75.2	4.4	43.7	13.6	5.3
6.1	2.33	na	0.00	2.0	0.2	0.21	2.19	3.07	93.2	5.5	52.4	10.8	5.3
3.4	1.88	na	0.16	4.8	3.9	0.87	9.07	3.71	65.0	4.0	16.5	9.2	6.4
5.7	0.31	na	0.07	6.6	14.4	1.47	18.58	3.43	62.9	1.6	10.4	19.6	7.2
6.5	0.25	na	0.13	6.6	4.4	1.50	12.46	4.56	60.4	1.5	16.8	25.2	8.1
8.7	0.17	na	0.00	5.8	2.3	1.13	9.18	3.57	51.3	2.9	21.5	12.7	7.8
8.8	0.00	na	0.00	3.4	3.3	0.66	6.91	2.93	77.7	4.1	25.7	9.4	6.1
7.3	1.86	na	0.00	9.1	2.2	2.59	13.50	3.99	55.1	4.7	28.5	6.6	9.6
4.5	1.83	7.6	0.26	3.2	560.7	0.51	4.28	2.41	61.3	5.3	39.6	7.8	10.0
10.0	na	0.0	na	3.5	0.0	0.35	0.40	6.03	-275.0	4.0	na	0.0	6.5
5.6	0.34	1.7	0.18	5.5	64.6	0.78	5.58	2.13	25.0	1.5	28.6	2.3	10.0
6.8	1.36	4.8	0.03	7.4	7.3	1.69	14.09	3.31	48.2	3.9	31.4	12.5	8.3
6.1	0.65	3.7	0.06	4.2	35.7	0.83	8.27	3.07	59.2	4.6	14.4	4.0	8.0

Name	City	State	Rating	2019 Rating	2018 Rating	Total Assets ($Mil)	One Year Asset Growth	Commercial Loans	Consumer Loans	Mortgage Loans	Securities	Capitalization Index	Leverage Ratio	Risk-Based Capital Ratio
BNC National Bank	Glendale	AZ	A-	B+	B-	1099.8	1.54	15.4	4.7	23.8	17.0	9.8	10.9	17.3
BNY Mellon Trust of Delaware	Wilmington	DE	B	B	B	154.5	24.48	0.0	0.0	11.3	0.0	10.0	39.1	122.4
BNY Mellon, N.A.	Pittsburgh	PA	B	B	B	30310.0	8.94	0.4	8.1	25.7	10.6	5.6	7.6	13.0
BOC Bank	Amarillo	TX	A-	A-	B+	106.2	71.28	53.7	0.1	6.8	5.0	10.0	15.2	16.7
▲ Bodcaw Bank	Stamps	AR	B+	B-	B	130.2	15.65	18.6	4.4	27.5	18.5	10.0	12.3	18.4
Boelus State Bank	Boelus	NE	C+	C+	C+	17.1	5.04	1.0	4.4	0.4	0.4	10.0	14.7	0.0
Bogota Savings Bank	Teaneck	NJ	C	C+	B	753.9	13.24	1.8	0.1	49.1	9.0	10.0	13.5	0.0
BOKF, N.A.	Tulsa	OK	B	B	B	45840.8	6.53	22.6	0.9	4.8	28.6	6.1	8.1	13.1
BOM Bank	Natchitoches	LA	B	B	B	624.1	30.84	23.5	2.7	21.3	2.1	7.6	9.4	13.8
Bonanza Valley State Bank	Brooten	MN	C+	C	C	72.1	9.96	8.5	2.6	27.7	7.3	6.7	8.7	12.3
Bonduel State Bank	Bonduel	WI	A-	B+	B+	72.5	19.14	5.5	4.2	10.2	32.1	10.0	20.0	40.5
Boone Bank & Trust Co.	Boone	IA	B+	A-	A-	165.0	9.79	6.9	1.2	2.7	37.2	6.9	9.5	0.0
▲ Boonville Federal Savings Bank	Boonville	IN	C-	D+	D	60.4	11.73	13.1	9.2	37.3	9.0	6.3	8.3	14.7
Border Bank	Greenbush	MN	B-	B-	B-	660.0	4.33	14.6	4.7	9.3	13.8	7.0	9.0	12.9
Boston Private Bank & Trust Co.	Boston	MA	B	B	B	9399.4	8.61	9.2	1.2	30.4	11.2	6.5	8.5	13.0
Boston Trust Walden Co.	Boston	MA	A-	A-	A-	52.2	1.46	0.1	0.0	0.0	2.8	10.0	52.7	78.3
Boundary Waters Bank	Ely	MN	C+	C+	C	131.7	18.45	3.0	1.0	9.4	3.3	10.0	11.0	15.1
Bradford National Bank of Greenville	Greenville	IL	A-	A-	B	406.7	27.75	4.7	1.2	10.6	58.0	10.0	11.6	18.9
Brady National Bank	Brady	TX	B-	B-	B-	140.1	16.19	12.7	1.9	8.1	43.4	6.6	8.6	16.4
Brainerd S&L Assn., A Federal Assn.	Brainerd	MN	D	D	D	70.3	5.23	0.3	1.2	42.6	3.0	5.1	7.1	12.3
Brannen Bank	Inverness	FL	B-	B-	C+	631.0	16.86	2.7	0.9	32.3	27.0	3.9	5.9	17.1
Branson Bank	Branson	MO	B-	B	B	268.1	13.71	14.8	2.1	25.1	3.9	5.4	8.9	0.0
Brantley Bank and Trust Co.	Brantley	AL	A-	B+	B+	95.9	38.58	9.8	2.3	6.7	46.1	10.0	11.9	0.0
Brattleboro S&L Assn.	Brattleboro	VT	C	C+	C	266.3	21.49	8.4	0.6	35.7	0.1	5.0	7.0	13.3
Brazos National Bank	Richwood	TX	B+	B+	B+	42.2	28.86	0.3	0.8	77.3	0.0	10.0	25.7	45.5
Breda Savings Bank	Breda	IA	A-	A-	A-	68.2	6.22	9.3	0.9	14.4	36.1	10.0	12.1	0.0
Bremer Bank, N.A.	Saint Paul	MN	B+	B+	B+	15345.3	17.52	16.9	0.9	7.0	21.1	6.4	8.4	13.5
Brenham National Bank	Brenham	TX	B+	A-	B	442.9	16.79	7.7	1.0	6.0	52.1	7.9	9.6	18.8
Brentwood Bank	Bethel Park	PA	B-	B	B	772.0	11.09	3.4	0.0	31.8	15.2	10.0	11.8	0.0
▼ Brickyard Bank	Lincolnwood	IL	C-	C-	D+	161.3	31.89	12.5	0.3	8.3	5.2	7.7	9.4	19.7
Bridge City State Bank	Bridge City	TX	B	B	B	263.9	25.55	4.0	0.7	7.8	42.8	6.8	8.8	22.9
Bridge Community Bank	Mount Vernon	IA	A-	B+	B+	112.5	13.78	23.3	3.5	18.6	7.5	8.9	10.6	0.0
Bridgewater Bank	Saint Louis Park	MN	A-	A-	A-	2768.4	24.30	16.4	0.2	8.8	13.5	8.6	11.2	13.9
Brighton Bank	Brighton	TN	E-	E-	E	46.5	13.53	7.8	0.9	41.5	10.4	5.3	7.3	14.8
Brighton Bank	Salt Lake City	UT	A-	A-	B+	283.7	35.96	14.1	0.3	3.7	12.8	8.1	9.7	0.0
Bristol County Savings Bank	Taunton	MA	C+	B-	C+	2745.8	20.45	11.5	10.8	28.3	9.5	7.2	10.3	12.6
Bristol Morgan Bank	Oakfield	WI	C-	C	C+	135.0	32.03	9.6	3.1	26.1	10.7	5.7	8.6	11.5
Broadway Federal Bank, F.S.B.	Los Angeles	CA	C-	C	C+	497.0	20.59	0.1	0.0	10.9	2.1	8.3	9.8	18.1
▼ Broadway National Bank	San Antonio	TX	B	B+	B	4630.7	21.22	13.5	3.1	10.7	36.8	7.0	9.0	0.0
Brookline Bank	Brookline	MA	B-	B	B	5855.8	17.61	25.2	0.5	10.1	7.3	7.1	9.4	12.6
Brookville Building and Savings Assn.	Brookville	OH	B	B	B-	47.8	6.28	8.2	0.9	49.7	11.5	10.0	18.6	0.0
Brown Brothers Harriman Trust Co.	Wilmington	DE	U	U	U	11.6	10.64	0.0	0.0	0.0	59.8	10.0	77.3	0.0
Brown Brothers Harriman Trust Co., N.A.	New York	NY	U	U	U	14.9	7.83	0.0	0.0	0.0	55.2	10.0	70.9	0.0
▲ Bruning Bank	Bruning	NE	B+	B	B-	414.4	17.61	11.7	0.7	1.0	26.7	7.6	11.5	0.0
Brunswick Bank and Trust Co.	New Brunswick	NJ	B-	B-	B-	304.4	34.14	5.4	0.0	15.8	11.1	10.0	12.5	16.9
Brunswick State Bank	Brunswick	NE	C-	C	C+	141.9	9.02	17.0	4.6	1.3	3.0	5.2	8.2	11.1
Bryant Bank	Tuscaloosa	AL	B+	A-	A-	2242.4	29.36	14.2	0.6	6.6	16.4	6.3	8.4	0.0
▲ Bryant State Bank	Bryant	SD	A-	B+	B	38.8	10.42	16.8	5.6	1.1	11.1	10.0	11.4	19.8
▼ Bryn Mawr Trust Co.	Bryn Mawr	PA	B	B+	B	5043.1	4.77	9.2	0.9	13.7	11.4	7.2	9.2	13.3
BTC Bank	Bethany	MO	B+	B+	B	622.8	12.25	10.5	1.7	10.8	10.7	10.0	13.5	0.0
BTH Bank, N.A.	Quitman	TX	B+	A-	B+	1926.1	6.59	34.8	0.7	15.6	20.0	10.0	12.8	0.0
▼ Buckeye Community Bank	Lorain	OH	B+	A-	B+	209.2	20.16	27.8	0.1	5.6	13.3	10.0	11.7	19.1
▲ Buckeye State Bank	Powell	OH	D	D-	D-	241.0	118.10	32.0	7.2	6.7	22.1	8.3	9.9	14.5
Buckholts State Bank	Buckholts	TX	A-	A-	A-	90.2	14.02	20.9	1.7	12.4	33.5	10.0	16.5	0.0
Buckley State Bank	Buckley	IL	B-	B-	C+	44.0	5.36	4.6	0.8	0.2	20.1	10.0	12.1	19.7
Buena Vista National Bank	Chester	IL	A-	A-	B+	237.9	14.62	4.9	5.9	18.8	29.3	10.0	11.6	0.0
Buffalo Federal Bank	Buffalo	WY	B-	B	B	142.1	14.41	11.3	3.9	16.4	15.5	7.7	10.4	0.0
▼ Burke & Herbert Bank & Trust Co.	Alexandria	VA	B-	B	B+	3356.7	15.12	4.5	0.1	12.7	31.5	9.7	10.8	16.7
Burling Bank	Chicago	IL	B+	A-	B	147.0	11.13	13.6	0.6	28.5	20.4	10.0	11.2	0.0
Burton State Bank	Burton	TX	B+	B+	B-	77.9	13.10	1.0	4.2	10.9	9.1	10.0	11.7	0.0

Asset Quality Index	Adjusted Non-Performing Loans as a % of Total Loans	as a % of Capital	Net Charge-Offs Avg Loans	Profitability Index	Net Income ($Mil)	Return on Assets (R.O.A.)	Return on Equity (R.O.E.)	Net Interest Spread	Overhead Efficiency Ratio	Liquidity Index	Liquidity Ratio	Hot Money Ratio	Stability Index
7.8	0.44	na	0.10	8.2	33.4	4.22	37.88	3.25	46.7	3.3	14.3	8.5	9.5
3.9	20.45	3.6	-0.01	9.5	4.4	4.35	6.84	1.25	39.7	8.7	111.4	0.0	8.3
6.8	0.09	0.3	0.00	5.3	225.0	0.99	7.70	1.14	60.5	2.3	35.6	28.2	8.3
8.5	0.00	na	0.00	7.4	0.9	1.58	12.43	4.00	54.3	4.5	32.0	9.6	8.5
7.1	1.18	na	0.08	6.0	1.2	1.27	11.20	4.20	50.7	0.8	21.9	47.1	6.5
8.7	0.00	0.0	0.00	3.5	0.1	0.56	3.84	2.28	64.9	4.1	77.5	19.2	6.7
9.6	0.22	na	-0.01	2.1	0.9	0.17	1.29	1.86	88.8	0.7	18.6	46.4	6.7
5.6	1.13	4.5	0.30	4.5	295.2	0.83	8.09	2.77	55.4	3.9	15.5	4.3	9.7
6.1	0.08	na	0.31	5.7	5.1	1.18	12.04	4.53	68.1	3.7	6.6	9.7	7.1
6.7	0.28	na	0.00	5.1	0.6	1.19	13.12	4.02	68.3	4.0	16.2	8.1	5.0
8.9	0.39	na	0.00	5.8	0.6	1.30	5.95	3.31	53.4	6.2	69.2	8.5	8.2
8.7	0.33	1.4	0.09	5.4	1.2	1.12	11.19	3.00	54.0 '	4.2	45.2	14.3	7.0
7.6	0.06	na	0.15	2.1	0.1	0.30	3.58	3.30	87.2	1.2	24.9	31.3	3.1
3.9	1.82	9.6	0.11	4.4	4.7	0.98	9.94	3.50	72.7	1.8	16.8	13.3	6.6
7.2	0.67	4.7	0.04	2.9	24.6	0.36	3.78	2.84	73.4	4.0	16.7	5.8	8.2
6.5	0.00	0.0	0.00	10.0	16.0	44.57	53.79	8.06	57.0	2.9	84.6	100.0	10.0
4.8	1.24	na	0.69	2.9	0.0	0.03	0.24	3.82	86.6	2.6	31.6	19.2	6.3
6.3	2.45	na	0.18	5.8	3.8	1.34	9.97	3.58	55.0	2.8	42.3	16.7	8.0
3.7	5.66	na	0.00	4.2	1.1	1.08	11.27	2.87	68.3	4.5	34.7	11.0	5.4
5.3	0.91	na	0.03	1.0	0.1	0.20	2.87	2.60	94.8	1.8	25.3	13.7	2.3
6.5	1.28	na	0.00	6.8	7.0	1.58	23.96	3.32	57.8	6.1	51.7	6.6	5.6
6.1	1.16	na	0.00	4.2	1.4	0.74	7.86	3.71	75.7	3.0	12.7	12.8	5.7
7.8	0.55	na	-0.02	5.7	0.7	1.15	8.77	4.38	63.3	3.2	54.0	23.9	6.7
6.7	0.21	na	0.03	3.0	0.8	0.46	5.73	3.08	81.6	4.2	21.0	8.3	3.9
8.4	0.05	na	0.00	10.0	2.1	7.52	27.47	3.59	74.1	0.6	13.3	53.3	8.0
8.8	0.00	na	0.00	7.5	0.8	1.74	15.00	3.55	51.6	4.9	41.2	10.7	8.1
6.9	0.56	2.9	0.11	6.0	133.3	1.24	13.31	3.33	55.8	3.3	15.7	5.2	8.2
6.7	2.19	na	0.06	5.2	4.3	1.42	12.56	3.38	62.8	5.1	58.1	14.0	7.2
8.8	0.29	na	0.00	3.7	3.9	0.70	5.76	2.97	66.5	3.4	14.3	11.2	7.5
7.0	2.30	na	0.01	2.1	0.3	0.27	2.60	2.51	89.8	2.4	44.6	31.8	4.7
5.9	1.64	na	0.01	3.9	1.5	0.82	8.19	2.87	67.7	6.7	66.1	6.1	5.2
8.3	0.00	na	-0.02	5.7	0.9	1.17	10.87	3.33	59.0	2.9	17.0	14.7	6.6
7.3	0.05	0.2	0.00	6.6	23.4	1.23	11.31	3.54	44.1	0.9	18.8	23.3	9.6
2.0	4.04	33.7	-0.01	4.6	0.5	1.47	21.59	4.38	84.3	1.7	19.7	22.2	1.3
6.1	2.06	na	0.00	10.0	4.5	2.31	21.14	4.76	50.9	6.0	35.5	1.1	7.7
7.0	0.57	2.5	0.05	1.4	-6.7	-0.25	-2.20	3.01	71.7	4.2	22.0	9.4	9.6
7.0	1.68	na	0.05	2.3	0.3	0.34	3.44	3.80	81.1	0.9	15.7	23.1	3.8
5.8	1.18	na	0.00	1.8	0.6	0.17	1.68	2.62	93.4	0.7	17.9	38.0	5.2
8.6	0.08	na	0.09	3.8	25.3	0.79	7.58	3.05	72.4	5.8	31.3	4.9	8.6
5.6	0.59	4.0	0.23	4.4	22.1	0.52	5.13	3.27	54.8	1.7	10.6	16.2	7.9
9.5	0.00	na	0.00	4.3	0.3	0.91	4.75	3.93	71.8	3.8	30.9	13.1	7.1
10.0	na	na	na	10.0	2.6	31.30	46.99	1.49	71.0	4.0	280.9	0.0	6.5
10.0	na	na	na	10.0	2.7	25.84	41.28	1.54	78.4	4.0	224.6	0.0	6.8
8.5	0.06	na	0.00	5.5	4.0	1.34	11.36	3.36	61.7	3.2	16.0	13.3	7.0
6.8	0.82	na	-0.01	2.9	0.9	0.45	3.50	3.48	81.1	1.4	23.3	24.9	7.1
2.2	1.49	na	1.34	4.4	0.7	0.68	8.27	3.46	49.0	0.8	17.6	41.5	5.8
8.4	0.43	na	-0.02	4.4	13.9	0.91	10.01	2.76	67.6	4.5	32.2	13.0	7.9
8.0	0.10	na	2.02	5.4	0.4	1.22	10.80	5.94	59.1	5.4	38.3	6.7	6.7
7.0	0.46	1.8	0.34	3.7	14.4	0.38	3.01	3.36	64.8	3.9	12.9	5.4	9.5
5.1	0.82	na	0.05	6.1	5.3	1.19	8.69	4.09	61.1	1.6	10.5	21.2	8.9
3.6	3.11	na	0.44	5.4	16.0	1.12	8.41	2.94	39.1	1.6	22.7	29.9	9.9
8.2	0.54	na	0.04	4.7	1.2	0.84	6.80	3.50	70.4	2.0	19.7	12.9	7.0
5.6	0.35	na	0.23	2.3	2.5	1.76	19.69	3.42	84.5	1.6	22.5	24.8	3.1
6.4	2.24	na	0.00	8.0	1.1	1.79	10.31	3.58	52.2	4.9	48.2	11.7	8.9
7.6	0.00	na	0.00	3.1	0.2	0.50	4.01	2.93	82.7	5.7	46.6	6.6	5.5
6.8	1.33	na	0.12	6.5	2.2	1.28	9.67	3.70	60.7	5.1	35.0	6.9	7.5
8.4	0.14	na	0.22	3.6	0.6	0.63	6.01	3.99	74.7	3.3	18.8	12.8	6.6
8.0	0.73	2.9	0.29	3.6	17.4	0.73	6.40	3.10	63.3	4.2	17.4	8.4	8.5
9.0	0.00	na	0.00	5.1	1.3	1.16	10.32	3.99	66.5	4.8	23.3	4.5	7.1
9.3	0.00	na	0.00	4.8	0.6	1.10	9.70	2.27	47.9	4.1	72.8	20.0	7.3

Name	City	State	2020 Rating	2019 Rating	2018 Rating	Total Assets ($Mil)	One Year Asset Growth	Asset Mix (As a % of Total Assets)				Capital- ization Index	Lever- age Ratio	Risk- Based Capital Ratio
								Comm- ercial Loans	Cons- umer Loans	Mort- gage Loans	Secur- ities			
Busey Bank	Champaign	IL	A-	A-	A-	10516.9	34.77	16.6	0.4	11.5	19.8	8.4	9.9	14.9
Business Bank of Texas, N.A.	Austin	TX	C+	B-	C	114.9	14.92	35.3	0.0	2.6	17.4	10.0	15.0	16.9
Butte State Bank	Butte	NE	B-	B-	C+	47.1	14.03	8.5	2.4	1.5	26.3	10.0	11.6	0.0
Byline Bank	Chicago	IL	B	B	B-	6490.1	19.46	28.8	0.1	4.1	23.3	9.2	10.5	14.5
Byron Bank	Byron	IL	C+	B-	C+	325.2	17.91	12.3	2.2	13.7	21.7	7.8	9.5	0.0
C3bank, N.A.	Encinitas	CA	B+	B+	B+	470.5	43.99	21.6	0.0	4.7	1.3	9.0	10.3	16.9
▼ Cache Bank & Trust	Greeley	CO	D+	C	C-	107.9	-5.90	6.2	1.4	4.1	22.0	10.0	12.7	0.0
Cache Valley Bank	Logan	UT	C+	B	B-	2770.9	92.36	35.4	0.3	3.9	0.8	0.9	9.4	0.0
▼ Cadence Bank, N.A.	Atlanta	GA	B-	B+	B+	18400.2	3.09	33.3	0.5	13.0	16.8	8.8	10.3	14.0
Caldwell Bank & Trust Co.	Columbia	LA	C	B-	D+	197.9	25.15	9.2	3.2	22.5	6.4	7.0	9.9	0.0
Calhoun County Bank, Inc.	Grantsville	WV	B-	B-	B-	165.0	6.79	2.1	13.4	50.6	5.1	8.5	10.0	17.9
▼ California Bank of Commerce	Walnut Creek	CA	C+	B-	C+	1972.9	80.20	37.8	0.1	0.2	2.6	6.5	8.5	12.9
California Business Bank	Irvine	CA	D	D	D	97.4	17.86	13.4	6.9	0.2	0.0	10.0	12.3	19.2
California First National Bank	Irvine	CA	A+	A	A	115.7	-20.43	0.0	0.0	0.0	0.1	10.0	50.5	93.8
California International Bank, N.A.	Westminster	CA	D	D	D	71.6	57.67	25.4	0.0	0.9	0.6	10.0	18.5	39.5
California Pacific Bank	San Francisco	CA	B+	A-	A	89.2	19.60	6.2	0.0	2.9	0.0	10.0	38.8	57.8
Callaway Bank	Fulton	MO	B-	B-	B-	431.5	11.31	13.7	1.0	20.1	12.6	5.6	9.3	0.0
▲ CalPrivate Bank	La Jolla	CA	B-	C+	B+	1243.4	24.38	31.1	0.6	4.3	2.1	7.2	9.1	14.8
Calvin B. Taylor Banking Co.	Berlin	MD	A	A	A-	697.7	25.74	6.9	0.3	17.9	10.7	10.0	13.6	0.0
Cambridge Savings Bank	Cambridge	MA	B-	B-	B-	5194.9	25.92	13.9	0.1	22.0	11.4	5.8	8.2	11.6
Cambridge State Bank	Cambridge	MN	C	B-	C	89.2	12.65	19.4	0.7	12.3	18.3	8.8	10.2	0.0
Cambridge Trust Co.	Cambridge	MA	B+	B+	B+	3986.8	40.29	10.7	1.0	33.9	10.2	6.7	8.7	13.2
Camden National Bank	Camden	ME	A-	B+	B+	5129.4	13.97	9.3	0.5	23.4	21.6	6.7	8.7	14.3
▼ Camp Grove State Bank	Camp Grove	IL	D+	D+	D+	17.2	-11.78	3.4	3.8	3.3	10.6	10.0	14.7	31.7
Campbell & Fetter Bank	Kendallville	IN	B-	B-	B-	332.3	6.66	6.7	5.1	39.4	23.8	8.3	9.9	24.2
▲ Campbell County Bank, Inc.	Herreid	SD	B	B	B+	137.5	-1.51	7.3	1.4	0.2	15.5	10.0	14.1	19.0
Campus State Bank	Campus	IL	C	C	C-	21.4	-1.48	0.0	14.5	12.9	7.4	10.0	12.0	0.0
▼ Canandaigua National Bank and Trust Co.	Canandaigua	NY	B	B+	B	3598.6	20.83	17.3	19.8	17.6	10.6	6.7	8.7	12.8
Canandaigua National Trust Co. of Florida	Sarasota	FL	U	U	U	4.1	10.28	0.0	0.0	0.0	12.4	10.0	92.2	393.3
Canton Co-operative Bank	Canton	MA	B-	B-	C+	138.9	13.07	2.4	0.0	28.9	19.7	10.0	14.8	26.9
Canyon Community Bank, N.A.	Tucson	AZ	D-	D	D	125.5	30.18	38.9	0.0	1.4	9.5	9.8	10.8	28.5
Cape Ann Savings Bank	Gloucester	MA	B+	A-	B+	747.8	10.54	4.2	0.1	39.2	13.9	10.0	22.2	40.5
Cape Cod Five Cents Savings Bank	Orleans	MA	B-	B-	B-	4172.7	15.34	6.5	0.6	49.1	8.3	7.3	9.2	16.3
Capital Bank	Houston	TX	B-	B-	B-	529.9	13.14	14.2	1.3	8.7	8.2	6.6	8.6	13.2
Capital Bank and Trust Co.	Irvine	CA	U	U	U	203.1	-0.97	0.0	0.0	0.0	57.9	10.0	72.1	174.5
▼ Capital Bank of Texas	Carrizo Springs	TX	B+	B+	B	89.5	2.81	3.0	0.4	2.5	13.2	10.0	11.5	0.0
Capital Bank, N.A.	Rockville	MD	B	B	B	1845.9	44.87	20.0	4.7	21.8	2.9	5.4	7.4	12.7
Capital City Bank	Tallahassee	FL	B+	B+	B	3578.0	22.88	9.5	7.6	11.8	14.8	6.9	8.9	16.6
Capital Community Bank	Provo	UT	B	B-	C+	474.1	1.17	22.6	21.7	0.8	2.5	10.0	11.3	15.7
Capital One Bank (USA), N.A.	Glen Allen	VA	C	B-	B-	111674.5	-7.13	7.0	72.3	0.0	13.1	10.0	16.2	22.3
Capital One, N.A.	McLean	VA	C	B-	B-	360261.2	13.23	7.8	22.9	0.1	23.5	5.4	7.4	13.4
Capitol Bank	Madison	WI	A-	A-	B+	489.5	28.97	17.1	0.2	6.1	13.0	7.7	10.4	13.0
Capitol Federal Savings Bank	Topeka	KS	B-	B	B	9508.5	1.60	1.0	0.1	66.6	16.4	10.0	12.4	0.0
▼ Capitol National Bank	Lansing	MI	C	B-	C	234.8	101.60	38.1	0.1	1.6	0.3	2.7	9.7	0.0
Capon Valley Bank	Wardensville	WV	B	B	B-	173.2	7.76	2.7	8.7	36.1	6.7	9.1	10.4	0.0
▼ CapStar Bank	Nashville	TN	B	B+	B-	3022.6	48.66	21.4	1.4	10.7	10.3	8.1	9.7	15.3
CapTex Bank	Fort Worth	TX	D-	D	D	215.3	15.98	15.0	8.3	13.0	2.7	9.2	11.0	14.3
Carmine State Bank	Carmine	TX	B	B	B	89.0	7.38	4.2	6.2	11.5	34.1	10.0	12.3	0.0
Carolina Bank & Trust Co.	Florence	SC	A-	A-	B+	578.8	20.33	18.6	1.2	16.3	9.1	10.0	13.2	22.3
Carroll Bank and Trust	Huntingdon	TN	B	B	B-	332.7	14.03	9.2	5.1	26.9	12.6	7.8	9.5	0.0
Carroll County Trust Co.	Carrollton	MO	C	C	C	158.2	1.09	3.6	1.8	5.0	45.8	5.6	10.8	0.0
Carrollton Bank	Carrollton	IL	B-	B-	B-	2506.5	30.56	34.6	0.4	13.2	6.3	4.8	6.8	11.0
Carrollton Federal Bank	Carrollton	KY	C+	C+	C+	34.0	5.81	0.1	4.2	48.4	5.1	10.0	16.2	0.0
Carson Bank	Mulvane	KS	B-	C+	C+	141.0	15.26	16.2	1.8	14.4	12.5	6.3	8.3	13.4
Carson Community Bank	Stilwell	OK	B+	B+	B+	157.2	238.03	14.0	3.3	6.9	31.7	9.0	10.6	0.0
▼ Carter Bankshares, Inc.	Martinsville	VA	C-	C	D+	4134.1	2.84	7.3	1.6	12.5	18.8	8.7	10.1	14.3
Carthage Federal S&L Assn.	Carthage	NY	B	B	B	282.4	12.47	2.6	2.4	51.4	10.5	10.0	11.1	27.1
Carver Federal Savings Bank	New York	NY	D-	D	D	673.1	14.12	6.3	0.4	15.1	16.8	8.1	9.7	15.2
Carver State Bank	Savannah	GA	C-	C	C-	48.4	17.30	34.2	2.1	20.3	6.3	7.3	9.2	0.0
▼ Casey County Bank, Inc.	Liberty	KY	B+	B+	B-	269.6	37.53	5.3	4.8	18.1	27.6	7.9	9.6	18.7

Asset Quality Index	Adjusted Non-Performing Loans as a % of Total Loans	Adjusted Non-Performing Loans as a % of Capital	Net Charge-Offs Avg Loans	Profitability Index	Net Income ($Mil)	Return on Assets (R.O.A.)	Return on Equity (R.O.E.)	Net Interest Spread	Overhead Efficiency Ratio	Liquidity Index	Liquidity Ratio	Hot Money Ratio	Stability Index
7.1	0.39	1.8	0.14	5.9	84.5	1.11	8.29	3.16	53.3	4.5	21.6	7.3	10.0
6.1	0.87	na	0.29	1.6	0.0	0.00	0.04	3.38	83.8	0.8	23.1	36.3	5.4
6.0	1.39	na	-0.05	6.2	0.5	1.36	10.93	3.76	67.7	1.6	35.6	16.1	7.3
4.2	1.03	7.7	0.53	4.2	28.1	0.62	4.73	3.87	59.4	3.0	11.4	9.2	8.9
3.8	2.98	na	0.22	5.2	2.8	1.28	12.43	2.97	61.6	1.7	21.5	23.5	6.1
7.4	0.00	na	0.00	6.3	4.6	1.47	13.58	3.55	55.4	3.1	17.3	8.5	5.9
8.8	0.00	na	0.00	0.6	-0.5	-0.66	-4.88	2.20	130.9	4.7	63.4	17.1	5.8
5.8	0.84	5.7	0.04	8.3	22.3	1.41	17.67	3.47	47.9	3.7	27.8	10.0	8.7
5.0	1.45	7.9	0.83	2.6	-396.7	-2.93	-23.58	3.67	126.4	3.6	19.3	7.9	9.2
3.4	1.80	na	0.53	4.3	1.2	0.92	9.03	4.54	70.6	0.8	19.8	52.5	4.1
5.2	0.69	na	0.06	4.2	0.9	0.75	7.81	3.94	72.5	2.8	15.9	15.3	5.9
7.9	0.04	na	0.23	2.8	3.3	0.27	3.17	2.99	74.6	4.4	29.6	12.6	7.3
7.7	0.00	na	0.02	0.0	-0.8	-1.09	-8.32	3.14	129.0	2.2	39.2	29.1	5.9
9.6	0.00	0.0	-0.03	10.0	3.5	3.76	7.79	4.43	35.7	4.3	96.0	28.3	9.5
8.4	0.00	na	-0.28	0.0	-1.1	-2.67	-11.87	3.44	180.3	2.1	49.8	64.7	6.0
5.1	3.69	5.2	0.00	10.0	1.2	1.89	4.70	4.63	45.1	4.5	60.2	12.9	9.4
6.2	0.78	na	0.04	5.1	3.2	1.05	10.99	3.73	69.5	3.8	8.1	9.3	5.3
7.1	0.17	1.3	0.00	4.0	7.4	0.81	8.57	4.11	64.4	3.6	15.0	9.6	5.8
8.6	0.62	na	-0.01	7.4	5.9	1.31	8.76	3.50	49.1	6.0	39.5	2.8	9.1
6.5	0.60	4.6	0.14	3.4	21.5	0.61	6.55	3.03	64.1	2.3	11.9	12.6	7.5
8.9	0.24	0.7	-0.01	1.2	-0.1	-0.09	-0.78	3.49	105.3	6.3	48.0	3.4	5.0
8.2	0.26	na	0.03	4.6	19.2	0.76	7.55	3.67	61.9	3.8	3.5	6.6	7.5
8.2	0.34	1.6	0.04	6.2	43.7	1.23	10.77	3.18	52.2	4.3	19.2	5.2	9.4
6.0	3.61	na	0.77	0.3	-0.1	-0.34	-2.29	3.10	101.0	1.8	48.1	26.1	4.0
9.1	0.00	0.2	0.01	4.0	1.9	0.80	8.30	2.92	65.8	5.2	35.5	6.5	5.5
4.5	0.17	na	0.00	9.3	2.2	2.04	13.31	4.95	52.0	1.9	17.3	12.7	10.0
6.6	0.40	2.2	0.00	4.0	0.1	0.87	7.32	3.26	75.7	4.4	36.4	9.8	5.1
4.1	1.10	na	0.16	5.6	27.3	1.09	11.95	3.33	60.3	3.4	4.9	11.3	8.0
10.0	na	na	na	5.0	0.1	1.55	1.69	0.49	95.3	4.0	na	0.0	6.4
6.1	2.69	na	0.00	3.1	0.4	0.43	2.83	3.01	81.1	4.7	46.9	13.3	7.4
8.7	0.00	na	0.00	0.0	-0.6	-0.76	-7.23	2.57	124.1	5.0	21.2	2.4	5.1
8.8	0.97	2.6	0.00	3.8	0.9	0.17	0.75	2.65	68.8	2.8	44.1	26.3	9.4
7.6	0.56	4.2	0.00	4.0	23.4	0.81	8.48	3.17	66.2	3.4	15.9	12.7	7.2
4.6	0.46	3.9	0.02	4.6	3.2	0.83	9.47	3.95	66.2	1.7	17.8	21.4	6.3
10.0	na	na	na	10.0	35.8	23.86	38.01	2.28	79.1	10.0	231.3	0.0	6.7
9.4	0.00	na	0.00	3.6	0.4	0.55	4.36	1.62	66.7	6.9	73.6	4.6	7.6
6.4	0.68	6.7	0.05	7.6	15.7	1.34	17.21	4.99	69.0	2.1	12.2	14.7	7.4
6.3	0.95	3.2	0.13	6.0	24.9	1.37	12.43	3.46	68.7	6.3	29.2	1.0	8.7
4.5	1.41	na	1.42	6.8	4.4	1.32	11.64	5.64	49.6	0.7	13.6	46.4	6.0
3.1	0.65	5.0	4.69	3.7	-383.6	-0.44	-3.01	10.60	44.5	1.4	28.2	72.0	7.6
4.6	1.15	3.7	0.88	2.5	436.2	0.17	1.38	3.41	73.1	6.5	50.1	4.7	7.7
8.6	0.03	na	0.00	5.7	3.6	1.08	9.48	2.96	57.3	2.0	28.7	21.7	7.2
9.8	0.19	1.1	0.00	3.5	42.1	0.60	4.83	2.09	51.7	1.6	14.1	23.5	9.8
4.2	1.71	9.3	-0.09	3.4	0.5	0.35	4.23	3.24	67.4	4.8	25.8	5.1	6.1
5.0	2.69	na	0.06	3.9	0.9	0.70	6.59	4.38	74.5	2.3	17.2	17.7	6.2
7.9	0.26	na	0.05	4.1	16.1	0.86	7.67	3.12	63.9	3.8	26.5	12.9	8.4
6.1	0.24	na	-0.02	0.2	-0.5	-0.35	-2.67	4.30	102.1	2.3	12.3	11.7	5.3
9.6	0.00	na	-0.09	3.9	0.6	0.88	7.08	2.87	65.2	3.2	80.7	41.5	7.1
7.6	1.21	na	-0.06	6.3	4.4	1.15	8.81	3.59	58.9	4.4	22.7	7.1	7.7
5.9	1.00	na	0.03	4.5	2.1	0.87	8.70	4.33	73.5	1.6	9.6	21.1	5.6
3.2	6.93	na	1.51	2.2	0.4	0.30	2.64	2.81	72.2	4.2	38.2	13.5	6.4
8.3	0.18	1.1	0.01	4.5	19.1	1.12	15.39	2.93	64.0	3.4	16.8	12.5	7.0
5.6	4.76	na	-0.01	3.7	0.2	0.70	4.34	4.13	79.6	3.2	18.5	13.3	6.7
8.2	0.04	1.6	-0.48	5.3	1.3	1.29	15.78	4.43	70.7	2.3	15.2	17.7	4.5
5.2	0.36	na	0.47	7.5	1.5	1.37	11.47	5.00	63.1	2.0	26.2	20.6	7.7
5.0	1.44	8.7	0.09	0.5	-48.8	-1.59	-13.77	2.82	144.2	2.2	21.8	19.8	7.7
9.5	0.25	na	0.02	3.8	1.4	0.69	6.33	2.64	65.9	1.6	26.6	27.3	6.0
1.7	1.91	21.1	-0.13	0.3	-3.3	-0.70	-6.80	2.86	128.0	1.2	28.5	26.1	4.5
3.7	2.19	na	0.38	3.2	0.2	0.43	4.48	4.66	83.5	1.1	17.6	18.8	3.3
5.5	1.62	na	0.02	5.0	1.8	1.00	9.24	3.42	62.7	2.8	23.7	16.0	6.1

Name	City	State	2019 Rating	2018 Rating	Total Assets ($Mil)	One Year Asset Growth	Commercial Loans	Consumer Loans	Mortgage Loans	Securities	Capitalization Index	Leverage Ratio	Risk-Based Capital Ratio
Casey State Bank	Casey	IL	C+	B-	B	364.1	11.04	17.6	6.3	8.5	17.1	8.6	10.1	13.8
▼ Cashmere Valley Bank	Cashmere	WA	A-	A	A-	1944.5	17.47	7.0	10.8	5.5	39.1	9.3	10.6	0.0
Cass Commercial Bank	Saint Louis	MO	A	A	B+	1105.9	28.27	38.1	0.0	0.0	0.0	10.0	14.5	21.2
Castle Rock Bank	Castle Rock	MN	A-	A-	B+	229.2	13.20	11.1	3.8	10.4	52.4	10.0	14.2	28.3
Castroville State Bank	Castroville	TX	B	B	B-	201.3	15.10	5.1	4.1	26.5	26.2	7.0	9.0	0.0
Cathay Bank	Los Angeles	CA	A-	A-	A-	19000.9	5.73	14.0	0.0	26.9	5.7	9.8	10.9	14.9
Catlin Bank	Catlin	IL	B	B-	C+	67.2	6.29	14.7	1.1	30.8	15.8	9.6	10.7	21.2
Catskill Hudson Bank	Kingston	NY	C	C	C	591.9	12.70	6.3	0.1	7.6	19.3	5.3	7.3	12.1
Cattaraugus County Bank	Little Valley	NY	C+	B-	C+	292.3	16.27	11.4	0.8	14.4	14.7	6.0	8.0	12.3
Cattle Bank & Trust	Seward	NE	A-	A-	B+	318.8	13.17	7.1	0.9	17.6	20.1	10.0	12.0	0.0
Cayuga Lake National Bank	Union Springs	NY	B-	B-	B	186.5	21.24	14.7	3.2	31.8	32.2	6.0	8.0	16.0
CB&S Bank, Inc.	Russellville	AL	B	B	B	2092.4	9.24	8.1	1.2	9.2	41.3	9.5	10.6	0.0
CBank	Cincinnati	OH	B-	B	B-	277.2	47.11	38.6	1.1	7.6	2.5	9.1	10.4	15.1
CBBC Bank	Maryville	TN	A-	B	B	406.9	13.70	5.3	0.4	6.1	29.6	10.0	14.9	21.5
CBC Bank	Saint Peters	MO	C-	C	C-	40.0	7.34	5.3	1.3	7.2	33.1	6.0	8.1	0.0
CBI Bank & Trust	Muscatine	IA	B+	B+	B-	681.3	18.23	12.2	1.2	12.2	18.6	8.6	10.1	15.5
CBW Bank	Weir	KS	A	A	A-	90.4	39.14	55.1	2.5	0.5	4.1	10.0	21.3	254.0
CCB Community Bank	Andalusia	AL	B+	A-	A-	567.6	11.19	10.3	1.2	13.5	3.9	7.8	10.3	0.0
Cecil Bank	Elkton	MD	E	E-	E-	195.0	11.96	11.3	0.1	11.5	31.9	3.1	5.1	13.4
Cecilian Bank	Cecilia	KY	B+	B+	B-	1208.7	31.19	9.0	4.2	18.1	26.5	6.9	9.3	0.0
Cedar Hill National Bank	Charlotte	NC	U	U	U	13.6	5.29	0.0	0.0	0.0	83.7	10.0	84.9	135.6
Cedar Rapids Bank and Trust Co.	Cedar Rapids	IA	B+	B+	B+	2017.6	26.49	26.3	0.4	4.2	12.9	7.5	9.7	12.9
▲ Cedar Rapids State Bank	Cedar Rapids	NE	C+	C-	C-	57.0	10.89	14.2	2.5	20.5	5.0	6.8	9.0	12.3
▲ Cedar Security Bank	Fordyce	NE	B+	B-	C+	52.3	7.72	10.7	2.4	8.8	3.4	10.0	14.6	0.0
Cedar Valley Bank & Trust	La Porte City	IA	C+	C+	C	85.3	14.42	11.7	4.5	26.3	13.8	4.7	8.0	0.0
CedarStone Bank	Lebanon	TN	B	B	B	261.4	26.01	10.5	2.3	26.1	18.6	8.1	9.7	14.2
▼ Celtic Bank Corp.	Salt Lake City	UT	C	B+	B-	4286.1	352.57	78.5	0.6	0.0	0.8	0.0	18.3	0.0
CenBank	Buffalo Lake	MN	B	B	B-	71.5	7.88	12.2	8.1	2.0	19.2	5.6	7.6	11.8
Cendera Bank, N.A.	Bells	TX	B+	B+	B	125.0	18.31	4.5	1.3	35.4	0.0	9.2	10.5	17.2
Cenlar FSB	Ewing	NJ	A-	A-	A-	1172.0	-1.64	0.0	0.0	37.3	49.0	7.1	9.0	22.9
Centennial Bank	Conway	AR	A-	A-	B+	16519.2	10.98	13.1	5.4	8.8	14.3	10.0	11.4	15.7
Centennial Bank	Trezevant	TN	B-	B-	C+	622.5	6.57	12.7	4.3	14.8	6.6	8.7	10.1	14.0
Center National Bank	Litchfield	MN	A-	A-	A-	215.1	9.23	16.3	5.0	6.9	30.5	9.8	10.9	17.8
Centera Bank	Sublette	KS	B-	B-	B	291.0	10.84	7.4	1.0	5.7	49.8	6.5	8.5	17.6
CenterBank	Milford	OH	B	B	B-	283.9	29.84	26.2	0.1	17.3	3.9	7.9	9.6	13.4
Centier Bank	Merrillville	IN	A-	B+	B+	5572.5	15.82	9.6	6.6	9.9	9.2	7.2	9.7	12.7
Centinel Bank of Taos	Taos	NM	A-	A-	B+	333.6	20.74	9.5	0.7	13.2	48.9	5.9	7.9	24.4
Central Bank	Little Rock	AR	B	B	B+	316.1	30.55	10.6	1.0	17.5	14.7	7.4	9.4	12.8
Central Bank	Tampa	FL	C+	C+	B-	285.4	50.96	24.0	0.0	17.6	2.5	5.3	8.6	0.0
▼ Central Bank	Storm Lake	IA	C+	B	C+	1479.4	61.93	24.3	1.4	14.7	4.3	1.4	9.8	0.0
▼ Central Bank	Savannah	TN	B-	B	C+	112.3	13.87	6.2	3.9	36.9	18.9	9.8	10.9	22.1
Central Bank	Houston	TX	B+	B+	B+	808.1	7.95	13.4	0.3	28.6	16.8	7.8	9.6	14.9
Central Bank	Provo	UT	A	A	B+	1469.1	22.95	9.1	1.0	3.9	24.0	10.0	14.6	0.0
Central Bank & Trust Co.	Lexington	KY	B+	A-	B	3120.3	15.52	20.6	4.1	14.7	8.5	9.3	10.6	16.7
▲ Central Bank and Trust	Lander	WY	B+	B	B-	191.8	25.12	16.5	1.6	17.5	23.0	6.7	8.7	20.1
Central Bank Illinois	Geneseo	IL	A-	B+	B	957.0	4.03	8.6	0.7	7.6	34.0	8.7	10.2	0.0
Central Bank of Audrain County	Mexico	MO	B	B	B	203.3	13.63	6.0	3.0	10.2	36.6	5.3	7.3	17.1
Central Bank of Boone County	Columbia	MO	B+	B+	B+	2372.7	9.39	9.0	4.4	9.8	32.5	6.4	8.4	14.1
Central Bank of Branson	Branson	MO	B+	B+	B	404.0	20.13	10.2	5.1	14.1	29.2	7.1	9.0	16.6
▼ Central Bank of Kansas City	Kansas City	MO	A-	A	A	288.3	33.38	39.4	0.0	0.5	0.0	10.0	13.9	15.8
Central Bank of Lake of the Ozarks	Osage Beach	MO	B+	B+	B+	988.8	20.52	7.0	4.6	13.1	33.4	5.9	7.9	16.2
Central Bank of Moberly	Moberly	MO	B	B	B	214.0	15.70	7.8	10.3	6.7	35.7	5.9	7.9	15.5
Central Bank of Oklahoma	Tulsa	OK	B	B	B	758.0	9.44	13.8	0.2	13.2	5.2	8.7	11.8	13.9
Central Bank of Sedalia	Sedalia	MO	B+	B+	B+	523.9	23.52	8.6	13.5	6.1	29.1	5.6	7.6	14.1
Central Bank of St. Louis	Clayton	MO	B+	B+	B+	2236.8	17.42	18.0	0.8	9.4	13.2	7.6	9.4	13.5
Central Bank of the Midwest	Lee's Summit	MO	B+	B+	B+	3588.0	102.61	14.9	5.4	4.9	22.4	6.5	8.6	13.8
Central Bank of the Ozarks	Springfield	MO	B+	B+	B+	1704.9	20.77	13.5	10.8	9.9	21.5	6.6	8.6	13.1
Central Bank of Warrensburg	Warrensburg	MO	B	B	B	291.5	15.25	8.2	1.8	7.6	27.9	6.7	8.8	17.8
Central Federal S&L Assn.	Cicero	IL	C-	C-	C	191.7	2.01	0.0	0.0	54.8	12.6	8.4	9.9	0.0
▲ Central National Bank	Junction City	KS	A-	B	B	1098.3	12.83	10.7	1.9	5.6	29.0	9.6	10.8	0.0

Asset Quality Index	Adjusted Non-Performing Loans as a % of Total Loans	as a % of Capital	Net Charge-Offs Avg Loans	Profitability Index	Net Income ($Mil)	Return on Assets (R.O.A.)	Return on Equity (R.O.E.)	Net Interest Spread	Overhead Efficiency Ratio	Liquidity Index	Liquidity Ratio	Hot Money Ratio	Stability Index
2.8	2.59	15.9	0.34	5.9	3.8	1.47	13.97	3.66	54.6	1.7	18.0	22.4	6.7
7.4	1.10	na	0.08	6.0	18.5	1.41	11.45	2.88	56.2	6.2	49.8	8.3	10.0
8.1	1.16	na	0.00	8.7	12.3	1.56	10.97	3.15	41.0	2.1	22.3	6.5	10.0
8.3	1.09	na	0.19	5.4	2.1	1.27	8.57	2.91	46.7	4.3	55.3	17.4	7.8
6.1	0.98	na	0.10	5.7	1.7	1.15	12.43	3.57	55.2	2.0	20.4	19.5	5.6
6.9	0.68	3.6	0.06	6.2	164.5	1.18	9.11	3.15	46.1	0.8	15.1	32.4	10.0
7.2	0.39	na	0.00	7.0	0.7	1.53	14.56	4.04	60.9	3.0	15.1	13.8	5.2
6.0	0.82	na	-0.01	2.6	1.6	0.41	5.43	2.75	85.1	3.0	21.5	14.9	3.3
5.1	2.46	na	-0.02	2.9	0.8	0.37	4.39	3.63	82.5	4.7	22.2	4.8	4.9
7.8	0.45	na	-0.09	5.5	2.9	1.25	10.01	3.29	63.1	1.7	18.8	21.9	8.4
7.7	0.59	na	0.04	3.7	1.0	0.78	9.17	3.31	75.5	3.0	19.2	14.6	4.4
5.5	2.37	na	-0.03	4.6	14.2	0.95	7.60	3.54	68.4	5.3	39.6	11.0	9.2
8.1	0.02	na	0.06	4.3	1.9	1.02	9.98	3.37	61.9	1.3	10.5	26.5	6.1
8.8	0.63	na	-0.01	7.0	4.3	1.48	9.31	3.44	51.9	3.5	41.1	17.7	7.9
9.9	0.00	na	0.00	1.6	0.0	0.10	1.04	2.02	101.8	7.2	64.5	0.9	3.9
4.7	1.91	na	0.04	4.7	4.1	0.87	8.10	3.63	69.6	3.1	28.7	15.9	7.7
6.6	2.38	na	0.00	9.5	1.6	2.04	13.59	2.68	77.7	6.6	48.1	1.3	8.7
6.1	0.57	na	0.11	6.7	5.8	1.44	13.53	4.11	57.6	1.7	19.7	19.7	8.6
3.7	3.99	21.4	-0.07	0.0	-1.0	-0.72	-13.21	1.82	141.4	4.4	51.8	15.6	0.0
7.9	0.49	na	0.05	5.3	9.4	1.11	10.54	3.48	64.9	2.4	16.0	17.3	9.0
10.0	na	na	na	9.5	0.4	3.78	4.47	2.28	76.6	10.0	436.1	0.0	7.0
7.0	0.79	4.5	0.09	9.7	30.9	2.25	21.27	3.15	39.8	4.1	25.7	8.7	8.6
8.1	0.00	na	0.08	5.5	0.5	1.37	15.91	3.67	64.1	0.7	8.2	29.5	4.1
7.1	1.01	na	-0.09	7.4	0.6	1.50	10.07	3.96	68.3	4.5	43.0	12.4	6.9
8.3	0.01	na	0.02	6.6	1.1	1.77	21.06	4.36	58.4	4.2	5.6	6.3	4.6
7.5	0.60	na	0.09	4.2	1.5	0.83	8.67	3.40	65.1	2.1	27.4	21.5	5.1
5.6	0.37	na	0.11	9.5	61.8	3.20	37.15	2.34	31.2	0.4	9.4	0.6	8.6
7.1	0.51	na	0.08	4.6	0.7	1.25	16.07	4.21	70.4	3.6	10.0	10.3	5.3
8.8	0.00	na	0.05	3.4	0.5	0.60	5.50	4.06	82.9	1.0	24.9	30.5	7.0
8.9	0.62	5.7	0.00	9.0	23.6	2.57	29.13	2.36	93.9	7.6	54.2	0.0	9.0
5.8	0.65	2.6	0.11	7.5	155.2	1.29	7.60	4.28	41.3	2.9	16.1	10.4	10.0
4.1	1.22	na	0.49	4.6	3.5	0.77	6.60	4.34	64.5	1.5	18.9	23.2	6.7
8.4	0.09	na	0.03	7.1	2.7	1.75	14.76	3.88	58.3	3.5	12.1	11.2	8.0
7.4	0.49	na	0.00	4.3	2.3	1.03	10.15	3.28	68.0	3.7	25.9	11.9	5.5
8.2	0.10	na	0.58	6.1	2.2	1.15	12.94	3.95	55.6	1.4	15.7	23.3	5.8
7.3	0.22	1.7	0.10	7.4	55.7	1.46	14.49	3.35	48.2	3.7	10.1	8.3	9.3
9.5	0.23	na	0.00	8.3	4.7	2.00	21.11	3.23	44.8	6.0	53.9	8.1	6.9
7.5	0.68	na	-0.03	5.6	2.5	1.24	12.43	2.97	49.6	1.3	32.7	52.3	6.3
4.7	1.07	na	0.00	3.4	1.2	0.66	8.18	3.41	73.1	0.9	19.6	36.4	4.8
7.2	0.16	na	0.01	6.6	11.2	1.27	11.94	3.82	64.7	2.5	4.8	15.7	8.2
6.0	4.39	na	-0.17	3.6	0.4	0.53	4.36	4.13	85.6	2.8	28.8	17.2	6.7
7.7	0.36	2.5	-0.01	5.8	7.7	1.28	12.68	4.94	71.9	1.5	12.6	21.8	7.6
8.7	0.25	na	0.03	9.8	18.9	1.88	12.17	4.39	51.7	5.2	41.2	11.8	10.0
5.5	2.25	9.9	0.07	4.1	16.7	0.75	6.83	3.54	76.5	3.7	16.2	10.9	9.0
8.1	0.02	na	-0.02	8.6	3.0	2.35	25.08	4.40	51.3	4.7	17.4	4.6	5.8
6.2	0.47	na	0.13	7.8	11.9	1.69	14.53	3.74	52.1	4.6	26.9	6.6	8.5
6.2	0.60	2.9	0.00	6.4	1.9	1.22	16.09	2.77	51.2	5.2	29.6	2.9	6.3
8.3	0.21	1.0	0.14	8.0	24.4	1.51	16.57	2.95	51.7	5.3	27.0	5.6	8.0
4.0	1.90	10.9	-0.06	7.2	3.9	1.35	14.16	3.36	58.9	4.2	22.5	6.7	7.1
4.9	2.77	13.6	-0.04	9.8	8.2	4.22	28.92	4.17	55.2	0.8	17.2	10.2	9.5
6.3	0.86	3.7	0.03	9.0	10.9	1.66	19.30	3.29	53.8	5.0	38.4	9.2	7.0
7.8	0.08	0.4	-0.10	5.9	1.9	1.22	14.43	2.90	56.6	4.7	21.9	3.3	6.4
3.6	0.50	1.9	0.00	8.3	8.4	1.52	8.23	3.94	46.6	1.5	8.5	17.1	8.6
6.2	0.19	1.2	0.11	8.3	5.1	1.44	17.04	3.27	52.0	4.0	21.8	7.9	7.1
7.3	0.22	1.4	0.03	8.9	29.6	1.78	16.69	3.32	49.5	4.1	8.0	6.5	7.0
5.2	0.65	2.0	0.17	6.1	26.8	1.13	8.47	3.60	58.2	5.1	22.1	4.0	8.5
7.7	0.04	0.3	0.08	6.5	14.7	1.25	13.86	3.21	60.0	4.8	21.4	4.8	7.3
4.6	0.39	1.3	0.20	5.5	2.3	1.12	8.25	3.06	60.4	4.1	22.6	7.9	8.3
7.3	3.46	na	0.00	1.8	0.2	0.16	1.61	2.50	94.5	2.7	38.0	22.2	5.4
7.7	1.09	3.6	0.32	6.0	11.4	1.42	12.95	3.41	62.6	4.5	19.2	6.3	9.1

Name	City	State	Rating	2019 Rating	2018 Rating	Total Assets ($Mil)	One Year Asset Growth	Asset Mix (As a % of Total Assets)				Capital-ization Index	Lever-age Ratio	Risk-Based Capital Ratio
								Comm-ercial Loans	Cons-umer Loans	Mort-gage Loans	Secur-ities			
Central National Bank	Waco	TX	A-	A-	B+	1105.7	19.03	16.5	0.8	25.3	7.1	6.4	8.4	14.4
Central National Bank of Poteau	Poteau	OK	A-	B+	B+	283.7	14.29	10.3	2.8	12.5	33.8	8.8	10.2	0.0
Central Pacific Bank	Honolulu	HI	A-	A-	A-	6642.2	11.30	15.6	7.5	25.6	17.6	6.6	8.6	13.6
Central Savings Bank	Sault Sainte Marie	MI	C+	B-	B-	345.9	27.55	10.7	4.8	16.9	28.9	9.6	10.8	0.0
▼ Central Savings, F.S.B.	Chicago	IL	C+	B	B-	116.2	12.16	0.0	0.0	29.2	2.6	10.0	23.5	33.6
Central State Bank	Calera	AL	A-	A-	A-	390.0	18.79	11.2	2.1	16.0	14.4	8.4	9.9	0.0
Central State Bank	Elkader	IA	B	B	B	380.5	17.54	16.0	1.6	18.8	11.5	6.1	8.1	11.8
Central State Bank	State Center	IA	C+	C	C+	356.6	15.97	18.0	1.2	3.1	23.8	5.8	11.3	0.0
Central State Bank	Clayton	IL	D+	C	C+	161.4	11.88	9.0	6.7	22.2	3.3	10.0	13.9	0.0
Central Trust Bank	Jefferson City	MO	B+	B+	B+	3403.4	28.66	7.4	6.0	7.8	53.3	4.6	6.6	15.0
▼ Central Valley Community Bank	Fresno	CA	B+	A	A	1950.1	23.12	14.8	2.0	1.8	32.4	7.3	9.2	15.8
CentreBank	Veedersburg	IN	A-	A-	A-	92.6	16.76	14.1	2.8	17.9	0.3	10.0	13.0	0.0
Centreville Bank	West Warwick	RI	C+	C+	D+	1898.0	50.96	4.0	0.1	28.4	13.4	10.0	15.2	0.0
▼ Centric Bank	Harrisburg	PA	B	B+	B+	1073.7	35.86	37.9	0.1	6.3	2.9	7.3	9.2	12.8
CenTrust Bank, N.A.	Northbrook	IL	C+	C+	C-	164.4	30.67	33.0	0.0	6.5	8.7	8.3	9.9	14.2
Century Bank	Lucedale	MS	B	B-	B-	421.5	27.48	9.9	8.9	12.0	25.4	7.7	9.9	0.0
Century Bank	Santa Fe	NM	B+	B+	B	1078.1	23.13	24.0	3.5	3.7	23.4	7.5	9.3	13.5
▲ Century Bank and Trust	Milledgeville	GA	B+	B-	B-	304.0	18.07	5.7	0.9	9.7	26.0	10.0	11.0	0.0
Century Bank and Trust	Coldwater	MI	A-	B	B	400.9	22.08	11.5	1.7	13.3	13.1	9.9	11.0	18.3
Century Bank and Trust Co.	Medford	MA	C+	C+	C+	6279.1	18.87	10.2	0.1	7.4	44.2	4.6	6.6	13.0
Century Bank of Florida	Tampa	FL	C+	C+	C	104.2	27.04	21.2	2.2	19.5	7.1	5.5	7.5	14.7
Century Bank of Georgia	Cartersville	GA	A-	A-	A-	253.7	27.77	15.5	1.3	10.8	15.6	6.8	8.9	20.1
▲ Century Bank of Kentucky, Inc.	Lawrenceburg	KY	B	C+	C	142.5	0.37	2.9	1.2	37.0	9.5	10.0	11.2	0.0
Century Bank of the Ozarks	Gainesville	MO	B+	A-	B	199.3	13.29	11.4	2.7	16.2	1.5	4.1	9.0	0.0
Century Next Bank	Ruston	LA	B-	B	B	504.9	3.18	16.0	2.8	28.1	0.1	9.2	10.7	0.0
Century S&L Assn.	Trinidad	CO	C	C+	C	98.5	9.03	0.0	0.4	17.5	58.0	10.0	14.2	0.0
Century Savings Bank	Vineland	NJ	C-	C+	C+	528.5	19.24	9.0	0.0	17.9	32.6	10.0	12.8	0.0
▲ CerescoBank	Ceresco	NE	B+	B	B	56.0	12.88	10.9	5.1	11.5	8.5	10.0	15.6	0.0
▲ CFBank, N.A.	Worthington	OH	A-	B	C+	1335.0	70.06	23.9	0.0	32.5	0.7	8.7	10.9	13.9
CFG Community Bank	Baltimore	MD	B	C+	C-	1725.1	57.11	27.7	0.0	1.4	5.0	5.6	10.3	0.0
cfsbank	Charleroi	PA	C+	C+	C	504.8	4.12	1.0	1.0	48.4	24.8	10.0	15.1	31.5
Chain Bridge Bank, N.A.	McLean	VA	C+	C+	C+	1089.1	53.11	9.4	0.3	16.6	47.4	4.5	6.5	23.1
▲ Chambers Bank	Danville	AR	B	B-	C+	1055.2	24.85	9.4	0.7	15.4	3.5	6.6	9.4	12.2
Chambers State Bank	Chambers	NE	B+	B+	B+	73.1	20.18	7.3	3.7	2.0	0.4	10.0	26.9	0.0
Champion Bank	Parker	CO	A-	A-	B-	94.1	28.51	5.6	0.0	5.3	0.0	10.0	19.6	68.7
Champlain National Bank	Willsboro	NY	B-	B-	C+	403.0	6.06	11.3	8.6	17.3	21.0	6.8	8.8	0.0
Chappell Hill Bank	Chappell Hill	TX	C	C+	C	43.1	29.22	4.3	2.8	26.2	3.7	6.5	8.5	15.8
Charis Bank	Justin	TX	C	C+	B	144.1	54.00	29.0	2.3	12.3	1.2	10.0	19.9	23.5
Charles River Bank	Medway	MA	C	C-	C-	281.6	11.81	6.3	2.4	36.0	15.9	5.7	7.7	13.6
Charles Schwab Bank, SSB	Westlake	TX	B+	B+	B+	307945.0	48.22	0.5	1.5	4.8	85.8	3.6	5.6	19.2
Charles Schwab Premier Bank, SSB	Westlake	TX	U	U	U	28309.0	109.28	0.0	0.0	0.0	92.8	3.5	5.5	28.4
Charles Schwab Trust Bank	Henderson	NV	U			11681.0	105.57	0.0	0.0	0.0	92.9	6.3	8.3	47.8
Charlevoix State Bank	Charlevoix	MI	B+	B+	B	259.4	26.39	10.8	2.4	15.4	22.0	6.0	8.0	0.0
Charlotte State Bank & Trust	Port Charlotte	FL	A-	A-	A-	458.7	20.93	3.2	0.1	15.7	25.6	7.5	9.3	0.0
Charter Bank	Johnston	IA	B+	B+	B+	188.3	15.27	15.3	2.4	18.7	29.5	9.4	10.6	16.5
Charter Bank	Corpus Christi	TX	B+	B	B	317.6	6.08	20.0	0.2	4.6	42.4	6.5	8.5	16.8
Charter Bank	Eau Claire	WI	A	A	A	1070.6	12.73	13.7	0.3	12.7	15.8	10.0	11.5	16.2
▲ Charter West Bank	West Point	NE	A-	B	B	347.7	16.65	13.0	2.3	25.7	7.1	8.0	10.1	0.0
Chasewood Bank	Houston	TX	D+	C-	C	104.4	17.46	4.9	0.1	7.6	17.0	7.9	9.6	0.0
Cheaha Bank	Oxford	AL	A	A	A	237.7	14.99	9.8	3.5	16.6	32.0	10.0	12.0	19.9
Chelsea Groton Bank	Norwich	CT	B+	A-	B	1434.9	23.73	8.9	0.5	42.5	11.1	10.0	14.8	20.8
Chelsea Savings Bank	Belle Plaine	IA	A-	A-	A-	175.8	48.50	9.7	1.2	9.9	46.3	10.0	13.9	0.0
Chelsea State Bank	Chelsea	MI	A-	A	A-	373.7	27.90	18.4	0.3	5.5	17.9	9.3	10.5	0.0
Chemung Canal Trust Co.	Elmira	NY	B-	B-	B-	2160.2	20.73	17.4	6.1	13.5	18.4	6.1	8.1	13.5
▲ Cherokee State Bank	Cherokee	IA	B+	B	B+	238.2	4.16	9.9	0.6	5.8	27.1	10.0	12.1	15.9
Chesapeake Bank	Kilmarnock	VA	B+	B+	A-	1170.7	24.45	16.6	0.7	9.2	35.2	7.4	9.3	14.9
Chesapeake Bank & Trust Co.	Chestertown	MD	B+	B+	B	121.7	11.64	7.6	0.7	33.6	22.3	8.0	9.7	0.0
Chesapeake Bank of Maryland	Baltimore	MD	C+	B-	B-	231.8	6.52	6.9	0.2	30.0	8.3	10.0	18.3	28.5
▼ Chester National Bank	Chester	IL	C+	B-	B-	67.5	9.92	1.7	2.2	50.5	11.7	10.0	11.9	26.0
Chesterfield State Bank	Chesterfield	IL	C	C-	D+	18.0	4.96	11.9	5.5	27.5	0.0	9.9	11.0	21.0

Asset Quality Index	Adjusted Non-Performing Loans as a % of Total Loans	as a % of Capital	Net Charge-Offs Avg Loans	Profitability Index	Net Income ($Mil)	Return on Assets (R.O.A.)	Return on Equity (R.O.E.)	Net Interest Spread	Overhead Efficiency Ratio	Liquidity Index	Liquidity Ratio	Hot Money Ratio	Stability Index
8.8	0.01	na	0.02	8.5	14.6	1.89	21.72	3.52	45.9	3.3	29.7	14.0	9.0
6.4	0.93	na	0.07	7.9	3.7	1.82	16.89	4.11	59.9	3.6	28.4	13.4	7.9
7.9	0.40	2.7	0.15	3.8	26.0	0.55	6.04	3.31	61.4	3.1	12.3	13.4	8.0
3.5	2.72	na	0.00	5.7	2.5	1.11	9.46	3.64	59.7	4.9	45.2	11.6	6.8
2.4	2.18	na	-0.01	2.5	0.2	0.28	1.12	3.15	88.1	0.8	23.7	37.6	7.5
8.8	0.12	na	0.01	7.1	4.2	1.55	14.50	4.09	58.8	2.3	23.2	18.3	7.9
6.9	0.11	0.8	0.00	5.5	3.6	1.34	13.70	3.73	50.9	2.6	14.9	9.1	6.1
3.6	2.81	na	0.02	5.8	3.7	1.48	12.24	2.90	44.3	1.5	33.8	51.4	8.5
0.5	8.08	na	0.08	7.4	1.9	1.58	10.81	3.42	56.5	1.5	25.8	27.9	9.1
8.0	0.39	1.9	0.06	6.6	35.9	1.53	21.12	2.38	61.1	4.7	9.2	3.6	6.9
6.8	1.14	3.2	-0.07	5.1	13.7	1.03	7.94	3.93	64.2	6.1	33.3	3.5	10.0
7.8	0.29	na	-0.01	9.3	1.1	1.74	13.25	4.38	59.8	4.6	38.0	11.4	6.7
7.9	1.01	3.9	0.23	2.7	-2.1	-0.16	-0.94	2.70	69.2	4.0	31.1	15.1	10.0
5.0	0.95	9.1	0.05	5.3	6.9	0.99	9.84	3.68	58.4	0.7	8.3	17.6	7.7
4.0	1.88	na	0.02	5.7	1.3	1.16	9.78	3.94	62.1	0.7	15.7	50.7	5.9
5.8	1.45	na	0.23	4.7	2.8	0.97	9.88	3.89	71.3	4.2	24.1	8.5	5.7
8.3	0.10	na	0.17	4.6	8.1	1.09	10.89	4.23	71.6	5.2	27.5	7.3	8.8
7.0	1.00	na	0.23	6.4	2.6	1.24	11.13	3.58	62.8	5.0	36.0	8.2	7.0
6.1	0.89	na	-0.01	6.6	3.8	1.37	11.72	3.36	62.1	5.7	33.5	2.2	7.0
9.5	0.12	0.6	-0.01	3.6	31.3	0.72	11.38	2.03	58.0	3.2	8.2	9.3	4.3
5.0	1.10	na	-0.11	3.1	0.5	0.66	8.27	3.46	85.4	3.3	30.8	15.5	4.0
8.6	0.29	na	0.01	6.6	2.3	1.31	13.74	4.19	54.0	5.2	34.8	6.5	6.1
5.1	3.35	na	-0.01	6.8	1.7	1.58	14.17	3.68	58.6	2.1	15.8	18.4	8.5
7.6	0.21	na	-0.01	9.2	2.2	1.55	16.34	4.87	56.9	4.0	12.7	8.2	7.7
4.5	1.15	na	0.04	5.3	3.9	1.01	9.05	4.33	67.2	1.5	10.6	9.5	7.3
8.2	3.21	na	0.01	1.9	0.1	0.16	1.09	2.32	94.2	2.7	63.8	40.1	7.1
7.1	1.33	na	0.79	1.2	0.3	0.07	0.55	2.63	95.7	6.0	47.2	5.9	7.2
8.4	0.24	na	0.08	5.2	0.5	1.15	7.16	3.29	55.9	3.9	31.0	12.5	7.0
7.9	0.29	na	0.07	8.7	23.4	2.94	30.64	2.65	42.8	0.7	7.8	30.8	8.1
5.5	0.29	na	0.20	8.1	19.3	1.72	15.22	3.65	50.3	1.8	21.5	24.6	10.0
8.4	1.01	na	-0.03	2.3	1.1	0.29	1.86	2.48	84.9	3.3	37.0	17.5	7.1
9.9	0.00	0.0	0.00	3.9	5.9	0.78	10.67	2.37	58.7	7.8	70.2	1.7	5.6
6.7	0.48	na	-0.02	5.6	8.5	1.09	10.97	3.85	63.4	1.5	16.0	26.5	9.0
6.9	0.18	na	0.12	8.2	0.8	1.59	5.77	3.90	43.4	0.9	24.4	31.4	7.6
9.7	0.00	0.0	0.00	9.4	0.9	1.69	7.70	2.06	68.5	4.8	82.8	17.4	9.0
5.0	0.97	na	0.03	4.7	2.8	0.96	11.08	3.84	64.1	2.0	11.4	14.1	5.4
6.3	0.00	na	0.43	3.7	0.2	0.70	7.82	4.02	80.7	2.6	36.7	22.9	4.7
7.2	0.00	na	0.00	0.0	-1.4	-1.39	-5.58	3.04	124.8	4.9	25.1	3.8	6.8
5.8	0.34	na	0.00	3.0	1.0	0.48	5.87	2.98	81.0	2.4	24.6	18.0	4.0
10.0	0.20	0.2	-0.01	6.0	1933.0	0.97	13.32	1.77	26.2	7.8	85.7	0.0	6.1
10.0	na	0.0	na	6.6	177.0	1.06	14.66	1.82	22.9	8.3	84.0	0.0	7.6
10.0	na	0.0	na	5.6	92.0	1.19	13.46	1.47	36.0	7.9	67.2	0.0	7.0
5.6	1.41	na	-0.02	8.1	3.0	1.84	20.72	3.96	56.6	6.6	48.9	2.2	6.1
8.8	0.19	0.7	-0.01	9.0	6.6	2.07	20.84	3.27	59.2	7.0	52.8	0.7	8.3
8.8	0.00	na	0.00	5.3	1.8	1.35	12.02	2.81	56.4	3.7	40.0	16.3	6.8
6.0	1.06	na	0.01	10.0	6.8	3.01	27.56	6.31	49.5	5.0	48.7	12.0	8.4
7.2	0.66	3.0	0.07	6.2	10.5	1.40	11.32	3.32	46.5	4.3	28.3	10.6	10.0
8.3	0.03	na	0.00	8.8	8.6	3.61	36.43	3.24	66.1	1.1	15.1	24.1	7.4
5.7	0.48	na	0.00	1.5	0.0	-0.05	-0.47	3.34	100.1	1.8	38.7	45.0	4.3
8.8	0.51	na	0.09	7.2	2.5	1.44	11.81	3.93	58.3	1.9	36.4	33.5	8.6
6.4	2.30	10.1	0.00	4.5	8.4	0.87	5.86	3.24	66.8	5.4	28.2	6.0	9.8
6.5	2.46	na	0.17	6.7	1.5	1.45	9.69	4.14	54.0	5.7	69.7	12.5	9.4
6.3	1.59	na	-0.02	6.0	3.5	1.33	11.58	3.50	60.2	6.1	42.3	3.5	8.4
4.5	1.20	8.0	0.27	4.4	13.3	0.90	9.58	3.32	66.2	4.5	18.5	6.5	7.2
5.1	1.83	na	0.03	6.8	2.4	1.37	10.98	3.63	51.7	3.2	26.6	10.1	7.9
8.8	0.18	0.9	-0.16	5.4	8.9	1.15	10.79	3.73	73.3	4.4	24.5	10.0	8.4
3.7	2.63	na	0.00	5.1	1.0	1.21	11.93	3.69	63.3	3.7	11.5	10.1	6.9
9.0	0.31	na	0.00	2.6	0.5	0.31	1.67	3.32	83.8	1.8	31.4	30.1	7.1
9.6	0.32	na	0.00	2.4	0.1	0.19	1.54	3.05	92.3	3.5	33.1	15.4	6.2
5.9	0.00	na	-0.09	3.4	0.1	0.63	5.72	3.52	82.4	2.6	37.6	18.9	4.3

Name	City	State	Rating	2019 Rating	2018 Rating	Total Assets ($Mil)	One Year Asset Growth	Asset Mix (As a % of Total Assets)				Capital- ization Index	Lever- age Ratio	Risk- Based Capital Ratio
								Comm- ercial Loans	Cons- umer Loans	Mort- gage Loans	Secur- ities			
Cheyenne State Bank	Cheyenne	WY	B-	B-	C+	44.0	9.36	3.3	0.7	16.2	2.5	10.0	15.5	23.5
Chicago Trust Co., N.A.	Lake Forest	IL	U	U	U	114.1	2.47	0.0	0.0	0.0	1.8	10.0	99.1	465.4
Chickasaw Community Bank	Oklahoma City	OK	C+	B	B+	263.2	30.24	13.8	1.6	32.5	8.1	10.0	12.1	19.0
Chillicothe State Bank	Chillicothe	MO	B	B	B	137.0	14.42	4.9	4.9	22.7	32.5	6.6	8.6	18.5
Chilton Trust Co., N.A.	Palm Beach	FL	U			16.6	na	0.0	0.0	0.0	55.6	10.0	90.4	341.0
Chino Commercial Bank, N.A.	Chino	CA	A-	B+	B	303.3	28.91	17.0	0.0	6.5	14.0	6.7	8.7	0.0
Chippewa Valley Bank	Hayward	WI	B-	B-	B-	599.9	34.26	11.1	0.3	14.2	7.3	5.4	7.4	11.7
Chisholm Trail State Bank	Park City	KS	C	C-	C	132.3	44.84	11.2	1.3	16.9	10.9	10.0	11.4	15.9
▼ Choice Financial Group	Fargo	ND	C+	B+	B+	2724.7	22.97	32.1	0.5	5.5	3.0	2.8	9.2	0.0
ChoiceOne Bank	Sparta	MI	B+	B+	B	1573.4	138.02	15.7	2.2	12.9	24.9	6.9	8.9	13.7
CIBC Bank USA	Chicago	IL	B-	B	B+	39464.7	24.33	24.7	0.6	4.2	15.4	9.0	10.7	14.2
CIBC National Trust Co.	Atlanta	GA	U	U	U	298.4	9.61	0.0	0.0	0.0	0.0	10.0	64.4	139.6
▲ CIBM Bank	Champaign	IL	B-	C	C+	785.6	13.46	10.0	0.1	27.4	13.4	9.8	10.9	15.7
Ciera Bank	Graham	TX	B+	B-	B	808.5	27.72	12.2	0.5	7.8	7.2	7.6	9.4	14.1
▲ Cincinnati Federal	Cincinnati	OH	B-	C+	B-	232.1	4.76	0.5	0.1	47.7	2.4	10.0	14.3	20.4
▲ Cincinnatus S&L Co.	Cincinnati	OH	B-	B-	B-	105.5	10.00	5.8	2.8	39.4	3.7	10.0	21.3	0.0
▼ CIT Bank, N.A.	Pasadena	CA	C+	B+	B+	55419.5	22.12	21.3	0.0	12.6	11.4	6.5	8.5	12.7
▼ Citibank, N.A.	Sioux Falls	SD	B	B+	B	1648667.0	11.93	9.6	9.9	5.2	25.0	6.5	8.5	15.8
Citicorp Trust Delaware, N.A.	Greenville	DE	U	U	U	23.8	9.35	0.0	0.0	0.0	0.9	10.0	95.9	492.9
Citizens & Northern Bank	Wellsboro	PA	B+	A-	A-	2336.2	43.60	13.7	0.7	24.4	13.9	8.1	9.7	15.7
Citizens 1st Bank	Tyler	TX	A+	A+	A+	728.5	3.37	1.2	0.7	8.1	60.6	10.0	21.1	50.2
Citizens Alliance Bank	Clara City	MN	B-	B-	B-	924.2	11.43	15.5	1.2	6.4	17.0	5.3	8.3	11.2
Citizens and Farmers Bank	West Point	VA	A-	A-	A-	2038.8	26.97	7.6	15.8	26.6	13.4	7.9	9.7	13.2
Citizens B&T Co. of Grainger County	Rutledge	TN	B+	A-	B+	236.0	14.76	2.8	1.5	10.5	62.2	10.0	15.8	0.0
Citizens Bank	Enterprise	AL	B	B	C+	175.5	19.13	9.8	1.2	16.8	11.7	7.7	9.4	0.0
▼ Citizens Bank	Greensboro	AL	B+	A-	A-	114.7	19.06	6.6	4.1	5.3	41.3	10.0	12.4	26.4
Citizens Bank	Batesville	AR	B-	B-	B-	1056.5	15.18	11.0	1.9	15.2	9.3	6.0	8.0	11.8
Citizens Bank	Sac City	IA	C-	C	C	61.0	10.62	15.1	2.2	10.1	27.4	6.8	8.8	15.6
Citizens Bank	Mooresville	IN	B	B	C+	576.3	17.98	5.1	36.3	5.0	18.3	8.5	10.0	15.1
Citizens Bank	Hickman	KY	B	B	B+	152.8	10.08	7.4	2.6	13.7	18.6	10.0	12.3	0.0
▼ Citizens Bank	Morehead	KY	C	B-	B-	180.8	26.46	5.7	3.8	29.2	16.9	4.6	6.6	13.5
Citizens Bank	Mount Vernon	KY	B	C+	C-	155.0	6.65	7.1	4.5	39.4	5.1	9.1	10.4	15.3
Citizens Bank	Butler	MO	B	B-	C+	172.6	13.79	10.8	2.0	24.0	1.4	5.1	7.4	11.1
▲ Citizens Bank	New Haven	MO	C+	C+	B-	252.0	9.61	10.4	1.2	15.5	6.8	7.0	11.4	12.5
Citizens Bank	Byhalia	MS	B+	B+	B	85.9	13.84	6.1	5.4	17.5	19.9	10.0	12.1	0.0
Citizens Bank	Columbia	MS	B-	B-	B-	471.1	10.73	10.5	3.7	20.2	8.7	8.3	9.9	16.9
Citizens Bank	Farmington	NM	A-	A-	B+	764.6	12.29	13.3	0.6	11.4	51.4	7.4	9.2	21.0
Citizens Bank	Corvallis	OR	B+	A	A-	985.1	22.33	12.9	0.3	3.4	20.6	7.6	9.4	21.0
Citizens Bank	Olanta	SC	B	B	B-	671.8	17.18	11.7	3.5	19.3	11.5	7.2	9.2	14.1
Citizens Bank	Carthage	TN	A	A	A	672.4	8.79	5.4	2.6	9.8	52.3	10.0	17.1	26.4
Citizens Bank	Elizabethton	TN	A	A	A-	1050.8	21.41	25.6	1.7	5.6	17.2	8.6	10.9	13.9
Citizens Bank	Hartsville	TN	A-	A-	B	275.3	14.74	5.9	2.7	19.8	17.2	7.9	9.6	13.9
Citizens Bank	Amarillo	TX	A-	A-	B	213.6	25.42	7.5	0.1	2.6	4.6	7.3	9.2	13.2
Citizens Bank	Kilgore	TX	B	B	B	475.6	13.62	23.6	0.7	6.4	5.2	10.0	12.6	20.1
Citizens Bank	Mukwonago	WI	A-	B+	B	900.1	17.07	12.2	0.1	5.9	16.7	10.0	12.3	0.0
▼ Citizens Bank & Trust	Guntersville	AL	B-	B	B-	686.1	26.64	14.4	1.6	11.6	21.8	7.0	9.0	16.2
Citizens Bank & Trust	Rock Port	MO	B	B	B	98.9	-0.22	15.2	2.6	6.7	35.7	10.0	11.8	0.0
Citizens Bank & Trust Co.	Van Buren	AR	A-	A-	A	452.4	12.78	8.9	3.9	14.2	29.3	10.0	12.1	0.0
Citizens Bank & Trust Co.	Campbellsville	KY	B	B	B	270.4	19.12	18.1	2.6	17.4	33.9	10.0	13.9	0.0
▼ Citizens Bank & Trust Co.	Covington	LA	B-	B	C	145.2	16.85	7.5	0.4	20.3	8.7	8.2	9.8	0.0
Citizens Bank & Trust Co.	Plaquemine	LA	B-	B	B-	371.0	18.26	13.7	0.8	16.0	7.5	9.4	11.0	14.5
Citizens Bank & Trust Co.	Vivian	LA	B-	B-	B-	162.2	13.98	6.0	2.0	26.7	33.7	10.0	11.2	0.0
Citizens Bank & Trust Co.	Hutchinson	MN	B	B-	C+	289.5	34.08	17.1	1.1	17.0	34.2	4.7	8.0	0.0
▼ Citizens Bank & Trust Co.	Marks	MS	E+	D	D+	136.9	-3.52	5.7	2.1	12.3	19.5	4.7	6.9	10.8
▲ Citizens Bank & Trust Co.	Big Timber	MT	B-	C+	C+	125.4	12.25	6.1	1.9	5.7	17.8	8.0	9.7	17.5
Citizens Bank & Trust Co.	Saint Paul	NE	D+	D+	C	220.1	4.48	8.7	1.6	5.9	12.2	7.1	11.1	0.0
Citizens Bank & Trust Co.	Atwood	TN	C-	C-	C-	25.1	1.81	2.2	11.8	21.9	41.8	9.0	10.3	26.7
Citizens Bank & Trust Co. of Ardmore	Ardmore	OK	B	B	B	253.9	15.73	8.4	2.2	27.5	24.5	7.1	9.0	0.0
Citizens Bank & Trust Co. of Jackson	Jackson	KY	C	C	D+	160.6	15.16	10.0	5.2	27.1	9.6	5.9	7.9	13.3
▼ Citizens Bank & Trust, Inc.	Trenton	GA	B+	A-	B+	110.7	4.45	3.0	7.4	33.5	29.0	9.6	10.7	22.0

Asset Quality Index	Adjusted Non-Performing Loans as a % of Total Loans	as a % of Capital	Net Charge-Offs / Avg Loans	Profitability Index	Net Income ($Mil)	Return on Assets (R.O.A.)	Return on Equity (R.O.E.)	Net Interest Spread	Overhead Efficiency Ratio	Liquidity Index	Liquidity Ratio	Hot Money Ratio	Stability Index
8.8	0.00	na	0.00	3.7	0.2	0.51	3.13	5.44	85.6	3.7	31.1	13.8	6.8
9.0	na	0.0	na	9.5	1.8	2.13	2.16	1.57	76.8	4.0	na	0.0	6.3
5.3	1.56	5.1	0.03	8.6	9.3	5.13	50.01	5.06	52.4	0.6	10.2	31.4	6.9
5.4	0.96	na	0.13	4.9	1.1	1.15	12.86	3.23	65.2	6.1	45.3	4.3	5.8
10.0	na	na	na	1.2	3.3	0.00	0.00	na	66.4	4.0	na	0.0	1.2
8.0	0.71	na	-0.08	6.0	2.1	1.03	10.73	3.55	58.5	5.0	29.8	3.4	5.7
5.7	0.42	na	0.00	5.7	5.0	1.24	15.95	3.35	58.0	2.9	19.0	5.9	5.8
7.7	0.08	0.5	0.02	4.2	0.9	1.06	9.33	4.37	69.5	4.1	20.9	6.3	5.5
4.8	0.56	5.3	0.03	9.0	32.4	1.66	14.40	4.00	46.9	2.0	8.7	10.8	10.0
6.1	0.55	2.2	0.06	6.2	13.4	1.42	12.66	4.31	64.9	5.4	32.2	7.8	9.4
4.4	1.34	4.1	0.18	3.6	145.9	0.53	2.97	2.75	44.6	5.1	30.5	5.6	10.0
6.5	na	0.0	na	10.0	22.9	11.01	16.46	0.77	60.2	3.9	124.2	100.0	5.7
6.3	0.43	2.2	-0.02	5.1	6.3	1.16	9.68	3.11	69.9	1.3	13.5	21.5	7.1
7.0	0.99	na	-0.06	7.7	9.5	1.72	15.97	3.91	56.8	2.2	28.7	20.3	9.5
8.5	0.66	2.1	0.00	4.3	1.6	0.94	7.18	2.66	79.2	1.8	14.1	20.1	6.8
7.3	1.99	na	-0.02	4.4	0.7	0.87	3.95	3.55	74.7	2.4	10.3	16.4	7.6
5.1	1.95	12.1	0.80	1.5	-481.6	-1.17	-13.02	2.50	95.2	2.1	21.7	14.5	8.2
6.6	1.20	4.4	1.10	3.6	5435.0	0.46	4.80	2.69	54.4	4.6	47.2	4.5	7.8
10.0	na	0.0	na	9.8	1.3	7.55	8.01	1.58	76.4	4.0	na	0.0	5.0
4.6	1.36	na	0.23	5.4	13.4	0.95	7.57	3.69	70.2	2.7	10.9	14.4	10.0
9.5	0.40	na	0.00	6.8	9.0	1.72	7.79	2.98	37.5	3.2	52.6	26.9	10.0
4.3	0.94	6.5	0.38	6.9	8.5	1.29	13.79	3.99	50.7	1.3	15.2	16.7	7.1
7.1	0.29	na	0.33	6.2	15.5	1.10	10.36	4.74	69.3	2.5	10.5	16.0	8.6
6.7	4.60	na	0.09	4.3	1.5	0.92	5.19	3.30	68.5	5.8	65.6	11.7	8.0
6.1	2.19	na	-0.09	4.3	1.0	0.83	8.37	3.53	73.3	3.6	27.9	13.0	5.3
7.7	0.29	2.1	0.19	4.9	0.7	0.94	6.80	2.88	51.9	3.3	47.2	21.2	7.4
5.9	0.91	na	0.08	4.5	6.6	0.87	9.51	3.79	67.9	3.6	18.2	11.8	8.1
3.2	2.61	na	0.60	4.3	0.4	1.09	11.85	3.35	61.9	2.8	31.1	18.3	4.5
6.5	0.43	na	0.03	5.0	4.1	1.02	9.22	3.35	66.9	4.1	19.7	8.8	7.3
7.5	0.37	na	0.14	4.1	1.3	1.12	8.84	3.63	70.1	1.6	11.8	21.3	6.7
5.2	0.71	na	0.07	2.8	0.5	0.39	4.72	3.69	86.4	4.4	19.6	6.7	4.0
5.3	0.62	na	-0.02	6.0	1.6	1.41	13.10	4.80	68.3	1.3	10.8	25.5	6.5
5.7	0.37	na	-0.03	6.9	1.9	1.50	18.06	4.55	63.7	3.8	20.8	10.5	5.8
5.4	0.22	1.3	1.51	4.7	1.8	1.00	8.67	3.54	59.4	2.8	16.0	10.9	7.9
8.7	0.38	na	0.18	4.1	0.4	0.68	5.43	4.44	77.9	5.5	51.0	9.2	6.3
4.6	1.74	na	0.05	6.2	5.0	1.45	15.64	3.85	64.9	2.1	21.3	19.2	6.8
5.6	2.44	na	0.00	7.6	10.2	1.83	17.56	3.54	49.8	5.1	45.0	10.8	7.3
7.5	0.70	na	-0.02	3.9	2.1	0.31	2.89	3.31	59.4	6.7	46.2	1.0	6.8
6.8	0.36	na	0.02	4.7	4.4	0.92	9.07	3.54	69.6	4.8	29.4	6.6	6.4
9.0	0.08	na	0.01	9.8	10.5	2.16	11.77	3.88	29.1	3.2	61.3	31.8	10.0
7.1	0.45	na	0.11	8.0	10.6	1.67	13.78	4.28	59.5	0.8	6.6	22.8	10.0
7.2	0.51	na	0.04	5.7	1.9	0.93	9.13	3.55	64.0	1.6	32.3	33.1	6.8
7.5	0.00	na	0.00	8.3	2.6	1.72	18.18	3.64	51.4	3.6	31.7	14.4	7.0
3.9	3.05	na	0.00	3.4	1.7	0.50	3.78	3.93	69.7	4.8	39.8	10.8	6.6
7.3	0.74	2.6	-0.04	6.6	8.7	1.36	10.82	3.36	54.1	3.9	20.5	9.8	7.7
7.0	0.41	na	0.03	3.9	4.4	0.91	9.70	3.47	69.0	3.1	21.2	14.1	5.9
8.6	0.42	na	0.70	4.3	0.9	1.22	10.05	3.02	73.7	3.4	19.3	12.4	7.4
6.1	1.64	6.0	0.06	8.9	5.3	1.62	12.68	3.96	48.9	3.0	22.7	15.0	9.1
8.4	1.29	na	0.04	4.7	1.9	0.98	6.58	3.16	61.3	4.5	37.6	11.5	7.9
7.3	0.34	na	0.01	3.8	0.7	0.66	6.54	3.90	79.4	3.0	27.7	15.9	5.4
4.1	1.93	na	0.13	4.4	2.1	0.77	7.37	3.62	67.2	2.5	14.3	16.4	6.7
5.6	2.48	na	0.07	3.8	1.1	0.96	7.57	3.62	83.1	4.0	28.3	11.3	6.6
5.6	2.12	na	0.00	7.8	3.9	2.05	25.07	3.92	47.7	5.0	27.1	4.5	6.0
0.3	7.99	na	4.83	0.1	-2.4	-2.18	-28.41	2.76	77.4	2.1	28.9	21.9	2.1
4.3	1.47	na	0.01	7.0	1.3	1.42	12.47	4.10	53.7	4.4	37.4	12.1	6.9
0.2	2.62	na	0.64	3.4	0.6	0.37	3.24	3.60	70.0	2.7	24.7	16.7	7.0
7.2	0.49	2.4	0.07	2.4	0.1	0.31	2.96	2.83	87.8	1.2	25.9	33.6	4.8
6.3	1.16	na	-0.01	5.4	2.5	1.36	14.72	3.74	67.3	3.4	28.6	14.4	6.1
4.0	1.49	na	0.18	3.7	0.8	0.71	7.67	3.78	80.0	1.6	19.1	24.2	3.8
7.0	0.96	na	0.07	4.9	0.7	0.80	7.21	4.75	76.3	4.6	34.8	10.4	6.9

Name	City	State	Rating	2019 Rating	2018 Rating	Total Assets ($Mil)	One Year Asset Growth	Comm- ercial Loans	Cons- umer Loans	Mort- gage Loans	Secur- ities	Capital- ization Index	Lever- age Ratio	Risk- Based Capital Ratio
								Asset Mix (As a % of Total Assets)						
Citizens Bank and Trust	Lake Wales	FL	B-	B-	C+	871.9	30.99	20.3	6.1	9.6	29.8	4.8	6.8	13.3
▼ Citizens Bank and Trust Co.	Kansas City	MO	C+	B	B-	1008.3	11.08	11.1	0.5	10.3	18.9	8.2	9.8	14.9
Citizens Bank and Trust Co.	Blackstone	VA	A-	A-	A-	465.6	15.99	8.2	2.5	21.5	31.7	10.0	12.6	0.0
Citizens Bank Co.	Beverly	OH	B+	A-	A-	266.8	17.05	12.2	1.8	29.5	20.0	10.0	11.7	0.0
Citizens Bank Minnesota	New Ulm	MN	B	B	B	535.7	27.20	8.3	1.2	17.9	25.1	5.9	8.3	11.7
▼ Citizens Bank of Ada	Ada	OK	B-	B	B-	224.2	18.88	17.5	2.7	16.1	17.2	7.6	9.4	0.0
Citizens Bank of Americus	Americus	GA	B+	B+	B	382.9	15.75	13.4	1.4	7.5	23.7	6.7	8.7	17.4
Citizens Bank of Cape Vincent	Cape Vincent	NY	C	C+	C+	76.5	9.41	1.2	2.5	39.0	38.5	7.5	9.3	0.0
Citizens Bank of Charleston	Charleston	MO	A	A-	B+	139.6	0.17	8.1	5.3	8.0	7.3	10.0	18.1	0.0
Citizens Bank of Chatsworth	Chatsworth	IL	D-	D	E+	41.6	33.38	34.3	1.2	3.7	20.2	6.7	8.8	15.5
Citizens Bank of Clovis	Clovis	NM	A-	A-	B+	388.1	11.85	5.4	0.5	3.7	31.2	10.0	11.8	0.0
Citizens Bank of Cochran	Cochran	GA	B-	B-	B-	117.5	11.65	8.5	4.0	28.4	16.9	8.0	9.7	16.3
▲ Citizens Bank of Cumberland County	Burkesville	KY	B+	B	B-	74.9	-1.37	3.9	13.6	25.0	8.5	10.0	14.0	0.0
▲ Citizens Bank of Edina	Edina	MO	A	B+	B+	76.7	4.98	8.5	2.8	5.9	4.6	10.0	12.2	0.0
▲ Citizens Bank of Edinburg	Edinburg	IL	C	C	C-	28.9	10.62	1.1	1.7	10.9	15.4	7.3	9.2	0.0
Citizens Bank of Edmond	Edmond	OK	B-	B-	C+	322.0	7.73	16.3	0.5	18.3	4.9	6.4	9.7	0.0
Citizens Bank of Eldon	Eldon	MO	B+	A-	A-	175.6	13.19	6.5	7.6	23.4	5.9	10.0	12.0	0.0
Citizens Bank of Fayette	Fayette	AL	A-	B+	B+	209.2	10.10	4.3	2.8	2.7	70.5	10.0	19.8	0.0
Citizens Bank of Florida	Oviedo	FL	B-	C+	C	432.6	22.07	15.6	1.0	7.1	15.6	6.0	8.0	13.2
Citizens Bank of Georgia	Cumming	GA	A-	B	B	406.3	23.33	12.6	1.0	8.4	25.5	8.4	9.9	17.8
Citizens Bank of Kansas	Kingman	KS	B-	B-	B-	450.9	19.11	9.0	1.0	16.5	32.1	7.1	9.0	14.5
▼ Citizens Bank of Kentucky	Paintsville	KY	C+	B	B	722.7	11.88	6.7	2.3	15.1	20.5	8.9	10.3	18.3
Citizens Bank of Lafayette	Lafayette	TN	B+	B+	B+	1014.8	9.16	7.6	4.3	12.7	27.9	10.0	11.4	18.9
Citizens Bank of Las Cruces	Las Cruces	NM	A	A-	B+	744.1	21.56	18.5	0.4	7.4	11.0	8.8	10.2	16.0
Citizens Bank of Morgantown, Inc.	Morgantown	WV	B	B-	B-	44.1	14.97	12.9	2.0	48.2	20.3	10.0	17.6	35.0
▲ Citizens Bank of Newburg	Rolla	MO	C	C	C	153.7	3.39	8.5	2.0	26.4	11.6	8.0	10.1	0.0
Citizens Bank of Philadelphia, Mississippi	Philadelphia	MS	C+	B-	B-	1374.0	30.93	8.7	1.0	6.9	42.4	5.2	7.2	13.3
▲ Citizens Bank of Rogersville	Rogersville	MO	B	B-	B-	97.6	5.68	19.7	4.0	25.5	7.6	7.7	10.6	0.0
Citizens Bank of Swainsboro	Swainsboro	GA	B+	B+	B	256.9	19.92	17.4	5.0	22.4	7.9	8.4	10.0	17.0
Citizens Bank of The South	Sandersville	GA	B+	B+	B	304.0	20.06	10.5	3.1	27.0	9.4	9.0	10.4	18.3
Citizens Bank of West Virginia, Inc.	Elkins	WV	B-	B-	C+	310.4	9.86	11.1	22.7	30.8	3.6	9.9	10.9	16.7
Citizens Bank of Weston, Inc.	Weston	WV	A-	B+	B-	211.1	3.16	26.8	3.5	19.8	20.5	10.0	11.8	18.3
Citizens Bank of Winfield	Winfield	AL	A	A	A	283.1	13.64	2.9	5.8	4.2	73.3	10.0	20.9	0.0
Citizens Bank, N.A.	Providence	RI	B-	B-	B-	179163.2	8.81	22.6	15.7	13.6	14.3	7.4	9.3	12.9
Citizens Bank, N.A.	Abilene	TX	B+	A-	B	123.0	15.08	17.6	5.1	15.0	15.8	4.7	9.0	0.0
▼ Citizens Building and Loan, SSB	Greer	SC	B-	B+	A-	149.8	7.46	0.0	0.2	52.0	14.2	10.0	19.8	0.0
Citizens Business Bank	Ontario	CA	A	A-	A	13813.4	21.92	12.9	0.1	3.0	20.3	8.1	9.7	15.8
Citizens Commerce Bank	Versailles	KY	C+	C-	C-	292.5	9.63	11.5	0.7	28.5	12.0	6.4	9.3	0.0
Citizens Community Bank	Hahira	GA	B+	A-	B+	160.3	17.53	8.6	3.4	17.8	26.2	10.0	11.8	20.5
Citizens Community Bank	Mascoutah	IL	B+	B+	B+	439.0	9.93	7.2	0.9	9.7	35.8	10.0	11.5	0.0
Citizens Community Bank	Pilot Grove	MO	B	B	B-	116.6	11.82	5.5	2.0	12.2	9.9	10.0	11.4	0.0
Citizens Community Bank	Winchester	TN	A-	B+	B-	262.5	11.23	12.7	3.2	16.8	15.1	10.0	12.8	21.3
Citizens Community Federal N.A.	Altoona	WI	B-	B-	B-	1622.5	9.97	13.7	2.7	12.2	10.4	8.3	9.9	15.0
Citizens Deposit Bank & Trust	Vanceburg	KY	B	B	B-	570.5	19.98	6.6	2.2	16.6	37.9	6.5	8.5	0.0
Citizens Deposit Bank of Arlington, Inc.	Arlington	KY	A-	A-	B+	267.6	14.79	19.5	4.8	15.8	22.8	10.0	13.7	0.0
Citizens Federal S&L Assn.	Covington	KY	B-	B	B+	42.9	8.44	0.0	0.0	51.6	17.1	10.0	26.3	64.3
Citizens Federal S&L Assn.	Bellefontaine	OH	C	C	C	158.9	17.38	0.0	0.1	61.9	15.0	10.0	11.6	23.2
Citizens Federal Savings Bank	Leavenworth	KS	C-	C	C	185.6	6.24	0.8	0.8	51.1	33.0	10.0	20.8	0.0
Citizens First Bank	The Villages	FL	A+	A+	A	2986.6	27.35	11.0	0.1	6.6	63.3	10.0	11.6	18.1
▼ Citizens First Bank	Clinton	IA	C	B-	C+	244.4	19.29	27.0	2.1	10.0	5.8	4.1	8.4	0.0
Citizens First Bank	Viroqua	WI	B	B-	C+	248.4	12.44	7.5	1.9	7.2	20.0	7.4	10.4	0.0
Citizens First National Bank	Storm Lake	IA	A	A	A-	243.2	20.94	11.2	3.5	3.7	43.2	9.5	10.7	20.3
Citizens First State Bank of Walnut	Walnut	IL	C+	C+	D+	53.3	12.68	6.7	3.4	20.0	22.9	6.6	8.6	16.9
Citizens Guaranty Bank	Irvine	KY	C-	D+	C-	217.4	8.70	10.8	8.2	39.8	6.3	3.5	6.5	10.2
Citizens Independent Bank	Saint Louis Park	MN	B-	B-	C+	345.2	16.75	18.4	5.4	11.1	15.8	9.0	10.3	19.0
Citizens National Bank	Greenleaf	KS	B-	B-	B-	194.6	14.65	6.8	2.1	10.0	55.9	9.1	10.4	0.0
Citizens National Bank	Sevierville	TN	A	A	A	1223.4	11.09	11.5	0.4	12.2	9.8	9.6	10.7	16.1
Citizens National Bank	Cameron	TX	B+	B	B	482.4	16.45	8.8	0.6	7.4	24.0	9.6	10.7	17.0
Citizens National Bank	Crockett	TX	B	B	B-	87.8	-1.27	12.3	6.0	7.0	13.9	10.0	12.0	0.0
Citizens National Bank at Brownwood	Brownwood	TX	A	A-	B+	238.0	10.46	10.2	5.7	12.0	43.4	10.0	11.7	24.0

Asset Quality Index	Adjusted Non-Performing Loans as a % of Total Loans	as a % of Capital	Net Charge-Offs Avg Loans	Profitability Index	Net Income ($Mil)	Return on Assets (R.O.A.)	Return on Equity (R.O.E.)	Net Interest Spread	Overhead Efficiency Ratio	Liquidity Index	Liquidity Ratio	Hot Money Ratio	Stability Index
5.6	0.84	na	0.02	5.2	9.5	1.58	18.95	3.52	72.0	5.1	19.9	2.0	5.4
6.4	2.03	6.4	0.15	2.5	1.7	0.24	2.20	2.98	80.9	3.8	23.9	13.0	7.8
9.1	0.75	2.0	0.00	6.1	4.2	1.26	9.74	3.44	57.9	4.2	38.6	13.6	7.8
8.8	0.07	na	0.00	5.3	1.8	0.96	7.64	3.83	64.4	3.6	14.1	11.0	8.1
8.6	0.11	0.6	0.00	4.9	3.7	1.01	10.44	3.05	62.5	3.7	24.4	11.3	5.8
4.5	1.97	na	0.17	3.0	0.7	0.44	4.46	4.22	88.7	4.1	17.9	8.4	5.0
7.2	0.54	na	0.15	5.4	2.7	1.01	10.95	3.40	56.1	4.9	33.0	7.8	6.5
6.0	1.26	na	0.15	2.6	0.3	0.46	4.69	3.34	81.5	5.1	28.9	4.2	4.8
8.0	0.60	na	0.04	8.5	1.7	1.53	8.73	3.63	48.7	2.4	25.2	18.2	9.2
0.9	2.63	na	0.37	0.0	-0.6	-2.20	-20.00	2.76	134.6	3.6	13.7	10.9	1.6
8.8	0.32	na	0.24	6.4	4.2	1.51	12.04	3.19	52.0	2.2	33.0	22.3	8.1
8.6	2.13	na	0.01	4.1	0.6	0.73	7.52	4.19	77.0	1.4	20.2	28.1	5.9
5.1	2.40	na	0.18	7.0	0.8	1.46	10.62	4.68	67.9	3.0	27.1	15.7	8.8
7.0	0.07	na	0.09	9.8	1.1	2.05	16.56	4.39	37.3	2.8	20.2	15.5	8.6
7.4	0.00	na	0.00	4.3	0.2	0.81	8.45	3.40	65.4	6.3	46.1	2.7	4.9
7.3	0.66	na	0.13	4.2	2.0	0.86	10.39	4.28	79.6	3.0	10.1	11.1	5.7
5.2	1.44	8.2	0.15	5.0	1.1	0.90	7.23	4.14	59.4	3.5	26.9	13.3	7.6
7.9	4.43	na	0.67	6.9	2.6	1.76	8.42	2.82	43.9	4.3	88.5	26.2	7.7
7.6	1.23	na	0.11	4.3	2.5	0.84	10.05	3.75	67.2	3.1	28.5	15.4	4.6
8.6	0.21	na	0.00	7.0	3.6	1.28	12.09	3.81	51.4	4.6	40.4	12.3	6.6
7.0	0.33	na	-0.05	4.2	2.7	0.88	6.63	3.80	77.7	4.9	29.5	6.3	7.4
5.0	1.53	na	0.17	3.3	3.4	0.65	4.92	2.94	76.8	2.6	33.7	19.6	8.0
4.9	1.94	8.8	0.08	5.8	8.2	1.12	9.00	3.64	61.6	2.8	30.3	23.6	9.8
8.4	0.19	na	0.00	9.7	15.7	3.07	29.03	4.09	54.6	4.7	18.8	4.7	8.6
8.9	0.71	na	0.20	4.1	0.2	0.66	3.75	4.91	73.1	2.2	26.6	19.6	7.1
5.4	0.97	na	0.16	2.9	1.2	1.02	10.25	3.48	75.4	0.8	15.2	19.9	4.1
5.0	1.59	na	0.10	3.2	5.1	0.52	5.82	2.75	78.5	3.1	7.7	12.7	6.0
6.2	0.34	na	0.07	6.4	1.1	1.56	13.94	4.06	64.8	2.4	12.3	14.2	7.4
5.9	0.56	na	0.11	6.2	2.1	1.19	11.46	4.49	66.6	2.6	19.7	16.7	6.6
6.7	0.50	na	0.23	4.8	1.9	0.88	8.22	4.04	68.9	2.9	25.8	15.6	6.2
3.2	1.42	na	0.07	6.8	3.2	1.41	14.23	4.21	59.0	3.2	8.2	11.9	6.6
5.5	2.43	na	0.01	8.4	2.3	1.47	12.80	3.83	50.5	4.7	30.5	7.5	7.7
9.2	2.50	na	0.69	8.9	3.6	1.84	8.18	3.89	39.1	2.4	49.9	42.8	8.1
4.2	1.49	6.4	0.52	3.5	614.4	0.47	3.72	2.94	59.7	4.5	20.8	4.3	10.0
7.2	0.00	na	0.03	8.1	1.7	2.02	15.47	4.42	56.2	1.6	9.9	20.9	9.3
9.8	0.72	na	0.02	3.2	0.5	0.47	2.34	2.87	78.2	1.0	28.1	55.1	8.1
7.1	0.17	0.6	0.00	8.7	130.9	1.39	8.86	3.69	40.1	5.1	20.8	2.8	10.0
7.9	0.21	2.5	0.00	3.9	1.7	0.82	8.08	3.42	71.5	1.3	7.8	24.9	5.8
6.5	0.76	na	0.45	5.3	1.4	1.19	9.62	3.99	70.0	4.3	39.8	13.7	8.0
5.9	2.98	na	0.02	5.3	3.4	1.07	9.09	2.94	49.6	1.8	16.9	20.4	6.7
8.1	0.45	na	-0.01	3.9	0.6	0.74	6.35	3.23	72.4	3.2	28.5	15.2	6.9
6.5	0.97	na	0.20	9.4	3.0	1.60	12.25	4.65	44.8	3.2	23.8	14.0	8.2
4.4	2.05	na	0.08	4.6	10.8	0.91	7.53	3.53	60.0	3.6	19.7	11.5	8.8
6.4	0.47	2.6	0.05	5.3	4.6	1.07	10.89	3.35	61.8	2.7	18.2	15.7	7.0
7.8	0.06	na	0.08	6.3	2.8	1.45	9.87	3.99	50.9	0.6	17.3	43.5	9.4
10.0	0.00	na	0.00	3.0	0.1	0.37	1.33	3.05	62.6	3.3	56.5	24.1	8.1
9.2	0.36	1.4	0.00	0.7	-0.3	-0.29	-2.46	2.44	115.3	0.9	18.3	34.1	5.9
10.0	0.12	na	0.01	1.8	0.2	0.17	0.81	2.56	94.3	3.6	42.5	17.8	7.2
9.6	0.36	0.5	-0.01	8.7	40.6	2.07	15.75	2.58	42.4	6.9	67.6	6.8	9.9
3.7	2.76	na	0.31	3.4	1.1	0.61	6.80	3.13	73.5	1.8	18.4	19.8	5.5
4.7	1.24	na	-0.06	6.1	2.8	1.54	13.29	3.81	63.8	1.9	27.7	15.5	7.6
8.4	0.00	na	0.03	9.1	3.3	1.98	17.48	3.19	50.9	5.2	48.1	11.2	8.1
7.6	0.62	na	-0.01	3.4	0.2	0.58	6.40	3.73	85.5	6.1	50.7	4.7	4.3
3.5	1.44	na	0.02	3.8	1.2	0.73	10.97	4.27	82.8	1.3	9.5	26.5	3.9
5.7	0.81	4.3	-0.16	3.3	1.3	0.54	4.82	3.27	80.2	5.8	35.7	2.6	6.2
9.2	0.00	na	-0.05	3.7	1.0	0.68	6.12	3.15	73.1	5.2	47.7	11.1	6.0
7.6	0.04	0.7	0.08	8.0	15.6	1.77	15.55	3.77	53.3	2.7	18.7	14.4	10.0
8.8	0.00	0.0	0.00	5.7	4.0	1.18	10.56	3.51	57.1	3.7	33.9	14.5	6.8
8.6	0.00	na	0.14	3.7	0.4	0.66	5.45	4.71	80.2	5.6	42.3	6.5	7.1
8.7	0.38	na	0.06	6.6	2.8	1.59	12.78	3.47	58.0	5.6	48.6	9.0	8.1

Name	City	State	Rating	2019 Rating	2018 Rating	Total Assets ($Mil)	One Year Asset Growth	Asset Mix (As a % of Total Assets)				Capital- ization Index	Lever- age Ratio	Risk- Based Capital Ratio
								Comm- ercial Loans	Cons- umer Loans	Mort- gage Loans	Secur- ities			
Citizens National Bank of Albion	Albion	IL	B	B	B+	323.0	1.31	9.4	3.7	14.7	22.5	10.0	17.4	26.1
▲ Citizens National Bank of Bluffton	Bluffton	OH	B+	B-	C	953.8	9.80	17.9	0.3	8.8	15.1	5.6	9.8	0.0
▲ Citizens National Bank of Cheboygan	Cheboygan	MI	B-	C+	C	399.2	21.36	8.9	1.6	13.5	33.4	5.2	7.2	14.2
Citizens National Bank of Crosbyton	Crosbyton	TX	B+	B+	B	54.0	10.17	4.1	2.1	1.6	4.7	10.0	16.8	48.8
Citizens National Bank of Hammond	Hammond	NY	C-	C-	D	26.2	3.83	5.0	11.9	40.1	18.5	7.7	9.4	0.0
Citizens National Bank of Hillsboro	Hillsboro	TX	B+	B+	B	198.1	20.03	11.6	2.8	6.0	58.4	10.0	12.6	33.2
Citizens National Bank of Lebanon	Lebanon	KY	B	B	B	133.1	7.29	4.1	2.6	11.6	51.7	10.0	11.1	29.0
Citizens National Bank of McConnelsville	McConnelsville	OH	B-	B	B	102.4	7.12	2.7	5.3	40.5	22.8	10.0	11.2	0.0
Citizens National Bank of Meridian	Meridian	MS	A-	A-	B+	1568.4	9.49	13.4	1.5	15.4	18.4	9.5	10.8	14.6
Citizens National Bank of Park Rapids	Park Rapids	MN	A-	A-	B-	310.0	17.12	11.8	7.3	23.6	10.4	8.8	10.2	0.0
Citizens National Bank of Quitman	Quitman	GA	B+	B+	B	110.4	11.51	4.1	12.7	14.4	12.9	10.0	12.9	20.8
Citizens National Bank of Somerset	Somerset	KY	B+	B+	B+	555.0	28.66	5.6	3.3	18.6	28.8	6.8	8.8	0.0
▲ Citizens National Bank of Texas	Waxahachie	TX	B	B-	C+	1538.9	32.43	14.1	0.6	9.6	0.7	7.1	9.1	13.4
Citizens National Bank of Woodsfield	Woodsfield	OH	C+	C+	C	144.8	2.61	4.2	1.1	27.0	53.0	4.9	6.9	24.7
Citizens National Bank, N.A.	Bossier City	LA	B+	B+	B	1185.7	18.22	12.0	0.5	10.7	13.2	8.7	10.1	15.7
Citizens Progressive Bank	Winnsboro	LA	C-	C	D+	189.8	16.32	7.9	3.0	17.4	6.1	5.8	8.8	0.0
Citizens Savings Bank	Anamosa	IA	A-	A-	B+	150.1	20.35	4.8	0.5	6.5	31.8	8.2	9.8	17.0
Citizens Savings Bank	Hawkeye	IA	B+	A-	B+	30.1	8.38	1.1	1.1	7.9	54.1	10.0	14.6	0.0
Citizens Savings Bank	Marshalltown	IA	C+	C+	C+	69.8	18.03	8.8	1.1	16.5	0.3	6.1	8.1	11.9
▲ Citizens Savings Bank	Spillville	IA	A-	A-	B+	116.6	6.15	3.7	0.4	3.7	38.1	10.0	17.2	0.0
Citizens Savings Bank	Bogalusa	LA	B-	B-	C+	251.3	7.40	2.1	4.5	37.8	7.7	10.0	14.1	0.0
Citizens Savings Bank	Clarks Summit	PA	B-	B-	B-	351.8	9.76	0.0	0.1	76.0	9.1	10.0	15.0	30.3
Citizens Savings Bank and Trust Co.	Nashville	TN	E+	E+	E+	106.3	6.62	8.8	1.7	12.2	4.7	2.4	6.2	9.4
Citizens State Bank	Vernon	AL	B	B	B-	77.5	8.41	9.3	4.5	10.5	53.1	10.0	13.9	36.4
Citizens State Bank	Monticello	IA	B+	A-	A-	434.1	4.66	6.2	0.9	3.8	42.9	10.0	11.1	0.0
Citizens State Bank	Sheldon	IA	A-	A-	B+	143.5	13.94	8.5	5.2	12.0	15.2	10.0	12.4	0.0
Citizens State Bank	Wyoming	IA	A-	B	B+	104.7	13.07	9.3	2.5	4.1	30.3	10.0	21.6	33.7
Citizens State Bank	Lena	IL	B	B	B	303.9	15.31	7.6	5.0	9.1	22.7	10.0	11.2	17.6
Citizens State Bank	Gridley	KS	B+	B+	B-	235.2	16.44	11.5	2.3	11.4	20.4	6.8	8.8	0.0
▲ Citizens State Bank	Hugoton	KS	B-	B-	B-	127.1	8.34	7.7	0.9	4.0	26.9	10.0	13.0	0.0
Citizens State Bank	Marysville	KS	A-	A-	B+	366.1	4.81	9.1	1.0	7.3	12.9	7.6	9.7	13.0
Citizens State Bank	Moundridge	KS	B+	B+	B	482.3	12.16	8.1	0.8	4.9	37.3	7.6	10.1	0.0
▲ Citizens State Bank	Carleton	NE	C-	D+	D	25.6	8.61	9.2	4.7	1.5	0.0	8.1	9.7	0.0
Citizens State Bank	Wisner	NE	C	C	B-	410.2	34.07	8.5	1.2	7.0	5.6	8.6	10.7	13.8
▼ Citizens State Bank	Anton	TX	D	C-	D	35.6	11.16	9.4	1.2	0.4	5.0	7.1	9.1	15.8
Citizens State Bank	Buffalo	TX	B	B+	B+	1182.2	20.77	4.1	1.3	3.7	77.0	9.7	10.8	0.0
Citizens State Bank	Corrigan	TX	A-	A-	B+	142.2	7.79	14.0	11.8	14.1	30.8	10.0	11.7	0.0
Citizens State Bank	Ganado	TX	D-	D	D-	61.0	9.75	1.4	1.8	6.2	59.9	6.0	8.0	29.0
Citizens State Bank	Miles	TX	A-	A-	A-	170.0	9.53	14.2	2.3	24.7	0.2	8.1	9.7	16.4
Citizens State Bank	Roma	TX	C+	B-	B-	94.3	8.17	3.6	10.3	17.7	35.9	6.7	8.7	19.1
Citizens State Bank	Sealy	TX	A-	A-	A-	330.7	7.61	6.8	2.3	27.2	38.4	10.0	11.1	0.0
Citizens State Bank	Somerville	TX	B+	B+	B	732.9	14.11	12.2	2.5	19.8	21.3	9.8	10.9	0.0
Citizens State Bank	Waco	TX	C+	C+	C+	183.0	28.03	4.9	2.2	36.5	19.8	6.5	8.5	20.1
Citizens State Bank	Cadott	WI	B	B-	B-	133.7	17.27	6.9	2.6	15.1	14.4	9.6	10.7	17.5
Citizens State Bank	Hudson	WI	B-	B-	B-	266.9	23.42	12.3	0.8	27.2	11.7	4.1	7.7	10.5
▲ Citizens State Bank and Trust Co.	Council Grove	KS	C-	D+	D+	59.9	25.21	18.6	1.6	9.1	4.6	4.3	7.9	10.7
Citizens State Bank and Trust Co.	Ellsworth	KS	B	B	B-	218.8	14.30	5.3	2.4	16.1	38.7	6.2	8.2	0.0
Citizens State Bank and Trust Co.	Hiawatha	KS	A-	A-	A-	99.2	20.47	4.2	2.1	12.3	33.8	10.0	14.9	23.4
Citizens State Bank at Mohall	Mohall	ND	B-	B-	C	62.6	3.89	10.3	3.2	13.1	21.7	10.0	11.9	17.5
Citizens State Bank Norwood Young Ameri	Norwood Young Ame	MN	C-	C	C	100.2	16.50	23.0	1.2	4.9	0.0	8.0	9.7	16.4
Citizens State Bank of Arlington	Arlington	SD	B+	B	B-	117.3	9.27	3.2	0.8	3.6	28.2	10.0	12.4	0.0
Citizens State Bank of Cheney, Kansas	Cheney	KS	B	B	C+	71.8	13.63	10.6	9.0	8.4	27.9	8.0	9.7	15.3
Citizens State Bank of Finley	Finley	ND	A-	A-	B-	137.0	3.27	6.7	1.5	0.5	27.3	10.0	14.1	0.0
Citizens State Bank of Hayfield	Hayfield	MN	D+	D+	D+	122.2	18.51	14.8	2.6	8.3	15.1	5.0	7.0	12.7
Citizens State Bank of La Crosse	La Crosse	WI	B	B	B	377.9	22.60	19.5	0.8	18.6	0.9	6.1	8.9	11.8
Citizens State Bank of Lankin	Lankin	ND	B-	C+	C+	51.2	6.50	9.3	6.6	3.3	29.6	8.6	10.1	15.5
Citizens State Bank of Loyal	Loyal	WI	B+	B+	B+	249.6	20.27	4.8	0.1	6.2	24.5	10.0	11.9	18.5
Citizens State Bank of Luling	Luling	TX	B	B	B	72.0	2.19	7.2	0.8	8.9	5.8	10.0	15.2	0.0
Citizens State Bank of Milford	Milford	IL	C-	C-	C-	49.5	18.96	6.7	1.7	0.5	12.2	6.9	8.9	13.4
Citizens State Bank of New Castle, Indiana	New Castle	IN	B	B	B	675.7	20.26	15.1	9.1	15.7	18.2	6.8	8.9	17.4

Asset Quality Index	Adjusted Non-Performing Loans		Net Charge-Offs Avg Loans	Profitability Index	Net Income ($Mil)	Return on Assets (R.O.A.)	Return on Equity (R.O.E.)	Net Interest Spread	Overhead Efficiency Ratio	Liquidity Index	Liquidity Ratio	Hot Money Ratio	Stability Index
	as a % of Total Loans	as a % of Capital											
5.0	2.20	na	0.59	4.8	2.2	0.92	5.23	2.99	58.0	2.6	27.7	17.8	8.3
7.1	0.88	na	0.00	8.8	14.9	2.16	21.11	4.03	54.7	3.5	9.1	6.3	9.1
7.0	1.37	na	-0.02	4.1	2.5	0.98	11.91	3.49	69.7	6.4	54.6	5.2	4.0
9.3	0.00	na	0.04	4.3	0.3	0.85	5.08	2.00	59.7	3.5	78.4	31.1	8.1
5.5	0.58	na	0.07	3.9	0.1	0.66	6.67	4.16	77.9	5.5	26.8	0.9	3.7
9.3	0.13	0.2	0.01	4.9	1.8	1.26	8.51	2.68	64.1	6.8	64.1	5.6	7.7
9.4	0.54	na	0.01	3.5	0.8	0.80	7.34	2.94	76.8	5.2	38.2	7.7	6.9
5.6	1.98	na	0.02	3.4	0.4	0.54	4.61	3.76	79.4	4.0	12.5	8.6	7.2
6.9	0.73	4.3	0.01	6.7	17.9	1.57	13.99	3.32	60.3	3.0	15.5	14.4	10.0
5.8	0.40	na	0.09	6.9	3.6	1.63	15.15	3.75	55.7	2.1	11.0	18.3	7.4
7.3	1.39	na	-0.15	5.5	0.8	1.03	7.90	3.74	64.4	1.6	23.2	24.9	7.6
6.4	0.72	na	0.08	6.1	5.8	1.55	15.76	3.49	60.8	3.8	32.6	13.6	6.5
6.9	0.53	na	-0.04	9.9	19.4	1.94	19.57	4.52	48.6	5.0	20.6	3.5	8.9
9.9	0.00	na	0.00	3.4	0.7	0.63	8.28	2.56	70.6	7.3	59.3	1.1	3.6
6.6	1.19	na	0.22	5.1	8.7	1.01	9.36	3.62	63.0	4.4	24.3	10.2	8.6
1.4	1.36	na	0.12	4.1	1.2	0.88	7.73	4.24	75.9	0.8	21.1	45.8	5.7
8.7	0.25	na	0.00	6.6	1.4	1.45	13.39	3.50	53.9	5.7	42.3	6.2	7.5
9.9	0.00	1.0	-0.11	3.6	0.2	0.75	5.09	2.56	69.3	6.4	78.7	8.8	6.9
8.5	0.00	na	0.00	5.2	0.6	1.26	15.55	3.68	63.7	4.2	23.7	8.8	4.5
5.5	0.08	na	0.00	6.7	1.2	1.41	7.74	3.53	48.3	3.7	49.2	11.4	9.2
4.5	7.49	na	0.04	3.9	1.3	0.68	4.76	4.34	78.7	1.8	24.9	23.0	7.6
9.2	0.78	3.4	-0.01	2.9	1.1	0.45	2.88	3.05	78.5	2.7	10.1	15.2	7.6
2.0	2.63	na	0.10	1.9	0.1	0.13	1.90	4.22	96.2	0.7	17.5	50.0	0.3
9.1	0.00	na	0.03	4.0	0.5	0.91	6.24	2.14	57.7	2.2	47.4	35.0	6.8
5.4	5.17	8.8	0.01	8.0	5.9	1.84	13.69	3.53	48.0	3.5	42.7	17.1	9.4
8.0	0.00	na	0.11	6.3	1.5	1.46	10.71	3.48	55.8	5.3	34.9	5.7	8.8
7.4	1.73	na	0.25	5.8	1.1	1.40	6.05	3.50	59.4	4.9	47.4	12.6	7.6
4.9	1.40	na	0.39	5.1	2.7	1.21	10.24	3.39	57.7	3.1	28.3	15.6	6.5
6.8	0.38	na	-0.02	4.8	1.4	0.86	9.09	3.61	64.8	4.9	32.1	6.9	5.6
4.6	2.70	na	-0.05	4.7	0.9	0.88	6.77	3.86	69.7	0.8	10.6	33.2	8.4
6.5	0.22	na	-0.03	9.0	5.3	1.93	18.36	3.46	39.4	1.3	12.7	26.3	8.7
5.5	0.72	na	0.00	5.9	4.0	1.14	9.48	3.56	60.7	4.9	33.4	7.5	7.6
6.7	0.00	na	0.00	4.6	0.2	1.03	10.63	4.00	71.5	0.7	13.8	36.5	3.7
2.7	1.83	10.7	0.00	4.6	3.0	1.01	8.85	3.43	71.6	1.5	16.3	21.8	7.7
7.0	0.50	na	0.38	0.4	-0.1	-0.42	-4.45	2.51	114.2	2.8	53.1	29.0	2.4
9.3	1.33	1.6	0.05	4.5	13.9	1.66	12.74	2.53	62.6	3.3	62.9	35.3	8.2
6.2	0.06	na	0.01	7.6	1.7	1.67	13.92	3.97	59.0	1.7	23.5	23.5	8.6
9.9	0.00	na	-0.09	0.0	-0.2	-0.39	-4.28	2.11	122.4	5.4	84.9	14.8	2.1
8.6	0.07	na	-0.04	9.6	2.7	2.19	22.94	4.06	47.6	1.2	28.2	39.4	7.7
6.3	0.79	2.7	0.47	2.7	0.2	0.31	3.37	4.29	90.0	2.1	45.4	42.1	4.6
9.3	0.00	na	0.01	6.6	3.6	1.54	13.52	3.29	47.0	3.5	50.9	21.0	7.5
4.7	1.26	na	0.13	8.7	8.7	1.68	14.88	4.58	52.9	3.2	20.5	13.7	7.8
3.5	2.57	na	0.52	6.2	1.9	1.49	16.71	3.63	44.5	4.3	23.8	7.6	4.7
4.9	1.33	na	-0.33	4.7	0.9	0.89	7.99	4.00	72.6	4.7	26.2	6.1	6.0
8.3	0.13	na	-0.02	4.6	1.6	0.85	11.17	3.57	65.7	3.1	12.6	13.0	4.6
6.4	0.14	na	0.00	7.6	0.7	1.75	19.62	5.07	60.3	0.8	16.4	36.1	5.2
7.1	1.20	na	0.01	5.0	2.1	1.26	12.90	3.25	63.4	3.8	13.0	9.5	6.1
7.3	2.25	7.2	0.01	5.1	0.8	1.09	6.85	3.38	69.6	5.2	25.7	2.0	8.2
6.3	0.80	na	0.07	4.2	0.4	0.90	7.48	3.72	75.7	2.3	10.9	17.0	5.8
1.8	3.82	na	0.23	7.8	1.3	1.83	13.88	3.97	56.2	4.9	32.9	7.4	6.9
7.5	0.20	na	-0.01	5.1	1.1	1.27	9.86	3.41	59.8	2.7	35.7	18.3	7.7
7.9	0.21	na	0.07	6.3	0.7	1.44	13.43	3.58	59.8	4.6	37.9	11.3	7.2
8.1	1.39	na	0.04	5.3	1.2	1.18	8.27	3.87	74.4	3.4	28.6	12.4	9.0
1.5	4.43	35.1	0.40	2.9	0.3	0.41	5.40	3.70	72.4	5.5	37.0	5.2	2.6
4.5	0.44	na	0.02	10.0	10.5	3.88	45.64	4.53	35.1	0.7	5.6	20.8	6.8
6.2	0.64	1.7	0.00	3.9	0.3	0.68	6.12	4.34	86.7	4.2	13.5	7.1	6.8
8.5	0.75	na	-0.01	5.3	2.0	1.18	9.11	3.51	63.1	5.4	31.7	3.7	7.2
7.3	0.09	na	-0.02	4.9	0.5	0.86	5.74	4.69	72.4	3.7	20.3	11.1	7.6
3.4	0.00	na	0.00	2.6	0.1	0.32	3.39	3.69	91.3	4.9	32.0	7.0	3.4
7.8	0.16	1.3	0.06	4.8	4.3	0.90	9.72	3.68	63.8	5.9	38.4	3.4	5.9

Name	City	State	2020 Rating	2019 Rating	2018 Rating	Total Assets ($Mil)	One Year Asset Growth	Commercial Loans	Consumer Loans	Mortgage Loans	Securities	Capitalization Index	Leverage Ratio	Risk-Based Capital Ratio
▼ Citizens State Bank of Ontonagon	Ontonagon	MI	C-	C	C+	64.2	13.60	2.9	5.6	12.4	23.9	9.7	10.8	0.0
▲ Citizens State Bank of Ouray	Ouray	CO	C	C	C-	149.5	27.54	21.0	0.6	19.5	10.8	6.3	8.3	15.7
▲ Citizens State Bank of Roseau	Roseau	MN	A-	B+	B	251.8	13.90	9.6	5.9	5.3	37.9	10.0	12.1	0.0
▲ Citizens State Bank of Tyler, Inc.	Tyler	MN	C	C-	D+	24.9	13.92	6.4	3.3	2.6	27.3	7.0	9.0	41.2
Citizens State Bank of Waverly	Waverly	MN	B	B+	B+	96.3	21.37	6.6	1.3	14.1	18.2	5.6	7.6	14.9
Citizens Tri-County Bank	Dunlap	TN	B	C+	C+	1019.6	12.34	5.8	9.5	19.1	20.5	7.5	9.4	0.0
▼ Citizens Trust Bank	Atlanta	GA	B	B+	B+	536.7	29.29	13.9	1.3	10.1	14.0	6.9	8.9	15.7
▲ Citizens Union Bank of Shelbyville	Shelbyville	KY	B+	B	B	1016.3	20.88	10.7	0.5	14.8	7.7	7.9	11.1	0.0
▼ Citizens' Bank, Inc.	Robertsdale	AL	B-	B	B	128.9	20.41	8.8	1.4	17.9	24.6	9.6	10.7	0.0
Citizens-Farmers Bank of Cole Camp	Cole Camp	MO	B+	B+	B+	144.8	7.33	4.8	7.0	26.7	26.8	10.0	15.7	0.0
City Bank	Lubbock	TX	B+	B+	B	3541.1	26.75	14.3	7.6	12.7	20.5	9.1	10.4	16.1
City Bank & Trust Co.	Natchitoches	LA	B	B	B	279.6	9.47	4.6	2.5	10.5	49.0	7.7	9.4	17.8
City Bank & Trust Co.	Lincoln	NE	C+	B	B	212.6	19.13	15.6	2.2	11.1	10.0	8.0	10.6	0.0
▼ City First Bank of D.C., N.A.	Washington	DC	D+	C+	C+	394.4	13.02	18.8	0.0	2.8	28.0	6.8	8.8	0.0
City National B&T Co. of Lawton, Oklahom	Lawton	OK	A	A	A-	403.0	10.20	5.8	2.4	18.2	19.9	10.0	13.0	22.0
City National Bank	Los Angeles	CA	B+	B+	B	72984.0	25.42	16.4	1.0	19.0	20.8	5.9	7.9	13.4
City National Bank	Corsicana	TX	B-	B-	B-	58.9	16.68	10.8	4.3	32.8	10.9	7.7	9.4	0.0
City National Bank of Colorado City	Colorado City	TX	B-	B-	B	170.2	25.90	3.7	6.0	33.1	19.5	6.0	8.0	13.7
City National Bank of Florida	Miami	FL	B-	B	B	17382.2	13.99	21.8	0.3	9.9	18.7	9.0	10.4	15.9
City National Bank of Metropolis	Metropolis	IL	B-	B	B	446.9	14.97	10.2	3.2	17.8	47.9	10.0	12.6	25.0
City National Bank of San Saba	San Saba	TX	C+	C+	C+	73.1	21.85	2.0	3.5	0.2	60.4	10.0	12.5	0.0
City National Bank of Sulphur Springs	Sulphur Springs	TX	A-	A-	B	872.9	12.64	8.6	5.0	26.5	23.0	8.3	9.9	0.0
City National Bank of Taylor	Taylor	TX	B+	A-	B+	223.6	11.88	5.0	0.5	30.7	20.6	9.2	10.5	26.1
City National Bank of West Virginia	Charleston	WV	A-	B+	B+	5447.5	11.33	6.7	1.0	29.9	20.5	7.5	9.3	15.0
City State Bank	Norwalk	IA	B	B	B	537.7	25.59	13.6	1.0	11.4	7.9	5.0	8.0	0.0
City State Bank	Fort Scott	KS	C+	C+	C+	47.6	18.90	6.9	3.6	22.5	13.6	6.7	8.7	0.0
Citywide Banks	Denver	CO	B+	B+	B+	2639.5	13.00	16.5	0.5	5.3	32.7	7.9	9.6	14.7
Civis Bank	Rogersville	TN	E-	E-	E-	95.0	6.92	7.3	1.1	21.0	12.3	0.0	2.5	5.7
Civista Bank	Sandusky	OH	A-	A-	A-	2810.7	24.28	15.2	0.5	11.9	13.0	7.9	9.6	14.5
Clackamas County Bank	Sandy	OR	A	A	A	278.6	20.56	3.4	0.3	9.6	23.4	10.0	11.0	22.7
Clare Bank, N.A.	Platteville	WI	B+	B+	B+	301.9	14.09	3.2	0.8	19.3	40.6	10.0	11.2	0.0
Claremont Savings Bank	Claremont	NH	C-	B-	C+	476.1	11.30	5.7	0.9	59.4	7.7	10.0	13.1	0.0
▼ Clarion County Community Bank	Clarion	PA	C	B-	B-	193.2	11.32	6.9	2.1	31.2	15.9	3.9	9.1	0.0
Clarkson Bank	Clarkson	NE	B+	B+	B	63.5	10.66	5.6	1.2	0.1	44.5	10.0	13.0	0.0
Classic Bank, N.A.	Cameron	TX	B	B-	C+	461.0	18.26	5.0	1.7	20.0	14.9	7.4	9.3	14.1
Claxton Bank	Claxton	GA	B-	C	C+	134.9	14.50	7.4	1.4	7.6	20.8	8.9	10.3	0.0
▼ Clay City Banking Co.	Clay City	IL	C-	C	C+	169.9	13.62	9.6	2.2	23.9	14.3	7.0	9.0	13.1
Clay County Bank, Inc.	Clay	WV	A-	A-	A-	104.9	9.64	1.3	12.7	37.2	18.2	10.0	14.4	0.0
Clay County Savings Bank	Liberty	MO	C	C+	C+	128.4	15.20	5.1	0.4	20.8	2.1	7.0	9.0	0.0
Clay County State Bank	Louisville	IL	B	B	C+	90.1	14.84	9.5	6.8	15.6	19.1	10.0	13.6	0.0
CLB The Community Bank	Jonesville	LA	C	C+	C	232.0	29.81	30.4	3.8	7.0	26.8	7.6	9.6	0.0
Clear Lake Bank and Trust Co.	Clear Lake	IA	B+	B+	B+	508.2	18.87	15.5	3.4	13.9	6.8	5.6	7.6	12.3
Clear Mountain Bank	Bruceton Mills	WV	A-	A-	B+	761.9	16.59	13.0	3.6	30.3	20.1	10.0	11.4	0.0
ClearPoint Federal Bank & Trust	Batesville	IN	U	U	U	114.4	11.15	0.0	0.0	0.0	93.5	10.0	16.0	0.0
▲ Cleo State Bank	Cleo Springs	OK	B	C+	B-	89.4	2.85	16.6	2.7	0.1	41.2	10.0	18.1	0.0
Cleveland State Bank	Cleveland	MS	B+	A-	B+	262.9	14.51	12.9	4.6	15.3	31.9	9.6	10.8	0.0
▼ Cleveland State Bank	Cleveland	WI	B-	B	B	153.2	17.74	10.9	3.8	21.4	22.5	7.4	11.2	0.0
Clinton Bank	Clinton	KY	B	B-	B-	61.6	-5.51	6.3	1.9	11.2	33.3	10.0	19.2	28.4
Clinton National Bank	Clinton	IA	C+	B-	B-	432.5	8.71	11.0	1.5	8.0	37.8	10.0	12.6	0.0
Clinton Savings Bank	Clinton	MA	B-	B	C+	629.8	7.72	7.5	1.5	30.8	16.4	9.8	10.9	16.8
CNB Bank	Carlsbad	NM	B+	B+	B+	483.4	8.15	15.7	7.9	13.5	31.8	6.7	8.7	14.9
CNB Bank	Clearfield	PA	B	B	B	4755.3	35.02	14.7	1.6	16.9	12.3	6.6	8.7	13.6
CNB Bank & Trust, N.A.	Carlinville	IL	C+	C+	C-	1484.1	12.31	13.4	1.6	7.2	22.6	5.4	8.2	0.0
CNB Bank, Inc.	Berkeley Springs	WV	C+	B-	B-	472.4	14.48	9.6	1.0	38.6	13.2	6.9	8.9	0.0
▲ CNB St. Louis Bank	Maplewood	MO	B	C+	C+	586.1	15.98	21.8	0.7	12.1	14.5	7.7	10.2	13.1
Coastal Bank & Trust	Jacksonville	NC	B	B-	B-	143.6	26.84	11.1	0.8	14.9	12.4	10.0	13.3	0.0
Coastal Carolina National Bank	Myrtle Beach	SC	B-	B-	B-	574.0	31.91	10.2	2.5	18.8	11.7	6.7	8.7	12.7
▼ Coastal Community Bank	Everett	WA	B+	A-	B+	1749.0	60.54	32.8	0.2	6.4	1.4	7.7	9.4	13.9
Coastal Heritage Bank	Weymouth	MA	C	C	C	908.8	7.01	8.2	1.6	46.9	6.0	8.0	9.7	0.0
▲ Coastal States Bank	Hilton Head Island	SC	C+	C-	D	1102.9	59.93	34.3	7.2	5.9	10.8	7.2	9.6	12.7

Asset Quality Index	Adjusted Non-Performing Loans		Net Charge-Offs Avg Loans	Profitability Index	Net Income ($Mil)	Return on Assets (R.O.A.)	Return on Equity (R.O.E.)	Net Interest Spread	Overhead Efficiency Ratio	Liquidity Index	Liquidity Ratio	Hot Money Ratio	Stability Index
	as a % of Total Loans	as a % of Capital											
6.7	3.90	na	0.12	0.3	-0.8	-1.74	-13.82	2.89	118.6	7.3	81.1	3.0	4.7
7.8	0.40	na	0.23	3.4	0.6	0.63	7.01	3.69	73.2	4.3	20.1	7.4	4.5
6.7	1.04	na	0.53	5.7	2.6	1.45	11.44	3.16	53.2	2.6	40.2	26.7	7.7
7.8	2.54	na	0.06	2.7	0.1	0.29	2.94	3.05	82.3	7.0	69.2	1.0	3.0
5.6	0.51	1.3	0.00	5.9	0.9	1.36	11.98	3.78	60.4	5.4	33.7	4.5	7.0
5.2	1.01	na	0.08	6.8	11.3	1.54	15.43	2.79	59.9	2.3	22.0	19.7	9.7
4.9	2.46	10.9	0.07	4.0	2.4	0.68	6.70	3.22	71.2	3.1	34.6	17.9	6.1
5.8	0.88	6.8	0.01	5.5	7.4	1.03	9.03	3.53	66.7	4.6	24.6	8.9	9.6
5.5	2.49	na	0.02	3.2	0.4	0.42	3.58	4.02	86.0	4.2	29.7	10.8	6.4
4.3	4.07	na	-0.03	6.5	1.4	1.32	8.47	3.50	48.9	3.2	27.0	14.6	8.1
7.1	0.63	3.4	0.20	5.9	32.0	1.25	10.88	3.98	62.3	4.4	24.2	8.0	8.9
8.4	0.52	na	0.02	4.8	2.6	1.33	13.16	3.22	66.6	7.0	65.4	3.9	6.1
7.3	0.18	na	0.01	2.2	0.1	0.09	0.82	2.91	86.4	2.6	11.7	15.8	7.4
5.3	1.64	9.2	0.10	1.6	0.3	0.12	1.33	2.50	95.0	1.1	28.4	24.8	5.0
7.9	0.66	2.8	0.43	8.1	5.0	1.73	13.21	4.20	82.2	5.8	36.2	3.1	8.7
7.4	0.36	2.9	0.11	4.1	322.7	0.63	7.36	2.65	65.6	5.6	25.6	2.3	7.6
8.6	0.00	na	0.01	3.4	0.2	0.53	5.30	3.81	86.8	2.0	31.6	26.9	5.5
4.9	0.98	na	0.21	6.8	2.0	1.75	22.14	4.45	60.5	1.6	9.6	21.4	4.2
6.6	0.93	5.4	0.06	3.7	90.4	0.71	6.15	2.81	51.9	4.1	20.9	7.9	9.1
6.1	2.25	7.8	0.09	3.3	3.0	0.98	7.30	2.44	73.1	2.0	41.3	28.5	6.3
9.9	0.00	na	0.48	3.1	0.3	0.57	4.40	2.92	78.1	6.9	74.9	4.7	6.6
6.8	0.22	na	0.13	8.3	11.1	1.80	15.10	4.51	59.3	3.8	31.2	12.9	9.1
6.8	0.77	na	0.15	4.5	1.5	0.96	8.61	3.62	76.7	6.4	46.8	2.6	7.2
6.1	1.18	4.3	0.10	9.2	68.8	1.75	14.71	3.24	46.9	3.1	15.4	13.9	9.9
8.5	0.07	na	0.00	4.8	4.1	1.07	12.66	2.88	68.0	2.9	21.3	14.9	6.6
8.8	0.00	0.0	0.00	4.9	0.4	1.11	12.03	4.07	69.5	3.2	34.8	17.5	5.0
6.2	0.66	2.9	0.11	4.8	15.8	0.86	5.80	4.02	60.9	5.4	26.7	5.2	8.3
3.7	5.26	na	0.48	0.4	-0.2	-0.29	-12.32	3.57	110.4	4.1	28.8	10.6	0.4
7.2	0.38	1.8	0.00	5.7	22.7	1.11	9.18	3.71	61.2	3.9	16.9	7.1	10.0
9.2	0.00	0.0	-0.15	6.3	2.6	1.39	11.18	3.84	66.7	5.6	39.5	5.4	8.3
8.5	2.14	na	0.00	4.7	2.6	1.17	9.27	2.58	58.9	5.7	42.9	6.5	7.4
7.2	1.03	na	0.09	1.3	-0.5	-0.15	-1.10	3.06	80.5	1.5	12.8	23.6	7.2
6.8	0.65	na	0.04	3.0	0.7	0.52	5.57	3.37	82.1	1.1	17.3	31.2	5.0
8.6	0.20	na	0.05	6.8	0.7	1.60	11.87	3.25	51.6	2.9	40.3	21.1	8.4
7.0	0.10	na	0.02	5.2	4.3	1.34	13.98	3.85	67.2	2.1	14.7	18.3	6.0
4.3	3.67	na	0.24	4.4	0.9	0.97	8.82	4.23	76.8	4.3	34.8	11.7	5.9
1.9	3.20	na	0.02	3.3	0.7	0.54	5.79	3.41	80.9	4.0	16.1	9.0	5.1
8.0	0.54	na	0.03	6.8	0.9	1.21	8.10	3.83	61.6	3.9	40.0	15.5	8.8
9.0	0.00	na	-0.05	3.2	0.5	0.57	6.18	3.32	82.5	5.3	34.6	5.5	5.5
4.4	1.53	na	-0.01	4.6	0.7	1.10	7.58	3.11	65.5	4.4	26.7	8.3	7.6
3.2	2.12	13.9	0.38	4.7	1.8	1.16	11.30	4.13	69.3	4.0	24.9	10.0	5.1
7.6	0.35	na	0.01	6.5	5.0	1.38	16.58	3.69	63.9	4.0	19.6	9.6	7.3
7.6	0.65	na	0.03	6.8	7.2	1.34	11.55	3.83	59.1	2.8	26.7	16.7	7.9
10.0	na	na	na	4.2	0.8	0.99	5.29	2.27	85.8	8.7	118.1	0.8	5.9
5.6	17.49	na	0.82	4.6	0.7	1.01	5.31	3.45	66.4	4.4	62.8	16.7	6.5
8.4	0.49	na	0.07	5.1	1.8	0.98	9.43	3.95	68.0	5.1	36.9	7.7	5.9
3.0	2.75	na	-0.31	8.5	2.2	2.04	18.38	3.89	52.2	5.2	36.1	5.4	6.9
7.0	0.49	na	0.04	4.4	0.5	0.99	5.04	3.69	69.5	2.8	19.7	15.5	7.1
8.2	0.88	2.7	0.00	2.7	1.4	0.47	3.34	2.80	83.7	5.2	40.9	9.1	7.3
5.3	1.57	8.0	0.01	3.4	2.7	0.59	5.25	2.99	76.2	2.0	25.8	16.4	7.5
7.5	0.25	na	0.00	9.2	8.9	2.54	27.91	4.27	45.6	5.1	28.5	3.9	6.9
5.8	1.01	6.2	0.16	4.5	26.8	0.85	9.44	3.57	62.4	4.4	15.8	6.4	8.1
3.2	3.00	na	0.29	5.4	10.6	1.01	9.80	3.66	58.7	2.5	22.4	18.4	8.0
6.8	0.84	na	-0.01	3.5	2.3	0.70	8.38	3.32	76.1	3.2	16.0	13.0	4.4
5.4	1.01	na	-0.01	6.0	6.4	1.54	14.74	3.63	54.4	2.4	9.7	14.0	6.5
8.7	0.60	na	0.00	3.9	0.8	0.83	5.57	4.30	80.2	3.6	24.3	11.7	7.2
6.6	0.46	na	0.10	4.0	2.8	0.73	7.40	3.59	68.3	2.2	21.2	18.7	6.0
7.0	0.30	2.5	0.01	5.3	11.1	1.01	10.95	3.90	58.2	4.5	11.5	3.3	7.8
5.8	0.75	na	-0.02	3.0	3.3	0.51	4.92	3.38	75.6	3.4	15.6	12.0	5.8
5.7	0.49	3.5	0.02	3.5	4.8	0.71	6.91	3.60	71.3	3.4	19.9	13.0	5.0

Name	City	State	Rating	2019 Rating	2018 Rating	Total Assets ($Mil)	One Year Asset Growth	Asset Mix (As a % of Total Assets)				Capital-ization Index	Lever-age Ratio	Risk-Based Capital Ratio
								Comm-ercial Loans	Cons-umer Loans	Mort-gage Loans	Secur-ities			
▲ Coffee County Bank	Manchester	TN	B+	B	B-	223.8	12.97	12.9	5.6	28.4	9.2	10.0	11.0	16.4
▲ Cogent Bank	Orange City	FL	D+	D-	E	634.8	161.21	40.2	0.3	8.9	17.9	6.9	8.9	13.3
Colchester State Bank	Colchester	IL	B	B	B	78.5	14.09	2.9	3.5	5.7	62.5	10.0	13.9	35.4
Coleman County State Bank	Coleman	TX	A-	B+	B-	147.2	20.74	14.1	1.6	11.7	11.9	7.0	9.0	15.8
Colfax Banking Co.	Colfax	LA	B	B	B	131.9	17.52	1.9	2.4	19.0	46.0	6.8	8.8	0.0
▲ Collins State Bank	Collins	WI	B+	B-	B-	113.0	20.84	8.6	3.3	22.1	17.8	6.8	8.9	13.6
Collinsville Bank	Collinsville	CT	C-	C+	C	185.7	12.02	13.7	2.3	39.1	6.8	4.5	8.0	0.0
Collinsville Building and Loan Assn.	Collinsville	IL	C+	C	C	131.3	8.66	0.0	0.0	71.4	19.1	10.0	25.7	0.0
Colonial Federal Savings Bank	Quincy	MA	B	B	B	333.5	7.27	0.0	0.5	44.3	29.4	10.0	14.3	0.0
Colonial Savings, F.A.	Fort Worth	TX	C-	C	C	1274.8	13.65	0.7	0.2	48.0	10.9	8.8	10.2	22.0
Colony Bank	Fitzgerald	GA	B-	B	B	1754.3	19.06	11.9	1.3	11.9	20.7	8.0	9.7	14.4
Colorado Bank and Trust Co. of La Junta	La Junta	CO	A-	B+	B	180.9	18.32	14.3	2.5	12.3	21.5	7.4	9.3	0.0
Colorado Federal Savings Bank	Greenwood Village	CO	B-	B	B-	2507.4	16.80	0.5	0.0	23.3	14.7	7.6	9.4	19.4
Columbia Bank	Fair Lawn	NJ	B-	B	B	8851.4	25.45	10.0	0.0	26.8	17.3	8.5	10.0	16.2
Columbia S&L Assn.	Milwaukee	WI	E-	E-	E-	24.4	8.42	0.0	1.8	40.1	0.0	6.0	8.0	13.0
Columbia State Bank	Tacoma	WA	B+	B+	B+	16224.7	17.97	17.6	0.2	2.6	26.4	7.2	9.1	14.1
▼ Columbus Bank and Trust Co.	Columbus	NE	C+	B-	C+	164.5	15.43	21.8	1.1	4.2	8.8	2.3	8.7	0.0
▼ Columbus State Bank	Columbus	TX	B-	B-	B-	124.2	18.33	0.2	0.2	0.5	40.6	10.0	12.1	38.9
Comenity Bank	Wilmington	DE	C-	D+	D+	10082.8	-27.13	0.0	84.2	0.0	1.1	10.0	17.6	21.7
Comenity Capital Bank	Draper	UT	C-	C-	C-	7742.6	-20.25	0.1	88.8	0.0	0.9	10.0	14.1	18.0
▼ Comerica Bank	Dallas	TX	B+	A-	A-	83608.0	14.70	30.3	0.6	2.5	18.1	6.8	8.8	13.0
Comerica Bank & Trust, N.A.	Ann Arbor	MI	U	U	U	70.3	1.57	0.0	0.0	0.0	0.0	10.0	100.	268.4
Commencement Bank	Tacoma	WA	B+	A-	B	511.4	36.23	35.8	0.5	3.2	3.3	7.7	9.5	16.8
▲ Commerce Bank	Edina	MN	B-	B-	B+	222.9	5.97	8.8	0.1	7.5	4.4	10.0	12.0	16.1
Commerce Bank	Kansas City	MO	A-	A	A-	31354.8	21.62	13.3	7.7	9.7	36.8	6.4	8.4	13.2
Commerce Bank	Corinth	MS	A-	A-	B+	147.0	17.83	14.6	5.1	26.9	20.8	9.4	10.6	0.0
Commerce Bank	Laredo	TX	A	A	A	559.3	8.38	6.9	0.8	16.3	49.8	10.0	16.9	36.3
Commerce Bank of Arizona, Inc.	Tucson	AZ	C-	D+	D	331.5	31.85	29.7	0.0	4.3	10.8	3.0	8.8	0.0
Commerce Bank Texas	Stockdale	TX	B-	B	B	57.7	4.48	11.0	0.2	15.5	25.2	10.0	13.4	0.0
Commerce Community Bank	Oak Grove	LA	B	B	B-	63.9	0.37	14.1	1.5	11.0	14.6	9.2	10.5	14.8
Commerce National Bank & Trust	Winter Park	FL	B+	A-	B	127.6	12.16	2.9	1.1	13.8	10.9	9.4	10.6	17.4
Commerce State Bank	West Bend	WI	B-	B-	C+	765.5	8.30	29.0	0.0	13.3	3.7	7.6	9.8	13.0
▲ Commerceone Bank	Birmingham	AL	C			313.2	78.99	22.8	0.2	5.0	6.7	10.0	16.7	21.6
CommerceWest Bank	Irvine	CA	B+	B+	B+	937.7	47.63	25.1	1.2	0.2	7.7	4.5	6.5	12.7
Commercial & Savings Bank of Millersburg	Millersburg	OH	B+	B+	B-	987.8	25.58	17.9	1.8	14.8	12.4	6.6	8.6	16.5
Commercial Bank	Crawford	GA	A-	A	A-	302.3	38.93	17.6	1.6	18.1	10.9	6.8	8.8	0.0
Commercial Bank	Parsons	KS	B+	B+	B+	386.3	17.59	14.2	7.1	10.8	43.2	6.0	8.0	16.2
Commercial Bank	West Liberty	KY	B-	B-	B	165.7	11.60	6.0	5.0	32.3	19.1	10.0	11.8	19.6
Commercial Bank	Alma	MI	B-	B-	C	547.6	7.04	10.1	1.4	29.6	5.5	6.8	8.8	15.4
Commercial Bank	Saint Louis	MO	C	C	C	258.2	17.25	24.6	1.5	13.1	19.5	5.1	7.1	12.3
Commercial Bank	De Kalb	MS	B-	B	B	181.2	9.79	13.0	12.0	11.7	32.0	7.8	9.5	0.0
Commercial Bank	Nelson	NE	B+	B	B	55.7	0.85	23.7	5.4	1.1	29.4	10.0	12.5	17.3
Commercial Bank	Honea Path	SC	B+	A-	B+	222.4	17.14	2.2	2.8	12.4	47.3	10.0	13.1	44.6
Commercial Bank	Harrogate	TN	B+	B+	B	1557.3	17.26	9.6	1.4	21.7	8.0	7.6	9.4	13.3
Commercial Bank	Mason	TX	B-	B-	C+	66.8	21.46	4.7	2.2	24.3	40.0	6.4	8.4	17.4
Commercial Bank & Trust Co.	Monticello	AR	B	B	B-	234.5	10.63	16.0	6.6	13.7	34.0	8.3	9.8	0.0
Commercial Bank & Trust Co.	Paris	TN	A-	A-	B+	953.4	20.77	14.4	3.1	14.9	23.2	7.5	9.3	18.0
▼ Commercial Bank & Trust of PA	Latrobe	PA	B+	B+	B+	424.1	-1.71	5.4	0.3	27.0	33.2	10.0	13.7	21.9
Commercial Bank of California	Irvine	CA	C+	B	C+	1587.5	56.14	19.5	2.6	0.9	5.5	2.3	8.0	0.0
Commercial Bank of Grayson	Grayson	KY	B	B	B	198.3	9.90	8.5	6.7	14.1	39.5	10.0	13.7	23.7
▲ Commercial Bank of Mott	Mott	ND	A	A-	B+	109.7	1.30	4.6	1.6	2.3	11.6	10.0	14.4	0.0
Commercial Bank of Oak Grove	Oak Grove	MO	B+	B+	B+	95.7	23.14	6.2	0.8	28.2	20.0	10.0	13.3	0.0
Commercial Bank of Ozark	Ozark	AL	C	C	C-	110.0	20.30	10.5	4.6	15.3	34.2	5.8	7.8	16.5
Commercial Bank of Texas, N.A.	Nacogdoches	TX	B+	B	B-	1008.1	28.13	18.0	3.5	14.6	20.6	8.3	9.8	15.1
Commercial Banking Co.	Valdosta	GA	A-	A-	B+	280.9	22.60	8.8	1.2	26.7	7.2	10.0	12.1	22.0
Commercial Capital Bank	Delhi	LA	C	B-	B-	232.9	33.89	7.2	2.9	15.6	3.8	8.7	11.6	0.0
Commercial National Bank of Brady	Brady	TX	A	A	A-	156.8	5.96	7.6	2.3	17.5	28.2	10.0	12.7	25.2
Commercial National Bank of Texarkana	Texarkana	TX	B+	B+	B+	257.4	20.47	18.3	2.1	18.3	30.1	6.1	8.1	14.9
Commercial Savings Bank	Carroll	IA	B	B	B-	217.8	13.58	12.4	2.4	27.5	8.4	5.9	7.9	12.1
Commercial State Bank	Republican City	NE	B+	B+	A-	63.0	0.73	2.7	0.5	0.0	54.6	10.0	30.3	0.0

Asset Quality Index	Adjusted Non-Performing Loans as a % of Total Loans	as a % of Capital	Net Charge-Offs Avg Loans	Profitability Index	Net Income ($Mil)	Return on Assets (R.O.A.)	Return on Equity (R.O.E.)	Net Interest Spread	Overhead Efficiency Ratio	Liquidity Index	Liquidity Ratio	Hot Money Ratio	Stability Index
5.3	2.43	na	0.08	9.8	3.8	2.37	20.51	4.45	45.3	1.4	11.7	25.3	8.6
6.8	0.22	na	-0.01	1.4	1.2	0.32	3.75	3.21	83.6	2.3	26.4	19.2	4.5
6.5	2.92	na	0.09	4.0	0.5	0.85	5.62	2.87	68.7	3.8	44.8	16.9	6.5
8.0	0.01	na	0.01	9.8	2.5	2.46	26.11	4.84	57.4	4.0	25.1	10.1	6.4
8.8	0.05	na	0.00	4.7	1.0	1.08	10.63	3.55	72.8	1.8	27.6	25.3	5.9
8.3	0.33	na	-0.05	8.0	1.6	2.12	23.42	3.81	61.3	4.9	34.6	8.1	5.4
4.5	1.71	na	0.00	1.8	0.1	0.09	1.05	3.03	94.2	2.1	12.3	17.5	4.7
10.0	0.00	na	0.00	2.8	0.4	0.37	1.41	2.22	77.8	2.1	33.4	27.2	7.4
10.0	0.00	na	0.00	3.2	1.2	0.50	3.46	2.47	75.2	2.8	44.4	26.8	7.9
0.4	19.29	25.2	0.18	0.5	-21.9	-2.49	-12.53	4.68	144.2	6.1	31.0	3.1	8.2
5.8	1.31	na	0.14	4.0	7.9	0.66	6.29	3.54	74.7	4.5	25.8	10.3	8.0
7.0	0.74	2.8	0.30	9.6	2.4	1.99	20.20	4.48	55.7	5.2	31.2	4.6	6.5
6.9	1.78	6.6	0.02	4.3	13.5	0.83	7.64	1.89	35.4	6.5	54.0	6.7	7.7
8.0	0.90	3.5	0.07	3.5	37.7	0.58	5.94	2.62	62.3	2.4	9.4	16.5	7.7
1.9	4.85	na	0.00	0.2	-0.1	-0.83	-9.48	4.53	118.9	0.8	23.6	38.5	2.1
6.5	0.54	1.9	0.16	5.2	98.4	0.88	5.81	3.73	57.2	6.4	32.3	1.4	10.0
4.7	1.13	na	0.59	6.0	1.5	1.34	12.45	4.29	57.5	1.6	9.9	21.9	6.7
10.0	0.00	na	0.00	2.8	0.5	0.62	4.98	1.87	76.6	6.9	106.6	11.2	6.1
1.3	2.83	13.7	7.07	10.0	220.7	2.52	18.26	20.03	47.3	0.4	16.7	64.1	9.5
1.5	2.23	14.4	6.35	3.7	-44.2	-0.69	-6.00	14.32	54.7	0.7	18.5	12.2	9.0
6.9	0.70	4.0	0.43	5.0	257.0	0.43	4.25	2.61	62.3	6.0	28.5	1.9	9.7
9.8	na	0.0	na	10.0	17.7	37.14	39.03	1.15	58.9	4.0	na	0.0	7.0
5.1	0.62	na	-0.11	4.6	2.7	0.77	7.41	3.30	62.7	1.7	14.0	21.5	6.8
3.8	1.35	na	-0.02	4.3	1.5	0.92	7.26	3.05	68.7	0.8	19.3	13.5	7.6
7.6	0.62	2.5	0.23	6.2	236.7	1.11	10.97	3.08	59.2	5.8	33.4	5.5	9.2
6.3	0.64	na	0.16	5.6	1.2	1.16	10.30	3.76	68.1	2.7	33.2	19.3	8.4
8.9	0.51	1.1	0.15	8.8	7.3	1.82	9.74	2.91	41.4	3.3	69.0	34.3	9.3
3.5	1.30	na	-0.19	3.5	1.4	0.64	6.76	4.25	88.4	3.9	26.0	10.6	5.3
7.5	0.00	0.0	0.00	2.8	0.1	0.22	1.23	3.96	92.1	3.5	34.1	15.6	8.2
5.8	1.41	na	0.22	4.9	0.5	0.96	9.10	4.02	68.7	2.5	39.8	26.5	5.9
8.8	0.00	na	0.00	4.2	0.7	0.73	6.49	3.36	79.0	1.9	28.7	25.6	8.7
6.0	0.70	na	0.36	4.8	4.7	0.85	8.67	3.47	47.7	0.9	10.6	21.8	6.0
8.5	0.00	0.0	0.00	3.0	1.4	0.69	3.89	3.32	60.9	3.6	30.2	14.0	4.5
8.5	0.00	0.0	0.74	4.6	4.1	0.71	8.53	3.26	47.4	3.7	28.8	8.9	5.4
6.0	0.90	na	-0.01	5.9	8.1	1.20	12.40	3.31	56.3	4.5	25.4	6.9	6.8
8.6	0.10	na	0.01	8.8	3.8	1.86	21.09	4.39	56.0	3.4	18.0	12.3	7.1
7.3	0.55	na	0.02	5.0	3.3	1.22	12.64	3.08	65.7	3.8	34.1	13.9	6.1
7.6	0.72	na	0.09	3.5	0.8	0.69	4.84	4.01	82.8	2.1	22.9	19.2	7.6
4.5	2.78	na	-0.01	4.2	3.5	0.86	8.87	3.16	60.1	1.8	19.3	5.0	6.8
4.7	1.12	na	-0.05	3.1	1.0	0.55	7.07	3.08	80.8	3.9	31.7	12.8	3.8
5.4	0.70	3.3	0.24	3.7	1.1	0.78	7.98	3.74	70.3	2.3	31.4	19.4	6.3
4.9	2.99	na	0.00	6.1	0.6	1.35	11.36	4.24	63.4	1.5	11.4	23.2	7.6
7.7	2.72	na	0.10	4.1	1.4	0.92	6.51	2.73	66.3	6.3	73.5	10.0	8.0
5.4	1.27	na	0.01	6.4	13.6	1.17	12.52	3.71	55.4	1.5	10.1	17.7	8.6
7.4	0.00	na	0.54	6.0	0.7	1.62	17.79	3.79	56.2	4.3	40.3	13.5	5.4
5.4	0.91	na	0.13	5.0	2.0	1.20	11.72	3.56	66.7	1.3	26.7	31.5	5.8
6.5	0.80	na	0.10	6.7	10.1	1.54	14.43	3.48	63.8	5.2	37.3	7.8	8.6
8.9	1.34	2.6	-0.16	4.5	3.2	1.04	6.69	4.18	64.6	5.3	35.6	5.9	8.8
8.2	0.40	na	0.01	3.2	4.2	0.43	5.05	3.32	73.9	6.0	34.2	4.6	7.5
7.1	0.79	3.4	0.08	4.2	1.1	0.77	5.31	3.79	78.2	6.3	48.7	4.2	7.8
7.1	1.46	na	0.26	9.0	1.6	1.96	13.50	3.53	45.3	1.0	12.7	29.5	10.0
6.7	1.19	na	0.01	3.7	0.5	0.75	5.31	2.89	69.3	3.1	34.8	18.0	6.9
4.0	1.36	na	0.00	3.2	0.7	0.86	9.83	3.33	81.0	3.7	26.1	12.1	3.8
7.6	0.77	na	0.07	5.8	7.6	1.15	11.31	4.13	54.9	4.3	18.9	7.8	7.5
8.0	1.04	na	0.17	6.3	2.5	1.26	9.34	4.68	62.4	3.6	25.7	12.5	7.6
3.1	1.32	na	0.07	7.4	2.5	1.67	15.09	4.32	60.9	1.2	28.3	36.8	8.1
8.9	0.00	na	0.03	7.0	1.8	1.58	11.82	3.89	63.0	4.7	33.8	9.2	9.2
8.6	0.06	0.6	0.02	6.8	2.8	1.57	17.19	4.06	61.9	3.7	25.0	11.4	6.2
6.1	0.54	na	0.12	5.2	1.8	1.16	14.29	3.13	57.5	1.7	21.9	23.0	5.6
9.3	0.00	na	0.01	6.3	0.6	1.39	4.50	3.10	40.9	4.4	91.5	21.5	7.7

Data as of September 30, 2020

Name	City	State	2019 Rating	2018 Rating	Rating	Total Assets ($Mil)	One Year Asset Growth	Asset Mix (As a % of Total Assets) Commercial Loans	Consumer Loans	Mortgage Loans	Securities	Capitalization Index	Leverage Ratio	Risk-Based Capital Ratio
Commercial State Bank	Wausa	NE	B-	B-	B-	156.3	21.01	24.1	5.7	3.7	4.3	6.6	9.3	12.2
Commercial State Bank	Palmer	TX	B-	C+	C	96.7	17.31	12.2	3.2	9.4	31.9	6.3	8.3	22.0
Commercial State Bank of Wagner	Wagner	SD	B-	B-	C+	206.6	10.46	6.9	2.5	7.3	26.0	8.3	9.9	0.0
Commercial Trust Co. of Fayette	Fayette	MO	B+	B+	B	152.3	16.55	5.2	5.4	37.7	7.1	7.2	9.1	0.0
Commodore Bank	Somerset	OH	D+	D+	D+	82.4	2.86	6.4	5.2	26.4	18.8	6.5	8.5	15.4
▲ Commonwealth Bank and Trust Co.	Louisville	KY	B+	B-	B-	1168.8	7.77	15.0	3.2	12.2	14.1	6.8	8.8	12.5
▼ Commonwealth Business Bank	Los Angeles	CA	B+	A-	A-	1399.4	20.68	14.1	0.2	1.1	6.4	10.0	11.7	16.5
Commonwealth Community Bank, Inc.	Hartford	KY	C+	B-	B	150.4	4.63	1.0	2.6	15.5	52.6	10.0	15.6	0.0
Commonwealth Cooperative Bank	Hyde Park	MA	B	B	B	189.5	-0.19	2.3	0.1	51.5	10.3	10.0	15.0	0.0
Commonwealth National Bank	Mobile	AL	D-	D+	D-	55.1	13.26	2.5	0.7	6.3	29.0	6.3	8.3	32.9
Community 1st Bank Las Vegas	Las Vegas	NM	C+	C+	C-	156.6	10.71	9.3	0.8	9.3	33.0	7.8	9.6	23.3
▼ Community Bank	Dunlap	IA	C+	B	B	95.3	6.95	4.0	3.4	15.1	8.4	10.0	12.7	17.4
Community Bank	Winslow	IL	A-	A-	B+	260.7	19.93	7.2	1.3	19.5	33.2	10.0	13.1	23.7
▼ Community Bank	Liberal	KS	B-	B-	C+	142.3	16.20	12.2	13.1	0.0	34.7	9.3	10.5	16.1
Community Bank	Topeka	KS	B+	B+	B	133.1	30.04	19.3	1.2	21.3	3.4	3.6	9.8	0.0
Community Bank	Zanesville	OH	B-	B-	C+	536.4	18.04	9.5	4.6	30.2	12.3	8.5	10.0	0.0
Community Bank	Alva	OK	B+	A-	A-	113.4	5.79	8.5	1.7	5.8	53.0	10.0	11.4	19.6
Community Bank	Bristow	OK	B+	A-	B+	93.5	6.08	6.6	3.3	29.1	11.8	7.3	9.2	0.0
▼ Community Bank	Joseph	OR	B	B+	B	476.3	13.03	7.0	0.3	2.0	48.0	7.2	9.1	23.8
▼ Community Bank	Carmichaels	PA	C+	B-	B-	1391.0	4.88	9.7	8.4	23.6	11.3	5.6	7.6	12.9
Community Bank	Avon	SD	C+	B-	B	57.0	5.32	11.3	5.2	6.3	36.6	10.0	15.2	0.0
▲ Community Bank	Lexington	TN	B+	B	B	179.2	9.29	15.7	5.3	28.5	6.3	7.9	9.7	13.3
Community Bank	Bridgeport	TX	B-	B-	C+	120.1	22.44	12.2	1.7	17.6	14.9	7.5	9.4	0.0
Community Bank	Longview	TX	A	A	A	238.3	8.00	11.8	2.7	31.7	0.0	10.0	11.4	0.0
Community Bank & Trust - Alabama	Union Springs	AL	D-	D	D-	49.1	7.72	8.1	4.3	11.1	41.2	5.9	7.9	21.2
Community Bank & Trust - West Georgia	LaGrange	GA	E+	E+	D-	84.4	10.55	20.9	1.1	15.7	9.0	0.0	3.0	7.4
Community Bank & Trust, Waco, Texas	Waco	TX	B+	A-	B+	525.4	14.20	26.0	1.9	21.7	25.2	10.0	13.9	24.2
Community Bank and Trust	Neosho	MO	B-	B-	B-	360.1	15.73	7.1	1.6	13.0	11.5	5.7	7.7	18.7
Community Bank and Trust Co.	Muscatine	IA	C-	D+	C	253.9	10.42	9.4	3.3	10.6	29.6	6.6	8.6	14.8
Community Bank Delaware	Lewes	DE	B-	B-	B	244.5	20.55	7.0	0.3	32.8	3.3	7.4	9.3	15.3
Community Bank Mankato	Vernon Center	MN	C+	C	C	366.1	16.22	13.1	2.3	13.3	0.2	6.2	8.3	12.1
Community Bank of Cameron	Cameron	WI	B	B	B-	144.3	18.17	2.5	2.8	29.6	8.7	6.7	8.8	13.3
Community Bank of Easton	Easton	IL	A-	A-	B+	37.9	4.64	24.0	9.7	2.9	1.3	10.0	21.6	0.0
Community Bank of El Dorado Springs	El Dorado Springs	MO	A	A	B+	118.7	11.78	3.3	2.0	11.2	31.9	10.0	14.9	0.0
Community Bank of Elmhurst	Elmhurst	IL	C+	B-	B-	175.9	20.67	19.3	0.2	13.9	30.5	3.0	8.9	0.0
Community Bank of Georgia	Baxley	GA	C+	C	C+	139.0	9.62	12.0	1.1	9.2	10.5	8.0	9.7	14.0
Community Bank of Louisiana	Mansfield	LA	B	B	B	584.1	17.65	14.4	1.2	9.6	42.6	6.6	8.6	0.0
Community Bank of Marshall	Marshall	MO	B+	B	B	187.3	22.36	11.9	2.4	11.3	42.0	7.8	9.5	17.4
▲ Community Bank of Memphis	Memphis	MO	B	B-	B-	52.4	15.92	2.9	3.4	14.8	17.2	10.0	12.1	0.0
Community Bank of Mississippi	Forest	MS	B-	B-	B-	3849.0	16.89	15.3	2.2	21.0	15.6	5.8	7.8	15.1
Community Bank of Missouri	Richmond	MO	B+	B+	B	64.9	22.22	10.3	1.2	16.6	2.9	10.0	13.1	17.1
▲ Community Bank of Oelwein	Oelwein	IA	B+	B	B	120.0	11.91	8.5	2.5	10.7	30.6	10.0	12.6	21.2
Community Bank of Oklahoma	Verden	OK	B-	B-	B-	63.3	54.40	15.2	3.9	2.7	35.2	7.7	9.5	0.0
Community Bank of Parkersburg	Parkersburg	WV	B+	B+	B+	272.6	7.61	7.1	6.2	54.5	9.3	9.6	10.7	0.0
Community Bank of Pickens County	Jasper	GA	B-	C+	C-	419.4	16.13	11.9	2.1	13.1	6.8	10.0	11.4	17.7
Community Bank of Pleasant Hill	Pleasant Hill	MO	B+	B+	B+	111.2	35.09	16.3	1.2	3.5	45.9	6.7	8.7	18.1
Community Bank of Raymore	Raymore	MO	B+	B+	B+	333.6	22.91	14.3	0.5	2.4	36.0	5.6	7.6	14.0
Community Bank of Santa Maria	Santa Maria	CA	B+	A-	B+	327.5	24.09	24.1	0.3	0.4	14.9	3.6	8.9	0.0
Community Bank of the Bay	Oakland	CA	B	B	B-	636.4	29.50	25.1	0.1	3.5	3.2	8.2	9.8	16.0
Community Bank of the Chesapeake	Waldorf	MD	B-	B-	B-	2135.4	15.16	10.4	0.1	13.1	10.8	7.4	9.5	12.8
Community Bank of the Midwest	Great Bend	KS	B+	B	B	209.3	18.08	18.7	2.2	6.3	31.8	10.0	11.7	18.9
Community Bank of the South	Merritt Island	FL	A-	A-	C+	201.4	30.58	16.9	0.6	3.3	19.6	7.1	9.1	27.8
Community Bank of Trenton	Trenton	IL	B	B	B-	96.8	14.51	10.4	4.1	25.2	17.4	9.6	10.8	15.9
Community Bank of Wichita, Inc.	Wichita	KS	C	C+	B-	97.2	15.57	31.1	4.2	19.3	5.9	3.0	8.4	0.0
Community Bank Owatonna	Owatonna	MN	C+	C+	C+	70.7	18.91	12.6	1.1	15.9	20.7	6.0	8.0	12.9
Community Bank, N.A.	De Witt	NY	B+	B+	B+	13647.9	19.81	7.2	8.8	20.3	23.6	6.1	8.1	15.8
Community Bankers' Bank	Midlothian	VA	C	C+	C-	168.8	19.93	6.1	0.7	4.2	12.2	9.3	11.5	0.0
Community Banking Co. of Fitzgerald	Fitzgerald	GA	B+	A-	B+	181.0	13.04	11.0	9.3	24.5	8.1	10.0	11.5	0.0
Community Banks of Shelby County	Cowden	IL	C+	C+	C+	52.3	12.67	5.6	2.6	10.3	28.7	9.5	10.7	0.0
▼ Community Commerce Bank	Claremont	CA	B	B+	B+	338.4	22.26	9.9	10.7	6.2	0.0	10.0	17.4	24.0

Asset Quality Index	Adjusted Non-Performing Loans		Net Charge-Offs Avg Loans	Profitability Index	Net Income ($Mil)	Return on Assets (R.O.A.)	Return on Equity (R.O.E.)	Net Interest Spread	Overhead Efficiency Ratio	Liquidity Index	Liquidity Ratio	Hot Money Ratio	Stability Index
	as a % of Total Loans	as a % of Capital											
5.3	0.40	na	0.06	6.5	1.8	1.58	16.90	3.65	55.4	1.1	13.4	28.1	6.1
5.2	1.73	na	0.10	6.1	1.1	1.68	19.00	4.09	67.1	5.6	50.1	8.0	4.1
4.1	4.94	na	0.08	9.5	3.2	2.21	20.15	4.26	44.7	0.9	11.1	32.7	8.1
6.9	0.28	na	0.02	5.3	1.4	1.32	13.81	3.10	62.9	3.8	31.7	13.2	6.1
3.0	1.12	na	0.04	1.8	0.1	0.23	2.52	3.56	91.2	5.5	32.8	3.8	3.4
8.1	0.19	1.4	-0.01	6.6	15.4	1.76	18.54	3.60	68.5	3.4	10.6	7.5	8.5
5.9	0.52	na	0.12	4.9	6.5	0.69	5.77	3.39	64.5	1.1	21.3	34.2	9.6
9.9	0.26	na	0.01	2.1	0.3	0.22	1.50	2.27	93.0	4.5	77.6	19.7	8.0
8.9	0.56	na	0.00	2.1	0.4	0.28	1.83	3.48	92.2	1.0	23.4	29.9	7.9
4.4	1.40	na	1.14	0.0	-0.5	-1.28	-13.42	3.33	140.8	4.0	35.8	13.5	2.2
9.1	0.25	0.7	-0.01	4.0	1.2	1.02	9.58	3.43	71.7	5.4	41.8	8.0	3.4
1.7	1.26	30.8	-0.08	4.0	0.6	0.83	6.27	4.13	76.8	4.3	20.4	7.5	7.1
8.6	0.70	na	-0.03	5.6	2.6	1.43	10.18	2.74	44.7	3.9	38.5	14.8	7.6
3.6	3.58	na	0.45	4.0	0.8	0.81	7.27	3.47	65.7	2.2	29.9	21.8	6.8
8.5	0.00	0.0	0.00	9.6	2.4	2.59	27.30	4.41	43.5	2.8	17.4	15.2	6.9
4.6	2.09	na	0.30	5.4	4.0	1.09	10.02	3.78	69.8	3.9	26.8	11.2	6.4
8.9	0.08	na	0.01	4.0	0.7	0.87	6.97	3.09	62.0	2.0	40.5	39.0	7.9
8.7	0.00	na	0.10	10.0	1.3	1.84	20.87	4.68	55.5	4.4	37.7	12.5	6.3
9.0	0.22	na	0.01	3.6	2.8	0.82	7.88	3.30	81.2	6.8	63.7	5.1	6.5
4.5	1.43	na	0.01	1.1	-13.4	-1.31	-12.53	3.32	124.0	3.9	11.0	9.3	8.4
3.7	5.32	na	-0.03	3.1	0.2	0.56	3.46	3.39	78.4	2.7	45.3	26.7	7.0
8.2	0.05	na	0.03	6.5	1.8	1.42	14.53	4.19	62.1	0.8	11.4	24.9	6.2
8.6	0.01	na	0.01	4.4	0.7	0.87	8.92	4.62	75.9	4.1	30.7	11.2	5.1
8.6	0.00	0.0	0.00	9.8	4.1	2.37	20.77	3.73	41.2	2.9	24.2	15.5	8.8
5.0	2.43	na	0.09	0.6	-0.2	-0.44	-5.15	3.24	115.5	3.3	49.4	19.9	2.3
2.1	2.16	33.0	0.05	1.3	0.2	0.30	9.95	4.41	96.5	5.0	26.3	4.2	0.4
8.3	0.70	2.8	-0.01	4.7	3.7	0.96	6.56	3.58	65.9	3.3	37.3	17.5	8.0
8.0	0.51	na	0.01	3.8	2.2	0.85	9.41	3.08	82.3	6.4	42.0	1.5	5.1
5.0	1.31	na	-0.16	2.6	1.2	0.62	5.69	3.39	78.9	5.1	41.9	9.8	4.4
7.7	0.45	na	0.00	4.2	1.4	0.81	8.55	3.14	66.9	0.8	17.9	44.2	5.6
4.1	0.96	na	0.20	6.2	3.1	1.17	14.28	3.95	57.2	2.2	13.1	18.0	4.8
6.5	0.64	na	0.03	6.4	1.6	1.55	17.64	4.15	61.4	3.2	22.6	12.6	6.3
7.5	0.00	na	0.00	9.8	0.7	2.65	12.36	4.30	17.9	3.3	27.6	14.4	9.3
8.4	1.47	na	0.01	6.5	1.2	1.50	9.05	2.94	50.8	4.8	55.1	14.9	9.6
6.5	1.40	na	0.11	3.4	0.7	0.57	5.51	3.76	76.3	5.1	35.2	7.5	4.5
3.9	2.44	na	0.01	6.9	1.1	1.05	11.25	3.71	52.1	1.5	19.9	25.8	7.6
6.8	0.55	na	0.20	6.9	7.2	1.70	17.20	3.62	54.4	2.2	20.7	18.3	6.3
8.8	0.27	na	-0.01	4.7	1.3	0.96	9.01	2.63	59.9	5.2	39.3	8.6	6.0
8.2	0.05	na	0.00	4.2	0.3	0.74	5.21	3.33	62.4	3.6	47.2	18.4	6.8
6.5	0.57	4.7	0.09	4.6	23.3	0.87	10.06	3.55	69.4	2.4	17.9	17.8	7.0
7.3	0.81	na	-0.03	8.6	0.8	1.73	12.93	4.93	61.4	3.8	20.4	10.6	7.1
8.8	0.00	na	-0.14	5.0	1.0	1.13	8.66	2.86	48.1	2.2	47.2	47.4	6.9
5.9	0.39	na	0.08	5.7	0.6	1.32	12.04	3.93	64.9	4.5	44.4	13.4	6.2
7.8	0.63	na	0.00	5.4	2.5	1.27	11.63	4.02	69.2	3.3	8.4	11.9	7.7
3.5	4.09	na	0.10	9.4	6.3	2.11	18.39	3.91	42.6	0.9	19.6	35.5	6.3
8.9	0.00	na	0.02	6.0	1.0	1.37	14.82	3.25	64.5	7.3	57.5	0.3	5.7
8.8	0.00	na	0.00	9.4	6.1	2.68	31.68	3.50	47.1	5.6	35.0	4.0	6.4
8.3	0.53	na	0.01	5.1	1.8	0.81	8.45	3.98	71.4	4.6	23.1	5.7	5.3
8.3	0.06	na	0.00	4.8	3.3	0.79	7.59	3.61	60.4	1.9	24.0	20.6	6.1
3.9	1.27	9.8	0.19	4.0	11.8	0.81	7.95	3.43	52.8	3.2	19.3	12.1	8.0
7.5	0.06	na	0.00	6.0	2.0	1.33	10.10	3.19	54.3	4.7	27.3	6.2	6.6
9.3	0.00	na	-0.04	6.0	1.6	1.21	11.99	3.59	56.5	6.3	54.5	5.9	5.9
4.7	1.81	8.3	-0.46	5.9	1.1	1.56	14.17	3.19	60.9	2.4	28.3	19.0	6.2
3.9	1.22	na	0.05	4.8	0.7	0.96	11.41	4.27	69.0	1.4	9.3	24.3	5.0
8.3	0.00	0.0	0.18	3.3	0.3	0.56	6.61	3.72	79.6	2.5	33.5	18.3	4.0
6.3	0.43	1.8	0.09	5.5	98.1	1.07	7.73	3.39	60.1	5.3	23.5	3.5	10.0
8.6	0.00	na	-0.04	2.6	0.5	0.40	3.33	2.53	84.6	1.8	34.5	14.1	7.0
5.5	1.24	na	0.06	6.2	1.5	1.14	8.98	4.21	56.7	2.5	19.7	17.2	7.9
6.3	0.93	na	-0.04	2.9	0.2	0.48	4.48	2.71	82.8	4.8	46.7	12.2	5.9
4.0	2.30	8.6	0.15	3.6	1.3	0.55	3.17	3.33	66.9	0.6	21.3	73.8	7.5

Name	City	State	2019 Rating	2018 Rating	Total Assets ($Mil)	One Year Asset Growth	Asset Mix (As a % of Total Assets)				Capital-ization Index	Lever-age Ratio	Risk-Based Capital Ratio
			Rating				Comm-ercial Loans	Cons-umer Loans	Mort-gage Loans	Secur-ities			
Community Development Bank, FSB	Ogema	MN	C	C+	B-	203.3	20.88	10.2	1.8	9.3	23.4	6.5	8.6	13.5
Community Federal Savings Bank	New York	NY	C-	C	D	380.7	116.77	38.8	2.0	7.8	3.1	9.8	10.9	24.8
Community Financial Bank	Prentice	WI	C+	C+	C+	49.4	6.19	5.5	1.4	28.8	0.0	8.8	10.2	19.3
Community Financial Services Bank	Benton	KY	C	C+	C+	1348.0	9.71	11.6	13.3	18.2	15.1	6.6	9.1	12.2
Community First Bank	Kansas City	KS	A-	B+	B	230.7	20.21	20.5	0.6	9.8	2.4	8.6	10.1	14.1
Community First Bank	New Iberia	LA	B	B	B	479.2	22.02	16.3	3.0	18.7	6.0	7.2	9.1	14.4
▲ Community First Bank	Menahga	MN	A	A-	A-	102.0	13.43	9.0	5.7	13.4	26.1	10.0	14.1	0.0
Community First Bank	Butler	MO	B	B	B	204.5	18.22	13.0	3.4	15.9	3.5	6.0	8.0	13.5
Community First Bank	Maywood	NE	D-	D-	D	124.1	1.74	8.0	2.5	5.6	14.0	5.7	10.2	0.0
Community First Bank	Walhalla	SC	C	C	C	518.2	23.41	6.9	24.7	13.3	8.0	4.9	9.2	0.0
Community First Bank	Kennewick	WA	B+	B+	B+	475.4	40.67	21.9	0.8	8.9	30.5	6.1	8.1	16.2
Community First Bank	Boscobel	WI	B+	B+	B+	487.8	14.09	12.4	1.2	13.0	23.1	8.5	10.0	15.4
Community First Bank	Rosholt	WI	B+	B	B-	102.6	23.23	8.8	1.3	12.5	30.3	8.1	9.8	0.0
Community First Bank of Indiana	Kokomo	IN	C+	B-	B-	396.0	32.83	25.9	0.8	9.5	0.7	2.0	8.8	0.0
Community First Bank of the Heartland	Mount Vernon	IL	B	B	B	251.3	23.55	21.2	0.3	7.6	7.6	6.6	8.6	13.2
Community First Bank, N.A.	Forest	OH	C	C-	C-	54.4	11.38	8.0	1.6	23.2	6.8	8.3	9.8	20.9
Community First Banking Co.	West Plains	MO	A-	A-	A-	228.3	19.76	9.0	3.3	23.0	20.5	9.2	10.5	0.0
Community First National Bank	Manhattan	KS	B-	C+	C+	318.5	8.17	18.5	1.7	20.4	0.0	7.0	9.4	12.5
Community National B&T of Texas	Corsicana	TX	A-	A-	B-	901.1	20.71	12.4	1.0	9.1	9.4	6.7	8.7	12.8
Community National Bank	Seneca	KS	B+	A-	A-	561.1	18.11	5.4	0.3	6.0	55.3	6.7	8.7	18.1
Community National Bank	Dayton	TN	C-	C	C+	276.0	3.77	7.5	1.1	13.6	24.6	8.3	9.9	0.0
Community National Bank	Hondo	TX	B+	B+	B	251.8	18.46	11.2	1.5	9.1	22.8	9.2	10.5	17.5
Community National Bank	Midland	TX	B+	B+	B	1370.8	-0.76	28.4	0.8	6.6	12.4	8.5	10.0	14.2
Community National Bank	Newport	VT	B-	B-	C+	868.2	19.16	21.5	0.5	19.9	4.0	7.0	9.0	15.0
Community National Bank & Trust	Chanute	KS	B-	B-	B-	1614.1	28.15	13.3	2.5	16.5	18.0	6.3	8.3	12.7
Community National Bank in Monmouth	Monmouth	IL	C	D+	D+	44.2	7.80	3.9	7.1	16.5	16.3	10.0	13.4	25.9
Community National Bank of Okarche	Okarche	OK	A	A	A	122.5	5.35	10.0	2.1	5.1	54.3	10.0	13.9	0.0
Community Neighbor Bank	Camden	AL	B+	A-	B+	123.3	19.14	17.8	5.7	14.0	8.0	10.0	13.3	0.0
Community Partners Savings Bank	Salem	IL	B-	B-	C	223.7	10.26	5.3	13.6	25.3	23.8	9.9	11.0	19.5
Community Point Bank	Russellville	MO	B-	B-	B-	149.4	7.34	5.4	2.9	18.4	14.1	7.8	9.5	14.6
▲ Community Resource Bank	Northfield	MN	A-	A-	A-	342.9	10.75	18.2	0.6	16.6	8.6	10.0	12.6	0.0
▲ Community Savings	Caldwell	OH	D+	D	D	53.2	3.77	0.0	25.6	47.1	6.6	10.0	13.8	29.8
▲ Community Savings Bank	Edgewood	IA	C	D	C-	478.4	15.25	16.2	2.0	7.4	19.8	7.1	9.1	13.6
Community Savings Bank	Chicago	IL	C-	C	C	425.6	7.35	0.0	0.0	32.8	31.1	10.0	15.6	0.0
▲ Community Savings Bank	Bethel	OH	B	B-	B	83.4	0.60	9.9	0.2	45.9	10.9	10.0	16.9	0.0
Community Spirit Bank	Red Bay	AL	B	B	B	159.0	6.62	16.4	4.9	23.0	16.2	9.0	10.3	16.5
▲ Community State Bank	Bradley	AR	C+	C	C-	27.7	22.60	36.0	5.0	10.6	3.7	8.5	10.0	15.2
Community State Bank	Lamar	CO	A	A-	A-	136.8	7.06	12.5	3.2	6.3	6.5	10.0	13.3	17.1
Community State Bank	Starke	FL	C	C+	C	160.8	27.82	11.5	3.6	15.4	26.3	5.9	7.9	15.9
Community State Bank	Ankeny	IA	B+	B+	B	938.8	16.95	18.9	0.1	7.4	19.4	7.3	9.9	12.7
Community State Bank	Paton	IA	B	B	B	46.7	8.08	5.9	2.1	1.4	47.5	10.0	19.3	38.3
Community State Bank	Spencer	IA	B+	B+	B+	228.5	9.23	18.6	1.4	4.8	36.8	7.4	9.3	0.0
▲ Community State Bank	Galva	IL	B	B-	C	260.7	9.89	15.6	1.5	9.0	18.6	7.3	10.6	0.0
▼ Community State Bank	Avilla	IN	A-	A-	B+	327.8	18.07	19.9	1.2	24.6	9.4	8.0	9.7	14.3
▲ Community State Bank	Brook	IN	B-	B-	C+	84.1	23.78	8.0	0.9	30.5	7.5	10.0	12.0	0.0
Community State Bank	Royal Center	IN	B-	B-	C+	139.9	13.34	7.8	2.4	13.0	21.5	9.2	10.4	17.5
Community State Bank	Coffeyville	KS	B+	A	A-	192.2	19.18	16.0	0.7	4.7	33.4	9.7	10.8	0.0
Community State Bank	Shelbina	MO	B	B-	B-	87.0	11.64	6.9	12.2	27.6	19.7	8.3	9.9	0.0
▲ Community State Bank	Colon	NE	C-	D+	D	35.2	94.26	4.7	1.0	1.3	6.8	7.2	9.2	0.0
▲ Community State Bank	Hennessey	OK	C	C-	D	73.6	7.00	12.7	3.1	5.8	47.8	5.5	7.5	20.8
Community State Bank	Poteau	OK	B-	B-	B-	306.2	13.12	8.5	2.9	17.7	17.2	6.9	8.9	14.4
Community State Bank	Union Grove	WI	B	B-	C+	519.8	32.84	21.2	0.3	6.9	18.7	6.1	8.1	15.0
▼ Community State Bank of Canton	Canton	OK	C+	B-	C+	52.4	9.23	14.3	6.7	4.5	21.6	8.8	10.6	0.0
Community State Bank of Missouri	Bowling Green	MO	B+	B+	B+	260.7	13.72	14.6	0.6	18.1	19.7	6.0	12.8	0.0
Community State Bank of Orbisonia	Orbisonia	PA	B-	B	B	381.8	16.30	3.8	8.3	52.2	14.6	8.9	10.3	0.0
▲ Community State Bank of Rock Falls	Rock Falls	IL	C-	C-	C	303.3	15.11	9.3	1.4	25.0	14.4	7.6	9.4	18.0
Community State Bank Of Southwestern In	Poseyville	IN	B	B	B-	92.2	9.49	9.9	1.8	22.4	0.9	8.2	9.8	17.8
Community Trust Bank	Irvington	IL	B-	B-	B-	86.9	11.20	10.5	1.0	9.0	35.4	10.0	13.1	24.6
Community Trust Bank, Inc.	Pikeville	KY	B-	B	B-	4990.9	15.63	10.7	16.7	16.7	18.6	10.0	12.1	0.0
Community Valley Bank	El Centro	CA	B+	A-	B+	251.8	32.81	23.4	0.0	4.7	0.6	6.0	9.8	0.0

Asset Quality Index	Adjusted Non-Performing Loans as a % of Total Loans	as a % of Capital	Net Charge-Offs Avg Loans	Profitability Index	Net Income ($Mil)	Return on Assets (R.O.A.)	Return on Equity (R.O.E.)	Net Interest Spread	Overhead Efficiency Ratio	Liquidity Index	Liquidity Ratio	Hot Money Ratio	Stability Index
4.2	1.42	6.3	-0.01	2.4	0.3	0.25	2.11	3.12	85.2	4.2	39.7	14.0	5.4
4.4	1.05	9.8	0.00	5.0	3.0	1.45	19.84	2.90	75.1	2.0	33.7	28.2	3.2
7.7	0.73	na	0.00	3.9	0.3	0.84	8.06	2.80	74.6	2.4	37.7	26.0	6.2
1.9	3.46	na	1.64	1.6	-0.1	-0.01	-0.11	3.14	68.5	1.4	15.7	20.2	7.0
8.4	0.15	na	0.00	9.8	2.8	1.72	17.01	4.69	51.3	0.6	9.2	43.9	7.1
5.6	0.43	na	0.02	5.4	4.0	1.20	12.34	3.95	67.2	2.2	25.9	19.2	7.1
8.2	0.03	na	-0.03	7.3	1.3	1.76	11.23	3.97	58.0	5.3	50.4	9.9	8.8
4.7	0.85	na	-0.01	7.4	2.6	1.76	20.58	3.84	49.5	1.8	26.2	23.5	6.7
0.4	4.55	na	0.06	1.1	-0.3	-0.27	-2.42	4.40	91.2	2.0	13.4	15.9	5.3
5.7	0.76	na	0.00	2.8	1.4	0.39	3.81	3.56	83.8	2.4	14.2	16.9	5.1
7.6	0.21	1.4	-0.01	4.8	3.8	1.21	12.51	3.44	75.4	5.7	30.3	1.0	6.0
4.7	1.20	5.7	0.02	5.8	4.9	1.44	11.93	4.08	63.5	3.6	27.3	12.5	7.4
8.7	0.00	na	0.01	6.0	1.1	1.52	14.65	4.14	68.3	6.4	44.3	1.9	6.2
5.8	0.79	na	-0.02	4.8	2.2	0.77	8.14	4.18	74.3	0.6	4.1	24.2	5.9
4.0	0.72	na	0.05	7.4	3.0	1.71	17.91	3.99	58.6	1.6	8.1	18.4	6.8
9.3	0.00	na	0.01	2.2	0.1	0.20	2.07	3.11	91.7	6.4	49.8	2.8	4.6
7.2	1.03	na	-0.01	5.8	2.3	1.44	12.67	3.45	62.6	2.8	25.0	14.8	8.4
7.1	0.33	na	0.00	4.9	2.5	1.04	11.24	3.56	69.6	1.4	9.5	23.3	5.8
7.2	0.39	na	0.01	7.1	8.8	1.40	12.46	4.37	60.3	4.2	23.9	8.5	7.8
5.1	3.35	na	0.01	8.9	7.3	1.93	20.59	3.17	49.1	6.2	50.3	5.2	7.5
1.9	7.90	na	0.47	2.1	-0.4	-0.19	-1.75	3.99	104.1	3.6	34.7	15.1	7.4
5.7	1.14	na	-0.06	5.9	2.5	1.45	12.84	4.17	64.1	4.9	38.6	9.8	7.1
5.8	0.93	5.2	-0.01	6.5	12.4	1.16	10.72	4.12	55.6	5.1	19.4	2.9	9.1
4.6	0.64	na	0.04	6.6	8.1	1.36	12.90	3.72	58.0	3.8	7.9	8.3	7.2
4.9	1.18	na	0.05	4.2	8.6	0.79	8.45	3.58	74.0	3.5	15.6	12.2	7.7
7.7	0.36	1.5	0.06	2.4	0.2	0.47	3.47	3.25	81.6	4.9	45.2	11.2	4.8
9.0	0.00	na	0.00	7.6	1.7	1.86	12.94	3.39	43.6	0.8	16.5	37.9	10.0
5.5	1.06	na	0.30	5.0	0.7	0.85	6.19	4.37	73.9	3.5	33.4	15.2	8.4
3.7	1.40	na	0.34	3.8	1.1	0.67	5.74	3.86	72.9	3.1	28.8	15.8	5.6
8.5	0.03	na	0.00	4.5	1.2	1.13	11.88	2.90	59.7	1.6	24.2	24.5	6.4
6.5	0.80	na	0.02	7.3	3.2	1.30	9.48	3.96	60.2	2.1	10.4	16.6	8.3
4.5	1.62	na	0.00	1.0	0.0	0.04	0.31	4.46	98.9	3.8	13.9	9.9	5.9
5.5	0.56	na	0.21	3.4	3.2	0.93	9.18	3.36	73.6	2.8	17.7	11.8	4.0
8.7	3.01	na	0.00	1.6	0.4	0.12	0.72	2.43	97.6	3.4	49.5	21.8	7.5
9.0	0.26	na	-0.01	4.1	0.5	0.79	4.63	3.82	76.6	2.1	20.3	19.1	7.9
7.5	1.55	na	0.01	4.9	1.3	1.10	10.33	4.53	73.2	1.5	18.2	25.6	6.1
5.9	0.00	na	0.03	7.3	0.3	1.76	14.73	4.74	62.6	1.1	27.3	37.4	5.3
8.0	0.02	0.1	-0.01	8.0	1.7	1.72	13.01	4.13	52.7	0.8	17.0	44.1	9.9
2.8	3.71	na	0.40	2.9	0.6	0.57	6.90	4.19	84.2	4.9	23.7	3.5	3.9
7.6	0.24	na	0.17	4.0	3.5	0.53	4.62	3.92	61.4	4.6	21.7	5.8	7.8
7.2	0.00	na	-0.02	4.7	0.4	1.02	4.88	2.85	57.9	4.7	65.4	15.7	7.2
8.3	0.32	na	-0.01	5.5	2.0	1.22	11.12	3.61	50.9	3.0	29.9	6.3	8.2
4.9	1.03	na	0.58	5.9	2.4	1.31	12.21	4.31	53.4	1.3	13.8	22.2	7.5
7.5	0.43	na	0.01	7.0	3.0	1.27	12.65	3.90	54.7	4.2	22.4	8.6	7.4
4.0	4.92	na	-0.07	7.2	0.8	1.42	11.93	4.06	53.3	1.6	31.8	26.1	5.4
4.2	2.38	11.8	0.00	4.2	0.9	0.84	7.55	3.87	79.0	4.7	26.6	6.3	6.4
6.3	3.24	na	0.00	8.8	2.3	1.74	15.05	3.89	45.0	4.7	14.3	3.8	7.7
6.1	1.21	na	0.14	9.0	1.1	1.78	18.91	3.92	39.0	3.0	15.4	9.9	5.9
7.6	0.58	na	0.00	1.9	0.1	0.30	3.56	2.68	86.5	2.7	47.8	20.2	4.1
3.9	3.96	na	0.51	4.5	0.5	0.93	13.04	3.78	73.0	6.5	45.1	1.5	3.1
4.1	1.64	10.9	0.09	4.2	2.4	1.08	11.63	4.34	77.9	1.8	28.0	25.2	6.0
5.0	1.97	na	-0.14	5.8	4.7	1.36	15.23	3.55	68.2	5.4	39.9	7.0	5.9
1.7	2.91	na	1.22	4.7	0.3	0.68	6.31	4.71	72.5	2.5	5.1	15.4	6.1
8.7	0.23	na	0.00	5.7	2.7	1.43	11.03	3.12	60.5	3.1	11.1	13.2	8.2
4.3	2.09	na	0.13	3.6	1.4	0.52	4.78	3.91	78.0	1.8	15.9	19.6	6.2
2.3	3.55	na	0.29	4.1	1.6	0.71	7.01	3.15	62.3	2.4	29.1	19.2	5.6
8.9	0.00	na	0.00	5.1	0.9	1.34	13.88	3.16	69.2	4.8	41.3	11.2	6.3
7.9	0.71	na	0.02	3.7	0.4	0.64	4.63	3.78	76.3	5.8	40.5	4.9	5.6
3.9	2.16	8.2	0.20	5.6	42.9	1.21	8.89	3.43	55.3	2.7	10.2	15.2	9.9
4.1	0.66	na	0.00	7.0	2.2	1.29	12.45	4.45	55.6	2.9	15.2	14.7	5.9

Name	City	State	2019 Rating	2018 Rating	Rating	Total Assets ($Mil)	One Year Asset Growth	Commercial Loans	Consumer Loans	Mortgage Loans	Securities	Capitalization Index	Leverage Ratio	Risk-Based Capital Ratio
Community West Bank, N.A.	Goleta	CA	C	C+	C-	1041.9	15.38	10.2	26.4	2.9	2.3	2.7	8.8	0.0
▼ CommunityBank of Texas, N.A.	Beaumont	TX	B+	A-	A-	3815.5	11.17	21.7	0.9	6.4	5.9	9.9	10.9	15.4
Compass Savings Bank	Wilmerding	PA	D-	D-	D+	52.5	2.07	0.4	0.9	73.3	9.4	6.4	8.4	17.5
Computershare Trust Co., N.A.	Canton	MA	U	U	U	33.5	9.42	0.0	0.0	0.0	0.0	10.0	94.4	302.2
Concorde Bank	Blomkest	MN	B-	C+	C+	66.8	17.91	7.4	2.4	16.3	6.6	8.4	9.9	14.5
Concordia Bank	Concordia	MO	B+	B+	B	87.2	18.40	11.0	1.3	18.1	3.0	8.6	10.1	0.0
Concordia Bank & Trust Co.	Vidalia	LA	B-	B	B	570.4	8.90	6.3	1.9	11.8	33.5	9.9	10.9	0.0
▼ Congressional Bank	Chevy Chase	MD	C-	C	C-	1567.2	42.20	50.4	1.2	8.5	2.1	9.9	11.3	14.9
Conneaut Savings Bank	Conneaut	OH	C	C	C	80.8	4.85	3.7	0.4	48.5	17.8	10.0	14.2	0.0
▲ Connect Bank	Star City	AR	A-	B+	A-	102.2	4.01	12.9	1.5	15.6	24.1	10.0	15.6	0.0
Connecticut Community Bank, N.A.	Norwalk	CT	C-	C	C	551.5	29.97	41.5	0.3	3.1	0.9	5.9	8.7	0.0
Connection Bank	Fort Madison	IA	B	B-	B-	346.8	12.61	18.1	1.9	28.1	6.2	6.1	8.2	12.0
▲ Connections Bank	Kirksville	MO	B+	B	C+	90.5	2.08	4.5	0.7	38.6	7.0	10.0	11.0	0.0
ConnectOne Bank	Englewood Cliffs	NJ	C+	C+	C	7449.1	20.90	16.1	0.0	7.3	6.1	8.4	10.4	13.7
Consumers National Bank	Minerva	OH	B	B	B-	751.3	33.31	16.1	2.9	13.5	18.7	6.1	8.1	12.6
Continental Bank	Salt Lake City	UT	B	B	B-	292.2	91.03	80.9	0.0	0.0	3.5	10.0	13.8	20.2
Converse County Bank	Douglas	WY	B+	B+	B	717.3	13.90	10.0	3.5	4.2	65.3	6.7	8.8	30.0
Conway Bank	Conway Springs	KS	D	D+	D+	102.8	4.20	19.3	0.8	14.9	8.6	5.3	7.3	14.8
Conway National Bank	Conway	SC	B+	B+	B	1453.2	16.25	8.4	3.4	11.8	52.8	7.4	9.3	20.4
Cooperative Bank	Roslindale	MA	C	C+	C+	472.4	7.56	4.6	0.7	42.8	9.5	7.6	9.4	14.2
Cooperative Bank of Cape Cod	Hyannis	MA	C+	C+	C+	1126.7	17.52	9.1	0.1	45.0	3.4	7.6	9.4	0.0
Copiah Bank	Hazlehurst	MS	B-	B-	B-	252.3	8.19	5.8	2.3	18.8	19.9	7.4	9.6	0.0
▼ Corder Bank	Corder	MO	D+	C	C-	21.6	10.05	10.3	4.5	16.5	18.1	8.7	10.1	18.4
▲ Core Bank	Omaha	NE	B-	C+	B-	703.2	16.97	26.4	0.3	17.3	5.5	6.1	8.1	11.9
COREBANK	Waynoka	OK	D+	C-	D	78.0	24.43	13.2	0.5	23.4	5.4	8.8	10.2	17.7
CoreFirst Bank & Trust	Topeka	KS	B-	C+	C+	1087.7	14.25	17.2	3.5	9.2	20.6	7.2	9.1	14.2
Corn City State Bank	Deshler	OH	B+	B+	B+	76.1	14.64	1.0	2.1	26.7	50.4	10.0	13.9	0.0
Corn Growers State Bank	Murdock	NE	D+	D+	D-	27.3	7.28	5.4	8.6	7.9	11.7	6.4	8.5	0.0
Cornerstone Bank	Atlanta	GA	D-	D	D+	222.2	15.24	23.1	0.3	11.3	16.4	6.2	8.2	16.4
Cornerstone Bank	Clarinda	IA	C-	C-	C-	40.5	-1.77	5.9	6.5	32.3	9.7	10.0	13.5	26.1
Cornerstone Bank	Overland Park	KS	B+	B+	B	278.5	20.50	21.6	0.5	16.9	5.4	4.6	8.7	0.0
Cornerstone Bank	Worcester	MA	C	C	C	1323.9	15.14	9.1	0.6	42.5	4.1	6.7	8.7	13.6
Cornerstone Bank	South West City	MO	B	B-	C+	154.6	9.97	12.4	8.6	24.5	12.3	10.0	13.1	22.2
Cornerstone Bank	Fargo	ND	B-	C	C	1095.4	12.95	17.3	2.1	8.5	14.4	5.8	7.8	11.8
Cornerstone Bank	York	NE	B+	B+	B+	1851.1	11.08	17.3	1.4	3.0	14.1	5.9	10.2	0.0
Cornerstone Bank	Mount Laurel	NJ	D+	D+	D	276.3	6.76	10.5	0.0	28.6	7.5	4.8	6.8	11.1
Cornerstone Bank	Watonga	OK	B-	C+	C	216.3	2.32	9.5	3.8	8.7	40.0	7.0	9.0	16.1
CornerStone Bank, N.A.	Lexington	VA	C	C+	B	189.7	12.36	14.1	1.6	22.9	6.8	6.8	9.4	0.0
Cornerstone Community Bank	Red Bluff	CA	B	B	B-	485.3	59.38	26.4	0.7	2.2	10.5	6.1	8.1	12.0
Cornerstone Community Bank	Grafton	WI	C+	C+	C+	235.8	14.51	19.0	0.2	9.1	0.0	2.0	9.0	0.0
Cornerstone National Bank & Trust Co.	Palatine	IL	B-	B-	B-	903.7	41.79	35.8	0.2	7.3	9.5	6.3	8.3	14.3
CornerStone State Bank	Montgomery	MN	B+	A-	B+	203.6	18.43	9.8	4.4	20.2	29.6	9.2	10.5	0.0
Cornhusker Bank	Lincoln	NE	B-	B-	B-	723.4	14.48	13.2	0.9	14.3	16.2	6.3	8.4	12.8
Cortland Savings and Banking Co.	Cortland	OH	B	B	C	808.3	15.91	15.1	0.5	9.8	20.7	6.8	8.8	14.0
CorTrust Bank N.A.	Mitchell	SD	C+	B-	B-	1346.8	10.84	15.5	3.0	7.9	25.7	6.9	8.9	14.3
▼ Corydon State Bank	Corydon	IA	B-	B+	B+	104.2	4.21	7.2	2.0	10.2	19.9	10.0	20.5	0.0
Cottonport Bank	Cottonport	LA	B+	B+	B+	411.4	13.57	9.3	2.7	13.0	10.1	10.0	11.9	0.0
▲ Cottonwood Valley Bank	Cedar Point	KS	B-	C+	C+	38.4	14.05	9.4	1.3	0.4	27.1	10.0	13.0	0.0
▲ Coulee Bank	La Crosse	WI	B-	C+	B-	434.8	12.44	22.6	1.6	8.7	16.5	6.8	9.1	12.3
▲ Country Bank for Savings	Ware	MA	B	B	B	1736.5	2.57	3.8	0.5	28.6	18.5	10.0	14.7	0.0
Country Club Bank	Kansas City	MO	B+	A-	A-	1968.2	40.93	25.5	0.6	7.8	19.5	5.6	8.7	0.0
Country Club Trust Co., N.A.	Kansas City	MO	U	U	U	14.5	-36.86	0.0	0.0	0.0	9.8	10.0	101.	0.0
COUNTRY Trust Bank	Bloomington	IL	U	U	U	32.6	5.54	0.0	0.0	0.0	59.9	10.0	100.	121.7
▲ Countryside Bank	Unadilla	NE	B	B	B	89.9	15.34	5.2	4.4	16.6	15.2	10.0	15.8	0.0
▲ County Bank	Rehoboth Beach	DE	B	B-	C-	475.7	25.81	14.1	5.3	8.8	7.5	9.6	10.7	15.4
▲ County Bank	Sigourney	IA	C+	C	C+	195.5	12.08	14.9	1.9	8.9	10.7	7.9	9.6	13.7
County Bank	Brunswick	MO	B-	B-	B-	104.5	13.01	13.1	4.5	18.1	16.2	5.6	7.6	13.6
County National Bank	Hillsdale	MI	B	B	B-	939.1	29.61	30.9	3.9	18.4	2.6	5.9	7.9	13.0
County Savings Bank	Essington	PA	C	C	C-	89.5	7.44	0.0	0.1	37.5	11.9	5.0	7.0	22.6
Countybank	Greenwood	SC	B-	B-	B-	544.0	25.13	15.5	0.9	19.8	19.3	5.3	7.3	14.0

Asset Quality Index	Adjusted Non-Performing Loans as a % of Total Loans	Adjusted Non-Performing Loans as a % of Capital	Net Charge-Offs Avg Loans	Profitability Index	Net Income ($Mil)	Return on Assets (R.O.A.)	Return on Equity (R.O.E.)	Net Interest Spread	Overhead Efficiency Ratio	Liquidity Index	Liquidity Ratio	Hot Money Ratio	Stability Index
6.1	0.42	na	-0.03	4.9	6.1	0.83	9.72	3.83	67.1	1.6	13.9	19.0	7.4
5.4	1.25	4.8	0.00	5.0	17.4	0.62	4.65	3.76	63.6	4.1	17.2	5.4	10.0
8.5	0.00	na	0.00	0.0	-0.4	-0.91	-10.33	1.38	154.8	0.8	17.1	36.2	3.2
6.5	na	na	na	9.5	4.5	19.05	20.32	0.58	61.6	4.0	na	0.0	6.9
5.2	1.61	na	-0.10	5.9	0.6	1.35	12.92	4.99	64.5	3.8	38.5	15.3	6.3
1.7	3.89	na	0.00	6.1	0.8	1.24	11.83	4.40	62.5	4.6	22.2	5.6	6.5
4.8	1.68	na	0.08	3.9	3.7	0.89	7.34	3.39	70.7	1.6	17.2	23.9	8.1
2.3	2.75	na	0.09	6.5	10.2	1.04	7.78	4.54	71.6	1.5	11.7	13.3	8.2
9.6	0.55	na	0.00	1.7	0.1	0.11	0.76	3.06	96.1	5.3	38.5	7.1	7.1
6.5	1.32	na	0.62	6.6	1.1	1.48	9.52	4.70	69.8	2.9	28.6	16.6	8.9
3.8	1.78	na	0.11	2.3	1.0	0.25	2.56	3.47	92.4	3.6	21.5	11.5	4.9
7.4	0.08	na	0.05	5.3	3.1	1.23	12.64	3.52	69.8	4.5	11.9	5.3	6.2
8.3	0.44	na	-0.01	5.0	0.7	0.95	7.63	4.31	64.7	0.7	10.6	39.6	7.1
3.1	1.34	8.3	0.00	4.9	51.0	0.92	7.32	3.54	49.1	1.0	9.5	17.9	9.3
7.6	0.38	na	0.03	4.9	5.5	1.06	12.13	3.83	62.6	3.7	13.2	10.2	5.6
5.7	2.10	na	0.48	4.6	1.1	0.66	5.86	4.67	75.0	0.3	13.3	93.7	6.4
9.3	0.01	na	-0.03	5.6	7.4	1.36	14.69	2.05	46.9	3.0	49.0	27.5	6.8
3.0	3.53	na	0.25	1.7	0.1	0.13	1.43	3.72	91.9	1.9	22.4	19.5	3.8
8.8	0.52	2.2	-0.02	5.3	10.5	1.04	10.65	2.91	58.1	5.2	47.5	13.6	8.0
6.2	1.03	na	0.00	2.4	1.1	0.33	3.35	3.25	83.8	2.3	15.3	17.3	6.1
6.6	1.11	6.9	-0.02	3.6	4.5	0.59	6.01	3.20	66.4	4.0	14.0	8.2	7.2
5.0	1.86	na	0.18	4.3	1.4	0.77	7.86	3.91	74.8	3.0	23.3	14.9	6.1
2.3	3.37	na	-0.50	3.8	0.1	0.64	5.91	3.68	77.9	4.6	41.2	9.9	4.5
5.8	1.81	na	-0.02	5.7	6.3	1.26	15.43	4.12	72.4	3.6	8.3	5.5	5.5
8.7	0.00	na	-0.02	2.0	0.2	0.34	3.12	3.11	84.1	1.3	32.9	61.1	5.5
4.3	2.50	na	0.05	4.5	8.4	1.09	11.97	3.47	68.7	4.8	12.8	3.3	7.9
9.5	0.14	na	0.06	4.4	0.8	1.41	9.40	2.38	61.3	2.6	36.7	22.4	8.1
5.1	0.67	na	-0.03	3.1	0.1	0.47	5.64	3.82	88.2	5.7	34.9	3.3	3.0
1.9	7.39	na	0.42	0.0	-1.9	-1.14	-12.54	3.03	128.4	1.2	21.1	31.4	2.7
5.6	2.15	na	0.03	1.4	0.1	0.22	1.62	2.92	92.3	2.3	37.4	27.9	5.6
6.8	0.58	na	0.07	6.2	2.7	1.42	15.55	3.74	47.0	2.0	14.7	19.1	6.3
7.9	0.53	3.4	0.00	1.3	-0.5	-0.05	-0.57	2.90	89.3	1.8	9.0	16.8	6.6
4.5	2.81	na	0.10	4.7	1.2	1.04	7.61	4.71	75.9	1.1	26.1	29.4	8.3
3.9	3.43	18.8	0.03	4.6	7.6	0.96	11.56	3.67	70.3	2.7	11.3	15.5	7.5
5.4	0.48	7.1	0.01	5.8	17.3	1.32	12.55	3.69	66.7	1.6	12.4	19.7	8.5
6.6	0.40	3.1	0.01	1.5	0.2	0.10	1.18	2.91	99.7	2.9	20.6	14.9	2.9
8.8	0.12	0.6	-0.06	4.9	2.1	1.27	14.62	3.78	71.2	4.8	32.7	7.8	4.2
4.0	2.49	na	0.02	2.8	0.3	0.24	2.51	3.54	82.7	1.2	15.3	28.6	5.1
8.3	0.03	na	0.00	5.4	2.8	0.93	11.85	3.51	49.7	1.9	27.2	14.8	5.8
5.5	0.43	na	0.00	7.5	2.4	1.44	16.07	3.97	52.4	2.9	4.3	12.7	5.9
5.3	0.53	na	-0.01	6.2	6.7	1.13	13.92	3.51	64.3	4.2	23.2	8.3	6.2
5.1	2.28	6.5	-0.07	4.8	1.7	1.20	10.38	3.35	68.4	4.9	33.4	7.7	6.5
6.8	0.58	na	0.02	4.9	6.2	1.20	13.75	3.47	70.0	3.4	20.8	9.7	6.6
6.2	1.43	na	0.00	5.3	6.2	1.08	11.46	3.31	60.4	3.9	17.6	8.1	6.0
6.5	0.50	na	0.36	3.2	4.3	0.45	4.44	3.93	75.5	4.0	19.4	9.8	7.5
0.0	15.36	na	4.56	2.7	0.5	0.63	2.93	3.39	34.5	2.2	43.9	27.6	6.7
6.4	1.10	na	0.14	4.8	2.9	0.98	8.19	3.78	70.5	3.5	29.0	14.1	6.4
9.4	0.00	na	-0.07	3.4	0.3	1.03	7.44	2.62	77.2	5.3	61.9	12.0	6.4
5.3	0.19	na	0.00	6.7	5.4	1.74	18.40	4.05	65.1	3.6	11.1	9.3	5.6
5.6	2.42	10.2	0.02	4.1	9.9	0.77	5.16	3.20	66.0	3.4	26.1	13.3	9.7
7.2	0.85	4.2	0.07	6.3	25.4	1.88	20.20	3.48	71.6	5.2	23.8	4.7	9.0
10.0	na	na	na	10.0	1.1	10.83	10.21	1.21	88.4	4.0	na	0.0	7.0
10.0	na	na	na	9.5	2.7	13.73	13.41	3.27	91.8	4.0	na	0.0	7.0
8.6	0.00	na	-0.01	4.2	0.7	1.01	6.12	3.16	69.0	5.2	42.3	9.2	7.6
6.3	3.42	na	-0.02	5.9	3.3	1.05	9.05	3.95	62.2	5.4	31.5	3.4	7.0
4.2	1.49	na	0.07	7.6	2.6	1.88	18.17	4.15	59.7	2.8	16.1	14.9	6.3
6.4	0.00	0.0	0.17	5.4	1.0	1.38	15.62	4.18	69.6	3.7	19.0	10.9	5.7
5.3	0.69	na	-0.01	6.5	8.1	1.23	14.54	3.87	61.4	4.2	12.6	7.3	6.2
10.0	0.27	na	0.00	2.4	0.2	0.25	3.53	3.13	88.6	6.2	54.3	5.1	3.4
5.4	0.82	na	0.14	5.5	5.2	1.39	17.48	3.39	78.1	5.3	21.9	0.8	5.4

Name	City	State	2019 Rating	2018 Rating	Rating	Total Assets ($Mil)	One Year Asset Growth	Commercial Loans	Consumer Loans	Mortgage Loans	Securities	Capitalization Index	Leverage Ratio	Risk-Based Capital Ratio
Covington County Bank	Collins	MS	C+	C+	C	81.1	6.47	12.1	3.4	4.3	33.7	8.0	9.6	17.6
Covington S&L Assn.	Covington	OH	B-	B-	B-	76.7	8.30	0.1	0.3	47.7	15.1	10.0	15.5	0.0
Cowboy Bank of Texas	Maypearl	TX	A-	A-	A-	96.4	10.75	0.6	3.9	25.2	12.1	10.0	11.3	17.3
▲ Cowboy State Bank	Ranchester	WY	C-	D	D-	52.5	5.05	4.5	4.5	8.3	18.2	6.4	8.4	15.0
Crawford County Trust and Savings Bank	Denison	IA	B	C+	C+	219.8	13.94	9.6	3.2	8.3	11.9	6.8	8.8	13.4
Credit First N.A.	Brook Park	OH	U	U	U	29.9	-3.64	0.0	0.0	0.0	0.0	10.0	101.	385.6
Credit One Bank, N.A.	Las Vegas	NV	U	U	U	731.0	33.43	0.0	56.4	0.0	3.6	10.0	38.5	0.0
Crescent Bank & Trust	New Orleans	LA	C-	C-	D	926.2	-5.88	2.8	73.9	2.8	7.5	10.0	13.8	17.4
Crest Savings Bank	Wildwood	NJ	C	C+	C+	553.2	13.84	2.6	3.7	51.3	0.9	5.5	7.5	14.1
Crews Bank & Trust	Arcadia	FL	A-	A-	A-	182.6	17.89	4.7	1.9	15.6	26.9	8.1	9.7	0.0
Crockett National Bank	San Antonio	TX	A	A	B+	691.5	6.12	5.5	0.1	35.0	4.2	10.0	13.7	20.2
▲ Croghan Colonial Bank	Fremont	OH	A-	B+	B+	1003.0	14.21	13.9	10.2	8.9	19.5	8.8	10.5	14.0
Cross County Bank	Wynne	AR	B+	B+	B+	302.5	10.49	11.0	1.0	10.7	2.7	7.7	11.5	0.0
Cross County Savings Bank	Middle Village	NY	C+	B	B	524.7	16.00	0.0	0.0	47.5	3.3	9.2	10.5	17.4
Cross Keys Bank	Saint Joseph	LA	B+	B+	B+	442.6	17.29	16.7	0.8	12.5	24.4	10.0	11.0	17.3
▼ Cross River Bank	Fort Lee	NJ	B+	A-	B	11779.4	488.97	68.2	10.8	0.8	0.3	6.5	8.5	17.0
CrossFirst Bank	Leawood	KS	C+	B-	C	5504.0	18.35	36.9	0.4	7.0	11.8	6.6	9.9	12.2
Crossroads Bank	Effingham	IL	A-	A-	A-	202.8	15.46	16.2	1.2	7.2	30.3	10.0	13.4	0.0
Crossroads Bank	Wabash	IN	B	B	C+	468.2	11.21	8.3	3.7	26.1	21.4	7.0	9.0	14.0
Crossroads Bank	Yoakum	TX	A	A	A-	253.2	20.15	13.7	6.1	20.5	36.3	9.7	10.8	0.0
Crowell State Bank	Crowell	TX	B	B-	B-	41.1	10.29	11.9	6.4	9.3	16.5	10.0	11.1	0.0
▲ Crown Bank	Edina	MN	C-	C-	B-	245.4	13.90	44.5	1.0	1.6	12.8	8.5	10.7	13.7
Crown Bank	Elizabeth	NJ	B-	C+	C-	550.5	5.31	7.1	0.1	2.0	7.3	10.0	21.0	0.0
Crystal Lake Bank & Trust Co., N.A.	Crystal Lake	IL	B	B	B	1287.3	9.93	36.3	13.7	2.6	9.7	6.1	9.1	11.8
CS Bank	Eureka Springs	AR	B-	B-	B-	401.6	23.60	7.6	3.9	19.6	7.8	5.4	7.4	13.5
CTBC Bank Corp. (USA)	Los Angeles	CA	B+	A-	A-	4181.3	17.35	6.2	0.0	30.5	6.6	10.0	13.7	0.0
Culbertson Bank	Culbertson	NE	C-	C	C-	13.7	-4.99	7.7	0.4	0.1	23.2	10.0	15.1	0.0
Cullman Savings Bank	Cullman	AL	A-	A-	B+	324.3	7.59	8.3	0.6	36.6	6.2	10.0	15.5	0.0
Cumberland Federal Bank, FSB	Cumberland	WI	A-	B+	A-	189.7	18.68	4.4	1.0	16.5	48.7	9.5	10.7	16.0
Cumberland Security Bank, Inc.	Somerset	KY	A	A	B+	264.1	16.94	8.4	4.3	26.2	10.1	10.0	12.8	19.0
Cumberland Valley National B&T Co.	London	KY	C+	C+	C+	622.0	18.34	12.6	1.7	12.1	10.6	7.1	9.1	14.9
Currie State Bank	Currie	MN	D	C-	C-	92.5	11.78	6.2	1.5	6.1	0.3	4.2	9.2	0.0
CUSB Bank	Cresco	IA	A-	B+	C+	524.4	7.60	9.9	4.7	7.3	18.6	10.0	14.0	0.0
Custer Federal State Bank	Broken Bow	NE	B-	B-	B	114.5	-1.35	8.1	1.8	15.4	21.4	10.0	11.8	0.0
Customers Bank	Phoenixville	PA	C+	B-	B	18757.1	59.99	36.1	6.8	2.6	6.0	5.8	9.3	11.6
Cypress Bank, SSB	Pittsburg	TX	B-	B-	C+	211.6	9.99	6.0	6.6	29.0	23.6	8.9	10.3	17.9
D.A. Davidson Trust Co.	Great Falls	MT	U	U	U	11.1	15.07	0.0	0.0	0.0	58.5	10.0	75.9	174.5
D.L. Evans Bank	Burley	ID	B+	A-	B+	2211.3	31.83	18.9	1.5	4.9	21.8	6.0	8.4	0.0
Dacotah Bank	Aberdeen	SD	B-	B-	B	3007.8	15.30	15.7	2.9	3.3	9.0	9.6	10.7	14.8
Dairy State Bank	Rice Lake	WI	B	B	B	613.0	21.03	10.2	0.8	6.5	53.8	10.0	11.1	24.2
Dakota Community Bank & Trust, N.A.	Hebron	ND	B+	B+	B	903.8	6.13	13.1	1.6	4.2	28.7	6.5	8.5	14.7
▲ Dakota Heritage Bank	Hunter	ND	B-	C+	B+	235.6	13.44	10.1	4.0	4.4	11.5	5.7	9.6	0.0
Dakota Prairie Bank	Fort Pierre	SD	A-	A-	B+	106.4	18.24	8.1	2.3	3.2	7.6	10.0	11.2	17.7
Dakota Western Bank	Bowman	ND	B+	B+	B	297.9	6.39	13.6	2.4	1.1	20.7	10.0	11.3	16.1
Dalhart Federal S&L Assn., SSB	Dalhart	TX	C	C	C+	119.8	8.23	0.4	2.0	46.5	29.4	10.0	11.5	28.4
Dallas Capital Bank, N.A.	Dallas	TX	C	C-	C	1031.5	4.37	17.6	0.0	7.3	8.4	2.9	9.3	0.0
Damariscotta Bank & Trust Co.	Damariscotta	ME	C+	C+	C	209.3	8.30	3.6	0.7	32.8	13.7	6.9	8.9	18.3
Danville State Savings Bank	Danville	IA	B+	B+	B+	162.5	11.27	4.2	4.1	20.6	33.7	10.0	12.0	0.0
Dart Bank	Mason	MI	B-	C+	B-	613.5	27.82	14.2	0.7	23.7	7.6	7.0	9.0	0.0
Davis Trust Co.	Elkins	WV	B-	B	B-	167.2	14.26	9.0	3.1	18.9	10.6	8.0	11.3	0.0
▼ De Witt Bank & Trust Co.	De Witt	IA	C+	B	B	206.7	17.75	16.6	2.1	9.1	21.5	2.9	9.2	0.0
▲ Dean Co-operative Bank	Franklin	MA	B-	C+	C+	368.7	11.25	8.3	0.9	46.0	12.7	6.6	8.6	15.6
▼ Dearborn Federal Savings Bank	Dearborn	MI	C+	B	B+	268.6	5.31	0.4	0.0	65.9	2.0	10.0	28.6	59.7
Decatur County Bank	Decaturville	TN	C+	C-	D+	164.0	24.20	21.3	3.8	17.5	12.3	5.1	7.1	11.3
Decorah Bank & Trust Co.	Decorah	IA	B+	A-	A-	555.7	13.69	16.1	2.3	8.2	21.3	9.0	10.3	14.9
▲ Dedham Institution for Savings	Dedham	MA	B	B	B	1720.2	12.78	4.7	0.0	36.3	16.9	10.0	12.1	16.3
Dedicated Community Bank	Darlington	SC	C+	C	C	84.5	19.20	20.2	2.2	14.6	12.4	5.6	10.9	11.4
Deerwood Bank	Waite Park	MN	B	B	C+	907.7	25.60	23.0	1.1	12.0	7.5	6.0	8.0	13.7
▲ Defiance State Bank	Defiance	IA	C+	C-	D+	35.4	5.91	6.9	6.9	8.3	6.5	8.5	10.0	14.0
▲ Del Norte Bank, A S&L Assn.	Del Norte	CO	B	B-	C+	117.5	9.56	11.8	1.1	22.5	5.3	6.5	8.6	0.0

Asset Quality Index	Adjusted Non-Performing Loans as a % of Total Loans	as a % of Capital	Net Charge-Offs Avg Loans	Profitability Index	Net Income ($Mil)	Return on Assets (R.O.A.)	Return on Equity (R.O.E.)	Net Interest Spread	Overhead Efficiency Ratio	Liquidity Index	Liquidity Ratio	Hot Money Ratio	Stability Index
6.3	0.86	2.8	-0.01	3.2	0.3	0.46	4.69	3.23	81.2	3.0	50.9	25.0	5.0
10.0	0.03	na	0.00	3.1	0.3	0.50	3.15	2.78	78.5	5.9	41.8	4.1	8.0
7.0	0.13	na	0.00	9.6	1.7	2.41	21.83	3.81	52.4	1.3	21.0	24.7	7.9
6.1	3.02	na	0.05	3.2	0.2	0.58	7.13	4.74	86.8	4.0	41.5	15.2	3.6
5.3	0.28	na	0.02	6.7	2.4	1.53	16.31	3.48	59.3	3.4	17.0	12.0	7.3
10.0	na	0.0	na	9.5	4.5	20.90	21.87	0.00	82.2	4.0	na	100.0	7.0
4.9	0.00	2.7	9.84	10.0	187.6	37.84	88.23	15.05	65.5	2.5	59.1	99.8	8.7
1.3	3.46	17.7	6.92	1.3	-8.1	-1.14	-8.27	12.55	48.6	0.7	19.8	61.2	6.6
8.5	0.28	na	-0.01	2.6	1.1	0.29	3.68	2.89	83.7	3.6	18.4	11.4	4.4
5.5	2.05	8.6	0.02	3.7	1.1	0.83	7.79	3.16	79.1	5.4	45.0	9.0	8.1
8.4	0.08	na	0.00	10.0	20.9	6.65	49.80	3.74	61.4	1.7	6.9	19.6	10.0
6.7	0.60	2.1	0.01	6.4	9.4	1.33	10.02	4.04	59.7	4.5	7.2	4.7	9.5
5.7	0.55	na	0.01	7.8	2.9	1.39	11.57	4.56	57.5	1.0	6.8	25.7	7.9
5.5	1.82	na	0.00	3.1	1.4	0.37	3.46	3.64	87.3	2.0	22.6	19.6	5.3
5.9	2.03	na	0.03	4.8	3.7	1.18	10.08	3.98	64.9	1.8	22.2	19.4	6.9
6.8	0.07	1.7	0.58	5.7	29.6	0.58	13.46	3.15	46.3	0.8	14.9	36.9	7.4
4.6	1.78	12.7	0.84	1.9	5.1	0.13	1.22	3.15	59.8	1.4	17.7	16.6	7.5
6.5	1.40	na	0.00	6.8	2.0	1.40	10.10	3.16	43.7	3.8	38.2	15.3	7.9
5.4	1.46	na	0.16	5.7	4.3	1.27	12.94	3.61	63.6	3.0	27.6	16.0	6.6
7.7	0.31	na	0.02	8.7	3.9	2.17	19.16	3.93	47.5	3.6	47.8	19.1	8.0
8.0	0.30	na	0.12	7.4	0.5	1.65	15.27	4.24	62.2	2.0	29.1	24.7	6.3
6.4	0.49	na	-0.01	4.2	2.2	1.33	13.69	4.08	68.1	0.8	15.1	28.6	4.7
3.8	2.99	9.1	-0.01	9.7	11.1	2.86	13.66	4.64	42.8	0.8	19.3	37.2	10.0
7.2	0.24	1.9	0.05	4.8	5.5	0.59	6.29	2.66	53.2	1.4	10.4	14.9	7.9
7.7	0.07	na	0.05	6.8	4.6	1.65	21.71	4.24	60.4	1.5	14.4	18.0	5.2
8.6	0.48	2.5	0.49	4.5	21.2	0.73	5.28	2.98	55.1	1.7	24.4	27.7	9.7
8.8	0.00	0.0	0.00	1.6	0.0	0.31	2.11	3.49	90.5	3.7	46.6	15.4	5.1
8.7	0.99	na	0.01	5.7	2.6	1.07	6.92	3.72	63.8	1.1	21.0	27.4	8.6
8.5	0.48	1.8	0.00	7.4	2.1	1.56	15.79	3.05	43.8	2.4	47.8	7.6	6.8
8.4	0.04	na	0.02	10.0	5.8	3.12	23.62	4.52	43.3	3.8	22.2	8.6	9.3
4.8	1.14	na	0.07	3.4	2.6	0.59	6.20	3.05	78.0	1.7	25.6	25.6	5.9
1.5	3.29	na	0.26	7.8	0.8	1.25	13.25	4.97	60.6	0.6	8.8	20.3	7.0
5.4	1.28	5.7	0.03	7.9	7.2	1.86	12.80	3.90	49.2	1.1	21.6	16.8	9.1
4.4	0.21	14.9	0.21	3.0	0.4	0.52	4.40	2.87	84.4	1.6	27.9	29.4	5.5
6.2	0.45	5.4	0.49	3.6	83.0	0.75	9.92	2.71	56.2	2.5	8.5	4.3	5.8
5.3	0.71	na	0.02	3.6	0.9	0.56	5.23	3.62	82.9	2.3	37.2	27.3	6.5
10.0	na	na	na	10.0	0.8	10.00	13.42	2.49	81.2	10.0	267.4	0.0	6.7
8.4	0.35	1.7	0.04	6.5	17.7	1.19	13.00	4.00	62.6	4.5	23.7	8.9	8.1
4.2	2.43	12.4	0.12	6.1	25.8	1.20	10.51	3.95	61.4	3.3	13.0	12.4	9.3
8.8	1.83	na	-0.02	3.9	3.1	0.72	5.68	2.61	67.3	5.6	51.5	9.9	7.4
7.5	0.23	na	0.01	7.8	13.0	1.98	22.64	3.54	56.2	4.0	29.8	9.0	8.1
5.5	0.70	na	0.00	6.6	2.3	1.37	12.43	4.10	64.3	2.1	17.7	19.0	8.4
6.8	0.02	na	0.32	5.6	0.9	1.18	10.16	4.24	67.1	1.9	21.4	20.6	7.8
3.0	2.33	na	0.25	8.0	3.9	1.73	15.33	3.97	47.9	1.6	9.3	19.1	8.9
9.1	0.28	na	0.04	2.3	0.4	0.40	3.46	3.50	87.3	2.2	44.4	38.0	6.0
7.9	0.00	na	-0.03	3.8	5.2	0.76	7.09	2.57	64.1	1.7	8.9	17.0	6.4
4.2	2.36	na	0.00	2.0	0.2	0.13	1.44	2.97	94.0	4.7	34.5	9.3	5.0
5.4	0.66	na	0.48	4.3	1.1	0.90	6.64	2.22	70.8	4.5	59.5	17.4	7.5
4.5	1.50	7.6	0.22	7.1	6.7	1.63	17.83	3.76	69.4	4.2	20.6	8.0	5.4
5.2	5.11	na	0.01	3.8	0.9	0.73	8.22	4.02	74.1	4.5	18.4	5.6	5.4
5.4	1.10	na	0.04	3.8	1.1	0.77	7.89	2.98	76.6	3.9	25.0	10.5	6.5
6.4	1.17	5.2	-0.01	4.3	2.2	0.81	9.34	3.56	72.3	4.1	21.0	8.7	4.9
9.3	2.65	na	0.00	2.4	0.4	0.20	0.68	2.69	89.0	4.2	38.3	13.5	7.7
6.1	0.36	na	0.30	3.9	1.0	0.82	11.87	4.92	71.0	2.3	15.3	15.9	3.8
5.8	0.17	2.0	0.20	7.5	6.7	1.69	14.19	3.65	55.2	3.9	19.9	9.8	9.6
9.0	0.23	1.3	-0.01	4.4	10.9	0.90	7.82	3.29	69.9	2.2	21.9	11.3	9.0
5.0	2.22	na	0.02	4.2	0.4	0.80	8.48	4.22	74.9	3.5	18.4	12.0	4.2
5.5	1.74	na	0.03	7.4	8.2	1.34	13.61	4.51	56.6	5.0	20.8	2.6	7.3
8.2	0.00	na	-0.14	4.5	0.3	1.02	10.69	3.62	73.0	3.3	40.0	18.3	4.2
7.4	0.42	na	0.00	6.6	1.1	1.32	14.62	4.40	61.9	1.5	17.9	19.8	5.4

Name	City	State	2020 Rating	2019 Rating	2018 Rating	Total Assets ($Mil)	One Year Asset Growth	Comm-ercial Loans	Cons-umer Loans	Mort-gage Loans	Secur-ities	Capital-ization Index	Lever-age Ratio	Risk-Based Capital Ratio
Delaware National Bank of Delhi	Delhi	NY	B-	B-	C+	336.6	10.43	8.7	1.3	22.7	24.3	8.5	10.0	0.0
Delta Bank	Vidalia	LA	B	B-	B-	368.7	19.40	8.9	2.1	18.6	18.4	5.2	8.4	0.0
▼ Delta National Bank and Trust Co.	New York	NY	D+	C	C	330.2	-19.29	31.1	12.8	0.0	22.2	10.0	15.3	0.0
DeMotte State Bank	Demotte	IN	B+	B+	B	475.4	11.49	13.6	0.8	11.8	35.8	10.0	11.9	19.5
Denali State Bank	Fairbanks	AK	B-	B-	B-	388.9	27.63	26.3	7.5	6.8	20.3	6.8	8.8	14.4
▲ Denison State Bank	Holton	KS	A	A-	B+	404.1	15.76	10.8	1.8	10.8	33.4	10.0	13.7	0.0
Denmark State Bank	Denmark	WI	B	B	B	629.0	20.47	18.0	1.5	7.5	5.5	7.0	9.0	13.6
Denver Savings Bank	Denver	IA	C+	C	C+	186.7	6.37	15.6	1.2	13.2	17.4	6.3	9.6	0.0
Department Stores National Bank	Sioux Falls	SD	B+	B+	B+	707.4	116.89	0.0	5.9	0.0	0.0	10.0	136.	241.1
Depository Trust Co.	New York	NY	U	U	U	3957.9	-3.75	0.0	0.0	0.0	0.0	10.0	16.9	91.7
Desjardins Bank, N.A.	Hallandale Beach	FL	B-	B-	B-	218.0	3.47	2.7	5.1	64.7	6.7	10.0	14.3	30.3
Deutsche Bank National Trust Co.	Los Angeles	CA	U	U	U	327.9	10.46	0.0	0.0	0.0	31.4	10.0	77.9	0.0
▼ Deutsche Bank Trust Co. Americas	New York	NY	A-	A	A-	46336.0	15.06	5.4	0.4	4.7	2.2	10.0	22.3	62.7
Deutsche Bank Trust Co. Delaware	Wilmington	DE	A+	A+	A-	124.2	-60.00	0.0	0.0	0.0	1.5	10.0	54.3	0.0
Deutsche Bank Trust Co., N.A.	New York	NY	U	U	U	162.5	7.69	0.0	0.0	0.0	65.3	10.0	97.3	0.0
▲ Devon Bank	Chicago	IL	C+	C	C-	372.4	28.93	15.6	2.1	15.0	24.7	5.7	7.7	11.6
Dewey Bank	Dewey	IL	C-	C-	D+	27.4	25.49	8.8	2.0	8.5	22.9	5.3	7.3	12.4
▲ DeWitt Savings Bank	Clinton	IL	B-	B-	B	132.0	12.47	0.5	18.2	23.9	32.1	10.0	11.6	25.3
Diamond Bank	Glenwood	AR	B	B	B-	686.1	7.32	8.1	2.2	17.5	20.1	8.5	10.0	16.6
▲ Dickinson County Bank	Enterprise	KS	D-	E+	D+	18.3	6.62	10.4	5.8	31.2	1.4	8.7	10.1	17.2
Dieterich Bank	Effingham	IL	B-	B-	C+	1090.8	53.82	6.4	1.3	7.7	26.0	6.5	8.6	12.2
▼ Dilley State Bank	Dilley	TX	B-	B+	B+	138.9	3.05	1.2	0.5	0.1	44.7	10.0	16.1	51.4
Dime Bank	Norwich	CT	B-	B-	C+	988.5	12.56	9.7	0.1	27.8	17.7	10.0	11.7	20.2
Dime Bank	Honesdale	PA	B	B-	C+	873.1	20.87	18.3	1.3	12.6	16.3	7.8	10.3	13.1
Dime Community Bank	Brooklyn	NY	B-	B-	B+	6612.1	3.03	9.7	0.0	2.8	8.0	8.5	10.0	13.9
Discover Bank	Greenwood	DE	D+	D+	C-	122784.4	12.47	0.1	70.6	1.4	23.6	8.8	10.2	15.2
Dixon Bank	Dixon	KY	B-	B	B	79.9	-3.42	2.3	2.4	4.0	35.3	10.0	26.0	0.0
DMB Community Bank	De Forest	WI	A-	A-	B+	537.2	8.72	0.7	0.4	20.1	12.2	10.0	12.3	19.4
DNB National Bank	Clear Lake	SD	B-	C+	C+	92.5	17.58	8.5	0.8	6.2	55.8	7.8	9.5	25.7
Dogwood State Bank	Raleigh	NC	D+	D+	C	647.2	96.19	39.1	0.3	7.5	9.1	10.0	15.7	21.3
Dollar Bank, Federal Savings Bank	Pittsburgh	PA	B	B	B	9828.2	9.22	10.6	2.8	46.1	12.4	10.0	11.5	20.4
Dolores State Bank	Dolores	CO	A-	A-	B+	301.4	11.66	4.2	4.8	29.7	26.4	10.0	13.6	23.9
Dominion Bank	Dallas	TX	C-	C	C+	342.0	234.56	57.2	0.6	2.7	1.0	10.0	20.8	26.5
Donley County State Bank	Clarendon	TX	C	C+	C	42.5	8.94	4.4	1.3	0.1	29.7	10.0	19.3	56.8
Douglas National Bank	Douglas	GA	A	A	A-	218.3	22.16	16.1	2.2	17.4	3.3	10.0	11.0	15.6
DR Bank	Darien	CT	D-	D-	D-	446.4	13.59	10.4	14.5	23.1	12.3	7.1	9.0	13.2
Drake Bank	Saint Paul	MN	C+	C+	B-	152.7	17.05	46.6	1.3	12.6	2.3	6.0	8.0	0.0
Drummond Community Bank	Chiefland	FL	A-	A-	A-	798.4	26.16	14.0	1.9	13.1	34.3	9.5	10.7	0.0
DSRM National Bank	Albuquerque	NM	U	U	U	3.9	0.62	0.0	0.0	0.0	53.4	10.0	86.0	0.0
Du Quoin State Bank	Du Quoin	IL	B+	B+	B+	119.8	10.53	5.3	1.6	14.0	70.2	6.9	8.9	0.0
Dubuque Bank and Trust Co.	Dubuque	IA	B+	B+	B+	1838.3	18.83	16.1	0.8	4.0	37.9	6.8	8.8	14.4
▼ Dundee Bank	Omaha	NE	B-	B-	C-	392.7	33.39	19.9	0.2	21.1	7.9	4.1	8.9	0.0
▼ Durand State Bank	Durand	IL	B-	B	B-	118.5	11.90	4.0	1.9	9.7	25.0	9.7	10.8	19.0
Durden Banking Co., Inc.	Twin City	GA	A	A	A-	202.0	12.88	9.3	5.1	26.4	20.9	10.0	15.2	27.6
Dysart State Bank	Dysart	IA	D+	D-	E	14.9	18.39	1.9	0.5	18.6	4.6	6.9	8.9	15.5
E*TRADE Bank	Arlington	VA	B	B	B	51565.8	12.35	0.0	0.9	1.5	94.7	5.2	7.2	36.3
E*TRADE Savings Bank	Arlington	VA	B	B	B	4809.5	25.85	0.0	9.6	0.0	58.6	10.0	33.5	146.2
Eagle Bank	Everett	MA	C	B-	C	501.4	9.06	10.5	0.0	28.9	14.4	9.6	12.0	0.0
Eagle Bank	Glenwood	MN	A	A	A	187.6	22.88	13.6	3.4	10.8	20.4	10.0	12.2	22.7
Eagle Bank	Polson	MT	B+	B+	C+	92.3	33.21	15.7	2.3	10.8	23.0	7.9	9.6	0.0
▲ Eagle Bank and Trust Co.	Little Rock	AR	A-	B	B-	448.3	6.55	3.3	0.4	31.9	32.8	10.0	13.7	0.0
Eagle Community Bank	Maple Grove	MN	D+	D	E	34.5	33.97	33.9	1.1	16.0	0.3	7.2	9.2	0.0
▲ Eagle Savings Bank	Cincinnati	OH	B+	B-	B	156.7	10.20	17.9	0.0	49.6	0.0	10.0	15.3	18.2
EagleBank	Bethesda	MD	A-	A	A	10088.9	12.17	16.4	0.0	3.2	9.5	10.0	12.5	16.3
Eaglemark Savings Bank	Carson City	NV	A-	A-	A-	80.5	50.75	0.0	46.2	0.0	0.0	10.0	15.9	24.4
Earlham Savings Bank	West Des Moines	IA	C	C	C+	339.0	12.65	12.9	1.5	10.2	40.6	6.1	8.1	18.1
East Boston Savings Bank	East Boston	MA	B	B	B-	6566.5	3.37	3.0	0.2	9.4	0.2	5.8	11.0	0.0
East Cambridge Savings Bank	Cambridge	MA	C+	C+	C+	1199.5	5.51	4.6	0.9	41.0	10.3	9.5	10.7	17.6
East West Bank	Pasadena	CA	A-	A-	A-	50396.2	16.54	20.5	0.0	16.7	9.0	7.4	9.3	13.4
East Wisconsin Savings Bank	Kaukauna	WI	D+	D+	D+	262.2	8.56	0.4	18.9	49.2	13.9	6.7	8.7	15.9

Asset Quality Index	Adjusted Non-Performing Loans as a % of Total Loans	Adjusted Non-Performing Loans as a % of Capital	Net Charge-Offs Avg Loans	Profitability Index	Net Income ($Mil)	Return on Assets (R.O.A.)	Return on Equity (R.O.E.)	Net Interest Spread	Overhead Efficiency Ratio	Liquidity Index	Liquidity Ratio	Hot Money Ratio	Stability Index
7.1	0.49	na	0.11	3.7	1.7	0.72	6.89	2.91	68.6	3.0	24.4	15.0	5.3
6.0	0.57	na	0.04	7.7	5.0	1.90	22.11	4.28	60.4	1.3	14.6	27.8	6.6
8.3	0.00	0.0	0.00	0.6	-1.6	-0.60	-3.97	1.69	119.1	2.4	39.9	12.3	7.3
5.7	2.05	na	0.07	4.9	3.6	1.03	8.54	3.78	67.6	5.3	40.4	7.9	6.8
4.8	0.77	4.9	0.20	4.6	2.3	0.88	9.30	4.41	70.8	4.8	21.2	4.1	5.1
8.5	0.34	na	-0.20	8.0	5.4	1.86	12.95	3.42	51.0	2.7	17.2	15.6	9.4
8.3	0.13	0.8	0.00	4.0	3.2	0.72	7.66	3.31	73.3	3.7	21.6	10.5	6.1
8.2	0.00	na	0.00	4.5	1.4	1.00	9.34	3.39	60.1	1.0	23.8	35.5	5.6
8.7	0.93	0.2	2.66	4.9	2.2	0.87	2.25	2.85	51.5	5.0	249.1	99.9	7.2
10.0	na	0.0	na	9.1	46.6	1.61	8.36	0.44	80.7	4.0	120.2	0.0	7.0
8.4	0.89	na	0.00	2.8	0.5	0.29	2.01	3.98	91.0	4.8	19.5	3.8	7.6
10.0	na	0.0	na	10.0	14.5	6.53	8.19	1.70	86.8	4.0	290.9	0.0	7.0
9.5	0.57	0.7	0.03	4.5	141.0	0.46	1.95	1.03	76.0	8.3	84.3	0.4	10.0
10.0	0.00	0.0	-13.36	9.4	3.5	1.71	1.78	0.56	63.4	4.0	na	100.0	7.0
10.0	na	0.0	na	10.0	5.2	4.88	5.22	1.76	87.5	4.0	na	0.0	7.0
4.4	1.89	na	0.08	4.0	2.2	0.86	10.44	3.41	77.6	3.6	25.7	12.5	4.0
4.3	1.00	na	-0.05	2.0	0.1	0.35	2.97	3.78	90.5	4.8	32.9	8.4	4.0
5.7	1.31	na	0.49	3.5	0.6	0.62	5.08	3.04	70.9	3.5	48.3	17.9	6.5
5.7	1.48	na	0.11	5.0	6.0	1.20	11.50	3.63	62.8	1.4	14.0	25.3	7.9
3.4	3.79	15.7	-0.06	1.7	0.0	-0.01	-0.09	3.66	94.3	2.1	36.9	23.9	4.8
5.1	1.36	6.2	0.01	4.0	5.1	0.79	8.31	2.91	65.2	5.0	27.5	8.3	6.7
10.0	0.26	na	-0.04	2.5	0.3	0.25	1.52	1.43	83.7	7.3	100.1	8.2	8.1
7.0	1.61	na	-0.04	3.4	4.8	0.68	6.00	2.79	72.5	3.0	26.0	14.9	6.6
4.3	2.45	na	0.12	5.2	6.4	1.07	9.76	3.83	62.1	2.9	9.5	13.3	7.3
6.9	0.22	2.0	0.00	4.0	40.8	0.84	8.02	2.93	53.6	1.5	10.7	17.3	8.2
1.7	2.71	11.1	3.23	5.8	313.4	0.37	4.42	8.42	36.0	1.5	24.1	12.1	10.0
7.6	5.37	na	-0.51	2.7	0.3	0.40	1.57	2.12	84.9	4.2	90.0	23.9	7.1
7.5	0.00	na	0.00	6.4	5.1	1.28	10.43	2.88	49.5	0.8	17.5	27.5	8.4
9.5	0.00	na	0.00	4.6	0.9	1.43	13.43	2.96	73.3	4.3	58.5	16.4	5.2
7.8	0.06	na	0.00	0.6	-0.2	-0.06	-0.36	3.11	97.8	2.2	16.4	11.3	6.5
7.3	0.96	5.2	0.13	3.5	43.7	0.61	5.37	2.64	72.5	3.4	17.3	7.9	9.0
6.5	0.98	na	0.08	7.0	2.6	1.24	8.41	3.98	55.3	5.0	33.7	7.0	8.8
7.9	0.03	na	0.00	0.2	-1.1	-0.64	-3.32	2.93	116.7	1.9	22.1	20.4	5.5
3.7	0.36	na	0.02	1.6	0.0	0.05	0.25	2.00	98.2	3.6	73.3	27.1	7.0
6.2	1.47	na	0.00	10.0	4.1	2.59	23.36	4.57	48.7	2.7	23.0	12.8	8.7
7.0	0.00	na	0.20	0.0	-1.1	-0.36	-3.87	2.67	110.0	1.4	31.9	40.4	5.7
8.0	0.14	na	-0.04	3.2	0.6	0.57	6.94	4.63	69.6	1.6	11.6	21.4	4.7
7.1	0.56	2.4	0.13	8.3	9.0	1.66	13.61	4.82	59.9	4.9	28.8	6.0	8.3
10.0	na	na	na	7.4	0.0	1.26	1.48	1.43	89.1	4.0	na	100.0	5.2
7.8	1.23	1.6	-0.02	4.9	1.0	1.19	8.80	3.73	71.5	3.8	69.4	25.9	7.7
4.9	3.22	11.9	0.07	6.6	15.9	1.23	13.32	3.08	55.9	6.5	36.5	2.4	7.9
5.2	0.39	na	0.00	7.9	5.3	2.06	22.42	3.75	57.8	0.7	4.9	27.8	5.3
5.7	2.56	5.4	-0.06	3.7	0.6	0.69	6.24	3.30	73.8	2.2	33.6	26.1	6.0
8.3	0.37	2.1	0.00	8.8	2.8	1.93	12.13	4.81	60.2	3.1	23.1	14.4	9.3
9.1	0.00	na	0.02	2.1	0.0	0.18	1.90	3.12	93.8	6.2	43.3	0.0	2.8
7.1	24.26	9.0	-1.28	4.3	304.2	0.83	11.08	2.38	58.1	3.6	85.2	0.0	6.7
7.5	0.11	0.0	0.00	2.6	22.9	0.69	1.74	2.34	90.0	4.1	130.3	0.0	8.4
8.9	0.12	na	0.00	3.4	2.2	0.61	5.32	3.45	75.8	1.8	28.2	20.2	6.9
8.5	0.01	0.1	0.00	7.1	2.2	1.73	12.95	3.45	56.6	5.6	32.2	2.8	8.9
8.4	0.05	na	-0.01	9.3	1.1	1.83	16.51	5.01	51.6	1.4	22.4	10.6	6.2
6.8	1.46	na	0.03	7.0	5.1	1.64	11.35	4.10	80.3	4.1	26.2	10.1	7.6
8.3	0.00	0.0	0.00	6.0	0.5	1.95	25.22	5.83	63.2	1.6	10.8	19.6	1.7
8.3	0.84	na	0.08	5.3	1.4	1.24	8.24	3.24	68.9	2.7	5.7	14.7	7.5
5.6	0.74	3.9	0.24	8.1	103.4	1.37	10.28	3.41	37.5	1.0	17.2	5.6	10.0
6.1	0.00	0.0	0.00	10.0	3.2	7.55	41.50	12.78	73.5	2.2	58.5	1.5	9.3
8.1	0.00	na	-0.05	2.3	0.8	0.33	3.88	2.98	85.9	6.1	51.3	6.8	4.2
7.2	0.09	0.5	0.00	5.1	47.2	0.98	9.00	3.12	47.0	1.7	12.5	14.3	8.7
9.1	0.14	1.0	0.00	3.2	4.4	0.50	5.01	3.07	75.6	2.0	21.1	21.8	7.6
6.8	0.93	5.2	0.16	6.2	412.2	1.15	11.39	3.06	44.9	2.0	22.6	17.9	10.0
6.7	0.39	na	0.04	1.6	0.4	0.19	2.08	2.54	94.8	2.1	24.8	19.3	4.9

Name	City	State	Rating	2019 Rating	2018 Rating	Total Assets ($Mil)	One Year Asset Growth	Asset Mix (As a % of Total Assets) Commercial Loans	Consumer Loans	Mortgage Loans	Securities	Capitalization Index	Leverage Ratio	Risk-Based Capital Ratio
Eastbank, N.A.	New York	NY	C+	B-	B	158.6	-10.82	0.8	0.0	11.7	13.6	10.0	20.9	30.0
▼ Eastern Bank	Boston	MA	B	B+	B	15453.7	34.30	17.3	1.8	10.9	14.3	8.1	9.7	14.1
Eastern Colorado Bank	Cheyenne Wells	CO	A-	A-	B+	519.7	20.34	8.6	0.3	8.1	17.3	10.0	12.0	17.5
Eastern Connecticut Savings Bank	Norwich	CT	D	D+	D	215.5	18.62	11.5	2.2	40.4	0.1	5.3	7.3	12.0
Eastern International Bank	Los Angeles	CA	C+	B	B	146.6	19.26	0.0	0.0	0.1	8.6	10.0	14.1	0.0
Eastern Michigan Bank	Croswell	MI	B	B	B-	481.4	20.31	18.1	2.8	6.3	17.7	9.4	10.6	20.4
Eastern National Bank	Miami	FL	D+	D+	C-	356.1	-0.30	12.5	0.4	21.9	1.0	5.5	7.5	11.4
Eastern Savings Bank, FSB	Hunt Valley	MD	B	B	B-	328.7	4.13	4.1	0.0	45.2	0.0	10.0	24.9	37.9
Easthampton Savings Bank	Easthampton	MA	B-	B-	B-	1640.6	15.45	10.9	0.6	27.9	9.4	6.5	8.5	14.2
Eaton Community Bank	Charlotte	MI	C+	B-	C+	407.7	9.75	3.9	1.4	32.2	32.1	10.0	14.2	0.0
▲ Eclipse Bank, Inc.	Louisville	KY	B-	C+	C+	211.6	32.56	5.7	1.5	19.2	8.8	8.3	10.3	13.5
Edgewater Bank	Saint Joseph	MI	C+	C+	C-	249.5	34.76	19.6	0.6	19.6	2.5	6.7	8.7	13.7
Edison National Bank	Fort Myers	FL	B-	B-	B-	373.5	23.68	10.7	1.5	19.4	6.1	6.0	8.1	22.7
Edmonton State Bank	Edmonton	KY	A	A-	B+	629.1	14.92	8.5	7.4	16.0	8.0	10.0	13.7	0.0
Edward Jones Trust Co.	Saint Louis	MO	U	U	U	106.5	11.90	0.0	0.0	0.0	0.1	10.0	94.1	369.6
EH National Bank	Beverly Hills	CA	C	C	C-	281.8	18.91	10.4	0.0	0.8	4.9	10.0	11.4	16.6
▼ El Dorado Savings Bank, F.S.B.	Placerville	CA	C+	B	B-	2448.4	13.29	0.0	0.0	22.6	58.9	9.1	10.4	35.9
▲ Elberfeld State Bank	Elberfeld	IN	B	B	B	88.5	10.34	11.4	0.6	8.4	19.0	10.0	11.2	0.0
Elberton Federal S&L Assn.	Elberton	GA	D+	C-	D+	26.5	9.99	0.0	0.9	72.3	13.0	10.0	19.1	0.0
Elderton State Bank	Elderton	PA	B	B+	B	315.5	7.06	14.1	0.9	12.1	5.8	10.0	11.4	0.0
Elgin State Bank	Elgin	IA	D-	D-	D-	24.9	8.95	5.5	2.7	16.7	19.4	5.5	7.5	16.4
Elizabethton Federal Savings Bank	Elizabethton	TN	A	A	A-	307.7	3.65	0.0	0.6	34.6	35.2	10.0	40.2	106.7
Elk State Bank	Clyde	KS	C+	C+	C+	98.2	1.14	6.1	1.4	10.6	32.6	9.5	10.6	19.4
Elkhorn Valley Bank & Trust	Norfolk	NE	B	B	B	869.2	9.78	14.6	2.8	5.7	20.9	10.0	12.6	17.2
▼ Elkton Bank & Trust Co.	Elkton	KY	B+	A-	A-	151.6	8.58	4.4	3.7	15.1	46.7	10.0	12.6	26.1
Elmira Savings Bank	Elmira	NY	C+	C+	C+	674.3	9.48	7.8	5.2	46.0	2.1	5.8	7.8	13.2
▲ Elysian Bank	Elysian	MN	A-	B+	B-	54.0	7.92	8.4	6.4	18.2	4.3	10.0	11.4	17.2
Embassy Bank for the Lehigh Valley	Bethlehem	PA	B	B	B	1365.2	17.51	8.3	0.1	47.1	8.9	6.1	8.1	13.0
Embassy National Bank	Lawrenceville	GA	A	A	A	109.3	4.76	9.1	0.0	2.1	0.0	10.0	17.2	26.4
▲ Emerald Bank	Burden	KS	C-	D+	C-	19.1	6.14	6.5	7.2	32.7	14.4	9.0	10.3	19.5
Emigrant Bank	New York	NY	B-	B-	B-	6380.6	12.69	33.0	0.6	12.9	5.9	10.0	18.9	21.0
Emigrant Mercantile Bank	New York	NY	U	U	U	3.4	-0.64	0.0	0.0	0.0	0.0	10.0	85.3	424.6
Empire State Bank	Newburgh	NY	C-	C	D+	495.4	17.44	15.3	0.0	34.4	1.4	7.1	9.1	15.5
▼ Emprise Bank	Wichita	KS	B	B+	B+	2077.4	16.78	14.0	2.3	17.0	22.2	5.3	7.3	12.1
Encore Bank	Little Rock	AR	C-	D+	C-	681.4	175.71	8.7	0.3	14.6	17.1	5.4	8.3	11.3
Endeavor Bank	San Diego	CA	D-	D	D	361.0	211.32	59.5	0.4	3.9	0.0	10.0	11.5	18.1
EnerBank USA	Salt Lake City	UT	B+	B+	A-	3166.8	18.10	0.0	95.5	0.0	1.0	3.5	10.4	0.0
Englewood Bank & Trust	Englewood	FL	A-	A-	A-	390.4	28.62	3.7	0.2	16.9	19.6	6.9	8.9	0.0
Ennis State Bank	Ennis	TX	B+	B+	B-	297.0	18.76	19.9	0.5	8.5	17.4	6.7	8.9	0.0
Enterprise Bank	Omaha	NE	B-	B-	C+	393.5	19.41	18.2	0.8	4.2	1.9	6.6	8.6	12.2
Enterprise Bank	Allison Park	PA	D-	D-	D	421.7	35.67	19.7	0.0	2.7	0.0	5.1	8.3	11.1
Enterprise Bank & Trust	Clayton	MO	B+	B+	B+	8344.8	14.09	37.3	0.3	3.3	16.1	7.8	9.5	13.3
Enterprise Bank and Trust Co.	Lowell	MA	B	B	B-	4060.6	29.37	21.5	0.2	10.6	12.3	7.2	9.1	14.2
Enterprise Bank of South Carolina	Ehrhardt	SC	C-	C-	D	385.4	15.33	10.2	3.2	15.6	28.2	5.9	7.9	16.1
▲ Envision Bank	Stoughton	MA	C	C	D	725.2	13.00	2.6	1.6	48.0	7.7	10.0	12.2	15.6
Ephrata National Bank	Ephrata	PA	B-	B	B-	1316.3	14.92	8.9	0.4	21.1	27.4	7.1	9.1	13.3
Equitable Bank	Grand Island	NE	C+	C+	C	402.2	19.46	18.3	1.1	17.4	4.2	5.3	8.7	11.2
Equitable Bank, S.S.B.	Wauwatosa	WI	D+	D	E	302.6	-4.45	1.1	0.1	44.6	6.5	8.6	10.0	0.0
Equitable S&L Assn.	Sterling	CO	B	B	B	161.6	-1.65	0.0	0.7	84.8	2.6	10.0	16.8	33.1
Equitable S&L Co.	Cadiz	OH	D	D+	D	13.7	3.07	0.0	0.3	51.0	1.0	10.0	18.7	0.0
▼ Equity Bank	Andover	KS	C	C+	B-	3862.2	-5.17	22.0	1.6	13.4	20.7	7.5	9.3	15.4
Ergo Bank	Markesan	WI	B-	B-	C	110.8	21.67	16.0	0.7	8.3	13.6	8.4	10.8	0.0
▲ ESB Bank	Caledonia	MN	B+	C+	C	129.8	14.53	13.0	3.5	9.4	8.0	6.0	9.4	0.0
ESB Financial	Emporia	KS	C	C+	B-	310.2	28.75	12.6	1.4	16.2	11.5	6.6	8.6	12.9
▼ Escambia County Bank	Flomaton	AL	C	C+	B-	79.9	7.37	8.5	5.0	14.4	55.1	10.0	14.4	0.0
Esquire Bank, N.A.	Jericho	NY	A	A	A-	869.5	14.92	36.6	5.0	5.6	12.7	10.0	12.2	16.9
ESSA Bank & Trust	Stroudsburg	PA	C+	C+	C+	1892.5	5.37	7.1	2.2	35.6	11.2	7.1	9.1	13.7
Essex Bank	Richmond	VA	B+	B+	B	1622.0	14.02	15.4	0.7	9.3	15.9	8.7	10.2	13.9
Essex Savings Bank	Essex	CT	C+	B-	B-	469.5	15.50	6.2	0.4	38.8	0.2	7.3	9.2	0.0
ETHIC	Boston	MA	D-	D	D-	270.1	24.83	0.9	13.1	36.9	0.0	7.6	9.4	15.4

Asset Quality Index	Adjusted Non-Performing Loans as a % of Total Loans	as a % of Capital	Net Charge-Offs Avg Loans	Profitability Index	Net Income ($Mil)	Return on Assets (R.O.A.)	Return on Equity (R.O.E.)	Net Interest Spread	Overhead Efficiency Ratio	Liquidity Index	Liquidity Ratio	Hot Money Ratio	Stability Index
7.8	0.00	0.0	0.00	1.2	-0.2	-0.14	-0.70	2.97	104.9	1.9	39.0	40.5	7.5
6.1	0.80	3.2	0.07	4.1	67.8	0.69	5.43	3.32	71.5	6.5	32.3	0.9	9.6
8.4	0.11	na	-0.04	7.0	6.2	1.72	14.92	4.21	55.4	1.7	19.3	22.1	9.4
1.8	3.39	na	0.03	1.7	0.3	0.19	2.49	3.29	93.0	1.6	9.0	21.6	3.1
7.5	0.00	na	0.00	2.1	0.2	0.22	1.50	2.97	88.6	1.7	36.8	46.0	7.5
7.2	0.65	1.3	0.00	4.9	3.2	1.03	10.87	3.01	61.7	6.5	45.0	1.6	4.9
1.6	7.11	42.1	0.40	0.0	-3.2	-1.26	-13.03	3.03	150.9	1.0	27.0	46.0	3.6
4.7	8.37	na	0.03	4.3	1.5	0.63	2.50	5.51	85.2	2.6	26.2	17.4	8.2
8.0	0.58	na	-0.01	3.9	8.5	0.74	8.46	2.77	62.4	1.9	23.5	26.1	6.4
8.7	1.19	na	-0.03	3.3	1.9	0.65	4.32	3.15	76.3	4.9	45.4	11.5	7.8
4.3	1.27	na	-0.02	3.9	1.1	0.77	7.03	3.37	71.7	0.7	14.7	35.2	6.7
4.3	1.02	11.1	-0.01	4.0	1.4	0.87	9.82	3.42	71.2	4.5	23.9	6.5	4.7
9.5	0.00	0.0	-0.08	3.8	2.3	0.84	10.50	2.97	72.9	6.6	50.6	2.7	4.7
7.7	0.49	na	-0.01	8.8	9.1	2.07	14.76	3.74	54.9	3.7	28.7	12.5	10.0
10.0	na	na	na	9.5	7.0	9.19	9.84	1.59	77.4	4.0	na	0.0	6.7
2.6	3.39	na	-0.01	1.0	-0.3	-0.15	-1.02	3.32	103.7	1.4	17.8	27.0	6.0
9.9	0.91	1.6	-0.03	3.2	8.8	0.51	4.63	2.00	70.5	6.6	80.4	11.0	8.2
6.9	4.20	na	0.00	4.6	0.6	0.93	7.93	3.51	70.3	4.8	44.3	11.7	6.3
9.3	0.84	na	0.00	0.9	0.0	-0.01	-0.05	3.24	102.5	1.7	27.6	27.4	6.7
4.0	4.17	na	0.21	6.5	2.8	1.24	10.84	3.51	50.3	2.2	13.4	18.0	7.5
8.8	0.01	na	0.00	1.4	0.0	0.03	0.44	3.11	102.7	5.4	41.5	4.7	1.5
10.0	0.00	na	0.00	5.7	2.3	1.04	2.56	2.64	47.9	4.5	87.5	22.2	8.7
7.0	2.46	na	-0.03	3.7	0.6	0.85	7.90	3.48	74.0	1.8	17.6	16.4	5.4
8.2	0.70	na	0.20	4.8	6.8	1.10	8.52	3.14	51.2	4.5	31.2	9.8	8.0
9.0	0.34	na	0.37	4.7	1.1	0.99	7.52	3.49	66.4	3.7	50.5	19.2	7.4
4.2	1.04	na	0.06	3.4	2.9	0.60	6.47	2.99	73.0	1.8	16.0	20.7	6.2
6.4	1.24	na	-0.19	9.3	1.0	2.41	21.53	4.39	53.4	6.1	36.1	0.7	7.7
9.1	0.23	1.3	0.00	4.6	9.5	0.99	12.16	3.05	55.0	3.2	9.2	12.9	7.2
6.6	0.84	na	0.00	6.2	0.6	0.72	4.40	3.87	81.1	1.4	24.5	29.4	10.0
4.3	3.21	na	0.10	3.8	0.1	0.70	6.78	4.05	88.0	3.8	38.4	13.2	3.7
3.1	5.15	18.9	0.05	4.6	28.4	0.65	3.35	3.89	69.7	1.4	18.8	9.3	10.0
10.0	na	0.0	na	0.1	0.0	-0.35	-0.41	1.13	141.4	4.0	na	0.0	6.4
5.6	0.69	na	0.18	2.4	1.2	0.35	4.10	3.12	69.0	1.7	11.8	19.2	4.5
5.5	1.28	na	0.05	5.0	15.1	1.03	11.92	3.46	63.4	4.6	24.2	6.0	9.1
8.6	0.10	na	0.05	2.6	3.2	0.84	7.98	2.82	72.7	1.4	33.9	9.8	4.0
8.0	0.00	na	0.00	0.7	0.3	0.13	1.48	2.89	79.9	4.3	17.6	7.1	2.2
5.2	0.02	2.0	1.17	9.4	33.8	1.61	17.77	6.81	40.2	0.2	5.8	9.7	9.0
7.9	0.45	1.4	-0.13	7.7	4.4	1.66	17.70	3.39	60.2	6.9	51.4	1.2	8.3
7.3	0.74	na	0.00	7.8	4.0	1.90	19.73	4.44	56.3	4.5	23.9	6.8	7.4
7.2	0.00	na	-0.01	4.4	2.4	0.83	9.29	2.83	58.3	0.7	15.0	40.0	5.5
0.4	6.09	na	0.10	4.1	1.9	0.69	8.78	3.55	71.8	0.8	18.0	3.3	3.7
6.1	0.63	3.3	0.06	5.6	53.5	0.90	7.27	3.68	47.2	3.4	17.4	5.4	9.9
6.0	1.02	6.1	0.01	4.8	23.1	0.83	9.20	3.68	63.3	4.2	8.4	4.6	8.2
2.3	4.06	na	-0.01	4.7	2.4	0.88	10.11	3.57	77.1	4.8	33.5	8.3	3.5
4.9	1.94	na	0.01	6.6	14.7	2.88	25.05	2.85	62.2	1.7	16.4	14.9	6.9
8.7	0.75	na	0.00	4.4	9.1	0.98	10.25	3.27	67.6	5.7	27.3	3.4	8.2
5.2	0.81	na	0.02	4.1	2.2	0.76	8.28	3.03	75.7	2.1	10.9	17.9	5.7
6.6	0.59	na	0.03	3.6	2.0	0.91	11.28	3.55	82.6	3.1	11.8	13.4	1.6
9.8	0.01	na	0.00	4.2	1.0	0.83	5.06	3.22	73.1	2.0	15.1	19.2	7.9
10.0	0.59	na	0.00	0.0	-0.1	-0.97	-5.08	2.43	141.3	3.8	44.6	14.6	6.7
4.1	1.93	11.2	0.07	1.5	-83.9	-2.79	-22.70	3.65	152.5	3.2	4.3	12.1	7.6
5.9	4.42	na	0.02	3.8	0.5	0.69	5.75	4.11	73.9	2.8	26.7	8.3	6.4
8.1	0.00	na	0.00	8.5	2.0	2.21	22.06	3.79	47.3	2.8	14.0	14.9	7.2
2.8	4.92	na	0.11	4.2	2.0	0.97	10.23	3.24	71.9	4.6	29.9	8.0	5.0
6.3	2.81	na	0.24	1.1	-0.1	-0.12	-0.76	3.13	103.0	3.5	68.9	26.9	7.5
6.0	0.28	na	0.03	9.3	9.9	1.59	12.80	4.48	51.6	5.7	28.2	0.4	8.5
5.4	1.85	na	0.02	3.6	11.0	0.76	7.79	2.65	69.2	1.6	9.3	7.9	7.5
7.5	0.39	2.9	0.03	4.7	10.5	0.91	8.62	3.50	59.7	1.4	18.9	26.2	8.6
1.7	3.17	na	0.00	2.1	0.4	0.12	1.06	2.95	95.0	4.3	26.6	8.6	6.7
6.2	0.62	na	0.18	0.0	-6.0	-3.12	-28.00	3.54	171.2	0.7	16.8	56.8	3.3

Name	City	State	Rating	2019 Rating	2018 Rating	Total Assets ($Mil)	One Year Asset Growth	Comm-ercial Loans	Cons-umer Loans	Mort-gage Loans	Secur-ities	Capital-ization Index	Lever-age Ratio	Risk-Based Capital Ratio
								Asset Mix (As a % of Total Assets)						
Eureka Homestead	Metairie	LA	C	C	C	104.6	-3.75	0.0	0.2	64.6	6.0	10.0	18.3	43.8
Eureka Savings Bank	La Salle	IL	C+	C+	C+	360.3	14.02	2.0	0.5	35.8	46.6	10.0	21.7	55.7
EvaBank	Cullman	AL	B	B-	B-	431.8	13.57	1.9	4.2	27.7	20.2	10.0	23.4	0.0
Evangeline Bank and Trust Co.	Ville Platte	LA	B+	B+	B	688.7	16.54	10.9	3.3	23.8	14.4	10.0	17.0	0.0
Evans Bank, N.A.	Hamburg	NY	B-	B-	C+	2040.3	41.70	20.8	0.0	19.1	7.9	6.6	8.6	13.6
Evercore Trust Co., N.A.	New York	NY	U	U	U	12.9	-44.07	0.0	0.0	0.0	78.1	10.0	98.8	0.0
Everence Trust Co.	Goshen	IN	U	U	U	9.7	8.45	0.0	0.0	0.0	56.0	10.0	107.	280.2
Everett Co-operative Bank	Everett	MA	B+	B+	B+	562.1	9.40	1.9	0.0	40.1	10.5	10.0	13.1	18.8
Evergreen Bank Group	Oak Brook	IL	B+	B+	B	1261.2	17.75	4.2	51.9	2.9	7.0	8.3	10.6	13.6
Evergreen Federal Bank	Grants Pass	OR	B	B	B	553.7	17.83	2.3	0.2	23.2	6.0	10.0	11.5	0.0
Evergreen National Bank	Evergreen	CO	C	C+	C+	135.3	14.25	15.1	0.4	15.0	15.8	6.6	8.6	0.0
EverTrust Bank	Pasadena	CA	B+	B+	A-	983.9	5.41	10.8	0.0	5.6	4.5	10.0	17.0	0.0
Evolve Bank & Trust	Memphis	TN	B-	B-	C+	646.9	24.70	23.7	0.5	31.1	2.6	7.3	9.2	13.5
Exchange Bank	Santa Rosa	CA	A	A	A-	3038.5	16.51	11.8	1.2	11.2	26.6	7.9	9.6	15.1
Exchange Bank	Milledgeville	GA	A-	A-	A-	298.1	16.28	3.9	0.9	17.4	35.1	10.0	12.6	21.3
Exchange Bank	Kearney	NE	B+	B+	B+	1129.1	20.89	8.8	0.6	11.1	25.2	6.0	9.8	0.0
Exchange Bank	Skiatook	OK	A-	A-	B+	127.9	22.19	19.8	1.2	10.0	26.4	9.1	10.4	0.0
Exchange Bank & Trust	Atchison	KS	A-	A-	B+	474.9	13.41	9.6	13.9	16.1	24.8	9.2	10.4	0.0
Exchange Bank and Trust Co.	Natchitoches	LA	A-	A-	A-	160.9	6.58	3.7	1.3	21.0	53.9	8.2	9.8	23.8
Exchange Bank and Trust Co.	Perry	OK	B-	B-	A-	326.6	11.09	8.9	4.3	19.0	31.9	8.7	10.1	17.3
Exchange Bank of Alabama	Altoona	AL	B+	B+	A-	329.4	14.25	5.7	2.5	14.5	20.6	10.0	13.3	23.7
Exchange Bank of Missouri	Fayette	MO	A-	B+	B	251.8	17.69	7.7	1.1	8.9	7.3	8.9	10.3	14.6
Exchange Bank of Northeast Missouri	Kahoka	MO	B-	C+	C	191.6	24.79	5.8	1.3	10.2	18.0	6.2	8.2	12.9
Exchange State Bank	Adair	IA	B+	B	B	38.4	10.01	6.6	1.9	6.6	19.4	10.0	13.1	23.9
Exchange State Bank	Collins	IA	B	B	B	118.6	5.66	13.8	0.9	13.0	6.6	7.6	9.8	0.0
Exchange State Bank	Springville	IA	B	B	B-	53.5	21.79	5.3	1.1	14.1	26.5	6.1	8.8	0.0
Exchange State Bank	Lanark	IL	B+	B	B	101.8	11.29	8.8	1.3	8.1	49.6	10.0	12.0	0.0
Exchange State Bank	Carsonville	MI	A-	A-	B+	191.7	14.68	6.5	2.1	10.3	31.8	10.0	11.4	0.0
Exchange State Bank of St. Paul, Kansas	Saint Paul	KS	B-	B-	B-	80.8	9.90	9.8	2.4	12.8	16.3	8.6	10.0	0.0
▼ Extraco Banks, N.A.	Temple	TX	C+	B	B-	1787.2	15.27	4.8	6.1	17.5	20.5	6.8	8.8	17.0
F & C Bank	Holden	MO	B-	C+	B	257.9	12.32	6.8	2.1	22.0	5.5	8.5	10.3	0.0
F & M Bank and Trust Co.	Manchester	GA	E-	E-	E-	81.5	19.90	28.0	2.3	10.5	0.9	1.1	4.5	8.1
F & M Bank Minnesota	Clarkfield	MN	B+	B	B-	131.9	3.54	4.1	0.3	1.6	24.6	6.2	8.6	11.9
F & M Community Bank, N.A.	Preston	MN	B	B	B	161.7	15.40	13.6	1.3	12.0	14.7	7.2	10.4	0.0
F&M Bank	Washington	GA	B+	B+	B+	305.6	14.35	8.2	2.3	16.7	31.3	10.0	15.9	0.0
F&M Bank	Falls City	NE	B+	B+	B+	111.4	0.96	3.8	2.2	10.2	31.4	8.3	9.8	0.0
F&M Bank	West Point	NE	B+	B+	B	330.2	19.25	9.5	1.0	8.4	7.8	6.7	9.7	0.0
F&M Bank	Edmond	OK	A-	A-	B+	530.1	10.49	10.5	1.9	14.8	26.3	8.6	10.1	0.0
▲ F&M Bank	Clarksville	TN	B-	C+	B-	1271.7	8.24	8.0	1.2	21.9	9.4	6.0	9.0	11.8
F&M Bank and Trust Co.	Hannibal	MO	B	B-	C+	142.9	8.17	9.4	2.5	31.5	14.1	7.9	9.6	0.0
Fahey Banking Co.	Marion	OH	B-	B+	B+	296.0	1.53	6.4	0.4	5.7	14.2	10.0	16.8	0.0
Fairfax State Savings Bank	Fairfax	IA	B-	B	B	192.5	14.33	9.7	2.0	10.8	28.3	10.0	11.4	0.0
Fairfield County Bank	Ridgefield	CT	B-	B	B	1732.0	12.83	18.4	0.1	18.2	14.0	9.7	12.6	0.0
Fairfield Federal S&L Assn. of Lancaster	Lancaster	OH	C	C+	C+	271.1	2.03	0.0	0.3	79.7	2.2	10.0	11.4	0.0
Fairfield National Bank	Fairfield	IL	B+	B+	B+	582.4	5.65	19.2	2.2	11.1	37.3	10.0	12.3	0.0
Fairmount State Bank	Fairmount	IN	C+	C+	C+	47.7	9.84	2.1	11.5	21.5	15.5	10.0	14.2	19.6
Fairview S&L Assn.	Fairview	OK	B+	B+	B+	48.9	5.61	6.9	2.1	25.9	1.0	10.0	20.1	0.0
Fairview State Banking Co.	Fairview	IL	C+	C+	C+	31.3	8.49	8.1	7.3	24.7	10.0	10.0	12.9	0.0
Falcon International Bank	Laredo	TX	A	A	A-	1469.9	16.64	10.1	1.4	7.6	17.6	10.0	11.9	19.4
Falcon National Bank	Foley	MN	B-	B	B	649.4	14.15	39.3	0.5	6.9	8.4	4.1	9.0	0.0
▲ Fall River Five Cents Savings Bank	Fall River	MA	C+	C	C	1216.9	14.21	14.3	1.2	31.0	15.9	6.1	8.2	13.4
▲ Falls City National Bank	Falls City	TX	A	B	B-	445.5	9.45	3.6	2.8	8.9	39.1	10.0	12.2	0.0
Family Bank	Pelham	GA	B+	B+	B	125.3	24.97	7.6	6.8	46.5	4.5	10.0	11.2	19.7
▼ Fannin Bank	Bonham	TX	B-	B	B	128.6	16.20	10.4	2.2	16.9	33.4	6.1	8.1	14.7
Farm Bureau Bank, FSB	Sparks	NV	C-	C-	D	763.5	-4.39	10.2	64.1	1.4	4.1	9.0	10.7	14.1
Farmers & Mechanics Bank	Galesburg	IL	B+	B+	B-	403.0	9.01	16.5	4.0	13.5	22.4	8.1	9.7	16.1
Farmers & Merchants Bank	Piedmont	AL	B+	B+	B	261.5	14.76	10.6	2.2	12.2	29.5	10.0	12.6	19.1
Farmers & Merchants Bank	Waterloo	AL	B+	B+	B+	93.2	5.24	1.3	1.6	0.2	81.4	10.0	20.7	46.4
Farmers & Merchants Bank	Stuttgart	AR	B+	B+	B+	1611.4	6.96	8.6	1.3	15.1	15.2	7.7	9.8	0.0
Farmers & Merchants Bank	Lodi	CA	A-	A-	A-	4301.3	20.52	16.5	0.3	7.3	14.9	7.7	9.5	13.1

Asset Quality Index	Adjusted Non-Performing Loans as a % of Total Loans	as a % of Capital	Net Charge-Offs Avg Loans	Profitability Index	Net Income ($Mil)	Return on Assets (R.O.A.)	Return on Equity (R.O.E.)	Net Interest Spread	Overhead Efficiency Ratio	Liquidity Index	Liquidity Ratio	Hot Money Ratio	Stability Index
10.0	0.00	na	0.00	1.6	0.1	0.11	0.60	1.51	98.7	1.0	29.5	69.5	7.3
7.5	2.59	na	0.10	3.2	1.6	0.63	2.72	2.47	72.5	6.2	69.7	10.2	6.6
4.4	5.03	na	0.45	10.0	6.8	2.33	8.73	6.09	38.9	1.7	36.4	33.7	8.6
6.8	1.06	na	0.17	4.1	3.2	0.67	3.76	3.94	72.3	1.3	15.5	27.2	8.4
5.2	1.36	9.6	0.00	3.6	6.7	0.49	5.76	3.35	74.5	3.4	7.3	10.1	7.8
10.0	na	na	na	9.3	0.3	1.86	2.08	1.49	93.1	4.0	na	0.0	6.3
10.0	na	na	na	9.5	0.3	5.46	5.25	3.08	98.1	4.0	na	100.0	6.7
9.1	0.37	2.2	0.00	4.6	3.8	0.95	7.23	3.02	58.6	1.1	19.6	31.2	8.3
5.7	0.22	1.6	0.45	6.8	11.2	1.24	11.65	4.63	45.8	0.8	16.8	36.2	8.6
8.8	0.73	na	0.00	4.2	2.9	0.74	6.17	3.58	65.7	4.8	30.1	7.2	7.5
4.4	1.67	na	0.02	3.0	0.4	0.42	4.49	3.86	88.5	6.3	37.3	0.2	5.0
2.6	2.59	na	0.81	5.9	6.6	0.93	4.52	3.25	47.5	1.1	29.4	56.4	9.5
4.4	1.29	9.3	0.06	8.2	7.8	1.89	21.79	4.24	85.2	2.8	10.8	12.6	5.5
8.1	0.85	3.9	0.03	6.8	24.5	1.14	11.41	3.50	60.1	5.7	29.6	5.1	9.0
7.9	1.03	na	0.09	5.9	2.3	1.10	8.14	4.03	66.0	4.4	37.3	12.1	8.0
6.8	0.23	1.1	-0.01	7.1	13.5	1.74	18.05	3.08	46.0	1.4	23.7	35.0	9.5
5.5	1.81	na	0.01	5.9	1.1	1.19	11.14	4.47	62.6	2.8	32.5	18.1	7.0
7.7	0.07	na	0.00	7.2	5.0	1.45	13.46	3.69	53.2	4.4	19.0	6.3	6.7
5.3	2.79	9.4	0.01	6.8	1.9	1.55	13.73	3.63	53.9	4.3	23.7	8.0	8.7
4.5	0.95	4.6	0.31	5.9	3.7	1.54	14.19	4.23	64.5	1.4	19.8	27.8	5.9
8.7	0.01	0.1	0.19	4.7	1.9	0.83	5.93	3.50	67.4	3.4	28.0	13.8	7.6
8.1	0.02	0.1	0.01	8.3	2.8	1.56	14.21	3.98	52.8	2.8	19.7	15.4	7.5
4.8	0.83	na	0.09	3.4	0.9	0.67	6.77	3.29	77.3	3.7	35.7	15.3	5.7
7.9	0.00	na	-0.01	7.7	0.5	1.79	11.72	4.00	55.4	4.3	40.9	13.7	7.0
8.2	0.00	na	0.58	4.2	0.9	0.98	9.75	3.21	62.8	2.4	14.6	16.7	6.8
6.4	1.20	na	-0.07	4.9	0.3	0.95	10.52	3.58	66.3	5.7	46.6	6.7	5.5
7.4	1.62	na	0.00	5.4	1.7	2.40	17.89	2.71	64.7	3.6	44.5	15.1	7.1
8.4	1.06	na	0.00	5.4	1.6	1.19	9.73	3.45	60.8	5.1	46.0	10.9	7.1
5.9	0.33	na	0.02	4.2	0.5	0.80	7.84	3.62	69.0	2.9	41.4	21.7	5.8
8.5	0.14	0.8	-0.01	3.2	7.9	0.64	6.46	3.31	73.4	5.9	33.1	4.4	8.5
4.5	1.36	na	0.00	9.1	3.9	2.10	19.85	4.93	55.8	3.7	12.5	10.2	8.3
3.4	2.78	na	-0.02	1.6	0.1	0.12	2.55	3.91	96.4	1.6	10.5	22.2	0.3
6.8	0.44	na	0.00	5.8	1.2	1.32	12.48	4.38	64.4	4.4	14.4	6.2	7.0
4.5	1.54	na	0.03	6.4	1.7	1.53	13.98	4.62	67.0	4.2	14.2	7.6	7.4
8.8	0.43	na	0.07	5.1	2.2	1.02	6.01	4.13	66.0	2.3	25.9	18.8	7.6
8.3	0.12	na	0.00	4.8	1.0	1.16	11.33	3.24	58.8	5.3	32.9	4.7	6.7
8.4	0.03	na	0.01	6.6	3.6	1.48	15.60	3.56	58.1	3.7	26.7	12.0	7.4
8.6	0.16	na	0.01	7.5	6.7	1.71	16.40	3.85	62.8	2.6	17.8	16.3	8.2
7.9	0.18	1.2	0.04	3.9	9.7	1.06	9.34	3.07	78.8	1.7	12.5	18.1	8.6
5.0	1.16	na	-0.05	5.3	1.1	1.09	10.86	3.47	64.0	3.8	19.1	10.3	5.8
4.6	2.03	na	0.05	3.9	2.1	0.98	5.78	3.31	67.0	0.7	11.8	27.1	8.3
9.0	0.24	na	-0.08	3.6	1.3	0.93	7.90	2.70	75.5	4.3	51.0	16.2	6.9
7.4	1.08	na	0.05	3.9	8.2	0.66	4.89	3.58	74.0	4.7	21.1	5.8	8.6
7.1	0.96	na	0.01	2.3	0.5	0.22	1.96	3.11	91.2	1.7	10.1	20.1	6.1
3.6	3.69	13.5	0.00	5.2	5.5	1.31	9.64	2.74	52.6	1.4	23.9	27.2	8.4
5.2	1.77	na	0.87	3.2	0.2	0.46	3.45	4.07	72.7	4.2	19.2	7.9	5.5
8.8	0.00	na	0.00	6.9	0.5	1.47	7.41	3.94	54.4	3.0	27.2	15.7	8.1
1.7	9.17	35.3	0.20	3.8	0.2	0.72	5.41	3.91	71.6	1.8	24.6	22.3	5.8
7.1	2.04	5.2	0.00	7.1	14.1	1.34	10.95	3.59	57.8	2.6	29.2	24.4	10.0
7.4	0.23	na	0.20	4.6	3.9	0.84	8.89	4.46	60.8	1.6	10.3	17.8	6.7
8.4	0.26	1.8	0.00	3.4	5.5	0.64	7.69	2.69	79.3	2.0	22.2	21.2	6.0
7.2	2.98	na	0.14	9.1	5.7	1.70	14.29	2.82	25.5	6.1	59.8	9.3	7.8
5.2	1.53	9.8	-0.01	5.2	0.9	1.02	8.75	4.75	71.4	1.4	16.1	25.7	6.4
4.6	0.57	8.4	0.55	3.9	0.7	0.79	9.01	4.32	77.8	2.8	35.5	15.1	5.6
3.1	0.85	na	0.71	1.8	0.1	0.01	0.08	4.15	71.2	0.5	10.7	31.8	5.8
5.6	0.57	na	0.09	5.8	3.5	1.19	9.69	3.45	62.5	4.4	14.8	6.2	7.9
8.7	0.72	na	0.15	4.2	1.5	0.79	6.00	4.03	73.2	4.1	30.7	11.5	7.2
10.0	3.03	na	3.09	3.9	0.7	0.96	4.51	2.12	48.7	3.7	88.6	31.9	7.2
7.0	0.45	na	0.06	4.7	10.7	0.91	6.88	3.89	68.1	3.4	15.6	12.4	9.5
8.4	0.27	0.9	0.01	8.5	44.4	1.49	14.55	3.87	49.1	4.1	17.1	9.1	9.5

Name	City	State	2019 Rating	2018 Rating	Total Assets ($Mil)	One Year Asset Growth	Asset Mix (As a % of Total Assets) Commercial Loans	Consumer Loans	Mortgage Loans	Securities	Capitalization Index	Leverage Ratio	Risk-Based Capital Ratio
Farmers & Merchants Bank	Eatonton	GA	B-	B-	C+	207.4	14.36	8.5	1.6	9.7	27.5	10.0	13.4	26.7
Farmers & Merchants Bank	Lakeland	GA	E-	E-	E-	598.9	22.01	14.1	4.4	15.6	12.4	3.3	5.5	10.2
Farmers & Merchants Bank	Salisbury	NC	A-	A-	B-	738.7	16.70	6.5	0.2	10.5	0.2	9.5	10.7	19.8
▲ Farmers & Merchants Bank	Tolna	ND	B	C+	C	110.5	1.96	8.5	3.2	2.6	28.4	8.6	10.1	15.1
Farmers & Merchants Bank	Miamisburg	OH	B+	B+	B+	222.5	25.06	18.5	1.0	12.6	16.8	6.9	9.0	12.5
Farmers & Merchants Bank	Duke	OK	C+	C+	C	19.8	8.52	6.8	1.4	0.0	18.1	9.6	10.7	0.0
Farmers & Merchants Bank	New Castle	VA	A-	A-	B+	67.0	9.80	2.2	4.3	26.1	35.3	10.0	19.2	0.0
Farmers & Merchants Bank	Timberville	VA	B-	C+	B-	1014.8	24.92	8.3	9.6	19.1	10.6	8.3	9.8	14.2
Farmers & Merchants Bank	Berlin	WI	B-	C+	C	391.5	25.10	12.3	2.2	19.2	10.9	8.5	10.2	13.8
Farmers & Merchants Bank & Trust	Burlington	IA	C	C-	C+	224.4	9.35	10.8	1.4	27.5	22.3	6.7	8.7	15.9
Farmers & Merchants Bank & Trust	Marinette	WI	B-	B-	C+	163.9	17.81	11.8	1.3	19.2	29.5	9.6	10.7	16.2
▲ Farmers & Merchants Bank of Colby	Colby	KS	A	A-	B+	282.8	15.59	10.3	0.3	0.8	24.6	9.7	13.3	0.0
Farmers & Merchants Bank of Hutsonville	Hutsonville	IL	B	B	B	46.4	1.66	5.4	8.7	25.0	6.0	10.0	18.5	0.0
Farmers & Merchants Bank of Long Beach	Long Beach	CA	B+	A-	A-	9682.9	27.46	6.0	0.5	6.2	34.5	10.0	12.7	20.4
Farmers & Merchants Savings Bank	Lone Tree	IA	B	B	B	93.6	2.17	13.4	1.0	19.2	16.0	10.0	12.1	15.8
▲ Farmers & Merchants Savings Bank	Manchester	IA	B+	B-	C+	677.4	13.01	44.9	0.4	5.3	4.0	9.0	12.3	14.2
Farmers & Merchants State Bank	Winterset	IA	A-	B+	B+	206.5	9.62	6.0	2.9	9.0	24.1	8.4	9.9	15.1
Farmers & Merchants State Bank	New York Mills	MN	B	B	B	73.6	19.94	9.5	3.0	5.4	40.9	10.0	14.0	28.6
Farmers & Merchants State Bank	Archbold	OH	B+	A-	A-	1802.1	16.17	13.2	3.0	7.8	13.4	6.2	9.3	11.9
Farmers & Merchants State Bank	Waterloo	WI	B+	B-	C+	204.9	12.58	3.8	0.9	22.2	7.3	7.9	11.2	0.0
▲ Farmers & Merchants Union Bank	Columbus	WI	B	C+	B-	413.3	4.47	13.0	0.8	7.3	9.2	10.0	12.1	15.2
▲ Farmers & Stockmens Bank	Clayton	NM	A-	B	B	432.0	98.17	36.6	0.5	5.3	0.7	10.0	11.7	17.5
Farmers & Traders Bank of Campton	Campton	KY	B-	B-	B-	54.9	17.67	1.0	3.9	23.4	46.0	7.9	9.6	13.7
Farmers & Traders Savings Bank	Bancroft	IA	B-	B-	B-	63.3	13.76	3.1	1.2	3.9	33.3	9.0	10.3	17.7
Farmers and Drovers Bank	Council Grove	KS	B+	A-	B+	203.1	11.68	4.6	8.1	14.1	36.1	10.0	24.9	0.0
Farmers and Mechanics FSB	Bloomfield	IN	D	C-	C-	81.3	9.85	11.9	0.1	34.9	36.2	10.0	14.6	0.0
Farmers and Merchants Bank	LaFayette	AL	A-	A-	B+	201.2	21.34	13.2	5.0	8.2	47.0	10.0	12.7	20.4
Farmers and Merchants Bank	Sylvania	GA	B	B	B	130.3	13.82	3.5	2.1	9.5	35.7	10.0	14.1	0.0
Farmers and Merchants Bank	Boswell	IN	B-	B	B	142.8	7.80	6.9	0.7	15.4	15.8	9.9	11.0	0.0
Farmers and Merchants Bank	Laotto	IN	A-	A-	B+	192.1	20.61	13.9	2.4	23.2	17.9	8.1	9.7	0.0
Farmers and Merchants Bank	Mound City	KS	D+	D+	D	43.5	9.44	15.8	5.2	30.2	9.5	5.5	7.5	13.6
▼ Farmers and Merchants Bank	Upperco	MD	C+	B-	C	488.7	12.47	12.3	0.0	8.4	13.0	6.4	8.4	12.1
Farmers and Merchants Bank	Baldwyn	MS	A-	A-	B+	395.6	15.59	9.7	6.8	15.2	31.5	10.0	14.1	0.0
Farmers and Merchants Bank	Axtell	NE	D+	D+	D+	8.3	7.03	5.5	3.1	0.3	54.7	7.2	9.1	26.7
▼ Farmers and Merchants Bank	Milford	NE	C+	B	B	919.3	36.80	1.8	2.6	3.1	47.1	7.3	9.2	20.9
▼ Farmers and Merchants Bank	Milligan	NE	B-	B	B-	128.1	8.13	11.1	0.9	3.0	0.0	9.4	11.2	14.5
▲ Farmers and Merchants Bank	Caldwell	OH	B	B-	C+	111.7	-0.17	7.9	6.6	42.3	19.9	10.0	14.9	0.0
Farmers and Merchants Bank	Arnett	OK	B	B	B	56.2	7.33	4.2	7.5	1.0	43.3	10.0	13.9	0.0
Farmers and Merchants Bank	Maysville	OK	B-	B-	C+	20.6	8.06	48.9	9.6	0.2	8.2	5.8	7.8	11.9
Farmers and Merchants Bank	Holly Hill	SC	B+	B+	B	334.5	6.76	4.5	1.9	7.8	30.9	10.0	14.6	44.1
Farmers and Merchants Bank	De Leon	TX	C+	C+	C	113.2	23.10	4.8	4.3	19.3	16.6	6.5	8.5	0.0
Farmers and Merchants Bank of Ashland	Ashland	NE	B	B	B	98.3	20.39	5.3	1.0	19.6	10.7	7.7	9.4	0.0
▲ Farmers and Merchants Bank of Kendall	Kendall	WI	B-	C+	B-	74.7	1.73	3.9	1.8	8.8	0.0	10.0	16.1	0.0
Farmers and Merchants Bank of St. Clair	Saint Clair	MO	B+	A-	B+	253.9	24.64	10.0	1.7	23.1	11.8	10.0	11.9	18.6
Farmers and Merchants National Bank	Nashville	IL	A-	A-	A-	215.6	17.51	5.2	1.0	13.1	27.7	9.8	10.9	0.0
Farmers and Merchants National Bank	Fairview	OK	A	A	A	120.4	5.95	5.2	2.1	8.5	54.8	10.0	12.4	0.0
▲ Farmers and Merchants State Bank	Bushnell	IL	B	B-	C+	78.3	12.69	8.5	4.8	10.0	17.0	6.7	8.7	18.5
Farmers and Merchants State Bank	Alpha	MN	C-	C-	C-	38.8	1.20	6.0	2.9	10.4	1.2	10.0	11.3	18.6
Farmers and Merchants State Bank	Appleton	MN	B-	B-	C+	52.9	14.37	10.2	2.1	2.5	9.0	10.0	12.8	15.5
Farmers and Merchants State Bank	Blooming Prairie	MN	C+	C+	C	100.9	14.08	13.2	1.8	10.4	0.2	5.8	7.8	14.7
▲ Farmers and Merchants State Bank	Pierz	MN	B+	B-	B-	265.8	19.33	13.0	1.9	10.4	24.7	7.0	9.2	0.0
Farmers and Merchants State Bank	Springfield	MN	C+	C+	C+	131.8	10.05	7.3	1.3	4.7	14.3	6.1	8.1	0.0
▲ Farmers and Merchants State Bank	Langdon	ND	B+	B	B+	117.3	10.33	6.9	2.1	0.9	28.2	10.0	14.8	0.0
Farmers and Merchants State Bank	Bloomfield	NE	A-	B	B-	142.9	6.00	6.5	3.5	0.0	22.9	10.0	13.6	15.1
Farmers and Merchants State Bank	Plankinton	SD	C	C	B-	123.2	8.40	10.4	3.8	6.5	4.6	8.1	11.1	13.4
Farmers and Merchants State Bank	Scotland	SD	C+	C+	B-	32.5	11.62	7.8	8.3	1.6	35.9	8.2	9.8	0.0
▼ Farmers and Merchants Trust Co.	Chambersburg	PA	B	B+	C+	1510.4	15.98	9.0	0.4	10.5	22.9	6.6	8.6	15.3
Farmers and Miners Bank	Pennington Gap	VA	B+	A-	B+	149.1	11.46	7.1	6.3	18.1	15.9	10.0	13.1	0.0
Farmers Bank	Greenwood	AR	B+	B+	B+	231.4	9.80	8.0	5.6	27.0	27.3	10.0	16.9	0.0
Farmers Bank	Ault	CO	A	A	A	262.1	3.42	9.7	0.5	5.1	15.8	10.0	13.1	0.0

Asset Quality Index	Adjusted Non-Performing Loans as a % of Total Loans	as a % of Capital	Net Charge-Offs Avg Loans	Profitability Index	Net Income ($Mil)	Return on Assets (R.O.A.)	Return on Equity (R.O.E.)	Net Interest Spread	Overhead Efficiency Ratio	Liquidity Index	Liquidity Ratio	Hot Money Ratio	Stability Index
5.8	5.37	na	-0.57	3.6	1.0	0.65	4.67	3.21	80.9	4.7	37.8	10.8	6.5
1.4	3.77	na	0.63	2.0	0.7	0.17	2.84	3.49	74.5	0.9	22.3	35.4	0.3
6.6	1.39	na	0.02	6.8	6.7	1.28	11.59	3.70	62.8	5.9	41.9	4.9	8.0
6.6	2.26	na	0.04	5.4	1.0	1.26	10.45	3.59	72.7	3.5	37.2	15.8	6.7
6.4	0.65	2.6	0.02	6.6	2.1	1.35	14.20	4.03	59.5	3.7	8.8	10.0	6.2
9.0	0.00	na	0.06	3.4	0.1	0.67	6.32	2.87	76.6	4.8	63.1	13.2	4.9
9.6	0.00	na	0.00	6.1	0.6	1.16	5.89	3.84	61.7	5.3	47.4	9.6	7.9
6.0	0.54	4.2	0.17	4.3	5.8	0.86	8.81	3.57	68.1	4.6	21.3	6.4	6.1
3.8	2.19	na	0.32	7.2	4.3	1.68	16.34	4.53	49.7	1.3	20.1	20.1	5.0
4.1	2.05	na	0.57	3.1	1.1	0.67	7.78	3.44	77.0	4.8	22.9	4.5	3.9
5.0	2.36	na	0.00	3.8	0.8	0.66	5.71	3.65	74.4	4.3	38.9	13.1	5.7
8.2	0.06	na	0.71	9.3	3.7	1.90	13.70	3.89	32.9	0.6	13.6	42.6	9.0
8.4	0.00	na	0.00	6.7	0.6	1.75	9.56	3.18	44.2	2.0	33.9	29.1	8.0
9.2	0.74	1.9	0.00	4.5	58.4	0.88	7.03	3.06	61.9	4.8	27.1	9.3	9.8
8.1	0.00	na	0.00	4.5	0.7	0.96	7.00	3.26	59.0	2.4	12.0	12.9	7.2
6.3	0.54	na	0.04	9.1	9.9	2.05	16.54	4.28	47.2	2.7	18.7	15.7	9.4
8.6	0.41	na	0.08	5.8	1.8	1.23	12.06	3.46	55.4	3.9	30.0	12.2	7.0
8.8	0.00	na	-0.01	3.7	0.4	0.77	4.90	3.24	73.1	4.6	44.8	12.8	7.0
6.1	0.78	4.1	0.03	5.2	12.6	0.99	7.92	3.66	61.5	3.9	15.1	10.1	9.4
7.6	0.00	na	0.00	7.8	2.2	1.51	13.66	3.34	53.6	4.0	15.1	8.4	7.3
4.9	3.76	12.0	-0.12	7.0	4.0	1.31	10.88	3.47	43.9	1.0	20.5	31.6	7.6
7.9	0.06	na	-0.01	9.7	6.0	2.43	23.21	5.13	65.1	4.7	19.8	4.7	7.6
7.8	0.97	1.8	0.06	4.1	0.4	1.13	9.75	3.77	81.1	2.6	38.6	25.2	5.5
7.5	0.08	na	-0.01	3.7	0.4	0.83	7.71	2.97	70.1	3.1	38.9	19.2	6.0
8.4	0.40	na	0.03	4.8	1.4	0.96	3.69	3.20	59.9	2.4	33.1	22.2	7.9
9.9	0.08	na	0.00	0.0	-0.8	-1.32	-7.98	1.92	232.7	4.3	50.5	15.4	7.4
7.5	0.93	2.3	0.04	5.6	1.6	1.17	8.45	3.62	61.8	3.2	42.7	19.6	7.2
7.8	2.98	na	0.05	4.0	0.7	0.78	5.29	3.13	72.1	4.4	55.1	16.9	7.0
8.4	0.35	1.2	-0.01	3.9	0.8	0.74	6.64	3.30	75.2	3.3	28.3	14.8	6.9
8.4	0.26	na	0.00	5.8	1.7	1.32	12.54	3.61	63.4	6.3	40.8	1.6	6.7
4.7	7.98	na	-0.01	5.6	0.4	1.27	16.44	4.25	66.7	1.9	24.8	20.9	3.7
5.8	0.54	na	-0.03	3.0	1.5	0.42	4.11	3.46	81.6	1.7	15.8	17.5	6.1
7.0	1.53	na	0.16	8.4	4.7	1.66	11.37	4.45	63.2	1.9	26.1	22.1	8.7
9.3	0.00	0.0	0.00	1.2	0.0	0.00	0.00	3.44	100.0	5.8	61.4	4.1	4.3
8.3	0.02	na	-0.02	3.2	5.2	0.85	11.28	1.84	79.7	2.9	63.3	7.4	5.8
3.8	0.00	na	0.00	6.6	1.3	1.42	11.56	3.84	56.3	0.7	16.3	24.1	8.5
4.4	3.18	na	0.12	5.7	0.9	1.05	7.08	4.69	64.8	4.2	21.7	8.0	8.2
8.5	0.00	na	0.08	3.9	0.3	0.84	5.80	2.46	64.5	3.8	44.9	16.8	7.6
7.6	0.00	na	0.06	9.2	0.3	2.14	26.90	4.92	59.3	4.3	32.5	9.2	5.0
7.6	5.10	na	0.01	3.1	1.1	0.39	2.97	2.31	81.0	6.2	59.0	8.6	7.0
5.9	0.50	na	-0.05	3.0	0.4	0.51	5.43	3.74	83.7	6.0	41.0	4.0	4.8
8.8	0.00	0.0	0.00	4.7	0.6	0.93	9.30	4.12	70.7	4.4	25.1	7.2	5.1
3.7	6.51	na	0.01	10.0	1.4	2.39	15.02	4.72	49.7	2.0	16.7	19.2	9.0
8.7	0.29	na	0.06	4.7	1.5	0.88	6.99	3.38	64.1	3.8	22.4	10.7	6.6
8.0	2.06	na	0.00	5.9	2.1	1.41	11.99	3.47	63.1	4.6	20.1	5.3	7.9
9.3	0.00	na	-0.01	7.3	1.5	1.70	12.55	3.88	57.7	3.6	39.6	17.1	9.3
8.7	0.03	na	0.04	5.0	0.6	0.98	10.73	3.02	67.5	5.9	39.1	3.7	4.7
3.4	2.22	na	0.03	3.0	0.1	0.43	3.83	3.19	80.6	2.2	38.4	23.5	1.0
4.0	1.55	na	0.02	8.2	0.8	1.97	15.05	3.99	46.9	4.3	18.5	7.1	8.5
5.6	0.66	4.7	0.00	8.9	1.5	2.10	26.51	4.55	53.6	5.1	28.2	4.4	4.9
6.4	3.39	na	0.34	8.6	3.6	1.98	19.70	4.12	52.2	4.5	29.2	8.7	7.8
4.4	0.84	na	0.00	5.0	1.1	1.17	13.96	3.65	64.3	3.8	19.6	9.2	4.3
5.6	2.46	na	0.00	9.4	2.0	2.40	16.04	4.01	38.1	2.5	25.0	17.6	9.7
7.0	0.16	na	0.04	8.2	1.5	1.48	10.73	4.01	54.1	4.6	15.7	4.6	8.5
1.4	2.04	na	0.18	9.8	2.0	2.30	20.69	4.69	42.2	0.8	14.2	15.0	8.0
4.9	3.32	na	0.30	2.7	0.1	0.22	2.01	3.10	84.8	4.9	40.6	10.4	5.3
6.0	1.74	na	0.02	4.2	9.4	0.91	9.56	3.61	67.3	5.3	21.2	2.5	7.9
7.2	1.74	na	0.11	4.2	0.7	0.67	4.92	4.09	81.3	4.5	51.2	15.5	7.6
8.1	0.50	2.0	0.13	5.1	2.1	1.20	6.87	4.16	73.9	3.7	15.6	10.3	8.0
8.5	0.00	na	0.00	9.1	3.8	1.95	14.83	4.10	49.3	1.8	13.6	20.0	9.7

Name	City	State	Rating	2019 Rating	2018 Rating	Total Assets ($Mil)	One Year Asset Growth	Asset Mix (As a % of Total Assets)				Capital-ization Index	Lever-age Ratio	Risk-Based Capital Ratio
								Comm-ercial Loans	Cons-umer Loans	Mort-gage Loans	Secur-ities			
Farmers Bank	Greensboro	GA	B-	B-	B-	113.0	18.55	7.5	0.7	15.4	49.9	10.0	13.7	26.4
Farmers Bank	Buhl	ID	A	A	A-	535.1	15.90	13.5	1.6	4.9	31.7	10.0	14.0	24.3
Farmers Bank	Nicholasville	KY	B	B	B	180.8	16.41	5.1	0.9	25.9	23.9	9.1	10.4	19.8
Farmers Bank	Carnegie	OK	D-	D-	C-	72.8	-19.76	6.0	2.5	28.1	5.2	1.0	4.2	8.8
Farmers Bank	Parsons	TN	C+	C+	C+	42.1	12.67	4.0	9.5	15.3	10.9	10.0	11.4	0.0
Farmers Bank	Portland	TN	A-	A-	A-	739.8	8.51	5.2	1.2	16.4	21.1	10.0	12.2	17.2
Farmers Bank	Windsor	VA	B+	B+	B	536.9	18.18	14.2	1.4	6.7	31.1	8.6	10.1	15.0
Farmers Bank & Trust	Atwood	KS	B-	B-	C+	117.0	17.21	7.6	0.9	2.6	31.8	6.5	8.6	14.1
Farmers Bank & Trust	Great Bend	KS	A	A	A	1039.3	19.23	5.3	0.2	12.0	45.0	10.0	17.2	20.0
Farmers Bank & Trust Co.	Magnolia	AR	B	B	B-	1797.3	12.09	14.9	1.3	16.7	13.8	7.7	9.5	13.3
Farmers Bank and Savings Co.	Pomeroy	OH	B	B	B-	367.1	9.57	8.7	4.5	32.9	13.7	7.9	9.6	0.0
Farmers Bank and Trust Co.	Blytheville	AR	B	B	B	313.6	11.35	16.6	2.8	16.2	4.8	6.9	9.0	13.9
Farmers Bank and Trust Co.	Marion	KY	B+	B+	B+	423.7	9.96	10.6	3.1	28.9	12.5	8.1	9.7	14.6
Farmers Bank and Trust Co.	Princeton	KY	A	A	A	156.5	15.04	9.0	1.4	15.2	16.7	10.0	12.7	0.0
Farmers Bank of Appomattox	Appomattox	VA	B+	B+	B	264.3	11.88	7.3	15.3	22.9	26.8	10.0	13.5	22.0
Farmers Bank of Green City	Green City	MO	C-	C	C-	63.7	14.96	17.2	4.4	12.5	17.3	6.4	8.4	12.7
Farmers Bank of Lohman	Jefferson City	MO	B-	B-	B-	75.1	10.72	4.0	2.7	14.2	54.3	10.0	14.6	34.3
Farmers Bank of Milton	Milton	KY	B	B	B	281.0	12.28	4.3	2.3	25.5	36.1	10.0	13.6	22.5
Farmers Bank of Mt. Pulaski	Mount Pulaski	IL	C	C	C	57.9	1.54	2.7	2.8	19.5	23.9	10.0	12.0	37.6
Farmers Bank of Northern Missouri	Unionville	MO	A-	B+	B+	423.6	14.63	5.0	1.5	8.2	36.0	10.0	11.8	0.0
Farmers Bank of Willards	Willards	MD	B	B	C	443.5	13.35	9.9	1.9	30.9	6.0	9.4	10.6	18.3
Farmers Bank, Frankfort, Indiana, Inc.	Frankfort	IN	B+	B-	C+	691.4	17.14	13.8	2.1	5.9	22.4	9.2	10.6	14.4
Farmers Building and Savings Bank	Rochester	PA	B	B	B+	111.0	11.76	0.2	0.0	38.3	24.8	10.0	19.5	54.1
Farmers National Bank	Prophetstown	IL	A	A	A	782.5	7.76	3.8	0.6	3.4	41.0	10.0	13.6	0.0
Farmers National Bank	Phillipsburg	KS	A-	A-	B+	149.1	3.17	16.8	3.0	7.5	20.8	10.0	16.5	22.4
Farmers National Bank of Canfield	Canfield	OH	B+	B+	B	2970.7	23.20	14.4	7.2	14.0	16.0	7.0	9.0	13.4
Farmers National Bank of Danville	Danville	KY	B	B+	B+	732.8	31.34	11.4	1.5	22.7	20.3	6.2	8.2	14.0
Farmers National Bank of Emlenton	Emlenton	PA	C+	B-	C+	1030.1	10.05	9.2	3.7	40.4	9.7	5.4	7.4	12.5
Farmers National Bank of Griggsville	Griggsville	IL	C-	C	C	106.4	16.63	4.7	6.2	14.3	3.9	7.4	10.6	0.0
Farmers National Bank of Lebanon	Lebanon	KY	B	B	C+	112.4	11.98	7.1	2.3	7.2	35.3	10.0	11.6	19.2
▲ Farmers Savings Bank	Colesburg	IA	B+	B	B+	226.8	6.79	6.6	2.3	4.8	33.8	10.0	11.6	0.0
▲ Farmers Savings Bank	Fostoria	IA	B	B	B	144.3	12.76	8.9	2.1	19.5	15.6	10.0	14.1	0.0
Farmers Savings Bank	Frederika	IA	B	B	B	49.4	8.09	4.0	2.9	8.9	13.4	10.0	18.4	0.0
Farmers Savings Bank	Marshalltown	IA	A-	A-	B+	126.4	13.50	9.6	1.2	9.4	15.8	10.0	14.9	0.0
▲ Farmers Savings Bank	Wever	IA	B-	C	C+	122.8	9.12	13.6	1.0	24.4	23.2	10.0	14.5	22.8
Farmers Savings Bank	Spencer	OH	A-	A-	B+	308.3	7.03	1.4	0.5	17.9	64.3	10.0	23.6	64.7
▲ Farmers Savings Bank	Mineral Point	WI	B+	B	B	360.3	16.69	10.4	5.6	10.5	41.7	6.8	8.8	16.8
Farmers Savings Bank & Trust	Traer	IA	A-	A-	B+	202.6	20.25	4.6	1.1	7.3	33.7	8.0	9.6	0.0
▲ Farmers Security Bank	Washburn	ND	B	B-	C-	61.2	9.70	8.2	2.2	1.9	22.7	9.5	10.7	0.0
Farmers State Bank	Dublin	GA	A-	A-	B+	138.5	10.90	10.0	6.2	17.0	15.9	10.0	14.3	19.4
Farmers State Bank	Lincolnton	GA	A	A	A-	148.3	16.46	5.9	5.9	20.5	18.7	10.0	15.0	25.6
Farmers State Bank	Algona	IA	A-	A-	B+	118.6	5.16	13.1	1.3	15.3	8.8	10.0	12.0	0.0
▲ Farmers State Bank	Lake View	IA	B	B	B-	36.4	8.72	7.7	4.9	11.8	22.5	10.0	11.9	0.0
Farmers State Bank	Marcus	IA	B+	B+	B+	69.3	9.00	7.6	2.8	5.3	33.4	10.0	14.1	0.0
Farmers State Bank	Marion	IA	A-	A	A	972.4	18.33	12.6	1.0	7.0	11.1	10.0	12.9	0.0
Farmers State Bank	Mason City	IA	A-	A-	B+	211.2	14.00	6.4	1.9	16.5	39.0	10.0	11.7	21.5
Farmers State Bank	Waterloo	IA	B+	B	B	1313.3	15.38	13.9	6.5	19.9	12.5	7.5	9.4	13.5
Farmers State Bank	Yale	IA	B	B	B-	56.3	12.96	7.7	2.1	13.4	33.8	10.0	11.2	0.0
Farmers State Bank	Elmwood	IL	C	C-	C-	59.5	7.55	5.7	1.2	21.5	33.9	6.6	8.6	16.7
Farmers State Bank	Pittsfield	IL	A-	A-	B+	285.7	13.12	3.7	0.9	3.7	17.9	10.0	13.2	16.7
Farmers State Bank	Lagrange	IN	B+	B+	B	947.3	20.48	6.5	1.8	29.6	17.6	6.7	8.7	14.9
Farmers State Bank	Dwight	KS	C	C-	C-	15.9	2.01	3.7	0.8	6.8	0.0	10.0	12.3	0.0
Farmers State Bank	Fairview	KS	C	D+	D	21.1	-0.45	1.9	4.5	8.3	5.2	9.3	10.5	16.4
Farmers State Bank	Holton	KS	B+	B+	B	62.7	9.73	3.3	1.0	21.4	26.6	10.0	12.7	0.0
Farmers State Bank	McPherson	KS	A-	A-	A-	135.4	12.38	9.8	3.5	15.6	38.3	7.8	9.5	13.8
Farmers State Bank	Phillipsburg	KS	D+	C	C-	36.0	-0.63	10.7	9.6	10.5	17.7	9.8	10.8	0.0
Farmers State Bank	Wathena	KS	B-	B	B	65.6	8.40	7.9	4.9	15.7	54.7	10.0	15.5	34.5
▼ Farmers State Bank	Westmoreland	KS	B-	B+	B+	206.5	11.62	10.6	2.2	11.1	20.4	7.8	13.2	0.0
Farmers State Bank	Booneville	KY	B-	B-	B-	56.7	11.10	5.2	4.6	15.1	52.6	10.0	11.4	16.6
Farmers State Bank	Cameron	MO	B-	B-	B-	268.4	10.52	3.9	2.8	40.8	8.9	6.7	8.7	13.1

Asset Quality Index	Adjusted Non-Performing Loans as a % of Total Loans	as a % of Capital	Net Charge-Offs Avg Loans	Profitability Index	Net Income ($Mil)	Return on Assets (R.O.A.)	Return on Equity (R.O.E.)	Net Interest Spread	Overhead Efficiency Ratio	Liquidity Index	Liquidity Ratio	Hot Money Ratio	Stability Index
7.5	0.00	na	-0.03	2.8	0.5	0.56	3.98	2.75	82.7	1.8	23.0	23.0	6.9
8.0	1.03	na	0.00	5.8	4.2	1.13	7.61	3.30	60.4	5.5	50.3	9.8	9.4
8.2	0.54	na	0.00	4.3	1.1	0.86	7.99	3.15	66.8	2.0	27.1	21.5	6.6
0.3	10.14	na	1.37	0.0	-0.8	-1.23	-31.24	2.14	152.0	0.8	22.4	47.6	0.4
5.2	1.78	na	0.07	3.6	0.2	0.63	5.15	3.37	71.9	3.8	57.3	18.8	6.1
8.2	1.15	na	0.01	7.2	7.4	1.40	11.36	4.35	61.8	1.7	23.0	24.4	8.4
7.5	0.32	na	0.09	5.0	3.8	1.07	8.37	3.52	71.4	3.3	33.3	16.2	8.0
5.9	2.89	na	-0.01	5.0	1.1	1.27	13.82	3.40	59.4	4.8	22.9	4.5	5.8
9.2	1.03	na	0.06	9.1	17.7	2.54	13.26	3.44	41.8	2.3	41.8	41.7	9.0
5.1	1.24	na	0.12	6.3	16.7	1.28	12.78	3.82	54.6	1.2	10.4	28.0	9.0
5.5	1.13	na	0.11	4.4	2.1	0.80	7.85	3.70	71.1	2.2	19.6	18.7	6.4
4.9	0.93	na	0.04	6.4	3.2	1.34	15.59	3.07	55.1	0.7	17.8	38.7	7.5
6.1	0.37	na	0.00	6.8	5.1	1.71	15.72	4.66	60.6	2.0	11.8	18.9	6.8
8.7	0.00	na	0.06	6.5	1.6	1.50	11.16	3.86	64.1	4.2	17.7	7.9	9.4
6.3	1.17	na	0.10	4.9	1.9	1.02	7.53	3.77	68.7	3.6	30.8	13.8	7.2
5.3	0.99	na	0.46	3.2	0.2	0.46	5.26	3.85	78.0	0.7	16.6	41.2	4.2
9.6	0.00	na	0.11	3.5	0.4	0.67	4.22	2.52	67.5	6.4	79.9	8.8	7.3
5.5	2.32	na	-0.03	4.6	1.8	0.91	6.35	3.52	69.2	2.7	33.5	19.3	7.5
9.6	0.10	0.7	0.30	2.2	0.1	0.24	1.87	2.45	88.2	4.5	62.8	16.4	6.7
8.4	0.38	1.7	0.11	6.6	4.6	1.54	11.58	3.70	51.4	4.6	32.4	9.0	7.7
6.1	0.87	na	0.38	4.7	2.6	0.83	7.75	4.01	66.3	2.4	27.5	17.6	6.0
6.6	0.39	na	-0.01	6.0	5.7	1.17	10.57	3.70	60.2	4.1	23.0	8.9	7.9
8.4	1.91	na	0.00	4.0	0.7	0.90	4.54	2.59	57.1	7.8	70.2	0.0	7.5
6.3	0.34	6.3	-0.02	7.0	9.1	1.60	11.26	3.15	41.0	1.6	34.7	36.8	9.9
6.3	0.39	na	0.25	6.8	1.5	1.38	7.70	3.57	55.2	3.0	21.3	14.7	8.6
6.5	0.55	3.5	0.08	7.0	29.7	1.42	13.16	3.67	53.5	1.7	10.7	10.8	9.0
5.3	1.09	na	0.12	4.1	4.0	0.76	8.11	3.66	74.9	4.8	21.4	4.2	6.2
6.5	0.42	na	0.05	3.1	4.8	0.65	7.46	3.09	67.3	3.2	8.9	12.4	6.7
2.4	1.77	na	0.05	7.2	1.3	1.70	15.85	4.22	57.9	1.2	19.0	27.4	7.8
6.8	1.66	na	0.02	3.9	0.6	0.82	7.05	3.73	75.1	4.9	41.6	11.1	5.4
5.5	1.78	na	0.40	5.6	2.1	1.29	10.20	3.54	52.6	1.8	37.2	37.9	8.0
5.5	0.17	na	0.45	4.0	0.7	0.67	4.72	3.36	58.9	3.0	24.4	15.0	7.8
8.7	0.17	na	-0.04	4.8	0.3	0.96	5.13	2.70	53.1	5.6	58.7	9.9	7.3
8.2	0.20	na	0.05	7.1	1.3	1.44	9.64	3.83	57.8	3.5	35.1	12.4	8.1
3.5	4.35	na	-0.63	4.8	0.9	1.07	7.03	3.68	70.4	4.3	36.0	12.4	8.0
7.2	5.70	na	-0.44	6.7	3.6	1.61	5.80	3.23	46.0	4.3	87.8	26.6	9.8
8.1	0.17	na	0.00	6.2	4.0	1.55	16.32	3.11	50.4	6.0	39.7	3.5	6.3
8.9	0.00	0.0	0.02	5.5	1.6	1.27	12.33	3.30	62.5	5.6	44.7	7.7	6.0
6.8	2.18	na	0.00	5.2	0.5	1.05	9.65	3.86	62.6	4.3	27.3	9.1	6.2
7.2	2.06	na	0.05	5.4	1.2	1.23	8.07	4.21	71.6	3.5	31.0	14.7	8.2
8.6	0.26	1.4	0.13	7.6	1.8	1.69	10.69	5.10	66.6	4.2	32.1	11.4	8.8
5.4	1.18	na	0.00	5.3	1.1	1.24	10.07	3.62	62.8	4.5	30.8	9.2	7.8
9.2	0.00	na	-0.03	4.1	0.2	0.84	7.38	3.30	62.0	6.9	69.3	3.9	6.2
5.8	3.47	na	0.05	6.9	0.9	1.75	12.20	3.36	50.5	5.7	48.1	7.0	7.3
8.4	0.14	na	0.00	6.4	9.9	1.46	10.93	3.18	55.5	3.8	23.4	10.9	9.6
7.2	1.25	na	0.05	5.1	1.6	1.07	8.17	3.43	61.4	2.6	43.9	29.4	7.3
8.0	0.00	na	0.03	7.6	16.3	1.82	19.18	3.82	44.3	1.4	13.9	14.5	8.5
8.6	0.00	na	0.00	5.3	0.5	1.15	9.85	3.50	61.2	3.5	48.1	18.9	6.1
7.4	1.39	na	-0.03	3.7	0.4	0.93	10.31	3.35	72.6	3.8	38.5	15.4	3.8
6.7	0.37	na	0.03	6.1	2.9	1.44	10.71	3.76	64.4	4.2	20.3	8.2	8.1
8.4	0.25	na	-0.01	7.5	10.1	1.54	16.62	3.81	54.4	4.0	27.0	10.1	6.9
8.1	0.00	na	0.00	2.6	0.1	0.44	3.56	3.39	85.6	5.2	58.7	10.2	5.1
7.4	0.37	na	-0.01	3.2	0.1	0.55	5.13	3.95	85.4	5.1	43.3	7.0	4.0
9.0	0.39	na	-0.04	5.9	0.5	1.10	8.24	3.86	65.7	2.5	28.8	18.7	7.3
8.8	0.15	na	-0.01	6.3	1.5	1.49	14.37	3.96	59.9	4.6	48.9	14.3	7.1
1.7	6.93	na	0.48	2.3	0.0	0.13	1.17	3.84	73.1	1.5	15.6	25.4	5.4
8.9	0.06	na	-0.38	2.9	0.2	0.35	2.05	3.54	90.0	5.8	55.2	8.0	7.6
3.9	4.81	na	0.65	3.4	1.0	0.68	4.86	3.20	61.5	2.5	31.1	19.8	7.3
6.6	2.02	5.4	0.23	4.5	0.5	1.19	9.68	3.84	81.0	3.4	41.4	18.1	6.3
7.4	0.21	1.6	0.03	4.4	1.6	0.83	8.50	3.87	75.7	3.5	21.4	12.1	5.6

Name	City	State	Rating	2019 Rating	2018 Rating	Total Assets ($Mil)	One Year Asset Growth	Comm-ercial Loans	Cons-umer Loans	Mort-gage Loans	Secur-ities	Capital-ization Index	Lever-age Ratio	Risk-Based Capital Ratio
Farmers State Bank	Victor	MT	B-	B	C+	527.4	23.96	7.8	2.3	11.9	26.6	6.5	8.6	13.7
Farmers State Bank	Dodge	NE	C+	C+	C+	307.7	12.13	18.6	0.9	2.2	4.7	6.2	8.2	12.1
Farmers State Bank	New Madison	OH	B	B	B	205.4	13.30	5.4	3.7	22.2	17.8	10.0	11.6	18.1
▼ Farmers State Bank	West Salem	OH	C	C+	C+	150.6	22.69	17.3	1.7	19.2	10.6	6.0	8.0	12.7
Farmers State Bank	Quinton	OK	B-	B-	C+	128.7	10.79	9.6	8.7	16.9	27.5	6.3	8.3	14.2
Farmers State Bank	Hosmer	SD	C+	B-	B-	23.4	25.36	33.2	4.5	0.0	5.8	8.9	13.5	14.1
Farmers State Bank	Parkston	SD	B	B	B	232.9	5.35	6.8	2.7	0.0	33.0	8.0	9.7	0.0
Farmers State Bank	Mountain City	TN	B-	B	B	161.6	11.84	6.5	4.1	25.7	28.6	10.0	15.1	25.1
▼ Farmers State Bank	Center	TX	C+	B-	B-	382.9	14.99	17.4	1.9	8.2	20.3	10.0	12.0	20.4
Farmers State Bank	Groesbeck	TX	B+	B+	B+	150.9	13.85	10.2	5.4	16.2	18.8	6.6	8.7	0.0
▼ Farmers State Bank	Winthrop	WA	C+	B-	C+	53.0	25.23	3.9	0.7	0.6	48.7	6.9	8.9	0.0
Farmers State Bank	Pine Bluffs	WY	C-	C-	C+	28.2	9.53	24.0	1.5	10.4	2.4	5.7	7.7	16.3
Farmers State Bank & Trust Co.	Mount Sterling	IL	B-	B-	C+	120.1	23.75	12.5	3.1	15.6	16.6	6.7	8.7	12.6
Farmers State Bank & Trust Co.	Church Point	LA	B	B-	B-	136.9	17.68	16.4	2.0	9.6	22.2	7.9	9.6	15.3
Farmers State Bank Hillsboro	Hillsboro	WI	A-	A	A-	192.7	15.57	2.7	1.5	8.0	40.5	10.0	18.6	0.0
Farmers State Bank of Aliceville, Kansas	Westphalia	KS	A-	A-	B+	164.8	13.58	5.0	6.5	15.4	15.4	10.0	15.0	0.0
Farmers State Bank of Alto Pass, Ill.	Harrisburg	IL	C-	C-	C+	318.1	35.49	32.0	1.3	15.2	5.7	5.9	8.5	11.7
Farmers State Bank of Blue Mound	Blue Mound	KS	B-	B-	B-	47.4	10.06	10.4	3.3	1.0	5.3	10.0	17.6	0.0
Farmers State Bank of Brush	Brush	CO	A	A-	B+	113.9	4.93	4.2	1.5	3.0	26.1	10.0	19.3	0.0
Farmers State Bank of Bucklin, Kansas	Bucklin	KS	C+	C+	C-	52.9	23.68	8.1	0.9	1.1	19.6	6.6	8.6	0.0
Farmers State Bank of Calhan	Calhan	CO	B+	B	B-	322.2	14.99	7.7	2.5	11.2	47.4	8.2	9.8	18.8
Farmers State Bank of Canton	Canton	SD	B-	B-	B-	49.8	4.18	3.2	4.0	25.5	14.3	10.0	11.8	18.3
Farmers State Bank of Emden	Emden	IL	B-	B	B	37.6	7.43	3.9	1.3	1.2	50.4	10.0	26.4	57.2
Farmers State Bank of Hamel	Hamel	MN	B+	B	B-	163.2	22.14	9.6	0.3	9.2	40.5	8.1	9.7	0.0
Farmers State Bank of Hartland	Hartland	MN	A-	B+	B-	189.8	10.07	18.4	1.0	2.7	14.6	8.4	10.6	0.0
Farmers State Bank of Hoffman	Hoffman	IL	B-	B	B	163.3	7.33	4.8	1.1	11.4	44.0	10.0	14.9	0.0
Farmers State Bank of Hoffman	Hoffman	MN	B	B	B-	31.7	4.18	6.5	3.2	8.9	31.8	10.0	12.4	0.0
Farmers State Bank of Medora	Medora	IL	C-	C	C	22.8	16.49	10.8	5.6	2.2	46.5	10.0	15.2	34.0
Farmers State Bank of Munith	Munith	MI	B	B-	B-	88.4	12.62	2.3	4.7	30.2	11.7	8.4	9.9	21.6
Farmers State Bank of Newcastle	Newcastle	TX	B-	B-	B-	53.2	10.69	16.1	2.3	6.7	31.6	7.7	9.5	15.3
Farmers State Bank of Oakley, Kansas	Oakley	KS	A	A-	B+	175.0	22.14	13.0	0.4	0.7	24.4	10.0	14.6	0.0
Farmers State Bank of Trimont	Trimont	MN	B	B	B-	64.7	5.23	9.3	1.9	3.8	27.8	10.0	16.9	22.3
Farmers State Bank of Turton	Turton	SD	B	B	B	30.3	-1.88	3.6	2.6	0.0	15.6	10.0	12.3	24.0
Farmers State Bank of Underwood	Underwood	MN	C+	B-	C+	84.6	17.48	18.1	3.6	12.7	9.2	6.4	8.4	12.2
▲ Farmers State Bank of Waupaca	Waupaca	WI	A	A-	A-	232.9	13.98	8.0	3.2	21.6	23.4	10.0	12.5	0.0
Farmers State Bank of Western Illinois	Alpha	IL	B+	A-	B+	152.5	5.57	4.8	2.3	5.6	24.7	10.0	12.2	0.0
Farmers State Bank, Allen, Oklahoma	Allen	OK	B-	B	B-	44.5	7.09	17.3	12.1	14.9	8.8	10.0	12.5	18.3
Farmers Trust & Savings Bank	Earling	IA	B+	B+	B	110.2	17.97	11.1	1.4	6.2	3.1	6.8	8.8	15.2
Farmers Trust & Savings Bank	Williamsburg	IA	A	A	A-	169.2	14.66	8.2	3.0	11.0	34.5	10.0	22.7	0.0
Farmers Trust and Savings Bank	Buffalo Center	IA	A-	A-	B+	267.2	3.26	14.9	1.1	5.4	0.8	9.4	12.4	0.0
Farmers Trust and Savings Bank	Spencer	IA	B-	C+	C+	498.1	8.87	11.9	0.7	7.3	15.1	6.1	8.8	11.8
▲ Farmers-Merchants Bank & Trust Co.	Breaux Bridge	LA	C-	D+	D	365.4	13.76	7.4	4.4	13.0	9.4	10.0	12.2	19.7
Farmers-Merchants Bank of Illinois	Joy	IL	B-	B	C+	250.2	30.87	1.2	1.0	5.1	4.8	5.9	9.5	0.0
Farmington State Bank	Farmington	WA	C-	C	C-	13.2	57.09	10.6	1.0	0.3	0.6	10.0	35.6	0.0
Fauquier Bank	Warrenton	VA	B	B	B-	839.4	15.66	10.6	1.6	27.6	10.1	6.7	8.7	13.6
Fayette County National Bank of Fayetteville	Fayetteville	WV	B+	B+	B	115.2	22.23	2.7	2.8	39.1	30.0	10.0	11.7	0.0
▼ Fayette Savings Bank, SSB	La Grange	TX	B-	B	B	272.1	33.69	9.0	1.6	40.2	7.6	6.1	8.1	12.4
Fayetteville Bank	Fayetteville	TX	B	B	B+	616.5	13.01	3.7	0.8	3.6	76.8	10.0	11.0	0.0
FBT Bank & Mortgage	Fordyce	AR	B+	B+	B	194.4	15.33	11.6	6.0	17.3	29.8	9.8	10.9	0.0
FCB Banks	Collinsville	IL	B	B	B	1936.0	15.13	4.5	4.1	33.7	14.7	6.2	8.2	14.7
FCN Bank, N.A.	Brookville	IN	B+	B+	B+	666.3	43.93	8.3	1.2	20.0	30.4	7.9	9.6	18.1
FDS Bank	Mason	OH	A+	A+	A+	136.7	27.14	0.3	0.3	0.0	60.7	10.0	54.2	49.3
Federal Savings Bank	Chicago	IL	A	A	A	1360.5	79.92	0.0	1.1	75.4	0.0	10.0	13.0	23.3
▲ Federated Bank	Onarga	IL	C+	C	C+	105.2	8.35	12.3	2.2	11.1	35.7	6.6	8.7	0.0
▼ Federation Bank	Washington	IA	C+	C+	C+	146.4	9.09	8.4	3.6	11.5	18.5	4.6	8.6	0.0
Feliciana Bank & Trust Co.	Clinton	LA	B+	B+	B-	134.4	5.53	7.6	1.8	29.7	17.8	10.0	11.1	0.0
Fidelity Bank	West Memphis	AR	A-	A-	B+	474.7	19.94	3.5	0.6	4.5	50.4	10.0	11.1	0.0
▲ Fidelity Bank	West Des Moines	IA	B+	B-	C+	99.4	-0.17	2.9	0.1	50.0	3.0	10.0	11.7	17.8
▲ Fidelity Bank	New Orleans	LA	B	B	B	1010.3	27.79	19.5	0.6	27.3	7.3	10.0	16.6	28.0
Fidelity Bank	Edina	MN	A-	A-	A	971.9	58.22	23.1	0.3	0.0	4.4	3.0	9.5	0.0

Asset Quality Index	Adjusted Non-Performing Loans as a % of Total Loans	as a % of Capital	Net Charge-Offs Avg Loans	Profitability Index	Net Income ($Mil)	Return on Assets (R.O.A.)	Return on Equity (R.O.E.)	Net Interest Spread	Overhead Efficiency Ratio	Liquidity Index	Liquidity Ratio	Hot Money Ratio	Stability Index
6.4	0.74	na	0.04	4.6	3.9	1.09	10.90	4.30	72.2	4.4	28.4	9.0	6.5
6.3	0.00	na	0.29	4.3	2.0	0.89	9.88	3.61	68.1	0.8	16.2	30.3	5.4
8.6	0.00	1.4	-0.01	4.4	1.4	0.95	8.43	3.37	70.1	1.6	14.9	23.5	6.9
7.1	0.58	na	0.00	2.6	0.3	0.33	3.88	3.94	92.2	5.2	21.6	1.4	4.3
6.4	1.85	na	0.34	5.0	1.4	1.53	19.50	5.10	75.7	5.4	37.1	6.0	4.2
7.3	0.26	na	0.00	5.3	0.2	1.07	7.26	5.07	68.3	1.0	28.5	35.4	5.0
8.5	0.02	na	0.00	4.6	1.5	0.91	8.96	3.26	64.9	4.6	39.5	11.8	5.8
7.3	2.80	na	0.05	3.7	0.7	0.59	3.82	4.01	78.8	3.2	24.4	13.7	7.2
5.7	0.99	na	1.63	2.6	1.3	0.47	3.61	3.45	77.6	4.7	43.1	12.2	5.8
8.3	0.56	na	0.01	5.6	1.3	1.23	12.64	4.16	70.5	4.3	27.8	9.2	6.5
8.7	0.00	na	0.05	2.9	0.1	0.41	4.28	2.12	75.5	8.1	93.7	0.0	4.1
8.5	0.00	na	0.01	3.6	0.2	0.95	12.09	4.69	85.9	4.2	22.6	8.1	2.9
4.4	2.61	na	0.04	6.3	0.9	1.22	13.45	3.51	53.3	2.5	32.2	19.9	4.9
4.7	1.13	na	-0.01	5.3	1.1	1.16	11.08	4.20	70.7	3.1	24.9	14.6	7.7
9.4	0.26	na	0.00	8.0	2.2	1.63	8.66	3.22	40.3	6.0	60.4	10.0	7.0
8.1	0.02	na	0.00	6.2	1.5	1.22	7.85	3.24	47.8	1.5	21.3	26.0	8.4
2.2	2.34	18.7	0.05	5.1	2.7	1.26	16.59	3.92	72.4	3.7	14.7	10.7	3.9
6.5	1.35	na	-0.23	4.8	0.3	0.97	5.27	4.71	78.0	3.2	21.0	13.5	7.4
8.7	0.00	na	0.00	8.7	1.3	1.58	8.05	4.07	55.7	2.8	29.9	17.4	8.9
8.8	0.00	na	0.00	3.4	0.3	0.77	6.97	3.22	78.6	5.7	53.1	8.4	5.8
8.5	0.34	na	0.03	6.0	3.3	1.48	13.33	3.80	62.6	4.3	35.9	12.0	6.5
8.4	0.30	na	0.43	3.1	0.2	0.40	3.33	3.64	86.1	4.6	25.8	6.6	5.8
9.6	0.00	na	0.00	3.4	0.2	0.62	2.27	2.53	69.4	3.5	60.6	23.2	7.0
9.6	0.00	na	0.00	5.2	1.5	1.38	12.76	3.16	58.0	6.0	58.8	9.3	6.2
6.9	1.66	na	0.05	8.7	2.9	2.18	18.53	4.22	51.3	3.7	24.5	4.9	8.2
9.2	0.86	na	0.06	3.7	0.8	0.67	4.28	2.84	72.8	5.9	51.9	7.9	8.0
8.8	0.00	na	0.00	4.6	0.3	1.10	8.12	3.38	67.0	4.4	53.8	15.5	7.1
4.4	0.03	na	0.13	1.2	0.0	-0.15	-0.93	3.06	100.0	5.6	84.4	12.5	4.8
4.8	2.08	na	-0.15	4.4	0.5	0.81	8.03	3.67	69.3	6.0	43.9	3.9	6.0
7.3	0.22	na	-0.05	6.1	0.5	1.27	13.34	3.88	58.9	5.7	27.8	0.0	5.9
7.3	0.00	na	0.00	8.3	2.0	1.66	10.89	4.14	45.3	1.0	8.6	29.6	8.8
7.2	1.35	na	-0.02	6.2	0.6	1.22	7.12	3.62	56.5	2.1	35.8	19.8	7.1
7.3	0.00	na	0.00	6.2	0.3	1.29	10.38	4.26	61.6	2.2	30.0	21.6	7.9
5.4	0.26	na	0.09	5.6	0.7	1.23	13.48	4.49	70.9	1.5	19.8	26.0	6.5
8.8	0.23	na	-0.02	7.8	2.6	1.60	12.26	4.26	56.9	4.6	38.7	11.8	7.4
8.6	0.52	na	0.02	4.2	1.0	0.89	6.77	3.65	72.2	5.8	39.9	4.7	7.4
6.1	0.17	3.2	0.17	5.6	0.4	1.22	9.50	4.68	72.1	2.0	26.0	21.3	7.9
8.4	0.00	na	-0.07	7.5	1.3	1.64	18.36	3.84	56.2	4.8	33.9	8.5	7.0
8.7	0.86	na	0.02	9.3	2.6	2.11	8.91	3.88	43.2	6.0	57.4	9.2	9.6
6.7	0.04	na	0.03	6.9	3.0	1.51	11.84	3.78	53.1	3.8	13.2	9.6	9.1
5.3	1.49	na	0.00	5.4	4.3	1.21	13.25	3.53	50.0	2.1	12.0	8.2	6.7
4.0	5.16	na	0.09	4.3	2.5	0.95	7.44	4.09	72.4	3.8	34.0	14.0	7.9
4.5	0.49	3.8	0.03	5.4	2.2	1.24	9.17	3.00	53.2	0.7	1.3	21.9	3.7
6.8	0.08	na	0.00	1.6	0.0	0.17	0.85	2.93	91.6	7.8	91.8	0.0	6.2
8.8	1.17	na	0.03	4.5	5.0	0.86	9.14	3.52	68.5	4.6	18.5	5.2	5.8
6.4	1.99	na	0.03	5.7	0.9	1.16	9.45	4.01	65.4	4.6	30.6	8.4	7.0
6.3	0.56	5.2	0.00	4.6	1.9	1.08	12.63	3.44	57.9	1.1	15.5	30.0	5.1
10.0	0.00	0.0	-0.01	4.8	8.3	1.94	15.57	2.31	52.5	3.0	62.8	40.9	7.7
5.8	5.74	na	0.16	6.4	2.3	1.64	15.36	4.07	66.9	3.5	44.8	18.9	6.0
6.3	0.82	5.5	0.03	5.0	12.9	0.93	10.89	2.62	59.1	3.4	19.6	13.0	7.4
7.0	0.67	2.2	-0.03	4.8	4.8	1.08	9.77	3.26	65.5	4.1	38.5	14.0	6.9
10.0	0.00	na	1.00	9.5	397.8	440.74	905.22	1.30	15.4	9.1	141.2	0.0	8.5
7.6	0.68	4.6	0.06	10.0	85.7	12.06	91.65	1.16	70.2	0.6	17.1	23.0	9.8
8.0	0.00	na	0.00	3.4	0.5	0.69	5.62	3.60	81.5	5.5	41.0	7.1	6.9
2.8	2.52	na	0.21	4.2	0.8	0.81	8.36	3.85	72.5	4.1	29.4	10.4	6.4
6.0	0.87	na	0.14	4.6	1.0	0.97	8.52	3.92	73.7	0.9	19.5	39.4	7.9
9.1	0.18	na	-0.01	5.7	5.2	1.52	12.52	3.13	55.7	1.6	24.8	26.2	7.6
7.3	0.52	na	0.00	7.1	4.1	5.98	48.68	2.33	65.9	0.8	7.8	31.8	8.1
8.4	0.65	na	0.15	7.7	13.6	2.01	11.71	5.40	71.7	3.6	13.7	8.3	8.6
6.8	0.00	na	0.05	8.5	9.7	1.96	13.63	4.49	51.9	0.8	6.4	0.3	9.0

Name	City	State	2019 Rating	2018 Rating	Total Assets ($Mil)	One Year Asset Growth	Asset Mix (As a % of Total Assets)				Capital-ization Index	Lever-age Ratio	Risk-Based Capital Ratio
			Rating				Comm-ercial Loans	Cons-umer Loans	Mort-gage Loans	Secur-ities			
Fidelity Bank	Fuquay-Varina	NC	A-	A-	B+	2719.0	32.16	14.9	0.4	4.1	20.6	6.5	8.5	15.9
Fidelity Bank & Trust	Dubuque	IA	B	B	B+	1468.0	21.85	13.0	1.3	8.3	16.3	6.9	8.9	13.6
Fidelity Bank of Texas	Waco	TX	B+	B+	B+	106.4	24.07	2.1	0.9	19.2	0.5	10.0	15.6	0.0
Fidelity Bank, N.A.	Wichita	KS	C+	B-	B-	2764.9	16.17	12.0	4.1	15.0	8.8	6.5	9.5	12.1
▲ Fidelity Co-operative Bank	Leominster	MA	C+	C+	C+	1129.5	12.72	15.3	0.2	28.6	13.0	6.9	8.9	13.1
Fidelity Deposit and Discount Bank	Dunmore	PA	B+	A-	B+	1705.9	68.15	14.5	6.3	20.1	20.0	6.9	8.9	16.4
Fidelity Federal S&L Assn. of Delaware	Delaware	OH	C-	C-	C-	116.6	9.04	0.0	1.1	33.4	35.2	10.0	19.6	45.6
Fidelity Personal Trust Co., FSB	Boston	MA	U	U	U	103.4	5.23	0.0	0.0	0.0	0.0	10.0	98.9	0.0
Fidelity State Bank and Trust Co.	Dodge City	KS	A-	A-	B+	193.7	13.75	2.0	0.3	1.1	27.2	10.0	19.4	84.1
Fidelity State Bank and Trust Co.	Topeka	KS	C+	C+	C	149.1	6.45	22.2	16.2	7.3	15.3	6.8	8.8	0.0
Field & Main Bank	Henderson	KY	B-	C+	C	533.7	16.85	16.6	0.8	20.1	6.1	6.4	8.4	12.8
Fieldpoint Private Bank & Trust	Greenwich	CT	C+	B	B	942.5	2.47	5.8	10.8	34.2	10.9	10.0	12.0	16.5
Fifth District Savings Bank	New Orleans	LA	B-	B-	B-	454.4	3.92	1.2	0.2	66.2	15.3	10.0	17.4	37.1
Fifth Third Bank, N.A.	Cincinnati	OH	B	B	B	200454.5	18.27	23.3	8.9	9.2	18.4	6.8	8.9	14.1
Finance Factors, Ltd.	Honolulu	HI	B-	B	B-	565.5	-3.84	0.0	1.0	31.8	15.7	10.0	12.6	19.1
Financial Federal Bank	Memphis	TN	A-	A-	B+	733.7	15.74	16.5	2.4	24.7	0.0	7.6	12.0	0.0
▲ Financial Security Bank	Kerkhoven	MN	B-	C+	C	123.7	22.71	26.8	0.6	8.5	2.7	5.1	8.9	11.0
FineMark National Bank & Trust	Fort Myers	FL	B-	B-	B-	2606.4	23.90	8.5	3.8	37.2	23.9	7.3	9.2	16.9
Finwise Bank	Murray	UT	B+	A-	B+	314.6	94.59	43.4	18.1	5.5	0.6	5.7	16.3	0.0
First & Farmers National Bank, Inc.	Somerset	KY	B-	B-	B+	571.5	8.82	5.6	2.7	28.8	32.5	9.2	10.4	15.6
First & Peoples Bank and Trust Co.	Russell	KY	B-	B	B	214.9	8.25	11.2	18.8	9.3	43.0	10.0	19.0	0.0
▼ First American Bank	Elk Grove Village	IL	C-	C+	B-	5878.9	30.76	13.1	2.0	5.5	52.5	4.6	6.7	14.7
First American Bank	Artesia	NM	A	A	A	1414.3	17.51	17.5	0.2	7.9	35.2	7.9	9.6	19.4
First American Bank	Stonewall	OK	B	B	B	31.2	-0.24	15.8	9.8	20.9	6.9	10.0	12.0	0.0
First American Bank and Trust	Vacherie	LA	A	A	A-	1050.7	15.87	6.6	1.3	24.2	22.3	10.0	13.7	23.6
▼ First American Bank and Trust Co.	Athens	GA	B+	A-	A-	712.6	28.48	9.7	0.4	15.3	17.2	8.5	10.0	18.8
First American National Bank	Iuka	MS	C+	B-	B-	322.0	16.37	8.4	7.1	21.4	30.4	9.1	10.4	0.0
First American State Bank	Greenwood Village	CO	B-	B-	B-	261.8	6.38	3.8	0.1	36.8	13.3	7.4	9.2	15.5
First American Trust, F.S.B.	Santa Ana	CA	U	U	U	4481.9	5.50	0.0	0.0	0.0	77.8	6.4	8.4	33.6
First Arkansas Bank and Trust	Jacksonville	AR	C+	B-	B-	831.6	10.47	18.6	10.5	9.5	21.3	10.0	13.8	0.0
▲ First Bank	Ketchikan	AK	B-	B-	C+	676.9	11.96	10.0	1.2	6.5	47.7	6.8	8.8	21.0
First Bank	Wadley	AL	B+	B+	B+	102.6	17.05	6.8	1.4	4.7	53.0	6.4	8.5	12.1
First Bank	Clewiston	FL	B	B	B-	482.1	24.89	15.8	1.7	12.8	12.8	6.6	8.6	14.7
First Bank	Dalton	GA	C+	B-	B-	458.0	14.63	15.6	1.4	14.0	14.6	5.3	10.1	0.0
First Bank	Waverly	IA	B+	B+	A-	606.0	16.49	15.9	1.1	8.9	6.1	9.3	10.5	16.9
First Bank	Sterling	KS	A-	B+	B+	160.9	15.59	14.7	0.6	11.5	30.7	9.7	11.0	0.0
▲ First Bank	Creve Coeur	MO	A-	B+	B	6621.5	8.34	16.2	0.3	11.3	30.7	9.0	10.3	17.5
First Bank	McComb	MS	C+	B	B	604.6	8.46	9.2	1.3	20.4	5.4	7.9	9.6	15.7
First Bank	Southern Pines	NC	A-	B+	B	7064.8	16.40	8.6	0.7	15.2	18.1	8.5	10.0	14.9
First Bank	Hamilton	NJ	B	B	B	2309.9	12.96	18.7	0.2	5.4	4.8	7.7	9.5	13.1
First Bank	Erick	OK	A-	A-	B+	85.1	18.20	32.1	3.7	8.8	3.1	10.0	12.5	15.8
First Bank	Burkburnett	TX	B-	B-	B-	544.2	16.02	19.6	0.9	25.8	1.3	9.8	10.9	16.9
First Bank	Strasburg	VA	B+	A-	B+	941.5	21.22	13.2	0.8	21.3	14.1	6.7	8.7	15.3
First Bank & Trust	Brookings	SD	B	B+	B+	2279.5	14.19	15.3	2.3	5.7	17.0	5.5	9.6	0.0
First Bank & Trust	Lubbock	TX	B+	B+	B	1289.2	11.30	15.6	0.9	13.2	28.3	8.5	10.0	14.5
First Bank & Trust	Seymour	TX	B-	B-	C	143.8	12.86	8.0	0.7	0.5	61.6	10.0	12.5	24.7
First Bank & Trust Co.	Duncan	OK	B+	B+	A-	624.3	10.84	7.7	2.3	22.2	5.8	10.0	15.4	22.1
First Bank & Trust Co.	Perry	OK	B+	A-	A	213.0	45.42	5.7	6.0	14.3	39.5	7.5	9.4	0.0
▼ First Bank and Trust	New Orleans	LA	C+	B-	B-	1171.5	19.56	16.6	2.6	18.9	3.5	6.6	8.6	12.5
First Bank and Trust Co.	Minden	NE	C+	C+	C+	76.6	11.83	7.5	2.6	14.4	30.7	9.1	10.4	19.2
First Bank and Trust Co.	Clinton	OK	B-	B	B-	57.5	5.86	3.5	8.8	15.1	31.9	10.0	12.6	0.0
First Bank and Trust Co.	Lebanon	VA	A	A	A	2239.4	16.18	16.6	2.5	14.5	0.9	9.7	10.8	19.0
First Bank and Trust Co. of Illinois	Palatine	IL	D+	C-	C	190.0	1.58	24.1	0.0	1.2	0.0	6.3	8.3	13.2
First Bank and Trust Co. of Murphysboro	Murphysboro	IL	D+	D	D+	84.6	6.87	10.6	4.9	20.6	17.3	5.3	8.3	0.0
First Bank and Trust of Childress	Childress	TX	C+	C+	C+	135.6	17.16	18.7	2.8	8.3	48.5	6.0	8.0	19.3
First Bank and Trust of Fullerton	Fullerton	NE	B+	B+	B	98.3	5.18	7.6	0.9	0.3	13.2	10.0	14.3	0.0
First Bank and Trust of Memphis	Memphis	TX	B+	B+	B	59.6	6.06	21.9	0.4	16.0	3.2	10.0	13.0	18.6
First Bank Blue Earth	Blue Earth	MN	A-	A-	B+	272.7	15.04	9.5	1.3	4.1	32.9	6.9	9.1	0.0
First Bank Elk River	Elk River	MN	C	C+	C	358.7	20.27	26.4	0.6	5.4	17.6	5.3	8.6	0.0
First Bank Hampton	Hampton	IA	A-	A-	B+	184.2	10.20	16.2	4.0	13.0	16.1	10.0	11.9	0.0

Asset Quality Index	Adjusted Non-Performing Loans		Net Charge-Offs Avg Loans	Profitability Index	Net Income ($Mil)	Return on Assets (R.O.A.)	Return on Equity (R.O.E.)	Net Interest Spread	Overhead Efficiency Ratio	Liquidity Index	Liquidity Ratio	Hot Money Ratio	Stability Index
	as a % of Total Loans	as a % of Capital											
7.6	1.30	na	-0.04	6.1	21.2	1.17	11.66	3.25	60.1	6.2	32.1	2.5	8.2
5.8	0.85	4.1	0.05	4.9	10.6	1.00	8.15	3.02	60.8	4.7	31.1	11.9	9.9
8.3	0.82	na	0.01	2.8	0.1	0.18	1.08	2.93	92.1	4.9	68.1	16.5	7.7
5.6	1.60	na	0.04	3.1	13.4	0.69	7.43	3.54	81.5	1.5	4.4	11.5	7.3
5.9	1.53	7.3	0.01	3.8	7.2	0.85	10.14	3.32	65.7	3.5	8.5	9.0	6.7
7.5	0.57	na	0.08	4.6	9.6	0.91	9.59	3.43	62.8	4.6	15.6	5.1	8.0
9.8	0.26	0.6	-0.02	1.5	0.1	0.17	0.82	2.99	97.8	6.3	60.6	8.0	7.4
10.0	na	na	na	9.5	31.5	41.30	44.32	2.33	43.5	4.0	na	100.0	7.0
9.9	0.60	0.6	0.00	6.3	1.6	1.20	5.99	2.71	54.3	7.6	84.5	3.4	8.9
6.6	0.22	na	-0.01	3.9	1.2	1.14	12.02	3.00	71.6	4.3	26.3	8.4	5.6
4.5	0.61	na	0.05	4.9	4.9	1.28	12.38	3.66	71.3	1.5	9.9	23.1	6.9
4.7	1.41	9.3	0.07	2.8	2.2	0.31	2.60	2.66	86.2	1.3	3.4	23.9	7.3
9.9	0.15	0.5	0.00	3.2	1.7	0.50	2.77	2.80	70.1	1.9	27.7	24.0	7.9
4.7	1.52	5.3	0.41	5.5	990.5	0.71	5.54	2.99	60.0	6.0	36.6	2.0	10.0
9.1	0.36	1.7	-0.08	3.4	2.2	0.50	4.11	3.51	81.3	1.3	21.1	28.9	8.4
5.7	0.37	na	0.00	7.7	9.1	1.79	14.66	2.90	47.3	0.3	3.3	68.0	10.0
6.0	0.35	na	0.00	6.1	1.3	1.45	17.60	3.92	61.3	3.5	4.7	10.4	4.9
8.9	0.09	0.5	0.00	4.3	17.6	0.99	10.66	2.57	63.4	4.8	15.9	3.5	7.4
3.9	1.09	na	2.01	10.0	6.7	3.86	27.76	11.67	51.1	1.4	11.6	17.6	8.2
6.3	0.40	na	0.01	3.9	3.0	0.71	5.54	3.68	76.3	2.9	30.8	17.6	8.2
6.8	0.85	na	0.22	3.2	0.7	0.43	2.28	3.67	81.4	4.7	33.9	9.1	7.6
6.0	1.51	6.3	0.01	1.8	24.0	0.57	8.55	2.43	92.6	5.2	23.5	4.4	6.0
8.8	0.45	na	-0.11	8.7	19.4	1.87	18.41	3.63	53.8	5.1	23.7	5.2	9.7
4.6	1.62	11.8	0.02	6.2	0.4	1.43	12.35	4.42	67.5	1.9	26.1	21.9	7.4
7.2	1.69	na	0.00	5.8	8.2	1.09	7.58	3.86	61.6	4.8	28.7	10.5	10.0
7.7	0.29	1.6	-0.04	5.2	5.1	1.08	10.40	3.24	62.1	4.8	23.2	4.5	7.0
5.3	1.61	na	0.09	3.9	1.9	0.83	7.25	4.43	82.6	4.5	35.5	10.9	5.9
9.1	0.00	na	0.00	3.7	1.4	0.72	8.16	3.37	65.8	0.8	19.6	46.2	4.6
10.0	na	0.0	na	6.6	30.8	1.04	10.67	1.52	34.8	8.8	108.9	0.0	7.0
3.1	2.96	na	0.34	7.2	10.9	1.78	10.37	4.23	70.1	4.3	21.4	7.4	8.4
8.6	0.29	na	-0.07	4.1	4.5	0.97	9.49	3.19	77.2	5.2	46.2	10.5	6.3
8.5	0.36	na	-0.03	5.2	0.8	1.12	11.01	3.95	68.8	5.8	60.9	11.0	6.6
7.0	1.32	4.8	-0.03	5.3	3.7	1.07	12.25	4.12	61.1	4.5	24.1	6.8	5.5
3.5	1.73	na	0.08	8.3	4.8	1.52	15.60	4.70	55.8	2.7	20.9	15.9	6.4
4.6	1.12	5.5	0.22	5.0	4.2	1.00	8.41	3.24	57.3	3.3	24.5	13.2	7.9
8.3	0.42	na	-0.03	5.8	1.5	1.29	9.99	3.72	57.3	2.2	20.5	18.7	8.1
8.5	0.57	2.6	0.04	8.4	96.7	1.98	18.84	2.93	46.2	5.5	32.3	6.9	9.7
5.2	0.62	na	0.11	3.3	2.6	0.58	5.99	2.93	77.5	4.3	31.6	9.8	7.5
6.2	0.85	3.1	0.09	6.4	59.8	1.21	8.76	3.68	55.2	4.1	20.6	9.0	10.0
4.2	0.62	5.1	0.17	4.3	13.3	0.80	7.77	3.19	53.7	1.5	8.9	15.5	7.8
8.1	0.07	na	-0.16	9.2	1.1	1.92	15.40	5.03	60.9	4.5	28.8	7.5	8.3
4.6	1.20	na	0.27	10.0	12.1	3.12	29.09	4.06	62.1	3.2	19.3	13.4	8.9
5.8	1.08	na	0.08	5.3	6.6	0.99	10.37	3.68	61.1	4.7	22.3	5.1	6.2
5.0	0.81	7.2	0.06	6.1	18.4	1.13	10.18	3.55	60.7	2.9	11.3	12.9	9.4
5.6	0.88	2.5	0.06	6.6	12.6	1.38	7.21	3.77	64.9	3.2	24.9	16.5	8.5
8.3	0.13	na	-0.06	3.1	0.7	0.70	4.30	2.06	93.3	6.9	72.9	6.1	6.3
3.3	4.63	na	0.01	8.8	9.2	2.01	13.02	4.42	58.8	3.5	17.6	11.9	10.0
4.5	2.77	na	0.44	7.1	2.9	1.86	17.98	4.13	63.4	3.9	35.9	14.2	8.6
2.5	1.86	na	-0.01	6.8	12.6	1.54	16.89	4.03	62.5	0.8	8.4	30.6	9.2
6.4	3.88	na	-0.01	3.9	0.5	0.94	8.38	3.36	73.6	3.6	31.3	14.0	5.8
8.7	0.00	na	0.06	3.2	0.2	0.53	3.88	3.55	86.9	3.6	32.3	14.5	6.2
8.1	0.16	1.9	-0.01	8.0	25.5	1.58	14.56	4.10	50.1	3.8	8.4	9.5	10.0
7.3	0.00	na	0.00	0.0	-1.8	-1.29	-14.12	4.22	165.5	0.9	22.3	37.5	4.5
3.2	2.01	na	0.06	3.0	0.3	0.42	4.75	3.74	81.7	3.0	20.1	14.4	3.5
7.8	0.72	na	0.01	3.6	0.8	0.78	8.97	2.26	69.8	0.6	12.1	48.3	4.7
7.4	0.00	na	-0.01	4.5	0.6	0.86	5.90	3.20	66.2	1.5	23.4	20.9	8.2
8.6	0.00	na	0.01	2.8	0.1	0.30	2.27	2.66	89.4	1.0	22.2	33.6	8.3
7.6	0.23	1.7	-0.03	6.5	3.0	1.56	15.28	3.23	52.0	3.2	20.4	13.8	7.9
7.6	0.33	na	0.00	3.1	1.6	0.66	6.92	2.71	81.5	3.7	21.1	9.4	4.4
8.0	1.54	na	0.05	7.0	2.1	1.52	12.63	3.62	50.0	2.6	21.7	10.4	8.3

Name	City	State	2019 Rating	2018 Rating	Rating	Total Assets ($Mil)	One Year Asset Growth	Commercial Loans	Consumer Loans	Mortgage Loans	Securities	Capitalization Index	Leverage Ratio	Risk-Based Capital Ratio
First Bank Kansas	Salina	KS	B+	B+	B	491.1	12.24	9.0	3.1	14.9	38.2	6.7	8.7	17.3
First Bank of Alabama	Talladega	AL	A-	A-	A-	683.8	22.30	10.3	1.4	11.8	25.1	10.0	11.5	17.7
▲ First Bank of Baldwin	Baldwin	WI	B	B-	C	221.4	18.54	7.9	1.1	8.1	32.4	7.2	9.1	17.7
First Bank of Bancroft	Bancroft	NE	B-	B-	B-	25.3	10.03	7.1	1.8	3.3	39.3	10.0	16.1	0.0
First Bank of Beloit	Beloit	KS	B-	B-	C+	88.1	17.34	11.7	1.6	14.7	28.0	10.0	12.7	21.1
First Bank of Berne	Berne	IN	A-	B+	B	864.4	22.97	4.0	0.8	14.4	20.8	7.4	9.2	14.4
First Bank of Boaz	Boaz	AL	A+	A+	A+	280.1	16.09	10.4	1.6	5.2	68.7	10.0	17.1	31.1
First Bank of Celeste	Celeste	TX	C+	C+	C	59.3	9.06	17.3	6.7	3.7	33.7	5.7	7.7	20.4
First Bank of Coastal Georgia	Pembroke	GA	B-	B-	B	129.5	14.37	2.1	0.4	9.7	63.7	10.0	13.8	32.9
First Bank of Greenwich	Cos Cob	CT	C+	B-	B-	483.9	23.55	17.0	0.2	33.1	2.9	6.4	8.4	13.4
First Bank of Highland Park	Highland Park	IL	C	C+	C+	1936.3	6.06	39.0	0.1	2.5	13.4	3.7	9.6	0.0
First Bank of Linden	Linden	AL	B-	B	B+	87.7	9.00	6.7	5.0	3.5	55.9	10.0	13.8	29.1
First Bank of Manhattan	Manhattan	IL	C+	B-	B	212.9	20.29	9.8	1.7	17.2	21.9	6.5	8.5	21.4
▼ First Bank of Muleshoe	Muleshoe	TX	C+	B-	B-	104.1	16.77	3.5	0.9	0.1	70.2	10.0	14.1	56.1
First Bank of Ohio	Tiffin	OH	B+	B+	B+	226.2	10.25	0.0	74.6	0.0	19.1	10.0	33.7	0.0
First Bank of Okarche	Okarche	OK	A	A	A-	119.3	7.76	7.3	1.6	1.4	38.8	10.0	11.8	0.0
First Bank of Owasso	Owasso	OK	A	A-	A-	530.1	22.66	14.1	0.4	8.6	2.1	8.7	10.1	15.2
First Bank of Pike	Molena	GA	C	C-	C-	60.5	10.82	6.7	10.3	23.8	18.2	6.0	8.0	14.8
First Bank of the Lake	Osage Beach	MO	C+	C	C	646.8	482.82	85.2	0.1	0.9	2.8	10.0	14.7	31.1
First Bank of Thomas	Thomas	OK	B+	B+	B+	46.6	0.91	5.1	1.4	10.3	17.0	10.0	15.5	30.7
First Bank of Utica	Utica	NE	C+	C+	C+	73.4	4.81	11.1	4.6	9.7	2.1	10.0	12.0	15.5
First Bank Richmond	Richmond	IN	B-	B-	C+	1054.1	10.52	12.8	1.3	11.5	23.2	10.0	13.9	20.1
▲ First Bank, Upper Michigan	Gladstone	MI	C	D+	D	528.2	11.23	18.8	8.8	16.0	10.8	8.3	10.1	13.6
First Bankers Trust Co., N.A.	Quincy	IL	B-	B-	C+	1079.1	19.03	8.5	3.7	5.7	46.7	6.5	8.5	16.8
First Bethany Bank & Trust	Bethany	OK	B+	B	B	255.1	13.93	9.5	0.4	10.6	36.3	7.4	9.3	0.0
▼ First Business Bank	Madison	WI	C+	B-	C+	2588.3	24.42	31.1	0.3	1.6	8.0	5.2	8.7	11.1
First Cahawba Bank	Selma	AL	B	B	B	156.0	22.76	19.5	3.4	13.4	11.1	8.7	10.2	16.1
First Capital Bank	Laurinburg	NC	D+	C-	C+	226.6	105.09	9.2	2.0	21.0	10.3	9.4	11.6	14.5
▼ First Capital Bank	Germantown	TN	B-	B-	B-	360.2	4.60	16.2	0.4	11.1	0.3	5.2	10.4	0.0
First Capital Bank	Quanah	TX	C-	C	C-	69.6	12.20	20.7	6.8	16.1	0.0	5.9	8.3	11.7
First Carolina Bank	Rocky Mount	NC	B	B	C+	934.2	57.49	7.9	0.1	6.6	21.8	10.0	12.5	15.7
First Central Bank	Cambridge	NE	C-	C-	C	114.2	2.61	16.1	3.4	3.2	9.9	5.5	10.2	0.0
First Central Bank McCook	McCook	NE	D	C-	C-	120.2	-0.69	19.4	2.6	3.7	8.8	6.4	11.4	0.0
First Central National Bank of Saint Paris	Saint Paris	OH	B-	B	B	97.1	4.14	4.9	2.2	12.7	8.6	10.0	17.6	22.6
▲ First Central Savings Bank	Glen Cove	NY	C-	D+	D+	681.2	14.46	10.0	0.0	21.8	6.2	6.1	8.6	11.9
First Central State Bank	De Witt	IA	A-	A-	A-	609.7	12.01	13.1	1.8	11.4	23.6	9.9	11.5	0.0
First Century Bank	Tazewell	TN	B+	B+	B+	469.1	13.77	6.4	1.2	24.6	1.2	7.0	9.0	14.3
First Century Bank, N.A.	Commerce	GA	A-	B	B	329.0	109.38	12.1	0.1	1.9	17.9	10.0	14.1	0.0
First Chatham Bank	Savannah	GA	C+	C-	D-	442.4	17.30	17.1	0.4	6.2	6.3	6.4	8.4	14.0
First Choice Bank	Cerritos	CA	B+	B+	B+	2256.1	36.27	30.7	0.0	9.0	1.8	2.8	10.3	0.0
First Choice Bank	Pontotoc	MS	A-	A-	B+	345.5	11.27	10.3	5.3	21.3	28.6	10.0	12.2	0.0
First Citizens Bank	Luverne	AL	A-	A-	A-	299.8	22.70	10.9	3.8	11.8	31.4	10.0	12.1	19.9
First Citizens Bank	Mason City	IA	A-	A-	A-	1497.2	17.25	16.6	1.0	7.7	20.2	10.0	11.7	16.3
First Citizens Bank of Butte	Butte	MT	B	B-	B-	83.9	20.57	16.7	5.3	16.1	11.5	8.2	9.8	0.0
First Citizens Community Bank	Mansfield	PA	B	B	B	1855.6	25.88	6.0	1.7	18.3	15.5	5.7	8.7	0.0
First Citizens National Bank	Dyersburg	TN	B+	B+	B+	1981.0	11.18	6.4	1.3	9.4	33.8	8.2	9.8	0.0
First Citizens National Bank of Upper Sand	Upper Sandusky	OH	B-	B-	B-	308.0	5.04	4.5	0.8	16.5	18.5	10.0	13.8	0.0
First Citizens State Bank	Whitewater	WI	A-	A-	A-	350.7	12.96	8.4	0.7	19.0	21.8	10.0	18.6	0.0
First Citrus Bank	Tampa	FL	C+	B-	C+	565.6	35.95	24.6	0.0	6.3	0.0	2.3	8.8	0.0
▲ First City Bank	Columbus	OH	B-	C+	C+	73.0	13.76	14.6	0.0	17.9	1.5	10.0	12.5	0.0
First Colony Bank of Florida	Maitland	FL	B+	B	B-	271.9	17.45	9.9	0.2	0.7	14.8	6.8	8.9	13.7
▼ First Colorado National Bank	Paonia	CO	C+	B	C+	77.9	6.85	4.0	0.3	1.3	0.0	10.0	19.6	208.1
First Columbia Bank & Trust Co.	Bloomsburg	PA	A-	A-	B+	845.1	12.11	5.9	0.6	26.3	23.0	10.0	11.1	0.0
First Command Bank	Fort Worth	TX	A-	A-	B+	911.7	15.91	13.5	21.9	0.0	48.3	5.9	7.9	14.0
First Commerce Bank	Marysville	KS	B+	B+	B-	114.6	16.72	13.9	4.8	26.7	6.7	8.3	9.9	0.0
First Commerce Bank	Lakewood	NJ	B	C+	C-	1051.4	4.70	11.5	0.0	21.2	6.6	10.0	14.0	20.4
First Commerce Bank	Lewisburg	TN	B	B	B	474.4	9.71	7.5	3.0	16.7	8.9	6.9	8.9	12.8
▼ First Commercial Bank	Jackson	MS	B-	B	B	529.4	34.86	26.1	1.0	13.5	4.1	7.8	11.3	13.2
First Commercial Bank (USA)	Alhambra	CA	A-	A-	B+	746.5	19.97	7.1	0.0	14.2	4.8	10.0	19.5	25.7
First Commercial Bank, N.A.	Seguin	TX	B	B	B	430.7	22.10	9.1	1.4	12.9	14.8	6.1	8.1	15.7

Asset Quality Index	Adjusted Non-Performing Loans as a % of Total Loans	as a % of Capital	Net Charge-Offs Avg Loans	Profitability Index	Net Income ($Mil)	Return on Assets (R.O.A.)	Return on Equity (R.O.E.)	Net Interest Spread	Overhead Efficiency Ratio	Liquidity Index	Liquidity Ratio	Hot Money Ratio	Stability Index
6.2	0.30	4.0	0.02	8.0	6.7	1.89	19.32	3.61	63.9	5.0	37.8	9.0	7.3
7.2	0.80	na	0.49	6.8	6.0	1.27	9.89	4.19	52.8	1.1	24.8	33.7	9.2
5.4	0.88	na	-0.11	5.7	2.2	1.42	12.90	3.81	60.5	6.1	38.8	2.2	6.6
6.5	9.25	na	-0.08	4.1	0.1	0.72	4.39	3.24	69.2	6.3	59.2	5.4	7.3
8.8	0.00	na	-0.41	5.3	0.7	1.14	8.66	3.86	61.7	4.3	19.0	7.4	7.0
6.4	0.52	na	0.02	9.5	15.4	2.57	25.45	3.71	43.8	5.5	30.7	2.3	8.0
9.5	0.09	0.1	-0.02	7.9	3.1	1.63	9.07	3.56	40.9	4.2	65.0	19.9	9.2
8.6	0.00	na	0.07	4.0	0.4	0.87	11.22	3.35	76.0	4.6	35.6	10.3	4.2
9.7	0.13	na	0.00	3.2	0.6	0.66	4.69	2.96	82.2	5.3	36.6	6.7	7.1
5.8	0.76	na	0.00	3.2	1.4	0.43	4.96	2.91	67.8	0.9	12.1	26.1	5.2
6.9	2.66	na	-0.03	3.1	6.0	0.42	4.34	2.22	72.4	0.9	15.5	25.7	7.6
8.5	0.00	na	0.20	2.9	0.3	0.44	2.96	3.30	84.1	3.1	70.7	34.2	7.2
7.4	1.04	na	0.00	3.0	0.7	0.48	5.07	3.15	84.0	5.1	31.5	5.8	5.5
9.9	0.06	0.0	-0.01	2.4	0.2	0.29	1.91	2.14	85.6	7.4	94.3	6.2	7.1
5.6	0.12	na	0.56	6.8	2.1	1.33	3.87	4.92	39.4	0.8	29.6	62.2	7.4
9.2	0.28	na	-0.08	6.6	1.2	1.41	12.34	2.78	50.3	5.4	73.6	14.5	9.0
7.2	0.00	0.0	0.01	10.0	10.3	2.79	26.76	4.57	38.5	2.3	14.9	11.2	9.6
5.3	0.43	na	0.12	3.6	0.2	0.55	6.48	5.16	85.1	4.1	38.6	13.8	3.0
7.3	0.19	na	0.06	9.2	9.3	3.07	72.07	5.54	39.4	0.5	5.4	44.1	6.0
7.7	1.27	3.8	0.21	5.9	0.5	1.29	8.12	3.51	62.2	4.1	46.1	15.3	8.5
4.2	1.28	6.9	0.14	4.1	0.4	0.67	5.65	3.83	73.4	1.1	12.5	29.2	6.6
8.4	0.13	na	0.02	3.5	7.9	1.00	7.11	3.32	57.4	1.8	17.4	16.7	7.2
2.7	3.16	na	0.09	8.0	7.3	1.97	15.03	4.10	59.5	2.6	18.2	15.8	9.3
5.4	2.48	10.0	0.52	4.2	6.5	0.86	8.55	2.79	60.4	2.8	14.2	11.2	7.5
8.3	0.23	na	0.00	5.8	3.2	1.78	18.09	2.97	61.1	3.5	30.0	12.9	6.3
3.2	1.65	11.7	0.08	4.0	14.0	0.80	8.39	3.46	63.7	3.1	7.6	4.7	7.9
8.4	0.00	na	0.11	4.2	0.7	0.70	6.48	4.51	75.2	4.5	27.5	7.8	5.4
7.4	0.46	na	-0.05	1.3	0.7	0.50	3.97	3.46	77.3	1.1	24.4	33.6	5.8
7.3	0.19	na	0.25	3.6	1.6	0.59	5.67	2.68	52.0	0.6	14.5	55.5	6.3
4.7	0.70	na	0.16	3.7	0.3	0.58	7.17	4.41	75.1	1.5	14.6	25.0	4.3
7.5	0.00	0.0	0.00	5.0	7.5	1.20	10.06	3.02	47.3	1.4	32.3	31.7	7.5
0.0	7.32	na	0.44	5.4	0.9	1.02	10.25	3.78	65.1	0.7	12.8	30.0	5.4
0.0	9.11	na	0.06	6.5	1.1	1.16	10.77	4.08	59.4	0.5	11.9	41.6	5.6
8.9	0.10	0.5	0.00	3.0	0.3	0.46	2.60	2.56	81.2	4.7	46.7	12.6	7.7
3.2	2.35	11.1	0.09	2.3	2.0	0.42	4.48	3.18	79.5	0.8	15.0	38.5	4.2
7.3	0.76	na	0.05	5.6	4.8	1.09	8.93	3.28	56.4	4.1	28.5	10.1	8.0
8.6	0.20	1.0	0.01	8.2	5.3	1.58	17.31	3.91	52.5	3.4	24.3	11.2	6.0
9.7	0.28	na	6.14	9.0	8.8	2.81	25.09	5.18	46.6	7.8	74.4	0.3	5.8
4.6	1.24	na	0.48	4.9	3.0	0.97	10.07	3.93	71.1	4.1	22.1	9.1	4.1
5.2	0.70	na	0.05	7.9	19.0	1.25	9.30	4.31	50.2	2.0	11.2	5.7	10.0
8.5	0.44	na	0.04	5.4	2.7	1.08	8.62	3.75	64.7	1.8	25.0	23.0	7.2
6.5	1.05	6.4	-0.01	5.8	2.4	1.16	8.76	3.77	62.8	2.7	29.3	18.0	7.7
6.0	1.77	na	-0.18	7.6	18.8	1.81	14.62	3.26	49.3	3.3	19.3	13.3	10.0
6.9	0.00	na	0.00	4.3	0.6	1.02	9.52	3.61	73.2	5.3	37.9	6.9	5.6
5.0	1.25	6.9	0.02	7.1	18.7	1.50	14.49	3.96	55.6	2.8	8.4	12.8	9.0
8.4	0.24	na	0.04	5.0	15.8	1.14	9.36	3.42	63.9	2.6	26.1	20.0	9.4
7.9	0.50	na	0.01	3.8	1.7	0.73	5.23	3.72	79.4	5.0	28.2	5.1	7.4
9.3	0.00	na	-0.08	5.9	3.1	1.20	6.37	3.35	54.8	4.0	41.5	15.4	8.4
6.3	0.53	na	0.14	5.3	3.6	0.97	11.42	3.59	61.9	4.1	21.3	8.4	5.3
7.4	0.00	0.0	0.01	3.7	0.4	0.79	7.23	3.70	80.8	2.7	10.4	14.9	6.2
7.0	0.72	na	-0.02	8.4	3.2	1.75	18.68	3.73	46.9	3.7	45.1	17.7	6.9
9.5	0.00	na	-0.40	0.7	-1.0	-1.71	-7.70	1.53	198.3	7.8	108.5	4.5	8.7
7.5	0.93	na	0.00	5.4	6.9	1.18	9.46	3.04	59.5	4.0	21.6	9.5	8.2
7.3	0.21	0.6	0.21	8.6	12.1	1.95	25.91	3.08	60.9	7.1	57.8	1.7	5.8
5.3	0.67	na	0.03	7.5	1.4	1.74	15.24	3.81	57.2	3.1	25.1	14.4	8.2
4.9	1.40	na	0.02	5.4	7.5	0.96	6.84	3.60	55.5	1.5	18.4	27.0	9.7
8.3	0.19	na	0.06	6.3	4.0	1.15	13.09	3.50	55.6	1.0	16.5	32.4	6.6
8.1	0.05	na	-0.01	3.0	1.7	0.51	4.19	3.17	87.1	0.8	8.4	19.2	7.2
7.3	0.00	na	0.00	5.6	4.9	0.94	4.82	2.90	51.5	0.7	16.3	45.4	8.9
5.2	1.26	na	-0.20	5.3	3.6	1.21	13.21	3.71	70.0	5.9	37.8	3.2	5.7

Name	City	State	Rating	2019 Rating	2018 Rating	Total Assets ($Mil)	One Year Asset Growth	Asset Mix (As a % of Total Assets)				Capital- ization Index	Lever- age Ratio	Risk- Based Capital Ratio
								Comm- ercial Loans	Cons- umer Loans	Mort- gage Loans	Secur- ities			
First Commonwealth Bank	Indiana	PA	B+	B+	B+	9264.5	13.92	16.8	8.6	12.8	12.8	6.7	8.7	14.1
First Community Bank	Batesville	AR	B-	B-	B-	1716.5	13.98	14.6	4.0	18.7	12.9	6.0	8.9	11.8
First Community Bank	Newell	IA	B	B	B-	98.0	2.52	5.6	2.6	6.3	14.4	8.0	9.7	14.5
First Community Bank	Harbor Springs	MI	B+	B+	B	390.9	23.11	15.1	0.5	7.6	6.7	6.6	8.6	13.2
First Community Bank	Lester Prairie	MN	B-	B-	B-	71.0	13.21	8.0	1.2	11.3	23.0	7.9	9.6	0.0
▲ First Community Bank	Glasgow	MT	B+	B	B-	335.6	9.67	8.4	1.3	10.5	23.9	9.6	10.7	15.4
First Community Bank	Beemer	NE	B-	B-	C+	165.9	13.33	11.9	1.7	6.5	12.1	7.8	9.6	15.2
▼ First Community Bank	Lexington	SC	B	B+	B+	1382.8	22.40	7.2	0.6	11.2	21.2	6.9	9.0	14.1
First Community Bank	Corpus Christi	TX	B+	A-	B+	532.0	26.14	23.0	2.0	14.4	14.0	9.0	10.3	17.7
First Community Bank	San Benito	TX	B	B	B	577.4	21.02	16.5	0.8	6.7	21.8	6.2	8.2	15.0
First Community Bank	Bluefield	VA	B	B	B	2947.3	33.84	6.0	4.0	28.4	3.1	7.9	9.6	14.5
First Community Bank	Milton	WI	A-	A-	B+	126.6	18.85	10.6	1.0	16.0	24.9	7.4	9.3	13.2
▼ First Community Bank and Trust	Beecher	IL	B+	A-	B+	177.0	13.30	14.5	1.9	6.6	16.5	10.0	11.7	0.0
First Community Bank of Central Alabama	Wetumpka	AL	B+	B+	B+	470.5	24.55	9.2	4.0	12.8	27.2	6.1	8.1	12.5
First Community Bank of Cullman	Cullman	AL	C+	C+	C	129.3	3.64	5.8	2.4	34.9	1.9	6.2	9.0	0.0
First Community Bank of East Tennessee	Rogersville	TN	B+	B	B-	187.0	13.20	8.1	1.7	18.2	8.7	10.0	11.8	0.0
First Community Bank of Hillsboro	Hillsboro	IL	B	B	C+	134.4	19.47	8.1	2.4	13.4	37.6	6.7	8.7	0.0
First Community Bank of Moultrie County	Sullivan	IL	B	B	C+	97.8	8.52	5.4	4.5	22.7	15.9	8.2	9.8	0.0
First Community Bank of Tennessee	Shelbyville	TN	A-	B+	B+	813.8	35.48	4.8	0.6	46.7	8.9	10.0	14.3	16.0
First Community Bank of the Heartland, Inc	Clinton	KY	B-	B-	C+	304.3	23.96	5.9	3.5	13.3	11.3	6.5	8.5	12.2
▼ First Community Bank of the Ozarks	Branson	MO	B	B+	B+	122.3	16.11	6.1	1.9	23.4	12.9	9.7	11.3	0.0
First Community Bank, Xenia-Flora	Xenia	IL	B	B	B-	48.8	18.61	3.2	5.8	22.6	25.4	9.5	10.7	0.0
First Community National Bank	Cuba	MO	D+	C-	D-	143.2	9.88	8.1	1.7	18.1	13.5	6.7	8.7	14.6
First Community Trust, N.A.	Dubuque	IA	U	U	U	12.8	5.08	0.0	0.0	0.0	38.4	10.0	88.4	0.0
First County Bank	Stamford	CT	C	C+	C+	1912.2	11.52	9.4	0.9	43.8	10.8	6.8	8.8	16.4
▲ First Credit Bank	Los Angeles	CA	B	B-	C	412.5	-9.28	1.6	0.0	8.1	3.7	10.0	45.8	59.9
▲ First Dakota National Bank	Yankton	SD	B+	B	B	2000.9	14.42	15.6	1.6	6.2	10.8	7.5	9.9	12.9
First Eagle Bank	Chicago	IL	A	A	A	559.8	5.88	5.6	0.0	19.2	29.0	10.0	17.3	0.0
First Electronic Bank	Salt Lake City	UT	A-	A-	B	37.5	-32.87	11.0	21.2	0.0	0.1	10.0	40.4	100.5
▲ First Enterprise Bank	Oklahoma City	OK	B+	B-	C-	196.9	26.24	14.8	0.4	13.7	0.0	9.3	10.7	0.0
First Exchange Bank	White Hall	WV	C-	C-	C-	313.4	8.33	10.8	3.4	39.2	7.0	6.8	8.9	0.0
First FarmBank	Greeley	CO	B-	C+	C-	294.4	16.35	11.3	0.3	10.2	10.2	6.3	8.3	12.1
First Farmers & Merchants Bank	Cannon Falls	MN	B+	B+	A-	385.3	21.16	13.1	2.0	8.2	11.4	10.0	12.3	18.4
First Farmers & Merchants National Bank	Fairmont	MN	B	B	B+	129.7	25.19	25.5	5.1	14.6	6.7	10.0	12.2	16.1
First Farmers & Merchants National Bank	Luverne	MN	B	B	B+	203.9	14.68	15.5	2.0	2.4	7.4	10.0	15.3	17.6
First Farmers & Merchants State Bank	Brownsdale	MN	B	B	B+	87.2	18.58	10.5	0.9	3.2	15.3	10.0	16.4	21.7
First Farmers & Merchants State Bank	Grand Meadow	MN	B	B	B+	72.6	2.14	10.4	0.4	5.4	6.0	8.1	9.8	13.8
First Farmers and Commercial Bank	Pikeville	TN	B-	B-	C+	161.6	23.04	11.0	3.2	15.8	11.8	8.1	9.7	14.7
First Farmers and Merchants Bank	Columbia	TN	B+	B+	B	1716.4	25.59	9.4	0.9	17.7	28.6	6.5	8.6	15.6
▼ First Farmers Bank & Trust Co.	Converse	IN	C+	B-	B-	2085.2	9.81	17.8	0.7	4.4	18.7	8.8	10.2	14.0
First Farmers National Bank of Waurika	Waurika	OK	B	B	B	48.3	9.43	1.6	2.6	0.6	47.5	10.0	20.0	0.0
First Farmers State Bank	Minier	IL	A-	A-	A-	196.8	14.34	6.9	0.3	6.1	16.5	10.0	12.0	21.7
First Federal Bank	Lake City	FL	A-	A-	A-	3061.2	38.83	7.2	1.9	28.6	23.9	8.3	9.9	16.8
▼ First Federal Bank	Dunn	NC	C	C+	C	204.5	10.57	7.9	0.4	32.9	21.4	9.9	10.9	19.8
First Federal Bank	Dickson	TN	A-	A-	A-	795.9	10.39	4.2	2.0	19.7	34.2	9.1	10.4	0.0
▲ First Federal Bank & Trust	Sheridan	WY	B+	B	C+	377.0	15.29	13.3	1.2	24.1	19.0	10.0	16.0	20.0
First Federal Bank Littlefield, Texas	Littlefield	TX	B-	B	B	51.2	1.81	12.5	10.4	15.9	0.0	10.0	19.8	25.2
First Federal Bank Of Kansas City	Kansas City	MO	C-	D+	C-	806.7	-1.54	0.0	2.8	56.6	9.0	10.0	14.9	0.0
First Federal Bank of Louisiana	Lake Charles	LA	C+	C+	C+	1022.4	16.58	6.4	1.6	25.2	14.7	10.0	11.6	22.2
First Federal Bank of Ohio	Galion	OH	C+	C+	C	247.5	3.65	0.1	0.9	33.1	33.3	10.0	14.6	33.1
▲ First Federal Bank of Wisconsin	Waukesha	WI	B	B-	C+	285.6	10.72	8.3	0.2	19.7	20.9	10.0	25.9	34.1
First Federal Bank, A FSB	Tuscaloosa	AL	C+	C	C-	176.9	25.37	0.0	0.4	74.2	0.5	10.0	14.7	23.3
First Federal Community Bank of Bucyrus	Bucyrus	OH	C+	C+	C+	212.8	19.75	9.3	4.3	47.1	5.6	6.4	8.4	12.1
First Federal Community Bank, N.A.	Dover	OH	B	B	B	536.2	21.00	14.5	2.0	23.5	3.8	6.3	8.3	13.8
First Federal Community Bank, SSB	Paris	TX	B	B	B	488.1	9.02	13.0	2.5	36.6	2.6	10.0	11.1	16.1
▼ First Federal S&L Assn.	Hazard	KY	C-	C+	C	87.7	5.75	0.0	1.2	72.6	0.2	10.0	21.9	0.0
First Federal S&L Assn.	Morehead	KY	C+	C+	C+	34.0	0.90	3.9	1.1	55.0	0.0	10.0	29.4	50.9
▲ First Federal S&L Assn.	Aberdeen	MS	C+	C+	B-	45.5	5.20	0.0	1.6	59.4	10.4	10.0	16.5	0.0
First Federal S&L Assn. of Bath	Bath	ME	B	B	B	154.5	13.78	2.5	1.1	63.0	3.2	10.0	15.7	30.0
First Federal S&L Assn. of Centerburg	Centerburg	OH	C+	C+	C+	24.4	2.96	0.0	0.6	58.2	2.0	10.0	20.0	0.0

Asset Quality Index	Adjusted Non-Performing Loans as a % of Total Loans	as a % of Capital	Net Charge-Offs Avg Loans	Profitability Index	Net Income ($Mil)	Return on Assets (R.O.A.)	Return on Equity (R.O.E.)	Net Interest Spread	Overhead Efficiency Ratio	Liquidity Index	Liquidity Ratio	Hot Money Ratio	Stability Index
5.4	0.70	3.9	0.25	4.7	52.4	0.79	6.35	3.38	58.2	4.6	5.3	3.7	9.5
5.4	1.38	na	0.14	5.2	12.8	1.04	11.60	3.70	64.3	1.1	13.7	31.8	7.4
6.3	0.05	na	0.00	5.1	0.8	1.11	8.84	3.51	65.2	4.3	32.3	10.8	7.6
7.4	0.03	na	-0.01	5.7	3.4	1.29	14.19	4.43	67.9	4.8	23.1	4.7	6.4
8.9	0.00	na	0.00	4.3	0.4	0.88	8.22	3.81	71.7	4.7	39.6	11.1	5.4
6.3	0.75	na	-0.12	6.0	2.9	1.19	10.47	4.01	66.8	3.4	20.9	10.8	7.1
6.7	0.48	na	-0.01	4.3	1.0	0.83	7.91	4.14	72.4	1.1	22.5	29.4	6.5
8.1	0.38	1.7	-0.02	4.2	7.3	0.78	7.02	3.47	68.8	4.5	20.6	7.3	8.6
6.4	0.56	2.9	0.09	5.8	4.8	1.31	11.78	4.99	72.2	3.6	22.7	11.9	7.6
7.8	0.00	na	0.06	6.7	5.6	1.39	16.15	4.41	64.6	3.7	25.6	11.5	6.5
4.4	1.61	na	0.20	7.0	25.2	1.18	8.37	4.34	57.9	4.5	16.9	6.4	10.0
8.8	0.12	na	0.01	8.3	1.9	2.10	21.70	3.63	50.1	4.1	37.1	13.8	7.7
3.7	3.94	na	-0.24	6.5	1.5	1.21	9.58	4.13	60.1	6.1	41.4	3.2	6.4
6.9	0.45	2.4	0.02	9.5	6.6	2.04	25.28	3.80	50.7	4.3	39.8	13.6	6.6
5.3	1.84	8.8	0.12	3.6	0.6	0.65	7.64	3.18	66.6	0.8	15.1	30.4	5.3
7.3	0.87	na	-0.69	3.9	0.9	0.65	5.19	3.77	85.4	4.5	25.7	6.9	7.0
8.4	0.44	na	0.00	5.4	1.2	1.37	14.76	3.07	55.0	4.4	18.6	6.3	5.4
8.1	0.17	na	0.01	5.0	0.8	1.17	11.28	3.56	67.2	5.3	34.8	5.8	6.4
7.9	0.10	2.2	0.09	8.3	34.5	7.09	58.10	2.90	57.0	0.5	8.5	32.2	8.4
5.1	0.88	na	0.07	4.3	2.4	1.16	11.73	4.42	71.9	1.4	14.5	23.6	5.9
7.1	0.75	na	0.63	3.7	0.6	0.67	6.07	3.71	75.0	3.8	18.7	10.4	6.6
7.8	0.31	na	0.15	6.2	0.5	1.46	12.57	3.50	59.8	4.2	45.7	15.2	7.4
5.5	2.12	na	-0.05	1.1	0.3	0.33	3.70	3.47	105.7	5.1	43.3	10.3	3.4
10.0	na	na	na	9.5	0.7	7.94	8.75	0.65	75.2	4.0	na	0.0	6.4
5.4	2.00	13.8	0.06	2.3	3.7	0.27	3.13	2.80	79.1	1.5	18.2	20.0	6.5
4.6	4.47	na	0.00	10.0	10.6	3.24	7.38	5.21	26.1	2.8	60.4	45.6	8.2
5.7	0.71	6.0	0.16	6.9	20.4	1.45	14.21	4.42	57.1	4.2	11.6	7.3	8.5
8.9	0.46	na	0.01	9.7	9.4	2.27	12.52	3.59	41.6	1.8	23.2	20.1	10.0
7.7	0.00	na	0.00	9.8	0.5	1.60	4.35	8.74	92.1	4.2	107.7	20.6	8.4
5.8	0.32	na	0.12	7.4	2.1	1.54	13.44	5.01	67.8	1.0	25.9	32.3	8.8
2.4	3.79	23.0	0.12	4.9	2.6	1.11	12.03	3.97	64.2	1.8	12.2	19.8	7.1
6.8	0.08	na	0.06	4.2	1.6	0.77	8.96	3.95	70.2	1.2	11.6	28.3	4.9
4.5	2.71	13.1	0.38	8.0	4.7	1.75	12.82	4.02	54.0	4.8	29.5	6.6	8.0
4.0	3.00	15.9	0.29	4.8	0.9	1.00	7.69	3.78	63.1	1.4	5.6	23.2	7.1
3.2	2.90	13.4	0.32	7.1	2.3	1.55	9.99	3.99	56.6	2.2	10.4	17.6	8.2
5.6	1.90	7.3	0.23	4.6	0.6	0.94	5.34	3.72	67.3	4.8	27.5	5.8	7.5
0.0	14.92	77.9	1.87	2.0	-0.3	-0.56	-5.28	3.54	76.0	2.6	19.4	14.9	6.4
5.2	1.49	na	0.03	4.7	1.0	0.87	8.71	3.77	62.6	0.8	16.2	33.0	4.6
8.7	0.19	0.9	-0.01	4.6	11.0	0.95	9.64	3.11	68.4	4.3	19.6	5.3	8.1
3.1	3.41	18.5	0.69	7.0	20.8	1.38	12.95	3.71	52.9	4.0	12.6	7.7	9.8
8.9	0.19	na	-0.17	5.3	0.5	1.33	6.29	3.46	60.6	3.1	48.5	22.2	7.7
7.4	0.00	0.0	0.00	7.5	2.6	1.81	15.11	3.51	56.2	2.6	18.5	16.3	8.1
6.0	0.65	2.8	0.01	8.6	50.8	2.47	23.28	3.63	52.8	1.8	20.5	8.5	10.0
5.4	1.52	na	0.00	2.6	0.6	0.38	3.47	3.77	93.4	2.8	27.1	16.7	6.1
7.3	0.86	na	-0.02	6.5	8.1	1.42	11.49	3.50	54.0	4.3	39.2	13.4	8.6
5.3	1.90	na	-0.05	6.7	3.7	1.53	9.80	3.54	67.4	3.8	20.8	10.6	7.3
7.7	0.00	0.0	0.12	2.8	0.1	0.20	1.02	4.30	80.8	1.0	22.4	34.8	6.8
9.0	0.35	na	0.06	3.3	5.6	0.95	7.07	2.21	73.7	2.0	29.4	24.8	7.1
8.5	0.80	na	0.01	3.0	3.6	0.50	4.05	2.81	80.9	4.3	25.2	11.0	7.6
9.5	1.11	na	0.30	2.0	0.7	0.37	2.56	2.79	92.6	6.3	54.8	6.3	7.2
8.4	0.88	na	-0.02	4.0	1.6	0.75	3.02	3.66	69.6	4.0	31.8	12.0	7.2
8.2	1.43	na	0.01	7.9	10.0	9.27	79.57	2.92	54.7	0.5	7.4	54.8	6.3
5.3	1.66	na	0.01	5.3	1.6	1.07	13.04	3.60	75.8	1.9	9.8	18.9	4.2
7.1	0.31	2.2	0.02	7.3	5.6	1.52	17.63	3.43	50.8	3.8	17.6	9.9	6.5
6.3	0.89	na	0.01	3.5	2.1	0.60	5.36	3.42	76.0	1.4	13.0	25.4	6.7
4.6	3.04	na	0.00	3.6	0.4	0.71	3.22	3.04	70.1	1.1	5.7	27.3	5.6
6.1	5.32	na	-0.02	2.4	0.1	0.23	0.78	3.30	91.6	1.6	23.4	25.9	6.5
9.8	0.00	na	0.00	3.2	0.2	0.61	3.68	1.93	70.5	1.9	39.3	39.3	6.9
5.5	5.18	na	0.08	3.9	0.7	0.64	4.07	4.40	76.4	3.7	25.5	11.8	7.8
9.9	0.00	na	0.00	3.3	0.1	0.58	2.78	3.44	79.6	2.4	34.0	19.2	6.5

Name	City	State	2020 Rating	2019 Rating	2018 Rating	Total Assets ($Mil)	One Year Asset Growth	Commercial Loans	Consumer Loans	Mortgage Loans	Securities	Capitalization Index	Leverage Ratio	Risk-Based Capital Ratio
First Federal S&L Assn. of Central Illinois,	Shelbyville	IL	B+	B+	B+	148.6	15.65	8.3	4.6	25.4	23.3	9.4	10.6	15.5
▼ First Federal S&L Assn. of Delta	Delta	OH	C-	C+	C-	187.5	14.75	1.9	0.3	40.2	16.3	10.0	11.4	32.7
▼ First Federal S&L Assn. of Greene County	Waynesburg	PA	C+	B-	C+	983.9	5.75	0.0	0.4	62.5	17.5	10.0	13.9	31.7
First Federal S&L Assn. of Greensburg	Greensburg	IN	C+	C+	C	160.4	7.95	0.6	1.9	37.6	28.0	8.2	9.8	22.0
▲ First Federal S&L Assn. of Lakewood	Lakewood	OH	C+	C-	C-	2130.0	11.01	6.7	3.9	55.0	4.7	8.9	10.3	0.0
First Federal S&L Assn. of Lorain	Lorain	OH	C-	C	C	458.1	3.90	0.0	0.2	61.5	15.8	10.0	14.6	31.1
▼ First Federal S&L Assn. of McMinnville	McMinnville	OR	B-	B	B	534.1	16.34	0.6	0.1	37.4	27.9	10.0	13.2	29.2
▲ First Federal S&L Assn. of Newark	Newark	OH	B-	C	C	232.5	4.84	0.0	0.2	41.4	10.0	10.0	15.9	0.0
First Federal S&L Assn. of Pascagoula-Mo	Pascagoula	MS	C	C	C	337.7	8.46	0.0	0.3	76.5	9.5	6.8	8.9	19.9
First Federal S&L Assn. of Port Angeles	Port Angeles	WA	B-	B-	C+	1556.8	26.17	2.9	7.5	22.3	23.3	9.3	10.5	16.0
First Federal S&L Assn. of Ravenswood	Ravenswood	WV	D+	D+	D	25.5	1.07	0.0	0.4	69.7	0.1	6.6	8.6	19.2
First Federal S&L Assn. of San Rafael	San Rafael	CA	B-	B-	B-	222.4	7.99	0.0	0.0	1.2	0.0	10.0	18.7	26.6
First Federal S&L Assn. of Valdosta	Valdosta	GA	C+	B-	C+	210.0	11.59	0.0	2.4	61.5	1.1	10.0	14.2	25.3
First Federal S&L Assn. of Van Wert	Van Wert	OH	B-	C+	C+	123.6	8.99	0.0	0.2	45.2	32.4	10.0	19.5	0.0
▲ First Federal S&L Bank	Olathe	KS	B	B	B	98.9	1.89	0.4	0.0	74.3	0.0	10.0	12.7	25.8
First Federal Savings Bank	Ottawa	IL	C-	C	C	375.1	3.02	2.0	0.9	45.5	3.9	10.0	11.1	0.0
First Federal Savings Bank	Evansville	IN	C	C	C	473.6	4.91	22.7	0.9	24.0	11.6	6.0	8.0	12.6
First Federal Savings Bank	Huntington	IN	B-	B-	B	392.9	11.74	22.3	2.5	10.4	18.8	9.5	10.7	17.3
First Federal Savings Bank	Rochester	IN	B	B-	C	484.3	13.90	1.2	0.1	61.9	0.0	9.2	10.4	20.7
First Federal Savings Bank of Angola	Angola	IN	B	B	B	137.1	6.53	0.4	2.7	58.6	0.0	10.0	19.7	0.0
▼ First Federal Savings Bank of Kentucky	Frankfort	KY	C-	C	C	242.4	-1.77	1.1	0.4	65.3	0.2	10.0	12.5	0.0
First Federal Savings of Middletown	Middletown	NY	C+	C+	C-	162.9	9.92	0.0	0.0	0.5	22.0	10.0	35.1	0.0
First Fidelity Bank	Fort Payne	AL	C+	C+	C+	117.3	15.41	11.7	1.9	23.0	36.0	7.1	9.1	19.0
▼ First Fidelity Bank	Oklahoma City	OK	B-	B	B	2114.4	19.41	14.3	12.4	6.7	16.4	3.5	8.3	0.0
First Fidelity Bank	Burke	SD	B+	B+	B	424.7	14.33	6.6	2.1	1.5	28.8	7.8	9.5	14.4
First Financial Bank	Bessemer	AL	C+	C+	B-	199.0	18.19	13.2	1.4	11.3	30.0	6.7	8.7	16.1
First Financial Bank	El Dorado	AR	B+	B+	B+	1517.1	41.61	10.2	1.6	4.9	4.3	8.7	10.2	0.0
First Financial Bank	Cincinnati	OH	B+	B+	B+	15851.3	10.01	19.0	0.6	8.8	19.8	8.2	10.0	13.5
First Financial Bank in Winnebago	Winnebago	MN	B+	B	B	50.5	6.34	17.3	2.3	7.8	19.1	10.0	14.5	19.2
First Financial Bank, N.A.	Terre Haute	IN	A-	A-	A-	4262.8	9.63	17.0	8.6	9.0	22.4	10.0	11.4	15.9
First Financial Bank, N.A.	Abilene	TX	A	A	A	10531.6	30.31	12.4	4.0	11.8	41.7	9.1	10.4	19.6
First Financial Northwest Bank	Renton	WA	B	B+	A-	1365.4	4.37	4.5	2.2	28.2	9.4	8.6	10.0	15.3
First Financial Trust & Asset Mgmt Co.	Abilene	TX	U	U	U	35.4	22.73	0.0	0.0	0.0	77.7	10.0	105.	324.9
First Financial Trust, N.A.	Wellesley	MA	U	U	U	10.9	7.51	0.0	0.0	0.0	14.5	10.0	99.0	0.0
First Florida Integrity Bank	Naples	FL	B-	B	B-	1901.2	24.66	17.2	0.2	6.9	13.9	6.6	8.6	14.0
First Foundation Bank	Irvine	CA	B-	B-	B-	6465.4	1.94	9.4	0.2	12.6	13.7	5.6	8.2	11.4
First Freedom Bank	Lebanon	TN	C+	B-	C+	621.1	28.23	27.3	4.4	9.1	0.0	2.0	9.6	0.0
First FSB of Champaign-Urbana	Champaign	IL	C+	B-	C+	199.0	18.69	7.3	0.8	20.1	0.0	7.6	9.4	0.0
First FSB of Lincolnton	Lincolnton	NC	B+	A-	B+	416.5	6.22	0.5	0.4	52.5	7.2	10.0	16.2	34.4
First FSB of Mascoutah	Mascoutah	IL	C+	C	C	125.0	14.69	4.2	1.1	41.8	28.8	10.0	11.6	22.2
First FSB of Twin Falls	Twin Falls	ID	A-	A-	B+	899.3	27.60	12.0	3.9	28.0	3.8	9.0	10.6	14.2
First FSB of Washington	Washington	IN	C-	C-	C-	78.1	1.52	7.6	2.9	49.5	4.3	10.0	11.8	22.6
First General Bank	Rowland Heights	CA	A	A-	B+	1066.8	8.55	8.2	0.0	3.9	0.7	10.0	14.9	0.0
▼ First Guaranty Bank	Hammond	LA	B-	B	B	2509.1	39.33	15.1	1.3	10.9	16.6	5.1	8.6	11.1
First Harrison Bank	Corydon	IN	B+	B+	B-	942.8	15.26	8.2	6.2	11.6	28.0	7.8	9.5	0.0
First Hawaiian Bank	Honolulu	HI	B+	B+	B	22310.8	8.30	12.6	6.0	16.0	25.5	5.8	7.8	13.3
First Heritage Bank	Shenandoah	IA	B-	B-	B-	49.4	27.36	23.2	2.5	16.9	16.6	8.1	10.3	0.0
First Heritage Bank	Centralia	KS	B+	B	B	202.9	17.46	31.0	0.8	6.9	25.9	6.5	8.5	0.0
First Home Bank	Saint Petersburg	FL	C+	B+	A-	1501.4	196.26	71.8	0.1	13.5	0.0	9.8	10.9	16.8
First Hope Bank, A National Banking Assn.	Hope	NJ	C+	C	C	621.6	21.05	10.3	0.2	10.6	17.3	6.2	8.2	14.2
First Horizon Bank	Memphis	TN	B	B-	B-	82688.7	89.95	20.1	1.0	13.0	9.6	6.2	8.3	11.9
First IC Bank	Doraville	GA	B+	B+	A	739.8	5.30	10.2	0.0	7.7	5.6	10.0	11.1	15.0
▼ First Independence Bank	Detroit	MI	C+	B-	B-	290.6	4.52	12.7	0.1	14.4	2.3	3.4	8.6	0.0
▲ First Independent Bank	Russell	MN	B-	C	C	328.8	16.05	10.8	2.3	8.9	31.2	9.1	10.4	15.3
First Independent Bank	Aurora	MO	B	B	B	105.9	12.19	9.0	3.5	20.8	31.5	10.0	11.3	0.0
First International Bank & Trust	Watford City	ND	B	B	B	4105.9	28.92	17.9	2.3	8.9	10.8	6.1	8.1	13.0
First Internet Bank of Indiana	Fishers	IN	B-	B-	B-	4330.7	5.81	13.8	6.7	4.9	13.8	6.5	8.5	13.2
First Interstate Bank	Billings	MT	B+	B+	B-	17009.4	16.18	13.1	6.1	7.7	20.6	6.2	8.2	12.9
First Iowa State Bank	Albia	IA	B+	B+	B+	167.2	19.88	8.8	1.1	10.8	29.5	10.0	12.1	0.0
First Iowa State Bank	Keosauqua	IA	B	B+	B+	141.1	4.36	16.1	2.8	15.9	19.3	9.1	10.6	0.0

Arrows denote recent upgrades ▲ or downgrades ▼

Asset Quality Index	Adjusted Non-Performing Loans as a % of Total Loans	as a % of Capital	Net Charge-Offs Avg Loans	Profitability Index	Net Income ($Mil)	Return on Assets (R.O.A.)	Return on Equity (R.O.E.)	Net Interest Spread	Overhead Efficiency Ratio	Liquidity Index	Liquidity Ratio	Hot Money Ratio	Stability Index
6.1	0.72	na	0.08	5.4	1.1	1.01	8.69	3.70	67.8	2.1	21.9	18.9	6.0
9.7	0.39	na	0.03	1.4	0.1	0.11	0.84	2.83	96.8	6.8	55.3	3.0	6.2
9.6	0.65	na	0.02	2.3	1.5	0.20	1.41	2.20	87.8	2.3	35.4	25.3	8.0
6.1	2.26	na	0.00	3.5	0.8	0.64	6.29	2.92	73.8	6.6	47.7	1.6	6.1
8.4	0.34	na	0.04	4.4	17.4	1.14	10.84	2.26	60.7	2.5	12.7	13.2	7.1
5.8	4.23	na	-0.14	1.4	0.4	0.13	0.87	2.48	105.7	3.1	27.2	15.1	7.2
9.7	0.57	na	0.00	2.9	1.4	0.39	2.74	3.04	76.0	5.6	50.3	9.4	8.3
7.3	2.59	na	0.00	3.5	1.1	0.63	3.95	3.21	74.9	1.8	29.0	26.4	7.3
7.2	1.07	na	0.07	2.4	0.8	0.32	3.55	2.79	85.4	0.7	17.9	50.3	4.7
8.2	0.50	na	0.10	3.4	6.7	0.65	6.02	3.20	72.8	2.3	23.3	14.4	8.7
8.8	0.30	na	0.00	3.5	0.1	0.60	7.02	2.99	75.5	1.0	19.9	33.4	4.8
7.2	0.00	na	0.00	2.8	0.6	0.35	1.81	3.36	85.3	1.1	17.1	30.7	7.6
5.4	3.10	na	-0.01	2.6	0.5	0.32	2.15	3.75	87.8	2.6	20.0	16.6	6.9
10.0	0.11	na	0.00	3.4	0.7	0.73	3.57	3.17	73.6	4.7	44.5	12.7	7.8
4.1	3.64	na	0.03	9.8	1.8	2.49	20.72	3.91	32.5	0.6	22.5	45.4	9.3
8.5	1.67	na	-0.05	1.8	0.2	0.08	0.66	1.96	90.3	3.3	42.1	19.3	6.4
5.9	0.43	3.0	0.02	2.8	1.7	0.49	5.19	3.02	82.1	3.4	9.1	10.1	5.1
3.7	2.11	na	-0.06	6.6	4.2	1.46	13.18	3.39	54.2	1.7	22.7	14.8	7.6
4.8	4.57	na	0.02	7.7	7.3	1.97	19.45	3.62	64.2	1.7	19.9	22.8	6.3
9.6	0.21	na	0.05	4.3	0.8	0.77	3.77	2.97	67.5	4.7	41.4	11.8	7.6
4.5	1.71	na	0.02	0.2	-13.0	-7.04	-46.08	2.97	330.1	1.0	8.1	30.7	6.1
9.9	0.00	na	0.00	3.0	0.7	0.57	1.61	3.00	70.6	5.5	81.9	15.0	7.4
6.7	0.79	na	-0.01	3.4	0.6	0.71	7.46	2.99	74.8	4.4	50.4	15.8	5.1
6.0	0.76	3.9	-0.01	4.7	16.5	1.11	11.94	3.37	62.3	5.0	17.2	2.5	8.7
6.9	0.11	na	0.02	8.1	5.4	1.79	18.11	4.18	55.1	4.7	27.7	6.9	7.2
7.9	0.25	na	0.08	4.5	2.0	1.43	16.50	3.54	80.6	5.3	28.2	3.1	3.8
5.0	3.61	na	0.30	8.0	18.5	1.67	14.35	3.70	64.1	1.6	23.6	27.9	10.0
5.3	0.82	3.2	0.10	5.9	121.7	1.07	7.25	3.63	56.3	3.7	13.7	5.1	9.9
8.2	0.95	na	0.00	5.3	0.5	1.32	8.93	3.87	67.6	3.7	23.9	11.6	8.0
6.7	0.66	na	0.09	6.2	36.1	1.16	8.60	3.89	60.6	4.4	14.3	6.4	10.0
7.0	0.79	2.7	0.07	9.5	138.6	1.88	13.34	3.91	44.2	5.0	19.4	3.3	10.0
7.5	0.31	na	-0.01	3.9	6.9	0.67	6.80	3.14	70.5	0.9	10.9	32.3	9.4
10.0	na	0.0	na	9.5	10.8	48.28	46.99	2.64	40.8	4.0	na	0.0	7.0
6.5	na	na	na	9.5	0.6	7.53	7.66	1.77	66.3	4.0	na	0.0	5.0
8.6	0.00	0.0	0.05	4.0	10.4	0.79	8.92	3.31	53.6	4.5	21.0	7.2	7.4
6.0	0.47	3.5	0.01	6.1	62.8	1.25	13.12	3.07	44.6	1.8	16.8	11.8	7.5
5.1	0.50	na	0.32	5.9	4.9	1.16	12.56	3.87	52.9	0.9	12.3	28.1	6.0
3.7	2.73	na	0.01	4.2	1.1	0.80	8.32	2.81	76.5	6.8	53.8	2.8	5.5
8.0	1.40	na	-0.02	3.9	2.2	0.72	4.37	3.06	66.4	1.8	33.7	31.4	8.6
9.6	0.00	na	0.00	3.0	0.5	0.52	4.30	2.53	73.3	1.8	27.0	23.7	6.3
8.3	0.26	na	-0.02	6.2	6.7	1.12	10.10	4.60	73.0	4.6	23.6	5.9	6.8
6.2	0.96	na	0.01	1.0	-0.1	-0.08	-0.65	2.91	102.0	1.7	25.0	24.7	6.4
7.0	0.14	na	0.00	9.8	13.8	1.83	12.42	3.60	29.8	0.6	7.5	40.8	10.0
4.4	1.51	11.6	0.08	4.3	16.0	0.93	9.25	3.40	64.8	1.5	17.7	23.6	7.4
6.8	0.74	na	0.06	5.2	7.0	1.07	9.63	3.46	63.6	6.2	42.0	3.0	6.8
6.9	0.34	1.7	0.29	5.2	128.5	0.79	6.43	2.78	51.7	4.2	22.1	10.1	10.0
8.3	0.03	na	0.00	7.1	0.6	1.74	16.55	4.58	58.1	3.3	17.6	12.9	5.7
8.3	0.08	na	0.00	6.0	2.2	1.43	15.36	3.50	58.4	1.7	21.4	10.7	6.3
5.7	0.26	na	0.59	3.9	7.6	0.93	16.21	2.91	76.4	3.1	2.6	12.2	7.6
5.7	0.75	4.8	0.25	3.3	2.5	0.57	6.39	3.09	79.2	5.1	30.1	5.2	5.0
5.0	1.08	6.1	0.28	6.8	663.9	1.54	15.22	2.99	49.9	3.8	15.0	4.7	9.9
4.9	1.70	na	0.16	6.4	5.1	0.93	8.35	3.26	58.8	1.7	22.2	23.4	10.0
6.4	0.40	na	1.62	4.4	0.6	0.72	8.97	4.08	91.3	1.5	12.2	18.3	5.0
3.7	2.19	na	0.19	5.3	2.9	1.27	11.10	3.84	60.1	3.4	33.1	15.9	7.6
7.0	1.79	na	0.14	3.8	0.5	0.71	5.99	3.17	72.7	4.3	51.5	16.3	6.1
5.2	1.64	8.8	0.06	6.5	45.1	1.58	17.71	4.05	65.0	3.9	16.7	9.5	8.3
7.7	0.33	na	0.06	3.7	22.9	0.72	9.02	1.74	55.7	0.9	18.2	34.4	6.5
5.8	0.46	2.6	0.14	6.3	128.0	1.10	8.86	3.60	55.7	5.1	22.3	4.2	9.7
6.2	0.19	na	0.13	7.9	2.1	1.78	13.54	4.10	52.8	4.5	36.2	11.2	8.3
4.5	1.50	na	-0.02	5.6	1.3	1.28	11.34	5.16	70.4	4.4	22.3	7.2	7.4

Name	City	State	2019 Rating	2018 Rating	Rating	Total Assets ($Mil)	One Year Asset Growth	Commercial Loans	Consumer Loans	Mortgage Loans	Securities	Capitalization Index	Leverage Ratio	Risk-Based Capital Ratio
First Jackson Bank, Inc.	Stevenson	AL	A-	A-	B+	339.0	22.72	7.3	3.2	14.7	14.3	10.0	11.1	0.0
First Kansas Bank	Hoisington	KS	B+	B+	B	211.3	16.21	4.4	1.1	12.9	60.7	6.3	8.3	22.7
First Kentucky Bank, Inc.	Mayfield	KY	B	B	B	483.6	8.45	6.6	4.9	23.2	24.8	6.9	8.9	14.2
First Keystone Community Bank	Berwick	PA	B	B	B	1133.2	11.29	7.9	0.5	19.8	27.9	7.5	9.3	14.4
First Liberty Bank	Oklahoma City	OK	B-	B-	B-	550.4	25.04	33.5	0.4	15.9	3.0	5.4	9.2	11.3
First Liberty National Bank	Liberty	TX	B+	A-	B+	391.3	20.93	10.8	3.6	17.4	26.3	9.1	10.4	20.4
First Merchants Bank	Muncie	IN	A-	A-	A-	13715.7	11.46	21.0	0.9	8.5	21.7	8.1	9.8	14.0
First Metro Bank	Muscle Shoals	AL	A	A	A	801.1	18.99	13.2	2.1	15.7	20.6	9.2	10.4	0.0
First Mid Bank & Trust, N.A.	Mattoon	IL	B+	B+	B+	4480.0	17.62	18.0	1.8	6.6	16.7	7.2	9.1	14.0
First Midwest Bank	Chicago	IL	B	B	B	20986.1	17.12	23.6	2.0	12.4	15.7	5.3	7.5	11.2
First Midwest Bank of Dexter	Dexter	MO	B-	B-	B-	417.8	26.39	33.5	1.8	11.0	2.7	7.4	10.1	12.8
First Midwest Bank of Poplar Bluff	Poplar Bluff	MO	B	B-	B-	480.7	9.09	22.6	3.3	23.2	4.7	7.7	9.6	13.1
First Midwest Bank of the Ozarks	Piedmont	MO	B-	B-	B-	139.7	11.98	18.4	4.6	12.3	15.5	8.2	10.0	13.5
First Minnetonka City Bank	Minnetonka	MN	A-	A-	B+	259.2	20.23	17.1	1.2	13.4	26.5	8.3	9.9	21.2
First Missouri Bank	Brookfield	MO	C	B-	B-	336.9	17.49	13.9	0.9	12.8	4.6	7.7	9.5	13.5
First Missouri Bank of SEMO	Kennett	MO	B+	B+	A-	192.7	-11.80	12.9	2.2	23.3	1.4	6.9	9.0	12.9
First Missouri State Bank	Poplar Bluff	MO	B	B+	B+	195.6	10.85	10.5	4.4	32.7	0.3	7.7	9.5	14.4
▲ First Missouri State Bank of Cape County	Cape Girardeau	MO	B	B-	B-	178.0	5.16	13.4	1.8	18.2	5.6	7.1	9.0	13.6
First Montana Bank, Inc.	Missoula	MT	B-	C+	B-	398.4	25.88	15.1	3.7	8.3	17.3	7.5	9.3	14.3
▲ First Mutual Bank, FSB	Belpre	OH	C+	C-	C-	92.6	3.02	3.0	0.8	42.4	23.9	6.3	8.3	0.0
First National B&T Co. of Ardmore	Ardmore	OK	B	B	B	581.3	4.01	16.2	3.3	8.4	27.5	8.1	9.7	0.0
First National B&T Co. of Bottineau	Bottineau	ND	B-	B-	B-	145.8	1.65	4.7	2.6	6.3	27.7	10.0	12.0	0.0
First National B&T Co. of Broken Arrow	Broken Arrow	OK	B+	B	C+	223.7	20.59	13.9	0.8	18.3	2.8	8.6	10.1	19.1
First National B&T Co. of Iron Mountain	Iron Mountain	MI	B-	C+	C+	398.8	22.62	18.1	2.0	10.9	27.0	6.3	8.3	0.0
First National B&T Co. of McAlester	McAlester	OK	B-	B	C+	523.4	11.54	7.0	1.8	9.0	22.4	9.2	10.5	16.0
First National B&T Co. of Miami	Miami	OK	B	B	C+	167.6	27.12	4.7	2.6	11.6	17.6	6.8	8.8	0.0
First National B&T Co. of Newtown	Newtown	PA	B+	B+	B-	1128.6	18.25	3.8	0.2	12.0	42.3	7.1	9.1	0.0
▼ First National B&T Co. of Okmulgee	Okmulgee	OK	B-	B	B+	263.1	-1.24	10.9	2.5	16.6	31.2	10.0	11.9	16.8
First National B&T Co. of Vinita	Vinita	OK	D+	C+	C	318.0	-28.07	17.4	4.2	7.4	20.3	5.3	7.8	11.2
First National B&T Co. of Weatherford	Weatherford	OK	B+	B+	B+	298.2	14.88	14.3	1.6	5.8	1.9	10.0	11.1	15.5
First National Bank	Hamilton	AL	A	A	A-	322.4	13.65	6.6	6.8	10.0	32.3	10.0	15.9	0.0
First National Bank	Paragould	AR	B+	A-	A-	1786.2	7.26	9.3	2.2	25.7	7.8	8.6	10.0	13.9
First National Bank	Mattoon	IL	C-	C-	C-	101.6	10.31	13.3	2.8	9.0	21.4	6.1	8.1	13.2
▼ First National Bank	Cloverdale	IN	C	C+	C+	357.4	20.67	10.3	1.2	14.6	18.4	6.7	8.7	21.4
First National Bank	Arcadia	LA	B-	B-	C-	268.9	5.12	11.1	1.0	17.6	0.9	3.1	9.2	0.0
First National Bank	Damariscotta	ME	B	B	B	2262.0	13.03	11.6	1.2	22.3	30.2	6.4	8.4	15.3
First National Bank	Alamogordo	NM	A	A-	B+	407.1	14.27	6.2	1.3	4.6	53.1	9.5	10.7	0.0
First National Bank	Heavener	OK	B+	B+	B+	94.1	11.71	7.0	2.9	15.3	9.6	6.7	8.7	0.0
First National Bank	Fort Pierre	SD	A-	A-	A	1459.7	10.07	12.6	11.4	6.5	9.6	10.0	18.8	25.7
First National Bank	Oldham	SD	A-	A-	A-	361.4	13.28	8.7	13.0	6.8	16.6	10.0	12.8	18.8
First National Bank	Rotan	TX	B-	C+	C	86.7	19.02	7.4	3.0	0.3	53.0	9.6	10.7	23.9
First National Bank	Spearman	TX	B+	A-	B+	245.8	8.90	14.6	2.4	6.5	25.4	10.0	13.5	20.3
First National Bank	Wichita Falls	TX	B	B	C+	866.4	63.52	10.2	0.9	23.9	7.4	7.4	9.3	13.2
First National Bank	Altavista	VA	B-	B-	B-	572.3	19.11	12.8	18.7	12.1	7.8	4.6	8.4	0.0
First National Bank & Trust of Elk City	Elk City	OK	A-	A-	B+	297.0	-2.74	10.4	0.6	12.2	37.8	10.0	11.8	0.0
First National Bank Alaska	Anchorage	AK	A	A	A	4718.6	22.72	14.3	0.3	2.4	36.8	10.0	11.6	21.8
First National Bank and Trust	Atmore	AL	B-	B-	B-	174.7	13.02	14.2	3.3	14.5	24.0	9.3	10.6	0.0
First National Bank and Trust	Phillipsburg	KS	B+	B	B-	245.6	13.57	12.6	4.2	9.5	22.7	10.0	14.9	0.0
First National Bank and Trust Co.	Clinton	IL	C	C+	B-	204.3	5.90	5.6	0.2	3.8	69.3	8.1	9.8	19.6
First National Bank and Trust Co.	Chickasha	OK	A-	B+	B-	799.9	21.34	13.4	0.8	5.5	31.5	10.0	11.8	0.0
First National Bank and Trust Co.	Shawnee	OK	C+	C+	C	327.8	29.60	6.2	0.6	5.6	34.8	10.0	12.0	28.1
First National Bank and Trust Co.	Beloit	WI	B-	B-	B-	1304.4	16.75	13.9	0.8	14.8	12.6	5.9	8.8	0.0
First National Bank at Darlington	Darlington	WI	B+	B+	B+	159.2	5.48	4.9	2.6	5.9	7.0	10.0	15.2	22.6
First National Bank at Paris	Paris	AR	B+	B+	B	208.5	13.83	9.8	8.2	17.0	10.8	10.0	11.0	16.7
First National Bank at Saint James	Saint James	MN	D+	D+	D	29.3	0.36	4.7	3.9	21.4	3.3	7.0	9.0	15.3
First National Bank Baird	Baird	TX	B-	C+	C+	525.4	30.74	25.1	1.2	12.1	2.4	7.5	9.3	13.9
▲ First National Bank in Amboy	Amboy	IL	B	B	B	231.5	12.22	8.3	2.3	9.0	43.2	9.6	10.7	0.0
First National Bank in Carlyle	Carlyle	IL	B	B	B	228.5	16.05	10.2	1.4	6.7	29.9	9.5	10.7	0.0
First National Bank in Cimarron	Cimarron	KS	B	B	B-	119.3	18.25	17.7	2.4	5.9	47.3	5.8	7.8	15.1
First National Bank in Cooper	Cooper	TX	B	B	B-	44.7	-0.17	4.3	4.9	23.9	28.5	10.0	15.2	0.0

Asset Quality Index	Adjusted Non-Performing Loans as a % of Total Loans	as a % of Capital	Net Charge-Offs Avg Loans	Profitability Index	Net Income ($Mil)	Return on Assets (R.O.A.)	Return on Equity (R.O.E.)	Net Interest Spread	Overhead Efficiency Ratio	Liquidity Index	Liquidity Ratio	Hot Money Ratio	Stability Index
8.6	0.10	na	0.04	6.5	2.8	1.24	10.76	3.42	47.8	1.5	33.8	41.2	6.9
9.7	0.00	0.0	-0.01	5.0	1.7	1.17	11.65	2.96	56.7	4.8	29.5	6.8	6.6
7.3	0.63	3.8	-0.01	4.5	3.9	1.11	11.55	3.39	68.1	2.3	25.6	15.3	6.5
5.5	1.97	na	0.02	5.0	9.0	1.16	9.90	3.42	62.1	3.8	8.1	7.5	8.7
8.2	0.00	na	0.54	5.2	3.8	1.02	11.68	3.95	60.7	0.7	12.5	33.7	5.8
6.8	0.37	na	0.45	5.1	3.6	1.29	11.70	4.32	67.4	4.8	29.5	6.7	7.0
6.5	0.64	2.9	0.11	5.5	110.5	1.11	7.92	3.30	52.3	4.3	20.1	4.3	10.0
8.8	0.13	na	0.03	7.2	7.1	1.25	11.66	3.11	50.8	2.7	29.3	18.0	8.2
5.5	0.69	3.5	0.10	4.6	27.3	0.87	7.20	3.36	55.5	2.6	10.5	8.3	9.0
4.4	0.98	5.5	0.39	4.3	84.8	0.57	4.76	3.26	63.5	4.3	14.7	6.9	10.0
4.1	1.26	na	0.02	7.8	5.2	1.73	16.81	4.26	54.7	1.8	11.1	19.7	6.4
4.8	0.62	na	0.07	7.6	6.7	1.87	19.42	4.04	54.9	1.5	10.6	21.1	6.9
2.5	2.45	na	0.05	5.5	1.1	1.12	10.70	3.87	65.7	1.5	16.3	25.0	6.2
9.0	0.00	na	0.00	5.5	2.5	1.35	12.47	3.18	60.2	5.7	43.3	6.5	6.6
2.5	2.25	na	0.00	5.6	3.2	1.23	13.43	3.61	60.1	3.0	12.1	13.8	7.2
6.7	0.17	1.3	0.05	4.4	1.3	0.92	9.67	3.92	61.0	2.5	10.3	16.1	6.5
5.1	0.71	5.7	0.03	7.4	2.5	1.78	19.36	3.77	51.4	1.1	11.1	26.9	7.2
5.1	0.76	5.5	-0.01	5.4	1.8	1.35	15.40	2.91	63.5	1.0	16.3	26.4	6.0
3.3	0.89	na	0.14	5.2	2.6	0.99	9.76	4.24	70.7	4.8	20.0	4.2	5.2
3.8	1.87	na	0.01	0.0	-0.1	-0.12	-0.88	3.22	119.5	5.4	43.7	8.4	6.4
4.6	1.09	na	0.01	4.6	4.3	1.01	10.40	3.65	71.4	3.4	15.0	12.0	7.5
4.1	2.98	na	-0.01	2.6	0.3	0.26	2.15	2.61	82.8	3.8	24.8	10.9	7.3
7.1	3.70	na	0.00	4.8	1.3	0.85	8.14	4.10	68.1	5.4	37.2	5.9	6.4
5.7	2.75	na	0.07	5.0	2.7	0.99	10.48	3.85	63.8	5.7	46.7	7.3	4.2
3.9	2.07	na	0.82	4.4	3.1	0.84	6.99	3.34	66.1	3.9	27.3	11.4	8.7
6.2	0.64	na	0.00	4.6	1.0	0.85	9.36	4.28	72.5	5.4	28.9	2.6	4.8
9.3	0.77	na	0.00	4.5	7.7	0.99	10.23	2.75	60.6	7.1	48.9	2.1	7.2
3.0	4.98	na	0.06	5.4	2.5	1.23	9.56	3.69	65.0	2.2	26.8	19.9	8.8
1.1	5.52	na	3.11	0.0	-7.9	-2.82	-34.73	3.55	84.1	1.7	16.3	15.9	3.2
5.5	1.39	na	0.06	5.7	2.7	1.22	10.01	4.07	60.8	1.6	25.5	25.9	7.9
8.7	0.27	na	0.17	5.9	3.0	1.31	7.49	3.47	62.6	6.2	59.4	8.3	8.5
7.9	0.21	1.3	0.30	4.8	12.1	0.93	8.77	3.17	61.4	1.2	8.1	28.2	8.9
4.6	1.37	na	0.15	3.0	0.4	0.55	6.10	3.19	83.6	2.3	31.7	21.7	4.6
7.8	0.58	na	-0.09	2.5	0.8	0.33	3.61	2.62	84.3	6.4	53.2	5.3	5.0
3.8	1.02	na	-0.02	7.4	3.2	1.58	16.69	5.58	70.3	2.6	5.0	14.9	7.7
6.3	0.74	5.5	0.08	5.8	20.7	1.27	14.72	3.12	50.4	1.5	22.3	19.1	7.9
6.5	1.99	na	0.02	6.5	4.7	1.60	12.90	3.71	60.5	5.9	43.6	5.5	8.0
8.5	0.00	na	0.21	6.6	0.8	1.13	13.10	5.23	70.6	3.6	27.7	12.9	5.7
6.3	0.62	1.6	3.08	10.0	21.8	2.09	10.09	7.81	40.5	3.9	19.2	10.5	9.5
6.2	0.61	2.9	3.54	6.7	2.8	1.09	8.18	7.85	54.0	3.6	18.3	11.2	6.4
4.3	2.58	na	1.18	5.6	1.1	1.81	16.82	3.68	70.3	5.1	42.0	9.7	5.3
4.1	3.34	na	0.14	6.1	3.7	2.11	14.81	4.08	63.5	1.3	19.3	27.1	9.1
6.0	0.53	na	0.01	5.3	6.6	1.23	13.15	4.16	71.9	1.4	13.0	25.6	7.4
5.7	0.33	na	0.06	3.7	2.6	0.64	7.59	3.39	79.1	4.5	22.4	6.4	5.4
7.4	1.69	na	0.05	7.9	4.5	1.95	15.51	3.59	53.1	1.8	28.0	25.4	9.2
7.9	1.25	3.5	0.01	7.7	44.3	1.40	10.22	3.56	52.2	5.3	21.6	2.7	10.0
4.4	1.88	na	-0.13	4.1	1.4	1.09	9.82	3.60	76.6	3.1	25.3	14.7	6.4
5.2	1.68	na	0.24	7.7	3.6	2.02	13.27	4.08	58.1	2.4	19.9	17.5	8.0
9.9	0.18	na	0.07	3.4	2.3	1.59	18.79	2.70	89.2	1.4	32.0	26.9	6.2
5.9	1.32	na	0.15	9.1	9.1	1.67	13.34	4.33	48.7	4.2	30.3	9.4	8.8
8.3	0.44	na	0.05	2.1	0.4	0.19	1.29	2.88	92.3	6.8	59.8	4.3	6.7
7.8	1.35	na	0.03	3.7	6.2	0.67	6.03	3.07	76.0	5.2	27.6	7.2	8.9
7.3	0.21	0.9	-0.02	4.7	1.0	0.87	5.68	3.22	65.8	2.6	34.9	20.5	8.1
5.0	0.88	na	0.09	8.0	2.6	1.77	13.14	4.48	60.9	1.3	12.7	26.3	8.9
3.3	1.50	na	0.00	2.8	0.1	0.30	3.37	4.28	92.2	3.0	30.2	16.7	4.3
3.9	1.30	na	0.07	5.0	3.4	0.93	10.77	4.35	71.0	2.5	20.8	17.1	4.4
8.8	0.24	na	-0.33	4.8	2.0	1.19	10.54	3.31	66.9	5.5	40.8	6.8	6.6
8.5	0.08	na	0.02	4.4	1.4	0.85	7.85	3.12	61.4	4.3	26.3	7.9	6.4
8.7	0.06	0.3	0.03	7.1	1.5	1.72	20.81	3.90	60.2	3.1	28.4	15.5	5.0
7.4	0.00	4.6	0.03	3.6	0.2	0.64	4.21	2.89	75.5	4.9	49.4	12.1	6.9

Name	City	State	Rating	2019 Rating	2018 Rating	Total Assets ($Mil)	One Year Asset Growth	Comm-ercial Loans	Cons-umer Loans	Mort-gage Loans	Secur-ities	Capital-ization Index	Lever-age Ratio	Risk-Based Capital Ratio
First National Bank in Creston	Creston	IA	B+	B+	B+	366.5	50.47	11.8	2.2	8.2	23.5	6.1	8.1	13.0
First National Bank in DeRidder	DeRidder	LA	B	B	B+	339.2	13.14	14.5	2.3	21.2	18.2	6.8	8.8	0.0
▼ First National Bank in Fairfield	Fairfield	IA	C	C+	C	163.5	12.38	7.3	0.8	11.1	12.3	8.6	10.0	15.9
First National Bank in Falfurrias	Falfurrias	TX	C+	C+	C+	84.4	10.47	17.2	3.7	2.2	40.1	8.7	10.1	0.0
First National Bank in Frankfort	Frankfort	KS	B	B	B-	51.9	9.54	6.6	2.9	8.8	41.9	8.8	10.2	0.0
First National Bank in Fredonia	Fredonia	KS	A-	A-	B+	100.4	13.97	7.6	6.4	9.7	59.2	10.0	16.0	0.0
First National Bank in Howell	Howell	MI	A-	B	B-	541.0	25.54	15.9	8.0	8.4	4.7	9.7	10.8	16.3
First National Bank in Marlow	Marlow	OK	C+	C+	C+	62.3	8.60	7.8	7.7	13.8	15.2	7.2	9.1	0.0
First National Bank in New Bremen	New Bremen	OH	B+	B+	B+	347.7	16.57	12.7	0.6	8.8	27.9	8.0	9.6	24.3
First National Bank in Okeene	Okeene	OK	C+	C	C+	79.7	-6.14	3.6	0.3	0.0	35.5	10.0	17.6	28.3
First National Bank in Olney	Olney	IL	A-	B+	B+	387.7	8.69	4.3	2.5	13.4	32.5	9.9	10.9	0.0
▼ First National Bank in Ord	Ord	NE	B-	B	C+	155.8	19.67	5.4	1.7	10.1	37.4	6.0	8.0	16.9
First National Bank in Philip	Philip	SD	A-	A-	B+	295.2	8.80	6.2	0.6	0.0	13.7	10.0	12.9	16.9
First National Bank in Pinckneyville	Pinckneyville	IL	A-	A-	A-	122.5	16.88	3.4	3.6	20.3	40.6	10.0	13.1	31.6
First National Bank in Port Lavaca	Port Lavaca	TX	B	B	B	364.3	10.19	6.4	1.6	29.8	38.2	8.6	10.0	0.0
First National Bank in Sioux Falls	Sioux Falls	SD	B+	A-	B	1424.9	16.68	16.5	0.7	19.6	20.0	10.0	12.1	17.8
First National Bank in Taylorville	Taylorville	IL	A-	A-	A	215.3	10.00	7.7	2.7	7.4	52.4	10.0	17.1	0.0
First National Bank in Tigerton	Tigerton	WI	C	C+	C+	24.8	5.76	1.2	2.6	27.4	19.9	10.0	13.6	0.0
First National Bank in Tremont	Tremont	IL	B-	B	B	135.6	10.47	8.0	2.1	21.4	26.0	10.0	11.4	0.0
First National Bank in Trinidad	Trinidad	CO	C+	B-	C+	241.3	14.82	1.4	0.7	27.2	35.7	9.8	10.9	0.0
▲ First National Bank Minnesota	Saint Peter	MN	B+	C+	C+	358.1	63.86	14.0	2.3	8.7	19.7	8.0	9.7	14.0
▼ First National Bank North	Walker	MN	A-	A	A-	685.6	21.34	7.5	6.9	19.3	15.2	8.0	9.7	0.0
First National Bank Northwest Florida	Panama City	FL	B+	B+	B+	190.9	4.69	7.3	0.0	7.5	3.7	9.0	10.4	34.6
First National Bank of Absecon	Absecon	NJ	C+	C+	C	161.3	9.71	14.1	0.2	29.3	25.1	9.0	10.4	0.0
First National Bank of Albany	Albany	TX	B+	A-	B+	587.5	-2.66	24.2	2.1	9.3	20.3	10.0	11.6	0.0
First National Bank of Allendale	Allendale	IL	B	B	B-	284.6	18.58	13.0	5.9	16.9	22.8	8.6	10.1	0.0
First National Bank of Alvin	Alvin	TX	B+	B+	B+	154.4	9.99	3.0	0.2	0.6	73.7	10.0	11.2	0.0
First National Bank of America	East Lansing	MI	B	B-	C	2825.8	20.97	0.3	0.2	85.3	1.6	8.3	9.9	18.9
First National Bank of Anderson	Anderson	TX	B	B	B	201.4	11.06	8.9	3.4	11.8	9.0	9.3	10.5	0.0
▼ First National Bank of Anson	Anson	TX	B-	B-	C+	71.3	16.72	8.1	9.5	19.0	20.6	6.1	8.1	18.2
First National Bank of Arenzville	Arenzville	IL	B-	B-	B-	101.2	16.42	11.5	4.0	10.6	14.3	7.2	9.7	0.0
First National Bank of Aspermont	Aspermont	TX	B+	B+	B+	69.8	15.57	6.6	2.8	5.8	60.4	10.0	14.7	0.0
First National Bank of Assumption	Assumption	IL	C	C	C-	24.1	15.39	7.6	3.3	8.8	21.6	8.2	9.8	0.0
First National Bank of Ava	Ava	IL	B	B	B	72.9	14.61	6.2	3.1	15.9	48.6	10.0	11.6	20.7
First National Bank of Bagley	Bagley	MN	C+	C+	C+	98.7	7.35	8.9	8.2	21.7	17.3	6.0	8.0	13.9
First National Bank of Ballinger	Ballinger	TX	B-	B-	B-	209.3	14.64	15.4	1.0	9.0	14.1	7.6	9.4	16.2
First National Bank of Bangor	Bangor	WI	A	A	B+	249.9	16.99	4.9	1.4	17.5	12.5	10.0	30.1	40.9
First National Bank of Bastrop	Bastrop	TX	A-	A-	B+	684.4	12.55	4.3	1.6	15.4	35.7	9.2	10.4	18.7
▲ First National Bank of Beardstown	Beardstown	IL	A-	A-	B+	141.3	9.67	3.9	5.6	10.3	13.1	10.0	11.6	0.0
First National Bank of Bellevue	Bellevue	OH	C+	C+	C+	284.9	17.96	15.9	1.1	5.9	13.4	4.5	9.1	0.0
First National Bank of Bellville	Bellville	TX	B+	B+	A-	801.7	12.84	2.8	1.5	9.3	65.7	10.0	11.2	0.0
First National Bank of Bemidji	Bemidji	MN	A-	A	A	816.1	21.72	8.0	7.8	8.4	43.5	10.0	12.1	0.0
First National Bank of Benton	Benton	LA	B+	A-	B+	67.3	9.56	1.9	1.8	36.6	15.0	10.0	17.4	43.9
First National Bank of Blanchester	Blanchester	OH	B+	B+	B+	67.6	9.52	1.6	3.8	44.2	12.9	10.0	11.5	23.8
First National Bank of Bosque County	Valley Mills	TX	B+	B+	B-	148.2	23.32	17.0	4.7	24.6	3.1	8.0	9.7	17.0
First National Bank of Brookfield	Brookfield	IL	B+	A-	B	255.9	24.70	1.6	5.6	12.5	4.9	7.9	9.6	14.7
First National Bank of Brooksville	Brooksville	KY	B-	B-	B-	68.2	12.71	1.6	2.2	30.6	43.3	9.6	10.7	0.0
First National Bank of Brownstown	Brownstown	IL	C+	C+	C	43.7	11.62	5.3	6.1	13.1	36.5	9.0	10.3	0.0
First National Bank of Buhl	Mountain Iron	MN	D	D	D-	30.8	18.52	11.6	8.8	38.7	0.0	5.1	7.1	15.7
First National Bank of Burleson	Burleson	TX	A-	A-	B+	223.3	13.32	12.8	2.2	3.5	30.3	8.4	9.9	0.0
First National Bank of Carmi	Carmi	IL	B-	B	B-	467.4	12.63	16.1	0.7	4.2	13.6	6.6	8.7	14.8
First National Bank of Central Texas	Waco	TX	B+	B+	B+	1033.5	20.74	21.5	0.9	12.5	3.4	6.3	8.3	12.5
First National Bank of Chadron	Chadron	NE	A-	A-	B	137.9	9.11	5.3	1.0	0.1	30.0	10.0	13.6	21.6
First National Bank of Chisholm	Chisholm	MN	C-	C-	D+	82.2	11.31	9.0	16.6	2.7	54.3	6.6	8.6	0.0
First National Bank of Clarksdale	Clarksdale	MS	A-	B+	A-	362.3	2.62	8.3	2.9	7.2	30.8	10.0	13.3	0.0
First National Bank of Coffee County	Douglas	GA	B+	B+	B+	288.5	40.01	11.2	0.7	12.4	5.5	7.5	9.4	18.1
First National Bank of Cokato	Cokato	MN	B	B	C+	78.8	29.51	29.2	2.4	14.9	16.8	6.1	8.1	16.7
▲ First National Bank of Coleraine	Coleraine	MN	B-	C+	C	96.6	8.83	3.7	2.8	13.6	42.2	6.0	8.0	20.6
First National Bank of Decatur County	Bainbridge	GA	B-	B-	B-	207.8	20.99	14.2	2.4	20.0	9.0	7.4	9.3	14.0
First National Bank of Dennison	Dennison	OH	B-	B	B-	263.1	12.58	8.1	16.1	12.1	32.9	8.7	10.1	0.0

Asset Quality Index	Adjusted Non-Performing Loans as a % of Total Loans	as a % of Capital	Net Charge-Offs Avg Loans	Profitability Index	Net Income ($Mil)	Return on Assets (R.O.A.)	Return on Equity (R.O.E.)	Net Interest Spread	Overhead Efficiency Ratio	Liquidity Index	Liquidity Ratio	Hot Money Ratio	Stability Index
7.9	0.30	na	0.00	4.8	2.0	0.83	8.52	3.45	77.0	3.5	21.5	12.0	7.5
7.0	0.77	na	0.02	4.2	1.8	0.73	8.52	3.60	76.4	4.5	27.9	8.0	5.2
0.8	9.23	na	0.59	1.3	0.1	0.05	0.52	3.12	96.0	3.4	26.4	7.4	4.0
7.1	1.05	na	0.14	3.7	0.6	0.93	9.41	2.79	69.1	5.6	45.8	7.2	4.5
6.0	1.95	na	-0.09	4.5	0.4	0.93	8.56	3.02	71.7	5.0	42.9	10.6	6.8
8.0	1.58	na	-0.05	5.4	0.9	1.28	7.31	3.12	60.4	3.9	58.4	20.3	8.3
5.9	0.42	na	-0.04	6.7	4.9	1.36	11.94	4.23	62.1	4.6	23.9	5.9	8.1
8.3	0.13	na	0.00	3.2	0.2	0.47	4.80	4.08	88.4	2.7	27.3	17.0	5.0
9.0	0.25	na	0.02	5.4	3.2	1.30	12.60	2.71	52.7	5.6	47.8	8.4	6.7
8.6	0.06	na	-0.05	5.0	0.7	1.13	6.71	3.25	53.8	2.4	40.6	28.6	7.2
5.0	2.11	na	0.04	5.6	3.5	1.27	10.21	3.16	58.6	4.0	28.0	11.0	7.6
8.9	0.03	0.2	-0.01	3.7	0.9	0.82	9.63	2.72	69.8	3.6	23.1	7.0	5.0
6.7	0.76	na	-0.02	8.1	3.9	1.82	13.45	3.58	46.6	2.3	21.2	7.2	9.5
8.0	1.83	na	-0.02	5.6	1.0	1.22	7.88	3.56	62.5	5.5	29.3	1.9	8.2
8.5	0.00	na	0.00	5.4	3.0	1.16	10.87	3.13	50.9	4.3	29.0	9.7	6.5
5.0	2.08	na	-0.08	6.0	11.8	1.15	8.88	3.54	66.4	4.5	5.1	3.9	9.9
9.1	0.16	na	-0.01	6.0	2.2	1.42	7.85	3.03	52.3	5.4	65.6	13.8	7.9
9.7	0.59	na	-0.01	2.3	0.0	0.21	1.52	2.94	90.0	5.0	46.1	8.8	6.4
8.2	0.38	na	-0.01	3.8	0.7	0.67	5.42	3.45	77.7	3.8	34.4	14.1	6.3
6.2	2.35	na	0.00	3.4	1.1	0.63	4.85	3.70	82.0	5.3	35.4	5.9	6.6
6.2	0.34	na	0.20	7.0	3.6	1.57	15.40	4.84	63.9	4.7	17.5	4.4	7.3
7.1	1.15	3.6	0.12	8.0	7.8	1.70	15.33	3.75	53.8	2.7	34.0	19.7	8.5
9.5	0.27	na	0.00	3.9	1.1	0.79	7.49	2.84	70.1	6.3	69.4	9.6	7.6
7.2	0.63	na	0.00	2.9	0.6	0.48	4.37	3.49	79.6	6.1	38.8	2.0	5.9
5.1	1.86	na	0.05	8.3	8.0	1.86	15.11	4.54	38.9	1.0	25.5	17.6	9.3
4.8	1.05	na	0.09	5.3	2.1	1.01	9.70	3.51	58.3	2.2	19.9	18.5	6.0
10.0	0.00	na	0.00	3.8	1.1	0.93	7.11	1.93	61.1	4.8	69.4	17.4	7.4
5.2	2.16	17.3	0.02	10.0	56.3	2.79	30.12	5.47	30.3	0.4	6.3	36.9	9.5
8.3	0.18	na	0.02	4.4	1.1	0.78	7.30	3.64	69.6	2.0	32.5	26.8	6.0
5.5	1.81	na	0.85	7.3	0.8	1.51	18.00	4.42	64.5	5.2	31.1	4.5	5.4
6.9	0.84	na	0.07	4.8	0.8	1.16	11.58	3.56	65.4	3.5	27.5	13.5	6.4
9.4	0.00	na	-0.38	5.4	0.7	1.35	7.67	2.97	57.5	3.7	54.7	19.1	7.8
8.0	0.81	na	0.04	4.0	0.2	0.91	8.80	3.19	68.5	6.4	62.1	3.4	4.0
5.2	4.26	11.6	0.10	5.1	0.5	1.02	8.05	3.79	65.6	5.0	46.4	11.0	7.5
6.4	0.50	na	0.01	4.9	0.8	1.17	13.61	4.16	69.2	4.1	24.9	9.5	5.0
3.7	3.33	na	0.00	5.9	2.0	1.30	12.66	4.10	63.3	2.2	27.4	20.1	6.8
8.3	1.65	na	0.00	9.8	4.2	2.33	7.62	4.15	23.0	5.4	31.6	3.6	9.4
7.2	0.55	na	0.06	7.5	8.2	1.66	15.19	3.98	58.9	3.5	28.9	14.0	9.0
8.3	0.00	na	0.07	5.3	1.3	1.24	10.47	3.66	68.0	4.3	26.0	8.4	7.4
4.2	1.46	na	0.00	5.8	2.3	1.17	11.95	3.90	61.5	1.7	21.4	7.7	6.1
8.6	0.02	0.0	0.01	5.5	11.3	1.99	13.37	2.71	54.2	2.7	55.0	35.7	8.7
6.0	2.53	6.8	0.06	8.2	12.4	2.22	15.61	3.39	45.7	3.4	39.5	17.8	9.9
6.3	7.33	na	0.11	3.5	-0.1	-0.14	-0.75	3.35	70.1	2.3	35.0	13.9	8.4
7.2	0.93	na	0.05	4.7	0.4	0.91	7.85	3.81	70.8	5.4	36.5	5.7	6.4
4.3	1.50	na	0.36	4.6	1.0	1.01	9.73	3.92	68.4	4.7	32.8	8.9	6.1
7.3	0.00	na	-0.15	4.9	2.2	1.24	12.31	3.18	60.8	2.7	30.0	18.0	6.3
7.4	1.29	na	0.13	3.5	0.4	0.69	5.84	3.37	79.3	4.4	21.5	6.7	6.0
5.2	0.64	na	0.45	3.5	0.2	0.59	5.56	2.97	71.9	5.4	50.6	9.8	5.0
3.4	0.73	na	0.01	2.7	0.1	0.46	5.25	4.29	88.9	3.4	29.6	14.6	2.3
9.2	0.00	na	0.07	6.2	2.3	1.46	14.05	3.62	52.2	7.0	62.8	3.5	6.5
5.6	0.95	6.1	-0.03	3.8	2.2	0.65	6.90	3.22	75.6	4.9	30.4	6.5	5.4
6.6	0.12	na	0.45	7.6	12.6	1.71	19.15	3.99	47.5	2.9	14.9	14.8	7.5
8.1	0.29	na	-0.01	5.7	1.1	1.13	7.19	3.65	65.7	4.0	41.1	15.4	8.4
7.7	0.07	0.9	-0.15	2.3	0.2	0.30	3.03	3.57	88.9	6.2	47.4	4.0	4.0
8.4	0.61	na	0.01	5.3	3.1	1.15	8.64	3.68	62.2	2.5	21.6	17.3	7.1
8.8	0.31	na	-0.05	5.1	2.4	1.18	12.77	4.23	68.4	5.4	35.2	5.1	6.1
8.3	0.02	na	0.17	6.1	0.8	1.39	16.14	3.98	58.9	5.0	29.3	5.2	5.3
9.3	0.00	na	0.00	4.0	0.5	0.79	8.99	2.94	67.3	5.3	48.0	9.8	4.2
5.3	0.88	na	0.02	4.0	1.0	0.66	7.32	3.68	70.3	2.0	24.9	20.0	4.5
7.3	0.12	na	0.15	3.6	1.1	0.58	6.19	3.73	79.4	5.6	42.6	6.7	5.6

Name	City	State	Rating	2019 Rating	2018 Rating	Total Assets ($Mil)	One Year Asset Growth	Commercial Loans	Consumer Loans	Mortgage Loans	Securities	Capitalization Index	Leverage Ratio	Risk-Based Capital Ratio
First National Bank of Dighton	Dighton	KS	B-	B-	B	63.3	17.80	9.3	1.8	2.4	29.5	10.0	18.5	29.0
▲ First National Bank of Dozier	Dozier	AL	B-	B-	B-	37.2	2.37	10.0	2.9	8.2	56.1	10.0	14.3	0.0
First National Bank of Dryden	Dryden	NY	B+	B+	B+	201.7	7.79	6.5	5.0	14.7	38.1	8.3	9.9	0.0
First National Bank of Dublin	Dublin	TX	B+	B+	B	107.3	16.41	13.3	8.9	3.3	1.4	8.5	10.0	15.2
First National Bank of Eagle Lake	Eagle Lake	TX	B-	B	B+	130.3	4.12	10.7	0.2	3.2	10.6	8.8	10.8	0.0
▲ First National Bank of East Texas	Gilmer	TX	B	B-	C+	417.1	0.52	11.8	5.6	19.3	23.0	10.0	11.2	0.0
First National Bank of Eastern Arkansas	Forrest City	AR	B+	B+	B+	490.2	17.22	8.0	1.7	6.5	31.5	8.1	9.7	0.0
First National Bank of Eldorado	Eldorado	TX	A-	A-	A-	65.1	10.38	24.1	3.1	16.2	20.1	10.0	17.9	0.0
First National Bank of Elmer	Elmer	NJ	B-	C	D+	326.6	14.44	14.3	0.2	28.8	2.8	6.5	8.5	13.5
First National Bank of Ely	Ely	NV	B+	B+	B	136.2	30.76	8.2	0.2	0.8	74.0	6.8	8.8	0.0
First National Bank of Evant	Evant	TX	A-	B+	B-	112.8	13.33	9.1	5.5	31.2	6.8	7.5	9.3	0.0
First National Bank of Fairfax	Fairfax	MN	B+	B+	B	32.2	10.47	13.2	0.5	0.7	31.5	10.0	36.1	0.0
▼ First National Bank of Fleming	Fleming	CO	C-	C	C-	24.3	10.05	4.8	1.8	3.4	10.3	10.0	11.1	0.0
▲ First National Bank of Fletcher	Fletcher	OK	A-	B+	B+	20.6	5.64	9.2	5.1	3.2	50.6	9.7	10.8	0.0
First National Bank of Floydada	Floydada	TX	A-	A-	B+	110.9	8.14	10.3	2.1	0.2	17.3	10.0	11.1	17.3
First National Bank of Fort Smith	Fort Smith	AR	A-	A-	A-	1766.1	28.36	14.3	0.7	9.6	6.6	6.9	9.8	0.0
First National Bank of Fort Stockton	Fort Stockton	TX	B+	B	B-	139.9	5.39	14.1	1.5	4.8	42.6	9.0	10.4	0.0
First National Bank of Frederick	Frederick	SD	C+	C+	C+	25.1	10.52	4.1	0.5	0.5	19.1	10.0	12.6	0.0
First National Bank of Germantown	Germantown	OH	C	C	C-	69.1	6.97	12.6	4.3	32.9	21.9	6.7	8.7	0.0
First National Bank of Giddings	Giddings	TX	B	B	B-	244.4	18.60	6.1	1.9	20.3	35.8	10.0	11.1	0.0
First National Bank of Gilbert	Gilbert	MN	D+	D+	C-	62.9	37.95	5.8	4.7	49.0	8.2	4.5	6.5	12.7
First National Bank of Gillette	Gillette	WY	B	B	B-	620.8	12.73	15.9	1.3	1.8	62.2	10.0	11.4	29.1
First National Bank of Gordon	Gordon	NE	A-	B+	B	237.1	15.23	5.6	2.1	0.1	43.9	10.0	12.3	23.8
First National Bank of Granbury	Granbury	TX	A-	A-	A-	720.4	15.90	3.8	2.4	18.8	42.5	10.0	11.2	0.0
First National Bank of Grayson	Grayson	KY	A-	A-	B	292.6	15.68	5.8	10.8	21.5	19.2	10.0	11.4	0.0
First National Bank of Griffin	Griffin	GA	C	C	C	322.5	14.07	8.8	1.1	5.6	33.0	4.8	6.8	15.7
First National Bank of Groton	Groton	NY	A-	A-	B+	195.7	8.25	9.3	7.4	22.8	42.8	10.0	14.2	0.0
First National Bank of Hartford	Hartford	AL	B	B	B	126.5	4.10	5.5	4.8	23.7	26.3	10.0	14.4	0.0
First National Bank of Harveyville	Harveyville	KS	C-	C-	D+	15.8	10.21	10.0	5.2	22.9	0.0	8.0	9.7	0.0
First National Bank of Hebbronville	Hebbronville	TX	A-	A-	A-	94.0	4.88	2.0	9.6	10.2	51.0	10.0	17.7	47.7
First National Bank of Henning	Ottertail	MN	A-	A-	B+	248.5	16.17	8.3	5.5	18.0	27.9	10.0	11.2	18.6
First National Bank of Hereford	Hereford	TX	B	B	C+	195.0	16.25	18.7	1.1	7.4	9.5	6.8	9.5	12.4
First National Bank of Hooker	Hooker	OK	B+	B	B+	82.0	10.29	8.1	2.8	12.6	28.1	10.0	13.9	22.7
First National Bank of Hope	Hope	KS	D	D-	D+	91.2	8.35	6.0	1.4	2.1	35.5	9.0	10.3	16.9
First National Bank of Hughes Springs	Hughes Springs	TX	B+	B	B+	299.0	13.27	18.7	4.4	17.1	7.4	10.0	12.2	21.5
First National Bank of Hugo	Hugo	CO	A-	A-	A-	135.0	10.41	1.9	1.8	4.1	24.5	10.0	11.0	0.0
First National Bank of Huntsville	Huntsville	TX	B+	B+	B	517.0	11.04	7.9	4.8	16.5	32.6	10.0	11.4	0.0
First National Bank of Hutchinson	Hutchinson	KS	B+	A-	B	855.8	19.75	15.2	1.3	8.1	16.1	8.0	11.4	13.3
First National Bank of Izard County	Calico Rock	AR	A	A	A	178.7	8.21	2.2	5.4	16.3	27.4	10.0	33.5	0.0
First National Bank of Jasper	Jasper	TX	B	B	B	267.5	9.79	6.5	3.9	7.6	58.9	10.0	13.7	43.5
First National Bank of Jeanerette	Jeanerette	LA	B	B	C+	322.7	22.43	12.9	2.4	22.7	4.8	8.5	10.0	15.5
First National Bank of Johnson	Johnson	NE	C+	C+	C+	77.3	7.53	1.8	2.5	4.7	44.2	10.0	19.5	0.0
First National Bank of Kansas	Burlington	KS	C+	C+	C+	91.0	7.12	5.6	2.1	8.9	67.7	6.2	8.2	22.7
First National Bank of Kemp	Kemp	TX	B-	B-	C+	107.4	12.10	16.0	1.2	16.0	21.8	7.5	9.3	0.0
First National Bank of Kentucky	Carrollton	KY	B+	B+	B+	141.4	16.76	6.2	1.9	34.6	10.7	8.6	10.1	16.6
First National Bank of Lacon	Lacon	IL	C+	C+	C	65.3	8.98	8.3	6.8	14.5	6.9	6.7	8.7	0.0
First National Bank of Lake Jackson	Lake Jackson	TX	B	B	B	272.4	6.78	1.6	0.4	0.1	80.6	7.5	9.3	38.9
First National Bank of Las Animas	Las Animas	CO	A	A	A	465.9	21.88	9.9	1.0	9.1	20.4	8.9	10.9	0.0
First National Bank of Lawrence County	Walnut Ridge	AR	B+	B+	B+	249.3	14.44	10.8	2.0	13.7	32.1	8.5	10.0	0.0
▼ First National Bank of Le Center	Le Center	MN	B+	A-	A-	132.5	-4.17	8.4	3.9	10.1	19.4	9.8	10.9	0.0
First National Bank of Lindsay	Lindsay	OK	B+	B+	B	77.5	19.53	28.3	3.0	13.1	14.3	10.0	11.2	0.0
First National Bank of Lipan	Lipan	TX	D+	C-	D+	27.3	27.51	3.5	10.7	6.8	10.1	5.4	7.4	25.7
First National Bank of Litchfield	Litchfield	IL	A-	B+	B+	106.6	10.22	11.4	3.0	9.5	11.6	10.0	12.7	17.3
First National Bank of Livingston	Livingston	TX	A-	B+	B+	423.8	5.50	6.8	2.8	15.3	42.2	10.0	13.3	44.8
First National Bank of Long Island	Glen Head	NY	B	B	B	4009.6	-3.63	6.7	0.0	34.4	16.1	7.9	9.6	0.0
First National Bank of Louisburg	Louisburg	KS	A-	A-	B+	150.1	25.17	8.2	0.6	23.3	41.6	9.8	10.9	0.0
First National Bank of Louisiana	Crowley	LA	A	A	A-	523.6	38.30	23.6	0.7	10.4	5.0	9.3	10.5	19.6
First National Bank of Manchester	Manchester	KY	B-	B	B	166.8	20.33	5.0	2.9	12.3	24.7	10.0	12.7	0.0
First National Bank of Manning	Manning	IA	B+	B+	B	70.6	13.26	8.8	1.3	7.5	11.1	10.0	18.3	33.5
First National Bank of McConnelsville	McConnelsville	OH	C+	C+	C+	174.5	16.40	1.0	4.1	31.2	20.6	4.6	6.6	16.7

Asset Quality Index	Adjusted Non-Performing Loans as a % of Total Loans	as a % of Capital	Net Charge-Offs Avg Loans	Profitability Index	Net Income ($Mil)	Return on Assets (R.O.A.)	Return on Equity (R.O.E.)	Net Interest Spread	Overhead Efficiency Ratio	Liquidity Index	Liquidity Ratio	Hot Money Ratio	Stability Index
8.2	0.61	na	0.57	3.0	0.3	0.59	3.15	3.12	65.1	6.1	42.0	3.3	4.7
9.5	0.00	na	0.00	3.4	0.2	0.65	4.36	2.87	72.2	4.0	72.6	20.5	7.1
5.1	2.97	na	0.23	4.7	1.6	1.11	10.73	3.03	56.9	6.6	46.8	1.7	5.9
7.5	0.09	na	0.06	5.6	0.9	1.21	11.57	4.74	72.5	4.9	31.5	6.7	7.1
5.6	0.71	3.6	0.04	3.4	0.6	0.59	5.39	4.22	74.4	5.1	29.3	4.6	6.6
5.2	0.77	na	0.21	5.4	4.0	1.20	10.34	3.91	64.3	1.8	23.7	22.6	8.2
7.2	0.30	na	0.42	4.6	3.6	1.03	10.12	3.10	66.5	3.6	34.6	15.1	6.8
8.3	0.15	2.8	0.03	9.9	1.1	2.25	13.18	5.52	51.8	5.3	21.6	1.2	9.2
4.9	1.59	na	0.02	3.6	1.2	0.52	5.85	3.75	75.8	3.7	6.8	9.4	4.9
9.2	2.65	na	0.04	4.6	1.0	1.13	10.05	2.46	55.6	7.7	69.4	0.0	5.1
8.2	0.19	na	0.03	7.2	1.3	1.59	16.37	4.58	67.7	4.5	33.2	10.3	7.1
9.4	0.32	na	-0.01	4.6	0.2	0.99	2.72	3.35	69.9	6.7	65.7	4.2	6.8
7.1	0.91	na	4.11	1.3	-0.2	-1.27	-10.69	4.35	64.0	0.9	25.3	42.8	5.4
8.8	0.42	na	0.22	2.8	0.1	0.42	3.49	3.91	90.2	6.0	65.3	6.9	6.2
7.5	0.00	na	-0.01	5.7	1.1	1.32	11.82	2.63	53.0	2.5	34.3	21.8	8.6
7.7	0.45	2.1	-0.08	8.7	17.3	1.46	13.31	3.52	51.6	5.3	29.1	7.2	9.6
8.5	0.00	0.0	0.02	5.3	1.4	1.35	12.19	4.14	70.1	3.0	32.5	17.1	6.9
9.2	0.00	na	0.00	2.1	0.0	0.22	1.50	3.35	91.3	6.6	68.2	5.3	6.1
6.5	0.59	na	0.00	4.0	0.4	0.78	8.58	3.62	72.2	4.6	24.4	5.8	4.5
7.3	0.86	na	0.23	4.4	1.7	0.98	8.58	3.21	60.8	3.3	30.5	15.1	6.6
5.1	1.04	na	0.03	4.0	0.3	0.81	11.95	3.93	69.0	3.5	27.0	13.0	2.9
6.8	3.26	na	0.31	4.5	4.7	1.03	8.15	2.30	55.3	5.7	68.0	12.6	6.5
6.5	1.86	na	0.45	6.6	2.5	1.48	11.44	3.93	47.5	2.6	21.9	16.2	7.4
7.2	2.40	7.0	0.01	5.8	6.7	1.34	11.38	3.70	60.9	5.2	53.5	12.4	7.6
6.3	0.97	na	0.04	8.0	3.2	1.53	13.08	3.96	59.5	4.7	33.7	9.4	7.2
7.2	0.38	1.7	0.02	3.7	1.8	0.77	9.74	3.46	78.4	6.5	52.3	4.2	2.8
6.4	1.09	na	0.34	5.4	1.5	1.04	7.04	4.12	61.0	4.1	21.9	9.2	7.8
6.2	2.42	na	0.62	3.3	0.6	0.59	4.00	4.13	82.1	1.9	28.8	25.0	7.7
7.7	0.00	na	0.00	3.1	0.1	0.50	5.22	3.77	83.4	2.3	38.5	21.4	3.7
8.4	0.94	na	0.02	5.4	0.9	1.25	6.87	3.37	67.4	2.3	50.8	36.7	8.6
6.8	0.44	na	0.00	7.0	3.0	1.72	14.08	3.55	58.2	3.1	27.0	15.4	7.7
6.9	0.13	na	-0.13	6.4	2.0	1.46	14.89	3.98	64.8	3.1	26.6	14.8	4.9
6.1	0.18	na	0.18	6.3	0.8	1.33	9.12	4.43	60.8	2.9	30.6	17.6	7.1
1.2	9.55	na	0.76	1.9	0.2	0.29	2.66	2.97	83.2	4.1	38.0	13.6	5.9
5.3	3.24	na	-0.69	8.7	4.5	2.08	16.83	5.28	61.8	4.3	23.8	8.0	8.5
7.1	0.49	3.4	0.05	5.5	1.2	1.26	10.32	3.97	64.4	5.6	32.4	2.9	8.1
8.4	0.00	na	0.01	4.1	3.1	0.82	6.41	3.06	70.7	4.6	35.8	10.7	8.3
8.5	0.04	na	0.00	4.6	6.1	0.98	8.20	3.40	66.6	4.5	23.2	6.3	8.0
8.9	1.62	2.0	0.00	6.1	1.7	1.29	3.80	3.96	59.5	4.7	66.6	17.3	8.6
9.3	0.15	0.3	0.02	3.8	1.5	0.79	5.59	2.92	70.0	4.3	36.9	12.6	7.1
4.5	1.42	na	0.08	5.5	2.8	1.26	12.07	4.42	65.7	3.3	24.1	13.5	7.3
6.7	4.47	na	0.20	2.4	0.2	0.28	1.38	2.38	86.0	6.8	70.9	5.1	6.9
8.1	1.20	na	-0.01	2.7	0.4	0.55	5.68	2.49	85.4	3.8	31.3	13.0	5.2
8.2	0.23	na	0.02	4.4	0.7	0.92	8.30	4.10	73.1	5.1	37.0	8.0	6.7
8.6	0.29	na	0.00	4.1	0.9	0.87	8.02	3.70	76.5	1.8	18.0	20.3	6.5
7.9	0.00	na	0.02	4.7	0.6	1.17	12.89	3.97	68.3	3.8	20.8	10.8	5.2
10.0	0.00	na	0.00	4.1	1.8	0.91	7.96	1.97	54.5	4.3	41.3	13.7	6.3
8.6	0.10	0.3	-0.01	9.5	7.0	2.23	17.86	4.41	49.5	3.7	19.3	11.0	9.0
8.0	0.33	na	0.00	4.3	1.7	0.95	8.95	3.40	74.1	1.9	29.1	25.1	6.7
3.0	5.17	26.1	-0.06	5.9	1.5	1.50	14.17	2.92	53.7	3.9	21.8	10.0	8.4
5.0	3.24	na	0.00	8.7	1.1	1.93	17.35	4.14	45.0	1.4	20.4	27.6	7.1
8.5	0.00	0.0	0.00	2.5	0.1	0.29	3.58	2.82	87.5	7.1	77.8	4.1	2.7
8.1	0.03	na	0.13	5.8	1.1	1.40	11.01	3.60	62.8	2.1	18.3	18.7	7.8
9.0	0.38	na	0.19	5.3	4.0	1.32	8.73	3.10	69.2	6.9	61.6	4.5	8.6
9.0	0.11	0.7	0.08	4.8	32.0	1.03	11.09	2.64	54.9	3.7	12.9	6.1	8.5
9.7	0.02	na	0.01	5.4	1.4	1.33	10.65	3.18	57.1	4.9	46.1	11.9	8.4
8.5	0.00	na	0.00	7.9	6.3	1.76	15.77	3.91	53.5	4.8	27.9	6.1	9.4
6.9	3.29	na	-0.06	3.7	0.8	0.72	5.13	3.07	78.4	1.9	36.3	32.9	7.2
8.7	0.00	0.0	0.00	4.8	0.5	0.99	5.49	3.05	58.3	5.3	52.2	10.6	7.5
5.1	0.48	2.1	0.01	2.9	0.6	0.46	4.30	2.88	83.0	5.0	28.2	4.8	5.6

Name	City	State	Rating	2019 Rating	2018 Rating	Total Assets ($Mil)	One Year Asset Growth	Asset Mix (As a % of Total Assets)				Capital-ization Index	Lever-age Ratio	Risk-Based Capital Ratio
								Comm-ercial Loans	Cons-umer Loans	Mort-gage Loans	Secur-ities			
First National Bank of McGregor	McGregor	TX	B+	B+	C+	686.7	40.47	11.3	2.5	24.2	4.2	7.6	9.4	13.7
First National Bank of McIntosh	McIntosh	MN	B-	B	B-	27.8	5.83	1.7	4.7	9.5	24.7	10.0	24.5	75.6
First National Bank of Mertzon	Mertzon	TX	B-	B-	C	514.0	7.52	4.1	0.7	1.3	46.9	5.4	7.4	46.3
First National Bank of Michigan	Kalamazoo	MI	B-	B-	B-	801.0	34.80	26.5	0.1	2.6	13.8	5.9	7.9	12.5
▲ First National Bank of Middle Tennessee	McMinnville	TN	A-	A-	B+	571.9	9.96	5.4	0.4	28.7	13.4	10.0	12.8	20.5
▼ First National Bank of Milaca	Milaca	MN	B+	A-	B	249.1	16.65	17.4	4.2	14.9	23.0	9.3	10.6	19.7
▲ First National Bank of Monterey	Monterey	IN	B	B	B	354.4	7.36	3.8	1.1	11.1	27.8	10.0	12.7	0.0
First National Bank of Moody	Moody	TX	B-	B-	B-	50.6	4.98	5.0	3.1	17.0	35.4	10.0	20.7	0.0
First National Bank of Moose Lake	Moose Lake	MN	A-	A-	B+	136.4	24.20	10.0	3.1	17.7	11.6	9.8	12.0	0.0
First National Bank of Mount Dora	Mount Dora	FL	A-	A-	B+	318.6	30.07	6.5	1.6	9.6	51.7	10.0	12.3	21.3
▼ First National Bank of Muscatine	Muscatine	IA	C+	B-	B	352.6	14.29	17.0	1.9	23.6	2.0	9.9	10.9	18.5
First National Bank of Nevada	Nevada	MO	B	B	B	105.2	10.22	6.7	1.6	10.6	32.9	10.0	15.4	26.9
First National Bank of Nokomis	Nokomis	IL	B	B	B	165.5	8.93	4.6	2.2	10.9	29.6	9.9	10.9	18.7
First National Bank of North Arkansas	Berryville	AR	B-	B	C+	223.3	14.13	9.1	9.8	27.2	0.0	9.6	10.8	0.0
First National Bank of Okawville	Okawville	IL	B-	B	B	70.7	18.12	1.9	1.3	5.7	49.3	10.0	11.2	19.3
First National Bank of Oklahoma	Oklahoma City	OK	B-	B-	B+	618.0	13.15	14.2	1.4	16.4	4.0	6.4	8.5	14.4
▲ First National Bank of Omaha	Omaha	NE	B	B-	B-	24143.2	9.23	10.4	25.7	5.5	17.9	8.6	10.0	14.0
First National Bank of Oneida	Oneida	TN	A-	A-	B+	252.2	15.08	7.2	2.6	24.2	16.9	9.5	10.7	19.4
First National Bank of Orwell	Orwell	VT	C-	C-	D+	84.4	11.96	3.7	2.3	47.9	0.0	6.5	8.5	0.0
First National Bank of Osakis	Osakis	MN	B-	B-	B	80.4	16.41	6.3	1.8	21.2	15.8	6.5	8.5	14.3
First National Bank of Ottawa	Ottawa	IL	C+	B	B-	859.4	126.84	37.2	0.1	17.3	4.6	4.1	9.3	0.0
First National Bank of Pana	Pana	IL	B+	A-	B+	225.3	20.14	12.5	1.3	15.3	13.0	9.4	10.6	0.0
▲ First National Bank of Pandora	Pandora	OH	B-	C+	C+	210.0	12.44	13.3	2.9	18.2	22.2	6.4	8.4	13.0
First National Bank of Pasco	Dade City	FL	B-	C+	C	214.6	19.34	17.7	2.6	8.9	16.7	10.0	11.1	0.0
First National Bank of Pennsylvania	Pittsburgh	PA	B-	B-	B-	37445.8	9.29	19.2	5.1	15.2	16.5	6.4	8.4	12.5
First National Bank of Peterstown	Peterstown	WV	B	B	B	76.0	12.26	3.4	3.8	34.1	21.0	10.0	11.4	0.0
First National Bank of Picayune	Picayune	MS	B+	B	B	234.2	15.99	9.7	5.5	23.0	24.3	10.0	13.5	22.8
First National Bank of Primghar	Primghar	IA	B-	B-	B-	35.8	8.95	6.1	1.3	0.7	15.4	10.0	17.8	26.9
First National Bank of Proctor	Proctor	MN	C-	C-	C-	27.2	7.99	1.1	3.7	33.8	9.1	6.9	8.9	0.0
First National Bank of Pulaski	Pulaski	TN	A-	A-	B+	990.8	13.58	6.2	2.3	12.8	24.9	8.8	10.5	0.0
First National Bank of Quitaque	Quitaque	TX	B	B	C	82.5	27.00	5.8	4.0	0.0	6.7	10.0	12.3	0.0
First National Bank of Raymond	Raymond	IL	B-	C+	B	166.7	11.40	5.0	1.9	6.5	47.7	8.5	10.0	17.8
First National Bank of River Falls	River Falls	WI	A-	A-	B+	327.1	16.91	8.1	1.1	11.2	38.8	8.9	10.3	21.4
First National Bank of Russell Springs	Russell Springs	KY	B	B	B	257.4	12.11	8.7	1.7	9.2	28.8	10.0	11.8	0.0
First National Bank of Sandoval	Sandoval	IL	B	B	B-	64.6	20.14	11.4	8.6	33.9	15.1	9.8	10.9	17.3
First National Bank of Scotia	Scotia	NY	C+	C+	C+	603.0	18.69	14.8	21.6	16.7	8.0	5.6	7.6	13.0
First National Bank of Scott City	Scott City	KS	B	B	C	135.2	16.26	8.5	5.0	6.7	26.7	10.0	11.8	0.0
▼ First National Bank of Sedan	Sedan	KS	D-	C-	D	61.9	13.12	7.6	1.8	9.3	15.8	9.8	10.8	0.0
First National Bank of Shiner	Shiner	TX	B+	B+	B+	888.9	10.14	3.3	0.7	4.6	76.2	10.0	11.4	0.0
First National Bank of Sonora	Sonora	TX	B-	B	B-	496.5	12.94	9.4	3.5	18.6	1.7	7.1	9.0	15.1
First National Bank of South Carolina	Holly Hill	SC	B	B	B	230.9	14.70	10.3	1.3	9.0	13.0	10.0	11.7	29.3
First National Bank of South Miami	South Miami	FL	C+	B-	B-	836.6	4.01	11.7	0.2	11.7	8.6	8.3	9.8	16.6
▼ First National Bank of South Padre Island	South Padre Island	TX	B-	B	B	69.4	22.92	5.1	0.3	26.4	4.0	8.5	10.0	0.0
First National Bank of Sparta	Sparta	IL	A-	A-	B+	90.7	15.14	13.2	8.4	19.7	36.2	10.0	12.4	25.6
First National Bank of Spearville	Spearville	KS	B+	B	B	41.8	10.57	11.7	4.0	0.0	5.4	10.0	15.0	0.0
First National Bank of St. Ignace	Saint Ignace	MI	C	C-	C-	340.3	18.72	2.9	1.4	6.6	46.3	4.4	6.4	15.5
First National Bank of Stanton	Stanton	TX	B+	B+	B-	240.0	9.47	4.0	1.2	1.9	64.4	8.9	10.3	28.8
First National Bank of Steeleville	Steeleville	IL	B+	B+	B+	234.9	14.88	6.1	3.6	17.6	48.0	10.0	13.2	28.6
First National Bank of Sterling City	Sterling City	TX	C	C	C-	196.1	7.85	2.1	2.0	5.1	59.3	7.1	9.1	35.5
First National Bank of Stigler	Stigler	OK	B+	B	B	128.0	12.93	8.3	1.9	5.1	48.4	5.8	7.8	20.7
First National Bank of Sycamore	Sycamore	OH	C+	C	C	172.5	13.25	6.8	1.4	19.8	34.2	8.7	10.1	19.2
First National Bank of Syracuse	Syracuse	KS	B	B	B	420.9	14.20	16.9	1.3	5.2	11.5	7.9	9.6	14.4
▼ First National Bank of Tahoka	Tahoka	TX	C	C+	B-	55.5	7.47	0.8	2.0	1.4	29.6	8.3	9.9	0.0
First National Bank of Tennessee	Livingston	TN	B+	A-	B+	1001.9	14.70	6.9	2.4	12.2	17.8	9.0	10.3	0.0
First National Bank of Tom Bean	Tom Bean	TX	C-	D+	D+	134.0	9.73	17.5	10.3	24.9	7.2	8.1	9.7	15.6
First National Bank of Trinity	Trinity	TX	B	B	B-	68.7	12.88	3.8	13.1	12.0	42.0	8.1	9.8	0.0
First National Bank of Wakefield	Wakefield	MI	C+	C+	C	57.2	11.13	1.5	8.7	16.4	24.4	6.7	8.8	0.0
First National Bank of Waseca	Waseca	MN	B+	B	B-	154.7	10.51	12.4	2.3	27.8	6.7	5.5	8.6	0.0
First National Bank of Waterloo	Waterloo	IL	B-	C+	C+	731.1	50.60	7.5	0.4	16.6	24.1	6.9	8.9	14.2
First National Bank of Wauchula	Wauchula	FL	C	C+	C	82.2	14.66	8.5	2.3	29.2	10.3	9.3	10.6	0.0

Asset Quality Index	Adjusted Non-Performing Loans		Net Charge-Offs Avg Loans	Profitability Index	Net Income ($Mil)	Return on Assets (R.O.A.)	Return on Equity (R.O.E.)	Net Interest Spread	Overhead Efficiency Ratio	Liquidity Index	Liquidity Ratio	Hot Money Ratio	Stability Index
	as a % of Total Loans	as a % of Capital											
4.5	1.50	na	0.18	4.6	3.8	0.83	8.35	4.33	69.4	0.7	22.1	32.2	6.4
9.1	0.25	na	0.03	2.7	0.1	0.33	1.32	2.21	86.7	5.8	72.2	11.3	7.3
10.0	0.00	0.0	-0.16	3.8	2.7	0.72	9.95	1.61	45.2	7.2	81.1	5.5	4.8
8.3	0.02	na	-0.05	3.5	2.7	0.51	5.96	2.89	66.9	0.9	19.0	23.9	5.7
8.9	0.08	na	-0.02	7.8	7.1	1.70	13.47	3.30	63.1	1.2	8.9	26.1	8.6
4.8	1.60	na	-0.06	6.4	2.6	1.49	12.89	4.00	63.4	5.8	38.2	3.9	7.7
8.7	0.64	na	0.00	4.1	2.3	0.88	6.76	3.16	66.8	4.1	34.9	12.7	7.7
5.5	3.74	na	-0.12	4.9	0.4	1.19	5.43	4.04	69.9	5.6	47.3	7.6	8.1
5.8	1.04	na	0.00	7.7	1.6	1.76	14.26	4.05	58.6	2.2	30.1	13.0	8.8
6.3	3.99	na	-0.02	5.9	2.8	1.32	9.01	3.47	72.8	6.9	63.4	4.3	8.0
3.5	3.29	na	0.13	4.9	2.4	0.94	8.33	2.93	61.6	4.0	27.8	11.2	5.9
5.7	2.24	na	0.03	3.8	0.7	0.94	5.98	3.44	74.1	6.0	57.7	9.6	7.7
6.9	0.93	na	-0.04	4.5	1.2	1.00	8.16	3.43	69.1	5.0	43.5	10.9	6.8
4.3	1.07	na	0.15	6.0	2.1	1.32	11.88	5.27	76.2	3.7	24.0	11.5	7.2
9.8	0.00	0.0	-0.03	2.8	0.2	0.39	3.37	2.74	82.7	6.7	71.6	5.6	6.0
4.7	0.98	9.2	0.12	6.6	7.4	1.60	19.07	3.80	50.8	1.5	16.9	24.4	7.3
4.9	1.07	4.4	1.73	6.1	187.9	1.08	10.16	5.64	53.6	4.3	13.8	3.0	9.3
7.1	0.45	na	-0.03	5.8	2.4	1.30	11.42	3.85	59.6	1.9	25.5	22.0	7.2
2.9	3.02	na	0.03	4.4	0.5	0.86	9.92	3.44	69.6	1.8	28.2	26.6	5.1
3.6	0.57	na	0.00	4.9	0.7	1.16	9.98	4.33	64.5	4.7	31.4	8.4	6.7
6.3	0.43	na	0.05	4.1	3.4	0.66	7.99	3.48	66.6	3.1	5.0	12.4	6.2
5.0	1.44	na	0.01	6.3	2.2	1.42	12.64	3.58	59.1	3.2	24.7	13.5	7.5
6.6	1.21	na	-0.03	4.7	1.6	1.03	11.75	3.84	70.1	2.6	13.9	15.6	4.8
6.5	0.74	na	-0.06	3.7	1.1	0.75	6.38	4.34	80.2	4.1	24.1	9.0	6.3
5.0	0.86	3.8	0.17	4.4	231.6	0.87	6.28	2.98	57.3	3.9	4.9	6.9	10.0
5.9	1.40	na	-0.01	3.5	0.4	0.73	6.21	3.26	75.0	4.1	41.9	14.6	6.2
5.0	2.09	na	0.12	10.0	4.1	2.49	17.12	4.56	50.3	2.8	31.3	18.3	9.4
7.5	0.00	0.0	0.00	4.5	0.2	0.85	4.60	3.82	71.0	3.1	46.2	22.0	7.3
7.2	0.59	na	0.00	1.6	0.0	0.04	0.43	3.10	97.7	6.1	53.5	5.8	4.2
7.9	0.34	1.6	0.05	5.3	7.5	1.07	9.96	3.45	62.1	2.2	28.1	20.1	7.4
6.9	2.54	na	0.06	3.9	0.4	0.66	5.17	2.99	73.8	3.2	49.5	21.5	7.4
6.2	1.04	na	-0.02	4.2	1.1	0.94	8.62	3.31	70.6	4.7	54.1	15.0	5.0
9.0	0.04	na	-0.01	5.6	3.3	1.43	12.90	3.42	61.8	6.0	39.6	3.2	7.0
8.4	1.00	na	0.01	4.1	1.6	0.83	6.71	3.44	70.7	2.1	12.1	18.4	6.8
5.4	0.72	na	0.02	7.0	0.8	1.79	15.61	4.45	54.5	2.8	15.1	15.2	6.6
5.3	0.20	3.7	0.06	3.9	2.6	0.65	8.77	3.56	75.0	5.1	22.0	2.3	4.1
5.9	0.92	na	0.30	4.1	0.8	0.82	6.61	3.62	68.1	5.4	38.7	6.9	5.8
8.4	0.00	na	0.22	0.0	-0.4	-0.78	-6.61	3.00	114.5	5.0	43.3	10.4	3.7
9.9	0.04	0.1	0.07	5.3	13.7	2.12	16.15	2.65	44.5	3.1	64.9	35.9	7.4
3.4	3.06	17.6	0.06	3.4	2.0	0.56	5.83	3.74	80.9	2.0	25.2	20.5	6.5
8.1	0.90	na	0.04	3.4	0.9	0.54	4.44	3.16	80.7	6.5	53.7	4.5	7.0
3.9	1.03	na	0.05	3.5	3.4	0.55	5.76	3.18	73.2	3.3	19.5	12.8	6.8
7.1	1.70	na	-0.12	3.8	0.4	0.80	7.37	3.56	78.5	6.4	58.7	4.9	5.5
7.8	0.50	na	0.04	7.1	1.1	1.62	12.48	4.11	62.3	5.2	32.5	5.2	7.5
7.7	0.00	0.0	-0.03	7.8	0.5	1.60	9.59	3.13	45.8	3.5	48.4	16.0	7.0
4.2	3.49	na	0.09	3.1	1.3	0.60	6.97	2.48	78.0	5.9	74.6	12.2	3.7
9.7	0.04	na	0.57	5.1	1.8	0.99	9.09	3.14	56.3	7.0	64.0	4.1	6.6
8.0	1.15	na	0.08	4.2	1.9	1.14	7.99	2.82	71.7	4.7	43.8	12.5	8.6
10.0	0.50	na	0.16	3.7	1.4	0.92	11.54	2.20	67.8	6.1	66.2	10.2	3.3
8.4	0.58	2.0	0.00	7.6	1.9	2.08	23.30	3.33	51.7	5.9	52.5	8.3	5.7
6.7	0.46	1.5	0.01	3.4	0.8	0.70	6.09	3.27	75.2	3.5	33.6	15.3	6.5
4.2	1.62	na	1.21	5.6	3.0	0.98	9.36	4.54	51.6	0.7	14.9	45.3	7.5
8.9	0.26	na	0.12	1.2	-0.2	-0.41	-3.87	2.43	118.5	4.8	72.2	16.4	5.4
7.9	1.57	na	0.03	4.3	4.9	0.70	6.10	3.06	65.2	5.7	51.5	11.5	9.0
2.5	1.41	na	0.42	5.1	1.0	1.12	11.43	4.78	78.9	1.2	18.2	29.6	4.4
7.4	0.20	na	0.22	4.4	0.5	0.98	9.41	4.14	78.0	5.0	42.4	10.6	5.4
7.0	1.24	na	0.01	3.2	0.2	0.49	5.23	3.60	83.7	5.2	65.6	13.2	3.7
7.3	0.39	na	0.00	6.8	1.8	1.61	16.58	4.18	63.3	4.3	15.6	6.6	7.1
5.9	1.11	na	-0.02	4.3	4.1	0.88	8.99	3.25	66.3	3.1	22.9	14.2	6.0
4.3	1.79	na	-0.01	2.4	0.2	0.29	2.79	4.50	95.8	1.9	24.7	21.8	6.0

Name	City	State	Rating	2019 Rating	2018 Rating	Total Assets ($Mil)	One Year Asset Growth	Comm-ercial Loans	Cons-umer Loans	Mort-gage Loans	Secur-ities	Capital-ization Index	Lever-age Ratio	Risk-Based Capital Ratio
▲ First National Bank of Waverly	Waverly	OH	C+	C	C	170.4	9.70	5.0	2.6	16.7	26.1	6.5	8.5	18.8
First National Bank of Waynesboro	Waynesboro	GA	A	A	A	161.0	18.68	6.7	8.2	27.2	11.2	10.0	16.3	31.9
First National Bank of Weatherford	Weatherford	TX	B-	B-	C+	389.3	40.97	12.7	1.2	8.5	3.3	6.3	8.3	14.6
First National Bank of Williamson	Williamson	WV	B-	B	B-	93.1	9.24	9.7	6.3	34.3	11.7	8.2	9.8	17.3
▲ First National Bank of Winnsboro	Winnsboro	TX	A-	B+	B	141.1	3.45	6.0	1.8	15.2	15.3	10.0	20.9	0.0
First National Bank Texas	Killeen	TX	B+	B+	B+	2717.3	33.65	2.5	11.6	12.7	36.0	6.6	8.6	22.8
First National Bank USA	Boutte	LA	B+	A-	B+	158.7	20.09	14.2	0.8	19.4	1.6	10.0	11.0	0.0
First National Bank, Ames, Iowa	Ames	IA	A-	A-	A-	986.1	12.98	7.2	0.5	11.9	30.8	5.5	8.8	0.0
First National Bank, Cortez	Cortez	CO	B	B	B-	113.2	3.07	4.8	3.2	9.8	12.6	10.0	11.0	17.4
First National Bankers Bank	Baton Rouge	LA	B-	B-	C+	876.4	-3.21	4.7	0.0	1.4	3.3	10.0	15.3	0.0
▲ First National Community Bank	Chatsworth	GA	A-	B	B	313.5	8.79	10.3	1.0	14.5	4.4	10.0	11.4	0.0
First National Community Bank	New Richmond	WI	C	C-	C+	275.1	32.95	7.7	2.6	14.9	24.1	6.1	8.1	14.1
First National Trust Co.	Pittsburgh	PA	U	U	U	38.1	21.39	0.0	0.0	0.0	0.0	10.0	79.7	139.8
▼ First Nations Bank	Chicago	IL	B+	A-	B+	408.6	13.82	3.1	0.3	6.4	2.2	10.0	12.5	17.8
First NaturalState Bank	McGehee	AR	B-	B-	C+	67.6	13.76	15.7	6.4	15.7	15.2	8.7	10.2	15.4
First Nebraska Bank	Valley	NE	B+	B+	B	313.2	10.37	10.6	1.1	9.6	19.6	6.4	9.9	0.0
▼ First Neighbor Bank, N.A.	Toledo	IL	C+	B-	C+	508.6	16.19	18.5	4.1	11.3	6.3	7.8	10.0	13.2
First Neighborhood Bank	Spencer	WV	C+	C+	B-	158.3	12.56	8.3	2.0	25.8	29.1	8.0	9.7	0.0
First New Mexico Bank	Deming	NM	A	A	A	234.4	15.05	20.5	1.5	7.4	28.3	10.0	13.3	0.0
First New Mexico Bank of Silver City	Silver City	NM	A	A	A	126.8	11.88	3.0	0.6	7.5	31.0	10.0	11.7	0.0
First New Mexico Bank, Las Cruces	Las Cruces	NM	A	A	A	134.8	19.03	8.5	1.4	15.5	15.4	10.0	13.2	0.0
First Northeast Bank of Nebraska	Lyons	NE	B+	A-	B	330.9	10.64	6.8	1.1	1.4	37.2	8.9	13.3	0.0
First Northern Bank and Trust Co.	Palmerton	PA	B	B	B-	835.3	16.43	9.7	0.4	26.1	16.1	10.0	13.4	0.0
First Northern Bank of Dixon	Dixon	CA	B+	A-	B+	1677.3	30.30	19.1	0.0	4.3	21.7	6.5	8.5	17.1
First Northern Bank of Wyoming	Buffalo	WY	B-	B-	C+	488.0	31.59	12.8	3.2	12.9	18.0	5.9	7.9	13.7
First Oklahoma Bank	Jenks	OK	C-	C	C-	917.1	23.97	27.7	0.3	13.8	0.1	1.5	8.5	0.0
First Option Bank	Osawatomie	KS	B	B	B	461.7	40.01	7.0	2.5	24.0	40.8	6.0	8.1	19.3
First Palmetto Bank	Camden	SC	A-	B+	B	806.8	11.14	12.2	0.7	14.2	9.4	8.7	10.1	18.8
First Peoples Bank	Pine Mountain	GA	B+	A-	B+	204.5	34.85	10.4	1.4	16.0	16.7	6.9	8.9	15.0
First Peoples Bank of Tennessee	Jefferson City	TN	C+	B-	C+	181.5	17.58	12.0	1.9	10.1	14.7	6.8	8.8	12.5
First Piedmont Federal S&L Assn. of Gaffn	Gaffney	SC	A	A	A	479.4	14.20	2.7	0.8	32.9	1.3	10.0	24.3	45.5
First Pioneer National Bank	Wray	CO	A-	A-	B+	213.6	18.86	4.4	2.8	2.2	23.7	10.0	12.8	22.6
First Port City Bank	Bainbridge	GA	B	B+	B+	298.8	38.33	16.7	1.0	19.5	11.0	5.3	7.3	12.5
First Premier Bank	Sioux Falls	SD	A-	A	A	2878.7	45.93	6.7	32.5	2.7	9.2	10.0	11.1	20.9
▲ First Progressive Bank	Brewton	AL	C+	C	C+	29.8	-1.57	9.5	2.8	14.5	56.9	10.0	28.0	0.0
First Pryority Bank	Pryor	OK	B	B	B	260.9	29.44	39.7	4.9	6.5	3.4	6.6	9.7	0.0
▲ First Reliance Bank	Florence	SC	B	C+	C+	779.9	19.13	7.5	8.6	19.8	4.6	8.4	10.0	14.8
First Republic Bank	San Francisco	CA	B	B	B	133225.8	19.99	8.5	3.9	42.4	14.9	6.4	8.4	12.9
First Resource Bank	Lino Lakes	MN	B-	B-	B-	264.2	24.26	26.5	0.1	19.9	2.4	5.9	7.9	13.0
First Resource Bank	Exton	PA	C+	C+	C-	395.3	22.65	20.7	0.2	21.0	3.9	5.7	7.7	15.4
First Robinson Savings Bank, N.A.	Robinson	IL	C+	B-	B-	390.5	15.52	10.7	3.8	17.8	34.1	6.0	8.0	17.5
First S&L Assn.	Mebane	NC	C+	C+	C+	58.4	5.69	0.0	0.0	55.7	17.1	10.0	21.7	51.5
▼ First Savanna Savings Bank	Savanna	IL	E+	D-	D	11.6	-1.65	0.0	10.3	53.6	4.3	4.7	6.7	14.0
First Savings Bank	Danville	IL	B-	C	B-	43.4	20.16	0.0	0.1	22.8	60.1	10.0	22.1	78.4
First Savings Bank	Jeffersonville	IN	B+	B+	B-	1760.6	44.48	14.5	0.8	24.2	11.6	7.6	9.4	13.1
First Savings Bank	Beresford	SD	A-	A-	A-	1013.0	19.97	11.9	13.0	7.3	13.2	10.0	15.3	23.1
First Savings Bank of Hegewisch	Chicago	IL	C+	B	B	723.0	7.40	0.0	0.1	45.1	24.2	10.0	15.3	47.5
First Seacoast Bank	Dover	NH	C-	C	C	477.1	19.15	11.5	0.5	45.5	11.9	9.5	10.7	16.3
First Secure Bank and Trust Co.	Palos Hills	IL	C+	B-	C	360.9	113.04	41.1	0.9	9.9	4.6	5.8	7.8	12.6
First Secure Community Bank	Sugar Grove	IL	C+	C+	C	436.2	20.82	27.6	2.7	3.0	18.5	4.8	8.3	10.9
First Security Bank	Searcy	AR	A+	A+	A+	6900.7	21.38	7.9	0.6	5.0	39.3	10.0	16.6	25.1
First Security Bank	Mapleton	IA	A-	A-	B+	73.3	11.67	4.5	3.7	3.6	23.3	10.0	12.7	19.5
First Security Bank	Mackinaw	IL	C-	D+	D	91.7	8.75	8.9	0.5	14.2	2.3	6.7	8.7	12.9
First Security Bank	Overbrook	KS	C+	C+	C+	73.7	11.62	10.5	1.3	23.4	3.4	5.3	7.3	11.4
▲ First Security Bank	Byron	MN	B-	C+	C	78.4	11.06	11.0	3.1	16.8	21.8	6.4	8.4	13.2
First Security Bank	Union Star	MO	C	C	C-	37.6	15.77	7.3	9.8	33.7	26.7	5.9	7.9	14.1
First Security Bank	Batesville	MS	B+	A-	B+	660.6	15.41	9.1	3.1	16.8	30.8	7.4	9.3	16.8
▲ First Security Bank	Beaver	OK	D+	D+	C-	117.6	2.32	10.1	1.3	7.2	9.2	7.0	9.0	12.5
First Security Bank & Trust Co.	Charles City	IA	C+	C	C-	539.7	9.34	6.4	1.1	13.4	24.3	7.2	9.1	15.0
First Security Bank - Canby	Canby	MN	A-	B+	B+	72.4	12.66	22.5	1.7	1.2	16.9	10.0	12.9	21.0

Asset Quality Index	Adjusted Non-Performing Loans as a % of Total Loans	as a % of Capital	Net Charge-Offs Avg Loans	Profitability Index	Net Income ($Mil)	Return on Assets (R.O.A.)	Return on Equity (R.O.E.)	Net Interest Spread	Overhead Efficiency Ratio	Liquidity Index	Liquidity Ratio	Hot Money Ratio	Stability Index
4.7	2.01	na	-0.11	3.8	0.9	0.73	8.47	3.31	77.9	4.5	22.3	6.4	4.2
8.2	0.30	1.6	0.09	8.0	1.6	1.41	8.48	4.30	58.7	4.2	36.8	13.1	8.7
6.0	0.03	na	-0.03	5.8	2.6	1.08	12.75	4.16	66.0	3.4	43.0	18.9	5.4
4.2	1.58	11.6	0.04	3.4	0.4	0.53	5.33	3.57	82.0	0.9	17.7	34.4	6.1
6.8	4.95	na	-0.01	5.7	1.0	0.92	4.35	4.53	72.9	3.1	27.9	15.6	8.6
8.2	0.11	na	0.99	5.8	25.4	1.36	15.26	3.23	86.3	7.3	47.9	0.8	7.2
5.1	1.08	6.0	0.26	4.3	1.0	0.89	7.54	3.63	76.9	2.9	24.0	15.2	8.1
5.2	2.92	13.5	0.10	4.7	7.1	0.98	10.06	2.99	56.0	4.6	28.2	7.6	7.1
5.4	1.75	na	0.01	4.7	0.7	0.86	7.58	4.00	74.9	4.0	27.0	10.6	6.2
4.0	2.96	na	0.10	3.1	3.6	0.50	3.19	2.81	79.8	6.1	33.6	0.0	8.1
7.0	0.85	na	-0.04	5.5	2.3	1.04	8.45	4.40	66.1	4.2	24.7	8.4	8.0
3.4	3.69	na	0.32	4.8	2.0	1.12	12.69	3.63	66.8	5.1	27.9	4.1	4.6
6.5	na	0.0	na	9.5	7.9	30.66	40.34	1.13	72.4	4.0	181.5	0.0	6.3
7.4	0.00	na	0.26	4.9	2.3	0.81	6.29	2.86	61.0	0.9	23.8	41.2	7.9
5.5	2.38	na	-0.24	4.1	0.4	0.77	7.68	3.75	72.5	3.0	13.6	14.0	5.7
4.6	0.37	na	0.07	6.8	3.7	1.64	15.82	3.83	65.2	4.5	19.0	5.8	6.8
2.6	3.35	na	0.15	5.0	2.9	0.79	7.53	3.64	63.8	1.5	16.4	25.1	7.5
9.1	0.05	na	-0.16	2.9	0.6	0.51	5.04	3.11	83.4	4.9	42.6	11.3	5.2
7.8	1.19	na	-0.03	7.3	2.3	1.44	10.46	3.97	55.4	6.6	46.6	1.6	8.3
9.7	0.12	na	0.00	8.0	1.4	1.50	12.65	4.21	62.4	7.3	64.5	2.0	8.1
9.1	0.00	na	-0.03	7.4	1.4	1.48	10.81	4.20	63.6	5.6	48.9	9.2	8.8
8.5	0.00	na	0.01	4.4	2.0	0.88	6.50	3.04	65.0	2.9	20.6	11.2	7.7
7.8	0.64	na	0.02	4.3	5.2	0.90	6.39	3.69	65.5	4.0	12.4	8.5	7.7
6.2	1.84	na	0.02	4.5	8.9	0.80	8.61	3.31	64.8	6.6	40.0	2.6	7.6
4.8	1.06	na	0.07	6.8	5.5	1.70	19.92	4.08	62.8	1.9	23.5	14.7	5.6
5.7	0.52	na	0.23	3.5	3.7	0.60	7.04	3.10	67.7	0.5	8.7	53.4	4.7
8.6	0.69	na	0.01	5.2	4.3	1.25	14.17	3.31	67.8	3.6	23.9	11.6	5.7
6.5	0.69	na	-0.07	5.4	6.2	1.09	10.18	3.22	59.5	2.2	29.1	21.3	7.9
6.1	1.08	na	0.00	4.5	1.1	0.74	8.14	4.07	69.5	4.8	33.1	8.5	6.2
5.0	2.55	na	1.68	1.3	-2.1	-1.74	-19.67	4.03	73.4	4.6	24.1	6.1	5.2
9.4	0.62	na	0.00	8.5	4.9	1.43	5.41	4.21	60.5	6.0	49.3	6.3	9.1
8.5	0.00	na	0.00	6.0	1.9	1.25	9.04	3.41	54.0	2.3	27.1	19.5	8.2
8.4	0.17	na	0.09	4.6	1.6	0.79	10.55	3.73	73.4	2.1	13.7	18.4	5.3
6.8	0.40	1.7	0.92	5.7	21.0	1.13	9.16	2.97	60.3	5.2	40.2	2.0	10.0
8.9	2.05	na	0.00	2.6	0.1	0.38	1.36	2.86	83.3	6.3	93.6	11.5	6.7
5.7	0.58	na	0.20	8.4	3.0	1.65	16.78	3.83	44.8	0.8	13.7	36.5	7.0
5.9	0.65	na	0.09	7.8	10.3	1.93	18.77	3.97	56.7	1.8	25.2	19.1	7.3
8.9	0.17	1.4	0.00	4.2	768.6	0.82	9.75	2.76	62.3	4.2	14.8	7.0	7.7
7.9	0.08	na	0.10	4.4	1.5	0.82	9.07	4.02	58.6	1.8	6.1	13.1	7.1
5.5	0.47	na	0.05	4.2	2.1	0.78	9.75	3.58	69.7	1.5	7.7	21.3	3.9
4.1	1.93	na	0.65	4.0	2.1	0.70	8.19	2.88	67.8	4.6	24.3	6.1	4.9
9.7	0.00	na	0.00	2.1	0.1	0.24	1.08	2.97	87.3	2.1	47.4	54.7	7.5
2.2	2.78	23.2	0.06	0.0	-0.2	-2.23	-27.42	3.49	154.8	1.5	25.8	25.7	2.5
10.0	0.59	na	0.00	3.3	0.3	1.03	4.28	2.14	77.9	4.4	97.9	25.1	6.6
5.7	1.19	na	0.11	9.0	30.1	2.70	28.37	3.80	66.8	1.4	14.8	14.9	8.8
5.9	0.97	3.2	3.34	10.0	17.5	2.48	15.62	8.50	43.8	4.0	17.8	9.4	8.8
10.0	0.19	na	0.02	2.3	1.1	0.21	1.32	1.95	84.9	3.7	58.7	23.1	8.3
8.1	0.25	na	0.01	2.1	1.2	0.35	3.29	3.13	87.4	4.3	20.2	7.4	5.4
4.7	0.53	8.6	0.00	4.4	1.6	0.80	10.74	2.51	57.5	0.8	15.9	36.9	5.2
4.5	1.49	na	0.01	2.6	0.9	0.29	3.17	2.95	79.5	1.3	24.3	28.8	5.0
9.1	0.13	0.3	0.07	8.6	86.2	1.85	9.89	3.57	43.0	5.4	29.4	6.7	10.0
7.0	0.00	na	0.00	6.4	0.8	1.45	8.64	3.67	58.0	3.9	39.5	15.5	8.0
2.3	1.74	na	0.06	3.1	0.4	0.61	6.30	3.58	70.7	2.3	17.6	17.8	5.4
8.4	0.00	0.0	-0.01	4.4	0.6	1.02	12.05	4.05	72.9	2.6	18.1	16.4	4.5
8.1	0.09	na	0.06	5.2	0.8	1.33	15.46	3.65	64.9	3.2	28.6	15.1	4.9
8.3	1.20	na	-0.01	4.7	0.3	0.92	10.97	4.20	69.3	4.0	17.3	9.2	3.7
4.8	2.16	na	0.06	5.1	4.8	0.96	9.33	3.62	69.2	4.5	22.2	6.5	8.0
3.2	1.13	na	0.54	7.1	1.4	1.61	16.56	4.06	48.5	0.9	22.3	43.6	7.2
4.3	3.04	na	1.19	3.7	3.5	0.88	7.92	3.21	75.0	4.7	29.0	6.3	6.5
5.8	1.71	na	0.01	8.1	1.0	1.97	12.95	4.13	50.7	5.6	34.0	3.6	8.5

Name	City	State	2019 Rating	2018 Rating	Rating	Total Assets ($Mil)	One Year Asset Growth	Commercial Loans	Consumer Loans	Mortgage Loans	Securities	Capitalization Index	Leverage Ratio	Risk-Based Capital Ratio
First Security Bank - West	Beulah	ND	A-	A-	B+	73.4	11.64	19.9	2.0	0.7	22.3	10.0	12.2	17.0
First Security Bank and Trust Co.	Oklahoma City	OK	D+	C-	C	60.3	10.81	19.6	2.3	35.5	2.7	5.8	9.1	11.6
First Security Bank of Deer Lodge	Deer Lodge	MT	B+	B+	B+	59.0	47.49	18.8	4.4	23.4	0.0	7.1	9.1	19.6
First Security Bank of Nevada	Las Vegas	NV	A	A	A	284.5	28.46	8.6	0.0	3.7	1.7	10.0	16.9	0.0
First Security Bank of Roundup	Roundup	MT	B-	B	B-	72.5	17.27	9.7	4.0	4.1	24.2	10.0	11.0	20.3
First Security Bank-Hendricks	Hendricks	MN	B+	B+	B+	40.7	32.02	18.0	2.0	4.8	28.2	9.5	10.6	22.4
First Security Bank-Sleepy Eye	Sleepy Eye	MN	A-	B+	B+	235.2	28.07	10.7	1.3	5.5	34.7	10.0	11.4	20.8
First Security State Bank	Evansdale	IA	B-	C+	C	100.1	0.55	31.1	26.6	5.7	3.9	10.0	12.4	16.9
First Security State Bank	Cranfills Gap	TX	B	B	B-	142.1	18.94	5.9	2.7	17.8	34.7	4.7	6.7	15.6
First Security Trust and Savings Bank	Elmwood Park	IL	B-	B-	C	308.8	-7.21	10.3	5.0	4.0	10.0	8.0	9.7	18.6
First Sentinel Bank	Richlands	VA	B-	B-	C+	315.1	11.53	9.2	35.1	19.6	0.5	5.9	8.5	11.6
First Service Bank	Greenbrier	AR	C+	C+	B-	420.7	24.16	13.5	0.8	21.0	4.2	5.7	9.7	0.0
First Shore Federal S&L Assn.	Salisbury	MD	B-	B	B	325.5	3.39	2.2	9.4	49.1	2.8	10.0	15.3	26.9
First Sound Bank	Seattle	WA	C-	C-	C-	152.8	37.18	33.5	1.0	4.5	3.7	6.8	11.4	0.0
▲ First Southeast Bank	Harmony	MN	C	D+	D	108.8	7.31	10.4	2.8	8.2	0.5	4.6	8.6	0.0
First Southern Bank	Florence	AL	B	B	B-	334.0	25.64	23.4	1.6	19.6	5.4	4.4	9.3	0.0
▲ First Southern Bank	Patterson	GA	E+	E	E-	191.0	54.65	23.7	1.6	9.4	6.9	6.9	9.5	0.0
First Southern Bank	Marion	IL	B+	A-	A-	758.7	7.94	10.1	6.5	12.2	24.2	10.0	11.9	0.0
First Southern Bank	Columbia	MS	B+	B+	B	223.3	13.22	11.2	5.7	14.5	17.8	8.9	10.4	0.0
First Southern National Bank	Lancaster	KY	B-	B	C+	996.8	11.04	9.6	1.9	22.1	12.2	6.7	8.7	16.4
First Southern State Bank	Stevenson	AL	B+	B+	B+	610.9	51.24	10.3	4.7	18.0	27.7	7.8	9.5	0.0
First Southwest Bank	Alamosa	CO	B	B-	C+	395.0	19.10	23.5	1.2	5.6	13.6	5.9	7.9	15.4
First State B&T Co. of Larned	Larned	KS	A-	A-	A-	179.4	16.29	9.2	0.6	2.0	28.3	10.0	12.7	0.0
First State Bank	Lonoke	AR	C-	C	C	258.4	2.76	6.1	0.4	13.6	27.7	8.8	10.2	0.0
First State Bank	Russellville	AR	A-	A-	A-	369.4	24.50	14.5	0.7	16.4	10.5	8.0	9.7	16.4
First State Bank	Wrens	GA	B	B	B-	192.8	24.26	14.8	2.1	27.9	9.5	6.4	8.5	12.0
▲ First State Bank	Belmond	IA	B+	B	B	113.8	19.62	10.8	2.8	9.0	44.9	10.0	11.0	0.0
First State Bank	Britt	IA	A	A	A	121.9	12.91	6.4	1.3	9.7	28.7	10.0	13.4	0.0
▲ First State Bank	Ida Grove	IA	A-	B	B	176.1	3.45	9.1	3.9	9.0	17.3	9.1	11.8	0.0
First State Bank	Lynnville	IA	A	A-	B	218.2	14.01	8.6	1.7	11.3	13.0	10.0	12.4	17.1
First State Bank	Nashua	IA	B+	B+	B+	54.7	3.43	11.7	3.8	24.5	6.9	9.9	11.0	0.0
First State Bank	Stuart	IA	B-	B-	B-	113.5	13.18	9.8	1.7	7.4	44.7	8.5	10.0	21.7
First State Bank	Sumner	IA	C+	C+	C	102.4	-1.47	10.8	2.1	11.5	35.1	10.0	13.0	22.4
First State Bank	Webster City	IA	A-	A-	A-	538.6	12.69	11.8	0.7	8.3	7.2	9.8	12.8	0.0
▲ First State Bank	Mendota	IL	B+	B-	B-	1319.7	16.10	11.2	0.9	22.0	7.7	8.1	9.7	13.6
First State Bank	Monticello	IL	B-	B-	C+	288.5	6.12	6.3	1.2	8.0	32.5	6.0	8.0	14.8
First State Bank	Ness City	KS	B+	B+	B+	70.5	18.58	8.2	1.9	0.0	58.1	10.0	17.1	31.1
First State Bank	Norton	KS	B-	B-	B-	478.7	7.69	10.7	2.4	1.8	41.0	9.0	10.3	0.0
First State Bank	Irvington	KY	B+	B+	A-	207.8	-6.95	5.7	4.2	32.6	17.7	10.0	12.3	18.6
First State Bank	Saint Clair Shores	MI	B	B	B	990.0	23.93	14.2	0.3	10.2	14.1	6.9	8.9	0.0
First State Bank	Holly Springs	MS	C	C	C+	123.7	4.40	10.7	1.5	14.5	35.3	10.0	11.3	0.0
First State Bank	Waynesboro	MS	B+	B+	B+	861.9	8.89	6.8	1.9	18.5	28.5	10.0	11.8	0.0
First State Bank	Buxton	ND	B+	B	B+	279.0	37.24	18.8	1.0	8.4	6.2	5.0	10.3	0.0
First State Bank	Farnam	NE	A-	A-	B+	145.4	-0.97	7.9	2.7	4.7	21.5	10.0	13.5	0.0
▲ First State Bank	Gothenburg	NE	C	C	C	684.2	26.92	11.5	0.7	2.2	24.1	7.5	11.1	0.0
First State Bank	Hordville	NE	B-	B-	C+	40.0	0.16	11.5	0.6	5.8	0.6	9.8	12.5	0.0
First State Bank	Loomis	NE	B+	B-	C+	161.2	9.79	9.6	3.0	4.8	11.4	9.2	12.0	14.4
First State Bank	Randolph	NE	B+	B+	B+	64.4	-1.54	4.3	1.5	1.4	6.8	10.0	13.9	0.0
First State Bank	Scottsbluff	NE	A-	A-	A-	334.6	7.17	13.1	1.3	7.0	16.9	5.6	9.1	0.0
First State Bank	Socorro	NM	B-	B	B	168.8	7.22	1.1	0.5	3.0	81.2	8.7	10.2	44.0
First State Bank	Winchester	OH	B	B	B-	584.2	17.12	1.6	7.5	16.5	30.1	7.8	9.5	16.6
First State Bank	Anadarko	OK	B+	B	A-	100.6	9.48	4.3	2.2	2.7	57.2	10.0	14.2	0.0
▼ First State Bank	Boise City	OK	C+	C+	C	92.4	11.23	10.7	5.2	2.0	13.4	4.0	9.6	0.0
First State Bank	Elmore City	OK	B-	C+	C-	19.5	34.62	17.3	1.4	47.9	0.9	9.8	10.9	23.2
▼ First State Bank	Noble	OK	C-	C+	C+	47.5	7.96	1.9	4.0	18.0	31.6	8.7	10.1	0.0
First State Bank	Oklahoma City	OK	C	C+	C	407.7	17.91	21.1	0.5	15.1	1.7	2.5	8.4	0.0
▲ First State Bank	Tahlequah	OK	C-	C-	C+	78.2	23.92	24.5	1.8	10.5	16.2	8.8	12.4	0.0
First State Bank	Valliant	OK	C	C-	D	79.4	13.67	8.9	4.7	18.6	8.5	6.2	8.2	14.3
▲ First State Bank	Watonga	OK	A-	B+	B+	76.2	1.95	12.6	2.9	2.2	34.6	10.0	11.3	0.0
First State Bank	Abernathy	TX	C+	C+	C+	40.3	-12.18	11.0	8.8	0.3	9.6	8.3	9.9	0.0

Asset Quality Index	Adjusted Non-Performing Loans		Net Charge-Offs / Avg Loans	Profitability Index	Net Income ($Mil)	Return on Assets (R.O.A.)	Return on Equity (R.O.E.)	Net Interest Spread	Overhead Efficiency Ratio	Liquidity Index	Liquidity Ratio	Hot Money Ratio	Stability Index
	as a % of Total Loans	as a % of Capital											
7.5	0.00	na	0.00	6.9	0.9	1.67	13.11	3.95	54.5	5.5	27.0	1.0	8.1
2.4	2.42	na	0.09	4.6	0.5	1.14	13.75	4.75	76.5	1.3	6.3	25.0	3.3
8.3	0.00	na	0.00	10.0	1.0	2.86	30.04	4.70	40.9	5.1	31.6	5.8	6.4
6.8	0.00	0.0	-0.01	8.3	2.7	1.37	7.07	3.78	49.5	6.0	38.0	2.2	9.5
4.0	2.80	na	-0.12	8.3	1.0	1.86	15.82	4.50	53.7	5.2	35.9	6.7	7.9
8.9	0.00	na	-0.09	8.2	0.5	2.00	17.23	3.69	47.1	6.0	52.6	5.8	7.0
8.0	0.55	na	0.43	5.8	2.1	1.33	9.77	3.72	58.5	5.6	35.9	3.9	7.8
3.0	1.01	na	0.31	4.5	0.6	0.77	6.34	3.61	59.9	1.9	25.6	19.2	8.2
9.1	0.01	na	0.07	4.4	1.0	1.04	13.13	3.36	72.6	6.4	59.1	7.0	4.7
5.5	1.25	na	-0.04	3.8	2.1	0.89	9.46	2.25	72.1	6.7	55.9	4.3	5.1
4.0	0.61	na	0.44	4.8	1.8	0.78	9.15	4.56	63.3	1.1	10.1	28.8	4.9
5.3	1.52	na	0.07	6.0	3.7	1.26	14.57	4.41	62.0	0.8	10.1	15.2	5.6
6.1	1.34	na	-0.03	3.0	1.0	0.42	2.72	2.98	80.1	1.8	22.2	22.5	7.7
3.6	1.43	na	0.13	1.8	0.1	0.07	0.63	3.92	98.2	4.6	24.6	6.2	4.5
3.2	1.45	na	0.31	5.2	0.9	1.19	13.36	4.24	68.9	1.8	19.2	16.5	5.7
8.0	0.24	na	0.00	6.5	3.2	1.40	15.45	4.03	53.4	3.1	10.0	12.9	5.1
5.8	1.78	na	0.01	0.9	0.0	-0.02	-0.21	4.15	103.1	4.2	23.6	8.2	1.5
4.9	1.07	na	0.09	7.2	7.5	1.37	10.13	3.83	49.5	3.2	22.8	13.7	9.0
8.3	0.16	na	-0.04	5.1	2.0	1.24	11.18	4.16	73.5	3.2	21.3	13.8	6.7
4.5	1.60	na	0.03	5.3	7.2	1.01	9.44	3.94	67.3	4.5	25.7	7.4	7.5
7.6	0.29	1.3	0.04	5.5	4.7	1.07	9.77	3.77	63.3	2.7	30.5	18.2	6.7
7.0	0.81	na	0.02	4.1	1.8	0.68	7.27	3.68	74.2	3.4	22.4	12.6	5.3
6.4	1.51	na	0.00	6.6	2.0	1.49	11.43	3.42	55.5	4.6	37.1	9.1	9.1
8.8	0.00	na	0.14	2.6	0.9	0.47	4.27	3.04	73.8	1.6	22.8	25.1	5.8
8.7	0.06	na	0.00	5.4	2.6	1.00	10.02	3.33	62.1	2.8	29.3	15.5	6.2
6.0	0.26	na	0.03	9.1	2.2	1.70	19.81	5.51	58.4	1.1	16.4	29.7	5.8
9.0	0.23	na	0.21	4.4	0.8	0.95	8.03	2.64	58.7	4.3	51.7	16.6	6.8
9.0	0.02	0.1	0.00	7.6	1.4	1.55	11.12	3.13	36.1	5.2	45.2	10.3	8.4
6.5	0.43	na	0.44	8.0	2.4	1.90	15.83	3.86	48.5	1.5	28.1	31.1	7.9
6.9	0.33	na	-0.11	8.6	2.8	1.83	13.63	4.21	49.6	3.2	22.9	10.5	9.0
8.5	0.00	0.0	0.33	8.8	0.7	1.71	15.50	3.31	42.8	1.5	25.8	28.8	7.4
8.8	0.00	na	-0.02	3.3	0.4	0.46	4.45	2.91	80.6	5.9	50.4	7.6	5.8
3.7	6.29	na	0.09	1.3	0.2	0.24	1.66	2.94	85.5	5.7	53.6	9.7	5.9
7.7	0.15	na	0.00	5.6	4.4	1.13	8.46	3.20	64.2	1.6	19.2	20.4	8.8
5.5	1.20	na	0.24	7.6	16.3	1.77	17.17	3.30	54.6	1.6	11.8	21.5	8.2
5.5	1.34	na	0.00	6.0	3.1	1.51	16.23	3.32	64.7	4.8	35.9	9.3	6.3
8.2	2.11	na	0.03	5.9	0.7	1.41	7.66	3.27	56.0	4.5	36.5	11.1	8.4
4.1	2.06	9.7	0.05	6.2	5.3	1.53	12.84	3.94	55.0	0.8	19.0	24.4	7.4
5.1	3.09	11.9	0.02	8.2	2.6	1.67	13.99	4.44	53.8	4.3	13.4	6.5	7.7
5.8	1.29	6.3	0.07	4.6	6.2	0.95	9.56	3.07	68.6	3.3	38.5	18.1	6.2
6.5	1.89	na	-0.02	2.3	0.4	0.39	3.36	3.06	94.2	2.7	19.4	15.9	6.8
5.6	1.55	na	0.33	3.9	4.3	0.68	5.19	3.36	65.3	2.1	22.4	19.5	8.6
6.7	0.24	1.8	0.00	5.7	2.8	1.40	12.87	3.48	59.7	1.4	5.4	18.3	7.7
6.7	0.63	na	-0.01	8.3	2.3	2.06	15.01	3.80	53.2	1.4	21.1	26.6	9.4
3.0	2.17	na	0.08	9.3	10.4	2.22	18.98	4.09	39.2	1.1	20.7	21.9	8.6
6.2	0.46	na	0.00	3.5	0.2	0.56	4.60	3.41	74.5	4.1	21.7	8.6	6.7
5.6	0.37	na	0.03	9.0	1.9	1.72	12.24	4.38	50.7	1.0	10.5	21.1	9.0
7.2	0.00	na	0.20	5.7	0.6	1.31	9.33	3.46	60.4	2.3	21.6	13.8	9.2
8.2	0.21	na	0.40	9.8	5.5	2.30	24.31	4.18	49.7	3.2	35.9	17.5	8.9
10.0	1.58	na	0.37	3.6	0.8	0.67	6.65	3.17	68.6	7.1	63.9	3.4	5.5
5.5	0.83	na	0.07	5.3	6.3	1.51	14.55	3.44	63.0	4.3	27.8	9.3	6.9
8.9	1.38	na	-0.09	5.7	1.4	1.92	13.55	2.91	60.0	4.9	43.7	11.4	5.4
4.2	0.41	na	0.31	8.6	1.5	2.27	27.68	4.13	45.6	0.6	10.3	21.1	5.6
7.3	0.39	na	0.00	9.3	0.5	3.19	27.49	2.64	88.2	5.1	25.0	2.3	6.3
6.4	1.45	na	0.04	2.0	0.1	0.26	2.39	4.10	100.3	5.9	41.9	4.1	5.1
7.1	0.05	na	0.01	4.4	2.4	0.85	9.46	3.31	69.6	0.7	9.3	36.6	5.0
3.4	3.28	na	0.05	3.6	0.4	0.82	7.36	3.35	70.5	2.3	30.8	20.9	5.9
5.7	0.49	na	0.16	3.3	0.3	0.59	6.74	4.38	85.7	2.7	29.1	18.0	4.6
8.3	1.18	na	0.22	5.8	0.6	1.12	9.43	4.03	64.3	4.8	51.1	12.8	8.0
4.0	0.89	na	-0.01	5.2	0.4	1.16	10.35	6.51	81.6	2.6	21.5	16.5	6.5

Name	City	State	2019 Rating	2018 Rating	Rating	Total Assets ($Mil)	One Year Asset Growth	Commercial Loans	Consumer Loans	Mortgage Loans	Securities	Capitalization Index	Leverage Ratio	Risk-Based Capital Ratio
First State Bank	Abilene	TX	C-	C	D+	44.6	22.70	17.7	1.1	1.9	7.3	4.5	6.5	29.3
First State Bank	Athens	TX	B+	A-	A-	532.9	15.76	9.7	2.6	26.4	26.5	9.8	10.9	0.0
First State Bank	Clute	TX	B	B-	B	269.1	29.06	22.4	6.4	13.7	15.0	6.4	8.5	0.0
First State Bank	Columbus	TX	C+	B-	B-	159.8	7.84	2.4	3.3	5.1	55.1	10.0	13.9	31.8
First State Bank	Gainesville	TX	B+	B+	B+	1310.9	15.31	13.2	1.4	9.7	31.6	7.1	9.1	15.7
First State Bank	Graham	TX	B+	B+	B+	176.8	18.87	23.3	1.6	12.8	14.6	6.4	8.4	15.9
First State Bank	Junction	TX	C+	C+	C-	60.1	21.00	5.5	2.2	11.8	25.0	6.6	8.6	0.0
First State Bank	Louise	TX	B+	A-	B+	613.4	22.76	14.6	0.6	7.9	12.5	4.1	8.7	0.0
First State Bank	Rice	TX	B-	B-	B-	171.8	14.87	17.9	2.5	10.7	19.8	10.0	11.5	0.0
First State Bank	Shallowater	TX	B	B-	B+	106.5	11.33	16.9	1.3	3.0	8.6	10.0	16.9	25.9
First State Bank	Spearman	TX	B	B	B-	149.6	3.30	9.4	0.8	4.1	7.7	8.8	10.2	0.0
First State Bank	Stratford	TX	A-	A-	A-	269.5	7.71	8.2	0.8	5.3	31.1	10.0	11.6	0.0
▲ First State Bank	New London	WI	B	B-	B-	494.6	62.94	8.6	2.7	11.3	28.4	7.2	9.7	0.0
First State Bank & Trust	Williston	ND	A-	A-	B	470.4	2.86	9.0	1.0	2.9	57.1	10.0	13.1	24.9
First State Bank & Trust Co.	Fremont	NE	B+	B+	B-	276.6	8.58	22.9	2.1	18.5	8.9	5.7	9.3	0.0
▲ First State Bank and Trust	Tonganoxie	KS	B	B-	C+	354.9	18.47	10.8	1.8	13.3	20.4	6.0	8.0	13.9
First State Bank and Trust	Bayport	MN	B	B	B-	310.9	17.25	10.4	4.9	27.5	18.4	6.5	8.5	15.7
▼ First State Bank and Trust Co.	Carthage	TX	B+	A-	A-	495.5	-1.92	1.9	4.7	18.3	58.2	10.0	16.2	0.0
First State Bank and Trust Co., Inc.	Caruthersville	MO	A-	A-	A-	424.5	10.67	9.2	3.0	12.5	18.9	9.6	11.7	0.0
First State Bank in Temple	Temple	OK	B-	C+	C+	24.5	-2.15	4.0	4.0	2.3	35.7	10.0	20.5	0.0
First State Bank Minnesota	Le Roy	MN	B-	B	B-	80.8	20.80	6.8	1.8	4.5	6.3	9.2	10.5	0.0
First State Bank Nebraska	Lincoln	NE	B	B	B-	669.5	12.71	16.1	1.1	11.9	8.4	6.5	8.5	12.8
First State Bank of Bedias	Bedias	TX	A	A	A	178.1	10.93	10.6	4.2	10.8	17.9	10.0	15.7	0.0
First State Bank of Beecher City	Beecher City	IL	B+	B+	B	81.7	12.45	7.2	11.5	20.5	6.1	10.0	14.2	19.8
First State Bank of Ben Wheeler, Texas	Ben Wheeler	TX	A-	A-	A-	166.9	10.17	6.1	2.9	16.6	47.4	10.0	13.4	0.0
▼ First State Bank of Bigfork	Bigfork	MN	D-	D+	D	90.1	11.80	11.1	10.8	33.8	0.9	8.8	10.3	0.0
First State Bank of Blakely	Blakely	GA	B+	A-	B+	545.0	4.68	9.0	2.2	12.4	14.9	10.0	14.5	0.0
First State Bank of Bloomington	Bloomington	IL	B-	C+	C+	142.5	17.26	15.7	1.7	19.1	18.1	6.1	8.1	16.5
▲ First State Bank of Brownsboro	Brownsboro	TX	B	B-	C+	117.2	14.66	5.3	7.0	18.9	45.7	8.4	10.0	18.0
First State Bank of Burnet	Burnet	TX	B+	A-	A-	283.8	15.28	7.4	1.4	7.6	59.3	10.0	12.3	0.0
First State Bank of Campbell Hill	Campbell Hill	IL	A-	B+	B	130.4	12.62	4.8	4.7	26.1	22.4	10.0	12.6	19.9
First State Bank of Cando	Cando	ND	C+	C+	C+	69.2	13.83	9.8	4.9	3.5	37.7	7.4	9.2	19.1
First State Bank of Decatur	Decatur	MI	B-	B	B	55.6	6.53	8.8	3.2	37.5	27.1	10.0	20.3	0.0
First State Bank of DeKalb County	Fort Payne	AL	B-	B-	C+	232.2	20.09	10.3	5.4	17.1	17.1	8.1	9.8	15.2
First State Bank of DeQueen	De Queen	AR	B-	B+	B+	296.4	11.71	10.4	3.7	13.7	17.1	6.3	9.3	0.0
▲ First State Bank of Dongola	Dongola	IL	B-	C+	C	28.6	13.98	4.5	10.3	25.3	10.5	9.0	10.3	19.0
First State Bank of Forrest	Forrest	IL	C-	C-	C-	236.7	3.26	16.9	4.6	30.7	6.4	6.3	8.3	12.7
▲ First State Bank of Forsyth	Forsyth	MT	B+	B	B-	138.8	16.78	6.2	3.4	8.8	41.3	10.0	11.5	0.0
First State Bank of Fountain	Fountain	MN	D+	D	D+	34.7	7.09	6.8	1.2	8.1	43.3	7.8	9.5	18.4
First State Bank of Golva	Golva	ND	B+	A-	B+	89.2	15.01	4.6	2.0	4.4	44.7	6.9	8.9	16.2
First State Bank of Harvey	Harvey	ND	B-	B	B-	86.5	6.81	3.6	3.3	4.8	49.3	9.0	10.3	0.0
First State Bank of Healy	Healy	KS	B	B-	C	80.1	3.85	9.4	0.8	1.1	38.5	10.0	21.2	0.0
First State Bank of Le Center	Le Center	MN	B+	B+	B	94.9	8.82	9.0	10.1	17.1	18.8	8.9	10.2	17.6
First State Bank of Livingston	Livingston	TX	B	B	B	376.8	12.31	2.1	2.4	4.2	47.0	10.0	14.2	0.0
▲ First State Bank of Malta	Malta	MT	D	D	D+	150.1	10.68	3.8	1.4	0.0	32.0	10.0	15.0	0.0
▲ First State Bank of Middlebury	Middlebury	IN	A-	B+	B-	671.0	12.93	20.0	1.8	20.0	17.3	10.0	11.2	17.5
First State Bank of Newcastle	Newcastle	WY	B	B	B	165.3	11.05	7.8	2.2	6.9	52.3	10.0	12.5	40.3
First State Bank of Odem	Odem	TX	A	A	A-	165.1	13.31	15.8	1.4	4.4	18.3	10.0	12.1	23.4
First State Bank of Olmsted	Olmsted	IL	B	B-	B-	61.1	20.14	14.8	3.6	25.0	22.2	10.0	12.1	20.0
First State Bank of Paint Rock	Paint Rock	TX	A-	A-	B	120.4	14.41	11.2	3.4	3.1	34.7	10.0	11.8	0.0
First State Bank of Porter	Porter	IN	B+	B+	A-	158.1	10.24	3.2	0.2	19.3	32.9	10.0	15.5	0.0
First State Bank of Purdy	Monett	MO	B-	B-	C	180.5	18.12	21.5	0.8	9.6	11.4	6.0	8.0	13.0
First State Bank of Randolph County	Cuthbert	GA	C-	D+	C-	83.3	7.63	12.4	3.4	4.5	44.0	7.5	9.3	0.0
First State Bank of Ransom	Ransom	KS	B	B	B	46.1	12.50	6.5	1.3	0.9	55.2	10.0	21.6	46.1
▲ First State Bank of Red Wing	Red Wing	MN	D+	D+	D+	87.4	15.09	5.3	11.2	9.6	40.6	6.2	8.2	20.8
First State Bank of Roscoe	Roscoe	SD	A-	A-	B+	125.3	14.07	7.7	0.5	0.1	4.5	10.0	11.3	17.3
▲ First State Bank of Rosemount	Rosemount	MN	D+	D-	D-	83.6	15.74	16.5	8.9	15.2	16.0	4.9	6.9	12.4
First State Bank of San Diego	San Diego	TX	C+	C+	C+	70.6	16.68	22.9	3.1	3.0	33.7	6.3	8.4	18.4
First State Bank of Sauk Centre	Sauk Centre	MN	A-	A-	B+	127.2	13.80	13.1	3.8	15.6	10.3	10.0	11.9	0.0
First State Bank of Shelby	Shelby	MT	B+	A	A	137.6	7.59	6.7	0.6	0.0	68.7	10.0	22.2	71.3

Asset Quality Index	Adjusted Non-Performing Loans		Net Charge-Offs	Profitability Index	Net Income ($Mil)	Return on Assets (R.O.A.)	Return on Equity (R.O.E.)	Net Interest Spread	Overhead Efficiency Ratio	Liquidity Index	Liquidity Ratio	Hot Money Ratio	Stability Index
	as a % of Total Loans	as a % of Capital	Avg Loans										
8.7	0.00	na	0.00	3.1	0.2	0.54	6.95	2.76	74.6	6.2	60.9	6.3	3.1
5.1	2.03	na	-0.01	5.9	4.4	1.15	10.22	3.84	62.6	4.3	25.1	8.3	7.6
5.7	0.47	na	0.09	6.3	2.6	1.38	16.18	3.67	64.0	4.7	31.3	8.2	5.4
9.5	0.02	na	0.01	3.1	0.9	0.78	5.41	2.40	73.8	3.1	63.5	36.6	7.4
6.7	0.67	3.8	0.04	5.0	12.0	1.30	13.34	3.76	73.5	5.8	33.4	6.1	8.4
8.7	0.00	na	0.06	7.7	2.3	1.85	19.52	4.31	59.8	2.7	33.4	19.4	7.0
7.4	0.20	na	0.17	4.4	0.4	0.93	10.34	3.58	68.9	4.4	27.3	8.6	5.4
8.4	0.13	na	0.04	10.0	10.3	2.44	26.72	5.43	52.0	4.6	24.3	5.9	7.6
8.2	0.13	na	0.01	3.4	0.6	0.49	3.83	3.91	85.5	3.7	24.2	11.4	6.7
4.1	1.54	5.2	0.45	9.3	1.5	1.97	9.98	4.63	62.0	2.4	21.1	17.7	9.5
8.6	0.00	na	0.16	5.2	1.3	1.13	13.07	3.79	68.0	1.8	28.0	26.7	5.8
8.6	0.00	na	0.00	6.8	3.1	1.61	13.06	3.40	56.8	3.1	36.4	18.1	8.4
5.0	3.35	na	0.03	4.9	3.5	1.00	9.31	4.22	66.7	4.6	29.0	7.7	7.0
5.9	0.10	na	3.27	5.2	3.8	1.06	7.17	3.39	49.9	5.5	49.3	10.1	8.8
8.0	0.12	na	-0.01	7.9	3.6	1.81	19.33	4.43	59.6	3.7	15.5	10.7	7.4
7.9	0.15	0.5	0.00	5.9	3.4	1.34	16.18	3.88	69.5	4.3	21.9	7.3	4.9
8.6	0.09	na	0.01	4.8	2.3	1.05	11.91	3.65	76.9	4.4	27.7	8.6	5.8
8.0	1.64	na	0.40	4.9	3.9	1.02	6.05	3.09	56.3	2.3	39.5	29.5	9.1
8.0	0.11	na	0.10	7.0	5.1	1.68	13.41	4.17	62.6	2.4	15.0	15.5	8.2
8.4	0.08	na	-0.03	4.1	0.2	0.86	4.22	3.92	70.7	1.9	34.9	25.4	6.4
4.7	2.78	na	0.65	6.0	0.7	1.33	12.35	3.59	61.6	6.0	37.3	2.5	6.9
7.2	0.22	na	0.00	5.5	6.6	1.37	14.57	3.33	57.2	2.5	11.2	14.1	6.9
7.4	1.03	4.4	-0.19	8.4	2.5	1.95	11.86	4.11	51.1	3.0	49.7	27.3	9.3
4.4	3.45	12.7	0.12	9.9	1.5	2.59	18.17	4.30	47.4	3.4	20.9	12.5	8.9
9.3	0.11	na	0.02	6.1	1.9	1.54	11.42	3.11	56.5	2.5	41.9	28.6	8.3
0.3	4.81	36.3	0.05	4.5	0.5	0.77	7.41	4.26	70.1	1.8	19.6	18.1	6.0
5.3	1.71	na	0.78	5.2	3.4	0.84	5.65	3.86	60.5	0.8	15.6	26.6	9.3
4.8	0.73	na	0.13	5.3	1.4	1.38	15.25	3.47	67.8	4.6	31.7	9.1	6.0
6.3	0.83	na	0.09	4.8	1.0	1.22	11.68	3.85	70.7	4.1	36.5	13.5	6.2
9.3	0.85	na	-0.04	4.6	2.2	1.11	7.91	3.24	59.8	6.1	66.8	10.4	8.0
5.8	1.58	8.4	0.01	6.6	1.2	1.31	10.89	3.74	57.6	5.3	36.6	6.5	6.6
7.2	0.03	na	0.32	4.4	0.6	1.11	11.12	3.44	71.6	3.6	38.5	16.6	5.4
9.3	0.44	na	0.05	3.4	0.2	0.55	2.55	3.53	81.9	5.1	60.9	13.2	7.5
4.0	0.65	na	0.33	6.4	2.1	1.30	11.47	4.94	55.5	3.8	37.0	14.9	6.7
5.5	0.66	na	0.15	5.4	2.9	1.30	14.06	3.82	60.5	0.7	12.1	18.6	6.3
7.1	1.46	na	-0.13	4.1	0.2	1.04	10.11	4.01	79.8	5.5	44.2	7.6	5.5
3.0	1.08	na	0.15	2.8	0.8	0.45	5.48	2.62	79.7	1.6	16.5	22.6	4.6
5.0	3.70	na	0.59	6.4	1.2	1.23	9.58	3.71	48.2	4.9	48.7	12.6	7.4
9.3	0.00	na	0.00	1.5	0.1	0.27	2.65	3.06	92.4	5.2	54.0	11.2	4.7
8.0	0.02	na	0.00	7.2	1.0	1.56	15.14	3.66	52.3	5.4	36.1	5.7	7.5
7.0	0.65	3.2	0.01	3.5	0.6	0.86	7.29	3.22	75.8	6.2	61.6	6.7	7.0
5.8	6.04	na	0.12	5.9	0.8	1.41	6.36	3.60	58.5	1.6	25.9	26.6	7.0
4.3	1.38	na	0.21	8.5	1.2	1.82	17.24	4.57	56.5	4.4	17.4	6.0	8.1
8.7	0.58	na	0.05	4.5	3.0	1.07	7.07	3.23	69.3	4.9	37.1	9.4	7.8
0.0	27.13	na	1.21	1.6	0.4	0.41	2.60	2.99	60.0	3.6	33.9	15.0	5.6
5.8	0.97	na	0.18	7.0	7.6	1.56	13.71	4.15	58.7	3.0	24.2	14.6	8.1
9.4	1.35	na	-0.02	3.2	0.8	0.64	4.58	2.59	71.4	3.7	54.8	21.3	7.3
8.8	0.00	na	-0.08	6.9	1.5	1.32	10.59	4.34	62.9	6.0	41.5	3.7	7.3
6.6	0.07	na	0.01	4.9	0.4	1.00	8.43	3.56	65.2	2.9	23.3	15.5	6.3
6.9	3.06	na	0.91	6.4	1.3	1.40	11.85	3.52	52.5	4.0	42.2	15.6	7.9
9.1	1.26	na	0.05	4.7	1.1	0.98	5.86	3.72	69.2	3.0	44.9	23.4	8.1
4.6	1.53	na	0.09	4.9	1.6	1.22	14.59	4.01	72.6	3.8	21.5	7.1	5.1
2.1	4.84	na	1.02	2.3	0.3	0.51	5.27	3.08	88.5	4.5	35.0	10.8	5.0
8.5	1.04	3.1	-0.01	5.3	0.4	1.19	5.20	2.97	59.2	5.7	64.9	10.9	6.8
8.7	0.02	na	-0.13	1.9	0.2	0.28	2.99	2.28	88.5	4.4	52.2	14.9	3.8
7.4	0.00	na	0.10	5.5	1.0	1.13	9.37	3.51	56.8	2.9	29.6	16.9	8.5
4.3	1.44	na	0.13	4.3	0.5	0.83	11.77	4.48	66.1	4.8	23.4	4.7	1.8
7.2	0.44	1.6	0.00	4.0	0.5	0.93	10.04	2.98	70.8	4.5	38.6	12.2	4.9
8.1	0.00	na	-0.01	5.8	1.0	1.10	8.10	3.48	57.6	3.4	24.1	12.8	8.2
10.0	0.40	na	0.55	4.4	0.8	0.84	3.66	2.71	60.5	6.6	99.5	11.9	8.7

Name	City	State	Rating	2019 Rating	2018 Rating	Total Assets ($Mil)	One Year Asset Growth	Commercial Loans	Consumer Loans	Mortgage Loans	Securities	Capitalization Index	Leverage Ratio	Risk-Based Capital Ratio
First State Bank of St. Charles, Missouri	Saint Charles	MO	A-	A-	A-	452.0	15.47	15.4	0.1	48.0	7.6	10.0	14.0	17.1
First State Bank of St. Peter	Saint Peter	IL	B+	B+	B+	30.0	4.68	1.5	4.0	3.3	38.5	10.0	17.1	40.4
First State Bank of Swanville	Swanville	MN	C+	C+	C+	25.6	2.84	14.6	3.1	11.3	0.8	10.0	15.6	24.5
First State Bank of Texas	Orange	TX	B-	B-	B-	208.6	22.84	24.5	7.2	12.5	12.7	7.9	10.3	0.0
First State Bank of the Florida Keys	Key West	FL	B	B	B-	1044.3	7.87	10.9	0.6	16.5	27.1	6.8	8.8	17.4
First State Bank of the South, Inc.	Sulligent	AL	B+	B+	B+	115.4	11.57	5.7	6.8	12.4	38.3	10.0	14.9	0.0
First State Bank of the Southeast, Inc.	Middlesboro	KY	C+	C+	B-	351.1	1.25	12.3	2.7	28.2	7.4	7.4	9.3	14.1
First State Bank of Uvalde	Uvalde	TX	B+	B+	B	1841.7	3.19	3.8	0.5	5.6	58.9	8.1	9.7	27.6
First State Bank of Van Orin	Van Orin	IL	C	C	C-	42.6	5.24	2.9	1.4	1.8	32.4	8.2	9.8	24.9
First State Bank of Warren	Warren	AR	C	B-	C+	120.7	12.55	18.6	1.6	4.4	39.6	8.9	10.3	0.0
First State Bank of Wyoming	Wyoming	MN	B+	A-	B+	210.0	15.64	8.2	1.5	12.1	54.1	10.0	16.4	0.0
▲ First State Bank Shannon-Polo	Shannon	IL	B-	C+	C+	186.7	13.01	9.5	2.2	8.2	32.6	6.2	8.9	0.0
First State Bank Southwest	Worthington	MN	A	A	A-	301.0	14.82	11.8	2.5	4.8	34.9	10.0	11.1	21.6
First State Bank, Pond Creek, Oklahoma	Pond Creek	OK	B	B	B-	50.3	4.84	18.9	3.0	20.2	9.4	10.0	12.0	0.0
First State Community Bank	Farmington	MO	A-	B+	B	3228.9	25.83	9.4	1.7	19.2	14.4	5.7	8.8	11.6
First Summit Bank	Ryan	OK	C	C	C+	25.8	-5.02	13.3	2.5	6.8	0.0	10.0	13.6	0.0
First Texas Bank	Georgetown	TX	B+	B+	B-	787.1	20.74	7.4	0.7	3.1	56.0	5.9	7.9	0.0
First Texas Bank	Killeen	TX	B	B	B-	371.7	17.78	5.3	0.3	11.0	44.1	8.0	9.6	0.0
First Texas Bank	Lampasas	TX	A-	A-	B-	161.9	17.29	5.5	1.1	15.2	37.4	8.8	10.2	0.0
First Texoma National Bank	Durant	OK	B+	A-	B+	208.2	13.16	5.7	4.7	23.0	22.0	9.1	10.4	16.3
First Tri-County Bank	Swanton	NE	C+	C	C	61.0	10.69	7.3	4.8	16.0	2.2	6.7	9.8	0.0
First Trust and Savings Bank	Coralville	IA	D+	C-	C+	57.2	24.05	4.4	1.3	3.1	72.2	9.5	10.6	25.1
First Trust and Savings Bank	Wheatland	IA	B-	B-	B-	213.4	13.59	16.2	3.1	7.7	3.2	4.9	9.9	0.0
First Trust and Savings Bank of Watseka	Watseka	IL	A-	A	A	270.9	5.82	9.5	1.2	5.8	34.0	10.0	15.2	0.0
First Trust Bank of Illinois	Kankakee	IL	C+	B	B	342.4	46.60	12.7	0.9	6.9	44.6	7.9	10.7	13.3
First United Bank	Park River	ND	B-	C+	C-	284.0	8.49	8.4	1.8	4.0	23.7	8.4	9.9	0.0
First United Bank	Dimmitt	TX	A-	A-	A-	1526.9	12.41	18.4	0.4	7.6	19.7	8.5	10.0	14.6
First United Bank & Trust	Oakland	MD	B-	B	B-	1669.8	17.41	15.7	2.1	20.4	13.0	8.0	9.6	15.4
First United Bank and Trust Co.	Madisonville	KY	A-	A-	A-	380.9	17.74	15.0	2.3	23.8	12.2	8.5	11.3	0.0
First United Bank and Trust Co.	Durant	OK	B	B	B	10218.4	30.18	13.1	1.7	21.3	11.2	5.5	9.0	11.3
First United National Bank	Fryburg	PA	B-	B	B	304.1	13.41	6.5	5.6	37.2	29.4	6.5	8.5	0.0
▼ First US Bank	Birmingham	AL	C+	B-	C+	852.6	10.50	6.8	22.1	8.9	11.0	7.1	9.1	12.8
First Utah Bank	Salt Lake City	UT	B	B-	C	631.3	44.26	26.1	0.5	0.9	5.3	6.9	8.9	14.1
First Vision Bank of Tennessee	Tullahoma	TN	B+	B+	B+	330.3	21.93	9.1	2.2	19.2	5.5	7.8	9.5	16.2
First Volunteer Bank	Chattanooga	TN	A-	A-	B+	1171.5	15.72	10.7	1.7	12.1	1.6	10.0	11.1	17.4
▲ First Western Bank	Booneville	AR	B	B-	C+	497.7	10.79	6.6	0.9	30.9	5.1	6.6	8.6	12.8
▼ First Western Bank & Trust	Minot	ND	C	B-	B+	1236.2	14.85	21.4	3.0	4.1	17.9	2.6	9.1	0.0
First Western Federal Savings Bank	Rapid City	SD	A-	A-	A-	59.7	-2.72	1.0	0.0	86.4	0.0	10.0	14.9	31.2
▲ First Western Trust Bank	Denver	CO	B-	C+	C+	1963.5	55.66	24.0	4.4	23.1	2.1	5.3	7.8	11.3
▼ First Westroads Bank, Inc.	Omaha	NE	A-	A	A	341.1	26.14	18.7	0.2	7.3	8.2	9.4	10.6	16.6
First Whitney Bank and Trust	Atlantic	IA	B+	B+	B+	253.8	14.06	17.5	1.2	4.7	31.8	5.6	10.2	11.4
▼ First, A National Banking Assn.	Hattiesburg	MS	B	B+	A-	5154.8	48.43	11.0	0.8	13.8	18.6	8.7	10.2	16.5
First-Citizens Bank & Trust Co.	Raleigh	NC	B+	B+	B+	48628.5	29.11	14.0	3.7	11.9	20.1	6.7	8.7	13.7
First-Lockhart National Bank	Lockhart	TX	B	B	B	319.6	16.27	2.6	0.6	17.1	18.5	7.0	9.0	16.8
▼ Firstar Bank	Sallisaw	OK	C+	B-	C+	772.0	21.89	22.0	2.4	17.8	5.9	2.7	8.1	0.0
FirstBank	Lakewood	CO	A-	A-	A-	23475.7	20.22	5.2	0.3	28.4	32.7	5.5	7.5	16.3
FirstBank	Antlers	OK	B	B	B-	527.7	67.04	8.8	11.1	25.3	6.1	6.1	8.2	0.0
FirstBank	Nashville	TN	B+	B+	B+	11053.0	81.65	14.9	2.2	15.8	10.5	10.0	12.4	15.6
▲ FirstBank of Nebraska	Wahoo	NE	A-	B+	B-	319.6	13.32	6.9	0.9	6.9	40.3	7.7	9.5	0.0
FirstBank Puerto Rico	San Juan	PR	C+	C-	D+	18644.4	48.88	9.1	11.3	19.6	18.6	10.0	13.8	19.8
FirstBank Southwest	Amarillo	TX	B+	B+	B	1175.6	16.53	16.8	2.7	8.0	34.5	6.5	8.5	14.7
FirstCapital Bank of Texas, N.A.	Midland	TX	B-	B-	C+	1891.8	11.87	23.8	0.7	13.7	4.5	5.0	10.0	0.0
FirsTier Bank	Kimball	NE	A-	A-	B+	490.4	21.80	42.8	1.6	2.9	4.7	6.5	12.0	0.0
FirstOak Bank	Independence	KS	A-	A-	B+	216.6	20.02	14.5	1.2	12.3	6.9	6.4	8.4	0.0
Firstrust Savings Bank	Conshohocken	PA	B+	B+	B+	4710.6	28.99	29.2	6.2	10.4	7.0	7.3	10.0	12.7
FirstState Bank	Lineville	AL	B+	A-	B+	288.7	17.72	4.4	3.9	8.8	35.7	9.7	10.8	0.0
▲ Fisher National Bank	Fisher	IL	A	A-	B+	149.7	17.14	6.5	2.0	32.2	21.4	10.0	12.7	21.3
Five Points Bank	Grand Island	NE	A-	A-	A	1537.4	28.02	21.5	1.0	5.5	27.7	5.8	9.4	0.0
Five Points Bank of Hastings	Hastings	NE	A-	A-	A	372.0	19.58	15.1	0.5	4.2	25.7	10.0	12.1	0.0
Five Star Bank	Rancho Cordova	CA	B+	B+	B	2057.2	44.53	18.7	0.3	1.5	5.8	5.5	7.5	12.2

Arrows denote recent upgrades ▲ or downgrades ▼

www.weissratings.com

Asset Quality Index	Adjusted Non-Performing Loans as a % of Total Loans	as a % of Capital	Net Charge-Offs / Avg Loans	Profitability Index	Net Income ($Mil)	Return on Assets (R.O.A.)	Return on Equity (R.O.E.)	Net Interest Spread	Overhead Efficiency Ratio	Liquidity Index	Liquidity Ratio	Hot Money Ratio	Stability Index
6.9	0.90	4.9	0.01	9.4	9.8	3.05	23.88	3.11	73.3	2.6	8.0	15.0	8.2
9.5	0.00	na	0.07	6.0	0.3	1.31	7.71	3.30	55.2	6.9	80.2	6.0	8.3
7.9	2.36	na	0.27	2.3	0.0	0.09	0.57	4.52	93.1	5.4	43.4	8.0	6.8
7.1	1.90	na	0.08	3.4	0.8	0.56	4.47	3.92	85.7	2.0	23.0	20.1	6.8
7.7	1.13	na	-0.05	4.4	8.3	1.10	12.27	3.37	67.5	5.2	22.9	4.2	8.7
8.7	0.00	na	0.07	3.9	0.6	0.71	4.56	4.02	76.4	3.4	53.6	24.1	7.6
3.2	2.39	17.7	0.76	4.8	3.6	1.36	14.87	3.77	60.2	1.7	18.0	21.3	4.2
9.7	0.33	na	0.02	4.4	12.7	0.93	8.68	1.99	43.4	3.0	57.3	55.9	7.5
7.5	0.70	na	-0.04	2.4	0.2	0.47	4.38	2.61	82.9	5.2	69.0	13.7	4.8
7.1	1.04	na	-0.02	2.3	0.2	0.28	2.62	2.65	89.2	4.5	44.4	13.5	5.7
8.3	2.39	na	-0.02	5.0	1.5	1.01	5.66	2.93	60.8	6.6	68.6	7.2	7.9
6.3	0.49	na	0.27	4.3	1.4	1.06	10.30	3.04	66.4	4.1	32.4	11.9	4.9
8.6	0.16	na	0.01	8.1	4.3	2.06	17.08	3.41	56.8	4.6	32.3	9.0	8.5
8.4	0.08	0.4	0.19	5.5	0.4	1.20	9.99	4.56	68.8	3.4	26.6	13.8	5.9
6.8	0.76	3.1	0.06	7.6	32.4	1.52	12.98	3.68	59.1	3.8	11.8	9.4	9.8
6.4	0.56	4.9	-0.05	1.9	0.0	0.06	0.44	4.35	98.6	1.4	16.5	25.9	6.1
9.8	1.35	na	0.01	5.9	6.6	1.22	14.58	2.81	50.9	7.0	66.4	4.4	6.1
9.3	1.01	na	0.00	4.1	2.0	0.81	7.87	3.24	66.1	7.1	60.9	2.7	6.6
9.5	0.26	na	-0.03	7.2	1.7	1.46	13.50	3.70	52.9	6.5	52.4	4.0	7.1
4.9	1.69	na	0.08	5.3	1.5	1.03	9.56	4.28	71.9	3.7	30.6	13.3	7.1
6.3	0.25	na	-0.01	3.9	0.3	0.70	6.45	3.76	76.4	4.2	20.7	8.0	4.9
6.0	3.50	na	0.00	1.2	0.0	0.08	0.70	2.57	106.9	2.6	58.1	26.0	4.8
4.3	0.48	3.8	0.00	5.5	1.8	1.20	11.90	3.91	63.6	1.4	10.1	25.1	6.6
8.7	0.76	1.4	0.03	5.5	2.0	1.02	6.47	2.56	51.8	4.9	36.3	9.0	8.8
4.5	2.04	na	0.00	3.4	1.6	0.65	6.39	2.84	75.1	3.7	34.8	15.0	6.2
4.3	0.79	na	-0.01	7.2	3.4	1.67	15.66	3.91	56.2	4.4	19.1	6.8	8.4
8.2	0.09	na	0.02	8.4	22.6	2.04	18.72	4.00	53.5	1.4	8.1	24.8	8.0
5.8	1.17	7.7	0.16	4.3	9.8	0.84	9.22	3.49	66.1	1.8	14.5	10.4	7.5
6.7	0.54	na	-0.01	5.8	3.8	1.40	11.80	4.22	66.8	4.0	6.7	7.7	8.6
5.7	1.05	4.8	0.14	5.9	82.9	1.22	13.00	3.93	68.0	1.5	10.5	17.7	7.1
6.4	0.64	na	0.07	3.4	1.2	0.57	6.20	3.13	79.1	4.8	35.1	9.2	4.9
4.6	0.49	3.3	0.24	3.1	2.5	0.40	3.91	4.70	81.6	2.7	11.1	15.1	5.3
5.4	1.40	na	0.01	5.3	3.6	0.90	9.23	4.05	71.0	1.8	21.0	21.6	7.8
8.3	0.13	na	0.02	7.2	3.2	1.40	14.65	3.60	60.9	1.7	25.4	24.5	5.7
7.4	0.64	na	0.06	6.1	5.9	0.72	6.03	4.25	57.7	4.4	25.0	10.5	10.0
8.0	0.26	na	0.00	5.9	4.3	1.18	13.84	4.15	62.1	2.1	9.9	18.2	4.8
5.0	1.66	6.4	0.14	5.1	9.2	1.02	10.52	3.53	63.1	1.7	18.4	18.7	8.8
9.8	0.18	0.5	0.00	10.0	1.2	2.51	17.11	5.26	50.9	0.4	6.6	59.7	8.0
6.2	0.62	na	0.00	7.5	20.7	1.79	21.53	3.16	62.6	1.9	15.8	10.7	6.6
7.4	0.02	0.1	0.03	6.1	2.9	1.19	10.18	3.31	57.8	5.2	29.5	4.1	8.8
8.5	0.00	na	0.00	9.0	3.6	2.01	19.18	3.09	34.6	3.2	30.2	16.0	8.0
4.4	1.38	5.8	0.06	6.0	43.0	1.23	8.68	3.78	50.2	4.3	21.3	9.2	10.0
6.0	1.00	5.4	0.07	5.0	359.2	1.07	11.33	3.30	68.7	4.9	20.1	3.8	8.6
8.4	0.00	na	0.01	4.1	1.9	0.82	8.70	3.36	72.6	3.9	31.5	12.9	5.7
3.6	0.98	na	0.29	6.2	6.1	1.08	10.67	4.45	58.8	2.1	10.9	16.8	7.9
9.6	0.14	1.2	0.03	6.4	192.5	1.20	14.77	3.14	50.0	6.4	39.0	3.5	8.2
6.1	0.40	na	0.09	7.9	7.1	1.83	19.89	5.71	66.2	1.4	22.3	28.2	7.0
6.2	0.48	2.7	0.05	4.9	20.0	0.35	2.95	3.55	69.3	3.3	16.6	12.0	10.0
6.3	0.71	na	-0.06	9.0	5.1	2.23	20.95	3.81	38.4	3.4	21.0	10.3	8.0
3.1	5.10	16.4	0.49	4.5	54.5	0.52	3.10	4.31	58.9	2.7	22.1	13.9	8.6
7.7	0.48	na	0.05	4.6	8.9	1.09	11.18	3.29	69.9	3.4	29.8	17.7	8.1
4.8	1.20	5.7	0.45	5.4	13.3	0.97	7.44	4.35	58.1	1.2	11.1	28.0	9.9
7.3	0.20	na	0.08	7.3	5.7	1.59	13.10	3.94	54.9	0.8	13.0	34.8	9.5
8.3	0.00	na	0.06	8.5	2.8	1.78	17.81	4.68	58.7	3.4	28.3	14.2	7.6
6.8	0.69	4.4	0.18	7.3	54.9	1.76	18.20	3.43	50.6	3.9	15.4	7.5	8.7
7.6	0.83	na	0.13	5.1	2.2	1.06	9.17	3.84	66.0	2.5	38.8	25.6	7.3
8.1	1.12	na	0.00	8.4	2.1	1.98	14.96	3.66	56.4	3.1	29.6	16.0	8.8
8.0	0.01	0.9	0.00	7.2	18.6	1.76	16.68	3.34	47.5	3.6	16.4	11.3	9.4
8.8	0.01	0.0	-0.01	6.0	3.7	1.32	11.46	3.29	49.6	4.8	22.8	4.5	8.1
7.2	0.09	0.8	0.13	9.4	28.3	2.10	26.99	3.64	35.4	5.3	22.7	3.4	8.3

Name	City	State	Rating	2019 Rating	2018 Rating	Total Assets ($Mil)	One Year Asset Growth	Asset Mix (As a % of Total Assets)				Capital- ization Index	Lever- age Ratio	Risk- Based Capital Ratio
								Comm- ercial Loans	Cons- umer Loans	Mort- gage Loans	Secur- ities			
Five Star Bank	Warsaw	NY	B-	B	B	4922.3	14.49	14.7	17.4	12.9	16.6	6.9	9.0	12.4
Flagler Bank	West Palm Beach	FL	B+	B+	B-	401.5	24.74	26.6	0.0	9.8	11.7	7.8	9.5	0.0
▼ Flagship Bank	Clearwater	FL	C	B	B-	299.7	158.87	30.9	0.5	2.7	1.7	2.4	10.3	0.0
Flagship Bank Minnesota	Wayzata	MN	B	B	C+	305.9	22.71	16.3	0.3	21.3	4.6	6.5	8.5	14.7
Flagstar Bank, FSB	Troy	MI	B+	B+	B+	29451.1	33.93	3.3	3.3	34.9	8.9	5.1	7.9	11.1
▲ Flanagan State Bank	Flanagan	IL	B-	B-	C+	215.3	14.66	5.5	1.9	24.6	26.0	10.0	11.5	0.0
Flatirons Bank	Boulder	CO	B	B	B+	258.7	44.63	24.8	0.2	25.4	27.0	5.9	7.9	0.0
Flatwater Bank	Gothenburg	NE	C-	C	B+	235.0	7.62	15.7	1.9	3.9	17.5	6.8	9.9	0.0
Fleetwood Bank	Fleetwood	PA	C+	C+	C+	295.6	15.77	6.5	0.1	36.1	20.0	6.6	8.7	0.0
Flint Community Bank	Albany	GA	C	C	C	281.3	7.54	13.5	1.3	27.5	1.1	5.5	7.6	11.4
Flint Hills Bank	Eskridge	KS	A-	A-	B+	144.4	12.49	6.3	2.5	12.2	43.9	10.0	12.0	0.0
Flora Bank & Trust	Flora	IL	B-	B-	B-	95.4	37.62	11.6	8.0	14.8	19.2	8.2	9.8	18.7
Florence Bank	Florence	MA	B	B	B	1680.2	18.69	3.1	0.0	36.9	23.5	9.0	10.4	0.0
Florida Business Bank	Melbourne	FL	A-	A-	B+	204.5	39.22	22.1	0.1	1.2	11.9	8.0	9.7	15.9
▲ Florida Capital Bank, N.A.	Jacksonville	FL	C+	C	C-	529.7	-1.30	9.4	0.0	37.0	3.3	10.0	11.1	16.2
Flushing Bank	Uniondale	NY	B-	B	B+	7065.5	-0.64	11.3	0.0	10.8	9.5	8.3	9.9	13.5
▲ FMB Bank	Wright City	MO	C-	D+	D+	41.0	8.85	13.7	3.3	14.6	28.7	6.2	8.2	0.0
FMS Bank	Fort Morgan	CO	C+	C+	B-	239.0	23.72	22.4	13.5	8.4	10.7	5.6	9.4	11.5
FNB Bank	Scottsboro	AL	B-	B-	C+	785.3	14.10	8.9	1.8	12.8	18.3	8.1	9.7	15.4
▲ FNB Bank	Fontanelle	IA	A-	B+	B+	215.8	7.54	5.0	1.0	7.8	10.3	10.0	13.2	0.0
FNB Bank	Goodland	KS	B+	B+	B+	213.2	11.17	8.4	0.9	1.7	20.0	10.0	12.8	18.2
FNB Bank, Inc.	Mayfield	KY	C+	B-	C+	551.6	8.07	12.2	9.4	17.7	18.4	6.3	8.3	12.2
▼ FNB Bank, Inc.	Romney	WV	B-	B	B-	230.8	15.01	10.3	3.9	28.1	15.2	7.1	9.1	14.7
FNB Community Bank	Vandalia	IL	A-	A-	B+	395.3	12.53	6.6	0.8	12.4	34.9	10.0	12.1	21.1
FNB Community Bank	Midwest City	OK	C+	C+	B-	507.4	9.46	8.1	3.8	6.0	35.2	7.6	9.4	17.6
FNB Coweta	Coweta	OK	C+	C+	C+	87.1	13.83	11.4	1.8	11.3	36.3	7.8	9.5	0.0
▼ FNB Oxford Bank	Oxford	MS	B	B+	A-	440.4	20.53	8.8	0.9	15.3	37.3	7.9	9.6	0.0
FNB South	Alma	GA	A	A	B+	454.0	17.39	13.4	5.0	14.8	7.5	10.0	15.1	24.6
FNB Washington	Washington	KS	B+	B+	B+	77.6	11.86	8.8	2.0	9.6	37.3	10.0	25.5	0.0
▲ FNBC Bank	Ash Flat	AR	B-	C	C	576.7	9.14	10.7	4.4	13.4	23.6	8.8	10.2	14.6
FNBC Bank and Trust	La Grange	IL	B	B	B-	584.8	12.42	7.9	0.3	15.5	26.7	7.3	9.2	19.1
▲ FNBT Bank	Fort Walton Beach	FL	A-	A-	B	519.2	15.08	5.2	0.7	11.0	0.8	8.7	10.1	20.0
FNCB Bank	Dunmore	PA	B	B	B-	1438.6	20.52	19.6	6.6	12.1	22.3	8.8	10.2	16.1
▲ FNNB Bank	Newton	IA	C	D+	C	93.8	13.93	22.4	0.7	8.9	13.8	6.1	8.1	14.8
Focus Bank	Charleston	MO	B+	B+	B-	784.3	2.59	11.2	1.9	25.7	5.1	7.7	10.8	0.0
Forcht Bank, N.A.	Lexington	KY	B-	B-	B-	1431.4	16.78	7.6	1.3	26.2	22.0	6.8	8.8	0.0
Ford County State Bank	Spearville	KS	B-	C+	B-	44.1	13.76	11.4	1.1	2.1	12.7	10.0	12.5	26.0
Foresight Bank	Plainview	MN	C+	B-	C	281.4	7.18	8.8	1.8	27.7	17.3	7.6	9.4	14.1
Forest Park National Bank and Trust Co.	Forest Park	IL	B-	B-	B-	290.4	22.23	10.3	0.1	15.8	9.1	5.5	7.5	12.1
▼ Fort Davis State Bank	Fort Davis	TX	C	C+	C+	99.0	8.21	7.1	3.5	5.2	25.9	6.9	8.9	17.7
Fort Jennings State Bank	Fort Jennings	OH	B	B	B	202.8	5.37	13.5	3.2	20.6	5.8	9.3	10.5	16.4
Forte Bank	Hartford	WI	B	B	B	273.7	19.12	12.9	0.4	15.8	7.7	8.1	10.0	0.0
▲ Fortifi Bank	Berlin	WI	B-	C+	C	529.9	20.88	17.5	1.6	12.3	10.2	6.5	8.5	12.1
▲ Fortis Private Bank	Denver	CO	C	C-	D+	1042.9	29.60	7.3	6.9	27.0	13.2	7.3	9.2	14.0
Fortress Bank	Peoria	IL	C+	C	C	552.5	23.71	21.0	1.2	14.9	10.9	5.7	8.0	11.5
▲ FortuneBank	Arnold	MO	C-	C-	C-	271.7	45.00	27.5	0.2	13.7	6.1	4.1	8.0	10.6
Forward Bank	Marshfield	WI	C+	C+	B-	718.5	21.11	16.4	2.8	14.8	15.7	5.6	7.6	11.7
Foundation One Bank	Omaha	NE	C	C+	C+	156.4	43.03	42.7	2.4	18.8	5.6	4.4	9.9	0.0
Founders Bank	Washington	DC	D-			61.6	na	0.1	0.0	16.8	14.0	9.8	48.4	0.0
▼ Fountain Trust Co.	Covington	IN	B+	A-	B+	503.8	30.51	6.2	1.4	20.0	34.8	8.6	10.1	19.4
Four Corners Community Bank	Farmington	NM	C-	C-	C-	437.6	17.97	22.2	0.5	4.5	14.3	8.3	10.7	0.0
▲ Four County Bank	Allentown	GA	A-	B+	B	77.7	9.52	9.4	9.3	20.4	15.1	10.0	13.9	0.0
Fourth Capital Bank	Nashville	TN	D-	D	D+	339.1	27.50	20.8	0.4	5.7	3.9	4.9	9.1	0.0
Fowler State Bank	Fowler	CO	B+	B	B	97.0	14.37	7.0	0.9	4.0	32.5	10.0	14.4	0.0
Fowler State Bank	Fowler	IN	A-	A-	A-	185.2	13.18	13.7	4.8	7.8	38.5	10.0	14.3	0.0
Fowler State Bank	Fowler	KS	D+	D+	D+	76.8	-0.49	7.6	1.5	3.1	19.0	7.1	9.1	17.8
Fox Valley Savings Bank	Fond du Lac	WI	B-	B	B	377.5	10.56	2.8	0.7	30.8	36.7	10.0	14.4	0.0
Foxboro Federal Savings	Foxborough	MA	B-	B-	B-	183.5	10.69	0.0	0.8	57.7	24.0	10.0	15.9	35.3
▲ Frandsen Bank & Trust	Lonsdale	MN	B+	B	B	1980.6	14.02	14.8	1.9	14.4	22.9	5.6	7.6	12.1
Franklin Bank	Pilesgrove	NJ	C	C+	C+	286.8	10.68	4.4	1.3	39.3	9.5	7.4	9.3	18.2

Asset Quality Index	Adjusted Non-Performing Loans as a % of Total Loans	as a % of Capital	Net Charge-Offs Avg Loans	Profitability Index	Net Income ($Mil)	Return on Assets (R.O.A.)	Return on Equity (R.O.E.)	Net Interest Spread	Overhead Efficiency Ratio	Liquidity Index	Liquidity Ratio	Hot Money Ratio	Stability Index
7.0	0.30	2.0	0.45	4.2	27.8	0.81	8.31	3.33	57.7	1.8	6.9	12.5	8.0
8.4	0.00	na	0.08	8.5	6.2	2.22	23.25	3.91	40.3	0.8	16.3	34.6	7.1
7.2	0.00	na	0.01	1.0	-1.0	-0.57	-3.92	3.26	99.6	4.1	20.6	8.7	6.5
8.1	0.34	na	-0.04	6.0	2.3	1.11	11.84	4.24	55.7	3.6	19.2	11.2	5.6
6.8	2.19	3.4	0.05	8.2	400.7	2.06	24.95	2.86	56.4	3.5	10.0	6.3	8.2
5.8	1.75	na	0.13	8.2	6.2	4.03	37.44	3.11	76.4	4.0	32.7	12.7	6.4
8.9	0.29	na	0.00	5.4	2.3	1.37	14.72	3.95	60.3	2.3	23.2	14.2	6.2
0.7	2.54	na	0.18	6.9	2.8	1.71	14.10	4.23	58.3	1.3	22.0	16.7	7.8
8.5	0.31	na	0.00	3.2	1.1	0.52	5.76	3.31	81.5	4.9	31.4	6.8	5.0
3.2	1.63	na	0.00	6.7	3.3	1.57	20.39	3.88	58.1	2.7	10.2	13.9	5.6
8.9	0.05	na	0.00	5.6	1.4	1.35	10.53	3.04	56.1	2.6	31.0	18.8	8.2
4.5	0.59	na	0.21	3.6	0.4	0.71	6.74	3.37	72.8	3.3	29.2	14.9	4.9
9.6	0.25	1.5	0.01	4.0	8.5	0.73	6.93	3.07	68.5	5.1	38.9	11.5	8.0
7.3	0.00	na	-0.06	6.5	1.6	1.21	11.82	3.75	52.4	3.7	27.5	12.1	7.3
6.5	1.50	na	0.35	7.8	8.7	2.46	25.22	3.26	65.9	1.1	10.6	11.7	6.7
6.5	0.50	3.7	0.07	3.8	32.7	0.61	6.52	2.90	58.7	1.2	7.9	13.1	7.9
6.8	1.53	na	-0.03	2.9	0.2	0.50	6.01	3.71	83.2	4.7	27.9	6.5	4.3
3.0	3.49	na	0.37	4.5	1.5	0.90	9.33	4.91	68.5	1.6	12.7	20.9	5.7
5.1	0.70	na	0.10	4.2	4.5	0.81	6.98	4.03	72.8	3.4	20.8	12.4	7.8
5.7	0.04	na	-0.05	5.7	2.0	1.26	8.46	3.70	65.8	2.9	14.9	14.4	9.2
7.3	0.16	0.6	0.00	5.1	1.9	1.23	9.15	4.13	69.4	3.8	9.7	9.3	8.1
6.3	1.73	na	0.03	3.2	2.2	0.54	5.37	3.43	77.4	2.7	11.1	9.4	7.6
7.0	1.83	na	1.84	2.6	0.1	0.06	0.58	3.60	67.5	1.7	20.0	22.7	6.1
7.4	0.52	na	-0.02	6.4	3.7	1.30	9.61	3.69	56.0	4.4	32.2	10.2	8.0
8.2	0.25	1.0	-0.04	3.4	2.6	0.68	6.78	3.21	75.0	4.7	25.4	5.6	6.3
6.1	2.06	na	0.00	3.7	0.5	0.74	7.55	3.66	73.8	4.8	43.6	11.5	5.1
8.8	0.34	na	0.04	4.0	2.5	0.82	7.62	3.14	62.1	3.1	30.8	11.5	7.0
8.2	0.01	na	-0.96	10.0	7.5	2.31	14.88	5.00	42.3	3.2	19.3	13.4	8.5
8.9	2.14	na	0.00	4.9	0.4	0.75	2.83	2.99	59.3	4.0	16.5	8.9	8.0
4.5	1.42	na	0.08	5.3	5.2	1.25	12.55	4.05	62.5	1.8	21.4	22.4	7.4
5.7	1.31	na	0.01	4.2	4.0	0.93	8.90	3.15	72.4	6.0	38.9	3.0	7.2
8.8	0.19	na	-0.06	6.3	5.7	1.55	14.92	2.61	65.0	6.8	60.8	4.7	8.3
5.9	1.39	na	-0.19	4.5	9.8	1.00	9.01	3.19	63.4	4.0	12.9	7.1	8.6
6.0	0.02	na	-0.02	2.9	0.5	0.71	8.02	3.41	84.9	4.7	27.8	6.6	3.1
5.0	0.90	na	0.04	4.9	6.9	1.18	10.98	3.45	66.9	1.0	9.5	27.7	8.0
6.3	1.07	3.6	0.03	3.2	5.4	0.54	4.35	3.62	82.7	4.6	25.0	9.3	9.1
5.6	2.32	na	0.82	3.7	0.2	0.54	4.11	3.47	79.2	4.9	46.2	11.3	6.2
4.2	4.20	na	-0.01	6.3	3.0	1.49	14.27	3.63	58.1	0.9	23.2	31.7	7.9
5.3	0.92	8.0	-0.09	4.8	2.1	1.06	13.25	4.22	75.7	4.4	18.7	6.2	4.8
6.9	0.33	na	0.09	2.5	0.2	0.28	2.81	3.64	92.3	5.6	51.9	8.5	5.6
5.2	0.84	na	0.04	5.3	1.5	0.99	9.04	4.27	63.2	2.6	20.6	16.3	7.3
7.8	0.50	2.7	0.00	4.3	1.8	0.93	8.87	3.49	66.8	4.1	21.4	8.9	5.7
4.8	0.95	na	0.23	5.4	4.2	1.11	12.43	3.85	61.7	3.0	20.3	10.0	5.5
8.5	0.05	na	0.00	3.3	4.7	0.67	7.78	2.93	64.0	5.0	30.5	6.4	5.1
3.8	0.69	na	0.04	5.1	3.7	0.99	9.80	3.67	65.1	1.8	16.7	18.2	6.2
4.8	0.06	na	0.01	4.8	1.7	0.96	12.64	3.84	73.4	0.6	7.5	28.2	3.2
4.7	0.75	na	0.03	5.3	5.7	1.13	11.47	3.67	66.7	3.9	21.1	9.9	6.1
6.9	0.00	na	0.05	3.8	0.8	0.76	7.55	3.02	68.8	0.7	11.1	37.0	4.8
10.0	0.00	na	0.00	0.0	-1.9	-9.25	0.00	0.67	1413.6	7.0	99.0	8.0	1.3
4.4	2.46	na	0.13	5.1	3.9	1.15	9.69	3.49	71.3	5.4	45.2	8.8	7.8
2.0	4.08	na	0.33	6.4	4.5	1.46	12.81	4.03	49.7	2.2	18.9	18.2	7.4
8.0	0.30	na	0.07	7.5	1.0	1.70	11.85	4.20	59.9	1.5	32.2	35.5	9.3
6.0	0.61	na	0.03	0.0	-2.6	-1.15	-12.00	3.08	127.1	2.7	31.5	18.7	0.8
8.4	0.34	na	-0.16	6.1	0.9	1.37	9.46	3.25	48.7	2.6	49.7	30.8	6.9
7.2	1.23	na	0.03	6.1	2.1	1.56	10.84	4.24	66.3	6.2	45.2	3.7	8.4
3.1	4.60	na	0.61	0.8	0.1	0.08	0.93	2.25	114.0	2.6	45.6	25.4	3.8
7.6	1.18	na	0.06	3.9	2.1	0.78	5.14	2.64	71.1	3.7	32.3	13.8	7.2
10.0	0.00	na	0.00	3.3	0.8	0.62	3.74	3.04	75.7	4.6	41.5	12.4	7.8
6.6	0.36	1.6	-0.01	7.5	24.2	1.78	14.79	4.55	58.9	5.1	17.2	1.9	10.0
7.7	0.75	na	0.07	2.5	0.5	0.25	2.55	3.12	89.7	4.8	32.2	7.8	4.6

Name	City	State	2019 Rating	2018 Rating	Rating	Total Assets ($Mil)	One Year Asset Growth	Asset Mix (As a % of Total Assets)				Capital-ization Index	Lever-age Ratio	Risk-Based Capital Ratio
								Comm-ercial Loans	Cons-umer Loans	Mort-gage Loans	Secur-ities			
Franklin Bank & Trust Co.	Franklin	KY	B+	A-	B+	628.2	15.79	27.7	1.0	13.9	0.5	7.7	11.7	0.0
Franklin Savings Bank	Farmington	ME	B+	B+	B+	481.1	8.37	12.4	3.0	35.7	2.2	10.0	23.8	30.4
Franklin Savings Bank	Franklin	NH	C+	C+	C+	603.3	15.45	9.0	0.3	25.5	22.3	7.8	9.5	16.8
Franklin State Bank	Franklin	MN	B-	B-	B	35.8	11.37	4.8	4.4	9.0	12.3	10.0	14.6	25.5
Franklin State Bank & Trust Co.	Winnsboro	LA	B+	B+	B	186.2	7.95	4.1	4.1	14.3	14.6	7.2	9.1	18.9
Frazer Bank	Altus	OK	C-	C-	C+	283.6	-4.83	16.9	1.0	8.9	21.1	8.3	9.8	14.9
Frederick Community Bank	Cissna Park	IL	A-	B+	B	157.6	12.17	10.5	2.0	6.0	29.8	8.6	10.1	0.0
Fredonia Valley Bank	Fredonia	KY	B+	B+	B+	89.9	10.89	6.1	2.7	41.3	19.4	10.0	17.0	0.0
Freedom Bank	Huntingburg	IN	A-	A-	A-	500.5	13.70	7.8	3.8	35.4	4.8	8.1	10.4	13.4
Freedom Bank	Overland Park	KS	B-	C+	B-	187.8	11.78	17.8	0.2	5.5	11.3	9.2	11.9	14.3
Freedom Bank	Columbia Falls	MT	B-	C+	C+	109.5	28.33	27.0	1.5	12.5	0.0	6.3	9.5	0.0
Freedom Bank	Maywood	NJ	B-	B-	B-	523.0	14.09	4.8	0.0	20.0	1.7	8.1	10.0	13.4
Freedom Bank	Freer	TX	C+	C	C-	63.5	35.94	13.0	1.8	8.5	15.4	8.0	10.3	0.0
▲ Freedom Bank of Southern Missouri	Cassville	MO	B+	B	B+	486.7	66.57	10.6	2.7	17.4	4.4	8.9	11.7	0.0
▲ Freedom Bank of Virginia	Fairfax	VA	B	B-	C+	751.6	48.13	24.0	2.2	16.0	14.7	10.0	11.6	15.2
Freedom Bank, Inc.	Belington	WV	C-	C-	D+	185.2	10.56	12.0	7.6	34.5	10.0	8.1	9.7	0.0
Freedom Financial Bank	West Des Moines	IA	B-	B	B	242.7	26.17	13.8	0.1	9.0	3.6	6.1	8.2	12.0
▼ FreedomBank	Elkader	IA	C+	C+	B	439.6	9.49	8.7	2.4	13.9	13.3	6.2	8.7	11.9
Freehold Bank	Freehold	NJ	C	C+	C+	309.8	7.87	3.6	0.0	20.5	38.8	10.0	12.9	0.0
Freeland State Bank	Freeland	MI	C-	C-	C-	53.3	3.24	0.0	0.4	8.9	47.1	10.0	17.3	0.0
▲ Freeport State Bank	Freeport	MN	B	B	B-	129.3	8.36	10.9	2.1	7.6	14.5	8.4	9.9	15.7
Fremont Bank	Fremont	CA	B+	B+	B+	5119.6	13.59	12.6	0.1	27.3	7.2	5.0	7.0	11.5
Fresno First Bank	Fresno	CA	A-	B+	B-	830.9	54.26	37.8	0.0	1.5	22.0	5.6	7.6	15.8
Friend Bank	Slocomb	AL	B+	B	B-	160.5	20.95	13.3	2.8	17.2	10.6	7.2	9.1	0.0
▼ Friendly Hills Bank	Whittier	CA	C+	B	B-	236.3	47.48	22.7	0.0	8.6	10.5	8.0	9.6	20.0
Friendship State Bank	Friendship	IN	A-	A-	B+	449.4	18.70	3.0	2.4	37.9	15.2	7.5	9.3	17.1
Frontier Bank	Lamar	CO	A-	A-	A	365.9	18.02	3.9	0.6	7.9	46.0	8.5	10.0	19.0
▲ Frontier Bank	Omaha	NE	B-	C+	C+	957.0	9.08	16.3	1.3	18.0	6.1	5.5	9.4	11.4
Frontier Bank	Sioux Falls	SD	B-	B-	C+	244.2	10.81	7.4	0.9	11.1	30.1	6.6	8.6	13.3
Frontier Bank of Texas	Elgin	TX	B+	B+	A-	440.4	22.09	11.4	1.5	17.1	5.4	8.7	10.1	15.1
Frontier Community Bank	Waynesboro	VA	C+	C+	C+	145.5	6.59	18.8	1.8	27.2	0.2	8.6	10.0	16.4
Frontier State Bank	Oklahoma City	OK	B-	C	C	614.4	3.98	11.2	0.4	13.0	12.4	10.0	12.7	17.9
Frost Bank	San Antonio	TX	B+	A-	B+	40175.5	21.11	20.9	1.2	2.5	31.4	5.9	7.9	13.8
Frost State Bank	Frost	MN	C	C-	C	51.9	-3.87	12.0	3.2	1.3	0.7	10.0	13.2	18.1
FSNB, N.A.	Lawton	OK	A	A	A	451.6	21.07	4.6	1.3	9.3	47.7	10.0	13.7	35.0
Fulton Bank, N.A.	Lancaster	PA	B	B	B	25401.4	17.79	16.1	1.9	14.3	12.3	8.7	10.1	14.1
▼ Fulton Savings Bank	Fulton	NY	B+	A	B+	413.3	9.18	0.4	0.8	31.7	34.0	10.0	27.3	56.7
FVCbank	Fairfax	VA	B+	B+	B	1791.0	14.66	15.3	1.0	6.2	6.2	5.6	11.0	0.0
G.W. Jones Exchange Bank	Marcellus	MI	B-	C+	C+	86.2	46.03	3.7	1.0	10.6	22.2	9.7	10.8	27.9
▼ Galion Building and Loan Bank	Galion	OH	D	C	C	67.5	8.32	8.3	1.3	54.3	12.1	9.9	10.9	0.0
Garden Plain State Bank	Wichita	KS	A	A	B+	125.1	24.39	11.1	1.5	8.9	28.9	10.0	13.6	22.0
Garfield County Bank	Jordan	MT	D	D	D	104.2	17.21	2.8	2.0	2.5	4.6	10.0	12.0	16.6
Garrett State Bank	Garrett	IN	B+	B	B-	288.0	16.77	7.8	2.1	49.5	12.4	8.2	9.8	19.9
Garrison State Bank and Trust	Garrison	ND	B	B	C+	154.8	8.27	5.7	3.8	2.3	23.7	10.0	11.8	0.0
Gary State Bank	Gary	MN	B-	B-	B-	15.4	2.53	9.1	5.7	0.8	0.0	10.0	14.1	20.6
▲ Gate City Bank	Fargo	ND	B	B	B	2632.2	13.17	3.9	27.4	44.5	5.4	10.0	11.1	0.0
Gates Banking and Trust Co.	Gates	TN	B	B	B+	50.8	3.65	9.1	0.4	2.7	60.1	9.6	10.7	20.4
Gateway Bank	Rison	AR	B-	B-	B-	84.1	10.57	12.4	3.4	32.7	2.9	9.5	11.0	0.0
Gateway Bank	Mendota Heights	MN	B+	A-	A-	242.4	25.34	33.6	2.3	11.5	0.8	6.1	8.1	13.9
Gateway Bank, F.S.B.	Oakland	CA	D	D	E	173.5	46.49	13.4	0.0	46.7	6.4	8.3	9.9	21.0
Gateway Commercial Bank	Mesa	AZ	B+	A-	A-	173.7	38.81	23.5	0.3	3.7	25.9	9.0	10.7	0.0
▲ Gateway First Bank	Jenks	OK	C+			1627.6	10.20	5.5	0.2	60.0	2.7	10.0	17.4	28.6
GBC International Bank	Los Angeles	CA	B-	B-	B-	705.1	21.04	24.4	0.0	0.4	0.5	6.7	9.9	0.0
Geddes Federal S&L Assn.	Syracuse	NY	C+	B-	B	581.8	4.18	0.0	0.1	79.2	6.6	10.0	15.8	0.0
Generations Bank	Rogers	AR	B	B	B-	613.8	16.94	13.4	2.1	22.4	14.2	8.1	10.7	13.4
Generations Bank	Exeter	NE	C	C-	C-	41.8	12.79	16.0	2.1	9.2	17.4	6.9	10.3	0.0
▲ Generations Bank	Seneca Falls	NY	D+	D+	D	368.8	14.09	5.7	24.3	36.3	6.7	6.5	8.5	13.0
Generations Commercial Bank	Seneca Falls	NY	U			50.2	304.99	0.0	0.0	0.0	12.1	10.0	12.3	62.1
Genesee Regional Bank	Rochester	NY	A-	A-	B-	746.4	25.13	32.2	0.6	11.6	11.7	7.9	10.4	0.0
Genoa Banking Co.	Genoa	OH	C+	C+	C+	465.0	18.53	12.0	4.3	24.5	10.7	5.8	7.8	13.8

Asset Quality Index	Adjusted Non-Performing Loans as a % of Total Loans	Adjusted Non-Performing Loans as a % of Capital	Net Charge-Offs Avg Loans	Profitability Index	Net Income ($Mil)	Return on Assets (R.O.A.)	Return on Equity (R.O.E.)	Net Interest Spread	Overhead Efficiency Ratio	Liquidity Index	Liquidity Ratio	Hot Money Ratio	Stability Index
7.7	0.30	na	0.05	5.0	4.2	0.93	8.04	3.64	59.0	1.3	10.4	26.1	7.6
7.2	0.96	na	0.01	4.7	3.0	0.85	3.72	4.46	75.5	3.7	8.1	9.5	8.1
6.6	0.93	na	0.00	3.6	2.9	0.67	6.86	3.41	73.4	2.7	25.2	14.1	5.9
6.3	3.46	na	-0.12	4.5	0.3	1.01	6.75	3.20	58.7	4.8	46.6	12.3	7.0
7.6	0.09	0.9	0.08	6.3	1.9	1.39	15.10	3.95	66.6	1.5	27.0	30.2	5.6
5.8	1.70	na	0.11	2.1	1.0	0.44	4.43	3.67	85.5	1.7	14.3	19.1	4.2
8.8	0.00	na	0.01	6.3	1.8	1.64	14.96	2.93	57.7	5.0	36.4	8.7	6.2
5.1	3.15	na	0.16	6.2	0.8	1.23	7.07	4.23	67.0	5.2	31.0	4.9	7.8
5.5	1.00	na	0.02	9.3	8.4	2.35	22.63	3.16	39.3	3.2	16.8	13.2	8.5
7.1	0.01	na	-0.01	4.7	1.2	0.89	7.50	3.64	69.3	4.7	5.1	2.6	6.2
4.6	0.65	na	-0.02	9.2	1.2	1.67	16.59	5.55	53.7	1.7	21.8	23.6	7.4
6.7	0.31	na	0.00	4.1	2.5	0.67	6.60	3.14	69.0	0.6	9.3	39.3	7.1
7.1	0.01	0.1	-0.05	3.5	0.4	0.82	5.94	4.42	79.4	2.9	40.6	22.4	5.4
5.8	0.68	na	0.14	7.0	4.6	1.73	14.43	4.03	57.6	2.0	23.5	19.3	7.1
5.7	0.64	4.9	0.04	4.5	5.0	1.06	9.90	3.38	70.7	1.4	22.4	23.2	5.7
2.4	4.30	na	0.21	4.2	0.7	0.54	5.39	3.76	70.1	4.1	22.7	9.0	5.2
6.2	0.43	na	0.92	3.7	1.3	0.77	8.64	3.08	51.7	0.9	23.3	27.5	6.0
1.7	1.33	na	0.16	5.9	4.2	1.31	10.88	4.19	55.6	3.2	16.5	11.6	7.9
9.5	0.07	0.1	0.00	1.8	0.4	0.19	1.46	1.64	88.4	2.0	32.4	27.9	6.6
9.1	11.80	na	-0.46	1.0	0.0	-0.03	-0.16	1.93	103.9	7.7	107.5	5.0	7.2
7.5	0.96	na	0.38	4.9	0.8	0.85	8.47	4.67	68.3	3.6	28.7	11.0	6.4
7.4	0.77	na	0.05	5.7	47.8	1.36	18.30	3.55	70.7	5.2	20.4	2.5	7.2
8.3	0.17	na	-0.01	9.2	8.3	1.65	19.36	4.08	45.7	3.3	21.6	5.7	5.8
6.4	0.50	na	0.12	7.6	1.9	1.72	18.15	4.09	60.6	4.4	32.6	10.6	6.4
8.5	0.08	na	0.02	3.1	0.6	0.43	4.19	2.68	76.1	6.0	40.8	3.8	5.1
7.6	0.47	na	0.11	6.3	3.9	1.25	12.30	4.11	67.6	3.7	32.4	13.9	6.4
9.2	0.03	0.1	-0.10	7.8	5.4	2.13	18.92	3.46	49.2	4.1	33.9	12.3	8.6
4.2	0.67	4.7	0.01	7.1	12.1	1.72	16.11	3.58	49.2	1.4	5.6	18.7	7.3
7.3	0.92	na	-0.01	4.2	1.8	1.03	11.22	3.39	71.1	1.7	21.6	16.4	5.8
8.4	0.09	na	0.02	5.1	3.2	1.02	9.96	3.71	61.9	0.9	22.5	33.3	6.5
8.6	0.00	na	0.00	3.1	0.5	0.45	4.51	2.92	76.8	1.2	16.1	29.9	6.2
3.8	2.56	17.6	0.08	4.6	6.6	1.48	11.46	2.75	51.3	0.8	24.0	62.3	6.2
7.2	0.52	2.9	0.71	4.3	251.2	0.92	8.40	3.12	62.0	6.8	42.7	2.4	9.2
2.6	2.43	na	1.45	4.5	0.3	0.75	5.85	3.13	39.1	0.7	23.8	56.8	7.0
9.8	0.04	0.1	1.08	9.5	8.2	2.51	16.33	3.33	76.5	7.3	63.0	1.7	8.8
5.1	1.03	5.4	0.09	4.2	153.0	0.87	7.28	2.96	62.3	4.5	19.8	5.2	9.9
9.8	1.35	na	0.08	3.5	1.4	0.46	1.63	3.92	84.9	7.3	74.2	3.6	9.0
5.4	0.52	na	0.02	5.0	12.2	0.97	8.11	3.38	52.6	1.7	12.3	15.7	9.2
7.5	0.84	na	0.22	4.1	0.5	0.94	8.34	4.00	78.1	7.4	75.2	1.6	4.4
6.5	0.76	na	0.08	0.6	-0.1	-0.27	-2.39	2.90	107.9	4.1	31.2	11.7	5.7
9.1	0.00	na	-0.03	6.1	1.1	1.25	8.37	2.97	56.0	5.5	58.6	12.2	7.9
0.6	6.14	na	-0.06	3.8	0.5	0.72	5.82	2.98	64.8	1.5	33.0	45.2	6.3
6.1	1.33	na	0.01	7.5	3.9	1.85	18.13	3.64	48.0	3.2	29.6	10.0	7.4
5.8	0.36	na	0.10	5.2	1.1	0.97	8.01	3.69	63.7	3.5	23.2	12.4	7.3
6.9	0.00	0.0	0.02	8.0	0.2	1.74	12.56	4.94	66.7	5.1	33.7	4.0	6.3
6.1	0.52	4.0	0.10	5.1	20.6	1.09	9.96	3.21	71.1	4.6	13.5	5.1	8.6
9.4	0.55	na	0.00	3.6	0.3	0.74	6.13	2.73	69.7	1.1	28.6	53.7	7.1
3.7	2.42	na	0.19	4.5	0.7	1.06	9.50	4.39	62.5	0.6	11.5	41.6	5.4
8.3	0.09	0.4	0.00	4.9	1.9	1.11	13.08	3.08	62.0	1.8	25.1	18.5	6.1
6.9	2.93	na	0.00	0.9	0.3	0.23	2.15	3.24	104.9	1.2	25.1	31.8	3.3
8.7	0.00	0.0	-0.02	5.2	1.3	1.06	9.35	3.34	52.8	4.3	34.3	11.5	6.7
3.4	2.47	9.8	0.08	6.3	76.1	6.75	45.88	2.38	59.8	0.8	13.4	33.3	6.4
7.1	0.26	na	0.01	4.3	4.5	0.90	8.89	3.19	56.8	0.7	15.8	48.2	6.4
9.9	0.38	1.9	0.00	2.9	1.7	0.39	2.42	1.93	73.4	0.8	16.8	39.5	8.6
5.7	0.94	na	0.15	5.4	4.6	1.07	11.24	3.76	66.1	1.0	12.3	29.4	6.5
4.2	2.54	na	0.04	4.1	0.2	0.71	6.01	3.79	74.8	2.4	19.3	11.4	5.6
1.8	2.23	14.9	-0.06	1.8	1.5	0.53	6.37	3.25	87.6	1.6	9.0	21.9	3.4
10.0	na	na	na	3.7	0.7	2.00	17.80	1.28	34.2	3.3	102.3	57.0	2.8
8.2	0.20	na	-0.03	8.9	9.5	1.91	17.67	3.84	49.8	1.1	6.8	18.1	7.2
8.5	0.04	na	0.07	3.9	2.4	0.74	9.10	3.74	69.9	1.7	14.5	16.9	4.5

Name	City	State	2019 Rating	2018 Rating	Rating	Total Assets ($Mil)	One Year Asset Growth	Asset Mix (As a % of Total Assets) Commercial Loans	Consumer Loans	Mortgage Loans	Securities	Capitalization Index	Leverage Ratio	Risk-Based Capital Ratio
Genoa Community Bank	Genoa	NE	B	B	C+	64.2	0.65	4.4	1.0	3.0	12.2	10.0	12.1	16.5
GENUBANK	Las Vegas	NV	B+	B+	B	138.9	6.23	11.7	0.0	2.0	0.0	10.0	12.3	0.0
Geo. D. Warthen Bank	Sandersville	GA	B-	B-	C+	223.0	25.57	13.5	6.6	18.4	12.0	6.2	8.3	0.0
Georgia Banking Co.	Sandy Springs	GA	C	C+	B	734.1	27.62	2.1	3.3	73.1	2.2	4.7	7.1	10.9
Georgia Community Bank	Dawson	GA	B	B	B	362.3	109.01	9.8	3.0	24.2	14.2	10.0	11.5	0.0
▲ Georgia Primary Bank	Atlanta	GA	B	C+	C-	278.7	26.82	25.3	0.3	4.1	15.4	7.1	9.1	13.0
Gerber State Bank	Argenta	IL	B-	B-	B-	84.1	8.87	8.2	1.1	10.4	50.0	10.0	12.0	25.0
German American Bank	Jasper	IN	A-	A-	A-	4842.9	11.49	14.9	0.9	10.2	21.3	7.6	9.4	13.6
German-American State Bank	German Valley	IL	B-	B	B	274.4	11.27	13.3	6.1	5.4	22.3	6.6	9.6	0.0
Germantown Trust & Savings Bank	Breese	IL	A	A	A-	435.9	10.59	4.2	1.0	13.4	45.2	10.0	12.1	0.0
▲ Gibraltar Bank	Parsippany	NJ	C+	C	C-	108.8	5.49	0.0	0.0	57.5	8.4	10.0	11.3	20.0
Gibsland Bank & Trust Co.	Gibsland	LA	C+	C	D+	459.0	2.44	17.6	2.1	12.7	11.1	9.6	10.7	14.8
Gifford State Bank	Gifford	IL	C+	C-	D+	166.0	7.04	5.5	3.5	26.4	1.9	6.6	9.5	0.0
Gilmer National Bank	Gilmer	TX	B	B	B-	244.9	8.00	8.0	9.7	20.1	13.8	10.0	13.5	21.0
Glacier Bank	Kalispell	MT	A-	A-	A-	17915.2	30.70	12.9	1.1	7.3	24.2	8.6	10.1	14.4
Glasford State Bank	Glasford	IL	B-	B-	C+	53.9	29.40	1.4	7.9	20.9	33.8	4.9	6.9	20.2
Glen Burnie Mutual Savings Bank	Glen Burnie	MD	C-	C-	C-	103.2	3.74	0.0	0.0	75.7	0.3	5.6	7.6	17.1
Glen Rock Savings Bank	Glen Rock	NJ	C-	D+	D+	267.0	-0.78	1.0	0.0	48.2	18.3	10.0	12.2	22.0
Glenmede Trust Co., N.A.	Philadelphia	PA	U	U	U	134.3	23.09	0.0	0.0	0.0	7.3	10.0	49.5	60.7
Glennville Bank	Glennville	GA	A-	A-	B+	297.6	16.36	5.2	3.3	19.7	24.0	10.0	11.1	20.0
Glens Falls National Bank and Trust Co.	Glens Falls	NY	B+	B+	B+	2979.2	17.92	5.5	23.1	20.8	17.3	6.8	8.8	15.2
Glenview State Bank	Glenview	IL	B-	B	B	1395.4	9.94	7.4	13.1	7.5	59.0	9.2	10.4	0.0
Glenwood State Bank	Glenwood	IA	B-	B-	C	255.0	16.02	8.1	1.9	9.5	36.9	8.7	10.1	0.0
Glenwood State Bank	Glenwood	MN	B-	C+	C	364.8	14.51	21.9	1.4	14.0	0.9	6.0	8.7	11.7
Global Bank	New York	NY	C+	C+	C	199.6	11.45	1.3	0.0	16.4	0.8	8.5	12.4	0.0
▲ Global Innovations Bank	Kiester	MN	C	D+	D	26.2	28.41	21.6	3.4	8.7	2.9	7.7	9.4	20.3
GN Bank	Chicago	IL	D-	D-	D	104.9	-22.76	2.2	0.5	20.9	25.9	8.2	9.8	19.2
GNB Bank	Grundy Center	IA	B+	B+	B	574.0	2.53	23.1	0.9	7.1	8.6	9.1	11.8	14.2
GNBank, N.A.	Girard	KS	B-	B-	C	839.0	16.52	17.2	1.7	7.7	20.3	8.1	10.4	0.0
▲ Gogebic Range Bank	Ironwood	MI	B	B-	C	150.3	20.16	20.1	4.6	8.8	19.5	8.0	9.6	0.0
Gold Coast Bank	Chicago	IL	B+	A-	B+	397.5	4.88	8.0	0.3	22.4	0.0	10.0	11.9	0.0
Golden Bank, N.A.	Houston	TX	A-	A-	A-	1141.5	15.09	8.2	0.1	8.5	9.8	10.0	12.8	17.5
Golden Belt Bank, FSA	Ellis	KS	B+	B+	B+	266.1	8.07	10.8	2.8	29.6	11.1	9.5	11.8	0.0
Golden Pacific Bank, N.A.	Sacramento	CA	D+	C	C-	168.9	28.05	16.9	0.6	4.1	5.2	6.1	8.1	0.0
▼ Golden State Bank	Glendale	CA	C-	C+	B-	444.6	26.11	9.3	0.1	5.9	0.0	2.4	7.4	0.0
Golden Valley Bank	Chico	CA	B+	B+	B+	414.0	20.40	26.1	0.0	6.9	25.1	5.6	7.6	15.7
Goldman Sachs Bank USA	New York	NY	C+	B	A-	277943.0	31.21	7.3	4.1	4.0	10.2	9.3	10.6	14.8
Goldman Sachs Trust Co., N.A.	New York	NY	U	U	U	76.2	14.05	0.0	0.0	0.0	33.0	10.0	50.8	227.2
▲ Goldwater Bank, N.A.	Phoenix	AZ	B-	C	C-	306.1	56.58	2.4	0.1	64.9	0.9	9.7	10.8	0.0
▲ Goodfield State Bank	Goodfield	IL	A	A-	B+	153.2	18.58	17.7	1.9	16.2	13.0	10.0	12.2	16.9
Goose River Bank	Mayville	ND	B+	B	C+	132.6	10.86	20.9	2.7	0.7	13.0	5.4	9.6	0.0
Goppert Financial Bank	Lathrop	MO	B	B	B-	195.4	10.76	8.9	0.5	8.0	27.3	8.4	10.0	0.0
Goppert State Service Bank	Garnett	KS	B	B	B	212.7	15.16	23.1	4.5	14.1	12.5	7.3	9.9	0.0
Gorham Savings Bank	Gorham	ME	C+	C+	C+	1397.0	14.21	16.3	0.3	16.0	14.2	5.3	9.2	0.0
Gorham State Bank	Gorham	KS	B-	C+	B-	32.1	13.92	13.1	3.3	10.0	2.2	10.0	12.0	20.0
▼ Gouverneur S&L Assn.	Gouverneur	NY	C	B-	B+	129.3	3.19	1.1	2.2	53.9	15.8	10.0	19.1	33.7
▼ Graham S&L, SSB	Graham	TX	B-	B	B+	145.7	5.13	2.7	0.7	40.3	12.0	9.8	10.9	21.0
Grand Bank	Tulsa	OK	B	B-	B-	452.0	16.67	20.0	0.2	12.9	9.5	8.4	10.8	13.7
Grand Bank for Savings, FSB	Hattiesburg	MS	B+	B+	B+	91.4	6.32	0.0	0.4	77.9	0.0	10.0	12.2	25.8
Grand Marais State Bank	Grand Marais	MN	B	B	B-	124.1	28.59	13.4	1.5	22.9	31.1	4.3	6.3	15.5
Grand Rapids State Bank	Grand Rapids	MN	B-	B-	B-	283.7	24.68	14.5	2.9	7.5	14.6	7.4	9.5	0.0
Grand Ridge National Bank	Grand Ridge	IL	A-	A	A-	265.4	18.63	19.1	0.0	6.7	0.2	8.6	11.4	0.0
▲ Grand River Bank	Grandville	MI	C+	C+	C+	455.0	41.90	18.0	0.0	12.6	1.0	8.4	9.9	13.8
Grand Rivers Community Bank	Grand Chain	IL	E-	E-	E-	25.6	-19.56	9.3	1.1	15.0	4.6	0.0	2.9	6.2
Grand Savings Bank	Grove	OK	B+	B+	B-	601.4	17.78	13.2	6.7	21.3	4.8	5.6	8.5	0.0
▲ Grand Timber Bank	McGregor	MN	B	B-	C+	52.3	18.94	8.4	7.3	26.8	12.2	10.0	13.7	23.2
Grand Valley Bank	Heber City	UT	B+	B+	B+	508.5	15.66	4.9	0.3	5.9	52.3	7.2	9.1	0.0
GrandSouth Bank	Greenville	SC	B	B	B	1011.4	14.00	21.2	3.6	10.7	10.2	7.2	9.8	12.7
Grandview Bank	Grandview	TX	A-	A-	B+	298.6	30.27	15.5	5.6	11.8	14.7	7.1	9.0	16.8
▼ Granger National Bank	Granger	TX	C+	B	B-	35.1	9.78	1.8	2.2	5.1	60.6	10.0	16.6	38.4

Asset Quality Index	Adjusted Non-Performing Loans as a % of Total Loans	as a % of Capital	Net Charge-Offs Avg Loans	Profitability Index	Net Income ($Mil)	Return on Assets (R.O.A.)	Return on Equity (R.O.E.)	Net Interest Spread	Overhead Efficiency Ratio	Liquidity Index	Liquidity Ratio	Hot Money Ratio	Stability Index
4.4	2.64	na	1.28	4.4	0.4	0.88	7.18	3.65	66.3	1.7	24.3	23.9	7.4
6.8	0.00	na	0.00	3.5	0.5	0.44	2.12	3.25	81.7	3.1	45.4	22.3	8.0
4.1	2.04	na	0.25	4.1	1.3	0.88	9.83	4.34	75.0	5.6	36.9	4.9	3.7
5.1	0.53	8.1	-0.03	4.7	3.7	0.86	11.35	3.14	72.4	0.4	1.2	35.0	4.0
4.7	3.36	na	0.17	5.3	3.6	1.39	11.39	3.72	66.1	1.4	25.7	30.1	6.7
7.4	0.05	na	-0.03	4.9	1.8	0.95	10.42	3.91	67.6	1.1	11.3	29.1	6.1
6.4	3.15	na	-0.05	3.6	0.4	0.75	5.76	3.08	72.8	5.0	35.9	8.3	6.6
6.5	0.71	3.5	0.03	6.3	43.0	1.25	9.94	3.70	56.9	5.1	25.1	6.0	10.0
3.8	2.35	15.0	0.08	4.8	1.7	0.88	8.75	3.33	66.3	2.6	17.5	16.3	6.5
8.5	0.00	na	-0.04	7.8	5.8	1.89	13.76	2.98	32.4	4.0	46.0	16.7	8.7
9.5	0.00	na	0.20	3.2	0.4	0.50	4.17	2.63	79.3	1.3	18.6	28.3	6.2
4.6	2.22	na	1.31	3.5	1.8	0.51	4.87	4.43	60.5	1.0	18.1	27.3	4.6
6.3	0.46	na	1.23	3.4	0.7	0.60	6.28	3.77	67.2	3.5	23.3	12.1	4.2
5.0	1.09	na	0.35	5.0	1.8	0.99	7.13	3.72	59.4	2.0	34.4	29.7	7.6
7.1	0.49	1.8	0.04	8.6	191.8	1.63	11.37	4.20	51.2	4.8	19.8	4.1	10.0
6.6	0.28	na	0.01	3.3	0.2	0.60	7.56	2.72	75.1	5.6	49.1	7.8	4.7
5.4	1.31	na	0.00	2.0	0.2	0.23	3.06	0.95	76.3	5.5	23.6	0.0	4.0
7.2	1.32	na	0.00	1.7	0.6	0.30	2.54	2.35	83.8	1.4	9.6	23.7	5.8
10.0	na	0.0	na	9.5	21.5	23.20	59.80	1.42	82.7	4.0	56.3	0.0	6.5
7.3	0.57	2.6	0.01	6.7	2.8	1.31	11.24	4.10	60.8	2.0	31.8	27.3	7.2
7.0	0.25	1.7	0.05	5.6	22.8	1.12	11.78	3.01	57.3	4.6	15.8	2.6	7.9
7.8	0.92	2.3	0.01	3.9	8.8	0.87	7.00	2.45	61.8	6.6	63.8	8.3	9.6
9.1	0.00	na	-0.01	3.8	1.3	0.70	6.76	2.98	68.9	6.5	57.9	5.7	5.5
4.4	1.25	na	0.00	6.7	3.9	1.51	16.76	3.92	60.0	2.5	7.8	14.8	7.0
7.1	0.23	na	0.00	3.4	0.9	0.56	4.71	3.86	74.5	0.5	5.9	51.6	6.8
8.4	0.00	na	0.09	6.6	0.3	1.49	14.30	4.21	59.0	5.2	38.2	7.6	2.9
2.9	8.50	na	0.33	0.0	-0.5	-0.59	-6.26	2.77	115.7	3.8	42.9	14.5	2.1
4.8	2.14	na	-0.03	6.7	6.5	1.54	11.73	4.09	60.7	1.0	8.8	19.7	8.2
3.4	2.43	na	0.30	5.5	6.5	1.09	9.43	3.84	62.6	3.8	21.1	10.6	7.8
4.7	2.00	na	-0.05	6.0	1.3	1.23	11.96	4.33	61.4	5.5	46.2	8.9	5.9
7.6	0.71	na	0.06	4.2	0.9	0.30	2.51	2.82	79.8	1.2	30.4	41.0	8.5
7.5	0.16	1.0	0.02	6.8	10.8	1.32	10.22	3.49	49.8	0.8	16.4	41.1	10.0
4.6	0.83	na	0.07	8.2	3.8	2.02	15.11	3.67	55.0	4.1	16.4	7.9	9.7
1.7	2.66	na	0.13	1.2	-0.2	-0.16	-1.56	3.56	101.8	3.6	26.8	12.5	4.6
4.5	0.48	na	0.00	1.8	-0.3	-0.09	-0.99	2.96	97.9	1.7	35.3	35.0	4.9
8.8	0.03	na	-0.06	4.9	3.1	1.06	13.51	3.42	57.1	4.8	31.2	7.2	5.4
7.5	2.33	6.7	0.75	3.0	675.0	0.33	3.06	1.14	46.9	3.5	71.6	12.9	9.1
10.0	na	0.0	na	10.0	35.1	52.99	71.50	0.74	44.8	4.0	240.7	0.0	5.0
7.9	0.52	3.0	-0.03	8.5	10.5	5.70	59.16	2.78	83.9	0.6	12.1	51.7	6.8
6.9	1.34	na	0.06	9.8	3.3	3.06	24.78	3.32	44.0	2.8	30.5	17.9	9.0
8.0	0.09	na	0.01	5.8	1.3	1.34	12.76	4.29	66.8	3.2	12.1	12.8	7.3
8.8	0.02	na	0.00	4.2	1.1	0.76	7.34	3.53	72.3	4.6	23.3	5.5	5.6
7.5	0.21	na	0.06	5.1	1.4	0.93	9.19	3.68	66.5	2.6	11.0	15.4	6.2
5.8	1.06	na	0.00	2.9	4.8	0.48	5.21	3.26	76.8	2.1	3.6	5.1	7.0
3.2	2.79	na	0.00	5.5	0.3	1.13	9.46	3.64	60.8	5.3	35.7	6.0	5.8
8.0	1.07	na	0.16	0.4	-0.7	-0.74	-3.58	4.12	139.7	4.6	22.3	6.0	7.0
7.9	0.29	na	0.03	3.2	0.6	0.53	4.74	3.25	77.6	1.7	35.6	35.2	7.7
4.6	1.26	na	0.00	5.8	3.2	1.06	9.85	4.19	47.3	0.8	10.7	26.8	7.4
7.3	1.11	na	0.00	3.9	0.5	0.74	6.13	5.84	85.1	0.6	14.4	42.3	7.4
9.1	0.00	na	0.00	7.2	1.4	1.83	25.07	3.79	54.1	4.9	21.2	3.5	5.1
8.4	0.00	0.0	0.00	6.9	3.3	1.75	18.05	4.41	64.6	5.2	29.7	4.3	5.5
5.9	0.49	na	-0.02	10.0	3.5	1.95	15.95	6.03	52.0	1.5	16.6	24.9	8.6
7.3	0.00	na	0.00	4.0	2.2	0.79	8.45	2.97	60.7	1.6	17.7	15.9	5.1
1.7	3.37	43.5	1.52	0.0	-1.1	-5.28	-108.29	3.18	160.7	1.8	30.2	27.6	0.0
7.0	0.34	na	0.06	7.6	5.7	1.33	14.87	4.67	58.9	1.6	13.3	21.9	7.0
4.1	5.01	na	0.29	8.4	0.6	1.89	13.11	4.42	60.0	5.6	36.2	4.6	8.9
8.7	0.05	na	0.14	5.6	3.8	1.08	10.31	3.58	62.0	5.7	52.0	9.6	6.3
7.8	0.24	1.2	0.14	4.8	6.0	0.84	8.44	4.54	68.4	1.6	15.5	21.4	6.9
6.6	0.70	4.5	0.15	8.0	3.1	1.49	15.69	4.13	52.9	4.5	31.7	9.9	6.4
8.7	2.87	na	0.18	2.1	0.1	0.22	1.22	2.93	92.3	5.6	81.3	13.3	7.2

Name	City	State	2020 Rating	2019 Rating	2018 Rating	Total Assets ($Mil)	One Year Asset Growth	Commercial Loans	Consumer Loans	Mortgage Loans	Securities	Capitalization Index	Leverage Ratio	Risk-Based Capital Ratio
▲ Granite Community Bank	Cold Spring	MN	B-	C+	C	151.2	22.03	22.9	1.3	6.7	5.9	6.0	8.3	11.7
Granite Falls Bank	Granite Falls	MN	A-	A-	B-	148.7	8.90	10.3	0.5	1.7	36.3	8.2	9.8	15.9
Granite Mountain Bank, Inc.	Philipsburg	MT	B-	B	B-	107.7	25.38	16.3	2.2	11.7	4.8	6.0	8.0	20.8
▲ Grant County Bank	Ulysses	KS	B+	B-	C+	258.2	13.52	11.4	2.1	21.9	29.4	10.0	12.6	0.0
Grant County Bank	Medford	OK	C-	C	C	59.7	6.29	3.5	5.2	1.3	37.4	10.0	15.4	0.0
Grant County Bank	Petersburg	WV	B	B	B-	286.0	10.90	10.9	2.4	25.9	10.8	10.0	12.8	0.0
Grant County State Bank	Swayzee	IN	B	B	C+	216.3	11.59	12.7	5.9	33.8	0.0	10.0	12.0	18.9
Grant County State Bank	Carson	ND	B+	A-	A-	36.5	9.66	1.1	0.1	0.0	0.0	10.0	12.3	0.0
Granville National Bank	Granville	IL	B-	B-	B-	101.4	14.26	3.1	4.2	22.0	38.1	8.3	9.9	0.0
Grasshopper Bank, N.A.	New York	NY	D			175.3	76.82	15.7	0.0	14.3	44.4	10.0	52.6	91.9
Gratz Bank	Gratz	PA	B	B	B	425.3	18.49	4.8	0.4	22.9	28.2	6.2	8.2	14.3
Great American Bank	Lawrence	KS	B+	B	B-	228.1	4.57	10.9	0.6	23.0	0.0	6.8	10.5	0.0
▲ Great Midwest Bank, S.S.B.	Brookfield	WI	A-	B+	B	911.1	7.02	0.0	0.1	59.0	5.7	10.0	15.4	0.0
Great Nations Bank	Norman	OK	C+	B-	B-	83.5	23.85	20.8	0.5	6.9	2.4	10.0	11.6	15.6
Great North Bank	Florence	WI	D+	D+	C-	143.3	0.68	23.6	2.6	14.2	21.2	6.9	8.9	14.2
Great Oaks Bank	Eastman	GA	B-	B-	C	197.8	27.20	23.6	1.7	16.2	12.4	6.1	8.1	14.2
Great Plains Bank	Eureka	SD	D	D+	D-	130.5	14.45	18.2	0.9	3.1	11.6	9.7	12.6	0.0
Great Plains National Bank	Hollis	OK	B	B	B+	952.7	17.62	27.5	3.0	18.6	6.4	7.0	9.0	14.0
▲ Great Plains State Bank	Petersburg	NE	B-	C	C	337.8	13.43	21.8	0.4	0.1	5.4	7.1	10.5	0.0
▲ Great Rivers Bank	Barry	IL	B	C+	C+	140.8	6.44	12.2	2.0	6.8	10.3	9.0	11.0	14.2
Great Southern Bank	Springfield	MO	A-	A-	B+	5447.3	9.47	6.2	2.6	12.5	8.2	9.3	11.5	14.5
Great Southern Bank	Meridian	MS	B	B	B	335.8	11.55	7.0	8.9	10.8	49.7	6.6	8.6	0.0
Great Western Bank	Sioux Falls	SD	C+	C+	C+	12589.4	-1.46	14.3	0.4	4.7	14.1	7.5	9.3	13.0
Greater Community Bank	Rome	GA	B+	B+	B	282.7	28.08	27.6	5.8	7.7	2.2	7.3	9.2	14.2
Greater State Bank	McAllen	TX	C	C	C	103.6	18.77	23.0	1.2	15.0	3.6	5.4	7.4	14.2
▲ Green Belt Bank & Trust	Iowa Falls	IA	B-	C	C-	555.2	11.79	11.6	1.4	5.5	8.3	6.2	8.8	11.9
Green Dot Bank	Provo	UT	A	A+	A	2794.6	110.82	0.1	0.6	0.0	11.1	6.9	8.9	86.7
Greene County Commercial Bank	Catskill	NY	U	U	U	684.2	14.90	0.0	0.0	0.0	97.7	7.9	9.6	44.8
▼ Greeneville Federal Bank, FSB	Greeneville	TN	C+	B-	B	157.4	2.23	12.4	1.1	28.8	0.9	10.0	14.5	22.1
Greenfield Banking Co.	Greenfield	IN	B+	A-	A-	686.5	18.95	10.2	0.6	4.8	17.4	8.4	9.9	0.0
▲ Greenfield Banking Co.	Greenfield	TN	D	D	C-	72.8	13.29	16.9	8.5	16.3	10.8	4.2	8.8	10.6
▼ Greenfield Co-operative Bank	Greenfield	MA	C+	B	B	732.4	11.49	6.7	0.4	36.3	18.2	9.7	10.8	0.0
Greenfield Savings Bank	Greenfield	MA	B	B	B	994.4	13.71	9.2	0.1	47.0	10.2	10.0	11.5	21.2
Greenleaf Bank	Greenleaf	WI	B	B	B	116.0	21.11	5.0	0.8	17.6	38.8	7.4	9.2	0.0
▼ Greenville Federal	Greenville	OH	C-	C	C+	212.7	14.21	11.6	0.7	44.2	2.1	7.4	9.2	14.5
Greenville National Bank	Greenville	OH	B+	B+	B+	526.5	8.67	6.8	9.6	18.4	14.1	9.4	10.6	0.0
Greenville Savings Bank	Greenville	PA	B-	B	B	264.6	8.73	1.2	0.7	58.8	12.5	10.0	13.7	0.0
Greenwoods State Bank	Lake Mills	WI	C+	C-	C	376.0	20.60	15.9	0.9	13.0	5.7	6.3	8.3	12.3
Grinnell State Bank	Grinnell	IA	B+	B	B	375.9	17.93	8.7	0.3	4.4	16.0	10.0	11.9	15.7
Grove Bank	Grove City	MN	B-	B-	B	34.7	11.10	16.1	2.4	18.7	0.8	8.6	10.1	0.0
Grove Bank & Trust	Miami	FL	B-	B-	B+	868.3	21.53	8.0	0.5	3.2	28.1	10.0	13.9	26.5
▲ Grundy Bank	Morris	IL	B+	B	B-	319.9	15.10	10.4	0.5	17.4	7.9	7.2	9.1	19.0
GSL Savings Bank	Guttenberg	NJ	D+	D+	D+	117.8	12.56	1.5	0.0	57.2	1.6	8.3	9.9	17.0
Guadalupe Bank	Kerrville	TX	A-	B+	B	206.3	22.25	11.0	1.1	25.6	0.1	6.7	8.7	0.0
Guaranty Bank	Springfield	MO	B-	C	C	1132.4	11.58	13.7	0.4	11.8	13.4	6.2	9.8	0.0
Guaranty Bank & Trust Co. of Delhi	Delhi	LA	B+	B+	B+	315.0	14.50	5.2	1.6	31.4	4.4	5.9	7.9	13.9
Guaranty Bank & Trust, N.A.	Mount Pleasant	TX	B+	B+	B	2662.9	14.51	14.8	2.0	14.6	13.9	7.4	9.7	12.9
Guaranty Bank and Trust Co.	New Roads	LA	A-	A-	B+	243.1	11.14	5.3	2.0	26.9	14.2	10.0	13.0	22.2
Guaranty Bank and Trust Co.	Belzoni	MS	B+	B	B-	1199.1	33.77	20.1	0.8	8.9	15.7	3.8	8.8	0.0
Guaranty State Bank and Trust Co.	Beloit	KS	C-	C+	C	315.7	10.73	9.6	1.2	7.3	13.3	10.0	12.4	0.0
Guardian Bank	Valdosta	GA	B+	B+	B	453.8	8.33	9.0	1.6	15.2	25.5	9.8	10.9	0.0
▲ Guardian Savings Bank	Granite City	IL	D	D	D+	37.2	-0.53	0.0	9.1	23.6	36.6	10.0	18.0	0.0
▲ Guardian Savings Bank, F.S.B.	West Chester	OH	A	B+	B	1090.9	8.80	0.0	0.0	59.1	0.0	10.0	12.2	26.6
Guilford Savings Bank	Guilford	CT	B-	B	B-	944.4	13.09	6.5	0.4	34.7	13.2	10.0	11.4	0.0
▲ Gulf Atlantic Bank	Key West	FL	D			24.0	na	0.1	2.8	31.6	21.1	10.0	49.7	96.2
Gulf Capital Bank	Houston	TX	D			145.3	na	66.8	0.3	0.0	4.2	10.0	62.6	819.3
Gulf Coast Bank	Abbeville	LA	B+	A-	B	464.8	25.52	32.2	6.3	13.0	7.0	9.5	12.5	0.0
Gulf Coast Bank and Trust Co.	New Orleans	LA	C+	B-	C+	2255.9	21.14	32.6	1.4	14.5	11.0	6.1	8.1	12.2
Gulfside Bank	Sarasota	FL	D-			147.0	76.79	20.1	0.1	10.2	26.6	9.8	14.9	0.0
Gunnison Bank and Trust Co.	Gunnison	CO	A-	A-	B	157.3	27.13	10.5	0.2	20.4	2.5	6.7	8.7	15.9

Asset Quality Index	Adjusted Non-Performing Loans as a % of Total Loans	as a % of Capital	Net Charge-Offs Avg Loans	Profitability Index	Net Income ($Mil)	Return on Assets (R.O.A.)	Return on Equity (R.O.E.)	Net Interest Spread	Overhead Efficiency Ratio	Liquidity Index	Liquidity Ratio	Hot Money Ratio	Stability Index
6.3	0.75	na	0.01	7.2	1.4	1.41	17.33	4.38	55.9	1.6	12.5	21.6	4.7
8.6	0.89	na	0.00	7.4	1.8	1.70	14.41	4.27	49.5	4.2	12.1	6.9	7.7
7.8	0.50	na	0.20	4.8	0.6	0.81	9.31	4.54	68.0	6.7	47.7	1.3	4.4
5.3	1.76	na	0.37	6.1	3.5	1.81	12.82	3.50	61.4	1.7	19.3	21.4	8.1
5.7	1.08	na	0.27	1.7	0.1	0.18	1.13	2.40	95.7	2.8	59.0	32.8	5.9
4.7	2.08	na	0.15	4.5	1.6	0.77	6.15	4.08	72.7	2.7	16.7	15.8	6.9
4.1	2.90	na	0.26	9.8	3.9	2.53	21.32	3.86	31.2	0.8	18.8	42.4	8.4
7.2	0.00	0.0	0.00	5.9	0.3	1.13	9.28	3.77	69.4	3.3	25.6	13.5	8.4
7.8	0.55	na	-0.03	3.5	0.4	0.59	4.99	2.71	71.4	6.3	55.1	6.7	6.5
9.8	0.00	na	0.00	0.0	-16.7	-18.71	-26.56	2.10	1069.7	4.0	108.7	0.0	1.5
7.8	0.29	1.5	0.00	4.9	3.1	1.07	11.80	3.11	61.0	4.7	33.1	8.9	5.5
6.4	0.00	na	0.00	9.2	3.7	2.20	16.30	4.76	54.2	1.1	5.0	27.8	9.9
6.8	1.80	na	0.00	6.4	9.1	1.39	8.99	2.65	53.8	0.7	17.3	39.9	8.9
6.4	1.01	na	0.08	2.8	0.3	0.53	4.13	3.41	83.2	1.1	29.1	52.3	6.5
1.9	4.11	25.3	1.54	1.9	1.2	1.07	11.50	3.07	84.9	1.4	34.5	43.0	4.6
8.5	0.09	na	0.01	4.1	1.2	0.85	9.54	4.17	76.8	3.4	18.4	12.3	4.9
0.8	4.34	na	-0.03	8.4	1.8	1.94	14.86	4.30	44.9	0.8	18.1	27.5	8.6
5.0	0.61	na	0.70	7.9	11.2	1.65	17.12	5.10	72.4	1.4	9.7	24.6	7.8
7.1	0.13	na	0.06	4.4	2.1	0.91	8.71	3.72	59.8	0.7	15.9	35.6	5.6
5.1	0.63	na	0.06	5.1	1.3	1.23	10.48	3.73	65.1	3.7	19.0	10.9	6.9
7.1	0.23	1.2	0.01	6.5	47.1	1.19	9.25	3.68	55.6	1.5	11.9	23.9	10.0
7.0	0.35	na	0.23	3.9	1.6	0.69	7.19	3.87	81.4	6.0	60.7	10.0	4.7
1.9	3.57	24.6	0.44	2.8	-714.5	-7.46	-70.75	3.59	330.1	4.0	9.7	5.5	9.9
7.8	0.06	0.4	0.19	5.4	2.2	1.13	12.54	4.58	63.3	3.2	19.1	13.0	6.0
6.9	0.10	na	0.04	3.0	0.3	0.44	5.30	4.32	82.7	1.2	16.3	28.7	3.7
5.3	1.29	na	1.08	5.0	4.8	1.17	12.75	3.38	46.7	2.2	19.1	17.3	6.7
10.0	5.65	na	4.64	9.5	38.0	2.09	21.00	0.88	21.3	3.8	102.3	0.1	8.2
10.0	na	na	na	6.7	6.3	1.26	13.96	2.18	12.5	5.1	5.6	0.1	7.0
2.4	4.96	na	0.80	2.6	0.2	0.20	1.35	4.26	81.3	1.7	15.5	21.5	7.7
5.7	1.05	na	0.17	4.9	4.4	0.89	9.16	3.25	62.2	6.6	46.7	1.4	7.0
3.4	2.18	na	-0.49	3.5	0.3	0.65	7.20	3.79	73.9	0.8	19.4	40.0	3.0
6.1	1.41	na	0.36	2.3	1.2	0.22	1.94	2.38	76.4	3.4	35.8	16.4	7.2
7.9	0.52	na	-0.03	4.2	5.8	0.83	7.10	3.30	69.9	1.8	19.7	20.2	7.2
9.2	0.00	na	0.00	4.6	0.9	1.14	11.12	3.17	68.2	6.5	56.7	5.3	6.0
8.0	0.14	na	0.17	2.3	0.4	0.23	2.33	2.66	85.5	1.2	18.7	30.0	5.1
4.8	1.47	8.2	0.02	5.9	4.5	1.19	11.13	3.29	60.2	4.0	24.3	9.9	8.1
9.0	0.14	na	0.03	3.0	0.9	0.45	3.23	2.63	77.4	2.0	25.9	20.7	7.4
4.6	1.41	na	-0.14	5.0	2.8	1.09	10.28	4.19	66.9	2.7	15.0	14.4	6.6
4.4	0.86	na	0.32	6.6	3.5	1.32	10.69	3.93	54.2	3.8	17.6	10.2	6.5
6.6	0.16	na	-0.04	4.1	0.2	0.60	3.73	2.62	68.0	5.2	42.7	9.0	7.5
9.2	0.20	0.4	-0.02	2.6	1.7	0.28	1.88	2.53	89.9	6.5	51.1	4.0	7.6
6.9	1.24	na	0.01	9.3	4.5	2.08	19.46	3.71	53.4	5.1	29.8	3.9	8.3
9.5	0.04	0.3	0.00	1.8	0.1	0.10	0.91	2.58	94.2	0.8	14.8	35.5	5.1
9.0	0.01	na	0.04	8.4	2.3	1.65	18.55	4.58	59.3	5.3	33.5	5.2	5.4
5.3	1.42	na	0.02	4.6	7.2	0.90	8.81	3.27	66.3	4.4	26.7	11.2	8.4
5.4	1.03	na	0.03	9.2	4.5	1.95	25.04	4.51	57.7	1.7	25.3	24.4	6.3
7.0	1.10	3.3	0.01	5.1	19.1	1.01	8.98	3.82	56.4	3.3	10.4	12.1	9.3
8.3	0.19	na	0.01	7.9	2.6	1.48	11.43	4.57	58.3	3.2	17.5	13.2	8.0
6.1	1.21	na	-0.01	6.7	13.1	1.53	15.25	4.05	61.6	2.2	11.2	17.7	9.4
3.0	2.78	14.4	0.12	5.4	2.6	1.14	8.72	3.74	60.9	3.2	20.8	12.0	6.8
4.5	1.85	na	0.10	6.0	4.8	1.45	13.20	3.55	59.4	2.3	25.0	18.6	7.6
9.6	1.04	na	0.02	0.8	0.0	0.11	0.56	2.32	95.5	3.9	69.0	21.6	5.7
7.5	1.03	na	-0.05	8.8	17.7	2.27	19.36	2.33	48.6	2.8	33.6	26.3	10.0
7.2	0.94	na	0.06	3.6	4.0	0.60	5.19	3.08	69.6	2.3	24.4	18.6	7.7
9.8	0.00	na	na	1.2	-1.2	0.00	0.00	na	808.0	3.4	98.2	33.3	2.0
8.1	0.00	na	0.00	0.0	-2.7	-3.33	-5.65	1.18	364.7	6.8	71.4	6.6	2.0
5.0	1.05	na	0.01	5.9	3.7	1.16	8.90	4.41	70.3	4.4	12.3	5.4	6.9
4.0	1.77	16.6	0.25	6.2	17.2	1.11	13.15	6.39	74.9	3.8	20.5	8.8	8.2
8.7	0.00	na	0.00	0.2	-0.3	-0.29	-1.60	3.55	89.5	5.4	32.6	4.1	1.1
8.9	0.07	na	-0.01	9.4	1.8	1.75	19.09	4.29	52.9	5.1	33.2	5.5	6.2

Name	City	State	2019 Rating	2018 Rating	Total Assets ($Mil)	One Year Asset Growth	Asset Mix (As a % of Total Assets) Commercial Loans	Consumer Loans	Mortgage Loans	Securities	Capitalization Index	Leverage Ratio	Risk-Based Capital Ratio
Gunnison S&L Assn.	Gunnison	CO	C+	B-	C+	102.5	-0.38	0.0	0.8	46.8	0.0	10.0	12.6	0.0
Guthrie County State Bank	Panora	IA	B	B-	C+	162.0	31.05	9.8	2.5	14.3	33.3	8.1	9.7	16.6
Habib American Bank	New York	NY	B+	B+	B+	1789.3	-2.48	2.9	0.4	8.8	16.1	7.3	9.2	17.4
Haddon Savings Bank	Haddon Heights	NJ	C	C	C	385.2	17.40	12.8	0.1	25.9	47.0	7.2	9.1	21.1
Halstead Bank	Halstead	KS	B	B	B-	139.0	18.15	14.4	6.6	15.4	14.6	6.0	8.9	0.0
Hamilton Bank	Hamilton	MO	B	B	C+	90.8	13.08	4.3	2.6	16.4	36.4	7.4	9.2	14.0
Hamler State Bank	Hamler	OH	A-	A-	B+	90.1	6.01	10.7	0.9	15.0	17.5	10.0	16.1	0.0
Hamlin Bank and Trust Co.	Smethport	PA	B+	A-	B+	412.3	6.13	1.2	4.0	48.0	23.2	10.0	20.2	0.0
Hancock Bank and Trust Co.	Hawesville	KY	B-	B-	C+	318.9	11.11	10.2	1.1	21.2	7.0	8.4	11.4	0.0
Hancock County Savings Bank, FSB	Chester	WV	B	B	B	399.2	6.88	0.2	2.9	74.9	10.5	10.0	18.1	35.3
▼ Hancock Whitney Bank	Gulfport	MS	C-	B-	C+	33173.7	8.66	24.4	2.7	9.7	21.6	5.9	7.9	11.8
Hanmi Bank	Los Angeles	CA	B	B+	A-	6103.8	10.72	19.8	0.1	6.3	11.9	9.7	10.9	14.8
Hanover Community Bank	Garden City Park	NY	B+	B+	B+	851.6	0.33	2.4	0.0	50.8	2.0	10.0	11.2	20.6
▼ Happy State Bank	Happy	TX	B+	A-	A-	5371.8	46.07	16.2	0.7	9.8	16.2	9.0	10.3	14.6
Harbor Bank of Maryland	Baltimore	MD	D	D-	D-	327.5	7.10	20.7	0.8	13.0	12.5	5.3	7.3	11.7
▲ HarborOne Bank	Brockton	MA	B-	C+	C	4432.9	16.08	8.5	7.0	26.7	6.3	10.0	11.4	15.1
Hardin County Bank	Savannah	TN	C+	C+	C+	561.8	11.79	27.6	2.9	13.8	10.6	3.9	9.0	0.0
Hardin County Savings Bank	Eldora	IA	B	B	B-	261.0	17.88	8.8	1.6	11.5	32.6	6.4	8.5	0.0
Harford Bank	Aberdeen	MD	B-	B-	C	472.8	21.31	17.4	1.9	15.7	8.8	7.8	9.5	15.9
Harleysville Bank	Harleysville	PA	B	B	B-	856.0	9.70	4.1	0.1	38.2	10.9	7.3	9.2	15.5
Harrison Building and Loan Assn.	Harrison	OH	B	B	B-	251.6	12.31	3.4	0.1	30.7	38.0	10.0	14.7	0.0
Harrison County Bank	Lost Creek	WV	B	B	B	132.6	15.43	5.9	4.7	26.7	40.2	8.5	10.0	0.0
Hart County Bank and Trust Co.	Munfordville	KY	B	B	B	30.1	11.74	23.3	1.1	0.0	20.4	10.0	22.4	28.9
Hartsburg State Bank	Hartsburg	IL	C+	C+	C	17.2	6.68	6.2	1.1	3.7	31.8	10.0	11.7	0.0
Harvard State Bank	Harvard	IL	C+	B-	B-	296.8	16.74	3.9	1.2	16.0	40.5	6.3	8.3	15.5
Harvest Bank	Kimball	MN	B-	B-	B	173.0	20.06	10.5	2.8	16.4	17.1	6.7	8.7	13.7
Harwood State Bank	Harwood	ND	C	C	C-	44.5	10.83	9.5	2.3	2.1	3.5	7.3	9.2	0.0
▼ Haskell National Bank	Haskell	TX	C+	B	B-	81.5	13.31	7.3	3.7	9.1	46.9	10.0	11.3	27.9
Hatboro Federal Savings, FA	Hatboro	PA	B	B	B	548.8	6.91	0.0	0.0	61.3	12.6	10.0	22.4	0.0
▲ Hatch Bank	San Marcos	CA	B-	C+	B	110.2	60.93	0.0	28.7	16.5	0.0	10.0	32.2	0.0
Havana National Bank	Havana	IL	C-	D+	C-	297.9	17.20	5.4	1.0	6.7	18.1	8.4	9.9	0.0
Haven Savings Bank	Hoboken	NJ	D	C-	C-	985.1	-2.38	2.1	0.0	51.2	13.5	8.8	10.2	0.0
Haverford Trust Co.	Radnor	PA	A	A	A	176.4	8.64	0.7	33.9	0.4	0.1	10.0	17.5	19.4
Haverhill Bank	Haverhill	MA	C+	C+	C	488.8	18.37	17.0	0.1	36.1	10.6	8.4	10.0	17.9
Haviland State Bank	Haviland	KS	B	B	B	40.3	2.90	8.9	1.1	0.7	20.5	10.0	14.8	0.0
Hawaii National Bank	Honolulu	HI	C+	C+	C	740.7	15.04	29.7	0.3	15.5	12.4	7.0	9.0	15.7
Hawthorn Bank	Jefferson City	MO	B+	A-	B	1661.4	15.25	13.9	1.7	14.2	11.2	9.0	10.3	15.0
Headwaters State Bank	Land O'Lakes	WI	B+	B+	B+	75.8	13.23	3.6	2.1	30.6	13.5	10.0	14.0	0.0
Heartland Bank	Somers	IA	A	A-	B+	181.3	14.10	21.2	1.4	7.6	15.1	10.0	12.4	16.6
▲ Heartland Bank	Geneva	NE	B	C+	C+	675.1	9.54	6.3	1.0	1.9	26.3	6.9	9.9	0.0
Heartland Bank	Whitehall	OH	B+	A-	B+	1517.1	33.50	13.9	0.5	21.3	9.9	7.0	9.0	13.8
Heartland Bank and Trust Co.	Bloomington	IL	A-	A-	A-	3184.1	12.99	11.3	0.4	8.2	23.7	8.2	9.8	14.5
Heartland National Bank	Sebring	FL	B+	A-	B+	516.6	24.40	4.7	1.2	7.8	21.3	6.4	8.4	0.0
Heartland State Bank	Edgeley	ND	C+	B-	C+	62.0	2.99	3.2	2.3	0.5	21.3	10.0	11.2	0.0
Heartland State Bank	Redfield	SD	B+	B-	B	94.5	6.49	9.5	1.3	0.1	10.6	8.5	11.1	13.8
Heartland Tri-State Bank	Elkhart	KS	B-	B-	C+	129.7	9.69	6.6	2.2	2.2	31.9	7.0	9.0	14.6
▲ Hebron Savings Bank	Hebron	MD	C	C-	D+	700.7	15.01	12.6	0.4	21.1	3.8	7.1	9.1	13.0
Helm Bank USA	Miami	FL	B	B	B	867.5	3.52	0.4	1.1	60.8	27.0	10.0	11.7	0.0
Henderson Federal Savings Bank	Henderson	TX	B	B	B	111.0	4.94	4.5	3.8	51.4	10.6	10.0	22.0	0.0
Henderson State Bank	Henderson	NE	C+	C-	C-	281.8	4.96	13.1	0.5	0.2	14.4	8.3	11.7	0.0
Hendricks County Bank and Trust Co.	Brownsburg	IN	B-	C+	B-	185.4	9.25	10.2	1.3	14.0	28.5	10.0	11.0	0.0
▲ Henry County Bank	Napoleon	OH	C	C	C	316.2	8.26	5.0	3.9	12.6	42.9	7.8	9.5	0.0
Heritage Bank	Marion	IA	D+	C-	D+	38.7	7.98	8.6	1.6	18.0	20.4	8.5	10.0	0.0
Heritage Bank	Topeka	KS	C-	C	C-	77.0	27.09	15.9	1.1	13.9	4.7	6.6	8.6	14.3
Heritage Bank	Wood River	NE	A	A	B+	553.0	7.31	6.3	0.8	2.7	57.4	10.0	15.5	0.0
Heritage Bank	Olympia	WA	B	B+	B	6681.9	21.25	18.0	3.7	3.7	12.5	6.6	8.6	13.2
Heritage Bank & Trust	Columbia	TN	B-	B-	C+	207.5	14.32	7.9	1.5	24.4	13.4	6.6	8.6	13.7
Heritage Bank Minnesota	West Concord	MN	C+	C+	B-	66.1	18.80	9.0	7.1	30.4	10.9	6.6	8.6	14.7
Heritage Bank of Commerce	San Jose	CA	A-	A-	A-	4605.4	44.77	17.2	0.3	2.1	13.0	8.0	9.7	15.2
Heritage Bank of Schaumburg	Schaumburg	IL	B-	B-	C	144.2	5.24	4.2	0.0	10.3	14.9	6.7	8.7	22.2

Asset Quality Index	Adjusted Non-Performing Loans as a % of Total Loans	as a % of Capital	Net Charge-Offs Avg Loans	Profitability Index	Net Income ($Mil)	Return on Assets (R.O.A.)	Return on Equity (R.O.E.)	Net Interest Spread	Overhead Efficiency Ratio	Liquidity Index	Liquidity Ratio	Hot Money Ratio	Stability Index
9.9	0.38	na	0.00	2.6	0.3	0.37	2.95	2.81	83.8	3.4	51.4	22.5	6.9
8.0	0.41	na	-0.09	5.2	1.4	1.29	11.50	4.12	67.6	5.0	27.4	4.8	5.8
7.5	0.52	2.8	0.00	5.2	12.3	0.87	9.71	2.10	52.6	2.5	41.0	43.0	8.0
8.5	0.72	na	0.19	2.1	0.6	0.22	2.22	1.67	83.7	1.8	34.9	14.3	4.6
7.6	0.24	na	0.06	6.0	1.5	1.48	16.05	4.25	63.8	2.4	12.0	9.3	5.6
5.8	0.23	na	0.01	6.5	1.0	1.52	15.22	4.13	63.4	4.5	38.1	12.0	6.5
8.7	0.11	na	0.01	5.6	0.9	1.38	8.45	3.36	52.5	2.4	23.0	18.0	8.7
7.4	0.41	na	0.18	2.7	-6.3	-2.10	-9.95	3.86	55.7	5.3	41.3	8.6	9.2
6.9	0.67	na	0.28	4.3	2.1	0.97	8.52	3.68	78.7	2.5	10.2	16.0	6.3
9.1	0.92	na	0.01	4.3	2.2	0.76	4.13	3.28	67.7	3.6	16.0	11.0	8.0
4.7	0.79	4.7	2.22	1.8	-138.3	-0.58	-5.38	3.30	61.4	4.6	17.5	5.3	9.8
4.2	1.49	7.6	0.83	4.1	33.8	0.78	6.92	3.32	56.3	1.5	19.3	23.4	8.7
9.1	0.19	na	0.10	3.9	3.7	0.58	5.58	3.40	73.1	0.7	12.5	38.5	7.4
5.0	1.43	6.8	0.09	5.8	45.3	1.33	9.58	4.35	61.1	2.5	12.5	6.9	9.7
2.7	3.25	na	0.00	1.1	0.2	0.09	1.31	3.18	96.0	1.5	18.3	24.8	2.1
4.6	1.43	6.7	0.08	4.3	28.1	0.90	6.88	3.03	66.0	3.1	10.8	10.2	8.2
3.9	1.48	10.8	0.06	5.6	4.7	1.16	12.85	3.90	61.2	0.9	7.1	24.4	5.5
8.5	0.23	1.4	0.03	4.9	2.1	1.17	13.91	2.95	57.5	2.2	36.3	20.6	5.3
4.2	1.46	11.1	0.00	4.0	2.0	0.62	6.14	3.53	64.2	1.9	14.4	17.6	5.5
5.6	1.25	na	0.00	4.7	5.7	0.93	9.86	2.82	57.7	4.2	23.4	8.3	6.3
6.9	2.61	na	0.00	3.8	1.3	0.75	4.51	3.31	71.7	5.0	57.0	14.3	7.5
8.6	0.00	na	0.01	4.5	0.8	0.80	7.48	3.63	70.7	5.8	48.0	7.3	6.0
8.6	0.00	na	0.00	4.1	0.2	0.70	3.10	3.59	80.6	4.5	45.8	13.7	7.6
8.4	0.00	na	-0.29	2.8	0.1	0.50	4.01	2.64	81.7	1.9	28.1	21.1	6.2
3.6	2.42	na	0.31	3.4	1.6	0.77	7.50	3.22	66.7	3.6	30.0	13.5	5.5
3.8	1.07	5.7	0.00	6.6	1.9	1.58	17.24	4.05	58.5	4.8	22.2	4.6	6.3
8.5	0.13	na	-0.02	3.3	0.2	0.50	5.29	2.96	78.0	4.0	51.1	16.7	4.3
9.1	0.10	na	-0.01	2.6	0.2	0.38	3.03	3.10	90.0	5.9	55.1	7.7	6.2
7.4	3.68	na	0.00	3.4	2.4	0.60	2.58	2.28	65.7	1.8	33.7	31.7	8.9
7.0	0.00	na	0.23	3.8	0.7	1.27	3.54	2.85	63.3	2.8	69.8	35.7	5.9
2.6	1.41	na	0.05	4.7	1.7	0.84	7.88	2.83	62.4	2.7	25.8	16.2	6.1
6.0	0.94	na	0.00	1.0	-0.7	-0.09	-0.84	2.07	102.5	0.8	17.9	39.4	7.5
6.8	0.00	0.0	0.00	10.0	8.0	6.31	37.33	1.05	77.8	3.0	72.9	82.7	9.7
8.8	0.20	na	-0.04	3.4	2.1	0.61	5.87	2.90	83.9	2.1	31.2	24.4	5.5
5.4	1.36	na	0.00	5.8	0.4	1.21	8.19	4.30	62.8	3.6	14.6	10.8	8.1
7.0	0.00	na	-0.01	2.9	2.0	0.37	3.90	3.75	85.7	4.8	24.6	4.6	5.8
7.3	0.63	3.5	0.01	4.7	10.9	0.91	8.63	3.58	63.0	2.7	10.6	12.5	8.9
7.9	0.90	na	0.15	4.5	0.5	0.96	6.25	4.02	75.2	5.4	51.3	9.9	8.2
8.0	0.09	na	-0.07	9.4	2.7	2.03	15.41	4.81	51.6	1.2	4.9	17.8	9.3
5.0	0.82	na	0.00	7.8	7.5	1.55	11.94	4.01	54.9	4.0	22.7	9.8	9.0
8.0	0.38	na	0.07	5.0	9.5	0.93	9.29	3.61	59.1	2.2	12.0	18.1	8.8
6.6	0.61	3.3	0.04	7.0	24.5	1.08	9.60	3.79	59.1	5.5	24.1	3.0	9.5
9.4	1.20	na	-0.01	4.8	3.0	0.85	9.67	2.65	61.6	6.6	67.3	7.5	5.7
6.9	0.00	na	0.00	3.2	0.2	0.51	4.05	3.72	83.6	2.4	18.8	14.7	7.3
6.3	0.00	na	-0.05	9.1	1.3	1.94	17.14	4.92	58.0	1.7	16.6	15.5	8.5
4.6	0.39	na	0.32	4.5	1.0	1.06	10.89	3.55	70.7	2.2	18.9	18.5	6.5
2.9	3.03	16.9	0.10	4.3	4.0	0.80	8.56	3.45	65.1	2.1	15.9	17.8	5.7
6.0	3.36	14.3	-0.04	4.2	4.9	0.77	6.36	3.53	72.4	2.7	41.4	25.0	8.1
6.1	2.40	na	0.47	3.9	0.6	0.72	3.24	3.34	63.7	0.9	23.2	41.2	7.7
3.7	1.68	na	-0.12	6.3	3.6	1.77	15.13	3.18	53.3	0.7	20.6	47.0	6.0
6.8	1.03	na	-0.03	3.1	0.8	0.56	4.84	3.99	85.2	4.6	38.3	11.6	6.3
6.2	2.40	na	0.00	3.3	1.5	0.63	6.34	3.11	75.8	1.3	22.9	26.0	5.2
7.4	0.44	na	0.10	1.8	0.1	0.18	1.71	3.28	94.2	5.8	50.9	7.3	4.4
5.9	1.24	6.5	0.00	2.8	0.2	0.43	4.77	3.50	82.3	1.6	27.5	29.1	4.1
9.2	0.09	na	0.01	6.7	4.4	1.10	6.96	2.72	55.4	5.9	38.9	2.7	10.0
3.9	1.54	6.8	0.09	4.2	26.7	0.58	4.41	3.70	61.3	4.7	19.5	5.2	9.9
7.7	0.18	na	-0.06	3.7	1.0	0.68	7.82	3.58	81.3	2.7	29.6	16.0	6.0
6.2	0.63	na	0.06	1.9	0.1	0.12	1.33	3.74	100.4	4.5	19.8	6.3	4.4
7.3	0.36	1.5	0.05	5.2	26.6	0.82	5.98	3.69	56.0	6.4	37.7	3.2	9.7
5.2	0.44	na	0.00	4.0	1.0	0.95	6.46	3.20	67.2	5.5	43.1	7.7	8.1

Name	City	State	2019 Rating	2018 Rating	Rating	Total Assets ($Mil)	One Year Asset Growth	Asset Mix (As a % of Total Assets)				Capital-ization Index	Lever-age Ratio	Risk-Based Capital Ratio
								Comm-ercial Loans	Cons-umer Loans	Mort-gage Loans	Secur-ities			
Heritage Bank of St. Tammany	Covington	LA	B-	B-	B-	145.0	10.46	3.7	0.2	42.8	6.5	10.0	14.6	22.8
Heritage Bank of the Ozarks	Lebanon	MO	B-	B-	B-	181.3	14.88	10.2	3.0	14.8	10.1	5.2	8.5	0.0
Heritage Bank, Inc.	Burlington	KY	B-	C+	C+	1157.6	25.50	17.1	0.5	7.8	19.1	6.0	8.0	12.2
▲ Heritage Bank, N.A.	Spicer	MN	C+	C	C-	485.5	12.64	20.8	4.3	13.8	12.5	6.0	9.7	11.7
Heritage Community Bank	Chamois	MO	C+	B-	B-	175.8	18.25	14.1	1.7	24.0	3.2	3.1	9.0	0.0
Heritage Community Bank	Greeneville	TN	B-	B-	B-	132.2	12.45	6.4	5.5	36.5	2.7	7.3	9.2	15.5
Heritage First Bank	Rome	GA	B-	B-	B-	169.6	16.63	15.1	2.6	14.0	7.2	7.5	9.9	13.0
Heritage Southeast Bank	Jonesboro	GA	C+	C+	B-	1530.9	18.94	17.7	1.2	8.0	10.3	7.1	9.1	13.3
Heritage State Bank	Lawrenceville	IL	D	C-	C-	79.2	-3.63	4.9	0.0	0.6	0.0	10.0	11.5	15.3
Herring Bank	Amarillo	TX	B-	C+	B-	508.5	13.44	13.2	10.1	8.3	7.3	5.9	8.8	11.7
Hershey State Bank	Hershey	NE	B+	B+	B+	81.3	4.85	11.8	5.1	15.3	5.0	10.0	13.6	19.5
Hertford Savings Bank, SSB	Hertford	NC	C	C	C	15.2	17.08	0.0	2.5	54.4	0.0	10.0	14.6	27.7
Hiawatha Bank and Trust Co.	Hiawatha	IA	B+	B	B-	89.5	70.52	6.6	2.4	30.8	8.3	9.7	10.8	0.0
Hiawatha National Bank	Hager City	WI	C	C	C	523.7	122.23	30.8	0.6	7.9	12.6	9.2	11.9	14.3
Hibernia Bank	New Orleans	LA	B-	B-	C	206.6	1.94	1.8	0.1	47.4	1.8	10.0	13.5	21.4
▼ Hickory Point Bank and Trust	Decatur	IL	B-	B	B-	770.3	20.43	12.2	0.4	4.6	15.0	8.0	9.7	15.1
Hicksville Bank	Hicksville	OH	B	B	B-	130.6	8.38	8.5	1.2	17.3	29.0	10.0	12.8	0.0
High Country Bank	Salida	CO	A-	A-	A-	360.6	26.25	11.9	0.8	23.8	8.4	6.8	9.4	0.0
High Plains Bank	Flagler	CO	B+	A-	A-	247.6	27.25	19.1	1.0	12.0	4.4	3.0	8.4	0.0
High Plains Bank	Keyes	OK	B	B	B-	143.6	-4.32	9.1	3.8	6.9	8.0	8.8	11.8	0.0
Highland Bank	Saint Michael	MN	B	B	B-	604.1	14.74	31.3	0.6	5.0	25.3	6.8	8.8	14.8
▲ Highland Federal S&L Assn.	Crossville	TN	B	C+	C	65.3	4.99	0.0	0.0	28.1	1.0	10.0	22.1	47.3
▲ Highland State Bank	Highland	WI	B+	B	C+	36.0	9.83	2.8	5.4	24.7	10.4	10.0	11.6	0.0
Highlands Community Bank	Covington	VA	B+	B+	B	169.1	11.25	12.9	14.6	20.2	27.2	10.0	12.2	0.0
Highpoint Community Bank	Hastings	MI	C+	C+	C+	382.1	15.35	11.4	2.8	24.8	12.0	7.2	9.1	18.4
Hill Bank & Trust Co.	Weimar	TX	B	B	B	152.4	6.38	0.6	0.7	3.4	61.6	10.0	16.4	0.0
▼ Hill-Dodge Banking Co.	Warsaw	IL	C+	B-	B-	45.0	8.30	13.4	3.1	5.9	4.5	10.0	13.6	0.0
Hills Bank and Trust Co.	Hills	IA	A-	A	A	3778.6	12.58	8.9	0.8	26.3	9.9	10.0	12.2	0.0
Hillsboro Bank	Plant City	FL	A	A	A	178.5	15.81	5.4	1.3	16.8	19.3	10.0	11.4	23.9
Hillsboro State Bank	Hillsboro	KS	D+	C-	D	20.8	13.75	9.2	1.3	11.5	7.3	6.8	8.8	21.2
Hilltop National Bank	Casper	WY	B+	A-	B+	890.1	17.18	9.6	1.8	11.3	37.0	10.0	11.7	0.0
Hingham Institution for Savings	Hingham	MA	A-	A-	B+	2719.2	9.63	0.2	0.0	37.4	0.0	8.9	10.4	14.1
Hinsdale Bank & Trust Co., N.A.	Hinsdale	IL	B	B	B	3829.6	44.01	33.3	9.3	4.9	8.6	6.1	8.5	11.8
HNB First Bank	Headland	AL	A-	A-	B+	181.0	14.77	17.5	2.7	15.8	8.4	7.9	9.6	14.6
HNB National Bank	Hannibal	MO	A	A	B+	587.7	16.30	8.0	1.3	15.4	4.8	10.0	12.9	0.0
Hocking Valley Bank	Athens	OH	B	B	B	309.1	14.29	8.6	0.8	25.4	20.6	8.3	9.9	0.0
Hodge Bank & Trust Co.	Hodge	LA	B+	B	B-	80.7	13.93	12.6	7.5	24.5	20.9	10.0	17.4	32.9
▲ Holcomb Bank	Rochelle	IL	B	C+	C	238.9	27.25	16.3	1.6	14.0	26.0	9.3	10.6	16.2
Holladay Bank & Trust	Salt Lake City	UT	B+	A-	A-	67.4	16.84	12.9	2.7	12.1	3.6	10.0	14.8	0.0
Holmes County Bank & Trust Co.	Lexington	MS	B-	B	B-	132.4	10.24	8.7	2.1	6.6	41.6	10.0	12.3	28.5
▲ Home Bank and Trust Co.	Eureka	KS	B	B-	C+	134.2	27.35	17.5	4.8	34.0	3.6	5.4	7.8	11.3
Home Bank of California	San Diego	CA	A	A	B+	205.9	17.07	0.7	0.0	22.1	0.9	10.0	12.2	0.0
▲ Home Bank SB	Martinsville	IN	B	B-	B-	364.4	13.29	6.5	0.8	26.6	27.9	10.0	11.6	0.0
Home Bank, N.A.	Lafayette	LA	B	B	B-	2574.1	16.28	16.4	1.5	16.2	9.9	7.7	9.4	15.3
▼ Home Banking Co.	Selmer	TN	C-	C+	C+	97.9	12.61	6.2	7.4	13.9	38.8	8.3	9.9	0.0
Home Exchange Bank	Jamesport	MO	A-	A-	A	177.5	2.41	3.3	0.4	3.0	48.2	10.0	11.6	0.0
Home Federal Bank	Shreveport	LA	B+	B+	B+	542.2	17.57	14.8	0.2	24.5	10.1	8.1	9.7	16.9
Home Federal Bank Corp.	Middlesboro	KY	B	B	B	426.7	9.10	6.2	1.9	38.0	19.1	9.9	10.9	18.4
Home Federal Bank of Hollywood	Hallandale Beach	FL	D-	D	D	54.6	-4.94	3.8	0.0	40.4	3.4	10.0	12.3	24.0
Home Federal Bank of Tennessee	Knoxville	TN	B-	B	B	2475.7	10.95	4.2	0.3	18.1	46.4	10.0	17.4	0.0
▲ Home Federal S&L Assn.	Bamberg	SC	C+	C+	C+	40.9	-3.91	0.0	3.5	61.6	0.0	10.0	13.4	0.0
Home Federal S&L Assn. of Grand Island	Grand Island	NE	B-	B-	C+	331.9	12.49	14.6	3.7	14.1	23.6	10.0	11.4	16.0
Home Federal S&L Assn. of Niles Ohio	Niles	OH	C	C+	C	106.8	12.17	3.9	0.1	40.0	13.4	10.0	11.6	0.0
Home Federal Savings Bank	Rochester	MN	B+	A-	B+	897.6	17.73	10.7	2.4	16.8	13.2	8.1	9.7	14.4
Home Loan Investment Bank, F.S.B.	Warwick	RI	D	D+	D	370.2	6.98	1.1	30.1	40.5	0.3	7.5	9.7	12.9
▲ Home Loan Savings Bank	Coshocton	OH	B+	B	B+	245.1	11.33	12.6	2.4	35.2	1.7	10.0	11.0	16.4
Home Loan State Bank	Grand Junction	CO	C+	C+	C	177.8	40.56	28.6	1.8	3.4	30.0	4.5	6.7	10.7
Home National Bank	Racine	OH	C	C-	C-	76.0	7.95	5.6	10.5	33.1	29.1	10.0	12.2	0.0
Home National Bank of Thorntown	Thorntown	IN	C+	B-	B-	129.5	13.43	16.1	2.1	15.7	41.6	7.2	9.1	16.7
Home S&L Assn. of Carroll County, F.A.	Norborne	MO	C+	C+	C+	86.0	0.38	1.8	3.1	46.6	5.9	10.0	20.9	38.5

Asset Quality Index	Adjusted Non-Performing Loans as a % of Total Loans	as a % of Capital	Net Charge-Offs Avg Loans	Profitability Index	Net Income ($Mil)	Return on Assets (R.O.A.)	Return on Equity (R.O.E.)	Net Interest Spread	Overhead Efficiency Ratio	Liquidity Index	Liquidity Ratio	Hot Money Ratio	Stability Index
7.9	0.59	na	0.00	3.5	0.6	0.62	4.26	3.37	79.2	1.2	20.8	30.4	6.9
7.4	0.31	na	0.12	4.3	1.0	0.73	8.40	3.86	76.3	1.6	19.9	17.1	5.5
6.1	1.44	6.2	0.07	4.6	8.0	0.98	11.52	3.38	60.8	3.5	21.4	12.5	7.3
4.3	1.11	na	0.12	6.9	5.3	1.57	16.28	4.61	70.0	2.2	16.1	13.2	6.0
5.3	0.44	3.4	-0.01	4.8	1.4	1.19	12.93	3.92	70.7	1.5	6.8	22.1	5.9
8.4	0.05	0.3	-0.48	3.7	0.7	0.68	7.33	3.66	79.0	1.3	17.0	28.7	5.8
4.2	1.51	9.7	0.14	3.6	0.8	0.69	6.56	4.40	78.3	2.2	26.1	19.6	5.6
4.9	1.79	na	0.09	3.2	4.4	0.41	3.46	3.86	74.7	3.2	19.8	14.0	7.3
0.2	7.51	na	3.53	0.5	-0.2	-0.35	-3.00	4.16	68.1	4.0	25.8	10.5	4.9
6.3	0.57	na	-0.10	4.9	4.3	1.17	14.20	4.29	78.8	3.8	15.3	9.7	5.4
4.3	2.57	na	-0.16	7.2	0.8	1.42	9.38	4.68	57.0	0.6	15.0	42.2	8.6
6.2	1.24	na	0.00	2.5	0.0	0.13	0.86	3.80	92.2	1.6	28.5	26.0	5.7
8.5	0.00	na	0.00	7.5	0.8	1.41	13.53	4.54	62.2	4.6	12.8	4.1	6.7
3.2	2.74	na	0.02	4.7	2.5	0.98	11.80	2.83	63.0	1.6	20.9	15.7	6.0
8.0	0.31	na	0.00	2.8	0.3	0.20	1.24	3.26	87.2	0.7	13.9	42.0	7.0
6.1	0.84	na	0.00	3.6	3.2	0.61	6.12	2.96	74.0	4.5	25.4	6.9	6.2
6.0	1.66	na	0.00	4.2	0.8	0.89	6.66	3.76	72.9	4.1	22.4	8.8	7.3
8.7	0.08	na	0.00	8.6	3.5	1.43	14.46	5.32	60.8	4.5	17.3	5.7	6.9
8.4	0.06	na	0.04	6.8	2.7	1.53	16.82	4.95	66.3	2.8	11.7	14.7	6.5
5.1	0.90	na	0.46	6.4	1.6	1.46	11.91	3.89	49.4	0.8	16.8	36.7	8.1
6.8	0.07	na	0.01	4.4	2.6	0.61	6.01	3.73	70.1	3.7	12.6	4.5	6.7
9.8	0.00	na	0.00	4.3	0.4	0.90	3.99	3.37	73.2	5.5	62.0	11.0	7.6
9.0	0.02	na	0.08	6.9	0.5	1.89	16.58	3.23	78.4	5.6	54.6	9.2	6.1
5.1	1.23	na	0.36	5.0	1.2	0.99	7.57	4.10	66.6	2.2	33.9	25.6	7.1
7.3	0.36	na	0.00	3.5	1.8	0.68	6.98	3.41	76.6	5.1	29.0	4.1	5.3
10.0	0.00	na	0.00	4.3	1.0	0.87	5.27	2.42	51.1	5.2	97.9	18.8	7.6
5.8	2.72	na	4.39	1.6	-0.1	-0.44	-2.90	3.51	49.9	5.9	54.8	7.1	5.5
7.2	0.67	4.9	0.06	5.9	30.2	1.16	9.21	3.00	54.8	4.2	27.7	10.7	10.0
9.3	0.13	na	0.01	5.7	1.3	1.02	8.16	3.24	59.6	5.6	59.3	11.7	8.6
6.7	10.39	na	0.00	2.5	0.1	0.37	3.73	2.97	84.9	6.5	62.4	3.0	3.6
9.3	1.17	na	0.17	4.7	7.3	1.14	9.54	2.66	63.0	6.2	55.6	6.9	7.8
7.7	0.15	1.0	0.04	9.0	33.7	1.68	17.40	3.13	26.1	0.7	12.2	30.8	8.6
4.6	0.80	5.0	0.05	4.7	12.3	0.45	3.84	3.16	61.6	1.9	14.9	11.8	8.3
8.3	0.06	0.6	-0.02	5.4	1.7	1.33	13.58	3.34	67.4	1.5	19.1	25.4	6.6
8.3	0.64	na	0.01	10.0	14.6	3.53	28.07	3.85	39.4	3.8	28.4	12.1	9.7
8.2	0.12	na	0.14	4.1	1.8	0.79	7.53	3.01	69.6	4.4	26.3	7.9	6.4
5.0	2.68	na	0.83	9.8	1.2	2.16	11.93	4.55	48.2	1.9	28.6	24.4	8.7
5.5	1.22	na	0.10	5.0	2.0	1.24	12.29	3.84	62.1	2.1	22.8	16.4	4.9
7.4	1.59	5.5	-0.02	5.6	0.4	0.83	5.26	4.36	71.0	2.8	33.4	18.7	8.4
4.9	7.88	na	0.10	3.1	0.6	0.65	5.01	3.20	77.7	3.6	33.8	15.2	6.6
8.4	0.53	na	0.03	7.8	1.7	1.94	25.84	3.55	60.7	1.7	14.4	21.5	4.9
7.5	0.00	na	0.00	9.2	2.7	1.89	14.80	4.49	49.4	0.8	15.1	36.4	9.7
7.6	0.40	na	-0.02	4.1	2.4	0.94	7.44	3.26	76.3	5.2	41.7	9.2	6.9
4.4	1.23	7.0	0.16	4.6	13.3	0.72	5.89	3.95	62.2	3.6	13.6	9.5	9.8
6.4	0.40	na	0.13	1.9	0.2	0.22	2.07	3.42	96.3	3.4	47.5	19.1	5.4
9.3	0.00	na	0.00	5.7	1.7	1.36	11.38	2.67	46.7	1.8	39.0	16.7	9.6
5.0	1.36	na	0.15	4.7	3.5	0.93	8.88	3.29	63.0	1.9	26.1	20.2	6.3
7.6	1.12	na	-0.01	4.3	2.6	0.85	7.50	3.53	74.5	2.0	21.3	19.7	7.0
3.7	5.69	na	0.00	0.0	-1.1	-2.61	-22.90	2.86	191.0	1.5	36.1	67.5	6.4
9.5	0.69	na	-0.09	2.9	7.0	0.39	2.24	2.18	79.6	4.9	51.7	15.7	8.9
6.0	2.12	na	0.03	2.8	0.1	0.32	2.40	3.52	88.1	0.7	18.0	54.4	6.1
7.0	0.58	na	0.09	3.2	1.3	0.56	4.89	3.43	80.6	4.4	20.2	6.7	6.6
7.7	0.71	na	0.00	2.5	0.4	0.45	3.65	2.35	75.6	0.8	18.9	44.8	6.3
6.8	0.38	na	0.12	6.5	7.6	1.22	11.52	3.50	60.4	4.5	19.1	6.1	7.0
2.1	3.71	na	0.58	4.9	3.0	1.14	12.24	4.31	62.8	0.5	9.5	43.8	6.6
5.8	0.91	na	0.75	8.2	2.7	1.50	13.33	4.00	49.7	2.5	17.6	16.0	8.2
5.1	1.68	na	0.00	4.7	1.0	0.87	11.48	3.58	69.6	4.7	19.2	4.7	4.0
1.9	5.62	24.3	0.45	4.8	0.5	0.96	7.66	4.70	74.3	2.0	14.3	19.1	7.5
5.5	1.05	4.3	0.03	3.8	0.8	0.80	8.10	3.43	71.6	3.1	16.9	13.9	5.5
7.3	1.34	na	0.13	2.7	0.3	0.43	2.07	2.74	83.8	2.6	35.5	22.1	7.0

Name	City	State	2020 Rating	2019 Rating	2018 Rating	Total Assets ($Mil)	One Year Asset Growth	Asset Mix (As a % of Total Assets)				Capital-ization Index	Lever-age Ratio	Risk-Based Capital Ratio
								Comm-ercial Loans	Cons-umer Loans	Mort-gage Loans	Secur-ities			
Home S&L Co. of Kenton, Ohio	Kenton	OH	B-	B	B	141.3	9.46	8.6	0.3	19.5	17.1	10.0	25.5	0.0
Home Savings Bank	Chanute	KS	B-	B-	B-	78.8	0.76	5.9	4.9	33.7	30.9	10.0	18.7	34.4
Home Savings Bank	Salt Lake City	UT	A-	A-	B+	132.6	4.31	0.0	0.0	30.0	2.2	10.0	13.6	0.0
▲ Home Savings Bank	Madison	WI	C	D+	D	177.8	15.49	2.6	0.2	37.8	0.7	6.9	8.9	15.9
▼ Home Savings Bank of Wapakoneta	Wapakoneta	OH	C	B-	B-	38.2	2.52	0.0	0.1	57.1	13.4	10.0	12.4	21.1
▲ Home Savings Bank, FSB	Ludlow	KY	D	D	D+	26.6	1.50	0.0	0.0	44.2	1.4	10.0	13.1	0.0
Home State Bank	Jefferson	IA	B-	B-	C+	277.7	6.77	17.2	1.4	3.9	9.7	4.7	8.9	0.0
Home State Bank	Royal	IA	B+	B+	B+	43.9	-4.48	2.2	0.5	2.3	36.2	10.0	31.2	45.5
Home State Bank	Litchfield	MN	B+	B+	B+	178.6	16.93	15.7	2.6	9.0	31.5	8.4	9.9	14.3
Home State Bank, N.A.	Crystal Lake	IL	B	B	B-	690.0	14.31	12.5	0.5	19.0	18.6	10.0	11.3	20.3
Home Trust & Savings Bank	Osage	IA	B+	B+	B+	257.5	7.83	5.5	1.5	16.2	29.7	9.3	10.5	17.2
HOMEBANK	Palmyra	MO	B	B-	B-	435.0	9.15	20.1	2.0	9.5	6.2	5.5	9.6	0.0
HomeBank of Arkansas	Portland	AR	D-	D+	C	73.8	3.81	10.9	2.9	22.2	0.0	8.6	10.1	15.4
HomeBank Texas	Seagoville	TX	A-	A-	B+	256.0	24.70	20.4	0.9	24.7	4.6	8.1	9.7	16.9
Homeland Community Bank	McMinnville	TN	C+	C+	C	184.6	21.48	4.9	2.6	20.4	24.1	6.4	8.4	0.0
Homeland Federal Savings Bank	Columbia	LA	B-	B-	C+	381.3	13.79	13.2	8.7	29.7	2.0	5.8	9.3	0.0
HomePride Bank	Mansfield	MO	D-	D-	D-	106.9	9.55	2.5	2.4	44.6	4.3	6.1	8.1	17.2
Homestead Bank	Cozad	NE	A-	B+	B	283.9	7.92	8.3	1.0	0.9	21.6	10.0	16.1	0.0
Homestead Savings Bank	Albion	MI	D	D-	E-	75.2	15.84	6.6	1.5	41.5	8.4	4.7	6.7	14.8
HomeStreet Bank	Seattle	WA	B-	C+	B-	7360.4	8.32	8.9	0.1	16.6	15.0	7.6	9.4	14.0
Hometown Bank	Oxford	MA	B-	B-	B-	1228.6	54.16	8.7	0.3	20.0	12.4	7.4	9.3	15.5
HomeTown Bank	Redwood Falls	MN	A-	A-	B+	451.9	27.87	17.1	1.9	14.1	30.0	7.2	9.1	16.3
Hometown Bank	Kent	OH	D+	C-	C-	232.8	13.75	21.0	0.9	22.9	5.5	4.9	8.1	10.9
Hometown Bank	Fond du Lac	WI	A	A-	B+	570.5	13.97	28.9	0.3	8.5	3.8	10.0	11.3	17.4
HomeTown Bank of Alabama	Oneonta	AL	A-	A-	A-	462.2	21.13	5.8	8.6	34.2	21.5	10.0	12.9	21.3
Hometown Bank of Corbin, Inc.	Corbin	KY	B-	B-	C+	215.3	21.33	13.9	2.8	23.4	21.4	6.2	8.2	14.3
Hometown Bank of Pennsylvania	Bedford	PA	C+	B-	B-	255.9	16.44	13.5	0.7	26.7	6.5	5.4	7.4	11.5
HomeTown Bank, N.A.	Galveston	TX	A-	A-	B+	756.2	19.49	11.9	1.4	11.3	25.9	10.0	11.5	17.7
Hometown Community Bank	Cyrus	MN	C+	C+	C	66.8	8.36	8.6	1.4	15.0	6.0	8.1	9.7	0.0
Hometown National Bank	LaSalle	IL	B+	B+	B+	300.3	37.15	22.9	0.5	5.0	18.8	7.2	9.1	13.8
HomeTrust Bank	Asheville	NC	C+	B-	B-	3673.8	0.57	15.4	3.8	13.7	8.2	6.7	10.1	12.3
Homewood Federal Savings Bank	Baltimore	MD	C+	B-	B-	61.6	0.86	3.9	2.2	53.1	0.8	10.0	26.8	49.2
▼ Hondo National Bank	Hondo	TX	B-	B+	B+	321.0	18.71	9.3	2.0	16.4	32.1	6.3	8.3	13.7
Honesdale National Bank	Honesdale	PA	A-	A-	A-	800.6	13.37	13.4	3.2	21.4	15.0	10.0	13.8	0.0
Honor Bank	Honor	MI	B-	B-	C+	292.2	17.24	20.9	1.5	13.6	5.7	6.7	8.7	12.9
▲ Hoosier Heartland State Bank	Crawfordsville	IN	B-	B-	B-	227.5	11.64	7.0	4.7	9.0	25.2	6.6	8.6	12.9
Hopeton State Bank	Hopeton	OK	C	D+	C	26.1	0.00	19.4	3.5	0.0	35.7	10.0	11.2	15.7
▲ Horatio State Bank	Horatio	AR	B	B	B-	235.3	8.10	5.9	18.4	26.9	9.7	10.0	11.9	0.0
Horicon Bank	Horicon	WI	C	C-	C+	1060.1	35.87	16.4	0.6	13.3	2.4	7.0	9.3	12.5
Horizon Bank	Michigan City	IN	B+	B+	B+	5775.9	11.31	11.5	6.9	12.5	20.9	5.7	8.6	11.6
Horizon Bank	Waverly	NE	A-	A-	B+	395.0	16.70	7.3	1.4	9.5	6.3	10.0	14.2	15.8
Horizon Bank, SSB	Austin	TX	B+	B+	B+	1463.8	24.24	30.1	0.1	8.1	7.3	5.3	7.3	11.5
Horizon Community Bank	Lake Havasu City	AZ	B-	B-	B-	454.6	31.90	24.9	0.3	5.8	14.9	5.0	7.0	13.2
Horizon Financial Bank	Munich	ND	B+	B+	B+	151.8	5.30	6.6	1.7	4.1	12.6	10.0	12.4	0.0
Houghton State Bank	Red Oak	IA	B+	B	B-	194.1	10.25	13.5	0.7	5.9	12.0	8.2	10.5	13.5
▼ Howard Bank	Baltimore	MD	C-	C+	C+	2558.8	11.59	21.3	2.1	15.4	15.0	8.7	10.1	14.1
Howard State Bank	Howard	KS	B+	B+	B-	56.1	10.19	2.6	3.3	4.5	36.2	10.0	11.2	0.0
▲ Hoyne Savings Bank	Chicago	IL	C-	C-	D+	450.3	1.55	0.0	0.0	29.1	38.2	10.0	16.7	0.0
HSBC Bank USA, N.A.	McLean	VA	C-	C	C	202543.0	11.23	12.8	0.7	9.2	25.7	8.7	10.2	21.2
HSBC Trust Co. (Delaware), N.A.	Wilmington	DE	U	U	U	55.1	-1.99	0.0	0.0	0.0	0.0	9.8	98.3	0.0
Huntingdon Savings Bank	Huntingdon	PA	C	C	C+	16.9	1.55	0.0	0.0	71.3	0.0	10.0	21.7	48.2
Huntingdon Valley Bank	Doylestown	PA	C	C-	C-	505.9	43.17	19.3	1.1	55.6	3.1	6.4	8.4	12.9
Huntington Federal Savings Bank	Huntington	WV	C	C+	B-	552.1	2.71	0.0	0.3	34.1	54.4	10.0	16.6	0.0
Huntington National Bank	Columbus	OH	B-	B-	B-	120113.5	10.41	21.8	15.4	12.1	19.8	7.0	9.0	13.6
Huron Community Bank	East Tawas	MI	B	B	B	273.8	16.46	16.4	1.0	9.1	15.0	8.7	10.2	0.0
▲ Huron State Bank	Rogers City	MI	B	B-	C	70.9	10.91	1.7	4.4	31.5	14.7	10.0	14.8	0.0
Huron Valley State Bank	Milford	MI	B	B	B	192.7	20.88	20.0	0.4	3.9	0.3	7.2	9.1	14.8
Hustisford State Bank	Hustisford	WI	B+	B+	B+	63.5	13.51	4.4	1.4	40.7	11.7	10.0	17.2	0.0
Hyden Citizens Bank	Hyden	KY	B-	B-	B-	135.0	6.65	7.3	3.3	21.2	36.8	7.3	9.2	13.3
Hyperion Bank	Philadelphia	PA	D+	D+	D	244.4	43.10	15.5	0.4	31.7	0.7	8.5	10.0	15.4

Asset Quality Index	Adjusted Non-Performing Loans as a % of Total Loans	as a % of Capital	Net Charge-Offs Avg Loans	Profitability Index	Net Income ($Mil)	Return on Assets (R.O.A.)	Return on Equity (R.O.E.)	Net Interest Spread	Overhead Efficiency Ratio	Liquidity Index	Liquidity Ratio	Hot Money Ratio	Stability Index
8.8	0.59	na	-0.04	2.9	0.5	0.48	1.85	2.66	78.4	1.7	37.3	30.0	7.8
8.9	0.05	na	0.00	3.7	0.4	0.61	3.01	3.52	76.4	2.4	32.9	20.2	7.8
7.6	0.28	na	0.00	5.4	0.9	0.89	6.43	3.40	63.7	0.7	21.0	51.2	8.2
7.0	0.60	na	0.00	3.8	2.3	1.78	19.68	2.92	79.3	1.8	18.8	17.1	4.6
9.8	0.00	na	0.00	0.4	-0.3	-1.22	-9.11	3.19	146.0	3.7	24.2	11.5	7.0
5.0	2.92	na	0.00	0.0	-0.2	-0.92	-6.63	2.04	139.7	2.3	45.4	31.1	5.8
4.5	1.34	na	0.01	6.4	3.1	1.46	16.48	3.92	62.2	2.0	18.6	9.2	6.8
7.5	0.00	na	0.01	8.0	0.7	1.95	6.17	3.66	45.7	5.9	58.0	7.7	9.0
8.7	0.10	0.5	-0.02	4.4	1.3	1.00	9.23	3.60	76.7	4.3	23.5	7.9	7.2
7.4	1.31	na	0.18	4.4	5.0	1.01	8.32	3.74	79.6	4.3	25.7	8.2	7.4
5.8	0.23	na	0.03	5.7	2.6	1.42	12.80	2.56	40.2	3.6	36.0	15.5	6.9
5.7	0.57	na	0.05	5.4	4.5	1.39	14.45	4.01	69.0	3.2	13.0	12.6	6.5
4.7	1.35	na	0.08	0.4	-0.2	-0.42	-3.96	3.96	112.3	1.2	28.9	48.9	4.8
8.5	0.00	na	0.00	9.0	3.7	2.07	20.54	4.32	50.2	2.5	23.3	17.1	7.5
4.2	1.74	na	0.01	3.9	1.0	0.82	9.29	3.17	73.6	2.6	34.3	21.0	4.6
4.1	1.39	na	0.06	5.8	3.5	1.26	13.32	4.60	65.1	0.6	10.2	43.5	6.5
5.2	1.15	9.0	0.09	0.5	-0.3	-0.38	-4.78	3.54	109.2	2.0	30.5	25.3	3.1
6.2	0.13	na	0.00	7.9	3.1	1.50	9.14	4.02	58.2	4.4	23.7	7.1	9.1
3.8	1.68	na	-0.06	2.8	0.3	0.52	7.42	3.69	88.7	5.3	34.1	5.2	2.3
5.0	1.24	5.9	0.01	4.8	54.2	1.02	9.75	3.25	65.3	3.1	15.3	10.8	8.5
6.0	1.31	na	0.11	4.2	6.8	0.82	7.52	3.30	67.9	3.7	30.0	16.3	6.8
6.4	0.35	na	-0.02	9.3	5.9	1.98	18.70	3.87	53.4	5.5	35.1	4.3	6.8
2.2	1.95	na	-0.01	3.3	1.0	0.58	7.34	3.19	82.5	1.3	14.0	27.6	3.6
7.8	0.36	na	-0.03	8.1	5.9	1.45	11.39	3.68	56.6	4.6	16.4	5.1	9.2
7.8	0.37	na	0.05	7.6	4.7	1.46	10.69	4.08	59.0	1.9	22.7	20.6	8.5
6.8	0.35	na	0.00	4.2	1.2	0.79	9.11	3.87	78.5	3.6	19.1	11.2	4.9
5.4	1.93	9.7	-0.07	2.8	0.7	0.41	5.19	2.70	81.4	2.1	27.9	20.9	5.0
8.7	0.23	na	0.00	7.2	7.4	1.43	11.75	3.96	53.5	2.6	32.7	19.7	7.9
6.8	0.00	na	-0.04	3.9	0.4	0.89	8.30	3.49	69.3	1.7	22.7	24.3	4.9
4.6	1.78	na	-0.02	4.9	1.8	0.90	8.87	3.28	68.1	4.6	32.5	8.8	6.0
6.0	0.91	4.7	0.13	2.9	11.1	0.41	3.74	3.01	76.8	3.0	13.3	11.1	9.2
9.2	1.73	na	0.00	2.1	0.0	0.06	0.21	2.61	91.5	1.5	34.6	53.0	7.2
2.0	5.57	na	0.03	3.3	1.1	0.48	5.30	3.37	76.8	3.2	30.7	15.9	4.7
8.0	0.48	na	0.10	6.1	7.0	1.25	8.71	3.88	61.7	3.7	21.3	10.9	8.9
5.2	0.35	na	0.02	5.2	2.2	1.07	12.01	4.06	61.0	4.6	13.1	4.2	5.5
5.7	1.94	na	0.06	4.1	1.5	0.87	9.39	3.95	80.8	4.6	24.6	5.9	5.4
8.5	0.00	0.0	-0.03	2.1	0.1	0.63	5.23	4.07	98.5	2.0	40.2	42.1	5.7
4.9	0.86	na	0.46	8.9	2.8	1.60	13.84	4.40	41.2	0.7	14.0	44.1	8.0
3.5	3.16	na	0.02	5.4	9.1	1.25	12.89	3.67	60.2	4.2	17.5	6.8	8.9
5.5	0.72	4.0	0.06	5.9	49.2	1.19	10.06	3.58	56.4	3.8	12.0	9.9	9.5
7.3	0.00	na	0.00	9.8	5.6	2.05	18.55	4.08	34.7	0.6	11.6	29.5	9.2
8.2	0.24	na	0.18	6.6	13.8	1.33	17.57	4.07	53.5	4.3	19.2	5.5	8.3
6.4	0.83	na	0.11	4.7	2.7	0.89	11.42	3.86	70.9	3.8	26.8	11.8	4.7
5.6	0.96	na	-0.01	4.4	0.9	0.83	6.70	3.68	70.6	2.7	18.3	14.4	7.5
4.8	0.19	na	0.00	6.4	1.7	1.20	8.92	3.93	56.5	3.8	9.8	9.5	7.7
5.1	0.90	na	0.04	0.6	-20.2	-1.09	-8.28	3.32	119.3	0.8	13.6	21.3	8.5
8.9	0.41	na	0.18	4.5	0.4	0.84	7.00	3.64	72.1	6.2	47.6	3.5	6.3
9.3	1.33	na	-0.14	1.6	0.4	0.12	0.71	2.18	98.7	3.7	61.0	25.4	6.2
7.1	2.47	6.5	0.30	0.5	-954.1	-0.64	-5.87	1.23	111.2	3.9	65.9	14.1	8.6
10.0	na	0.0	na	7.0	0.5	1.16	1.19	0.65	54.5	4.0	na	0.0	2.3
7.0	1.71	na	0.00	3.1	0.1	0.43	1.98	3.11	78.8	1.2	26.7	31.3	8.0
5.3	0.54	na	0.20	5.0	3.8	1.24	16.02	2.58	69.5	3.4	12.4	9.3	3.1
10.0	0.45	na	-0.23	2.2	0.9	0.22	1.39	2.01	86.3	3.6	69.0	28.9	8.0
4.4	1.52	6.8	0.56	4.7	621.2	0.73	6.81	3.12	52.4	4.6	13.0	0.8	9.9
4.8	1.95	na	-0.02	4.4	1.6	0.84	7.61	3.61	70.7	5.2	31.6	4.8	6.5
6.1	4.36	na	-0.69	4.0	0.4	0.77	5.08	3.38	77.1	5.2	55.4	11.8	6.1
5.3	0.21	1.9	0.13	4.6	1.1	0.84	8.70	3.70	63.6	2.7	19.7	14.4	5.7
6.1	6.21	na	0.02	5.1	0.4	0.92	5.17	3.88	66.5	2.5	31.4	15.8	7.8
6.2	0.81	4.8	0.02	4.1	0.9	0.96	9.58	3.74	78.3	1.9	20.1	20.1	5.9
5.0	1.58	na	0.00	2.0	0.5	0.33	3.19	3.48	82.4	0.8	19.9	39.7	3.7

Name	City	State	2019 Rating	2018 Rating	Total Assets ($Mil)	One Year Asset Growth	Comm-ercial Loans	Cons-umer Loans	Mort-gage Loans	Secur-ities	Capital-ization Index	Lever-age Ratio	Risk-Based Capital Ratio
							Asset Mix (As a % of Total Assets)						
Idabel National Bank	Idabel	OK	B+	B+	B+	151.1	14.59	6.5	6.2	16.7	39.3	8.2	9.8	0.0
Idaho First Bank	McCall	ID	C+	C+	C-	916.7	327.66	72.8	0.6	3.8	1.6	6.7	8.7	13.5
Idaho Trust Bank	Boise	ID	C+	C	C	180.3	23.68	25.9	2.9	0.7	0.3	6.5	8.5	13.9
▲ Illini State Bank	Tonica	IL	B+	B	B-	145.3	15.81	11.0	0.7	11.9	24.9	10.0	12.6	0.0
Illinois Bank & Trust	Rockford	IL	B+	B+	B+	1500.0	72.12	23.3	1.0	6.8	31.3	6.3	8.3	13.1
Impact Bank	Wellington	KS	B-	B-	B-	149.4	8.30	11.8	1.9	2.9	24.3	8.5	10.0	15.7
INB, N.A.	Springfield	IL	B-	B-	C+	1432.2	20.84	13.0	0.1	10.0	7.3	5.9	7.9	13.3
InBank	Raton	NM	C-	C+	B	614.7	68.42	25.3	1.0	4.9	15.5	7.3	9.4	12.8
▲ Incommons Bank, N.A.	Mexia	TX	B	B-	B-	188.5	6.40	12.5	3.9	22.8	19.6	7.1	9.0	15.8
IncredibleBank	Wausau	WI	B-	B-	B-	1696.0	22.97	33.7	4.7	6.7	12.3	4.6	7.1	10.8
Independence Bank	Havre	MT	A	A-	B+	912.8	15.96	8.5	2.0	6.1	7.0	10.0	12.5	16.2
Independence Bank	Independence	OH	B	B	B	182.2	7.26	28.8	0.4	4.5	16.1	10.0	13.3	0.0
▲ Independence Bank	East Greenwich	RI	B	B	B	68.9	6.26	70.0	0.3	2.2	0.0	10.0	27.3	0.0
Independence Bank of Kentucky	Owensboro	KY	B+	B+	B+	2903.0	13.03	8.8	0.3	13.9	41.0	5.7	7.7	13.0
▲ Independence State Bank	Independence	WI	C-	D	D	80.6	17.78	12.6	1.0	8.7	15.3	5.7	8.0	11.5
Independent Bank	Grand Rapids	MI	B-	B-	B-	4168.1	17.42	12.6	11.3	22.3	23.6	6.8	8.8	13.8
▲ Independent Bank	Memphis	TN	B	B-	C+	1177.5	11.51	11.9	40.9	4.1	0.5	6.5	10.9	12.1
▲ Independent Bank	McKinney	TX	A-	B+	B+	17111.8	14.43	12.4	0.4	8.4	6.3	8.1	11.0	13.4
Independent Farmers Bank	Maysville	MO	B+	B	B	131.3	6.52	6.5	3.4	11.8	46.3	8.3	9.8	17.9
Industrial & Commerc. Bank of China (USA	New York	NY	B-	B	B	2986.8	5.84	30.4	0.0	10.5	0.4	10.0	13.6	15.9
Industrial Bank	Washington	DC	D+	C-	D+	553.8	30.30	9.8	0.1	17.9	17.1	4.8	6.9	12.9
▲ Industry State Bank	Industry	TX	A-	B+	A-	904.8	8.27	5.7	1.2	4.6	71.9	10.0	11.0	0.0
Inez Deposit Bank	Inez	KY	C+	C+	C	148.8	5.83	1.1	2.4	21.2	32.0	10.0	12.8	45.3
Infinity Bank	Santa Ana	CA	D	D	D	190.0	72.52	48.9	2.1	1.0	12.8	10.0	13.3	16.5
InFirst Bank	Indiana	PA	C+	B-	B-	458.9	9.20	10.3	0.8	52.1	7.6	7.6	9.4	14.1
▲ Inland Bank and Trust	Oak Brook	IL	B	B	B	1252.2	12.57	8.9	0.1	13.6	17.6	10.0	12.6	15.2
▼ InsBank	Nashville	TN	B-	B	B-	583.7	8.77	28.9	1.5	5.9	3.3	8.8	11.1	14.0
INSOUTH Bank	Brownsville	TN	B-	B	B-	369.5	8.25	19.2	2.4	17.5	9.0	4.8	9.3	0.0
Institution for Savings	Newburyport	MA	B-	A-	C+	3869.7	7.20	1.0	0.3	55.8	4.6	9.3	10.5	14.4
Integrity Bank & Trust	Monument	CO	B	B	B-	263.7	22.66	11.9	0.7	12.6	8.7	6.0	8.0	13.1
▼ Integrity Bank Plus	Wabasso	MN	C-	C+	C+	72.0	13.32	8.9	1.2	7.4	21.0	9.1	10.4	16.2
Interamerican Bank, A FSB	Miami	FL	C+	C	C-	229.6	15.27	2.2	0.3	22.7	0.0	10.0	12.9	20.9
Interaudi Bank	New York	NY	B+	B+	B	2093.7	2.05	8.0	0.2	18.3	22.3	6.6	8.6	22.2
InterBank	Oklahoma City	OK	C-	C-	C+	3556.2	-1.35	23.2	0.5	5.2	0.0	4.8	10.5	0.0
Intercity State Bank	Schofield	WI	A	A	B+	202.9	7.72	14.0	1.2	20.4	6.8	10.0	22.1	31.2
Intercredit Bank, N.A.	Miami	FL	D	D+	C	384.6	2.26	10.5	1.5	24.8	11.4	9.6	10.7	15.5
International Bank of Amherst	Amherst	WI	A-	A-	A-	83.6	15.52	8.7	0.7	10.3	26.3	10.0	13.0	0.0
International Bank of Chicago	Chicago	IL	C+	B-	C	754.1	16.26	11.1	0.0	19.3	22.9	9.4	10.6	19.0
International Bank of Commerce	Brownsville	TX	A	A	A	1284.7	21.73	16.7	0.4	2.8	21.3	10.0	14.5	23.7
International Bank of Commerce	Laredo	TX	A	A	A	9963.5	16.86	12.7	0.5	8.0	21.3	10.0	13.3	19.1
International Bank of Commerce	Zapata	TX	A	A	A	441.2	11.00	6.0	1.3	16.8	53.3	10.0	16.5	36.7
International Bank of Commerce Oklahoma	Oklahoma City	OK	A-	A-	A-	1636.3	15.86	21.7	0.1	1.0	24.1	10.0	12.9	17.7
▼ International City Bank	Long Beach	CA	B-	B+	A-	440.9	34.76	5.7	0.0	2.6	53.4	6.8	8.8	22.2
▼ International Finance Bank	Miami	FL	C	C+	C+	809.1	7.43	32.7	2.2	21.9	5.3	3.5	6.9	10.3
▼ Interstate Bank	Perryton	TX	C+	B	C+	194.4	-3.86	22.6	1.2	9.4	28.8	9.4	10.6	0.0
Interstate Federal S&L Assn. of McGregor	McGregor	IA	C-	C-	C	8.2	4.40	0.0	0.6	69.1	0.0	10.0	20.8	47.4
▲ Intracoastal Bank	Palm Coast	FL	B+	B	B	482.1	42.33	9.6	0.1	1.5	16.5	6.3	8.5	11.9
INTRUST Bank, N.A.	Wichita	KS	B-	B	B	7326.1	42.47	22.9	3.5	2.6	23.6	4.8	6.9	11.6
Investar Bank, N.A.	Baton Rouge	LA	B-	B	B	2319.0	14.80	16.7	1.0	12.8	12.6	8.2	10.2	13.5
Investment Savings Bank	Altoona	PA	C	C+	C+	106.8	5.23	0.6	0.7	34.9	39.4	10.0	20.6	0.0
Investors Bank	Short Hills	NJ	B-	B	B+	26574.5	-0.55	4.7	1.4	17.6	15.5	6.8	8.8	13.2
▲ Investors Community Bank	Chillicothe	MO	B+	B+	B+	79.1	12.20	3.0	3.7	17.8	58.7	10.0	12.5	32.7
Investors Community Bank	Manitowoc	WI	B-	B-	B-	1488.6	5.82	10.7	0.0	1.0	20.1	10.0	13.6	17.3
Inwood National Bank	Dallas	TX	A-	A-	A-	3469.1	17.22	7.3	0.2	9.3	31.4	7.1	9.1	0.0
Ion Bank	Naugatuck	CT	C	B-	C+	1639.1	22.71	19.4	10.6	20.4	3.8	6.8	8.8	13.8
▲ Iowa Falls State Bank	Iowa Falls	IA	B-	B-	B-	139.2	3.19	13.0	2.0	11.8	30.8	10.0	11.5	0.0
▼ Iowa Prairie Bank	Brunsville	IA	D-	D	D+	69.0	14.66	8.4	2.1	0.6	49.2	3.7	5.7	12.1
Iowa Savings Bank	Carroll	IA	B	B	B	222.7	13.98	15.4	0.6	4.8	11.8	5.5	8.6	0.0
Iowa State Bank	Algona	IA	B+	A-	A-	352.8	9.72	13.0	1.4	8.4	18.7	10.0	11.9	19.2
Iowa State Bank	Clarksville	IA	D-	D-	D+	397.8	4.50	10.9	0.7	2.5	13.3	6.5	8.5	13.5

Asset Quality Index	Adjusted Non-Performing Loans as a % of Total Loans	as a % of Capital	Net Charge-Offs Avg Loans	Profitability Index	Net Income ($Mil)	Return on Assets (R.O.A.)	Return on Equity (R.O.E.)	Net Interest Spread	Overhead Efficiency Ratio	Liquidity Index	Liquidity Ratio	Hot Money Ratio	Stability Index
5.8	0.00	na	0.67	8.4	2.1	2.04	20.28	4.04	47.8	1.7	28.0	28.3	7.8
7.9	0.00	na	0.00	2.9	1.9	0.39	8.50	2.41	69.7	2.4	4.2	15.0	5.2
8.4	0.01	na	0.13	3.7	0.9	0.67	5.72	3.77	78.8	4.9	25.4	4.4	6.8
7.7	0.30	na	0.00	5.2	1.3	1.31	8.33	3.10	53.7	4.3	27.8	4.9	8.1
7.1	0.53	2.9	0.46	5.1	10.9	1.04	10.71	3.62	60.0	5.3	25.3	4.7	7.1
4.4	1.97	na	0.57	3.7	1.0	0.89	8.44	3.61	79.0	3.4	32.4	15.2	6.9
6.3	0.65	na	0.02	4.2	9.5	0.98	11.72	3.11	70.9	3.1	25.2	3.2	7.0
5.4	1.21	na	-0.01	1.6	1.3	0.34	2.81	4.10	90.4	2.7	17.0	15.5	5.8
6.2	0.57	na	0.02	5.4	1.5	1.08	11.48	4.78	74.7	4.0	15.3	8.6	5.7
4.7	1.05	6.2	0.12	6.5	17.6	1.50	17.12	3.94	63.7	3.4	15.6	9.8	7.9
6.1	1.47	na	0.07	9.8	12.1	1.88	14.61	4.43	40.1	0.7	10.4	14.9	9.9
7.8	0.51	na	0.03	4.0	1.0	0.74	5.39	2.91	66.2	0.8	19.1	40.5	7.4
4.8	3.99	5.2	3.17	7.8	0.7	1.29	4.50	5.16	70.3	2.1	46.3	54.2	8.2
9.9	0.17	1.0	0.07	6.5	32.3	1.56	19.42	3.68	54.9	3.3	11.2	4.6	7.5
3.7	1.84	na	0.01	3.8	0.4	0.67	7.40	3.69	75.3	3.6	27.3	12.9	4.4
4.6	1.88	7.4	0.15	6.9	39.7	1.38	14.11	3.51	58.9	4.7	27.0	5.6	8.7
5.2	0.60	na	0.23	6.5	10.7	1.24	10.26	4.50	65.9	1.7	5.4	11.9	8.8
6.7	0.25	1.5	0.03	7.8	169.7	1.41	8.52	3.70	45.0	2.5	12.7	8.7	10.0
6.9	0.63	na	0.23	6.1	1.2	1.21	11.19	4.17	62.9	3.5	28.7	14.0	6.3
3.6	1.94	10.7	0.00	2.7	3.5	0.16	1.06	2.70	70.3	0.5	8.9	38.4	9.3
1.5	3.06	na	0.01	2.8	0.9	0.21	2.81	3.59	86.8	3.5	21.7	11.9	4.8
9.3	0.46	0.7	0.13	6.2	13.0	1.94	15.23	2.61	56.2	3.0	62.4	37.2	8.8
6.2	2.35	na	0.21	2.1	0.2	0.22	1.59	2.45	90.0	4.5	54.3	16.0	6.5
7.3	0.83	4.2	0.00	0.0	-0.6	-0.46	-2.85	3.41	102.3	3.2	17.0	0.0	1.5
5.3	1.87	na	0.42	3.3	1.3	0.40	4.07	3.56	77.0	1.5	9.4	22.2	6.0
4.9	1.93	8.3	0.17	5.7	10.6	1.21	9.55	2.98	69.6	1.9	18.5	19.7	8.2
3.9	0.94	6.9	0.06	3.5	2.3	0.54	4.88	2.81	60.3	0.6	10.2	47.5	7.0
4.7	0.75	na	0.09	5.9	2.8	1.05	10.90	4.55	72.9	2.6	4.2	15.0	6.3
9.6	0.11	0.6	0.00	2.4	3.0	0.11	1.05	1.94	62.5	1.4	23.1	33.5	9.3
8.0	0.82	na	0.03	5.8	1.8	1.03	12.27	4.71	66.8	4.6	21.5	5.5	5.2
0.2	7.50	na	0.00	5.1	0.6	1.16	9.93	4.34	71.0	3.8	18.9	10.4	7.9
4.3	6.01	na	-0.05	3.0	0.8	0.50	3.71	3.79	88.9	4.0	28.5	11.1	7.7
9.5	0.33	1.7	0.05	4.6	10.9	0.69	8.33	1.91	63.1	3.2	58.9	43.2	7.2
0.8	3.64	24.3	0.03	7.6	46.0	1.74	13.71	3.80	47.7	4.1	11.3	8.1	10.0
6.0	2.24	na	0.03	9.5	2.6	1.71	7.80	3.58	41.2	3.7	31.1	13.6	9.0
5.5	0.69	4.6	0.12	1.2	0.2	0.05	0.51	3.18	95.4	0.9	20.5	30.6	5.8
9.3	0.01	na	0.00	7.2	1.0	1.74	12.88	3.82	53.2	6.2	51.6	4.6	8.5
1.9	4.86	na	-0.10	3.6	3.6	0.67	5.74	2.86	73.6	1.2	28.1	30.1	8.4
8.7	0.07	0.4	0.07	9.8	16.8	1.90	12.18	3.75	43.3	3.9	45.2	19.5	9.3
7.1	0.13	0.7	0.07	7.6	93.0	1.32	8.19	3.54	53.4	4.2	31.5	14.4	9.4
8.9	0.57	1.2	0.41	4.8	2.9	0.93	4.94	3.20	67.5	3.9	51.9	18.4	8.2
7.9	0.09	0.3	0.18	4.0	7.3	0.63	3.96	3.51	69.7	4.3	11.9	6.5	7.0
10.0	0.02	na	-0.02	1.1	-1.0	-0.32	-2.66	2.67	132.4	2.3	42.2	22.8	6.6
5.0	1.34	13.3	0.00	2.9	2.5	0.41	5.92	3.20	63.7	1.7	10.8	20.7	5.6
3.0	4.90	na	0.75	4.1	1.3	0.87	7.94	3.23	76.9	3.2	39.4	18.5	7.3
9.9	0.62	1.1	0.00	1.3	0.0	0.02	0.08	3.01	97.4	1.8	28.8	22.5	5.8
7.9	0.67	na	0.00	7.1	5.0	1.63	18.79	3.59	44.4	4.4	42.7	13.5	6.6
5.0	2.61	14.7	0.23	4.5	42.8	0.86	12.75	2.80	63.9	2.7	25.5	8.5	5.9
5.5	0.91	5.0	0.03	3.7	12.0	0.71	6.20	3.60	66.1	1.7	12.1	22.1	8.7
9.9	0.42	na	0.00	2.4	0.2	0.26	1.22	2.61	87.4	4.6	59.1	16.5	7.6
5.6	0.68	5.0	0.08	4.1	146.2	0.72	8.39	2.73	52.6	2.3	12.7	8.5	8.4
9.3	0.35	na	0.06	5.1	0.7	1.22	8.66	3.57	62.2	5.7	68.1	8.2	7.8
2.7	5.60	20.6	0.01	4.5	8.5	0.79	5.57	2.91	62.7	1.7	25.4	22.7	10.0
8.7	0.02	0.1	0.00	8.1	48.5	1.94	19.25	3.15	39.7	5.0	31.3	10.3	9.7
4.9	1.53	na	0.03	2.7	3.8	0.33	4.16	3.13	77.0	3.5	17.4	4.8	5.9
3.6	1.13	na	1.10	4.0	0.7	0.70	6.09	3.77	61.6	4.8	45.8	12.2	7.3
5.8	1.34	na	0.62	0.0	-0.7	-1.48	-19.76	2.84	191.1	4.4	31.8	10.4	1.6
8.0	0.53	na	0.02	6.0	2.3	1.41	15.74	3.08	57.2	4.4	26.6	6.8	6.9
6.3	3.24	na	0.02	5.5	2.6	1.06	7.91	3.78	60.5	3.0	16.3	13.9	8.1
0.0	10.16	na	0.77	2.7	1.0	0.35	4.00	2.41	56.7	1.5	34.2	32.0	3.9

Name	City	State	Rating	2019 Rating	2018 Rating	Total Assets ($Mil)	One Year Asset Growth	Asset Mix (As a % of Total Assets)				Capital-ization Index	Lever-age Ratio	Risk-Based Capital Ratio
								Comm-ercial Loans	Cons-umer Loans	Mort-gage Loans	Secur-ities			
Iowa State Bank	Des Moines	IA	A	A	A	450.1	14.27	11.0	0.2	10.8	29.8	10.0	15.1	0.0
Iowa State Bank	Hull	IA	B+	A-	B+	697.0	17.64	8.9	0.9	3.4	11.4	9.4	12.9	0.0
Iowa State Bank	Sac City	IA	A	A-	B+	150.9	13.99	11.1	4.7	20.7	4.6	10.0	11.9	0.0
Iowa State Bank and Trust Co.	Fairfield	IA	B	B	B	155.0	16.95	12.2	1.7	16.9	6.5	7.7	9.5	15.1
Iowa State Savings Bank	Creston	IA	C+	C	C-	231.1	11.48	3.6	1.1	9.3	23.3	7.8	9.5	0.0
Iowa Trust & Savings Bank	Emmetsburg	IA	A-	B+	B+	358.9	14.17	5.1	0.4	7.6	19.8	10.0	12.7	17.7
Iowa Trust and Savings Bank	Centerville	IA	A	A	B+	203.3	18.54	7.2	1.6	5.0	48.4	8.7	10.1	0.0
Ipava State Bank	Ipava	IL	B+	B+	B+	181.7	27.52	9.8	3.0	17.1	14.2	6.1	8.1	15.5
Ipswich State Bank	Ipswich	SD	B	B	B	59.7	11.82	5.4	0.7	0.0	19.6	10.0	15.4	25.0
▼ Ireland Bank	Malad City	ID	B+	B+	B-	300.5	20.89	17.6	0.9	2.6	26.1	8.6	10.1	20.2
Iron Workers Savings Bank	Aston	PA	C-	C	C	186.8	5.57	0.5	0.0	44.3	14.1	7.8	9.6	0.0
Iroquois Farmers State Bank	Iroquois	IL	B-	B-	B-	120.6	6.40	2.4	2.8	11.1	17.9	6.8	8.8	13.8
Iroquois Federal S&L Assn.	Watseka	IL	B-	B-	B-	726.0	7.05	11.6	1.1	17.3	22.2	9.4	10.6	0.0
Isabella Bank	Mount Pleasant	MI	B-	B-	B-	1921.9	9.21	11.9	3.9	16.3	18.9	6.4	8.4	13.0
Islanders Bank	Friday Harbor	WA	B+	A-	B+	340.4	15.45	4.1	0.8	15.5	15.9	6.1	8.2	15.1
Israel Discount Bank of New York	New York	NY	B	B+	B+	10669.5	9.98	26.3	0.1	0.8	24.8	9.5	10.7	15.7
Itasca Bank & Trust Co.	Itasca	IL	B+	B+	B-	696.3	20.22	30.4	0.3	9.6	26.2	4.9	9.0	0.0
ITS Bank	Johnston	IA	U	U	U	8.6	6.97	0.0	0.0	0.0	26.1	10.0	93.1	0.0
▼ Iuka State Bank	Salem	IL	C	C	D+	112.4	15.22	8.7	11.3	10.6	11.0	6.3	9.0	0.0
▲ Ixonia Bank	Ixonia	WI	B-	B-	C+	506.5	36.51	26.2	0.1	19.2	11.5	8.9	10.2	16.1
Jacksboro National Bank	Jacksboro	TX	B+	B+	B+	256.8	8.90	6.9	2.8	8.6	53.6	10.0	12.7	25.4
Jackson County Bank	Seymour	IN	B-	B-	B-	677.1	14.08	8.4	0.9	20.9	13.1	6.7	8.7	13.0
Jackson County Bank	McKee	KY	A	A	A-	155.5	16.31	1.7	9.1	18.1	30.4	10.0	25.1	0.0
▲ Jackson County Bank	Black River Falls	WI	D	D-	C-	193.1	-3.65	0.5	0.9	12.2	42.3	6.6	8.6	20.5
Jackson Federal S&L Assn.	Jackson	MN	C	C	C	39.2	5.69	5.3	3.8	26.6	41.2	10.0	23.9	41.1
Jackson Parish Bank	Jonesboro	LA	B-	B-	B-	69.4	7.04	4.4	4.5	12.6	61.9	10.0	15.1	0.0
▼ Jackson Savings Bank, SSB	Sylva	NC	C-	B-	C+	34.7	6.41	0.0	0.5	54.4	0.0	10.0	19.5	44.6
James Polk Stone Community Bank	Portales	NM	A-	A-	B+	278.6	19.20	6.2	3.7	18.5	28.9	8.0	9.7	0.0
Janesville State Bank	Janesville	MN	A-	B+	B+	79.7	9.76	4.9	2.6	18.3	8.0	10.0	12.6	0.0
Jarrettsville Federal S&L Assn.	Jarrettsville	MD	C	C+	B-	124.3	-2.84	2.8	0.0	50.7	8.1	10.0	14.6	0.0
JD Bank	Jennings	LA	B+	B+	B	1076.8	23.67	12.8	3.0	15.0	20.3	8.0	9.7	16.7
▼ Jeff Bank	Jeffersonville	NY	B	B+	B	594.7	16.13	5.8	0.5	18.4	25.4	9.3	10.6	0.0
Jefferson Bank	Greenville	MS	A-	A-	B+	148.8	18.49	12.8	0.2	2.9	23.8	10.0	15.0	18.7
Jefferson Bank	San Antonio	TX	B+	B+	B+	2225.9	19.46	11.2	1.0	20.4	18.1	6.7	8.8	14.2
Jefferson Bank and Trust Co.	Saint Louis	MO	B	B	B	697.5	12.61	16.8	1.4	4.5	18.3	8.7	11.0	13.9
Jefferson Bank of Missouri	Jefferson City	MO	B+	B+	B+	766.9	18.10	13.7	19.8	18.6	10.3	7.3	9.2	14.9
Jefferson Security Bank	Shepherdstown	WV	B-	B-	C+	376.4	17.45	5.3	0.9	31.8	26.6	7.0	9.0	15.9
Jersey Shore State Bank	Williamsport	PA	B-	B-	B-	1314.7	5.75	3.2	11.5	18.5	9.3	5.7	7.7	11.8
Jersey State Bank	Jerseyville	IL	B	B+	B+	188.5	21.68	8.1	0.6	6.5	37.3	10.0	12.2	0.0
Jewett City Savings Bank	Jewett City	CT	B-	B	B-	348.2	18.61	13.6	1.1	35.1	5.6	10.0	14.2	22.2
Jim Thorpe Neighborhood Bank	Jim Thorpe	PA	C+	C+	C+	221.9	10.08	4.6	0.5	21.6	23.1	8.3	9.9	19.4
John Deere Financial, F.S.B.	Madison	WI	A-	A-	A-	3957.4	0.89	4.1	14.0	0.0	0.0	9.5	16.0	0.0
John Marshall Bank	Reston	VA	B+	B+	B+	1861.0	23.02	12.0	0.1	12.9	7.1	9.5	11.1	14.6
Johnson Bank	Racine	WI	A-	A-	A-	6078.1	15.63	23.6	1.3	15.5	9.7	10.0	11.1	17.0
Johnson City Bank	Johnson City	TX	B+	A-	A-	142.3	16.19	11.8	6.5	21.3	9.6	10.0	11.2	0.0
Johnson County Bank	Mountain City	TN	B	B	B	133.1	10.79	3.1	3.6	31.7	31.6	10.0	14.8	0.0
Johnson State Bank	Johnson	KS	B-	B	B	88.0	12.15	6.2	1.6	3.8	43.0	10.0	14.5	0.0
Jonah Bank of Wyoming	Casper	WY	B+	B	B-	526.6	57.41	19.7	0.3	7.0	4.2	5.3	9.5	0.0
Jones Bank	Seward	NE	A-	B+	B-	358.0	10.76	12.0	1.2	6.7	35.8	9.7	10.8	0.0
Jonesboro State Bank	Jonesboro	LA	B+	A-	A	406.5	29.11	2.1	0.8	3.2	87.0	10.0	11.3	21.4
Jonesburg State Bank	Jonesburg	MO	B	B	B-	117.8	18.59	9.5	2.1	20.6	1.5	6.1	8.1	15.1
Jonestown Bank and Trust Co.	Jonestown	PA	C	C+	C	721.1	14.37	4.9	24.5	17.8	4.2	2.9	8.4	0.0
JPMorgan Chase Bank, Dearborn	Dearborn	MI	U	U	U	61.7	1.79	0.0	0.0	0.0	0.0	10.0	99.2	511.5
▼ JPMorgan Chase Bank, N.A.	Columbus	OH	B	B+	B+	2869536.0	21.22	6.8	6.7	7.7	18.6	5.9	7.9	16.8
Junction National Bank	Junction	TX	B	B	B+	81.4	18.00	5.5	2.0	6.8	58.9	6.6	8.6	28.7
Juniata Valley Bank	Mifflintown	PA	B-	B-	B-	774.1	16.26	8.7	0.9	17.3	38.4	6.5	8.5	0.0
Kahoka State Bank	Kahoka	MO	B-	B-	C+	57.8	15.07	4.6	4.4	26.1	26.0	8.1	9.7	0.0
▼ Kalamazoo County State Bank	Schoolcraft	MI	C	C+	C	111.9	17.42	7.2	13.2	11.5	46.1	9.7	10.8	22.2
Kansas State Bank	Ottawa	KS	B+	B+	B-	154.1	6.20	11.3	1.7	14.8	44.0	6.9	8.9	0.0
▼ Kansas State Bank Overbrook Kansas	Overbrook	KS	B	B+	B+	72.4	14.67	9.4	3.0	6.7	47.9	10.0	12.5	21.3

Asset Quality Index	Adjusted Non-Performing Loans		Net Charge-Offs Avg Loans	Profitability Index	Net Income ($Mil)	Return on Assets (R.O.A.)	Return on Equity (R.O.E.)	Net Interest Spread	Overhead Efficiency Ratio	Liquidity Index	Liquidity Ratio	Hot Money Ratio	Stability Index
	as a % of Total Loans	as a % of Capital											
9.0	0.32	na	-0.07	6.7	4.9	1.59	9.41	3.35	62.2	6.0	48.9	6.6	9.6
5.5	0.89	na	0.05	6.3	6.7	1.34	9.60	3.31	54.1	4.0	23.7	9.6	9.1
8.0	0.03	na	0.01	8.6	2.1	1.91	14.98	3.55	45.7	3.5	22.3	12.4	9.1
7.4	0.79	na	0.00	4.9	1.1	0.97	9.82	3.53	63.9	3.1	23.5	14.5	5.8
6.9	0.28	na	0.02	3.8	1.2	0.70	6.10	3.75	68.0	3.9	27.2	11.3	5.9
7.1	0.00	na	-0.01	6.2	3.8	1.49	11.36	3.64	56.3	1.3	26.5	25.7	8.6
9.1	0.00	na	0.00	7.2	2.4	1.68	14.50	3.53	52.6	5.2	48.3	11.0	7.7
8.8	0.01	0.3	-0.17	6.5	2.0	1.55	19.80	3.60	65.3	3.9	26.9	11.3	5.5
8.6	0.00	na	0.00	5.0	0.5	1.16	7.41	3.15	60.4	2.2	34.1	26.4	7.9
7.5	1.05	na	-0.03	4.6	1.6	0.79	7.53	4.32	76.6	5.9	41.4	4.2	5.9
8.5	0.35	na	0.00	1.9	0.1	0.10	1.05	2.86	96.0	2.2	22.9	18.7	5.3
5.6	0.93	na	0.21	3.4	0.6	0.71	7.82	3.03	72.8	3.9	28.6	11.5	5.1
8.4	0.23	na	0.06	3.5	3.6	0.67	5.94	2.78	72.0	1.2	16.5	25.3	7.4
5.0	2.15	9.2	-0.02	4.3	12.7	0.93	10.23	2.91	66.8	3.0	22.2	15.3	7.7
5.3	2.34	9.8	-0.01	6.6	2.7	1.17	12.35	3.67	58.4	6.4	45.9	2.9	7.6
8.3	0.17	1.0	0.06	4.0	56.7	0.73	6.87	2.53	57.9	2.4	32.5	19.5	8.8
5.1	1.42	na	0.03	5.3	4.6	0.96	10.25	3.67	61.7	2.0	25.7	20.5	6.5
10.0	na	na	na	10.0	0.4	6.55	7.05	6.31	14.6	4.0	na	100.0	5.8
1.5	4.05	na	0.32	3.6	0.5	0.57	6.24	3.86	72.0	1.7	20.7	21.2	5.0
8.3	0.01	na	0.08	7.6	6.4	1.92	17.40	3.55	74.5	1.9	22.1	15.7	6.4
7.8	1.07	na	0.05	4.4	1.8	0.97	7.03	3.67	78.2	5.0	48.1	12.3	7.5
5.5	1.44	na	0.00	4.3	4.7	0.97	10.07	3.16	69.1	4.1	22.7	9.2	6.5
8.5	0.88	na	0.15	6.5	1.4	1.23	4.69	3.74	60.9	5.1	55.2	13.4	8.2
4.9	12.33	na	4.68	0.0	-2.6	-1.69	-17.79	2.32	109.3	3.3	52.4	11.6	4.3
9.3	0.00	0.0	0.00	2.1	0.1	0.45	1.83	3.16	92.8	3.2	38.9	18.6	6.2
8.5	0.92	na	-0.11	2.6	0.2	0.37	2.36	2.68	85.9	5.8	50.7	7.3	6.4
7.3	0.82	7.7	0.00	1.6	0.0	-0.01	-0.06	2.70	96.9	2.0	43.1	42.8	6.7
5.6	1.25	na	0.16	7.3	3.3	1.73	16.27	4.81	64.7	5.8	32.6	1.2	7.2
8.4	0.00	na	0.00	8.3	1.2	2.05	16.35	3.95	48.1	3.4	15.5	12.1	9.1
9.3	0.60	na	-0.02	2.5	0.3	0.26	1.81	2.41	85.4	2.5	38.0	25.3	7.6
4.9	2.38	10.9	0.02	4.2	5.7	0.78	7.21	4.26	73.7	5.6	37.5	8.3	8.4
3.1	4.63	na	0.02	4.6	3.7	0.89	8.34	3.68	68.8	5.9	41.2	4.1	7.3
7.4	0.33	na	0.20	8.0	2.0	1.93	11.45	4.10	51.2	0.6	16.2	45.1	7.3
8.0	0.56	3.9	0.05	4.8	17.7	1.15	13.56	3.46	69.0	4.5	31.0	13.0	7.8
8.3	0.02	0.2	0.01	5.2	5.5	1.10	9.48	2.94	51.1	1.3	8.1	23.2	7.6
5.1	0.37	2.5	0.09	9.8	10.8	2.02	22.24	3.77	43.3	3.9	20.4	8.3	7.7
4.9	2.36	na	0.01	4.0	2.0	0.79	9.16	3.31	69.7	4.5	21.8	6.1	4.5
4.7	1.20	9.2	0.06	4.6	9.6	1.00	12.64	2.88	61.9	2.8	12.1	12.2	6.6
8.2	2.18	na	-0.01	4.3	1.2	0.95	6.88	3.04	67.8	6.2	50.2	5.6	7.1
5.4	1.67	9.6	0.05	3.1	1.0	0.40	2.63	3.55	83.3	4.3	16.2	7.0	7.0
8.2	0.49	2.0	0.00	2.9	0.8	0.56	5.16	2.92	84.3	4.6	28.8	7.6	5.2
5.8	0.15	na	1.06	10.0	92.0	3.65	19.69	6.04	30.6	0.0	0.0	99.5	10.0
7.4	0.04	0.1	0.00	5.5	14.8	1.15	10.13	3.38	49.7	0.8	13.4	26.1	9.1
7.2	0.70	4.1	-0.19	5.7	48.2	1.10	9.34	3.14	61.3	4.8	14.8	3.6	9.8
7.3	1.23	na	0.11	4.7	1.0	1.06	8.88	3.42	68.8	3.3	46.0	20.0	7.4
6.7	2.84	na	-0.06	4.2	0.8	0.84	5.29	3.42	67.8	2.7	42.5	27.2	7.7
5.4	3.13	na	-0.36	3.5	0.4	0.62	3.96	2.99	77.2	4.4	38.6	12.7	8.0
6.1	1.00	na	0.46	9.3	5.5	1.86	19.68	4.47	48.6	6.0	38.9	3.2	5.9
8.1	0.19	na	-0.18	6.5	3.8	1.52	12.53	3.71	57.8	3.6	21.3	11.6	7.6
9.6	2.20	na	-0.18	4.3	6.1	2.23	17.92	2.62	83.0	3.2	86.7	64.2	8.6
8.1	0.57	na	0.00	6.7	1.3	1.62	19.72	3.98	61.2	4.1	31.2	11.4	6.1
3.6	0.94	6.4	0.08	3.5	3.1	0.60	6.86	3.38	70.1	3.0	11.0	13.7	5.8
10.0	na	0.0	na	6.4	0.5	1.00	1.01	1.34	0.0	4.0	na	100.0	5.7
6.3	1.68	5.1	0.57	4.1	11693.0	0.57	6.23	2.21	59.7	6.9	61.6	3.0	8.4
9.7	0.32	na	-0.27	4.8	0.7	1.16	12.17	2.58	61.8	5.1	73.5	14.9	5.7
6.3	0.38	na	-0.11	3.4	4.4	0.81	7.80	3.10	77.1	5.0	34.2	7.8	6.4
7.8	0.20	na	0.44	3.3	0.2	0.52	5.15	3.14	78.0	2.0	32.4	27.6	4.7
8.2	0.01	na	0.10	2.6	0.3	0.41	3.45	3.27	85.7	6.8	60.6	5.0	5.6
9.2	0.00	na	0.01	5.4	1.6	1.32	13.95	3.34	60.2	4.2	10.9	7.1	6.4
3.7	6.62	na	-0.02	3.9	0.3	0.56	4.05	3.13	75.5	3.2	49.2	21.8	7.8

Name	City	State	2019 Rating	2018 Rating	2018 Rating	Total Assets ($Mil)	One Year Asset Growth	Commercial Loans	Consumer Loans	Mortgage Loans	Securities	Capitalization Index	Leverage Ratio	Risk-Based Capital Ratio
KansasLand Bank	Quinter	KS	D+	C-	C+	53.9	2.31	5.9	1.8	9.1	19.7	6.9	8.9	16.3
Kanza Bank	Kingman	KS	C+	B-	B-	264.2	19.51	10.7	0.7	20.3	14.2	6.7	8.7	0.0
Karnes County National Bank	Karnes City	TX	B	B	C	394.4	-3.28	3.2	0.7	3.4	65.3	10.0	11.5	36.6
Katahdin Trust Co.	Patten	ME	B-	B-	B-	938.7	11.09	21.6	0.7	17.6	10.6	6.9	9.0	14.5
Kaw Valley Bank	Topeka	KS	C+	B-	C+	341.8	8.19	18.2	2.2	18.0	4.4	8.5	11.2	0.0
Kaw Valley State Bank	Eudora	KS	B-	B-	C	57.1	12.25	5.6	5.2	19.8	46.3	7.1	9.0	21.1
Kaw Valley State Bank and Trust Co.	Wamego	KS	A-	A-	A	206.1	11.88	10.0	1.8	14.1	33.5	10.0	11.2	0.0
Kearney Trust Co.	Kearney	MO	B+	A-	A-	237.6	20.01	8.4	2.8	13.5	23.7	7.4	9.3	15.6
Kearny Bank	Fairfield	NJ	B-	B-	B-	7286.6	10.05	3.2	0.1	19.1	21.0	10.0	11.8	20.2
Kearny County Bank	Lakin	KS	A	A-	B+	229.8	13.13	20.5	1.9	10.7	23.6	10.0	15.9	0.0
KEB Hana Bank USA, N.A.	New York	NY	D	D	D	218.2	-8.06	9.7	0.0	1.5	14.7	10.0	15.2	25.6
Kendall Bank	Valley Falls	KS	D+	C-	C	52.0	44.12	19.5	1.6	9.1	0.0	10.0	19.8	33.5
▲ Kennebec Federal S&L Assn. of Waterville	Waterville	ME	C	C	C-	92.5	-5.93	0.0	0.1	76.6	3.0	7.6	9.4	17.1
Kennebec Savings Bank	Augusta	ME	B+	A-	B+	1252.1	11.52	7.3	0.3	54.8	7.1	10.0	13.0	0.0
Kennebunk Savings Bank	Kennebunk	ME	B-	B	B	1548.6	17.55	8.8	0.1	22.2	8.0	8.5	10.6	0.0
Kennett Trust Bank	Kennett	MO	B-	B	C+	102.6	-4.39	11.4	3.5	33.9	26.2	10.0	12.2	0.0
▲ Kensington Bank	Kensington	MN	C	C-	C+	307.3	12.53	16.3	1.5	7.3	7.8	5.2	8.4	11.1
Kentland Bank	Kentland	IN	A	A	A-	323.1	5.56	12.5	1.4	6.9	28.5	10.0	14.0	19.5
Kentland Federal S&L Assn.	Kentland	IN	D	D	D	3.7	-10.57	0.7	0.0	92.3	1.5	10.0	14.2	0.0
▼ Kentucky Bank	Paris	KY	B	B+	B+	1196.6	10.84	8.1	1.9	20.2	24.4	6.7	8.8	0.0
Kentucky Farmers Bank Corp.	Ashland	KY	A	A	A	228.1	21.78	9.5	4.2	25.6	35.0	10.0	20.3	31.9
Kerndt Brothers Savings Bank	Lansing	IA	C+	B-	C+	316.2	10.03	11.3	0.9	7.9	22.1	8.0	10.1	0.0
Key Community Bank	Inver Grove Heights	MN	C+	C+	C+	66.5	29.55	23.1	2.2	6.2	0.0	7.2	9.2	0.0
Key National Trust Co. of Delaware	Wilmington	DE	U	U	U	5.1	9.19	0.0	0.0	0.0	0.0	10.0	99.6	466.5
KeyBank N.A.	Cleveland	OH	B	B	B	168973.7	16.39	26.3	6.6	7.6	21.7	6.6	8.7	13.0
KeySavings Bank	Wisconsin Rapids	WI	C-	C-	C-	89.4	15.72	0.7	1.2	43.0	30.3	10.0	12.7	29.3
▼ Keystone Bank, N.A.	Austin	TX	D+	C	C	338.6	89.46	27.7	0.6	17.5	6.8	8.5	10.0	15.8
Keystone Savings Bank	Keystone	IA	B	B-	B	177.8	20.60	8.3	1.5	14.4	24.2	7.9	9.6	13.5
▼ Killbuck Savings Bank Co.	Killbuck	OH	B+	A-	A-	640.5	14.86	10.5	0.9	17.5	28.6	8.3	9.8	15.5
Kindred State Bank	Kindred	ND	C	C	D+	32.3	13.51	8.6	8.2	4.0	1.9	7.0	9.0	17.1
Kingston National Bank	Kingston	OH	B-	B	B	409.1	8.78	11.4	2.6	20.0	20.0	6.1	8.1	11.9
Kingstree Federal S&L Assn.	Kingstree	SC	C+	C+	C+	39.0	15.62	0.6	0.3	37.8	18.0	10.0	14.8	0.0
Kinmundy Bank	Kinmundy	IL	B+	B	B-	53.1	9.37	8.3	15.9	26.5	16.4	10.0	11.2	19.2
Kirkpatrick Bank	Edmond	OK	A-	B+	B-	894.5	12.10	12.0	1.1	6.4	21.0	9.6	10.7	16.1
Kirkwood Bank and Trust Co.	Bismarck	ND	B	B	B-	293.3	16.36	14.8	3.1	10.8	12.1	5.4	9.3	0.0
Kish Bank	Belleville	PA	B-	C+	C+	1045.8	16.16	15.2	0.6	23.0	13.2	5.9	7.9	12.0
Kitsap Bank	Port Orchard	WA	A-	A-	B	1475.3	23.84	13.8	0.3	6.6	29.9	7.2	9.1	16.1
Kleberg Bank, N.A.	Kingsville	TX	B-	B-	C	654.7	16.19	13.9	11.0	11.4	21.8	6.5	8.5	15.3
▲ KodaBank	Drayton	ND	B+	B	C+	301.9	102.74	12.6	4.6	6.9	12.0	10.0	13.0	0.0
Kress National Bank	Kress	TX	B	B	B-	36.2	-6.48	13.8	3.3	0.6	19.8	10.0	13.9	23.0
KS Bank, Inc.	Smithfield	NC	B	B-	B-	478.1	18.34	9.4	0.3	19.1	13.3	6.9	8.9	14.6
▲ KS StateBank	Manhattan	KS	A-	A-	A-	2235.1	6.55	14.2	0.3	17.9	16.5	8.5	10.0	0.0
La Monte Community Bank	La Monte	MO	B+	B+	B+	38.1	18.68	2.1	1.9	12.3	26.6	8.0	9.7	0.0
Labette Bank	Altamont	KS	B+	B+	B+	443.2	11.76	4.5	2.2	21.9	24.1	8.8	10.2	0.0
Ladysmith Federal S&L Assn.	Ladysmith	WI	C+	B-	C	69.3	30.18	15.6	5.6	42.9	15.0	7.1	9.1	18.2
▲ Lafayette State Bank	Mayo	FL	D	E+	E-	143.9	36.41	14.0	2.2	13.0	9.3	5.1	7.1	12.9
Lake Area Bank	Lindstrom	MN	B	B	B	430.4	19.37	11.5	0.1	22.3	20.6	5.5	10.4	11.4
Lake Bank	Two Harbors	MN	B+	B	C	150.2	12.43	8.2	1.4	31.1	12.0	5.9	7.9	13.7
Lake Central Bank	Annandale	MN	A	A	A-	192.5	21.89	11.9	0.5	12.2	33.6	10.0	11.9	16.5
Lake City Bank	Warsaw	IN	A-	A-	A-	5543.1	12.28	33.2	1.9	3.3	11.6	9.8	11.0	14.8
Lake City Federal Bank	Lake City	MN	B-	B	C	76.1	9.87	1.6	2.7	46.0	14.2	10.0	12.4	0.0
Lake Community Bank	Long Lake	MN	B+	B+	B	142.8	19.02	11.4	0.5	6.3	12.6	10.0	11.4	16.9
▼ Lake Country Community Bank	Morristown	MN	D+	C	C-	30.6	12.42	9.7	1.2	11.4	41.9	6.9	8.9	26.1
▼ Lake Elmo Bank	Lake Elmo	MN	B+	A-	B	454.1	20.64	12.1	1.9	23.9	11.2	6.9	8.9	17.2
▼ Lake Forest Bank & Trust Co., N.A.	Lake Forest	IL	B	B+	B+	5427.4	26.32	47.8	6.6	1.9	7.0	6.5	8.5	12.2
Lake Region Bank	New London	MN	B-	B-	B-	132.6	16.35	17.7	3.3	7.8	34.3	7.7	9.5	20.6
Lake Shore Savings Bank	Dunkirk	NY	B-	B	B	682.8	14.39	5.1	0.2	23.7	12.0	10.0	11.7	0.0
Lake-Osceola State Bank	Baldwin	MI	C+	C+	C+	347.4	23.98	10.2	16.0	15.1	7.4	6.4	8.4	14.9
Lakeland Bank	Oak Ridge	NJ	B+	B+	B+	7512.6	15.80	9.8	0.1	8.2	11.8	6.8	9.1	12.3
Lakeside Bank	Chicago	IL	A-	A-	A-	2084.3	17.37	9.0	0.0	6.7	1.4	8.8	10.2	14.0

Arrows denote recent upgrades ▲ or downgrades ▼

Asset Quality Index	Adjusted Non-Performing Loans as a % of Total Loans	as a % of Capital	Net Charge-Offs Avg Loans	Profitability Index	Net Income ($Mil)	Return on Assets (R.O.A.)	Return on Equity (R.O.E.)	Net Interest Spread	Overhead Efficiency Ratio	Liquidity Index	Liquidity Ratio	Hot Money Ratio	Stability Index
0.3	21.64	82.7	0.05	0.3	-0.1	-0.29	-2.88	3.04	104.8	1.3	28.8	34.6	3.5
8.6	0.21	na	-0.02	3.6	1.2	0.66	6.62	3.74	74.5	3.1	19.9	14.2	5.9
6.9	9.55	na	-0.14	3.5	1.9	0.60	5.09	2.34	74.0	6.7	66.4	6.4	5.7
5.3	0.66	4.5	0.02	4.7	6.8	0.98	10.29	3.47	64.3	0.5	5.1	12.5	6.7
3.6	2.49	na	0.74	4.8	2.3	0.98	8.71	4.18	60.4	1.6	17.4	22.9	7.5
6.0	1.16	na	0.03	5.2	0.5	1.19	11.09	3.66	69.6	5.3	36.5	6.4	5.7
5.5	1.96	na	-0.06	6.1	2.1	1.36	11.38	3.17	58.3	5.3	41.3	8.7	8.3
8.8	0.05	na	0.57	5.4	2.1	1.22	12.33	3.53	55.2	5.1	39.7	9.2	6.5
5.4	1.06	4.4	0.00	3.6	34.5	0.67	4.61	2.63	63.2	1.8	16.8	19.7	8.9
5.7	1.75	na	0.00	8.8	3.6	2.09	12.60	4.01	54.6	3.4	22.0	11.8	9.7
7.3	0.91	na	-0.07	0.0	-3.3	-1.89	-12.17	2.91	165.8	5.1	37.7	8.1	5.8
8.1	0.04	0.1	0.00	0.8	0.0	-0.02	-0.15	4.23	101.0	5.0	36.6	8.6	4.1
7.2	0.31	na	0.09	2.7	0.3	0.37	4.07	3.31	87.0	1.6	10.7	20.8	4.5
8.6	0.47	na	0.11	4.8	7.2	0.80	6.25	3.33	60.4	3.5	13.8	5.3	10.0
8.3	0.49	na	-0.02	3.3	5.0	0.48	4.49	3.64	70.9	5.3	18.1	1.2	8.1
8.6	0.53	na	0.06	3.6	0.7	0.85	6.82	3.54	83.2	1.1	27.3	25.8	6.5
3.0	1.59	na	0.00	3.0	1.1	0.48	4.67	3.65	82.8	3.8	17.6	10.2	5.4
8.7	0.28	na	0.01	6.1	2.7	1.16	7.84	4.15	63.3	3.1	36.2	18.0	9.0
6.6	1.57	na	0.00	0.6	0.0	-0.40	-2.90	3.97	110.2	1.1	7.0	28.1	6.1
6.6	0.69	4.4	0.04	4.1	7.9	0.87	8.83	3.30	74.1	2.0	16.5	12.1	8.6
7.3	0.32	na	0.09	8.5	3.1	1.92	9.02	4.72	61.9	4.7	45.7	12.8	8.9
3.3	1.11	na	0.13	4.2	2.1	0.91	7.64	3.59	71.4	3.6	33.6	14.9	6.9
7.2	2.54	na	0.00	3.8	0.3	0.74	7.75	3.63	77.2	5.9	40.1	3.8	4.5
10.0	na	0.0	na	10.0	0.3	8.91	9.14	6.25	48.9	4.0	na	0.0	6.3
5.2	0.99	5.4	0.39	4.4	877.6	0.73	6.69	2.83	56.6	5.7	26.2	2.3	9.6
9.5	0.43	na	0.00	1.1	0.0	0.06	0.45	2.43	104.1	5.0	48.7	11.7	6.3
7.5	0.25	na	-0.01	1.2	0.4	0.19	1.41	3.41	86.0	1.5	18.4	25.2	6.6
7.3	0.80	na	-0.09	4.3	1.1	0.96	8.71	3.89	70.5	4.4	44.1	13.9	5.5
8.9	0.19	na	0.00	5.1	4.7	1.05	9.88	3.21	63.5	4.8	35.4	9.5	7.6
5.3	0.19	na	0.06	4.1	0.2	0.93	10.77	3.63	72.8	6.2	45.7	3.2	3.4
8.6	0.15	na	0.01	3.8	2.0	0.68	8.14	3.17	73.7	1.5	15.9	24.7	5.4
4.9	4.31	na	0.00	2.4	0.1	0.21	1.31	2.36	87.4	1.7	36.4	39.3	6.9
5.6	0.02	na	0.16	10.0	0.8	1.98	14.62	4.61	47.2	4.2	25.8	9.3	8.8
7.3	0.00	na	0.27	6.3	10.1	1.56	14.13	3.55	54.2	3.2	11.5	11.0	7.9
8.4	0.26	na	0.00	4.8	1.9	0.94	9.87	3.18	69.0	4.0	19.7	9.5	5.7
8.6	0.17	na	0.00	3.9	6.2	0.82	10.15	3.39	70.3	2.6	8.3	15.7	7.0
8.3	0.03	0.1	0.00	5.7	16.0	1.64	14.64	4.09	69.6	6.9	41.4	1.4	9.3
4.7	0.61	na	0.29	4.1	4.0	0.89	7.55	3.73	74.2	4.1	29.1	10.2	7.5
5.5	2.07	na	0.05	9.1	4.3	1.91	15.71	4.00	53.3	2.0	13.3	18.2	8.4
8.6	0.41	na	0.04	3.7	0.2	0.73	5.52	3.72	78.9	2.5	41.1	28.1	6.1
6.5	0.90	na	-0.01	5.3	3.4	1.01	10.86	3.61	66.6	1.9	17.1	16.6	5.7
7.3	0.55	3.9	0.04	8.5	39.3	2.36	24.55	3.16	42.7	0.9	18.4	33.3	9.5
8.8	0.00	na	-0.01	3.2	0.1	0.48	4.63	3.22	80.0	3.9	30.0	12.0	5.5
6.9	0.80	na	0.01	4.8	2.7	0.84	7.25	3.57	70.0	2.9	19.0	15.0	6.9
5.7	1.69	na	0.08	3.4	0.3	0.61	6.09	3.47	70.5	1.7	27.8	27.1	3.6
2.0	3.91	24.2	0.52	4.9	1.2	1.22	16.22	4.58	76.3	5.2	29.6	4.2	0.7
4.8	2.06	na	0.25	8.6	10.4	3.55	31.65	4.49	61.2	2.5	22.8	14.9	7.4
8.3	0.07	na	na	3.5	0.2	0.00	0.00	na	54.1	1.6	16.9	21.5	5.8
8.2	0.00	1.0	0.00	9.7	3.4	2.68	19.30	4.52	51.6	6.0	39.1	2.7	8.4
7.3	0.42	2.4	0.11	8.4	60.6	1.53	13.27	3.18	42.5	1.7	7.5	20.3	10.0
7.2	1.16	na	0.01	3.2	0.2	0.40	3.10	3.32	84.4	3.4	29.4	14.5	7.2
7.6	0.05	na	0.36	6.5	1.2	1.26	10.50	3.69	57.8	4.2	30.5	10.6	7.4
7.5	0.00	na	0.58	1.6	0.0	0.14	1.38	2.84	104.8	5.5	62.7	11.3	4.3
6.7	0.93	4.1	-0.07	6.0	4.3	1.38	14.20	3.60	62.4	4.8	25.8	5.2	6.5
6.0	0.75	4.9	0.12	9.2	62.7	1.63	18.01	2.89	45.2	3.1	17.4	5.1	7.7
4.4	1.84	na	0.02	4.8	1.1	1.15	11.70	3.74	75.2	7.1	57.7	2.2	5.6
7.3	0.75	na	0.01	3.7	3.5	0.71	5.77	3.22	68.7	2.9	22.9	15.2	8.2
3.9	1.33	7.2	0.05	4.9	2.2	0.94	10.81	3.64	65.5	4.2	31.4	9.6	4.6
5.1	0.64	4.5	0.02	4.5	43.2	0.82	7.04	3.18	53.9	2.3	9.9	12.9	9.4
6.2	0.89	4.6	0.03	5.6	21.4	1.41	13.70	3.46	49.9	1.3	17.2	16.0	10.0

Name	City	State	2019 Rating	2018 Rating	Total Assets ($Mil)	One Year Asset Growth	Asset Mix (As a % of Total Assets)				Capital-ization Index	Lever-age Ratio	Risk-Based Capital Ratio
			Rating				Comm-ercial Loans	Cons-umer Loans	Mort-gage Loans	Secur-ities			
▼ Lakeside Bank	Lake Charles	LA	C+	B-	B-	260.9	23.76	14.4	1.8	13.3	4.3	8.8	10.2	19.1
Lakeside Bank	Rockwall	TX	C	C+	C+	147.6	76.01	22.4	0.8	4.3	0.0	10.0	18.6	56.2
Lakeside Bank of Salina	Salina	OK	B	B	B	46.4	19.14	11.6	24.1	21.8	10.5	9.8	10.9	0.0
▼ Lakeside State Bank	Oologah	OK	D+	C	C	73.2	10.93	4.3	8.7	15.4	27.1	6.7	8.7	0.0
Lakeview Bank	Lakeville	MN	B	B	B	139.3	34.99	32.2	0.2	20.9	5.3	6.2	8.2	16.4
Lamar Bank and Trust Co.	Lamar	MO	A-	A-	B+	189.6	16.49	11.7	2.7	16.1	6.7	8.5	10.9	0.0
Lamar National Bank	Paris	TX	B-	C+	C+	266.6	53.19	21.0	1.1	20.4	3.3	9.0	10.3	19.1
Lamesa National Bank	Lamesa	TX	C+	B-	B	371.2	6.84	3.3	0.2	0.0	54.4	7.5	9.3	21.6
Lamont Bank of St. John	Saint John	WA	B+	B+	B	55.8	9.64	6.5	12.6	0.3	28.7	10.0	14.0	0.0
Landmark Bank	Clinton	LA	C+	C+	C	158.9	14.85	10.0	2.2	24.8	25.6	7.2	9.1	0.0
Landmark Community Bank	Pittston	PA	D+	D+	D+	373.2	16.13	16.3	7.8	13.2	15.9	8.4	9.9	14.6
Landmark Community Bank	Collierville	TN	B	B	B	954.7	-1.46	8.2	0.9	43.5	12.4	8.6	10.1	15.5
Landmark National Bank	Manhattan	KS	B+	B	B+	1145.9	13.95	23.6	0.1	15.4	25.7	8.8	10.2	16.9
Laona State Bank	Laona	WI	C+	B-	B	233.1	13.37	7.4	3.4	25.0	30.1	9.2	10.5	0.0
LaSalle State Bank	La Salle	IL	C+	C+	C+	155.7	10.37	11.2	1.2	9.6	32.5	7.7	9.4	17.6
▼ Latimer State Bank	Wilburton	OK	B-	B	B-	69.4	0.23	8.0	3.2	5.0	12.9	10.0	20.1	60.6
Lauderdale County Bank	Halls	TN	B-	B-	C+	57.2	13.73	22.3	6.6	12.2	30.2	8.9	10.3	0.0
Laurens State Bank	Laurens	IA	B+	B+	B+	74.5	9.32	5.2	1.7	6.9	24.5	10.0	11.5	0.0
Lawrenceburg Federal Bank	Lawrenceburg	TN	B-	B	B	74.3	4.22	0.0	2.6	71.5	0.0	10.0	21.0	0.0
LCA Bank Corp.	Park City	UT	A-	A	A	217.8	33.72	33.6	0.0	0.0	0.5	7.3	16.9	0.0
LCNB National Bank	Lebanon	OH	B+	B	B	1722.8	4.94	7.2	2.1	17.5	10.8	7.3	10.1	12.7
Lea County State Bank	Hobbs	NM	A-	A-	B	463.7	34.15	22.1	2.9	1.2	60.7	8.4	9.9	22.1
▼ Lead Bank	Garden City	MO	C-	C	C+	493.4	38.30	11.9	34.6	10.5	2.4	5.6	7.6	14.4
Leader Bank, N.A.	Arlington	MA	A	A	A	1999.6	29.39	7.3	0.0	42.5	4.0	10.0	11.6	17.4
Leaders Bank	Oak Brook	IL	C+	C+	C-	361.7	7.77	20.7	0.9	6.2	6.4	10.0	11.7	18.3
Ledyard National Bank	Norwich	VT	B+	B+	B	651.8	29.21	12.5	2.0	19.5	33.8	6.3	8.3	16.0
Lee Bank	Lee	MA	C	C+	C	448.6	12.05	10.4	0.2	34.2	8.2	6.7	9.0	0.0
Lee Bank and Trust Co.	Pennington Gap	VA	A-	B+	B	161.1	11.55	27.2	3.4	20.5	8.4	10.0	16.0	24.2
Lee County Bank	Fort Madison	IA	A-	A-	A-	207.9	10.64	13.4	4.5	45.4	0.9	10.0	11.8	0.0
Legacy Bank	Wiley	CO	B+	B+	B+	425.9	15.78	13.2	0.5	6.4	18.9	10.0	13.7	16.6
Legacy Bank	Altoona	IA	C+	C	C-	139.3	23.87	23.1	1.8	21.8	7.5	4.6	6.6	13.1
Legacy Bank	Wichita	KS	C+	C+	C	542.6	16.62	14.1	0.4	17.2	9.2	8.4	10.0	0.0
Legacy Bank	Hinton	OK	B-	B-	B-	797.1	74.39	45.1	0.8	8.3	8.0	6.2	8.3	12.9
▲ Legacy Bank	Grundy	VA	C+	C	C-	321.0	5.96	6.4	4.2	7.6	31.7	10.0	22.2	40.2
Legacy Bank & Trust Co.	Rogersville	MO	B	B	B	525.0	84.30	23.5	1.0	17.7	0.2	5.9	8.3	11.7
Legacy Bank of Florida	Boca Raton	FL	B	B	C+	542.9	18.57	22.4	0.1	11.4	4.5	5.9	10.3	11.7
Legacy National Bank	Springdale	AR	C+	B-	C+	640.9	17.52	14.1	1.1	16.0	4.5	2.9	8.7	0.0
Legacy State Bank	Loganville	GA	C+	C-	D	132.2	19.38	15.6	0.2	7.3	11.5	7.9	9.6	14.6
Legacy Trust Co., N.A.	Houston	TX	U	U	U	30.4	-3.81	0.0	0.0	0.0	19.4	10.0	89.5	106.7
Legence Bank	Eldorado	IL	B	B	B	576.8	20.86	19.1	6.6	3.6	23.0	6.6	8.6	16.3
Legend Bank, N.A.	Bowie	TX	B+	B+	B	853.7	11.54	13.5	0.7	12.1	19.7	7.9	9.6	15.1
Legends Bank	Linn	MO	A	A-	B+	443.4	15.13	6.3	7.3	18.6	17.5	10.0	13.9	0.0
Legends Bank	Clarksville	TN	B+	B+	B	567.9	12.19	15.8	2.0	10.0	16.0	7.5	9.3	13.5
▼ Leighton State Bank	Pella	IA	B+	A-	B+	207.7	10.25	12.7	1.0	16.7	13.2	9.2	10.4	15.2
Lemont National Bank	Lemont	IL	D+	D+	D+	57.8	11.33	0.0	0.0	8.5	42.3	4.1	6.1	27.6
Lena State Bank	Lena	IL	B+	B+	B	94.2	4.77	11.3	0.5	3.0	35.5	10.0	11.5	0.0
▼ Level One Bank	Farmington Hills	MI	B-	B	B	2443.8	62.26	31.0	0.1	12.6	10.4	5.8	7.8	12.5
Lewis & Clark Bank	Oregon City	OR	B+	B+	B-	327.4	22.45	25.9	0.0	6.0	0.0	10.0	12.9	20.4
Lewisburg Banking Co.	Lewisburg	KY	B+	B+	B	150.4	11.75	7.8	4.8	26.8	20.9	7.7	9.5	0.0
Lexicon Bank	Las Vegas	NV	D-			252.7	969.42	48.9	0.0	1.7	5.1	9.8	12.6	0.0
Liberty Bank	Geraldine	AL	B	B	B	158.0	6.78	5.9	5.7	17.8	25.1	10.0	11.3	19.2
▼ Liberty Bank	South San Francisco	CA	C+	B	B-	300.0	10.64	6.5	0.1	1.2	12.9	7.9	11.8	0.0
Liberty Bank	Middletown	CT	B+	A-	B	6822.0	28.85	14.7	0.2	14.8	13.7	9.5	11.6	14.6
Liberty Bank	Liberty	IL	B+	B+	B-	114.9	13.46	7.8	5.4	16.3	13.3	10.0	12.0	19.4
Liberty Bank	Ironton	OH	C+	B-	B-	56.0	7.39	3.0	4.0	42.0	8.6	10.0	15.9	31.1
Liberty Bank	Poulsbo	WA	C	C-	C	176.3	50.28	27.0	2.2	13.7	5.0	6.1	8.1	15.2
Liberty Bank and Trust Co.	New Orleans	LA	B-	B-	C+	756.8	20.54	10.4	3.2	22.2	19.3	6.0	8.0	14.2
Liberty Bank for Savings	Chicago	IL	C+	C+	C+	868.5	5.19	0.0	0.0	46.7	39.4	10.0	23.1	58.6
Liberty Bank Minnesota	Saint Cloud	MN	A-	A	A	268.8	21.06	0.1	2.3	32.2	23.0	10.0	11.7	24.3
Liberty Bank, Inc.	Salt Lake City	UT	E+	E+	E+	10.9	22.83	1.5	37.0	13.2	7.5	3.5	5.5	12.0

Asset Quality Index	Adjusted Non-Performing Loans as a % of Total Loans	as a % of Capital	Net Charge-Offs Avg Loans	Profitability Index	Net Income ($Mil)	Return on Assets (R.O.A.)	Return on Equity (R.O.E.)	Net Interest Spread	Overhead Efficiency Ratio	Liquidity Index	Liquidity Ratio	Hot Money Ratio	Stability Index
8.6	0.22	na	0.02	3.1	0.8	0.48	4.31	3.47	76.5	2.4	35.0	24.4	6.7
8.5	0.04	na	0.00	0.8	-0.1	-0.11	-0.54	2.83	95.8	6.8	57.6	3.9	5.0
3.2	2.83	na	0.12	8.0	0.5	1.45	12.38	5.39	56.9	1.4	13.1	25.8	6.5
5.1	5.03	na	0.26	1.5	0.0	-0.04	-0.44	3.45	97.1	4.5	33.4	10.5	3.6
5.4	0.52	4.6	0.11	9.0	1.6	1.71	19.90	5.11	54.1	3.3	22.8	10.9	5.6
6.4	0.55	na	0.02	7.1	2.1	1.59	14.65	3.97	57.4	4.2	19.4	7.8	8.2
3.7	2.82	16.0	0.03	4.4	2.2	1.22	13.14	4.00	69.0	4.6	32.4	9.4	5.7
7.3	2.89	na	-1.34	2.9	1.5	0.50	5.30	1.38	61.1	3.7	60.0	23.7	4.5
7.6	1.11	na	2.58	5.3	0.4	1.03	7.40	4.37	34.8	5.9	30.4	0.0	7.1
4.1	1.95	na	0.03	3.7	0.8	0.72	7.38	4.13	80.1	2.5	30.7	16.8	4.9
7.2	0.32	na	0.05	1.9	0.8	0.31	3.13	3.18	87.2	3.7	12.0	10.2	4.6
5.9	0.86	5.9	0.05	4.9	7.4	1.06	10.81	3.03	54.8	0.8	14.9	26.3	6.5
5.7	1.40	5.4	0.14	7.6	14.4	1.80	14.46	3.78	58.6	4.0	3.5	7.4	9.4
3.2	4.24	na	0.05	4.1	1.4	0.82	7.37	2.85	54.2	4.6	46.8	13.9	6.6
7.5	0.78	na	-0.03	3.9	1.0	0.94	9.19	3.01	72.3	3.7	18.2	11.0	5.3
7.3	3.99	5.7	0.04	3.3	0.4	0.64	3.20	2.06	68.1	3.5	89.9	35.2	7.2
6.6	1.11	na	0.06	3.3	0.2	0.44	4.02	3.79	81.5	2.5	43.0	28.9	5.0
9.2	0.00	na	0.02	4.7	0.6	1.05	8.74	2.81	62.2	5.6	61.8	10.6	7.2
5.9	0.95	na	0.00	3.5	0.3	0.52	2.50	3.11	79.5	0.9	21.4	37.6	7.6
7.3	0.41	na	1.18	6.9	1.4	0.94	7.37	6.83	48.4	0.3	12.3	0.0	8.0
5.7	0.58	na	0.02	5.5	14.3	1.13	8.28	3.68	64.4	3.8	4.9	8.9	10.0
8.9	0.04	0.3	0.13	5.4	5.5	1.74	16.28	3.02	65.0	5.9	49.7	7.0	6.8
1.3	1.08	na	0.07	6.1	3.3	1.02	13.08	19.41	92.2	0.6	7.4	6.9	4.5
8.4	0.26	1.6	0.24	9.9	52.8	3.84	35.14	2.72	31.1	3.4	12.0	11.2	10.0
7.1	1.44	na	0.01	2.0	0.6	0.20	1.64	2.56	89.1	0.9	23.0	44.5	7.1
7.0	0.53	2.5	0.05	4.6	5.1	1.16	12.36	3.16	69.1	1.5	5.1	7.8	6.6
5.4	1.26	na	0.05	3.4	1.8	0.57	6.76	3.35	77.4	4.6	18.9	5.5	4.5
6.6	0.37	5.9	0.09	5.1	1.2	1.03	6.73	4.04	68.0	1.8	18.2	20.7	7.1
8.5	0.11	na	0.29	6.7	2.3	1.52	13.10	4.01	48.1	4.8	8.9	2.6	8.4
4.1	3.59	na	-0.02	8.4	5.6	1.87	12.17	4.10	45.9	1.7	22.6	22.0	9.5
3.6	3.20	na	0.01	5.0	1.2	1.21	17.25	3.89	74.5	5.1	28.7	4.1	3.7
3.4	2.36	na	0.00	5.3	3.9	1.02	9.55	3.76	60.0	2.7	19.0	14.6	6.9
3.3	2.68	33.8	-0.06	4.8	3.0	0.62	9.68	4.58	71.6	4.5	7.8	4.2	4.5
5.9	2.87	6.2	-0.02	4.4	2.6	1.12	4.90	2.80	60.9	3.8	51.0	18.7	6.4
8.0	0.10	na	0.02	9.4	7.5	2.45	28.96	4.28	40.6	0.7	10.7	34.6	5.9
6.7	0.35	na	0.00	5.1	4.1	1.07	10.12	3.38	57.7	1.1	6.1	27.6	6.4
4.3	1.10	na	0.02	5.8	4.8	1.06	11.73	3.65	58.8	1.9	4.7	15.5	6.2
7.4	0.00	na	0.00	3.8	0.8	0.91	9.17	3.57	71.1	1.7	16.6	21.2	4.7
10.0	na	na	na	9.5	2.3	9.85	10.96	1.22	76.1	4.0	na	0.0	6.7
4.7	2.22	na	0.06	6.3	6.3	1.58	14.32	5.05	65.6	4.2	23.2	8.4	8.1
5.8	0.60	na	0.08	6.5	9.5	1.55	13.57	4.43	64.1	3.0	19.5	14.3	8.4
7.8	0.19	na	0.05	8.9	5.2	1.65	11.62	4.05	46.4	2.7	12.9	15.4	8.6
6.9	0.10	1.5	0.01	5.4	4.3	1.07	10.99	3.98	65.6	2.4	12.4	8.1	7.0
6.1	0.10	na	0.10	4.1	1.0	0.66	5.33	3.64	66.2	2.9	25.5	15.6	8.4
10.0	0.00	0.0	0.00	1.6	0.0	0.01	0.21	2.50	99.3	7.7	85.5	1.3	2.1
8.7	0.01	0.0	0.46	6.0	0.8	1.11	9.32	2.98	55.5	1.9	30.7	26.9	5.7
5.1	1.07	8.3	0.14	3.9	14.0	0.83	8.74	3.17	64.0	1.3	14.9	26.3	8.2
7.2	0.06	na	0.03	3.8	1.2	0.55	4.46	3.93	72.8	3.7	18.6	10.6	7.1
4.7	1.99	na	0.01	6.1	1.5	1.36	13.39	3.78	65.9	2.9	18.0	14.8	7.6
8.4	0.00	na	0.00	0.0	-1.2	-0.91	-8.69	1.79	140.5	4.7	39.9	11.2	0.8
7.3	0.00	na	0.44	4.6	1.1	0.94	7.97	4.76	72.2	2.9	36.9	19.6	6.6
6.4	1.18	na	0.00	3.2	1.0	0.46	3.78	3.47	81.3	4.0	26.5	10.4	7.2
8.2	0.47	2.3	0.13	3.4	17.9	0.38	2.97	2.49	73.0	5.0	30.3	10.0	9.7
5.4	0.90	na	0.00	6.8	1.1	1.35	11.07	3.59	50.9	3.9	33.5	13.6	7.0
6.1	1.84	na	0.00	2.4	0.1	0.20	1.23	3.62	94.0	4.5	31.6	9.8	7.1
7.1	0.00	na	-0.01	3.0	0.4	0.36	4.66	3.91	83.1	4.5	17.7	5.5	3.9
4.7	1.96	8.0	0.28	3.6	3.5	0.68	7.56	3.90	79.0	1.9	20.7	15.0	5.0
10.0	0.71	na	0.00	2.8	2.6	0.41	1.69	2.35	80.1	4.7	60.8	16.4	8.4
8.6	0.00	na	0.04	7.8	3.4	1.87	15.31	2.78	70.2	6.9	54.9	2.1	7.9
5.6	1.61	na	0.16	0.0	-0.8	-10.04	-133.51	2.48	244.2	1.5	44.9	62.2	2.2

Name	City	State	2019 Rating	2018 Rating	Total Assets ($Mil)	One Year Asset Growth	Comm- ercial Loans	Cons- umer Loans	Mort- gage Loans	Secur- ities	Capital- ization Index	Lever- age Ratio	Risk- Based Capital Ratio
Liberty Capital Bank	Addison	TX	A-	A-	B+	326.5	22.04	20.6	0.0	14.1	0.0	7.5	9.3	16.0
Liberty First Bank	Monroe	GA	B+	B+	B+	166.6	24.48	6.7	0.4	11.0	41.1	8.0	9.6	0.0
Liberty National Bank	Sioux City	IA	B+	B+	B	495.1	14.62	17.7	0.5	11.2	11.6	7.4	9.2	13.2
Liberty National Bank	Ada	OH	A-	B+	B	406.3	18.63	12.7	0.1	11.6	9.3	10.0	12.2	17.5
Liberty National Bank	Lawton	OK	A-	A-	A-	732.1	29.61	14.3	1.2	9.0	14.6	7.3	9.2	16.1
Liberty National Bank in Paris	Paris	TX	A-	A-	A-	332.9	12.73	7.6	6.3	27.5	28.9	10.0	15.3	0.0
Liberty Savings Assn., FSA	Fort Scott	KS	C	C	C+	31.4	-0.94	0.4	3.3	21.0	58.8	10.0	20.9	0.0
Liberty Savings Bank, F.S.B.	Wilmington	OH	B	B-	B-	800.8	12.87	0.1	1.9	61.1	22.1	7.7	9.5	20.2
Liberty State Bank	Powers Lake	ND	A-	A-	A-	102.5	7.64	3.5	2.2	7.3	48.6	10.0	11.8	0.0
Liberty Trust & Savings Bank	Durant	IA	A	A	A	156.3	6.04	7.9	2.2	8.4	30.9	10.0	20.5	0.0
Libertyville Bank & Trust Co., N.A.	Libertyville	IL	B	B	B	2044.2	21.35	32.7	10.1	3.4	9.5	5.8	8.2	11.6
Libertyville Savings Bank	Fairfield	IA	B	B-	C+	389.2	6.07	10.4	1.1	10.3	27.5	8.8	10.2	15.9
Lifestore Bank	West Jefferson	NC	B	B	B	352.1	15.46	6.8	0.6	23.8	21.8	9.7	10.8	18.5
▲ LimeBank	Bolivar	MO	C	C	C+	72.0	10.16	2.9	2.4	28.5	4.6	6.6	8.6	14.3
Limestone Bank, Inc.	Louisville	KY	B-	C	C-	1284.7	14.09	17.0	2.8	12.3	15.8	7.6	9.9	13.0
Lincoln 1st Bank	Lincoln Park	NJ	D-	D	D	311.1	1.40	3.4	0.1	38.4	22.2	4.8	6.9	13.6
Lincoln FSB of Nebraska	Lincoln	NE	B-	C+	C-	347.9	11.96	0.0	0.0	48.8	25.8	10.0	13.2	26.0
Lincoln National Bank	Hodgenville	KY	B+	A-	B+	348.3	11.10	5.6	4.8	39.3	8.1	10.0	12.3	22.8
Lincoln Savings Bank	Reinbeck	IA	B	B	B	1485.1	10.59	16.6	0.7	12.0	7.0	8.3	9.9	13.6
Lincoln State Bank	Hankinson	ND	B	B	C+	89.7	18.36	8.7	5.2	2.8	40.3	8.6	10.1	0.0
▼ LincolnWay Community Bank	New Lenox	IL	C-	C	C+	257.3	14.26	16.8	0.0	14.5	1.6	9.8	10.8	15.5
▼ Lindell Bank & Trust Co.	Saint Louis	MO	A-	A	A-	541.2	5.05	13.7	0.4	16.2	35.4	10.0	11.4	0.0
▲ LINKBANK	Camp Hill	PA	D-	E	E-	367.5	88.39	35.1	0.5	10.2	1.3	10.0	16.5	18.2
Lisle Savings Bank	Lisle	IL	B+	A-	B	577.3	14.14	0.5	0.0	39.5	41.3	10.0	22.6	0.0
Litchfield Bancorp	Litchfield	CT	C-	C+	C	290.0	14.54	11.3	1.4	33.7	9.3	5.8	7.8	12.7
Litchfield National Bank	Litchfield	IL	C+	C+	C+	123.6	15.15	4.7	5.3	17.5	19.2	6.0	8.0	0.0
Little Horn State Bank	Hardin	MT	C+	B-	B-	117.0	7.28	19.9	1.9	10.0	2.4	7.0	9.2	12.5
Live Oak Banking Co.	Wilmington	NC	B+	A-	A-	8059.8	76.03	41.8	0.0	0.6	9.5	5.6	7.6	13.2
Llano National Bank	Llano	TX	A-	A-	B	220.6	18.68	3.3	2.9	13.6	40.4	10.0	12.1	0.0
▲ LNB Community Bank	Lynnville	IN	B+	C+	C+	130.9	12.21	4.7	3.1	39.5	8.3	8.9	10.2	0.0
Logan Bank & Trust Co.	Logan	WV	B-	B-	B-	298.5	11.26	13.0	3.3	19.6	40.0	7.0	9.0	0.0
Logan County Bank	Scranton	AR	B+	B+	B+	87.5	6.75	3.1	7.9	21.0	56.5	10.0	20.2	47.1
Logan State Bank	Logan	IA	C-	C-	D+	72.0	8.19	11.5	3.3	10.9	0.9	5.1	7.1	12.2
▲ Logansport Savings Bank	Logansport	IN	A	A-	A-	223.5	20.12	15.3	0.7	14.7	22.5	10.0	11.4	17.1
Lone Star Bank	Houston	TX	B	B-	B-	153.3	13.36	9.0	0.1	19.3	0.0	9.5	10.6	16.0
Lone Star Capital Bank, N.A.	San Antonio	TX	C+	B-	B-	293.2	14.45	13.8	1.0	14.7	12.8	8.9	10.3	14.2
Lone Star National Bank	McAllen	TX	B+	B+	B+	2540.3	16.94	8.9	0.9	7.5	31.8	10.0	11.2	0.0
▲ Lone Star State Bank of West Texas	Lubbock	TX	B-	C+	C	1000.7	3.36	30.3	0.7	4.1	7.1	10.0	11.4	15.5
▲ Longview Bank	Ogden	IL	C+	C	C+	218.6	5.40	12.4	1.3	10.3	7.7	6.5	8.5	12.6
Longview Bank & Trust	Chrisman	IL	C+	C	C-	202.6	8.58	8.6	1.0	6.5	1.1	6.1	8.2	11.8
Lorraine State Bank	Lorraine	KS	C+	C+	C+	24.5	9.24	4.2	8.2	9.7	13.4	10.0	17.1	0.0
Lovelady State Bank	Lovelady	TX	B-	B-	C	47.8	8.34	8.6	10.2	12.8	12.8	10.0	11.0	0.0
Lowell Five Cent Savings Bank	Tewksbury	MA	B+	A-	B	1396.6	18.23	7.7	0.2	23.8	7.6	10.0	11.8	17.4
Lowry State Bank	Lowry	MN	B-	C+	C	57.4	4.78	14.5	4.9	23.1	0.1	6.2	8.2	12.8
Loyal Trust Bank	Johns Creek	GA	D			67.3	na	50.3	0.0	0.0	3.8	10.0	39.0	41.1
▲ Luana Savings Bank	Luana	IA	A-	B+	B+	1739.6	16.24	1.3	1.1	21.4	12.5	7.7	9.5	13.1
▼ Lumbee Guaranty Bank	Pembroke	NC	B-	B	B-	409.3	18.23	7.8	1.8	10.7	30.6	9.4	10.6	0.0
Lusitania Savings Bank	Newark	NJ	B+	B+	B+	355.0	7.92	0.0	0.3	37.3	23.8	10.0	14.9	37.4
Lusk State Bank	Lusk	WY	A-	A-	B+	61.4	16.75	4.7	3.0	0.3	13.7	10.0	12.8	15.2
Luther Burbank Savings	Santa Rosa	CA	B-	B	B+	7067.7	-1.27	0.0	0.0	26.0	8.9	9.0	10.4	20.3
Luzerne Bank	Luzerne	PA	C+	C+	C+	524.0	13.63	9.1	5.6	13.1	5.4	5.4	8.0	11.3
Lyndon State Bank	Lyndon	KS	C	C	C	81.3	9.77	4.8	3.1	34.4	9.7	8.0	9.7	15.4
Lyon County State Bank	Emporia	KS	B	B	B	162.8	14.87	8.6	1.9	19.4	45.5	6.8	8.8	23.8
▲ Lyons Federal Bank	Lyons	KS	B	B	B	136.7	16.50	4.4	3.3	17.0	4.5	10.0	12.5	0.0
Lyons National Bank	Lyons	NY	B	B	B	1383.0	20.00	15.7	2.2	25.3	15.3	5.5	7.5	12.5
Lytle State Bank of Lytle, Texas	Lytle	TX	B+	B+	B+	94.1	8.96	6.1	17.6	2.7	51.2	10.0	16.1	0.0
M C Bank & Trust Co.	Morgan City	LA	B	B-	B	334.3	8.15	15.8	1.5	10.0	21.6	10.0	22.0	0.0
M.Y. Safra Bank, FSB	New York	NY	D	D+	D	363.5	-15.83	0.0	6.9	24.7	25.1	10.0	11.6	23.8
M1 Bank	Macks Creek	MO	C+	B-	B-	430.1	51.78	45.5	0.0	1.9	0.0	1.7	8.2	0.0
MA Bank	Macon	MO	B	B	C+	310.4	11.61	9.3	2.2	6.5	28.1	8.5	10.0	0.0

Asset Quality Index	Adjusted Non-Performing Loans as a % of Total Loans	as a % of Capital	Net Charge-Offs Avg Loans	Profitability Index	Net Income ($Mil)	Return on Assets (R.O.A.)	Return on Equity (R.O.E.)	Net Interest Spread	Overhead Efficiency Ratio	Liquidity Index	Liquidity Ratio	Hot Money Ratio	Stability Index
8.5	0.00	na	0.00	6.4	3.3	1.45	15.62	3.48	53.5	5.0	27.4	4.4	6.9
8.6	0.94	na	0.00	4.5	1.3	1.12	10.96	3.48	68.6	4.4	53.5	16.3	6.2
7.8	0.05	na	0.00	8.3	6.0	1.67	14.63	4.25	48.4	2.4	9.6	16.2	8.0
7.8	0.40	na	-0.03	5.8	3.5	1.20	9.39	3.93	63.5	2.6	13.4	14.3	6.7
6.7	0.35	2.1	0.01	6.1	6.8	1.31	12.85	3.93	62.8	2.7	25.7	16.5	8.0
8.7	0.23	na	0.16	5.9	3.0	1.28	8.07	3.47	55.1	4.3	28.5	9.8	8.2
10.0	0.00	na	0.00	2.0	0.1	0.24	1.17	2.52	88.9	4.3	90.9	23.1	6.6
5.8	1.90	na	0.01	7.5	16.6	2.85	31.06	2.46	34.3	0.8	24.5	39.4	7.5
8.9	0.00	na	0.00	7.3	1.2	1.68	13.13	3.42	44.9	2.8	39.2	21.7	9.3
8.7	0.00	na	0.00	6.9	1.5	1.32	6.13	3.66	53.6	6.2	55.2	5.3	9.4
6.4	0.49	3.6	0.00	4.5	7.3	0.51	5.74	2.52	52.3	2.2	16.0	10.2	7.4
5.8	0.90	na	0.12	4.7	2.8	1.02	8.36	3.83	70.5	5.2	43.9	10.1	7.6
6.1	1.32	6.6	0.05	5.1	3.0	1.20	10.86	3.19	63.9	3.2	39.8	18.9	6.4
4.7	0.89	na	0.00	2.7	0.1	0.19	1.77	5.03	85.9	2.2	19.7	18.3	6.7
8.1	0.26	na	0.05	4.1	7.8	0.80	7.33	3.46	64.7	1.6	14.2	23.3	8.6
3.7	3.16	na	0.23	0.2	-0.3	-0.11	-1.52	2.01	116.0	0.6	13.2	24.3	1.8
8.7	0.56	na	0.00	5.8	3.8	1.54	10.87	2.71	62.0	2.0	30.9	25.5	7.5
8.6	0.29	na	0.00	4.9	2.1	0.84	6.45	3.78	66.0	3.0	25.4	15.1	8.0
4.3	2.00	12.2	0.33	4.8	9.3	0.89	7.88	3.74	69.1	1.7	17.2	16.3	9.0
7.6	0.33	na	-0.06	5.1	0.7	1.20	11.05	3.58	66.8	4.1	25.4	9.8	5.8
1.3	2.97	na	0.02	7.0	2.5	1.30	12.06	4.29	60.0	1.5	18.6	25.2	7.4
8.4	0.47	na	-0.18	6.3	5.5	1.33	7.23	3.45	64.4	4.8	27.1	5.6	9.2
8.0	0.02	0.5	0.00	0.0	-1.7	-0.78	-6.65	3.08	91.0	1.1	11.6	29.7	5.0
7.7	4.18	na	-0.01	3.2	2.2	0.55	2.33	2.14	69.5	3.9	60.7	22.1	9.0
4.7	1.32	na	0.00	1.9	0.5	0.23	2.97	3.16	94.4	3.5	22.4	12.4	4.0
3.6	0.66	na	0.13	3.1	0.6	0.63	7.59	3.24	80.2	4.1	36.6	13.5	4.6
4.2	1.26	na	-0.01	6.4	1.0	1.18	12.36	4.89	63.2	2.7	9.7	14.9	6.6
5.2	2.34	9.4	0.40	3.4	19.2	0.39	5.13	2.90	70.6	0.8	18.7	30.0	7.6
7.8	1.02	na	0.02	5.9	1.9	1.23	9.66	4.15	67.1	5.0	55.2	13.7	8.1
6.7	0.52	na	-0.01	5.5	1.4	1.46	14.06	3.47	70.1	5.9	38.2	3.2	6.1
9.2	0.06	na	0.01	4.0	1.9	0.87	9.17	2.82	67.4	4.4	40.8	13.3	5.4
8.7	0.91	na	0.12	4.7	0.7	1.09	5.29	2.88	53.8	3.3	53.4	21.6	7.4
7.0	0.00	na	0.00	4.5	0.5	1.00	14.16	3.65	70.5	1.2	7.6	12.9	3.8
8.4	1.06	na	0.00	8.4	3.1	1.93	15.90	3.74	53.1	4.9	34.5	8.2	8.0
5.7	0.37	na	0.01	4.5	1.0	0.87	7.56	3.77	68.2	0.7	17.6	48.4	6.9
5.0	1.60	na	0.00	3.3	1.0	0.48	3.53	3.80	83.3	1.9	21.9	18.8	7.1
5.7	2.33	7.6	0.18	4.9	20.1	1.09	8.70	3.39	68.8	2.7	22.3	17.0	9.5
5.8	0.94	na	0.12	5.2	7.5	0.98	8.28	3.20	53.1	1.5	17.7	27.0	10.0
3.3	1.82	na	0.08	6.3	2.0	1.23	14.22	3.59	54.3	1.8	17.2	21.0	6.1
5.1	0.75	na	0.08	6.8	2.0	1.33	14.94	3.36	52.3	2.7	22.2	16.1	5.3
6.9	0.00	na	-0.07	6.1	0.2	1.17	6.96	3.41	53.2	2.0	25.5	19.4	5.0
5.5	1.44	na	0.04	4.1	0.3	0.76	6.73	4.94	81.1	5.0	50.3	11.6	6.0
6.9	1.51	na	0.01	3.2	4.1	0.42	3.57	3.25	74.9	4.3	22.4	9.9	9.2
3.9	0.50	na	-0.22	8.8	0.8	1.86	22.26	4.31	59.3	4.0	21.9	9.5	6.1
8.2	0.00	na	0.00	0.0	-2.5	-7.42	-14.40	3.50	264.7	2.1	43.4	38.7	2.0
8.5	0.06	na	0.00	8.2	23.5	1.94	21.27	2.47	33.2	0.6	15.8	9.9	9.2
4.6	3.37	na	0.00	3.6	1.6	0.58	5.07	3.56	80.0	3.7	27.1	12.4	6.4
9.8	0.72	na	0.00	4.2	2.0	0.78	5.13	2.55	57.0	4.3	60.2	18.5	8.0
7.9	0.00	na	0.00	7.3	0.7	1.65	12.12	3.86	59.9	4.8	36.8	4.8	8.6
7.6	0.10	0.7	0.01	4.0	35.5	0.67	6.38	2.05	44.5	0.7	13.6	49.2	8.5
4.0	1.08	5.5	0.04	4.2	3.1	0.85	7.61	3.18	64.7	3.8	21.4	10.8	6.9
5.5	0.00	na	-0.03	3.1	0.2	0.41	3.82	4.26	90.6	3.6	20.0	11.6	6.1
9.4	0.03	na	0.01	4.8	1.3	1.14	11.16	3.48	72.5	6.5	50.6	3.5	6.4
8.0	0.25	na	0.02	5.4	1.2	1.22	9.36	3.16	62.2	2.6	25.8	17.0	7.1
7.9	0.37	na	0.03	4.1	7.8	0.81	10.64	3.36	65.4	3.2	10.8	12.0	7.0
7.1	1.39	na	0.74	3.8	0.5	0.76	4.57	3.54	76.5	5.0	50.0	11.8	7.1
6.7	2.80	na	0.03	5.0	2.2	0.90	3.90	4.30	63.7	2.7	28.4	17.5	8.1
8.5	0.03	na	0.29	0.0	-5.7	-1.89	-16.50	1.95	177.0	0.8	17.5	33.2	5.0
8.2	0.00	na	0.00	7.6	4.4	1.60	17.99	3.62	37.1	1.0	26.7	32.0	5.0
4.5	2.75	11.0	0.43	4.3	2.5	1.13	10.25	3.18	69.3	2.8	23.8	15.8	5.9

Name	City	State	2020 Rating	2019 Rating	2018 Rating	Total Assets ($Mil)	One Year Asset Growth	Asset Mix (As a % of Total Assets) Commercial Loans	Consumer Loans	Mortgage Loans	Securities	Capitalization Index	Leverage Ratio	Risk-Based Capital Ratio
Mabrey Bank	Bixby	OK	B	B-	B-	1411.6	20.77	23.5	1.9	17.4	18.1	5.8	8.0	0.0
Macatawa Bank	Holland	MI	A	A	A	2508.4	17.05	29.2	0.2	6.9	13.0	7.8	9.5	17.3
Machias Savings Bank	Machias	ME	B+	B+	B	1800.1	19.80	19.1	1.0	21.7	5.6	10.0	11.9	16.5
Macon Bank and Trust Co.	Lafayette	TN	B-	B	B	483.4	16.21	3.4	3.8	10.2	42.1	10.0	11.7	0.0
Madison County Bank	Madison	NE	A	A-	B+	436.8	3.49	1.3	1.5	15.5	15.1	10.0	17.6	19.9
Madison County Community Bank	Madison	FL	B-	B-	C+	149.4	17.82	9.5	1.6	7.4	38.1	6.4	8.5	18.0
Madison Valley Bank	Ennis	MT	B+	B	B-	239.7	30.72	8.2	3.5	16.1	5.9	6.3	8.4	0.0
▲ Magnolia Bank, Inc.	Magnolia	KY	A	A-	B+	400.5	24.76	4.9	0.7	41.6	6.8	10.0	13.2	0.0
▲ Magnolia State Bank	Eastman	GA	B	C	D+	177.5	8.30	15.7	4.2	21.7	8.7	10.0	11.3	0.0
Magnolia State Bank	Bay Springs	MS	B-	B-	B-	375.3	11.54	11.6	3.5	20.2	9.4	6.9	9.0	13.9
Magyar Bank	New Brunswick	NJ	C	C	C	754.0	19.62	13.2	0.6	27.8	6.0	6.3	8.3	13.2
Mahopac Bank	Brewster	NY	B	B	B	1615.1	20.38	16.2	1.8	17.6	17.5	6.2	8.2	13.1
Main Bank	Albuquerque	NM	B+	B+	B	207.9	25.03	28.1	0.1	4.0	1.5	5.5	7.5	13.3
Main Street Bank	Marlborough	MA	C	C+	C	1192.7	15.48	9.6	1.1	29.2	13.6	7.8	10.4	0.0
Main Street Bank	Bingham Farms	MI	B-	B-	B-	337.5	15.76	18.4	0.4	28.5	0.9	5.5	8.8	0.0
▲ Main Street Bank Corp.	Wheeling	WV	B-	C+	C	511.6	12.29	13.6	3.4	35.2	11.9	7.4	9.3	0.0
▲ Maine Community Bank	Biddeford	ME	B	B	B-	984.8	95.14	12.7	0.5	37.9	7.3	10.0	12.5	0.0
Mainstreet Bank	Cook	NE	B-	B-	B-	100.6	6.48	3.8	2.2	11.6	22.7	8.5	10.0	15.4
MainStreet Bank	Fairfax	VA	B+	B+	C+	1630.7	32.19	16.1	3.2	7.5	8.6	8.1	10.2	13.4
▼ Mainstreet Community Bank of Florida	Deland	FL	C+	C+	C+	637.2	37.09	16.9	0.8	7.1	10.7	2.6	8.1	0.0
Malaga Bank F.S.B.	Palos Verdes Estates	CA	A-	A-	B+	1282.4	4.15	1.0	0.0	8.1	0.0	10.0	12.5	21.1
Malvern Bank	Malvern	IA	C+	C	C-	160.9	13.40	26.8	14.1	13.0	0.5	6.7	8.7	12.9
Malvern Bank, N.A.	Paoli	PA	B	B	B	1209.8	-4.29	10.5	0.2	22.8	3.8	10.0	13.3	17.0
Malvern National Bank	Malvern	AR	C	C	C	610.1	8.11	7.4	0.7	7.7	29.3	7.4	9.3	14.2
Manasquan Bank	Manasquan	NJ	B-	B	B	2116.9	22.49	14.9	0.1	29.4	2.8	3.7	8.6	0.0
Manhattan Bank	Manhattan	MT	B+	B+	B+	219.9	19.34	6.6	1.8	16.6	30.3	6.6	8.6	15.3
Manson State Bank	Manson	IA	B-	B-	B-	37.9	12.32	13.2	1.5	6.9	36.4	10.0	11.4	0.0
Manufacturers and Traders Trust Co.	Buffalo	NY	C+	C+	C+	138246.2	10.56	16.2	8.8	12.0	5.3	6.3	8.3	12.6
▼ Manufacturers Bank	Los Angeles	CA	B-	B	B	4011.5	-10.70	27.3	0.0	0.5	22.5	8.1	9.8	13.4
Manufacturers Bank & Trust Co.	Forest City	IA	A-	A-	A-	393.4	10.43	15.5	1.7	10.1	19.8	9.2	13.3	0.0
▼ Maple Bank	Champlin	MN	D-	D+	C	99.7	70.63	37.2	0.4	6.1	3.8	1.7	8.8	0.0
▲ Maple City Savings Bank, FSB	Hornell	NY	C	C-	C-	93.9	11.53	7.1	1.5	56.1	11.2	6.3	8.3	14.7
MapleMark Bank	Dallas	TX	D-	D	D	712.2	39.24	31.1	0.9	14.9	10.2	8.3	10.0	13.6
Maquoketa State Bank	Maquoketa	IA	A-	A-	A-	383.7	12.27	8.1	2.7	4.5	33.6	10.0	16.1	0.0
Marathon Bank	Wausau	WI	C+	B-	B-	172.3	15.78	7.4	0.3	23.5	9.4	8.0	12.6	13.3
Marblehead Bank	Marblehead	MA	C-	C	C-	244.4	13.72	5.8	0.3	45.1	3.3	6.5	8.5	15.0
Marblehead Bank	Marblehead	OH	C	C	C	54.9	9.39	2.9	7.1	18.0	62.3	8.9	10.3	0.0
Maries County Bank	Vienna	MO	A-	A-	B+	513.1	10.78	4.1	7.3	13.0	37.1	10.0	15.1	0.0
▲ Marine Bank	Springfield	IL	B-	C	C-	684.2	8.47	9.2	0.4	6.6	10.6	7.2	10.7	0.0
Marine Bank & Trust Co.	Vero Beach	FL	B-	B-	C+	397.3	43.02	19.2	0.2	30.3	4.1	5.4	7.4	13.7
Mariner's Bank	Edgewater	NJ	C	C	C-	408.9	4.34	10.6	1.5	13.6	1.1	7.8	9.7	13.2
Marion Bank and Trust Co.	Marion	AL	C+	B-	B	306.0	6.25	14.5	2.9	9.6	37.0	9.2	10.4	0.0
Marion Center Bank	Indiana	PA	C	C	C	343.6	7.35	12.9	3.2	27.1	20.1	5.2	7.2	11.8
Marion County State Bank	Pella	IA	B	B	B+	560.3	78.09	19.1	1.8	12.3	24.2	6.5	8.5	13.1
▲ Marion National Bank	Marion	KS	B-	C+	C	25.0	11.13	5.0	0.8	8.2	39.0	10.0	12.9	0.0
▼ Marion State Bank	Marion	LA	B-	B	B	194.1	7.45	11.7	3.2	16.8	12.8	10.0	11.0	15.7
Marion State Bank	Marion	TX	B+	A-	B+	119.0	6.61	9.2	6.3	0.0	37.4	10.0	13.7	0.0
Marlin Business Bank	Salt Lake City	UT	B+	A-	A-	995.7	-7.70	52.6	0.0	0.0	0.7	10.0	13.3	18.2
Marquette Bank	Orland Park	IL	C+	C+	B-	1796.0	12.34	1.7	0.0	12.4	21.2	5.9	7.9	13.6
▲ Marquette Farmers State Bank	Marquette	KS	C	C-	C	30.1	4.48	7.2	3.4	12.3	20.6	10.0	16.4	0.0
Marquette Savings Bank	Erie	PA	B-	B	B+	1033.7	12.87	8.4	0.2	38.8	33.0	10.0	16.5	0.0
Mars Bank	Mars	PA	C	C	C	457.4	13.39	6.0	0.1	32.8	21.5	6.6	8.6	16.1
Marseilles Bank	Marseilles	IL	B-	B-	B	66.1	3.99	0.6	8.6	26.5	48.9	8.1	9.7	0.0
▼ Marshall County State Bank	Newfolden	MN	C	B	B	32.2	1.17	1.0	4.3	9.3	21.3	10.0	17.5	98.8
Martha's Vineyard Savings Bank	Edgartown	MA	B+	B+	B+	1030.4	23.83	6.0	0.4	44.3	6.9	10.0	11.7	0.0
Martinsville First Savings Bank	Martinsville	VA	C	C+	C+	39.4	1.07	0.0	0.3	45.8	9.2	10.0	16.8	0.0
Mascoma Bank	Lebanon	NH	C+	C+	C+	2226.6	18.18	10.7	0.4	38.6	8.1	6.6	8.6	13.3
Mason Bank	Mason	TX	A	A	A-	128.2	7.39	7.2	4.6	8.8	57.5	10.0	17.7	42.0
Mason City National Bank	Mason City	IL	B+	B+	B	73.2	2.37	1.1	1.3	9.6	47.7	10.0	17.5	0.0
▼ Maspeth Federal S&L Assn.	Maspeth	NY	B+	A-	A-	2027.4	3.07	0.0	0.0	47.2	2.0	10.0	32.5	45.7

Asset Quality Index	Adjusted Non-Performing Loans as a % of Total Loans	as a % of Capital	Net Charge-Offs Avg Loans	Profitability Index	Net Income ($Mil)	Return on Assets (R.O.A.)	Return on Equity (R.O.E.)	Net Interest Spread	Overhead Efficiency Ratio	Liquidity Index	Liquidity Ratio	Hot Money Ratio	Stability Index
8.0	0.14	na	-0.02	5.0	11.0	1.11	13.74	3.95	67.0	1.7	13.1	13.9	7.2
8.4	0.61	na	0.25	6.5	22.1	1.28	12.30	2.84	53.1	6.5	37.8	2.6	8.9
5.9	2.16	na	0.06	4.7	10.7	0.87	6.96	4.12	63.9	3.2	15.9	6.1	9.4
8.9	0.15	na	0.03	3.3	2.0	0.60	4.92	2.93	79.4	2.8	49.2	29.7	6.9
7.2	0.04	na	0.00	8.0	5.3	1.65	9.20	3.76	52.2	4.9	15.4	2.9	8.9
6.1	1.03	4.4	0.02	4.2	0.9	0.87	9.68	3.45	67.5	4.4	41.5	13.6	4.7
6.5	0.33	na	0.00	6.5	2.9	1.96	21.76	4.50	61.0	5.7	42.8	6.1	4.9
8.5	0.06	0.8	0.05	9.4	37.7	14.52	131.79	2.90	61.7	0.6	9.7	43.6	8.5
4.4	2.36	na	0.21	4.1	1.2	0.91	7.87	4.84	79.1	3.6	26.3	12.4	6.1
6.1	0.62	na	0.17	3.6	2.1	0.77	8.05	3.44	77.8	2.1	22.8	19.1	5.3
4.1	2.10	na	0.04	2.8	1.8	0.33	4.16	3.39	77.5	2.8	10.0	13.0	4.5
6.0	0.76	4.4	0.00	4.2	8.7	0.80	8.03	3.44	63.6	3.6	10.3	5.3	7.1
7.4	0.00	na	0.00	8.1	2.7	1.73	22.32	3.50	46.4	2.1	18.2	18.8	6.6
6.0	1.55	na	0.20	3.0	3.8	0.45	3.90	3.25	71.0	3.7	18.4	10.5	8.2
5.8	0.50	na	0.01	7.5	4.1	2.01	14.78	4.76	67.5	0.5	4.0	34.0	5.7
4.0	2.07	na	-0.07	4.8	3.2	0.85	9.02	3.46	64.0	1.5	20.8	22.0	6.5
8.8	0.89	na	0.00	4.4	6.2	0.85	7.72	3.50	65.4	1.6	4.1	11.1	7.1
7.7	1.22	na	0.00	3.3	0.5	0.60	5.78	3.80	81.7	2.7	23.1	16.2	6.5
7.1	0.10	0.7	0.20	4.2	8.6	0.79	7.49	3.30	56.4	0.8	18.1	32.4	8.2
6.8	0.46	na	0.00	4.2	3.3	0.78	9.05	3.38	66.0	4.0	27.2	8.0	6.0
7.2	0.00	na	0.00	8.0	13.9	1.45	11.59	2.98	31.1	1.2	6.4	22.7	10.0
2.9	0.32	na	0.43	4.0	0.9	0.76	8.42	3.60	70.9	0.8	16.6	27.2	4.7
5.5	2.18	na	-0.01	4.0	6.7	0.72	5.68	2.44	58.5	1.9	9.9	16.2	9.4
8.0	0.36	na	0.47	3.1	2.8	0.64	6.78	3.13	75.1	1.9	24.7	19.1	6.6
8.0	0.34	2.7	0.00	2.6	3.8	0.26	2.91	3.00	63.1	2.1	15.6	18.9	7.0
7.9	0.02	1.5	-0.01	5.4	1.9	1.26	13.23	3.85	63.8	5.7	38.1	4.8	6.1
4.6	4.64	na	0.04	3.3	0.2	0.77	6.02	3.05	72.0	6.2	58.5	6.1	6.3
3.5	1.50	7.5	0.21	6.0	868.7	0.88	7.49	3.21	54.7	4.8	20.9	1.6	10.0
8.4	0.69	2.8	0.00	3.3	13.4	0.42	4.61	1.91	61.3	3.3	39.8	11.7	7.3
8.1	0.17	na	0.11	8.4	5.5	1.93	14.01	3.73	56.8	3.2	23.3	13.9	9.3
4.9	0.84	4.0	1.46	1.8	0.0	0.04	0.45	3.65	72.3	1.1	18.0	9.7	4.9
4.5	1.01	na	0.10	3.4	0.5	0.73	7.96	3.69	78.0	2.2	13.8	13.3	4.7
8.2	0.26	na	0.00	0.2	0.1	0.03	0.25	2.45	102.1	1.5	19.5	25.2	5.9
7.1	1.21	na	0.18	5.6	3.2	1.16	7.00	3.23	59.6	5.5	45.0	8.3	8.7
7.7	0.87	na	-0.04	3.1	0.7	0.54	4.12	3.25	79.8	3.0	29.0	14.3	6.8
6.7	0.50	na	0.00	2.0	0.4	0.20	2.44	3.34	92.2	4.4	16.9	6.0	3.9
8.7	0.39	na	0.00	3.0	0.3	0.70	6.14	3.13	83.9	6.0	58.2	7.4	5.6
7.8	0.89	na	0.30	5.1	3.7	0.99	6.28	3.97	68.6	3.3	26.9	13.9	8.4
4.0	1.02	na	0.01	5.0	6.2	1.23	11.29	3.11	69.1	3.0	19.5	8.9	7.9
8.5	0.00	na	0.00	4.1	2.1	0.81	10.42	3.63	64.7	3.9	13.4	9.4	3.9
2.8	2.04	na	0.02	3.7	2.6	0.85	9.00	3.34	69.7	1.7	12.8	20.5	5.6
1.8	5.76	24.5	0.40	1.9	0.3	0.12	1.04	3.01	87.1	1.7	32.3	32.3	6.6
4.1	1.82	na	0.15	2.8	1.1	0.42	5.65	3.40	78.3	2.5	21.0	16.9	4.1
3.8	0.64	na	-0.01	7.4	6.1	1.55	14.26	3.64	54.4	5.2	29.7	4.3	8.8
8.1	0.00	na	0.00	3.5	0.1	0.56	3.37	3.03	75.3	5.6	59.1	10.1	7.2
6.1	0.75	3.5	0.13	3.8	0.9	0.63	5.61	4.22	78.5	2.5	24.6	17.6	6.4
8.1	0.24	na	0.39	4.4	0.9	1.08	7.65	3.23	65.1	1.8	29.7	27.9	8.7
7.1	0.90	na	3.46	3.1	-15.3	-1.92	-16.14	7.44	65.3	0.4	21.6	44.7	9.5
3.1	2.12	12.0	0.04	3.3	6.2	0.49	4.66	3.39	78.4	4.0	20.2	9.9	7.4
2.5	4.87	na	-0.06	3.6	0.2	1.11	6.49	3.44	82.3	3.4	56.7	22.2	5.4
9.3	0.46	na	0.10	3.5	4.4	0.60	3.43	2.95	73.5	4.5	39.2	14.8	9.2
9.4	0.02	na	0.00	2.8	1.5	0.47	5.11	2.73	84.1	4.5	23.7	6.5	4.7
6.2	0.14	na	0.37	3.5	0.4	0.72	6.85	2.63	68.7	2.8	47.2	26.6	5.6
9.5	0.04	na	0.00	1.9	0.0	-0.02	-0.11	1.66	101.2	6.9	75.8	4.7	7.7
8.1	0.36	2.2	0.09	4.5	6.0	0.87	7.18	3.46	64.1	4.7	19.0	3.6	8.3
3.7	8.30	na	0.14	0.8	-0.1	-0.20	-1.18	2.11	123.9	3.1	59.0	28.5	7.5
8.7	0.32	1.9	0.01	3.6	10.7	0.69	7.52	3.40	75.0	4.0	12.2	8.4	6.9
8.9	0.76	na	0.03	6.5	1.4	1.53	8.15	3.61	57.2	5.5	73.6	14.3	9.2
6.8	0.41	na	0.00	4.5	0.5	1.04	5.49	2.97	63.0	5.4	58.9	11.0	8.2
6.2	3.24	7.9	-0.01	4.5	9.0	0.60	1.84	2.85	62.9	2.1	16.3	19.2	10.0

Name	City	State	2020 Rating	2019 Rating	2018 Rating	Total Assets ($Mil)	One Year Asset Growth	Asset Mix (As a % of Total Assets)				Capital-ization Index	Lever-age Ratio	Risk-Based Capital Ratio
								Comm-ercial Loans	Cons-umer Loans	Mort-gage Loans	Secur-ities			
Massena S&L	Massena	NY	B	B	B	179.9	8.69	1.5	7.9	68.1	0.0	10.0	12.7	21.2
MassMutual Trust Co., FSB	Enfield	CT	U	U	U	90.8	0.80	0.0	0.0	0.0	82.4	10.0	35.1	44.8
Mauch Chunk Trust Co.	Jim Thorpe	PA	C+	C+	C+	507.9	10.47	7.4	0.6	18.8	45.1	5.4	7.4	12.6
Maxwell State Bank	Maxwell	IA	B	B+	B+	30.3	6.10	3.1	0.6	4.0	62.3	10.0	13.6	0.0
Maynard Savings Bank	Maynard	IA	B+	A-	B+	61.3	1.53	4.3	4.0	23.1	18.5	10.0	15.4	0.0
Mayville Savings Bank	Mayville	WI	B-	B-	B-	69.5	4.50	6.3	1.0	45.0	4.3	10.0	11.0	21.3
Mayville State Bank	Mayville	MI	C+	B-	C+	97.1	14.34	4.4	4.2	26.6	28.0	9.0	10.3	0.0
mBank	Manistique	MI	B	B	B-	1520.9	12.49	21.3	1.3	13.8	7.0	7.0	9.0	14.2
▲ MCBank	Goldthwaite	TX	B	C	C+	367.8	16.34	7.6	2.3	10.1	49.2	10.0	11.3	24.1
McClain Bank	Purcell	OK	A-	A-	A-	253.4	13.01	9.1	1.6	19.5	4.8	9.5	10.7	0.0
McClave State Bank	McClave	CO	B	B	B-	44.1	0.50	11.6	1.4	3.5	10.2	10.0	13.9	0.0
McCurtain County National Bank	Broken Bow	OK	A-	A-	B+	301.4	17.48	3.9	5.9	26.7	6.0	10.0	12.1	0.0
McGehee Bank	McGehee	AR	A-	A-	A-	146.6	6.90	11.4	1.0	1.9	18.0	9.1	13.5	0.0
McHenry Savings Bank	McHenry	IL	D	E+	E	261.6	13.63	8.1	23.2	20.0	16.4	6.5	8.5	13.5
McIntosh County Bank	Ashley	ND	C+	C	C-	97.1	12.17	5.2	1.9	0.2	25.3	10.0	11.5	16.8
▲ McKenzie Banking Co.	McKenzie	TN	B-	B-	B+	155.2	19.76	11.6	6.0	17.8	6.0	10.0	13.3	0.0
MCNB Bank and Trust Co.	Welch	WV	C-	C+	C-	322.7	8.35	7.8	0.9	16.7	13.2	10.0	11.2	0.0
MCS Bank	Lewistown	PA	C+	C+	C+	158.9	8.06	9.6	6.9	35.1	5.9	10.0	12.5	0.0
Meade County Bank	Brandenburg	KY	B+	B+	B+	252.7	18.79	6.0	3.2	32.5	14.2	6.5	8.5	15.1
Meadows Bank	Las Vegas	NV	A-	B+	B-	1113.5	17.14	27.4	0.0	2.1	1.2	8.9	11.7	0.0
Mechanics and Farmers Bank	Durham	NC	C-	C-	D	316.5	18.43	10.0	0.4	5.6	16.4	5.5	7.5	13.5
Mechanics Bank	Walnut Creek	CA	B-	B-	B	18539.3	7.17	8.6	14.3	10.1	27.2	6.1	8.1	14.9
Mechanics Bank	Water Valley	MS	B	B	B-	251.3	7.51	12.3	2.0	27.0	14.3	9.2	10.5	0.0
Mechanics Bank	Mansfield	OH	B-	B-	C+	647.4	16.69	4.7	1.1	65.4	9.3	6.4	8.4	17.6
▲ Mechanics Cooperative Bank	Taunton	MA	A-	B+	B-	665.6	8.77	14.0	1.1	27.6	10.7	10.0	11.3	17.3
▼ Medallion Bank	Salt Lake City	UT	D+	C+	C-	1282.7	10.37	6.2	87.8	0.0	3.6	10.0	15.5	17.5
▲ Mediapolis Savings Bank	Mediapolis	IA	B-	C+	D+	192.5	11.99	8.5	1.5	16.5	10.7	8.0	10.4	0.0
Mega Bank	San Gabriel	CA	C+	B	B	403.6	15.35	17.4	1.9	18.9	0.0	9.0	10.7	0.0
Melvin Savings Bank	Melvin	IA	C+	B-	B	77.9	10.80	6.8	1.5	2.6	32.0	10.0	17.4	0.0
MEMBERS Trust Co.	Tampa	FL	U	U	U	41.4	3.05	0.0	0.0	0.0	70.6	10.0	89.6	573.3
Menard Bank	Menard	TX	B-	B-	B-	74.1	77.19	1.4	0.5	4.5	65.3	6.5	8.5	0.0
Mer Rouge State Bank	Mer Rouge	LA	C	C+	C+	44.8	14.26	20.0	0.8	4.2	11.1	9.7	11.5	0.0
Meramec Valley Bank	Ellisville	MO	C+	C	C-	147.0	21.57	21.9	1.0	16.4	2.3	6.0	8.0	11.7
Mercantile Bank of Louisiana, Missouri	Louisiana	MO	A-	A-	A-	114.7	4.18	3.7	1.0	11.5	12.7	10.0	20.4	0.0
Mercantile Bank of Michigan	Grand Rapids	MI	A-	A-	A-	4402.6	19.23	27.7	0.4	8.3	7.1	7.9	9.6	13.5
▲ Mercer County State Bank	Sandy Lake	PA	B-	C+	B-	474.6	8.51	12.2	0.7	20.2	26.8	7.1	9.1	0.0
▼ Mercer Savings Bank	Celina	OH	C	C+	C+	135.7	1.78	1.6	0.7	52.4	2.5	8.1	9.8	15.9
Merchants & Citizens Bank	McRae	GA	B-	B-	B-	114.1	10.35	3.3	2.8	14.1	38.6	10.0	14.5	35.5
Merchants & Farmers Bank	Eutaw	AL	C+	C+	B-	89.1	24.29	10.0	7.8	12.6	20.8	6.5	8.5	0.0
▼ Merchants & Farmers Bank	Holly Springs	MS	C+	B	C	115.9	12.84	7.6	3.6	10.3	40.1	8.9	10.3	0.0
Merchants & Farmers Bank & Trust Co.	Leesville	LA	B	B	B-	418.3	1.92	7.2	0.9	24.0	28.8	10.0	11.9	0.0
Merchants & Marine Bank	Pascagoula	MS	B-	B-	B	632.1	10.11	11.6	3.4	12.6	15.8	10.0	12.3	22.9
Merchants & Planters Bank	Clarendon	AR	C-	C-	C+	41.2	6.53	20.6	1.5	1.2	47.8	10.0	12.9	0.0
Merchants & Planters Bank	Newport	AR	C+	C+	C+	302.9	13.43	8.5	3.7	8.1	16.1	7.2	10.3	0.0
Merchants and Farmers Bank	Dumas	AR	B-	B-	B-	180.0	12.10	17.5	2.4	10.2	6.7	7.2	9.8	12.7
Merchants and Farmers Bank of Salisbury	Salisbury	MO	C+	C+	C	103.8	10.12	1.5	1.9	13.8	28.3	6.7	8.7	15.8
Merchants and Manufacturers Bank	Joliet	IL	C+	C+	C+	329.1	16.08	25.8	39.9	5.6	2.3	5.1	8.3	11.0
Merchants and Planters Bank	Raymond	MS	B+	B	C	98.8	5.29	12.6	1.2	14.2	22.8	8.9	10.3	0.0
Merchants Bank	Rugby	ND	B	B	C+	184.7	8.95	9.1	1.6	2.7	24.8	6.6	8.8	12.2
Merchants Bank of Alabama	Cullman	AL	B+	B+	B-	352.4	16.11	10.8	3.1	18.4	21.4	7.9	9.6	19.5
Merchants Bank of Commerce	Redding	CA	B+	B+	B	1739.3	18.18	15.5	1.4	5.2	19.4	8.5	10.0	15.3
▼ Merchants Bank of Indiana	Carmel	IN	B-	B+	A	9308.8	51.48	5.3	0.1	1.1	2.9	1.6	8.0	0.0
Merchants Bank, N.A.	Winona	MN	B	B	B	2613.3	40.93	22.4	1.6	10.6	4.6	6.8	8.8	13.0
▲ Merchants Commercial Bank	Saint Thomas	VI	B-	C	C-	288.1	12.67	9.8	0.4	15.9	50.4	6.8	8.8	0.0
Merchants National Bank	Hillsboro	OH	B	B-	B-	1064.2	14.04	8.6	2.6	29.6	2.1	6.2	8.3	12.6
▲ Merchants State Bank	Freeman	SD	B-	B-	C+	189.2	10.60	8.5	1.4	1.7	15.4	10.0	13.2	0.0
Meredith Village Savings Bank	Meredith	NH	B	B	B	1148.8	14.71	8.4	8.8	42.5	5.5	9.2	10.5	17.3
▲ Meridian Bank	Malvern	PA	B-			1758.7	56.06	28.9	0.0	23.8	6.3	9.8	11.5	0.0
Merit Bank	Huntsville	AL	C-	C	C+	142.2	121.83	23.4	0.9	4.8	14.7	10.0	12.3	0.0
Merrick Bank Corp.	South Jordan	UT	C	C	C	4082.5	3.94	0.0	87.9	0.0	2.7	10.0	24.2	30.7

Asset Quality Index	Adjusted Non-Performing Loans as a % of Total Loans	as a % of Capital	Net Charge-Offs Avg Loans	Profitability Index	Net Income ($Mil)	Return on Assets (R.O.A.)	Return on Equity (R.O.E.)	Net Interest Spread	Overhead Efficiency Ratio	Liquidity Index	Liquidity Ratio	Hot Money Ratio	Stability Index
4.6	3.17	na	0.24	3.4	0.8	0.58	4.46	3.00	74.0	0.8	13.4	34.5	6.9
10.0	na	na	na	10.0	3.0	4.83	14.37	0.87	83.6	4.0	138.1	100.0	7.0
7.6	1.56	na	0.55	2.7	2.2	0.61	6.55	3.05	76.4	4.3	24.7	7.3	5.5
9.6	0.00	na	0.00	3.9	0.2	0.83	4.50	2.59	60.9	6.1	90.1	11.4	7.1
8.0	0.16	2.1	0.67	5.4	0.6	1.28	8.22	3.35	58.6	4.0	38.1	14.5	6.8
6.9	1.34	6.0	-0.03	3.5	0.3	0.58	5.25	2.98	70.7	3.7	30.6	13.5	5.9
8.6	1.03	na	0.21	3.0	0.4	0.52	4.79	3.10	84.7	6.5	57.2	3.7	5.7
5.6	1.00	5.0	0.01	5.2	11.0	1.01	9.31	4.37	70.2	3.4	19.0	7.4	8.7
5.2	3.02	na	0.08	4.9	3.0	1.16	9.61	3.75	69.8	6.0	56.4	9.0	6.5
5.8	0.24	na	0.71	6.8	2.3	1.22	11.38	4.16	62.5	4.8	28.8	6.5	7.4
6.3	0.00	na	0.43	7.9	0.5	1.42	10.51	4.90	59.7	0.5	13.6	46.3	7.1
6.7	1.39	na	0.04	6.3	2.4	1.13	9.12	3.12	52.6	4.7	50.7	14.4	7.7
5.1	1.09	3.0	0.06	8.0	2.0	2.01	14.43	4.19	54.0	2.0	5.2	18.0	9.2
3.3	1.07	na	0.03	1.3	0.3	0.17	1.86	3.18	90.6	0.8	18.3	27.1	1.6
5.6	2.62	na	0.27	6.3	1.0	1.40	11.87	3.76	57.1	4.1	27.1	10.4	7.9
4.5	2.74	na	0.17	10.0	2.2	1.99	15.09	6.30	63.1	5.2	51.2	11.9	8.9
1.6	7.86	na	0.24	3.4	1.6	0.67	5.98	3.55	77.5	3.2	19.4	13.4	6.5
5.2	1.16	na	0.41	2.5	0.4	0.34	2.68	3.19	79.5	1.2	12.7	21.7	6.4
8.8	0.00	0.4	0.00	5.1	1.9	1.03	11.67	3.38	59.3	3.0	22.4	14.7	5.2
6.8	0.67	na	0.01	9.0	12.3	1.57	13.21	4.48	46.6	1.5	7.3	17.7	10.0
5.6	2.30	na	-0.01	2.3	0.4	0.19	2.40	3.51	83.9	1.8	28.6	26.5	2.5
5.3	0.46	2.0	0.21	3.2	42.2	0.32	2.36	3.57	67.7	5.3	27.2	5.2	8.5
4.6	1.64	12.0	0.04	4.8	1.8	1.00	9.19	3.87	70.1	1.6	18.1	24.1	6.1
7.2	0.72	na	0.02	3.8	3.0	0.67	8.29	2.96	73.0	3.5	16.8	11.6	5.5
8.6	0.13	na	0.00	5.8	5.3	1.11	11.07	3.72	61.0	1.2	8.3	22.5	6.7
0.6	7.31	na	3.34	3.1	-11.8	-1.23	-7.11	9.15	33.3	0.2	8.0	0.0	8.8
4.8	1.41	na	0.03	4.8	1.6	1.18	11.37	3.43	55.6	2.6	27.2	18.0	6.1
8.5	0.00	na	0.00	1.5	-0.3	-0.11	-1.05	2.62	81.5	0.6	12.6	58.2	6.8
8.5	0.00	na	1.31	2.9	0.3	0.49	2.83	2.66	68.9	6.4	76.8	8.2	7.1
9.3	na	0.0	na	7.7	0.5	1.69	1.86	1.74	97.3	4.0	na	0.0	7.0
9.9	0.00	na	0.00	3.4	0.3	0.69	6.21	2.85	73.7	5.3	69.3	13.2	5.4
8.6	0.06	na	-0.05	1.3	0.0	-0.09	-0.73	3.49	115.2	2.8	38.4	21.1	5.2
8.4	0.13	na	0.00	3.9	1.2	1.08	14.26	3.62	68.3	3.6	13.3	10.8	4.1
7.3	5.87	na	-0.04	5.4	1.0	1.23	5.77	3.66	62.6	4.4	29.7	9.1	9.6
7.9	0.48	2.1	-0.01	5.9	34.4	1.15	10.34	3.28	56.2	3.4	16.6	10.3	10.0
4.5	3.61	na	0.03	4.8	3.8	1.11	11.27	3.67	67.5	3.7	23.7	11.4	6.4
6.9	0.50	3.8	0.00	2.1	0.2	0.16	1.70	2.73	88.0	3.6	15.2	11.0	5.4
8.0	0.22	na	0.15	2.8	0.4	0.51	2.85	3.13	84.6	3.4	49.5	21.7	7.3
4.1	1.66	na	0.04	2.9	0.2	0.33	3.58	3.95	91.1	1.9	26.7	23.0	4.1
5.2	0.95	na	1.17	2.4	0.3	0.38	3.33	3.63	94.4	2.6	34.5	20.7	5.8
6.1	1.69	na	0.07	4.3	3.2	1.03	8.02	3.74	74.4	3.4	26.9	11.4	7.1
5.7	1.88	na	0.01	2.8	3.8	0.82	6.54	3.05	86.0	4.9	42.1	10.8	7.2
8.5	0.51	na	0.17	1.5	0.0	0.14	1.06	3.07	90.4	5.4	47.6	8.9	4.0
2.7	2.33	na	0.28	4.1	1.8	0.82	7.91	3.74	74.8	1.6	10.0	21.0	5.9
4.1	2.07	na	0.01	4.7	1.1	0.91	9.32	4.08	70.0	1.9	18.8	20.0	5.9
8.9	0.17	na	0.36	3.0	0.4	0.55	5.73	3.42	83.2	4.3	33.0	11.3	5.1
3.6	1.35	na	0.00	4.5	1.7	0.73	9.43	3.96	73.2	3.0	9.3	8.3	4.2
8.3	0.09	na	-0.03	5.2	0.8	1.06	9.87	3.70	71.2	4.2	21.4	8.0	6.1
7.1	0.00	na	-0.03	7.4	1.9	1.45	15.31	3.88	50.4	2.3	16.2	17.7	6.5
7.3	0.71	na	0.08	5.4	2.5	1.04	10.28	3.77	64.5	4.3	39.1	13.2	6.1
5.5	1.03	na	0.07	4.9	10.6	0.89	7.54	3.76	58.4	4.9	24.7	7.2	9.3
7.7	0.08	1.3	0.00	9.6	122.7	2.05	24.22	2.62	26.8	1.4	5.1	3.8	8.6
5.0	1.25	6.8	0.07	5.8	16.5	1.00	9.81	3.99	61.2	4.2	20.7	9.3	8.5
4.4	3.09	na	0.25	8.1	3.4	1.56	16.44	3.80	47.5	5.8	47.0	1.8	4.4
5.5	0.73	na	0.03	6.3	9.5	1.26	12.98	3.79	57.3	3.4	14.4	10.4	8.6
4.2	0.99	na	-0.01	7.9	2.5	1.77	13.31	3.98	49.9	2.3	11.5	15.6	8.7
6.5	0.73	4.3	0.00	4.4	6.5	0.82	7.52	3.63	70.3	3.4	8.2	10.2	7.4
6.7	0.74	na	0.01	7.6	19.1	1.81	15.68	3.46	67.0	1.4	8.3	5.4	8.2
8.2	0.12	na	0.32	0.0	-1.5	-1.74	-11.07	3.37	121.1	5.3	38.8	7.7	5.4
2.2	2.95	8.2	10.31	10.0	186.9	6.02	26.94	17.25	27.8	1.0	23.6	15.5	9.5

Name	City	State	2019 Rating	2018 Rating	Total Assets ($Mil)	One Year Asset Growth	Asset Mix (As a % of Total Assets)				Capital- ization Index	Lever- age Ratio	Risk- Based Capital Ratio
							Comm- ercial Loans	Cons- umer Loans	Mort- gage Loans	Secur- ities			
Merrimack County Savings Bank	Concord	NH	B-	B-	B-	1052.4	15.09	16.8	8.1	28.6	7.3	7.4	9.3	14.3
MetaBank, N.A.	Sioux Falls	SD	B+	B+	B+	6095.9	-1.52	33.3	3.7	1.0	22.3	5.6	7.6	15.3
Metairie Bank and Trust Co.	Metairie	LA	B-	B-	B-	486.0	19.87	13.8	1.0	27.9	8.0	7.1	9.1	0.0
Metamora State Bank	Metamora	OH	C	C	C	90.0	8.83	8.8	1.1	22.5	13.4	6.9	8.9	12.5
Methuen Co-operative Bank	Methuen	MA	C+	C	C-	105.5	13.14	11.9	1.1	39.5	14.3	8.3	9.8	0.0
Metro Bank	Pell City	AL	A	A-	B+	849.5	11.48	7.2	1.7	9.1	18.1	10.0	15.1	0.0
Metro City Bank	Doraville	GA	A	A	A	1742.6	5.76	8.4	0.0	47.6	1.0	10.0	12.5	20.5
Metro Phoenix Bank	Phoenix	AZ	A	A-	B+	323.8	44.69	33.6	0.0	4.0	0.6	10.0	11.4	0.0
Metropolitan Bank	Oakland	CA	A-	B	B-	187.9	4.50	1.7	0.1	20.5	2.4	10.0	12.4	0.0
▼ Metropolitan Capital Bank & Trust	Chicago	IL	D+	D+	D-	228.5	-0.64	43.7	0.3	3.6	14.4	8.4	9.9	15.3
Metropolitan Commercial Bank	New York	NY	A-	A-	A-	4000.3	23.42	11.7	1.1	2.9	4.6	7.0	9.0	12.9
Metz Banking Co.	Nevada	MO	A-	B+	B+	85.5	13.40	7.5	1.0	11.8	16.3	9.9	11.0	0.0
Mi Bank	Bloomfield Hills	MI	D			111.0	118.50	27.3	0.4	1.5	0.0	10.0	17.6	23.8
▼ Miami Savings Bank	Miamitown	OH	C+	A-	B+	138.4	7.69	4.9	0.3	31.5	3.2	0.0	16.2	0.0
Mid America Bank	Jefferson City	MO	B+	A-	B+	587.7	16.17	14.6	2.0	15.5	9.2	7.9	9.8	0.0
Mid Penn Bank	Millersburg	PA	B-	B-	B-	3052.1	35.73	29.9	0.2	13.1	5.0	5.4	7.4	11.7
▲ Mid-America Bank	Baldwin City	KS	B+	B-	B-	283.4	24.99	5.5	0.8	34.8	1.4	7.0	9.0	12.5
▼ Mid-Central National Bank	Wadena	MN	C	B-	B-	137.9	18.79	2.3	12.7	39.8	0.7	10.0	12.0	23.9
▼ Mid-Missouri Bank	Springfield	MO	B-	B	B	774.1	17.16	8.1	1.0	18.4	3.8	6.2	8.2	12.4
Mid-Southern Savings Bank, FSB	Salem	IN	B-			218.1	4.37	2.4	0.7	29.7	36.6	9.8	17.7	0.0
MidAmerica National Bank	Canton	IL	B	B-	B-	464.5	9.47	7.3	6.8	10.0	27.8	9.4	10.6	0.0
MidCountry Bank	Minneapolis	MN	B-	B-	C+	840.8	4.81	17.8	0.1	10.6	6.4	10.0	12.4	15.7
Middlefield Banking Co.	Middlefield	OH	B	B	B-	1363.6	6.51	18.6	0.8	17.1	8.3	6.2	9.5	11.9
Middlesex Federal Savings, F.A.	Somerville	MA	D+	C	C-	461.5	8.32	2.5	0.0	33.3	8.2	7.5	9.3	14.4
Middlesex Savings Bank	Natick	MA	B-	B	B	5642.8	14.20	9.3	0.2	21.1	26.8	10.0	12.3	18.1
Middletown State Bank	Middletown	IL	B-	B-	B	40.8	9.10	1.6	2.0	31.4	12.4	6.8	8.8	0.0
Middletown Valley Bank	Middletown	MD	B-	B-	B-	660.4	36.46	28.0	0.1	15.8	10.2	5.4	9.0	0.0
MidFirst Bank	Oklahoma City	OK	B	B	B	28168.4	30.34	9.3	0.5	46.6	12.9	6.1	8.1	16.4
Midland Community Bank	Kincaid	IL	B+	B+	B	75.2	20.62	11.2	2.6	31.0	28.5	8.9	10.4	14.1
Midland Federal S&L Assn.	Bridgeview	IL	D	D+	D+	119.0	2.84	0.3	0.3	27.8	39.6	6.9	8.9	35.4
Midland States Bank	Effingham	IL	B-	B-	B-	6691.0	17.12	18.2	12.8	7.5	9.1	6.1	9.0	11.8
▼ MidSouth Bank	Dothan	AL	B-	B+	B+	477.4	14.75	17.9	0.6	7.6	11.4	8.2	11.1	0.0
Midstates Bank, N.A.	Council Bluffs	IA	C+	B-	C+	606.7	5.50	8.3	0.6	7.6	32.9	6.6	8.6	14.4
Midwest Bank	Monmouth	IL	C	C+	B-	579.1	10.88	10.1	2.6	6.7	27.3	7.1	9.1	15.7
Midwest Bank	Detroit Lakes	MN	B+	B+	B	611.6	20.21	19.2	1.9	13.3	3.1	6.6	8.6	12.6
Midwest Bank N.A.	Pierce	NE	B+	B+	B+	883.2	12.06	10.8	1.7	2.3	22.1	7.3	9.2	13.8
Midwest BankCentre	Saint Louis	MO	C+	C+	B-	2275.4	13.35	24.2	2.5	16.6	13.3	5.7	8.1	11.6
▲ Midwest Community Bank	Freeport	IL	B+	B-	B-	381.2	54.79	2.6	0.1	51.3	0.2	8.2	9.8	14.2
Midwest Heritage Bank, FSB	West Des Moines	IA	A	A	A	310.7	9.09	9.6	13.2	23.0	11.7	10.0	12.8	19.5
Midwest Independent BankersBank	Jefferson City	MO	B+	B+	B+	249.1	-9.27	1.8	0.0	1.1	10.9	10.0	15.9	22.3
Midwest Regional Bank	Festus	MO	C	C	C	867.3	34.60	31.7	0.2	5.0	7.4	6.8	8.8	12.6
▼ MidWestOne Bank	Iowa City	IA	C+	B	B	5323.6	14.72	15.1	1.2	7.6	25.7	7.4	9.3	13.0
Mifflinburg Bank & Trust Co.	Mifflinburg	PA	B	B	B-	506.8	12.10	13.1	2.2	17.3	19.4	7.7	9.5	0.0
Milford Bank	Milford	CT	C-	C+	C	479.1	6.85	12.3	3.1	40.2	2.9	9.1	10.4	16.4
Milford Building and Loan Assn., SB	Milford	IL	D+	D+	C-	30.9	2.63	0.0	0.1	56.4	0.0	6.9	8.9	19.7
Milford Federal Bank	Milford	MA	C+	C+	C+	438.4	4.73	0.5	1.2	72.1	1.8	10.0	11.7	20.4
▲ Millbury National Bank	Millbury	MA	C	C	C	101.5	5.92	4.6	1.3	26.5	14.5	8.7	10.1	16.5
Milledgeville State Bank	Milledgeville	IL	B+	A-	A-	155.2	4.43	14.4	0.6	5.4	23.0	9.7	10.8	16.3
▲ Millennial Bank	Leeds	AL	C-	D	E	114.5	44.84	21.6	0.5	8.1	13.2	3.4	9.8	0.0
Millennium Bank	Des Plaines	IL	A-	A-	A-	217.5	50.11	14.6	0.0	3.9	0.0	9.3	10.5	16.6
Millennium Bank	Ooltewah	TN	C+	B-	B	491.4	161.40	15.8	0.5	10.5	6.9	5.2	9.3	0.0
Millville Savings Bank	Millville	NJ	C+	C+	C	143.3	9.48	0.0	0.0	20.7	47.0	10.0	13.5	28.7
Millyard Bank	Nashua	NH	D			68.5	na	35.5	0.0	5.4	0.0	10.0	35.7	54.6
Milton Savings Bank	Milton	PA	B	B	B	69.0	10.85	0.0	1.6	52.8	17.3	10.0	23.1	65.1
Minden Exchange Bank & Trust Co.	Minden	NE	A	A	A-	158.3	9.41	6.3	2.1	1.0	27.7	10.0	19.6	0.0
▼ Mineola Community Bank, SSB	Mineola	TX	C	C+	C+	299.0	13.45	3.3	1.4	46.3	17.7	9.7	10.8	0.0
▼ Miners and Merchants Bank	Thomas	WV	C	B-	B-	59.1	9.22	0.9	1.5	22.7	52.9	10.0	15.2	0.0
Miners Exchange Bank	Coeburn	VA	C+	B-	B-	86.4	-14.30	4.1	6.3	36.2	13.1	10.0	13.0	23.6
▲ Miners National Bank of Eveleth	Eveleth	MN	B-	C+	C-	76.3	8.95	3.7	4.2	29.6	20.0	6.7	8.7	0.0
Miners State Bank	Iron River	MI	B	B	B-	158.5	14.45	9.8	0.3	12.9	16.3	7.5	9.4	0.0

Asset Quality Index	Adjusted Non-Performing Loans as a % of Total Loans	as a % of Capital	Net Charge-Offs Avg Loans	Profitability Index	Net Income ($Mil)	Return on Assets (R.O.A.)	Return on Equity (R.O.E.)	Net Interest Spread	Overhead Efficiency Ratio	Liquidity Index	Liquidity Ratio	Hot Money Ratio	Stability Index
7.8	0.27	1.6	0.02	4.0	5.7	0.76	7.71	3.52	71.2	3.7	5.5	8.1	6.7
4.8	1.09	4.1	1.25	7.1	84.8	1.55	12.88	4.05	60.9	0.8	14.8	1.1	8.9
8.6	0.21	na	0.02	4.2	2.6	0.79	8.28	3.92	74.4	4.5	21.7	6.1	5.5
7.1	1.58	na	0.00	2.9	0.3	0.42	4.52	3.81	87.9	2.9	23.3	14.9	4.6
7.2	0.66	na	0.00	2.8	0.3	0.39	3.74	2.92	83.9	4.2	41.7	14.3	5.4
8.3	0.45	na	0.10	7.7	8.6	1.42	9.33	3.74	52.7	3.2	39.5	18.8	9.0
6.1	1.18	5.8	0.00	9.8	27.1	2.18	17.14	4.06	43.3	1.6	12.1	23.2	10.0
8.3	0.00	na	0.00	8.8	3.8	1.68	14.23	4.58	44.5	3.9	22.9	10.0	7.4
7.4	1.02	na	0.00	5.0	0.8	0.58	4.64	3.49	73.0	1.6	21.8	25.2	8.7
4.1	3.22	na	-0.03	1.4	-0.9	-0.60	-5.89	4.24	120.3	2.1	43.7	29.2	4.8
7.1	0.24	na	0.02	5.9	29.5	1.05	11.05	3.31	53.9	4.0	26.3	2.6	8.3
8.8	0.01	na	0.08	5.1	0.8	1.25	10.96	3.45	64.6	3.0	38.8	19.7	7.5
8.0	0.00	na	0.00	0.0	-0.8	-1.20	-5.83	2.75	123.6	3.5	20.4	12.0	1.5
7.4	0.70	na	-0.02	4.6	0.9	0.93	5.69	2.87	64.6	2.5	38.0	26.2	8.2
5.4	1.23	na	0.06	7.6	7.7	1.83	18.14	3.56	50.7	4.4	23.5	6.9	8.9
5.4	0.52	4.6	0.00	4.4	20.0	1.00	10.28	3.32	64.3	3.2	8.5	9.2	7.1
8.2	0.00	na	0.00	7.8	3.0	1.50	16.70	3.51	54.7	1.0	24.9	34.2	6.1
6.2	0.08	na	na	1.9	0.0	0.00	0.00	na	87.5	3.4	30.3	14.5	5.8
4.9	0.95	7.8	0.07	4.9	5.2	0.96	11.21	3.44	71.6	2.1	19.9	9.7	5.8
7.2	2.47	na	0.02	3.5	1.1	0.70	3.77	3.26	76.9	4.8	53.8	14.7	7.8
5.1	1.86	na	0.17	5.6	3.6	1.09	8.47	3.86	61.7	4.1	11.3	7.3	7.9
6.4	1.61	na	0.00	3.3	4.6	0.60	4.46	3.87	69.7	3.0	12.2	11.0	8.4
5.6	0.82	5.0	0.39	4.4	7.3	0.76	6.82	3.63	55.7	2.1	8.3	17.3	9.1
7.1	0.32	2.6	0.00	1.9	0.5	0.14	1.69	3.13	87.7	0.8	15.6	23.6	4.9
6.9	1.33	6.2	0.01	3.0	18.1	0.45	3.62	2.59	71.4	4.5	38.9	15.0	9.3
7.0	0.00	na	0.00	7.6	0.5	1.72	19.02	3.05	41.8	2.1	30.2	24.2	5.0
7.1	0.34	na	0.00	3.2	2.2	0.48	4.85	3.32	71.3	2.8	10.5	11.0	5.8
6.6	0.32	3.6	0.10	6.6	278.7	1.53	22.57	3.27	49.4	1.7	15.3	7.1	8.6
8.3	0.04	na	0.05	9.0	0.9	1.72	16.31	3.05	45.6	2.2	32.3	24.4	6.4
5.9	3.91	na	0.00	0.5	-0.5	-0.56	-5.97	2.24	110.7	6.5	72.0	9.0	4.5
4.0	1.31	7.9	0.60	3.7	20.6	0.43	3.48	3.59	69.3	4.3	11.0	5.7	8.9
8.7	0.20	na	-0.03	3.6	2.3	0.68	5.90	3.18	79.7	4.0	28.2	11.0	6.8
2.0	4.17	na	0.02	4.0	3.8	0.82	8.13	3.56	73.9	4.6	33.9	9.8	7.6
1.6	3.20	13.0	0.76	3.7	2.9	0.71	5.84	3.35	68.9	2.7	18.6	10.8	7.1
4.8	1.00	8.0	0.72	6.8	5.0	1.21	13.08	3.60	46.9	3.2	21.5	13.6	7.9
6.7	0.74	na	-0.01	7.2	8.9	1.41	14.61	3.52	54.1	1.3	17.4	25.8	7.6
7.8	0.32	2.2	0.04	3.3	10.5	0.63	6.67	2.82	74.0	2.7	6.3	14.5	7.4
7.6	0.22	na	-0.06	9.2	13.1	6.26	69.13	2.58	68.9	0.6	5.8	20.7	6.5
7.5	0.36	1.0	0.03	10.0	5.1	2.20	17.23	3.92	64.4	4.8	21.9	4.6	9.1
8.7	0.00	na	-0.12	5.5	2.3	1.09	7.64	2.33	71.4	5.3	46.3	7.6	7.8
5.4	0.43	na	0.23	3.5	3.7	0.63	7.38	2.61	63.3	0.7	13.0	30.2	4.6
5.0	1.17	6.4	0.18	2.2	-6.0	-0.16	-1.38	3.46	80.3	4.1	22.8	10.9	8.5
5.1	1.52	na	0.04	5.3	4.2	1.18	11.86	3.19	56.2	3.7	15.9	10.5	6.3
6.2	0.76	na	0.00	2.2	0.8	0.23	2.25	3.40	87.1	4.4	8.4	5.4	6.0
3.9	0.72	na	0.00	2.6	0.1	0.24	2.73	2.36	76.4	1.7	35.8	41.5	4.6
8.8	0.42	na	0.00	2.7	1.2	0.39	3.29	2.74	86.2	2.9	14.0	14.4	6.7
4.1	1.53	8.2	-0.01	2.8	0.3	0.36	3.84	3.93	86.0	0.9	19.2	37.2	5.1
7.4	0.60	na	0.50	5.3	1.4	1.24	10.94	3.38	47.0	1.2	31.8	47.8	8.6
8.6	0.00	na	0.10	2.4	0.3	0.42	4.26	4.88	92.4	2.7	23.5	16.1	3.1
7.3	0.03	0.2	0.25	9.5	3.7	2.74	25.14	3.20	53.7	0.7	18.1	41.1	7.6
6.0	2.12	na	-0.09	2.9	0.6	0.19	2.16	3.87	93.0	1.9	22.7	18.1	6.0
9.5	1.51	2.4	-0.20	2.7	0.4	0.35	2.46	2.75	84.4	6.8	63.6	5.4	7.2
8.3	0.00	0.0	0.00	0.0	-1.9	-6.34	-14.04	1.82	384.7	5.3	32.1	4.3	2.0
9.8	0.02	na	0.00	3.6	0.3	0.66	2.79	3.04	73.1	5.9	54.9	7.0	7.2
8.2	0.00	na	0.01	6.4	1.5	1.29	6.40	3.41	57.5	4.4	8.4	5.0	9.5
6.3	0.57	na	0.01	2.7	0.8	0.38	3.30	3.08	84.4	2.2	27.9	20.3	6.7
9.3	1.00	na	0.00	1.9	0.0	0.07	0.46	2.40	97.8	7.1	75.7	3.4	7.3
7.3	2.27	na	0.19	2.7	0.2	0.31	2.31	5.09	91.8	4.4	33.8	10.8	5.7
9.1	0.04	na	0.01	5.1	0.5	0.96	10.60	5.16	68.1	5.3	34.3	5.8	4.6
8.7	0.16	0.5	-0.02	4.1	1.0	0.86	8.70	3.83	72.9	3.2	34.7	17.0	5.4

Name	City	State	2019 Rating	2018 Rating	Total Assets ($Mil)	One Year Asset Growth	Asset Mix (As a % of Total Assets) Commercial Loans	Consumer Loans	Mortgage Loans	Securities	Capitalization Index	Leverage Ratio	Risk-Based Capital Ratio
Minnesota Bank & Trust	Edina	MN	B	B	B	1007.9	39.49	27.7	1.6	4.0	31.4	6.3	8.3	12.6
Minnesota First Credit and Savings, Inc.	Rochester	MN	C+	C+	C+	25.5	-4.36	1.8	37.4	49.1	0.0	10.0	16.3	23.8
Minnesota Lakes Bank	Delano	MN	B-	B-	C+	160.9	54.65	25.7	1.1	4.9	6.8	2.8	7.9	0.0
Minnesota National Bank	Sauk Centre	MN	B+	B+	B	235.9	11.38	9.9	2.8	13.4	25.8	7.8	9.5	15.5
MinnStar Bank N.A.	Lake Crystal	MN	B	B-	B-	146.3	14.92	15.3	0.6	16.7	2.0	7.8	9.5	13.8
Minnwest Bank	Redwood Falls	MN	B+	B+	B	2213.8	10.93	10.4	0.7	2.5	5.2	9.5	10.7	15.0
Minster Bank	Minster	OH	B+	B+	B+	604.2	18.58	13.9	0.5	6.7	23.6	6.0	8.0	17.1
MINT National Bank	Kingwood	TX	B-	B-	C+	366.8	46.82	29.4	0.4	7.6	0.0	4.6	13.1	0.0
▼ Mission Bank	Kingman	AZ	C+	B-	B-	162.1	30.44	5.0	0.4	2.6	38.9	5.1	7.1	15.7
▼ Mission Bank	Bakersfield	CA	B+	B+	B	1184.2	47.96	18.5	0.0	2.8	9.2	4.0	8.7	0.0
▼ Mission National Bank	San Francisco	CA	B	B+	B	243.9	0.35	1.0	0.1	22.8	0.0	10.0	15.3	0.0
▼ Mission Valley Bank	Sun Valley	CA	B+	A-	B+	465.8	37.68	34.1	0.0	1.2	6.5	8.0	9.7	15.7
Mississippi River Bank	Belle Chasse	LA	B+	A-	B+	122.3	10.61	21.2	0.7	10.5	5.2	10.0	13.4	36.5
Missouri Bank	Warrenton	MO	A-	A-	A-	364.6	70.33	6.3	1.0	20.5	19.1	9.6	11.3	0.0
Mitchell Bank	Milwaukee	WI	C	C+	C-	57.4	17.55	10.3	0.0	8.1	0.0	10.0	15.1	62.0
▼ Mizuho Bank (USA)	New York	NY	B-	B	B	7960.8	31.10	29.9	0.0	0.0	0.0	10.0	17.8	21.7
▲ MNB Bank	McCook	NE	C+	C+	C	393.2	8.81	7.7	0.5	5.5	27.5	10.0	14.6	0.0
▼ Modern Bank, N.A.	New York	NY	C-	C	C+	886.1	13.21	52.3	0.0	3.9	12.5	6.8	9.7	12.4
Monona Bank	Monona	WI	B	B-	C+	1034.8	10.11	15.6	0.6	12.2	7.1	6.6	9.6	12.2
Monroe Federal S&L Assn.	Tipp City	OH	C-	C	C	117.5	13.43	11.2	0.7	30.4	14.2	9.1	10.4	0.0
Monroe Savings Bank	Williamstown	NJ	B-	B-	C+	98.0	5.42	0.4	11.3	49.6	13.3	10.0	13.7	27.4
Monson Savings Bank	Monson	MA	B-	B-	B-	504.2	15.59	13.2	0.6	26.0	10.3	6.0	8.7	0.0
Montecito Bank & Trust	Santa Barbara	CA	B	B+	B+	1885.6	22.61	16.5	0.9	12.8	23.2	6.0	9.4	0.0
Monterey County Bank	Monterey	CA	D+	C-	D+	210.9	22.94	20.8	0.1	4.9	18.2	7.5	9.3	15.2
Montezuma State Bank	Montezuma	IA	B-	B-	C+	46.9	25.25	12.3	7.6	8.4	14.9	10.0	11.9	0.0
Montgomery Bank	Sikeston	MO	B-	C+	C+	1120.0	20.53	20.2	0.4	18.8	4.5	5.5	7.5	11.9
Monticello Banking Co.	Monticello	KY	B	B	B	899.3	17.68	8.0	2.6	18.5	17.6	6.4	9.3	0.0
Montrose Savings Bank	Montrose	MO	B+	B	B	46.4	9.88	7.0	3.5	14.2	19.8	10.0	14.5	0.0
Moody National Bank	Galveston	TX	A-	A-	A-	1420.3	18.88	11.7	0.5	4.9	25.0	10.0	13.6	0.0
Morgan Stanley Bank, N.A.	Salt Lake City	UT	A-	A	A	169782.0	22.80	5.1	4.8	0.1	43.7	9.6	10.7	20.4
Morgan Stanley Private Bank, N.A.	New York	NY	A-	A	A	110164.0	39.83	3.9	12.8	30.5	17.2	6.2	8.2	23.7
▼ Morganton Savings Bank, S.S.B.	Morganton	NC	B	B+	B-	110.7	16.13	0.2	0.1	29.6	5.9	10.0	23.4	0.0
Morgantown Bank & Trust Co., Inc.	Morgantown	KY	B-	B-	B-	223.9	9.11	7.6	3.6	38.2	14.1	6.5	8.5	0.0
▲ Morris Bank	Dublin	GA	B	C+	C-	1165.4	21.58	14.0	2.0	13.3	14.3	7.7	11.4	0.0
▼ Morris County National Bank	Naples	TX	C	C	C	94.5	5.39	9.2	6.6	16.4	23.3	9.2	10.5	17.4
Morris Plan Co. of Terre Haute, Inc.	Terre Haute	IN	A-	A-	A-	118.4	29.45	0.1	94.5	1.8	2.0	10.0	23.4	25.2
Morton Community Bank	Morton	IL	B+	B	B	4511.7	16.55	13.8	1.9	8.0	24.1	7.5	9.3	13.6
Mound City Bank	Platteville	WI	B	C+	B-	421.5	13.51	3.1	0.6	15.6	14.7	9.9	10.9	16.7
▲ Mount Vernon Bank	Mount Vernon	GA	B	B	B+	151.1	15.24	13.0	1.9	11.7	20.3	9.3	10.5	0.0
Mount Vernon Bank and Trust Co.	Mount Vernon	IA	A-	A-	A-	149.9	14.84	7.1	3.6	27.9	29.7	10.0	13.1	0.0
Mountain Commerce Bank	Knoxville	TN	B+	B+	B+	1127.0	23.94	16.1	0.9	19.4	6.9	8.3	10.2	13.5
▲ Mountain Pacific Bank	Everett	WA	C+		C	510.1	47.94	21.1	0.3	7.3	1.3	6.0	10.2	0.0
Mountain Valley Bank	Walden	CO	B	B	B-	274.8	16.73	11.9	1.4	16.7	16.5	7.1	9.1	0.0
Mountain Valley Bank	Dunlap	TN	C+	C+	C-	114.7	7.92	6.5	6.6	37.3	15.2	6.8	8.8	16.2
Mountain Valley Bank, N.A.	Elkins	WV	B+	A-	B	168.3	15.69	10.7	1.7	24.9	21.6	10.0	13.1	0.0
Mountain View Bank of Commerce	Westminster	CO	C+	C	C	158.0	25.94	20.1	0.0	5.8	0.0	6.6	8.6	12.6
▼ MountainOne Bank	North Adams	MA	B-	B	B-	907.5	0.96	15.8	0.6	23.0	9.8	10.0	12.4	17.2
▲ Movement Bank	Danville	VA	D+	D	E	66.6	46.29	7.1	1.4	14.1	10.9	10.0	11.4	21.6
MRV Banks	Sainte Genevieve	MO	B+	B	B-	457.2	18.57	25.9	0.3	7.5	2.3	4.7	9.1	0.0
Mt. McKinley Bank	Fairbanks	AK	B+	A-	B+	528.8	15.11	13.5	0.3	4.9	42.5	10.0	18.3	0.0
Mt. Victory State Bank	Mount Victory	OH	C	C	C	20.2	11.25	4.7	6.4	14.2	13.7	8.9	10.3	0.0
Muenster State Bank	Muenster	TX	A	A	A-	182.3	10.44	6.1	2.4	8.4	63.5	10.0	15.3	0.0
MUFG Union Bank, N.A.	San Francisco	CA	C	C+	B	132479.1	-1.66	14.7	2.7	22.7	18.3	9.8	10.8	16.4
Muncy Bank and Trust Co.	Muncy	PA	B	B	B	520.7	5.57	6.7	2.1	41.1	15.6	8.3	9.8	0.0
Municipal Trust and Savings Bank	Bourbonnais	IL	A	A	A-	324.4	2.03	3.2	0.4	23.4	7.4	10.0	15.4	30.1
▲ Murphy Bank	Fresno	CA	A-	B+	B+	319.6	3.32	28.1	19.0	12.9	0.0	8.6	11.4	0.0
▼ Murphy-Wall State Bank and Trust Co.	Pinckneyville	IL	C	B-	B-	153.7	19.55	7.7	4.0	15.1	29.4	8.5	10.0	18.0
Murray Bank	Murray	KY	B	B	B	347.0	11.15	10.5	2.9	23.4	17.0	7.5	9.3	15.0
▲ Mutual Federal Bank	Chicago	IL	B-	C	C-	98.2	36.70	0.0	0.0	61.0	0.2	10.0	16.3	18.8
Mutual S&L Assn.	Metairie	LA	B-	B-	B-	45.6	-8.79	0.0	0.3	76.8	0.0	10.0	30.2	57.8

Asset Quality Index	Adjusted Non-Performing Loans as a % of Total Loans	as a % of Capital	Net Charge-Offs Avg Loans	Profitability Index	Net Income ($Mil)	Return on Assets (R.O.A.)	Return on Equity (R.O.E.)	Net Interest Spread	Overhead Efficiency Ratio	Liquidity Index	Liquidity Ratio	Hot Money Ratio	Stability Index
4.6	1.07	4.1	1.01	6.1	8.0	1.24	9.57	3.69	52.6	5.4	25.6	4.2	8.0
6.8	0.11	na	0.07	3.1	0.1	0.44	2.75	5.28	89.3	2.0	10.8	12.7	6.3
4.7	0.08	8.0	-0.08	5.5	1.5	1.44	15.13	4.23	71.4	5.8	34.5	2.2	5.3
7.4	0.34	1.3	0.02	5.3	2.0	1.25	10.52	3.79	67.9	4.7	30.6	7.9	7.1
8.5	0.08	na	-0.01	6.7	1.8	1.74	18.50	4.08	61.7	2.6	12.4	14.0	5.2
5.7	1.70	6.9	0.11	6.0	18.0	1.13	10.05	3.80	58.0	2.4	19.3	8.8	9.1
8.7	0.19	na	-0.01	6.2	5.5	1.30	15.55	3.04	57.6	5.3	34.8	5.8	6.0
6.4	0.14	na	0.00	7.1	2.7	1.27	11.37	3.65	55.1	0.5	6.6	51.3	6.9
7.8	0.56	na	-0.04	3.1	0.5	0.45	5.42	3.37	85.7	7.0	64.0	4.0	4.4
8.4	0.02	na	0.04	8.3	10.1	1.32	14.89	4.00	53.4	5.8	26.7	2.0	8.1
8.9	0.00	na	0.00	1.7	-0.8	-0.44	-3.05	3.25	111.2	1.5	32.9	31.7	7.6
7.6	0.32	na	0.58	4.3	1.7	0.52	5.16	4.16	71.0	5.0	26.3	4.2	7.5
4.1	4.85	na	0.17	7.4	1.3	1.46	10.03	3.55	60.1	6.2	50.0	5.1	8.8
8.9	0.07	na	0.01	7.1	4.2	1.76	15.95	4.20	57.8	3.8	17.4	10.1	8.1
8.4	9.19	na	0.13	1.7	0.0	0.10	0.57	2.84	95.7	7.7	80.4	0.7	6.6
8.1	0.00	0.0	0.00	2.7	10.3	0.17	0.94	0.81	91.9	0.8	18.8	6.6	9.2
4.9	3.25	9.5	-0.02	4.7	2.9	1.05	6.73	3.45	61.8	3.3	27.7	14.4	7.8
8.0	0.00	na	0.00	1.8	0.9	0.15	1.53	1.87	74.2	0.2	2.4	81.5	5.8
6.8	0.18	na	0.00	4.9	7.6	1.01	9.10	3.46	62.1	3.1	11.3	9.5	8.8
5.1	1.62	na	0.14	2.1	0.2	0.26	2.33	3.05	92.9	3.1	23.6	13.2	6.0
7.2	0.32	2.8	0.00	3.4	0.4	0.51	3.67	2.99	74.2	2.2	31.1	22.7	6.9
7.7	0.32	na	-0.01	4.0	2.6	0.71	7.99	3.26	68.5	2.6	18.9	16.1	6.0
6.4	0.79	na	-0.01	4.3	9.6	0.73	7.11	3.63	74.3	5.4	25.3	4.1	7.4
2.6	3.57	na	-0.23	1.7	1.3	0.92	9.01	3.73	106.6	4.7	39.7	11.5	4.6
3.4	4.19	na	0.03	4.8	0.3	0.99	7.39	3.28	56.1	5.9	48.4	5.7	6.0
7.4	0.19	na	0.10	4.4	8.3	1.09	13.14	3.26	68.1	4.7	18.0	5.0	6.6
6.5	0.81	na	0.05	5.0	6.2	0.98	9.82	3.52	66.9	1.6	18.9	23.5	6.7
7.8	0.64	na	0.01	7.1	0.6	1.65	10.92	4.06	54.8	4.9	38.1	9.6	7.0
5.0	2.94	9.7	0.15	6.0	10.8	1.12	8.00	3.39	59.3	2.4	27.2	24.5	10.0
7.8	0.85	3.2	0.11	6.8	1358.0	1.12	10.70	1.72	20.1	3.9	56.9	0.0	9.1
7.8	0.29	2.6	0.00	6.3	878.0	1.19	14.10	1.94	29.5	3.0	33.1	0.0	7.7
9.1	0.71	na	-0.03	2.2	-0.1	-0.07	-0.30	3.31	73.7	2.5	31.8	19.7	7.2
7.9	0.06	na	0.05	3.7	1.0	0.59	6.92	3.50	78.8	2.0	11.8	18.6	5.2
4.8	1.54	na	0.38	9.1	12.9	1.67	13.60	4.73	51.7	3.8	24.1	12.8	10.0
2.0	4.43	20.8	0.09	4.3	0.7	1.06	9.66	3.76	71.1	1.9	19.9	20.3	5.1
5.0	0.69	na	1.56	10.0	2.6	3.20	13.16	10.90	29.0	0.2	3.3	66.8	8.8
5.3	0.97	7.0	0.09	5.8	43.5	1.38	13.09	3.02	43.9	2.0	19.8	10.6	9.9
4.5	3.98	na	0.02	7.0	4.3	1.41	12.68	3.18	52.0	3.0	27.6	14.7	6.6
4.8	1.11	na	0.01	4.8	1.1	1.08	9.55	3.79	75.3	3.5	43.2	18.1	7.2
8.8	0.00	na	0.02	5.6	1.3	1.21	8.76	3.31	56.6	5.2	43.6	8.5	8.0
8.3	0.30	2.3	0.00	5.2	6.2	0.76	7.60	3.40	43.6	1.4	13.7	26.6	9.1
5.1	0.37	na	0.03	5.8	3.5	1.10	10.64	3.56	54.0	1.5	11.7	23.9	6.7
6.5	0.72	na	0.09	4.9	1.7	0.89	9.28	3.84	65.3	1.9	26.8	21.1	6.3
4.9	1.34	na	0.16	3.5	0.4	0.52	5.77	4.48	78.9	2.3	12.6	17.1	4.7
8.9	0.04	na	0.06	4.7	1.0	0.88	6.81	3.81	71.3	4.9	29.7	6.3	7.3
7.2	0.09	na	-0.01	4.3	0.8	0.73	8.70	3.81	67.2	1.1	16.7	31.7	4.7
6.9	1.29	na	0.15	3.3	3.7	0.54	4.28	3.48	66.9	1.0	15.4	21.4	7.9
6.3	4.83	na	-0.07	2.8	0.3	0.71	5.91	4.70	93.8	6.0	43.5	4.3	3.6
8.4	0.00	na	-0.01	8.0	5.3	1.55	17.18	3.96	40.9	2.4	18.3	14.6	5.7
9.4	0.94	na	0.00	4.3	3.3	0.88	4.56	3.34	70.9	5.7	51.4	9.2	8.6
8.8	0.00	na	0.05	2.8	0.1	0.45	4.29	3.15	80.5	4.8	55.6	12.0	4.2
7.8	2.14	na	0.00	6.9	2.6	1.96	11.84	3.03	44.0	6.0	62.1	10.4	8.9
6.3	1.08	4.6	0.38	0.8	-322.8	-0.33	-2.92	2.25	91.2	5.0	33.8	6.2	8.7
6.3	1.10	na	0.10	5.3	4.2	1.12	11.06	3.79	64.4	2.1	10.7	18.0	7.3
7.9	0.19	na	0.00	10.0	6.4	2.65	17.62	3.55	33.8	3.5	40.0	14.3	9.8
6.4	0.13	1.7	0.07	8.5	4.5	1.92	17.15	4.37	48.7	0.5	15.2	73.7	8.4
1.1	4.50	na	-0.01	4.0	0.7	0.69	6.10	3.82	73.6	3.4	20.9	8.7	6.4
7.0	0.37	na	0.24	5.2	3.1	1.26	13.01	3.24	59.4	2.8	21.0	15.8	6.1
5.2	1.89	na	0.00	5.5	1.0	1.58	9.13	3.56	86.2	1.4	13.4	25.7	6.7
9.8	0.14	na	0.00	3.0	0.2	0.50	1.74	3.20	80.1	0.7	13.5	49.9	7.5

Name	City	State	Rating	2019 Rating	2018 Rating	Total Assets ($Mil)	One Year Asset Growth	Asset Mix (As a % of Total Assets) Commercial Loans	Consumer Loans	Mortgage Loans	Securities	Capitalization Index	Leverage Ratio	Risk-Based Capital Ratio
▲ Mutual Savings Assn.	Leavenworth	KS	A	A-	B	239.6	11.53	3.4	1.9	27.8	34.3	10.0	28.1	47.6
Mutual Savings Bank	Franklin	IN	B-	B-	B-	202.7	17.33	7.9	1.8	17.0	23.3	5.7	9.5	11.5
Mutual Savings Bank	Hartsville	SC	D	C-	C-	50.1	-1.55	5.0	3.4	33.1	0.3	10.0	25.3	40.9
MutualOne Bank	Framingham	MA	A-	A-	B+	974.1	-0.93	22.4	0.7	16.1	6.3	10.0	18.3	0.0
▲ MVB Bank, Inc.	Fairmont	WV	A-	B+	B	2210.7	12.89	17.7	0.2	8.2	13.5	9.5	10.6	15.9
Nano Banc	Irvine	CA	C	C+	C+	1366.7	50.12	21.0	0.0	3.2	0.5	5.6	8.4	11.4
Nantahala Bank & Trust Co.	Franklin	NC	D	E+	E-	192.2	18.53	9.1	0.9	21.3	9.9	5.0	7.0	11.8
Napoleon State Bank	Napoleon	IN	A-	A-	B+	321.8	17.87	9.3	6.2	18.5	5.0	9.1	10.7	0.0
Nashville Savings Bank	Nashville	IL	B	B	B	71.4	17.60	8.6	5.2	22.0	7.3	10.0	12.5	0.0
Natbank, N.A.	Hollywood	FL	B	B	B-	184.8	4.08	1.1	1.3	76.8	1.3	10.0	17.1	33.9
National Advisors Trust Co.	Kansas City	MO	U	U	U	14.2	7.53	0.0	0.0	0.0	13.4	10.0	91.8	326.3
▲ National Bank & Trust	La Grange	TX	B	B-	B-	215.2	1.94	3.1	4.3	25.3	52.7	10.0	12.5	0.0
National Bank of Adams County	West Union	OH	B	B	B-	97.6	18.89	2.2	2.6	21.4	22.8	8.7	10.1	0.0
National Bank of Andrews	Andrews	TX	C-	C+	B-	242.7	8.12	26.8	2.4	7.9	14.5	8.2	9.8	13.9
National Bank of Blacksburg	Blacksburg	VA	A-	A	A	1431.2	12.75	6.8	2.3	11.6	34.1	10.0	13.3	21.4
▲ National Bank of Commerce	Superior	WI	A-	B	B	1073.5	69.43	22.0	1.7	12.0	13.4	10.0	11.0	15.3
National Bank of Coxsackie	Coxsackie	NY	C-	C	C	408.8	21.85	10.7	2.6	28.6	28.1	6.7	8.7	18.0
National Bank of Indianapolis	Indianapolis	IN	B	B	B	2667.0	24.09	17.9	1.1	10.4	18.3	5.5	7.5	13.7
National Bank of Malvern	Malvern	PA	B+	B+	B	172.4	13.72	9.2	0.4	18.5	16.1	10.0	14.1	0.0
National Bank of Middlebury	Middlebury	VT	B-	B	B-	474.4	23.90	9.1	2.2	27.4	19.9	6.6	8.7	16.9
▼ National Bank of New York City	Flushing	NY	C+	B	B+	207.5	-9.04	1.1	0.0	21.8	1.6	10.0	18.6	25.2
National Bank of St. Anne	Saint Anne	IL	B-	B-	B-	95.7	28.02	10.4	3.5	13.3	3.2	6.7	8.7	12.6
▼ National Bank of Texas at Fort Worth	Fort Worth	TX	C	B-	B	342.8	20.15	13.7	4.3	32.6	0.0	8.1	9.7	18.2
▼ National Capital Bank of Washington	Washington	DC	C	B-	B	592.5	15.21	13.1	0.1	27.2	17.9	6.8	8.8	15.8
▲ National Cooperative Bank, N.A.	Hillsboro	OH	B-	B-	B	2846.6	8.60	21.8	1.3	18.5	7.5	9.5	10.9	14.5
National Exchange Bank and Trust	Fond du Lac	WI	A	A	A	2360.3	21.47	13.6	0.9	5.6	24.1	10.0	17.1	25.2
National Grand Bank of Marblehead	Marblehead	MA	B+	A-	A-	408.6	20.13	3.6	0.4	60.6	15.3	8.6	10.0	0.0
National Iron Bank	Salisbury	CT	C	C	C	196.9	38.67	10.5	0.9	51.3	9.3	5.5	7.5	17.1
National United	Gatesville	TX	B	B	B	748.6	16.13	9.0	5.3	11.1	17.5	8.3	9.9	14.8
Nationwide Trust Co., FSB	Columbus	OH	U	U	U	207.1	7.22	0.0	0.0	0.0	56.3	10.0	25.2	63.7
▲ Native American Bank, N.A.	Denver	CO	C	C-	C-	202.5	60.05	60.9	0.2	0.4	4.3	6.5	8.5	0.0
NBC Oklahoma	Oklahoma City	OK	B-	B-	C+	750.1	10.87	23.3	0.7	10.2	10.3	6.3	8.3	12.7
▲ NBH Bank	Greenwood Village	CO	B+	B	B	6600.5	10.33	24.2	0.3	12.9	13.6	7.4	9.2	13.6
▲ NBKC Bank	Kansas City	MO	A	B+	B+	1118.6	37.37	5.0	1.4	32.7	11.8	10.0	18.1	24.9
▼ NBT Bank, N.A.	Norwich	NY	B	B+	B	10761.6	12.20	14.3	14.8	15.1	17.5	8.3	9.9	14.8
Nebraska Bank of Commerce	Lincoln	NE	C+	C	C	162.8	7.22	19.5	0.3	11.8	6.1	6.8	8.9	13.2
Nebraska State Bank	Bristow	NE	C	C	C	19.3	6.18	11.5	2.1	1.2	0.0	10.0	13.5	25.3
▲ Nebraska State Bank	Lynch	NE	C	C	C-	18.0	19.49	3.9	1.7	1.8	0.0	10.0	12.8	0.0
Nebraska State Bank	Oshkosh	NE	A-	A-	B+	56.6	12.52	5.3	0.0	0.0	0.0	10.0	16.1	0.0
Nebraska State Bank and Trust Co.	Broken Bow	NE	B+	B	B	280.7	13.62	7.2	2.6	7.7	5.6	5.1	9.2	0.0
NebraskaLand National Bank	North Platte	NE	B-	B	B	868.2	16.14	15.1	0.6	7.3	21.6	9.9	10.9	0.0
Needham Bank	Needham	MA	B-	B-	B-	2568.8	9.52	9.2	0.3	37.9	6.5	8.0	11.7	0.0
Neffs National Bank	Neffs	PA	B+	A-	A-	395.8	6.84	3.0	2.9	22.8	47.7	10.0	18.0	0.0
▼ Neighborhood National Bank	San Diego	CA	D-	D	D+	135.4	98.81	33.7	0.0	3.8	0.1	9.6	10.7	26.9
Neighborhood National Bank	Mora	MN	B+	A-	B+	260.6	16.08	16.7	3.2	16.8	33.1	9.3	10.6	17.5
Neighbors Bank	Clarence	MO	C+	C-	C+	78.5	152.68	0.4	0.5	35.8	6.2	10.0	11.8	20.4
Nekoosa Port Edwards State Bank	Nekoosa	WI	A-	A-	B+	226.1	5.28	7.6	2.4	32.1	19.1	10.0	14.0	26.8
Nelsonville Home & Savings Bank	Nelsonville	OH	B-	B-	B-	33.0	7.60	1.7	3.3	52.7	3.0	10.0	12.3	28.2
Neuberger Berman Trust Co. of Delaware	Wilmington	DE	U	U	U	7.1	4.50	0.0	0.0	0.0	0.0	10.0	90.5	223.1
Neuberger Berman Trust Co., N.A.	New York	NY	U	U	U	23.5	-12.09	0.0	0.0	0.0	0.0	10.0	61.6	130.3
Nevada Bank and Trust Co.	Caliente	NV	B-	C+	C+	192.9	35.43	8.2	3.4	2.0	45.2	6.0	8.0	0.0
▼ New Albin Savings Bank	New Albin	IA	A-	A	A	274.8	7.70	2.1	1.0	11.5	70.7	10.0	16.7	54.2
New Carlisle Federal Savings Bank	New Carlisle	OH	C+	C+	C+	167.1	28.24	22.2	1.2	29.7	1.4	4.6	9.2	0.0
New Century Bank	Belleville	KS	B	B	B+	60.7	1.59	2.6	2.7	35.4	0.0	9.0	10.3	16.5
New Covenant Trust Co., N.A.	Jeffersonville	IN	U	U	U	6.5	-2.95	0.0	0.0	0.0	4.1	10.0	92.7	285.5
New Era Bank	Fredericktown	MO	A-	A-	A-	440.3	25.59	6.4	0.9	20.1	13.2	7.2	9.1	0.0
New Foundation Savings Bank	Cincinnati	OH	C-	C+	C	29.7	55.82	5.5	0.2	70.8	1.0	6.4	8.4	0.0
New Frontier Bank	Saint Charles	MO	B-	B-	C	115.2	18.21	14.3	0.1	6.2	16.9	6.4	8.4	12.3
New Haven Bank	New Haven	CT	C	C+	C	155.5	6.74	10.8	5.8	33.5	2.4	7.9	9.6	16.1
New Horizon Bank, N.A.	Powhatan	VA	C-	C+	C+	98.2	12.03	19.2	1.0	12.6	9.4	8.9	10.3	15.3

Asset Quality Index	Adjusted Non-Performing Loans as a % of Total Loans	as a % of Capital	Net Charge-Offs / Avg Loans	Profitability Index	Net Income ($Mil)	Return on Assets (R.O.A.)	Return on Equity (R.O.E.)	Net Interest Spread	Overhead Efficiency Ratio	Liquidity Index	Liquidity Ratio	Hot Money Ratio	Stability Index
8.0	1.82	na	-0.33	8.2	3.0	1.68	5.70	3.64	55.0	4.0	50.9	17.6	8.3
8.7	0.00	na	0.02	4.8	1.5	1.06	11.08	3.43	70.8	3.2	27.5	15.0	5.6
8.3	1.25	na	0.00	0.2	-0.1	-0.33	-1.31	3.10	118.3	0.7	15.5	45.8	6.4
7.4	2.10	na	0.04	8.0	9.7	1.32	7.29	3.51	46.7	1.0	16.8	31.9	9.4
6.3	1.25	6.4	0.16	9.4	31.3	1.99	19.05	3.61	54.9	4.4	18.6	5.7	9.4
8.0	0.98	na	0.00	2.6	4.5	0.59	6.68	3.84	75.9	6.9	37.2	0.1	8.0
2.9	2.34	na	0.00	1.2	0.0	-0.02	-0.27	3.57	102.9	3.7	28.4	12.9	1.8
6.5	0.24	na	0.01	7.7	3.3	1.45	13.56	3.82	54.1	2.4	25.5	18.0	7.2
7.4	0.20	na	0.00	4.8	0.5	0.91	7.12	2.71	58.2	2.2	32.3	24.2	6.5
9.8	0.13	na	0.01	4.0	1.0	0.68	4.06	3.94	77.4	2.0	20.1	13.8	7.8
9.2	na	na	na	9.5	1.7	17.05	19.82	1.15	85.9	4.0	na	100.0	6.2
9.3	0.08	na	-0.04	4.0	1.6	1.03	7.43	2.67	64.1	3.5	47.4	19.3	6.7
4.2	1.27	na	-0.01	4.0	0.5	0.72	6.81	2.83	66.8	5.4	44.9	8.1	6.4
1.9	3.49	na	0.04	9.6	3.6	2.07	20.48	4.81	60.6	4.6	28.6	7.4	8.0
8.3	0.62	2.2	0.07	5.4	11.5	1.12	8.05	2.97	54.4	5.6	26.9	3.8	10.0
6.3	0.50	na	0.14	6.3	10.8	1.42	11.51	4.23	57.8	3.9	14.6	9.8	10.0
7.2	0.61	2.7	-0.01	3.3	1.6	0.60	6.64	3.37	73.5	5.0	20.0	2.6	2.3
8.2	0.56	2.7	0.01	4.7	16.6	0.91	11.50	2.72	61.1	5.9	29.4	3.4	7.0
6.0	1.22	na	0.00	4.1	1.0	0.80	5.50	3.35	65.7	3.4	18.6	12.1	7.7
7.2	0.21	1.4	-0.08	4.4	3.1	0.98	10.71	3.33	69.7	5.3	28.9	3.0	5.1
5.1	2.05	na	0.02	1.4	-0.4	-0.26	-1.45	2.53	80.7	0.5	15.2	55.0	8.0
4.4	0.43	na	0.00	6.3	0.8	1.15	10.57	3.82	61.1	1.5	18.9	25.9	6.7
6.9	1.17	na	0.33	2.4	0.9	0.38	3.67	3.52	86.2	2.7	31.8	18.7	5.7
8.5	0.93	na	0.02	2.6	1.7	0.39	4.30	3.34	78.1	4.3	19.1	7.3	5.9
7.8	0.39	2.0	-0.02	3.9	18.3	0.87	8.01	3.19	71.5	4.4	25.6	8.5	9.2
7.9	1.53	na	1.26	6.1	15.3	0.92	4.93	3.61	49.9	6.1	30.6	3.0	10.0
9.3	0.63	na	-0.01	4.8	2.6	0.92	8.27	2.99	60.4	4.6	29.8	8.4	6.1
9.6	0.00	na	0.00	2.8	0.5	0.41	5.28	2.87	82.9	4.3	28.2	9.4	3.5
5.2	1.91	na	0.04	5.1	5.7	1.08	10.46	3.79	64.8	4.6	33.2	9.6	6.4
10.0	na	na	na	9.0	20.8	14.21	45.44	0.71	86.5	8.5	102.7	0.0	8.2
3.6	2.31	na	-0.01	3.1	0.7	0.56	6.22	3.65	83.0	0.5	16.5	57.9	4.6
4.6	1.19	8.4	0.01	4.0	6.2	1.13	13.45	3.89	76.0	3.2	22.6	13.9	5.4
6.4	0.79	3.3	0.04	6.7	66.3	1.43	12.92	3.45	60.5	4.1	13.7	8.3	8.5
7.4	0.82	na	-0.06	9.5	109.9	15.55	99.62	2.06	51.8	2.8	38.9	26.6	10.0
6.0	0.67	3.0	0.24	4.5	67.0	0.87	7.37	3.39	56.6	4.6	11.6	2.6	8.8
8.4	0.02	na	0.00	3.1	0.6	0.52	5.97	2.98	68.1	1.4	21.0	27.8	5.5
8.3	0.00	na	-0.06	3.3	0.1	0.68	5.02	3.75	68.2	2.0	52.3	28.4	4.3
5.8	0.00	na	0.00	4.4	0.2	1.32	10.20	3.42	57.5	5.1	58.6	7.7	3.9
6.3	0.69	na	0.00	9.8	1.6	3.69	23.41	4.15	39.2	1.9	12.2	19.2	9.2
7.6	0.09	na	0.04	6.3	2.8	1.43	14.71	3.54	57.8	1.6	22.6	18.5	6.9
8.7	0.00	0.0	0.00	3.9	4.9	0.80	7.12	2.99	69.8	1.8	17.3	14.5	7.5
6.1	1.36	9.0	0.14	3.3	10.1	0.53	4.54	2.74	66.4	0.9	9.7	31.1	9.1
9.5	1.00	na	0.00	4.3	2.5	0.87	4.66	2.90	62.4	4.1	52.2	17.8	8.9
3.7	3.74	na	0.30	0.0	-2.0	-2.36	-24.49	2.49	169.0	2.8	43.4	25.2	5.0
7.1	0.27	1.2	-0.03	4.9	2.1	1.15	9.90	3.69	72.3	4.2	28.1	10.0	7.2
9.6	0.05	na	0.00	6.7	2.7	6.59	56.86	1.12	69.4	6.7	52.0	1.6	6.7
8.6	1.27	na	-0.05	5.9	2.4	1.40	9.87	2.83	49.0	2.1	41.5	34.7	8.4
9.2	0.00	na	0.00	3.9	0.2	0.69	5.69	3.30	65.2	2.8	32.0	18.3	6.5
10.0	na	na	na	9.9	0.1	1.71	1.86	23.26	97.3	4.0	359.0	0.0	5.8
10.0	na	na	na	10.0	0.8	5.19	8.91	19.90	96.3	4.0	124.3	0.0	6.5
9.0	0.20	na	-0.03	3.4	0.8	0.64	6.73	3.18	76.6	7.5	65.3	0.7	5.2
9.7	0.23	na	-0.09	5.4	2.4	1.18	6.62	2.22	35.4	4.1	69.6	21.7	9.3
3.7	1.01	na	0.02	4.0	0.9	0.82	9.36	3.34	73.2	1.5	11.1	23.7	5.0
6.7	0.18	na	0.23	6.5	0.6	1.27	12.83	5.23	75.3	0.7	13.6	46.4	6.3
10.0	na	na	na	9.5	0.1	2.28	2.57	1.41	95.2	4.0	na	0.0	5.7
8.7	0.00	0.2	0.01	6.8	4.6	1.53	14.48	2.97	47.5	5.1	35.7	7.6	7.6
8.6	0.40	na	0.00	6.9	0.1	2.40	25.54	2.79	83.8	1.7	12.8	21.5	4.3
4.0	1.55	na	-0.02	4.1	0.9	1.04	11.54	3.92	72.9	3.6	20.6	11.3	5.7
8.3	0.00	na	0.02	2.2	0.3	0.21	1.99	2.87	84.3	0.6	9.9	45.0	6.4
6.3	0.42	na	0.04	2.5	0.1	0.20	1.90	4.25	90.3	1.2	15.4	28.6	6.0

Name	City	State	Rating	2019 Rating	2018 Rating	Total Assets ($Mil)	One Year Asset Growth	Commercial Loans	Consumer Loans	Mortgage Loans	Securities	Capitalization Index	Leverage Ratio	Risk-Based Capital Ratio
New Market Bank	Elko New Market	MN	C+	C+	C+	157.5	31.73	22.2	0.7	10.3	16.0	5.0	7.0	14.6
New Mexico Bank & Trust	Albuquerque	NM	B+	A-	A-	2005.5	24.76	14.5	0.3	4.3	37.3	6.0	8.0	12.9
New Millennium Bank	Fort Lee	NJ	C+	C+	C	461.9	2.95	19.5	0.0	12.8	0.6	7.2	9.1	14.1
New OMNI Bank, N.A.	Alhambra	CA	A-	A-	A-	523.7	8.48	2.8	0.1	31.9	0.7	10.0	14.6	23.5
▲ New Peoples Bank, Inc.	Honaker	VA	C	C	C-	747.9	5.97	12.9	2.9	28.6	5.9	7.2	9.1	15.7
New Republic Bank	Roanoke Rapids	NC	C-	C-	C	69.8	10.01	3.6	0.3	48.1	0.0	7.8	9.5	14.8
New Tripoli Bank	New Tripoli	PA	B	B	B+	518.0	3.78	7.9	0.3	44.4	17.1	10.0	11.4	0.0
New Valley Bank & Trust	Springfield	MA	D			210.3	363.33	49.6	0.0	8.5	9.0	10.0	14.2	22.9
New Washington State Bank	New Washington	IN	B+	B+	B-	386.9	13.88	12.4	9.0	14.5	10.5	7.2	9.5	0.0
New York Community Bank	Hicksville	NY	B	B	B+	54908.2	4.56	3.2	0.0	0.5	9.5	7.2	9.4	12.7
▼ NewBank	Flushing	NY	B+	A-	B+	477.1	6.50	23.5	0.0	0.1	0.0	9.9	11.0	0.0
Newburyport Five Cents Savings Bank	Newburyport	MA	C+	C+	B-	1185.6	17.11	12.1	2.3	27.1	9.4	10.0	12.3	16.5
Newfield National Bank	Newfield	NJ	C+	C+	C	811.1	17.87	6.1	0.2	16.1	28.1	6.2	8.2	16.7
NewFirst National Bank	El Campo	TX	B+	B	B	817.1	12.30	18.5	0.5	7.1	5.2	8.3	10.8	0.0
▼ Newport Federal Bank	Newport	TN	C+	B	B	234.0	9.29	0.4	1.1	34.4	43.5	9.5	10.7	0.0
Newton Federal Bank	Covington	GA	C-	C+	B-	888.0	186.16	31.1	4.8	10.7	2.8	6.5	9.0	12.1
Newtown Savings Bank	Newtown	CT	C+	C+	C+	1570.0	17.19	10.6	1.4	34.0	10.2	5.5	7.5	14.6
NexBank	Dallas	TX	B+	B+	A-	9037.4	-11.03	3.7	0.1	36.0	12.2	6.6	8.6	14.0
NexTier Bank, N.A.	Butler	PA	B+	B+	B	1693.4	21.29	12.7	7.1	21.0	6.1	3.8	8.8	0.0
Nicolet National Bank	Green Bay	WI	B+	B+	B+	4694.8	51.51	21.8	0.7	9.7	11.4	5.7	8.3	11.6
▲ Ninnescah Valley Bank	Cunningham	KS	B	B	B	34.3	9.91	6.4	2.1	4.9	57.0	10.0	12.3	0.0
Noah Bank	Elkins Park	PA	D+	C-	C	359.0	-19.19	11.6	0.0	0.8	1.2	5.7	7.7	13.8
▼ NobleBank & Trust	Anniston	AL	C+	B-	B-	323.3	21.17	24.5	1.6	12.5	16.4	3.3	8.5	0.0
Nodaway Valley Bank	Maryville	MO	A	A	A-	1118.7	22.72	10.4	0.8	5.2	19.9	10.0	11.5	16.4
Nokomis Savings Bank	Nokomis	IL	C-	C	C+	33.9	17.96	8.3	3.1	16.1	36.0	10.0	14.3	0.0
Normangee State Bank	Normangee	TX	B	B-	C+	130.6	7.68	2.4	8.8	24.8	33.5	10.0	15.6	32.3
North Adams State Bank	Ursa	IL	B-	B-	B-	43.8	13.82	15.0	4.6	15.8	16.1	10.0	13.4	0.0
▲ North Alabama Bank	Hazel Green	AL	B+	B-	C+	132.4	15.92	7.8	1.7	8.5	7.7	6.3	9.6	0.0
North American Banking Co.	Roseville	MN	A-	A-	B+	735.7	23.29	20.5	0.3	5.1	19.0	5.8	7.8	13.2
▲ North American Savings Bank, F.S.B.	Kansas City	MO	A	A-	A-	2539.8	-2.03	0.3	0.0	72.4	6.2	10.0	13.8	19.5
North Arundel Savings Bank	Pasadena	MD	C	C	C	44.7	2.88	0.0	1.5	58.9	3.5	10.0	12.9	27.9
North Brookfield Savings Bank	North Brookfield	MA	C+	B-	B-	338.1	5.69	4.0	2.0	46.8	15.6	10.0	11.7	0.0
▼ North Cambridge Co-operative Bank	Cambridge	MA	C+	C+	C+	89.6	-2.13	0.0	0.1	53.1	8.0	10.0	23.5	0.0
▲ North Central Bank	Hennepin	IL	A-	B	B	135.0	8.07	6.4	3.9	19.8	25.9	10.0	12.7	0.0
North Country Savings Bank	Canton	NY	B-	B-	B-	295.8	11.68	0.8	2.1	69.3	0.7	10.0	14.2	25.4
North County Savings Bank	Red Bud	IL	C+	C+	C+	60.0	10.37	0.0	2.4	36.8	18.9	6.3	8.3	0.0
North Dallas Bank & Trust Co.	Dallas	TX	B	B	B	1452.4	13.43	7.6	0.5	16.5	33.7	10.0	11.4	0.0
▲ North Easton Savings Bank	South Easton	MA	C	C	C	1251.6	10.24	7.3	2.2	36.1	18.8	6.1	8.1	14.5
North Georgia National Bank	Calhoun	GA	B-	B-	B-	145.2	18.27	11.1	0.9	13.5	22.8	9.3	10.6	0.0
North Salem State Bank	North Salem	IN	B	B	B-	472.0	29.13	9.8	3.0	14.7	6.5	6.2	8.2	12.0
▲ North Shore Bank of Commerce	Duluth	MN	B+	B	B	360.4	25.07	9.7	0.4	30.0	10.1	9.4	10.6	0.0
North Shore Bank, a Co-operative Bank	Peabody	MA	B-	B-	C+	1508.5	66.33	13.6	0.2	23.7	8.3	8.6	10.0	15.7
North Shore Bank, FSB	Brookfield	WI	B-	B	B-	2430.6	18.64	2.7	19.2	14.1	15.8	9.4	10.6	0.0
North Shore Trust and Savings	Waukegan	IL	D+	C	C	238.8	6.37	0.4	0.2	39.1	30.1	10.0	18.3	0.0
North Side Bank and Trust Co.	Cincinnati	OH	B+	A-	B+	910.8	27.35	27.2	0.7	11.1	19.6	7.5	10.5	13.0
North Side Federal S&L Assn. of Chicago	Chicago	IL	D-	D+	D	47.2	19.10	10.3	0.0	39.8	12.9	7.2	9.2	24.1
North Star Bank	Roseville	MN	B+	B+	B	328.0	11.69	19.8	1.6	3.0	21.6	7.4	9.9	0.0
North State Bank	Raleigh	NC	B	B	B-	1241.6	31.03	17.3	0.2	20.6	2.8	5.6	7.6	11.6
North Valley Bank	Thornton	CO	A	A	A	195.7	9.98	6.2	0.1	38.8	0.0	10.0	11.9	18.0
North Valley Bank	Zanesville	OH	C+	B-	B-	307.0	47.13	19.4	3.0	15.7	12.3	3.6	8.7	0.0
Northbrook Bank & Trust Co., N.A.	Northbrook	IL	B	B	B	3377.3	17.57	29.9	8.3	3.2	11.3	6.0	9.1	11.8
Northeast Bank	Lewiston	ME	C+	C+		1256.8	11.91	0.7	0.1	5.8	5.4	10.0	14.0	21.2
Northeast Bank	Minneapolis	MN	A-	A-	A-	666.7	30.69	29.5	0.1	6.5	14.8	6.8	8.8	13.8
NorthEast Community Bank	White Plains	NY	B	B	B-	951.3	-7.76	8.7	0.0	0.7	0.8	9.0	14.4	14.2
Northeast Georgia Bank	Lavonia	GA	A-	A-	A-	524.6	13.94	10.0	4.1	6.2	19.5	10.0	11.1	0.0
Northeast Missouri State Bank	Kirksville	MO	A-	A-	A-	116.7	5.40	2.8	3.2	10.4	43.4	10.0	12.2	25.2
Northeast Security Bank	Sumner	IA	B+	A-	A-	319.4	19.09	10.4	0.6	9.8	26.0	9.7	10.8	17.4
Northern Bank & Trust Co.	Woburn	MA	A	B+	B-	2677.2	24.62	38.3	0.0	8.8	1.6	10.0	12.0	15.4
Northern California National Bank	Chico	CA	B+	B+	B	312.3	17.96	8.5	0.4	4.9	26.7	7.0	9.0	0.0
▼ Northern Interstate Bank, N.A.	Norway	MI	B-	B	B-	179.1	13.69	8.2	3.9	21.4	30.1	9.3	10.6	0.0

Asset Quality Index	Adjusted Non-Performing Loans as a % of Total Loans	as a % of Capital	Net Charge-Offs Avg Loans	Profitability Index	Net Income ($Mil)	Return on Assets (R.O.A.)	Return on Equity (R.O.E.)	Net Interest Spread	Overhead Efficiency Ratio	Liquidity Index	Liquidity Ratio	Hot Money Ratio	Stability Index
5.2	1.80	na	0.03	6.2	1.5	1.48	19.40	4.22	68.5	5.6	29.0	1.5	3.7
8.4	0.35	2.2	0.72	6.5	13.8	1.01	11.29	3.71	51.3	5.3	24.1	4.0	7.8
3.6	0.94	na	0.09	4.3	2.1	0.65	6.83	3.27	60.2	0.8	20.9	51.3	5.9
8.9	0.08	na	0.00	5.8	3.9	1.07	7.26	3.89	59.8	0.7	22.7	64.9	8.1
4.8	1.18	7.8	0.09	2.8	1.9	0.35	3.63	3.74	82.5	2.2	17.0	18.0	6.2
6.8	0.55	na	0.00	1.9	0.2	0.32	3.27	3.89	93.3	0.5	8.1	54.5	4.9
7.3	0.94	na	0.00	4.5	4.1	1.08	9.29	3.45	58.6	2.4	16.2	17.2	8.2
8.1	0.00	na	0.00	0.0	-0.7	-0.67	-4.81	2.19	113.9	3.6	10.3	10.6	1.5
7.0	0.48	na	0.02	6.7	4.3	1.56	15.76	4.13	66.2	5.1	27.6	4.1	7.3
6.1	0.14	0.7	0.04	4.4	348.6	0.86	6.48	2.23	42.5	0.8	11.4	22.2	10.0
8.5	0.10	na	0.42	5.0	3.1	0.91	8.13	2.43	66.4	2.4	41.5	30.7	6.5
8.5	0.14	na	0.10	2.1	2.9	0.34	2.88	3.25	76.5	3.1	15.1	12.6	8.6
6.4	0.77	4.1	0.04	3.2	3.0	0.54	5.96	2.98	78.6	5.9	39.9	4.2	5.3
4.1	1.44	na	0.01	10.0	15.4	2.55	23.08	4.80	47.7	5.0	22.2	3.0	8.7
8.1	0.87	na	0.00	3.2	0.8	0.47	4.26	2.53	72.2	1.9	35.5	31.9	6.5
4.7	0.87	na	-0.03	2.6	2.1	0.38	3.72	2.99	80.7	2.5	22.9	15.7	6.4
5.5	1.50	8.7	0.13	3.1	5.1	0.45	6.10	2.88	69.2	4.9	26.8	7.6	6.0
6.2	1.38	15.4	0.03	5.5	74.1	1.07	18.27	2.31	28.0	4.9	18.1	1.6	5.9
6.1	0.52	na	0.14	4.6	9.6	0.82	8.57	3.20	62.6	4.1	11.5	6.1	8.3
6.3	0.38	1.9	0.04	7.8	43.0	1.38	11.52	3.48	52.0	4.6	30.6	5.9	10.0
8.9	0.29	na	0.10	4.2	0.3	1.03	7.81	3.82	74.4	5.4	59.7	11.1	7.1
0.5	3.68	na	1.31	0.1	-2.1	-0.74	-9.17	2.58	152.3	0.7	16.9	51.0	2.7
6.2	0.44	na	1.15	4.2	1.9	0.85	9.20	4.31	74.6	3.7	21.0	10.9	4.2
8.1	0.07	na	0.01	8.6	15.2	1.97	14.79	3.88	54.7	5.3	29.9	7.7	10.0
7.5	1.48	na	0.02	1.3	0.0	-0.04	-0.24	2.19	96.1	3.2	52.5	22.5	6.5
5.0	4.50	na	0.47	4.5	0.8	0.87	5.33	4.03	62.7	3.7	44.2	17.7	6.3
8.1	0.15	na	0.09	4.3	0.2	0.69	4.74	3.87	73.7	4.2	34.8	12.0	6.5
7.1	0.66	na	-0.05	5.8	1.0	1.03	9.32	4.88	69.6	1.3	23.3	27.8	7.3
7.6	0.00	0.4	0.00	8.5	11.3	2.08	25.75	3.30	47.6	3.5	31.0	14.3	7.5
6.7	1.16	5.2	0.12	10.0	89.1	4.61	38.95	3.86	44.3	0.6	5.6	31.6	10.0
8.3	1.40	5.5	0.00	0.7	-0.1	-0.28	-2.15	3.40	102.0	1.4	31.5	35.5	6.0
8.8	0.34	1.4	0.00	2.6	1.1	0.45	3.82	2.98	87.8	3.7	25.3	11.7	6.6
9.9	0.40	na	0.00	1.6	0.0	0.02	0.07	2.85	82.8	3.1	52.3	24.3	7.6
7.1	1.67	na	0.01	6.0	1.4	1.48	10.12	3.51	62.2	4.6	40.0	11.8	8.7
8.6	0.56	na	0.07	2.7	0.7	0.33	2.65	3.46	85.5	4.7	15.7	4.3	6.5
9.8	0.00	0.0	0.00	2.8	0.2	0.41	4.75	2.39	80.7	3.2	56.9	25.1	3.7
9.5	0.00	na	0.05	3.7	6.3	0.61	4.99	2.47	70.0	6.2	53.2	9.1	8.3
6.9	0.75	na	0.06	2.9	4.2	0.48	4.91	3.40	77.3	4.8	26.3	9.1	6.1
8.0	1.23	na	-0.08	3.5	0.6	0.62	5.57	3.79	80.5	4.3	25.2	8.2	6.2
5.7	1.14	na	-0.05	6.0	3.6	1.16	14.09	3.71	60.1	2.7	26.0	16.7	5.3
8.0	0.50	1.7	-0.04	8.8	6.0	2.47	27.72	4.98	66.5	5.3	28.7	2.7	5.8
7.2	0.66	na	0.00	4.2	8.0	0.74	7.11	3.64	64.8	3.4	19.5	13.2	7.9
6.7	0.42	2.1	0.00	3.6	9.8	0.58	4.95	3.05	79.2	4.7	24.9	8.8	8.4
9.9	1.97	na	-0.01	0.7	-0.1	-0.04	-0.21	2.13	102.5	4.6	61.3	17.0	7.3
8.7	0.10	na	0.04	5.7	6.9	1.10	10.09	2.83	52.1	3.0	13.5	13.8	7.4
3.4	5.61	na	0.00	0.5	-0.1	-0.32	-3.56	3.15	113.5	4.2	33.6	11.7	3.9
7.9	1.51	na	0.00	6.2	3.4	1.46	14.00	3.81	60.2	4.6	37.4	11.0	6.8
6.5	0.53	na	0.07	5.3	10.4	1.23	16.40	3.58	69.1	4.8	16.6	3.8	7.2
8.8	0.00	na	0.00	10.0	3.9	2.76	23.21	5.31	45.9	3.8	13.2	9.6	9.2
5.7	0.71	na	0.02	3.0	1.0	0.49	5.55	3.43	85.0	4.1	18.3	7.2	4.2
5.6	0.77	4.5	0.25	5.8	20.4	0.93	9.62	2.79	45.0	2.1	20.5	10.6	7.6
3.3	4.03	na	0.08	10.0	20.9	2.24	16.97	5.11	46.2	1.2	19.6	31.8	10.0
8.0	0.28	1.3	0.00	6.1	6.5	1.43	14.81	3.86	59.8	4.4	15.1	4.4	7.8
5.3	0.49	na	0.00	6.8	8.7	1.26	8.67	4.48	61.4	0.7	10.8	36.8	8.4
8.2	0.65	na	0.06	5.2	4.6	1.19	11.11	3.24	65.0	4.8	33.9	8.4	8.2
8.2	0.08	na	0.02	6.0	1.4	1.56	10.20	3.31	54.9	3.9	47.9	17.5	9.1
8.4	0.01	na	0.00	5.1	2.4	1.06	8.53	3.12	59.2	4.0	29.4	11.4	7.5
7.8	0.34	na	-0.01	9.6	34.5	1.84	16.47	4.17	35.1	1.2	14.5	17.7	10.0
8.8	1.50	na	-0.01	4.8	2.7	1.19	12.94	2.91	49.4	4.9	31.7	6.1	5.7
3.3	4.55	na	-0.01	4.5	1.3	1.00	8.81	3.82	70.6	5.7	43.3	6.8	6.6

Name	City	State	2019 Rating	2018 Rating	Rating	Total Assets ($Mil)	One Year Asset Growth	Comm-ercial Loans	Cons-umer Loans	Mort-gage Loans	Secur-ities	Capital-ization Index	Lever-age Ratio	Risk-Based Capital Ratio
Northern Sky Bank	Crookston	MN	B	B-	C+	82.4	6.85	9.6	2.1	14.5	18.3	9.0	10.3	18.4
Northern State Bank	Ashland	WI	B+	B+	B-	285.2	20.87	8.6	0.9	22.6	21.5	6.4	8.4	17.5
Northern State Bank of Gonvick	Gonvick	MN	B-	B	B-	37.9	9.88	2.9	4.8	6.0	43.5	10.0	16.7	95.5
▼ Northern State Bank of Thief River Falls	Thief River Falls	MN	B	B+	B-	379.9	11.28	5.3	4.2	9.7	23.2	8.0	9.7	25.2
Northern State Bank of Virginia	Virginia	MN	B-	B-	C	84.2	13.02	17.7	2.0	25.9	13.9	7.2	9.1	14.7
Northern Trust Co.	Chicago	IL	B+	B+	B	151628.9	22.45	2.7	0.2	3.7	38.6	5.2	7.2	15.6
Northfield Bank	Woodbridge	NJ	B-	B	B	5596.2	16.34	3.9	0.0	5.1	21.1	9.8	11.9	0.0
Northfield Savings Bank	Berlin	VT	C	B-	B-	1220.5	15.82	12.2	0.1	40.4	15.9	9.5	10.7	0.0
Northmark Bank	North Andover	MA	B+	A-	B+	417.3	14.12	11.9	0.5	33.9	6.7	10.0	11.9	0.0
Northpointe Bank	Grand Rapids	MI	B+	B	B	3155.1	51.19	0.1	0.0	54.7	0.0	7.0	9.0	0.0
▲ Northrim Bank	Anchorage	AK	B+	B	B	2083.0	29.88	34.7	0.3	7.8	10.3	6.9	8.9	13.4
▲ Northside Community Bank	Gurnee	IL	A-	B	B-	278.0	15.43	9.6	0.1	6.4	1.7	10.0	19.9	27.7
▼ NorthStar Bank	Estherville	IA	B+	A-	B+	193.9	2.09	5.7	1.2	12.6	8.6	10.0	11.8	18.5
Northstar Bank	Bad Axe	MI	B-	C+	C-	777.0	16.56	16.9	1.5	9.7	6.2	3.3	8.5	0.0
Northumberland National Bank	Northumberland	PA	C+	C+	C+	590.1	8.55	11.2	0.8	32.7	28.4	8.4	10.0	18.2
▲ Northview Bank	Sandstone	MN	A-	B	C+	378.3	16.33	8.1	3.4	19.3	15.2	10.0	11.1	0.0
▼ Northway Bank	Berlin	NH	C	B	C+	1097.3	22.52	9.5	1.3	17.0	16.1	7.5	9.3	16.8
Northwest Bank	Spencer	IA	B+	B+	B+	1987.3	19.24	22.6	1.6	13.5	8.3	5.7	8.5	11.5
Northwest Bank	Boise	ID	A-	A-	A-	1052.1	33.36	47.6	0.0	0.3	9.8	4.5	9.3	0.0
Northwest Bank	Warren	PA	B-	B	B	13927.3	29.86	9.0	10.8	30.6	10.2	7.8	9.5	14.5
Northwest Bank & Trust Co.	Davenport	IA	B-	B-	B-	229.3	43.10	19.1	0.4	6.9	4.5	5.9	7.9	15.6
Northwest Bank of Rockford	Rockford	IL	B-	B	B-	338.5	18.42	31.0	3.4	10.8	14.8	2.7	8.3	0.0
Northwest Community Bank	Winsted	CT	C	B-	B-	427.8	2.80	8.4	2.5	45.0	14.5	10.0	11.6	0.0
Northwestern Bank	Orange City	IA	A-	A-	B+	245.4	11.30	6.8	0.8	10.5	8.1	10.0	14.0	0.0
Northwestern Bank	Chippewa Falls	WI	A-	A	A-	517.6	15.33	26.1	0.7	7.0	16.5	9.3	10.7	14.4
Northwestern Bank, N.A.	Dilworth	MN	C+	C+	C+	166.2	13.47	14.5	3.1	9.9	8.8	5.4	9.6	0.0
Northwestern Mutual Wealth Mgmt Co.	Milwaukee	WI	U	U	U	334.3	6.82	0.0	0.0	0.0	92.4	10.0	62.9	0.0
▲ Northwoods Bank of Minnesota	Park Rapids	MN	B+	B-	B-	135.4	11.69	7.5	1.3	21.3	36.2	8.5	10.0	0.0
▼ Norway Savings Bank	Norway	ME	B+	A	B+	1458.7	17.58	12.5	5.1	26.4	5.6	10.0	13.6	0.0
▲ Norwood Co-operative Bank	Norwood	MA	B+	B	B	628.9	10.03	4.7	0.0	33.5	8.0	10.0	13.7	0.0
NSB Bank	Mason City	IA	A-	A-	A-	237.1	13.02	29.2	1.1	6.4	10.8	9.0	10.3	14.8
NVE Bank	Englewood	NJ	B	B	B	709.9	7.23	2.6	0.0	30.6	14.2	10.0	15.7	29.4
NXT Bank	Central City	IA	B	B-	B-	248.9	-5.35	12.0	0.4	11.1	11.6	10.0	12.2	17.5
O'Bannon Banking Co.	Buffalo	MO	B-	B-	B-	241.5	12.68	7.3	1.7	23.0	10.7	5.8	8.5	0.0
Oak Bank	Fitchburg	WI	B+	B	B+	405.6	28.33	22.1	0.8	11.0	10.7	8.4	9.9	16.3
Oak Valley Community Bank	Oakdale	CA	B+	B+	B+	1449.0	31.60	17.0	0.1	1.7	15.7	6.0	8.0	12.9
Oak View National Bank	Warrenton	VA	C+	B-	C+	295.0	15.41	16.4	1.1	32.0	1.0	7.1	9.2	0.0
Oakdale State Bank	Oakdale	IL	C+	C+	C+	23.4	11.57	6.0	6.3	21.4	1.8	10.0	11.6	18.8
OakStar Bank	Springfield	MO	B-	B-	C+	1279.0	26.23	22.0	1.3	17.3	1.4	5.3	10.2	0.0
Oakwood Bank	Dallas	TX	D+	D	D+	589.8	57.94	19.5	0.4	8.2	3.3	5.0	9.5	11.0
Oakwood Bank	Pigeon Falls	WI	C-	C	C+	102.8	15.81	8.1	0.4	9.9	1.3	4.5	8.4	10.8
Oakworth Capital Bank	Birmingham	AL	B+	A-	A-	844.4	30.52	39.1	1.7	1.9	9.1	3.9	9.7	0.0
Ocean Bank	Miami	FL	B-	B+	B+	4594.5	6.70	9.7	0.5	5.1	9.1	8.9	10.7	14.1
▼ OceanFirst Bank, N.A.	Toms River	NJ	B-	B	B	11597.6	42.58	6.9	0.8	24.9	9.2	6.4	8.4	12.4
Oconee Federal S&L Assn.	Seneca	SC	B+	B+	B+	522.1	-0.35	1.7	1.2	55.6	17.3	10.0	15.7	29.9
Oconee State Bank	Watkinsville	GA	C	C+	C+	469.4	31.89	16.7	0.9	9.3	12.1	7.5	9.3	14.3
Odin State Bank	Odin	MN	D+	D	D	51.7	12.90	7.9	6.4	13.2	13.9	7.7	10.0	0.0
Ohana Pacific Bank	Honolulu	HI	B-	B	B	196.7	12.98	10.3	0.0	12.7	2.4	9.3	10.6	16.6
Ohio State Bank	Bexley	OH	D-			179.2	165.70	7.0	0.0	18.0	11.4	9.8	26.8	0.0
Ohio Valley Bank Co.	Gallipolis	OH	B-	B	C+	1121.7	8.85	10.0	9.4	27.6	10.9	9.6	10.7	0.0
Ohnward Bank & Trust	Cascade	IA	A-	A-	A-	342.4	15.56	17.7	1.9	9.9	13.9	8.3	11.9	0.0
Oklahoma Bank and Trust Co.	Clinton	OK	A-	A-	B+	168.4	5.65	6.0	0.7	8.3	52.1	10.0	14.6	34.4
Oklahoma Capital Bank	Tulsa	OK	B	B	B	178.2	-1.70	18.3	1.2	10.2	7.8	10.0	16.4	0.0
Oklahoma Heritage Bank	Stratford	OK	C+	C+	C-	91.8	7.28	11.0	4.6	27.0	12.3	8.4	9.9	16.0
Oklahoma State Bank	Buffalo	OK	B+	B+	B	57.6	8.30	8.9	10.2	5.8	22.6	8.5	10.0	17.3
Oklahoma State Bank	Guthrie	OK	D+	D+	C-	175.1	15.81	28.4	0.8	13.7	1.6	9.1	10.5	14.2
Oklahoma State Bank	Vinita	OK	A-	A-	B	213.2	42.99	7.0	2.0	16.3	20.2	10.0	14.0	21.0
Old Dominion National Bank	North Garden	VA	D+	D	D	715.1	100.72	41.0	0.1	11.1	1.1	10.0	12.8	16.6
Old Exchange National Bank of Okawville	Okawville	IL	B+	B+	B-	84.0	22.64	5.1	0.5	7.1	44.1	8.4	9.9	22.8
Old Fort Banking Co.	Old Fort	OH	B	B	B	689.0	22.69	21.5	0.4	13.7	19.8	5.4	7.4	14.9

Asset Quality Index	Adjusted Non-Performing Loans as a % of Total Loans	Adjusted Non-Performing Loans as a % of Capital	Net Charge-Offs Avg Loans	Profitability Index	Net Income ($Mil)	Return on Assets (R.O.A.)	Return on Equity (R.O.E.)	Net Interest Spread	Overhead Efficiency Ratio	Liquidity Index	Liquidity Ratio	Hot Money Ratio	Stability Index
7.2	0.00	na	0.00	6.7	1.0	1.72	11.39	3.81	45.1	4.0	33.0	12.9	6.3
8.3	0.61	na	0.02	5.7	2.8	1.38	15.20	3.27	59.0	5.3	32.8	5.0	5.8
9.3	1.95	na	-0.02	2.6	0.1	0.36	2.03	1.72	80.3	7.2	87.1	5.1	7.2
8.1	0.25	na	-0.02	3.7	2.1	0.79	7.78	2.19	66.7	6.7	57.4	4.3	6.5
8.2	0.00	na	0.00	5.3	0.7	1.22	11.23	4.29	70.0	3.3	22.6	13.3	5.6
9.5	0.40	1.1	-0.01	5.2	976.5	0.98	12.62	1.25	69.4	7.2	54.8	3.0	5.9
6.5	0.43	3.0	0.01	3.7	24.5	0.63	4.95	2.52	56.4	3.5	19.5	10.9	9.4
9.1	0.33	na	0.00	2.9	3.9	0.46	3.97	3.25	75.8	2.4	10.9	17.1	8.4
8.9	0.00	na	0.00	4.6	2.4	0.81	6.62	3.29	68.1	1.5	21.9	26.0	7.3
6.1	0.52	3.9	0.00	9.8	81.4	3.97	44.39	2.57	65.7	0.8	12.2	27.5	9.0
5.4	0.94	na	0.04	8.9	24.6	1.76	17.50	4.20	65.0	4.2	12.1	7.1	8.8
7.4	0.00	na	-0.01	5.8	1.7	0.83	3.90	3.49	66.3	1.9	20.5	18.2	8.6
3.7	0.00	na	-0.02	5.6	1.8	1.26	9.37	3.18	60.8	4.2	31.5	11.3	9.1
5.2	2.77	na	0.06	4.5	3.9	0.74	7.77	3.59	69.0	3.6	23.5	9.3	7.0
7.3	0.41	na	0.00	3.5	3.1	0.74	7.14	2.97	74.8	3.7	23.6	11.1	6.5
6.3	0.82	na	0.02	8.6	5.3	2.02	16.22	4.64	60.2	4.3	27.6	8.1	8.5
7.6	0.61	na	0.00	2.5	2.9	0.39	3.55	3.02	82.8	4.5	15.3	5.9	8.1
6.9	0.68	na	0.01	5.7	15.6	1.12	12.29	3.21	64.3	2.9	7.3	13.7	8.3
5.8	1.42	7.6	0.22	5.8	6.1	0.82	8.45	3.77	53.0	2.7	17.6	7.4	9.0
4.5	1.15	6.6	0.31	3.8	44.1	0.46	4.10	3.66	66.3	4.6	16.5	5.2	8.9
5.3	1.73	na	0.06	6.3	2.3	1.51	17.35	3.27	69.6	5.1	34.4	7.1	4.5
5.3	0.54	4.2	1.15	2.5	0.7	0.30	3.49	3.45	70.6	2.3	14.1	17.7	5.2
8.3	0.67	na	0.01	2.5	0.9	0.28	2.35	2.91	77.7	4.0	19.2	9.0	6.3
5.3	2.49	na	0.03	9.3	3.0	1.72	12.08	3.42	44.7	3.2	22.2	12.4	9.1
5.8	0.85	na	0.00	9.3	8.1	2.28	19.16	4.23	42.3	4.7	19.5	4.4	8.7
5.8	0.48	na	0.02	4.3	1.1	0.88	8.60	5.05	79.6	3.1	20.2	8.2	5.7
10.0	na	na	na	10.0	78.5	28.53	49.28	1.46	86.3	5.0	342.7	100.0	6.7
5.8	1.73	na	0.02	5.6	1.4	1.44	12.79	4.16	65.3	5.1	32.0	6.1	6.6
7.8	0.56	na	0.02	5.0	6.8	0.67	4.66	3.91	74.5	4.6	17.4	5.7	10.0
8.3	0.53	3.5	0.00	5.1	4.8	1.02	7.93	3.07	56.7	1.8	16.2	20.7	8.4
7.6	0.09	0.8	0.00	9.0	3.3	1.93	18.14	4.25	43.6	3.5	4.3	10.6	8.2
7.6	1.26	na	0.00	3.9	3.6	0.69	4.33	2.69	68.7	4.5	30.0	8.9	8.6
7.2	0.02	na	0.00	3.9	1.4	0.73	5.96	3.11	63.6	1.5	11.6	23.6	6.9
5.5	0.39	na	0.20	4.8	1.5	0.86	9.80	3.86	67.7	2.2	18.9	18.3	4.9
6.7	0.57	na	0.00	7.3	3.9	1.40	13.37	3.19	47.8	3.2	19.3	8.7	7.3
8.4	0.07	0.6	0.00	5.3	9.5	0.96	10.76	3.63	58.4	5.2	16.5	1.7	7.7
8.8	0.01	0.1	0.00	3.8	1.4	0.68	7.68	3.08	69.1	1.9	15.1	19.8	5.4
6.2	0.90	na	0.00	5.8	0.2	0.97	8.10	4.24	64.2	3.4	37.2	15.0	5.0
6.7	1.28	na	0.07	4.5	7.6	0.89	8.42	3.64	69.8	2.3	6.6	13.1	8.7
8.0	0.04	na	0.00	1.9	1.5	0.38	3.73	3.03	80.2	2.7	21.0	15.9	5.5
3.9	2.56	na	0.00	5.0	0.9	1.29	9.71	3.82	62.9	1.0	20.6	33.4	7.1
8.2	0.00	na	0.00	4.6	4.9	0.85	8.38	3.18	69.4	3.8	16.6	10.1	6.9
5.5	0.85	5.1	0.14	3.4	20.0	0.61	5.47	3.47	71.9	1.6	15.8	19.8	9.4
4.2	1.47	7.6	0.26	3.4	39.2	0.47	3.62	3.30	64.1	3.7	15.6	7.7	9.4
8.2	0.65	na	0.00	4.2	3.3	0.88	5.20	3.24	65.9	2.1	25.6	20.0	9.0
3.5	1.86	na	-0.15	3.2	1.7	0.50	5.93	3.39	80.9	4.5	25.8	7.2	5.3
1.8	3.54	na	1.16	3.4	0.2	0.59	5.68	3.60	64.9	2.0	29.3	19.9	4.3
8.7	0.02	na	0.00	3.7	0.9	0.60	5.68	2.87	67.3	1.0	25.1	36.5	7.0
8.9	0.00	na	0.00	0.1	-0.5	-0.48	-1.58	2.53	87.0	6.3	44.0	2.4	0.9
4.8	1.40	6.7	0.34	3.8	4.8	0.60	5.09	3.92	75.0	3.1	11.5	11.7	8.8
6.9	0.06	na	0.00	5.9	2.8	1.17	9.36	3.84	57.5	2.0	19.1	17.4	8.1
8.3	0.08	na	-0.18	5.8	1.8	1.44	9.30	3.16	55.2	1.9	27.5	23.9	8.9
6.8	0.24	na	0.09	3.4	0.6	0.49	2.93	3.44	76.1	1.3	30.5	37.7	6.3
5.4	0.73	4.6	0.16	3.5	0.5	0.70	6.88	4.31	83.2	0.9	20.1	34.4	4.6
4.1	2.07	na	0.07	10.0	1.0	2.28	22.81	4.85	54.2	2.2	17.0	18.2	7.2
4.1	1.69	na	0.21	2.2	0.6	0.48	4.00	3.86	82.6	1.5	11.5	24.1	5.3
8.6	0.76	na	-0.05	6.0	1.7	1.35	10.22	4.19	62.4	2.0	39.3	31.4	8.3
6.1	0.96	na	0.12	1.0	0.9	0.20	1.41	2.93	85.7	3.5	8.9	9.9	6.0
9.3	0.10	na	0.00	4.7	0.8	1.30	11.58	2.82	60.3	4.4	65.3	17.2	6.5
8.6	0.02	na	0.01	6.6	7.8	1.64	20.48	3.13	54.9	4.4	22.4	6.8	6.3

Name	City	State	2020 Rating	2019 Rating	2018 Rating	Total Assets ($Mil)	One Year Asset Growth	Commercial Loans	Consumer Loans	Mortgage Loans	Securities	Capitalization Index	Leverage Ratio	Risk-Based Capital Ratio
▲ Old Mission Bank	Sault Sainte Marie	MI	A-	B	B	135.5	12.16	12.4	2.7	8.5	40.0	10.0	11.2	23.1
Old Missouri Bank	Springfield	MO	C+	C+	C	604.0	15.75	15.9	1.6	14.7	3.8	5.7	9.1	11.5
Old National Bank	Evansville	IN	B-	B-	B-	22360.7	9.97	15.9	4.7	11.4	25.0	6.7	8.7	13.2
▼ Old Plank Trail Community Bank, N.A.	Mokena	IL	C+	B	B	1994.3	20.43	33.6	12.9	1.7	9.1	5.9	8.1	11.7
Old Point National Bank of Phoebus	Hampton	VA	C+	C+	C-	1249.1	19.62	13.5	9.8	12.1	13.0	6.6	8.7	12.7
Old Point Trust & Financial Services, N.A.	Newport News	VA	U	U	U	7.0	6.58	0.0	0.0	0.0	15.8	10.0	89.5	360.6
Old Second National Bank	Aurora	IL	A-	A-	A-	2981.1	14.17	18.3	0.1	6.5	15.0	9.9	10.9	15.5
▲ Olpe State Bank	Olpe	KS	B	B	B-	44.3	7.63	6.2	1.9	16.3	23.8	10.0	14.5	30.5
Olympia Federal S&L Assn.	Olympia	WA	C+	B-	B-	771.7	9.82	0.9	0.4	60.4	7.4	10.0	13.9	0.0
OmniBank	Bay Springs	MS	C-	D+	D-	52.7	12.45	12.2	6.6	18.3	6.2	6.8	8.8	15.4
▲ ONB Bank	Rochester	MN	A-	B	B	131.7	14.88	21.1	1.2	14.9	3.8	9.4	10.6	15.1
▲ One American Bank	Sioux Falls	SD	C+	C	C	301.3	122.95	4.7	12.2	38.6	0.4	10.0	18.2	21.4
One Bank of Tennessee	Cookeville	TN	B	B	B-	1264.8	45.49	8.8	2.3	20.0	26.0	5.4	7.4	15.2
▼ One Community Bank	Oregon	WI	B+	A	B+	1309.4	149.67	11.3	0.2	13.9	5.2	4.2	10.4	0.0
▼ One Florida Bank	Orlando	FL	C-	C	B-	794.2	125.97	30.5	0.1	5.7	0.8	10.0	14.6	19.1
One South Bank	Blakely	GA	C+	C+	C+	157.2	9.56	10.1	0.8	13.0	0.4	8.7	10.2	17.2
▼ One World Bank	Dallas	TX	C+	B	C+	133.9	14.89	32.0	0.0	1.2	1.9	7.7	11.6	0.0
OneUnited Bank	Boston	MA	D-	D	D-	683.7	5.14	0.2	0.4	3.5	22.3	3.5	5.5	12.7
Oostburg State Bank	Oostburg	WI	A-	B+	B	292.4	22.04	16.7	0.6	15.1	20.6	10.0	11.9	15.2
Open Bank	Los Angeles	CA	A-	A-	B+	1340.0	16.35	12.4	0.1	9.4	7.0	9.3	10.5	14.5
Opportunity Bank of Montana	Helena	MT	A-	B	B	1243.0	22.79	9.1	1.7	13.0	12.9	10.0	11.5	16.2
OptimumBank	Plantation	FL	D+	C-	C	208.4	75.84	10.6	2.4	15.4	5.9	5.3	8.7	0.0
Optum Bank, Inc.	Salt Lake City	UT	A+	A+	A	12560.6	17.78	2.6	0.0	0.0	73.7	10.0	11.9	23.3
Optus Bank	Columbia	SC	C	C	D	161.5	124.23	35.4	0.5	4.3	7.2	6.4	8.4	0.0
Orange Bank & Trust Co.	Middletown	NY	B-	B-	C+	1715.9	38.89	17.7	1.3	6.3	19.1	5.7	7.7	13.3
Oregon Coast Bank	Newport	OR	B+	A-	B+	317.0	27.51	9.3	1.3	10.9	39.1	9.0	10.7	0.0
Oregon Pacific Banking Co.	Florence	OR	B+	B+	B	534.8	48.45	34.1	0.2	6.4	6.1	3.4	8.1	0.0
Oriental Bank	San Juan	PR	D	C-	D+	9976.3	58.74	11.5	19.2	24.2	4.3	7.9	9.6	14.9
Origin Bank	Choudrant	LA	C+	B	B-	7073.6	31.83	24.1	0.3	9.3	11.9	6.3	8.8	12.0
▼ Ormsby State Bank	Ormsby	MN	B	B+	B+	25.9	-2.28	4.8	3.7	1.6	26.3	10.0	16.4	0.0
Orrstown Bank	Shippensburg	PA	B	B-	B-	2781.0	20.32	22.3	1.0	14.7	17.2	6.5	8.5	14.3
Osgood State Bank	Osgood	OH	B+	B+	B	322.8	22.13	35.9	1.4	8.0	20.6	7.4	9.3	13.4
Ossian State Bank	Ossian	IN	B-	B	C+	121.6	13.61	7.5	1.0	5.3	17.5	7.8	9.6	16.6
▲ Ottawa Savings Bank	Ottawa	IL	B	B	B	310.4	2.09	8.3	8.8	43.1	7.0	10.0	14.6	21.0
Ottoville Bank Co.	Ottoville	OH	A-	A-	A-	85.5	9.15	6.8	0.5	9.8	32.1	10.0	20.4	0.0
Our Community Bank	Spencer	IN	C+	C+	C	73.7	1.96	1.2	0.6	56.0	10.7	10.0	11.4	0.0
Owen County State Bank	Spencer	IN	B-	B	B-	270.9	15.15	8.4	3.4	26.6	24.1	9.2	10.5	0.0
Owingsville Banking Co.	Owingsville	KY	C	C-	D+	73.4	5.24	1.3	4.8	34.1	21.6	8.2	9.8	0.0
Oxford Bank	Oxford	MI	B	B	C+	723.7	51.78	40.0	0.6	4.5	10.4	5.8	7.8	14.9
Oxford Bank & Trust	Oak Brook	IL	B	C+	C-	717.6	23.04	5.2	12.5	4.8	29.4	7.8	9.6	0.0
Oxford University Bank	Oxford	MS	B	B	B	189.3	15.67	9.6	3.7	29.9	17.0	7.9	9.6	0.0
Ozark Bank	Ozark	MO	B	B	B-	276.3	15.23	7.6	0.8	22.8	18.2	8.0	9.7	0.0
Ozarks Federal S&L Assn.	Farmington	MO	B-	B-	B-	265.0	5.44	0.0	0.2	58.9	8.0	10.0	14.1	23.2
Ozona National Bank	Ozona	TX	B	B	B	313.4	14.69	9.4	0.8	8.9	26.1	9.0	10.3	27.8
Pacific Alliance Bank	Rosemead	CA	B+	B+	B+	358.7	29.60	8.5	0.0	13.8	9.1	8.9	11.6	0.0
Pacific City Bank	Los Angeles	CA	A	A	A	2021.1	18.93	16.3	1.1	11.4	6.4	10.0	11.2	16.6
▲ Pacific Coast Bankers' Bank	Walnut Creek	CA	A	A-	B+	1300.4	47.79	0.8	0.0	0.1	6.8	7.8	9.5	15.2
Pacific Crest Savings Bank	Lynnwood	WA	B+	B+	B-	251.4	11.49	0.0	0.0	17.5	10.3	10.0	11.0	16.7
Pacific Enterprise Bank	Irvine	CA	B-	B	B+	619.2	27.22	41.8	0.0	3.0	0.0	8.2	9.8	18.4
Pacific Mercantile Bank	Costa Mesa	CA	C	B-	B	1617.5	12.50	37.7	5.3	2.1	1.7	7.7	9.5	16.0
Pacific National Bank	Miami	FL	C	B-	B-	742.1	26.60	8.8	0.1	11.5	20.3	7.5	9.4	16.2
Pacific Premier Bank	Irvine	CA	B+	A-	A-	19841.1	67.98	9.2	0.2	1.2	18.3	9.0	10.3	15.4
Pacific Valley Bank	Salinas	CA	B-	B	C+	420.2	23.46	26.9	0.2	3.6	0.0	5.1	9.1	0.0
Pacific West Bank	West Linn	OR	C-	C	C+	197.1	89.12	36.5	0.2	7.5	7.8	10.0	16.7	0.0
Pacific Western Bank	Beverly Hills	CA	B-	B+	B	28403.9	6.45	16.2	1.3	0.6	16.0	7.5	9.7	13.0
Paducah Bank and Trust Co.	Paducah	KY	A-	A-	A	792.4	11.11	18.5	1.0	18.3	14.8	9.2	10.5	15.6
▼ Palmetto State Bank	Hampton	SC	A-	A	B+	632.4	15.06	10.2	2.9	9.4	50.9	10.0	12.3	25.8
Palo Savings Bank	Palo	IA	B	B	B+	44.1	14.24	4.3	3.0	23.3	28.6	10.0	11.5	0.0
▲ Pan American Bank & Trust	Melrose Park	IL	C	C	C	376.0	-0.68	5.8	0.2	19.8	12.0	7.3	9.2	13.6
▼ Panola National Bank	Carthage	TX	B-	B-	B-	125.3	8.74	3.1	4.5	26.2	44.9	8.7	10.1	24.9

Asset Quality Index	Adjusted Non-Performing Loans as a % of Total Loans	as a % of Capital	Net Charge-Offs Avg Loans	Profitability Index	Net Income ($Mil)	Return on Assets (R.O.A.)	Return on Equity (R.O.E.)	Net Interest Spread	Overhead Efficiency Ratio	Liquidity Index	Liquidity Ratio	Hot Money Ratio	Stability Index
6.5	1.19	na	0.23	6.3	1.5	1.55	13.06	4.02	61.3	5.6	54.6	10.8	6.8
4.7	0.68	na	-0.01	5.2	4.6	1.07	11.28	3.75	57.1	0.5	2.8	39.9	6.6
4.5	1.18	4.4	0.04	4.6	161.7	1.02	7.28	3.21	64.5	4.8	18.8	4.2	10.0
6.0	0.49	4.0	0.05	2.5	0.6	0.05	0.49	2.63	73.8	3.3	18.5	8.8	7.2
5.8	0.63	4.4	0.10	3.0	4.9	0.57	6.16	3.22	80.7	3.9	19.6	10.4	6.7
10.0	na	na	na	9.5	0.4	8.42	9.21	0.86	85.2	4.0	na	0.0	5.0
6.0	1.00	5.4	0.06	7.0	24.8	1.18	9.86	3.55	56.9	4.2	15.5	7.8	10.0
8.6	0.00	na	0.01	4.5	0.3	1.04	6.79	3.02	72.0	4.2	50.9	15.9	7.1
8.5	0.78	na	0.03	3.0	2.4	0.42	3.03	3.22	80.6	1.8	18.0	21.1	8.5
4.9	1.02	6.2	-0.04	2.4	0.1	0.36	3.78	3.84	100.3	4.9	34.3	8.3	4.0
8.3	0.15	na	0.11	6.1	1.4	1.49	13.53	4.47	61.2	1.9	17.6	18.5	7.1
6.3	0.12	0.5	1.57	7.5	29.8	22.35	174.56	5.51	52.4	0.6	8.4	38.0	5.8
8.7	0.09	na	0.07	4.2	7.9	0.89	11.15	3.17	71.5	4.1	35.1	15.7	6.9
7.0	0.11	na	0.00	9.1	11.8	1.55	13.24	3.79	47.1	2.9	7.3	10.6	9.2
8.4	0.09	na	0.00	0.6	-1.6	-0.36	-2.04	2.91	99.1	5.2	31.7	5.3	6.5
4.7	1.23	na	0.33	3.3	0.6	0.52	5.03	4.19	81.2	1.8	21.6	22.4	5.3
4.8	0.40	na	-0.05	3.0	0.4	0.40	3.11	2.86	90.2	0.8	14.9	35.1	8.1
4.4	0.56	3.0	0.00	0.2	-0.6	-0.11	-1.68	1.99	102.7	1.3	29.7	39.3	2.9
7.9	0.93	na	0.00	6.9	2.7	1.36	10.65	3.82	58.6	4.6	34.6	8.7	8.0
7.2	0.03	na	0.00	6.6	10.0	1.07	9.67	3.71	55.9	1.2	15.4	26.1	9.8
6.3	0.83	na	0.01	8.7	17.6	1.99	15.69	4.24	62.6	4.0	19.0	9.8	9.8
6.7	0.00	0.0	1.17	0.9	-0.6	-0.51	-6.42	3.25	83.2	4.1	29.6	10.8	3.9
8.8	0.00	0.0	0.12	9.5	200.0	2.24	15.35	2.44	31.1	8.6	98.2	0.0	10.0
4.8	2.47	9.3	0.11	4.5	2.9	3.14	35.61	2.74	76.3	1.8	39.3	53.3	2.5
6.5	1.22	6.4	0.14	3.7	8.4	0.77	9.43	3.46	67.1	5.1	23.0	4.5	6.4
5.5	1.08	na	0.00	6.8	4.1	1.95	17.27	3.96	53.7	4.3	38.7	12.8	6.8
6.0	0.70	na	0.00	4.2	2.4	0.70	7.57	3.94	67.4	5.0	17.1	2.4	6.4
0.9	4.71	23.9	0.99	5.0	54.6	0.76	7.08	4.82	63.5	3.4	27.0	15.6	7.5
5.9	0.59	4.8	0.26	3.3	18.5	0.40	4.24	3.19	58.6	1.6	13.8	9.1	7.1
8.6	0.00	na	0.00	3.9	0.2	0.84	4.96	2.97	71.9	3.6	70.7	22.0	8.1
6.7	0.43	3.3	0.00	4.6	19.7	1.00	10.89	3.40	64.6	3.9	5.5	8.3	7.4
8.1	0.83	na	0.00	5.3	2.7	1.17	11.94	4.05	59.8	3.7	16.1	10.4	6.2
6.2	0.87	4.5	0.00	3.4	0.7	0.72	7.56	3.13	77.5	6.3	52.6	5.5	6.2
6.5	0.71	na	0.05	4.2	1.7	0.75	5.09	3.72	69.1	1.4	14.0	25.0	7.4
9.1	0.00	na	0.00	5.0	0.7	1.11	5.22	3.43	59.4	2.4	32.1	21.3	8.4
7.7	0.92	na	0.05	2.6	0.3	0.49	4.30	3.80	87.8	2.7	23.3	12.8	6.1
7.7	0.41	na	0.00	3.6	1.1	0.59	5.76	3.57	79.4	3.7	36.0	15.1	6.1
5.1	0.88	10.0	0.15	3.0	0.2	0.39	5.76	4.27	83.5	1.5	21.5	26.9	2.7
5.2	1.21	na	0.00	4.6	4.8	0.96	12.90	3.23	58.9	4.7	17.4	4.5	5.6
4.6	1.02	na	0.02	5.7	10.4	2.09	20.75	3.77	64.9	3.8	31.7	12.0	6.4
7.5	0.09	0.7	0.10	4.6	1.2	0.87	8.70	3.63	67.4	1.6	26.1	26.9	5.8
8.9	0.09	na	-0.01	4.8	2.3	1.15	11.44	3.51	67.0	2.5	9.8	16.0	5.9
7.6	1.00	5.0	0.00	2.7	0.6	0.30	2.30	2.59	85.9	1.8	21.4	21.5	7.5
5.7	4.32	na	0.25	4.3	1.5	0.68	6.09	3.59	79.4	6.8	60.6	4.9	7.1
7.6	0.00	na	0.00	4.3	1.6	0.68	5.25	2.81	63.2	0.9	26.8	67.0	7.5
7.2	0.22	1.6	0.08	5.6	10.8	0.76	6.48	3.49	52.7	0.9	15.9	30.7	9.8
9.8	0.00	0.0	-0.01	8.9	24.5	2.62	26.89	1.41	47.0	5.6	28.9	5.4	8.4
5.1	1.21	na	-0.03	4.3	1.7	0.94	8.27	2.99	64.4	1.1	27.1	29.4	7.8
7.6	0.21	na	0.06	3.9	2.0	0.48	5.05	4.35	71.1	0.5	9.4	47.4	6.2
4.3	1.31	na	0.55	3.4	5.6	0.46	4.63	3.32	61.4	3.1	20.7	14.7	7.0
8.8	0.00	0.6	0.12	1.4	0.0	0.01	0.06	2.25	91.3	1.9	38.3	37.1	6.3
5.9	0.20	0.8	0.12	3.7	6.2	0.05	0.33	4.01	62.3	4.9	27.2	7.6	10.0
6.0	0.29	na	0.00	4.6	2.3	0.80	8.36	3.66	68.1	3.9	17.9	9.5	5.4
8.5	0.03	na	0.02	0.0	-0.9	-0.68	-3.38	3.23	116.2	4.2	18.5	7.9	6.7
6.5	0.52	1.9	0.47	3.7	-1342.1	-6.63	-45.15	4.23	223.3	4.7	27.9	5.0	10.0
6.5	0.53	2.9	0.03	6.3	8.8	1.54	13.82	3.76	60.5	1.6	13.5	12.5	8.9
8.9	1.44	na	0.67	5.3	5.0	1.16	8.92	3.01	58.8	5.9	55.4	9.2	8.6
8.7	0.06	na	0.01	4.0	0.2	0.69	5.72	2.87	73.1	3.5	55.5	20.1	6.9
7.6	0.04	na	0.00	2.8	1.7	0.59	6.50	3.42	86.4	1.2	23.0	26.8	5.3
8.7	0.58	na	0.01	3.3	0.6	0.62	5.18	3.20	84.1	5.8	56.4	10.0	6.4

Name	City	State	2019 Rating	2018 Rating	Total Assets ($Mil)	One Year Asset Growth	Asset Mix (As a % of Total Assets)				Capital-ization Index	Lever-age Ratio	Risk-Based Capital Ratio
			Rating				Comm-ercial Loans	Cons-umer Loans	Mort-gage Loans	Secur-ities			
Paper City Savings Assn.	Wisconsin Rapids	WI	B+	B+	B	204.1	21.81	0.6	2.3	37.5	0.3	10.0	12.8	21.5
Paradise Bank	Boca Raton	FL	A	A	A	347.7	9.05	21.2	0.3	11.8	7.6	9.4	10.6	14.7
▼ Paragon Bank	Memphis	TN	B-	B	B-	499.0	20.66	30.2	3.9	15.1	10.5	8.4	9.9	16.5
Paramount Bank	Saint Louis	MO	C	C-	C-	217.3	71.53	1.7	1.3	70.2	0.0	6.2	8.2	0.0
Park Bank	Holmen	WI	B-	B-	B-	66.2	15.56	8.3	3.5	22.1	20.3	10.0	14.9	29.7
Park Bank	Madison	WI	B-	B-	B-	1169.5	11.98	19.0	0.4	13.7	6.8	7.7	10.1	13.1
Park National Bank	Newark	OH	C+	C+	C+	9209.6	6.09	13.0	17.8	16.1	11.2	6.0	8.0	11.9
Park Ridge Community Bank	Park Ridge	IL	A	A	A-	382.7	19.38	9.2	0.0	12.0	17.0	10.0	12.4	18.6
Park State Bank	Duluth	MN	B+	B	B-	228.0	63.83	45.2	0.9	17.2	3.5	6.0	8.0	15.1
Park State Bank & Trust	Woodland Park	CO	B	B-	C+	123.4	20.03	4.8	0.9	16.6	7.2	8.0	9.7	15.2
Parke Bank	Sewell	NJ	A	A	A-	2075.9	29.90	5.6	0.5	31.2	1.1	10.0	12.3	0.0
Parkside Financial Bank & Trust	Clayton	MO	B+	B+	B	664.5	26.11	37.9	0.1	1.9	3.6	7.8	9.6	14.0
Parkway Bank and Trust Co.	Harwood Heights	IL	B-	B-	B-	2787.0	6.34	13.4	0.0	1.3	8.0	8.6	10.9	13.8
Partners Bank	Helena	AR	C	C+	C+	325.2	58.47	16.0	0.6	8.8	14.4	6.6	10.5	12.2
Partners Bank	Spencer	WI	B+	B+	B	237.8	10.84	14.6	1.8	13.9	25.6	10.0	13.3	0.0
Partners Bank of California	Mission Viejo	CA	B-	B	B	438.1	53.89	35.5	0.0	7.5	0.7	6.8	8.8	16.2
▼ Partners Bank of New England	Sanford	ME	B	B+	B-	669.3	14.19	9.4	0.7	40.1	3.6	10.0	11.2	15.9
Passumpsic Bank	Saint Johnsbury	VT	C+	C	C-	810.6	19.39	8.7	6.9	30.7	5.0	9.8	10.9	17.6
▼ Pataskala Banking Co.	Pataskala	OH	D-	D	D	37.8	12.19	3.1	5.7	24.1	23.7	4.8	6.9	13.5
Pathfinder Bank	Oswego	NY	U	U	U	1197.0	13.75	18.0	5.1	18.9	24.0	6.3	8.4	12.4
Pathway Bank	Cairo	NE	C-	C-	C-	197.7	15.59	7.1	1.0	4.8	14.4	7.0	10.6	0.0
Patriot Bank	Millington	TN	B	B	B	467.6	29.23	8.1	1.4	17.6	38.4	6.3	8.3	12.4
Patriot Bank, N.A.	Stamford	CT	D+	D+	D+	923.1	-5.05	14.6	5.1	19.7	5.2	6.8	9.4	12.3
Patriot Community Bank	Woburn	MA	B+	B+	B+	197.7	5.64	2.2	0.0	18.5	0.0	10.0	14.2	24.6
Patriots Bank	Garnett	KS	B	B	C+	145.0	15.23	6.2	3.0	15.0	15.1	7.3	9.7	0.0
Patterson State Bank	Patterson	LA	B-	B-	B	286.4	26.15	11.0	1.5	34.0	26.4	6.6	8.6	19.8
Pauls Valley National Bank	Pauls Valley	OK	B-	B-	C+	275.9	12.18	16.0	8.7	3.9	31.5	8.6	10.1	0.0
Pavillion Bank	Richardson	TX	B	B	B	81.0	7.18	9.8	0.8	21.4	3.5	10.0	12.5	20.1
Payne County Bank	Perkins	OK	A	A	A	192.5	11.95	10.1	5.5	21.8	28.1	10.0	16.9	0.0
PBK Bank, Inc.	Stanford	KY	A-	B+	B+	130.9	11.21	2.6	5.4	20.6	6.6	10.0	12.5	0.0
▲ PCSB Bank	Clarinda	IA	B-	C+	B-	275.2	8.40	9.9	3.1	7.1	23.9	9.1	10.4	0.0
PCSB Bank	Yorktown Heights	NY	B-	B-	B-	1790.0	8.13	5.6	0.0	13.8	19.3	10.0	12.4	18.2
Peach State Bank & Trust	Gainesville	GA	B+	B+	B	409.3	55.19	13.7	2.2	9.0	18.7	6.5	8.5	14.9
▼ Peapack-Gladstone Bank	Bedminster	NJ	B	B+	B+	5952.2	20.96	17.4	0.7	9.2	10.0	8.0	9.7	14.6
Pearland State Bank	Pearland	TX	B+	A-	B+	199.5	5.77	7.4	0.7	4.9	64.6	10.0	11.0	0.0
Pecos County State Bank	Fort Stockton	TX	B	B	B	307.5	17.37	8.4	3.9	7.8	57.4	6.2	8.2	20.8
▼ Pee Dee Federal Savings Bank	Marion	SC	D+	C	D+	35.6	-2.28	11.0	5.0	3.9	47.3	10.0	18.1	0.0
Pegasus Bank	Dallas	TX	B+	A-	B-	761.5	4.85	31.7	2.6	12.3	6.6	6.6	8.7	12.5
Pendleton Community Bank, Inc.	Franklin	WV	C+	B	B	506.2	49.16	12.7	3.5	23.2	13.7	6.5	8.5	13.7
Penn Community Bank	Doylestown	PA	B-	B-	B-	2525.8	9.84	6.0	0.1	29.8	21.7	10.0	11.7	18.1
PennCrest BANK	Altoona	PA	C+	B-	B-	199.9	9.34	0.5	6.7	52.0	25.3	10.0	15.0	0.0
Pennian Bank	Mifflintown	PA	B-	B-	B	601.8	12.20	10.5	0.2	20.3	27.7	7.5	9.3	16.5
Pennsville National Bank	Pennsville	NJ	C	C	C	225.9	11.38	5.2	0.7	15.6	62.0	6.3	8.3	0.0
Pentucket Bank	Haverhill	MA	C+	B-	C+	890.5	12.20	14.1	0.2	37.2	8.2	9.3	11.2	0.0
People's B&T Co. of Clinton County	Albany	KY	B-	B-	C	43.2	5.57	14.0	23.9	25.0	4.4	8.8	10.2	0.0
People's B&T Co. of Pickett County	Byrdstown	TN	B-	B-	C	132.6	6.06	15.2	9.5	22.4	11.9	10.0	12.2	0.0
People's Bank of Commerce	Medford	OR	B+	B	B-	500.6	37.58	27.5	0.3	9.7	4.6	4.6	9.8	0.0
▼ People's Bank of Seneca	Seneca	MO	C	B-	B-	269.7	31.51	19.2	1.9	26.1	4.7	2.5	8.7	0.0
People's United Bank, N.A.	Bridgeport	CT	B	B	B	60603.1	16.95	18.3	0.2	16.5	13.6	6.7	8.7	12.3
▼ PeopleFirst Bank	Joliet	IL	B-	B	C+	172.1	24.27	9.1	0.1	6.8	3.2	9.6	11.5	0.0
Peoples B&T Co. of Madison County	Berea	KY	B+	B	B	465.8	15.72	3.6	2.4	19.0	32.7	10.0	11.5	0.0
▲ Peoples B&T Co. of Pointe Coupee Parish	New Roads	LA	A-	B	B-	344.2	7.33	9.9	1.7	34.3	1.1	10.0	13.8	0.0
Peoples Bank	Magnolia	AR	C+	C+	C+	213.7	5.60	4.6	22.5	40.2	7.4	9.1	10.4	18.4
Peoples Bank	Sheridan	AR	A	A	A	179.9	6.29	14.0	3.3	7.1	31.9	10.0	14.6	0.0
Peoples Bank	Eatonton	GA	D-	E+	E	169.2	30.10	5.0	2.6	17.3	7.9	10.0	12.6	0.0
▼ Peoples Bank	Lyons	GA	B-	B-	B-	131.6	27.68	13.9	1.4	12.4	1.8	6.0	8.0	14.2
Peoples Bank	Willacoochee	GA	B	B	B	84.0	13.29	2.7	3.7	10.8	19.9	10.0	12.6	0.0
Peoples Bank	Clive	IA	C	C-	C	362.6	8.20	8.3	1.0	8.7	22.8	5.4	8.7	0.0
Peoples Bank	Rock Valley	IA	C	C	C-	668.3	12.72	15.0	1.5	4.6	6.5	9.0	11.6	14.2
▼ Peoples Bank	Brownstown	IN	C	B-	C+	238.7	15.04	2.1	4.6	18.4	55.6	8.3	9.8	0.0

Asset Quality Index	Adjusted Non-Performing Loans		Net Charge-Offs Avg Loans	Profitability Index	Net Income ($Mil)	Return on Assets (R.O.A.)	Return on Equity (R.O.E.)	Net Interest Spread	Overhead Efficiency Ratio	Liquidity Index	Liquidity Ratio	Hot Money Ratio	Stability Index
	as a % of Total Loans	as a % of Capital											
6.7	1.55	6.2	0.02	5.6	1.6	1.15	8.80	2.50	62.6	2.9	42.9	23.1	7.2
7.4	0.51	3.4	0.05	6.7	3.4	1.31	12.54	4.18	66.9	4.6	21.2	5.3	8.5
8.0	1.04	na	0.02	3.8	2.3	0.67	6.50	3.29	72.7	2.5	6.8	6.9	5.1
9.3	0.00	na	0.00	6.9	7.5	6.77	82.35	1.51	71.0	0.2	10.5	62.8	5.6
5.0	9.58	na	0.63	3.8	0.3	0.72	4.70	4.16	83.4	5.2	25.6	2.6	5.8
3.8	1.33	na	-0.11	5.2	8.4	0.98	9.74	3.40	60.2	4.5	3.9	3.9	8.8
3.0	2.01	13.3	0.03	6.5	89.6	1.31	13.04	3.84	57.7	4.2	6.9	6.3	8.7
7.6	0.21	na	0.00	9.3	5.5	2.07	15.39	4.03	41.3	4.1	19.6	8.8	9.6
7.0	0.18	na	0.01	9.8	3.8	2.63	24.48	5.36	48.9	2.3	11.8	17.0	7.2
4.6	2.35	11.0	0.00	5.3	1.0	1.22	11.88	4.54	77.3	6.0	39.7	3.3	5.5
6.6	1.63	6.2	0.00	8.8	21.2	1.54	14.16	3.34	29.3	1.5	25.3	31.2	10.0
7.1	0.10	na	-0.21	5.7	4.9	1.06	10.56	3.02	60.6	2.9	25.0	4.4	6.9
3.3	3.28	13.5	0.01	5.7	20.5	1.04	9.08	3.00	47.7	1.2	14.9	22.0	9.3
8.3	0.01	na	0.01	3.2	1.2	0.62	5.73	3.90	72.5	0.5	5.6	48.8	5.9
6.3	1.07	na	-0.01	4.3	1.5	0.87	5.78	3.26	66.3	2.9	29.0	15.0	7.3
7.9	0.15	na	-0.03	4.2	1.6	0.61	6.30	4.75	54.6	4.0	18.9	4.2	5.9
8.8	0.28	na	0.05	2.1	-1.4	-0.28	-2.51	3.56	78.3	2.9	11.0	11.9	7.6
4.0	1.17	na	0.09	6.5	9.0	1.63	13.25	3.23	62.3	2.0	24.6	6.3	7.4
4.9	2.24	na	0.03	1.9	0.0	0.08	1.04	4.24	96.6	6.3	44.5	2.6	1.7
4.5	1.86	na	0.08	3.6	5.5	0.65	7.97	3.03	61.7	1.0	19.4	20.9	6.1
2.1	2.25	na	-0.07	6.0	1.8	1.30	11.81	3.69	61.4	2.0	23.4	19.7	7.0
7.8	0.15	na	0.07	7.9	6.1	1.98	21.03	3.40	58.4	0.6	4.2	36.7	5.4
1.7	3.00	na	0.12	1.0	-1.3	-0.17	-1.80	2.81	99.4	0.8	11.8	21.8	5.6
5.9	3.01	9.2	0.00	5.7	1.6	1.10	7.72	2.47	55.8	1.8	37.7	41.0	8.2
6.8	2.30	na	0.00	4.7	1.1	1.05	10.60	4.36	74.9	1.9	14.1	19.5	6.7
5.4	1.46	na	0.23	3.5	1.2	0.62	6.57	3.49	75.5	2.6	19.6	16.6	4.8
5.2	0.56	na	0.18	4.0	1.3	0.68	6.29	3.60	77.5	2.8	39.9	23.4	6.0
6.5	0.67	na	0.00	5.4	0.6	0.97	7.43	4.62	72.7	2.8	29.9	17.5	6.9
8.2	0.50	2.6	0.01	8.8	3.1	2.22	12.14	4.39	46.4	3.0	38.1	19.2	9.2
6.1	1.15	na	0.00	8.7	1.4	1.46	11.26	4.76	65.7	5.1	34.4	6.7	8.7
4.8	1.55	8.7	0.04	4.6	2.0	1.00	9.49	3.50	64.3	5.4	40.3	7.7	5.9
7.7	0.46	na	0.00	3.3	6.9	0.53	4.19	2.75	69.4	2.0	22.4	19.0	8.2
8.6	0.00	na	0.05	4.5	2.1	0.83	9.27	3.79	67.9	5.5	39.7	6.3	5.0
6.7	0.47	3.0	0.22	3.9	26.6	0.62	6.20	2.39	58.0	3.4	15.4	9.0	8.5
9.7	0.26	na	0.00	5.4	2.2	1.43	11.22	2.46	51.2	3.9	67.8	25.0	7.9
7.8	0.18	na	0.25	6.4	3.6	1.59	17.53	3.51	58.1	3.4	22.1	12.5	5.8
8.5	1.23	na	0.00	0.8	-0.1	-0.22	-1.21	3.26	106.7	5.9	86.8	12.5	5.7
8.0	0.00	0.0	0.21	3.8	3.5	0.63	7.33	2.91	65.8	5.1	31.1	5.3	5.7
3.7	2.00	na	0.04	5.2	3.5	0.98	9.83	4.07	68.6	3.4	13.7	11.9	6.1
8.9	0.46	1.9	0.03	3.2	11.3	0.62	5.01	2.76	71.9	3.1	23.8	12.5	8.3
8.9	0.18	na	0.05	2.1	0.3	0.23	1.46	3.02	87.1	4.6	35.7	10.6	7.4
5.8	0.92	7.7	-0.02	3.5	2.9	0.68	6.78	3.07	74.7	3.8	20.4	10.4	6.6
6.7	1.70	na	0.64	2.8	0.8	0.49	5.15	2.96	78.2	7.3	67.0	2.7	4.2
6.0	0.76	na	0.00	1.8	0.7	0.10	0.91	2.96	83.7	2.8	13.3	14.7	7.4
3.7	0.72	na	0.14	5.0	0.3	1.00	10.04	4.82	75.6	0.7	17.5	49.8	5.3
4.2	2.97	na	0.17	6.6	1.2	1.27	10.24	4.80	63.8	1.0	23.1	35.1	6.8
7.8	0.01	0.1	0.00	6.3	4.4	1.32	12.49	4.45	62.8	4.7	15.9	3.0	6.5
6.1	0.75	na	0.06	7.4	2.6	1.35	15.72	4.13	50.1	1.3	9.4	18.7	5.4
4.9	0.97	4.5	0.11	4.3	382.2	0.85	6.50	3.09	59.7	2.7	7.4	6.7	10.0
3.9	1.80	na	0.06	5.3	1.1	1.00	8.17	3.63	67.8	1.8	27.9	22.1	6.7
5.1	2.84	7.2	0.02	6.3	4.1	1.25	8.86	3.88	58.4	4.4	23.8	7.2	8.0
5.5	1.05	na	0.12	8.7	3.7	1.50	11.05	4.31	49.9	0.8	15.8	35.1	9.3
3.4	1.63	na	0.68	6.1	2.5	1.55	14.98	4.38	56.8	0.8	22.2	30.6	6.2
8.7	0.16	na	0.00	9.6	2.4	1.87	12.69	4.17	41.4	4.1	22.1	8.6	9.6
5.2	2.10	na	0.17	1.8	0.5	0.41	3.32	3.42	89.2	5.5	37.1	5.6	1.6
4.5	0.04	11.2	0.16	5.4	0.9	0.98	11.83	4.16	62.8	2.6	28.0	18.2	5.3
8.6	1.68	na	0.04	3.2	0.4	0.58	4.43	3.08	82.7	3.0	43.6	21.4	7.1
2.7	2.10	na	0.07	4.6	2.6	1.00	7.63	3.95	67.9	2.1	23.6	17.6	3.9
2.8	1.04	na	0.00	8.9	9.6	1.98	15.42	3.93	51.1	1.6	10.2	16.5	9.7
7.3	1.21	3.8	1.40	2.6	0.9	0.54	5.18	2.78	76.9	6.7	69.8	7.0	5.1

Name	City	State	2019 Rating	2018 Rating	Rating	Total Assets ($Mil)	One Year Asset Growth	Asset Mix (As a % of Total Assets) Commercial Loans	Consumer Loans	Mortgage Loans	Securities	Capitalization Index	Leverage Ratio	Risk-Based Capital Ratio
Peoples Bank	Munster	IN	B-	B-	B	1478.7	11.28	12.3	1.9	19.8	20.1	6.2	8.2	13.7
Peoples Bank	Coldwater	KS	B+	B+	B	52.5	0.86	5.1	1.3	8.3	37.2	10.0	12.7	0.0
Peoples Bank	Pratt	KS	C-	C+	B-	468.8	34.37	7.7	1.1	7.8	36.2	8.4	9.9	16.0
Peoples Bank	Lebanon	KY	C	B-	B-	93.5	57.27	28.3	2.5	8.4	18.8	1.8	8.8	0.0
▼ Peoples Bank	Marion	KY	D+	D+	C-	87.9	22.50	33.5	4.6	5.5	1.8	2.0	8.4	0.0
Peoples Bank	Taylorsville	KY	A-	B+	B	116.3	13.19	2.8	2.7	21.6	26.0	10.0	12.1	22.0
▲ Peoples Bank	Chatham	LA	C	D+	C-	88.6	-2.75	11.9	6.2	27.5	2.1	10.0	11.0	16.1
▲ Peoples Bank	Chestertown	MD	B	B-	B-	286.7	16.44	5.0	0.2	27.6	9.8	7.9	9.6	0.0
Peoples Bank	Cuba	MO	B+	B+	B+	230.0	11.38	6.4	2.5	33.3	18.5	8.5	10.0	0.0
Peoples Bank	Mendenhall	MS	D+	C-	C	426.6	37.18	29.9	2.8	12.5	8.0	7.8	9.6	16.4
Peoples Bank	Ripley	MS	B	B	B+	475.0	11.71	8.3	5.3	15.0	51.5	8.4	9.9	20.7
Peoples Bank	Newton	NC	B+	A	A-	1457.5	19.30	11.8	0.5	14.1	15.3	8.7	10.1	15.2
Peoples Bank	Gambier	OH	C-	C	C	62.8	9.44	2.2	3.4	34.9	32.2	8.0	9.7	19.6
Peoples Bank	Marietta	OH	B	B	B	4906.5	11.69	23.0	11.6	13.1	18.1	6.2	8.2	13.7
▼ Peoples Bank	Iva	SC	B-	B	B	341.0	16.23	8.5	2.0	14.3	32.1	9.9	10.9	18.1
▲ Peoples Bank	Clifton	TN	C+	C-	D+	219.9	5.32	30.5	7.0	13.5	4.8	6.0	10.1	0.0
Peoples Bank	Sardis	TN	A-	A-	B+	102.1	18.10	4.7	4.2	26.1	7.1	6.9	8.9	0.0
Peoples Bank	Lubbock	TX	B+	A-	A-	692.0	27.46	12.9	2.3	7.8	16.0	5.9	9.6	0.0
Peoples Bank	Paris	TX	B-	B-	B-	151.3	2.05	4.2	1.4	30.6	7.8	8.7	10.1	0.0
Peoples Bank	Bellingham	WA	B+	A-	A-	2319.3	20.65	12.8	6.6	8.7	4.6	7.0	11.2	0.0
Peoples Bank & Trust	Buford	GA	B	B	B	373.9	11.92	7.8	0.7	8.9	40.6	8.9	10.3	0.0
▲ Peoples Bank & Trust	Pana	IL	C	C-	C+	480.0	11.82	19.6	0.2	3.7	24.4	6.6	8.6	13.1
Peoples Bank & Trust Co.	Troy	MO	B-	B-	C+	558.4	22.57	9.7	0.9	8.1	31.6	6.9	9.0	13.9
Peoples Bank & Trust Co.	Ryan	OK	C+	B-	B	82.4	76.11	43.3	0.2	2.0	0.8	9.7	12.4	0.0
Peoples Bank & Trust Co.	Manchester	TN	A-	A-	B+	117.0	16.29	8.9	4.3	27.0	7.8	10.0	11.7	0.0
Peoples Bank & Trust Co. of Hazard	Hazard	KY	E-	E	E+	250.1	6.35	13.8	2.0	19.2	27.4	3.4	5.4	10.3
Peoples Bank and Trust Co.	McPherson	KS	B+	B+	B+	713.6	16.49	21.3	2.4	4.1	30.9	5.5	9.0	11.4
Peoples Bank Co.	Coldwater	OH	A	A	A-	600.7	6.60	5.2	1.7	11.7	42.2	10.0	11.3	20.5
Peoples Bank MT. Washington	Mount Washington	KY	A-	A-	B	97.6	13.00	8.2	0.2	6.4	12.6	10.0	11.6	15.9
Peoples Bank of Alabama	Cullman	AL	B-	B-	B-	998.7	20.89	20.7	1.9	7.9	8.9	5.1	8.5	0.0
Peoples Bank of Altenburg	Altenburg	MO	B-	B-	C+	71.3	12.49	6.4	1.5	28.2	13.2	8.3	9.8	16.7
Peoples Bank of Deer Lodge	Deer Lodge	MT	C	C-	C-	38.5	8.74	15.1	4.6	15.3	19.3	7.9	9.6	0.0
Peoples Bank of East Tennessee	Madisonville	TN	A-	A-	B+	273.5	19.82	7.6	2.9	26.3	14.2	9.2	10.5	0.0
Peoples Bank of Georgia	Talbotton	GA	B-	B-	C+	108.9	32.89	10.9	8.0	27.9	16.6	8.4	9.9	0.0
Peoples Bank of Graceville	Graceville	FL	B+	A-	A-	108.1	13.36	5.2	1.6	11.9	50.7	9.8	10.9	41.6
Peoples Bank of Greensboro	Greensboro	AL	C+	B-	B-	101.0	10.88	9.5	6.2	11.8	34.2	7.3	9.2	17.2
▲ Peoples Bank of Kankakee County	Bourbonnais	IL	B-	C+	C	275.3	24.62	10.6	2.4	8.3	41.1	5.6	7.6	15.3
Peoples Bank of Kentucky, Inc.	Flemingsburg	KY	B	B	B-	346.2	8.64	8.3	6.7	19.0	7.1	10.0	11.1	15.2
Peoples Bank of Macon	Macon	IL	C+	C+	C+	22.6	9.25	9.1	5.9	4.6	37.7	10.0	12.9	0.0
Peoples Bank of Middle Tennessee	Shelbyville	TN	A-	A-	A-	157.7	2.30	3.0	4.7	17.5	25.4	10.0	12.9	0.0
▼ Peoples Bank of Moniteau County	Jamestown	MO	D+	C-	D+	64.4	12.80	3.1	3.7	17.9	35.5	6.7	8.7	13.6
▲ Peoples Bank of Red Level	Red Level	AL	C	C	C	15.5	3.06	0.6	18.0	11.5	21.3	10.0	12.7	0.0
▲ Peoples Bank of the South	La Follette	TN	B	C	C	176.0	16.33	7.5	1.3	28.9	0.1	10.0	12.2	16.8
Peoples Bank of Wyaconda	Kahoka	MO	B+	B+	B	103.9	7.99	3.6	4.4	17.6	19.6	10.0	11.1	0.0
▼ Peoples Bank, Biloxi, Mississippi	Biloxi	MS	C-	C	C-	686.4	11.64	7.6	0.6	8.2	36.5	10.0	12.4	22.5
Peoples Community Bank	Greenville	MO	A	A-	B+	540.8	11.95	7.4	6.5	34.1	19.4	10.0	16.8	0.0
Peoples Community Bank	Mazomanie	WI	A-	A-	B+	333.1	12.75	8.5	1.1	6.8	19.2	10.0	11.9	0.0
Peoples Community Bank SB	Monticello	IN	C	C+	C-	31.8	16.28	0.3	2.9	60.9	1.6	10.0	40.9	0.0
Peoples Exchange Bank	Monroeville	AL	B	B	B-	82.0	18.18	16.0	5.8	12.2	21.9	10.0	12.8	0.0
Peoples Exchange Bank	Winchester	KY	B	B	B-	453.5	9.24	6.4	1.3	30.8	3.1	7.3	9.2	0.0
Peoples Federal S&L Assn.	Sidney	OH	B-	B-	B-	122.0	5.91	2.2	1.4	48.7	6.0	10.0	12.7	23.3
Peoples First Savings Bank	Mason	OH	C+	C	B-	67.7	-4.91	0.0	0.2	45.1	0.4	10.0	11.9	19.6
Peoples Independent Bank	Boaz	AL	B+	B	B	360.5	18.00	12.7	1.2	7.1	36.0	6.6	8.6	13.0
▼ Peoples National Bank of Checotah	Checotah	OK	B+	A-	A-	150.6	8.37	2.0	10.5	9.4	45.5	10.0	16.2	41.2
Peoples National Bank of Kewanee	Kewanee	IL	B+	B+	B+	410.2	13.74	3.9	1.2	5.2	43.3	10.0	11.8	20.4
Peoples National Bank, N.A.	Mount Vernon	IL	B-	C+	B-	1468.1	21.17	22.1	0.3	5.3	3.7	5.5	9.0	11.4
Peoples S&L Co.	Bucyrus	OH	C+	C+	B-	147.6	5.45	0.0	1.0	33.2	37.0	10.0	20.0	0.0
Peoples S&L Co.	West Liberty	OH	B-	B-	B-	62.0	23.24	1.3	2.1	59.9	4.4	10.0	12.7	0.0
Peoples Savings Bank	Crawfordsville	IA	B	B	B-	36.4	4.09	7.5	0.9	7.5	47.8	8.9	10.3	0.0
Peoples Savings Bank	Indianola	IA	B	B	B	388.4	18.23	18.2	0.6	6.4	29.1	10.0	11.2	17.1

Asset Quality Index	Adjusted Non-Performing Loans		Net Charge-Offs / Avg Loans	Profitability Index	Net Income ($Mil)	Return on Assets (R.O.A.)	Return on Equity (R.O.E.)	Net Interest Spread	Overhead Efficiency Ratio	Liquidity Index	Liquidity Ratio	Hot Money Ratio	Stability Index
	as a % of Total Loans	as a % of Capital											
4.3	1.70	13.2	0.02	5.2	12.8	1.21	12.14	3.57	65.1	3.9	21.8	11.5	8.0
8.4	0.15	na	0.00	4.4	0.4	0.97	6.78	3.57	72.6	1.4	21.6	18.3	7.0
2.2	3.66	na	0.00	7.4	6.2	1.83	15.35	4.06	54.9	1.6	23.6	26.0	7.1
8.4	0.00	na	0.00	4.6	0.6	1.03	11.71	3.97	72.2	2.1	18.4	18.7	4.2
4.7	0.92	na	0.47	5.1	0.6	0.96	11.22	4.36	65.7	1.2	11.1	27.1	4.3
5.7	3.58	na	-0.03	6.9	1.5	1.71	13.57	4.12	60.2	4.5	31.2	9.5	7.9
3.7	1.02	na	0.28	4.2	0.5	0.77	7.27	4.20	71.3	0.5	17.0	61.0	5.1
4.7	1.71	na	-0.06	5.1	1.9	0.95	8.64	3.59	75.9	5.2	34.8	6.1	6.7
5.3	1.81	na	0.06	7.1	2.7	1.61	15.47	3.97	60.3	3.7	17.0	10.6	7.8
1.3	3.47	na	0.17	10.0	8.0	2.95	30.10	4.62	57.1	1.4	9.5	23.5	6.7
8.4	0.02	na	0.60	4.2	3.1	0.93	8.44	3.10	63.6	3.3	49.6	23.2	5.5
8.5	0.35	2.2	0.04	4.9	10.0	1.00	9.12	3.77	71.6	5.4	26.7	4.9	9.8
8.9	0.01	na	0.03	2.4	0.2	0.33	3.26	3.49	91.2	3.9	34.3	13.6	5.2
4.3	1.11	5.8	0.04	4.0	17.4	0.50	4.11	3.27	65.1	2.7	8.2	8.4	9.5
6.0	1.92	na	0.32	3.2	1.5	0.62	5.22	3.02	78.2	4.3	42.2	14.2	7.0
5.8	1.46	na	0.26	5.2	1.8	1.07	11.28	4.75	63.9	0.7	14.7	37.4	5.3
7.2	0.62	na	0.04	4.1	0.5	0.71	7.68	3.75	77.0	1.7	28.5	21.4	6.0
8.3	0.19	na	0.00	6.9	6.4	1.37	14.04	4.02	61.0	2.9	28.0	16.6	7.0
7.9	0.26	na	0.12	6.7	1.9	1.67	16.66	3.58	66.0	2.7	23.3	10.9	6.7
7.7	0.34	2.6	0.00	4.3	9.9	0.65	5.79	3.24	63.3	4.4	22.9	9.0	9.2
7.7	1.01	na	-0.04	4.7	3.0	1.11	10.14	3.51	68.2	3.0	49.6	27.1	6.6
3.1	1.82	na	-0.41	8.2	5.3	1.62	15.96	4.14	55.3	2.2	26.6	16.8	5.6
5.7	1.30	na	-0.02	5.2	5.9	1.47	15.42	3.43	68.1	4.6	21.3	5.4	6.7
2.8	1.42	na	0.29	8.3	1.4	2.64	28.42	3.43	56.0	0.7	15.3	53.8	6.5
8.1	0.05	na	0.02	5.0	0.8	0.91	7.56	4.14	71.1	3.9	32.9	13.1	7.2
0.3	9.40	69.4	0.29	0.6	0.0	0.01	0.21	2.99	97.6	2.3	34.6	25.0	1.2
6.0	0.19	na	0.01	6.0	6.7	1.30	11.51	3.77	59.3	3.5	10.4	10.9	7.9
8.9	0.04	na	0.00	8.7	7.4	1.78	14.61	3.06	40.2	5.6	43.9	7.1	8.9
7.6	2.07	na	-0.01	6.3	1.0	1.50	12.05	4.41	67.7	5.0	28.4	4.6	8.6
4.8	1.32	5.7	-0.66	6.9	11.0	1.56	16.64	4.04	69.1	4.6	24.3	6.0	7.4
7.2	0.41	na	0.00	4.5	0.4	0.78	7.43	3.66	78.4	5.2	32.7	5.7	6.8
3.8	1.97	na	-0.01	5.9	0.4	1.39	13.68	4.55	68.9	5.7	34.8	3.3	4.5
5.3	1.01	na	0.19	6.3	2.3	1.26	11.43	4.59	66.0	4.1	26.9	10.3	6.8
4.3	0.99	na	0.22	4.8	0.6	0.86	8.41	5.18	73.2	0.8	14.6	20.1	5.2
8.4	1.51	na	0.00	5.0	1.0	1.21	9.92	2.63	57.4	4.6	65.8	17.8	7.5
4.8	1.80	na	0.05	4.8	1.0	1.40	14.77	3.41	70.7	3.4	44.9	19.4	5.5
5.8	1.18	na	0.00	5.7	3.6	1.86	24.76	3.07	60.1	4.7	37.9	10.8	4.5
4.9	1.32	na	0.05	5.8	2.9	1.14	9.89	3.98	60.6	1.2	7.8	27.5	7.3
9.1	0.00	na	0.00	2.8	0.1	0.41	3.11	2.45	79.9	4.6	43.0	10.0	6.2
8.0	0.56	2.6	0.00	6.1	1.2	1.06	8.12	3.52	60.4	1.7	27.8	25.3	8.0
3.0	3.34	na	0.22	3.0	0.3	0.59	6.41	2.87	78.2	4.8	44.8	11.7	3.1
3.5	6.67	na	0.78	4.7	0.1	0.80	6.24	5.48	75.8	6.9	71.7	2.5	5.2
4.2	2.09	na	0.03	9.2	2.5	2.00	15.65	4.83	57.6	1.7	20.0	22.8	9.7
8.5	0.00	na	-0.01	5.0	0.7	0.90	8.14	3.51	59.9	2.0	16.8	19.2	6.9
6.7	1.76	na	2.73	0.3	-3.3	-0.66	-4.63	3.06	87.8	4.4	22.9	7.2	6.7
7.7	0.75	na	0.06	10.0	11.8	2.99	16.79	4.94	39.8	2.0	19.7	19.5	9.9
6.3	3.91	na	-0.05	6.5	3.3	1.36	10.82	3.34	55.1	4.7	31.8	8.5	7.5
9.2	0.64	na	0.00	2.3	0.1	0.39	0.92	3.68	89.0	4.7	42.3	11.7	6.1
5.9	2.40	na	-0.01	4.3	0.4	0.66	4.82	4.56	79.3	3.3	35.4	12.7	7.4
8.2	0.40	na	0.03	5.1	3.5	1.09	11.56	3.67	69.8	2.2	15.6	18.2	6.3
8.1	0.62	na	0.00	3.9	0.6	0.65	4.99	3.52	77.6	4.0	24.0	9.8	7.5
9.1	0.00	na	0.00	2.9	0.2	0.42	3.65	2.91	87.3	1.7	13.7	20.5	6.6
8.2	0.54	1.4	0.02	4.6	2.5	1.01	9.25	3.76	70.7	5.5	46.8	9.2	6.2
8.6	0.37	na	0.12	4.7	1.2	1.04	5.99	3.04	69.2	5.4	65.7	13.6	8.8
6.0	3.36	na	1.37	3.4	1.6	0.55	4.08	3.49	67.1	5.2	53.6	12.2	7.7
4.3	1.51	12.0	0.29	4.6	10.6	1.07	12.20	3.75	69.2	3.2	9.3	12.1	7.2
7.8	0.49	na	0.03	1.6	0.1	0.09	0.44	2.77	96.6	5.6	73.4	13.5	7.3
9.2	0.00	na	0.00	3.8	0.3	0.69	5.11	3.69	77.6	2.6	16.6	16.4	6.7
7.0	0.00	na	0.00	4.1	0.2	0.83	8.18	3.01	66.8	6.7	69.7	5.3	6.6
6.1	0.21	na	0.34	4.9	3.6	1.42	13.68	3.40	61.1	3.4	28.9	12.3	6.1

Name	City	State	2019 Rating	2018 Rating	Total Assets ($Mil)	One Year Asset Growth	Asset Mix (As a % of Total Assets)				Capital-ization Index	Lever-age Ratio	Risk-Based Capital Ratio
							Comm-ercial Loans	Cons-umer Loans	Mort-gage Loans	Secur-ities			
Peoples Savings Bank	Montezuma	IA	B-	B-	B-	43.4	11.37	9.4	6.4	13.3	28.5	10.0	11.4	0.0
Peoples Savings Bank	Wellsburg	IA	C	C	C	102.7	8.65	16.5	2.3	6.9	20.7	5.0	9.3	0.0
Peoples Savings Bank	New Matamoras	OH	B	B	B	66.5	4.80	2.6	3.4	28.2	52.2	10.0	11.8	0.0
Peoples Savings Bank	Urbana	OH	C	C	C	133.0	10.18	1.8	1.7	50.2	2.9	8.5	10.0	0.0
Peoples Savings Bank of Rhineland	Rhineland	MO	B-	B-	B-	329.9	21.62	16.0	1.7	22.6	8.4	7.2	9.4	12.7
Peoples Security Bank and Trust Co.	Scranton	PA	B+	B+	B	2805.1	18.26	18.0	3.1	11.9	9.1	9.2	10.4	14.5
Peoples State Bank	Ellettsville	IN	B	B	B	356.5	19.24	8.4	0.9	9.8	35.4	7.9	9.6	0.0
▲ Peoples State Bank	Cherryvale	KS	C+	C-	C-	17.8	0.98	13.6	4.0	17.0	6.4	10.0	25.9	27.0
▼ Peoples State Bank	Manhattan	KS	D	C+	C+	262.1	0.60	12.8	1.1	10.9	2.9	6.4	9.2	0.0
▼ Peoples State Bank	Fairmount	ND	D-	D+	D+	31.5	13.66	26.1	2.7	4.1	26.7	4.8	6.8	13.2
Peoples State Bank	Westhope	ND	B+	B+	B+	67.7	9.94	6.7	2.7	0.1	21.2	10.0	13.9	0.0
Peoples State Bank	New Lexington	OH	B-	B-	C+	163.0	21.45	7.0	8.1	33.5	6.3	6.2	8.2	15.3
Peoples State Bank	Blair	OK	B-	B-	C+	17.5	4.28	34.5	7.2	2.9	9.6	6.7	8.7	14.3
Peoples State Bank	Rocksprings	TX	A-	A-	B+	83.5	3.22	1.7	1.8	12.8	41.3	10.0	13.2	27.4
Peoples State Bank	Shepherd	TX	B-	B-	B-	137.0	14.40	3.3	3.8	6.6	35.9	7.3	9.2	22.6
▼ Peoples State Bank	Prairie Du Chien	WI	C-	C	C+	875.9	10.55	9.0	0.5	9.4	36.6	8.4	10.0	17.6
Peoples State Bank	Wausau	WI	B+	B+	B	1103.1	16.27	17.1	0.4	13.3	17.3	7.5	9.4	15.7
Peoples State Bank of Colfax	Colfax	IL	B+	B+	B	41.4	19.08	7.0	5.8	16.2	7.2	10.0	11.1	22.1
Peoples State Bank of Hallettsville	Hallettsville	TX	B-	B-	B-	308.1	11.33	4.8	1.4	12.2	34.1	10.0	11.2	0.0
Peoples State Bank of Munising	Munising	MI	B+	A-	B+	175.5	20.39	15.6	4.4	10.8	20.3	8.1	11.2	0.0
▲ Peoples State Bank of Newton, Illinois	Newton	IL	B	B-	B-	498.2	7.86	12.8	2.1	11.0	30.7	8.9	10.4	0.0
Peoples State Bank of Plainview	Plainview	MN	B	B-	B-	321.9	14.17	11.1	2.8	14.7	27.9	6.3	8.3	14.7
Peoples State Bank of Velva	Velva	ND	D+	C-	C	126.3	9.58	13.7	2.4	10.0	7.8	7.7	9.4	13.4
▼ Peoples State Bank of Wells	Wells	MN	C+	B-	C	57.4	4.15	3.7	1.4	10.3	4.3	5.0	10.2	11.0
Peoples Trust & Savings Bank	Boonville	IN	B-	B	B	211.6	8.20	4.9	0.6	32.3	25.4	10.0	15.1	0.0
Peoples Trust and Savings Bank	Riverside	IA	B	B	B-	30.7	9.66	5.4	0.7	12.3	39.4	8.5	12.7	0.0
Peoples Trust Co. of St. Albans	Saint Albans	VT	B-	B	B-	335.3	23.16	7.2	1.9	18.4	15.3	9.1	10.4	19.0
PeoplesBank	Holyoke	MA	C+	B-	B-	3233.5	10.47	10.9	2.7	25.0	11.9	6.7	9.0	12.3
PeoplesBank, A Codorus Valley Co.	York	PA	B+	B+	B+	2105.5	12.85	16.8	0.6	11.1	9.4	7.5	9.4	14.9
PeoplesSouth Bank	Colquitt	GA	B	B	B-	931.7	14.17	9.9	2.6	13.2	26.1	6.6	8.7	15.1
PeoplesTrust Bank	Hamilton	AL	B-	B-	B-	118.8	13.81	18.2	5.5	12.2	15.4	8.6	11.3	0.0
Perennial Bank	Darwin	MN	B	B	B-	126.5	22.55	5.5	4.5	11.5	35.5	6.3	8.3	25.0
Perpetual Federal Savings Bank	Urbana	OH	A	A	A-	391.1	-0.15	4.8	1.0	47.6	1.8	10.0	19.8	34.7
Perryton National Bank	Perryton	TX	B+	A-	B+	178.1	2.31	11.6	4.3	5.0	53.2	10.0	14.5	0.0
Persons Banking Co.	Forsyth	GA	D+	D+	D	378.3	19.45	10.1	1.1	12.1	31.9	4.2	6.2	12.4
Peru Federal Savings Bank	Peru	IL	B-	B-	B-	170.8	13.35	4.9	1.4	30.2	39.9	10.0	12.8	29.0
Peshtigo National Bank	Peshtigo	WI	B-	B-	B	247.2	14.70	10.1	1.6	14.5	28.3	8.0	9.7	0.0
Petefish, Skiles & Co.	Virginia	IL	A-	A-	B+	225.7	13.91	6.6	7.0	13.8	21.5	9.7	11.0	0.0
Petit Jean State Bank	Morrilton	AR	A-	A-	B+	201.6	7.84	17.2	2.3	11.3	30.4	10.0	14.6	0.0
Phelps County Bank	Rolla	MO	B	B	B	434.0	15.62	7.8	1.4	24.6	22.5	5.5	7.5	16.3
▲ Phenix-Girard Bank	Phenix City	AL	A	B+	B	221.2	16.07	1.7	0.3	9.6	48.5	10.0	14.4	0.0
Philadelphia Trust Co.	Philadelphia	PA	B+	B+	B+	22.8	2.90	1.1	19.1	1.9	0.0	10.0	71.5	0.0
Philo Exchange Bank	Philo	IL	B+	B+	B	116.0	19.05	2.8	1.4	7.5	25.3	9.1	10.4	17.2
Phoenixville Federal Bank and Trust	Phoenixville	PA	B-	B-	B-	521.3	14.18	4.8	0.0	40.3	8.4	10.0	11.4	0.0
Pickens S&L Assn., FA	Pickens	SC	C+	B-	B-	109.3	14.26	1.6	0.9	38.9	35.0	8.9	10.3	22.9
Piedmont Bank	Peachtree Corners	GA	A-	B	C+	1367.7	32.97	22.2	0.6	5.2	4.2	8.2	10.2	13.5
Piedmont Federal Savings Bank	Winston-Salem	NC	C-	C+	C+	903.1	2.41	1.8	0.0	56.4	26.4	10.0	26.0	0.0
Piermont Bank	New York	NY	D			128.3	208.89	16.7	0.0	4.8	15.9	10.0	24.6	39.5
▼ Piggott State Bank	Piggott	AR	B-	B	B	101.4	19.55	7.2	3.7	17.1	32.1	5.8	7.8	16.4
Pike National Bank	McComb	MS	B+	B+	B+	282.1	9.97	11.7	3.4	15.6	24.7	10.0	13.1	23.1
▼ Pikes Peak National Bank	Colorado Springs	CO	C+	B-	C+	108.3	16.97	9.0	0.2	3.5	0.0	10.0	12.9	35.9
Pilgrim Bank	Pittsburg	TX	B	B	B-	589.4	6.07	6.5	0.8	11.3	30.4	10.0	11.5	18.5
Pilot Bank	Tampa	FL	C+	C	C-	586.9	37.74	42.8	14.6	3.2	12.1	2.8	9.8	0.0
Pilot Grove Savings Bank	Pilot Grove	IA	A-	A-	A-	693.0	12.24	9.5	3.0	27.0	4.6	8.5	10.0	15.6
Pine Country Bank	Little Falls	MN	B+	B+	B-	210.3	17.48	11.8	0.6	5.2	13.5	6.7	8.7	0.0
Pine Island Bank	Pine Island	MN	B+	B+	B+	117.1	9.98	7.8	1.2	27.3	7.5	7.4	9.2	14.8
Pine River State Bank	Pine River	MN	B-	B-	C+	147.3	23.43	9.3	1.8	15.3	15.6	5.3	7.3	17.3
Pineland Bank	Alma	GA	B	B	B-	340.6	18.24	11.3	1.9	10.6	8.3	8.1	9.7	0.0
Pineries Bank	Stevens Point	WI	B+	B+	B	120.6	18.47	6.8	2.1	29.8	8.3	7.2	9.1	19.8
Pinnacle Bank	Jasper	AL	A-	A-	A-	277.9	17.93	19.9	1.8	6.1	45.1	10.0	11.5	18.6

Asset Quality Index	Adjusted Non-Performing Loans		Net Charge-Offs Avg Loans	Profitability Index	Net Income ($Mil)	Return on Assets (R.O.A.)	Return on Equity (R.O.E.)	Net Interest Spread	Overhead Efficiency Ratio	Liquidity Index	Liquidity Ratio	Hot Money Ratio	Stability Index
	as a % of Total Loans	as a % of Capital											
7.5	0.21	na	-0.04	3.8	0.3	0.80	6.97	3.68	71.9	6.0	57.6	7.3	5.1
2.7	2.85	na	0.13	3.4	0.6	0.74	7.66	3.40	77.2	1.4	22.4	28.9	4.7
7.9	1.36	na	0.19	3.3	0.3	0.61	4.71	3.49	78.9	6.6	55.5	2.9	6.8
3.9	2.34	na	0.03	3.0	0.3	0.36	4.70	3.59	87.0	1.8	21.8	22.3	3.8
5.7	0.60	na	0.02	4.5	2.1	0.88	9.07	3.71	66.7	3.8	8.5	8.9	5.3
6.6	0.49	2.6	0.15	4.9	21.9	1.11	9.10	3.39	57.5	3.7	12.8	9.4	9.5
8.8	0.09	na	0.00	5.4	3.6	1.46	13.82	3.20	64.8	4.8	36.1	9.7	6.7
3.0	1.21	na	0.67	10.0	0.5	3.37	12.55	6.23	42.4	2.1	25.2	19.2	8.0
1.7	5.00	na	0.14	0.7	-1.7	-0.84	-8.05	3.61	107.2	1.2	21.1	30.2	5.3
5.0	0.49	na	0.00	2.6	0.1	0.34	4.63	3.49	85.1	4.7	10.7	3.3	1.7
8.5	0.00	na	-0.02	5.4	0.6	1.27	8.89	3.59	63.0	5.0	45.1	11.0	8.6
4.2	1.52	na	0.01	3.6	0.7	0.59	6.35	3.73	80.1	3.4	26.8	13.6	4.7
8.0	0.00	na	-0.01	4.7	0.1	0.73	8.11	5.17	84.2	5.2	38.3	4.7	5.4
9.3	0.00	na	0.00	6.4	0.9	1.53	11.28	2.96	47.7	4.8	46.8	12.4	8.5
8.7	0.00	na	0.03	3.8	0.8	0.83	8.75	3.25	74.8	3.7	41.2	16.9	5.4
1.8	6.00	na	0.48	4.1	6.4	1.01	8.79	3.17	64.6	4.0	33.4	12.9	7.5
6.7	0.98	na	0.24	5.0	7.9	1.01	10.26	3.41	55.4	3.7	16.7	9.8	8.5
8.5	0.20	na	0.04	7.8	0.4	1.38	11.99	3.90	51.3	5.6	50.8	8.6	6.7
9.4	0.24	na	0.00	4.0	2.0	0.90	7.40	2.36	55.0	2.8	56.3	32.6	6.6
5.6	0.93	na	0.12	6.1	1.4	1.19	9.25	4.17	59.5	3.5	17.6	11.7	8.0
4.8	1.14	na	0.15	6.0	4.3	1.20	10.44	3.57	53.0	3.6	22.9	11.4	7.1
5.9	0.71	na	-0.04	7.2	4.0	1.78	18.91	3.60	57.1	3.3	27.0	12.8	6.5
1.3	7.91	na	-0.05	4.7	1.0	1.07	11.07	3.89	73.4	1.8	13.7	20.1	6.0
5.3	0.00	na	0.00	6.6	0.7	1.57	13.33	3.73	58.2	1.8	19.2	20.8	7.7
9.2	0.48	na	0.00	3.8	1.1	0.73	4.29	3.51	75.5	3.3	37.9	18.0	8.2
4.5	3.65	na	-0.65	2.9	0.1	0.48	3.82	2.95	82.2	5.4	47.9	8.8	5.6
4.8	2.65	na	0.03	3.7	1.7	0.74	6.42	3.47	73.9	5.4	41.4	8.1	6.7
7.2	0.55	4.1	0.05	3.5	12.4	0.54	5.64	2.93	64.0	4.4	13.2	4.2	7.7
5.1	1.26	8.4	1.20	3.1	4.3	0.28	2.88	3.18	66.5	3.0	13.2	13.8	8.2
5.5	1.46	na	-0.04	6.5	8.4	1.30	14.26	4.18	59.1	4.0	31.0	12.1	6.9
4.5	1.20	na	0.00	5.1	0.7	0.79	6.34	3.61	68.0	1.8	28.9	26.9	7.4
7.9	0.00	na	-0.02	4.5	1.0	1.12	11.53	2.85	63.4	7.3	61.2	1.8	5.3
8.7	0.53	na	-0.03	6.7	3.7	1.23	6.29	2.58	41.3	0.8	17.9	41.9	9.2
7.6	1.59	na	0.02	4.7	1.4	1.03	7.00	3.01	51.6	4.9	61.2	15.8	9.0
7.2	1.18	3.2	0.05	2.3	1.3	0.50	7.41	3.71	87.9	4.5	30.3	9.1	1.1
7.3	2.74	na	0.18	3.2	0.6	0.51	3.68	2.56	69.8	4.1	47.1	16.3	6.9
8.4	0.43	na	0.08	3.6	1.3	0.76	6.79	3.49	78.1	5.3	39.3	7.7	7.0
6.1	0.42	na	0.05	8.0	3.2	2.02	15.65	3.98	56.8	3.8	12.3	9.5	8.2
7.2	1.84	na	0.14	7.3	2.0	1.35	9.32	3.50	46.2	2.5	35.3	23.4	8.4
7.8	0.33	na	0.01	8.3	6.1	2.07	25.51	3.51	57.6	5.1	26.6	3.1	4.7
9.6	0.57	na	0.04	6.6	2.8	1.74	11.23	3.56	59.9	5.9	42.4	4.6	7.9
8.3	0.00	0.0	0.00	9.5	0.6	3.68	5.22	1.72	85.0	4.9	181.2	71.9	7.0
6.5	1.15	na	-0.08	4.5	0.9	1.05	8.53	3.28	67.8	4.5	32.5	10.0	7.5
7.9	1.25	na	0.00	2.9	1.6	0.43	3.62	3.08	75.4	3.3	18.8	12.8	7.3
7.7	0.88	na	0.01	3.0	0.4	0.52	4.60	3.13	83.4	3.8	47.4	17.7	6.4
7.0	0.23	na	0.00	7.8	12.0	1.38	12.48	4.15	49.9	1.3	16.9	29.5	8.7
10.0	0.25	na	0.00	1.8	0.7	0.10	0.38	2.26	93.6	2.2	42.0	32.1	8.1
8.7	0.00	na	0.00	0.0	-5.0	-6.98	-20.76	2.45	308.9	2.7	48.7	15.0	1.5
8.9	0.00	na	0.00	3.3	0.4	0.59	6.54	3.38	72.6	3.5	31.1	14.7	6.4
6.7	3.29	na	0.06	4.6	1.6	0.81	5.98	3.97	74.8	2.5	26.2	18.0	7.8
7.3	1.66	4.2	-0.02	2.3	0.0	-0.01	-0.10	4.19	97.0	7.0	63.5	3.8	7.7
8.3	0.37	na	0.00	4.8	5.1	1.19	8.84	3.65	68.2	2.7	28.9	17.9	8.3
5.8	0.72	na	0.15	5.0	4.5	1.13	12.81	3.42	52.1	1.8	15.3	10.2	5.5
6.4	0.21	1.9	0.10	7.7	8.2	1.66	15.28	3.22	51.3	3.9	20.8	10.1	8.6
5.2	1.86	na	0.11	6.8	2.0	1.38	14.90	4.29	58.8	4.4	29.0	7.0	5.8
5.2	0.96	4.4	-0.04	8.8	1.8	2.08	19.63	3.98	45.8	0.9	10.0	21.4	8.0
7.3	1.18	na	0.06	3.8	0.7	0.73	8.85	3.65	80.2	6.0	47.6	6.1	4.5
4.7	1.68	9.5	0.16	3.9	1.5	0.64	6.20	4.63	77.2	4.0	22.0	9.8	5.3
8.8	0.00	na	0.12	4.4	0.8	0.98	10.05	2.80	64.5	3.3	42.9	19.4	6.4
8.8	0.16	0.4	-0.06	6.1	2.4	1.22	9.98	3.69	63.5	3.6	30.8	13.7	7.7

Name	City	State	Rating	2019 Rating	2018 Rating	Total Assets ($Mil)	One Year Asset Growth	Comm- ercial Loans	Cons- umer Loans	Mort- gage Loans	Secur- ities	Capital- ization Index	Lever- age Ratio	Risk- Based Capital Ratio
▼ Pinnacle Bank	Gilroy	CA	B+	A-	B	625.8	56.63	24.5	0.1	4.6	0.2	7.0	9.0	14.8
Pinnacle Bank	Elberton	GA	B+	B+	B+	1517.4	58.00	12.7	1.9	8.2	8.7	5.7	9.3	11.6
Pinnacle Bank	Marshalltown	IA	A	A	B+	226.4	11.69	20.6	2.2	5.6	16.9	10.0	15.8	22.4
Pinnacle Bank	Lincoln	NE	A-	A-	A-	6215.0	19.66	9.1	1.1	8.7	14.4	8.2	9.8	13.7
Pinnacle Bank	Nashville	TN	B+	B+	B+	33637.2	22.69	23.9	1.1	6.3	13.4	6.9	8.9	12.6
Pinnacle Bank	Fort Worth	TX	A-	A-	B+	1705.7	14.96	11.0	1.1	11.3	22.7	7.7	9.4	16.0
Pinnacle Bank - Wyoming	Cody	WY	A-	A-	B+	1152.5	20.59	8.3	1.4	11.6	23.0	7.9	9.6	14.0
Pinnacle Bank, Inc.	Vanceburg	KY	B-	B-	B-	49.0	-1.92	5.0	4.5	34.0	12.2	10.0	15.2	0.0
Pioneer Bank	Sioux City	IA	B	B	B	211.2	17.72	17.6	0.7	22.8	5.0	5.5	8.8	0.0
Pioneer Bank	Mapleton	MN	C+	C	C+	676.5	3.90	18.9	1.4	8.9	13.5	7.4	9.3	17.6
Pioneer Bank	Roswell	NM	B-	B-	B-	832.3	1.54	10.5	1.5	15.8	26.4	8.5	10.0	19.3
▼ Pioneer Bank	Albany	NY	B-	B	B+	1627.4	12.38	15.0	0.1	22.1	5.7	10.0	11.6	16.7
Pioneer Bank	Stanley	VA	B	B	C-	251.8	14.42	7.9	9.9	24.8	4.3	10.0	11.1	16.1
Pioneer Bank & Trust	Spearfish	SD	A	A	A	798.6	19.00	13.9	1.7	4.9	35.1	9.9	11.0	18.4
Pioneer Bank, SSB	Austin	TX	C	C+	C	1834.1	8.70	11.8	2.1	12.6	17.1	6.0	8.0	12.5
Pioneer Commercial Bank	Albany	NY	U	U	U	398.8	12.30	0.0	0.0	0.0	4.8	6.9	8.9	36.4
Pioneer Community Bank, Inc.	Iaeger	WV	B	B	B	130.2	14.68	21.2	2.4	44.2	6.8	10.0	13.1	0.0
Pioneer Federal S&L Assn.	Dillon	MT	B-	B-	B	99.3	10.12	3.8	1.6	51.8	17.4	10.0	17.7	0.0
Pioneer Savings Bank	Cleveland	OH	C	C	C+	42.1	7.79	0.0	0.6	36.5	29.9	10.0	15.8	36.2
▲ Pioneer State Bank	Earlville	IL	C+	C	C	117.0	8.70	6.6	0.9	13.0	11.4	10.0	11.5	0.0
Pioneer Trust Bank, N.A.	Salem	OR	A+	A	A	629.9	17.46	23.1	0.2	5.6	14.4	10.0	11.6	20.4
▼ Piqua State Bank	Piqua	KS	B-	B	C+	31.7	14.91	8.4	2.2	9.3	32.5	9.8	10.9	25.4
Piscataqua Savings Bank	Portsmouth	NH	C+	B-	B-	320.7	9.93	0.0	0.5	54.7	25.1	10.0	15.4	0.0
Pitney Bowes Bank, Inc.	Salt Lake City	UT	A-	A-	B+	777.5	4.56	26.1	0.0	0.0	48.9	7.7	9.4	0.0
Pittsfield Co-operative Bank	Pittsfield	MA	B	B	B	361.3	11.98	7.9	0.5	40.5	15.2	10.0	12.6	0.0
▲ Plains Commerce Bank	Hoven	SD	C	C	D+	1117.3	60.82	10.6	0.5	35.7	5.0	10.0	11.4	0.0
▲ Plains State Bank	Plains	KS	C	C	C	252.8	20.00	24.9	1.3	15.6	17.6	7.0	9.6	12.5
▲ Plains State Bank	Humble	TX	B-	C	C-	652.2	16.08	22.9	0.3	4.6	7.2	7.1	10.3	0.0
PlainsCapital Bank	Dallas	TX	A-	A-	A-	13674.0	23.24	12.0	0.2	22.8	12.1	8.8	10.2	15.5
Planters and Citizens Bank	Camilla	GA	C+	B-	B-	123.3	23.58	11.0	2.0	4.6	30.6	8.8	10.2	0.0
Planters Bank & Trust Co.	Indianola	MS	B	B	B	1222.7	12.07	13.3	1.7	11.2	35.2	7.8	9.5	17.3
Planters Bank, Inc.	Hopkinsville	KY	A-	B+	B+	1299.1	14.69	10.0	0.8	13.4	17.0	8.7	11.2	13.9
Planters First Bank	Hawkinsville	GA	B-	B-	C+	371.9	22.39	14.1	1.3	7.8	12.1	6.8	8.8	13.6
Plaquemine Bank and Trust Co.	Plaquemine	LA	B-	B-	B-	173.8	9.01	12.5	2.6	9.6	30.7	10.0	11.1	23.2
Platinum Bank	Oakdale	MN	B+	B	B	396.2	43.19	44.5	0.9	7.2	2.8	5.5	7.5	13.9
Platte Valley Bank	North Bend	NE	A-	A-	B+	86.8	0.38	13.0	2.9	3.1	16.7	10.0	13.7	0.0
Platte Valley Bank	Scottsbluff	NE	B-	B-	C+	833.4	12.34	17.4	6.5	18.3	8.8	5.2	8.8	0.0
Platte Valley Bank	Torrington	WY	B	B	C+	500.9	10.80	31.7	5.0	13.2	6.6	6.1	10.6	0.0
Pleasants County Bank	Saint Marys	WV	C+	C	B-	65.6	1.38	5.7	8.2	28.1	7.9	10.0	11.1	0.0
Plumas Bank	Quincy	CA	A-	B	B	1114.8	25.55	14.2	8.8	1.1	14.2	7.5	9.3	15.3
Plus International Bank	Miami	FL	D	C-	D+	71.2	-13.87	25.7	0.0	30.1	3.1	10.0	19.3	31.4
PNB Community Bank	Niceville	FL	B-	B-	C	120.4	15.19	4.0	0.7	23.8	19.1	9.3	10.5	0.0
PNC Bank, N.A.	Wilmington	DE	B-	B-	B-	457454.2	15.58	21.7	6.2	7.7	20.0	5.9	7.9	13.2
Poca Valley Bank, Inc.	Walton	WV	C+	B-	C+	438.3	16.51	16.7	5.7	31.6	10.9	6.0	8.0	13.2
Pocahontas State Bank	Pocahontas	IA	B+	B+	B+	105.0	0.09	4.9	0.4	3.3	47.3	10.0	25.5	0.0
▼ Pointbank	Pilot Point	TX	B+	B+	B	652.5	20.09	16.0	2.1	7.1	24.2	8.3	9.9	18.9
Points West Community Bank	Windsor	CO	A-	A-	B+	753.7	197.02	10.7	1.2	5.8	30.1	6.7	8.7	0.0
POINTWEST Bank	West	TX	B	B	B-	117.0	18.99	4.0	6.5	21.7	22.9	8.0	9.7	22.3
Ponce Bank	Bronx	NY	C+	C+	C+	1260.8	14.78	7.3	0.8	32.5	1.2	10.0	11.5	16.9
Pony Express Bank	Liberty	MO	B+	B	B	220.7	23.27	23.8	1.5	12.3	10.3	7.1	9.1	13.1
Poppy Bank	Santa Rosa	CA	A	A	A	3157.3	34.51	11.0	0.0	8.7	8.0	8.9	10.3	18.0
Popular Bank	New York	NY	C-	C+	C	10220.5	1.24	4.9	2.2	11.2	14.2	10.0	12.0	17.2
Port Austin State Bank	Port Austin	MI	B+	B+	B+	61.3	17.01	3.3	3.1	31.5	11.5	10.0	16.9	0.0
Port Richmond Savings	Philadelphia	PA	A-	A-	B	101.2	25.75	20.2	0.0	51.9	0.0	10.0	15.9	0.0
Port Washington State Bank	Port Washington	WI	B	B	B-	736.4	22.52	11.0	2.2	13.6	21.1	6.5	8.5	14.0
Portage Community Bank	Ravenna	OH	B	B	B	434.4	22.15	10.9	1.2	25.8	16.5	9.6	10.7	18.1
Portage County Bank	Almond	WI	B-	B-	B	184.1	13.51	10.3	0.5	14.8	11.2	8.6	10.1	16.2
Potter State Bank of Potter	Potter	NE	B	B	B-	41.9	0.15	13.5	2.0	1.4	21.7	10.0	15.4	0.0
Powell State Bank	Powell	TX	C	C-	D	31.3	2.52	10.7	13.8	5.2	26.7	9.6	10.8	0.0
Powell Valley National Bank	Jonesville	VA	B	B	B+	386.0	30.88	10.0	2.9	21.5	7.7	10.0	11.0	17.9

Asset Quality Index	Adjusted Non-Performing Loans as a % of Total Loans	as a % of Capital	Net Charge-Offs Avg Loans	Profitability Index	Net Income ($Mil)	Return on Assets (R.O.A.)	Return on Equity (R.O.E.)	Net Interest Spread	Overhead Efficiency Ratio	Liquidity Index	Liquidity Ratio	Hot Money Ratio	Stability Index
7.1	0.02	na	-0.03	5.6	2.5	0.63	6.15	4.12	68.3	4.0	18.6	9.3	6.7
7.9	0.23	1.1	0.07	5.5	10.5	1.08	10.41	4.47	64.1	4.5	25.8	10.4	9.0
7.7	0.12	na	0.04	10.0	3.4	2.08	12.09	4.32	37.2	4.4	19.6	1.6	9.3
8.3	0.20	1.6	0.00	6.9	59.1	1.36	13.08	3.35	53.3	4.1	17.8	9.0	9.0
6.7	0.33	1.4	0.18	5.4	211.8	0.90	5.96	2.99	47.3	2.1	21.5	6.9	10.0
7.2	0.05	0.7	0.07	5.8	14.0	1.17	8.69	3.90	58.7	4.7	31.4	11.7	9.0
8.3	0.42	2.5	0.01	8.0	12.2	1.54	15.40	3.73	50.1	3.7	26.4	14.6	8.7
5.2	1.22	na	0.28	3.8	0.2	0.59	3.47	4.46	80.2	0.9	12.7	30.1	7.0
8.4	0.01	0.1	-0.09	4.9	1.7	1.15	12.78	3.57	62.9	2.3	15.7	17.8	6.0
3.0	3.23	na	0.45	3.8	3.0	0.59	5.35	3.77	68.0	3.1	18.5	13.6	7.0
7.4	1.96	na	0.13	3.7	4.8	0.78	7.68	2.87	73.8	5.0	38.2	8.9	6.4
6.0	1.40	8.2	-0.19	3.0	3.4	0.30	2.69	3.10	78.3	5.2	22.3	3.5	6.4
5.4	1.13	na	0.27	4.8	1.9	1.03	9.08	4.34	69.2	4.1	16.3	8.5	6.7
8.8	0.21	0.9	0.04	8.7	9.7	1.77	15.40	3.59	43.3	4.9	35.9	8.9	8.1
6.8	0.56	3.9	0.13	2.7	6.7	0.49	5.61	2.46	74.6	1.8	28.2	37.0	6.8
10.0	na	0.0	na	3.8	1.4	0.57	6.99	0.97	21.1	8.5	102.6	0.0	5.8
7.0	0.68	na	0.11	3.6	0.7	0.71	5.33	4.16	83.8	3.8	20.9	10.5	6.7
9.8	0.00	na	0.00	3.4	0.4	0.63	3.44	3.61	77.7	4.2	43.7	14.7	6.4
6.0	5.07	na	-0.09	1.7	0.1	0.33	1.98	2.55	101.9	2.3	53.1	51.6	6.4
5.8	2.29	na	-0.04	3.1	0.5	0.61	5.06	3.95	82.2	4.0	22.0	9.9	6.8
8.6	0.00	na	-0.01	9.8	10.1	2.27	18.77	3.72	36.0	5.8	35.2	2.5	9.2
9.4	0.00	na	0.11	3.2	0.1	0.32	2.65	4.12	77.5	6.8	63.3	3.2	6.1
10.0	0.32	na	0.00	2.8	1.2	0.53	3.49	2.15	83.6	2.9	39.6	20.9	7.7
6.8	1.65	4.3	2.51	10.0	49.0	8.45	83.87	8.90	6.4	7.8	72.8	0.0	7.2
7.0	1.86	na	-0.01	3.5	1.5	0.58	3.74	3.44	73.0	2.5	28.8	17.0	7.3
3.7	2.33	na	0.13	8.8	52.6	8.10	65.96	3.93	54.9	0.7	9.2	28.5	9.9
6.5	0.33	na	-0.01	4.0	1.6	0.87	8.48	3.97	68.6	2.1	11.1	16.7	5.5
5.6	1.26	na	0.08	6.7	5.8	1.24	11.85	4.09	54.7	0.8	17.1	28.3	7.8
6.0	0.84	4.5	0.27	9.6	269.5	3.03	24.11	3.22	60.5	2.1	20.5	10.9	10.0
8.9	0.02	na	0.12	2.8	0.4	0.44	3.92	3.34	80.7	6.6	52.2	3.7	5.3
6.0	1.43	6.6	0.29	4.3	7.8	0.87	8.48	3.05	67.3	3.1	31.2	19.8	7.8
7.7	0.71	na	0.02	7.9	14.9	1.61	14.60	3.85	46.6	1.7	8.6	15.1	9.9
5.2	0.95	4.5	0.14	4.1	2.7	0.97	10.33	4.19	78.9	3.9	18.5	10.0	5.8
6.1	2.36	na	0.11	3.8	0.9	0.68	6.11	3.53	71.4	2.5	34.5	21.6	6.4
8.0	0.15	1.0	0.01	6.8	3.6	1.49	18.81	3.84	55.0	4.8	17.9	3.8	4.9
8.4	0.04	na	0.00	5.3	0.7	1.03	7.60	3.46	58.9	5.9	41.2	4.6	8.0
4.3	0.80	na	0.08	6.5	8.2	1.37	14.89	3.81	54.7	1.8	17.1	20.2	6.9
5.5	1.27	na	0.71	9.5	6.4	1.78	16.80	5.73	49.0	1.0	11.1	27.3	7.5
3.7	2.04	na	0.03	3.6	0.3	0.69	6.27	3.45	76.3	4.4	34.0	11.1	6.0
7.5	0.44	na	0.09	8.8	10.6	1.46	14.10	4.17	49.4	5.5	22.3	1.8	9.3
4.1	5.86	na	0.00	0.0	-1.0	-1.84	-9.26	3.78	133.7	0.8	26.0	62.2	6.8
7.6	1.04	na	-0.12	3.4	0.5	0.54	4.88	4.07	83.9	5.4	42.3	8.3	5.9
4.9	1.39	6.0	0.31	3.4	1451.2	0.48	4.70	2.57	61.9	6.4	37.8	1.4	9.3
5.4	0.90	na	0.11	3.4	1.5	0.48	5.37	3.81	81.8	3.3	22.1	13.0	4.9
8.7	0.00	na	0.00	8.9	1.5	2.01	7.00	3.38	26.9	4.7	80.6	17.8	6.3
8.7	0.16	na	-0.03	5.0	5.3	1.15	10.82	3.74	70.4	5.0	30.3	5.5	7.5
7.5	1.02	na	0.09	7.2	8.6	1.57	17.33	3.16	59.1	2.9	15.2	14.4	8.8
9.0	0.00	0.0	0.08	4.2	0.8	1.02	10.21	3.16	72.2	6.3	60.3	7.8	5.2
4.6	1.57	na	0.00	2.9	3.8	0.44	3.67	3.63	80.7	0.9	8.3	23.8	7.7
6.7	0.00	na	0.02	8.0	2.4	1.65	14.23	4.35	50.6	3.0	20.8	5.8	8.6
7.2	1.25	na	0.02	7.4	33.8	1.61	18.98	2.85	40.8	1.8	25.5	27.6	9.4
5.1	0.71	2.5	0.16	1.4	-17.1	-0.22	-1.28	3.15	70.5	1.6	16.5	17.0	7.3
8.8	0.05	na	-0.06	5.8	0.6	1.38	7.86	3.47	57.1	5.1	42.1	10.1	8.0
8.6	0.33	na	0.00	8.2	1.3	1.87	11.10	3.74	48.7	2.6	4.0	15.0	7.7
7.7	0.41	na	0.13	5.1	5.6	1.10	12.18	3.10	61.9	3.9	20.5	9.8	5.2
5.1	1.48	na	0.00	4.0	2.3	0.76	6.62	3.18	74.4	2.4	24.8	17.7	6.7
8.6	0.10	na	0.00	4.5	1.3	0.97	8.99	3.75	72.2	2.9	35.8	12.5	5.8
8.6	0.00	na	-0.13	4.1	0.2	0.77	4.99	3.97	76.1	3.5	56.1	20.9	7.2
3.8	3.44	na	0.59	2.6	0.1	0.24	2.22	3.99	80.7	4.9	37.4	9.7	4.5
6.8	0.74	4.0	0.03	3.7	1.6	0.62	5.02	3.52	78.9	2.6	28.8	18.0	7.7

Name	City	State	2020 Rating	2019 Rating	2018 Rating	Total Assets ($Mil)	One Year Asset Growth	Comm-ercial Loans	Cons-umer Loans	Mort-gage Loans	Secur-ities	Capital-ization Index	Lever-age Ratio	Risk-Based Capital Ratio
Prairie Bank of Kansas	Stafford	KS	C+	C	C+	122.1	17.85	11.8	1.5	4.7	25.4	6.2	8.3	0.0
Prairie Community Bank	Marengo	IL	C-	C	C-	157.4	25.83	17.9	0.7	13.5	3.7	6.4	8.4	15.4
Prairie State Bank & Trust	Springfield	IL	A-	A-	A-	769.9	11.17	11.0	0.7	15.7	18.6	9.5	10.6	0.0
▼ Prairie Sun Bank	Milan	MN	C-	C-	D	62.4	24.36	7.9	3.4	3.8	16.9	3.3	8.3	0.0
Preferred Bank	Los Angeles	CA	A-	B+	B+	5087.7	13.13	23.9	0.0	10.3	4.5	8.1	9.8	14.5
Preferred Bank	Casey	IL	C-	C-	C-	66.1	12.15	17.5	4.4	16.7	15.6	6.7	8.7	0.0
Preferred Bank	Rothville	MO	B-	B-	B-	127.9	19.31	4.8	1.8	9.9	50.1	5.6	7.6	22.7
Premier Bank	Dubuque	IA	B	B	B	393.6	15.84	19.0	0.9	15.0	17.0	6.1	8.1	13.2
Premier Bank	Rock Valley	IA	C	C+	C	578.8	-0.29	12.0	1.7	4.5	9.9	9.8	11.0	14.9
▲ Premier Bank	Maplewood	MN	B+	B-	C+	974.2	12.43	13.0	0.3	4.9	7.2	9.0	10.3	15.1
▼ Premier Bank	Omaha	NE	B+	B+	B	340.8	11.23	19.0	0.4	7.4	5.9	5.2	10.9	0.0
▲ Premier Bank	Youngstown	OH	B	B	B	6947.1	109.08	17.5	1.8	19.3	8.3	6.1	9.1	11.8
▲ Premier Bank Minnesota	Farmington	MN	B+	B	B	302.3	15.06	14.9	0.2	4.8	14.1	7.7	9.5	14.0
▼ Premier Bank of Arkansas	Marion	AR	B+	A-	A-	175.4	6.58	13.3	1.2	17.5	2.6	10.0	14.1	18.2
Premier Bank of the South	Cullman	AL	B	B	B	240.0	22.74	16.3	6.1	25.1	14.8	6.2	8.2	13.6
Premier Bank Rochester	Rochester	MN	B	B-	C+	256.9	8.90	10.9	0.1	8.7	9.8	6.6	8.6	12.3
Premier Bank, Inc.	Huntington	WV	B	B	B-	1311.2	6.79	12.7	1.0	18.5	16.8	8.7	10.8	0.0
Premier Community Bank	Marion	WI	B-	B-	C+	366.5	18.11	7.3	2.3	9.3	13.8	6.7	9.0	12.3
Premier Valley Bank	Fresno	CA	B+	A-	B+	1042.4	17.34	18.6	0.5	2.2	29.4	6.4	8.4	12.7
PremierBank	Fort Atkinson	WI	B	B	C+	489.2	15.42	10.3	1.0	14.8	31.1	8.1	9.7	16.7
Prescott State Bank	Prescott	KS	B-	B-	B-	14.2	11.36	9.1	2.9	14.7	11.8	10.0	15.7	0.0
▲ Presidential Bank, FSB	Bethesda	MD	A-	B	B-	744.1	18.04	5.9	2.3	34.7	3.7	9.7	10.8	16.9
Prevail Bank	Medford	WI	C+	C+	B+	834.4	42.27	7.0	0.1	42.2	18.4	10.0	13.8	25.2
Primary Bank	Bedford	NH	C+	C+	C	532.0	101.72	38.8	0.0	3.7	0.3	8.7	10.1	16.7
▼ Prime Alliance Bank	Woods Cross	UT	C+	B-	C+	519.9	8.92	35.5	0.0	0.4	15.0	7.6	10.3	13.0
Prime Meridian Bank	Tallahassee	FL	B	B+	B+	620.6	28.24	24.5	1.1	19.7	9.8	7.1	9.1	15.0
▲ Prime Security Bank	Karlstad	MN	B	B-	C	103.0	25.54	24.0	0.4	13.2	5.5	6.7	8.7	12.3
Primebank	Le Mars	IA	B	B	B+	519.9	9.87	13.2	1.3	15.8	9.3	10.0	11.2	15.1
PrimeSouth Bank	Waycross	GA	B+	B	B	845.1	26.27	11.5	3.3	22.6	8.1	7.1	9.1	13.6
Princeville State Bank	Princeville	IL	C-	C	C-	111.9	29.65	14.6	2.6	5.1	34.5	6.1	8.1	12.3
Principal Bank	Des Moines	IA	B+	B+	B+	4375.7	16.73	0.0	0.0	30.3	65.0	5.0	7.0	12.7
PrinsBank	Prinsburg	MN	A	A-	B+	179.5	31.99	6.7	2.3	2.5	2.6	10.0	12.9	20.3
Priority Bank	Fayetteville	AR	C+	B-	C+	97.6	14.43	2.5	1.1	70.3	2.0	6.8	8.8	0.0
PriorityOne Bank	Magee	MS	B+	B	B+	785.5	14.21	10.8	3.4	16.0	15.8	7.9	9.7	0.0
Private Trust Co., N.A.	Cleveland	OH	U	U	U	21.6	-6.69	0.0	0.0	0.0	61.5	10.0	88.5	950.3
▼ Produce State Bank	Hollandale	MN	B	B+	B-	107.6	80.65	13.5	4.4	4.7	7.7	5.1	7.1	12.7
▼ Professional Bank	Coral Gables	FL	C	C+	C+	2076.6	115.68	18.9	0.6	17.4	4.8	6.5	8.5	12.7
Profile Bank	Rochester	NH	C	C	C	251.0	13.99	5.7	1.0	27.8	21.5	10.0	11.6	19.4
Profinium, Inc.	Truman	MN	B	B	C+	486.7	24.56	12.0	0.5	7.5	15.6	6.1	8.4	0.0
Progress Bank and Trust	Huntsville	AL	B	B	B	1548.4	28.05	25.4	1.2	14.5	3.4	6.5	9.4	12.1
Progressive Bank	Monroe	LA	C+	B	B	732.5	27.97	17.2	0.8	14.3	9.1	6.6	9.3	12.2
Progressive National Bank	Mansfield	LA	C-	C+	D+	89.4	23.61	6.6	2.5	22.3	14.8	6.3	8.3	0.0
Progressive Ozark Bank	Salem	MO	A-	A-	A-	138.0	22.70	6.1	5.5	42.7	3.7	7.8	9.6	0.0
ProGrowth Bank	Nicollet	MN	B	B	C+	156.1	31.63	18.8	0.8	10.3	35.8	7.0	9.0	16.7
PromiseOne Bank	Duluth	GA	A-	A-	B+	541.9	24.43	12.7	0.0	1.7	13.7	10.0	11.0	18.3
Prospect Bank	Paris	IL	B-	B-	B-	626.9	14.87	13.8	0.5	8.1	30.3	6.7	8.7	13.1
Prosper Bank	Coatesville	PA	C-	C	C-	258.3	17.74	2.5	0.0	38.5	9.5	6.7	8.7	15.0
Prosperity Bank	El Campo	TX	A-	A-	A-	33278.1	50.69	11.3	0.4	13.6	22.9	8.3	9.9	14.2
Providence Bank	Columbia	MO	B-	B	B	1192.6	11.86	23.9	2.2	10.1	11.2	10.0	12.8	15.6
Providence Bank	Rocky Mount	NC	A-	A-	B	576.7	19.41	9.7	1.3	8.3	4.3	10.0	11.6	15.3
Providence Bank & Trust	South Holland	IL	B+	B+	B	1199.5	15.88	20.5	0.0	4.7	13.6	6.9	9.8	0.0
Providence Bank of Texas	Southlake	TX	B	B	B-	182.5	19.65	8.6	0.5	13.7	0.0	10.0	11.6	17.0
Provident Bank	Jersey City	NJ	B-	B-	B-	12845.4	29.52	9.8	0.2	13.2	12.2	5.5	9.3	11.4
Provident Savings Bank, F.S.B.	Riverside	CA	C+	C+	C+	1184.0	7.12	0.1	0.0	24.6	16.9	8.0	9.6	18.2
▲ Provident State Bank, Inc.	Preston	MD	B	B-	C+	542.0	18.52	13.1	0.5	17.3	10.8	7.2	9.5	12.6
▼ Prudential Bank	Philadelphia	PA	C+	B-	B	1223.3	-5.10	1.1	0.1	18.5	36.4	9.3	10.5	18.1
Prudential Bank & Trust, FSB	Hartford	CT	U	U	U	28.3	10.75	0.0	0.0	0.0	67.3	10.0	90.7	203.6
▲ PS Bank	Wyalusing	PA	B+	B	B	441.1	8.74	13.6	0.6	19.1	21.8	8.2	9.8	0.0
Pueblo Bank and Trust Co.	Pueblo	CO	B+	B+	A-	536.1	23.99	15.9	0.1	4.9	17.5	8.7	10.1	16.8
Pulaski Savings Bank	Chicago	IL	D	D	D-	48.5	-0.88	0.0	0.5	75.1	0.8	5.5	7.5	17.1

Asset Quality Index	Adjusted Non-Performing Loans as a % of Total Loans	Adjusted Non-Performing Loans as a % of Capital	Net Charge-Offs Avg Loans	Profitability Index	Net Income ($Mil)	Return on Assets (R.O.A.)	Return on Equity (R.O.E.)	Net Interest Spread	Overhead Efficiency Ratio	Liquidity Index	Liquidity Ratio	Hot Money Ratio	Stability Index
4.4	3.25	na	0.01	3.2	0.5	0.51	5.49	3.19	77.1	2.3	22.8	18.1	4.2
1.7	4.94	26.0	0.31	1.9	0.2	0.20	2.10	3.08	84.2	2.3	31.2	21.3	4.2
7.7	0.35	2.2	0.10	6.1	8.1	1.48	13.30	3.48	62.6	4.0	17.5	8.7	8.4
4.1	0.29	na	-0.02	6.3	0.7	1.72	17.54	4.39	57.7	2.5	20.9	11.4	4.9
6.3	1.21	6.5	0.12	8.4	48.6	1.33	13.41	3.60	32.5	0.9	18.2	30.8	9.5
2.9	0.68	na	0.11	1.8	0.1	0.21	2.32	3.25	90.5	1.6	26.7	28.3	3.7
8.8	0.06	na	0.05	4.3	1.3	1.46	17.59	2.77	74.2	6.5	56.2	5.4	4.5
7.2	0.51	2.0	0.00	5.0	3.6	1.29	14.89	2.97	62.1	4.0	17.5	5.5	5.3
2.3	1.26	na	0.03	9.1	8.4	1.92	16.02	3.55	38.5	0.8	15.5	32.0	9.2
5.7	0.84	na	0.40	8.5	9.4	1.40	13.51	3.87	40.0	4.0	20.5	9.6	7.6
7.3	0.00	0.0	0.00	7.1	3.2	1.29	11.50	4.01	60.6	3.2	19.7	11.5	7.3
5.1	1.00	5.0	0.05	4.9	28.3	0.66	5.11	3.97	58.2	3.7	6.5	9.6	10.0
5.6	0.89	na	0.35	7.1	3.4	1.57	15.82	4.17	51.6	4.0	20.5	9.5	7.7
6.4	0.91	4.9	-0.01	4.9	1.2	0.89	6.23	4.08	68.4	2.6	11.7	15.6	8.2
7.8	1.02	na	0.04	5.1	1.9	1.10	12.84	4.11	71.8	3.6	16.9	11.3	4.7
6.8	0.20	na	0.24	5.6	2.4	1.27	13.66	3.79	52.7	2.2	16.7	18.0	6.4
4.9	0.86	4.7	0.44	8.0	13.5	1.42	10.05	4.17	51.8	4.0	15.4	9.6	8.8
4.9	3.18	na	0.01	4.0	1.8	0.72	7.39	3.59	74.3	4.9	32.2	6.1	5.7
6.7	0.77	1.6	1.57	3.6	0.8	0.11	0.78	3.86	62.8	5.1	23.1	4.6	8.5
5.2	3.97	na	0.01	5.3	3.5	1.05	8.40	3.52	63.0	4.8	24.1	4.5	7.3
8.7	0.00	na	0.02	3.6	0.1	0.54	3.33	3.85	83.3	2.8	50.3	23.7	6.0
6.2	1.29	na	0.08	7.7	14.0	2.81	26.83	3.63	66.8	3.1	11.9	13.0	6.9
8.0	1.43	na	0.02	2.2	1.2	0.19	1.12	2.68	72.8	2.6	29.6	18.5	7.7
4.4	0.95	6.8	0.00	3.5	1.8	0.58	5.40	2.94	60.7	1.3	17.3	28.0	5.0
1.7	6.38	34.8	1.21	5.0	0.8	0.19	1.79	4.28	22.4	0.7	22.3	48.2	8.7
6.5	0.27	2.1	0.34	4.3	3.2	0.73	8.31	3.24	55.3	3.9	17.8	9.4	6.4
8.0	0.59	na	0.00	5.8	1.0	1.35	15.81	4.72	60.5	2.7	7.4	10.4	5.0
5.0	1.21	na	1.06	4.9	3.9	1.03	8.76	3.48	50.8	1.5	15.6	20.2	9.6
7.0	0.91	na	-0.24	5.4	5.4	0.92	8.92	4.00	66.3	2.6	14.2	15.9	8.4
3.3	3.02	na	-0.01	3.6	0.6	0.80	9.14	3.09	68.4	3.7	39.9	13.5	4.1
9.8	0.56	1.8	-0.18	5.3	25.7	0.83	10.88	2.16	33.9	4.4	74.4	5.0	7.1
5.7	0.00	na	-0.59	8.9	2.2	1.79	12.60	3.69	56.3	4.2	44.2	14.9	8.1
3.4	2.06	na	-0.06	9.1	1.7	2.48	27.83	4.21	68.5	0.6	9.1	33.2	7.0
5.5	0.65	na	0.02	7.2	9.7	1.72	16.87	4.38	63.7	2.3	16.5	15.2	7.4
7.1	na	na	na	10.0	3.5	20.07	21.80	2.04	49.2	4.0	na	0.0	5.8
5.1	1.10	na	-0.01	5.5	0.9	1.18	13.05	3.71	62.7	6.2	44.3	3.6	5.9
7.1	0.64	na	0.03	2.7	5.0	0.35	4.25	3.44	67.2	3.4	21.1	13.4	6.4
8.2	1.40	na	0.00	2.2	0.4	0.24	2.08	3.09	91.6	3.8	37.6	15.3	5.2
5.8	0.77	na	-0.11	4.9	3.6	1.09	10.83	3.20	65.0	3.0	17.8	10.3	5.6
7.8	0.34	1.6	0.01	5.9	12.8	1.24	11.00	3.85	59.7	1.3	12.1	17.8	8.7
7.7	0.30	na	0.45	2.7	1.4	0.28	3.01	3.60	77.6	3.9	18.6	9.6	6.0
9.1	0.16	na	0.01	3.1	0.4	0.65	7.86	3.34	86.4	2.7	31.4	18.6	4.3
7.0	0.40	na	0.03	7.0	1.5	1.56	15.80	4.52	70.9	5.0	14.6	1.9	7.1
8.8	0.05	na	-0.04	4.1	0.8	0.77	8.79	3.41	75.0	5.2	29.6	4.4	4.2
6.0	3.18	na	0.12	7.9	6.8	1.80	15.59	2.98	56.2	1.0	26.9	40.4	9.5
3.5	2.88	na	-0.02	4.3	4.9	1.09	11.67	2.97	61.5	0.8	14.1	19.6	6.5
4.6	1.99	na	-0.19	1.8	0.1	0.07	0.78	2.84	86.5	2.0	26.1	21.2	4.9
6.8	0.28	0.9	0.16	8.0	400.9	1.65	8.88	3.69	41.9	4.0	10.0	8.3	10.0
5.7	1.16	na	0.22	3.6	6.7	0.79	5.36	3.40	72.9	1.0	7.4	22.1	9.1
7.1	0.01	na	0.02	7.0	5.5	1.36	10.87	3.52	44.6	0.8	18.5	32.0	8.3
7.1	0.70	na	-0.03	6.6	9.7	1.16	9.82	4.14	59.3	4.6	25.8	8.5	10.0
6.5	1.63	na	0.01	3.7	0.7	0.56	4.49	3.67	79.1	1.5	26.6	29.1	7.3
4.2	0.88	4.1	0.05	4.1	56.5	0.70	5.51	3.05	61.2	3.8	9.2	6.5	9.5
5.8	1.56	na	0.00	3.5	4.8	0.56	5.56	3.10	71.2	3.8	6.3	8.8	7.7
6.8	0.59	na	0.09	4.7	3.5	0.93	9.45	3.62	66.1	3.1	13.5	13.3	5.7
5.7	2.19	9.7	0.03	2.9	7.4	0.81	7.59	1.92	68.7	2.6	42.8	16.1	9.0
9.8	na	na	na	10.0	5.5	30.28	34.16	1.98	18.0	4.0	na	100.0	6.4
7.2	0.33	na	0.04	5.6	3.7	1.19	12.03	3.24	58.0	2.9	24.3	15.3	6.1
8.3	0.32	na	-0.21	4.3	3.1	0.86	7.70	3.98	74.2	5.3	28.9	3.0	7.7
5.4	2.12	13.6	0.00	1.3	0.0	0.12	1.62	3.06	95.8	4.0	15.9	9.1	2.0

Name	City	State	2019 Rating	2018 Rating	Rating	Total Assets ($Mil)	One Year Asset Growth	Comm-ercial Loans	Cons-umer Loans	Mort-gage Loans	Secur-ities	Capital-ization Index	Lever-age Ratio	Risk-Based Capital Ratio
Putnam 1st Mercantile Bank	Cookeville	TN	A-	A-	B+	144.2	13.37	18.4	2.3	20.3	13.1	9.2	10.5	0.0
Putnam County Bank	Hurricane	WV	B-	B-	C+	640.3	7.59	3.3	0.7	30.3	27.3	10.0	15.0	34.2
Putnam County National Bank of Carmel	Carmel	NY	B	B	B-	195.2	17.11	2.0	0.3	19.3	8.1	10.0	20.9	0.0
▲ Putnam County State Bank	Unionville	MO	B+	B	B+	239.4	8.77	10.9	1.6	7.4	2.2	10.0	13.6	0.0
▲ PyraMax Bank, FSB	Greenfield	WI	C	D+	D	505.1	15.04	11.7	0.1	15.5	11.3	8.4	9.9	15.9
QNB Bank	Quakertown	PA	B-	B-	B-	1405.2	13.84	15.8	0.4	13.3	31.6	6.1	8.1	13.5
Quad City Bank and Trust Co.	Bettendorf	IA	B+	B+	B	2223.1	33.69	23.7	0.5	6.6	12.8	5.9	7.9	12.1
▲ Quail Creek Bank, N.A.	Oklahoma City	OK	C	C-	C	751.3	8.96	2.8	0.8	20.9	18.2	7.3	9.2	15.6
Quaint Oak Bank	Southampton	PA	B	B	C+	421.4	44.06	32.3	0.0	18.5	2.6	7.4	9.2	15.0
Quantum National Bank	Suwanee	GA	A-	A	A	651.8	27.65	16.2	0.0	8.8	1.2	5.6	10.7	0.0
Quarry City S&L Assn.	Warrensburg	MO	B-	C+	B-	65.3	13.85	0.8	1.3	33.5	0.0	10.0	14.8	21.2
Queensborough National Bank & Trust Co.	Louisville	GA	C-	C-	C	1561.3	29.12	14.2	0.9	10.8	21.0	6.2	8.2	14.6
Queenstown Bank of Maryland	Queenstown	MD	A-	A-	B+	558.5	17.89	5.3	1.2	30.8	8.5	10.0	12.5	20.7
Quoin Financial Bank	Miller	SD	A-	A-	A-	186.0	8.37	14.1	1.3	6.6	13.1	10.0	12.5	18.4
▼ Quontic Bank	New York	NY	C	B	B	1382.2	252.00	63.3	0.0	19.5	0.5	0.0	10.6	0.0
R Bank	Round Rock	TX	B-	B-	C+	670.5	22.58	26.3	0.4	12.8	9.2	7.5	9.3	13.4
Rabun County Bank	Clayton	GA	B+	B+	B	215.8	17.59	2.2	4.3	29.4	3.0	10.0	11.8	0.0
Raccoon Valley Bank	Perry	IA	B-	C+	C+	330.4	15.94	15.4	0.4	7.2	16.2	6.5	8.5	12.2
Radius Bank	Boston	MA	C-	C+	C+	2186.6	61.25	35.6	15.5	7.9	12.2	5.6	7.6	12.1
Ramsey National Bank	Devils Lake	ND	A	A	A-	267.0	1.16	15.7	0.6	8.3	12.9	10.0	13.9	0.0
Randall State Bank	Randall	MN	B	B-	C+	51.9	10.68	9.4	2.1	20.2	0.1	10.0	11.1	0.0
Range Bank, N.A.	Marquette	MI	B-	B-	C+	475.5	22.17	17.9	0.8	15.0	21.4	6.3	8.3	14.4
▲ Raritan State Bank	Raritan	IL	C+	C+	C+	199.1	9.23	9.5	5.3	24.8	22.6	10.0	11.2	0.0
▲ Raymond Federal Bank	Raymond	WA	C-	C-	D+	63.7	9.02	0.0	0.6	71.3	12.2	8.9	10.3	24.0
Raymond James Bank, N.A.	Saint Petersburg	FL	B+	A-	A-	30610.5	19.08	25.2	10.7	16.1	25.0	5.7	7.7	14.3
Raymond James Trust, N.A.	Saint Petersburg	FL	U	U	U	42.2	19.50	0.0	0.0	0.0	2.6	10.0	82.6	224.2
▲ Rayne Building and Loan Assn.	Rayne	LA	B-	B-	B	61.5	13.62	6.8	1.2	22.0	32.1	10.0	26.0	0.0
Rayne State Bank & Trust Co.	Rayne	LA	A	A	A-	460.5	20.54	22.6	0.4	13.9	19.0	10.0	11.5	21.8
▼ RBC Bank (Georgia), N.A.	Raleigh	NC	B+	A-	B+	4876.7	6.47	0.0	2.3	28.8	60.8	8.4	10.0	33.9
RCB Bank	Claremore	OK	B	B	B	3519.7	12.83	8.4	4.3	8.5	19.3	6.3	8.3	13.5
Reading Cooperative Bank	Reading	MA	B-	B-	B-	630.7	6.62	7.3	0.0	43.2	10.1	7.2	9.1	14.3
Readlyn Savings Bank	Readlyn	IA	A-	A-	A-	81.7	8.57	9.6	1.3	20.3	15.3	10.0	15.3	22.4
Red River Bank	Alexandria	LA	A-	A-	A-	2490.9	28.47	16.6	0.9	17.4	18.8	8.9	10.2	16.6
Red River State Bank	Halstad	MN	B	B	B+	101.0	9.44	42.5	11.4	7.2	5.2	7.9	9.6	15.7
Red Rock Bank	Sanborn	MN	A-	A-	B	37.8	-3.12	7.5	3.9	13.5	5.6	6.8	8.8	0.0
Redstone Bank	Centennial	CO	B+	A-	B+	202.9	28.62	12.0	0.1	11.3	31.9	10.0	11.2	21.6
Redwood Capital Bank	Eureka	CA	B+	B+	B	492.2	31.30	20.5	0.2	5.9	7.4	6.5	8.5	15.3
Regal Bank	Livingston	NJ	C	C	C	550.0	5.03	5.0	0.0	2.3	4.5	7.8	9.5	0.0
Regent Bank	Tulsa	OK	C+	C+	C+	897.0	38.01	27.6	0.5	11.4	1.2	5.9	9.3	11.7
Regional Missouri Bank	Marceline	MO	C+	C	C	429.8	77.20	10.0	2.8	15.0	17.2	8.2	11.1	0.0
Regions Bank	Birmingham	AL	B	B	B-	144473.0	13.27	20.3	4.3	13.6	19.6	7.3	9.2	13.4
Reliabank Dakota	Estelline	SD	B-	B-	B-	538.1	18.28	14.7	1.2	6.8	27.4	5.5	8.5	11.4
Reliance Bank	Faribault	MN	B-	B-	B	184.4	11.83	27.3	1.0	11.3	10.5	5.8	9.2	0.0
▲ Reliance Savings Bank	Altoona	PA	B-	C+	C+	619.6	10.88	8.1	1.2	21.5	22.3	8.6	10.1	14.9
▼ Reliance State Bank	Story City	IA	B	B+	A-	248.6	8.28	6.8	0.9	9.9	25.3	6.8	10.0	0.0
▲ Reliant Bank	Brentwood	TN	B+	B	B+	3036.4	63.69	15.3	6.9	13.6	9.0	8.0	10.5	13.3
Relyance Bank, N.A.	Pine Bluff	AR	B+	B	C+	985.3	13.70	12.8	0.9	9.3	9.3	8.4	11.5	13.7
Renasant Bank	Tupelo	MS	B+	A-	A-	14793.1	13.61	17.6	1.6	16.7	8.7	8.0	9.6	13.5
Republic Bank & Trust Co.	Louisville	KY	A	A-	A-	6229.1	2.23	12.3	4.0	19.0	9.7	10.0	11.9	15.9
▼ Republic Bank of Arizona	Phoenix	AZ	C+	B+	B+	182.4	71.93	18.6	4.2	8.5	18.1	7.8	10.1	0.0
Republic Bank of Chicago	Oak Brook	IL	B+	B+	B	2267.6	11.84	21.6	0.1	5.8	11.8	8.9	10.3	14.1
Republic Banking Co.	Republic	OH	B	B-	B-	53.0	8.53	5.8	9.5	38.0	4.1	10.0	16.3	0.0
Republic First Bank	Philadelphia	PA	D+	D+	C	4949.3	60.83	16.6	0.0	10.2	23.3	6.0	8.0	12.7
▲ Resource Bank	Covington	LA	A-	B	C+	887.9	17.09	2.6	0.8	18.1	7.2	9.3	10.9	0.0
Resource Bank, N.A.	DeKalb	IL	C	C	C+	624.6	18.55	9.9	0.6	13.2	31.4	6.1	8.1	14.7
Reynolds State Bank	Reynolds	IL	A-	A	A	107.7	0.90	0.5	0.1	0.1	61.3	10.0	19.4	56.0
Rhinebeck Bank	Poughkeepsie	NY	C+	C	D+	1112.4	17.61	17.7	32.2	5.6	9.6	8.0	9.7	13.6
▲ Richland County Bank	Richland Center	WI	A	B	B-	110.5	11.05	7.0	3.3	9.2	44.0	10.0	17.3	0.0
▲ Richland State Bank	Bruce	SD	A-	B+	B+	39.8	10.43	16.5	4.4	2.9	29.4	9.9	10.9	17.2
▼ Richton Bank & Trust Co.	Richton	MS	B-	B	B	62.4	9.37	14.9	2.5	7.6	30.4	10.0	14.2	30.0

Asset Quality Index	Adjusted Non-Performing Loans as a % of Total Loans	as a % of Capital	Net Charge-Offs Avg Loans	Profitability Index	Net Income ($Mil)	Return on Assets (R.O.A.)	Return on Equity (R.O.E.)	Net Interest Spread	Overhead Efficiency Ratio	Liquidity Index	Liquidity Ratio	Hot Money Ratio	Stability Index
6.4	0.00	na	0.13	6.2	1.4	1.35	12.12	3.57	57.3	1.3	26.6	32.4	7.2
6.5	3.88	na	-0.74	3.5	3.1	0.68	4.56	2.47	63.9	2.1	41.9	36.9	7.5
6.3	5.73	na	-0.01	4.1	0.9	0.76	3.44	2.92	68.7	6.5	54.4	5.0	6.7
5.2	0.10	na	-0.04	8.9	2.7	1.57	11.73	3.31	35.2	0.8	18.7	46.2	8.9
6.5	0.55	na	-0.06	2.7	1.5	0.43	3.86	2.71	78.4	3.9	30.6	9.5	5.0
5.5	1.64	na	0.02	4.2	8.5	0.87	9.87	2.95	65.2	4.3	18.4	7.7	7.2
7.6	0.35	2.4	0.32	4.4	13.0	0.80	9.56	3.10	45.1	5.7	27.9	3.9	7.2
4.4	1.69	na	0.14	7.3	9.1	1.66	17.17	3.65	50.2	3.6	34.7	15.3	8.5
7.0	0.09	3.1	0.00	4.8	2.4	0.90	9.96	3.16	68.6	0.6	8.0	43.8	4.9
7.3	0.00	0.0	0.00	10.0	10.4	2.49	23.94	5.15	43.4	3.3	13.2	9.1	8.1
5.5	1.70	na	0.00	3.6	0.3	0.66	4.42	3.14	80.6	1.9	22.0	20.1	6.8
2.7	2.89	22.1	0.07	4.8	9.2	0.87	9.55	3.67	69.5	3.8	19.9	9.7	7.8
6.7	1.74	na	0.07	6.8	4.3	1.10	8.49	3.59	53.7	2.5	27.9	18.7	8.8
8.2	0.42	1.8	0.02	9.1	2.5	1.84	15.25	4.52	51.2	1.6	16.3	20.7	7.4
6.3	0.13	na	0.00	3.8	2.8	0.50	7.98	2.26	80.9	1.0	9.0	28.8	7.7
8.1	0.10	0.7	0.00	3.9	3.1	0.66	6.18	3.86	79.6	1.4	12.2	25.7	6.4
8.1	0.68	na	0.00	4.3	1.2	0.77	6.14	3.46	73.9	5.5	37.1	5.6	8.0
8.2	0.33	na	0.00	6.5	3.8	1.61	18.52	3.54	58.8	1.8	16.6	20.3	5.9
3.8	0.94	10.4	0.16	2.8	4.3	0.31	4.52	2.87	76.6	3.0	10.4	7.9	4.9
8.2	0.00	na	0.00	8.6	4.0	2.04	14.66	3.61	52.8	4.2	14.9	7.5	9.8
5.1	2.52	na	0.30	7.9	0.5	1.32	11.65	5.24	57.4	3.9	32.3	13.0	8.3
4.5	1.52	na	0.06	3.6	1.8	0.58	5.97	3.28	71.9	5.1	32.0	5.6	5.0
2.9	2.75	na	0.43	4.3	1.1	0.73	6.44	3.31	59.4	1.8	27.2	25.5	6.8
9.5	0.55	na	-0.01	2.1	0.1	0.14	1.38	3.59	95.2	2.1	24.8	19.7	5.5
7.8	0.18	1.3	0.60	4.6	59.7	0.28	3.49	2.49	45.9	5.9	31.1	1.0	8.8
10.0	na	0.0	na	9.5	4.1	13.79	17.06	0.63	87.4	4.0	425.5	0.0	6.3
8.1	1.03	na	0.00	3.4	0.2	0.55	1.96	3.66	69.4	2.8	71.0	58.1	7.2
8.6	0.00	na	0.00	6.4	4.9	1.48	12.27	3.93	61.8	4.3	25.1	8.1	9.0
9.9	0.34	1.2	0.25	5.4	30.4	0.89	8.83	2.19	49.1	7.9	72.9	1.2	7.2
7.7	0.33	1.8	0.08	4.8	28.3	1.12	10.27	3.40	67.5	3.7	18.6	9.8	8.9
8.4	0.07	na	0.00	4.3	3.7	0.79	8.76	3.50	67.8	2.1	18.1	11.9	5.8
8.6	0.20	1.3	0.00	6.8	0.9	1.50	9.64	3.18	44.0	2.5	32.7	20.0	9.6
8.4	0.34	1.9	0.12	6.1	21.6	1.29	11.91	3.21	57.4	4.9	29.0	10.1	8.9
3.9	1.07	10.1	-0.05	7.8	1.4	1.92	19.26	4.50	54.3	0.7	8.7	32.2	6.6
7.2	0.00	na	0.17	4.7	0.3	0.82	6.98	3.52	61.2	4.7	42.8	12.1	6.8
8.0	0.00	na	0.00	4.2	1.1	0.79	5.36	4.27	68.0	3.7	50.3	18.9	8.1
7.5	0.45	na	0.00	6.4	3.6	1.11	12.56	3.65	57.7	4.2	21.1	8.2	5.6
6.9	0.25	na	0.00	2.6	1.4	0.35	3.58	2.91	83.0	1.3	23.8	29.9	6.5
4.5	1.02	na	0.35	4.6	5.4	0.89	10.02	4.29	54.0	1.2	15.4	27.6	5.4
6.4	0.69	na	-0.01	8.5	6.0	2.03	17.19	4.08	50.5	3.0	22.3	10.4	8.2
4.8	1.31	5.2	0.63	4.4	542.0	0.54	4.11	3.30	55.9	5.8	26.1	2.1	10.0
5.5	0.75	na	0.22	6.3	5.4	1.42	15.56	3.67	62.7	3.0	6.4	13.2	6.6
4.7	0.70	na	0.50	4.6	1.3	0.97	10.13	3.51	62.6	1.9	22.5	18.6	5.4
6.4	2.13	na	0.03	4.2	4.2	0.96	8.93	2.86	64.8	3.0	14.8	12.8	6.5
3.7	1.92	9.1	0.51	5.5	1.9	1.07	8.74	3.47	48.4	4.4	28.0	8.5	8.1
7.4	0.27	1.7	0.01	6.1	28.3	1.36	11.55	4.38	56.3	0.8	11.8	31.3	8.7
4.9	1.19	na	0.28	5.3	6.8	1.00	7.82	3.93	63.6	2.9	5.8	13.7	8.0
6.0	0.56	2.2	0.04	4.7	59.9	0.56	3.52	3.51	70.0	3.9	9.1	9.1	10.0
6.7	0.73	3.6	0.58	7.7	63.2	1.42	11.60	4.23	55.6	2.4	13.3	5.8	9.9
8.1	0.23	na	-0.06	3.1	0.4	0.36	3.29	3.26	83.5	2.2	36.1	27.8	6.2
4.4	2.45	14.1	0.11	6.2	17.7	1.08	10.43	3.71	54.4	3.3	24.1	13.5	9.5
5.9	0.17	na	-0.01	8.8	0.7	1.75	11.10	4.41	44.4	2.6	11.9	15.7	8.1
6.9	0.69	5.3	0.01	1.5	2.9	0.10	1.51	2.59	96.3	5.3	24.5	4.1	3.8
7.2	1.21	na	0.00	6.2	7.5	1.20	10.56	4.16	64.2	3.4	25.2	13.4	8.0
3.3	3.23	na	0.05	5.0	6.1	1.39	15.37	3.57	72.9	4.4	25.5	7.8	6.1
10.0	0.00	na	-0.28	4.8	0.8	1.04	5.08	2.13	38.7	7.7	95.9	4.9	8.9
4.5	0.65	na	0.17	3.1	4.2	0.53	5.37	3.47	65.4	3.0	13.5	14.1	6.6
9.0	0.05	na	0.01	7.2	1.5	1.86	10.11	3.52	59.3	6.3	59.7	7.8	8.1
8.2	0.00	na	0.00	8.8	0.8	2.95	23.51	3.74	60.8	4.7	62.5	15.2	8.0
8.8	0.00	na	0.00	2.4	0.0	0.09	0.55	3.66	97.4	6.1	62.5	7.8	7.6

Name	City	State	2020 Rating	2019 Rating	2018 Rating	Total Assets ($Mil)	One Year Asset Growth	Asset Mix (As a % of Total Assets)				Capital- ization Index	Lever- age Ratio	Risk- Based Capital Ratio
								Comm- ercial Loans	Cons- umer Loans	Mort- gage Loans	Secur- ities			
Richwood Banking Co., Inc.	Richwood	OH	B-	B-	B-	838.8	13.90	10.7	0.6	18.1	14.6	6.9	8.9	13.4
Riddell National Bank	Brazil	IN	C	C+	C	256.2	9.87	15.1	5.0	31.2	9.6	6.5	9.1	12.2
Ridgewood Savings Bank	Ridgewood	NY	B-	B	C+	6256.8	9.06	0.5	0.1	31.9	23.0	10.0	12.6	0.0
Riley State Bank of Riley, Kansas	Riley	KS	B	B	B	102.7	13.58	11.2	3.3	6.1	30.8	8.9	10.2	0.0
▼ Rio Bank	McAllen	TX	C	B-	C+	659.8	19.00	16.1	1.0	6.4	23.4	6.4	8.4	13.6
Rio Grande S&L Assn.	Monte Vista	CO	C	C+	C+	122.8	13.27	2.6	1.8	49.7	8.4	9.2	10.5	0.0
River Bank	La Crosse	WI	B	B	B-	777.1	50.29	7.1	0.3	10.4	7.0	7.7	10.7	13.1
River Bank & Trust	Prattville	AL	B+	A-	B+	1781.6	56.43	16.7	2.3	15.4	23.3	6.3	8.3	13.3
▼ River City Bank	Sacramento	CA	B-	B+	B+	3147.3	27.90	10.8	0.0	4.8	14.6	2.5	8.4	0.0
River City Bank	Rome	GA	B+	A-	B	185.9	14.46	12.2	1.1	11.6	17.6	10.0	11.1	17.7
River City Bank, Inc.	Louisville	KY	B+	B+	A-	373.7	19.70	1.7	0.7	22.9	11.8	10.0	12.4	22.6
River Falls State Bank	River Falls	WI	A-	B+	B-	116.1	24.61	2.8	2.5	31.0	15.4	10.0	12.8	0.0
River Valley Community Bank	Yuba City	CA	B-	B	B-	531.0	26.66	16.1	0.0	2.1	34.2	5.4	7.4	13.9
RiverBank	Pocahontas	AR	C	B-	C+	97.8	-6.76	6.3	1.3	9.9	5.8	10.0	12.0	19.2
RiverBank	Spokane	WA	C	C+	C	179.0	26.21	15.6	0.2	7.7	3.2	4.8	9.4	0.0
RiverHills Bank	Vicksburg	MS	A-	B+	B-	369.9	9.26	10.9	1.3	8.3	39.0	10.0	11.5	0.0
RiverHills Bank	Milford	OH	B	B-	C+	240.9	37.62	10.0	0.3	7.4	25.1	7.1	9.1	12.6
Riverland Bank	Jordan	MN	C	C+	C+	178.8	25.41	25.6	0.8	20.2	0.5	7.1	11.1	0.0
▲ Rivers Edge Bank	Marion	SD	B-	C	C	218.6	5.16	8.9	2.3	6.4	1.2	6.5	8.6	12.4
Riverside Bank	Sparkman	AR	B	B	B-	63.5	5.37	17.3	7.1	46.3	1.9	6.6	8.6	13.2
Riverview Bank	Marysville	PA	C-	C	C	1356.7	22.27	24.7	0.5	12.0	7.3	6.4	8.4	12.4
Riverview Community Bank	Vancouver	WA	A-	A	A-	1423.9	21.48	13.3	0.2	6.2	8.9	8.2	9.8	17.5
▼ Riverwind Bank	Augusta	AR	C+	B	B-	124.9	21.81	7.8	2.4	13.3	23.7	7.6	9.4	0.0
RiverWood Bank	Baxter	MN	B-	C+	C	491.2	13.42	14.0	5.1	11.9	21.6	6.1	8.1	13.4
RNB State Bank	Rawlins	WY	C+	C+	C+	219.8	22.16	11.4	1.6	4.3	29.9	6.6	8.6	0.0
Roanoke Rapids Savings Bank, SSB	Roanoke Rapids	NC	C	C+	C-	74.6	4.23	0.1	1.7	34.7	13.1	10.0	24.3	0.0
Robert Lee State Bank	Robert Lee	TX	C+	B-	C+	43.8	-2.45	3.8	5.8	18.3	46.6	10.0	13.6	0.0
Robertson Banking Co.	Demopolis	AL	A-	A-	A-	373.1	10.79	13.7	1.1	16.3	10.5	8.1	9.7	14.6
▼ Rochelle State Bank	Rochelle	GA	C	C+	B-	32.8	20.41	3.8	5.4	0.3	46.8	10.0	14.5	28.5
Rochester State Bank	Rochester	IL	C+	C	C	108.8	14.39	1.8	1.3	8.4	69.1	7.9	9.6	0.0
▼ Rock Canyon Bank	Provo	UT	B+	B+	B+	662.4	40.59	19.2	0.2	7.3	0.0	5.0	9.5	0.0
Rockefeller Trust Co., N.A.	New York	NY	U	U	U	16.8	12.67	0.0	0.0	0.0	0.6	10.0	85.9	356.7
Rockhold Bank	Bainbridge	OH	E	D-	D	45.9	12.39	16.1	0.7	41.1	0.0	5.4	7.4	11.4
Rockland Savings Bank, FSB	Rockland	ME	C-	C+	D+	90.4	8.29	8.8	1.3	50.2	0.1	8.5	10.0	0.0
Rockland Trust Co.	Rockland	MA	B+	B+	B+	13161.9	14.05	15.1	0.2	16.8	8.5	7.5	9.3	14.1
Rockwood Bank	Eureka	MO	A-	A-	B	270.7	8.15	7.0	1.0	20.1	0.0	4.1	8.1	0.0
Rocky Mountain Bank	Billings	MT	B	B	B	617.2	16.87	14.0	1.5	6.0	36.9	6.3	8.3	13.6
Rocky Mountain Bank	Jackson	WY	B+	B+	B+	410.8	26.90	14.5	7.2	13.7	3.8	7.7	9.5	16.7
Rocky Mountain Bank & Trust	Florence	CO	B-	C+	C-	87.3	18.74	24.2	0.7	12.2	20.1	7.5	9.3	0.0
Rolette State Bank	Rolette	ND	D-	D-	D	42.2	5.21	11.0	2.1	2.4	9.0	5.1	8.4	0.0
▲ Rolling Hills Bank & Trust	Atlantic	IA	C-	D+	C	348.1	14.78	7.7	0.7	3.2	1.3	5.4	9.7	0.0
Rollstone Bank & Trust	Fitchburg	MA	C	C+	B-	764.5	10.67	9.0	0.1	17.1	27.3	9.9	10.9	15.8
Rondout Savings Bank	Kingston	NY	C	C	C+	428.3	9.90	9.3	0.3	44.8	9.7	8.7	10.1	17.6
Root River State Bank	Chatfield	MN	C+	C+	C+	76.7	10.80	7.9	0.4	8.1	38.3	10.0	11.4	21.2
Roscoe State Bank	Roscoe	TX	A-	A-	B+	188.4	13.16	5.3	1.1	12.9	50.5	8.7	10.1	0.0
Rosedale Federal S&L Assn.	Baltimore	MD	C+	B	B	1017.9	5.86	5.0	0.0	40.5	12.7	10.0	24.6	0.0
Round Top State Bank	Round Top	TX	A-	A-	A-	681.8	14.33	6.3	1.9	22.5	22.6	10.0	11.2	0.0
Roundbank	Waseca	MN	B+	B	B	371.4	15.29	13.1	1.0	21.5	22.8	9.0	11.0	14.1
Rowley Savings Bank	Rowley	IA	C-	C-	D	16.3	6.01	5.3	4.8	7.0	0.0	6.9	8.9	0.0
▲ Roxboro Savings Bank, SSB	Roxboro	NC	A-	B+	B+	254.1	13.16	0.8	0.3	22.5	41.5	10.0	21.1	47.6
Royal Bank	Elroy	WI	B+	B+	B	550.7	22.32	11.2	3.7	15.5	19.0	7.9	9.6	15.7
Royal Banks of Missouri	Saint Louis	MO	B+	B-	C	847.9	26.93	13.2	0.6	3.3	6.6	9.2	11.9	14.4
Royal Business Bank	Los Angeles	CA	A	A	A	3358.0	19.26	5.6	0.1	38.5	6.6	10.0	14.2	19.3
▼ Royal Savings Bank	Chicago	IL	B	B+	B+	512.0	29.76	3.0	0.2	44.4	6.2	6.7	8.7	14.0
RSI Bank	Rahway	NJ	C+	B-	B-	603.9	11.33	4.7	0.1	36.7	21.6	10.0	15.3	0.0
RSNB Bank	Rock Springs	WY	A	A	A-	393.8	9.04	8.0	0.7	4.0	56.0	10.0	11.5	0.0
Rushford State Bank (Inc.)	Rushford	MN	C-	C-	D+	63.9	13.98	4.9	2.8	14.8	7.6	5.8	7.8	13.6
Rushville State Bank	Rushville	IL	A-	A-	B+	116.4	10.60	6.7	1.5	3.6	48.7	10.0	13.2	0.0
▼ S&T Bank	Indiana	PA	C+	B	B+	9173.8	21.42	19.4	0.9	12.1	7.8	7.0	9.0	12.9
▲ Sabal Palm Bank	Sarasota	FL	B	B-	C+	382.4	60.68	23.6	0.2	16.5	2.0	6.4	8.4	14.8

Asset Quality Index	Adjusted Non-Performing Loans as a % of Total Loans	as a % of Capital	Net Charge-Offs Avg Loans	Profitability Index	Net Income ($Mil)	Return on Assets (R.O.A.)	Return on Equity (R.O.E.)	Net Interest Spread	Overhead Efficiency Ratio	Liquidity Index	Liquidity Ratio	Hot Money Ratio	Stability Index
5.6	0.74	na	0.07	3.7	4.3	0.72	6.88	3.66	68.7	2.9	11.2	14.1	6.5
4.0	1.34	na	0.03	5.3	2.1	1.11	13.72	3.71	66.4	1.7	18.3	22.4	4.8
7.2	0.86	4.2	0.03	3.1	22.8	0.50	3.84	2.12	73.6	3.0	34.2	22.5	9.2
5.7	1.42	na	-0.04	3.9	0.6	0.80	7.58	3.02	69.0	2.5	19.8	17.1	6.6
2.6	1.91	na	0.36	4.6	3.9	0.85	8.16	4.73	71.7	4.5	26.7	7.2	7.0
4.9	1.40	na	0.01	3.0	0.4	0.46	4.36	4.09	83.0	1.7	19.8	22.9	5.9
5.7	0.91	na	0.00	7.1	8.7	1.59	13.90	3.15	43.9	0.9	5.3	28.2	8.6
7.4	0.45	2.3	0.02	5.4	12.3	1.05	9.42	3.88	53.1	3.7	21.0	12.2	9.0
7.4	0.00	0.0	-0.02	5.6	21.8	1.03	11.63	2.73	35.6	4.9	11.6	3.0	7.9
8.2	0.64	na	0.00	4.0	0.7	0.53	4.48	4.30	70.1	4.6	31.9	9.1	6.2
6.8	0.95	5.5	0.00	5.8	3.1	1.19	9.31	3.83	65.2	3.4	39.4	17.6	7.5
8.9	0.00	na	-0.02	7.5	1.7	2.14	15.73	3.54	55.9	5.5	36.4	5.0	8.0
9.0	0.22	na	0.02	3.8	2.9	0.79	9.42	3.03	64.2	5.4	39.5	7.2	5.5
2.6	3.37	na	0.05	7.3	0.9	1.15	9.95	3.62	48.4	0.6	13.3	50.1	7.4
8.3	0.43	na	0.00	2.5	0.3	0.26	2.87	3.57	92.6	3.9	28.9	11.8	4.9
7.0	1.01	na	0.15	6.6	4.3	1.63	14.82	3.40	50.3	2.8	37.1	20.4	7.9
5.3	2.59	na	0.00	6.7	2.4	1.53	23.04	4.41	68.0	1.2	18.4	4.6	6.2
7.5	0.23	na	0.00	3.4	1.0	0.79	6.85	3.69	74.8	0.7	11.7	43.1	6.7
5.0	0.79	na	0.00	5.1	1.9	1.16	11.51	3.90	61.5	3.9	17.4	8.2	7.1
6.7	0.19	3.3	0.01	9.7	1.1	2.29	25.40	3.57	54.0	0.7	13.5	43.1	6.3
7.5	0.93	na	0.20	0.8	-22.4	-2.40	-26.48	3.41	149.4	3.8	5.0	9.0	5.9
7.7	0.56	1.8	0.02	5.4	6.5	0.67	5.25	3.83	62.8	5.3	28.5	7.3	10.0
7.2	0.37	na	1.50	2.9	0.5	0.52	5.32	3.26	72.9	3.1	42.3	20.0	4.7
5.4	0.46	na	0.21	4.8	3.1	0.88	10.01	3.64	64.2	3.1	22.6	13.7	5.5
7.4	0.49	na	0.02	3.6	1.0	0.69	7.38	3.90	81.7	4.6	30.3	7.4	5.0
8.7	0.54	na	0.16	2.4	0.2	0.32	1.24	4.02	87.3	3.2	31.4	16.1	6.9
8.8	0.92	na	0.55	2.3	0.1	0.41	3.01	3.25	89.2	2.3	31.9	22.0	6.6
8.5	0.19	1.0	0.01	5.8	3.4	1.25	12.79	3.53	60.8	2.0	19.6	19.3	7.5
6.5	0.00	0.0	6.35	0.5	0.0	-0.05	-0.32	2.39	131.5	2.9	59.0	30.5	5.6
8.3	1.15	na	-0.02	3.3	0.6	0.80	6.92	2.54	78.1	7.9	81.2	0.9	5.8
8.0	0.10	1.1	-0.01	10.0	9.4	2.11	22.45	5.58	59.2	2.7	23.3	13.2	7.3
10.0	na	na	na	10.0	1.4	11.27	13.34	0.47	78.1	4.0	na	0.0	6.5
3.7	1.41	na	0.01	0.4	-0.2	-0.53	-6.93	3.89	112.7	1.7	14.4	20.0	1.5
6.5	2.53	na	0.13	0.8	-0.2	-0.27	-2.45	3.09	108.2	1.2	23.4	32.2	5.5
5.1	1.22	5.8	0.07	5.7	89.7	0.97	6.87	3.40	54.8	4.6	18.4	5.2	10.0
7.5	0.08	na	-0.03	9.1	3.6	1.85	13.36	4.11	53.6	4.4	23.5	6.8	7.5
4.7	2.73	6.4	0.15	4.3	3.4	0.77	8.50	3.73	67.3	4.5	27.7	7.7	6.5
6.7	0.04	na	0.69	2.7	0.4	0.13	1.16	3.44	55.9	3.9	31.8	8.6	6.0
6.9	0.22	na	0.03	4.3	0.5	0.82	7.75	4.25	77.4	5.4	35.7	5.7	5.1
3.3	5.13	na	2.26	1.0	-0.3	-0.84	-9.09	4.42	81.0	2.2	14.1	12.9	4.3
2.9	1.90	na	0.00	5.1	2.5	1.00	8.63	3.21	60.0	3.8	20.7	10.2	7.5
7.5	0.84	na	0.19	2.8	2.7	0.49	4.78	2.57	76.7	1.3	29.2	14.1	7.1
6.9	1.17	na	0.01	2.8	1.2	0.38	3.79	3.02	83.4	1.6	12.7	22.0	5.6
9.3	0.00	na	-0.01	2.8	0.2	0.44	3.66	3.33	82.8	5.4	46.1	8.7	6.3
9.3	0.25	na	0.02	5.8	2.0	1.45	12.95	3.65	66.1	3.8	43.6	16.7	7.4
5.2	5.51	na	0.02	2.3	1.5	0.21	0.82	2.56	79.0	2.9	31.3	22.6	9.4
8.8	0.08	na	0.05	5.9	6.2	1.28	11.11	3.18	53.5	1.9	31.3	27.2	7.7
5.7	1.11	na	0.08	7.8	5.5	2.11	18.42	3.90	61.4	2.8	22.3	13.1	7.9
9.4	0.00	na	-0.04	2.5	0.0	0.32	3.58	2.54	87.6	7.4	86.4	1.8	4.0
8.6	2.13	na	0.00	6.0	2.7	1.50	7.19	3.11	56.3	3.8	59.4	23.2	8.0
6.1	0.37	na	0.11	7.8	5.8	1.53	14.77	4.43	54.7	4.2	26.0	9.4	7.4
3.8	0.84	na	0.03	4.9	5.7	1.02	6.75	3.11	57.0	1.4	14.7	25.1	8.1
7.9	0.61	1.7	0.05	7.3	26.4	1.13	7.00	3.70	48.8	0.7	12.1	41.9	10.0
6.3	0.56	na	0.47	3.9	1.7	0.53	4.86	3.63	63.9	0.6	11.0	37.5	6.3
6.9	2.20	7.8	0.04	2.3	1.0	0.23	1.54	2.54	82.9	4.0	36.7	14.1	8.0
9.5	0.24	na	-0.10	7.1	8.9	3.13	24.24	3.35	52.3	5.7	47.0	7.7	8.5
4.9	3.88	na	0.11	3.4	0.3	0.60	7.37	3.93	79.3	2.6	29.1	18.6	3.9
6.3	2.23	na	0.04	5.9	1.2	1.40	9.88	3.14	55.8	5.1	44.9	10.5	8.6
3.9	1.38	7.3	1.65	3.0	0.9	0.01	0.10	3.40	53.6	3.7	9.1	9.4	9.7
8.7	0.00	na	-0.06	5.7	2.7	1.17	14.42	4.18	56.0	4.2	26.2	9.4	5.1

Name	City	State	2019 Rating	2018 Rating	Total Assets ($Mil)	One Year Asset Growth	Asset Mix (As a % of Total Assets) Commercial Loans	Consumer Loans	Mortgage Loans	Securities	Capitalization Index	Leverage Ratio	Risk-Based Capital Ratio
Sabine State Bank and Trust Co.	Many	LA	B+	B+	B	1103.5	15.33	11.2	1.4	8.9	7.5	8.2	9.8	14.2
Saco & Biddeford Savings Institution	Saco	ME	C+	B	B	1100.7	6.72	3.3	0.5	50.7	13.5	10.0	11.3	0.0
Sacramento Deposit Bank	Sacramento	KY	A-	A-	B+	119.7	8.91	4.9	4.8	19.0	26.8	10.0	11.2	17.9
Safra National Bank of New York	New York	NY	B+	B+	B+	9512.5	23.43	9.1	0.0	0.1	49.6	6.4	8.5	20.5
Sage Capital Bank	Gonzales	TX	B+	B+	B	483.2	18.85	8.2	0.4	9.5	8.9	8.0	9.7	15.0
Sainte Marie State Bank	Sainte Marie	IL	D	D	D+	16.4	-4.09	5.0	0.9	0.8	3.8	10.0	22.6	27.2
Saints Avenue Bank	New London	MO	C-	C-	D+	118.9	27.21	19.8	15.8	14.2	8.1	4.0	7.2	10.5
Salem Co-operative Bank	Salem	NH	C	C	C+	472.7	2.92	5.5	0.0	54.6	13.1	10.0	14.8	27.6
Salem Five Cents Savings Bank	Salem	MA	B+	A-	B	5524.6	5.37	14.0	2.3	26.1	14.8	9.9	10.9	15.9
Salisbury Bank and Trust Co.	Lakeville	CT	B	B	B-	1292.8	12.98	15.9	0.6	27.6	7.4	6.9	8.9	13.6
Sallie Mae Bank	Salt Lake City	UT	D+	D+	D+	30564.3	-1.47	0.0	76.7	0.0	6.8	8.7	10.3	13.9
Salyersville National Bank	Salyersville	KY	B	B	B+	118.8	8.81	6.9	2.2	16.0	25.6	10.0	14.7	28.8
Samson Banking Co., Inc.	Samson	AL	A-	A-	B+	94.2	17.98	7.8	5.1	17.4	49.2	10.0	12.5	0.0
San Luis Valley Federal Bank	Alamosa	CO	B	B	B	324.3	13.91	5.0	1.6	39.6	17.4	10.0	15.5	24.3
Sanborn Savings Bank	Sanborn	IA	B-	C+	C+	68.7	2.03	5.6	3.3	14.4	12.3	8.4	9.9	0.0
Sandhills Bank	North Myrtle Beach	SC	C	C	C	214.2	9.28	11.0	1.5	32.3	8.5	6.3	8.3	0.0
Sandhills State Bank	Bassett	NE	C+	C+	C	320.2	8.42	16.2	0.8	1.7	12.2	6.3	8.4	12.6
Sandy Spring Bank	Olney	MD	B-	B-	B	12666.0	50.34	15.6	0.2	14.5	10.6	8.1	9.8	13.4
▼ Sanger Bank	Sanger	TX	B+	A	A	160.2	13.25	7.9	2.4	14.2	15.3	10.0	14.2	29.7
Sanibel Captiva Community Bank	Sanibel	FL	B	B-	B-	566.7	23.15	16.3	0.9	37.4	1.9	5.9	7.9	11.8
Santa Anna National Bank	Santa Anna	TX	B+	B+	B+	53.3	-1.77	19.3	8.6	0.9	37.1	10.0	11.9	0.0
Santa Cruz County Bank	Santa Cruz	CA	A	A	A-	1448.7	100.41	33.2	0.1	4.1	4.3	8.9	10.3	16.5
▼ Santander Bank, N.A.	Boston	MA	C	C+	C+	86157.4	3.13	16.7	10.4	8.6	18.6	10.0	12.1	16.6
Saratoga National Bank and Trust Co.	Saratoga Springs	NY	B+	B+	B+	799.4	32.45	8.5	20.3	22.1	11.7	6.6	8.6	13.5
Sauk Valley Bank & Trust Co.	Sterling	IL	B-	B-	B-	569.6	26.53	18.8	0.3	7.0	25.6	6.6	8.6	13.0
▼ Savanna-Thomson State Bank	Savanna	IL	B-	B	B	105.0	11.79	9.5	0.4	6.4	30.9	10.0	11.0	19.2
▼ Savannah Bank, N.A.	Savannah	NY	C	B-	B-	157.0	7.24	9.5	0.7	20.2	41.3	6.4	8.4	18.0
Savers Co-operative Bank	Southbridge	MA	B-	B-	B-	653.4	12.39	6.8	3.6	31.6	8.0	8.5	10.5	0.0
SaviBank	Burlington	WA	C	C+	C+	387.9	25.19	27.5	7.2	8.2	2.3	1.8	8.0	0.0
Savings Bank	Primghar	IA	A-	A-	B	222.5	3.15	12.1	3.4	6.3	11.8	9.7	12.8	0.0
Savings Bank	Wakefield	MA	C+	B-	C+	655.6	6.56	3.1	0.1	48.2	5.8	10.0	11.8	0.0
Savings Bank	Circleville	OH	C+	B-	B-	390.5	11.44	8.4	3.0	34.6	30.3	8.9	10.3	20.6
Savings Bank of Danbury	Danbury	CT	B+	A-	B+	1247.7	13.77	11.2	0.1	43.1	5.0	10.0	11.8	0.0
Savings Bank of Mendocino County	Ukiah	CA	A	A	A	1286.0	15.92	7.5	0.4	4.8	37.5	10.0	15.5	0.0
Savings Bank of Walpole	Walpole	NH	B-	B-	C+	545.1	23.38	12.9	1.5	33.4	17.8	5.3	7.3	15.1
▲ Savoy Bank	New York	NY	B	C	D+	587.9	54.02	39.5	0.0	8.7	0.5	10.0	11.1	15.0
Sawyer Savings Bank	Saugerties	NY	D+	D+	C-	256.0	1.97	5.1	0.1	44.8	20.3	8.9	10.2	18.1
Schaumburg Bank & Trust Co., N.A.	Schaumburg	IL	B-	B	B	1430.0	17.22	27.0	13.2	2.7	10.6	5.7	7.9	11.5
Schertz Bank & Trust	Schertz	TX	B+	A-	B+	521.8	28.20	9.0	0.3	4.6	1.7	6.1	11.0	0.0
Schuyler Savings Bank	Kearny	NJ	C	C	C	126.0	4.71	0.0	0.1	62.3	7.9	10.0	16.1	0.0
Scott State Bank	Bethany	IL	B	B	B-	182.0	11.70	9.8	2.5	12.2	36.0	10.0	14.2	0.0
Scottsburg Building and Loan Assn.	Scottsburg	IN	C+	C+	C+	86.5	-3.51	1.2	0.1	43.0	36.3	10.0	16.0	35.0
Scribner Bank	Scribner	NE	A-	A-	B+	72.6	10.64	7.6	1.3	2.5	8.6	10.0	14.0	21.2
Seacoast National Bank	Stuart	FL	B+	B+	B+	8287.4	20.27	16.5	2.3	13.7	18.1	10.0	11.2	16.8
Seamen's Bank	Provincetown	MA	C	C+	C	472.0	17.51	5.7	0.1	33.4	14.0	8.1	9.7	0.0
Seattle Bank	Seattle	WA	B-	B	B-	730.7	10.41	15.1	0.6	8.8	0.0	8.3	9.9	20.9
Sebree Deposit Bank	Sebree	KY	D-	D+	D+	22.4	2.42	3.6	5.3	31.1	15.2	9.6	10.7	0.0
Second Federal S&L Assn. of Philadelphia	Philadelphia	PA	D	D	D	19.6	33.61	0.0	0.0	56.5	14.7	10.0	29.9	50.1
Securian Trust Co., N.A.	Saint Paul	MN	U	U	U	15.7	-1.90	0.0	0.0	0.0	77.4	10.0	89.4	98.3
Security Bank	Stephens	AR	B+	B+	B	70.2	1.22	4.1	5.3	51.7	5.1	8.4	10.0	18.5
Security Bank	Laurel	NE	A-	A-	B-	256.1	15.53	11.8	2.0	2.8	30.4	10.0	12.1	18.3
Security Bank	Tulsa	OK	B-	B-	B+	686.1	20.96	34.6	0.8	6.4	2.7	8.3	9.9	15.4
Security Bank	Dyersburg	TN	B-	B-	B	226.7	11.78	9.2	1.3	5.3	57.6	8.2	9.8	15.7
Security Bank	New Auburn	WI	B-	B	C+	133.8	20.18	12.1	1.3	10.7	8.1	9.9	12.0	0.0
Security Bank & Trust Co.	Glencoe	MN	B+	B+	B+	699.4	22.70	8.9	0.6	4.5	24.3	6.3	8.3	16.3
Security Bank and Trust Co.	Maysville	KY	B+	B+	B+	58.5	7.60	2.2	1.3	14.9	23.4	10.0	18.6	0.0
Security Bank and Trust Co.	Miami	OK	B-	B-	B-	91.6	-3.00	11.9	4.3	27.6	15.5	7.7	9.6	0.0
Security Bank and Trust Co.	Paris	TN	B+	B+	B+	703.4	47.85	31.9	1.6	11.8	12.2	4.4	8.1	10.7
Security Bank Minnesota	Albert Lea	MN	B+	B+	B+	151.5	12.97	51.9	2.4	2.8	6.0	7.4	9.4	12.9
Security Bank of Crawford	Crawford	TX	C+	C+	C	82.4	6.61	10.1	2.7	40.0	0.0	7.2	9.1	0.0

Asset Quality Index	Adjusted Non-Performing Loans		Net Charge-Offs	Profitability Index	Net Income ($Mil)	Return on Assets (R.O.A.)	Return on Equity (R.O.E.)	Net Interest Spread	Overhead Efficiency Ratio	Liquidity Index	Liquidity Ratio	Hot Money Ratio	Stability Index
	as a % of Total Loans	as a % of Capital	Avg Loans										
8.3	0.32	na	0.17	5.6	9.2	1.17	12.02	3.99	71.5	5.6	26.8	4.0	9.6
7.8	0.52	na	0.04	2.8	3.2	0.40	3.60	2.69	80.9	1.2	16.1	18.7	8.6
7.4	0.81	na	0.05	7.4	1.5	1.70	14.68	4.18	57.0	2.9	41.9	22.3	8.3
9.4	0.00	0.0	0.00	4.1	48.4	0.69	6.67	1.22	60.7	1.5	26.3	7.1	8.3
8.4	0.07	na	-0.01	5.5	4.0	1.12	10.35	3.89	61.8	2.2	25.0	19.2	6.9
7.4	0.00	na	-0.29	0.0	-0.2	-1.70	-7.37	2.68	158.0	1.8	29.3	22.9	4.4
6.8	0.00	na	0.42	2.4	0.2	0.20	2.67	3.74	89.7	2.0	16.6	9.8	3.2
9.3	0.60	na	0.01	2.4	1.2	0.34	2.27	2.77	81.9	1.9	23.2	21.0	7.6
7.2	0.59	3.8	-0.01	6.0	49.3	1.22	11.46	2.66	54.1	3.2	15.6	13.3	9.3
7.0	0.71	na	0.01	4.8	9.8	1.08	10.44	3.36	56.5	4.1	9.0	7.3	8.7
1.1	5.71	19.5	1.47	10.0	476.6	2.03	27.81	4.88	28.0	0.9	20.7	9.4	9.7
8.8	0.22	na	0.00	4.5	0.8	0.88	5.89	3.50	71.8	1.4	22.3	28.4	7.3
8.9	0.00	na	0.07	5.5	0.9	1.33	9.69	3.33	63.6	4.8	53.0	13.0	7.5
8.5	0.75	na	0.00	4.2	1.7	0.77	4.65	3.90	75.1	4.5	31.3	9.7	7.6
6.9	0.88	na	0.00	6.0	0.8	1.49	14.63	3.79	53.7	3.9	23.1	10.3	6.0
8.1	0.19	na	0.00	2.8	0.6	0.41	4.33	3.31	83.4	1.7	21.0	23.0	4.7
4.0	0.54	na	-0.02	4.9	2.8	1.22	10.87	4.03	65.6	1.6	7.7	15.8	6.5
4.4	0.71	4.1	0.01	4.4	46.1	0.54	4.41	3.39	56.8	2.2	10.2	13.2	9.9
9.1	0.17	na	0.00	4.9	1.1	0.97	6.65	3.59	68.9	3.2	44.6	21.1	8.3
4.8	0.68	na	0.03	9.7	6.5	1.70	23.90	4.65	51.7	4.5	11.7	4.9	6.0
8.0	0.01	na	0.32	7.8	0.6	1.50	12.64	4.69	59.1	2.7	35.5	20.1	7.9
7.6	0.05	0.4	0.01	8.7	13.5	1.44	11.43	3.99	47.6	3.8	9.2	9.8	9.8
5.6	1.07	3.8	0.44	0.4	-1786.0	-2.76	-18.57	2.62	176.3	5.5	27.7	2.9	9.1
7.0	0.18	1.7	0.04	6.1	6.4	1.17	13.07	3.02	43.6	2.9	12.4	14.1	6.8
3.8	1.84	13.0	0.11	4.3	3.4	0.87	9.83	3.32	63.3	2.6	14.9	9.1	5.6
5.3	1.91	na	0.00	3.1	0.4	0.55	3.78	3.03	78.0	5.6	33.5	2.9	7.0
7.4	0.70	3.4	0.04	2.7	0.4	0.36	3.99	2.89	85.6	2.0	20.9	19.4	5.5
6.1	0.84	na	0.03	3.6	2.8	0.61	5.63	3.00	74.1	2.9	20.0	15.1	6.9
6.3	1.01	na	0.05	3.1	0.9	0.34	3.79	3.78	81.2	1.3	10.0	23.0	5.3
7.0	0.00	0.6	-0.03	7.4	2.7	1.62	12.79	3.04	43.5	2.0	13.5	18.7	9.1
9.1	0.31	na	0.00	2.4	1.2	0.26	2.09	3.06	82.0	1.9	23.4	20.3	8.0
6.2	1.70	na	0.05	3.2	1.4	0.49	4.43	3.18	77.6	3.6	25.0	11.8	6.2
5.2	1.78	12.5	0.09	4.3	8.1	0.91	7.70	3.26	59.2	1.5	10.6	20.3	9.2
9.0	0.28	na	-0.02	7.3	11.7	1.32	7.93	3.56	52.8	6.8	47.4	4.1	10.0
6.2	0.60	3.6	0.07	3.5	2.3	0.63	8.05	3.09	74.7	4.9	29.3	5.6	5.3
4.8	0.70	na	0.07	5.5	3.3	0.85	10.28	3.79	56.6	0.4	7.2	57.5	7.0
5.9	1.85	na	-0.26	1.8	0.6	0.31	2.95	2.77	90.8	1.0	26.8	33.5	5.3
6.4	0.44	3.3	0.45	2.7	0.5	0.05	0.50	2.34	68.5	2.0	21.5	15.5	7.2
6.8	0.41	na	0.35	7.4	4.9	1.39	12.08	3.90	47.7	0.8	16.9	35.3	8.1
8.4	1.41	na	0.00	2.0	0.2	0.18	1.13	2.61	90.3	1.5	24.8	27.5	7.3
8.7	0.40	na	0.09	4.0	1.3	0.95	6.46	3.07	73.0	6.1	47.6	5.5	7.5
10.0	0.46	na	0.00	2.4	0.2	0.29	1.84	2.38	86.1	1.7	37.5	45.5	7.5
8.4	0.24	na	-0.01	8.8	0.9	1.63	11.28	3.42	65.7	6.0	41.9	3.8	8.0
6.1	0.79	3.5	0.11	5.3	50.3	0.87	6.46	3.70	58.6	3.3	20.6	6.2	9.9
3.1	5.24	na	0.02	2.6	1.1	0.34	3.16	2.83	83.9	4.2	42.3	14.6	5.2
6.0	2.59	na	0.07	3.9	6.9	1.26	12.47	2.81	77.7	0.6	12.7	40.6	8.9
8.8	0.00	na	0.01	0.0	-0.1	-0.70	-5.88	3.10	122.7	2.2	38.7	23.4	4.6
9.9	0.00	na	0.00	0.3	0.0	-0.32	-1.01	3.53	90.7	1.4	40.0	44.8	6.0
10.0	na	0.0	na	3.7	-0.1	-0.57	-0.60	2.89	101.7	4.0	na	0.0	5.3
8.7	0.13	na	0.00	5.8	0.8	1.46	14.99	3.87	62.0	0.7	21.0	49.6	6.0
8.2	0.35	na	0.36	7.8	4.1	2.27	17.70	4.38	60.4	4.6	26.7	7.0	8.0
4.2	1.47	na	-0.04	7.2	8.1	1.60	15.45	3.29	42.5	1.1	18.3	29.7	9.1
7.5	1.63	na	0.00	4.2	1.6	1.00	8.79	3.28	75.7	1.9	22.9	20.9	6.9
2.3	3.67	na	0.07	8.1	1.4	1.55	12.56	3.45	51.4	2.0	25.7	11.9	6.6
6.5	0.41	2.2	0.00	6.6	7.8	1.65	17.96	3.18	52.2	4.5	28.3	8.1	7.1
9.4	0.20	na	-0.01	5.0	0.5	1.18	6.17	3.25	64.2	5.3	50.1	10.3	8.3
4.9	0.54	na	0.50	6.0	1.3	1.82	18.19	4.06	66.0	1.6	13.7	19.1	6.0
8.3	0.15	na	0.01	7.3	7.8	1.73	21.10	3.38	50.2	4.0	11.5	8.1	7.2
6.9	0.29	na	0.44	5.9	1.4	1.35	13.47	4.26	54.6	1.8	17.0	19.9	7.1
7.6	0.31	na	-0.03	3.4	0.4	0.70	7.92	4.16	80.1	0.8	21.9	39.7	4.5

Name	City	State	Rating	2019 Rating	2018 Rating	Total Assets ($Mil)	One Year Asset Growth	Commercial Loans	Consumer Loans	Mortgage Loans	Securities	Capitalization Index	Leverage Ratio	Risk-Based Capital Ratio
								Asset Mix (As a % of Total Assets)						
Security Bank of Kansas City	Kansas City	KS	A-	A-	A-	3519.5	9.10	7.7	0.3	1.4	31.8	10.0	13.4	0.0
Security Bank of Pulaski County	Waynesville	MO	C+	C+	C+	123.8	14.57	11.2	4.4	18.5	20.8	6.2	8.2	13.7
Security Bank of Southwest Missouri	Cassville	MO	B+	B+	B	92.0	16.59	7.1	4.8	26.9	15.3	9.7	10.8	0.0
Security Bank of the Ozarks	Eminence	MO	C+	C+	C	111.2	18.53	9.3	7.1	14.2	14.7	5.7	7.7	11.6
Security Bank USA	Bemidji	MN	B+	B+	B-	193.4	20.10	19.9	3.9	16.2	6.7	6.3	8.5	0.0
Security Bank, s.b.	Springfield	IL	C	C	C-	183.2	-6.68	8.3	3.0	18.5	12.0	6.4	8.4	0.0
Security Federal Bank	Aiken	SC	C+	B-	B-	1130.8	14.10	8.0	2.1	8.3	46.1	8.1	9.7	19.6
Security Federal Bank	Elizabethton	TN	B-	B-	B-	62.3	-0.63	2.2	1.6	30.7	16.5	10.0	16.2	27.8
Security Federal Savings Bank	Jasper	AL	C+	C+	C	38.3	11.02	0.0	6.3	30.9	14.3	10.0	12.1	0.0
Security Federal Savings Bank	Logansport	IN	B-	B-	B-	320.0	15.17	9.0	0.9	30.1	8.1	9.8	10.9	17.2
Security Financial Bank	Durand	WI	B-	B-	B	607.4	21.66	19.7	0.1	6.3	11.7	7.1	9.0	12.7
Security First Bank	Lincoln	NE	B-	C+	C+	1221.3	8.62	8.4	7.9	8.4	18.8	6.6	8.6	12.4
Security First Bank of North Dakota	Center	ND	A	A-	B+	200.1	9.77	12.2	3.2	7.1	3.4	9.0	13.6	0.0
Security First National Bank of Hugo	Hugo	OK	B+	A-	B+	129.6	14.79	4.7	1.5	22.7	7.5	6.6	8.6	0.0
▼ Security FSB of McMinnville	McMinnville	TN	B+	A-	B+	245.7	12.83	14.1	5.2	23.5	15.4	9.0	10.3	15.2
▼ Security National Bank	Witt	IL	B-	B	B-	90.5	10.85	10.4	1.8	16.8	13.8	7.7	9.4	15.8
Security National Bank of Enid	Enid	OK	B+	B+	B+	347.9	9.16	5.9	1.0	21.8	36.2	6.2	8.2	14.5
▼ Security National Bank of Omaha	Omaha	NE	B+	A	A-	1041.6	21.77	30.8	5.1	6.2	15.9	6.6	10.9	0.0
Security National Bank of Sioux City, Iowa	Sioux City	IA	A-	A-	B+	1266.9	22.13	8.5	1.4	12.0	23.1	8.7	10.2	0.0
Security National Bank of South Dakota	Dakota Dunes	SD	A	A	A-	226.2	15.80	4.8	1.6	13.0	25.2	9.6	10.7	0.0
Security National Trust Co.	Wheeling	WV	U	U	U	6.8	3.27	0.0	0.0	0.0	60.0	10.0	109.	147.7
Security Savings Bank	Gowrie	IA	B+	A-	B+	135.4	6.99	7.3	2.3	11.9	20.7	10.0	11.5	15.9
Security Savings Bank	Monmouth	IL	B-	B-	C+	212.1	6.90	4.9	5.9	9.9	18.7	9.9	10.9	0.0
Security Savings Bank	Canton	SD	C+	C+	B-	447.1	-0.95	5.3	0.8	5.9	7.6	8.0	9.7	14.5
Security State Bank	McRae	GA	A-	A-	B+	48.2	3.39	16.2	2.3	7.5	24.1	10.0	15.3	32.0
▼ Security State Bank	Algona	IA	B+	A-	B+	118.2	16.93	14.6	0.9	2.0	5.8	10.0	16.9	0.0
Security State Bank	Radcliffe	IA	C-	C-	C-	105.0	11.52	9.2	1.6	13.0	19.2	6.8	8.8	18.4
▼ Security State Bank	Sutherland	IA	B+	B+	B-	258.8	15.61	10.7	2.4	4.7	0.3	5.3	10.1	0.0
Security State Bank	Waverly	IA	B+	A-	B+	86.6	6.10	2.6	2.4	11.0	39.8	10.0	12.2	0.0
Security State Bank	Scott City	KS	A	A-	B+	330.4	9.41	15.2	2.5	2.1	12.3	10.0	14.7	0.0
▲ Security State Bank	Wellington	KS	C+	C+	C	53.7	1.24	5.6	0.8	6.6	48.2	10.0	13.8	0.0
Security State Bank	Cheyenne	OK	A-	A-	A-	231.6	38.16	7.7	3.6	13.2	31.8	10.0	11.2	15.7
▼ Security State Bank	Alexandria	SD	B-	B	B-	93.5	8.36	8.9	3.3	2.0	25.5	8.6	10.1	0.0
Security State Bank	Emery	SD	B+	B+	B	56.1	10.69	17.9	2.3	0.0	0.6	10.0	13.7	29.2
Security State Bank	Tyndall	SD	B-	B	C+	228.9	-0.47	9.0	0.5	1.8	6.9	7.3	10.3	0.0
Security State Bank	Farwell	TX	A	A-	A-	153.5	1.35	17.5	1.0	12.0	18.4	10.0	15.5	21.1
Security State Bank	Pearsall	TX	A-	A-	B	690.2	9.26	4.6	0.8	2.8	32.8	10.0	12.7	0.0
Security State Bank	Winters	TX	B-	B-	C+	62.7	1.64	9.1	7.5	8.0	27.0	8.3	9.9	19.7
Security State Bank	Centralia	WA	A	A	A-	567.6	16.28	9.7	1.0	3.9	2.7	10.0	11.5	29.9
Security State Bank	Iron River	WI	B-	B-	C	120.8	15.86	25.4	1.2	12.3	14.4	10.0	17.3	0.0
Security State Bank	Basin	WY	B-	B	B+	392.6	9.50	9.5	2.9	7.8	36.9	9.8	10.8	18.9
Security State Bank & Trust	Fredericksburg	TX	A	A	A	1337.0	22.63	11.7	1.7	8.9	19.7	10.0	11.6	0.0
Security State Bank of Aitkin	Aitkin	MN	A-	A-	B+	114.9	13.02	20.9	2.0	8.8	20.9	10.0	11.8	0.0
Security State Bank of Fergus Falls	Fergus Falls	MN	B+	B+	B-	147.0	21.15	13.0	0.3	5.5	20.9	6.8	8.8	12.9
Security State Bank of Hibbing	Hibbing	MN	B	B	C+	162.2	19.92	20.1	1.7	10.2	17.4	8.0	9.7	21.7
Security State Bank of Kenyon	Kenyon	MN	D-	D-	D-	59.8	8.41	5.2	1.5	14.3	1.1	9.1	11.0	14.2
Security State Bank of Marine	Marine On Saint Croi	MN	A-	A-	B+	170.7	17.80	7.2	1.8	30.4	2.1	7.8	9.5	18.4
▲ Security State Bank of Oklahoma	Wewoka	OK	B	C	C	284.8	11.33	17.7	9.7	14.2	19.2	10.0	11.7	16.0
Security State Bank of Oklee	Oklee	MN	B+	B+	B	34.9	13.94	3.1	5.4	13.9	22.6	10.0	15.9	44.1
Security State Bank of Wanamingo	Wanamingo	MN	B+	B+	B	68.7	3.12	9.1	1.1	2.7	18.3	10.0	12.1	0.0
▲ Security State Bank of Warroad	Warroad	MN	C-	D	D+	116.3	14.14	16.0	10.8	2.0	34.8	10.0	15.3	0.0
▼ Security State Bank, Wishek, North Dakota	Wishek	ND	B	B+	B	92.5	27.04	5.3	2.2	0.5	34.1	6.9	9.0	20.2
Security Trust & Savings Bank	Storm Lake	IA	B-	B-	B-	253.4	9.29	5.4	0.9	7.0	33.5	8.7	10.2	23.9
SEI Private Trust Co.	Oaks	PA	U	U	U	200.3	9.10	0.0	0.0	0.0	52.7	10.0	93.1	305.7
Seiling State Bank	Seiling	OK	B	B	B-	127.4	12.76	12.7	2.3	9.4	26.4	6.9	8.9	14.2
Select Bank	Forest	VA	C+	B-	B-	323.8	32.70	38.9	1.8	24.4	0.4	5.9	7.9	18.4
▼ Select Bank & Trust Co.	Dunn	NC	B-	B	B	1764.6	39.09	8.4	0.2	11.2	5.0	7.6	9.6	13.0
Senath State Bank	Senath	MO	A	A	A-	80.9	7.53	6.6	7.9	27.9	3.9	10.0	15.0	0.0
SENB Bank	Moline	IL	B-	B-	B-	339.8	14.26	16.1	0.9	15.5	20.2	5.7	8.4	11.5
Seneca Savings	Baldwinsville	NY	C	C	C	231.2	9.82	13.7	0.4	40.1	18.8	8.6	10.1	0.0

Asset Quality Index	Adjusted Non-Performing Loans as a % of Total Loans	Adjusted Non-Performing Loans as a % of Capital	Net Charge-Offs Avg Loans	Profitability Index	Net Income ($Mil)	Return on Assets (R.O.A.)	Return on Equity (R.O.E.)	Net Interest Spread	Overhead Efficiency Ratio	Liquidity Index	Liquidity Ratio	Hot Money Ratio	Stability Index
6.2	2.10	4.4	0.14	5.3	24.4	1.00	6.16	2.99	54.8	5.8	37.8	7.4	10.0
5.6	0.79	4.7	0.12	3.8	0.7	0.78	8.79	4.04	75.7	1.6	15.6	18.5	4.6
4.0	0.39	na	-0.02	9.2	1.3	2.05	17.80	4.29	57.7	3.5	28.4	13.6	8.0
4.2	1.40	na	-0.01	5.1	0.9	1.18	13.05	4.75	71.9	3.0	19.4	14.2	5.1
6.1	0.36	2.7	0.05	7.9	2.7	1.95	22.60	4.01	60.4	4.7	23.7	5.3	5.9
2.9	3.16	17.2	0.04	2.6	0.4	0.26	2.83	2.85	87.6	6.3	47.7	4.2	5.0
8.0	0.80	na	-0.01	3.3	5.0	0.63	5.92	3.28	72.7	4.0	28.4	10.9	8.9
6.4	3.47	na	0.01	3.1	0.2	0.51	3.17	3.15	83.0	0.9	22.1	34.9	7.1
9.2	0.61	na	0.41	2.5	0.1	0.32	2.67	2.89	86.3	2.9	52.1	28.3	5.2
6.8	0.97	na	0.02	3.5	1.5	0.64	5.80	3.50	76.0	4.1	18.1	8.7	6.1
4.4	1.02	na	0.01	6.2	6.1	1.48	13.88	3.69	58.2	4.1	19.1	6.8	7.4
5.2	1.47	na	0.17	4.1	7.4	0.84	8.87	3.27	67.0	3.1	21.4	15.0	7.8
7.8	0.34	na	-0.01	7.1	2.3	1.63	11.45	4.43	68.8	3.9	4.0	7.7	9.4
3.1	2.55	na	-0.01	9.8	1.6	1.73	20.61	5.34	56.2	1.8	19.7	21.0	6.5
7.9	0.27	1.8	0.05	4.9	1.7	0.93	8.91	3.48	66.1	1.8	18.3	20.3	6.6
5.3	1.99	6.4	0.15	3.5	0.4	0.54	5.46	3.46	74.0	4.0	38.7	14.7	5.0
6.2	0.84	5.3	0.00	7.2	4.2	1.63	17.08	3.51	48.3	4.4	15.2	6.0	7.4
8.0	0.33	1.8	0.05	5.2	7.2	0.98	8.25	3.57	66.7	5.0	16.3	2.9	9.7
7.4	1.46	na	0.12	6.8	11.0	1.29	11.75	2.61	58.9	5.5	33.1	7.2	9.1
8.9	0.00	na	0.00	7.5	2.2	1.32	12.32	2.27	54.7	3.3	37.6	16.4	8.4
10.0	na	na	na	9.5	0.8	21.78	18.49	1.82	80.6	4.0	na	0.0	5.7
8.3	0.13	na	0.17	4.8	1.1	1.09	9.51	3.32	64.0	3.5	24.0	12.2	7.8
6.9	0.38	na	0.01	3.4	0.9	0.56	5.06	2.87	75.0	2.5	31.8	20.0	6.3
3.7	0.58	na	0.01	3.5	2.5	0.75	7.22	2.99	74.8	2.4	23.3	17.6	6.2
8.9	0.08	na	0.01	4.9	0.4	1.04	6.35	4.31	75.6	5.5	48.6	8.5	7.7
4.7	0.53	na	-0.07	8.2	1.2	1.51	8.87	3.58	46.7	3.3	33.4	16.3	8.7
3.5	1.40	na	0.02	2.2	0.2	0.26	2.78	2.41	87.5	5.9	53.1	8.4	4.5
6.9	0.00	na	-0.03	9.8	4.1	2.22	21.61	3.94	37.9	1.3	6.3	20.2	7.8
9.0	0.01	0.1	0.02	4.7	0.7	1.11	9.20	2.88	55.7	6.2	50.6	4.7	6.9
6.1	0.98	na	-0.01	6.0	3.1	1.31	8.80	3.29	46.7	0.6	15.0	40.0	8.7
5.8	3.00	na	0.14	2.7	0.2	0.48	3.27	3.34	85.7	5.8	45.4	6.0	6.0
5.4	1.69	na	0.40	7.6	2.0	1.47	10.46	3.93	52.0	1.3	14.1	26.9	8.9
7.8	0.22	na	0.00	3.8	0.5	0.77	7.19	3.23	73.5	2.4	34.4	23.7	6.1
8.8	0.00	0.0	0.00	4.0	0.3	0.69	4.96	2.83	63.4	5.6	68.4	11.8	7.4
4.1	2.58	na	0.00	7.1	2.7	1.58	15.53	4.24	58.2	1.7	23.5	22.6	7.2
8.5	0.00	na	0.00	9.1	2.6	2.21	15.89	3.66	44.7	1.7	13.1	20.5	9.2
8.6	1.42	na	0.02	5.5	5.6	1.09	8.41	3.02	52.2	1.1	22.4	32.2	8.0
8.4	0.15	na	0.90	4.1	0.4	0.92	9.24	4.12	71.8	5.6	37.6	5.2	5.2
8.8	0.13	na	0.01	6.1	4.4	1.10	8.92	2.74	65.2	6.9	64.1	4.8	10.0
3.9	4.30	na	0.00	4.9	0.8	0.95	5.44	3.38	64.9	2.3	33.8	21.7	6.4
5.5	2.04	na	0.27	4.1	2.5	0.87	7.85	3.09	65.0	2.2	32.7	23.2	6.3
6.5	1.15	na	0.04	6.2	12.4	1.33	10.97	4.02	63.5	4.4	24.4	10.4	10.0
5.6	3.86	na	-0.10	7.3	1.4	1.79	14.56	4.15	51.7	5.5	34.0	3.9	7.9
6.5	1.16	na	-0.01	7.6	1.9	1.88	17.17	4.33	57.7	4.1	10.6	7.5	6.6
5.3	1.25	na	0.01	4.9	1.0	0.91	9.70	3.99	64.7	5.7	45.5	6.9	4.8
0.0	15.40	na	0.66	2.6	0.1	0.29	2.61	3.97	91.9	2.9	18.7	14.6	5.7
8.7	0.47	na	0.00	8.4	2.1	1.79	17.89	3.74	55.2	5.0	39.6	9.7	7.5
4.5	1.53	na	0.10	9.7	3.9	1.91	16.00	4.89	44.4	1.0	19.1	30.6	7.0
8.8	0.00	na	0.11	4.6	0.3	0.99	5.93	2.23	68.4	6.3	60.7	5.6	7.9
8.6	0.00	na	0.00	5.8	0.7	1.34	10.75	3.81	64.0	4.2	26.5	9.6	7.7
6.0	3.00	na	-0.01	2.3	0.4	0.47	2.93	3.85	75.1	5.0	45.7	11.4	4.7
9.0	0.00	0.5	0.01	4.3	0.6	0.96	9.82	2.41	71.9	5.6	57.1	9.9	6.2
8.9	0.10	na	-0.07	3.5	1.3	0.75	6.29	2.42	65.8	6.1	65.0	9.9	6.4
10.0	na	na	na	9.5	61.3	42.61	45.66	2.22	56.4	4.0	na	100.0	7.0
8.5	0.02	na	-0.09	5.2	1.3	1.34	14.62	4.00	66.3	0.9	13.1	33.1	5.8
5.4	0.52	na	0.30	4.0	1.5	0.67	8.25	3.54	65.2	0.6	5.3	36.5	4.3
4.4	1.12	5.8	0.07	3.9	5.1	0.46	3.44	3.63	69.8	2.2	20.6	19.1	9.7
8.1	0.00	1.1	0.00	8.4	1.1	1.75	11.86	4.30	56.3	6.1	40.5	3.0	9.6
6.0	0.11	na	0.02	4.2	2.3	0.96	9.83	3.62	74.3	3.9	14.2	9.4	5.8
5.9	0.57	na	0.16	2.7	0.7	0.42	4.89	3.17	76.6	1.6	15.9	20.6	4.4

Name	City	State	2019 Rating	2018 Rating	Rating	Total Assets ($Mil)	One Year Asset Growth	Asset Mix (As a % of Total Assets)				Capital-ization Index	Lever-age Ratio	Risk-Based Capital Ratio
								Comm-ercial Loans	Cons-umer Loans	Mort-gage Loans	Secur-ities			
Sentry Bank	Saint Joseph	MN	B	B-	C+	281.4	22.51	19.1	2.4	14.0	18.2	4.2	8.2	0.0
ServisFirst Bank	Birmingham	AL	A-	A-	A-	11393.6	26.53	29.3	0.5	4.5	8.0	6.8	8.8	13.2
Settlers Bank	Marietta	OH	A-	A-	B+	135.6	7.02	4.5	3.4	36.0	3.5	10.0	12.5	0.0
Settlers bank	Windsor	WI	C+	C+	B-	369.5	17.53	29.7	2.2	9.1	2.3	7.3	9.6	12.8
Severn Savings Bank, FSB	Annapolis	MD	B+	A-	B+	936.5	13.88	8.1	0.2	26.4	8.0	10.0	13.6	0.0
Sevier County Bank	Sevierville	TN	E	E-	E-	395.0	21.17	8.9	0.5	11.1	17.6	6.1	8.1	14.2
Sewickley Savings Bank	Sewickley	PA	B-	B-	B-	317.1	-0.67	2.9	0.1	5.0	57.5	10.0	28.5	67.3
▲ Seymour Bank	Seymour	MO	B	B	B	168.0	13.10	4.3	4.9	19.5	24.5	10.0	11.2	0.0
Shamrock Bank, N.A.	Coalgate	OK	A-	A-	A-	372.3	18.22	7.1	3.5	14.4	31.7	9.6	10.7	0.0
Sharon Bank	Springfield	PA	D+	D+	D+	182.6	5.34	2.3	0.1	29.6	17.8	6.9	9.3	0.0
▲ Shelby County State Bank	Harlan	IA	B+	B-	C+	296.1	10.27	6.4	1.4	4.7	15.1	9.5	10.6	15.2
Shelby County State Bank	Shelbyville	IL	A-	B+	B	270.2	4.98	6.3	2.4	16.2	14.8	8.2	10.0	0.0
Shelby Savings Bank, SSB	Center	TX	A-	A-	B+	338.9	12.15	13.0	4.1	12.4	12.2	10.0	12.3	17.0
▼ Shelby State Bank	Shelby	MI	C+	B-	B-	331.4	22.92	8.3	1.1	12.3	28.0	5.0	7.0	12.4
Shell Lake State Bank	Shell Lake	WI	A-	A-	A	241.0	12.82	4.2	3.1	27.5	40.4	10.0	15.3	0.0
Sherburne State Bank	Becker	MN	B	B	C+	178.7	40.79	16.7	1.0	9.8	11.8	5.4	7.4	11.8
▲ Sherwood Community Bank	Creighton	MO	B-	C+	C	54.6	11.95	8.9	1.5	21.0	21.2	7.6	9.4	0.0
Sherwood State Bank	Sherwood	OH	B-	C+	C	79.7	9.31	7.0	4.8	35.1	15.1	9.9	10.9	0.0
Shinhan Bank America	New York	NY	C-	C	C+	1820.9	15.14	18.0	0.2	15.0	2.7	10.0	12.1	16.8
Shore United Bank	Easton	MD	B+	B+	B+	1827.2	16.96	11.7	1.5	19.0	8.7	8.6	10.1	14.3
Sibley State Bank	Sibley	IA	B	B	C	85.4	5.91	8.4	1.0	2.9	14.4	10.0	12.1	17.2
▼ Sicily Island State Bank	Sicily Island	LA	C	B-	B-	63.7	1.04	12.6	4.0	28.7	4.8	10.0	13.2	21.3
Sidney Federal S&L Assn.	Sidney	NE	E+	E+	D-	19.4	23.96	12.0	1.8	47.6	9.4	4.8	6.9	12.6
Sidney State Bank	Sidney	MI	C	C	C	93.5	16.58	3.9	4.0	42.4	17.8	6.1	8.1	15.6
Signature Bank	Rosemont	IL	A-	A-	B+	1204.8	35.18	46.4	0.0	2.0	6.7	7.2	9.1	14.1
Signature Bank	New York	NY	B+	B+	B+	63760.3	29.00	24.7	0.3	0.8	14.8	6.3	8.6	12.0
Signature Bank of Arkansas	Fayetteville	AR	B-	B	B	752.3	14.00	12.2	3.2	17.3	9.4	8.0	10.8	13.4
Signature Bank of Georgia	Sandy Springs	GA	C-	C-	D	184.7	27.54	5.3	0.1	2.5	10.1	9.3	10.5	17.6
Signature Bank, N.A.	Toledo	OH	A-	A-	B+	1221.8	27.51	31.2	0.5	6.4	2.3	7.2	9.1	15.4
▼ Silex Banking Co.	Silex	MO	B	B+	B+	75.7	7.09	6.8	0.5	9.1	27.6	10.0	16.0	0.0
Silicon Valley Bank	Santa Clara	CA	B+	A-	B+	95182.4	41.94	14.8	0.2	3.8	41.4	4.4	6.5	11.8
Silver Lake Bank	Topeka	KS	B+	B+	B	343.8	18.62	19.6	1.0	17.3	12.1	8.7	10.5	0.0
Silvergate Bank	La Jolla	CA	A-	A-	B+	2620.4	22.83	1.0	0.0	33.0	36.0	8.3	9.8	23.5
Simmesport State Bank	Simmesport	LA	B-	B-	C+	132.8	37.37	5.8	14.6	33.6	3.6	10.0	11.4	19.1
Simmons Bank	Pine Bluff	AR	B+	B+	B	21394.5	20.76	13.7	1.5	9.6	12.4	8.3	9.9	14.4
Simply Bank	Spring City	TN	B-	C+	C-	408.6	11.02	13.6	1.3	17.3	9.6	4.7	8.6	0.0
Siouxland Bank	South Sioux City	NE	C+	C+	C	82.1	48.30	12.1	2.0	11.9	0.3	5.4	7.4	16.8
SJN Bank of Kansas	Saint John	KS	C+	B	B+	207.4	19.39	12.1	1.5	3.3	38.8	5.8	7.8	13.6
▼ Skowhegan Savings Bank	Skowhegan	ME	B	B+	B	696.0	15.30	5.1	6.9	31.8	13.0	10.0	13.8	22.5
Skyline National Bank	Independence	VA	B-	B-	C+	816.6	17.64	13.6	0.9	23.1	3.7	8.0	9.7	13.3
Sloan State Bank	Sloan	IA	B+	B+	B+	58.6	8.48	4.5	8.9	13.8	39.7	10.0	11.3	0.0
Slovenian S&L Assn. of Canonsburg	Strabane	PA	A-	A-	B+	477.4	10.75	0.0	0.2	32.3	58.1	10.0	14.7	0.0
▼ Slovenian S&L Assn. of Franklin-Conemau	Conemaugh	PA	C-	C+	C+	155.9	6.54	0.0	2.1	47.7	24.4	10.0	11.0	0.0
▲ Smackover State Bank	Smackover	AR	B	B	B	187.2	2.75	2.4	3.8	21.1	43.8	10.0	13.8	0.0
▲ Small Business Bank	Lenexa	KS	B-	C+	C	74.1	12.54	39.3	5.1	13.2	0.0	10.0	13.8	0.0
SmartBank	Pigeon Forge	TN	B	B	B	3387.5	41.57	18.5	0.3	10.7	6.3	8.0	9.7	13.4
▼ SNB Bank, N.A.	Shattuck	OK	C	C+	C	138.6	20.95	18.9	5.9	1.8	12.5	4.8	8.0	0.0
Solera National Bank	Lakewood	CO	B+	A-	B+	404.7	45.66	30.1	3.7	6.0	12.9	7.6	11.4	0.0
▲ Solomon State Bank	Solomon	KS	A-	A-	A-	201.5	-0.75	3.4	1.6	45.9	7.2	10.0	16.8	0.0
Solon State Bank	Solon	IA	B+	A-	A-	112.7	17.32	18.4	1.5	10.0	30.3	10.0	22.1	0.0
Solutions Bank	Forreston	IL	B+	B+	B+	335.7	51.60	4.7	0.3	6.2	43.2	9.0	10.4	0.0
Solutions North Bank	Stockton	KS	A-	B+	B+	269.6	9.26	7.8	2.1	5.0	23.5	10.0	11.8	16.0
▼ Solvay Bank	Solvay	NY	B-	B	B	1066.0	9.94	13.2	7.0	24.7	26.3	6.9	9.0	0.0
Somerset Savings Bank, SLA	Bound Brook	NJ	C+	B-	C+	609.6	4.67	0.0	0.0	50.2	31.2	10.0	20.1	0.0
Somerset Trust Co.	Somerset	PA	B-	B-	B-	1596.5	21.84	24.8	3.0	12.0	20.9	6.0	8.0	11.9
Somerville Bank	Somerville	OH	B-	B-	C+	235.3	19.97	8.6	1.1	13.2	24.7	7.6	9.4	0.0
Sonabank	Glen Allen	VA	B+	A-	B+	3156.5	16.75	15.6	0.7	18.4	6.6	10.0	12.3	16.2
▼ Sooner State Bank	Tuttle	OK	B+	A	A-	291.3	39.28	3.0	1.6	16.3	17.9	7.0	9.0	0.0
Sound Banking Co.	Lakewood	WA	B+	B+	B-	67.0	17.73	4.3	0.4	18.9	0.0	7.2	9.1	0.0
Sound Community Bank	Seattle	WA	B-	B-	C+	867.8	21.31	10.3	8.9	21.5	1.5	6.7	10.4	0.0

Asset Quality Index	Adjusted Non-Performing Loans as a % of Total Loans	as a % of Capital	Net Charge-Offs Avg Loans	Profitability Index	Net Income ($Mil)	Return on Assets (R.O.A.)	Return on Equity (R.O.E.)	Net Interest Spread	Overhead Efficiency Ratio	Liquidity Index	Liquidity Ratio	Hot Money Ratio	Stability Index
7.7	0.10	na	0.00	6.9	2.5	1.26	11.28	3.66	49.7	2.3	28.7	18.2	6.8
7.4	0.27	2.5	0.34	8.5	120.8	1.57	16.78	3.40	30.2	4.4	20.3	6.8	8.5
6.7	1.27	na	0.04	5.1	0.9	0.90	6.99	3.21	62.4	3.5	33.9	15.5	8.3
4.1	0.72	na	-0.02	5.0	3.2	1.19	13.11	3.36	56.6	1.5	13.6	22.7	4.9
6.2	1.98	7.5	-0.14	4.4	4.8	0.74	5.33	3.28	75.7	3.2	27.2	14.5	8.8
8.4	0.50	na	0.00	1.1	1.3	0.48	5.40	3.07	93.5	1.8	24.7	23.4	1.6
10.0	0.06	0.0	0.00	2.6	0.8	0.35	1.17	1.37	73.1	4.3	108.5	32.6	8.0
8.6	0.57	na	-0.02	4.2	1.1	0.86	7.43	3.88	74.5	2.2	32.1	20.2	7.3
8.0	0.24	na	0.16	5.4	3.3	1.24	10.71	4.14	67.3	3.5	39.5	17.4	7.8
6.0	1.82	na	-0.02	0.0	-1.0	-0.75	-7.92	2.29	117.5	2.0	26.9	21.8	4.4
6.3	0.60	na	-0.01	6.8	2.7	1.30	10.72	3.65	53.0	4.9	28.8	5.9	7.4
5.4	1.67	na	0.00	5.5	2.4	1.25	11.99	3.52	66.0	4.2	22.6	8.6	7.1
7.8	0.73	2.8	0.02	5.5	3.2	1.32	10.64	4.00	70.9	1.7	25.6	24.9	7.6
4.4	2.59	11.6	0.15	3.5	1.5	0.63	7.59	3.49	80.3	5.3	31.8	4.5	4.3
8.9	0.62	na	0.00	5.9	2.5	1.48	8.70	3.48	56.3	5.3	43.0	9.1	8.5
7.5	0.15	na	0.01	9.9	2.7	2.36	30.73	4.40	45.1	4.1	32.9	11.9	5.9
7.3	0.22	na	0.01	4.0	0.4	0.90	9.40	4.00	78.0	6.0	40.0	3.3	5.1
4.5	2.10	na	0.09	3.9	0.4	0.74	6.66	4.31	77.6	3.8	21.0	10.8	5.9
7.3	0.12	0.8	-0.01	1.4	-0.1	-0.01	-0.04	2.96	93.2	1.0	14.1	30.1	8.3
6.0	0.79	na	0.06	5.3	12.5	1.01	8.75	3.34	58.5	4.2	15.8	7.8	8.8
6.0	1.28	na	0.08	4.7	0.5	0.79	6.37	3.03	64.2	1.6	15.0	22.4	7.2
1.8	5.38	na	0.19	3.9	0.4	0.73	5.51	3.99	79.6	0.7	14.9	41.7	7.3
6.1	0.45	na	-0.02	1.8	0.1	0.43	5.95	3.13	90.8	1.8	20.7	21.1	0.3
4.9	1.74	10.0	0.14	3.9	0.5	0.67	8.32	3.80	76.8	4.1	28.1	10.6	4.7
8.0	0.27	na	-0.04	9.0	12.4	1.51	15.86	3.75	48.1	3.3	20.2	7.7	8.7
7.9	0.51	3.0	0.05	4.6	355.4	0.83	9.80	2.76	39.4	5.2	22.1	3.4	7.4
7.5	0.03	0.2	0.15	3.6	3.0	0.56	5.09	3.65	71.9	0.9	16.6	23.5	7.6
5.2	3.70	na	-0.01	2.3	0.7	0.51	4.59	3.04	85.2	5.3	43.1	8.8	5.3
8.2	0.14	0.8	-0.04	6.2	10.4	1.23	12.63	3.20	50.2	4.3	23.8	9.4	8.5
9.2	0.00	na	-0.01	3.4	0.3	0.59	3.64	3.01	75.5	6.0	53.2	6.1	8.1
9.2	0.31	1.7	0.24	6.4	583.2	1.00	13.71	2.79	51.9	7.6	55.9	0.1	6.3
5.6	3.16	na	0.00	6.3	3.2	1.27	11.99	3.89	51.3	1.5	11.5	22.7	7.0
9.6	0.33	1.2	0.00	5.3	19.3	1.12	9.94	3.14	64.4	7.4	49.1	0.0	8.1
3.5	2.59	na	0.07	6.3	1.2	1.40	11.97	4.43	57.7	1.0	25.9	49.3	7.2
4.8	1.21	4.9	0.42	6.3	221.8	1.38	9.70	3.51	55.0	3.1	20.6	11.8	10.0
5.3	1.95	na	0.02	5.4	3.7	1.25	14.03	4.40	69.4	2.2	16.1	18.0	5.9
9.0	0.00	na	-0.02	3.5	0.3	0.62	7.50	2.31	70.2	4.8	55.9	13.4	3.8
3.2	3.71	na	0.36	5.2	1.8	1.18	13.33	3.77	59.9	3.3	16.8	12.4	6.2
7.1	0.75	na	0.01	2.6	1.4	0.29	1.96	3.65	78.6	4.6	28.5	7.6	8.6
4.9	1.20	na	0.03	3.9	4.2	0.74	6.85	3.95	75.5	2.7	8.4	14.7	6.7
4.5	0.63	na	0.00	7.0	0.7	1.58	13.05	3.29	50.5	5.8	44.7	5.8	8.3
7.2	1.75	na	0.14	6.0	3.7	1.06	7.21	2.56	32.3	3.1	69.9	53.1	8.3
7.8	0.01	na	0.03	1.3	-0.1	-0.05	-0.43	2.55	100.9	3.1	49.7	25.7	6.3
9.3	0.02	na	0.04	4.2	1.3	0.94	6.87	2.73	62.2	2.0	35.1	29.7	7.7
7.3	1.26	na	0.07	4.1	0.3	0.67	4.41	4.55	82.9	4.7	18.1	4.7	5.7
7.7	0.09	0.8	0.01	4.5	17.6	0.78	6.44	3.69	63.9	2.8	22.7	13.9	8.8
2.8	1.48	na	0.49	2.7	0.4	0.45	5.25	2.88	70.2	0.6	11.4	35.3	4.4
7.5	0.30	na	0.01	6.6	4.2	1.56	13.33	3.61	44.0	1.3	10.3	16.4	8.4
8.1	0.01	na	0.39	5.9	2.3	1.51	8.91	3.13	46.8	1.7	27.3	25.2	8.2
4.6	1.71	13.4	0.02	9.9	1.9	2.39	9.56	5.18	47.6	6.1	54.9	7.6	9.0
7.6	0.78	na	0.01	5.0	4.4	2.37	25.30	3.78	63.1	3.7	46.6	14.0	6.6
8.4	0.00	na	-0.02	6.8	3.3	1.70	13.49	3.92	60.1	1.8	10.3	19.4	7.2
7.9	0.80	na	0.03	3.8	5.5	0.72	7.72	2.64	64.0	3.4	20.5	13.1	8.0
10.0	0.04	na	0.00	2.1	1.0	0.22	1.08	2.03	86.2	5.2	52.2	12.3	8.4
5.7	1.04	6.5	0.16	3.8	8.3	0.75	8.98	4.07	77.3	3.3	16.9	9.0	6.7
5.8	0.91	5.3	0.02	4.2	1.8	1.10	10.96	3.11	70.5	2.8	36.5	19.9	5.8
6.9	0.67	2.6	0.05	4.5	17.0	0.77	5.29	3.43	56.3	2.2	9.5	17.6	9.4
8.2	0.28	na	0.05	4.9	1.9	0.88	8.85	3.99	76.7	4.5	36.5	11.1	7.3
9.0	0.00	na	0.00	8.2	0.8	1.93	20.50	4.47	56.0	2.9	39.7	21.7	6.3
4.9	1.12	na	0.12	5.1	5.8	0.98	9.86	3.77	66.6	1.7	16.5	21.3	6.9

Name	City	State	2019 Rating	2018 Rating	Total Assets ($Mil)	One Year Asset Growth	Asset Mix (As a % of Total Assets) Comm- ercial Loans	Cons- umer Loans	Mort- gage Loans	Secur- ities	Capital- ization Index	Lever- age Ratio	Risk- Based Capital Ratio
South Atlantic Bank	Myrtle Beach	SC	B-	B-	C+	931.9	31.34	14.1	0.6	21.8	12.1	6.1	8.1	11.9
South Central Bank, Inc.	Glasgow	KY	B+	B+	B	1367.3	15.82	13.4	1.5	14.4	14.8	9.7	10.8	14.8
South Central State Bank	Campbell	NE	A-	A-	B+	141.5	4.37	4.6	0.8	0.5	20.0	10.0	12.6	15.4
South Coast Bank & Trust	Brunswick	GA	B	B	B	178.3	29.58	7.6	0.8	18.6	10.2	6.9	8.9	13.5
South Georgia Bank	Glennville	GA	A	A	A	180.8	14.66	5.0	3.5	16.4	19.6	10.0	11.8	20.5
South Georgia Banking Co.	Tifton	GA	A-	A-	B+	497.9	12.37	7.3	1.7	10.7	15.8	10.0	11.5	18.9
South Lafourche Bank & Trust Co.	Larose	LA	C	C-	D	146.2	0.29	16.7	4.3	35.6	7.7	8.4	10.0	17.4
South Louisiana Bank	Houma	LA	A-	A-	B+	647.3	32.78	21.8	1.4	7.0	8.5	10.0	12.4	0.0
South Ottumwa Savings Bank	Ottumwa	IA	B+	A-	B+	535.4	35.82	7.8	1.2	17.6	33.8	8.6	10.0	16.8
South Shore Bank	South Weymouth	MA	C+	C+	C+	1847.1	19.91	17.7	0.3	22.7	13.9	6.8	8.8	14.1
South State Bank, N.A.	Winter Haven	FL	B+	B+	B+	37716.3	116.65	12.0	2.4	13.2	9.4	6.5	8.5	12.8
South Story Bank & Trust	Slater	IA	B	B	C+	294.2	46.26	14.4	0.6	17.6	4.5	7.8	10.6	13.2
SouthCrest Bank, N.A.	Atlanta	GA	B	B	B-	631.4	20.94	4.2	0.3	8.2	34.7	7.6	9.4	0.0
SouthEast Bank	Farragut	TN	B	B	B	2010.4	17.58	7.4	55.7	5.4	0.0	6.9	8.9	13.4
▲ Southeast First National Bank	Summerville	GA	C	C	C+	55.2	-7.85	7.2	2.4	15.4	32.5	10.0	13.6	0.0
Southeastern Bank	Darien	GA	A	A	A-	500.5	18.87	10.2	1.8	13.6	24.3	9.5	10.7	0.0
Southern Bancorp Bank	Arkadelphia	AR	B	B-	B-	1602.3	9.61	14.4	2.2	15.6	11.1	6.9	8.9	14.1
Southern Bank	Sardis	GA	C+	B-	B-	87.5	10.92	1.7	6.8	26.2	20.6	10.0	11.5	0.0
Southern Bank	Poplar Bluff	MO	B+	B+	B+	2526.5	12.89	13.2	1.4	17.7	7.0	7.7	9.9	13.1
Southern Bank and Trust Co.	Mount Olive	NC	B+	A-	A-	3623.7	26.96	14.0	0.7	11.5	24.2	5.8	7.8	12.7
▼ Southern Bank Co.	Gadsden	AL	C	C	C-	103.2	6.86	15.1	0.9	6.7	34.3	9.1	10.4	0.0
Southern Bank of Tennessee	Mount Juliet	TN	B+	B+	B+	336.3	16.46	9.4	1.6	21.6	7.8	10.0	12.0	16.0
Southern First Bank	Greenville	SC	B+	B+	B+	2479.0	12.60	9.1	1.0	28.9	3.6	8.5	10.1	13.7
Southern Heritage Bank	Jonesville	LA	B+	A-	B+	332.5	10.40	13.1	4.1	30.6	20.1	10.0	11.0	0.0
Southern Hills Community Bank	Leesburg	OH	C	C	C-	170.9	7.12	3.2	3.3	36.8	11.1	10.0	14.8	23.2
Southern Illinois Bank	Johnston City	IL	B+	B+	B+	135.7	15.81	7.1	1.4	13.8	27.8	10.0	11.5	18.3
Southern Independent Bank	Opp	AL	B+	B+	B	289.8	19.76	16.4	2.0	14.1	31.0	8.9	10.3	0.0
Southern Michigan Bank & Trust	Coldwater	MI	B	B	B	931.4	15.16	16.9	0.3	6.9	19.1	7.0	9.0	13.5
Southern States Bank	Anniston	AL	B-	B-	B+	1300.1	15.30	17.6	0.8	6.6	7.2	7.4	10.1	12.8
▲ SouthernTrust Bank	Marion	IL	C+	C	C	193.0	244.31	16.9	1.6	21.2	13.5	7.6	11.4	0.0
▼ SouthFirst Bank	Sylacauga	AL	D+	D+	C+	89.4	13.30	9.7	0.5	28.2	10.4	9.6	10.8	22.1
SouthPoint Bank	Birmingham	AL	C+	B-	B-	557.1	36.77	29.8	0.7	10.6	13.0	1.6	10.1	0.0
Southside Bank	Tyler	TX	B+	A-	A-	7186.0	9.92	7.9	1.3	10.4	38.4	9.8	10.8	18.9
SouthStar Bank, S.S.B.	Moulton	TX	B+	A-	A-	1095.8	27.34	4.7	0.3	18.8	7.0	6.5	9.7	12.2
SouthTrust Bank, N.A.	George West	TX	C+	B-	B-	460.6	14.81	13.8	0.9	7.9	17.9	8.6	10.0	19.2
▼ Southwest Bank	Odessa	TX	B	B+	B+	536.3	19.59	44.3	0.5	6.1	8.8	4.9	6.9	13.1
Southwest Bank of Weatherford	Weatherford	OK	B+	B+	B+	76.8	1.35	8.2	4.1	13.3	16.8	10.0	12.9	22.2
Southwest Capital Bank	Albuquerque	NM	C-	C	C	374.7	8.85	15.7	0.1	5.0	11.8	9.4	10.6	0.0
Southwest Missouri Bank	Carthage	MO	B	B	B	887.5	18.63	10.8	6.7	18.9	34.8	6.5	8.5	16.1
Southwest National Bank	Wichita	KS	C+	B-	B-	518.6	15.73	16.4	36.5	5.2	8.4	2.8	8.8	0.0
▼ Southwestern National Bank	Houston	TX	B	B+	B	757.3	46.51	7.5	0.0	2.3	2.3	8.0	10.1	13.4
Southwind Bank	Natoma	KS	B+	B	B-	141.3	8.62	11.1	3.1	11.6	43.6	8.7	10.2	18.4
▼ Spectra Bank	Fort Worth	TX	D+	C	B-	91.7	10.49	18.8	0.3	1.6	1.2	4.1	6.1	11.6
Spencer County Bank	Santa Claus	IN	B-	B	B-	121.2	11.05	6.8	5.3	26.0	19.4	10.0	12.6	0.0
▼ Spencer Savings Bank, SLA	Elmwood Park	NJ	C+	B-	B-	3219.5	6.11	1.2	0.1	21.3	10.2	10.0	11.0	16.9
Spirit of Texas Bank, SSB	Conroe	TX	B+	B+	B	2922.5	49.14	22.8	0.4	12.7	4.1	7.8	9.9	13.2
▲ SpiritBank	Tulsa	OK	B-	C	C	659.7	5.63	23.4	2.1	10.6	6.6	8.5	10.3	13.8
▼ Spiro State Bank	Spiro	OK	C-	C+	C	57.0	10.72	4.2	3.2	7.0	50.4	9.7	10.8	0.0
Spratt Savings Bank	Chester	SC	C+	C+	C+	145.0	20.83	4.1	0.5	12.1	40.6	10.0	20.4	56.1
▼ Spring Bank	Bronx	NY	B	B+	B+	325.0	68.20	31.2	0.4	8.0	11.2	7.1	10.8	0.0
Spring Bank	Brookfield	WI	B-	B-	C	355.9	12.71	20.7	0.0	11.3	4.7	7.5	11.4	0.0
Spring Hill State Bank	Longview	TX	B+	B+	B-	211.1	3.21	8.3	4.9	45.4	2.6	10.0	12.3	25.1
Spring Valley Bank	Wyoming	OH	A	A-	A-	91.8	14.28	1.2	0.1	41.6	0.1	10.0	37.4	41.8
Spring Valley City Bank	Spring Valley	IL	B+	B+	B+	208.3	9.76	14.4	2.5	15.7	36.0	10.0	14.1	28.8
Springfield First Community Bank	Springfield	MO	B+	B+	B-	804.1	15.70	17.0	0.5	10.1	6.9	8.4	10.3	13.7
Springfield State Bank	Springfield	KY	B+	A-	B+	348.8	8.51	4.8	2.1	25.0	38.9	10.0	15.2	25.3
Springfield State Bank	Springfield	NE	B+	B+	B	77.3	28.88	4.1	2.3	5.4	27.0	6.7	8.7	0.0
Springs Valley Bank & Trust Co.	Jasper	IN	B-	B-	B-	494.2	9.09	9.3	2.5	19.8	12.4	9.0	10.4	14.7
Spur Security Bank	Spur	TX	C	C+	C+	49.9	10.87	2.6	2.9	0.6	62.4	10.0	11.5	33.2
SSB Bank	Pittsburgh	PA	C-	C	C	227.4	13.01	19.3	1.1	25.9	3.3	6.5	8.6	13.1

Asset Quality Index	Adjusted Non-Performing Loans		Net Charge-Offs	Profitability Index	Net Income ($Mil)	Return on Assets (R.O.A.)	Return on Equity (R.O.E.)	Net Interest Spread	Overhead Efficiency Ratio	Liquidity Index	Liquidity Ratio	Hot Money Ratio	Stability Index
	as a % of Total Loans	as a % of Capital	Avg Loans										
8.4	0.10	na	0.00	4.4	5.7	0.91	9.82	3.82	73.8	3.0	20.1	11.3	6.1
6.5	0.92	4.4	0.01	5.5	11.8	1.19	11.29	3.19	64.1	2.7	13.1	15.7	8.7
8.2	0.01	na	0.00	5.1	1.5	1.39	11.65	3.37	61.5	3.6	17.9	11.0	8.0
7.4	0.30	na	0.00	4.6	1.3	1.08	11.54	3.60	71.0	1.7	26.3	25.4	6.3
8.6	0.00	0.0	-0.15	9.6	2.7	2.10	16.89	4.51	56.3	1.9	30.8	27.9	9.0
7.5	0.21	na	0.03	5.0	3.4	0.93	6.73	3.79	69.5	4.2	34.2	12.1	7.7
3.9	1.98	na	6.04	0.3	-4.4	-3.92	-30.70	3.64	75.3	1.5	23.8	27.1	5.0
6.7	1.25	na	0.37	6.2	4.4	1.05	7.92	3.66	64.1	3.7	40.5	16.5	8.8
7.1	0.53	na	0.17	4.9	4.6	1.14	9.27	3.25	60.1	3.0	32.2	16.7	8.6
6.6	0.72	na	0.00	2.7	4.4	0.34	3.49	3.00	72.1	4.5	21.4	7.1	7.7
6.3	0.45	2.3	0.01	4.2	63.9	0.33	2.25	3.26	68.3	4.4	21.4	6.4	10.0
4.4	0.88	na	0.02	4.9	2.0	0.98	7.37	4.25	64.1	1.6	13.6	13.7	6.9
5.6	1.01	4.8	-0.03	4.8	5.2	1.17	11.44	3.53	69.1	4.9	34.5	8.4	6.0
2.9	1.15	na	0.06	4.3	10.7	0.75	8.73	3.31	62.6	0.6	4.3	23.9	7.5
9.4	0.07	na	-0.01	2.6	0.2	0.46	3.40	3.15	83.9	4.7	37.6	10.9	5.5
7.5	0.40	na	-0.45	6.3	4.1	1.14	10.00	3.75	61.5	5.3	29.9	3.3	8.3
5.2	1.46	na	0.16	4.7	11.0	0.94	8.25	3.89	62.0	2.7	14.1	13.2	9.0
4.0	3.75	na	0.17	2.8	0.3	0.40	3.40	4.11	89.8	2.2	29.3	21.4	5.6
6.7	0.76	na	0.04	6.7	23.5	1.28	12.44	3.75	55.4	1.5	3.1	18.6	9.3
7.3	0.42	3.2	-0.01	5.0	21.9	0.89	9.49	3.50	60.9	4.9	21.3	4.8	7.7
4.5	3.02	12.7	0.23	2.1	0.2	0.20	1.67	4.13	96.6	2.0	37.0	31.5	5.0
8.5	0.24	1.3	0.02	3.9	1.9	0.78	6.10	3.42	78.8	1.4	23.8	29.0	7.2
7.3	0.65	4.1	0.11	4.7	10.9	0.62	6.07	3.68	50.5	3.7	11.3	8.5	8.8
5.2	0.90	na	0.18	7.1	4.1	1.68	14.84	4.57	64.9	2.7	18.1	15.9	8.0
6.2	3.19	na	-0.05	2.1	0.2	0.19	1.24	4.05	95.1	3.2	34.8	17.0	6.4
7.1	1.18	na	-0.15	4.9	0.9	0.98	8.03	3.76	64.8	4.8	29.0	6.5	6.6
6.1	1.32	na	0.01	4.6	1.9	0.93	8.65	2.88	58.0	2.3	45.2	34.6	6.0
6.8	0.65	1.6	0.00	4.4	5.7	0.86	8.08	3.33	65.3	3.5	22.5	11.6	7.7
3.7	1.27	na	-0.02	5.0	9.5	1.03	8.81	3.71	62.3	1.5	14.6	21.1	8.1
4.5	1.38	na	0.00	7.8	1.3	1.92	22.01	5.76	50.0	1.3	20.4	28.9	4.5
5.3	1.45	na	-0.08	0.6	-0.2	-0.35	-3.00	3.57	110.6	3.1	39.1	19.3	5.2
7.1	0.25	2.4	0.04	6.9	5.3	1.57	17.68	3.94	69.3	1.3	11.8	25.8	6.0
7.9	0.19	0.6	0.04	4.8	59.0	1.11	8.29	3.14	50.8	2.1	21.6	13.7	10.0
8.0	0.45	na	-0.02	5.8	9.0	1.28	12.34	4.49	63.0	1.1	7.8	21.8	8.0
7.5	0.46	na	-0.01	3.5	1.8	0.55	5.14	3.62	83.4	3.9	35.6	14.0	6.0
6.3	0.26	na	0.27	6.5	5.8	1.43	19.15	4.10	66.8	4.1	16.1	8.4	6.1
4.9	2.90	11.4	0.00	5.1	0.6	1.04	7.96	3.79	66.8	4.3	47.0	14.5	7.7
1.9	6.00	na	0.75	0.9	-2.4	-0.86	-8.46	3.77	97.2	5.0	40.4	8.2	5.6
6.3	1.24	na	0.08	4.5	6.0	0.95	10.43	3.64	72.5	4.4	28.4	8.8	5.5
5.8	0.72	na	0.12	5.6	5.0	1.38	14.92	4.27	60.3	1.3	11.5	20.4	6.3
7.1	0.21	na	0.00	2.8	1.0	0.21	1.90	3.82	54.6	0.9	20.2	32.6	8.2
6.6	0.75	na	0.02	5.3	1.3	1.25	11.26	3.64	58.5	4.4	33.5	10.8	6.7
4.8	1.76	na	4.27	0.0	-1.1	-1.84	-26.07	3.43	98.3	2.8	47.6	27.4	2.9
4.8	3.02	na	0.07	3.8	0.6	0.72	5.45	3.07	74.6	2.8	34.3	18.9	6.7
5.3	1.16	5.8	-0.11	2.7	8.9	0.38	3.43	2.48	71.8	2.2	21.6	20.0	8.4
6.9	0.35	2.4	0.08	5.3	21.2	1.05	8.17	4.10	62.4	1.5	8.5	23.7	9.1
4.1	1.72	na	-0.13	5.3	5.1	1.06	9.48	3.92	66.7	0.6	10.6	36.0	6.4
9.2	0.00	na	0.01	2.0	0.1	0.19	1.51	3.18	93.6	6.5	69.0	6.3	6.0
10.0	0.99	na	0.01	2.8	0.4	0.40	1.87	2.23	79.0	5.4	85.0	16.3	7.0
4.3	1.31	na	0.11	5.2	1.0	0.46	4.84	3.49	69.7	0.9	24.0	33.8	6.9
4.6	0.55	na	0.00	6.3	3.0	1.20	10.53	3.41	43.6	0.8	16.8	37.4	7.6
6.3	0.33	na	0.03	5.9	1.8	1.17	9.61	3.88	61.0	1.9	23.7	20.8	7.6
8.6	1.62	na	0.00	10.0	3.2	4.98	12.74	6.00	23.7	1.3	29.7	39.5	9.5
8.0	0.83	na	0.00	4.6	1.6	1.05	7.08	2.99	60.7	3.8	39.9	15.9	8.2
6.8	0.06	na	0.00	6.4	7.0	1.28	7.74	3.78	45.3	2.5	15.5	15.6	8.2
8.5	0.84	na	-0.04	4.7	2.6	1.01	6.70	3.20	60.8	2.3	36.9	27.1	8.2
6.4	2.15	na	0.00	4.0	0.4	0.80	8.12	2.61	67.1	6.8	53.5	0.8	6.0
5.6	1.18	na	0.32	4.5	3.3	0.93	8.58	3.68	68.2	2.0	18.3	16.5	6.3
9.6	0.00	na	0.00	2.0	0.1	0.36	3.07	2.14	95.4	3.1	74.4	35.0	5.1
2.3	3.10	22.0	0.00	3.4	1.1	0.65	8.23	2.29	66.2	0.8	22.8	40.1	4.4

Name	City	State	2019 Rating	2018 Rating	Total Assets ($Mil)	One Year Asset Growth	Asset Mix (As a % of Total Assets)				Capital-ization Index	Lever-age Ratio	Risk-Based Capital Ratio
				Rating					Comm-ercial Loans	Cons-umer Loans	Mort-gage Loans	Secur-ities			

Name	City	State	Rating	2019 Rating	2018 Rating	Total Assets ($Mil)	One Year Asset Growth	Comm-ercial Loans	Cons-umer Loans	Mort-gage Loans	Secur-ities	Capital-ization Index	Lever-age Ratio	Risk-Based Capital Ratio
SSB Community Bank	Strasburg	OH	C+	C+	C+	132.8	28.26	9.0	1.2	26.2	0.0	5.5	8.0	11.4
▼ St. Ansgar State Bank	Saint Ansgar	IA	B+	A-	A-	135.8	15.55	11.1	1.5	9.0	15.1	9.3	10.6	0.0
St. Charles Bank & Trust Co., N.A.	Saint Charles	IL	B-	B	B	1785.0	40.21	32.0	17.8	3.0	5.2	5.7	8.7	11.5
St. Clair County State Bank	Osceola	MO	A	A	A-	156.6	9.66	7.4	3.7	16.7	8.6	10.0	13.8	0.0
St. Clair State Bank (Inc.)	Saint Clair	MN	A-	B+	B+	101.6	6.71	8.9	5.7	10.6	1.4	8.7	10.7	13.9
St. Henry Bank	Saint Henry	OH	A	A	A	348.3	16.50	6.8	0.5	11.4	21.7	10.0	13.7	0.0
St. Johns Bank and Trust Co.	Saint Louis	MO	B-	C+	C+	329.8	12.48	8.3	0.5	7.8	15.5	7.0	9.0	0.0
St. Landry Bank and Trust Co.	Opelousas	LA	C	C+	B	327.6	17.05	3.5	0.5	3.1	48.5	6.2	8.2	0.0
St. Landry Homestead FSB	Opelousas	LA	B-	B	B	241.9	9.97	3.0	2.0	42.8	17.0	10.0	21.4	40.4
St. Louis Bank	Saint Louis	MO	C	C	C	633.3	44.72	29.5	0.3	5.0	7.1	6.7	9.1	12.3
St. Martin National Bank	Saint Martin	MN	B	B	B	25.1	16.53	5.5	2.7	20.1	18.6	10.0	14.4	0.0
Stafford Savings Bank	Stafford Springs	CT	B+	A-	B-	319.7	7.81	0.0	0.3	18.8	10.6	10.0	41.9	31.8
Standard Bank, PaSB	Monroeville	PA	B	B	B	1066.1	7.62	7.8	0.1	36.9	16.4	10.0	11.0	17.9
Standing Stone Bank	Lancaster	OH	C+	C+	C	106.2	3.67	16.3	16.1	20.0	15.4	6.7	8.7	15.3
Stanley Bank	Overland Park	KS	A-	A-	B+	147.0	21.91	33.2	2.1	3.5	0.0	10.0	13.9	0.0
Stanton State Bank	Stanton	NE	C+	C+	C	52.5	7.92	12.9	3.6	12.9	19.8	7.6	9.4	16.8
Star Bank	Maple Lake	MN	C-	C	B-	328.7	16.71	9.1	2.0	8.2	2.0	6.6	8.6	12.8
STAR Financial Bank	Fort Wayne	IN	B+	B+	B	2560.9	26.00	23.8	1.2	9.5	16.6	7.4	9.3	14.0
Starion Bank	Bismarck	ND	B+	B+	A-	1518.3	9.10	14.7	1.8	6.4	24.7	8.6	10.1	16.0
State Bank	La Junta	CO	A-	B	B	118.3	12.21	4.7	2.0	7.9	20.4	10.0	14.0	23.6
State Bank	Spencer	IA	C+	C+	C	75.1	8.15	11.7	3.3	17.5	9.9	6.4	8.4	14.5
State Bank	Spirit Lake	IA	C+	C+	B-	74.3	3.25	4.9	1.3	13.4	36.2	10.0	12.3	0.0
State Bank	Freeport	IL	B	B+	B	301.5	14.79	21.6	0.2	3.0	23.1	7.3	9.9	0.0
State Bank	Waterloo	IL	B-	C	C	229.1	20.40	4.8	0.9	14.1	22.3	6.0	8.5	11.7
State Bank	Wonder Lake	IL	D+	C	C	258.4	15.33	15.8	0.8	19.4	20.8	7.2	9.1	0.0
State Bank	Fenton	MI	A-	B+	B	1284.7	31.47	20.9	0.4	22.2	5.5	7.4	9.3	14.7
State Bank	Richmond	MO	B	B	B	36.8	10.84	6.3	3.2	20.8	34.8	5.9	7.9	21.5
State Bank	Green River	WY	D-	D-	D+	29.5	4.41	3.1	1.3	8.2	0.0	7.9	9.6	0.0
State Bank & Trust	Winfield	AL	B-	B-	B-	281.7	17.08	4.6	6.2	14.7	58.8	8.2	9.8	0.0
State Bank & Trust Co.	Nevada	IA	B+	A-	B+	185.3	15.77	14.8	0.5	9.9	18.3	5.2	8.9	0.0
State Bank & Trust Co.	Golden Meadow	LA	B-	C+	D+	122.4	3.55	15.7	3.9	16.6	22.6	10.0	11.8	19.0
State Bank & Trust of Kenmare	Kenmare	ND	B-	B-	C	138.6	8.52	12.9	2.5	7.2	34.6	8.4	9.9	16.3
State Bank and Trust Co.	Defiance	OH	B+	B+	B+	1212.9	16.97	16.7	1.1	17.9	10.7	8.8	10.4	14.0
State Bank Financial	La Crosse	WI	B-	B	B	429.9	24.25	15.8	0.5	4.2	21.8	6.6	8.6	15.0
▲ State Bank Northwest	Spokane Valley	WA	A-	B-	C+	190.9	39.59	32.4	0.1	10.3	2.6	8.9	10.3	18.5
▼ State Bank of Arcadia	Arcadia	WI	B-	B	B-	194.6	12.15	4.9	1.3	17.3	10.1	9.3	10.5	26.3
State Bank of Bellingham	Bellingham	MN	B-	C	C	52.4	7.12	7.5	0.3	0.0	29.9	10.0	12.2	17.5
State Bank of Bement	Bement	IL	C+	B-	B-	119.9	14.94	19.3	10.6	8.8	15.5	9.7	11.1	0.0
State Bank of Bern	Bern	KS	A-	A-	B+	100.9	6.66	4.4	2.1	0.9	48.2	10.0	16.7	0.0
State Bank of Bottineau	Bottineau	ND	B-	B-	C+	79.5	0.76	8.7	2.5	18.2	1.6	4.2	9.7	0.0
State Bank of Brooks	Corning	IA	C	C	C	20.7	12.68	1.8	4.2	9.5	37.1	10.0	11.3	41.7
▲ State Bank of Burrton	Burrton	KS	C	C	C-	10.8	1.09	16.3	3.5	16.9	23.9	10.0	11.4	0.0
State Bank of Bussey	Bussey	IA	C	C	C-	45.9	4.88	6.6	1.3	30.3	2.2	6.6	8.6	0.0
State Bank of Canton	Canton	KS	B	B	C+	32.4	6.65	12.5	1.0	1.3	27.3	10.0	20.0	46.1
State Bank of Cerro Gordo	Cerro Gordo	IL	C+	B-	B-	39.4	26.74	13.2	3.6	8.2	33.0	8.8	10.2	21.7
State Bank of Ceylon	Ceylon	MN	D	D+	D+	17.9	26.50	2.1	4.2	27.3	7.4	8.4	11.2	13.6
State Bank of Chandler	Chandler	MN	B	B-	B-	48.9	1.45	9.6	3.7	2.4	8.7	10.0	12.4	17.5
State Bank of Cherry	Cherry	IL	A-	A-	A-	104.3	15.05	8.1	4.9	13.4	13.9	10.0	12.5	0.0
State Bank of Chilton	Chilton	WI	B-	B	B	349.2	24.35	14.5	0.9	10.8	4.0	9.0	10.4	15.0
State Bank of Cochran	Cochran	GA	B+	B+	B	232.3	11.72	4.6	6.6	18.0	10.6	10.0	15.3	29.4
State Bank of Cold Spring	Cold Spring	MN	C+	C+	C+	72.9	15.16	5.6	5.0	21.0	10.3	6.7	8.7	0.0
State Bank of Cross Plains	Cross Plains	WI	B-	C+	C	1507.8	14.42	16.3	1.0	12.4	10.6	5.1	9.6	0.0
State Bank of Danvers	Benson	MN	A-	B+	B	53.3	15.39	4.4	0.9	0.1	41.1	10.0	12.4	24.3
State Bank of Davis	Davis	IL	B+	B+	B	176.5	9.44	20.0	0.8	2.1	40.2	9.2	10.5	0.0
State Bank of De Kalb	De Kalb	TX	B+	B+	B+	324.3	24.70	21.5	1.1	14.9	0.0	8.2	10.1	0.0
State Bank of Downs	Downs	KS	B-	C+	C-	105.3	13.90	16.2	1.6	21.4	4.9	10.0	12.1	0.0
State Bank of Eagle Butte	Eagle Butte	SD	C-	C-	D+	77.9	17.72	5.2	16.9	2.5	48.1	6.6	8.6	16.4
State Bank of Easton	Easton	MN	C-	C-	D+	21.7	7.09	17.8	5.4	3.2	5.9	10.0	13.1	0.0
▼ State Bank of Fairmont	Fairmont	MN	C-	C+	B-	116.8	3.66	23.6	5.3	3.2	12.9	9.6	10.9	14.7
State Bank of Faribault	Faribault	MN	B	B	B-	262.0	25.42	11.4	2.8	13.6	18.9	7.3	9.2	15.0

Asset Quality Index	Adjusted Non-Performing Loans as a % of Total Loans	as a % of Capital	Net Charge-Offs Avg Loans	Profitability Index	Net Income ($Mil)	Return on Assets (R.O.A.)	Return on Equity (R.O.E.)	Net Interest Spread	Overhead Efficiency Ratio	Liquidity Index	Liquidity Ratio	Hot Money Ratio	Stability Index
3.8	1.70	na	0.00	6.4	1.4	1.59	20.32	3.86	62.6	1.9	25.7	22.6	4.9
8.6	0.00	na	-0.09	5.3	1.1	1.19	10.59	3.45	61.1	5.0	30.2	5.9	6.9
5.0	0.82	5.4	0.14	3.1	4.3	0.34	3.03	2.95	54.7	1.7	11.8	13.1	7.4
8.2	0.03	na	0.00	7.9	1.6	1.42	10.30	3.86	50.8	2.8	24.1	16.0	8.9
8.0	0.08	na	0.03	7.8	1.4	1.94	18.38	3.34	41.2	2.2	31.2	23.9	9.2
8.9	0.27	na	0.00	9.3	5.4	2.19	14.85	3.48	40.5	5.5	42.8	8.0	9.5
7.6	0.01	na	0.03	3.4	1.3	0.54	5.60	3.63	79.7	5.0	21.4	2.7	4.9
6.5	4.09	na	4.54	1.5	0.5	0.20	2.27	1.91	76.5	6.3	56.0	6.8	2.7
7.0	3.13	na	0.00	1.7	0.0	0.01	0.03	3.16	87.0	2.0	35.2	29.0	7.5
3.7	0.79	na	-0.04	3.2	2.8	0.64	7.71	3.08	70.8	0.5	10.2	46.7	4.6
9.0	0.00	na	0.00	7.8	0.3	1.88	12.46	3.79	56.5	6.2	56.6	5.7	6.3
10.0	0.86	0.4	0.07	4.5	1.2	0.51	1.27	2.18	76.5	7.7	128.7	8.1	9.9
7.5	0.65	na	0.02	3.6	4.9	0.64	4.66	2.95	65.4	3.5	23.2	13.8	9.3
6.4	0.20	na	0.15	3.8	0.6	0.67	7.54	3.50	78.3	1.8	22.3	6.5	5.1
8.4	0.03	na	0.02	5.3	1.0	0.96	6.03	3.03	58.5	5.6	46.3	8.1	7.4
7.8	0.87	na	0.01	3.2	0.2	0.65	6.70	3.16	79.8	5.7	36.6	3.7	5.2
0.9	4.24	na	0.41	6.5	3.2	1.39	14.47	4.48	65.8	4.3	26.4	8.7	7.4
6.4	0.96	5.1	0.05	4.6	16.2	0.91	9.02	3.36	68.2	5.1	18.3	2.3	8.2
5.4	1.18	5.9	0.01	5.8	15.9	1.45	13.07	3.46	57.7	3.0	24.2	15.7	10.0
6.4	2.12	na	0.00	5.2	0.9	0.99	6.73	4.46	67.1	4.6	28.9	7.6	8.1
8.5	0.05	na	0.01	4.7	0.6	1.06	12.49	3.78	72.9	2.8	29.2	17.4	4.3
5.0	4.72	na	2.02	2.2	0.1	0.23	1.75	2.74	78.1	3.2	51.5	23.2	4.8
6.1	0.63	4.1	0.12	6.2	2.5	1.16	11.11	3.07	48.2	2.5	15.9	16.6	7.2
7.6	1.06	na	-0.31	3.7	1.1	0.68	7.75	2.84	75.6	2.8	32.7	18.6	4.7
3.4	2.45	na	0.09	2.0	0.4	0.20	1.80	3.57	94.4	4.3	23.9	7.9	5.9
8.3	0.06	na	0.05	7.1	12.9	1.47	15.02	3.58	52.9	3.3	11.7	10.0	8.5
5.8	0.85	4.3	0.01	4.2	0.3	0.94	10.58	3.43	75.4	6.6	47.1	0.7	5.5
9.4	0.00	na	0.00	0.0	-0.7	-3.25	-29.51	3.04	214.4	5.2	63.8	12.9	3.9
5.4	2.29	na	0.15	4.0	2.1	1.08	9.64	2.87	68.9	2.4	49.5	46.1	5.5
5.0	1.34	8.4	0.03	6.9	1.8	1.40	14.96	3.25	45.8	4.4	24.2	4.6	6.8
4.3	2.61	13.1	0.29	3.4	0.6	0.61	4.99	3.82	80.9	2.8	22.4	15.6	5.6
2.8	1.39	na	0.01	3.7	0.8	0.78	7.18	2.87	71.0	3.0	37.8	19.1	5.9
6.4	0.80	4.4	0.10	6.1	10.7	1.27	10.24	3.44	63.6	2.7	15.1	15.1	10.0
6.3	1.35	2.8	0.03	3.6	2.5	0.82	8.11	2.74	70.9	4.6	25.0	6.3	6.1
8.1	0.44	na	0.00	8.2	2.6	1.97	18.52	5.26	61.8	3.8	16.7	10.4	7.4
7.3	1.04	na	-0.01	3.7	1.2	0.86	7.10	2.48	64.5	6.0	50.3	6.6	7.0
5.0	2.37	na	0.00	3.7	0.4	0.97	7.76	2.68	90.8	2.1	46.9	35.6	8.5
5.8	0.13	na	0.04	3.1	0.4	0.48	4.07	3.52	83.9	4.4	31.5	10.4	6.2
8.6	0.93	na	-0.03	6.7	1.0	1.43	8.32	3.66	47.3	4.5	62.0	17.8	8.4
7.1	0.00	na	0.00	5.3	0.8	1.27	12.96	4.37	66.2	2.0	5.2	17.4	6.7
6.5	0.76	na	-0.10	2.7	0.1	0.48	4.13	2.38	77.0	7.1	87.5	4.1	5.0
8.9	0.00	na	0.61	2.6	0.0	0.45	3.93	3.84	82.3	3.8	32.6	11.5	5.2
7.4	0.68	na	-0.01	2.6	0.1	0.27	3.04	3.83	91.8	4.1	31.3	11.5	4.5
8.6	0.00	na	0.00	3.5	0.1	0.54	2.50	2.91	79.9	7.5	77.5	1.6	7.4
8.4	0.00	na	0.00	2.1	0.1	0.21	1.65	2.75	92.2	6.3	61.7	5.9	5.4
3.7	2.96	na	-0.03	3.9	0.1	1.02	8.48	4.26	77.7	0.7	16.1	14.7	2.9
6.2	0.00	na	-0.03	5.3	0.4	0.98	7.73	3.85	64.8	3.6	21.8	11.7	7.0
7.3	0.60	na	0.00	6.0	1.0	1.34	9.97	3.72	54.2	2.5	32.6	20.5	8.3
4.1	2.25	na	-0.10	5.1	2.9	1.16	10.98	3.29	57.2	2.8	21.1	10.3	8.0
5.1	3.63	na	-0.26	9.5	3.6	2.13	13.85	3.87	54.8	4.6	40.4	11.9	9.4
4.5	2.76	na	0.01	4.7	0.6	1.23	13.39	3.42	64.5	5.7	44.6	6.1	4.8
6.2	0.80	5.2	0.01	5.9	11.8	1.11	9.87	3.63	60.0	4.6	17.2	5.6	9.1
9.0	0.03	na	0.01	7.2	0.6	1.65	12.56	3.29	50.4	5.6	45.8	7.0	8.1
4.8	3.06	9.9	0.29	6.1	1.6	1.25	11.42	2.62	55.8	2.1	28.2	21.2	7.3
4.7	0.45	na	-0.03	8.3	4.6	1.96	20.29	3.90	57.8	3.2	22.6	13.9	8.5
6.5	4.62	na	0.06	6.3	1.1	1.45	11.74	3.66	57.5	4.5	27.7	7.3	7.8
4.5	0.75	na	1.36	3.1	0.2	0.33	3.38	4.76	78.1	1.4	7.7	24.0	3.8
4.6	2.05	na	-0.02	4.9	0.2	1.32	10.37	3.57	67.5	2.1	28.7	19.4	4.3
1.7	4.22	21.9	0.21	4.9	1.1	1.20	11.17	3.61	58.2	2.4	22.1	17.8	6.4
8.6	0.07	na	-0.01	5.0	2.0	1.14	11.03	4.15	73.7	4.3	29.9	9.9	6.1

Name	City	State	Rating	2019 Rating	2018 Rating	Total Assets ($Mil)	One Year Asset Growth	Comm-ercial Loans	Cons-umer Loans	Mort-gage Loans	Secur-ities	Capital-ization Index	Lever-age Ratio	Risk-Based Capital Ratio
State Bank of Geneva	Geneva	IL	C	C-	D+	96.6	20.31	10.8	0.6	11.7	11.2	6.8	8.8	16.0
State Bank of Graymont	Graymont	IL	B	B	B	234.8	10.87	9.2	1.6	6.8	22.7	10.0	11.5	0.0
State Bank of Herscher	Herscher	IL	B+	B+	B	164.3	12.37	16.2	0.1	4.9	32.0	10.0	12.0	0.0
State Bank of India (California)	Los Angeles	CA	B+	B+	B	886.7	5.63	20.1	0.0	0.0	10.6	10.0	16.5	20.6
State Bank of Industry	Industry	IL	B	B	B	54.9	6.60	7.0	4.1	15.2	19.0	10.0	14.4	23.6
State Bank of Jeffers	Jeffers	MN	B	B	B-	30.1	9.23	8.8	3.7	1.3	17.2	10.0	12.4	15.4
State Bank of Lake Park	Lake Park	MN	C+	C+	C	42.5	11.73	7.1	5.9	25.0	13.6	8.0	9.7	0.0
State Bank of Lakota	Lakota	ND	B-	B-	C+	57.7	15.67	6.2	4.4	9.1	13.5	7.5	9.3	15.2
State Bank of Lincoln	Lincoln	IL	A-	A-	B+	349.4	1.34	8.4	0.3	4.0	39.9	8.2	9.8	19.2
▲ State Bank of Lismore	Lismore	MN	C+	C	C	63.5	3.11	7.7	2.4	0.0	0.1	7.9	9.9	13.2
State Bank of Lizton	Brownsburg	IN	B+	B+	B	604.8	20.14	15.3	0.7	8.6	11.2	7.1	9.6	12.6
State Bank of Medora	Medora	IN	B	B	B	92.0	1.03	4.7	4.4	17.3	54.3	10.0	15.1	0.0
State Bank of Missouri	Concordia	MO	B	B	B	114.3	15.77	8.1	1.7	21.7	25.6	6.2	8.2	18.4
State Bank of Nauvoo	Nauvoo	IL	D-	D	C-	33.2	-0.48	6.5	8.5	30.6	0.0	6.9	8.9	16.4
▲ State Bank of New Richland	New Richland	MN	C+	C	C-	113.3	-2.23	4.7	1.4	15.5	10.3	8.4	10.3	13.7
State Bank of Newburg	Newburg	WI	A-	A-	B	206.5	10.61	5.3	0.6	29.4	9.2	10.0	19.0	0.0
State Bank of Odell	Odell	NE	D+	C	C	30.0	12.70	2.2	8.3	2.4	2.7	6.9	8.9	19.0
▲ State Bank of Pearl City	Pearl City	IL	B-	B-	C	63.8	9.63	1.9	36.3	6.9	15.0	10.0	11.0	0.0
State Bank of Reeseville	Reeseville	WI	B-	B-	B-	115.6	13.63	8.0	1.7	13.6	47.4	7.7	9.5	18.1
State Bank of Saunemin	Saunemin	IL	B	B-	B-	38.2	8.26	13.5	2.3	3.1	27.3	10.0	11.7	0.0
State Bank of Schaller	Schaller	IA	B+	B	B	35.5	16.87	4.5	2.0	2.1	56.7	10.0	12.9	0.0
▲ State Bank of Scotia	Scotia	NE	B	B-	B-	51.1	8.83	5.5	1.9	6.8	6.2	10.0	21.3	27.1
State Bank of Southern Utah	Cedar City	UT	A	A	A	1601.1	28.11	11.8	2.2	3.2	18.5	10.0	11.5	0.0
State Bank of Southwest Missouri	Springfield	MO	B-	B-	C+	168.8	28.62	19.2	4.1	28.9	8.9	4.2	6.2	11.5
State Bank of Spring Hill	Spring Hill	KS	C+	C+	C	48.5	7.51	5.7	0.9	4.5	47.6	6.9	8.9	26.1
State Bank of St. Jacob	Saint Jacob	IL	B+	B+	B+	71.3	9.56	5.5	11.0	13.6	28.6	10.0	15.6	34.6
State Bank of Table Rock	Table Rock	NE	C	C-	D+	107.7	15.02	10.4	2.8	10.1	1.8	4.1	7.9	0.0
▲ State Bank of Taunton	Taunton	MN	C+	B-	D+	48.4	1.52	4.7	0.5	5.2	10.6	10.0	11.1	15.7
▲ State Bank of Texas	Dallas	TX	A-	B+	B+	958.5	16.46	2.9	0.5	5.0	5.8	10.0	16.7	0.0
State Bank of the Lakes, N.A.	Antioch	IL	B-	B	B	1538.4	16.45	29.6	20.0	2.3	8.1	5.5	8.2	11.4
State Bank of Toledo	Toledo	IA	D	D	D+	132.6	16.13	5.9	4.3	24.3	0.7	5.2	9.3	0.0
State Bank of Toulon	Toulon	IL	B-	B-	B-	262.7	14.62	10.6	1.1	5.4	30.2	8.0	9.8	13.3
State Bank of Wapello	Wapello	IA	B	B	B-	40.9	7.17	3.3	4.0	9.2	18.6	10.0	13.6	28.0
State Bank of Wheaton	Wheaton	MN	A-	A-	B+	89.9	6.71	4.8	0.7	0.7	0.7	10.0	23.8	31.0
State Bank of Whittington	Benton	IL	B	B	C+	146.1	9.85	9.6	13.3	14.6	28.1	9.0	10.3	16.0
State Bank of Wynnewood	Wynnewood	OK	B+	B+	A-	94.4	2.04	7.8	1.9	8.9	49.2	10.0	15.8	0.0
State Central Bank	Bonaparte	IA	D+	D+	D+	42.7	13.09	19.5	1.9	11.0	26.2	7.5	9.3	0.0
State Exchange Bank	Mankato	KS	B-	B-	C+	39.1	13.13	5.5	3.2	4.7	45.1	10.0	12.6	0.0
State Exchange Bank	Lamont	OK	D	D+	D-	71.8	8.60	26.8	0.9	5.0	2.7	6.5	11.3	0.0
State National Bank of Big Spring	Big Spring	TX	B+	A-	B	430.8	7.70	5.3	0.5	1.2	50.9	10.0	11.1	24.9
▲ State National Bank of Groom	Groom	TX	B-	C	C	42.3	14.11	9.7	1.6	4.0	8.4	10.0	11.4	15.7
State Nebraska Bank & Trust	Wayne	NE	A-	A-	B+	172.6	9.97	17.9	2.2	10.7	27.4	10.0	13.0	20.3
State Savings Bank	Creston	IA	B-	B-	B+	136.2	9.19	10.8	4.6	19.5	0.0	5.4	9.4	0.0
State Savings Bank	Rake	IA	D-	D-	D-	76.3	0.97	13.4	0.6	0.5	1.5	9.0	11.9	14.2
State Savings Bank	West Des Moines	IA	B+	B+	B+	172.4	14.60	13.4	0.6	13.5	0.3	7.6	9.4	13.5
▲ State Savings Bank	Frankfort	MI	D+	D+	C-	306.8	37.24	12.1	0.6	19.6	6.9	5.7	8.7	0.0
State Savings Bank of Manistique	Manistique	MI	B	B	B	142.5	8.87	7.1	4.7	14.7	43.4	10.0	11.2	0.0
State Street B&T Co. of California, N.A.	Long Beach	CA	U	U	U	16.9	6.31	0.0	0.0	0.0	0.0	10.0	100.	312.5
State Street Bank and Trust Co.	Quincy	IL	B	B	B-	266.4	18.71	5.4	23.2	20.7	15.2	6.7	8.7	12.5
State Street Bank and Trust Co.	Boston	MA	B+	B+	B+	268733.0	11.34	1.6	0.0	0.0	40.7	5.2	7.2	17.4
State Street Bank and Trust Co., N.A.	New York	NY	U	U	U	40.4	17.43	0.0	0.0	0.0	0.0	10.0	100.	282.5
Stearns Bank Holdingford N.A.	Holdingford	MN	A-	A-	A-	94.8	-8.12	84.1	0.7	0.9	3.4	10.0	18.5	21.0
Stearns Bank N.A.	Saint Cloud	MN	A-	A-	A-	2203.2	1.40	57.6	0.1	0.9	0.9	10.0	20.7	27.0
Stearns Bank Upsala N.A.	Upsala	MN	A-	A-	A-	75.9	-14.41	80.8	0.2	0.8	4.5	10.0	17.5	20.4
Stephenson National Bank and Trust	Marinette	WI	B	B	C+	633.9	19.33	17.8	4.1	13.2	25.1	5.8	9.2	0.0
Sterling Bank	Poplar Bluff	MO	A-	A-	A-	1273.2	1.66	30.8	0.7	3.4	3.8	9.9	10.9	15.1
Sterling Bank	Barron	WI	B	B	B	288.9	15.64	9.5	0.4	10.2	20.1	6.2	8.2	15.0
▼ Sterling Bank and Trust, FSB	Southfield	MI	B+	A	A-	3934.2	18.39	0.0	0.0	55.8	6.2	8.4	9.9	21.3
Sterling Federal Bank, F.S.B.	Sterling	IL	D+	D+	C-	487.5	7.38	5.5	0.3	23.6	39.1	6.0	8.1	16.6
Sterling National Bank	Pearl River	NY	B	B	B	30539.2	1.73	19.1	0.0	6.0	14.2	8.6	10.5	13.9

Asset Quality Index	Adjusted Non-Performing Loans as a % of Total Loans	as a % of Capital	Net Charge-Offs Avg Loans	Profitability Index	Net Income ($Mil)	Return on Assets (R.O.A.)	Return on Equity (R.O.E.)	Net Interest Spread	Overhead Efficiency Ratio	Liquidity Index	Liquidity Ratio	Hot Money Ratio	Stability Index
7.8	0.20	na	0.00	2.9	0.3	0.47	4.97	3.55	84.2	2.6	32.4	19.4	4.4
5.0	3.03	15.3	0.08	4.3	1.4	0.86	7.02	2.98	59.8	4.0	24.2	10.0	6.8
4.8	3.29	15.2	0.36	4.7	1.0	0.87	6.65	3.90	63.2	4.4	27.5	8.3	7.4
7.1	0.27	na	-0.02	4.3	4.9	0.73	4.43	3.07	63.8	0.7	12.7	40.9	8.8
8.4	0.09	na	0.02	4.7	0.5	1.17	8.12	3.02	60.3	1.0	26.3	42.1	8.2
8.4	0.03	na	0.00	3.9	0.2	0.68	5.41	2.94	68.9	5.8	52.1	7.2	6.3
4.3	3.03	na	0.45	5.1	0.4	1.19	12.17	4.35	70.2	4.1	44.6	15.4	5.4
7.0	0.38	na	0.03	5.4	0.5	1.20	12.60	3.57	64.8	2.6	27.4	18.1	5.6
5.9	2.13	na	0.09	4.6	2.1	0.83	7.69	3.33	66.8	4.9	30.0	6.4	8.3
5.2	0.00	na	0.01	5.1	0.6	1.18	11.91	4.00	63.8	1.1	19.0	32.2	5.0
4.5	1.72	10.7	0.01	5.1	4.6	1.07	10.41	3.52	63.6	3.8	17.5	9.1	7.1
9.8	1.11	na	-0.05	3.5	0.4	0.58	3.93	2.44	72.6	3.5	62.6	23.9	7.5
6.2	1.00	5.7	0.05	5.9	1.2	1.48	16.92	3.41	60.4	5.2	33.9	6.2	6.0
1.7	3.85	24.2	1.85	2.2	0.0	0.18	1.91	3.80	74.8	5.0	35.8	7.9	2.6
3.5	0.86	na	0.01	9.8	2.3	2.65	26.77	4.25	38.2	0.9	9.1	16.4	8.0
7.3	3.14	na	-0.01	8.7	2.3	1.57	8.23	3.53	42.9	1.3	27.2	25.4	9.0
5.7	0.54	na	0.67	1.2	0.0	-0.07	-0.69	3.16	98.4	6.9	67.1	3.5	3.6
6.8	0.19	na	0.05	3.3	0.3	0.71	5.92	3.70	78.9	3.9	43.0	16.0	5.9
9.1	0.06	na	-0.01	3.5	0.6	0.70	7.61	2.79	72.4	2.7	54.7	12.3	6.0
8.6	0.00	na	0.00	6.1	0.5	1.67	13.41	3.07	65.2	4.6	40.7	12.2	6.4
8.3	0.28	na	0.10	6.5	0.4	1.39	10.24	3.64	58.8	5.6	44.4	7.4	7.7
6.0	0.94	na	0.09	6.3	0.5	1.20	5.55	3.79	52.3	1.2	22.9	30.6	8.2
7.2	1.15	na	0.01	8.4	15.1	1.43	11.46	3.98	49.6	5.4	38.6	10.4	10.0
6.6	0.24	na	0.01	6.3	1.7	1.48	22.83	2.97	62.5	4.2	15.7	7.3	3.5
9.7	0.00	na	0.00	2.8	0.1	0.37	3.92	2.80	82.1	6.4	56.7	4.6	4.2
5.6	0.60	na	0.02	5.9	0.7	1.47	8.89	3.25	44.0	5.7	59.4	9.5	7.6
4.3	0.55	na	0.01	3.2	0.4	0.56	7.08	3.38	80.8	2.7	22.4	16.2	4.5
8.4	0.00	na	-0.05	2.8	0.3	0.75	6.92	3.82	88.9	3.4	15.9	12.1	5.5
5.4	1.00	na	-0.04	10.0	21.7	3.19	20.15	4.91	27.9	0.7	18.3	42.8	10.0
4.1	0.81	4.8	0.45	3.4	6.1	0.57	4.62	2.74	58.2	2.2	16.3	10.7	8.3
1.4	4.88	na	0.03	7.2	1.5	1.68	18.03	4.23	61.6	4.2	26.3	7.8	6.6
5.2	0.60	na	0.13	4.3	2.0	1.08	9.31	3.45	63.6	3.2	25.0	14.3	5.8
9.1	0.00	0.0	0.05	4.2	0.3	0.97	6.95	2.85	65.2	7.3	64.6	0.0	6.9
7.3	0.17	na	0.00	9.8	1.7	2.58	10.83	4.29	42.2	2.5	33.2	20.2	9.8
5.0	0.35	na	0.20	5.2	1.3	1.24	11.47	4.32	70.2	5.3	32.5	4.3	6.4
8.8	0.24	na	0.01	5.0	1.3	1.80	10.98	3.45	63.7	2.9	44.9	24.7	8.6
1.6	31.61	na	-0.74	1.5	0.1	0.31	2.58	3.32	88.1	6.7	47.1	0.3	3.8
8.2	0.24	na	0.53	3.9	0.2	0.87	6.50	3.34	66.9	4.4	31.2	9.9	5.7
1.7	7.41	na	0.56	6.2	0.8	1.61	13.81	4.20	57.5	0.5	10.7	38.0	7.2
9.8	0.00	na	0.01	4.8	3.5	1.09	9.20	2.42	51.9	7.4	80.1	4.3	6.8
6.4	1.87	na	0.19	4.3	0.3	1.00	8.95	4.16	75.5	4.4	26.7	8.2	5.3
5.7	1.54	na	0.03	7.0	1.7	1.35	10.25	3.72	52.7	4.3	12.1	6.5	8.4
3.8	1.69	11.5	-0.07	8.0	1.7	1.77	18.50	3.62	49.4	1.9	17.0	19.8	7.8
0.3	4.83	na	1.83	4.2	0.5	0.88	7.59	3.01	40.2	0.6	16.6	52.4	5.5
6.2	0.45	na	0.02	6.2	1.7	1.34	14.10	3.84	61.7	4.0	18.0	9.2	7.2
5.8	0.91	na	-0.06	3.4	1.2	0.64	6.68	3.70	81.7	5.2	29.3	4.1	4.6
8.0	1.60	na	0.31	4.5	1.0	1.05	8.44	4.12	65.9	6.2	57.6	7.5	6.4
10.0	na	0.0	na	8.9	0.9	7.56	7.61	0.33	53.4	4.0	na	0.0	6.3
6.6	0.20	na	0.02	7.7	3.5	1.86	20.19	3.84	58.9	4.3	27.5	8.9	6.1
8.6	0.00	0.0	0.16	4.7	1908.0	0.97	9.79	1.12	71.1	6.7	57.7	0.2	8.7
10.0	na	0.0	na	10.0	5.3	18.78	19.09	0.35	54.5	4.0	na	0.0	6.3
7.6	0.57	na	1.48	4.3	0.4	0.56	3.24	3.79	14.7	0.6	10.5	39.6	7.8
5.3	4.17	7.7	1.14	7.7	21.5	1.25	6.33	5.99	37.5	1.0	20.5	10.1	9.4
7.5	1.21	na	1.30	4.0	0.2	0.39	2.32	3.64	16.5	0.6	13.6	46.1	8.0
4.8	0.92	na	0.02	6.4	7.2	1.67	16.14	3.70	59.7	3.9	18.5	9.9	7.6
7.8	0.13	0.9	0.33	7.4	14.3	1.51	12.74	3.71	48.7	1.3	16.8	17.5	9.4
8.0	0.33	na	0.00	7.2	3.7	1.82	21.56	3.48	54.6	3.5	38.4	16.5	6.2
3.7	3.49	20.7	0.04	4.1	3.6	0.13	1.30	3.22	63.7	2.1	32.3	36.4	8.6
5.3	5.02	na	0.05	1.2	0.5	0.13	1.42	2.63	96.8	3.2	44.9	20.7	4.2
4.5	0.99	4.0	0.57	4.9	173.9	0.76	5.04	3.26	45.8	3.6	9.5	4.5	10.0

Name	City	State	Rating	2019 Rating	2018 Rating	Total Assets ($Mil)	One Year Asset Growth	Asset Mix (As a % of Total Assets) Commercial Loans	Consumer Loans	Mortgage Loans	Securities	Capitalization Index	Leverage Ratio	Risk-Based Capital Ratio
Sterling State Bank	Austin	MN	C+	C+	C+	427.9	21.14	19.9	1.1	7.7	31.1	5.8	7.8	17.3
Stifel Bank	Clayton	MO	B	B	B	2641.3	25.55	28.4	11.5	0.9	44.2	5.3	7.3	19.3
Stifel Bank and Trust	Saint Louis	MO	B+	B+	B+	14176.4	1.98	25.6	8.3	28.1	29.2	5.2	7.2	13.0
Stifel Trust Co. Delaware, N.A.	Wilmington	DE	U	U	U	284.2	1881.1	0.0	0.0	0.0	74.8	6.3	8.3	43.7
Stifel Trust Co., N.A.	Saint Louis	MO	U	U	U	817.8	46.48	0.0	0.0	0.0	78.5	5.5	7.5	37.2
▲ Stillman BancCorp, N.A.	Stillman Valley	IL	B+	B	B-	535.0	15.25	6.4	1.1	6.7	57.2	6.4	8.4	22.2
Stock Exchange Bank	Caldwell	KS	C+	C+	C	61.1	12.74	5.8	3.0	41.1	11.2	6.9	8.9	0.0
Stock Exchange Bank	Woodward	OK	A-	A	A-	260.6	5.44	9.5	3.6	6.4	33.0	10.0	15.8	0.0
Stock Growers Bank	Forman	ND	A-	A-	A-	277.2	47.70	4.6	1.8	1.2	44.7	7.9	9.6	0.0
Stock Yards Bank & Trust Co.	Louisville	KY	A	A	A	4360.9	23.54	30.9	1.0	8.7	9.8	7.6	9.4	13.4
Stockgrowers State Bank	Ashland	KS	B+	B+	B	141.5	5.30	6.0	0.8	1.4	33.0	10.0	13.5	0.0
Stockgrowers State Bank	Maple Hill	KS	B+	B+	B+	89.3	9.84	8.4	1.4	17.6	33.6	10.0	12.2	17.0
Stockman Bank of Montana	Miles City	MT	A-	A-	A-	4759.5	24.77	8.9	0.6	5.5	26.4	7.8	9.5	15.0
Stockmans Bank	Altus	OK	B-	C+	C-	327.5	27.15	4.3	0.5	6.6	1.7	7.5	9.7	0.0
Stockmens Bank	Colorado Springs	CO	B+	B	B-	401.4	11.50	12.9	0.6	17.4	2.5	6.7	9.7	0.0
Stockmens Bank	Cascade	MT	B-	B-	B-	39.4	1.23	5.1	2.1	4.7	6.8	10.0	12.0	35.7
Stockmens National Bank in Cotulla	Cotulla	TX	B+	B+	B+	97.3	1.59	1.9	3.5	3.3	16.6	10.0	11.7	0.0
Stone Bank	Mountain View	AR	C+	C+	C	541.1	14.67	18.7	0.6	7.2	9.0	9.5	10.7	14.9
StonehamBank	Stoneham	MA	C-	C+	C+	678.9	10.28	13.3	0.1	31.8	11.1	8.3	9.9	15.5
Stoughton Co-operative Bank	Stoughton	MA	C	C-	C-	122.5	2.84	0.8	2.0	61.9	15.9	6.8	8.8	0.0
Strasburg State Bank	Strasburg	ND	C	C+	C+	76.2	15.66	2.4	0.4	0.0	15.8	5.9	7.9	11.7
Streator Home Savings Bank	Streator	IL	C+	B-	B-	166.7	2.31	0.0	1.2	21.8	67.2	10.0	25.5	0.0
▼ Stride Bank, N.A.	Enid	OK	C-	C+	C-	1171.6	71.30	22.3	12.7	3.8	5.6	4.8	6.9	13.4
Stroud National Bank	Stroud	OK	B-	B-	C+	84.6	11.71	13.3	5.5	19.6	28.8	10.0	11.4	0.0
Studio Bank	Nashville	TN	D			395.1	101.03	11.9	1.1	18.2	11.6	10.0	12.9	18.0
Sturdy Savings Bank	Cape May Court Hou	NJ	C	C+	C+	1066.7	19.38	6.3	0.0	22.7	34.0	6.2	8.2	15.5
Sturgis Bank & Trust Co.	Sturgis	MI	B-	B-	C+	604.7	27.82	11.1	1.2	27.2	12.6	5.3	7.3	12.3
Success Bank	Bloomfield	IA	B+	B-	C+	220.1	11.39	9.5	1.6	13.6	4.9	8.5	11.2	0.0
Sugar River Bank	Newport	NH	B-	B-	B-	337.7	7.83	7.4	1.9	42.9	20.9	10.0	13.9	0.0
Sullivan Bank	Sullivan	MO	B-	B-	B-	591.8	12.28	12.1	2.3	31.1	9.1	7.9	9.6	13.9
▼ Sumitomo Mitsui Trust Bank (U.S.A.) Ltd.	Hoboken	NJ	B	B+	B-	3827.8	31.14	0.0	0.0	0.0	0.0	6.8	8.8	26.9
Summit Bank	Oakland	CA	A-	A-	B+	317.4	26.48	21.4	0.0	1.9	0.1	10.0	11.6	15.8
Summit Bank	Eugene	OR	C+	B-	B-	758.7	52.15	31.7	0.2	1.2	1.2	1.9	8.5	0.0
Summit Community Bank, Inc.	Moorefield	WV	B+	B+	B	2945.4	26.86	11.2	1.2	15.1	13.3	7.3	9.6	12.8
▲ Summit National Bank	Hulett	WY	B-	C	D+	86.2	15.92	6.6	2.4	4.2	10.4	8.6	10.0	16.9
Summit State Bank	Santa Rosa	CA	B	B	B+	833.8	22.47	17.2	0.0	7.0	7.2	6.1	8.1	12.6
Sumner Bank & Trust	Gallatin	TN	B	B	B-	183.8	1.18	8.9	0.6	21.0	8.3	8.7	10.2	14.9
Suncrest Bank	West Sacramento	CA	B+	B+	B+	1290.4	29.37	13.7	0.0	2.9	25.2	7.8	9.5	14.7
Sundance State Bank	Sundance	WY	B	B-	C	207.8	7.47	14.2	3.3	7.6	32.3	9.6	10.7	15.5
Sundown State Bank	Sundown	TX	B+	B+	B	179.2	12.44	21.4	0.5	0.6	7.1	9.2	10.5	14.7
▲ Sunflower Bank, N.A.	Denver	CO	B	C	C	4875.7	21.10	26.4	0.3	13.1	10.6	6.8	9.6	12.3
SunMark Community Bank	Hawkinsville	GA	A-	B+	B+	344.3	28.64	13.2	1.7	16.3	6.2	8.5	10.0	0.0
Sunnyside Federal S&L Assn. of Irvington	Irvington	NY	D+	D+	D+	97.0	10.33	7.4	4.7	19.8	49.4	10.0	12.3	28.6
Sunrise Bank	Cocoa Beach	FL	B+	A-	B+	273.1	16.97	10.5	0.7	10.3	11.7	9.3	10.9	0.0
▲ Sunrise Bank Dakota	Onida	SD	C-	D+	D+	55.2	5.68	3.1	1.5	4.3	26.3	10.0	12.3	23.2
Sunrise Banks, N.A.	Saint Paul	MN	B+	B	B	1437.8	27.93	20.7	5.8	10.0	10.7	7.3	9.2	14.9
Sunset Bank & Savings	Waukesha	WI	C	C+	C+	141.1	8.17	8.6	0.8	33.9	6.6	9.5	10.7	0.0
▲ SunSouth Bank	Dothan	AL	D	E	E	125.9	17.54	31.0	1.6	9.8	42.1	5.0	7.0	14.7
▼ Sunstate Bank	Miami	FL	C+	B	C+	510.5	11.45	4.9	0.2	25.9	15.9	7.6	9.4	13.2
Sunwest Bank	Irvine	CA	B	B+	B+	1976.2	46.76	36.3	1.7	2.0	5.0	2.8	9.9	0.0
Superior National Bank & Trust Co.	Hancock	MI	B+	A-	B+	655.2	11.79	8.1	6.9	17.5	35.1	6.0	8.0	0.0
Superior Savings Bank	Superior	WI	B	B	B-	76.2	14.92	2.0	0.8	48.8	4.0	10.0	18.2	0.0
Surety Bank	Deland	FL	B	B-	B-	156.4	19.10	6.3	0.1	5.6	13.5	8.4	10.0	22.2
Surrey Bank & Trust	Mount Airy	NC	A	A-	B+	425.4	28.27	28.3	0.6	5.5	3.1	10.0	11.7	22.0
Susquehanna Community Bank	West Milton	PA	B+	B+	B+	477.1	0.72	9.0	3.1	7.4	33.9	5.9	9.8	0.0
Sutton Bank	Attica	OH	B+	B	B	779.2	38.81	13.4	0.6	3.7	17.0	7.0	9.0	22.8
Swedish-American State Bank	Courtland	KS	B-	C+	C-	43.7	5.27	12.0	2.2	8.1	14.9	10.0	12.3	19.2
Sweet Water State Bank	Sweet Water	AL	C+	B-	C+	105.0	7.30	14.7	3.9	8.2	12.7	9.1	10.6	0.0
Sycamore Bank	Senatobia	MS	B	B	B	262.7	15.49	5.5	2.6	19.8	20.6	7.3	9.2	0.0
▲ Synchrony Bank	Draper	UT	C+	C	C	85130.0	-7.40	1.4	81.3	0.0	11.8	10.0	13.0	17.9

Asset Quality Index	Adjusted Non-Performing Loans as a % of Total Loans	as a % of Capital	Net Charge-Offs Avg Loans	Profitability Index	Net Income ($Mil)	Return on Assets (R.O.A.)	Return on Equity (R.O.E.)	Net Interest Spread	Overhead Efficiency Ratio	Liquidity Index	Liquidity Ratio	Hot Money Ratio	Stability Index
8.7	0.06	0.2	-0.04	3.3	1.9	0.65	7.28	3.32	81.6	4.7	20.8	5.0	4.5
7.6	0.01	na	0.00	4.5	18.3	0.93	13.29	2.45	38.4	5.5	25.1	1.5	7.0
8.1	0.15	1.3	0.00	8.6	165.0	1.50	21.51	2.75	28.3	5.9	24.4	0.3	7.0
10.0	na	na	na	6.1	1.1	0.77	7.31	0.89	72.1	8.7	109.7	0.0	7.0
10.0	na	na	na	6.1	5.9	1.01	13.22	1.45	54.3	8.6	107.6	0.0	7.0
9.3	0.01	na	-0.05	6.0	5.9	1.57	15.40	2.75	61.3	4.5	52.4	15.7	6.6
5.2	0.33	na	-0.19	4.6	0.4	0.88	9.49	4.11	74.9	1.1	18.0	30.9	4.3
8.7	0.79	1.9	0.50	5.3	2.0	1.01	6.26	3.09	55.1	4.5	33.7	10.5	8.6
8.6	0.20	na	0.01	7.7	3.2	1.93	18.35	4.32	49.4	4.8	40.7	11.0	8.4
7.6	0.35	2.8	0.07	7.4	42.7	1.39	14.33	3.39	52.7	4.4	8.9	5.0	9.5
8.5	0.04	na	-0.02	4.0	1.0	0.89	6.20	3.42	71.6	1.7	26.7	26.0	7.8
7.9	0.20	na	0.01	6.4	1.0	1.57	12.17	4.04	55.6	2.8	17.0	15.3	7.7
6.7	0.80	4.2	0.02	8.4	71.5	2.23	21.55	3.48	49.6	4.0	21.9	8.0	9.9
3.6	1.07	na	0.01	4.8	2.5	1.08	11.29	4.25	75.5	0.9	19.8	32.4	6.3
7.8	0.18	na	0.04	5.5	3.1	1.05	10.37	3.79	58.1	3.8	18.6	10.1	6.1
8.0	0.73	na	0.00	3.2	0.2	0.72	6.17	2.83	76.2	4.9	74.5	15.8	6.3
9.7	0.00	0.0	-0.05	3.3	0.4	0.50	4.67	2.02	71.8	7.1	90.4	6.0	6.6
4.0	2.37	na	0.57	3.9	3.0	0.76	7.10	2.90	60.8	0.7	12.3	33.7	6.8
6.3	1.10	na	-0.01	2.5	1.8	0.37	3.68	3.07	74.9	2.7	17.2	15.9	6.5
7.4	0.44	na	0.00	2.7	0.4	0.40	4.58	2.62	81.3	1.4	27.1	30.5	4.5
8.9	0.00	na	0.00	3.0	0.2	0.35	4.38	2.42	76.6	4.5	47.6	13.6	4.5
10.0	1.98	na	0.10	2.4	0.4	0.31	1.21	2.10	84.9	4.8	97.0	21.9	7.6
2.6	2.64	na	0.09	3.5	3.7	0.49	7.16	3.46	77.7	1.8	29.1	3.6	6.8
4.7	2.88	na	0.14	3.9	0.5	0.82	6.75	4.68	81.0	4.7	30.2	7.5	5.7
8.8	0.00	na	0.00	0.2	-0.8	-0.35	-2.67	2.87	94.5	2.6	24.5	3.3	1.7
6.3	1.43	na	0.17	2.7	2.5	0.36	3.63	3.34	83.7	6.7	37.1	1.3	5.9
5.7	1.26	na	0.03	5.2	4.7	1.14	14.55	3.44	60.9	1.6	9.8	7.5	5.6
5.5	0.52	na	0.09	6.6	2.3	1.45	12.71	4.30	61.7	1.9	16.3	16.9	8.4
8.0	1.04	na	0.14	3.3	1.5	0.62	4.38	3.46	79.2	4.2	31.2	11.0	7.3
4.3	1.48	na	0.08	5.9	5.6	1.31	13.34	3.57	58.5	2.3	9.1	16.9	6.7
10.0	0.00	0.0	0.00	3.1	9.7	0.34	3.69	0.25	83.8	8.8	108.5	0.0	7.5
8.4	0.83	na	0.00	5.9	2.1	0.94	7.76	4.37	65.9	4.3	31.2	10.4	7.6
4.2	0.92	na	0.50	5.4	4.4	0.91	11.21	4.19	55.3	4.8	19.9	4.0	5.6
6.7	0.48	3.0	0.09	5.3	22.1	1.08	10.39	3.72	54.3	3.1	12.4	11.0	9.3
4.5	1.24	na	0.12	4.5	0.6	0.87	8.40	4.26	68.5	4.4	28.6	8.8	5.9
6.5	0.34	na	0.00	6.4	7.6	1.31	14.47	3.79	52.3	1.0	10.4	18.7	6.4
8.9	0.05	na	0.01	4.6	1.1	0.82	8.15	3.66	69.5	3.9	17.6	9.5	6.1
6.1	0.53	2.5	0.10	5.6	8.8	1.00	7.44	3.79	52.7	6.0	36.7	5.8	9.7
4.2	1.73	na	0.13	5.8	1.9	1.27	11.04	3.99	51.4	2.6	28.2	18.3	6.7
7.9	0.29	na	-0.03	4.8	1.3	0.93	9.19	3.60	70.4	2.6	22.5	16.6	6.5
6.3	0.65	4.8	0.04	4.9	38.9	1.14	10.77	3.33	70.3	3.8	5.7	5.4	7.9
5.8	0.55	na	-0.02	7.3	4.0	1.75	16.25	4.55	66.9	4.3	21.6	7.4	7.0
7.2	2.57	na	0.00	0.3	-0.2	-0.34	-2.86	2.10	119.1	3.4	55.1	21.9	5.0
7.6	0.00	na	0.00	3.8	1.5	0.79	7.10	3.41	72.6	2.6	24.2	15.3	7.6
1.7	15.51	na	0.10	2.9	0.2	0.47	3.78	3.26	84.2	3.1	39.0	16.2	5.4
7.3	0.50	4.2	0.08	7.6	18.5	2.08	22.59	4.59	71.5	1.1	20.2	1.6	7.0
6.2	1.11	na	0.01	2.9	0.4	0.43	3.67	3.07	83.6	1.6	21.4	24.7	6.4
7.7	0.20	na	0.10	2.3	0.8	0.89	12.58	2.81	88.3	1.8	30.5	28.9	0.8
7.3	0.90	na	0.00	3.3	1.5	0.42	3.75	2.45	74.7	1.9	39.0	40.1	7.5
4.9	0.85	6.2	0.18	7.1	14.6	1.12	10.30	3.73	57.1	3.5	8.1	2.6	10.0
6.1	1.59	na	0.03	4.9	4.5	1.00	10.43	3.40	66.6	5.1	50.6	12.1	6.5
6.8	2.63	5.6	0.01	4.8	0.5	0.97	5.24	2.86	66.4	5.4	38.5	6.5	7.4
4.9	3.17	na	-0.01	8.3	2.1	1.99	18.84	3.71	65.0	4.8	54.2	14.6	7.2
8.5	0.42	na	-0.01	6.3	3.1	1.12	8.58	3.46	58.9	3.6	32.4	12.4	8.6
7.5	0.16	na	0.03	4.8	4.1	1.20	10.80	3.46	65.7	4.2	21.4	8.2	6.9
6.2	1.43	4.0	0.08	9.5	16.5	2.91	31.35	2.74	47.5	4.5	47.2	0.9	7.2
5.3	0.05	na	0.00	7.2	0.6	1.70	13.63	4.44	62.9	1.7	17.4	22.4	5.2
4.0	1.89	na	0.50	3.4	0.4	0.48	4.24	4.99	88.2	1.8	28.1	26.9	6.3
6.4	0.69	3.1	0.04	4.3	1.5	0.77	8.17	3.91	73.7	3.9	16.9	9.0	5.5
2.6	1.19	6.9	5.18	7.4	730.0	1.13	9.90	10.73	37.3	1.6	27.0	28.1	9.8

Name	City	State	2019 Rating	2018 Rating	Total Assets ($Mil)	One Year Asset Growth	Asset Mix (As a % of Total Assets) Comm- ercial Loans	Cons- umer Loans	Mort- gage Loans	Secur- ities	Capital- ization Index	Lever- age Ratio	Risk- Based Capital Ratio
Synergy Bank	Houma	LA	B+	B	C+	665.5	20.39	19.9	2.0	10.6	22.5	9.1	10.4	0.0
▼ Synovus Bank	Columbus	GA	B	B+	B+	52991.3	11.39	20.8	3.2	12.0	14.3	6.8	8.9	12.3
Synovus Trust Co., N.A.	Columbus	GA	U	U	U	108.4	11.17	0.0	0.0	0.0	18.7	10.0	97.0	128.5
Systematic Savings Bank	Springfield	MO	D+	D	D	49.6	34.62	4.2	0.3	38.0	4.5	10.0	11.3	21.9
T Bank, N.A.	Dallas	TX	A-	B+	B-	511.1	45.60	45.8	1.5	0.9	4.2	8.8	10.2	17.5
Table Grove State Bank	Table Grove	IL	B	B	B-	44.8	-3.38	1.8	9.3	1.5	21.2	10.0	12.5	0.0
Table Rock Community Bank	Kimberling City	MO	B-	B-	C+	106.6	18.39	5.5	5.0	26.4	8.6	6.4	8.4	0.0
Talbot State Bank	Woodland	GA	C-	C-	D	56.3	-6.12	0.0	0.5	51.1	19.6	10.0	11.5	29.5
Tampa State Bank	Tampa	KS	C+	C+	C+	61.5	10.07	12.1	2.6	16.6	27.4	8.1	9.9	0.0
Tandem Bank	Tucker	GA	D			86.6	317.04	41.1	0.1	7.2	1.9	10.0	22.6	46.4
▼ Tarboro Savings Bank, SSB	Tarboro	NC	D+	C+	B-	58.5	18.56	0.0	0.0	50.5	0.0	10.0	11.4	0.0
▲ Taylor County Bank	Campbellsville	KY	A	A-	B+	206.0	13.18	11.0	3.6	17.9	18.5	10.0	13.9	0.0
Taylorsville Savings Bank, SSB	Taylorsville	NC	C+	B-	C+	117.3	8.95	2.2	0.8	46.6	5.6	9.6	10.8	19.4
TBK Bank, SSB	Dallas	TX	B-	B	B-	5817.6	16.01	41.6	0.3	2.4	4.2	6.2	11.3	11.9
TC Federal Bank	Thomasville	GA	C+	C+	C+	339.2	9.18	10.1	0.3	31.7	5.5	10.0	11.9	16.7
TCF National Bank	Sioux Falls	SD	B+	B+	B	47532.4	4.04	22.1	2.8	13.8	16.0	6.4	8.4	13.5
TCM Bank, N.A.	Tampa	FL	B-	B-	C+	263.6	-15.52	23.0	66.0	0.0	1.0	10.0	18.9	21.5
TD Bank USA, N.A.	Wilmington	DE	B-	B-	C+	25341.5	50.73	1.1	33.0	0.0	14.5	10.0	12.0	31.4
▼ TD Bank, N.A.	Wilmington	DE	C	B-	C+	388336.9	24.85	10.2	7.7	7.9	44.7	5.6	7.6	16.2
Tecumseh Federal Bank	Tecumseh	NE	B-	B	B	47.8	-2.39	2.0	1.2	39.5	15.1	10.0	21.9	0.0
Tejas Bank	Monahans	TX	A	A-	B+	192.2	4.69	20.4	2.4	1.8	27.8	8.3	9.9	18.5
Templeton Savings Bank	Templeton	IA	A-	A-	A-	138.5	11.48	8.1	2.2	12.4	18.4	10.0	13.7	0.0
▼ Tempo Bank	Trenton	IL	D+	C-	C-	102.1	7.59	1.5	1.0	72.0	0.0	7.0	9.0	0.0
Tennessee State Bank	Pigeon Forge	TN	A-	A-	B	789.9	19.15	4.9	2.9	16.3	20.5	8.8	10.2	17.0
Tensas State Bank	Newellton	LA	B+	B+	B	163.6	4.97	7.5	1.3	14.0	28.8	10.0	12.8	0.0
Terrabank, N.A.	Miami	FL	C	C+	C+	504.0	18.53	6.9	0.4	16.9	32.5	5.9	7.9	15.5
Terre Haute Savings Bank	Terre Haute	IN	C	C	C	420.6	27.24	9.9	1.1	20.2	20.5	6.3	8.3	13.6
Territorial Savings Bank	Honolulu	HI	B+	B+	B+	2107.1	1.03	0.5	0.0	68.3	14.9	10.0	11.6	26.9
Teutopolis State Bank	Teutopolis	IL	A	A	A	277.9	12.74	8.6	2.3	8.6	28.3	10.0	13.3	0.0
Texan Bank, N.A.	Houston	TX	C	C	C	405.8	23.27	20.0	0.2	3.5	0.8	6.3	10.4	0.0
▲ Texana Bank, N.A.	Linden	TX	B-	C-	D+	232.9	7.81	18.5	1.6	30.2	5.7	7.4	9.2	13.3
Texas Advantage Community Bank, N.A.	Alvin	TX	B	B-	B-	160.0	29.66	34.4	1.3	4.2	6.4	6.4	8.4	17.9
Texas Bank	Henderson	TX	B-	B-	B	586.8	19.96	10.6	4.5	14.7	27.8	8.2	9.8	0.0
Texas Bank and Trust Co.	Longview	TX	A-	A-	B+	3116.1	18.23	17.6	1.4	19.7	7.2	9.8	10.9	15.6
Texas Bank Financial	Weatherford	TX	A-	B+	B+	504.9	20.01	2.0	0.1	71.0	0.5	9.4	10.6	17.3
Texas Brand Bank	Dallas	TX	B+	B+	B+	301.7	43.28	28.9	0.1	4.9	0.9	8.6	10.0	17.0
Texas Capital Bank, N.A.	Dallas	TX	C+	B-	B-	38388.6	14.57	19.6	0.2	2.8	3.5	5.4	7.4	11.4
Texas Champion Bank	Corpus Christi	TX	C	C-	D+	386.3	21.34	25.8	1.0	3.7	3.7	6.7	11.5	0.0
▼ Texas Citizens Bank, N.A.	Pasadena	TX	D	C-	C-	557.5	7.01	28.9	1.7	4.7	0.8	8.5	10.0	14.6
▼ Texas Community Bank	Laredo	TX	A-	A	A-	1551.0	8.19	13.3	1.1	10.8	14.4	9.7	10.8	20.5
Texas Exchange Bank, SSB	Crowley	TX	A-	A	A	2115.3	96.04	23.2	0.0	0.0	24.0	10.0	12.8	20.2
Texas Financial Bank	Eden	TX	A-	A-	B+	112.8	10.45	4.4	0.8	0.5	38.4	8.7	10.2	0.0
Texas First Bank	Texas City	TX	A-	A-	A-	1668.5	52.15	15.5	0.5	8.2	30.0	7.5	9.3	0.0
Texas Gulf Bank, N.A.	Houston	TX	B+	B-	B+	678.3	-2.28	17.0	0.6	16.4	27.7	8.1	10.4	0.0
Texas Heritage Bank	Boerne	TX	B	B	B-	176.3	20.37	20.5	1.1	16.5	0.1	6.1	8.1	14.6
Texas Heritage National Bank	Daingerfield	TX	B-	B	B	246.9	72.55	19.0	3.1	17.6	7.6	6.1	10.6	0.0
Texas National Bank	Mercedes	TX	B	B	B	419.7	42.22	29.7	1.1	12.8	9.0	7.1	9.1	15.2
Texas National Bank	Sweetwater	TX	C+	C+	C+	154.8	8.41	8.7	1.7	5.8	57.1	7.7	9.5	0.0
Texas National Bank of Jacksonville	Jacksonville	TX	B	B	B-	617.8	10.51	14.7	2.7	26.2	2.2	8.7	10.1	15.5
Texas Partners Bank	San Antonio	TX	B-	B	B	1046.6	28.64	35.2	0.4	7.9	5.8	5.1	7.9	11.1
Texas Regional Bank	Harlingen	TX	B-	B-	C+	1448.1	46.69	15.5	0.7	6.2	34.3	4.9	8.8	11.0
Texas Republic Bank, N.A.	Frisco	TX	A-	A-	B+	370.8	24.60	15.1	0.2	23.0	0.0	9.2	10.5	0.0
Texas Security Bank	Dallas	TX	B+	A-	A-	934.7	91.30	36.5	0.1	7.9	21.1	8.9	10.3	15.4
▼ Texas State Bank	San Angelo	TX	A-	A	A-	340.6	24.20	11.9	0.9	10.9	35.3	9.6	10.7	21.0
TexasBank	Brownwood	TX	A	A	B+	586.4	17.88	9.4	1.1	12.1	9.6	10.0	12.3	20.0
Texico State Bank	Texico	IL	D-	D-	D-	11.3	38.04	30.8	1.6	18.1	0.0	6.0	10.1	11.7
TexStar National Bank	Universal City	TX	B+	B+	B	395.8	40.31	14.0	0.5	4.8	7.8	7.4	9.3	17.9
▲ Thayer County Bank	Hebron	NE	C+	C	C-	71.1	10.53	17.5	2.5	13.0	19.9	10.0	11.2	0.0
The Bank	Oberlin	KS	D+	D+	C-	372.5	12.67	5.9	0.3	0.8	15.7	10.0	12.6	23.0
The Bank	Jennings	LA	B+	A-	B+	298.2	22.57	13.7	11.2	26.1	6.3	9.0	10.7	0.0

Asset Quality Index	Adjusted Non-Performing Loans		Net Charge-Offs Avg Loans	Profitability Index	Net Income ($Mil)	Return on Assets (R.O.A.)	Return on Equity (R.O.E.)	Net Interest Spread	Overhead Efficiency Ratio	Liquidity Index	Liquidity Ratio	Hot Money Ratio	Stability Index
	as a % of Total Loans	as a % of Capital											
5.9	2.93	na	-0.15	5.9	5.6	1.20	11.03	3.62	58.0	2.9	34.0	18.3	7.0
6.5	0.82	4.2	0.24	4.4	242.0	0.63	6.05	3.21	60.6	2.6	15.9	8.0	9.7
6.6	na	0.0	na	9.5	7.0	9.08	9.38	0.79	76.5	4.0	na	0.0	6.3
9.4	0.10	na	0.04	1.1	0.0	0.13	1.03	3.28	95.9	1.8	38.7	44.0	4.8
6.2	0.42	na	0.07	8.8	5.9	1.71	14.59	3.57	62.8	0.6	14.1	47.6	9.3
6.7	0.04	na	0.00	5.8	0.5	1.33	10.56	4.17	72.1	4.5	23.9	6.2	7.4
5.8	0.64	na	0.13	5.7	0.8	1.12	12.56	4.25	66.3	4.8	26.1	5.0	5.1
5.4	4.78	na	0.01	0.2	-0.1	-0.13	-1.03	3.60	122.4	1.9	42.0	41.9	5.3
7.1	0.15	na	-0.04	4.4	0.6	1.22	12.09	3.30	73.0	1.8	21.7	22.2	5.9
8.2	0.00	na	0.00	0.0	-1.2	-2.56	-8.53	3.61	147.7	2.5	25.2	2.1	1.5
8.7	0.00	na	0.19	1.0	-0.1	-0.18	-1.50	2.55	107.1	1.3	29.8	42.8	6.5
7.0	0.90	na	0.16	8.5	2.8	1.92	12.96	4.26	58.3	4.2	33.2	11.5	9.1
5.5	3.51	na	0.00	3.3	0.4	0.51	5.32	3.54	84.4	1.7	24.9	22.4	6.0
4.0	1.19	7.8	0.10	5.9	39.9	1.01	7.44	5.65	66.4	1.0	8.8	17.9	10.0
6.5	0.90	na	-0.10	2.6	0.8	0.32	2.62	3.35	80.6	2.5	13.5	16.2	7.0
5.0	1.23	6.7	0.12	3.4	133.8	0.38	3.41	3.46	75.2	3.3	20.2	8.4	9.3
4.2	0.25	na	3.47	2.7	-1.8	-0.83	-4.36	7.06	81.7	0.2	11.7	99.7	6.6
4.7	1.47	4.5	5.33	5.1	112.1	0.65	5.04	8.00	40.6	3.3	71.2	0.0	7.0
5.6	0.82	3.1	0.39	2.5	791.4	0.29	2.53	2.04	61.7	3.1	55.0	1.0	8.4
9.4	0.27	na	-0.05	2.8	0.1	0.34	1.59	3.26	89.8	3.9	44.5	16.3	7.1
8.1	0.21	na	0.08	9.1	2.8	1.91	17.04	3.84	45.7	5.8	39.6	4.8	8.5
7.5	0.04	3.2	0.00	5.3	1.0	1.00	6.53	3.35	59.6	4.3	40.5	13.7	8.4
5.8	1.21	na	0.01	0.0	-2.1	-2.84	-30.07	2.26	111.8	1.7	25.3	25.3	5.5
6.1	0.48	na	-0.45	5.5	7.8	1.46	13.27	3.89	68.7	4.8	28.9	6.2	6.9
5.1	2.88	na	0.20	5.3	1.5	1.27	9.34	3.81	63.9	2.2	34.0	24.7	7.9
8.9	0.69	na	0.15	2.4	1.2	0.32	3.70	3.20	84.2	3.4	39.1	16.8	5.4
5.8	0.66	na	0.02	2.6	1.1	0.38	3.98	2.90	86.6	3.6	35.8	15.8	4.2
10.0	0.19	1.0	0.01	4.5	13.5	0.86	7.92	2.90	57.9	2.5	16.9	17.1	9.0
8.8	0.00	na	0.00	8.2	3.2	1.61	11.85	3.48	40.7	5.5	40.9	7.2	8.0
4.2	0.89	na	-0.06	4.1	2.2	0.77	6.83	3.79	74.3	1.0	17.4	32.4	5.3
7.4	0.08	1.4	0.06	7.2	3.1	1.83	20.96	4.19	74.9	0.9	7.5	26.0	4.1
8.2	0.00	na	0.00	4.8	1.1	1.03	11.30	3.86	65.6	1.8	28.1	24.0	4.7
5.0	0.76	na	0.08	4.6	4.4	1.06	10.62	4.02	70.3	2.0	26.1	20.6	6.5
7.1	0.58	3.4	0.03	6.6	28.0	1.29	10.87	3.38	56.5	3.8	21.3	11.5	9.9
6.0	0.63	na	0.00	10.0	11.3	3.20	31.94	5.18	54.9	0.6	10.5	43.4	8.5
7.2	0.00	na	-0.01	4.9	2.0	0.94	9.11	4.14	58.9	1.0	15.7	31.9	7.2
5.6	0.63	5.7	0.68	2.8	16.0	0.06	0.75	2.41	67.8	4.0	34.0	1.4	7.2
3.8	1.96	na	-0.05	2.6	0.7	0.27	2.41	3.89	82.4	4.2	15.0	7.5	5.2
0.7	6.40	34.8	0.51	2.1	0.5	0.12	1.33	4.07	88.9	2.7	15.3	13.7	5.5
8.7	0.01	0.1	0.03	5.7	12.4	1.10	9.65	3.30	57.9	2.9	31.3	23.1	9.9
9.3	0.00	0.0	0.14	6.0	14.3	1.50	13.59	2.25	50.0	3.1	72.0	29.4	9.7
9.3	0.33	na	0.45	5.2	0.9	1.03	10.15	3.10	65.7	4.4	41.5	13.4	6.6
7.0	1.17	na	0.00	6.9	18.5	1.59	14.75	3.97	57.5	5.5	34.3	7.9	9.6
5.8	1.40	na	0.05	6.1	7.5	1.49	13.86	3.78	62.8	3.9	18.6	9.9	8.2
8.1	0.10	na	0.12	5.7	1.6	1.24	14.46	4.52	64.6	3.1	19.5	14.1	5.8
4.6	0.69	na	0.30	3.5	0.9	0.62	6.04	3.99	71.8	1.8	22.3	22.0	6.2
7.7	0.09	na	-0.02	8.8	5.5	1.96	23.98	5.65	58.0	1.4	12.4	25.4	5.2
9.3	0.00	na	0.13	3.4	0.8	0.68	6.31	2.96	75.7	5.8	49.2	8.1	6.2
5.1	0.55	4.5	0.30	5.4	4.4	1.00	9.82	3.94	59.2	0.7	12.2	42.9	7.0
8.0	0.05	0.5	1.76	3.8	1.9	0.27	3.08	3.57	59.4	4.8	15.1	4.0	7.7
8.0	0.78	na	0.04	4.3	9.0	0.98	10.14	4.34	71.0	4.3	38.8	15.5	7.6
7.6	0.00	na	0.00	8.2	3.9	1.49	13.82	4.41	55.2	1.4	20.9	27.7	7.9
8.4	0.07	na	0.01	4.6	4.9	0.81	9.80	2.81	63.3	2.4	25.1	12.4	6.7
9.2	0.00	na	0.00	5.6	3.1	1.29	11.12	3.02	64.5	6.4	48.7	3.9	7.7
8.6	0.17	na	-0.01	9.5	8.8	2.16	17.06	4.14	56.2	4.5	33.1	10.2	10.0
6.6	0.48	na	0.00	3.7	0.1	0.95	10.92	3.67	85.2	6.2	43.8	0.0	1.6
8.5	0.03	na	0.04	3.9	2.2	0.86	8.37	3.24	64.3	1.5	33.9	28.5	6.3
3.7	4.85	na	0.07	4.3	0.5	0.93	8.26	3.27	61.0	2.9	19.5	15.2	5.6
0.9	10.42	na	0.03	8.0	4.6	1.65	12.54	3.30	51.8	4.1	24.9	8.0	9.4
4.5	1.14	na	0.14	6.6	2.6	1.26	11.60	5.09	61.2	1.9	25.7	19.2	6.7

Name	City	State	Rating	2019 Rating	2018 Rating	Total Assets ($Mil)	One Year Asset Growth	Asset Mix (As a % of Total Assets)				Capital-ization Index	Lever-age Ratio	Risk-Based Capital Ratio
								Comm-ercial Loans	Cons-umer Loans	Mort-gage Loans	Secur-ities			
▲ The Bank of Soperton	Soperton	GA	B+	B	C+	108.7	18.57	15.4	7.4	23.1	3.2	8.2	9.8	15.4
▼ The Bankers Bank	Oklahoma City	OK	C	B-	B-	204.0	-36.15	4.2	0.5	1.5	0.5	10.0	13.0	0.0
▲ The Farmers State Bank and Trust Co.	Jacksonville	IL	B	B-	C	217.1	10.37	4.8	6.6	10.7	40.4	10.0	11.4	0.0
The Provident Bank	Amesbury	MA	B+	B+	B+	1497.2	38.90	38.6	0.5	3.1	2.3	9.2	12.6	14.3
Think Mutual Bank	Rochester	MN	B+	B+	B+	1903.3	14.49	2.6	10.9	43.8	30.3	10.0	15.5	0.0
▲ Third Coast Bank, SSB	Humble	TX	B-	C	C-	1774.7	90.04	40.3	0.2	6.0	0.8	7.8	10.1	13.2
Third Federal S&L Assn. of Cleveland	Cleveland	OH	C+	B-	B-	14614.2	0.82	0.0	0.0	76.8	3.1	9.1	10.4	20.0
Thomaston Savings Bank	Thomaston	CT	C	C+	C+	1349.6	20.39	15.4	2.5	22.2	19.4	8.5	10.0	0.0
Thomasville National Bank	Thomasville	GA	A-	A-	A-	1167.6	22.40	22.2	1.5	21.9	4.9	6.8	8.8	12.7
▼ Three Rivers Bank of Montana	Kalispell	MT	B-	B+	A-	210.8	24.42	27.5	2.1	8.5	7.7	6.6	9.8	0.0
Thrivent Trust Co.	Appleton	WI	U	U	U	70.3	9.48	0.0	0.0	0.0	36.4	10.0	34.3	134.7
▲ Thumb Bank & Trust	Pigeon	MI	B-	C+	C+	322.1	20.35	13.7	1.1	7.3	16.9	5.9	7.9	12.2
▼ TIAA, FSB	Jacksonville	FL	C-	C+	B-	42826.9	4.05	2.4	0.0	37.1	10.8	5.3	7.3	12.3
TIB The Independent BankersBank, N.A.	Farmers Branch	TX	B-	B	B-	3618.6	37.41	3.1	1.9	0.9	8.0	5.4	7.4	17.3
▲ Tilden Bank	Tilden	NE	B	C+	C	91.8	8.64	4.4	2.1	1.8	5.2	9.1	10.4	15.2
Timberland Bank	Hoquiam	WA	A	A	A	1563.3	25.58	12.6	0.2	8.5	5.6	10.0	11.1	21.0
Timberline Bank	Grand Junction	CO	B-	B-	B-	487.1	58.18	33.6	0.8	8.9	15.4	5.2	7.2	11.7
▼ Tioga Franklin Savings Bank	Philadelphia	PA	C-	C	B-	88.1	94.49	46.6	0.5	31.0	1.1	6.6	8.6	15.6
Tioga State Bank	Spencer	NY	A-	A-	B+	531.1	10.22	17.1	1.3	24.3	22.4	10.0	12.2	20.9
▲ Tipton Latham Bank, N.A.	Tipton	MO	B+	B	B	150.6	8.05	13.2	3.0	20.1	19.0	9.8	11.0	0.0
Titan Bank, N.A.	Mineral Wells	TX	A-	A-	A-	326.0	129.14	19.6	0.0	14.2	12.5	7.0	9.0	0.0
Titonka Savings Bank	Titonka	IA	C+	C+	B-	196.7	8.62	4.2	1.4	9.2	35.9	10.0	11.3	21.2
▼ TNB Bank	Tuscola	IL	C	C+	C	95.2	10.87	4.2	1.8	7.7	10.5	10.0	11.4	20.3
TNBANK	Oak Ridge	TN	C	C	C	276.9	17.60	9.7	1.0	15.9	9.9	5.3	8.4	11.2
Today's Bank	Huntsville	AR	C+	C+	C	284.0	17.29	10.3	1.4	18.7	18.5	6.4	8.5	12.8
Tolleson Private Bank	Dallas	TX	A-	A-	B	620.9	14.63	12.5	4.1	40.8	7.4	6.4	8.4	13.1
Tomahawk Community Bank, SSB	Tomahawk	WI	B	B	B-	169.0	17.33	10.2	4.4	30.9	6.1	10.0	12.4	20.5
Tompkins State Bank	Avon	IL	B	B-	B-	252.4	16.21	13.9	1.3	7.3	25.6	6.5	8.5	13.2
Tompkins Trust Co.	Ithaca	NY	B+	B+	B+	2366.9	15.53	7.7	1.2	24.1	28.2	6.3	8.4	14.5
▼ Torrington Savings Bank	Torrington	CT	C+	B	B-	860.1	4.44	2.2	0.1	53.6	12.8	10.0	19.3	43.6
Touchmark National Bank	Alpharetta	GA	B	B	B-	449.5	10.26	26.4	0.0	1.5	4.1	10.0	11.3	25.5
Touchstone Bank	Prince George	VA	C+	B-	C+	527.1	11.77	11.0	0.8	20.9	15.4	6.5	9.2	0.0
Towanda State Bank	Towanda	KS	E+	E+	E+	10.9	6.96	0.5	6.3	49.5	14.4	3.5	5.5	12.4
Tower Community Bank	Jasper	TN	C+	C+	C-	233.7	12.38	10.7	2.8	18.9	5.7	4.1	9.1	0.0
Town & Country Bank	Salem	MO	A-	A-	A-	615.0	18.10	5.6	2.9	30.5	17.3	9.2	10.4	18.5
Town & Country Bank	Ravenna	NE	A-	A-	A-	170.9	0.44	6.4	1.5	2.0	25.7	10.0	13.3	0.0
Town & Country Bank	Las Vegas	NV	B+	B+	B+	244.6	49.95	15.0	0.0	2.4	0.0	8.9	10.3	0.0
Town & Country Bank and Trust Co.	Bardstown	KY	A-	A	A-	361.7	14.73	7.9	1.0	18.7	14.1	10.0	11.6	0.0
Town and Country Bank	Springfield	IL	B-	B-	B-	866.8	4.93	14.9	0.4	15.5	14.3	7.3	9.2	13.3
Town and Country Bank Midwest	Quincy	IL	A-	A-	B+	191.4	1.66	24.9	1.2	13.7	6.0	10.0	12.1	0.0
Town Bank, N.A.	Hartland	WI	B	B	B	2949.1	23.24	28.4	17.1	4.4	10.3	5.9	7.9	11.8
Town Center Bank	New Lenox	IL	C+	C+	C	155.7	53.32	35.8	1.6	0.8	10.2	8.1	9.7	14.1
Town-Country National Bank	Camden	AL	A-	A-	B	120.8	10.35	14.6	12.6	12.7	27.2	10.0	18.3	0.0
TowneBank	Portsmouth	VA	B+	A-	A-	14795.4	23.08	15.3	2.2	12.8	9.0	6.9	8.9	15.3
Toyota Financial Savings Bank	Henderson	NV	C-	C	C+	1896.2	87.44	23.7	0.2	51.6	0.4	8.0	9.7	26.0
TPNB Bank	Paris	MO	B+	B+	B+	86.0	6.96	4.3	1.2	8.0	44.1	10.0	14.6	24.5
Tradition Capital Bank	Wayzata	MN	B-	C+	B-	1232.9	45.00	23.6	0.8	10.0	10.2	4.5	8.6	10.7
Traditional Bank, Inc.	Mount Sterling	KY	A-	A-	A-	1961.2	21.21	11.8	0.3	20.3	21.5	7.4	9.4	12.9
Traditions Bank	Cullman	AL	B+	B+	B	465.1	24.97	16.4	6.9	28.5	4.9	7.5	9.3	14.4
▼ Traditions First Bank	Erin	TN	C+	B-	B-	175.4	15.52	4.5	1.4	16.6	22.4	6.0	8.0	12.5
TrailWest Bank	Lolo	MT	B+	B+	B	822.6	23.10	11.2	1.8	26.3	3.0	6.8	8.8	14.4
Transact Bank, N.A.	Denver	CO	D	D	D	22.0	-18.11	0.0	0.0	0.0	5.0	10.0	17.4	105.5
TransPecos Banks, SSB	Pecos	TX	C+	C+	B-	408.3	68.32	42.5	1.4	19.4	11.9	6.1	8.1	12.5
Transportation Alliance Bank, Inc.	Ogden	UT	C	C	C+	958.4	26.57	69.4	2.7	0.0	4.6	4.7	12.8	0.0
Tri City National Bank	Oak Creek	WI	B+	A-	B+	1732.5	19.86	5.3	0.2	8.9	26.8	9.1	10.4	0.0
Tri Counties Bank	Chico	CA	A-	A	A-	7447.9	16.68	8.5	1.1	7.3	19.7	8.3	9.9	15.1
Tri Valley Bank	Talmage	NE	C-	C	C	115.0	135.99	10.8	1.4	11.4	3.3	4.9	7.8	11.0
▲ Tri-County Bank	Brown City	MI	A	A-	A-	380.2	19.30	12.7	1.1	6.6	8.7	10.0	11.6	0.0
▲ Tri-County Bank	Stuart	NE	B	B-	C+	164.6	19.74	10.7	2.2	14.2	27.6	6.5	8.5	12.4
Tri-County Bank & Trust Co.	Roachdale	IN	B-	B	B	217.8	0.48	5.8	4.1	15.6	39.0	10.0	12.5	0.0

Asset Quality Index	Adjusted Non-Performing Loans as a % of Total Loans	as a % of Capital	Net Charge-Offs / Avg Loans	Profitability Index	Net Income ($Mil)	Return on Assets (R.O.A.)	Return on Equity (R.O.E.)	Net Interest Spread	Overhead Efficiency Ratio	Liquidity Index	Liquidity Ratio	Hot Money Ratio	Stability Index
7.2	0.39	na	0.39	7.4	1.1	1.51	15.33	5.13	67.4	1.6	26.3	27.4	7.5
6.1	0.93	na	0.26	0.7	-11.7	-6.74	-43.40	3.11	223.9	0.8	20.8	27.4	6.5
5.6	2.31	na	0.02	4.0	1.2	0.69	5.91	3.19	68.7	6.0	38.9	3.1	6.1
4.6	1.99	na	0.09	4.6	7.5	0.76	5.76	4.11	63.7	2.8	4.4	4.4	9.2
8.3	0.07	na	0.05	4.5	11.6	0.87	5.31	2.88	67.8	6.5	38.5	2.9	9.4
5.6	0.94	na	0.06	4.7	11.5	0.95	11.69	4.24	66.8	0.8	7.2	21.9	6.3
7.5	1.14	7.0	-0.04	3.2	55.2	0.49	5.25	1.60	64.2	0.7	7.2	30.5	7.7
6.2	1.75	na	0.01	3.0	5.0	0.55	5.68	3.02	78.5	3.2	28.8	17.1	6.8
7.9	0.27	na	0.00	9.8	14.5	1.80	19.49	3.68	45.7	3.2	9.0	10.4	9.6
3.9	0.85	8.8	0.04	6.2	1.6	1.10	10.58	4.82	64.1	3.2	17.8	13.1	7.1
6.5	na	na	na	2.1	0.3	0.54	1.06	-0.06	99.2	4.1	148.1	100.0	3.6
6.9	0.58	na	-0.02	4.9	2.6	1.12	12.78	3.73	69.4	2.8	28.3	16.9	4.7
3.7	1.84	14.7	0.11	0.7	-469.3	-1.47	-18.37	1.91	149.3	1.4	14.2	19.4	6.9
8.7	0.04	0.2	0.15	3.6	17.4	0.68	8.30	1.56	69.3	5.8	59.7	5.7	6.6
5.8	2.19	na	-0.02	5.4	0.7	1.09	10.23	3.81	69.4	5.2	29.1	4.0	7.3
7.8	0.56	2.2	0.00	9.2	17.9	1.67	13.42	3.76	49.5	5.3	27.8	6.4	10.0
4.8	0.88	na	-0.03	4.7	3.6	1.15	14.85	4.23	71.9	4.9	9.4	2.2	3.9
4.6	1.07	na	0.00	1.9	0.0	0.01	0.14	3.51	81.1	0.4	10.1	58.0	4.8
7.5	1.12	na	0.03	5.7	4.2	1.11	8.99	4.04	63.5	3.6	14.6	8.9	8.1
5.7	1.74	na	-0.19	5.8	1.8	1.67	15.37	3.12	52.3	1.3	29.3	35.3	7.0
8.6	0.02	1.3	0.00	9.6	5.0	2.57	31.14	3.52	41.7	6.0	36.0	1.8	6.8
7.0	2.69	na	0.35	2.9	1.0	0.73	6.07	2.93	78.3	4.1	51.4	17.3	5.3
5.9	2.42	na	0.33	0.8	-0.1	-0.19	-1.56	2.48	106.2	3.0	45.5	22.9	6.6
4.7	1.30	na	0.06	4.1	1.3	0.66	7.83	3.74	75.2	2.6	21.4	16.1	4.4
6.7	0.27	na	0.01	3.0	1.4	0.69	7.75	3.52	85.7	0.9	21.6	39.6	5.2
8.5	0.01	na	0.00	8.9	9.7	2.16	24.98	2.86	46.8	4.3	16.9	7.1	7.5
8.0	0.63	na	0.00	4.7	1.2	0.96	7.43	3.97	69.4	4.9	28.8	5.7	7.2
7.8	0.06	na	0.02	5.2	2.3	1.25	12.16	3.57	64.0	2.5	14.9	12.7	6.3
6.8	0.76	5.7	0.13	7.5	23.6	1.41	19.47	3.31	66.7	3.7	8.2	6.0	6.3
9.9	0.72	na	0.01	1.1	-4.7	-0.74	-3.74	2.58	79.1	3.2	37.7	18.3	8.8
4.9	0.70	na	0.13	4.6	2.3	0.70	6.13	2.62	57.2	0.6	11.8	50.2	7.5
5.8	0.98	na	0.04	3.0	1.6	0.44	4.43	3.93	78.3	3.5	25.5	12.7	5.7
0.3	7.64	85.5	0.11	0.0	-0.1	-0.81	-14.26	3.55	122.3	3.9	24.0	10.0	0.8
7.5	0.14	na	0.01	4.3	1.6	0.96	10.12	4.46	78.6	2.6	10.9	15.4	4.6
6.3	0.50	3.1	0.04	6.3	6.3	1.44	12.11	3.67	64.0	3.6	17.8	11.3	9.0
7.4	0.00	0.5	-0.11	7.1	1.8	1.45	10.67	3.96	57.9	2.5	24.6	17.6	8.6
5.6	3.99	na	0.00	7.2	2.3	1.50	13.76	4.00	53.5	5.2	40.0	8.4	7.9
8.5	0.63	1.8	0.00	6.2	3.1	1.22	10.06	3.85	66.3	5.3	30.9	3.7	8.0
5.7	0.47	3.9	0.10	4.1	4.9	0.76	7.64	3.49	66.3	3.5	11.4	11.0	6.8
6.2	0.66	na	-0.01	10.0	5.6	3.87	31.38	4.17	34.6	4.1	25.8	9.5	8.8
6.5	0.33	2.3	0.02	3.7	12.4	0.59	5.54	2.59	59.7	3.2	15.4	6.4	7.6
3.4	2.92	na	-0.08	3.3	0.6	0.61	5.72	3.55	78.5	1.9	17.0	19.9	6.4
6.0	1.47	na	-0.02	9.7	1.8	2.12	11.25	5.01	58.4	2.0	40.7	34.6	9.1
7.3	0.29	1.3	0.00	5.1	95.5	1.11	9.16	2.98	66.8	3.3	21.7	9.3	9.8
9.3	0.22	1.2	-0.04	2.2	3.2	0.28	2.47	1.37	58.4	0.6	15.9	20.1	7.2
5.7	2.98	8.1	0.00	4.4	0.6	0.98	6.54	3.14	66.3	4.5	36.5	11.4	8.2
8.3	0.08	0.5	0.03	5.4	8.6	1.09	12.79	3.82	52.8	2.4	13.8	11.3	7.1
7.7	0.62	na	0.01	6.5	21.8	1.63	16.44	3.31	51.0	2.1	22.3	16.1	9.3
6.2	0.40	2.6	0.53	6.6	4.0	1.25	12.84	5.38	61.9	1.6	18.6	17.7	5.0
8.7	0.00	na	0.00	3.3	0.8	0.59	6.54	3.31	79.3	2.1	30.2	23.6	5.1
8.2	0.20	na	-0.12	6.0	7.7	1.39	15.63	3.56	59.1	4.2	26.0	7.4	7.2
9.9	0.00	na	0.00	0.0	-2.0	-11.15	-51.82	1.35	326.0	7.2	83.9	3.0	5.3
4.1	0.60	11.5	1.03	3.9	1.9	0.74	10.55	6.48	71.2	0.9	11.8	11.7	3.5
3.8	0.82	na	2.34	4.4	4.2	0.63	5.41	7.80	69.3	0.7	15.2	33.1	7.4
6.6	1.71	5.8	-0.09	4.4	10.2	0.86	7.63	3.42	74.0	6.5	34.0	1.4	8.9
7.1	0.58	2.4	-0.01	5.6	43.1	0.82	6.14	4.06	58.8	5.5	25.4	3.8	10.0
5.0	0.66	na	0.00	4.6	0.6	1.07	16.04	2.63	54.7	1.3	20.3	29.2	3.7
7.5	0.40	2.1	0.15	9.8	5.1	1.98	15.97	4.56	50.6	4.6	25.7	6.1	7.7
8.4	0.38	na	0.00	5.8	1.4	1.17	13.52	4.54	66.6	4.2	29.9	10.5	5.4
6.9	0.68	na	0.00	3.1	0.9	0.57	4.41	3.11	78.0	6.0	61.5	10.1	6.9

Name	City	State	2019 Rating	2018 Rating	Rating	Total Assets ($Mil)	One Year Asset Growth	Asset Mix (As a % of Total Assets)				Capital- ization Index	Lever- age Ratio	Risk- Based Capital Ratio
								Comm- ercial Loans	Cons- umer Loans	Mort- gage Loans	Secur- ities			
Tri-County Trust Co.	Glasgow	MO	B-	B-	B	63.4	8.19	11.6	5.7	23.3	25.3	7.9	11.4	0.0
Tri-State Bank of Memphis	Memphis	TN	D+	C-	C-	101.2	13.06	5.9	6.6	7.0	23.4	6.0	8.0	14.9
Tri-Valley Bank	Randolph	IA	B-	B-	C+	66.6	11.29	9.9	1.5	11.4	28.1	10.0	11.0	0.0
Triad Bank	Frontenac	MO	B	C+	C	573.8	49.33	27.8	0.3	13.1	3.3	5.2	8.8	11.1
Triad Bank, N.A.	Tulsa	OK	B+	B	B-	210.6	15.92	17.9	2.2	28.2	0.0	8.0	9.6	0.0
Triad Business Bank	Greensboro	NC	D			241.3	na	49.6	0.0	2.4	7.5	10.0	37.1	59.7
TriCentury Bank	De Soto	KS	A-	A-	B+	120.4	19.48	10.5	0.8	19.1	0.0	9.1	11.2	0.0
Trinity Bank, N.A.	Fort Worth	TX	A	A-	A	342.1	15.95	41.7	0.1	4.5	26.4	9.6	10.8	20.6
TriStar Bank	Dickson	TN	C+	C+	C	358.7	17.87	12.2	5.9	19.8	13.6	6.0	8.0	12.2
TriState Capital Bank	Pittsburgh	PA	B-	B-	B-	9414.7	32.34	31.1	25.8	0.3	8.6	5.0	7.0	12.5
Triumph Bank	Memphis	TN	C+	C+	B-	925.2	10.14	20.3	0.5	22.7	15.7	6.6	9.7	12.2
Triumph State Bank	Trimont	MN	C+	C+	C+	75.8	3.88	11.0	3.9	1.5	8.4	8.3	9.8	0.0
Troy Bank & Trust Co.	Troy	AL	B+	B+	B+	1081.7	14.33	13.7	2.5	14.2	24.2	8.1	10.0	0.0
TruBank	Indianola	IA	B	B-	B	342.5	12.08	9.0	0.7	9.0	14.8	9.0	10.3	0.0
Truist Bank	Charlotte	NC	B+	B+	B+	488016.0	112.29	15.7	11.0	11.5	17.6	6.7	8.7	13.1
TruPoint Bank	Grundy	VA	B-	B-	C	490.9	9.28	17.1	4.8	13.6	18.8	7.7	9.5	16.0
Trust Bank	Lenox	GA	C+	C	C	41.2	7.19	3.4	6.4	14.5	4.8	9.6	10.7	19.2
Trust Co. of Toledo, N.A.	Holland	OH	U	U	U	6.3	11.40	0.0	0.0	0.0	31.1	10.0	97.3	299.4
Trustar Bank	Great Falls	VA	D			277.5	169.12	29.7	0.1	11.9	0.0	10.0	19.1	26.7
TrustBank	Olney	IL	B+	B+	B+	279.6	19.43	13.0	2.1	15.0	6.6	6.4	10.3	0.0
▼ TrustCo Bank	Glenville	NY	B+	A-	B+	5735.5	9.83	1.1	0.2	65.2	8.2	8.1	9.8	19.8
Trustmark National Bank	Jackson	MS	B+	B+	B	15556.1	14.53	14.6	1.0	12.2	16.5	7.0	9.0	12.6
TrustTexas Bank, SSB	Cuero	TX	C+	B-	B-	356.1	3.83	3.8	0.9	26.3	37.1	10.0	12.0	0.0
▼ Truxton Trust Co.	Nashville	TN	A-	A	A	687.0	33.33	13.0	3.4	12.4	22.8	7.7	9.4	15.5
TS Bank	Treynor	IA	D+	D	D+	414.2	15.58	8.0	0.8	2.7	52.7	7.0	9.0	13.8
TSB Bank	Lomira	WI	B+	A-	B+	161.6	13.44	12.5	0.8	13.7	9.4	8.8	11.3	0.0
▼ Tucumcari Federal S&L Assn.	Tucumcari	NM	C-	C+	C+	35.0	2.64	0.2	0.6	50.9	19.3	10.0	14.9	34.3
Turbotville National Bank	Turbotville	PA	A-	B+	B+	160.9	6.84	7.3	1.5	24.5	19.8	10.0	16.7	0.0
Turtle Mountain State Bank	Belcourt	ND	C	C	D+	85.9	156.65	17.4	2.7	1.5	2.8	6.7	8.7	0.0
▲ Tustin Community Bank	Tustin	CA	B	B	B+	87.6	18.07	14.2	31.0	5.8	0.0	10.0	12.5	0.0
Twin City Bank	Longview	WA	B-	B-	C+	69.3	20.59	31.6	0.1	12.5	0.0	7.1	9.1	0.0
Twin River Bank	Lewiston	ID	B+	B+	B-	121.3	17.74	19.8	2.9	9.7	2.6	6.7	8.7	17.3
Twin Valley Bank	West Alexandria	OH	C+	C+	C+	95.3	19.90	12.5	2.1	17.6	21.5	6.3	8.5	0.0
▲ Two Rivers Bank	Blair	NE	A-	B+	B	144.7	1.23	8.3	1.7	13.2	26.0	10.0	13.5	20.5
Two Rivers Bank & Trust	Burlington	IA	B-	B-	B-	931.6	10.47	22.6	1.0	15.4	11.0	7.2	9.1	12.8
U.S. Bank N.A.	Minneapolis	MN	B	B	B-	530496.7	11.12	15.7	10.8	16.1	25.0	6.5	8.5	13.4
U.S. Bank Trust Co., N.A.	Portland	OR	U	U	U	19.9	5.95	0.0	0.0	0.0	0.0	10.0	101.	499.1
U.S. Bank Trust N.A.	Wilmington	DE	U	U	U	671.9	2.90	0.0	0.0	0.0	0.0	10.0	98.2	492.9
U.S. Bank Trust N.A. SD	Sioux Falls	SD	U	U	U	110.4	8.83	0.0	0.0	0.0	0.0	10.0	99.5	414.3
U.S. Century Bank	Doral	FL	C+	B-	B-	1491.0	16.19	11.4	0.1	16.0	12.7	6.7	8.7	14.3
UBank	Jellico	TN	B	B	B	75.5	12.59	19.2	7.2	16.1	9.5	10.0	12.9	0.0
UBank	Huntington	TX	B+	B+	B-	311.6	29.75	11.9	1.8	15.8	7.1	6.5	9.1	0.0
UBS Bank USA	Salt Lake City	UT	A-	A	A	77831.3	36.90	8.6	34.5	23.5	10.8	6.6	8.6	34.4
Uinta Bank	Mountain View	WY	B-	B-	B-	250.4	14.52	10.7	0.5	2.7	59.1	5.8	7.8	21.3
Ulster Savings Bank	Kingston	NY	B-	C+	C-	1133.6	19.98	4.0	2.0	36.1	11.2	7.9	9.6	15.4
▲ Ultima Bank Minnesota	Winger	MN	B	C+	C	200.7	6.06	16.6	1.5	6.2	0.0	6.5	10.3	0.0
UMB Bank & Trust, N.A.	Saint Louis	MO	U	U	U	3.0	0.20	0.0	0.0	0.0	0.0	10.0	99.9	103.0
UMB Bank, N.A.	Kansas City	MO	C+	B-	B-	30130.1	25.73	24.9	1.1	4.8	32.6	6.1	8.1	12.7
Umpqua Bank	Roseburg	OR	B-	B+	B+	29427.9	1.81	17.2	1.1	14.4	9.9	7.6	9.4	14.1
UNB Bank	Mount Carmel	PA	C-	C-	D+	156.4	6.51	1.9	0.9	40.9	33.0	7.5	9.3	0.0
UniBank	Lynnwood	WA	A-	A-	B+	393.0	16.56	22.1	0.0	0.3	14.7	10.0	14.4	21.2
UniBank for Savings	Whitinsville	MA	C+	B-	B-	2098.6	18.98	8.0	19.6	18.6	8.5	6.3	8.4	14.4
▼ UNICO Bank	Mineral Point	MO	D+	C	C+	383.3	13.51	8.4	3.6	28.8	8.9	4.5	7.7	10.8
Unified Bank	Martins Ferry	OH	A-	B+	B	694.9	2.99	14.5	1.2	15.1	22.8	9.0	10.3	16.2
Unified Trust Co., LLC	Lexington	KY	U	U	U	13.6	-20.94	0.0	0.0	0.0	0.0	10.0	51.4	0.0
Union Bank	Lake Odessa	MI	C-	C	C	245.2	27.79	21.5	0.9	7.3	6.3	5.8	7.8	12.0
▼ Union Bank	Greenville	NC	C+	B	B	971.0	23.29	11.4	0.4	12.5	24.8	7.0	9.0	14.7
Union Bank	Halliday	ND	C+	C+	C+	171.5	11.80	4.7	5.2	9.3	18.3	7.7	9.4	0.0
▼ Union Bank	Jamestown	TN	C-	C+	B-	212.9	7.44	6.8	3.6	16.8	38.2	10.0	11.4	22.7
Union Bank	Morrisville	VT	B	B	B	1008.3	19.44	11.4	0.3	20.3	8.8	5.4	7.4	13.6

Asset Quality Index	Adjusted Non-Performing Loans as a % of Total Loans	Adjusted Non-Performing Loans as a % of Capital	Net Charge-Offs Avg Loans	Profitability Index	Net Income ($Mil)	Return on Assets (R.O.A.)	Return on Equity (R.O.E.)	Net Interest Spread	Overhead Efficiency Ratio	Liquidity Index	Liquidity Ratio	Hot Money Ratio	Stability Index
4.8	2.98	na	0.22	4.7	0.5	1.04	8.79	3.97	68.3	0.8	21.1	40.8	7.5
3.0	5.56	na	0.29	0.9	-0.9	-1.20	-10.38	2.73	122.1	3.7	32.3	13.9	5.9
5.9	2.15	na	0.10	2.6	0.1	0.29	2.42	3.65	80.5	3.3	29.2	13.1	5.6
7.0	0.01	na	-0.01	6.1	4.5	1.25	14.77	3.99	50.4	2.0	12.3	5.5	5.7
4.7	1.34	na	0.02	6.4	1.9	1.39	12.80	4.85	65.2	4.7	20.3	5.0	6.6
8.4	0.00	na	0.00	0.0	-3.3	-5.22	0.00	2.34	286.9	6.7	45.3	0.5	2.0
8.6	0.00	0.0	0.00	5.4	0.9	1.01	8.99	3.19	56.8	3.4	20.6	12.8	7.0
8.5	0.12	na	-0.01	6.8	3.5	1.42	12.03	3.47	50.1	4.2	36.9	12.9	8.0
7.4	0.32	na	0.20	4.2	2.0	0.78	9.48	4.02	70.3	1.8	20.5	22.3	4.8
6.8	0.09	1.0	0.00	3.3	35.2	0.53	7.79	1.63	53.7	2.3	15.8	11.5	5.3
4.1	2.12	12.5	0.00	4.9	6.4	1.00	10.56	2.54	64.2	0.8	16.7	34.8	6.3
5.4	1.50	na	0.03	3.5	0.2	0.41	3.95	3.98	80.4	5.2	38.8	8.5	5.6
5.3	2.12	10.0	0.21	5.0	7.3	1.00	8.74	3.48	63.8	3.1	26.0	17.6	8.2
7.8	0.01	na	0.12	4.8	2.5	1.00	8.77	3.58	64.7	1.7	20.2	23.6	6.6
6.1	0.59	2.4	0.32	4.8	2986.0	0.82	6.19	3.17	66.0	5.3	25.8	2.7	10.0
7.9	0.14	0.9	0.04	3.4	2.3	0.65	6.49	3.40	74.3	3.5	14.4	11.5	5.2
2.7	3.66	na	-0.09	6.1	0.4	1.36	12.62	5.50	80.8	4.2	37.8	13.1	5.5
10.0	na	0.0	na	10.0	2.4	63.09	70.21	1.36	64.1	4.0	na	0.0	5.5
8.3	0.00	na	0.00	0.0	-3.4	-2.13	-9.29	2.61	155.7	3.0	19.8	14.5	1.5
5.2	0.68	na	-0.01	7.0	3.2	1.63	14.11	3.98	69.2	4.4	10.3	5.4	8.1
8.1	0.80	4.7	0.01	5.2	39.6	0.99	9.85	2.86	56.6	3.6	23.1	13.5	8.5
6.5	0.49	2.8	0.02	4.8	110.8	0.99	8.62	3.17	67.5	4.4	8.3	5.4	9.2
8.9	0.78	na	0.01	1.1	0.4	0.16	1.32	3.27	103.8	4.6	48.3	13.9	6.9
7.3	0.72	3.6	0.01	8.2	7.0	1.53	15.21	3.20	56.1	4.9	33.8	5.3	7.5
6.6	0.09	na	1.07	1.8	3.0	1.01	11.33	3.03	83.3	2.4	50.8	25.4	3.3
4.8	1.04	na	1.70	3.3	0.1	0.08	0.73	3.56	62.6	1.9	24.4	16.3	6.9
6.2	2.27	na	0.01	1.4	0.0	0.03	0.21	3.20	97.9	0.8	19.6	50.9	6.4
5.8	3.16	na	0.01	7.6	1.9	1.65	9.75	3.41	44.2	2.7	35.1	19.7	9.0
6.1	4.25	na	1.43	2.8	0.1	0.19	3.43	1.86	86.4	6.6	76.0	7.2	3.2
6.8	0.06	na	0.62	4.4	0.5	0.82	6.11	5.51	75.1	1.1	26.7	40.1	6.5
8.4	0.66	na	0.00	7.4	0.8	1.57	16.41	5.22	65.5	3.3	14.3	12.3	5.5
8.6	0.00	na	0.00	8.9	1.9	2.20	25.09	4.67	53.7	5.7	41.6	5.8	5.5
7.4	0.16	2.0	0.15	3.2	0.4	0.65	7.01	3.86	80.9	3.7	18.5	10.7	4.5
8.8	0.00	0.6	0.02	5.5	1.9	1.74	12.92	3.58	64.5	3.4	23.1	10.3	7.9
4.4	1.43	na	0.01	4.9	6.5	0.96	9.58	3.65	63.9	4.6	12.9	4.2	6.6
5.1	1.17	4.8	0.57	5.2	3403.4	0.89	9.00	2.79	58.2	5.4	35.6	2.3	9.6
10.0	na	0.0	na	10.0	0.9	5.88	5.86	4.44	17.0	4.0	na	0.0	6.3
9.3	na	0.0	na	9.5	12.5	2.49	2.54	0.77	32.8	4.0	na	0.0	7.0
10.0	na	0.0	na	9.5	6.5	8.01	8.13	0.66	21.3	4.0	na	0.0	7.0
8.4	0.63	2.2	0.01	3.5	6.6	0.63	5.37	3.28	68.2	3.0	27.2	18.5	9.2
7.6	0.34	na	0.28	5.2	0.6	1.15	8.69	4.66	73.5	1.0	12.0	30.5	7.3
5.1	1.29	na	-0.06	5.3	2.2	0.99	10.16	4.85	73.0	3.2	15.3	12.9	5.4
6.8	0.17	1.4	0.01	7.2	686.7	1.25	12.87	2.04	18.7	5.1	29.8	0.0	9.0
9.1	0.00	na	0.00	4.3	1.7	0.94	10.44	2.31	50.8	2.0	41.4	30.8	5.1
4.7	2.79	14.1	0.09	3.5	5.1	0.65	6.21	3.15	77.8	3.2	27.4	15.8	6.6
4.7	1.24	na	0.01	9.9	3.5	2.32	22.82	5.23	55.1	1.0	3.5	26.4	8.3
10.0	na	na	na	2.3	0.0	0.13	0.13	5.93	99.9	4.0	0.0	0.0	6.7
7.8	0.59	3.2	0.16	3.4	136.4	0.66	7.20	2.95	65.6	5.2	22.5	1.5	7.6
7.4	0.17	2.4	0.30	2.3	-1663.5	-7.62	-72.64	3.28	250.4	3.9	16.0	8.6	10.0
9.3	0.05	na	0.00	1.7	0.3	0.28	2.82	2.33	94.3	3.9	34.7	13.8	5.4
7.1	0.26	na	-0.01	8.6	4.5	1.64	11.24	4.31	51.2	0.9	8.8	14.3	9.0
4.3	1.19	7.8	0.16	3.0	5.8	0.37	4.60	2.59	73.1	5.4	27.7	5.6	6.4
2.0	2.53	na	0.15	3.6	1.9	0.72	8.49	3.59	78.9	1.6	14.9	22.8	3.9
7.5	0.35	na	0.09	5.7	7.6	1.44	12.14	3.83	55.9	4.6	27.1	6.7	7.5
10.0	na	na	na	9.5	4.8	39.90	59.39	0.98	80.3	4.0	38.6	0.0	6.0
2.7	3.75	na	-0.24	4.0	1.3	0.79	8.77	4.03	78.9	4.4	15.4	6.0	5.0
7.8	0.09	0.4	0.03	3.1	3.5	0.51	5.12	3.48	65.1	3.6	29.3	12.4	7.4
5.8	0.40	na	0.16	3.3	0.6	0.45	4.40	3.76	81.0	4.5	25.2	7.0	5.4
3.8	6.95	na	1.00	1.3	-0.1	-0.06	-0.48	3.27	92.3	2.3	43.1	32.8	5.3
6.2	0.62	5.2	0.01	6.2	9.3	1.34	16.70	3.64	63.6	4.0	17.6	7.8	6.9

Name	City	State	2019 Rating	2018 Rating	Total Assets ($Mil)	One Year Asset Growth	Asset Mix (As a % of Total Assets) Commercial Loans	Consumer Loans	Mortgage Loans	Securities	Capitalization Index	Leverage Ratio	Risk-Based Capital Ratio
Union Bank & Trust Co.	Monticello	AR	B	B-	C-	244.2	15.52	21.5	4.4	18.4	13.2	**7.8**	9.7	13.2
Union Bank & Trust Co.	Livingston	TN	B+	B+	B-	96.2	15.25	9.4	4.9	26.1	22.7	**10.0**	12.3	23.1
Union Bank and Trust Co.	Minneapolis	MN	B	B-	B-	184.7	9.83	10.8	0.1	0.1	17.2	**6.5**	8.5	0.0
Union Bank and Trust Co.	Lincoln	NE	A-	A-	B+	5433.6	23.58	17.6	11.7	3.6	13.7	**7.8**	9.5	13.5
Union Bank Co.	Columbus Grove	OH	B+	B	B-	995.4	13.70	17.3	0.9	15.1	18.3	**7.3**	9.2	14.9
Union Bank of Mena	Mena	AR	A-	B+	B	305.4	13.90	7.0	11.5	28.0	27.5	**8.2**	9.8	20.0
Union Bank, Inc.	Middlebourne	WV	B+	B+	B	309.7	16.24	6.1	2.2	13.9	42.9	**7.3**	9.2	0.0
Union Banking Co.	West Mansfield	OH	B+	B+	B+	61.1	6.21	0.2	0.2	4.5	86.1	**9.1**	10.4	40.9
Union County Savings Bank	Elizabeth	NJ	C	C+	B-	1819.6	2.82	0.0	0.1	5.0	75.4	**10.0**	13.8	52.5
Union Federal S&L Assn.	Kewanee	IL	C+	B-	B-	159.7	6.36	2.4	0.3	48.5	2.0	**10.0**	13.7	0.0
Union National Bank	Elgin	IL	B+	B+	A-	444.3	41.38	32.4	0.0	2.4	1.1	**8.0**	9.7	19.8
Union S&L Assn.	Connersville	IN	B-	B-	C+	176.4	7.24	2.7	11.7	36.7	1.7	**8.8**	10.2	0.0
Union Savings Bank	Danbury	CT	B+	B+	B	2735.1	24.62	6.9	0.2	23.7	13.8	**10.0**	11.0	0.0
UNION Savings BANK	Freeport	IL	C-	C	C	170.7	12.45	5.6	2.2	37.9	17.6	**7.7**	9.5	17.0
▲ Union Savings Bank	Cincinnati	OH	A	A-	B+	3372.2	9.94	0.3	0.4	54.4	0.0	**9.2**	10.5	17.1
Union State Bank	Pell City	AL	D+	D+	D-	235.2	14.08	4.8	1.0	4.7	19.4	**5.0**	7.0	13.1
Union State Bank	Greenfield	IA	C	C-	C-	83.3	3.79	4.1	1.6	18.0	10.7	**8.0**	10.6	0.0
Union State Bank	Winterset	IA	B-	C+	C+	112.3	25.68	8.6	1.8	23.1	25.5	**5.6**	7.6	15.0
Union State Bank	Arkansas City	KS	B	B	B	537.3	60.08	10.5	4.5	16.0	20.1	**7.0**	9.0	13.4
▲ Union State Bank	Clay Center	KS	B	B-	B-	153.5	6.56	7.6	0.9	11.6	41.9	**10.0**	11.2	0.0
▼ Union State Bank	Olsburg	KS	C	C+	B	34.2	10.68	10.5	3.6	3.6	17.3	**10.0**	11.9	27.9
Union State Bank	Uniontown	KS	C	C	D+	56.0	13.35	10.9	3.9	22.9	9.7	**6.2**	8.2	14.5
Union State Bank of Browns Valley	Browns Valley	MN	B-	B-	C+	24.6	16.41	6.5	1.6	0.5	4.9	**9.6**	10.7	0.0
Union State Bank of Everest	Everest	KS	B	B-	C+	346.0	12.42	9.6	2.7	17.5	21.7	**7.8**	9.5	14.5
Union State Bank of Fargo	Fargo	ND	C+	B-	B-	144.8	35.32	12.8	3.9	14.9	3.4	**3.8**	8.9	0.0
Union State Bank of Hazen	Hazen	ND	C	C	B-	187.9	27.09	6.4	4.3	12.6	27.4	**6.1**	8.1	0.0
Union State Bank of West Salem	West Salem	WI	C+	B-	B-	97.8	15.32	9.9	4.0	22.0	20.9	**9.9**	11.0	0.0
Unison Bank	Jamestown	ND	B+	B	B+	389.5	21.43	9.6	8.1	18.3	22.0	**7.8**	9.5	14.7
United Bank	Atmore	AL	B+	B	B-	870.6	25.79	21.6	2.3	8.8	16.5	**6.9**	8.9	15.1
United Bank	Springdale	AR	B+	B+	B+	222.4	10.49	14.4	0.5	33.9	1.5	**9.6**	10.8	15.7
United Bank	Zebulon	GA	A	A	A	1786.7	22.46	9.3	2.0	9.7	21.0	**8.5**	10.0	20.1
United Bank	Vienna	VA	B	B	B	25903.6	31.26	11.9	4.7	17.0	10.6	**9.3**	10.7	14.4
▼ United Bank & Trust	Marysville	KS	B+	A-	A-	707.4	16.18	11.3	1.4	6.4	6.9	**9.6**	10.8	0.0
▼ United Bank & Trust N.A.	Marshalltown	IA	B	B+	A-	111.5	8.42	7.8	0.7	6.9	30.3	**7.7**	9.6	0.0
▲ United Bank and Trust Co.	Hampton	IA	A	A	A-	180.1	9.25	5.1	3.2	10.6	35.0	**10.0**	14.5	0.0
United Bank of El Paso del Norte	El Paso	TX	C+	C	C+	299.9	17.76	29.3	0.4	3.0	7.4	**9.2**	10.5	15.1
United Bank of Iowa	Ida Grove	IA	A-	A-	A-	1850.7	11.90	5.6	2.8	6.7	17.9	**7.8**	10.1	0.0
United Bank of Michigan	Grand Rapids	MI	B-	C+	C-	781.7	12.42	8.2	1.1	11.2	0.6	**5.7**	9.5	0.0
United Bank of Philadelphia	Philadelphia	PA	E-	E-	E-	54.6	10.22	18.4	1.1	7.1	3.2	**9.4**	10.6	21.2
United Bank of Union	Union	MO	C+	C	C-	424.8	13.98	16.1	0.8	15.0	18.1	**8.9**	10.4	14.1
United Bankers' Bank	Bloomington	MN	B-	B-	B-	1028.8	23.31	5.9	0.6	0.8	13.3	**8.2**	9.8	14.9
United Business Bank	Walnut Creek	CA	B+	A-	B+	2270.1	28.27	13.7	0.3	7.3	5.0	**8.4**	9.9	14.4
United Citizens Bank & Trust Co.	Campbellsburg	KY	A-	B+	B	128.3	16.35	6.7	1.3	21.1	12.4	**10.0**	11.8	20.9
United Citizens Bank of Southern Kentucky	Columbia	KY	A-	A-	B+	171.1	-0.23	9.5	6.1	31.6	6.6	**10.0**	12.7	17.6
United Community Bank	Blairsville	GA	A-	A-	A-	17126.7	33.96	22.6	0.9	9.7	18.1	**7.6**	9.4	14.2
United Community Bank	Milford	IA	B-	B	B-	223.8	7.08	11.0	1.4	10.3	1.0	**7.2**	9.5	12.7
United Community Bank	Chatham	IL	B	B-	B	2999.6	15.32	13.4	1.3	11.9	27.4	**6.6**	8.6	14.4
▲ United Community Bank	Raceland	LA	B	C+	C-	594.1	11.23	25.2	0.5	8.8	7.2	**10.0**	13.9	0.0
▼ United Community Bank	Perham	MN	B	B+	B	311.1	19.49	17.4	3.0	10.0	24.7	**8.3**	9.9	0.0
United Community Bank of North Dakota	Leeds	ND	B	B	B-	360.8	2.58	21.0	1.4	4.2	11.3	**8.0**	9.7	13.5
United Community Bank of W Kentucky	Morganfield	KY	A	A	A-	316.5	18.51	14.0	4.8	15.6	29.0	**10.0**	12.2	19.2
United Cumberland Bank	Whitley City	KY	B	B-	C+	328.4	10.45	10.6	9.9	26.0	19.1	**10.0**	12.5	0.0
United Farmers State Bank	Adams	MN	B-	B	B+	162.8	4.72	6.9	1.0	3.7	3.2	**8.6**	12.1	13.9
▼ United Fidelity Bank, FSB	Evansville	IN	B	B+	B+	1181.4	22.34	4.2	0.1	10.4	56.6	**6.2**	8.2	21.3
▲ United Midwest Savings Bank, N.A.	De Graff	OH	C+	C-	D+	356.3	26.59	39.1	14.3	9.7	0.1	**10.0**	11.4	16.1
United Minnesota Bank	New London	MN	C-	C	D+	39.8	24.51	15.2	8.1	22.4	3.8	**4.9**	6.9	12.5
United Mississippi Bank	Natchez	MS	C+	C+	C+	389.0	9.14	17.5	3.1	11.4	20.4	**5.7**	9.9	0.0
United National Bank	Cairo	GA	B-	B	B	236.2	5.38	17.5	3.7	14.0	4.5	**10.0**	14.2	18.6
▼ United Orient Bank	New York	NY	C	B	B	83.8	-2.94	1.0	0.0	21.2	2.4	**10.0**	16.3	0.0
United Pacific Bank	City of Industry	CA	B-	B	B	173.3	20.69	6.0	0.0	1.7	0.1	**10.0**	14.6	21.1

Asset Quality Index	Adjusted Non-Performing Loans as a % of Total Loans	as a % of Capital	Net Charge-Offs Avg Loans	Profitability Index	Net Income ($Mil)	Return on Assets (R.O.A.)	Return on Equity (R.O.E.)	Net Interest Spread	Overhead Efficiency Ratio	Liquidity Index	Liquidity Ratio	Hot Money Ratio	Stability Index
6.5	0.65	na	0.05	7.2	3.0	1.72	17.19	3.95	56.5	1.0	11.2	25.7	7.2
5.6	2.30	na	1.00	9.7	1.4	1.99	16.01	4.74	51.7	4.1	34.6	12.9	8.2
9.3	0.00	na	-0.01	3.7	0.7	0.62	6.58	3.25	82.4	7.5	68.8	1.4	5.1
6.5	0.47	3.1	0.07	5.6	38.4	0.99	10.57	3.12	60.4	1.6	15.1	15.4	9.4
6.6	0.39	1.6	0.03	8.1	12.9	1.79	14.54	3.87	57.2	4.2	20.6	7.6	8.8
7.2	0.44	na	0.07	8.6	4.2	1.90	18.16	4.27	56.4	3.6	26.1	12.1	8.3
6.2	0.86	na	0.07	5.6	2.8	1.33	10.32	3.43	57.5	5.4	31.1	3.7	8.0
9.8	1.45	na	0.00	3.2	0.2	0.50	3.72	2.28	73.0	2.0	30.4	24.7	7.8
10.0	1.23	0.4	0.00	2.3	4.1	0.30	2.17	0.35	113.4	4.0	107.6	62.9	8.7
5.6	2.90	na	-0.01	1.1	-0.4	-0.35	-2.44	2.99	111.7	3.2	20.8	13.7	7.5
5.5	0.38	3.2	-0.01	5.3	2.9	1.00	10.11	2.45	47.8	0.7	10.4	42.3	6.3
4.3	1.13	na	0.04	3.6	0.8	0.60	5.88	3.32	77.9	1.5	16.0	24.2	6.3
6.4	1.22	na	0.01	4.0	14.0	0.74	6.36	2.94	69.5	4.3	13.3	6.8	8.7
7.6	0.10	na	0.10	2.0	0.1	0.11	1.12	3.10	93.0	4.4	29.0	8.9	4.5
7.4	0.88	na	-0.04	9.4	86.4	3.56	34.43	2.49	42.6	1.9	26.9	31.8	10.0
4.9	2.67	na	-0.51	1.1	0.3	0.17	2.24	3.01	107.7	6.0	44.8	4.6	2.5
5.8	0.21	na	0.09	5.8	0.8	1.34	8.59	4.30	61.8	1.0	19.4	30.0	8.9
9.1	0.00	na	0.00	4.5	0.8	0.97	11.72	3.71	73.2	4.5	30.7	9.2	4.5
7.6	0.08	na	0.04	4.2	3.5	0.90	7.52	3.51	74.7	3.1	20.8	13.9	7.8
7.3	1.93	na	0.14	4.2	1.0	0.90	7.40	3.20	63.4	2.2	7.3	13.7	6.8
2.4	19.36	na	0.10	0.7	-0.1	-0.21	-1.58	2.63	69.5	5.9	52.6	7.0	4.6
4.2	0.00	na	0.43	4.8	0.4	1.06	12.56	4.83	77.0	4.0	19.7	9.1	4.1
9.0	0.00	na	0.06	5.1	0.2	1.23	11.21	2.87	55.4	5.7	66.8	8.8	5.4
4.7	1.51	na	0.09	5.2	2.9	1.17	10.50	4.20	64.9	4.0	10.6	8.0	7.3
6.0	0.48	1.6	0.00	2.1	0.2	0.23	1.83	3.44	82.5	2.7	21.2	15.7	5.9
2.3	3.99	na	0.29	4.1	1.1	0.82	8.50	3.87	70.7	3.7	33.2	14.0	4.8
4.0	3.19	na	0.14	3.9	0.5	0.66	5.58	3.86	72.1	4.4	32.7	10.2	5.6
7.4	0.31	na	0.01	7.5	4.1	1.47	14.13	4.09	53.0	1.7	13.0	14.9	7.7
6.1	0.75	na	0.02	8.8	10.3	1.71	18.35	3.64	53.6	4.7	29.8	7.6	6.3
6.3	0.93	na	-0.03	5.3	2.1	1.30	11.73	3.88	70.7	0.8	16.9	26.7	7.7
7.3	0.97	na	-0.06	9.5	27.3	2.23	21.59	3.61	52.5	6.6	44.7	4.3	9.7
4.7	0.74	3.1	0.13	6.0	210.7	1.20	7.10	3.24	53.8	3.7	11.4	9.9	10.0
5.3	1.47	na	1.05	4.9	4.9	0.94	7.98	3.13	55.3	3.8	24.5	9.2	8.5
5.5	2.86	14.3	-0.01	5.6	0.9	1.18	11.64	3.13	60.5	5.5	42.8	8.0	7.1
8.6	0.30	na	-0.01	6.8	2.2	1.65	10.91	3.39	47.9	4.8	50.1	13.4	9.3
6.4	0.05	na	0.36	6.1	2.4	1.14	10.44	4.90	60.5	3.3	15.4	11.2	6.6
5.4	0.91	4.3	0.09	5.8	18.5	1.36	12.34	2.99	58.0	2.1	25.8	26.0	10.0
6.4	0.57	na	0.15	4.9	5.7	1.02	10.51	3.49	64.0	4.5	17.5	6.0	6.6
0.3	10.89	na	-0.04	0.2	-0.1	-0.36	-5.37	4.16	101.2	4.9	27.9	5.1	0.2
3.7	2.53	na	-0.03	7.3	5.5	1.81	16.98	3.67	55.9	1.7	11.5	20.4	7.2
7.9	1.14	3.0	0.04	3.9	5.4	0.72	6.61	2.46	69.9	4.0	40.4	0.4	8.0
6.3	0.49	na	0.00	4.2	10.2	0.62	5.15	4.05	66.4	4.1	22.1	10.4	9.0
5.6	1.82	na	-0.02	6.2	1.2	1.26	10.29	4.05	64.2	4.5	26.8	7.3	7.4
7.8	0.62	na	0.06	8.3	2.2	1.63	13.40	4.22	54.7	1.3	12.5	26.2	8.2
6.7	0.72	3.1	0.22	6.1	115.3	1.05	8.61	3.62	55.2	4.3	21.9	7.2	9.7
6.4	3.12	na	0.00	7.1	2.7	1.62	14.91	4.42	56.7	3.3	9.9	11.9	8.2
4.9	1.46	7.8	0.20	4.2	15.2	0.72	7.17	2.79	61.1	4.2	19.5	7.2	8.2
4.6	2.17	11.5	0.39	6.5	7.2	1.67	11.86	4.41	60.8	3.4	20.1	12.5	7.5
6.4	0.82	na	0.01	4.2	2.0	0.94	8.53	3.50	74.0	3.8	36.1	14.5	6.8
6.9	0.65	2.4	0.01	8.2	5.0	1.85	17.54	4.68	44.9	3.6	7.6	10.3	6.3
8.3	0.43	na	0.02	7.6	3.3	1.48	11.38	3.90	55.2	2.6	24.2	13.0	8.7
5.0	2.36	na	0.12	7.1	3.8	1.59	12.29	4.14	62.9	2.2	25.1	19.0	8.5
3.7	0.87	na	0.01	9.4	2.7	2.29	19.06	3.98	43.6	3.4	14.9	10.5	9.3
7.9	1.96	3.5	0.03	2.7	1.9	0.23	1.98	2.27	97.1	4.1	23.6	8.4	10.0
3.0	3.14	na	0.97	8.5	3.7	1.53	14.00	4.16	69.9	0.7	13.9	46.5	6.9
8.2	0.04	na	0.19	5.3	0.4	1.32	19.20	3.94	70.2	5.1	32.4	6.3	2.5
5.0	1.99	na	0.08	4.4	2.7	0.99	9.13	4.04	80.3	3.2	15.5	13.1	6.3
3.7	2.79	na	0.27	8.2	2.5	1.47	10.08	4.55	53.2	1.4	2.9	19.7	8.5
7.7	0.00	0.0	0.00	1.7	-0.3	-0.46	-2.77	5.06	108.2	2.1	18.1	18.9	7.6
7.2	0.02	na	0.00	3.0	0.5	0.43	2.81	2.83	80.1	0.9	23.7	48.9	7.7

Name	City	State	2019 Rating	2018 Rating	Total Assets ($Mil)	One Year Asset Growth	Asset Mix (As a % of Total Assets)				Capitalization Index	Leverage Ratio	Risk-Based Capital Ratio
			Rating				Commercial Loans	Consumer Loans	Mortgage Loans	Securities			
United Prairie Bank	Mountain Lake	MN	B-	C+	C+	746.9	25.36	15.0	0.6	3.6	11.4	6.6	8.6	12.2
United Republic Bank	Elkhorn	NE	D+	D+	C-	143.6	4.26	10.2	0.2	12.3	10.7	6.2	10.8	0.0
United Roosevelt Savings Bank	Carteret	NJ	C-	C-	D+	179.6	24.75	16.4	0.1	42.3	10.3	8.8	10.2	17.9
United Savings Bank	Philadelphia	PA	B-	B-	B-	413.6	11.60	3.3	0.0	25.2	14.3	10.0	15.3	0.0
United Security Bank	Fresno	CA	B+	B+	B+	1133.1	18.49	7.3	5.5	4.2	7.8	10.0	11.2	0.0
United Security Bank	Auxvasse	MO	B+	B+	B+	67.8	10.61	8.5	6.2	30.4	26.6	10.0	13.6	0.0
United Southern Bank	Umatilla	FL	B	B	B-	648.0	21.48	10.2	1.1	11.2	30.0	6.9	8.9	0.0
United Southern Bank	Hopkinsville	KY	B+	B+	B-	241.3	10.51	5.8	2.3	20.6	15.5	10.0	11.7	0.0
United Southwest Bank	Cottonwood	MN	C-	C	C-	50.4	6.22	1.8	1.8	0.3	21.5	6.1	8.1	16.8
▼ United State Bank	Lewistown	MO	B-	B	B-	192.3	4.65	8.4	1.2	6.7	6.6	8.1	10.3	13.4
United Texas Bank	Dallas	TX	B-	B-	B-	1026.0	58.94	10.6	0.1	3.8	45.8	8.0	9.7	0.0
▼ United Trust Bank	Palos Heights	IL	E-	E+	E	34.2	30.08	2.7	1.1	21.7	0.2	3.5	5.5	11.0
United Valley Bank	Cavalier	ND	B	B-	B-	417.7	15.99	15.4	2.3	6.0	14.8	6.3	8.4	12.7
Unity Bank	Clinton	NJ	B+	A-	B+	1924.4	16.02	11.9	0.1	26.3	2.5	5.2	9.6	0.0
▲ Unity Bank	Augusta	WI	C-	D+	C-	591.3	16.77	10.2	2.3	11.7	4.8	5.9	7.9	12.2
▲ Unity National Bank of Houston	Houston	TX	D	D-	D-	133.6	37.61	27.3	0.4	10.9	4.5	5.2	8.2	0.0
Universal Bank	West Covina	CA	C+	C+	B	423.8	4.26	0.4	0.0	3.9	1.8	10.0	14.6	0.0
▲ University Bank	Ann Arbor	MI	A-	B+	B+	613.9	60.22	2.3	0.0	37.4	0.9	10.0	11.2	0.0
University National Bank of Lawrence	Lawrence	KS	B	B	C+	83.7	4.31	9.8	0.6	39.0	2.1	7.0	9.0	17.3
Univest Bank and Trust Co.	Souderton	PA	B-	B	B	6360.6	19.27	20.4	0.4	13.2	5.8	6.3	9.1	11.9
Upper Peninsula State Bank	Escanaba	MI	A-	A-	A-	244.0	21.33	9.7	4.8	12.7	12.6	10.0	15.3	0.0
▲ Upstate National Bank	Rochester	NY	C+	C	C+	192.2	22.57	8.3	0.0	31.8	7.3	6.5	8.5	13.1
US Metro Bank	Garden Grove	CA	B	A-	B+	733.7	44.63	16.9	0.0	0.5	0.0	8.9	10.2	14.1
▼ USAA Federal Savings Bank	San Antonio	TX	C+	C+	C+	103029.7	16.37	0.0	36.5	4.1	46.9	6.2	8.2	16.8
USAA Savings Bank	Las Vegas	NV	U	U	U	1647.1	-5.77	0.0	0.0	0.0	15.1	10.0	22.8	95.8
▲ Utah Independent Bank	Salina	UT	A	A-	B+	120.8	45.36	20.4	4.3	9.2	12.1	10.0	13.7	0.0
▲ Uwharrie Bank	Albemarle	NC	C+	C+	C+	787.2	19.47	15.9	1.6	10.7	26.2	5.5	7.5	12.3
Valley Bank of Commerce	Roswell	NM	A	A	A-	198.0	16.58	26.1	0.4	5.2	0.1	8.0	9.7	20.4
Valley Bank of Kalispell	Kalispell	MT	B	B	C+	164.6	22.41	15.4	3.5	15.2	13.7	7.6	9.4	0.0
Valley Bank of Nevada	North Las Vegas	NV	C	D+	D	200.6	40.11	25.0	0.3	0.8	3.5	4.8	6.8	14.6
▲ Valley Bank of Ronan	Ronan	MT	C-	D+	C+	129.1	23.87	17.1	4.1	9.4	2.4	8.1	9.7	17.5
▲ Valley Central Bank	Liberty Township	OH	C+	C-	C	155.3	-6.57	2.1	0.4	50.7	2.7	10.0	23.6	0.0
Valley Exchange Bank	Lennox	SD	B-	B	B	64.6	-3.23	4.0	1.0	0.9	8.3	10.0	12.4	31.2
Valley National Bank	Wayne	NJ	B-	C+	B-	40734.8	20.74	15.4	5.2	11.0	9.2	6.7	8.7	12.5
Valley Premier Bank	Hawley	MN	B	B	B	123.7	11.37	15.6	3.6	10.6	29.5	8.2	9.8	0.0
Valley Republic Bank	Bakersfield	CA	B+	B+	B-	1194.0	30.49	25.6	0.1	3.2	17.6	5.9	10.5	0.0
Valley State Bank	Russellville	AL	B	B	B	128.8	3.80	10.0	2.8	19.9	38.8	10.0	17.6	0.0
▲ Valley State Bank	Belle Plaine	KS	B+	B	B	159.9	18.60	12.4	9.2	16.3	17.8	10.0	12.0	0.0
Valley State Bank	Syracuse	KS	B	B-	B-	181.5	18.90	12.0	5.1	11.1	9.0	4.6	8.9	0.0
Valliance Bank	Oklahoma City	OK	C	C	C	567.5	24.23	28.1	0.1	10.3	3.4	3.7	9.0	0.0
Valor Bank	Edmond	OK	B+	B	B	127.4	33.60	7.4	0.1	56.4	0.0	6.2	8.3	12.0
ValueBank Texas	Corpus Christi	TX	A	A	B+	278.7	14.38	5.5	0.4	11.1	13.6	8.5	10.0	0.0
Van Wert Federal Savings Bank	Van Wert	OH	C	C+	C+	118.5	1.84	0.3	0.6	47.7	10.2	10.0	20.9	0.0
Vanguard National Trust Co., N.A.	Malvern	PA	U	U	U	100.2	-8.49	0.0	0.0	0.0	65.2	10.0	75.3	269.3
Vantage Bank	Kent	MN	C	C-	D+	42.4	30.79	15.0	5.3	22.8	0.0	6.8	8.8	12.8
Vantage Bank Texas	San Antonio	TX	B	B		2467.9	23.68	17.7	0.3	4.8	3.7	8.8	11.1	14.0
▲ Vast Bank, N.A.	Tulsa	OK	B-	B-	B-	773.9	18.85	28.2	1.8	10.0	2.9	6.8	8.8	12.4
VCC Bank	Richmond	VA	D+	D	D	236.9	10.61	19.5	0.0	8.8	9.1	6.6	10.7	0.0
VeraBank, N.A.	Henderson	TX	B+	B	B	2888.1	20.40	11.0	2.8	13.6	23.6	7.6	9.4	16.2
Vergas State Bank	Vergas	MN	C+	B-	B-	51.3	2.32	3.9	2.6	8.5	10.6	10.0	14.5	0.0
Veritex Community Bank	Dallas	TX	B	B	B	8696.7	9.27	21.5	0.2	6.0	12.6	4.9	10.6	0.0
Vermilion Bank & Trust Co.	Kaplan	LA	B-	B-	C+	133.6	21.69	6.6	4.1	16.8	16.2	8.1	9.8	18.2
Vermilion Valley Bank	Piper City	IL	A	A-	B+	147.1	12.56	4.8	1.0	9.1	24.5	10.0	15.8	24.0
Vermillion State Bank	Vermillion	MN	A+	A+	A+	692.9	17.05	16.9	1.2	11.8	42.1	10.0	14.7	0.0
Vermont State Bank	Vermont	IL	D	D	D	29.5	-1.32	6.3	18.6	30.5	8.9	10.0	12.5	19.0
Versailles S&L Co.	Versailles	OH	B	B	B-	60.4	10.04	1.5	1.8	48.7	0.1	10.0	19.8	0.0
▲ Verus Bank of Commerce	Fort Collins	CO	A	A-	B+	281.6	4.72	7.3	0.0	8.9	0.0	10.0	13.0	0.0
Victory Bank	Limerick	PA	B-	B-	C	430.9	61.22	21.8	2.1	7.9	2.7	5.9	7.9	13.0
▼ Vidalia Federal Savings Bank	Vidalia	GA	C	C+	B-	202.7	0.57	0.0	1.7	27.9	49.0	10.0	15.6	0.0
Viking Bank	Alexandria	MN	B	B	B-	242.8	30.80	17.3	2.1	14.6	3.3	6.6	9.8	0.0

Asset Quality Index	Adjusted Non-Performing Loans as a % of Total Loans	Adjusted Non-Performing Loans as a % of Capital	Net Charge-Offs Avg Loans	Profitability Index	Net Income ($Mil)	Return on Assets (R.O.A.)	Return on Equity (R.O.E.)	Net Interest Spread	Overhead Efficiency Ratio	Liquidity Index	Liquidity Ratio	Hot Money Ratio	Stability Index
4.5	1.16	na	0.03	6.2	7.9	1.53	14.80	4.23	64.7	2.1	21.1	11.6	7.1
6.4	0.00	na	0.00	3.3	0.7	0.65	4.62	3.42	67.1	0.7	18.9	39.7	2.9
7.9	0.26	2.1	0.00	2.0	0.4	0.29	3.12	2.93	75.9	2.9	13.5	14.1	4.7
9.9	0.01	na	0.00	3.1	1.6	0.53	3.20	2.24	69.7	3.7	47.0	18.3	7.7
4.8	1.99	na	0.28	6.0	6.4	0.84	6.81	3.44	57.8	5.9	33.3	4.9	10.0
6.8	1.09	na	0.02	5.4	0.7	1.38	9.79	4.01	65.9	2.7	27.5	17.2	7.9
5.4	1.50	na	0.00	4.7	4.1	0.91	9.31	3.68	67.9	6.1	39.1	2.2	6.7
5.4	2.46	na	0.05	4.9	1.6	0.94	7.76	3.79	71.8	3.4	31.9	15.1	6.8
5.9	0.00	na	0.18	2.2	0.1	0.22	2.63	2.96	90.8	6.7	59.5	3.3	4.0
3.1	2.34	15.4	0.09	6.6	2.0	1.46	14.63	3.85	56.2	3.0	19.0	14.2	7.1
9.0	0.00	1.5	0.00	6.1	28.1	4.51	49.31	2.67	44.3	3.5	66.1	18.8	7.0
3.8	1.94	na	0.01	0.0	-0.8	-3.41	-46.38	3.34	205.8	1.8	32.0	30.0	1.7
6.0	0.55	na	-0.05	4.9	3.2	1.08	10.32	3.79	68.8	3.6	11.6	10.4	6.8
7.1	0.60	na	0.01	6.8	16.2	1.25	12.82	3.88	52.2	1.8	14.0	12.2	8.6
2.4	1.87	na	0.04	4.4	4.2	0.98	11.52	3.96	72.4	1.6	15.3	18.3	5.7
3.7	1.78	na	0.01	1.3	0.2	0.25	2.98	4.18	94.4	0.8	18.8	43.3	3.1
7.4	0.67	na	-0.04	2.4	0.6	0.20	1.34	3.17	91.9	1.4	22.3	27.9	7.9
7.1	4.88	2.0	-0.01	9.0	20.2	8.08	85.16	3.48	68.6	6.7	44.7	0.3	6.8
7.9	0.11	na	-0.01	5.4	0.8	1.25	13.00	4.25	71.7	3.5	21.7	12.0	6.3
5.2	0.58	4.2	0.11	4.0	26.4	0.60	5.20	3.32	58.4	4.0	7.5	5.2	9.7
7.8	0.53	2.4	0.06	7.6	2.7	1.52	10.06	3.52	55.7	2.8	30.5	9.4	8.4
7.7	0.00	na	0.00	3.7	1.3	0.99	9.52	3.01	62.1	0.4	13.5	69.1	5.7
5.4	0.36	na	0.02	4.6	3.7	0.79	7.40	3.36	56.1	1.0	21.1	31.2	3.0
5.0	5.35	3.7	1.44	2.0	-103.1	-0.15	-1.47	4.20	85.8	5.9	63.3	3.2	6.7
10.0	na	0.0	0.00	9.5	125.6	10.79	51.17	0.72	74.9	4.0	103.3	36.7	4.3
7.7	0.36	na	0.02	9.3	1.7	2.17	15.79	2.67	54.8	6.1	44.0	4.2	9.5
5.0	1.72	9.3	-0.02	3.6	3.7	0.69	8.49	3.36	74.6	4.9	25.8	4.5	5.0
6.7	0.53	na	0.01	9.4	3.3	2.17	23.06	3.57	39.7	5.9	48.5	7.0	7.6
4.7	0.99	na	0.23	9.0	1.8	1.70	16.87	5.47	56.7	3.1	36.6	18.3	5.9
4.6	2.50	9.3	0.05	2.6	0.4	0.31	3.64	3.09	82.2	5.8	35.5	2.8	4.4
2.6	5.14	na	0.07	5.9	1.0	1.15	11.08	4.65	71.3	6.3	45.3	3.1	5.9
9.0	0.53	na	0.01	3.5	0.8	0.70	2.97	3.92	80.6	1.0	10.6	18.5	7.1
8.7	0.00	na	0.00	2.5	0.1	0.12	0.99	2.41	92.4	6.7	68.4	4.7	6.3
3.6	0.84	4.7	0.15	5.0	295.9	0.98	8.40	3.03	48.2	1.6	9.1	11.8	9.7
7.3	0.00	na	0.00	4.9	1.0	1.19	11.51	3.70	69.9	5.8	46.2	6.9	6.3
8.4	0.45	na	0.00	5.8	9.8	1.24	12.49	3.13	46.3	5.2	21.5	3.3	8.4
8.9	0.20	na	-0.01	3.9	0.9	0.89	5.06	3.16	67.0	1.2	17.0	29.4	8.0
6.7	0.99	na	0.18	5.0	1.1	0.96	7.63	3.97	64.2	1.7	22.5	21.7	7.0
5.6	0.06	7.6	0.00	7.3	2.2	1.68	18.45	3.61	61.6	0.9	22.6	35.8	6.4
5.3	0.53	na	0.00	3.7	3.0	0.78	8.57	3.78	69.1	0.8	17.7	24.5	5.1
9.0	0.00	na	0.00	8.4	1.6	1.90	23.37	3.66	69.4	0.5	2.4	39.4	5.6
9.1	0.00	na	0.01	6.2	2.1	1.06	9.96	3.98	74.0	5.8	44.5	6.1	7.1
9.9	0.08	na	0.00	2.5	0.3	0.27	1.30	2.43	86.7	3.4	43.7	18.8	7.6
10.0	na	na	na	6.5	0.7	1.02	1.33	0.83	98.7	4.0	252.7	0.0	6.7
7.1	0.33	na	0.00	7.7	0.7	2.59	28.19	3.53	55.7	2.0	19.2	19.5	4.6
5.0	0.82	na	0.09	5.3	18.1	1.03	8.56	3.96	65.5	1.8	17.6	22.3	9.4
5.8	0.57	4.0	0.34	4.3	3.8	0.68	7.46	3.63	62.7	0.7	15.7	43.7	6.3
1.6	2.21	na	0.37	2.8	0.7	0.42	4.05	2.56	58.8	0.5	12.0	57.5	5.8
6.4	0.98	3.7	0.07	5.3	22.6	1.13	10.32	3.50	59.2	6.0	34.6	5.0	8.4
8.5	0.05	1.4	0.00	2.1	0.1	0.18	1.22	2.23	91.3	4.6	75.2	17.8	7.3
3.9	1.41	7.9	0.09	5.0	56.3	0.89	5.83	3.54	49.4	1.7	15.5	18.0	9.9
4.6	3.28	na	-0.03	5.9	1.3	1.42	13.90	3.81	61.3	3.1	39.0	19.4	6.0
7.3	0.05	na	0.04	7.8	1.9	1.76	10.64	3.31	40.1	2.7	22.2	16.3	9.6
8.2	0.76	2.4	-0.04	9.5	12.0	2.47	15.75	3.25	27.4	5.8	53.5	9.0	9.8
0.0	9.59	na	2.14	0.1	-0.1	-0.57	-4.48	3.15	103.1	0.6	18.8	55.9	3.3
9.5	0.00	na	0.00	3.6	0.3	0.60	2.96	3.04	73.5	3.6	40.7	16.9	7.3
7.3	0.00	na	0.00	9.3	3.4	1.62	12.71	4.10	42.9	1.5	16.6	9.1	9.7
8.2	0.07	na	0.05	3.7	1.8	0.68	8.85	3.47	62.7	4.5	30.8	9.3	3.9
8.8	0.86	na	0.29	0.7	-0.3	-0.22	-1.36	1.88	109.8	3.7	77.6	30.7	7.4
4.7	0.13	na	0.08	6.0	2.4	1.40	9.44	3.50	54.7	3.3	26.3	14.2	9.1

Name	City	State	Rating	2019 Rating	2018 Rating	Total Assets ($Mil)	One Year Asset Growth	Commercial Loans	Consumer Loans	Mortgage Loans	Securities	Capitalization Index	Leverage Ratio	Risk-Based Capital Ratio
Villa Grove State Bank	Villa Grove	IL	B+	B+	B+	73.8	2.18	8.5	2.4	40.4	9.6	10.0	11.8	0.0
Village Bank	Saint Libory	IL	B	B	B-	98.4	10.26	7.0	6.5	20.2	16.8	7.4	9.3	0.0
Village Bank	Auburndale	MA	B	B	B	1455.2	16.46	4.3	0.3	39.5	12.1	8.9	10.2	17.2
Village Bank	Saint Francis	MN	B-	C+	C	393.0	30.13	26.2	0.7	5.8	19.2	5.4	7.4	14.8
Village Bank	Midlothian	VA	B-	C	C-	728.2	30.64	30.6	4.6	12.9	5.0	6.8	8.8	14.1
Village Bank & Trust, N.A.	Arlington Heights	IL	B	B	B	2087.0	18.93	50.4	12.5	2.5	9.6	6.3	8.3	12.2
▲ Vinings Bank	Smyrna	GA	B-	C+	B-	699.3	86.11	28.2	0.1	0.4	38.5	5.4	7.4	11.9
Vintage Bank Kansas	Leon	KS	B	B	B	162.2	14.61	8.5	2.3	12.8	26.8	7.6	9.4	0.0
Vinton County National Bank	McArthur	OH	B	B	B	1154.2	14.72	6.0	16.0	25.4	15.6	8.8	10.2	16.7
Virginia Commonwealth Bank	Richmond	VA	C	C+	C+	1247.0	12.59	17.8	0.5	23.6	7.1	8.4	10.5	13.7
Virginia National Bank	Charlottesville	VA	A-	A-	B-	821.2	24.37	18.0	7.6	12.9	17.2	7.7	9.5	15.4
Virginia Partners Bank	Fredericksburg	VA	C+	C+	C+	594.3	34.53	18.1	0.5	15.4	11.2	7.7	9.5	13.1
Vision Bank, N.A.	Ada	OK	B-	B-	B-	829.8	21.98	9.1	5.4	19.8	22.7	6.4	8.4	0.0
▼ VisionBank	Topeka	KS	C	C+	B-	225.9	23.48	27.8	2.0	14.1	2.2	2.6	8.2	0.0
VisionBank	Saint Louis Park	MN	A-	A-	B+	169.8	83.03	42.8	0.3	13.1	0.0	6.6	8.6	12.6
▲ VISIONBank	Fargo	ND	D+	D	D	228.3	15.53	30.2	4.4	16.0	0.0	7.0	9.0	14.2
VisionBank of Iowa	Ames	IA	B-	B	B-	566.4	15.84	8.0	0.2	10.0	2.6	7.4	10.0	12.8
VIST Bank	Wyomissing	PA	B+	B+	B	1982.7	9.10	11.2	0.2	17.6	20.1	6.5	8.5	13.3
Vista Bank	Dallas	TX	C+	B-	B+	1235.1	43.02	26.0	0.5	7.9	2.4	9.3	10.5	14.5
Volunteer Federal Savings Bank	Madisonville	TN	B	B	B-	237.6	10.69	0.7	3.8	41.4	10.4	10.0	13.2	27.0
Volunteer State Bank	Portland	TN	B	B	B	864.5	18.50	14.0	0.7	10.4	1.1	7.3	9.2	13.6
Wabash Savings Bank	Mount Carmel	IL	D-	D-	D-	9.3	2.15	1.5	6.9	30.4	4.9	10.0	12.1	26.8
Wadena State Bank	Wadena	MN	B+	B+	A-	211.0	20.22	14.8	2.7	12.3	21.6	7.0	9.0	0.0
Waggoner National Bank of Vernon	Vernon	TX	A	A	A-	327.8	14.32	7.1	4.2	5.7	39.4	10.0	13.4	0.0
Wahoo State Bank	Wahoo	NE	C-	C	B-	104.2	15.08	10.5	3.7	30.8	15.9	4.7	6.7	11.9
Wake Forest Federal S&L Assn.	Wake Forest	NC	A-	A	A-	107.5	2.94	0.0	0.5	31.9	2.0	10.0	23.2	0.0
Wakefield Co-operative Bank	Wakefield	MA	C	C	C	276.1	10.81	2.7	0.0	52.4	11.5	5.6	7.6	14.6
Walden Savings Bank	Montgomery	NY	B-	B	C+	715.5	18.58	7.1	0.5	27.4	20.5	7.0	9.0	16.9
Waldo State Bank	Waldo	WI	B	B	B	100.8	22.51	11.3	1.6	33.0	10.4	10.0	11.4	0.0
Walker State Bank	Walker	IA	B	B	B-	44.8	4.13	5.2	1.9	9.0	31.7	9.5	10.7	0.0
Wallis Bank	Wallis	TX	B+	A-	A-	1153.3	47.91	35.6	0.2	0.9	0.9	8.2	9.8	14.2
Wallkill Valley Federal S&L Assn.	Wallkill	NY	C	C	C-	351.5	6.66	5.0	1.1	46.5	10.7	8.5	10.0	16.0
▲ Walpole Co-operative Bank	Walpole	MA	B	B	B	562.1	10.15	5.9	0.0	21.5	10.9	10.0	18.0	0.0
Walters Bank and Trust Co.	Walters	OK	B	B	B	57.4	7.42	3.9	5.1	18.5	25.6	10.0	21.6	59.0
▼ Walton State Bank	Walton	KS	E+	D-	D-	9.7	7.25	12.1	3.6	10.6	22.6	5.3	7.3	23.6
Wanda State Bank	Wanda	MN	B+	B+	B+	155.6	11.45	2.5	1.3	2.6	19.4	10.0	15.4	0.0
Warren Bank and Trust Co.	Warren	AR	B-	B-	B	133.1	4.21	5.1	4.8	16.5	54.1	10.0	17.1	41.4
Warren-Boynton State Bank	New Berlin	IL	A-	A-	B+	183.1	5.10	12.0	2.1	16.2	25.6	10.0	13.5	20.4
▲ Warrington Bank	Pensacola	FL	C	C	C-	95.8	8.89	2.0	0.2	1.2	58.5	10.0	16.8	0.0
Warsaw Federal S&L Assn.	Cincinnati	OH	D+	D	D	57.5	3.64	0.0	0.0	57.5	16.7	9.2	10.5	0.0
▲ Washington Business Bank	Olympia	WA	A-	B+	B-	107.6	17.58	36.4	0.0	12.6	0.1	9.2	10.4	15.6
Washington County Bank	Blair	NE	B+	B+	B	481.2	10.99	10.4	1.5	6.2	11.6	7.0	9.8	12.5
Washington Federal Bank, N.A.	Seattle	WA	B+	A-	A-	18791.4	14.09	10.0	0.4	28.4	15.8	6.9	8.9	13.7
Washington Financial Bank	Washington	PA	B	B	B	1337.1	12.43	5.8	0.4	29.2	16.5	10.0	12.4	20.1
▲ Washington Savings Bank	Effingham	IL	B	B-	B-	433.1	8.55	8.7	1.1	26.2	24.7	10.0	15.7	24.8
▲ Washington Savings Bank	Lowell	MA	C+	C	C	256.3	1.66	1.1	0.1	52.4	9.4	8.0	9.7	18.1
Washington State Bank	Washington	IA	A-	A-	B+	401.1	21.51	9.3	0.7	28.1	23.2	10.0	11.4	19.5
Washington State Bank	Washington	IL	C+	B-	C+	64.8	4.06	3.0	4.6	31.9	41.0	8.8	10.2	0.0
Washington State Bank	Washington	LA	C+	B-	B	239.7	16.75	11.3	1.9	12.8	7.8	7.2	9.1	0.0
Washington Trust Bank	Spokane	WA	B+	A-	A-	9233.0	35.74	23.7	1.3	8.8	25.0	6.1	8.1	14.1
Washington Trust Co. of Westerly	Westerly	RI	B+	B+	B+	5848.4	12.50	7.5	0.3	27.2	15.6	6.7	8.7	13.0
Washita State Bank	Burns Flat	OK	B-	C+	B	91.6	-13.76	11.3	4.4	11.2	37.1	10.0	12.3	0.0
Washita Valley Bank	Fort Cobb	OK	B	B	B+	45.1	6.74	6.0	8.2	1.2	23.8	10.0	16.6	0.0
Waterford Bank, N.A.	Toledo	OH	B-	B+	B	1287.9	61.89	32.1	2.1	3.1	6.4	1.8	8.2	0.0
Waterford Commercial and Savings Bank	Waterford	OH	B	B	B	54.3	16.93	2.2	11.5	27.9	16.0	10.0	13.0	0.0
Waterman State Bank	Waterman	IL	C	C-	D+	62.3	85.78	33.4	0.7	17.3	13.5	10.0	11.7	20.0
Watermark Bank	Oklahoma City	OK	D			164.4	108.06	39.9	1.0	8.0	2.0	10.0	16.8	19.4
WaterStone Bank, SSB	Wauwatosa	WI	A	A	A	2218.9	10.82	2.6	0.0	38.1	7.0	10.0	16.9	22.3
Watertown Savings Bank	Watertown	MA	C	C+	C+	1364.0	8.40	2.2	0.1	32.2	38.5	8.8	10.2	24.8
▲ Watertown Savings Bank	Watertown	NY	A-	B	B-	840.6	21.66	12.5	1.3	12.6	16.8	10.0	12.8	0.0

Asset Quality Index	Adjusted Non-Performing Loans as a % of Total Loans	as a % of Capital	Net Charge-Offs Avg Loans	Profitability Index	Net Income ($Mil)	Return on Assets (R.O.A.)	Return on Equity (R.O.E.)	Net Interest Spread	Overhead Efficiency Ratio	Liquidity Index	Liquidity Ratio	Hot Money Ratio	Stability Index
9.1	0.08	na	0.03	5.8	0.8	1.34	11.52	3.52	61.4	4.3	28.8	9.7	7.7
7.2	0.14	na	0.01	4.8	0.8	1.16	12.43	3.10	62.0	5.8	37.3	3.3	5.2
8.5	0.57	3.5	0.01	4.1	7.9	0.76	7.30	2.94	66.4	1.7	23.4	29.2	8.2
6.2	1.48	na	-0.17	4.5	2.4	0.90	10.90	3.56	78.6	5.1	35.3	7.1	5.6
5.1	1.40	na	0.02	5.5	6.0	1.22	14.06	3.36	64.0	3.4	11.1	11.6	5.7
4.5	1.05	5.9	0.14	4.3	8.2	0.54	5.52	2.80	50.8	1.8	8.6	11.1	7.9
6.1	0.52	4.2	0.00	4.4	5.1	1.21	17.52	2.92	61.8	5.7	37.4	4.2	4.8
5.0	2.00	na	0.01	4.8	1.3	1.06	10.03	3.87	66.1	3.7	24.9	9.7	7.2
6.7	0.48	na	0.12	4.4	7.6	0.94	8.32	3.46	68.6	2.8	19.3	16.0	8.9
4.6	1.96	na	0.04	1.4	-3.5	-0.39	-3.64	3.44	90.9	1.3	12.9	25.7	7.8
7.5	0.33	na	0.05	5.2	6.3	1.07	10.77	3.12	59.7	3.8	19.8	10.2	6.4
8.4	0.11	na	0.01	3.6	2.8	0.78	7.66	3.31	68.9	0.9	24.2	33.4	5.8
4.6	1.59	9.4	0.23	5.0	7.0	1.19	13.33	3.76	68.3	1.9	20.9	20.3	6.0
6.4	0.06	na	0.58	5.1	1.6	1.01	12.28	4.07	58.1	2.5	13.7	16.3	3.4
8.1	0.09	na	0.00	9.6	3.0	2.81	36.76	4.91	32.9	0.4	4.4	54.4	7.0
2.0	2.21	16.6	0.06	3.8	0.9	0.58	6.01	3.81	75.5	2.6	18.2	16.4	4.9
5.3	0.50	na	-0.01	4.4	4.3	1.03	10.22	2.91	62.1	2.6	14.7	7.5	7.8
6.6	0.57	3.0	-0.02	3.9	10.4	0.75	6.92	3.25	65.1	3.7	6.5	5.1	7.4
7.9	0.29	1.5	0.20	3.8	6.9	0.90	10.22	4.02	58.9	2.6	25.1	16.3	7.0
9.4	0.08	na	0.00	3.9	1.2	0.70	5.18	3.54	76.5	4.8	34.5	9.1	7.3
6.6	0.28	0.7	0.01	4.7	5.5	0.92	5.48	4.23	67.0	2.5	26.2	17.2	8.9
4.4	0.61	na	0.03	0.0	-0.1	-1.19	-9.51	2.76	143.2	3.0	59.9	24.6	4.7
5.7	2.12	na	0.08	8.0	2.7	1.91	17.93	4.14	53.6	5.5	42.8	7.8	6.8
7.4	1.53	na	0.22	9.4	5.0	2.16	15.95	3.66	51.1	2.5	24.8	17.3	9.3
7.3	1.44	na	0.00	2.3	0.2	0.23	3.09	3.26	91.8	4.6	20.6	5.4	3.9
9.4	0.00	na	0.00	5.7	0.8	1.04	4.43	3.19	57.8	2.6	44.2	28.5	8.8
5.7	0.88	8.0	0.00	3.4	1.3	0.66	8.70	2.79	72.0	1.3	20.6	24.5	4.1
6.5	2.64	na	0.15	3.4	3.2	0.65	6.78	3.18	75.4	5.3	33.0	4.8	6.2
6.2	1.83	na	-0.06	4.9	0.7	0.99	8.20	3.56	67.1	2.1	31.9	20.8	6.9
8.8	0.00	na	0.00	5.7	0.4	1.28	11.63	3.42	56.3	3.9	37.0	14.3	6.7
6.0	0.46	2.2	0.56	8.1	11.9	1.69	17.26	4.39	58.2	1.3	9.8	26.7	9.0
5.3	2.85	na	0.15	2.8	1.2	0.45	3.98	3.70	80.0	2.6	16.6	14.4	6.8
6.3	1.05	na	-0.03	4.1	2.9	0.72	3.96	3.07	67.4	1.0	13.1	31.9	8.3
8.8	0.00	na	0.01	4.3	0.4	1.01	4.42	3.52	73.9	5.5	46.1	8.0	7.6
3.5	3.75	na	0.00	1.6	0.0	0.04	0.56	2.89	96.8	5.8	57.5	6.3	1.0
5.6	0.91	5.8	0.04	4.7	1.2	1.05	6.51	2.69	55.2	4.1	46.2	16.1	7.7
8.3	4.31	na	0.03	3.0	0.5	0.53	2.85	2.81	81.9	3.8	53.9	19.3	7.6
7.4	1.90	na	0.01	6.0	1.6	1.16	8.42	3.73	60.8	2.6	22.5	16.9	8.7
9.9	0.00	na	0.00	2.5	0.2	0.26	1.47	2.20	85.7	7.4	84.6	3.2	6.3
7.0	1.85	na	0.19	0.0	-0.5	-1.38	-11.27	1.90	129.1	2.1	37.3	30.8	6.5
8.2	0.00	na	0.00	6.7	1.0	1.39	12.90	4.06	56.1	2.7	13.5	15.5	6.2
6.8	0.61	na	0.03	6.8	4.4	1.29	12.75	3.54	53.7	3.5	12.7	11.3	6.4
8.0	0.50	2.2	-0.01	4.6	105.9	0.80	7.19	2.87	63.0	3.5	24.9	14.6	10.0
7.6	0.98	5.1	0.01	3.5	6.5	0.70	5.47	2.85	72.1	4.7	16.0	4.8	9.1
6.4	3.52	9.0	-0.03	4.0	2.4	0.78	4.73	2.62	64.6	3.9	35.0	13.8	7.6
5.8	1.33	9.2	0.00	3.4	1.1	0.58	6.41	2.99	76.5	1.7	17.6	22.3	5.2
8.0	0.49	na	0.05	5.4	3.5	1.23	10.74	3.16	55.4	1.4	25.8	20.2	7.4
5.5	1.09	na	0.05	3.1	0.2	0.50	4.60	2.52	70.4	3.8	28.9	12.5	5.2
3.4	1.87	na	0.07	2.3	0.4	0.21	2.17	3.27	93.5	1.7	27.4	27.4	5.2
8.6	0.26	1.6	-0.03	4.8	58.3	0.95	10.54	3.32	61.5	6.4	32.5	1.5	7.9
7.5	0.47	3.0	0.03	6.4	52.0	1.22	13.20	2.39	54.3	1.7	16.9	9.9	8.8
5.4	3.06	na	-0.01	3.8	0.9	1.35	10.61	2.23	63.0	1.4	31.3	41.3	4.2
7.4	0.19	na	1.12	6.2	0.4	1.05	6.34	4.57	61.8	3.4	38.8	17.4	7.4
6.6	0.40	na	0.02	5.6	9.2	1.05	11.90	3.54	57.6	3.4	15.7	12.7	8.2
8.0	0.00	na	0.00	4.2	0.3	0.77	5.67	3.86	78.3	4.5	32.5	10.0	6.9
6.9	1.34	na	0.00	5.2	0.6	1.55	15.83	2.71	66.1	3.1	17.8	13.6	2.7
8.1	0.00	na	0.00	0.0	-0.7	-0.76	-3.89	3.63	87.6	4.3	22.5	7.0	1.5
8.4	0.81	2.7	-0.01	9.9	53.3	3.35	19.76	2.86	63.4	1.4	12.5	25.7	10.0
10.0	0.49	na	0.00	2.2	2.6	0.26	2.58	2.35	87.4	5.1	54.6	15.1	7.3
5.3	1.02	na	0.11	5.3	6.3	1.08	7.34	3.46	58.9	5.0	19.7	2.7	8.1

Name	City	State	2019 Rating	2018 Rating	Total Assets ($Mil)	One Year Asset Growth	Asset Mix (As a % of Total Assets)				Capital- ization Index	Lever- age Ratio	Risk- Based Capital Ratio
			Rating				Comm- ercial Loans	Cons- umer Loans	Mort- gage Loans	Secur- ities			
Watkins Savings Bank	Watkins	IA	B+	B+	B+	79.3	14.04	0.7	1.1	5.9	52.5	10.0	16.7	0.0
Wauchula State Bank	Wauchula	FL	A-	B+	B	800.9	15.75	5.3	0.5	12.4	22.6	10.0	11.4	0.0
Waukesha State Bank	Waukesha	WI	A	A	A	1225.0	24.20	21.1	0.6	18.8	15.6	7.7	10.7	0.0
Waukon State Bank	Waukon	IA	A	A	A-	343.0	15.84	12.5	1.9	15.3	9.4	8.3	10.9	0.0
Waumandee State Bank	Waumandee	WI	B	B	B	309.8	67.73	15.5	1.9	16.4	9.6	5.7	8.3	11.5
Waycross Bank & Trust	Waycross	GA	B+	B+	B	220.3	22.81	4.8	0.4	7.5	32.6	8.3	9.9	24.5
▲ Wayland State Bank	Mount Pleasant	IA	A-	A-	A-	123.3	12.27	10.1	2.0	11.3	28.3	10.0	16.3	27.3
Wayne Bank	Honesdale	PA	B+	B+	B+	1843.0	51.49	12.3	8.8	15.1	10.7	6.8	8.9	12.4
▲ Wayne Bank and Trust Co.	Cambridge City	IN	B	B-	B-	189.2	15.18	13.1	4.3	21.0	13.1	10.0	11.5	15.7
▲ Wayne County Bank	Waynesboro	TN	C+	C+	C+	344.7	9.68	14.2	6.8	15.7	8.7	10.0	14.4	0.0
Wayne Savings Community Bank	Wooster	OH	B	B	B-	552.0	11.64	10.6	0.4	26.9	11.8	6.8	8.8	14.1
Waypoint Bank	Cozad	NE	B+	A-	B+	306.7	13.74	6.8	1.4	1.4	17.7	10.0	11.3	15.3
WCF Financial Bank	Webster City	IA	C-	C	C	135.0	7.42	0.4	3.9	36.5	25.0	10.0	15.5	28.4
WebBank	Salt Lake City	UT	A-	B+	B+	2782.2	212.90	85.4	9.2	0.0	0.5	10.0	29.2	36.5
Webster Bank, N.A.	Waterbury	CT	B	B	B	33034.5	10.38	22.4	0.5	16.9	28.2	6.5	8.5	13.5
Webster Five Cents Savings Bank	Webster	MA	B-	B	B	982.4	11.33	11.3	0.9	19.9	13.8	9.3	11.7	0.0
Welch State Bank of Welch, Oklahoma	Welch	OK	A-	A-	A	291.5	5.67	5.8	2.6	13.9	20.6	8.6	10.1	0.0
Welcome State Bank	Welcome	MN	B+	B+	C+	33.8	11.77	13.0	7.2	10.8	2.7	9.9	10.9	16.0
▼ Wellington State Bank	Wellington	TX	C+	B	B	458.9	18.87	7.5	2.0	5.5	23.4	8.3	10.5	13.6
Wellington Trust Co., N.A.	Boston	MA	U	U	U	86.2	-1.22	0.0	0.0	0.0	0.0	10.0	49.8	46.01
Wells Bank	Platte City	MO	A-	A-	A-	272.3	18.90	7.1	0.7	21.6	4.5	6.1	9.3	0.0
Wells Fargo Bank South Central, N.A.	Houston	TX	B+	A-	B	7110.9	27.10	0.0	0.0	10.5	0.0	8.6	10.1	69.9
Wells Fargo Bank, N.A.	Sioux Falls	SD	B-	B	B	1750196.0	2.44	9.6	6.1	16.9	23.0	6.5	8.5	15.8
Wells Fargo Delaware Trust Co., N.A.	Wilmington	DE	U	U	U	234.4	-1.93	0.0	0.0	0.0	0.0	10.0	99.4	490.4
Wells Fargo National Bank West	Las Vegas	NV	B+	A-	A-	18248.0	23.42	0.0	0.0	53.7	0.0	10.0	11.0	37.7
Wells Fargo Trust Co., N.A.	Salt Lake City	UT	U	U	U	1296.2	0.85	0.0	0.0	0.0	0.0	10.0	94.2	419.2
▲ Wells River Savings Bank	Wells River	VT	C-	C-	D+	199.8	8.10	7.4	5.4	41.1	21.5	8.9	10.3	16.3
▲ Wenona State Bank	Wenona	IL	C+	C+	C+	39.8	15.86	7.7	3.6	4.2	39.1	10.0	12.3	0.0
WesBanco Bank, Inc.	Wheeling	WV	B+	A-	B+	16516.3	31.50	11.9	1.9	14.1	17.1	7.8	9.5	14.5
▼ West Alabama Bank & Trust	Reform	AL	B+	A-	B+	718.3	12.92	6.7	1.6	11.5	37.6	10.0	12.1	0.0
West Bank	West Des Moines	IA	B+	B+	B+	2773.3	12.90	20.2	0.1	2.2	13.5	6.0	9.3	11.8
West Central Bank	Ashland	IL	B-	B-	C	198.5	9.04	15.8	7.0	21.8	14.2	8.6	10.1	0.0
▼ West Central Georgia Bank	Thomaston	GA	A-	A	A-	134.0	11.83	4.2	4.4	16.7	44.5	10.0	25.3	0.0
West Gate Bank	Lincoln	NE	A-	B+	B+	897.4	21.09	12.6	0.2	24.9	2.9	8.7	10.2	0.0
West Iowa Bank	West Bend	IA	A-	A-	B+	139.0	2.59	9.0	1.2	7.9	13.9	10.0	13.5	0.0
West Michigan Community Bank	Hudsonville	MI	C+	B-	C+	706.2	18.12	30.3	0.7	8.1	5.2	3.3	9.5	0.0
West Plains Bank	Ainsworth	NE	A-	A-	B+	127.0	11.63	12.4	1.5	0.8	24.0	10.0	14.1	0.0
West Plains Bank and Trust Co.	West Plains	MO	A-	A-	B+	487.0	25.89	12.0	3.1	7.3	15.3	9.4	10.6	14.7
West Plains S&L Assn.	West Plains	MO	B	B-	B	85.7	3.35	2.5	1.0	59.7	8.7	10.0	21.3	0.0
West Point Bank	Radcliff	KY	B	B	B+	300.2	1.66	0.5	1.6	28.6	19.3	7.7	9.5	15.8
▲ West Pointe Bank	Oshkosh	WI	B-	C+	C	297.3	4.94	17.0	0.1	18.6	10.8	10.0	17.4	22.3
West Shore Bank	Ludington	MI	B-	B-	B-	562.9	16.06	17.3	3.7	16.2	14.3	6.1	8.1	12.9
West Suburban Bank	Lombard	IL	C+	B-	B-	2646.0	16.90	22.6	0.3	4.7	38.2	6.5	8.5	15.2
▼ West Texas National Bank	Midland	TX	B+	A-	B+	1358.7	3.96	29.2	0.5	15.0	21.7	9.2	10.5	16.5
▲ West Texas State Bank	Snyder	TX	B+	B-	C-	156.0	17.20	6.1	3.5	4.8	41.6	10.0	11.2	22.0
West Town Bank & Trust	North Riverside	IL	C	B-	C	333.8	21.28	45.2	0.1	10.2	4.3	8.9	10.3	15.1
West Union Bank	West Union	WV	B	B-	C+	214.3	12.05	4.6	8.8	7.2	49.5	7.0	9.0	16.0
▲ West Valley National Bank	Goodyear	AZ	D+	D-	D	152.3	98.67	26.2	0.2	2.4	1.7	4.6	6.6	16.2
West View Savings Bank	Pittsburgh	PA	B-	B-	C+	328.2	-8.07	0.0	0.0	24.6	66.8	7.7	9.5	17.5
WestAmerica Bank	San Rafael	CA	B+	B+	B+	6517.4	16.60	5.8	3.9	0.4	70.2	5.6	7.6	12.7
Westbury Bank	Waukesha	WI	B-	B-	B-	887.6	3.97	15.4	0.7	14.7	10.9	7.1	9.0	13.3
Westchester Bank	White Plains	NY	A-	A-	A-	1200.9	35.51	23.0	0.2	3.0	7.4	9.3	10.5	14.4
Western Alliance Bank	Phoenix	AZ	A-	A-	A-	33350.7	26.59	22.5	0.0	6.4	13.5	6.6	9.1	12.2
Western Bank	Lordsburg	NM	A	A	B+	239.3	26.67	7.7	1.1	4.7	53.4	8.4	10.0	22.9
Western Bank	Lubbock	TX	B-	B-	B-	385.8	10.94	14.6	0.5	12.3	11.7	4.4	8.9	0.0
Western Bank of Clovis	Clovis	NM	B+	B+	B+	76.4	7.57	13.4	0.4	2.3	13.2	10.0	13.0	0.0
Western Bank, Artesia, New Mexico	Artesia	NM	B	B-	C+	249.0	16.66	37.4	1.1	1.8	31.3	6.5	8.5	14.2
Western Commerce Bank	Carlsbad	NM	B+	A-	B+	556.3	6.05	25.7	0.5	17.2	22.3	5.7	7.7	14.8
Western Dakota Bank	Timber Lake	SD	C	C	D+	44.6	17.83	7.5	2.5	0.0	3.0	5.9	7.9	15.4
Western Heritage Bank	Las Cruces	NM	C+	C+	C-	284.5	11.76	31.6	0.8	5.7	5.5	8.4	9.9	14.7

Asset Quality Index	Adjusted Non-Performing Loans as a % of Total Loans	as a % of Capital	Net Charge-Offs Avg Loans	Profitability Index	Net Income ($Mil)	Return on Assets (R.O.A.)	Return on Equity (R.O.E.)	Net Interest Spread	Overhead Efficiency Ratio	Liquidity Index	Liquidity Ratio	Hot Money Ratio	Stability Index
9.3	0.00	na	0.00	4.6	0.5	0.90	5.13	2.61	56.0	4.4	74.4	18.7	8.1
5.7	2.33	9.3	0.15	7.8	9.9	1.69	14.87	3.69	54.3	4.5	43.3	13.2	8.7
8.7	0.12	0.7	0.00	9.1	18.9	2.22	19.36	4.05	53.2	5.2	15.2	1.0	10.0
8.5	0.05	na	0.01	7.9	4.0	1.65	14.64	3.37	46.0	4.0	29.2	11.4	9.3
6.5	2.63	na	0.05	4.6	1.5	0.87	8.52	3.80	65.5	1.5	17.1	18.9	6.0
7.8	0.52	na	0.03	6.0	2.1	1.38	12.73	2.75	72.7	6.0	56.4	8.9	7.4
5.3	3.57	na	1.10	6.2	1.1	1.21	6.80	3.47	45.8	6.6	59.4	5.9	8.4
5.3	0.82	na	0.08	5.0	11.0	1.01	10.05	3.52	57.9	1.5	8.0	23.4	8.5
6.7	0.47	na	0.00	4.9	1.7	1.30	11.27	4.25	70.5	3.9	17.2	8.3	6.4
3.6	4.40	na	0.10	5.7	2.7	1.09	7.45	4.69	62.5	1.0	23.8	34.9	7.3
5.8	0.54	na	0.02	6.4	5.1	1.29	13.69	3.69	51.3	3.5	15.9	10.2	6.4
4.9	1.93	na	-0.01	7.6	3.9	1.77	13.95	3.95	54.5	3.5	20.6	11.8	9.0
9.0	0.47	na	0.14	1.0	-0.1	-0.06	-0.37	2.90	95.7	2.9	40.2	21.9	7.2
5.6	0.00	na	1.93	9.8	26.0	1.81	19.45	4.46	33.5	0.4	4.5	9.9	8.8
5.7	1.39	6.0	0.22	4.7	179.5	0.75	7.57	3.05	59.0	4.3	18.9	4.9	9.4
7.8	0.32	1.6	0.00	3.9	5.6	0.80	6.45	3.39	70.8	4.7	12.5	3.5	7.5
8.2	0.17	na	0.04	7.3	3.8	1.71	16.58	4.56	63.7	1.3	14.8	25.0	8.0
6.9	0.00	na	0.03	8.7	0.5	1.98	18.12	4.04	56.8	4.6	27.7	7.1	7.8
5.3	0.49	na	0.19	3.2	1.9	0.55	4.76	4.15	79.0	2.3	16.8	17.7	6.3
10.0	na	na	na	10.0	4.6	7.96	16.42	-81.65	97.0	4.0	10.4	0.0	7.0
6.1	0.48	3.8	0.00	9.7	4.4	2.29	24.28	4.62	47.4	4.4	11.2	5.8	7.4
6.8	13.36	10.6	-0.02	5.0	13.1	0.26	2.39	1.70	63.2	7.7	97.9	0.0	7.6
5.5	1.56	6.1	0.36	2.6	416.0	0.03	0.33	2.53	75.2	6.3	44.1	1.9	9.2
10.0	na	0.0	na	8.3	2.5	1.42	1.44	0.59	61.5	4.0	na	0.0	5.0
10.0	0.10	1.0	0.00	10.0	382.9	2.56	29.94	2.25	13.5	2.9	50.8	0.0	5.7
10.0	na	0.0	na	2.5	6.9	0.71	0.75	0.76	87.2	4.0	na	0.0	7.6
7.0	0.36	na	0.01	2.0	0.4	0.25	2.33	3.65	94.0	5.4	33.4	4.6	5.6
6.8	1.48	na	0.90	3.1	0.2	0.56	4.32	2.92	74.2	6.3	57.5	5.5	5.8
6.0	0.37	1.7	0.08	4.1	74.6	0.61	3.86	3.43	57.2	4.2	11.7	7.1	9.7
8.0	1.46	na	0.08	4.6	4.7	0.91	6.71	3.16	64.7	2.5	40.1	28.4	8.3
5.3	0.79	6.6	-0.01	6.2	25.2	1.26	14.25	3.25	41.8	3.2	10.5	6.5	8.4
4.3	0.13	na	0.11	4.5	1.6	1.11	10.14	3.89	72.2	1.8	23.3	22.4	6.0
9.3	0.23	na	0.00	5.5	1.0	1.05	3.94	3.73	67.0	6.6	77.4	8.7	8.3
7.7	0.10	na	0.01	9.3	17.4	2.64	26.74	4.53	53.1	2.8	19.8	15.5	8.2
7.9	0.05	na	-0.01	6.3	1.3	1.24	8.77	3.64	54.8	4.4	27.9	8.6	8.2
8.0	0.23	na	-0.02	6.0	6.5	1.30	13.57	3.75	54.7	3.0	12.1	8.7	6.4
7.6	0.79	na	0.16	6.0	1.0	1.03	7.11	3.35	57.3	3.7	30.9	13.3	8.5
5.7	1.01	na	0.14	6.0	4.6	1.39	12.16	3.48	62.2	1.8	22.5	8.7	8.4
7.2	0.92	na	0.00	4.2	0.5	0.77	3.60	3.20	65.5	1.5	32.2	36.1	7.7
6.2	0.94	4.2	-0.01	6.1	2.8	1.33	14.09	3.61	51.1	5.4	37.6	6.4	6.5
3.5	3.29	na	0.06	6.0	2.7	1.21	6.97	3.72	53.9	0.7	15.0	47.2	8.5
4.9	0.89	4.5	0.02	3.8	2.8	0.76	8.36	3.63	79.5	4.3	19.7	7.5	5.3
5.6	1.96	10.4	0.07	2.7	7.6	0.41	4.52	2.62	75.4	6.5	42.3	4.4	6.6
6.3	1.26	6.1	0.86	4.5	7.5	0.73	6.29	3.44	57.3	6.3	39.2	4.3	8.9
5.2	5.61	na	0.29	5.9	1.9	1.68	13.90	3.19	55.9	4.6	46.3	13.8	6.1
1.2	3.34	na	1.63	3.6	-0.9	-0.40	-3.47	3.90	80.8	0.7	11.4	23.7	7.2
7.7	0.47	na	0.18	5.1	1.7	1.12	11.75	3.71	63.5	5.5	33.4	3.7	5.0
5.7	1.41	12.6	0.00	3.7	1.1	1.32	19.00	4.29	74.9	5.9	46.3	6.2	4.0
10.0	0.00	na	0.00	3.5	1.4	0.52	6.00	1.73	56.8	4.1	30.9	7.5	5.3
8.5	0.55	0.8	0.18	6.5	57.0	1.27	12.10	2.94	47.9	7.8	70.8	1.4	8.7
3.4	1.25	9.7	0.06	4.4	5.6	0.86	9.16	3.17	65.3	4.4	16.2	6.3	6.8
8.3	0.18	0.8	0.13	6.3	9.9	1.18	10.89	3.27	47.2	4.5	28.4	10.4	9.6
6.6	0.65	5.2	0.06	8.2	317.9	1.40	13.77	4.05	39.8	4.2	17.2	4.9	10.0
7.5	1.87	na	0.28	7.4	3.0	1.82	16.34	3.70	58.2	6.8	58.4	4.4	8.5
8.4	0.00	na	-0.02	5.8	4.1	1.46	16.24	4.25	62.5	1.2	18.4	29.9	5.7
6.7	3.43	8.6	0.00	4.8	0.5	0.83	6.22	3.86	69.4	3.4	17.8	12.2	7.8
5.1	1.38	na	0.22	8.9	3.7	1.99	21.50	3.47	41.1	5.6	47.2	8.7	7.3
8.8	0.57	na	-0.01	8.7	7.7	1.84	25.13	4.16	48.2	4.3	25.3	8.0	7.3
8.8	0.00	na	0.05	3.6	0.2	0.69	8.75	3.86	77.7	6.2	56.2	5.6	2.9
8.0	0.09	na	0.10	3.3	1.1	0.53	4.82	4.82	69.9	2.1	20.1	18.9	6.2

Name	City	State	2019 Rating	2018 Rating	Rating	Total Assets ($Mil)	One Year Asset Growth	Commercial Loans	Consumer Loans	Mortgage Loans	Securities	Capitalization Index	Leverage Ratio	Risk-Based Capital Ratio
▲ Western National Bank	Duluth	MN	C+	C	C	120.0	12.47	9.4	2.0	17.2	1.0	7.6	9.4	15.0
Western National Bank	Chester	NE	B-	B	B	133.7	0.29	9.0	2.2	14.5	0.2	5.8	9.4	0.0
▲ Western National Bank of Cass Lake	Cass Lake	MN	C+	C	C	34.9	3.27	0.1	1.7	23.3	0.5	6.5	8.5	18.0
▼ Western Nebraska Bank	Curtis	NE	C-	C-	D+	139.0	15.45	18.2	1.8	5.1	12.0	2.8	9.4	0.0
Western State Bank	Garden City	KS	A-	A-	A	533.2	14.27	15.7	0.4	4.5	24.7	10.0	11.8	16.6
Western State Bank	Devils Lake	ND	B	B	B-	1445.6	16.33	49.9	0.9	7.7	2.1	7.2	10.0	12.6
Western States Bank	Laramie	WY	B	B-	C	544.6	15.10	14.1	0.6	8.1	11.0	9.3	11.6	0.0
Westfield Bank	Westfield	MA	C+	B-	B	2480.8	14.26	16.9	0.2	27.5	7.7	6.8	8.8	13.7
Westfield Bank, FSB	Westfield Center	OH	B	B	B	1868.8	25.11	30.6	10.1	14.6	8.1	5.8	9.3	0.0
Westmoreland Federal S&L Assn.	Latrobe	PA	C-	C	C+	172.4	0.53	0.0	0.0	42.2	36.7	10.0	24.4	0.0
WestSide Bank	Hiram	GA	B-	B-	C-	184.9	33.89	10.4	0.3	6.4	3.6	6.9	9.0	0.0
Westside State Bank	Westside	IA	C+	B-	B-	130.3	8.92	17.6	3.3	24.7	5.1	6.2	8.5	11.9
WestStar Bank	El Paso	TX	A-	A-	A-	2301.9	23.51	23.1	0.1	2.3	14.8	8.1	9.9	13.5
▲ WEX Bank	Midvale	UT	A-	B+	B+	2459.4	-18.89	72.9	0.0	0.0	0.0	10.0	12.8	15.7
Wheatland Bank	Spokane	WA	B+	B+	B-	560.3	23.55	12.7	0.3	5.1	6.6	8.1	9.7	13.9
Wheaton Bank & Trust Co., N.A.	Wheaton	IL	B	B	B	2653.0	33.67	33.0	15.7	3.1	14.4	5.5	7.7	11.3
Wheaton College Trust Co., N.A.	Wheaton	IL	U	U	U	3.6	-0.88	0.0	0.0	0.0	93.0	9.8	94.4	0.0
Wheeler County State Bank	Alamo	GA	B+	B+	B+	107.1	16.09	10.6	5.2	14.9	10.8	10.0	15.5	0.0
Whitaker Bank, Inc.	Lexington	KY	B	B	B	1304.3	11.66	4.9	2.5	15.2	43.2	10.0	13.8	0.0
White State Bank	South English	IA	B	B	B-	43.3	7.93	11.8	2.4	10.2	31.7	10.0	13.7	0.0
Whitesville State Bank	Whitesville	WV	C+	C+	B-	113.7	3.44	4.3	14.2	24.1	38.6	8.8	10.2	19.4
▲ Wilcox County State Bank	Abbeville	GA	B+	B	C+	124.0	11.74	5.0	5.0	31.6	15.4	9.3	10.6	0.0
Wilkinson County Bank	Irwinton	GA	B	B	B	50.9	8.60	3.2	5.3	37.8	39.1	10.0	16.4	0.0
Willamette Community Bank	Albany	OR	C+	C+	B-	209.8	35.36	21.2	0.1	1.2	12.0	4.9	10.4	0.0
Willamette Valley Bank	Salem	OR	A	A-	B+	383.5	44.48	9.6	0.1	34.9	0.0	10.0	16.4	0.0
William Penn Bank,	Bristol	PA	B+	B+	B+	731.2	75.02	0.8	0.5	48.0	16.9	10.0	11.9	0.0
▼ Williamstown Bank, Inc.	Williamstown	WV	B	B+	B+	177.2	6.21	7.6	12.9	32.9	7.6	10.0	11.7	0.0
Williamsville State Bank & Trust	Williamsville	IL	C-	C	C	101.7	3.61	9.0	3.4	26.1	40.1	10.0	12.9	30.3
Wilmington Savings Bank	Wilmington	OH	B-	B	C+	170.8	5.49	0.7	1.3	57.8	4.9	10.0	17.2	24.0
Wilmington Savings Fund Society, FSB	Wilmington	DE	B+	A-	B+	13796.5	12.58	15.4	2.6	13.0	17.8	9.0	10.3	14.5
▼ Wilmington Trust, N.A.	Wilmington	DE	B-	B-	B	4573.0	22.28	0.0	0.0	0.8	0.1	10.0	12.5	62.2
Wilson & Muir Bank & Trust Co.	Bardstown	KY	B-	B-	B	599.3	8.94	13.6	2.0	15.2	31.1	5.6	7.6	14.8
Wilson Bank and Trust	Lebanon	TN	A-	A-	A-	3245.8	18.38	5.9	1.1	17.8	17.7	7.9	11.1	0.0
Wilson State Bank	Wilson	KS	C-	C+	C	100.5	15.71	17.9	2.8	21.8	22.0	5.4	7.9	11.3
Winchester Co-operative Bank	Winchester	MA	B-	B	B	739.1	8.23	0.7	0.2	53.8	11.2	10.0	12.4	0.0
Winchester Savings Bank	Winchester	MA	C+	C+	C+	594.7	7.66	0.8	0.1	54.0	7.9	10.0	12.3	0.0
Windsor Federal S&L Assn.	Windsor	CT	B-	B-	B-	647.2	21.77	16.4	0.1	21.4	11.7	8.0	10.1	0.0
WinFirst Bank	Winchester	KY	B+	B+	B+	145.8	1.43	1.7	0.3	45.8	2.2	10.0	13.5	0.0
Winnsboro State Bank & Trust Co.	Winnsboro	LA	C+	C	C+	265.7	16.82	7.0	2.9	11.8	14.7	6.5	8.5	13.3
Winter Hill Bank, FSB	Somerville	MA	C	C	C	350.8	-4.28	0.8	0.4	44.7	12.7	8.6	10.1	17.3
Winter Park National Bank	Winter Park	FL	B	B	C	516.2	50.73	12.8	0.3	1.2	35.1	7.8	9.5	16.9
Wintrust Bank, N.A.	Chicago	IL	B	B	B	8238.3	27.83	42.7	5.5	4.6	5.4	5.8	8.6	11.6
Wisconsin Bank & Trust	Madison	WI	B	B+	B+	1262.1	22.29	23.2	0.9	3.8	22.5	7.9	9.6	14.1
Wisconsin River Bank	Sauk City	WI	B	B	B-	158.1	11.40	7.8	0.4	28.4	4.8	8.5	10.0	0.0
WNB Financial, N.A.	Winona	MN	B+	B+	B+	495.6	18.71	11.6	1.6	15.4	31.3	8.6	10.1	0.0
Wolf River Community Bank	Hortonville	WI	A-	A-	A-	238.0	20.41	12.3	1.6	20.2	10.9	10.0	11.1	0.0
Wood & Huston Bank	Marshall	MO	A	A-	B+	833.1	13.59	15.0	2.0	13.9	18.4	10.0	11.3	15.3
Woodford State Bank	Monroe	WI	B+	B+	B	291.8	18.51	12.7	0.8	10.1	27.1	5.0	8.3	0.0
Woodforest National Bank	The Woodlands	TX	B+	B+	B+	8413.0	33.38	27.2	0.7	5.6	19.2	5.6	7.6	11.6
Woodland Bank	Grand Rapids	MN	B	B	B	118.7	10.12	17.1	4.6	22.1	7.3	8.7	10.2	0.0
Woodlands Bank	Williamsport	PA	B	B-	B-	498.0	17.37	13.0	0.2	19.6	15.2	7.7	9.6	0.0
Woodlands National Bank	Onamia	MN	A-	A-	B+	303.0	46.98	26.0	3.8	4.2	24.0	7.3	9.2	19.7
▼ Woodruff Federal S&L Assn.	Woodruff	SC	C	B-	C+	105.9	11.83	0.0	0.0	41.1	2.4	10.0	29.3	0.0
Woodsboro Bank	Woodsboro	MD	C	C	C	309.7	18.97	14.0	0.4	20.5	19.1	5.9	7.9	13.9
Woodsfield Savings Bank	Woodsfield	OH	C-	C-	C-	77.8	12.79	2.8	9.8	37.4	15.1	5.9	7.9	15.3
Woodsville Guaranty Savings Bank	Woodsville	NH	C+	C+	C+	562.8	11.15	11.3	1.7	43.4	12.2	6.7	8.8	0.0
WoodTrust Bank	Wisconsin Rapids	WI	B	B	B-	522.9	25.12	12.9	1.3	6.8	22.4	7.3	9.8	0.0
▼ Woori America Bank	New York	NY	B	B+	A-	2134.6	3.96	9.9	0.1	16.8	7.4	10.0	13.6	0.0
Worthington Federal Savings Bank, FSB	Worthington	MN	B	B	B	86.2	10.89	0.8	3.4	58.4	12.9	10.0	15.5	39.8
Worthington National Banks	Arlington	TX	B	B	B-	389.7	32.96	16.6	1.2	19.3	0.0	6.6	8.6	0.0

Asset Quality Index	Adjusted Non-Performing Loans as a % of Total Loans	as a % of Capital	Net Charge-Offs Avg Loans	Profitability Index	Net Income ($Mil)	Return on Assets (R.O.A.)	Return on Equity (R.O.E.)	Net Interest Spread	Overhead Efficiency Ratio	Liquidity Index	Liquidity Ratio	Hot Money Ratio	Stability Index
3.4	1.08	na	0.07	3.6	0.6	0.65	5.51	4.24	81.7	1.9	25.1	21.6	5.6
6.5	0.15	1.0	0.00	6.1	1.6	1.54	13.85	3.39	53.1	0.7	12.2	37.2	7.5
7.3	0.32	na	0.11	3.8	0.2	0.82	8.92	2.23	78.3	3.6	45.6	17.7	4.8
4.9	0.64	5.0	0.00	4.1	0.8	0.86	8.55	3.77	70.6	1.4	10.5	19.9	4.5
5.4	1.53	7.2	0.01	9.2	7.8	2.06	16.65	4.70	50.0	3.2	14.3	13.1	8.8
4.6	1.62	na	0.22	8.4	14.3	1.38	13.57	4.94	48.5	1.6	5.2	14.9	9.6
4.9	2.59	na	0.24	5.5	4.1	1.09	8.91	4.21	67.0	3.2	21.7	13.5	7.7
6.5	0.95	5.8	0.05	2.7	7.3	0.42	4.47	2.82	71.7	2.1	13.3	16.0	7.0
5.5	0.65	4.3	0.01	3.9	9.9	0.78	7.16	3.13	64.5	2.6	15.2	16.2	8.0
9.6	1.32	2.2	0.00	0.9	-0.2	-0.16	-0.65	1.22	112.3	5.1	76.5	16.3	7.4
8.8	0.00	na	-0.17	4.2	0.9	0.76	6.93	4.50	70.3	4.9	38.4	10.2	5.3
8.1	0.00	na	0.09	3.7	0.6	0.64	7.38	3.79	80.1	1.7	12.5	20.2	5.6
7.8	1.24	na	0.05	9.7	38.1	2.43	19.63	4.09	47.2	4.1	20.2	9.8	10.0
5.3	0.03	7.7	1.77	10.0	78.0	4.18	36.39	21.05	81.4	1.2	23.6	1.1	8.9
8.3	0.04	na	-0.01	6.4	5.0	1.30	12.96	4.06	68.9	4.9	18.4	3.3	6.8
5.7	0.60	3.9	0.02	4.8	13.6	0.76	7.52	2.63	48.9	2.7	11.5	7.6	7.5
10.0	na	na	na	3.5	-0.1	-1.63	-1.74	1.07	107.6	4.0	na	0.0	4.2
6.9	0.78	na	0.08	4.3	0.7	0.95	5.94	3.97	73.4	2.0	28.5	23.0	8.4
4.3	5.33	13.5	-0.13	4.2	7.5	0.81	5.08	3.56	74.5	5.9	40.8	7.6	8.3
7.9	0.00	na	-0.07	7.4	0.5	1.49	9.35	3.37	46.3	4.2	46.0	15.2	7.0
6.6	0.52	2.3	0.15	3.3	0.5	0.64	5.92	3.83	85.9	3.8	51.6	18.5	5.2
5.5	1.41	na	-0.01	6.2	1.0	1.13	10.53	4.27	66.3	1.4	12.8	24.8	6.8
7.2	1.44	na	0.92	5.0	0.3	0.77	4.55	4.31	73.5	3.9	28.8	11.9	7.8
5.6	0.59	na	0.00	3.1	0.5	0.38	3.35	3.87	84.2	4.7	22.6	5.0	5.3
8.5	0.26	na	0.00	10.0	20.8	8.83	64.75	3.73	60.4	1.5	6.1	14.5	9.2
7.2	1.23	na	0.03	2.3	0.6	0.14	0.98	3.14	92.9	2.9	28.1	16.3	8.5
7.4	0.22	na	0.07	3.3	0.4	0.27	2.22	3.97	83.9	4.4	25.7	7.7	7.5
5.7	3.32	na	0.36	1.0	-0.1	-0.06	-0.46	2.82	101.4	6.1	53.6	6.9	5.9
5.3	5.59	na	-0.15	2.9	0.6	0.48	2.67	2.59	78.6	3.1	18.7	14.0	8.2
7.0	0.44	1.8	0.07	4.7	57.3	0.58	3.92	3.92	55.5	4.4	16.3	4.7	9.5
10.0	4.74	0.7	-0.06	3.9	18.0	0.46	3.88	4.10	88.2	8.8	111.0	0.1	7.3
4.1	2.18	12.4	0.34	7.2	7.2	1.66	19.33	3.76	54.4	5.5	33.5	4.0	6.7
8.6	0.02	0.3	-0.01	7.0	30.4	1.34	11.45	3.51	56.6	3.3	18.5	13.1	9.8
4.0	1.68	11.3	0.16	4.5	0.7	0.98	10.81	3.80	70.6	2.3	9.2	16.8	5.6
8.2	0.28	na	0.00	2.7	1.8	0.33	2.65	1.93	78.8	1.8	37.7	35.8	8.0
9.3	0.47	na	0.00	2.5	1.2	0.27	2.31	2.52	81.3	1.8	23.4	23.0	7.3
5.0	1.70	7.5	0.00	3.5	2.7	0.59	5.43	3.13	74.8	4.3	21.6	7.9	7.1
6.8	1.17	na	0.02	5.3	1.5	1.36	10.06	3.27	55.0	0.7	11.0	39.8	8.6
3.8	0.96	9.9	0.06	3.9	1.4	0.73	7.95	3.84	76.8	1.3	24.0	28.3	4.8
9.3	0.13	na	0.00	2.6	0.9	0.33	3.45	3.00	87.2	1.8	17.6	14.8	5.7
9.1	0.00	na	0.00	4.8	4.3	1.31	11.96	2.56	44.9	6.8	50.8	1.4	5.6
6.2	0.47	3.8	0.12	5.2	30.6	0.53	5.62	2.72	60.1	2.3	8.4	8.7	7.8
4.4	1.50	6.0	0.92	4.7	6.6	0.77	6.46	3.92	61.7	5.1	21.2	3.2	8.2
3.8	1.18	na	-0.06	5.2	1.3	1.08	10.44	3.30	56.3	0.8	18.4	31.2	7.0
6.6	0.87	na	0.00	5.5	5.5	1.60	11.91	3.35	67.4	4.8	32.1	8.0	7.7
6.8	1.92	na	0.00	6.5	2.2	1.32	11.12	4.13	53.4	4.2	24.4	8.4	7.6
8.4	0.49	na	0.10	7.4	11.0	1.83	16.53	3.83	58.6	2.6	8.1	15.2	8.9
6.9	0.66	na	0.03	8.0	3.9	1.95	20.97	3.89	55.9	3.7	31.5	13.6	7.1
6.1	1.69	8.7	0.93	6.8	91.9	1.62	19.83	3.21	74.7	7.0	41.7	0.9	7.6
4.7	1.07	na	0.03	4.8	0.8	0.88	8.35	4.61	71.8	2.2	11.9	16.7	6.6
4.7	1.95	na	0.00	5.8	3.9	1.13	10.91	3.50	65.4	4.6	15.5	4.4	6.4
8.1	0.17	0.9	0.18	5.4	2.1	1.07	9.56	3.35	58.6	4.6	43.2	2.8	6.3
9.0	1.37	na	0.00	1.7	0.1	0.10	0.35	1.58	101.2	2.6	53.6	47.1	7.4
7.9	0.40	na	-0.02	2.5	0.7	0.33	3.70	3.24	83.5	4.8	32.4	8.1	4.3
4.3	1.45	na	0.03	3.1	0.3	0.53	6.58	3.62	81.1	4.9	36.2	9.2	3.7
8.3	0.19	na	0.01	3.5	2.4	0.61	6.48	3.25	78.6	4.0	17.7	7.9	5.8
5.0	1.76	na	0.00	9.5	11.5	3.26	30.90	3.03	39.9	6.1	39.6	2.2	7.9
6.7	0.73	na	0.01	3.1	5.7	0.36	2.65	3.05	71.7	2.1	19.3	17.0	9.5
9.6	0.39	1.6	0.00	4.0	0.4	0.69	4.36	3.18	67.1	4.8	40.3	11.2	7.5
8.6	0.11	na	0.01	4.8	2.3	0.89	9.36	3.94	65.8	3.1	29.0	15.6	5.5

Name	City	State	Rating	2019 Rating	2018 Rating	Total Assets ($Mil)	One Year Asset Growth	Asset Mix (As a % of Total Assets)				Capital-ization Index	Lever-age Ratio	Risk-Based Capital Ratio
								Comm-ercial Loans	Cons-umer Loans	Mort-gage Loans	Secur-ities			
Wray State Bank	Wray	CO	D+	C-	D+	169.5	11.18	12.2	3.7	9.4	10.5	8.4	9.9	13.8
Wrentham Co-operative Bank	Wrentham	MA	C+	C+	C+	133.3	15.88	0.1	1.7	51.0	5.2	10.0	12.7	0.0
WSB Municipal Bank	Watertown	NY	U	U	U	143.2	30.97	0.0	0.0	0.0	85.6	10.0	11.3	0.0
Wyoming Bank & Trust	Cheyenne	WY	A	A	A-	248.8	14.10	6.5	0.2	5.5	34.8	10.0	11.2	21.8
Wyoming Community Bank	Riverton	WY	B	B	B	180.0	19.71	13.4	4.2	8.5	33.8	6.8	8.8	0.0
Yakima Federal S&L Assn.	Yakima	WA	B+	A-	A-	1917.5	6.37	0.0	0.0	33.6	41.6	10.0	25.0	0.0
▼ Yampa Valley Bank	Steamboat Springs	CO	B	A-	B-	425.9	33.42	13.9	1.3	14.3	19.2	3.4	9.0	0.0
Yellowstone Bank	Laurel	MT	A	A	A	937.6	20.20	14.8	0.8	9.2	19.3	10.0	15.3	0.0
YNB	Yukon	OK	B-	C+	C	217.9	-5.90	7.5	4.0	19.1	21.8	6.6	8.6	13.5
Yoakum National Bank	Yoakum	TX	A-	A-	A-	243.5	10.44	4.9	4.2	15.4	48.2	10.0	14.2	0.0
York State Bank	York	NE	B-	B-	C	156.8	5.20	10.8	1.5	4.4	9.2	8.6	10.9	13.9
▲ York Traditions Bank	York	PA	B+	B	B-	647.9	20.31	16.6	0.0	22.3	12.5	8.6	10.1	15.3
Yorktown Bank	Pryor	OK	B	B-	B-	111.2	-6.18	14.4	1.2	24.5	0.1	10.0	11.7	17.6
Young Americans Bank	Denver	CO	D-	D-	D-	21.6	5.37	0.0	0.3	0.0	0.5	5.3	7.3	198.0
▲ Zapata National Bank	Zapata	TX	B+	B	B-	87.4	7.63	5.6	5.7	16.9	19.6	10.0	13.6	0.0
▼ Zavala County Bank	Crystal City	TX	B-	B+	B+	80.3	16.02	1.7	3.4	0.2	62.7	10.0	12.2	52.4
Zions BanCorp., N.A.	Salt Lake City	UT	A-	A-	A-	78356.9	11.36	22.4	0.7	9.7	19.5	6.3	8.3	13.8

Asset Quality Index	Adjusted Non-Performing Loans as a % of Total Loans	as a % of Capital	Net Charge-Offs Avg Loans	Profitability Index	Net Income ($Mil)	Return on Assets (R.O.A.)	Return on Equity (R.O.E.)	Net Interest Spread	Overhead Efficiency Ratio	Liquidity Index	Liquidity Ratio	Hot Money Ratio	Stability Index
1.2	3.96	na	0.32	4.9	1.0	0.84	7.30	4.16	65.0	1.5	7.9	22.9	6.4
9.9	0.42	na	0.00	2.6	0.4	0.37	2.81	2.66	86.4	4.4	44.8	14.0	6.8
10.0	na	na	na	4.7	0.9	0.95	7.93	1.24	3.3	5.2	16.0	1.1	5.8
8.8	0.02	na	0.00	9.9	5.4	3.28	27.83	3.37	77.5	6.1	53.4	4.6	8.6
6.7	0.88	3.6	-0.04	4.5	1.2	0.99	10.37	4.10	72.6	4.5	34.3	10.8	6.2
10.0	0.16	na	0.00	4.2	11.3	0.82	3.21	2.07	54.0	4.0	76.6	30.4	10.0
8.4	0.20	na	0.00	9.2	5.5	1.98	21.56	4.49	50.4	4.4	26.3	7.7	7.3
8.5	0.19	na	0.01	9.8	17.0	2.58	15.07	4.03	40.2	5.0	29.6	5.7	10.0
6.8	0.49	na	0.05	3.8	1.6	0.95	10.55	4.01	81.3	3.2	17.8	13.1	4.8
9.0	0.03	0.1	0.00	5.1	2.1	1.23	8.02	2.93	60.4	4.5	54.9	16.0	8.6
3.9	0.73	na	0.02	5.6	1.2	1.06	7.61	3.74	64.1	3.7	16.9	10.9	8.2
7.5	0.35	na	0.32	6.3	6.1	1.38	13.47	3.42	56.1	3.5	12.2	10.2	6.3
7.7	0.00	na	0.00	4.7	0.8	0.92	6.41	3.84	70.4	2.5	22.8	17.3	7.3
10.0	15.52	na	10.06	0.0	-1.0	-6.15	-81.38	2.07	396.7	8.1	106.5	0.5	0.9
6.9	4.01	na	-1.63	7.3	1.2	1.80	13.04	2.81	68.6	2.2	47.3	40.2	8.1
9.7	0.05	na	0.06	3.1	0.3	0.57	4.43	2.20	80.7	5.6	73.2	12.2	7.0
6.2	1.02	5.3	0.22	3.8	254.8	0.46	4.52	3.20	64.0	5.4	25.4	2.0	8.9

Section II

Weiss
Recommended Banks by State

A compilation of those

U.S. Commercial Banks and Savings Banks

receiving a Weiss Safety Rating
of A+, A, A-, or B+.

Institutions are ranked by Safety Rating
in each state where they have a branch location.

Section II Contents

This section provides a list of Weiss Recommended Banks by State and contains all financial institutions receiving a Safety Rating of A+, A, A-, or B+. Recommended institutions are listed in each state in which they currently operate one or more branches. If a company is not on this list, it should not be automatically assumed that the firm is weak. Indeed, there are many firms that have not achieved a B+ or better rating but are in good condition with adequate resources to weather an average recession. Not being included in this list should not be construed as a recommendation to immediately withdraw deposits or cancel existing financial arrangements.

Institutions are ranked within each state by their Weiss Safety Rating, and then listed alphabetically by name. Institutions with the same rating should be viewed as having the same relative safety regardless of their ranking in this table.

- **State**
  The state in which the institution currently operates one or more branches. With the adoption of interstate branching laws, some institutions operating in your area may actually be headquartered in another state. Even so, there are no restrictions on your ability to do business with an out-of-state institution.

- **Institution Name**
  The name under which the institution was chartered. A bank's name can be very similar to, or the same as, the name of other banks which may not be on our Recommended List, so make sure you note the exact name.

- **Telephone**
  The telephone number for the institution's headquarters, or main office.

- **Safety Rating**
  Weiss rating assigned to the institution at the time of publication. Our ratings are designed to distinguish levels of insolvency risk and are measured on a scale from A to F based upon a wide range of factors. Highly rated companies are, in our opinion, less likely to experience financial difficulties than lower rated firms. See *About Weiss Safety Ratings* for more information and a description of what each rating means.

Weiss Safety Ratings are not deemed to be a recommendation concerning the purchase or sale of the securities of any bank that is publicly owned.

Alabama

Name	Telephone	Name	Telephone
Rating: A+		Farmers & Merchants Bank	(256) 766-2579
		Farmers & Merchants Bank	(256) 447-9041
First Bank of Boaz	(256) 593-8670	First Bank	(256) 395-2255
Rating: A		First Community Bank of Central Alabama	(334) 567-0081
		First Southern State Bank	(256) 437-2171
Cheaha Bank	(256) 835-8855	First State Bank of the South, Inc.	(205) 698-8116
Citizens Bank of Winfield	(205) 487-4277	FirstBank	(615) 313-0080
First Metro Bank	(256) 386-0600	FirstState Bank	(256) 396-2187
First National Bank	(205) 921-7435	Friend Bank	(334) 886-2367
Metro Bank	(205) 884-2265	Merchants Bank of Alabama	(256) 734-8110
Metro City Bank	(770) 455-4989	North Alabama Bank	(256) 828-9500
Phenix-Girard Bank	(334) 298-0691	Oakworth Capital Bank	(205) 263-4700
Rating: A-		Peoples Independent Bank	(256) 593-8844
		Renasant Bank	(800) 680-1601
Armed Forces Bank, N.A.	(913) 682-9090	River Bank & Trust	(334) 290-1012
Bank of Vernon	(205) 695-7141	South State Bank, N.A.	(863) 551-5500
Bank OZK	(501) 978-2265	Southern Independent Bank	(334) 493-2265
Brantley Bank and Trust Co.	(334) 527-3206	Traditions Bank	(256) 735-2121
Centennial Bank	(501) 328-4663	Troy Bank & Trust Co.	(334) 566-4000
Central State Bank	(205) 668-0711	Truist Bank	(336) 733-2000
Citizens Bank of Fayette	(205) 932-8911	Trustmark National Bank	(601) 208-5111
Cullman Savings Bank	(256) 734-1740	United Bank	(251) 446-6000
Farmers and Merchants Bank	(334) 864-9941	West Alabama Bank & Trust	(205) 375-6261
First Bank of Alabama	(256) 362-2334	Woodforest National Bank	(832) 375-2505
First Citizens Bank	(334) 335-3346		
First Jackson Bank, Inc.	(256) 437-2107		
First National Bank of Pulaski	(931) 363-2585		
HNB First Bank	(334) 693-3352		
HomeTown Bank of Alabama	(205) 625-4434		
Pinnacle Bank	(205) 221-4111		
Robertson Banking Co.	(334) 289-3564		
Samson Banking Co., Inc.	(334) 898-7107		
ServisFirst Bank	(205) 949-0302		
Town-Country National Bank	(334) 682-4155		
Rating: B+			
Ameris Bank	(404) 814-8114		
AuburnBank	(334) 821-9200		
BancorpSouth Bank	(662) 680-2000		
BankPlus	(662) 247-1811		
BankSouth	(334) 677-2265		
Bryant Bank	(205) 464-4646		
Capital City Bank	(850) 402-7700		
CCB Community Bank	(334) 222-2561		
Citizens Bank	(334) 624-8888		
Citizens Bank & Trust, Inc.	(706) 657-5678		
Community Neighbor Bank	(334) 682-4215		
Exchange Bank of Alabama	(205) 589-6334		

Alaska

Name	Telephone	Name	Telephone

Rating: A

First National Bank Alaska	(907) 777-4362

Rating: B+

Mt. McKinley Bank	(907) 452-1751
Northrim Bank	(907) 562-0062

Arizona

Name	Telephone	Name	Telephone

Rating: A

Metro Phoenix Bank	(602) 346-1800
Western Bank	(575) 542-3521

Rating: A-

Academy Bank, N.A.	(877) 712-2265
Alerus Financial, N.A.	(701) 795-3369
Armed Forces Bank, N.A.	(913) 682-9090
Bank of Colorado	(970) 206-1160
Bell Bank	(701) 298-1500
BNC National Bank	(602) 508-3760
First Savings Bank	(605) 763-2009
FirstBank	(303) 232-2000
Glacier Bank	(406) 756-4200
Johnson Bank	(262) 619-2700
KS StateBank	(785) 587-4000
Meadows Bank	(702) 471-2265
Stearns Bank N.A.	(320) 253-6607
Western Alliance Bank	(602) 389-3500
Zions BanCorp., N.A.	(801) 844-7637

Rating: B+

1st Bank Yuma	(928) 783-3334
Arizona Bank & Trust	(602) 381-2090
Bank of America, N.A.	(704) 386-5681
Comerica Bank	(214) 462-4000
Enterprise Bank & Trust	(314) 725-5500
First National Bank Texas	(254) 554-4236
First-Citizens Bank & Trust Co.	(919) 716-7050
Gateway Commercial Bank	(480) 358-1000
Northern Trust Co.	(312) 630-6000
Pacific Premier Bank	(949) 864-8000
TrustBank	(618) 395-4311
Unison Bank	(701) 253-5600
Washington Federal Bank, N.A.	(206) 204-3446

Arkansas

Name	Telephone	Name	Telephone
		Logan County Bank	(479) 938-2511
		Premier Bank of Arkansas	(870) 739-7300
Rating: A+		Relyance Bank, N.A.	(870) 535-7222
		Security Bank	(870) 786-5416
First Security Bank	(501) 279-3400	Simmons Bank	(870) 541-1000
		Southern Bank	(573) 778-1800
Rating: A		Truist Bank	(336) 733-2000
		United Bank	(479) 756-8811
Bank of England	(501) 842-2555		
First National Bank of Izard County	(870) 297-3711		
FSNB, N.A.	(580) 357-9880		
Peoples Bank	(870) 942-5707		
Rating: A-			
Arkansas County Bank	(870) 946-3551		
Bank of Delight	(870) 379-2293		
Bank of Lake Village	(870) 265-2241		
Bank OZK	(501) 978-2265		
Centennial Bank	(501) 328-4663		
Citizens Bank & Trust Co.	(479) 474-1201		
Connect Bank	(870) 628-4286		
Eagle Bank and Trust Co.	(501) 223-2000		
Fidelity Bank	(870) 735-8700		
First National Bank of Fort Smith	(479) 788-4600		
First State Bank	(479) 498-2400		
Great Southern Bank	(417) 895-5234		
McGehee Bank	(870) 222-3151		
Petit Jean State Bank	(501) 354-4988		
Sterling Bank	(573) 778-3333		
Union Bank of Mena	(479) 394-2211		
Rating: B+			
BancorpSouth Bank	(662) 680-2000		
Bank of America, N.A.	(704) 386-5681		
Bank of Bearden	(870) 687-2233		
Bank of Salem	(870) 895-2591		
Bodcaw Bank	(870) 533-4486		
Commercial National Bank of Texarkana	(903) 831-4561		
Cross County Bank	(870) 238-8171		
Farmers & Merchants Bank	(870) 673-6911		
Farmers Bank	(479) 996-4171		
FBT Bank & Mortgage	(870) 352-3107		
First Financial Bank	(870) 863-7000		
First Missouri Bank of SEMO	(573) 717-7177		
First National Bank	(870) 215-4000		
First National Bank at Paris	(479) 963-2121		
First National Bank of Eastern Arkansas	(870) 633-3112		
First National Bank of Lawrence County	(870) 886-5959		
First National Bank Texas	(254) 554-4236		
Focus Bank	(573) 683-3712		
Grand Savings Bank	(918) 786-2203		

California

Name	Telephone	Name	Telephone
		American Continental Bank	(626) 363-8988
Rating: A+		Avidbank	(408) 200-7390
		Axos Bank	(858) 350-6200
California First National Bank	(800) 735-2465	Bank of America, N.A.	(704) 386-5681
		Bank of Feather River	(530) 755-3700
Rating: A		Bank of San Francisco	(415) 744-6700
		Bank of Santa Clarita	(661) 362-6000
Bank of Hemet	(951) 248-2000	Bank of Stockton	(209) 929-1600
Citizens Business Bank	(909) 980-4030	Bank of the Sierra	(559) 782-4900
Exchange Bank	(707) 524-3000	Banner Bank	(509) 527-3636
First General Bank	(626) 820-1234	C3bank, N.A.	(760) 759-1130
Home Bank of California	(858) 270-5881	California Pacific Bank	(415) 399-8000
Pacific City Bank	(213) 210-2000	Central Valley Community Bank	(559) 298-1775
Pacific Coast Bankers' Bank	(415) 399-1900	City National Bank	(800) 773-7100
Poppy Bank	(707) 636-9000	Comerica Bank	(214) 462-4000
Royal Business Bank	(213) 627-9888	CommerceWest Bank	(949) 251-6959
Santa Cruz County Bank	(831) 457-5000	Commonwealth Business Bank	(323) 988-3000
Savings Bank of Mendocino County	(707) 462-6613	Community Bank of Santa Maria	(805) 922-2900
		Community Valley Bank	(760) 352-7777
Rating: A-		CTBC Bank Corp. (USA)	(424) 277-4612
		Enterprise Bank & Trust	(314) 725-5500
American First National Bank	(713) 596-2888	EverTrust Bank	(626) 993-3800
American Plus Bank, N.A.	(626) 821-9188	Farmers & Merchants Bank of Long Beach	(562) 437-0011
Armed Forces Bank, N.A.	(913) 682-9090	First Choice Bank	(562) 345-9092
Bank of America California, N.A.	(925) 988-4801	First IC Bank	(770) 451-7200
Bank of Marin	(415) 763-4520	First Northern Bank of Dixon	(707) 678-3041
Cathay Bank	(213) 625-4791	First-Citizens Bank & Trust Co.	(919) 716-7050
Chino Commercial Bank, N.A.	(909) 393-8880	Five Star Bank	(916) 851-5440
East West Bank	(626) 768-6000	Flagstar Bank, FSB	(248) 312-5400
Farmers & Merchants Bank	(209) 367-2300	Fremont Bank	(510) 505-5226
First Bank	(314) 995-8700	Golden Valley Bank	(530) 894-1000
First Commercial Bank (USA)	(626) 300-6000	Habib American Bank	(212) 532-4444
FirstBank	(303) 232-2000	Merchants Bank of Commerce	(800) 421-2575
Fresno First Bank	(559) 439-0200	Mission Bank	(661) 859-2500
Golden Bank, N.A.	(713) 777-3838	Mission Valley Bank	(818) 394-2300
Heritage Bank of Commerce	(408) 947-6900	Northern California National Bank	(530) 879-5900
Malaga Bank F.S.B.	(310) 375-9000	Northern Trust Co.	(312) 630-6000
Metropolitan Bank	(510) 834-1933	Oak Valley Community Bank	(209) 844-7500
Murphy Bank	(559) 225-0225	Pacific Alliance Bank	(626) 773-8888
New OMNI Bank, N.A.	(626) 284-5555	Pacific Premier Bank	(949) 864-8000
Open Bank	(213) 892-9999	Pinnacle Bank	(408) 842-8200
Plumas Bank	(530) 283-7305	Premier Valley Bank	(559) 438-2002
Preferred Bank	(213) 891-1188	Redwood Capital Bank	(707) 444-9800
Silvergate Bank	(858) 362-6300	Signature Bank	(646) 822-1500
Summit Bank	(510) 839-8800	Silicon Valley Bank	(408) 654-7400
Tri Counties Bank	(530) 898-0300	State Bank of India (California)	(213) 225-5700
Western Alliance Bank	(602) 389-3500	Sterling Bank and Trust, FSB	(248) 355-2400
Zions BanCorp., N.A.	(801) 844-7637		
Rating: B+			
1st Capital Bank	(831) 264-4000		

California

Name	Telephone	Name	Telephone
Suncrest Bank	(916) 830-3597		
United Business Bank	(925) 476-1800		
United Security Bank	(559) 248-4944		
Valley Republic Bank	(661) 371-2000		
Wallis Bank	(979) 478-6151		
WestAmerica Bank	(415) 257-8057		

Colorado

Name	Telephone	Name	Telephone
		Citywide Banks	(303) 365-3800
Rating: A		Farmers State Bank of Calhan	(719) 347-2727
		First-Citizens Bank & Trust Co.	(919) 716-7050
Community State Bank	(719) 336-3272	FNB Bank	(785) 890-2000
Farmers Bank	(970) 834-2121	Fowler State Bank	(719) 263-4276
Farmers State Bank of Brush	(970) 842-5101	Golden Belt Bank, FSA	(785) 726-3157
First National Bank of Las Animas	(719) 456-1512	Grand Valley Bank	(435) 654-7400
North Valley Bank	(303) 452-5500	High Plains Bank	(719) 765-4000
Verus Bank of Commerce	(970) 204-1010	Legacy Bank	(719) 829-4811
		NBH Bank	(720) 554-6650
Rating: A-		Northern Trust Co.	(312) 630-6000
		Pueblo Bank and Trust Co.	(719) 545-1834
Academy Bank, N.A.	(877) 712-2265	Redstone Bank	(720) 880-5000
Alamosa State Bank	(719) 589-2564	Solera National Bank	(303) 209-8600
Alpine Bank	(970) 945-2424	Stockmens Bank	(719) 955-2800
AMG National Trust Bank	(303) 694-2190	TCF National Bank	(952) 745-2760
Armed Forces Bank, N.A.	(913) 682-9090	United Business Bank	(925) 476-1800
Bank of Colorado	(970) 206-1160	Waypoint Bank	(308) 784-2515
Bank of Estes Park	(970) 586-4485		
Champion Bank	(303) 840-8484		
Colorado Bank and Trust Co. of La Junta	(719) 384-8131		
Commerce Bank	(816) 234-2000		
Dolores State Bank	(970) 882-7600		
Eastern Colorado Bank	(719) 767-5652		
Farmers & Stockmens Bank	(575) 374-8301		
First National Bank	(605) 223-2521		
First National Bank of Hugo	(719) 743-2415		
First Pioneer National Bank	(970) 332-4824		
First State Bank	(308) 632-4158		
FirstBank	(303) 232-2000		
FirsTier Bank	(308) 235-4633		
FirstOak Bank	(620) 331-2265		
Frontier Bank	(719) 336-4351		
Glacier Bank	(406) 756-4200		
Gunnison Bank and Trust Co.	(970) 641-0320		
High Country Bank	(719) 539-2516		
Independent Bank	(972) 562-9004		
Kirkpatrick Bank	(405) 341-8222		
Points West Community Bank	(970) 686-0878		
State Bank	(719) 384-5901		
Zions BanCorp., N.A.	(801) 844-7637		

Rating: B+

Name	Telephone
5Star Bank	(719) 574-2777
Adams Bank & Trust	(308) 284-4071
ANB Bank	(303) 394-5143
Bank of America, N.A.	(704) 386-5681
Bank of Burlington	(719) 346-5376
Bankers' Bank of the West	(303) 291-3700
Central Trust Bank	(573) 634-1302

Connecticut

Name	Telephone	Name	Telephone
Rating:	**A**		
Bessemer Trust Co., N.A.	(212) 708-9100		
Rating:	**B+**		
Bank of America, N.A.	(704) 386-5681		
Chelsea Groton Bank	(860) 823-4800		
Liberty Bank	(860) 638-2922		
Northern Trust Co.	(312) 630-6000		
Savings Bank of Danbury	(203) 743-3849		
Signature Bank	(646) 822-1500		
Stafford Savings Bank	(860) 684-4261		
Union Savings Bank	(203) 830-4200		
Washington Trust Co. of Westerly	(401) 348-1200		

Delaware

Name	Telephone	Name	Telephone
Rating: A+			
Deutsche Bank Trust Co. Delaware	(302) 636-3301		
Rating: A			
Applied Bank	(888) 839-7952		
Calvin B. Taylor Banking Co.	(410) 641-1700		
FSNB, N.A.	(580) 357-9880		
Rating: A-			
Bank of Ocean City	(410) 213-0173		
Morgan Stanley Private Bank, N.A.	(212) 762-1803		
Rating: B+			
Bank of America, N.A.	(704) 386-5681		
Shore United Bank	(410) 822-1400		
Wilmington Savings Fund Society, FSB	(302) 792-6000		

District of Columbia

Name	Telephone	Name	Telephone
Rating:	**A-**		
EagleBank	(240) 497-2075		
Presidential Bank, FSB	(301) 652-1616		
Rating:	**B+**		
Bank of America, N.A.	(704) 386-5681		
City National Bank	(800) 773-7100		
FVCbank	(703) 436-4740		
John Marshall Bank	(703) 584-0840		
MainStreet Bank	(703) 481-4567		
Northern Trust Co.	(312) 630-6000		
Truist Bank	(336) 733-2000		

Federated States of Micronesia

Name	Telephone	Name	Telephone

Rating: **A-**

Bank of the Federated States of Micronesia

Florida

Name	Telephone	Name	Telephone
		Commerce National Bank & Trust	(407) 622-8181
Rating: A+		First Colony Bank of Florida	(407) 740-0401
Citizens First Bank	(352) 753-9515	First National Bank Northwest Florida	(850) 769-3207
		First National Bank of Coffee County	(912) 384-1100
Rating: A		First-Citizens Bank & Trust Co.	(919) 716-7050
Amerasia Bank	(718) 463-3600	Flagler Bank	(561) 432-2122
Esquire Bank, N.A.	(516) 535-2002	Heartland National Bank	(863) 386-1300
Hillsboro Bank	(813) 707-6506	Interaudi Bank	(212) 833-1000
Metro City Bank	(770) 455-4989	Intracoastal Bank	(386) 447-1662
Paradise Bank	(561) 392-5444	Northern Trust Co.	(312) 630-6000
Republic Bank & Trust Co.	(502) 584-3600	Peoples Bank of Graceville	(850) 263-3267
Southeastern Bank	(912) 437-4141	PrimeSouth Bank	(912) 283-6685
		Raymond James Bank, N.A.	(727) 567-8000
Rating: A-		Renasant Bank	(800) 680-1601
1st Source Bank	(574) 235-2000	Safra National Bank of New York	(212) 704-5500
American National Bank	(954) 491-7788	Seacoast National Bank	(772) 221-2760
Armed Forces Bank, N.A.	(913) 682-9090	South State Bank, N.A.	(863) 551-5500
Bank OZK	(501) 978-2265	Sunrise Bank	(321) 784-8333
Busey Bank	(217) 351-6500	Truist Bank	(336) 733-2000
Centennial Bank	(501) 328-4663	TrustCo Bank	(518) 377-3311
Charlotte State Bank & Trust	(941) 624-5400	Trustmark National Bank	(601) 208-5111
Community Bank of the South	(321) 452-0420	United Bank	(251) 446-6000
Crews Bank & Trust	(863) 494-2220	Woodforest National Bank	(832) 375-2505
Drummond Community Bank	(352) 493-2277		
Englewood Bank & Trust	(941) 475-6771		
First Federal Bank	(386) 755-0600		
First National Bank of Mount Dora	(352) 383-2111		
Florida Business Bank	(321) 253-1555		
FNBT Bank	(850) 796-2000		
ServisFirst Bank	(205) 949-0302		
Stearns Bank N.A.	(320) 253-6607		
Thomasville National Bank	(229) 226-3300		
United Community Bank	(706) 745-2151		
Wauchula State Bank	(863) 773-4151		
Rating: B+			
American Momentum Bank	(979) 774-1111		
Ameris Bank	(404) 814-8114		
BAC Florida Bank	(305) 789-7000		
BancorpSouth Bank	(662) 680-2000		
Bank of America, N.A.	(704) 386-5681		
Bank of Central Florida	(863) 701-2685		
Bank of Tampa	(813) 872-1216		
BankUnited, N.A.	(786) 313-1010		
Capital City Bank	(850) 402-7700		
CCB Community Bank	(334) 222-2561		
City National Bank	(800) 773-7100		
Comerica Bank	(214) 462-4000		

Georgia

Name	Telephone	Name	Telephone
Rating: A		Atlantic Capital Bank, N.A.	(404) 995-6050
		Bank of America, N.A.	(704) 386-5681
Douglas National Bank	(912) 384-2233	Bank of Camilla	(229) 336-5225
Durden Banking Co., Inc.	(478) 763-2121	Bank of Dawson	(229) 995-2141
Embassy National Bank	(770) 822-9111	Bank of Dudley	(478) 277-1500
Farmers State Bank	(706) 359-3131	Bank of Monticello	(706) 468-6418
First National Bank of Waynesboro	(706) 554-8100	Capital City Bank	(850) 402-7700
FNB South	(912) 632-7262	Century Bank and Trust	(478) 453-3571
FSNB, N.A.	(580) 357-9880	Citizens Bank & Trust, Inc.	(706) 657-5678
Metro City Bank	(770) 455-4989	Citizens Bank of Americus	(229) 924-4011
South Georgia Bank	(912) 654-1051	Citizens Bank of Swainsboro	(478) 237-7001
Southeastern Bank	(912) 437-4141	Citizens Bank of The South	(478) 552-5116
United Bank	(770) 567-7211	Citizens Community Bank	(229) 794-2111
		Citizens National Bank of Quitman	(229) 263-7575
Rating: A-		City National Bank	(800) 773-7100
		Community Banking Co. of Fitzgerald	(229) 423-4321
Armed Forces Bank, N.A.	(913) 682-9090	F&M Bank	(706) 678-2187
Bank of Dade	(706) 657-6842	Family Bank	(229) 294-2821
Bank of Madison	(706) 342-1953	First American Bank and Trust Co.	(706) 354-5000
Bank OZK	(501) 978-2265	First IC Bank	(770) 451-7200
BankSouth	(706) 453-2943	First National Bank of Coffee County	(912) 384-1100
Century Bank of Georgia	(770) 387-1922	First Peoples Bank	(706) 663-2700
Citizens Bank of Georgia	(770) 886-9500	First State Bank of Blakely	(229) 723-3711
Commercial Bank	(706) 743-8184	FirstBank	(615) 313-0080
Commercial Banking Co.	(229) 242-7600	First-Citizens Bank & Trust Co.	(919) 716-7050
East West Bank	(626) 768-6000	Greater Community Bank	(706) 295-9300
Exchange Bank	(478) 452-4531	Guardian Bank	(229) 241-9444
Farmers State Bank	(478) 275-3223	Liberty First Bank	(770) 207-3000
First Century Bank, N.A.	(770) 297-8060	Northern Trust Co.	(312) 630-6000
First National Community Bank	(706) 695-9646	Oconee Federal S&L Assn.	(864) 882-2765
First Volunteer Bank	(423) 668-4509	Peach State Bank & Trust	(770) 536-1100
Four County Bank	(478) 962-3221	Pinnacle Bank	(615) 744-3705
Glennville Bank	(912) 654-3471	Pinnacle Bank	(706) 283-2854
Northeast Georgia Bank	(706) 356-4444	PrimeSouth Bank	(912) 283-6685
Peoples Bank of East Tennessee	(423) 442-7262	Rabun County Bank	(706) 782-4571
Piedmont Bank	(770) 246-0011	RBC Bank (Georgia), N.A.	(919) 206-1060
PromiseOne Bank	(678) 385-0800	Renasant Bank	(800) 680-1601
Quantum National Bank	(770) 945-8300	River City Bank	(706) 236-2123
Security State Bank	(229) 868-6431	South State Bank, N.A.	(863) 551-5500
ServisFirst Bank	(205) 949-0302	Southern First Bank	(864) 679-9000
South Georgia Banking Co.	(229) 382-4211	State Bank of Cochran	(478) 934-4501
SunMark Community Bank	(478) 783-4036	The Bank of Soperton	(912) 529-4431
Thomasville National Bank	(229) 226-3300	Truist Bank	(336) 733-2000
United Community Bank	(706) 745-2151	Wallis Bank	(979) 478-6151
West Central Georgia Bank	(706) 647-8951	Waycross Bank & Trust	(912) 283-0001
		Wheeler County State Bank	(912) 568-7191
Rating: B+		Wilcox County State Bank	(229) 467-2511
American Pride Bank	(478) 784-1448		
Ameris Bank	(404) 814-8114		

Georgia

Name	Telephone	Name	Telephone
Woodforest National Bank	(832) 375-2505		

Guam

Name	Telephone	Name	Telephone

Rating: B+

Name	Telephone
First Hawaiian Bank	(808) 525-6340

Hawaii

Name	Telephone	Name	Telephone

Rating: A-

Central Pacific Bank	(808) 544-0500

Rating: B+

American Savings Bank, F.S.B.	(808) 627-6900
First Hawaiian Bank	(808) 525-6340
Territorial Savings Bank	(808) 946-1400

Idaho

Name	Telephone	Name	Telephone

Rating: A

Name	Telephone
Altabank	(801) 756-7681
Bank of Commerce	(208) 525-9108
Farmers Bank	(208) 543-4351

Rating: A-

Name	Telephone
Bell Bank	(701) 298-1500
First FSB of Twin Falls	(208) 733-4222
Glacier Bank	(406) 756-4200
Northwest Bank	(208) 332-0700
Zions BanCorp., N.A.	(801) 844-7637

Rating: B+

Name	Telephone
Bank of America, N.A.	(704) 386-5681
Bank of Jackson Hole	(307) 733-8064
bankcda	(208) 665-5999
Banner Bank	(509) 527-3636
Columbia State Bank	(253) 305-1900
D.L. Evans Bank	(208) 678-8615
First Interstate Bank	(406) 255-5000
Ireland Bank	(208) 766-2211
Twin River Bank	(208) 746-4848
Washington Federal Bank, N.A.	(206) 204-3446
Washington Trust Bank	(509) 353-4204

Illinois

Name	Telephone	Name	Telephone
		Heartland Bank and Trust Co.	(309) 662-4444
Rating: A		Lakeside Bank	(312) 435-5100
		Lindell Bank & Trust Co.	(314) 645-7700
Bank of Advance	(573) 722-3517	Millennium Bank	(847) 296-9500
Farmers National Bank	(815) 537-2348	North Central Bank	(815) 925-7373
Federal Savings Bank	(312) 738-8422	Northside Community Bank	(847) 244-5100
First Eagle Bank	(312) 850-2900	Old Second National Bank	(630) 892-0202
Fisher National Bank	(217) 897-1136	Petefish, Skiles & Co.	(217) 452-3041
Germantown Trust & Savings Bank	(618) 526-4202	Prairie State Bank & Trust	(217) 993-6260
Goodfield State Bank	(309) 965-2221	Reynolds State Bank	(309) 372-4242
Municipal Trust and Savings Bank	(815) 935-8000	Rushville State Bank	(217) 322-3323
Park Ridge Community Bank	(847) 384-9200	Shelby County State Bank	(217) 774-3911
Royal Business Bank	(213) 627-9888	Signature Bank	(847) 268-1001
Teutopolis State Bank	(217) 857-3166	State Bank of Cherry	(815) 894-2345
Vermilion Valley Bank	(815) 686-2258	State Bank of Lincoln	(217) 735-5551
		State Bank of Texas	(972) 252-6000
Rating: A-		Sterling Bank	(573) 778-3333
		Town and Country Bank Midwest	(217) 222-0015
AMG National Trust Bank	(303) 694-2190	Warren-Boynton State Bank	(217) 488-6091
Apple River State Bank	(815) 594-2351		
Armed Forces Bank, N.A.	(913) 682-9090	**Rating:** B+	
Bank of O'Fallon	(618) 632-3595		
Bank of Pontiac	(815) 844-6155	Albany Bank and Trust Co., N.A.	(773) 267-7300
Bradford National Bank of Greenville	(618) 664-2200	American Community Bank & Trust	(815) 338-2300
Buena Vista National Bank	(618) 826-2331	Anna State Bank	(618) 833-2151
Busey Bank	(217) 351-6500	Anna-Jonesboro National Bank	(618) 833-8506
Cathay Bank	(213) 625-4791	Bank of America, N.A.	(704) 386-5681
Central Bank Illinois	(309) 944-5601	Bank of Bourbonnais	(815) 933-0570
Commerce Bank	(816) 234-2000	Bank of Hillsboro, N.A.	(217) 532-3991
Community Bank	(815) 367-5011	BankChampaign, N.A.	(217) 351-2870
Community Bank of Easton	(309) 562-7420	Bankers' Bank	(608) 833-5550
Crossroads Bank	(217) 347-7751	BankFinancial, N.A.	(800) 894-6900
Farmers and Merchants National Bank	(618) 327-4401	Belmont Bank & Trust Co.	(773) 589-9500
Farmers State Bank	(217) 285-5585	Blackhawk Bank & Trust	(309) 787-4451
First Bank	(314) 995-8700	Burling Bank	(312) 408-8400
First Farmers State Bank	(309) 392-2623	CBI Bank & Trust	(563) 263-3131
First Financial Bank, N.A.	(812) 238-6000	Central Bank of St. Louis	(314) 862-8300
First Merchants Bank	(765) 747-1500	Citizens Community Bank	(618) 566-8800
First National Bank	(605) 482-8293	Du Quoin State Bank	(618) 542-2111
First National Bank in Olney	(618) 395-8541	Evergreen Bank Group	(630) 413-9580
First National Bank in Pinckneyville	(618) 357-9393	Exchange State Bank	(815) 493-2631
First National Bank in Taylorville	(217) 824-2241	Fairfield National Bank	(618) 842-2107
First National Bank of Beardstown	(217) 323-4105	Farmers & Mechanics Bank	(309) 343-7141
First National Bank of Litchfield	(217) 324-2105	Farmers State Bank of Western Illinois	(309) 629-4361
First National Bank of Sparta	(618) 443-2187	First Community Bank and Trust	(708) 946-2246
First State Bank of Campbell Hill	(618) 426-3396	First Federal S&L Assn. of Central Illinois, S.B.	(217) 774-3322
First Trust and Savings Bank of Watseka	(815) 432-2494	First Financial Bank	(877) 322-9530
FNB Community Bank	(618) 283-1141	First Mid Bank & Trust, N.A.	(217) 234-7454
Frederick Community Bank	(815) 457-2111		
Grand Ridge National Bank	(815) 249-6414		

Illinois

Name	Telephone	Name	Telephone
First National Bank of Brookfield	(708) 485-2770		
First National Bank of Pana	(217) 562-3961		
First National Bank of Steeleville	(618) 965-3441		
First Nations Bank	(773) 594-5900		
First Southern Bank	(618) 997-4341		
First State Bank	(815) 538-2265		
First State Bank of Beecher City	(618) 487-5161		
First State Bank of St. Peter	(618) 349-8343		
Gold Coast Bank	(312) 587-3200		
Grundy Bank	(815) 942-0130		
Hometown National Bank	(815) 223-7300		
Illini State Bank	(815) 442-8211		
Illinois Bank & Trust	(815) 637-7000		
Ipava State Bank	(309) 753-8202		
Itasca Bank & Trust Co.	(630) 773-0350		
Kinmundy Bank	(618) 547-3533		
Lena State Bank	(815) 369-4901		
Liberty Bank	(217) 645-3434		
Lisle Savings Bank	(630) 852-3710		
Mason City National Bank	(217) 482-3246		
Midland Community Bank	(217) 237-4324		
Midwest Community Bank	(815) 235-6137		
Milledgeville State Bank	(815) 225-7171		
Morton Community Bank	(309) 266-5337		
Northern Trust Co.	(312) 630-6000		
Old Exchange National Bank of Okawville	(618) 243-5234		
Peoples National Bank of Kewanee	(309) 853-3333		
Peoples State Bank of Colfax	(309) 723-2111		
Philo Exchange Bank	(217) 684-2600		
Providence Bank & Trust	(708) 333-0700		
Quad City Bank and Trust Co.	(563) 344-0600		
Republic Bank of Chicago	(630) 570-7700		
Royal Banks of Missouri	(314) 212-1500		
Simmons Bank	(870) 541-1000		
Solutions Bank	(815) 938-3121		
Southern Bank	(573) 778-1800		
Southern Illinois Bank	(618) 983-8433		
Spring Valley City Bank	(815) 663-2211		
State Bank of Davis	(815) 865-5125		
State Bank of Herscher	(815) 426-2156		
State Bank of St. Jacob	(618) 644-5555		
Stillman BancCorp, N.A.	(815) 645-2266		
TCF National Bank	(952) 745-2760		
TrustBank	(618) 395-4311		
Union National Bank	(847) 888-7500		
Villa Grove State Bank	(217) 832-2631		
Woodforest National Bank	(832) 375-2505		

Indiana

Name	Telephone	Name	Telephone
		Horizon Bank	(219) 874-9245
		LNB Community Bank	(812) 922-3231

Rating: A

Name	Telephone
Alliance Bank	(219) 567-9151
Kentland Bank	(219) 474-5155
Logansport Savings Bank	(574) 722-3855
Republic Bank & Trust Co.	(502) 584-3600
Stock Yards Bank & Trust Co.	(502) 582-2571
Union Savings Bank	(513) 247-0300

Name	Telephone
New Washington State Bank	(812) 293-3321
Providence Bank & Trust	(708) 333-0700
STAR Financial Bank	(260) 467-5500
State Bank and Trust Co.	(419) 783-8950
State Bank of Lizton	(317) 858-1039
Truist Bank	(336) 733-2000
WesBanco Bank, Inc.	(304) 234-9419
Woodforest National Bank	(832) 375-2505

Rating: A-

Name	Telephone
1st Source Bank	(574) 235-2000
Busey Bank	(217) 351-6500
Centier Bank	(219) 755-6100
CentreBank	(765) 294-2228
Civista Bank	(419) 625-4121
Community State Bank	(260) 897-3361
Farmers and Merchants Bank	(260) 637-5546
First Bank of Berne	(260) 589-2151
First Financial Bank, N.A.	(812) 238-6000
First Merchants Bank	(765) 747-1500
First State Bank of Middlebury	(574) 825-2166
Fowler State Bank	(765) 884-1200
Freedom Bank	(812) 683-8998
Friendship State Bank	(812) 667-5101
German American Bank	(812) 482-1314
Lake City Bank	(574) 267-6144
Morris Plan Co. of Terre Haute, Inc.	(812) 238-6063
Napoleon State Bank	(812) 852-4002

Rating: B+

Name	Telephone
Bank of America, N.A.	(704) 386-5681
Bank of Wolcott	(219) 279-2185
Bankers' Bank	(608) 833-5550
Bippus State Bank	(260) 356-8900
DeMotte State Bank	(219) 987-4141
Farmers & Merchants State Bank	(419) 446-2501
Farmers Bank, Frankfort, Indiana, Inc.	(765) 654-8731
Farmers State Bank	(260) 463-7111
FCN Bank, N.A.	(765) 647-4116
First Financial Bank	(877) 322-9530
First Harrison Bank	(812) 738-2198
First Savings Bank	(812) 283-0724
First State Bank of Porter	(219) 926-2136
Flagstar Bank, FSB	(248) 312-5400
Fountain Trust Co.	(765) 793-2237
Garrett State Bank	(260) 357-3133
Greenfield Banking Co.	(317) 462-1431
Greenville National Bank	(937) 548-1114

Iowa

Name	Telephone	Name	Telephone
Rating: A		Iowa Trust & Savings Bank	(712) 852-3451
		Lee County Bank	(319) 372-2243
Bank 1st	(563) 422-3883	Luana Savings Bank	(563) 539-2166
Citizens First National Bank	(712) 732-5440	Manufacturers Bank & Trust Co.	(641) 585-2825
Farmers Trust & Savings Bank	(319) 668-2525	Maquoketa State Bank	(563) 652-2491
First State Bank	(641) 843-4411	Mount Vernon Bank and Trust Co.	(319) 895-8835
First State Bank	(641) 527-2535	New Albin Savings Bank	(563) 544-4214
Heartland Bank	(515) 467-5561	Northwestern Bank	(712) 737-4911
Iowa State Bank	(515) 288-0111	NSB Bank	(641) 423-7638
Iowa State Bank	(712) 662-4721	Ohnward Bank & Trust	(563) 852-7696
Iowa Trust and Savings Bank	(641) 437-4500	Pilot Grove Savings Bank	(319) 469-3951
Liberty Trust & Savings Bank	(563) 785-4441	Readlyn Savings Bank	(319) 279-3321
Midwest Heritage Bank, FSB	(515) 278-6541	Savings Bank	(712) 957-6815
Pinnacle Bank	(641) 752-2393	Security National Bank of Sioux City, Iowa	(712) 277-6500
United Bank and Trust Co.	(641) 456-5587	Templeton Savings Bank	(712) 669-3322
Waukon State Bank	(563) 568-3451	United Bank of Iowa	(712) 364-3393
		Washington State Bank	(319) 653-2151
Rating: A-		Wayland State Bank	(319) 385-8189
		West Iowa Bank	(515) 887-7811
Audubon State Bank	(712) 563-2644		
Bellevue State Bank	(563) 872-4911	**Rating:** B+	
Breda Savings Bank	(712) 673-2321		
Bridge Community Bank	(319) 895-8200	American National Bank	(402) 399-5000
Chelsea Savings Bank	(319) 444-3144	American Savings Bank	(319) 882-4279
Citizens Savings Bank	(319) 462-3561	American State Bank	(641) 342-2175
Citizens Savings Bank	(563) 562-3674	Atkins Savings Bank & Trust	(319) 446-7700
Citizens State Bank	(712) 324-2519	Availa Bank	(712) 792-3567
Citizens State Bank	(563) 488-2211	BANK	(319) 523-5200
CUSB Bank	(563) 547-2040	Bank of America, N.A.	(704) 386-5681
Farmers & Merchants State Bank	(515) 462-4242	Bankers' Bank	(608) 833-5550
Farmers Bank of Northern Missouri	(660) 947-2474	BankFirst	(402) 371-8005
Farmers Savings Bank	(641) 752-2525	Blackhawk Bank & Trust	(309) 787-4451
Farmers Savings Bank & Trust	(319) 478-2148	Boone Bank & Trust Co.	(515) 432-6200
Farmers State Bank	(641) 424-3053	BTC Bank	(660) 425-7285
Farmers State Bank	(319) 377-4891	CBI Bank & Trust	(563) 263-3131
Farmers State Bank	(515) 295-7221	Cedar Rapids Bank and Trust Co.	(319) 862-2728
Farmers Trust and Savings Bank	(641) 562-2696	Charter Bank	(515) 331-2265
First Bank Hampton	(641) 456-4793	Cherokee State Bank	(712) 225-3000
First Central State Bank	(563) 659-3141	Citizens Savings Bank	(563) 427-3255
First Citizens Bank	(641) 423-1600	Citizens State Bank	(319) 465-5921
First National Bank	(605) 482-8293	Clear Lake Bank and Trust Co.	(641) 357-7121
First National Bank, Ames, Iowa	(515) 232-5561	Community Bank of Oelwein	(319) 283-4000
First Security Bank	(712) 881-1131	Community State Bank	(515) 331-3100
First Security Bank-Sleepy Eye	(507) 794-3911	Community State Bank	(712) 262-3030
First State Bank	(515) 832-2520	Danville State Savings Bank	(319) 392-4261
First State Bank	(712) 364-3181	Decorah Bank & Trust Co.	(563) 382-9661
FNB Bank	(641) 745-2141	Dubuque Bank and Trust Co.	(563) 589-2000
Great Southern Bank	(417) 895-5234	Exchange State Bank	(641) 742-3201
Hills Bank and Trust Co.	(319) 679-2291		

Iowa

Name	Telephone	Name	Telephone
F&M Bank	(402) 372-5331	Watkins Savings Bank	(319) 227-7773
Farmers & Merchants Savings Bank	(563) 927-4475	West Bank	(515) 222-2300
Farmers Savings Bank	(563) 856-2525		
Farmers State Bank	(319) 287-3961		
Farmers State Bank	(712) 376-4154		
Farmers Trust & Savings Bank	(712) 747-2000		
Fidelity Bank	(515) 221-0022		
First Bank	(319) 352-1340		
First Iowa State Bank	(641) 932-2144		
First National Bank in Creston	(641) 782-2195		
First National Bank of Manning	(712) 655-3557		
First State Bank	(641) 444-3226		
First State Bank	(641) 435-4943		
First Whitney Bank and Trust	(712) 243-3195		
GNB Bank	(319) 824-5431		
Grinnell State Bank	(641) 236-3174		
Hiawatha Bank and Trust Co.	(319) 378-5979		
Home Federal Savings Bank	(507) 535-1309		
Home State Bank	(712) 933-5511		
Home Trust & Savings Bank	(641) 732-3763		
Houghton State Bank	(712) 623-4823		
Iowa State Bank	(712) 439-1025		
Iowa State Bank	(515) 295-3595		
Laurens State Bank	(712) 845-2627		
Leighton State Bank	(641) 628-1566		
Liberty National Bank	(712) 224-4425		
Maynard Savings Bank	(563) 637-2289		
Northeast Security Bank	(563) 578-3251		
NorthStar Bank	(712) 362-3322		
Northwest Bank	(712) 580-4100		
Pocahontas State Bank	(712) 335-3567		
Principal Bank	(800) 672-3343		
Quad City Bank and Trust Co.	(563) 344-0600		
Security National Bank of Omaha	(402) 344-7300		
Security Savings Bank	(515) 352-3333		
Security State Bank	(515) 295-9501		
Security State Bank	(319) 352-3500		
Security State Bank	(712) 446-3324		
Shelby County State Bank	(712) 755-5112		
Sloan State Bank	(712) 428-3344		
Solon State Bank	(319) 624-3405		
South Ottumwa Savings Bank	(641) 682-7541		
St. Ansgar State Bank	(641) 713-4501		
State Bank & Trust Co.	(515) 382-2191		
State Bank of Schaller	(712) 275-4261		
State Savings Bank	(515) 457-9533		
Success Bank	(641) 664-2006		

Kansas

Name	Telephone	Name	Telephone
		Western State Bank	(620) 275-4128

Rating: A

Name	Telephone
CBW Bank	(620) 396-8221
City National B&T Co. of Lawton, Oklahoma	(866) 385-3444
Denison State Bank	(785) 364-3131
Farmers & Merchants Bank of Colby	(785) 460-3321
Farmers Bank & Trust	(620) 792-2411
Farmers State Bank of Oakley, Kansas	(785) 672-3251
Garden Plain State Bank	(316) 721-1500
Kearny County Bank	(620) 355-6222
Midwest Heritage Bank, FSB	(515) 278-6541
Mutual Savings Assn.	(913) 682-3491
NBKC Bank	(816) 965-1400
Security State Bank	(620) 872-7224

Rating: A-

Name	Telephone
Academy Bank, N.A.	(877) 712-2265
Armed Forces Bank, N.A.	(913) 682-9090
Bank of Prairie Village	(913) 713-0300
Central National Bank	(785) 238-4114
Citizens State Bank	(785) 562-2186
Citizens State Bank and Trust Co.	(785) 742-2101
Commerce Bank	(816) 234-2000
Community First Bank	(913) 371-1242
Eastern Colorado Bank	(719) 767-5652
Exchange Bank & Trust	(913) 367-6000
Farmers National Bank	(785) 543-6541
Farmers State Bank	(620) 241-3090
Farmers State Bank of Aliceville, Kansas	(785) 489-2468
Fidelity State Bank and Trust Co.	(620) 227-8586
First Bank	(620) 278-2161
First National Bank in Fredonia	(620) 378-2151
First National Bank of Louisburg	(913) 837-5191
First State B&T Co. of Larned	(620) 285-6931
First State Bank of St. Charles, Missouri	(636) 940-5555
FirstOak Bank	(620) 331-2265
Flint Hills Bank	(785) 449-2266
Great Southern Bank	(417) 895-5234
Kaw Valley State Bank and Trust Co.	(785) 456-2021
KS StateBank	(785) 587-4000
Pinnacle Bank	(402) 434-3127
Security Bank of Kansas City	(913) 281-3165
Solomon State Bank	(785) 655-2941
Solutions North Bank	(785) 425-6721
Stanley Bank	(913) 681-8800
State Bank of Bern	(785) 336-6121
TriCentury Bank	(913) 583-3222
Union Bank and Trust Co.	(402) 323-1828

Rating: B+

Name	Telephone
Adams Bank & Trust	(308) 284-4071
Alliance Bank	(785) 271-1800
ANB Bank	(303) 394-5143
Bank of America, N.A.	(704) 386-5681
Bank of Blue Valley	(913) 234-2334
Bank of Protection	(620) 622-4224
Bank of Tescott	(785) 283-4217
Bank7	(405) 810-8600
Bankers' Bank of Kansas	(316) 681-2265
Bankwest of Kansas	(785) 899-2342
Central Bank of the Midwest	(816) 525-5300
Citizens State Bank	(620) 836-2888
Citizens State Bank	(620) 345-6317
Commercial Bank	(620) 421-1000
Community Bank	(785) 440-4400
Community Bank of the Midwest	(620) 792-5111
Community National Bank	(785) 336-6143
Community State Bank	(620) 251-1313
Cornerstone Bank	(913) 239-8100
Country Club Bank	(816) 931-4060
Enterprise Bank & Trust	(314) 725-5500
Exchange Bank	(308) 237-7711
Farmers and Drovers Bank	(620) 767-5138
Farmers State Bank	(785) 364-4691
First Bank Kansas	(785) 825-2211
First Commerce Bank	(785) 562-5558
First Heritage Bank	(785) 857-3341
First Kansas Bank	(620) 653-4921
First National Bank and Trust	(785) 543-6511
First National Bank of Hutchinson	(620) 663-1521
First National Bank of Spearville	(620) 385-2636
First State Bank	(785) 798-3347
First-Citizens Bank & Trust Co.	(919) 716-7050
FNB Bank	(785) 890-2000
FNB Washington	(785) 325-2221
Golden Belt Bank, FSA	(785) 726-3157
Grant County Bank	(620) 356-4142
Great American Bank	(785) 838-9704
Howard State Bank	(620) 374-2127
Kansas State Bank	(785) 242-3600
Labette Bank	(620) 784-5311
Landmark National Bank	(785) 565-2000
Mid-America Bank	(785) 594-2100
NBH Bank	(720) 554-6650

Kansas

Name	Telephone	Name	Telephone
Peoples Bank	(620) 582-2166		
Peoples Bank and Trust Co.	(620) 241-2100		
Silver Lake Bank	(785) 232-0102		
Simmons Bank	(870) 541-1000		
Southwind Bank	(785) 885-4234		
Stockgrowers State Bank	(785) 256-4241		
Stockgrowers State Bank	(620) 635-4032		
United Bank & Trust	(785) 562-2333		
Valley State Bank	(620) 488-2211		

Kentucky

Name	Telephone	Name	Telephone
		First Financial Bank	(877) 322-9530
Rating: A		First Harrison Bank	(812) 738-2198
		First National Bank of Kentucky	(502) 732-4406
Cumberland Security Bank, Inc.	(606) 679-9361	First State Bank	(270) 547-2271
Edmonton State Bank	(270) 432-3231	FirstBank	(615) 313-0080
Farmers Bank and Trust Co.	(270) 365-5526	Franklin Bank & Trust Co.	(270) 586-7121
Guardian Savings Bank, F.S.B.	(513) 942-3500	Fredonia Valley Bank	(270) 545-3301
Jackson County Bank	(606) 287-8484	Heartland Bank	(614) 416-4601
Kentucky Farmers Bank Corp.	(606) 929-5000	Independence Bank of Kentucky	(270) 686-1776
Magnolia Bank, Inc.	(270) 324-3226	Lewisburg Banking Co.	(270) 755-4818
Republic Bank & Trust Co.	(502) 584-3600	Lincoln National Bank	(270) 358-4116
Stock Yards Bank & Trust Co.	(502) 582-2571	Meade County Bank	(270) 422-4141
Taylor County Bank	(270) 465-4196	Peoples B&T Co. of Madison County	(859) 986-6860
United Community Bank of W Kentucky	(270) 389-3232	River City Bank, Inc.	(502) 585-4600
		Security Bank and Trust Co.	(606) 564-3304
Rating: A-		Security Bank and Trust Co.	(731) 642-6644
		South Central Bank, Inc.	(270) 651-7466
Armed Forces Bank, N.A.	(913) 682-9090	Springfield State Bank	(859) 336-3939
Bank of the Bluegrass & Trust Co.	(859) 233-4500	Truist Bank	(336) 733-2000
Citizens Deposit Bank of Arlington, Inc.	(270) 655-6921	United Southern Bank	(270) 885-0056
City National Bank of West Virginia	(304) 769-1100	WesBanco Bank, Inc.	(304) 234-9419
First Financial Bank, N.A.	(812) 238-6000	WinFirst Bank	(859) 744-1900
First National Bank of Grayson	(606) 474-2000	Woodforest National Bank	(832) 375-2505
First United Bank and Trust Co.	(270) 821-5555		
German American Bank	(812) 482-1314		
Paducah Bank and Trust Co.	(270) 575-5700		
PBK Bank, Inc.	(606) 365-7098		
Peoples Bank	(502) 477-2244		
Peoples Bank MT. Washington	(502) 538-7301		
Planters Bank, Inc.	(270) 886-9030		
Sacramento Deposit Bank	(270) 736-2212		
Town & Country Bank and Trust Co.	(502) 348-3911		
Traditional Bank, Inc.	(859) 498-0414		
United Citizens Bank & Trust Co.	(502) 532-7392		
United Citizens Bank of Southern Kentucky, Inc.	(270) 384-2265		
Rating: B+			
Bank of Clarkson	(270) 242-2111		
Bank of Edmonson County	(270) 597-2175		
Bank of Maysville	(606) 564-4001		
Casey County Bank, Inc.	(606) 787-8394		
Cecilian Bank	(270) 862-3294		
Central Bank & Trust Co.	(859) 253-6013		
Citizens Bank of Cumberland County	(270) 864-2323		
Citizens National Bank of Somerset	(606) 679-6341		
Citizens Union Bank of Shelbyville	(502) 633-4450		
Commercial Bank	(423) 869-5151		
Commonwealth Bank and Trust Co.	(502) 259-2200		
Elkton Bank & Trust Co.	(270) 265-9841		
Farmers Bank and Trust Co.	(270) 965-3106		

Louisiana

Name	Telephone	Name	Telephone

Rating: A

Name	Telephone
First American Bank and Trust	(225) 265-2265
First National Bank of Louisiana	(337) 783-4014
FSNB, N.A.	(580) 357-9880
Rayne State Bank & Trust Co.	(337) 334-3191

Rating: A-

Name	Telephone
American Bank & Trust Co.	(337) 948-3056
Exchange Bank and Trust Co.	(318) 352-8141
Guaranty Bank and Trust Co.	(225) 638-8621
Peoples B&T Co. of Pointe Coupee Parish	(225) 638-3713
Red River Bank	(318) 561-4000
Resource Bank	(985) 801-1800
South Louisiana Bank	(985) 851-3434

Rating: B+

Name	Telephone
BancorpSouth Bank	(662) 680-2000
Bank of Sunset and Trust Co.	(337) 662-5222
BankPlus	(662) 247-1811
Beauregard Federal Savings Bank	(337) 463-4493
Citizens National Bank, N.A.	(318) 747-6000
Cottonport Bank	(318) 253-9612
Cross Keys Bank	(318) 766-3246
Evangeline Bank and Trust Co.	(337) 363-5541
Feliciana Bank & Trust Co.	(225) 683-8565
First National Bank of Benton	(318) 965-9691
First National Bank USA	(985) 785-8411
Franklin State Bank & Trust Co.	(318) 435-3711
Guaranty Bank & Trust Co. of Delhi	(318) 878-3703
Gulf Coast Bank	(337) 893-7733
Hodge Bank & Trust Co.	(318) 259-7362
Home Federal Bank	(318) 841-1170
JD Bank	(337) 824-3424
Jonesboro State Bank	(318) 259-4411
Mississippi River Bank	(504) 392-1111
Sabine State Bank and Trust Co.	(318) 256-7000
Southern Heritage Bank	(318) 339-8505
Synergy Bank	(985) 851-3341
Tensas State Bank	(318) 467-5401
The Bank	(337) 824-0033
Woodforest National Bank	(832) 375-2505

Maine

Name	Telephone	Name	Telephone

Rating: A

Bath Savings Institution	(207) 442-7711

Rating: A-

Camden National Bank	(207) 236-8821

Rating: B+

Bank of America, N.A.	(704) 386-5681
Franklin Savings Bank	(207) 778-3339
Kennebec Savings Bank	(207) 622-5801
Machias Savings Bank	(207) 255-3347
Norway Savings Bank	(207) 743-7986

Maryland

Name	Telephone	Name	Telephone

Rating: A

Name	Telephone
Calvin B. Taylor Banking Co.	(410) 641-1700

Rating: A-

Name	Telephone
Bank of Ocean City	(410) 213-0173
Cathay Bank	(213) 625-4791
Clear Mountain Bank	(304) 379-2265
EagleBank	(240) 497-2075
Presidential Bank, FSB	(301) 652-1616
Queenstown Bank of Maryland	(410) 827-8881

Rating: B+

Name	Telephone
ACNB Bank	(717) 334-3161
Bank of America, N.A.	(704) 386-5681
BayVanguard Bank	(410) 477-5000
Chesapeake Bank & Trust Co.	(410) 778-1600
Essex Bank	(804) 419-4329
First-Citizens Bank & Trust Co.	(919) 716-7050
Firstrust Savings Bank	(610) 238-5001
FVCbank	(703) 436-4740
John Marshall Bank	(703) 584-0840
PeoplesBank, A Codorus Valley Co.	(717) 846-1970
Severn Savings Bank, FSB	(410) 260-2000
Shore United Bank	(410) 822-1400
Sonabank	(804) 528-4754
Truist Bank	(336) 733-2000
WesBanco Bank, Inc.	(304) 234-9419
Woodforest National Bank	(832) 375-2505

Massachusetts

Name	Telephone	Name	Telephone

Rating: A

Name	Telephone
Leader Bank, N.A.	(781) 646-3900
Northern Bank & Trust Co.	(781) 937-5400

Rating: A-

Name	Telephone
Bank of New England	(603) 894-5700
Boston Trust Walden Co.	(617) 726-7250
Cathay Bank	(213) 625-4791
East West Bank	(626) 768-6000
Hingham Institution for Savings	(781) 749-2200
Mechanics Cooperative Bank	(508) 823-7744
MutualOne Bank	(508) 820-4000

Rating: B+

Name	Telephone
Bank of America, N.A.	(704) 386-5681
Cambridge Trust Co.	(617) 876-5500
Cape Ann Savings Bank	(978) 283-0246
Community Bank, N.A.	(315) 445-2282
Everett Co-operative Bank	(617) 387-1110
Lowell Five Cent Savings Bank	(978) 452-1300
Martha's Vineyard Savings Bank	(774) 310-2001
National Grand Bank of Marblehead	(781) 631-6000
Northern Trust Co.	(312) 630-6000
Northmark Bank	(978) 686-9100
Norwood Co-operative Bank	(781) 762-1800
Patriot Community Bank	(781) 935-3318
Rockland Trust Co.	(781) 982-6110
Salem Five Cents Savings Bank	(978) 745-5555
State Street Bank and Trust Co.	(617) 786-3000
The Provident Bank	(877) 487-2977
TrustCo Bank	(518) 377-3311

Michigan

Name	Telephone	Name	Telephone

Rating: A

Name	Telephone
Macatawa Bank	(616) 820-1444
Tri-County Bank	(810) 346-2745

Rating: A-

Name	Telephone
1st Source Bank	(574) 235-2000
Alden State Bank	(231) 331-4481
Alerus Financial, N.A.	(701) 795-3369
Bank of Ann Arbor	(734) 662-1600
Century Bank and Trust	(517) 278-1500
Chelsea State Bank	(734) 475-1355
Exchange State Bank	(810) 657-9333
First Merchants Bank	(765) 747-1500
First National Bank in Howell	(517) 546-3150
Mercantile Bank of Michigan	(616) 242-7760
Old Mission Bank	(906) 635-9910
State Bank	(810) 629-2263
University Bank	(734) 741-5858
Upper Peninsula State Bank	(906) 789-7000

Rating: B+

Name	Telephone
Bank of America, N.A.	(704) 386-5681
Charlevoix State Bank	(231) 547-4411
ChoiceOne Bank	(616) 887-7366
Comerica Bank	(214) 462-4000
Farmers State Bank	(260) 463-7111
First Community Bank	(231) 526-2114
Flagstar Bank, FSB	(248) 312-5400
Horizon Bank	(219) 874-9245
Nicolet National Bank	(920) 430-1400
Northern Trust Co.	(312) 630-6000
Northpointe Bank	(616) 940-9400
Peoples State Bank of Munising	(906) 387-2006
Port Austin State Bank	(989) 738-5235
Sterling Bank and Trust, FSB	(248) 355-2400
Superior National Bank & Trust Co.	(906) 482-0404
TCF National Bank	(952) 745-2760

Minnesota

Name	Telephone	Name	Telephone
Rating: A+		National Bank of Commerce	(715) 394-5531
		North American Banking Co.	(651) 636-9654
Bank of Alma	(608) 685-4461	Northeast Bank	(612) 379-8811
Vermillion State Bank	(651) 437-4433	Northview Bank	(320) 245-5261
Rating: A		ONB Bank	(507) 280-0621
		Red Rock Bank	(507) 648-3871
Charter Bank	(715) 832-4254	Security State Bank of Aitkin	(218) 927-3765
Community First Bank	(218) 564-4171	Security State Bank of Marine	(651) 433-2424
Eagle Bank	(320) 634-4545	St. Clair State Bank (Inc.)	(507) 245-3636
First State Bank Southwest	(507) 376-9747	State Bank of Danvers	(320) 843-3828
Lake Central Bank	(320) 274-8216	State Bank of Wheaton	(320) 563-8142
PrinsBank	(320) 978-6351	Stearns Bank Holdingford N.A.	(320) 746-2261
		Stearns Bank N.A.	(320) 253-6607
Rating: A-		Stearns Bank Upsala N.A.	(320) 573-2111
		VisionBank	(952) 920-8400
1st United Bank	(507) 334-2201	Woodlands National Bank	(320) 384-6191
21st Century Bank	(763) 479-2178		
Alerus Financial, N.A.	(701) 795-3369	**Rating:** B+	
American Heritage National Bank	(320) 732-6131		
Bank of Maple Plain	(763) 479-1931	American National Bank	(402) 399-5000
Bell Bank	(701) 298-1500	American National Bank of Minnesota	(218) 824-7900
BNC National Bank	(602) 508-3760	Arlington State Bank	(507) 964-2256
Bridgewater Bank	(952) 893-6868	Bank Forward	(701) 769-2121
Castle Rock Bank	(651) 463-7590	Bank of America, N.A.	(704) 386-5681
Center National Bank	(320) 693-3255	Bank of Elk River	(763) 441-1000
Citizens National Bank of Park Rapids	(218) 732-3393	Bank of Zumbrota	(507) 732-7555
Citizens State Bank of Roseau	(218) 463-2135	BANKWEST	(763) 477-5231
Community Resource Bank	(507) 645-4441	Bremer Bank, N.A.	(651) 288-3751
Elysian Bank	(507) 267-4326	City National Bank	(800) 773-7100
Farmers State Bank of Hartland	(507) 845-2233	CornerStone State Bank	(507) 364-2265
Farmers Trust and Savings Bank	(641) 562-2696	ESB Bank	(507) 725-3329
Fidelity Bank	(952) 831-6600	F & M Bank Minnesota	(320) 669-4431
First Bank Blue Earth	(507) 526-3241	Farmers & Merchants Savings Bank	(563) 927-4475
First Citizens Bank	(641) 423-1600	Farmers and Merchants State Bank	(320) 468-6422
First Minnetonka City Bank	(952) 935-8663	Farmers State Bank of Hamel	(763) 478-6611
First National Bank	(605) 482-8293	First Farmers & Merchants Bank	(507) 263-3030
First National Bank North	(218) 547-1160	First Financial Bank in Winnebago	(507) 893-3155
First National Bank of Bemidji	(218) 751-2430	First National Bank Minnesota	(507) 931-4000
First National Bank of Henning	(218) 367-2735	First National Bank of Fairfax	(507) 426-7242
First National Bank of Moose Lake	(218) 485-4441	First National Bank of Le Center	(507) 357-2273
First Security Bank - Canby	(507) 223-7231	First National Bank of Milaca	(320) 983-3101
First Security Bank-Sleepy Eye	(507) 794-3911	First National Bank of Waseca	(507) 835-2740
First State Bank of Sauk Centre	(320) 352-5771	First Security Bank-Hendricks	(507) 275-3141
Granite Falls Bank	(320) 564-2111	First State Bank of Le Center	(507) 357-2225
Great Southern Bank	(417) 895-5234	First State Bank of Wyoming	(651) 462-7611
HomeTown Bank	(507) 637-1000	Frandsen Bank & Trust	(507) 744-2361
Janesville State Bank	(507) 234-5108	Gateway Bank	(651) 209-4800
Liberty Bank Minnesota	(320) 252-2841	Home Federal Savings Bank	(507) 535-1309
Manufacturers Bank & Trust Co.	(641) 585-2825		

Minnesota

Name	Telephone	Name	Telephone
Home State Bank	(320) 593-2001		
KodaBank	(701) 454-3317		
Lake Bank	(218) 834-2111		
Lake Community Bank	(952) 473-7347		
Lake Elmo Bank	(651) 777-8365		
Midwest Bank	(218) 847-4771		
Minnesota National Bank	(320) 352-5211		
Minnwest Bank	(507) 637-5731		
Neighborhood National Bank	(320) 679-3100		
North Shore Bank of Commerce	(218) 722-4784		
North Star Bank	(651) 489-8811		
Northern State Bank	(715) 682-2772		
Northern Trust Co.	(312) 630-6000		
Northwoods Bank of Minnesota	(218) 732-7221		
Park State Bank	(218) 722-3500		
Pine Country Bank	(320) 632-9740		
Pine Island Bank	(507) 356-8328		
Platinum Bank	(651) 332-5200		
Premier Bank	(651) 777-7700		
Premier Bank Minnesota	(651) 463-4440		
Roundbank	(507) 835-4220		
Security Bank & Trust Co.	(320) 864-3107		
Security Bank Minnesota	(507) 373-1481		
Security Bank USA	(218) 751-1510		
Security State Bank of Fergus Falls	(218) 736-5485		
Security State Bank of Oklee	(218) 796-5157		
Security State Bank of Wanamingo	(507) 824-2265		
Sunrise Banks, N.A.	(651) 265-5600		
TCF National Bank	(952) 745-2760		
Think Mutual Bank	(507) 288-3425		
Wadena State Bank	(218) 631-1860		
Wanda State Bank	(507) 550-1678		
Welcome State Bank	(507) 728-8251		
West Bank	(515) 222-2300		
WNB Financial, N.A.	(507) 454-8800		

Mississippi

Name	Telephone	Name	Telephone

Rating: A

FSNB, N.A.	(580) 357-9880

Rating: A-

Bank of Commerce	(662) 453-4142
Bank of Vernon	(205) 695-7141
BNA Bank	(662) 534-8171
Citizens National Bank of Meridian	(601) 484-5269
Commerce Bank	(662) 286-5577
Farmers and Merchants Bank	(662) 365-1200
First Choice Bank	(662) 489-1631
First National Bank of Clarksdale	(662) 627-3261
Jefferson Bank	(662) 332-7545
RiverHills Bank	(601) 636-1445

Rating: B+

BancorpSouth Bank	(662) 680-2000
Bank of Forest	(601) 469-3663
Bank of Franklin	(601) 384-2305
Bank of Kilmichael	(662) 262-7844
Bank of Wiggins	(601) 928-5233
BankPlus	(662) 247-1811
Citizens Bank	(662) 838-2146
Cleveland State Bank	(662) 843-9461
First Financial Bank	(870) 863-7000
First National Bank of Picayune	(601) 749-3200
First Security Bank	(662) 563-9311
First Southern Bank	(601) 736-6378
First State Bank	(601) 735-3124
Grand Bank for Savings, FSB	(601) 264-1467
Guaranty Bank and Trust Co.	(662) 247-1454
Merchants and Planters Bank	(601) 857-8044
Pike National Bank	(601) 684-7575
PriorityOne Bank	(601) 849-3311
Renasant Bank	(800) 680-1601
Truist Bank	(336) 733-2000
Trustmark National Bank	(601) 208-5111
Woodforest National Bank	(832) 375-2505

Missouri

Name	Telephone	Name	Telephone
Rating: A		New Era Bank	(573) 783-3336
		Northeast Missouri State Bank	(660) 665-6161
Adrian Bank	(816) 297-2194	Pinnacle Bank	(402) 434-3127
Bank of Advance	(573) 722-3517	Progressive Ozark Bank	(573) 729-4146
Bank of Grain Valley	(816) 373-1905	Rockwood Bank	(636) 938-9222
Bank of Old Monroe	(636) 665-5601	Security Bank of Kansas City	(913) 281-3165
Cass Commercial Bank	(314) 506-5544	Sterling Bank	(573) 778-3333
Citizens Bank of Charleston	(573) 683-3373	Town & Country Bank	(573) 729-3155
Citizens Bank of Edina	(660) 397-2266	Town and Country Bank Midwest	(217) 222-0015
Community Bank of El Dorado Springs	(417) 876-6811	Wells Bank	(816) 858-2121
HNB National Bank	(573) 221-0050	West Plains Bank and Trust Co.	(417) 256-2147
Legends Bank	(573) 897-2204		
NBKC Bank	(816) 965-1400	**Rating: B+**	
Nodaway Valley Bank	(660) 562-3232	Alliance Bank	(573) 334-1010
North American Savings Bank, F.S.B.	(866) 599-9800	Alliant Bank	(660) 291-3041
Peoples Community Bank	(573) 224-3267	Alton Bank	(417) 778-7211
Senath State Bank	(573) 738-2646	BancorpSouth Bank	(662) 680-2000
St. Clair County State Bank	(417) 646-8128	Bank of America, N.A.	(704) 386-5681
Wood & Huston Bank	(660) 886-6825	Bank of Blue Valley	(913) 234-2334
		Bank of Odessa	(816) 230-4512
Rating: A-		BTC Bank	(660) 425-7285
Academy Bank, N.A.	(877) 712-2265	Central Bank of Boone County	(573) 874-8100
Armed Forces Bank, N.A.	(913) 682-9090	Central Bank of Branson	(417) 334-4125
Bank Northwest	(816) 583-2154	Central Bank of Lake of the Ozarks	(573) 348-2761
Bank of Missouri	(573) 547-6541	Central Bank of Sedalia	(660) 827-3333
Bank of Monticello	(573) 767-5264	Central Bank of St. Louis	(314) 862-8300
Bank of New Madrid	(573) 748-5551	Central Bank of the Midwest	(816) 525-5300
Bank of St. Elizabeth	(573) 493-2313	Central Bank of the Ozarks	(417) 881-3100
Bloomsdale Bank	(573) 483-2514	Central Trust Bank	(573) 634-1302
Busey Bank	(217) 351-6500	Century Bank of the Ozarks	(417) 679-3321
Central Bank of Kansas City	(816) 483-1210	Citizens Bank of Eldon	(573) 392-3381
Commerce Bank	(816) 234-2000	Citizens-Farmers Bank of Cole Camp	(660) 668-4416
Community First Banking Co.	(417) 255-2265	Commercial Bank of Oak Grove	(816) 690-4416
Exchange Bank & Trust	(913) 367-6000	Commercial Trust Co. of Fayette	(660) 248-2222
Exchange Bank of Missouri	(660) 248-3388	Community Bank of Marshall	(660) 886-9621
Farmers Bank of Northern Missouri	(660) 947-2474	Community Bank of Missouri	(816) 470-2265
First Bank	(314) 995-8700	Community Bank of Pleasant Hill	(816) 540-2525
First State Bank and Trust Co., Inc.	(573) 333-1700	Community Bank of Raymore	(816) 322-2100
First State Bank of St. Charles, Missouri	(636) 940-5555	Community State Bank of Missouri	(573) 324-2233
First State Community Bank	(573) 756-4547	Concordia Bank	(660) 463-7911
Great Southern Bank	(417) 895-5234	Connections Bank	(660) 665-7703
Home Exchange Bank	(660) 684-6114	Country Club Bank	(816) 931-4060
Lamar Bank and Trust Co.	(417) 682-3348	Enterprise Bank & Trust	(314) 725-5500
Lindell Bank & Trust Co.	(314) 645-7700	Farmers and Merchants Bank of St. Clair	(636) 629-2225
Maries County Bank	(573) 422-3323	First Mid Bank & Trust, N.A.	(217) 234-7454
Mercantile Bank of Louisiana, Missouri	(573) 754-6221	First Missouri Bank of SEMO	(573) 717-7177
Metz Banking Co.	(417) 667-4550	First-Citizens Bank & Trust Co.	(919) 716-7050
Missouri Bank	(636) 456-3441		

Missouri

Name	Telephone	Name	Telephone
Focus Bank	(573) 683-3712		
Freedom Bank of Southern Missouri	(417) 846-1719		
Great American Bank	(785) 838-9704		
Hawthorn Bank	(573) 761-6100		
Independent Farmers Bank	(816) 449-2182		
Investors Community Bank	(660) 646-3733		
Jefferson Bank of Missouri	(573) 634-0888		
Kearney Trust Co.	(816) 628-6666		
La Monte Community Bank	(660) 347-5656		
Mid America Bank	(573) 635-0019		
Midwest Independent BankersBank	(573) 636-9555		
Montrose Savings Bank	(660) 693-4424		
MRV Banks	(573) 883-8222		
NBH Bank	(720) 554-6650		
Northern Trust Co.	(312) 630-6000		
Parkside Financial Bank & Trust	(314) 290-8600		
Peoples Bank	(573) 885-2511		
Peoples Bank of Wyaconda	(660) 727-2941		
Pony Express Bank	(816) 781-9200		
Putnam County State Bank	(660) 947-2477		
Royal Banks of Missouri	(314) 212-1500		
Security Bank of Southwest Missouri	(417) 847-4794		
Simmons Bank	(870) 541-1000		
Southern Bank	(573) 778-1800		
Springfield First Community Bank	(417) 882-8111		
State Street Bank and Trust Co.	(617) 786-3000		
Stifel Bank and Trust	(314) 342-2000		
Stockmens Bank	(719) 955-2800		
Tipton Latham Bank, N.A.	(660) 433-2004		
TPNB Bank	(660) 327-4181		
United Security Bank	(573) 386-2233		

Montana

Name	Telephone	Name	Telephone
Rating: A			
Bank of Commerce	(208) 525-9108		
Independence Bank	(406) 265-1241		
Yellowstone Bank	(406) 628-7951		
Rating: A-			
1st Bank	(406) 436-2611		
Bank of Montana	(406) 829-2662		
Glacier Bank	(406) 756-4200		
Opportunity Bank of Montana	(406) 442-3080		
Stockman Bank of Montana	(406) 234-8420		
Rating: B+			
American Bank	(406) 587-1234		
Belt Valley Bank	(406) 277-3314		
Eagle Bank	(406) 883-2940		
First Community Bank	(406) 228-8231		
First Federal Bank & Trust	(307) 674-0464		
First Interstate Bank	(406) 255-5000		
First Security Bank of Deer Lodge	(406) 846-2300		
First State Bank of Forsyth	(406) 346-2112		
First State Bank of Shelby	(406) 434-5567		
Madison Valley Bank	(406) 682-4215		
Manhattan Bank	(406) 284-3255		
TrailWest Bank	(406) 273-2400		

Nebraska

Name	Telephone	Name	Telephone
		American Exchange Bank	(402) 994-4000
Rating: A		American National Bank	(402) 399-5000
		Bankers' Bank of the West	(303) 291-3700
American Interstate Bank	(402) 289-2551	BankFirst	(402) 371-8005
Heritage Bank	(308) 583-2262	Bruning Bank	(402) 353-2555
Madison County Bank	(402) 454-6511	Cedar Security Bank	(402) 357-3508
Minden Exchange Bank & Trust Co.	(308) 832-1600	CerescoBank	(402) 665-3431
		Chambers State Bank	(402) 482-5222
Rating: A-		Clarkson Bank	(402) 892-3411
		Commercial Bank	(402) 225-3381
Auburn State Bank	(402) 274-4342	Commercial State Bank	(308) 799-3995
Bank of Dixon County	(402) 755-2224	Cornerstone Bank	(402) 363-7411
Bank of Elgin	(402) 843-2228	Exchange Bank	(308) 237-7711
Bank of Prague	(402) 663-4317	F&M Bank	(402) 245-2491
Cattle Bank & Trust	(402) 643-3636	F&M Bank	(402) 372-5331
Central National Bank	(785) 238-4114	First Bank and Trust of Fullerton	(308) 536-2492
Charter West Bank	(402) 372-5147	First Nebraska Bank	(402) 359-2281
Farmers and Merchants State Bank	(402) 373-4321	First Northeast Bank of Nebraska	(402) 687-2640
First National Bank of Chadron	(308) 432-5552	First State Bank	(308) 876-2451
First National Bank of Gordon	(308) 282-0050	First State Bank	(402) 337-0323
First Savings Bank	(605) 763-2009	First State Bank & Trust Co.	(402) 721-2500
First State Bank	(308) 632-4158	Hershey State Bank	(308) 368-5555
First State Bank	(308) 569-2311	Midwest Bank N.A.	(402) 329-6221
First Westroads Bank, Inc.	(402) 330-7200	Nebraska State Bank and Trust Co.	(308) 872-2466
FirstBank of Nebraska	(402) 443-4117	Northwest Bank	(712) 580-4100
FirsTier Bank	(308) 235-4633	Premier Bank	(402) 558-8000
Five Points Bank	(308) 384-5350	Security National Bank of Omaha	(402) 344-7300
Five Points Bank of Hastings	(402) 462-2228	Springfield State Bank	(402) 253-2222
Great Southern Bank	(417) 895-5234	Stockmens Bank	(719) 955-2800
Homestead Bank	(308) 784-2000	Washington County Bank	(402) 426-2111
Horizon Bank	(402) 786-2555	Waypoint Bank	(308) 784-2515
Jones Bank	(402) 643-3602		
Nebraska State Bank	(308) 772-3234		
Pinnacle Bank	(402) 434-3127		
Pinnacle Bank - Wyoming	(402) 697-5990		
Platte Valley Bank	(402) 652-3221		
Points West Community Bank	(970) 686-0878		
Scribner Bank	(402) 664-2561		
Security Bank	(402) 256-3247		
South Central State Bank	(402) 756-8601		
State Nebraska Bank & Trust	(402) 375-1130		
Town & Country Bank	(308) 452-3225		
Two Rivers Bank	(402) 426-9500		
Union Bank and Trust Co.	(402) 323-1828		
West Gate Bank	(402) 434-3453		
West Plains Bank	(402) 387-2381		
Rating: B+			
Adams Bank & Trust	(308) 284-4071		
Adams State Bank	(402) 988-2255		

Nevada

Name	Telephone	Name	Telephone

Rating: A

Name	Telephone
Bank of George	(702) 851-4200
First Security Bank of Nevada	(702) 853-0900
Royal Business Bank	(213) 627-9888

Rating: A-

Name	Telephone
American First National Bank	(713) 596-2888
Armed Forces Bank, N.A.	(913) 682-9090
Cathay Bank	(213) 625-4791
Eaglemark Savings Bank	(775) 886-3000
East West Bank	(626) 768-6000
First Savings Bank	(605) 763-2009
Glacier Bank	(406) 756-4200
Meadows Bank	(702) 471-2265
Plumas Bank	(530) 283-7305
Western Alliance Bank	(602) 389-3500
Zions BanCorp., N.A.	(801) 844-7637

Rating: B+

Name	Telephone
Bank of America, N.A.	(704) 386-5681
City National Bank	(800) 773-7100
Enterprise Bank & Trust	(314) 725-5500
First National Bank of Ely	(775) 289-4441
GENUBANK	(702) 912-0700
Northern Trust Co.	(312) 630-6000
Pacific Premier Bank	(949) 864-8000
Town & Country Bank	(702) 252-8777
Washington Federal Bank, N.A.	(206) 204-3446
Wells Fargo National Bank West	(702) 952-6650
Wilmington Savings Fund Society, FSB	(302) 792-6000

New Hampshire

Name	Telephone	Name	Telephone
Rating:	**A-**		
Alerus Financial, N.A.	(701) 795-3369		
Bank of New England	(603) 894-5700		
Camden National Bank	(207) 236-8821		
Rating:	**B+**		
Bank of America, N.A.	(704) 386-5681		
Cambridge Trust Co.	(617) 876-5500		
Ledyard National Bank	(802) 649-2050		
Lowell Five Cent Savings Bank	(978) 452-1300		
The Provident Bank	(877) 487-2977		

New Jersey

Name	Telephone	Name	Telephone

Rating: A

Name	Telephone
Bessemer Trust Co.	(212) 708-9100
Metro City Bank	(770) 455-4989
Pacific City Bank	(213) 210-2000
Parke Bank	(856) 256-2500

Rating: A-

Name	Telephone
AMG National Trust Bank	(303) 694-2190
Armed Forces Bank, N.A.	(913) 682-9090
Cathay Bank	(213) 625-4791
Cenlar FSB	(609) 883-3900

Rating: B+

Name	Telephone
Bank of America, N.A.	(704) 386-5681
Bank of Princeton	(609) 921-1700
Cross River Bank	(201) 808-7000
CTBC Bank Corp. (USA)	(424) 277-4612
First IC Bank	(770) 451-7200
Firstrust Savings Bank	(610) 238-5001
Habib American Bank	(212) 532-4444
Lakeland Bank	(973) 697-2000
Lusitania Savings Bank	(973) 344-5125
NewBank	(718) 353-9100
State Street Bank and Trust Co.	(617) 786-3000
Truist Bank	(336) 733-2000
TrustCo Bank	(518) 377-3311
Unity Bank	(908) 730-7630
William Penn Bank,	(215) 269-1200
Wilmington Savings Fund Society, FSB	(302) 792-6000

New Mexico

Name	Telephone	Name	Telephone

Rating: A

Name	Telephone
Citizens Bank of Las Cruces	(575) 647-4100
First American Bank	(575) 746-8000
First National Bank	(575) 437-4880
First New Mexico Bank	(575) 546-2691
First New Mexico Bank of Silver City	(575) 388-3121
First New Mexico Bank, Las Cruces	(575) 556-3000
Valley Bank of Commerce	(575) 623-2265
Western Bank	(575) 542-3521

Rating: A-

Name	Telephone
AimBank	(806) 385-4441
Bank of Clovis	(575) 769-9000
Bank of Colorado	(970) 206-1160
Centinel Bank of Taos	(575) 758-6700
Citizens Bank	(505) 599-0100
Citizens Bank	(806) 350-5600
Citizens Bank of Clovis	(575) 769-1911
Farmers & Stockmens Bank	(575) 374-8301
First Savings Bank	(605) 763-2009
James Polk Stone Community Bank	(575) 356-6601
Lea County State Bank	(575) 397-4511
WestStar Bank	(915) 532-1000
Zions BanCorp., N.A.	(801) 844-7637

Rating: B+

Name	Telephone
American Heritage Bank	(575) 762-2800
Bank of America, N.A.	(704) 386-5681
Century Bank	(505) 995-1200
City Bank	(806) 792-7101
CNB Bank	(575) 234-2500
Enterprise Bank & Trust	(314) 725-5500
First National Bank Texas	(254) 554-4236
First-Citizens Bank & Trust Co.	(919) 716-7050
Main Bank	(505) 880-1700
NBH Bank	(720) 554-6650
New Mexico Bank & Trust	(505) 830-8100
United Business Bank	(925) 476-1800
Washington Federal Bank, N.A.	(206) 204-3446
Western Bank of Clovis	(575) 769-1975
Western Commerce Bank	(575) 887-6686

New York

Name	Telephone	Name	Telephone
		Saratoga National Bank and Trust Co.	(518) 583-3114
Rating: A		Signature Bank	(646) 822-1500
		Sterling Bank and Trust, FSB	(248) 355-2400
Amerasia Bank	(718) 463-3600	Tompkins Trust Co.	(607) 273-3210
Bessemer Trust Co., N.A.	(212) 708-9100	TrustCo Bank	(518) 377-3311
Esquire Bank, N.A.	(516) 535-2002	Wayne Bank	(570) 253-1455
Metro City Bank	(770) 455-4989	Woodforest National Bank	(832) 375-2505
Pacific City Bank	(213) 210-2000		
Royal Business Bank	(213) 627-9888		

Rating: A

Name	Telephone
Amerasia Bank	(718) 463-3600
Bessemer Trust Co., N.A.	(212) 708-9100
Esquire Bank, N.A.	(516) 535-2002
Metro City Bank	(770) 455-4989
Pacific City Bank	(213) 210-2000
Royal Business Bank	(213) 627-9888

Rating: A-

Name	Telephone
Alpine Capital Bank	(212) 328-2555
Armed Forces Bank, N.A.	(913) 682-9090
Bank OZK	(501) 978-2265
Cathay Bank	(213) 625-4791
Centennial Bank	(501) 328-4663
Deutsche Bank Trust Co. Americas	(212) 250-2500
East West Bank	(626) 768-6000
First National Bank of Groton	(607) 898-5871
Genesee Regional Bank	(585) 249-1540
Metropolitan Commercial Bank	(212) 659-0600
Morgan Stanley Private Bank, N.A.	(212) 762-1803
Preferred Bank	(213) 891-1188
Tioga State Bank	(607) 589-7000
Watertown Savings Bank	(315) 788-7100
Westchester Bank	(914) 368-9919

Rating: B+

Name	Telephone
Bank of America, N.A.	(704) 386-5681
Bank of Greene County	(518) 943-2600
BankUnited, N.A.	(786) 313-1010
Citizens & Northern Bank	(570) 724-3411
City National Bank	(800) 773-7100
Community Bank, N.A.	(315) 445-2282
CTBC Bank Corp. (USA)	(424) 277-4612
First IC Bank	(770) 451-7200
First National Bank of Dryden	(607) 844-8141
Fulton Savings Bank	(315) 592-4201
Glens Falls National Bank and Trust Co.	(518) 793-4121
Habib American Bank	(212) 532-4444
Hamlin Bank and Trust Co.	(814) 887-5555
Hanover Community Bank	(516) 248-4868
Interaudi Bank	(212) 833-1000
Lakeland Bank	(973) 697-2000
Maspeth Federal S&L Assn.	(718) 335-1300
NewBank	(718) 353-9100
Northern Trust Co.	(312) 630-6000
Peoples Security Bank and Trust Co.	(570) 955-1700
Safra National Bank of New York	(212) 704-5500

North Carolina

Name	Telephone	Name	Telephone

Rating: A

Name	Telephone
FSNB, N.A.	(580) 357-9880
Surrey Bank & Trust	(336) 783-3900

Rating: A-

Name	Telephone
AMG National Trust Bank	(303) 694-2190
Bank OZK	(501) 978-2265
Benchmark Community Bank	(434) 676-9054
BlueHarbor Bank	(704) 662-7700
Farmers & Merchants Bank	(704) 633-1772
Fidelity Bank	(919) 552-2242
First Bank	(910) 692-6222
Providence Bank	(252) 443-9477
Roxboro Savings Bank, SSB	(336) 599-2137
United Community Bank	(706) 745-2151
Wake Forest Federal S&L Assn.	(919) 556-5146

Rating: B+

Name	Telephone
American National Bank and Trust Co.	(434) 792-5111
Bank of America, N.A.	(704) 386-5681
First FSB of Lincolnton	(704) 735-0416
First-Citizens Bank & Trust Co.	(919) 716-7050
Live Oak Banking Co.	(910) 779-5867
Peoples Bank	(828) 464-5620
Pinnacle Bank	(615) 744-3705
Signature Bank	(646) 822-1500
South State Bank, N.A.	(863) 551-5500
Southern Bank and Trust Co.	(919) 658-7000
Southern First Bank	(864) 679-9000
TowneBank	(757) 638-7500
Truist Bank	(336) 733-2000
Woodforest National Bank	(832) 375-2505

North Dakota

Name	Telephone	Name	Telephone

Rating: A

Name	Telephone
Commercial Bank of Mott	(701) 824-2593
Ramsey National Bank	(701) 662-4024
Security First Bank of North Dakota	(701) 794-8758

Rating: A-

Name	Telephone
Alerus Financial, N.A.	(701) 795-3369
Bell Bank	(701) 298-1500
BNC National Bank	(602) 508-3760
Citizens State Bank of Finley	(701) 524-1921
First Security Bank - West	(701) 873-4301
First State Bank & Trust	(701) 577-2113
Liberty State Bank	(701) 464-5421
Stock Growers Bank	(701) 724-3216

Rating: B+

Name	Telephone
American State Bank & Trust Co	(701) 774-4100
Bank Forward	(701) 769-2121
Bremer Bank, N.A.	(651) 288-3751
Dakota Community Bank & Trust, N.A.	(701) 878-4416
Dakota Western Bank	(701) 523-5803
Farmers and Merchants State Bank	(701) 256-5431
First State Bank	(701) 847-2600
First State Bank of Golva	(701) 872-3656
Frandsen Bank & Trust	(507) 744-2361
Goose River Bank	(701) 788-3110
Grant County State Bank	(701) 622-3491
Horizon Financial Bank	(701) 682-5331
KodaBank	(701) 454-3317
Peoples State Bank	(701) 245-6407
Starion Bank	(701) 223-6050
Unison Bank	(701) 253-5600

Northern Mariana Islands

Name	Telephone	Name	Telephone

Rating: B+

Name	Telephone
First Hawaiian Bank	(808) 525-6340

Ohio

Name	Telephone	Name	Telephone
		Greenville National Bank	(937) 548-1114
Rating: A+		Heartland Bank	(614) 416-4601
		Home Loan Savings Bank	(740) 622-0444
FDS Bank	(513) 573-2265	Killbuck Savings Bank Co.	(330) 276-4881
		LCNB National Bank	(513) 932-1414
Rating: A		Minster Bank	(419) 628-2351
		North Side Bank and Trust Co.	(513) 542-7800
Guardian Savings Bank, F.S.B.	(513) 942-3500	Northern Trust Co.	(312) 630-6000
Peoples Bank Co.	(419) 678-2385	Osgood State Bank	(419) 582-2681
Perpetual Federal Savings Bank	(937) 653-1700	State Bank and Trust Co.	(419) 783-8950
Republic Bank & Trust Co.	(502) 584-3600	Sutton Bank	(419) 426-3641
Spring Valley Bank	(513) 761-6688	TCF National Bank	(952) 745-2760
St. Henry Bank	(419) 678-2358	Truist Bank	(336) 733-2000
Stock Yards Bank & Trust Co.	(502) 582-2571	Union Bank Co.	(419) 659-2141
Union Savings Bank	(513) 247-0300	Union Banking Co.	(937) 355-6511
		WesBanco Bank, Inc.	(304) 234-9419
Rating: A-		Woodforest National Bank	(832) 375-2505
Bank of Magnolia Co.	(330) 866-9392		
CFBank, N.A.	(614) 505-5805		
City National Bank of West Virginia	(304) 769-1100		
Civista Bank	(419) 625-4121		
Croghan Colonial Bank	(419) 332-7301		
Farmers Savings Bank	(330) 648-2441		
First Bank of Berne	(260) 589-2151		
First Merchants Bank	(765) 747-1500		
Hamler State Bank	(419) 274-3955		
Liberty National Bank	(419) 634-5015		
Ottoville Bank Co.	(419) 453-3313		
Settlers Bank	(740) 373-9200		
Signature Bank, N.A.	(419) 841-7773		
Unified Bank	(740) 633-0445		
Rating: B+			
Bank of America, N.A.	(704) 386-5681		
Buckeye Community Bank	(440) 233-8800		
Citizens Bank Co.	(740) 984-2381		
Citizens National Bank of Bluffton	(419) 358-8040		
Commercial & Savings Bank of Millersburg	(330) 674-9015		
Corn City State Bank	(419) 278-0015		
Eagle Savings Bank	(513) 574-0700		
Farmers & Merchants Bank	(937) 866-2455		
Farmers & Merchants State Bank	(419) 446-2501		
Farmers National Bank of Canfield	(330) 533-3341		
FCN Bank, N.A.	(765) 647-4116		
First Bank of Ohio	(419) 448-9740		
First Commonwealth Bank	(724) 463-8555		
First Financial Bank	(877) 322-9530		
First National Bank in New Bremen	(419) 629-2761		
First National Bank of Blanchester	(937) 783-2451		
Flagstar Bank, FSB	(248) 312-5400		

Oklahoma

Name	Telephone	Name	Telephone
Rating: A		Carson Community Bank	(918) 696-7745
		Community Bank	(918) 367-3343
City National B&T Co. of Lawton, Oklahoma	(866) 385-3444	Community Bank	(580) 327-5500
Community National Bank of Okarche	(405) 263-7491	Fairview S&L Assn.	(580) 227-3735
Farmers and Merchants National Bank	(580) 227-3773	First Bank & Trust Co.	(580) 336-5562
First Bank of Okarche	(405) 263-7215	First Bank & Trust Co.	(580) 255-1810
First Bank of Owasso	(918) 272-5301	First Bank of Thomas	(580) 661-3515
FSNB, N.A.	(580) 357-9880	First Bethany Bank & Trust	(405) 789-1110
Payne County Bank	(405) 547-2436	First Enterprise Bank	(405) 681-0771
Rating: A-		First National B&T Co. of Broken Arrow	(918) 251-5371
		First National B&T Co. of Weatherford	(580) 772-5574
American Exchange Bank	(405) 756-3101	First National Bank	(918) 653-3200
BancFirst	(405) 270-1086	First National Bank of Hooker	(580) 652-2448
Bank of Commerce	(918) 789-2567	First National Bank of Lindsay	(405) 756-4433
Bank of Hydro	(405) 663-2214	First National Bank of Stigler	(918) 967-4665
Bank of the Panhandle	(580) 338-2593	First State Bank	(405) 247-2471
Bank of the West	(580) 661-3541	First Texoma National Bank	(580) 924-4242
Bank, N.A.	(918) 423-2265	First-Citizens Bank & Trust Co.	(919) 716-7050
Central National Bank of Poteau	(918) 647-2233	Grand Savings Bank	(918) 786-2203
Commerce Bank	(816) 234-2000	Idabel National Bank	(580) 286-7656
Exchange Bank	(918) 396-2345	Oklahoma State Bank	(580) 735-2545
F&M Bank	(405) 715-1100	Peoples National Bank of Checotah	(918) 473-2237
First Bank	(580) 526-3332	Security First National Bank of Hugo	(580) 326-9641
First National Bank & Trust of Elk City	(580) 225-2580	Security National Bank of Enid	(580) 234-5151
First National Bank and Trust Co.	(405) 224-2200	Simmons Bank	(870) 541-1000
First National Bank of Fletcher	(580) 549-6106	Sooner State Bank	(405) 381-2326
First National Bank of Fort Smith	(479) 788-4600	Southwest Bank of Weatherford	(580) 774-0900
First State Bank	(580) 623-4945	State Bank of Wynnewood	(405) 665-2001
Great Southern Bank	(417) 895-5234	Triad Bank, N.A.	(918) 254-1444
International Bank of Commerce Oklahoma	(405) 841-2100	Valor Bank	(405) 212-9800
Kirkpatrick Bank	(405) 341-8222		
Liberty National Bank	(580) 351-2265		
McClain Bank	(405) 527-6503		
McCurtain County National Bank	(580) 584-6262		
Oklahoma Bank and Trust Co.	(580) 323-2345		
Oklahoma State Bank	(918) 256-5585		
Prosperity Bank	(979) 543-2200		
Security State Bank	(580) 497-3354		
Shamrock Bank, N.A.	(580) 927-2311		
Stock Exchange Bank	(580) 256-3314		
Welch State Bank of Welch, Oklahoma	(918) 788-3373		
Rating: B+			
American Bank and Trust Co.	(918) 481-3000		
Anchor D Bank	(580) 423-7541		
Bank of America, N.A.	(704) 386-5681		
Bank of Cordell	(580) 832-5600		
Bank7	(405) 810-8600		

Oregon

Name	Telephone	Name	Telephone

Rating: A+

Name	Telephone
Pioneer Trust Bank, N.A.	(503) 363-3136

Rating: A

Name	Telephone
Clackamas County Bank	(503) 668-5501
Willamette Valley Bank	(503) 485-2222

Rating: A-

Name	Telephone
Bank of the Pacific	(360) 537-4052
Northwest Bank	(208) 332-0700
Riverview Community Bank	(360) 693-6650
Zions BanCorp., N.A.	(801) 844-7637

Rating: B+

Name	Telephone
Baker-Boyer National Bank	(509) 525-2000
Bank of America, N.A.	(704) 386-5681
Banner Bank	(509) 527-3636
Citizens Bank	(541) 766-2299
Columbia State Bank	(253) 305-1900
First Interstate Bank	(406) 255-5000
First-Citizens Bank & Trust Co.	(919) 716-7050
Lewis & Clark Bank	(503) 212-3200
Oregon Coast Bank	(541) 265-9000
Oregon Pacific Banking Co.	(541) 997-7121
Pacific Premier Bank	(949) 864-8000
People's Bank of Commerce	(541) 776-5350
Washington Federal Bank, N.A.	(206) 204-3446
Washington Trust Bank	(509) 353-4204

Pennsylvania

Name	Telephone	Name	Telephone

Rating: A

Name	Telephone
Haverford Trust Co.	(610) 995-8700
Parke Bank	(856) 256-2500
Union Savings Bank	(513) 247-0300

Rating: A-

Name	Telephone
First Columbia Bank & Trust Co.	(570) 784-1660
Honesdale National Bank	(570) 253-3355
Port Richmond Savings	(215) 634-7000
Slovenian S&L Assn. of Canonsburg	(724) 745-5000
Turbotville National Bank	(570) 649-5118

Rating: B+

Name	Telephone
ACNB Bank	(717) 334-3161
American Bank	(610) 366-1800
Apollo Trust Co.	(724) 478-3151
Bank of America, N.A.	(704) 386-5681
Bank of Landisburg	(717) 789-3213
Bank of Princeton	(609) 921-1700
Citizens & Northern Bank	(570) 724-3411
Commercial Bank & Trust of PA	(724) 539-3501
Community Bank, N.A.	(315) 445-2282
Fidelity Deposit and Discount Bank	(570) 802-3081
First Commonwealth Bank	(724) 463-8555
First National B&T Co. of Newtown	(215) 860-9100
Firstrust Savings Bank	(610) 238-5001
Hamlin Bank and Trust Co.	(814) 887-5555
National Bank of Malvern	(610) 647-0100
Neffs National Bank	(610) 767-3875
NexTier Bank, N.A.	(724) 543-1125
Northern Trust Co.	(312) 630-6000
Peoples Security Bank and Trust Co.	(570) 955-1700
PeoplesBank, A Codorus Valley Co.	(717) 846-1970
Philadelphia Trust Co.	(215) 979-3434
PS Bank	(570) 746-1011
Susquehanna Community Bank	(570) 568-6851
Truist Bank	(336) 733-2000
Unity Bank	(908) 730-7630
VIST Bank	(610) 208-0966
Wayne Bank	(570) 253-1455
WesBanco Bank, Inc.	(304) 234-9419
William Penn Bank,	(215) 269-1200
Wilmington Savings Fund Society, FSB	(302) 792-6000
Woodforest National Bank	(832) 375-2505
York Traditions Bank	(717) 741-1770

Rhode Island

Name	Telephone	Name	Telephone
Rating:	**B+**		
Bank of America, N.A.	(704) 386-5681		
Washington Trust Co. of Westerly	(401) 348-1200		

South Carolina

Name	Telephone	Name	Telephone

Rating: A

Name	Telephone
Bank of Clarendon	(803) 433-4451
First Piedmont Federal S&L Assn. of Gaffney	(864) 489-6046

Rating: A-

Name	Telephone
AMG National Trust Bank	(303) 694-2190
Bank of South Carolina	(843) 724-1500
Bank OZK	(501) 978-2265
Carolina Bank & Trust Co.	(843) 413-9978
First Bank	(910) 692-6222
First Federal Bank	(386) 755-0600
First Palmetto Bank	(803) 432-2265
Palmetto State Bank	(803) 943-2671
ServisFirst Bank	(205) 949-0302
United Community Bank	(706) 745-2151

Rating: B+

Name	Telephone
Ameris Bank	(404) 814-8114
Arthur State Bank	(864) 427-1213
Bank of America, N.A.	(704) 386-5681
Bank of Greeleyville	(843) 426-2161
Bank of Travelers Rest	(864) 834-9031
Commercial Bank	(864) 369-7326
Conway National Bank	(843) 248-5721
Farmers and Merchants Bank	(803) 496-3430
First-Citizens Bank & Trust Co.	(919) 716-7050
Oconee Federal S&L Assn.	(864) 882-2765
Pinnacle Bank	(615) 744-3705
South State Bank, N.A.	(863) 551-5500
Southern First Bank	(864) 679-9000
Truist Bank	(336) 733-2000
Woodforest National Bank	(832) 375-2505

South Dakota

Name	Telephone	Name	Telephone

Rating: A

Name	Telephone
Pioneer Bank & Trust	(605) 717-2265
Security National Bank of South Dakota	(605) 232-6060

Rating: A-

Name	Telephone
American Bank & Trust	(605) 352-9122
Bryant State Bank	(605) 628-2171
Dakota Prairie Bank	(605) 223-2337
First National Bank	(605) 482-8293
First National Bank	(605) 223-2521
First National Bank in Philip	(605) 859-2525
First Premier Bank	(605) 357-3000
First Savings Bank	(605) 763-2009
First State Bank of Roscoe	(605) 287-4451
First Western Federal Savings Bank	(605) 341-1203
Quoin Financial Bank	(605) 853-2473
Richland State Bank	(605) 627-5671

Rating: B+

Name	Telephone
Citizens State Bank of Arlington	(605) 983-5594
Department Stores National Bank	
First Dakota National Bank	(605) 665-7432
First Fidelity Bank	(605) 775-2641
First Interstate Bank	(406) 255-5000
First National Bank in Sioux Falls	(605) 335-5200
Heartland State Bank	(605) 475-5500
Liberty National Bank	(712) 224-4425
MetaBank, N.A.	(605) 782-1767
Minnwest Bank	(507) 637-5731
Security State Bank	(605) 449-4261
Sunrise Banks, N.A.	(651) 265-5600
TCF National Bank	(952) 745-2760

Tennessee

Name	Telephone	Name	Telephone
		Citizens B&T Co. of Grainger County	(865) 828-5237
		Citizens Bank of Lafayette	(615) 666-2195

Rating: A

Name	Telephone
Bank of Cleveland	(423) 478-5656
Citizens Bank	(615) 735-1490
Citizens Bank	(423) 543-2265
Citizens National Bank	(865) 453-9031
Elizabethton Federal Savings Bank	(423) 543-5050
First Bank and Trust Co.	(276) 889-4622
FSNB, N.A.	(580) 357-9880
Republic Bank & Trust Co.	(502) 584-3600

Rating: A-

Name	Telephone
Andrew Johnson Bank	(423) 783-1000
Bank of Lincoln County	(931) 433-1708
CBBC Bank	(865) 977-5900
Citizens Bank	(615) 374-2265
Citizens Community Bank	(931) 967-3342
Commercial Bank & Trust Co.	(731) 642-3341
Farmers Bank	(615) 325-2265
Financial Federal Bank	(901) 756-2848
First Community Bank of Tennessee	(931) 684-5800
First Federal Bank	(615) 446-2822
First Financial Bank, N.A.	(812) 238-6000
First Jackson Bank, Inc.	(256) 437-2107
First National Bank of Middle Tennessee	(931) 473-4402
First National Bank of Oneida	(423) 569-8586
First National Bank of Pulaski	(931) 363-2585
First Volunteer Bank	(423) 668-4509
Peoples Bank	(731) 858-2661
Peoples Bank & Trust Co.	(931) 728-3381
Peoples Bank of East Tennessee	(423) 442-7262
Peoples Bank of Middle Tennessee	(931) 684-7222
Planters Bank, Inc.	(270) 886-9030
Putnam 1st Mercantile Bank	(931) 528-6372
ServisFirst Bank	(205) 949-0302
Tennessee State Bank	(865) 453-0873
Truxton Trust Co.	(615) 515-1700
United Community Bank	(706) 745-2151
Wilson Bank and Trust	(615) 444-2265

Rating: B+

Name	Telephone
American B&T of the Cumberlands	(931) 823-2265
BancorpSouth Bank	(662) 680-2000
Bank of America, N.A.	(704) 386-5681
Bank of Crockett	(731) 663-2031
Bank of Frankewing	(931) 363-1796
Bank of Gleason	(731) 648-5506
Bank of Marion	(276) 783-3116

Name	Telephone
Citizens B&T Co. of Grainger County	(865) 828-5237
Citizens Bank of Lafayette	(615) 666-2195
City National Bank	(800) 773-7100
Coffee County Bank	(931) 728-1975
Commercial Bank	(423) 869-5151
Community Bank	(731) 968-6624
First Century Bank	(423) 626-7261
First Citizens National Bank	(731) 285-4410
First Community Bank of East Tennessee	(423) 272-5800
First Farmers and Merchants Bank	(931) 388-3145
First National Bank of Eastern Arkansas	(870) 633-3112
First National Bank of Tennessee	(931) 823-1261
First Vision Bank of Tennessee	(931) 454-0500
FirstBank	(615) 313-0080
First-Citizens Bank & Trust Co.	(919) 716-7050
Guaranty Bank and Trust Co.	(662) 247-1454
Legends Bank	(931) 503-1234
Mountain Commerce Bank	(865) 694-5725
Pinnacle Bank	(615) 744-3705
Reliant Bank	(615) 221-2020
Renasant Bank	(800) 680-1601
Security Bank and Trust Co.	(731) 642-6644
Security FSB of McMinnville	(931) 473-4483
Simmons Bank	(870) 541-1000
Southern Bank of Tennessee	(615) 758-6600
Truist Bank	(336) 733-2000
Trustmark National Bank	(601) 208-5111
Union Bank & Trust Co.	(931) 823-1247

Texas

Name	Telephone	Name	Telephone
Rating: A+		Citizens Bank	(806) 350-5600
		Citizens State Bank	(979) 885-3571
Citizens 1st Bank	(903) 581-1900	Citizens State Bank	(325) 468-3311
Rating: A		Citizens State Bank	(936) 398-2566
		City National Bank of Sulphur Springs	(903) 885-7523
Austin Bank, Texas N.A.	(903) 586-1526	Coleman County State Bank	(325) 625-2172
Bessemer Trust Co., N.A.	(212) 708-9100	Commerce Bank	(816) 234-2000
Citizens Bank of Las Cruces	(575) 647-4100	Community National B&T of Texas	(903) 654-4500
Citizens National Bank at Brownwood	(325) 643-3545	Cowboy Bank of Texas	(972) 435-2131
Commerce Bank	(956) 724-1616	East West Bank	(626) 768-6000
Commercial National Bank of Brady	(325) 597-2961	First Command Bank	(888) 763-7600
Community Bank	(903) 236-4422	First National Bank of Bastrop	(512) 321-2561
Crockett National Bank	(210) 467-5391	First National Bank of Burleson	(817) 295-0461
Crossroads Bank	(361) 293-3572	First National Bank of Eldorado	(325) 853-2561
Falcon International Bank	(956) 723-2265	First National Bank of Evant	(254) 471-5531
Falls City National Bank	(830) 254-3573	First National Bank of Floydada	(806) 983-3717
First Financial Bank, N.A.	(325) 627-7200	First National Bank of Granbury	(817) 573-2655
First State Bank of Bedias	(936) 395-2141	First National Bank of Hebbronville	(361) 527-3221
First State Bank of Odem	(361) 368-2651	First National Bank of Livingston	(936) 327-1234
FSNB, N.A.	(580) 357-9880	First National Bank of Winnsboro	(903) 342-5275
International Bank of Commerce	(956) 547-1000	First Savings Bank	(605) 763-2009
International Bank of Commerce	(956) 765-8361	First State Bank	(806) 396-5521
International Bank of Commerce	(956) 722-7611	First State Bank of Ben Wheeler, Texas	(903) 833-5861
Mason Bank	(325) 347-5911	First State Bank of Paint Rock	(325) 732-4386
Metro City Bank	(770) 455-4989	First Texas Bank	(512) 556-3691
Muenster State Bank	(940) 759-2257	First United Bank	(806) 647-4151
Security State Bank	(806) 481-3327	Golden Bank, N.A.	(713) 777-3838
Security State Bank & Trust	(830) 997-7575	Grandview Bank	(817) 866-3316
Tejas Bank	(432) 943-4230	Guadalupe Bank	(830) 792-1950
TexasBank	(325) 649-9200	HomeBank Texas	(972) 287-2030
Trinity Bank, N.A.	(817) 763-9966	HomeTown Bank, N.A.	(409) 763-1271
ValueBank Texas	(361) 888-4451	Independent Bank	(972) 562-9004
Waggoner National Bank of Vernon	(940) 552-2511	Industry State Bank	(979) 357-4437
Rating: A-		International Bank of Commerce Oklahoma	(405) 841-2100
		Inwood National Bank	(214) 358-5281
AimBank	(806) 385-4441	Liberty Capital Bank	(469) 375-6600
American First National Bank	(713) 596-2888	Liberty National Bank in Paris	(903) 785-5555
American National Bank of Mount Pleasant	(903) 572-1776	Llano National Bank	(325) 247-5701
Amistad Bank	(830) 775-0295	Moody National Bank	(409) 632-5016
Armed Forces Bank, N.A.	(913) 682-9090	Open Bank	(213) 892-9999
Arrowhead Bank	(325) 247-5741	Peoples State Bank	(830) 683-2119
Bank of DeSoto, N.A.	(972) 780-7777	Pinnacle Bank	(817) 810-9110
Bank of Texas	(432) 221-6100	PlainsCapital Bank	(214) 525-9000
Bank OZK	(501) 978-2265	PromiseOne Bank	(678) 385-0800
BOC Bank	(806) 779-2461	Prosperity Bank	(979) 543-2200
Buckholts State Bank	(254) 593-3661	Roscoe State Bank	(325) 766-3311
Cathay Bank	(213) 625-4791	Round Top State Bank	(979) 249-3151
Central National Bank	(254) 776-3800		

Texas

Name	Telephone	Name	Telephone
Security State Bank	(830) 334-3606	Citizens National Bank of Hillsboro	(254) 582-2531
Shelby Savings Bank, SSB	(936) 598-5688	Citizens State Bank	(979) 596-1421
State Bank of Texas	(972) 252-6000	City Bank	(806) 792-7101
T Bank, N.A.	(972) 720-9000	City National Bank of Taylor	(512) 671-2265
Texas Bank and Trust Co.	(903) 237-5500	Comerica Bank	(214) 462-4000
Texas Bank Financial	(817) 596-9998	Commercial Bank of Texas, N.A.	(936) 715-4100
Texas Community Bank	(956) 722-8333	Commercial National Bank of Texarkana	(903) 831-4561
Texas Exchange Bank, SSB	(817) 297-4331	Commonwealth Business Bank	(323) 988-3000
Texas Financial Bank	(325) 869-5511	Community Bank & Trust, Waco, Texas	(254) 753-1521
Texas First Bank	(409) 948-1990	Community National Bank	(432) 262-1600
Texas Republic Bank, N.A.	(972) 334-0700	Community National Bank	(830) 426-3066
Texas State Bank	(325) 949-3721	CommunityBank of Texas, N.A.	(409) 861-7200
Titan Bank, N.A.	(940) 325-9821	Ennis State Bank	(972) 875-9676
Tolleson Private Bank	(214) 252-3033	Farmers State Bank	(254) 729-3272
WestStar Bank	(915) 532-1000	Fidelity Bank of Texas	(254) 755-6555
Yoakum National Bank	(361) 293-5225	First Bank & Trust	(806) 788-0800
Zions BanCorp., N.A.	(801) 844-7637	First Bank and Trust of Memphis	(806) 259-3556

Rating: B+

Name	Telephone	Name	Telephone
		First Community Bank	(361) 888-9310
		First IC Bank	(770) 451-7200
Amarillo National Bank	(806) 378-8000	First Liberty National Bank	(936) 336-6471
American Momentum Bank	(979) 774-1111	First National Bank	(806) 659-5544
American National Bank & Trust	(940) 397-2300	First National Bank of Albany	(325) 762-2222
American National Bank of Texas	(972) 524-3411	First National Bank of Alvin	(281) 331-3151
Anahuac National Bank	(409) 267-3106	First National Bank of Aspermont	(940) 989-3505
Anchor D Bank	(580) 423-7541	First National Bank of Bellville	(979) 865-3181
Austin Capital Bank SSB	(512) 693-3600	First National Bank of Bosque County	(254) 932-5345
Austin County State Bank	(979) 865-4200	First National Bank of Central Texas	(254) 772-9330
BancorpSouth Bank	(662) 680-2000	First National Bank of Dublin	(254) 445-4400
Bandera Bank	(830) 796-3711	First National Bank of Fort Stockton	(432) 336-8541
Bank and Trust, SSB	(830) 774-2555	First National Bank of Hughes Springs	(903) 639-2521
Bank of America, N.A.	(704) 386-5681	First National Bank of Huntsville	(936) 295-5701
Bank7	(405) 810-8600	First National Bank of McGregor	(254) 840-2836
Benchmark Bank	(972) 673-4000	First National Bank of Shiner	(361) 594-3317
Big Bend Banks, N.A.	(432) 729-4344	First National Bank of Stanton	(432) 756-3361
Brazos National Bank	(979) 265-1911	First National Bank Texas	(254) 554-4236
Brenham National Bank	(979) 836-4571	First State Bank	(903) 676-1900
BTH Bank, N.A.	(903) 763-2264	First State Bank	(940) 665-1711
Burton State Bank	(979) 289-3151	First State Bank	(979) 648-2691
Capital Bank of Texas	(830) 876-5221	First State Bank	(940) 549-8880
Cendera Bank, N.A.	(903) 965-7755	First State Bank and Trust Co.	(903) 693-6606
Central Bank	(832) 485-2300	First State Bank of Burnet	(512) 756-2191
Charles Schwab Bank, SSB	(775) 689-6800	First State Bank of Uvalde	(830) 278-6231
Charter Bank	(361) 241-7681	First Texas Bank	(512) 863-2567
Ciera Bank	(940) 549-2040	First Texoma National Bank	(580) 924-4242
Citizens Bank, N.A.	(325) 695-3000	FirstBank Southwest	(806) 355-9661
Citizens National Bank	(254) 697-6653	First-Citizens Bank & Trust Co.	(919) 716-7050
Citizens National Bank of Crosbyton	(806) 675-2376	Frontier Bank of Texas	(512) 281-1500

Texas

Name	Telephone	Name	Telephone
Frost Bank	(210) 220-4011	West Texas State Bank	(325) 573-5441
Guaranty Bank & Trust, N.A.	(903) 572-9881	Woodforest National Bank	(832) 375-2505
Happy State Bank	(806) 558-2265	Zapata National Bank	(956) 765-4302
Horizon Bank, SSB	(512) 637-5730		
Jacksboro National Bank	(940) 567-5551		
Jefferson Bank	(210) 734-4311		
Johnson City Bank	(830) 868-7131		
Legend Bank, N.A.	(940) 872-2221		
Lone Star National Bank	(956) 984-2991		
Lytle State Bank of Lytle, Texas	(830) 709-3601		
Marion State Bank	(830) 420-2331		
NBH Bank	(720) 554-6650		
NewFirst National Bank	(979) 543-3349		
NexBank	(972) 934-4700		
Northern Trust Co.	(312) 630-6000		
Pearland State Bank	(281) 485-3211		
Pegasus Bank	(214) 353-3000		
Peoples Bank	(806) 794-0044		
Perryton National Bank	(806) 435-9641		
Pointbank	(940) 686-7000		
Sabine State Bank and Trust Co.	(318) 256-7000		
Sage Capital Bank	(830) 672-8585		
Sanger Bank	(940) 458-4600		
Santa Anna National Bank	(325) 348-3108		
Schertz Bank & Trust	(210) 945-7400		
Security National Bank of Omaha	(402) 344-7300		
Simmons Bank	(870) 541-1000		
Southside Bank	(903) 531-7111		
SouthStar Bank, S.S.B.	(361) 596-4611		
Spirit of Texas Bank, SSB	(936) 538-1000		
Spring Hill State Bank	(903) 759-0751		
State Bank of De Kalb	(903) 667-2553		
State National Bank of Big Spring	(432) 264-2100		
Stockmens National Bank in Cotulla	(830) 879-2331		
Sundown State Bank	(806) 229-2111		
Texas Brand Bank	(214) 219-0003		
Texas Gulf Bank, N.A.	(713) 595-7400		
Texas Security Bank	(469) 398-4800		
TexStar National Bank	(210) 659-4000		
Truist Bank	(336) 733-2000		
Trustmark National Bank	(601) 208-5111		
UBank	(936) 422-3000		
VeraBank, N.A.	(903) 657-8521		
Wallis Bank	(979) 478-6151		
Washington Federal Bank, N.A.	(206) 204-3446		
Wells Fargo Bank South Central, N.A.	(713) 802-2717		
West Texas National Bank	(432) 685-6500		

Utah

Name	Telephone	Name	Telephone
Rating: **A+**			
Optum Bank, Inc.	(866) 234-8913		
Rating: **A**			
Altabank	(801) 756-7681		
Bank of Utah	(801) 409-5001		
Central Bank	(801) 375-1000		
Green Dot Bank	(801) 344-7020		
State Bank of Southern Utah	(435) 865-2300		
Utah Independent Bank	(435) 529-7459		
Rating: **A-**			
BMW Bank of North America	(801) 461-6500		
Brighton Bank	(801) 943-6500		
First Electronic Bank	(801) 572-4004		
Glacier Bank	(406) 756-4200		
Home Savings Bank	(801) 523-3878		
LCA Bank Corp.	(435) 658-4824		
Morgan Stanley Bank, N.A.	(801) 236-3600		
Pitney Bowes Bank, Inc.	(801) 832-4440		
UBS Bank USA	(801) 741-0310		
WebBank	(801) 456-8350		
WEX Bank	(801) 568-4345		
Zions BanCorp., N.A.	(801) 844-7637		
Rating: **B+**			
Bank of America, N.A.	(704) 386-5681		
D.L. Evans Bank	(208) 678-8615		
EnerBank USA	(801) 832-0700		
Finwise Bank	(801) 545-6000		
Grand Valley Bank	(435) 654-7400		
Holladay Bank & Trust	(801) 272-4275		
Marlin Business Bank	(888) 479-9111		
NBH Bank	(720) 554-6650		
Rock Canyon Bank	(801) 426-0150		
Washington Federal Bank, N.A.	(206) 204-3446		

Vermont

Name	Telephone	Name	Telephone

Rating: B+

Name	Telephone
Community Bank, N.A.	(315) 445-2282
Ledyard National Bank	(802) 649-2050
TrustCo Bank	(518) 377-3311

Virginia

Name	Telephone	Name	Telephone
		TowneBank	(757) 638-7500
		Truist Bank	(336) 733-2000
		Woodforest National Bank	(832) 375-2505

Rating: A

Name	Telephone
Calvin B. Taylor Banking Co.	(410) 641-1700
First Bank and Trust Co.	(276) 889-4622
Metro City Bank	(770) 455-4989
Surrey Bank & Trust	(336) 783-3900

Rating: A-

Name	Telephone
AMG National Trust Bank	(303) 694-2190
Armed Forces Bank, N.A.	(913) 682-9090
Bank of Charlotte County	(434) 542-5111
Benchmark Community Bank	(434) 676-9054
Citizens and Farmers Bank	(804) 843-2360
Citizens Bank and Trust Co.	(434) 292-8100
City National Bank of West Virginia	(304) 769-1100
EagleBank	(240) 497-2075
Farmers & Merchants Bank	(540) 864-5156
Fidelity Bank	(919) 552-2242
Lee Bank and Trust Co.	(276) 546-2211
MVB Bank, Inc.	(844) 682-2265
National Bank of Blacksburg	(540) 951-6205
Presidential Bank, FSB	(301) 652-1616
Virginia National Bank	(434) 817-8621

Rating: B+

Name	Telephone
American National Bank and Trust Co.	(434) 792-5111
Bank of America, N.A.	(704) 386-5681
Bank of Clarke County	(540) 955-2510
Bank of Marion	(276) 783-3116
Bank of Southside Virginia	(434) 246-5211
Chesapeake Bank	(804) 435-1181
City National Bank	(800) 773-7100
Essex Bank	(804) 419-4329
Farmers and Miners Bank	(276) 546-4692
Farmers Bank	(757) 242-3150
Farmers Bank of Appomattox	(434) 352-7171
First Bank	(540) 465-9121
First-Citizens Bank & Trust Co.	(919) 716-7050
FVCbank	(703) 436-4740
Highlands Community Bank	(540) 962-2265
John Marshall Bank	(703) 584-0840
MainStreet Bank	(703) 481-4567
Pinnacle Bank	(615) 744-3705
Shore United Bank	(410) 822-1400
Sonabank	(804) 528-4754
South State Bank, N.A.	(863) 551-5500
Southern Bank and Trust Co.	(919) 658-7000
Summit Community Bank, Inc.	(304) 530-1000

Washington

Name	Telephone	Name	Telephone

Rating: A

Name	Telephone
Bessemer Trust Co., N.A.	(212) 708-9100
Security State Bank	(360) 736-0763
Timberland Bank	(360) 533-4747

Rating: A-

Name	Telephone
1st Security Bank of Washington	(800) 683-0973
Armed Forces Bank, N.A.	(913) 682-9090
Bank of the Pacific	(360) 537-4052
Cashmere Valley Bank	(509) 782-2624
Cathay Bank	(213) 625-4791
East West Bank	(626) 768-6000
Glacier Bank	(406) 756-4200
Kitsap Bank	(360) 876-7834
Northwest Bank	(208) 332-0700
Riverview Community Bank	(360) 693-6650
State Bank Northwest	(509) 789-4335
UniBank	(425) 275-9700
Washington Business Bank	(360) 754-1945
Zions BanCorp., N.A.	(801) 844-7637

Rating: B+

Name	Telephone
American Continental Bank	(626) 363-8988
Baker-Boyer National Bank	(509) 525-2000
Bank of America, N.A.	(704) 386-5681
Banner Bank	(509) 527-3636
Coastal Community Bank	(425) 257-9000
Columbia State Bank	(253) 305-1900
Commencement Bank	(253) 284-1800
Community First Bank	(509) 783-3435
First Interstate Bank	(406) 255-5000
First-Citizens Bank & Trust Co.	(919) 716-7050
Islanders Bank	(360) 378-3658
Lamont Bank of St. John	(509) 648-3636
Northern Trust Co.	(312) 630-6000
Pacific Crest Savings Bank	(425) 670-9600
Pacific Premier Bank	(949) 864-8000
Peoples Bank	(360) 715-4200
Sound Banking Co.	(253) 588-0100
Sterling Bank and Trust, FSB	(248) 355-2400
Twin River Bank	(208) 746-4848
United Business Bank	(925) 476-1800
Washington Federal Bank, N.A.	(206) 204-3446
Washington Trust Bank	(509) 353-4204
Wheatland Bank	(509) 458-2265
Yakima Federal S&L Assn.	(509) 248-2634

West Virginia

Name	Telephone	Name	Telephone

Rating: A-

Name	Telephone
Bank of Monroe	(304) 772-3034
Citizens Bank of Weston, Inc.	(304) 269-2862
City National Bank of West Virginia	(304) 769-1100
Clay County Bank, Inc.	(304) 587-4221
Clear Mountain Bank	(304) 379-2265
MVB Bank, Inc.	(844) 682-2265
Unified Bank	(740) 633-0445

Rating: B+

Name	Telephone
Bank of Romney	(304) 822-3541
Community Bank of Parkersburg	(304) 485-7991
Fayette County National Bank of Fayetteville	(304) 574-1212
First-Citizens Bank & Trust Co.	(919) 716-7050
Mountain Valley Bank, N.A.	(304) 637-2265
Summit Community Bank, Inc.	(304) 530-1000
Truist Bank	(336) 733-2000
Union Bank, Inc.	(304) 758-2191
WesBanco Bank, Inc.	(304) 234-9419
Woodforest National Bank	(832) 375-2505

Wisconsin

Name	Telephone	Name	Telephone
		Wolf River Community Bank	(920) 779-7000

Rating: A+

Name	Telephone
Bank of Alma	(608) 685-4461
Bank of Prairie Du Sac	(608) 643-3393

Rating: A

Name	Telephone
American National Bank-Fox Cities	(920) 739-1040
Badger Bank	(920) 563-2478
Bank of Deerfield	(608) 764-5411
Bank of Mauston	(608) 847-6200
BLC Community Bank	(920) 788-4141
Bluff View Bank	(608) 582-2233
Charter Bank	(715) 832-4254
Farmers State Bank of Waupaca	(715) 258-1400
First National Bank of Bangor	(608) 486-2386
Hometown Bank	(920) 907-0788
Intercity State Bank	(715) 359-4231
National Exchange Bank and Trust	(920) 921-7700
Richland County Bank	(608) 647-6306
WaterStone Bank, SSB	(414) 761-1000
Waukesha State Bank	(262) 549-8500

Rating: A-

Name	Telephone
Apple River State Bank	(815) 594-2351
Bank of Brodhead	(608) 897-2121
Bank of Lake Mills	(920) 648-8336
Bank of Wisconsin Dells	(608) 253-1111
Bonduel State Bank	(715) 758-2141
Capitol Bank	(608) 836-1616
Citizens Bank	(262) 363-6500
Cumberland Federal Bank, FSB	(715) 822-2249
DMB Community Bank	(608) 846-3711
Farmers State Bank Hillsboro	(608) 489-2621
First Citizens State Bank	(262) 473-2112
First Community Bank	(608) 868-7644
First National Bank of River Falls	(715) 425-2401
Great Midwest Bank, S.S.B.	(262) 784-4400
International Bank of Amherst	(715) 824-3325
John Deere Financial, F.S.B.	(608) 821-2000
Johnson Bank	(262) 619-2700
National Bank of Commerce	(715) 394-5531
Nekoosa Port Edwards State Bank	(715) 886-3104
Northwestern Bank	(715) 723-4461
Oostburg State Bank	(920) 564-2336
Peoples Community Bank	(608) 795-2120
River Falls State Bank	(715) 425-6782
Shell Lake State Bank	(715) 468-7858
State Bank of Newburg	(262) 675-2306

Rating: B+

Name	Telephone
Bank First, N.A.	(920) 652-3100
Bank of Cashton	(608) 654-5121
Bank of Milton	(608) 868-7672
Bankers' Bank	(608) 833-5550
Bay Bank	(920) 490-7600
Black River Country Bank	(715) 284-9448
Bremer Bank, N.A.	(651) 288-3751
Citizens State Bank of Loyal	(715) 255-8526
Clare Bank, N.A.	(608) 348-2727
Collins State Bank	(920) 772-4433
Community First Bank	(715) 677-4523
Community First Bank	(608) 375-4117
Farmers & Merchants State Bank	(920) 478-2181
Farmers Savings Bank	(608) 987-3321
First National Bank at Darlington	(608) 776-4071
First-Citizens Bank & Trust Co.	(919) 716-7050
Flagstar Bank, FSB	(248) 312-5400
Frandsen Bank & Trust	(507) 744-2361
Headwaters State Bank	(715) 547-3383
Highland State Bank	(608) 929-4515
Home Federal Savings Bank	(507) 535-1309
Hustisford State Bank	(920) 349-3241
Nicolet National Bank	(920) 430-1400
Northern State Bank	(715) 682-2772
Northern Trust Co.	(312) 630-6000
Oak Bank	(608) 441-6000
One Community Bank	(608) 835-3168
Paper City Savings Assn.	(715) 423-8100
Partners Bank	(715) 659-2430
Peoples State Bank	(715) 842-2191
Pineries Bank	(715) 341-5600
Royal Bank	(608) 462-8401
Starion Bank	(701) 223-6050
TCF National Bank	(952) 745-2760
Tri City National Bank	(414) 761-1610
TSB Bank	(920) 269-7777
WNB Financial, N.A.	(507) 454-8800
Woodford State Bank	(608) 325-7766

Wyoming

Name	Telephone	Name	Telephone

Rating: A

RSNB Bank	(307) 362-8801
Wyoming Bank & Trust	(307) 632-7733

Rating: A-

AMG National Trust Bank	(303) 694-2190
Bank of Commerce	(307) 324-2265
Bank of Star Valley	(307) 885-0000
First State Bank	(308) 632-4158
FirsTier Bank	(308) 235-4633
Glacier Bank	(406) 756-4200
Lusk State Bank	(307) 334-2500
Pinnacle Bank - Wyoming	(402) 697-5990
Points West Community Bank	(970) 686-0878
Zions BanCorp., N.A.	(801) 844-7637

Rating: B+

ANB Bank	(303) 394-5143
Bank of Jackson Hole	(307) 733-8064
Central Bank and Trust	(307) 332-4730
Converse County Bank	(307) 358-5300
First Federal Bank & Trust	(307) 674-0464
First Interstate Bank	(406) 255-5000
Hilltop National Bank	(307) 265-2740
Jonah Bank of Wyoming	(307) 237-4555
Rocky Mountain Bank	(307) 739-9000

Section III

Rating Upgrades
and Downgrades

A list of all

U.S. Commercial Banks and Savings Banks

receiving a rating upgrade or downgrade
during the current quarter.

Section III Contents

This section identifies those institutions receiving a rating change since the previous edition of this publication, whether it be a rating upgrade, rating downgrade, newly-rated company or the withdrawal of a rating. A rating upgrade or downgrade may entail a change from one letter grade to another, or it may mean the addition or deletion of a plus or minus sign within the same letter grade previously assigned to the company. Ratings are normally updated once each quarter of the year. In some instances, however, an institution's rating may be downgraded outside of the normal updates due to overriding circumstances.

1. **Institution Name**   The name under which the institution was chartered. A company's name can be very similar to, or the same as, that of another, so verify the company's exact name, city, and state to make sure you are looking at the correct company.

2. **New Safety Rating**   Weiss rating assigned to the institution at the time of publication. Our ratings are designed to distinguish levels of insolvency risk and are measured on a scale from A to F based upon a wide range of factors. Highly rated companies are, in our opinion, less likely to experience financial difficulties than lower rated firms. See *About Weiss Safety Ratings* for more information and a description of what each rating means.

3. **State**   The state in which the institution's headquarters or main office is located.

4. **Date of Change**   Date that rating was finalized.

Rating Upgrades

Name	State	Date of Change	Name	State	Date of Change
Rating:		**A**	Citizens State Bank of Roseau	MN	12/07/20
			Community Resource Bank	MN	12/07/20
American National Bank-Fox Cities	WI	12/07/20	Connect Bank	AR	12/07/20
Badger Bank	WI	12/07/20	Croghan Colonial Bank	OH	12/07/20
Bank of England	AR	12/07/20	Eagle Bank and Trust Co.	AR	12/07/20
Bank of Grain Valley	MO	12/07/20	Elysian Bank	MN	12/07/20
Bluff View Bank	WI	12/07/20	Farmers & Stockmens Bank	NM	12/07/20
Citizens Bank of Edina	MO	12/07/20	First Bank	MO	12/07/20
Commercial Bank of Mott	ND	12/07/20	First National Bank of Beardstown	IL	12/07/20
Community First Bank	MN	12/07/20	First National Bank of Fletcher	OK	12/07/20
Denison State Bank	KS	12/07/20	First National Bank of Middle Tennessee	TN	12/07/20
Falls City National Bank	TX	12/07/20	First National Bank of Winnsboro	TX	12/07/20
Farmers & Merchants Bank of Colby	KS	12/07/20	First National Community Bank	GA	12/07/20
Farmers State Bank of Waupaca	WI	12/07/20	First State Bank	IA	12/07/20
Fisher National Bank	IL	12/07/20	First State Bank	OK	12/07/20
Goodfield State Bank	IL	12/07/20	First State Bank of Middlebury	IN	12/07/20
Guardian Savings Bank, F.S.B.	OH	12/07/20	FirstBank of Nebraska	NE	12/07/20
Logansport Savings Bank	IN	12/07/20	FNB Bank	IA	12/07/20
Magnolia Bank, Inc.	KY	12/07/20	FNBT Bank	FL	12/07/20
Mutual Savings Assn.	KS	12/07/20	Four County Bank	GA	12/07/20
NBKC Bank	MO	12/07/20	Great Midwest Bank, S.S.B.	WI	12/07/20
North American Savings Bank, F.S.B.	MO	12/07/20	Independent Bank	TX	12/07/20
Pacific Coast Bankers' Bank	CA	12/07/20	Industry State Bank	TX	12/07/20
Phenix-Girard Bank	AL	12/07/20	KS StateBank	KS	12/07/20
Richland County Bank	WI	12/07/20	Luana Savings Bank	IA	12/07/20
Taylor County Bank	KY	12/07/20	Mechanics Cooperative Bank	MA	12/07/20
Tri-County Bank	MI	12/07/20	Murphy Bank	CA	12/07/20
Union Savings Bank	OH	12/07/20	MVB Bank, Inc.	WV	12/07/20
United Bank and Trust Co.	IA	12/07/20	National Bank of Commerce	WI	12/07/20
Utah Independent Bank	UT	12/07/20	North Central Bank	IL	12/07/20
Verus Bank of Commerce	CO	12/07/20	Northside Community Bank	IL	12/07/20
			Northview Bank	MN	12/07/20
Rating:		**A-**	Old Mission Bank	MI	12/07/20
			ONB Bank	MN	12/07/20
21st Century Bank	MN	12/07/20	Peoples B&T Co. of Pointe Coupee Parish	LA	12/07/20
American Bank & Trust	SD	12/07/20	Presidential Bank, FSB	MD	12/07/20
American Exchange Bank	OK	12/07/20	Resource Bank	LA	12/07/20
Arkansas County Bank	AR	12/07/20	Richland State Bank	SD	12/07/20
Auburn State Bank	NE	12/07/20	Roxboro Savings Bank, SSB	NC	12/07/20
Bank of Brodhead	WI	12/07/20	Solomon State Bank	KS	12/07/20
Bank of Dixon County	NE	12/07/20	State Bank Northwest	WA	12/07/20
Bank of Magnolia Co.	OH	12/07/20	State Bank of Texas	TX	12/07/20
Bank of Missouri	MO	12/07/20	Two Rivers Bank	NE	12/07/20
Bank of Monticello	MO	12/07/20	University Bank	MI	12/07/20
Bell Bank	ND	12/07/20	Washington Business Bank	WA	12/07/20
Bellevue State Bank	IA	12/07/20	Watertown Savings Bank	NY	12/07/20
Bryant State Bank	SD	12/07/20	Wayland State Bank	IA	12/07/20
Central National Bank	KS	12/07/20	WEX Bank	UT	12/07/20
CFBank, N.A.	OH	12/07/20			
Charter West Bank	NE	12/07/20	**Rating:**		**B+**
Citizens Savings Bank	IA	12/07/20			

Rating Upgrades

Name	State	Date of Change	Name	State	Date of Change
American National Bank & Trust	TX	12/07/20	KodaBank	ND	12/07/20
American National Bank of Minnesota	MN	12/07/20	LNB Community Bank	IN	12/07/20
BANK	IA	12/07/20	Mid-America Bank	KS	12/07/20
Bank First, N.A.	WI	12/07/20	Midwest Community Bank	IL	12/07/20
Bank of Romney	WV	12/07/20	NBH Bank	CO	12/07/20
Bankers' Bank	WI	12/07/20	North Alabama Bank	AL	12/07/20
BayVanguard Bank	MD	12/07/20	North Shore Bank of Commerce	MN	12/07/20
Belmont Bank & Trust Co.	IL	12/07/20	Northrim Bank	AK	12/07/20
Belt Valley Bank	MT	12/07/20	Northwoods Bank of Minnesota	MN	12/07/20
Bodcaw Bank	AR	12/07/20	Norwood Co-operative Bank	MA	12/07/20
Bruning Bank	NE	12/07/20	Premier Bank	MN	12/07/20
Cedar Security Bank	NE	12/07/20	Premier Bank Minnesota	MN	12/07/20
Central Bank and Trust	WY	12/07/20	PS Bank	PA	12/07/20
Century Bank and Trust	GA	12/07/20	Putnam County State Bank	MO	12/07/20
CerescoBank	NE	12/07/20	Reliant Bank	TN	12/07/20
Cherokee State Bank	IA	12/07/20	Shelby County State Bank	IA	12/07/20
Citizens Bank of Cumberland County	KY	12/07/20	Stillman BancCorp, N.A.	IL	12/07/20
Citizens National Bank of Bluffton	OH	12/07/20	The Bank of Soperton	GA	12/07/20
Citizens Union Bank of Shelbyville	KY	12/07/20	Tipton Latham Bank, N.A.	MO	12/07/20
Coffee County Bank	TN	12/07/20	Valley State Bank	KS	12/07/20
Collins State Bank	WI	12/07/20	West Texas State Bank	TX	12/07/20
Commonwealth Bank and Trust Co.	KY	12/07/20	Wilcox County State Bank	GA	12/07/20
Community Bank	TN	12/07/20	York Traditions Bank	PA	12/07/20
Community Bank of Oelwein	IA	12/07/20	Zapata National Bank	TX	12/07/20
Connections Bank	MO	12/07/20			
Eagle Savings Bank	OH	12/07/20	**Rating: B**		
ESB Bank	MN	12/07/20	American Heritage Bank	OK	12/07/20
Farmers & Merchants Savings Bank	IA	12/07/20	Balboa Thrift and Loan Assn.	CA	12/07/20
Farmers and Merchants State Bank	MN	12/07/20	Bank of Abbeville & Trust Co.	LA	12/07/20
Farmers and Merchants State Bank	ND	12/07/20	Bank of Holly Springs	MS	12/07/20
Farmers Savings Bank	WI	12/07/20	Bank of Turtle Lake	ND	12/07/20
Farmers Savings Bank	IA	12/07/20	Blackhawk Bank	WI	12/07/20
Fidelity Bank	IA	12/07/20	Campbell County Bank, Inc.	SD	12/07/20
First Community Bank	MT	12/07/20	Century Bank of Kentucky, Inc.	KY	12/07/20
First Dakota National Bank	SD	12/07/20	Chambers Bank	AR	12/07/20
First Enterprise Bank	OK	12/07/20	Citizens Bank of Rogersville	MO	12/07/20
First Federal Bank & Trust	WY	12/07/20	Citizens National Bank of Texas	TX	12/07/20
First National Bank Minnesota	MN	12/07/20	Cleo State Bank	OK	12/07/20
First State Bank	IL	12/07/20	CNB St. Louis Bank	MO	12/07/20
First State Bank	IA	12/07/20	Community Bank of Memphis	MO	12/07/20
First State Bank of Forsyth	MT	12/07/20	Community Savings Bank	OH	12/07/20
Frandsen Bank & Trust	MN	12/07/20	Community State Bank	IL	12/07/20
Freedom Bank of Southern Missouri	MO	12/07/20	Country Bank for Savings	MA	12/07/20
Grant County Bank	KS	12/07/20	Countryside Bank	NE	12/07/20
Grundy Bank	IL	12/07/20	County Bank	DE	12/07/20
Highland State Bank	WI	12/07/20	Dedham Institution for Savings	MA	12/07/20
Home Loan Savings Bank	OH	12/07/20	Del Norte Bank, A S&L Assn.	CO	12/07/20
Illini State Bank	IL	12/07/20	Elberfeld State Bank	IN	12/07/20
Intracoastal Bank	FL	12/07/20	Farmers & Merchants Bank	ND	12/07/20
Investors Community Bank	MO	12/07/20	Farmers & Merchants Union Bank	WI	12/07/20

Rating Upgrades

Name	State	Date of Change	Name	State	Date of Change
Farmers and Merchants Bank	OH	12/07/20	Peoples State Bank of Newton, Illinois	IL	12/07/20
Farmers and Merchants State Bank	IL	12/07/20	Premier Bank	OH	12/07/20
Farmers Savings Bank	IA	12/07/20	Prime Security Bank	MN	12/07/20
Farmers Security Bank	ND	12/07/20	Provident State Bank, Inc.	MD	12/07/20
Farmers State Bank	IA	12/07/20	Sabal Palm Bank	FL	12/07/20
Fidelity Bank	LA	12/07/20	Savoy Bank	NY	12/07/20
First Bank of Baldwin	WI	12/07/20	Security State Bank of Oklahoma	OK	12/07/20
First Credit Bank	CA	12/07/20	Seymour Bank	MO	12/07/20
First Federal Bank of Wisconsin	WI	12/07/20	Smackover State Bank	AR	12/07/20
First Federal S&L Bank	KS	12/07/20	State Bank of Scotia	NE	12/07/20
First Missouri State Bank of Cape County	MO	12/07/20	Sunflower Bank, N.A.	CO	12/07/20
First National Bank in Amboy	IL	12/07/20	The Farmers State Bank and Trust Co.	IL	12/07/20
First National Bank of East Texas	TX	12/07/20	Tilden Bank	NE	12/07/20
First National Bank of Monterey	IN	12/07/20	Tri-County Bank	NE	12/07/20
First National Bank of Omaha	NE	12/07/20	Tustin Community Bank	CA	12/07/20
First Reliance Bank	SC	12/07/20	Ultima Bank Minnesota	MN	12/07/20
First State Bank	WI	12/07/20	Union State Bank	KS	12/07/20
First State Bank and Trust	KS	12/07/20	United Community Bank	LA	12/07/20
First State Bank of Brownsboro	TX	12/07/20	Walpole Co-operative Bank	MA	12/07/20
First Western Bank	AR	12/07/20	Washington Savings Bank	IL	12/07/20
Freedom Bank of Virginia	VA	12/07/20	Wayne Bank and Trust Co.	IN	12/07/20
Freeport State Bank	MN	12/07/20			
Gate City Bank	ND	12/07/20	**Rating:** **B-**		
Georgia Primary Bank	GA	12/07/20	Abacus Federal Savings Bank	NY	12/07/20
Gogebic Range Bank	MI	12/07/20	Allied First Bank,sb	IL	12/07/20
Grand Timber Bank	MN	12/07/20	American Exchange Bank	OK	12/07/20
Great Rivers Bank	IL	12/07/20	Apex Bank	TN	12/07/20
Heartland Bank	NE	12/07/20	Bank of Gibson City	IL	12/07/20
Highland Federal S&L Assn.	TN	12/07/20	Bank of Hamilton	ND	12/07/20
Holcomb Bank	IL	12/07/20	Bank of Kaukauna	WI	12/07/20
Home Bank and Trust Co.	KS	12/07/20	Bank of Whittier, N.A.	CA	12/07/20
Home Bank SB	IN	12/07/20	Blue Ridge Bank, N.A.	VA	12/07/20
Horatio State Bank	AR	12/07/20	CalPrivate Bank	CA	12/07/20
Huron State Bank	MI	12/07/20	CIBM Bank	IL	12/07/20
Incommons Bank, N.A.	TX	12/07/20	Cincinnati Federal	OH	12/07/20
Independence Bank	RI	12/07/20	Cincinnatus S&L Co.	OH	12/07/20
Independent Bank	TN	12/07/20	Citizens Bank & Trust Co.	MT	12/07/20
Inland Bank and Trust	IL	12/07/20	Citizens National Bank of Cheboygan	MI	12/07/20
Lyons Federal Bank	KS	12/07/20	Citizens State Bank	KS	12/07/20
Magnolia State Bank	GA	12/07/20	Commerce Bank	MN	12/07/20
Maine Community Bank	ME	12/07/20	Community State Bank	IN	12/07/20
MCBank	TX	12/07/20	Core Bank	NE	12/07/20
Morris Bank	GA	12/07/20	Cottonwood Valley Bank	KS	12/07/20
Mount Vernon Bank	GA	12/07/20	Coulee Bank	WI	12/07/20
National Bank & Trust	TX	12/07/20	Dakota Heritage Bank	ND	12/07/20
Ninnescah Valley Bank	KS	12/07/20	Dean Co-operative Bank	MA	12/07/20
Olpe State Bank	KS	12/07/20	DeWitt Savings Bank	IL	12/07/20
Ottawa Savings Bank	IL	12/07/20	Eclipse Bank, Inc.	KY	12/07/20
Peoples Bank	MD	12/07/20	F&M Bank	TN	12/07/20
Peoples Bank of the South	TN	12/07/20	Farmers and Merchants Bank of Kendall	WI	12/07/20

Rating Upgrades

Name	State	Date of Change	Name	State	Date of Change
Farmers Savings Bank	IA	12/07/20	Summit National Bank	WY	12/07/20
Financial Security Bank	MN	12/07/20	Texana Bank, N.A.	TX	12/07/20
First Bank	AK	12/07/20	Third Coast Bank, SSB	TX	12/07/20
First City Bank	OH	12/07/20	Thumb Bank & Trust	MI	12/07/20
First Federal S&L Assn. of Newark	OH	12/07/20	Vast Bank, N.A.	OK	12/07/20
First Independent Bank	MN	12/07/20	Vinings Bank	GA	12/07/20
First National Bank of Coleraine	MN	12/07/20	West Pointe Bank	WI	12/07/20
First National Bank of Dozier	AL	12/07/20			
First National Bank of Pandora	OH	12/07/20			

Rating: C+

Name	State	Date of Change
First Security Bank	MN	12/07/20
First State Bank of Dongola	IL	12/07/20
First State Bank Shannon-Polo	IL	12/07/20
First Western Trust Bank	CO	12/07/20
Flanagan State Bank	IL	12/07/20
FNBC Bank	AR	12/07/20
Fortifi Bank	WI	12/07/20
Frontier Bank	NE	12/07/20
Goldwater Bank, N.A.	AZ	12/07/20
Granite Community Bank	MN	12/07/20
Great Plains State Bank	NE	12/07/20
Green Belt Bank & Trust	IA	12/07/20
HarborOne Bank	MA	12/07/20
Hatch Bank	CA	12/07/20
Hoosier Heartland State Bank	IN	12/07/20
Iowa Falls State Bank	IA	12/07/20
Ixonia Bank	WI	12/07/20
Lone Star State Bank of West Texas	TX	12/07/20
Main Street Bank Corp.	WV	12/07/20
Marine Bank	IL	12/07/20
Marion National Bank	KS	12/07/20
McKenzie Banking Co.	TN	12/07/20
Mediapolis Savings Bank	IA	12/07/20
Mercer County State Bank	PA	12/07/20
Merchants Commercial Bank	VI	12/07/20
Merchants State Bank	SD	12/07/20
Meridian Bank	PA	12/07/20
Miners National Bank of Eveleth	MN	12/07/20
Mutual Federal Bank	IL	12/07/20
National Cooperative Bank, N.A.	OH	12/07/20
PCSB Bank	IA	12/07/20
Peoples Bank of Kankakee County	IL	12/07/20
Plains State Bank	TX	12/07/20
Rayne Building and Loan Assn.	LA	12/07/20
Reliance Savings Bank	PA	12/07/20
Rivers Edge Bank	SD	12/07/20
Sherwood Community Bank	MO	12/07/20
Small Business Bank	KS	12/07/20
SpiritBank	OK	12/07/20
State Bank of Pearl City	IL	12/07/20
State National Bank of Groom	TX	12/07/20

Name	State	Date of Change
1st Colonial Community Bank	NJ	12/07/20
1st State Bank of Mason City	IL	12/07/20
Alva State Bank & Trust Co.	OK	12/07/20
American Eagle Bank	IL	12/07/20
AmeriState Bank	OK	12/07/20
Arbor Bank	NE	12/07/20
Bank of Bartlett	TN	12/07/20
BayCoast Bank	MA	12/07/20
Belmont Savings Bank, SSB	NC	12/07/20
Cedar Rapids State Bank	NE	12/07/20
Citizens Bank	MO	12/07/20
Coastal States Bank	SC	12/07/20
Community State Bank	AR	12/07/20
County Bank	IA	12/07/20
Defiance State Bank	IA	12/07/20
Devon Bank	IL	12/07/20
Fall River Five Cents Savings Bank	MA	12/07/20
Federated Bank	IL	12/07/20
Fidelity Co-operative Bank	MA	12/07/20
First Federal S&L Assn.	MS	12/07/20
First Federal S&L Assn. of Lakewood	OH	12/07/20
First Mutual Bank, FSB	OH	12/07/20
First National Bank of Waverly	OH	12/07/20
First Progressive Bank	AL	12/07/20
Florida Capital Bank, N.A.	FL	12/07/20
Gateway First Bank	OK	12/07/20
Gibraltar Bank	NJ	12/07/20
Grand River Bank	MI	12/07/20
Heritage Bank, N.A.	MN	12/07/20
Home Federal S&L Assn.	SC	12/07/20
Legacy Bank	VA	12/07/20
Longview Bank	IL	12/07/20
MNB Bank	NE	12/07/20
Mountain Pacific Bank	WA	12/07/20
One American Bank	SD	12/07/20
Peoples Bank	TN	12/07/20
Peoples State Bank	KS	12/07/20
Pioneer State Bank	IL	12/07/20
Raritan State Bank	IL	12/07/20
Security State Bank	KS	12/07/20
SouthernTrust Bank	IL	12/07/20

Rating Upgrades

Name	State	Date of Change	Name	State	Date of Change
State Bank of Lismore	MN	12/07/20	Nebraska State Bank	NE	12/07/20
State Bank of New Richland	MN	12/07/20	New Peoples Bank, Inc.	VA	12/07/20
State Bank of Taunton	MN	12/07/20	North Easton Savings Bank	MA	12/07/20
Synchrony Bank	UT	12/07/20	Pan American Bank & Trust	IL	12/07/20
Thayer County Bank	NE	12/07/20	Peoples Bank	LA	12/07/20
United Midwest Savings Bank, N.A.	OH	12/07/20	Peoples Bank & Trust	IL	12/07/20
Upstate National Bank	NY	12/07/20	Peoples Bank of Red Level	AL	12/07/20
Uwharrie Bank	NC	12/07/20	Plains Commerce Bank	SD	12/07/20
Valley Central Bank	OH	12/07/20	Plains State Bank	KS	12/07/20
Washington Savings Bank	MA	12/07/20	PyraMax Bank, FSB	WI	12/07/20
Wayne County Bank	TN	12/07/20	Quail Creek Bank, N.A.	OK	12/07/20
Wenona State Bank	IL	12/07/20	Southeast First National Bank	GA	12/07/20
Western National Bank	MN	12/07/20	State Bank of Burrton	KS	12/07/20
Western National Bank of Cass Lake	MN	12/07/20	Warrington Bank	FL	12/07/20

Rating: C

Name	State	Date of Change
1st Trust Bank, Inc.	KY	12/07/20
American Bank & Trust Co., Inc.	LA	12/07/20
American Bank of Oklahoma	OK	12/07/20
Asian Pacific National Bank	CA	12/07/20
Aspire Bank	ND	12/07/20
Bank of Anguilla	MS	12/07/20
Bank of Pensacola	FL	12/07/20
Bank of the South	FL	12/07/20
BankNorth	ND	12/07/20
Bison State Bank	KS	12/07/20
Citizens Bank of Edinburg	IL	12/07/20
Citizens Bank of Newburg	MO	12/07/20
Citizens State Bank of Ouray	CO	12/07/20
Citizens State Bank of Tyler, Inc.	MN	12/07/20
Commerceone Bank	AL	12/07/20
Community Savings Bank	IA	12/07/20
Community State Bank	OK	12/07/20
Envision Bank	MA	12/07/20
First Bank, Upper Michigan	MI	12/07/20
First Southeast Bank	MN	12/07/20
First State Bank	NE	12/07/20
FNNB Bank	IA	12/07/20
Fortis Private Bank	CO	12/07/20
Global Innovations Bank	MN	12/07/20
Hebron Savings Bank	MD	12/07/20
Henry County Bank	OH	12/07/20
Home Savings Bank	WI	12/07/20
Kennebec Federal S&L Assn. of Waterville	ME	12/07/20
Kensington Bank	MN	12/07/20
LimeBank	MO	12/07/20
Maple City Savings Bank, FSB	NY	12/07/20
Marquette Farmers State Bank	KS	12/07/20
Millbury National Bank	MA	12/07/20
Native American Bank, N.A.	CO	12/07/20

Rating: C-

Name	State	Date of Change
1st Equity Bank	IL	12/07/20
Andes State Bank	SD	12/07/20
Bank of Hazlehurst	GA	12/07/20
Bank of the Rockies	MT	12/07/20
Bank of Washington	MO	12/07/20
Boonville Federal Savings Bank	IN	12/07/20
Citizens State Bank	NE	12/07/20
Citizens State Bank and Trust Co.	KS	12/07/20
Community State Bank	NE	12/07/20
Community State Bank of Rock Falls	IL	12/07/20
Cowboy State Bank	WY	12/07/20
Crown Bank	MN	12/07/20
Emerald Bank	KS	12/07/20
Farmers-Merchants Bank & Trust Co.	LA	12/07/20
First Central Savings Bank	NY	12/07/20
First State Bank	OK	12/07/20
FMB Bank	MO	12/07/20
FortuneBank	MO	12/07/20
Hoyne Savings Bank	IL	12/07/20
Independence State Bank	WI	12/07/20
Millennial Bank	AL	12/07/20
Raymond Federal Bank	WA	12/07/20
Rolling Hills Bank & Trust	IA	12/07/20
Security State Bank of Warroad	MN	12/07/20
Sunrise Bank Dakota	SD	12/07/20
Unity Bank	WI	12/07/20
Valley Bank of Ronan	MT	12/07/20
Wells River Savings Bank	VT	12/07/20

Rating: D+

Name	State	Date of Change
Alma Bank	NY	12/07/20
Cogent Bank	FL	12/07/20
Community Savings	OH	12/07/20
First Security Bank	OK	12/07/20

Rating Upgrades

Name	State	Date of Change	Name	State	Date of Change
First State Bank of Red Wing	MN	12/07/20			
First State Bank of Rosemount	MN	12/07/20			
Generations Bank	NY	12/07/20			
Movement Bank	VA	12/07/20			
State Savings Bank	MI	12/07/20			
VISIONBank	ND	12/07/20			
West Valley National Bank	AZ	12/07/20			

Rating: D

Name	State	Date of Change
Buckeye State Bank	OH	12/07/20
First State Bank of Malta	MT	12/07/20
Greenfield Banking Co.	TN	12/07/20
Guardian Savings Bank	IL	12/07/20
Gulf Atlantic Bank	FL	12/07/20
Home Savings Bank, FSB	KY	12/07/20
Jackson County Bank	WI	12/07/20
Lafayette State Bank	FL	12/07/20
SunSouth Bank	AL	12/07/20
Unity National Bank of Houston	TX	12/07/20

Rating: D-

Name	State	Date of Change
Dickinson County Bank	KS	12/07/20
LINKBANK	PA	12/07/20

Rating: E+

Name	State	Date of Change
First Southern Bank	GA	12/07/20

Rating Downgrades

Name	State	Date of Change	Name	State	Date of Change
Rating: A-			Ireland Bank	ID	12/07/20
			Killbuck Savings Bank Co.	OH	12/07/20
Alpine Capital Bank	NY	12/07/20	Lake Elmo Bank	MN	12/07/20
Cashmere Valley Bank	WA	12/07/20	Leighton State Bank	IA	12/07/20
Central Bank of Kansas City	MO	12/07/20	Maspeth Federal S&L Assn.	NY	12/07/20
Community State Bank	IN	12/07/20	Mission Bank	CA	12/07/20
Deutsche Bank Trust Co. Americas	NY	12/07/20	Mission Valley Bank	CA	12/07/20
First National Bank North	MN	12/07/20	NewBank	NY	12/07/20
First Westroads Bank, Inc.	NE	12/07/20	NorthStar Bank	IA	12/07/20
Lindell Bank & Trust Co.	MO	12/07/20	Norway Savings Bank	ME	12/07/20
New Albin Savings Bank	IA	12/07/20	One Community Bank	WI	12/07/20
Palmetto State Bank	SC	12/07/20	Peoples National Bank of Checotah	OK	12/07/20
Texas Community Bank	TX	12/07/20	Pinnacle Bank	CA	12/07/20
Texas State Bank	TX	12/07/20	Pointbank	TX	12/07/20
Truxton Trust Co.	TN	12/07/20	Premier Bank	NE	12/07/20
West Central Georgia Bank	GA	12/07/20	Premier Bank of Arkansas	AR	12/07/20
			RBC Bank (Georgia), N.A.	NC	12/07/20
Rating: B+			Rock Canyon Bank	UT	12/07/20
			Sanger Bank	TX	12/07/20
American Bank	MT	12/07/20	Security FSB of McMinnville	TN	12/07/20
American Continental Bank	CA	12/07/20	Security National Bank of Omaha	NE	12/07/20
Axos Bank	CA	12/07/20	Security State Bank	IA	12/07/20
Bank of Bourbonnais	IL	12/07/20	Security State Bank	IA	12/07/20
Bank of Dudley	GA	12/07/20	Sooner State Bank	OK	12/07/20
Bank of Marion	VA	12/07/20	St. Ansgar State Bank	IA	12/07/20
Bank of Southside Virginia	VA	12/07/20	Sterling Bank and Trust, FSB	MI	12/07/20
Bank of the Sierra	CA	12/07/20	TrustCo Bank	NY	12/07/20
Bank7	OK	12/07/20	United Bank & Trust	KS	12/07/20
Bankwest of Kansas	KS	12/07/20	West Alabama Bank & Trust	AL	12/07/20
Buckeye Community Bank	OH	12/07/20	West Texas National Bank	TX	12/07/20
Capital Bank of Texas	TX	12/07/20			
Casey County Bank, Inc.	KY	12/07/20	**Rating: B**		
Central Valley Community Bank	CA	12/07/20			
Citizens Bank	AL	12/07/20	Atlantic Union Bank	VA	12/07/20
Citizens Bank & Trust, Inc.	GA	12/07/20	Bank of Brookhaven	MS	12/07/20
Coastal Community Bank	WA	12/07/20	Bank of Kirksville	MO	12/07/20
Comerica Bank	TX	12/07/20	Bank of York	SC	12/07/20
Commercial Bank & Trust of PA	PA	12/07/20	BankNewport	RI	12/07/20
Commonwealth Business Bank	CA	12/07/20	BNB Bank	NY	12/07/20
CommunityBank of Texas, N.A.	TX	12/07/20	Broadway National Bank	TX	12/07/20
Cross River Bank	NJ	12/07/20	Bryn Mawr Trust Co.	PA	12/07/20
Elkton Bank & Trust Co.	KY	12/07/20	Canandaigua National Bank and Trust Co.	NY	12/07/20
First American Bank and Trust Co.	GA	12/07/20	CapStar Bank	TN	12/07/20
First Community Bank and Trust	IL	12/07/20	Centric Bank	PA	12/07/20
First National Bank of Le Center	MN	12/07/20	Citibank, N.A.	SD	12/07/20
First National Bank of Milaca	MN	12/07/20	Citizens Trust Bank	GA	12/07/20
First Nations Bank	IL	12/07/20	Community Bank	OR	12/07/20
First State Bank and Trust Co.	TX	12/07/20	Community Commerce Bank	CA	12/07/20
Fountain Trust Co.	IN	12/07/20	Eastern Bank	MA	12/07/20
Fulton Savings Bank	NY	12/07/20	Emprise Bank	KS	12/07/20
Happy State Bank	TX	12/07/20	Farmers and Merchants Trust Co.	PA	12/07/20

Rating Downgrades

Name	State	Date of Change	Name	State	Date of Change
First Community Bank	SC	12/07/20	Cleveland State Bank	WI	12/07/20
First Community Bank of the Ozarks	MO	12/07/20	Columbus State Bank	TX	12/07/20
First, A National Banking Assn.	MS	12/07/20	Community Bank	KS	12/07/20
FNB Oxford Bank	MS	12/07/20	Corydon State Bank	IA	12/07/20
Jeff Bank	NY	12/07/20	Dilley State Bank	TX	12/07/20
JPMorgan Chase Bank, N.A.	OH	12/07/20	Dundee Bank	NE	12/07/20
Kansas State Bank Overbrook Kansas	KS	12/07/20	Durand State Bank	IL	12/07/20
Kentucky Bank	KY	12/07/20	Fannin Bank	TX	12/07/20
Lake Forest Bank & Trust Co., N.A.	IL	12/07/20	Farmers and Merchants Bank	NE	12/07/20
Mission National Bank	CA	12/07/20	Farmers State Bank	KS	12/07/20
Morganton Savings Bank, S.S.B.	NC	12/07/20	Fayette Savings Bank, SSB	TX	12/07/20
NBT Bank, N.A.	NY	12/07/20	First Capital Bank	TN	12/07/20
Northern State Bank of Thief River Falls	MN	12/07/20	First Commercial Bank	MS	12/07/20
Ormsby State Bank	MN	12/07/20	First Federal S&L Assn. of McMinnville	OR	12/07/20
Partners Bank of New England	ME	12/07/20	First Fidelity Bank	OK	12/07/20
Peapack-Gladstone Bank	NJ	12/07/20	First Guaranty Bank	LA	12/07/20
Produce State Bank	MN	12/07/20	First National B&T Co. of Okmulgee	OK	12/07/20
Reliance State Bank	IA	12/07/20	First National Bank in Ord	NE	12/07/20
Royal Savings Bank	IL	12/07/20	First National Bank of Anson	TX	12/07/20
Security State Bank, Wishek, North Dakota	ND	12/07/20	First National Bank of South Padre Island	TX	12/07/20
Silex Banking Co.	MO	12/07/20	FNB Bank, Inc.	WV	12/07/20
Skowhegan Savings Bank	ME	12/07/20	Graham S&L, SSB	TX	12/07/20
Southwest Bank	TX	12/07/20	Hickory Point Bank and Trust	IL	12/07/20
Southwestern National Bank	TX	12/07/20	Hondo National Bank	TX	12/07/20
Spring Bank	NY	12/07/20	InsBank	TN	12/07/20
Sumitomo Mitsui Trust Bank (U.S.A.) Ltd.	NJ	12/07/20	International City Bank	CA	12/07/20
Synovus Bank	GA	12/07/20	Latimer State Bank	OK	12/07/20
United Bank & Trust N.A.	IA	12/07/20	Level One Bank	MI	12/07/20
United Community Bank	MN	12/07/20	Lumbee Guaranty Bank	NC	12/07/20
United Fidelity Bank, FSB	IN	12/07/20	Manufacturers Bank	CA	12/07/20
US Metro Bank	CA	12/07/20	Marion State Bank	LA	12/07/20
Williamstown Bank, Inc.	WV	12/07/20	Merchants Bank of Indiana	IN	12/07/20
Woori America Bank	NY	12/07/20	Mid-Missouri Bank	MO	12/07/20
Yampa Valley Bank	CO	12/07/20	MidSouth Bank	AL	12/07/20
			Mizuho Bank (USA)	NY	12/07/20

Rating: B-

Name	State	Date of Change	Name	State	Date of Change
			MountainOne Bank	MA	12/07/20
Atascosa Bank	TX	12/07/20	Northern Interstate Bank, N.A.	MI	12/07/20
Auburn Banking Co.	KY	12/07/20	OceanFirst Bank, N.A.	NJ	12/07/20
Bank & Trust Co.	IL	12/07/20	Panola National Bank	TX	12/07/20
Bank Leumi USA	NY	12/07/20	Paragon Bank	TN	12/07/20
Bank of Alapaha	GA	12/07/20	PeopleFirst Bank	IL	12/07/20
Bank of Morton	MS	12/07/20	Peoples Bank	SC	12/07/20
Burke & Herbert Bank & Trust Co.	VA	12/07/20	Peoples Bank	GA	12/07/20
Cadence Bank, N.A.	GA	12/07/20	Piggott State Bank	AR	12/07/20
Central Bank	TN	12/07/20	Pioneer Bank	NY	12/07/20
Citizens Bank & Trust	AL	12/07/20	Piqua State Bank	KS	12/07/20
Citizens Bank & Trust Co.	LA	12/07/20	Richton Bank & Trust Co.	MS	12/07/20
Citizens Bank of Ada	OK	12/07/20	River City Bank	CA	12/07/20
Citizens' Bank, Inc.	AL	12/07/20	Savanna-Thomson State Bank	IL	12/07/20
Citizens Building and Loan, SSB	SC	12/07/20	Security National Bank	IL	12/07/20

Rating Downgrades

Name	State	Date of Change
Security State Bank	SD	12/07/20
Select Bank & Trust Co.	NC	12/07/20
Solvay Bank	NY	12/07/20
State Bank of Arcadia	WI	12/07/20
Three Rivers Bank of Montana	MT	12/07/20
United State Bank	MO	12/07/20
Wilmington Trust, N.A.	DE	12/07/20
Zavala County Bank	TX	12/07/20

Rating: C+

Name	State	Date of Change
American Bank of Baxter Springs	KS	12/07/20
American Express National Bank	UT	12/07/20
Arvest Bank	AR	12/07/20
b1Bank	LA	12/07/20
Bank of Herrin	IL	12/07/20
Bank of Ontario	WI	12/07/20
BankIowa of Cedar Rapids	IA	12/07/20
Beacon Business Bank, N.A.	CA	12/07/20
Blissfield State Bank	MI	12/07/20
BMO Harris Bank N.A.	IL	12/07/20
California Bank of Commerce	CA	12/07/20
Central Bank	IA	12/07/20
Central Savings, F.S.B.	IL	12/07/20
Chester National Bank	IL	12/07/20
Choice Financial Group	ND	12/07/20
CIT Bank, N.A.	CA	12/07/20
Citizens Bank and Trust Co.	MO	12/07/20
Citizens Bank of Kentucky	KY	12/07/20
Columbus Bank and Trust Co.	NE	12/07/20
Community Bank	IA	12/07/20
Community Bank	PA	12/07/20
Community State Bank of Canton	OK	12/07/20
De Witt Bank & Trust Co.	IA	12/07/20
Dearborn Federal Savings Bank	MI	12/07/20
El Dorado Savings Bank, F.S.B.	CA	12/07/20
Extraco Banks, N.A.	TX	12/07/20
Farmers and Merchants Bank	MD	12/07/20
Farmers and Merchants Bank	NE	12/07/20
Farmers State Bank	WA	12/07/20
Farmers State Bank	TX	12/07/20
Federation Bank	IA	12/07/20
First Bank and Trust	LA	12/07/20
First Bank of Muleshoe	TX	12/07/20
First Business Bank	WI	12/07/20
First Colorado National Bank	CO	12/07/20
First Farmers Bank & Trust Co.	IN	12/07/20
First Federal S&L Assn. of Greene County	PA	12/07/20
First Independence Bank	MI	12/07/20
First National Bank of Muscatine	IA	12/07/20
First Neighbor Bank, N.A.	IL	12/07/20
First State Bank	OK	12/07/20
First US Bank	AL	12/07/20
Firstar Bank	OK	12/07/20
FreedomBank	IA	12/07/20
Friendly Hills Bank	CA	12/07/20
Granger National Bank	TX	12/07/20
Greeneville Federal Bank, FSB	TN	12/07/20
Greenfield Co-operative Bank	MA	12/07/20
Haskell National Bank	TX	12/07/20
Hill-Dodge Banking Co.	IL	12/07/20
Interstate Bank	TX	12/07/20
Lakeside Bank	LA	12/07/20
Liberty Bank	CA	12/07/20
Mainstreet Community Bank of Florida	FL	12/07/20
Merchants & Farmers Bank	MS	12/07/20
Miami Savings Bank	OH	12/07/20
MidWestOne Bank	IA	12/07/20
Mission Bank	AZ	12/07/20
National Bank of New York City	NY	12/07/20
Newport Federal Bank	TN	12/07/20
NobleBank & Trust	AL	12/07/20
North Cambridge Co-operative Bank	MA	12/07/20
Old Plank Trail Community Bank, N.A.	IL	12/07/20
One World Bank	TX	12/07/20
Peoples State Bank of Wells	MN	12/07/20
Pikes Peak National Bank	CO	12/07/20
Prime Alliance Bank	UT	12/07/20
Prudential Bank	PA	12/07/20
Republic Bank of Arizona	AZ	12/07/20
Riverwind Bank	AR	12/07/20
S&T Bank	PA	12/07/20
Shelby State Bank	MI	12/07/20
Spencer Savings Bank, SLA	NJ	12/07/20
Sunstate Bank	FL	12/07/20
Torrington Savings Bank	CT	12/07/20
Traditions First Bank	TN	12/07/20
Union Bank	NC	12/07/20
USAA Federal Savings Bank	TX	12/07/20
Wellington State Bank	TX	12/07/20

Rating: C

Name	State	Date of Change
1st Bank of Sea Isle City	NJ	12/07/20
Adrian State Bank	MN	12/07/20
ANZ Guam, Inc.	GU	12/07/20
Apple Bank for Savings	NY	12/07/20
Banesco USA	FL	12/07/20
Berkshire Bank	MA	12/07/20
Capitol National Bank	MI	12/07/20
Celtic Bank Corp.	UT	12/07/20
Citizens Bank	KY	12/07/20

Rating Downgrades

Name	State	Date of Change	Name	State	Date of Change
Citizens First Bank	IA	12/07/20	Bank of Vici	OK	12/07/20
Clarion County Community Bank	PA	12/07/20	BankPacific, Ltd	GU	12/07/20
Equity Bank	KS	12/07/20	BBVA USA	AL	12/07/20
Escambia County Bank	AL	12/07/20	Blue Foundry Bank	NJ	12/07/20
Farmers State Bank	OH	12/07/20	Brickyard Bank	IL	12/07/20
First Federal Bank	NC	12/07/20	Carter Bankshares, Inc.	VA	12/07/20
First National Bank	IN	12/07/20	Citizens State Bank of Ontonagon	MI	12/07/20
First National Bank in Fairfield	IA	12/07/20	Clay City Banking Co.	IL	12/07/20
First National Bank of Tahoka	TX	12/07/20	Congressional Bank	MD	12/07/20
First Western Bank & Trust	ND	12/07/20	First American Bank	IL	12/07/20
Flagship Bank	FL	12/07/20	First Federal S&L Assn.	KY	12/07/20
Fort Davis State Bank	TX	12/07/20	First Federal S&L Assn. of Delta	OH	12/07/20
Gouverneur S&L Assn.	NY	12/07/20	First Federal Savings Bank of Kentucky	KY	12/07/20
Home Savings Bank of Wapakoneta	OH	12/07/20	First National Bank of Fleming	CO	12/07/20
International Finance Bank	FL	12/07/20	First State Bank	OK	12/07/20
Iuka State Bank	IL	12/07/20	Golden State Bank	CA	12/07/20
Kalamazoo County State Bank	MI	12/07/20	Greenville Federal	OH	12/07/20
Marshall County State Bank	MN	12/07/20	Hancock Whitney Bank	MS	12/07/20
Mercer Savings Bank	OH	12/07/20	Home Banking Co.	TN	12/07/20
Mid-Central National Bank	MN	12/07/20	Howard Bank	MD	12/07/20
Mineola Community Bank, SSB	TX	12/07/20	Integrity Bank Plus	MN	12/07/20
Miners and Merchants Bank	WV	12/07/20	Jackson Savings Bank, SSB	NC	12/07/20
Morris County National Bank	TX	12/07/20	Lead Bank	MO	12/07/20
Murphy-Wall State Bank and Trust Co.	IL	12/07/20	LincolnWay Community Bank	IL	12/07/20
National Bank of Texas at Fort Worth	TX	12/07/20	Modern Bank, N.A.	NY	12/07/20
National Capital Bank of Washington	DC	12/07/20	National Bank of Coxsackie	NY	12/07/20
Northway Bank	NH	12/07/20	One Florida Bank	FL	12/07/20
Peoples Bank	IN	12/07/20	Peoples Bank, Biloxi, Mississippi	MS	12/07/20
People's Bank of Seneca	MO	12/07/20	Peoples State Bank	WI	12/07/20
Professional Bank	FL	12/07/20	Prairie Sun Bank	MN	12/07/20
Quontic Bank	NY	12/07/20	Slovenian S&L Assn. of Franklin-Conemaugh	PA	12/07/20
Rio Bank	TX	12/07/20	Spiro State Bank	OK	12/07/20
Rochelle State Bank	GA	12/07/20	State Bank of Fairmont	MN	12/07/20
Santander Bank, N.A.	MA	12/07/20	Stride Bank, N.A.	OK	12/07/20
Savannah Bank, N.A.	NY	12/07/20	TIAA, FSB	FL	12/07/20
Sicily Island State Bank	LA	12/07/20	Tioga Franklin Savings Bank	PA	12/07/20
SNB Bank, N.A.	OK	12/07/20	Tucumcari Federal S&L Assn.	NM	12/07/20
Southern Bank Co.	AL	12/07/20	Union Bank	TN	12/07/20
TD Bank, N.A.	DE	12/07/20	Western Nebraska Bank	NE	12/07/20
The Bankers Bank	OK	12/07/20			
TNB Bank	IL	12/07/20			

Rating: D+

Name	State	Date of Change
Union State Bank	KS	12/07/20
United Orient Bank	NY	12/07/20
Vidalia Federal Savings Bank	GA	12/07/20
VisionBank	KS	12/07/20
Woodruff Federal S&L Assn.	SC	12/07/20

Name	State	Date of Change
1st Bank in Hominy	OK	12/07/20
Amerant Bank, N.A.	FL	12/07/20
Bank of Wyandotte	OK	12/07/20
Cache Bank & Trust	CO	12/07/20
Camp Grove State Bank	IL	12/07/20
City First Bank of D.C., N.A.	DC	12/07/20
Corder Bank	MO	12/07/20
Delta National Bank and Trust Co.	NY	12/07/20
Keystone Bank, N.A.	TX	12/07/20

Rating: C-

Name	State	Date of Change
Bank of Labor	KS	12/07/20
Bank of Orrick	MO	12/07/20

Rating Downgrades

Name	State	Date of Change
Lake Country Community Bank	MN	12/07/20
Lakeside State Bank	OK	12/07/20
Medallion Bank	UT	12/07/20
Metropolitan Capital Bank & Trust	IL	12/07/20
Pee Dee Federal Savings Bank	SC	12/07/20
Peoples Bank	KY	12/07/20
Peoples Bank of Moniteau County	MO	12/07/20
SouthFirst Bank	AL	12/07/20
Spectra Bank	TX	12/07/20
Tarboro Savings Bank, SSB	NC	12/07/20
Tempo Bank	IL	12/07/20
UNICO Bank	MO	12/07/20

Rating: D

Name	State	Date of Change
Beneficial State Bank	CA	12/07/20
Citizens State Bank	TX	12/07/20
Galion Building and Loan Bank	OH	12/07/20
Peoples State Bank	KS	12/07/20
Texas Citizens Bank, N.A.	TX	12/07/20

Rating: D-

Name	State	Date of Change
First National Bank of Sedan	KS	12/07/20
First State Bank of Bigfork	MN	12/07/20
Iowa Prairie Bank	IA	12/07/20
Maple Bank	MN	12/07/20
Neighborhood National Bank	CA	12/07/20
Pataskala Banking Co.	OH	12/07/20
Peoples State Bank	ND	12/07/20

Rating: E+

Name	State	Date of Change
Citizens Bank & Trust Co.	MS	12/07/20
First Savanna Savings Bank	IL	12/07/20
Walton State Bank	KS	12/07/20

Rating: E-

Name	State	Date of Change
United Trust Bank	IL	12/07/20

Appendix

RECENT BANK FAILURES
2020

Institution	Headquarters	Date of Failure	At Date of Failure	
			Total Assets ($Mil)	Safety Rating
First State Bank	Barboursville, WV	4/06/2020	152.40	E- (Very Weak)
Ericson State Bank	Ericson, NE	2/14/2020	113.02	C- (Fair)
Almena State Bank	Almena, KS	10/23/2020	70.04	D- (Weak)

2019

Institution	Headquarters	Date of Failure	At Date of Failure	
			Total Assets ($Mil)	Safety Rating
City National Bank of NJ	Newark, NJ	11/1/19	142.5	E- (Very Weak)
Resolute Bank	Maumee, OH	10/25/19	27.1	E+ (Very Weak)
Enloe State Bank	Cooper, TX	5/31/19	36.5	C (Fair)

2017

Institution	Headquarters	Date of Failure	At Date of Failure	
			Total Assets ($Mil)	Safety Rating
Washington Federal Banks for Savings	Chicago, IL	12/15/17	166.4	A (Excellent)
Farmers & Merchants State Bk of Argonia	Argonia, KS	10/13/17	34.2	E- (Very Weak)
Fayette County Bank	Saint Elmo, IL	05/26/17	34.8	E- (Very Weak)
Guaranty Bank (MHC)	Milwaukee, WI	05/05/17	1,010.0	E- (Very Weak)
First NBC Bank	New Orleans, LA	04/28/17	4,740.0	E- (Very Weak)
Proficio Bank	Cottonwood Heights, UT	03/03/17	80.3	E- (Very Weak)
Seaway Bank and Trust Co	Chicago, IL	01/27/17	361.2	E- (Very Weak)
Harvest Community Bank	Pennsville, NJ	01/13/17	126.4	E- (Very Weak)

2016

Institution	Headquarters	Date of Failure	At Date of Failure	
			Total Assets ($Mil)	Safety Rating
Allied Bank	Mulberry, AR	09/23/16	66.3	E- (Very Weak)
Woodbury Banking Company	Woodbury, GA	08/19/16	22.5	E- (Very Weak)
First Cornerstone Bank	King of Prussia, PA	05/06/16	107.0	E- (Very Weak)
Trust Co Bank	Memphis, TN	04/29/16	20.7	E- (Very Weak)
North Milwaukee State Bank	Milwaukee, WI	03/11/16	67.1	E- (Very Weak)

2015

Institution	Headquarters	Date of Failure	At Date of Failure	
			Total Assets ($Mil)	Safety Rating
Bank of Georgia	Peachtree City, GA	10/02/15	294.2	E- (Very Weak)
Hometown National Bank	Longview, WA	10/02/15	4.9	E+ (Very Weak)
Premier Bank	Denever, CO	07/10/15	31.7	E- (Very Weak)
Edgebrook Bank	Chicago, IL	05/08/15	90.0	E- (Very Weak)
Doral Bank	San Juan, PR	02/27/15	5,900.0	E+ (Very Weak)
Capitol City Bank & Trust Co	Atlanta, GA	02/13/15	272.3	E- (Very Weak)
Highland Community Bank	Chicago, IL	01/23/15	54.7	E- (Very Weak)
First National Bank of Crestview	Crestview, FL	01/16/15	79.7	E- (Very Weak)

How Do Banks and Credit Unions Differ?

Since credit unions first appeared in 1946, they have been touted as a low-cost, friendly alternative to banks. But with tightening margins, pressure to compete in technology, branch closures, and the introduction of a host of service fees — some even higher than those charged by banks — the distinction between banks and credit unions has been gradually narrowing. Following are the key differences between today's banks and credit unions.

	Banks	**Credit Unions**
Access	Practically anyone is free to open an account or request a loan from any bank. There are no membership requirements.	Credit unions are set up to serve the needs of a specific group who share a "common bond." In order to open an account or request a loan, you must demonstrate that you meet the credit union's common bond requirements.
Ownership	Banks are owned by one or more investors who determine the bank's policies and procedures. A bank's customers do not have direct input into how the bank is operated.	Although they may be sponsored by a corporation or other entity, credit unions are owned by their members through their funds on deposit. Therefore, each depositor has a voice in how the credit union is operated.
Dividends and Fees	Banks are for-profit organizations where the profits are used to pay dividends to the bank's investors or are reinvested in an effort to increase the bank's value to investors. In an effort to generate more profits, bank services and fees are typically more costly.	Credit unions are not-for-profit organizations. Any profits generated are returned to the credit union's members in the form of higher interest rates on deposits, lower loan rates, and free or low-cost services.
Management and Staffing	A bank's management and other staff are employees of the bank, hired directly or indirectly by its investors.	Credit unions are frequently run using elected members, volunteer staff, and staff provided by the credit union's sponsor. This helps to hold down costs.
Insurance	Banks are insured by the Federal Deposit Insurance Corporation, an agency of the federal government.	Credit unions are insured by the National Credit Union Share Insurance Fund, which is managed by the National Credit Union Administration, an agency of the federal government.

Glossary

This glossary contains the most important terms used in this publication.

ARM
Adjustable-Rate Mortgage. This is a loan whose interest rate is tied to an index and is adjusted at a predetermined frequency. An ARM is subject to credit risk if interest rates rise and the borrower is unable to make the mortgage payment.

Average Recession
A recession involving a decline in real GDP that is approximately equivalent to the average of the postwar recessions of 1957-58, 1960, 1970, 1974-75, 1980, 1981-82, 1990-1991, 2001, and 2007-2009. It is assumed, however, that in today's market, the financial losses suffered from a recession of that magnitude would be greater than those experienced in previous decades. (See also "Severe Recession.")

Bank Holding Company
A company that holds stock in one or more banks and possibly other companies.

Bank Insurance Fund (BIF)
A unit of Federal Deposit Insurance Corporation (FDIC) that provided deposit insurance for banks, other than thrifts. BIF was formed as part of the 1989 savings and loan association bailout bill to keep separate the administration of the bank and thrift insurance programs. There were thus two distinct insurance entities under the FDIC: BIF and savings association insurance fund (SAIF). (See also Federal Deposit Insurance Corporation.")

Brokered Deposits
Deposits that are brought into an institution through a broker. They are relatively costly, volatile funds that are more readily withdrawn from the institution if there is a loss of confidence or intense interest rate competition. Reliance on brokered deposits is usually a sign that the institution is having difficulty attracting deposits from its local geographic markets and could be a warning signal if other institutions in the same areas are not experiencing similar difficulties.

Capital
The cushion an institution has of its own resources to help withstand losses. The basic component of capital is stockholder's equity which consists of common and preferred stock and retained earnings. (See also "Core Capital")

Cash & Equivalents
Cash plus highly liquid assets which can be readily converted to cash.

Core (Tier 1) Capital
A measurement of capital defined by the federal regulatory agencies for evaluating an institution's degree of leverage. Core capital consists of the following: common stockholder's equity, preferred stockholder's equity up to certain limits, and retained earnings net of any intangible assets.

Critical Ranges
Guidelines developed to help you evaluate the levels of each index contributing to a company's Weiss Safety Rating. The sum or average of these grades does not necessarily have a one-to-one correspondence with the final rating for an institution because the rating is derived from a wider range of more complex calculations.

Deposit Insurance Fund (DIF)	In 2005 Congress passed legislation merging the SAIF and BIF into one insurance fund called the deposit insurance fund (DIF). The same law also raised the federal deposit insurance level from $100,000 to $250,000. (See also "Emergency Economic Stabilization Act.")
Emergency Stabilization Act	In 2008 Congress passed the Emergency Economic Stabilization Act that temporarily increased the basic limit on deposit insurance for all ownership categories from $100,000 to $250,000. This increase was set to expire in 2013 but has been extended permanently.
Equity	Total assets minus total liabilities. This is the "capital cushion" the institution has to fall back on in times of trouble. (See also "Capital.")
FDIC	Federal Deposit Insurance Corporation. The provider of insurance on deposits. This agency also plays an active role when banks are found to be insolvent or in need of federal assistance. It is the governing body of the Deposit Insurance Fund (DIF) that now incorporates both the Bank Insurance Fund (BIF) and the Savings Association Insurance Fund (SAIF). (See also "Deposit Insurance Fund.")
Federal Home Loan Bank (FHLB)	A quasi-governmental agency (reporting to the Federal Housing Finance Board) whose chartered purpose is to promote the issuance of mortgage loans by providing increased liquidity to lenders. This agency raises money by issuing notes and bonds and then lends the money to banks and other mortgage lenders.
Federal Reserve	America's central bank, regulating all banks that offer transaction accounts. It works hand-in-hand with the FDIC, providing examination and regulation of its member banks.
Safety Rating	Weiss Safety Ratings, which grade institutions on a scale from A (Excellent) to F (Failed). Ratings are based on many factors, emphasizing capitalization, asset quality, profitability, liquidity, and stability.
FSB	Federal Savings Bank. A thrift institution operating under a federal charter.
Goodwill	The value of an institution as a going concern, meaning the value which exceeds book value on a balance sheet. It generally represents the value of a well-respected business name, good customer relations, high employee morale and other intangible factors which would be expected to translate into greater than normal earning power. In a bank acquisition, goodwill is the value paid by a buyer of the institution in excess of the value of the institution's equity because of these intangible factors.
Hot Money	Individual deposits of $100,000 or more plus those deposits received through a broker. These types of deposits are considered "hot money" because they tend to chase whoever is offering the best interest rates at the time and are thus relatively costly and fairly volatile sources of funds.
Loan Loss Reserves	The amount of capital an institution sets aside to cover any potential losses due to the nonrepayment of loans.
N.A.	National Association. A commercial bank operating under a federal charter.

Net Charge-offs	The amount of foreclosed loans written off the institution's books since the beginning of the year, less any previous write-offs that were recovered during the year.
Net Interest Spread	The difference between the interest income earned on the institution's loans and investments and the interest expense paid on its interest-bearing deposits and borrowings. This "spread" is most commonly analyzed as a percentage of average earning assets to show the institution's net return on income-generating assets. Since the margin between interest earned and interest paid is generally where the company generates the majority of its income, this figure provides insight into the company's ability to effectively manage interest spreads. A low Net Interest Spread can be the result of poor loan and deposit pricing, high levels of nonaccruing loans, or poor asset/liability management.
Net Profit or Loss	The bottom line income or loss the institution has sustained in its most recent reporting period.
Nonaccruing Loans	Loans for which payments are past due and full repayment is doubtful. Interest income on these loans is no longer recorded on the income statement. (See also "Past Due Loans.")
Nonperforming Loans	The sum of loans past due 90 days or more and nonaccruing loans. These are loans the institution made where full repayment is now doubtful. (See also "Past Due Loans" and "Nonaccruing Loans.")
Past Due Loans	Loans for which payments are at least 90 days in arrears. The institution continues to record income on these loans, even though none is actually being received, because it is expected that the borrower will eventually repay the loan in full. It is likely, however, that at least a portion of these loans will move into nonaccruing status. (See also "Nonaccruing Loans.")
OCC	Office of the Comptroller of the Currency. This agency of the U.S. Treasury Department is the primary regulator of national banks.
Overhead Expense	Expenses of the institution other than interest expense, such as salaries and benefits of employees, rent and utility expenses, and data processing expenses. A certain amount of "fixed" overhead is required to operate a bank, so it is important that the institution leverage that overhead to the fullest extent in supporting its revenue-generating activities.
RBCR	See "Risk-Based Capital Ratio."
Resolution Trust Corp. (RTC)	The now-defunct federal agency that was formed to handle the liquidation of insolvent savings and loans.
Restructured Loans	Loans whose terms have been modified in order to enable the borrower to make payments which he otherwise would be unable to make. Modifications could include a reduction in the interest rate or a lengthening of the time to maturity.

Risk-Based Capital Ratio	A ratio originally developed by the International Committee on Banking as a means of assessing the adequacy of an institution's capital in relation to the amount of credit risk on and off its balance sheet. (See also "Risk-weighted Assets.")
Risk-Weighted Assets	The sum of assets and certain off-balance sheet items after they have been individually adjusted for the level of credit risk they pose to the institution. Assets with close to no risk are weighted 0%; those with minor risk are weighted 20%; those with low risk, 50%; and those with normal or high risk, 100%.
R.O.A	Return on Assets calculated as net profit or loss as a percentage of average assets. This is the most commonly used measure of bank profitability.
R.O.E.	Return on Equity calculated as net profit or loss as a percentage of average equity. This represents the rate of return on the shareholders' investment.
S.A.	Savings Association.
Savings and Loan (S&L)	A financial institution that traditionally offered primarily home mortgages to individuals and served small depositors. However, in 1980, savings and loans were given power to diversify into other areas of lending. Also known as a thrift.
Savings and Loan Holding Company	A company that holds stock in one or more savings and loans and possibly other companies.
Savings Association Insurance Fund (SAIF)	Fund created in 1989 by Congress to replace the FSLIC as the provider of deposit insurance to thrifts. This fund is administered by the Federal Deposit Insurance Corporation (FDIC). (See also "Bank Insurance Fund.")
Savings Bank	A financial institution created to serve primarily the small saver and to lend mortgage money to individuals. Though savings banks have expanded their services, they are still primarily engaged in providing consumer mortgages and accepting consumer deposits. Also known as a thrift.
Severe Recession	A drop in real GDP which is significantly greater than that of an average postwar recession. (See also "Average Recession.")
Stockholder's Equity	See "Equity."
Thrift	Generic term for an institution formed primarily as a depository for consumer savings and a lender for home mortgages, such as a savings and loan or a savings bank.
Total Assets	Total resources of an institution, primarily composed of cash, securities (such as municipal and treasury bonds), loans, and fixed assets (such as real estate, buildings, and equipment).
Total Equity	See "Equity."

| **Total Liabilities** | All debts owed by an institution. Normally, the largest liability of a bank is its deposits. |
| **Trust Company** | A financial institution chartered to provide trust services (legal agreements to act for the benefit of another party), which may also be authorized to provide banking services. |